American Metal Toys' Royce Reyff in 1942.
Courtesy Stan Reyff.

To Achilles Papaliolios
Longtime friend,
for putting me in touch -
via the magic of his brother Costas' computer -
with Stan Reyff,
son of Royce Reyff,
co-owner of American Metal Toys

TABLE OF CONTENTS

Acknowledgments.. vi
Introduction...vii

Sections

Action Figures.. 375
Aircraft...167/563
Animal-Drawn.. 175
Battery-Operated.. 276
BB Guns.. 555
Comic Character... 442
Disney... 486
Erector Sets... 647
Figure Kits.. 414
Fisher-Price... 622
German Composition Civilian Figures......... 705
Guns... 519
Japanese Tin Airplanes... 167
Japanese Tin Cars... 154
Marbles.. 684
Matchbox.. 143
Mechanical Banks... 208
Miscellaneous... 655
Movies, Radio, Television...................................... 468
Paper Toys... 216
Pez.. 421
Plastic Dollhouse Furniture.................................... 634
Premiums.. 425
Ramp Walkers... 507
Schoenhut... 611
Ships.. 594
Soldiers... 331
Steam Toys.. 644
Tin Wind-Up.. 239
Vehicles.. 1
Western-Style Guns... 543
White-Knob Windups... 515

Company Histories

A.C. Gilbert.. 647
Acme.. 4
All American Toy Company.................................... 4
Althof, Bergmann.. 175
American Metal Toys... 366
Animate Toy.. 239
Arcade.. 5
Auburn.. 363
Aurora.. 415

Baldwin.. 657
Banner... 19
Barclay... 20, 331/567
Barr.. 31
Beaut.. 32
Best.. 33
Big Bang.. 667
Bliss.. 177
Buddy L... 36
Built-Rite... 219
C.A.W. 41
Carpenter... 178
Champion.. 45
Chein.. 241
Courtland (Walt Reach).. 244
Cozzone... 673
Cracker Jack.. 430
Craftoy.. 50
Crandall... 674
Daisy.. 555
Dayton... 50
Dent... 51
Dinky.. 52
Disney... 486
Doepke... 53
Dunwell.. 55
Dyna Model (Dyna-Mo)... 56
Erie.. 57
Ertl... 58
Fallows.. 181
Fisher-Price.. 622
G.I. Joe... 375
George Brown... 183
Gibbs.. 184
Girard... 247
Grey Iron.. 356
Harris... 186
Hartland... 385
Hess... 61
Hubley... 62
Ideal.. 639
Ives... 193
Jane Francis... 69
Judy Company... 69
Kansas Toy... 70
Kenner... 391

...continued

Kenton	77/195	
Keystone	79	
Kilgore	81	
Kingsbury	82	
Lansing Slik-Toys	83	
Liberty Playthings	599	
Lincoln White Metal	84	
Lindstrom	87	
M & L	87	
Manoil	345	
Markam/King	561	
Marx	253	
Matchbox	143	
Mattel	407	
McLoughlin	228	
Metal Cast	92	
Metalcraft	93	
Midgetoy	94	
Midwest	95	
Miniature Vehicles Castings, Inc.	98	
Neff-Moon	98	
North & Judd	98	
Nylint	99	
Ohio Art	688	
Orkin & Orkin Craft	603/604	
Pez	421	
Plasco	638	
Plasticville (Bachmann Bros.)	689	
Pratt & Letchworth	199	
Pyro	103	
Ralstoy	103	
Renwal	105	

Savoye	106
Schieble	107
Schoenhut	611
Schuco	265
Smitty (Smith-Miller)	108
Strauss	267
Structo	115
Sun Rubber	117
Technofix	269
Thomas Toys	118
Tilliam	607
Tip Top	118
Toledo Metal Wheel ("Blue Streak")	119
Tonka	121
Tootsietoys	126
T.P.S	270
Unique Art	273
Wannatoys	608
Wilkins	203
Williams, A.C.	139
Wolverine	701
Wyandotte	140

Museums	719
Bibliography	720
Auctioneers	721
Leading Collectors and Dealers	722

ACKNOWLEDGMENTS

Over the years, as this book has grown bigger, the number of contributors has continued to increase. This kind of project could never be done properly without them, and they have my total gratitude. I know just how hard the work they do is, and once again I find myself impressed, as well as grateful for their cheerful willingness to do it.

So once again, thanks to all. To longtime friend Jim Harmon, whose promptness is only matched by his expertise. To Barbara and Jonathan Newman for coming through once again, and to Don Hultzman, who, despite now having his own book on the subject, once again pitched in with his usual energy and assiduity.

Jim and Patsy Carlson, who had previously aided the late Blossom Abell, took over the full project at the last minute. Perry Eichor continued his much-appreciated efforts, as did the very-busy Bill Bertoia. James Schleyer both con-

tributed and expanded greatly on his previous work, as did the always-willing Barry Goodman. Also coming through in the same stellar fashion as they had in the past were Ron Smith, Dave Leopard, Joe and Sharon Freed, Fred Maxwell, Thomas G. Nefos, David Welch and John J. Murray.

Weighing in early and well were newcomers Mary Brett, Randy Welch, Jim Buskirk, Richard Leach, Bob Smith, W.S. Harrison III, James Theobald, Kent Comstock, Mark McManus, John Gibson, Aaron Roy and Raymond V. Brandes. Photographs are a terribly important part of this book. So whether for a single shot or a horde, I'm as grateful as can be to many of the above plus the following: Timothy Luke of Christie's East, Scott Smiles, Tim Oei, Bob Emmons, Don Patman, Brian Seligman, Harold Haseley, Bill Conover, Rod Carnahan and Barry S. Josephs.

A nod too, to Jeffrey L. Hubbard, for straightening out the first chunk of the Nylint listing, to Stanley Block for his expertise on marbles, and to George Parola for providing prices on the rare (and expensive!) Barclay red podfoot soldiers.

Gramercy all, as well as to all those I've forgotten (I invariably do; nothing personal, let me assure you), to my agent Al Zuckerman for getting me the original "Collecting Toys" contract way back when, and to Books Americana publisher Dan Alexander for his continuing courtesy, friendliness and professionalism.

INTRODUCTION

On August 15, 1977 I signed a contract for the first edition of this book. When it was published in late 1978 it listed almost 4000 toys, the largest book of its kind ever published. Since then each new edition has represented considerable bulking-up. Last time out a bit over 14,000 toys made it in; this one includes over 15,900.

As a result, the book has become so big that I've decided to try a couple of experiments in an attempt to conserve space. I've dropped the Britains soldiers section for this edition at least. Though I've added seven new sections, one, German Composition Civilian Figures, is planned as a one-time-only appearance. It is an area that I think has a limited base, but is important enough to be included just this once, as a reference as well as a price guide. So if you're interested in these toys, but tend to toss out old editions of "Collecting Toys" as new ones emerge, hang onto this, as the section will not reappear, unless enough readers convince me otherwise.

I think it's important to state here for new readers that <u>the numbers running under the various condition categories (usually C6, C8, C10, but not always) are the amounts in dollars the toys are worth.</u>

There has been some mild concern voiced of late by dealers and collectors about the health of his hobby. Judging by what I've found as I've gone over all these prices, there's no real reason for concern. Only one category has dropped in average price since the last edition (and that may be due to my adding a number of cheaper toys), all the others rising. However, most of the increases haven't been as spectacular as at times in the past. My seat-of-the-pants feeling as I worked is that there has been a considerable amount of stasis, and that it's the rarer toys which have generally had the most eyebrow-raising increases in price, perhaps greatly contributing to the overall increases. This suggests that the hobby may have reached a point of maturity where prices for the more common toys have begun to be far more stable than in the past. However, since even the recent severe recession prompted no noticeable panicky bailouts, it appears, barring an all-out depression, this hobby will remain a healthy one.

Something that hasn't changed at all is that, when it comes to prices, this book must be thought of as a <u>guide,</u> and not as the absolute last word on the price of a toy. Prices may inflate or deflate in the months it takes to publish a book. Even on the same day a toy can vary in price, depending on the dealer, the buyer, the geographical area in which it's being sold, and whether it's being offered in the first, expectant rush of a toy show or in its last, draggy minutes, when the dealer finds himself confronted with having to pack up all that stuff again. Employed by itself "Collecting Toys" should at least prevent serious mistakes from being made. Used with the assistance of a few current prices found in ads, lists, or on dealer tables, it can get the prospective buyer or seller much nearer to the current (always fuzzily defined) market price.

Finally, for those who wish to consider this field as an investment, and it can be a good one, it should be stressed that mint or near-mint conditions provide considerably more financial safety than any of the other conditions, as this is the only category sure to attract all collectors and dealers of any particular toy.

CONDITION OF A TOY
AND ITS RELATION TO PRICE

CONDITION CODE:

C6 - Good. Evident overall wear, well played with, but acceptable to many collectors

C8 - Very Good Minor wear overall, very clean

C10 - Mint (like new)

Note: Mint in Box commands a higher price. Condition below C6 brings considerably lower prices.

Richard O'Brien
January, 1995

VEHICLES

(Also see Tin Wind-Up)
Average mint price of vehicles in the last edition was $488.23 this edition
it is $590.17 an increase of 21%.

CAST IRON AUTOMOTIVE TOYS

by C.B.C. Lee

The manufacture of cast iron toys began shortly after the Civil War and had about reached its zenith by the beginning of the twentieth century. The first toy automobiles began to appear soon after their real life prototypes began chugging along the horse-carriage roads, by which time some of the great 19th century toy makers had already gone out of business. Among those that continued into the automotive era were Hubley, Dent, Wilkins, and Kenton. During the first three decades of this century, others came to the forefront, such as Arcade, Kilgore, A.C. Williams, and Champion. Others also made toy cars and trucks in smaller numbers or for a short period of time, such as Grey Iron, Freidag, and North and Judd. Many of these firms made no identifying marks on their toys, and it has only been in recent years that many very familiar toys have been correctly attributed, as catalogues, patents, and old advertisements have gradually come to light. Probably the greatest American toymaker of all was Ives, but this firm is thought to have made only one toy car, a clockwork-driven horseless carriage runabout with figure, measuring 6-1/2" long and 6" to the top of the jockey cap on the driver.

Value does not have much relationship to either age or size, however, having more to do with scarcity, complexity and nicety of design, detail, and "desirability". As with anything else in a free market, it is simply the rule of supply and demand.

Demand and "desirability" are affected by a number of factors. One of these is nostalgia.

As a general guide to factors affecting desirability, there are a few broad easy clues, however. Accuracy of scale and proportion, the use of many different cast parts, cast-in or decal logos and details, hand-painting (by the original maker, but NOT by some later child or collector!!), etc. all enhance the value. In most cases, a 4-inch roadster with a separate chassis, separate nickel-plated radiator and head-lights, and a separate cast figure will be worth much more than a two-piece one with the halves riveted together.

Values are very volatile, both up and down, and may be badly obsolete even by the time this is printed. The lawyers long ago defined the "fair market value" as the price paid by a (knowledgeable) willing buyer to a (knowledgeable) willing seller.

A WORD OF CAUTION!!!

In recent years several American makers have begun to make cast-iron or brass copies of old toys, and more recently many more have been coming in from Taiwan and perhaps other sources. These are marketed as decorator pieces, and sell quite cheaply. Many unscrupulous dealers are using these pieces to cheat unwary new collectors. They usually rust them hurriedly - and sometimes make other modifications of tip-off parts (axles or screws) to fool the uninitiated. The Makers, "IRON ART", "UTEXIQUAL" and others here and abroad are running an honest enough business, but the dishonest dealers are using the products to turn a quick profit at the expense of naive buyers.

The fakes are usually easy to spot once one has gained a little experience. They are usually held together by a long screw, which is threaded all the way to the hub, as are standard stove bolts in your local hardware store (only a few genuinely old toys are assembled with a screw rather than a long peaned rivet, and the few screws used often had only about 1/4-inch threaded at the tip (the Hubley Packard is an important exception). Modern axles are usually a hollow rolled piece of sheet-metal, much like a long shear-pin, though a few are rods with threaded ends and sheet metal acorn nuts. The castings themselves are the most dependable give away, but require a little experience; a blind man could tell in an instant. The old castings are thinner, lighter, and smoother, the modern ones being gritty, thick and coarse of detail.

CLINT SEELEY (8/28/27-3/6/84), a New England doctor, used the pen-name C.B.C. LEE when writing about toys, which he did prolifically. He contributed to books and magazines not only in this country but also in England, France, Italy, New Zealand, Australia and Japan and was in touch with collectors on five continents. His extensive research on the subject, and his generosity in sharing what he'd learned, will keep his name alive as long as interest remains in the hobby he so loved.

TOOTSIETOYS, DIE-CAST AND SLUSH

by C.B.C. Lee

Die-casting was an outgrowth of the invention of the Linotype machine, introduced at the Columbian Exposition at Chicago in 1893. A trade-journal publisher in that city named Samuel Dowst began to adapt the type-casting machine to making small promotional miniatures, collar buttons, and so on related to the Laundry Journal he also published. By the turn of the century, however, the die-casting business had become his principal business, and he was producing a myriad of small party favors, candy premiums, political items and penny jewelry. Amongst these were several charms and miniatures of automotive, trains, and aircraft. By 1911, he produced a small 47 mm. limousine with free-turning wheels. By 1914 a 77 mm. Ford touring car was marketed, and a matching pick-up truck was made two years later. All three of these stayed in the catalogue until the late 20s, and the truck as late as 1932. In 1922 a line of doll furniture was developed, and was trade-named Tootsietoy after the daughter of the company's president at the time, Tootsie Dowst. The name later was used to identify nearly all of the toys the company sold. However, it continued to make items for other buyers, and still makes the metal marker pieces used in the deluxe Monopoly game. Tootsietoys continue to be made today, the present name of the Company being the Strombecker Corporation.

As with other collectibles, the value of obsolete toys today is not greatly related to age. The oldest Tootsietoys were made in such large numbers and for so long a period that they are not hard to find today. Others, some of which were unpopular in their day, were not sold in great numbers and are rare today. The 1932 Funnies series of six pieces drawn from the contemporary comic strips is an example of this. These were made in a boxed set of 6, having cams on the axles, which imparted action to the figures as the toy was pushed along the floor, and having details and figures hand-painted in up to seven different colors. This boxed set sold for $1.00. The six pieces were also made in simpler non-action versions with simple paint and sold for 10¢ each. For reasons hard to understand today, these toys were not popular. Consequently they are very hard to find, and are more valuable. Some of the individual pieces must have been better liked by their owners and were played to death or lost, making them even scarcer. So, though all were made in about equal numbers, some are rarer than others. Uncle Walt Wallet in a roadster is the most valuable, Uncle Willie and Mamie in a boat is at the other end, worth about half as much.

In regular production cars, LaSalles and a sort of pseudo-Lincoln have the greatest value, while other Fords, Yellow Cabs, and early Mack trucks are about one-third of that. A 1925 delivery truck, often called "Federal" by collectors, was made in stock versions having legends on the side panels saying: MILK, MARKET, LAUNDRY, GROCERY, BAKERY, and FLORIST. Their rarity is in about that order, MILK being worth the least. This same line of small trucks were also made in small numbers with custom private liveries, and over a dozen such versions with store names on the sides are presently know to exist. There were probably more. These, too vary in value according to scarcity, the most common being HORSCHSCHILD KOHN & CO. One which had the J.C.Penney logo is worth twice that, and a few might find a buyer at even higher prices.

Other manufacturers also made die-cast toys, and a few of these are desirable enough to have some value. Barclay made a small series of separate body/chassis vehicles in the late 1930s, and a west coast firm, TIP-TOP Toys, which are of fair value. So are a few of the finer die-cast Manoils and ERIEs. Many others are in little demand, such as JANE FRANCIS, GOODIE, METAL MASTERS and IT'S A BEAUT.

Slush casting was a process simple enough to be done in tiny factories, and even in home-industries during the depression. A few large manufacturers made toys in this way, most notably Barclay, Manoil, Savoye, Kansas Toy and Novelty, and others, but many were made by anonymous and small unidentifiable and local operations, using molds made and marketed by a few firms. Many slush-cast toys are of very little value today, but there are exceptions. Foremost among these were dealer promotional replicas of real cars, made by Banthrico and National Products. Other very accurate and detailed slush models, similar in size and scale to the contemporary Tootsietoys, can be valuable, most notable among these being certain nicely cast models of the Reo Victoria, Packard, Chrysler Imperial, Cord coupe, late 20s, Buick and Model A Ford; these, and others made with an extra mold part resulting in detailed radiator grilles, were made by the Lincoln White Metal Works. Other small accurate replicas, with the names cast on the door sides, were made by Tommy Toy.

As with other toys, condition is very important. Paint wear can drop the value to half, and broken or missing parts can drop it to nearly nothing. Repairing can occasionally partially rescue an exceptionally rare piece, but more often depresses the value. Reproductions are beginning to appear on the market, and will also tend to depress the values of the real thing. As with anything else in a free market, cost is largely a matter of supply and demand, both of which can wax and wane cyclically. Let the buyer beware.

RUBBER TOY VEHICLES

by Dave Leopard

For about 20 years (roughly 1935-1955), American kids enjoyed playing with rubber toys and Moms were told that these toys would not mar the furniture or floors. Then, almost as suddenly as they came on the market, they disappeared again, but left a rich legacy for toy collectors. The Auburn Rubber Company of Auburn, Indiana was not the first to introduce rubber toys to the American market but they were no doubt the largest and had the greatest impact on the toy field. After introducing some toy soldiers in 1935, Auburn brought out its first vehicle in 1936 - a beautiful coffin-nosed Cord sedan. Today, the Auburn Cord is one of the most highly prized rubber toys and is seldom seen offered for sale. Auburn followed the Cord with a wealth of vehicles, including trucks, farm tractors and implements, motorcycles, racers, fire engines, military vehicles, aircraft, ships, and trains. In all, I have catalogued about 90 different varieties of Auburn rubber vehicles and I'm sure there are more than that. To my knowledge, 1952 was Auburn's last year of marketing rubber toys exclusively. The 1953 Auburn catalog contained a vinyl motorcycle, which I believe was their first vinyl toy. By 1955, their toy line was mostly vinyl with a few rubber varieties hanging on. The 1956 catalog is exclusively vinyl, except for two rubber fire engines, which were no doubt the last rubber toys to be marketed by Auburn. Auburn continued in the toy business in Auburn, Indiana and later in Deming, New Mexico until they went out of business in 1969.

The Sun Rubber Company of Barberton, Ohio was the second largest producer of rubber toys and, like Auburn, produced a full line of toys, in addition to vehicles, including dolls, balls, and baby squeak toys. I have catalogs that confirm Sun's line of rubber toy vehicles, beginning in 1936 and ending in 1955, which pretty well puts them on the same course with Auburn - about 20 years of rubber toys. The Sun 1936 catalog contains a good selection of cars, trucks, and racers. In later years, they added a few airplanes and military vehicles but unlike Auburn never produced any motorcycles, ships, or trains. Among the most famous of the Sun Rubber vehicles are the Walt Disney characters, Mickey Mouse and Donald Duck driving a tractor, firetruck, roadster, or airplane. The Disney tractor and firetruck are the only examples of each produced by Sun. By 1955, Sun's catalog line largely consisted of athletic balls, with the Disney toys included as the only vehicle toys. Sun existed as a company until 1974 but they did not manufacture rubber toy vehicles past 1955. I have catalogued 32 varieties of Sun Rubber toy vehicles, which I believe accounts for all the toys they made.

Auburn and Sun made the vast majority of rubber toys we see today but there were a significant number of rubber toys made by other companies mostly prior to World War II. Several companies from the rubber industry produced some rubber toy vehicles, including Firestone, Seiberling, Barr, and Rainbow. All of the Rainbow, Barr, and Seiberling toys appear to have been made in 1935-1936, or at least based on real cars from those years. All of the Seiberling or Barr toys I have seen are 1935 Fords. The Firestone toys include a 1935 Ford, a 1936 Ford, and a 1939 Mercury. Rainbows are mostly based on a 1935 Oldsmobile. Some of these toys were mass-marketed via dimestores, just like Auburn and Sun toys were, but some were sold (or given away?) at expositions and exhibits. All of the Firestone toys seem to be marked with some significant event being celebrated, like the Texas Centennial in 1936. I have catalogued only 14 varieties of toys produced by these four companies.

Many rubber toys were produced as "promotionals" for the automobile industry and are not marked to indicate who manufactured them. A number of Chrysler, DeSoto, Dodge, and Plymouth vehicles were produced during the mid-thirties as promotionals and are highly prized as collectibles.

A few rubber vehicles were produced as very inexpensive toys, perhaps sold in sets, and can take the form of either a solid rubber or hollow vehicle. These toys often had the wheels molded in, so they could not turn. Some of these solid rubber toys are two-dimensional and are referred to as "flat" toys. Although they were originally sold as cheap toys, they are actively sought by collectors and constitute a small but important segment of the field.

DAVE LEOPARD is a retired Air Force Colonel, now employed by the State of South Carolina Budget and Control Board, Division of Human Resource Management.

Dave is a collector of small, American made toy cars and trucks and is an authority on rubber toys. He currently writes the "Little Wheels" column monthly for "U.S. Toy Collector Magazine" and has written his own book on rubber toy vehicles.

A.C. WILLIAMS (*see Williams, A.C.*)

ACME

Acme seems to have produced only two toy vehicles, both in clockwork; a 1903 curved-dash Oldsmobile roadster and a delivery truck with a pressed-steel canopied roof. In 1905 Jacob Lauth, the owner of the Chicago firm, turned to production of the real thing, under the name Lauth-Juergens Co.

	C6	C8	C10
Acme Curved Dash Olds, clockwork, circa 1905, 11" long	650	1000	1600

ACME Curved Dash Olds, 11" long. Courtesy Wilkinson Collection, Detroit Antique Toy Museum.

ACME

Many Acme vehicles are exactly like Thomas Toys. The reason is that New York's Ben Shapiro was a financial partner in Thomas Toys, and Thomas Toys' Islyn Thomas made up toys for Shapiro at his request, with the Acme imprint substituted for that of Thomas. Acme was located at 121 East 24th Street in Manhattan.

	C6	C8	C10
Acme No. 138 Airline Limousine, plastic, 4" long	5.00	7.50	10.00
"Aerocar PT 560 Made in U.S.A. Plas-Tex", 7-1/2", plastic	30	45	60

ALL AMERICAN TOY COMPANY

All American was founded by Clay Steinke in Salem, Oregon about 1948. It continued till 1955, with its location the Jorgenson Building on Ferry Street. At its peak it employed 42 people and in its existence sold a total of 26,000 toys. Their most popular toy was the Timber Toter, despite its formidable 1950 price of twenty dollars. Bill Hellie purchased the defunct company; molds, dies, parts. All American now sells parts and is producing new limited editions (see Leading Collectors and Dealers)

	C6	C8	C10
All American C-5 Cattle Liner, 38" long	300	450	600

A page from an ALL AMERICAN TOY COMPANY catalog.

	C6	C8	C10
All American CL-8 Cargo Liner, 38" long	375	525	750
All American D-3 Dyna-Dump, 20" long	305	458	610
All American HD-6 Play-Loader, 11" long	No Price Found		
All American Play-Dozer, 9" long	No Price Found		
All American HH-9 Heavy Hauler, 38" long	250	375	500
All American L-2 Timber Toter, with logs, 38" extended length	285	425	570
All American LJ-4 Timber Toter, Jr., with lumber, 20" long	212	318	425
All American MS Midget Skagit, battery-powered, 18" long	300	450	600
All American S-1 Scoop-a-Veyor, 16" long	237	355	475
All-Nu "Field Kitchen", slush lead, "Made In USA", approx 2-1/2" long	No Price Found		
All-Nu Searchlight, "Made In USA", slush lead, approx. 2-3/4" long	No Price Found		
All-Nu Sound Detector, "Made In USA", slush lead, approx. 2-3/4" long	No Price Found		
All-Nu Tank "USA", "Made In USA", slush lead, 3" long	No Price Found		

	C6	C8	C10
American Metal Toys			
Tank, throwing flame, flame touching hull	40	60	80
Tank, throwing flame, flame not touching hull	45	67	90
Tank, throwing flame, "No.25"	60	90	120
Tank, "22" on side	50	75	100
American National Army Truck, Mack "Giant", 26-1/2" long	800	1400	2000

	C6	C8	C10
American National "Juvenile Auto" dump truck pedal car, red and yellow tin, 57" long	2000	3500	5000
American National Packard Coupe, 1920s, steerable front wheels 30" long	900	1600	2200
American National Velie, child's pedal car, circa 1918	1000	1400	2000
Animate Toy "Baby Tractor", friction, "patented June 20, 1916"	100	150	200

ALL-NU Searchlight, "Field Kitchen", Tank, Sound Detector. (Head of soldier missing on Field Kitchen.) Photo by Bill Kaufman. Courtesy Evelyn Besser.

ANIMATE TOY "Baby Tractor", circa 1916. Courtesy Good Old Days Store. Photo by Bill Kaufman.

ARCADE MANUFACTURING COMPANY
A Brief History
by C.B.C. Lee
(based on information from Dave Davison)

In 1869 a foundry in Freeport, IL. was organized as a two-man partnership under the name of Novelty Iron and Brass Foundry, but was dissolved in 1885, when a new, larger factory was incorporated under the name of Arcade Manufacturing Co.. It made industrial castings and household items, but no toys. After a disastrous fire in 1892 and management changes in 1893, toys began to appear in its catalogue, and by the early 1900's the line had become so extensive that a 50-page catalogue was issued showing a large line of notions and novelties, small stoves, banks and a few trains, including a unique pile-driver. But it was not until an enterprising young lawyer married the daughter of one of the officers and joined the firm in 1919 that the firm rapidly became one of the major makers of cast iron toys. Struck by the large numbers of Yellow Cabs in the streets of Chicago (my reference doesn't say he was hit or injured by them), the young man approached the Yellow Cab Company with a novel proposition: in return for the sole right to make toy replicas of the cab, the Yellow Cab Company would have the exclusive right to use the toy in its advertising. Success was instantaneous.

Arcade went on to duplicate this pattern with miniature Buicks, Chevrolets, Ford cars, McCormack-Deering and Harvester farm equipment, and several makes of trucks and buses. Arcade's slogan "They look real" was well justified by its products. In the booming 1920s the company's sales swelled so much that a new and larger plant was built in 1927. Two years later, the stock market crash heralded the great depression, and hard times hit the small car business just as it did the large ones. Cheap competition and dwindling demand for toys costing more than a dime had brought the company to the brink of bankruptcy by 1933. But, once again, the enterprising management gave the firm new life with an exclusive arrangement to provide souvenir replicas of the fairground buses made by G.M.C. for the Chicago Century of Progress. The depression caused a cheapening of quality, but World War II gave the firm business in military material. After the war, the company returned to making industrial and household hardware and a few toys, but cheaper toys of die-cast zamac, plastic, rubber and lithographed tin eclipsed the costlier cast iron toys. In 1946 the firm was sold to

Rockwell Manufacturing Co. of Pittsburgh. Death and retirement soon finished the change of the old firm, and it followed its guiding directors into oblivion when Rockwell moved to Alabama.

Though the source is gone, the toys live on in collections across the land. Arcade is a prestigious name in cast iron automotive toys exceeded by none and approached by very few of its old competitors. No serious collection of cast iron toy cars, trucks, buses, or farm and construction equipment can pretend to be representative without its inclusion.

(The year noted is the year the toy was introduced)

ARCADE AR4. Courtesy Dick & Nancy Dice.

ARCADE AR10. Courtesy Mapes Auctioneers & Appraisers.

	C6	C8	C10
(AR1)A.C.F.Bus, 1927, 11-1/2" long.....	1500	2800	4000
(AR2)Allis-Chalmers Tractor and Trailer, 1936 , No.2650, total length 13" long............................	230	345	460
(AR3)Allis-Chalmers Tractor and Dump Trailer, 1937, No.2657, 12-3/4" long with trailer.....................	230	345	460
(AR3A)Allis-Chalmers Tractor and Dump Trailer, 1937, No 2660, 8-1/4" long..	110	165	220
(AR4)Allis-Chalmers Tractor Trailer, 1937, No 2650, 13" long w/trailer......	94	142	188
(AR5)Allis-Chalmers "WC" Tractor, 1941, 7-3/4" long..................................	250	400	540
(AR6)Ambulance, 1932, No.187, 7-3/4" long..	650	1100	1500
(AR7)Ambulance, 1932, No.188, 6" long.	375	562	750
(AR8)Ambulance, 1936, (white-painted version of No. 2620X Chevrolet Panel Delivery Truck), 4" long....................	340	510	680
(AR9)Anthony Dump Truck, 1927, 8-1/8" long..	1200	2000	3000
(AR10)Austin Autocrat Road Roller, 1928, No. 291, 7" long......................	312	468	625
(AR11)Austin Delivery Truck, 1932 No. 173, 3-3/4" long...........................	50	75	100
(AR12)Austin Racer, 1932, No. 175X, 3-3/4" long..	47	70	95
(AR13)Austin Roadster, 1932, No. 174, 3-3/4" long..	137	205	275
(AR14)Austin "Roll-A-Plane", 8" long..	900	1400	2000
(AR15)Austin Stake Truck, 1932, No.176X, 3-3/4" long.......................	150	225	300

	C6	C8	C10
(AR16)Austin Wrecker, 1932, No. 177X, 3-3/4" long........................	150	225	300
(AR17)Avery Tractor, 1923, stack, no hood, 4-1/2" long................	30	45	60
(AR18)Avery Tractor, 1926, has hood, no stack, 4-1/2" long...........................	125	188	250
(AR19)Borden's Milk Bottle Truck, 1936, No. 2640X, 6-1/4" long...........	1000	1500	2500
(AR20)Brinks Express Truck, 1932, 11-3/4" long, auctioned in excellent, 1994, for $20,000			
(AR21)Buick Coupe, 1927,8-1/2" long....	2200	3700	6000
(AR22)Buick Sedan, 1927, 8-1/2" long....	2200	3700	6000
(AR23)Bus, Double-Decker, 1929, No. 316X, 8-1/2" long.......................	500	750	1000
(AR24)Bus, Double-Decker, 1936, No.317, "Chicago Motor Coach" stamp, 8-1/4" long..............................	450	675	900
(AR25)Car Carrier, 1931, No.238, cargo has four 25¢ cars or three 50¢ cars, 24-1/2" long..............	1700	2700	3900

ARCADE AR17.
Photo by
Orville C. Britton.

	C6	C8	C10

(AR26)Car Carrier, 1932, No.296, carries either 2 No.114 Ford sedans and one 113X Ford Coupe, or one No.213 Ford Stake Truck and one each of the others, 24-1/2" long......... 1300 2200 3300

(AR27)Car Transport, 1937, No.3107, came with 2 No.1501 sedans, No.1502 stake truck and No.1503 wrecker, 18-1/2" long.......................... 1000 1600 2300

(AR28)Car Transport, 1937, No. 2977, holds 2 sedans, 2 trucks, 11-1/2" long.................................... 375 525 750

ARCADE AR21. Courtesy Phillips New York.

(AR29)Carry Car Truck and Trailer Set, 1934, No.2970, carries three Austins 14-1/4" long.................................. 650 1000 1500

(AR30)Caterpillar Tractor, 1930, No.271, 7-1/2" long........................... 550 900 1300

(AR31)Caterpillar Tractor, 1931, No.269X, 6-7/8" long....................... 600 950 1400

(AR31A)Caterpillar Tractor, 1931, No.268X 5-5/8" long...................... 500 800 1200

(AR32)Caterpillar Tractor, 1931, No.267X, 3-7/8" long........................ 262 393 525

ARACADE AR23. Courtesy Phillips New York.

(AR33)Caterpillar Tractor, 1931, No.266X, 3" long............................. 50 75 100

(AR34)Caterpillar Tractor, 1936, No.270Y, later 2700Y, 7-3/4"long........ 750 1100 170

(AR35)Century of Progress Bus, 1933, No. 3200, later No. 3250 (1934), 14-1/2" long................................. 315 472 630

(AR36)Century of Progress Bus, 1933, No. 3210, 12" long............................. 232 198 465

(AR37)Century of Progress Bus, 1933, No. 3220, 10-1/2" long...................... 250 375 500

(AR38)Century of Progress Bus, 1933, No. 3230, 7-5/8" long........................ 155 232 310

(AR38A)Century of Progress Bus,1933, won't pivot or detach, approx. 5-1/2" long....................................... 187 280 375

	C6	C8	C10

(AR38B)Century of Progress Yellow Cab, 6-1/2" long................................. 1200 2000 3000

(AR39)Checker Cab, 1923, paint variation of No.1 Yellow Cab, 9" long...2500 4200 6250

(AR40)Checker Cab, 1932, No. 157, (came with and without "Checker" on visor), 9-1/4" long......................... 5000 8000 12000'

(AR41)Chevrolet Coupe, 1929, No.121X, 8-1/4" long........................1200 2100 2725

(AR42)Chevrolet Coupe, 1934,rumble seat, No.1150X, 4-3/8" long.............. 155 232 310

(AR43)Chevrolet Panel Delivery Truck, 1936, No.2620X, 4" long....... 125 188 250

(AR44)Chevrolet Sedan, 1929, No.122X, 8-1/4" long........................1000 1600 2200

ARCADE AR37. Courtesy Mapes Auctioneers & Appraisers.

ARCADE AR22. Courtesy James S. Maxwell/Virginia Caputo. Photo by Virginia Captuo.

ARCADE AR41. Courtesy James S. Maxwell/Virginia Caputo. Photo by Virginia Caputo.

ARCADE Buicks and Chevrolets: on top are Chevy 1924 coupe and 1928 sedan and coupe. The latter were later made with double-striping around the waistline, rarer and more valuable. Bottom row: the famous Arcade Buicks, Sedan and 4-passenger coupe. Photo by C.B.C. Lee.

ARCADE made other brands of cars and trucks: Top, 1922 Dodge coupe: 1931 Reo Royal coupe 9-1/4"; Mack high-lift coal truck, one of a very large range of various trucks; Bottom: Yellow panel truck; White panel delivery; International-Harvester panel truck; each of these vans was issued in various private liveries, the best know being the I-H Hathaway Bakery, which was done in versions using either decal transfers or colored rubber stamping. Photo by C.B.C. Lee.

	C6	C8	C10
(AR45)Chevrolet Sedan, 1934, No.1170X, 4-1/4" long	50	75	100
(AR46)Chevrolet Stake Truck, 1925, 9" long	1000	1500	2100
(AR47)Chevrolet Stake Truck, 1936, No.2610, 4-1/4" long	No Price Found		
(AR48)Chevrolet Superior Roadster, 1925, 7" long	600	900	1225
(AR49)Chevrolet Superior Sedan, 1925, 7" long	No Price Found		
(AR50)Chevrolet Superior Touring Car, 1925, 7" long	700	1100	1600
(AR51)Chevrolet Utility Coupe, 1925, 7" long	325	488	650
(AR52)Chevrolet Wrecker Truck, 1936, No.2630X, 4-1/4" long	150	225	300
(AR53)"Chief" Fire Chief Coupe, 1934, No.1230, 6-3/4" long	1500	2500	3400
(AR54)"Chief" Fire Chief Coupe, 1934, No.1240, 5" long	500	800	1100
(AR55)"Coast To Coast GMC" Transcontinental Bus, 1937, No.4378X, 9" long	330	495	660
(AR56)Corn Harvester, 1939, No.702, 6 1/2" long	200	300	400
(AR57)Corn Harvester, 1939, No.4180, 5" long	150	225	300
(AR58)Corn Planter, 1939, 4-1/2" long	62	93	125
(AR59)Coupe, "1922" on spare tire, 9" long	1500	2500	4000
(AR60)Coupe, like above, no 1922 date on spare	800	1400	2100
(AR61)Coupe, 1932, No.109, no Arcade markings, rumble seat opens. 6" long	187	280	375
(AR62)Deluxe Sedan, 1941, No.1590X, same as Yellow Cab No.1590Y,			

	C6	C8	C10
but with top lights and sun roof ground off, 8-1/2" long	350	525	700
(AR63)DeSoto Sedan, 1936, No.1460X, 4" long	170	255	340
AR64)Double Decker Bus, 1939, No. 3180, 8" long	350	525	700
(AR65)Dump Truck, 1936, No.2320, 4-1/2" long	75	112	150
(AR66)Dump Truck, 1941, No. 3910X, 7" long	550	950	1300
(AR67)Dump Truck Trailer, 1931, No.234, 12-7/8" long	700	1150	1700
(AR68)Dump Wagon, 1923, driver, no cab, 7" long	425	638	850
(AR69)Express Truck, 1929, No.207X, 8" long	No Price Found		
(AR70)Express Truck, 1929, No.209X, 6" long	No Price Found		
(AR71)Express Truck, 1929, No.214X, 5" long	No Price Found		
(AR72)Fageol Bus, 1925, 12" long	375	525	750

ARCADE AR46. Courtesy Lloyd W. Ralston Auctions.

ARCADE AR 68. Driver in photo may be wrong. Courtesy Sotheby's New York.

ARCADE AR64. Courtesy Ed Hyers Antique Toys.

ARCADE AR 72. Courtesy Good Old Days Store. Photo by Bill Kaufman.

	C6	C8	C10
(AR73)Fageol Bus, 12-1/2" long	430	645	860
(AR74)Fageol Bus, 8" long	300	450	600
(AR74A)Fageol Bus, 5" long	162	243	325
(AR75)Farm Mower, 1939, No.4210X, 4" long	60	90	120
(AR76)Farmall "A" Tractor, 1941, No.7050, 7-1/2" long	400	600	800
(AR77)Farmall "M" Tractor, 1941, No.7070, 7 1/4" long	300	450	600
(AR78)Farmall Tractor, 1929, No.279, 6" long	350	525	700
(AR78A)Fire Chief Car, 1941, 5-5/8" long	160	240	320
(AR79)Fire Engine, 1923, pumper, 7-1/2" long	250	375	500
(AR80)Fire Engine, 1936, No.1740, pumper, 9" long	200	300	400
(AR81)Fire Engine, 1936, No.1810, 6-1/4" long	No Price Found		
(AR82)Fire Engine, 1936, No.2340, 4-1/2" long	90	135	180
(AR83)Fire Engine, 1941, No.6990, 13-1/2" long	900	1350	1800
(AR84)Fire Ladder Truck, 1936, No.1820, 7" long	200	300	400
(AR85)Fire Trailer Truck, 1934, No.1940, ladder truck,16-1/4" long	575	862	1150

	C6	C8	C10
(AR86)Ford Carry Car Truck and Trailer, 1934, No.2400	No Price Found		
(AR87)Ford Coupe, 1923, 6" long	200	300	400
(AR88)Ford Coupe, 1924, 6-1/2" long	300	450	600
(AR89)Ford Coupe, 1934, No.1610X, rumble seat opens, 6-3/4" long	175	262	350
(AR90)Ford Coupe, 1930s, No.1190X, 4-3/4" long	100	150	200
(AR91)Ford Dump Truck, 1929, No.219X, 7-1/2" long	275	412	550
(AR92)Ford Express Truck, 1929, No.210X, 8-1/4" long	270	405	540
(AR93)Ford Fordor Sedan, 1924, removable chauffeur, 6-1/2" long	340	510	680
(AR94)Ford Sedan, 1923, 6-1/2" long	150	225	300
(AR95)Ford Sedan, 1934, No.1620X, 6-7/8" long	No Price Found		
(AR96)Ford Sedan, 1934, "Century of Progress", 6-7/8" long	1000	1700	2400
(AR97)Ford Sedan, 1930s, No.1200 4 3/4" long	150	225	300
(AR97A)Ford Sedan, 1934, "Century of Progress", 4-3/4" long	No Price Found		
(AR98)Ford Sedan with Trailer, 1937, No.1970, 12" long (trailer 5-1/2" long)	650	1000	1500
(AR99)Ford Stake Truck, 1925, 8-3/4" long	1000	1500	2200

ARCADE AR 73. Courtesy Lloyd W. Ralston Auctions.

ARCADE AR 85. Courtesy Mapes Auctioneers & Appraisers.

	C6	C8	C10
(AR100)Ford Stake Truck, 1927, 9" long	650	1000	1500
(AR101)Ford Stake Truck, 1934, No.2010X, 4-3/4" long	No Price Found		
(AR102)Ford Touring Car, 1923, 6-1/2" long	225	338	450
(AR103)Ford Touring Car Bank, 1923, 6-1/2" long	1100	1800	2700
(AR104)Ford Tractor and Plow, 1941, No.7220, tractor 6-1/2" long, overall length 8-3/4"	225	338	450
(AR105)Ford Truck, 1923, cab,C-cab, 8-1/2" long	400	600	800
(AR106)Ford Wrecker, 1929, No.215 8-1/4" length to end of hoist	850	1400	1850
(AR107)Ford Wrecker, 1930, No.218, 4-1/2" long	125	188	250
(AR108)Fordson Tractor, 1923, 5-3/8" long	200	300	400
(AR109)Fordson Tractor, 1928, No. 274, 4-3/4" long	112	168	225
(AR110)Fordson Tractor, 1928, No.273, 3-7/8" long	50	75	100
(AR111)Fordson Tractor, 1934, rubber shells, No.2730X, 3-1/2" long	75	112	150
(AR112)Greyhound Cruiser Coach Bus, 1941,No. 4400, 9-1/8" long	238	357	475
(AR113)"Greyhound Lines" Bus, 1937, No. 3850 SP, 7-3/4" long	306	460	612
(AR114)"Greyhound Lines Great Lakes Exposition", 1936, No. 437,11" long	437	655	875

	C6	C8	C10
(AR115)"Greyhound Lines Great Lakes Exposition", 1936, No.436,6-3/4" long.	450	675	900
(AR116)Greyhound Super Coach, 1937, No.4380, 9" long	320	480	640
(AR117)"Ice" Truck, circa 1941, No.1933, 6-3/4" long	270	355	540
(AR118)International Delivery Truck, 1932, No.226, 9-3/4" long	1000	1500	2000
(AR119)International Delivery Truck, 1936, No.3020, 9-1/2" long	1700	2600	3950
(AR120)International Dump Truck, 1931, No.236-0, 10-3/4" long	100	1750	2360
(AR121)International Dump Truck, 1936, No.3030, 10-1/2" long	650	1100	1500
(AR122)International Dump Truck, 1937, No.3710, 9-1/2" long	950	1500	2050
(AR123)International Dump Truck, 1940, No.1670, chassis and dump box are steel, 11-5/8" long	300	450	600
(AR 124)International Dump Truck, 1941, No.7100, 11-1/8" long	600	900	1200
(AR125)International Harvester Company Public Utility Truck, 1932, No.197, 11-1/4" long	No Price Found		
(AR126)International Pickup Truck, 1941, No.7000, 9-1/2" long	500	775	1080
(AR127)International Stake Truck, 1931, No.237-0, 12" long	1000	1700	2400
(AR128)International Stake Truck, 1936, No. 3090, 12" long	750	1200	1700
(AR129)International Stake Truck, 1937, No.2600, 9-1/2" long	650	1000	1500
(AR130)International Stake Truck, 1941, No.7090, 11-1/2" long	1100	1700	2500

ARCADE. Top to Bottom: AR96, AR97A. Photo by John M. Ianuzzi.

	C6	C8	C10
(AR131)International Wrecker, 1940, No.1650, wrecker crane body and crane are steel, 13" long	410	615	820
(AR132)Ladder Truck, 1936, No.1700 length with ladders 12-1/2" long	325	488	650
(AR133)Ladder Truck, 1936, No.2350, 4-3/4" long	75	112	150
(AR134)"Mack" Bus, 1929, No.318, 13-1/4" long, auctioned 1994, excellent, for $15,000			
(AR135)Mack Cement Mixer, 1931, 6-11/16" long, drum revolves		No Price Found	
(AR136)Mack Chemical Truck, 1928, fire engine No.245R, has ladders, 15" long	2000	3500	5500
(AR137)Mack Chemical Truck, 1929, fire ladder truck, 15" long	400	600	800
(AR138)Mack Chemical Truck, 1929, fire engine with ladders, 10" long	500	800	1100
(AR139)Mack Dump Truck, 1925, 12" long	800	1300	1750
(AR140)Mack Dump Truck, 1929, No. 248X, 8-1/2" long	500	800	1175
(AR141)Mack High Dump Truck, 1931, No. 244X, 10" long	1100	1700	2500
(AR142)Mack High Dump Truck, 1931, No. 259X, 8-1/2" long	800	1300	1800

ARCADE AR96. Courtesy Chic Gast.

ARCADE AR94. Courtesy Ed Hyers Antique Toys.

	C6	C8	C10
(AR143)Mack Fire Apparatus Truck, 1929, No.242, ladder truck, 21" long	1300	2000	2900
(AR144)Mack Hoist Truck, 1932, No.198, body 8" long	900	1500	2130
(AR145)Mack Ice Truck, 1930, No.257, 7" long	375	562	750
(AR146)Mack Ice Truck, 1931, No. 226, 8-1/2" long	450	675	900
(AR147)Mack Ice Truck, 1932, No.257, with driver, glass "ice" and tongs. 10 3/4" long	2000	3200	4450
(AR148)Mack Side Dump Truck, 1932, No.1960, 9" long	1200	2000	2800

ARCADE AR110. Coutesy Mapes Auctioneers & Appraisers.

	C6	C8	C10
(AR149)Mack Stake Truck, 1929, No. 246X, 12" long		No Price Found	
(AR150)Mack Stake Truck, 1929, No.253, 8-3/4" long	800	1400	2000
(AR151)Mack Tank Truck, 1925, 13-1/4" long	1000	1600	2200
(AR152)Mack Tank Truck, 1925, "American Gasoline", 13-1/4" long	1200	1850	2500
(AR153)Mack Tank Truck, 1925, "Lubrite", 13-1/4" long	1200	2000	3000
(AR154)Mack Tank Truck, 1930, No.241,sheet metal tank, "Gasoline" "Mack", 13" long	1500	2500	3600
(AR155)Mack Wrecker, 1930 No.255, 12-1/2" long	1800	2800	4400
(AR156)McCormick-Deering Farmall Tractor, 1937, 6-1/4" long	300	450	600
(AR157)McCormick-Deering Thresher, 1927,12" long	550	900	1250
(AR158)McCormick-Deering Thresher, 1930, 9-1/2" long	320	480	640

ARCADE AR143. Courtesy Christie's East

	C6	C8	C10
(AR159)McCormick-Deering Tractor, 1925, 7-1/4" long	350	525	700
(AR160)Milk Truck, 1931, No.256, box is wood, 13-5/8" long	No Price Found		
(AR161)Model A Coupe, 1928, No. 116X, rumble seat, 5" long	200	300	400
(AR162)Model A Coupe, 1928, No.106,rumble seat,6-3/4" long	500	750	1000
(AR163)Model A Coupe, 1928, No.113X, 4-1/8" long	125	188	250
(AR164)Model A Fordor, 1928, No. 207, 6-3/4" long	375	525	750
(AR165)Model A Tudor, 1928, No.108, 6-3/4" long	425	638	850
(AR166)Model T Stake Truck, 1927, 9" long	600	1000	1450
(AR167)Model T Stake Truck, 1927, 5-3/4" long	130	195	260
(AR168)Model T Wrecker, 1927, 11" long	600	950	1400
(AR168A)"Mullins Red Cap"auto trailer	105	158	210
(AR169)Nash Wrecker, 1936,4-1/2" long	250	375	500
(AR170) National Trailways Bus,1937, No.3870, 9-1/4" long	550	850	1200
(AR171)New York World's Fair Bus, 1939,No.3780, 10-1/2" long	540	800	1180
(AR172)New York World's Fair Bus, 1939, No.3770, 8-1/2" long	300	450	600
(AR173)New York World's Fair Bus, 1939, No. 3750, 7" long	175	262	350
(AR174)New York World's Fair Tractor-Train, 1939, No.7270, tractor and one car, tractor 3-1/4" long, car 4-1/4" long.	290	435	580
(AR175)New York World's Fair Tractor-Train,1939, No.7290, same as above with three cars	450	675	900
(AR176)Oliver Plow, 1923, 6-1/2" long	250	375	500
(AR177)Oliver Plow, 1941, No.4230X, 6-1/4" long	138	208	275
(AR178)Oliver Superior Spreader, No.7140, 1941, 10-1/4" long	No Price Found		
(AR179)Oliver Tractor, 1937, No.356, 7-1/2" long	212	318	425

	C6	C8	C10
(AR180)Oliver Tractor, 1941, No.3560, 7-1/2" long	75	112	150
(AR181)"Plymouth" Coupe, 1934, No.1340X, 4-1/2" long	100	150	200
(AR182)"Plymouth" Sedan, 1934, No.1330X, 4-3/4" long	450	675	900
(AR183)"Plymouth" Stake Truck, 1934, No.1840X, 4-3/4" long	No Price Found		
(AR184)"Plymouth" Wrecker, 1934, No. 1830X, 4-3/4" long	125	188	250
(AR185)Pontiac Sedan, 1934, No.1350X, 4-1/4" long	175	262	350
(AR186)Pontiac Sedan, 1935,6-1/2" long.	350	525	700
(AR187)Pontiac Stake Truck, 1935, No.2390X, 6-1/4" long	300	450	600
(AR188)Pontiac Stake Truck, 1936, No.2780X, 4-1/4" long	No Price Found		
(AR189)Pontiac Wrecker, 1936, No.2000X, 4-1/4" long	125	188	250
(AR190)Racer, pre 1923, 7-3/4" long	400	600	800
(AR191)Racer, Bullet Racer, 1931, No.139X, 7-5/8" long	950	1550	2200
(AR192)Racer, 1931, No.138X, 6-3/4" long	150	225	300
(AR193)Racer, 1932, No.140X 10-1/2" long, plastic or celluloid windshield, auctioned in 1994 in excellent condition for $11,500.00			
(AR194)Racer, 1932, No.137X, 5-5/8" long	150	225	300
(AR195)Racer, 1937, No1440X, 8" long	No Price Found		

ARCADE AR151. Courtesy Mapes Auctioneers & Appraisers.

ARCADE AR153. Courtesy Sotheby's New York

ARCADE AR155. Courtesy James S. Maxwell/Virginia Caputo. Photo by Virginia Caputo.

	C6	C8	C10
(AR196)Racer, 1937, No.1457, 5-3/4" long	140	210	280
(AR197)Red Baby Dump Truck, 1923, No.2, 10-3/8" long	675	1012	1350
(AR198)Red Baby Truck, 1923, No.1, 10-3/4" long	1200	2200	2775
(AR199)Red Baby "Weaver" Wrecker, 1929, 12" long	700	1200	1800
(AR200)Reo Coupe, 1931, No.1247, 9-3/8" long	2500	4200	7500
(AR201)Reo Coupe, 1931, smaller size	1200	2000	3000
(AR202)Sand Loading Shovel, 1932, No.298 (later No.299)	1500	2800	3550
(AR203)Scraper, 1929, No.287, 8-1/4" long	42	63	85
(AR204)Sedan, 1937, No.1501X 4-3/4" long	100	150	200
(AR205)Sedan and Trailer, 1937, No.1497X, car 5 5/8" long, trailer 2-1/2" long	375	525	750
(AR206)Side Dump Trailer, 1932, No.290, fastens to trucks or tractors, 7" long	No Price Found		
(AR207)"Silver Arrow", 1934, 7-1/4" long	225	338	450
(AR208)Stake Trailer Truck, 1931 No.233, 11-5/16" long	700	1200	1700
(AR209)Stake Truck, 1929, No.208X, 6" long	200	300	400

	C6	C8	C10
(AR210)Stake Truck, 1929, No.213X, 5" long	125	188	250
(AR211)Stake Truck, 1932,No.208, no Arcade markings, 6" long	600	1000	1400
(AR212)Stake Truck, 1937, No.1502X, 4-1/4" long	200	300	400

ARCADE AR162. Courtesy Ed Hyers Antique Toys.

ARCADE AR161. Courtesy Ed Hyers Antique Toys.

ARCADE. Top, Left to Right: AR171,AR112 Second Row, Left to Right: AR116, AR37 Third Row, Left to Right: AR36,AR172 Bottom Row, Left to Right: AR173, AR38. Courtesy Sotheby's New York.

	C6	C8	C10
(AR213)Steam Shovel, 1932, No.292 Industrial Derrick, body 6" long........	750	1125	1500
(AR214)Tandem Disc Harrow, 1939, No.704, 6-3/4" long.............	60	90	120
(AR215)Tank, Army, 1937, No.400, 8" long.....................	500	825	1130
(AR216)Tank, Army, 1941, No.3960, shoots, 4" long.....................	82	123	165
(AR217)Texas Centennial Bus, 1936, 10-3/4" long (*Extremely Rare*)............	1000	1700	2300
(AR218)"Trac-Tractor", International Harvester, 1937, No.277,8-1/4" long....	800	1400	2000
(AR219)Trac Tractor, 1941,No.7120, 7-1/2" long......................	500	800	1200
(AR220) Unused			
(AR221) Unused			
(AR222)Tractor, 1941, No. 7200, 6-1/2" long................	No Price Found		
(AR223)Tractor, 1941, No.4060X, black rubber wheels,6 1/4" long........	No Price Found		
(AR224)Tractor, 1941, No.7341X, wood wheels, 6-1/4" long..................	No Price Found		
(AR225)Tractor, 1941, No.7321X, 4-1/4" long....................	No Price Found		
(AR226)Tractor, 1941, No.7260X, wooden wheels, 3-1/8" long.............	No Price Found		
(AR227)Tractor, 1941, No.7240X, rubber wheels, 3-1/8" long.................	No Price Found		
(AR228)Tractor and Dump Trailer, 1941, No.7300, 15-1/2" long.............	500	850	1200
(AR229)Trailer, Farm, 1929, No.286, 6-3/8" long.......................	40	60	80
(AR230)Trailer, Farm, 1929, No.288, 4-5/8" long.....................	35	52	70
(AR231)Trailer, Farm, 1929, No.289, 3-3/4" long....................	30	45	60
(AR232)Transport Trailer Truck, 1934, No.1800, 7-1/2" long..............	500	850	1200
(AR233)W&K Truck Trailer, 1923, 8-1/2" long.......................	No Price Found		
(AR234)Two-Wheeled Jack, 1932, No.216, 5-1/2" long.................	30	45	60
(AR235)White Bus, No. 319,1928, 13-1/4" long......................	1800	3000	4250
(AR236)White Delivery Truck, 1929, No.252X, 8-1/4" long........................	2000	3800	6000

(AR237)White Deliver Van, 1929, No.251, 13-1/2" long, auctioned 1994, excellent for $11,000 and $16,000.

	C6	C8	C10
(AR238)White Dump Truck, 1929, No.249, 11-1/2" long, auctioned 1994, excellent for $23,000.			

	C6	C8	C10
(AR239)White Dump Truck, 1931, No.258X, 13-1/2" long.....................	No Price Found		
(AR240)White Tank Truck, 1931, No.254X, "Gasoline",14-1/8" long....	1000	1500	2000
(AR241)Wrecker, 1929, No.217,1928, body 8" long......................	375	562	750
(AR242)Wrecker, 1932, No.225, no Arcade markings...........................	600	950	1350
(AR243)Wrecker, 1934, No.2020X, 7" long.....................	337	505	675
(AR244)Wrecker, 1937, No.1493X, 6-1/2" long.....................	150	225	300
(AR245)Wrecker, 1937, No.1503X, 4-3/4" long.....................	100	150	200
(AR246)Wrecker, 1941, No.3900X, 8-1/2" long.....................	85	128	170
(AR246A)Yellow Baby Dump Truck, 1923, 10-1/2" long.....................	700	1100	1700
(AR247)Yellow Baby Wrecker, 1929, 12" long	650	1100	1600
(AR248)Yellow Cab, 1922, No.1, 9-1/4" long.....................	600	900	1400
(AR249)Yellow Cab, 1923, No.2, 8" long.....................	800	1350	2000
(AR250)Yellow Cab, 1927, No.1, 9" long.....................	600	900	1400
(AR251)Yellow Cab, 1927, No.5, 8-1/2" long.....................	425	638	850

ARCADE AR197. Courtesy Phillips New York.

ARCADE AR198. Courtesy James S. Maxwell/Virginia Caputo. Photo by Virginia Caputo.

ARCADE AR208. Courtesy James S. Maxwell/Virgina Caputo. Photo by Virginia Caputo.

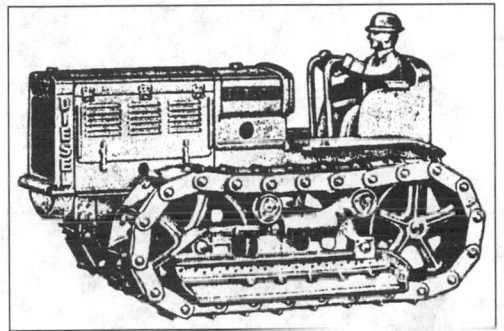

ARACDE AR218

ARCADE AR219. Courtesy Thomas G. Nefos, National Toy Connection

	C6	C8	C10
(AR258)Yellow Cab Bank, 1927..........	750	1125	1500
(AR259)Yellow Cab Panel Delivery Truck, 1925, 8-1/4" long,w/driver, auctioned 1994, near mint for $10,500			
(AR260)Yellow Coach Double-Decker Bus, 1925, 14" long............	1850	3400	5400
(AR261)Yellow Parlor Coach Bus, 1926, 13" long............	100	1600	2400
(AR262)Yellow Parlor Coach Bus, 1926, 9-1/2" long...............	600	925	1250
Argo FrictionCars, Taxi, Police car each, 3-1/2" long...........	15	22	30
Argo Friction Cars, Passenger car, Tank each, 3-1/2" long..............	5	8	10

	C6	C8	C10
(AR252)Yellow Cab, 1927, No.2 8" long.......................	600	900	1400
(AR253)Yellow Cab, 1927, No.3, 5-1/4" long...................	650	975	1300
(AR254)Yellow Cab, 1934, Ford Sedan, 6-7/8" long........	650	1000	1500
(AR255)Yellow Cab, 1936, No.1580Y, 8-1/4" long..........	1500	2500	3500
(AR256)Yellow Cab, 1941, No.1590Y, 8-1/2" long..........	500	800	1200
(AR257)Yellow Cab Bank, 1923, 8" long.......................	750	1300	1750

ARCADE AR249.
Courtesy Sotheby's New York.

ARCADE AR237. Courtesy James S. Maxwell/Virginia Caputo. Photo by Virginia Caputo.

ARCADE AR236. Courtesy James S. Maxwell/ Virginia Caputo. Photo by Virginia Caputo.

ARCADE AR259. Courtesy Phillips New York.

ARCADE AR250. Courtesy Wilkinson Collection, Detroit Antique Toy Museum.

ARCADE. "Yellow Cab", 9" long, c. 1928. Courtesy Mapes Auctioneers & Appraisers.

ARCADE AR259. Side-mounted tire, original tires missing. Courtesy James S. Maxwell/Virginia Caputo. Photo by Virginia Caputo.

AUBURN RUBBER

This company also manufactured rubber tires for other companies, including Wyandotte. The following list and its codings were compiled by David Leopard. Vehicles are broken down by types.

	C6	C8	C10
AA01 '36 Cord, four door coffin-nose sedan, 6" long	65	98	130
AA02 '37 Olds, 4 door sedan, 4-1/2" long	22	33	45
AA03 '38 Olds, 4 door sedan, 5-3/4" long	30	45	60
AA04 '40 Olds, 4 door sedan, open fenders, 6" long	27	41	55
AA05 '40 Olds, 4 door sedan, fender skits, 6" long	25	38	50
AA06 '48 Buick, 2 door sedanette, fastback, 7-1/4" long	40	60	80
AA07 '39 Buick, Y Job Experimental Roadster, 9-3/4" long	No Price Found		
AA08 '35 Ford Coupe, 4" long	27	41	55
AA09 '35 Ford 2 door slantback sedan, 4" long	27	41	55
AA10 '50 Cadillac, 4 door sedan, 7-1/4" long	40	60	80

	C6	C8	C10
AA11 '50 Cadillac, 4 door sedan 5-3/4" long	No Price Found		
AA12 '39 Plymouth, 2 door trunk back sedan, 4-1/4" long	22	33	45
AA13 '46 Lincoln convertible, 2 door, square headlights, 4-1/2" long	20	30	40
AA14 '46 Lincoln convertible, 2 door round headlights, 4-1/2" long	20	30	40
AA15 Late 40's Fururistic Sedan, fin down back, 5" long	20	30	40
AT01 '37 International Cabover Stake Truck, 5-3/8" long	22	33	45
AT01A '37 Same as above, "U.S. Army" decal, khaki	22	33	45
AT02 Same as AT01 with rounded bumper, minor variations	22	33	45

	C6	C8	C10
AT03 '37 International Cabover Stake Truck, 4-1/4" long	20	30	40
AT03A Same as above, khaki	20	30	40
AT04 Same as above with rounded bumper, minor variations	20	30	40
AT05 '37 International Cabover Stake Truck, 3-3/4" long	20	30	40
AT06 Same as above with rounded bumper, minor variations	20	30	40
AT07 '37 International Cabover Stake Truck, milk version, 4-1/4" long	No Price Found		
AT08 '37 International Cabover Stake Truck, ambulance version	No Price Found		
AT09 Cab-Forward Box Truck, smooth sides, futuristic, 5-1/2" long	22	33	45
AT10 Cabover Box Truck, smooth sides, futuristic, 4-1/8" long	20	30	40
AT11 '47 Chevy Cab Forward Box Truck, 5-3/4" long	22	33	45
AT12c. '50 Pickup Truck open fenders 4-1/2" long	20	30	40
AT13c. '50 Pickup Truck, fender skirts, 4-1/2" long	20	30	40

	C6	C8	C10
AT14 '38 GMC "Carry Car" Auto Transport, 11-1/2" long	42	63	85
AT15 '38 GMC Cab/Open Squared-off Trailer, 9" long	42	63	85
AT16 Updated Carry Car Transport, cab changed, trailer same 11-3/4" long	42	63	85
AT17 '35 Ford Stake Body Truck, 4-3/4" long	27	41	55
AE01 Ahrens-Fox Fire Engine, 5-1/2" long	75	112	150
AE02c. 40s Fire Engine, hose and ladders, 7-3/4" long	27	41	55
AE03c. 40s Pumper, Boiler, 7-3/4" long	27	41	55
AE04c. 40s Fire Engine, ladders, no hose, 7-3/4" long	27	41	55
AR01 Open Racer, V-6, high fin, 10-1/2" long	55	82	110
AR02 Open Racer, V-6, low fin, 10-1/2" long	40	60	80

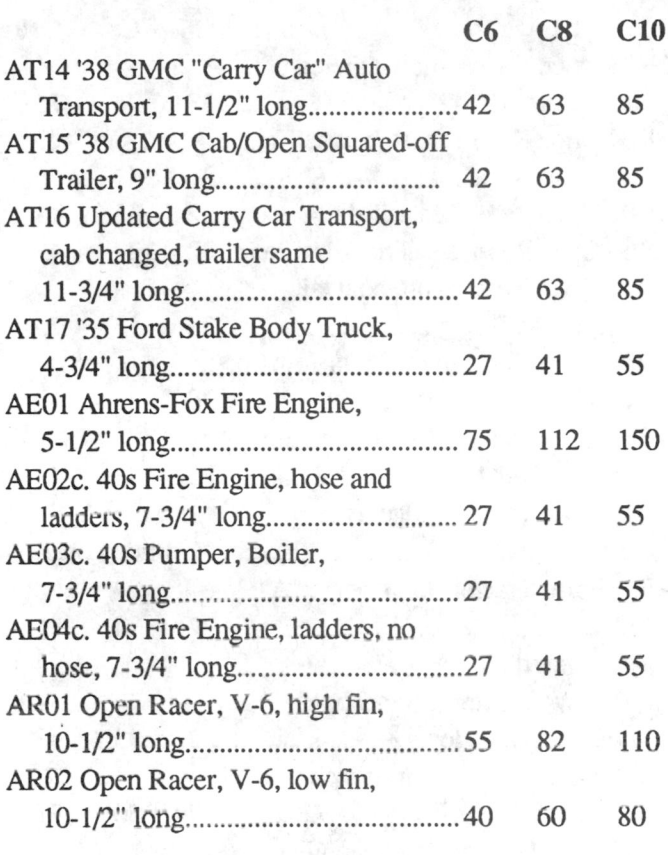

AUBURN AT01A. Photo by Ed Poole.

AUBURN AA03. Photo by Dave Leopard.

AUBURN, Left to Right: AA05, AA04. Photo by Dave Leopard.

AUBURN AA12. Photo by Dave Leopard.

AUBURN AA01. Photo by Max Heiss.

AUBURN AA06. Photo by Dave Leopard.

	C6	C8	C10
AR03 Open Racer, short, tapered tail, large tires, 10-1/2" long	37	56	75
AR04 Open Racer, short, boat tail 6-1/2" long	27	41	55
AR05 Open Racer, boat tail, 4-3/4" long	22	33	45
AR06 Open Racer, small fin,6-1/4" long	22	33	45
AR07 Open Racer short, boat tail, early, 6-1/2" long	35	52	70
AR08 Open Racer, no fenders, low fin, long back, 5-1/4" long	20	30	40
AR09 Open Racer, boat tail, no side pipes, 4-3/4" long	22	33	45
AR10 Open Racer, midget type, early, 5" long	No Price Found		
AF01 Farm Tractor, John Deere "A", 5" long	22	33	45
AF02 Unused			
AF03 Farm Tractor, Minneapolis-Moline "Z", 4" long	22	33	45
AF04 Farm Tractor, Minneapolis-Moline "R", early style, 7-1/2" long	37	56	75
AF05 Farm Tractor, Minneapolis-Moline "R", later style, 7-1/4" long	37	56	75
AF06 Farm Tractor, Oliver Row Crop "70", 8" long	37	56	75
AF07 Unused			
AF08 Farm Tractor, McCormick-Deering IH Farmall "M", 4" long	22	33	45
AF09 Farm Tractor, Graham-Bradley, 4-1/2" long	25	38	50

AUBURN. Left to Right: AA13, AA14. Photo by Dave Leopard.

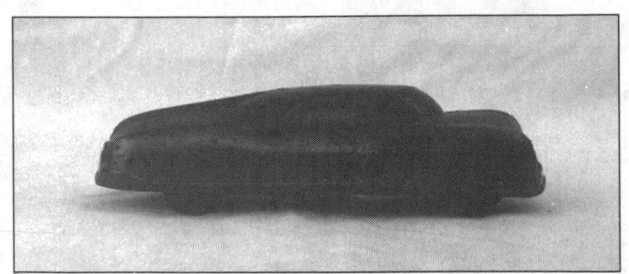

AUBURN AA15. Photo by Dave Leopard.

	C6	C8	C10
101 Trailer, 2 wheel, Graham-Bradley, 5-3/4" long	22	33	45
A102 Trailer, 4 wheel, Graham-Bradley, 4-3/4" long	22	33	45
A103 Harvester, open top, 5-1/2" long	27	41	55
A104 Manure Spreader, David Bradley, 4-3/4" long	20	30	40
A105 Reliable Front-Lift Seeder,5" long	22	33	45
A106 Plow Seeder, 3-1/2" long	No Price Found		
A107 Side-Cutter Sickle Bar Mower, David Bradley, 3-3/4" long	20	30	40
A108 Two Furrow Plow, David Bradley, 4-3/4" long	20	30	40
A109 Cultipacker (Disc Harrows?), David Bradley, 4-3/8" long	22	33	45
A110 Harrow, 4-1/2" long	20	30	40
A111 Disc Harrows, 4-1/2" long	22	33	45
A112 Unused			
AM01 Tank, Marmon-Harrington, 4-1/2" Long	22	33	45
AM02 Tank, Marmon-Harrington, 3-1/4" long	15	22	30
AM03 Tractor and Cannon, olive green, 11-1/2" long	No Price Found		
"Austin" Car, cast iron, early1930s	112	168	225
"Austin " Racer, cast iron,4" long	67	100	135
"Austin" Stakebody, 1920s, cast iron, 3-3/4" long	100	150	200
Auto Express 546, with drivers and barrels, 6" long	250	375	500
Auto Express 546, cast iron, 7" long	125	187	250
Auto, Raked Cab, cast iron, early 1930s, approx. 4" long	70	105	140
Auto Trailer, carries three cars, all two-door,circa 1932,12-1/2" long	80	120	160
Auto Trailer, 1920s, with coupe, two-door sedan, and four-door sedan on trailer, 22" long	240	360	480
Auto with House Trailer, late 1930s, cast iron, 13-1/2" long	400	600	800

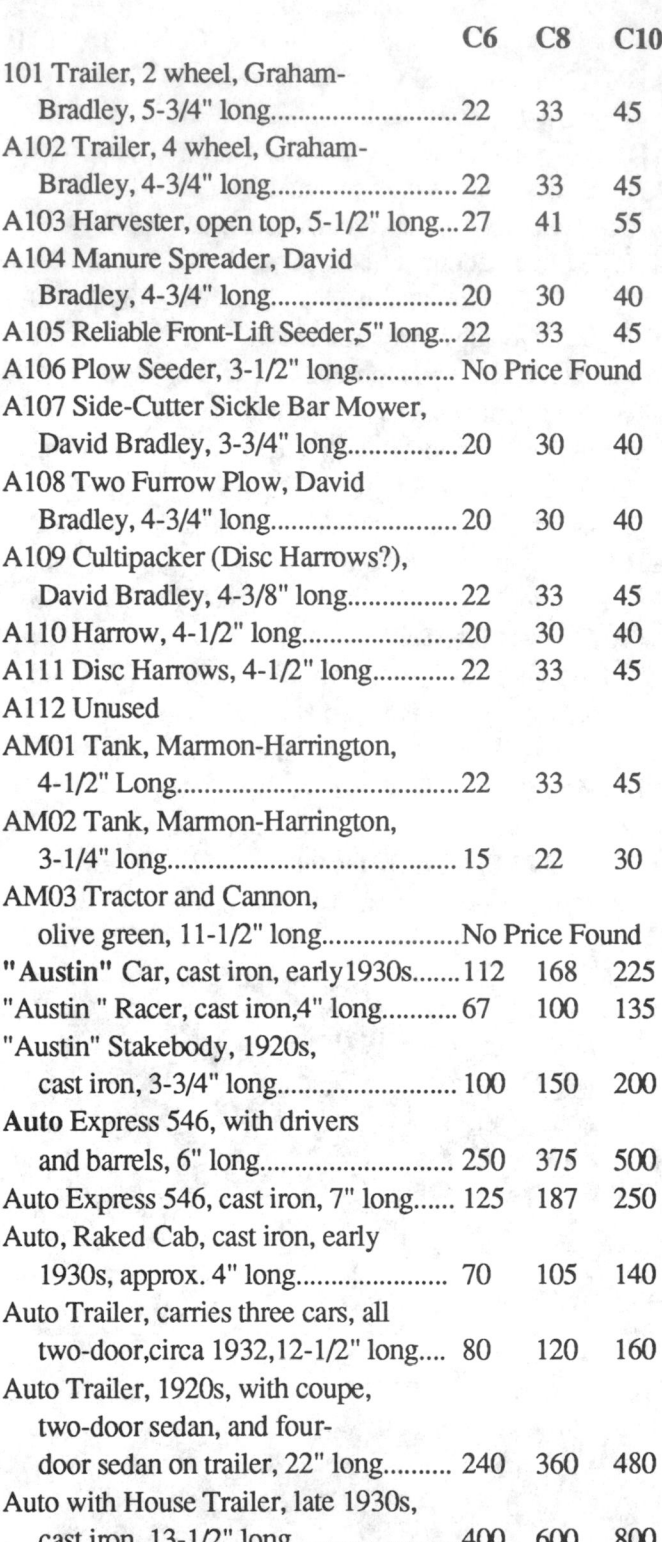

AUBURN AT09. Photo by Dave Leopard.

AUBURN AT11. Photo by Dave Leopard.

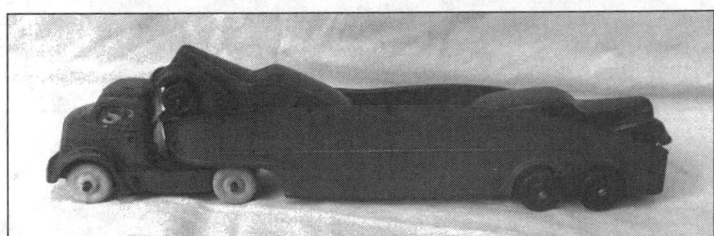

AUBURN AT14. Photo by Dave Leopard.

AUBURN AE02. Photo by Dave Leopard.

AUBURN AR04. Photo by Dave Leopard.

AUBURN AR03. Photo by Dave Leopard.

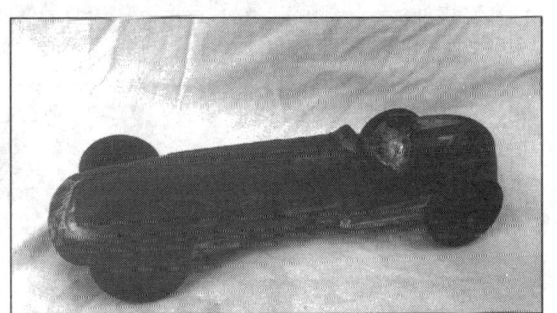

AUBURN AF05. Photo by Dave Leopard.

BANNER

Banner was begun by Emanuel M. Pressner (8/4/99-1/1/74) and Bernard Schiller in 1945 or 1946 at 150 Bruckner Blvd. in the Bronx, New York. Pressner had been a toy importer before the war. When the war cut off imports, he went to work for Columbia Protektosite, which, among other things, cast Beton's plastic toy soldiers. (Though his family has no recollection of this, in 1942 Pressner was noted in a toy trade magazine as being secretary of Beton.) Schiller was eventually edged out. Banner moved to 80 Beckwith Avenue in Paterson, New Jersey in 1950, where it remained. The firm's original toys seem to have been small plastic cars and trucks, with the leading items for years being tea sets and metalicized plastic forks, knives

and spoons. Other items included plastic sand molds. The stamped steel Banner used was made up of "off-falls" - the blanks formed when holes were cut in steel to allow for car windows and television tubes.

The company, which at its peak periods had as many as 200 employees, went into Chapter 11 bankruptcy in 1965, came out of it, and then was sold in 1967 to Tal-Cap, a toy conglomerate in Minnesota. During its heyday, Banner produced at least tens of thousands of toys a week, according to former vice-president Joseph Stern. Banner got its name, according to Stern, because Pressner (his father-in-law) wanted a company with a name "high up in the alphabet".

	C6	C8	C10
Banner American Express Truck, tin, 11" long	150	225	300
Banner American Express Van	50	75	100
Banner Dodge, 1950, plastic, 4"	5	8	10
Banner Dump Truck, Ford, plastic	17	26	35
Banner Garbage Truck, Ford, plastic,			

	C6	C8	C10
1954, 4" long	15	22	30
Banner International Harvester Metro 1950 van, plastic, 4" long	12	18	25
Banner Jewel Tea Van	175	263	350
Banner LaFrance Fire Truck, plastic, 1950, 4" long	12	18	25

	C6	C8	C10
Banner North American Van Lines Truck and Trailer, 15" long	100	150	200
Banner Service Station (cardboard) with 3 plastic trucks, circa late 40s - early 50s	25	38	50
Banner Stake Truck, GMC, plastic, 4" long	12	18	25
Banner Station Wagon, 1948, Oldsmobile, plastic, 4" long	12	18	25

	C6	C8	C10
Banner Tanker, plastic, 7" long	15	22	30
Banner "Toy Truck" Van, 9" long	59	78	118
Banner Tractor, Wheelhorse, plastic, 3" long	14	21	28
Banner Wonder Bread Truck, circa 1950s, tin litho, 11" long	87	130	175

BARCLAY VEHICLES

Barclay vehicles can be roughly dated by their tires. The earliest are metal. About 1934 rubber tires on wooden hubs were introduced. About 1936 nail axles began to replace the wooden hubs. Black tires are post War (after 1945). A number of unmarked vehicles were in possession of late Barclay-All Nu designer Frank Krupp. Most of these were too early to have been All-Nu and were checked with four early Barclay employees. The number of Xs in parenthesis after the toy's description indicate how many thought it had been Barclay. However, it is possible, since these are based on memories of several decades, that not all are Barclay. An X? indicates the employee believed it was Barclay but was not sure. Those not marked with Xs have been identified in other ways.

Barclay, Left to Right: BV80, BV10, BV26, BV59. Photo by Bill Kaufman. Courtesy Evelyn Besser.

Barclay, Left to Right: BV65, BV52. Photo by Bill Kaufman. Courtesy Evelyn Besser.

Barclay, Left to Right: BV54, BV30, BV81. Photo by Bill Kaufman. Courtesy Evelyn Besser.

Barclay, Left to Right: BV32, BV33, BV41. Photo by Bill Kaufman. Courtesy Evelyn Besser.

	C6	C8	C10
(BV 1) Ambulance, No.194 ,small cross, 3-1/2" long	26	39	52
(BV 2) Ambulance, No.194, large cross, 3-1/2" long	20	30	40
(BV 3) Ambulance, No.50, 5" long	35	52	70
(BV 4) No.151 Army Truck with Gun, 2-3/4" long	13	19	27
(BV 5) No.151 Army Truck with Anti-Aircraft Gun, 2-1/2" long	10	15	21
(BV 6) No. 152 Armored Army Truck, 2-7/8" long	9	13	18
(BV 7) No. 197 Army Tank Truck, circa 1935-36, 3-1/8" long	17	25	34

	C6	C8	C10
(BV 8) Army Car with two silver bullhorns, approx. 2-1/2" long (this may be the same as BV 86)	22	33	44
(BV 9) Army Tractor (Mineapolis-Moline "Jeep"), 2-3/4" long	14	21	28
(BV 10) Austin Coupe, circa 1931, No.43, 2" long	17	26	35
(BV 11) No.330 Auto Transport Set, 2 50's cars, 4-1/2" long	31	46	63
(BV 12) "Beer" Truck, circa 1940, No.376, wood barrels, 4" long	37	56	75
(BV 13) Beer Truck No. 377 with barrels	35	52	70

Barclay BV8. Photo by Stan Alekna.

Barclay Left to Right: BV12, BV13. Photo by Craig A. Clark.

Barclay, Top, Teft to Right: BV11, BV49, BV14, BV13: Bottom, Left to Right: BV82, sedan for BV61 set. Photo by Bill Kaufman. Courtesy George Buhler.

Barclay, Top, Left to Right: BV60, BV63, BV25, BV28,BV71; Bottom, Left to Right: BV37, BV61, BV55, BV24. Photo by Bill Kaufman. Courtesy George Buhler.

	C6	C8	C10
(BV 14) Bus, futuristic, "Made in U.S.A.", 3" long	18	27	36
(BV 15) Cannon Car, gunner low 3 5/16" long	12	18	25
(BV 16) No.198, Anti-Aircraft Gun Truck, in 1931 Barclay catalog, 3-1/8" long	20	30	40
(BV 17) Cannon Car, slight casting differences from headlight version, 3-1/4" long	19	28	38
(BV 18) Cannon Car, battery-powered headlight, in 1935 catalog, 3-1/2"long.	80	130	225
(BV 18A) Same casting as above but with no fitting for bulb	22	33	44
(BV 19) No. 48 Anti-Aircraft Gun Truck, one man, 4" long	22	33	45
(BV 20) No. 48, Anti-Aircraft Gun Truck, two men, 4" long	16	24	32
(BV 21) Cannon Truck, with moveable cannon, 4" long	20	30	40
(BV 22) Unused			
(BV 23) Chrysler Airflow, circa 1936, 4" long	30	45	60
(BV24) "Coast to Coast" diecast bus, "Barclay Toy", two piece, No.405, 2-7/8" long	42	63	85
(BV 25) Coupe, 1930s, "Made in U.S.A.", 3" long	12	18	25
(BV 26) Coupe, circa 1935 XXX, 2-1/2" long	50	75	100
(BV 27) Coupe, 1934, XXX,4-1/4" long	40	60	80

	C6	C8	C10
(BV 28) Coupe, 2 piece, 1930s, "Barclay Toy", 2-7/8" long	42	63	85
(BV 29) Unused			
(BV 30) Coupe, 1934, XXX,4-1/4" long	40	60	80
(BV 31) No. 40 Cord Front Drive Coupe, circa 1931, 3-5/8" long	25	38	50
(BV 32) No. 302 Streamline Car, circa 1936, 3-1/8" long	25	38	50
(BV 33) "Delivery" Truck, No.309, XXX, 2-15/16" long	15	22	31
(BV 34) Double Decker Bus, 4" long	60	90	120
(BV 35) Unused			
(BV 36) Unused			
(BV 37) "Express" stake truck, 1930s, 2-15/16" long	22	33	45
(BV 38) Fire Engine No. 390?, moveable ladder, circa 1950s	15	22	30
(BV 39) Field Kitchen, 2-1/4" long	9	13	18
(BV 40) Fire Engine, 2 firemen, black metal wheels, 1930s, No. 41, 2-3/4" long	16	24	33
(BV 41) Fire Engine, French-looking (Barclay often copied foreign toys) XXX, 4" long	16	24	33
(BV 42) Ford, 1931, 2-1/4" long	15	22	30
(BV 43) "Golden Arrow Racer", X?X, 4 1/2" long	20	30	40
(BV 44) Mack Pick Up Truck,3-1/2" long	15	22	30

	C6	C8	C10
(BV 45) "Milk & Cream" Truck, stamped No. 377, white rubber tires, 3-5/8" long	30	45	60
(BV 45A) Milk Truck No. 377, black rubber tires, 3-5/8" long	22	33	45
(BV 46) Motorcycle with flat rider, full-dimensional sidecar, No.55, 2-3/4" long	47	70	95
(BV 47) "Oil-Fuel" Truck, No. 308, circa 1936, 3-9/16" long	12	18	25
(BV 48) "Parcel Delivery", slush lead, No. 45, circa 1931, 3-5/8" long	65	98	130
(BV 49) "Police" Car, No. 317, slush mold, circa 1930s, (Radio Police), 1939 Packard, 3-5/8" long	31	46	63
(BV 49A) Police Car No. 317, diecast 3-5/8" long	15	22	30
(BV 50) Race Car, 3" long	12	18	24
(BV51) Racer, closed cockpit, 5-1/2"long	17	26	35
(BV 52) Racer, closed cockpit, circa 1939, 7" long	30	45	60
(BV 53) Racer, No. 53, early slush lead, 1920s-30s, approx. 2" long	24	36	48
(BV 54) Racer, two passengers, XXX, 4-1/4" long	55	82	110
(BV 55) Racer with tail fin, "Made U.S.A.", 3-1/2" long	17	26	35
(BV 56) Renault Tank, Circa 1937, No. 47, 4" long	22	33	45
(BV 57) Searchlight Truck, white rubber tires, circa 1940, 4-1/16" long	87	130	175
(BV 57A) Searchlight Truck, second version	87	130	175
(BV 58) Sedan, 4 door, circa 1936 maybe Chrysler, 5" long	17	26	35
(BV 59) Sedan, 2-door circa 1935, rubber wheels,XX, 3-1/8" long	37	56	75
(BV 60) Sedan, two-piece, No.401, 2-door, 1930s, "Barclay Toy", diecast, 2-7/8" long	42	63	85
(BV 61) Sedan and "Tourist Trailer", Made in U.S.A.", 1930s, 6-1/2" long	35	52	70
(BV 62) Silver Arrow Race Car, 5-1/2" long	22	33	45
(BV 63) Station Wagon, No.404, diecast, 1930s, 2-piece, "Barclay Toy", 2-15/16" long	37	56	75
(BV 64) Steam-Roller, traction type, sluch lead with tin roof, No.44 circa 1931, 3-1/4" long	30	45	60
(BV 65) Large Steamline Racer, No.363, in 1935 catalog, 6-7/8" long	45	68	90
(BV 66) Tank "4562", one man in turret, 3-7/8" long	17	26	35
(BV 67) Tank "4562", two men in turret, 3-7/8" long	21	31	42
(BV 68) Tank T41, 4-1/2" long	15	22	30
(BV 69) Tank, man in turret, diecast, black rubber tires, 2-5/8" long	12	18	25
(BV 70) Tank (based on US M2 light tank), 2-1/4" long	15	22	30
(BV 71) Taxi, circa 1940s, slush, 3-1/4" long	14	21	28
(BV 71A) Taxi, No. 318, diecast, 3-1/4" long	50	75	100
(BV 72) Tractor, caterpillar type,slush lead, XX, approx. 2-5/8" long	17	26	35
(BV 73) Unused			
(BV 74) Trailer Truck variously "Railway Express", or with Moving Company name, circa 1950s	5	8	10
(BV 75) Transport Set No.330, 2 cars 1960s, 4 1/2" long	25	40	75
(BV 76) U.S. Army Truck, No. 204, no hitch, red wood hubs,2-1/2" long	19	28	38
(BV 77) "U.S. Army" Truck, white rubber wheels, wire or peg hitch,2-1/2" long	17	25	34
(BV 78) "U.S. Motor Unit" Truck, circa 1940, white rubber tires, came 3 ways; no hitch, wire hitch, peg hitch, 3-1/4" long	17	26	35
(BV 79) Wheel-A-Rific speedway track, two lead racers, black rubber wheels, 10' of plastic track, sold for $1.00, circa 1970	17	26	35
(BV 80) Wrecker, No.46, circa 1931, 3-1/2" long	30	45	60
(BV 81) Wrecker, circa 1934, XXX, 3-15/16" long	30	45	60
(BV 82) Wrecker, two-piece, No.403, diecast, 1930s, "Barclay Toy" 2-7/8" long	42	63	85
(BV 83) Cannon Truck, moveable cannon, 4" long	37	56	75
(BV 84) Milk Truck in shape of bottle, No. 567	150	225	300
(BV 85) "Milk" Van Truck, bottle on side, 2 7/8" long	20	30	41
(BV 86) Officer's Car, with megaphone on top, 2-1/2" long	22	33	44

Barclay BV51. Photo by Craig A. Clark.

Barclay, Top, Left to Right: BV57, BV21 cannon missing, BV39; Middle, Left to Right: BV67, BV66, BV70; Bottom, Left to Right: BV68, BV5, BV69, cannon 4" long, Post WWII. Photo by Ed Poole.

Barclay BV83. Photo by Ed Poole.

Barclay BV34 (tire in photo not correct). Photo by James Apthorpe.

Barclay BV45. Courtesy Toy Soldier Review.

Barclay, Top, Left to Right: Howitzer, 4 wheels, loop hitch horzontal, Howitzer, 4 wheels, loop hitch vertical, BV78 with wire hitch, BV78 with peg hitch: Bottom, Left to Right: BV7, BV77, peg hitch, BV77, wire hitch, BV76, no hitch. Photo by Ed Poole.

Barclay, Top; Left to Right: BV15, BV6, BV4, BV9; Middle, Left to Right: BV56, BV19, BV20; Bottom, Left to Right: BV16, BV18, BV17. Photo by Ed Poole

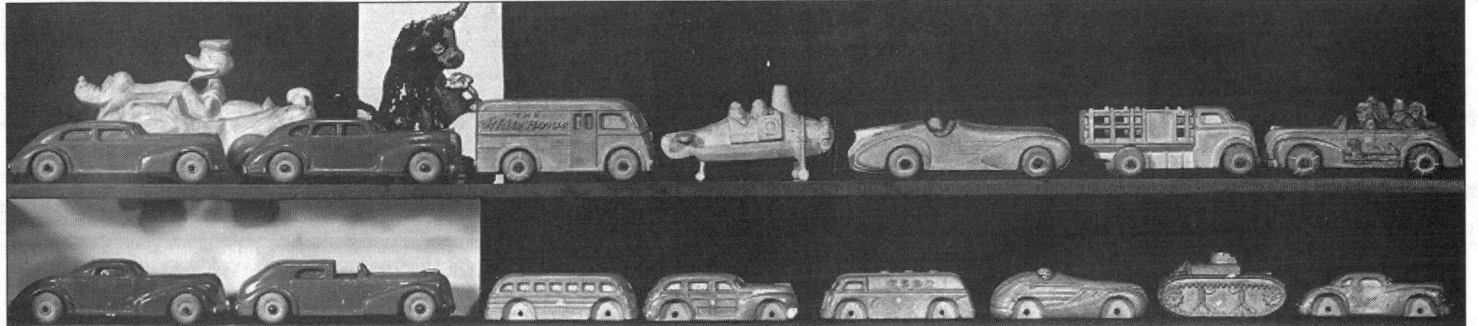

In 1984, 45 plaster castings retained by Barclay's chief of maintenance when he cleaned out the shut-down factory in 1971 were shown to the author in the course of his research. Included were soldiers, Disney figures, vehicles and an autogiro, many never produced. Some of the toys in this photo may now identify previously unmarked vehicles as being made by Barclay.

Barclay BV85.

Barclay BV90A. Photo by Perry R. Eichor.

	C6	C8	C10
(BV 87) Side Dump, approx. 1-1/2" long	7	11	15
(BV 88) Convertible with vactioners	47	70	95
(BV 89) 100/4 Build & Paint Auto Set, 6 vehicles, parts, paints, 1930s	No Price Found		
(BV 89A) Build and Paint Auto Set, No. 5004, circa 1934	No Price Found		
(BV 90) 2004 Build & Paint Set, truck, coupe, sedan, parts, paints, early	180	270	360
(BV 90A) 2004 Build & Paint Set, same number only 2 vehicles	No Price Found		
(BV 91) "U.S. Mail" Truck, 1960s, approx. 2" long	10	17	24
(BV 92) Moving Truck, circa 1960s, approx. 2" long	7	11	15
(BV 93) Log Truck, circa 1960s, approx. 2" long	7	11	15

	C6	C8	C10
(BV 94) Dump Truck, circa 1960s, approx. 2" long	7	11	15
(BV 95) Racing Car, circa 1968, approx. 2" long	5	8	10
(BV 96) "Police" Car (like BV86 and BV97), approx. 2" long	5	8	10
(BV 97) "Chief" Police Car (like BV86 and BV96), approx. 2" long	5	8	10
(BV 98) Vintage Car, approx. 2" long	15	22	30
(BV 99) Oil Truck, Circa 1960s, approx. 2" long	9	13	18
(BV 100) Pepsi-Cola Truck, 1960s, approx. 2" long	9	13	18
(BV 101) Racing Car, circa 1968, no fenders, approx. 2" long	5	8	10
(BV 102) Volkswagen, 1960s, approx. 2" long	12	18	24
(BV 103) U.S. Army Truck, circa 1968, approx 2" long	7	11	15
(BV 104) Hospital Truck, circa 1968, approx. 2" long	9	13	18
(BV 105) Army Truck, open bed, circa 1968, approx. 2" long	7	11	15
(BV 106) Army Oil Truck, circa 1968, approx 2" long	9	13	18
(BV 107) Double Transport Set No. 440, four cars on upper and lower racks, 1960s, hinged for unloading, 4-1/2"	37	56	75
(BV 108) Two-door Sedan, 1960s, 1-5/8" long	2	3	5
(BV 109) No. 203 Tractor, peg hitch, 2-1/8" long	11	16	22
(BV 110) Open Coupe with drive in cab, early 30s	15	22	30

BV90, showing from Top to Bottom: BV140, BV145, BV144A. Photo by Rogers Sanders.

Barclay, Left to Right: BV92, BV93, BV94, BV87. Courtesy Toy Soldier Review.

Barclay, Left to Right: BV95, BV96, BV97, BV98. Courtesy Toy Soldier Review.

Barclay, Left to Right: BV99, BV100, BV101, BV102. Courtesy Toy Soldier Review.

Barclay BV107. Courtesy Toy Soldier Review.

Barclay BV137A. Photo By Craig A. Clark.

Barclay BV151. Photo by Craig A. Clark.

	C6	C8	C10
(BV 111) "Esso Gas" Truck 1930s, 5" long	20	30	40
(BV 112) No.361 Steamline Large Coupe	17	26	35
(BV 113) 1935 DeSoto Airflow, 5-3/16" long	17	26	35
(BV 114) Car Carrier, two small cars, early 1930s	25	38	50
(BV 115) No.371 Racing Car, large, 1930s, 4-1/4" long	16	24	32
(BV 116) No.7 Tractor, circa late 20s-early 30s	15	22	30
(BV 117) No.1105 (or 1705) "Towing Service" Truck, large	20	30	40
(BV 118) 1929 Buick Sedan?, 3" long	27	41	55
(BV 119) No.312 "Towing" Truck, in 1936 catalog, 3-3/8" long	17	26	35
(BV 120) No. 306 Racer, in 1936 catalog	15	22	30

	C6	C8	C10
(BV 121) No.303 Streamline Racer, 4-3/8" long	15	22	30
(BV 122) No.208 Hook and Ladder, in 1935 catalog, 3" long	16	24	32
(BV 123) No.301 Coupe Streamline, 3-1/4" long	50	75	100
(BV 124) No.207 Stake Truck, in 1935 catalog, 3-1/8" long	39	58	78
(BV 125) No.362 Streamline Sedan large, in 1935 catalog	41	61	82
(BV 126) No.368 Fire Truck, 1930s, "Fire Dept. No. 99", 5-3/4" long	20	30	40
(BV 127) No.1703 1935 Chrysler Airflow Sedan, large	17	26	35
(BV 128) No.42 small Tractor, in 1931 magazine, 2-3/16" long	12	18	25
(BV 129) No.39 New Imperial Chrysler Coupe, circa 1931	15	22	30

Barclay BV27-BV110.

Barclay BV84.

Barclay, Left to Right: BV 31, BV 48, BV 43.

Barclay BV 79.
Courtesy
Toy Soldier Review.

Barclay BV 126.

	C6	C8	C10
(BV 130) No.5 Racer, in 1931 magazine, Golden Arrow	15	22	30
(BV 131) No.206 Delivery Truck "Bakery Fine Cake Pies", circa 1934, 3-1/8" long	90	135	180
(BV 132) No.51 Coupe, circa 1931, 2-3/16" long	17	26	35
(BV 133) No. 210 Fire Truck, circa 1934, 3-1/8" long	25	38	50
(BV 134) No.209 Fire Engine, circa 1934, 3-1/8" long	25	38	50
(BV 135) No. 311 Sedan, circa 1936	21	32	43
(BV 136) No.309 "Delivery" Truck, circa 1936, 3-1/2" long	12	18	25
(BV 137) No.50 Fire Truck, circa 1931, 2-3/8" long	22	33	45
(BV 137A) Like BV 137, but with gold hydraulics on both sides, wood hubs, rubber tires, 2-7/16" long	25	38	50
(BV 138) No.56 Double-Decker Bus, circa 1931, 3-1/4" long	22	33	45
(BV 139) No.58 Auburn Speedster, circa 1931	17	26	35
(BV 140) Sedan, circa 1934	37	56	75
(BV 141) No.205 Tow Car, in 1935 catalog, 3-1/16" long	20	30	40

	C6	C8	C10
(BV 142) No.338 Contractor Set, tractor, two hoppers, 1930s, (has hole hitch for wire, unlike BV 109's peg hitch)6-1/4" long...			No Price Found
(BV 143) Large Steamline Coupe,1930s	15	22	30
(BV 144) "Gasoline" Truck, small, circa 1931, 3 tank top, 2-5/16" long	30	45	60
(BV 144A) Gas Truck, circa 1935, 200 series?, 4 tank top, 3" long	25	38	50
(BV 145) Coupe, cast rear tire, circa 1935, 200 series?, 3-1/8" long	21	31	42
(BV 146) Coupe, removable spare tire, in 1935 catalog, 4-1/2" long	30	45	60
(BV 147) Dump Truck, spring action, ratchet, in 1935 catalog, 4" long	20	30	40
(BV 148) Sport Coupe, removable spare tire, in 1935 catalog,2 7/8" long	32	48	65
(BV 149) Racing Car, large, raised exhaust pipe, driver, in 1935 catalog	17	26	35
(BV 150) Race Car, open, driver,4" long	70	105	140

Barclay BV 116.

Barclay BV125.

Barclay's trucks in "Bottle" blister packs sell for about $15 in mint. Photo from the Barclay files. Courtesy Toy Soldier Review.

Barclay BV 118.

Barclay BV128.

Barclay BV 137.

Barclay BV 144.

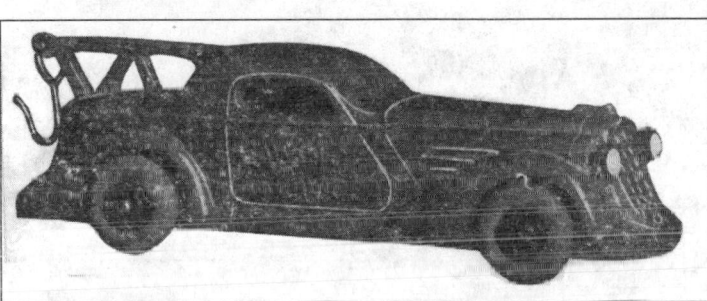

Barclay BV 117.

	C6	C8	C10
(BV 151) Stake Truck, in 1935 catalog, 4-3/8" long	36	54	72
(BV 152) 2 Car Transport Set, approx. 4-3/4" long	42	63	85
(BV 153) 4-Car Transport Set, open-cab Mack Truck, 4 2-1/2" cars, in 1935 catalog, 10-1/4" long			No Price Found
(BV 154) Roadster, open, driver, dummy spare tire on each side, in 1935 catalog, 4-1/2" long			No Price Found
(BV 155) Streamline Coupe, in 1937 catalog, 5" long			No Price Found
(BV156) "White Horse" Van, (some have sticker reading "Welcome I.C.M.A. compliments the White Motor Co."), approx. 3" long	55	82	110

Barclay, Top, Left to Right: BV 53, BV 71, BV 49, BV 87, BV 74; Bottom, Left to Right: BV 46; BV 4, BV 6, BV68.

Barclay BV 127.

Barclay BV 152. Photo by Craig A. Clark.

Barclay BV 155. Photo by Craig A. Clark.

Barclay BV 129.

Barclay BV 138.

Barclay BV 130.

Barclay BV 136.

Barclay BV 131

Barclay BV 143.

Barclay BV 133.

Barclay BV 139.

Barclay BV 124.

Barclay, Left to Right: BV 148, BV 147. Photo by Fred Maxwell.

Barclay BV 153. Photo by Dave Leopard.

28

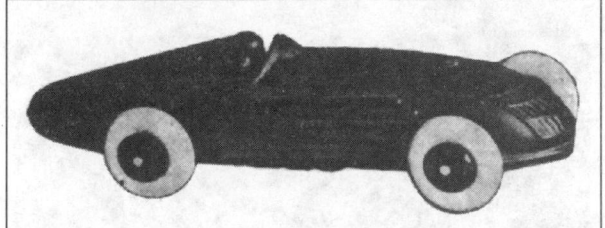

Barclay BV 121.

Barclay BV 122.

Barclay BV 142.

Barclay BV 132.

Barclay BV123.

Barclay BV 141.

Barclay BV 135.

Barclay
BV 144A.

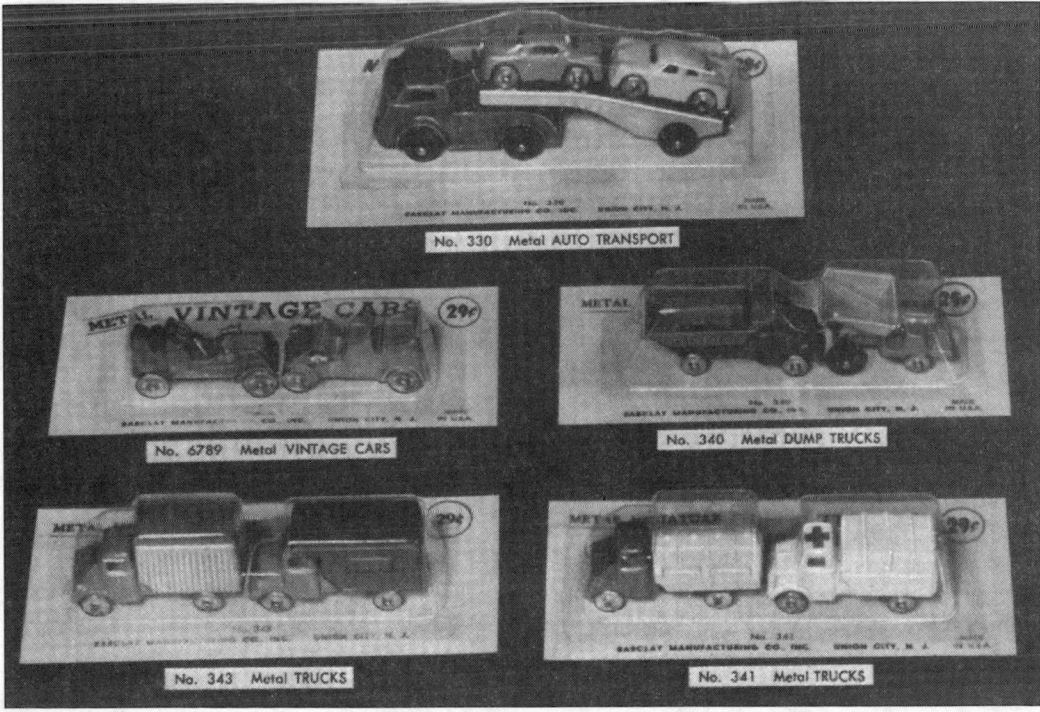

Barclay Blister pack sets, circa 1968. The No. 330 Auto Transport (BV 75) is worth about $75 in mint. The other are worth about $40 in mint. Courtesy Toy Soldier Review.

325 TRAILER TRUCK

339 MINIATURE AUTOS

349 MINIATURE FOREIGN CARS

347 SPORTS CARS

Barclay blister pack vehicles, circa 1968. Value is about $25 in mint, except for the No. 339 pack of seven autos, which would go for about $60 in mint. Photo from the Barclay files. Courtesy Toy Soldier Review.

BARR, Left to Right:
BA02, BA01.
Photo by Dave Leopard

BARR RUBBER

Barr Rubber was located in Sandusky, Ohio. The following list, with its codings, was compiled by Dave Leopard. Vehicles are broken down by type.

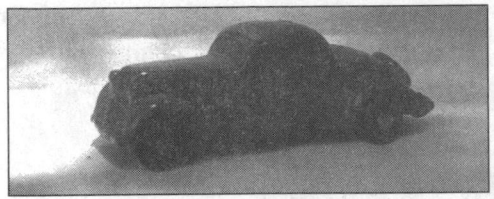

*BARR BA01.
Photo by
Dave Leopard.*

RUBBER TOY CARS

Miniature reproductions in molded rubber of the famous V-8 in four different models. Tiny details such as door handles, radiator grills, etc., are all skillfully reproduced. Wheels are sturdily mounted on plated hubs; colors are varied; and finishes are sparkling and non-cracking. Due to their rubber construction, these beautiful little cars cannot harm the child or mar the furniture.

*Write for samples and
literature.*

WORLD'S LARGEST MANUFACTURER OF TOY BALLOONS
The **BARR RUBBER PRODUCTS CO.** SANDUSKY OHIO

*BARR RUBBER ad from the November 1935 Playthings magazine.
Courtesy Playthings.*

	C6	C8	C10
BA01 '35 Ford Coupe, 4" long	27	41	55
BA02 '35 Ford 2 door slantback sedan, 4" long	27	41	55
BT01 '35 Ford Stake Body Truck 4-3/4" long	27	41	55
BT02 '35 Ford Panel Truck/Ambulance, 4-1/4" long	27	41	55
BT03 '35 Ford Army Truck, 4-3/4" long	32	48	65

*BARR BT02, both versions.
Photo by Dave Leopard.*

*BARR, Left to Right:
BT03, BT01.
Photo by Dave Leopard.*

BEAUT MFG. CO.

Beaut Mfg. Co., North Bergen, New Jersey, was founded in 1946 by Eugene Buhler and Irving Reader, former machinist and salesman, respectively, for Barclay Mfg. Co. The company put out five toys: a taxi cab, a police car, a fire engine, a sedan and a child's wagon. The company was successful at first, employing ten people, and selling to Woolworth's and many overseas buyers. It ceased its toy-making activities (it continued until 1982 as a general machine shop) around 1950, because of competition from plastic toys.

BEAUT "Police" car (left) and "Taxi". Photo by Bill Kaufman. Courtesy George Buhler.

	C6	C8	C10		C6	C8	C10
BEAUT "Fire" car, No.4, approx. 3-3/4"	10	15	20	BEAUT Sedan, approx. 3-3/4"	10	15	20
BEAUT "Police" car, approx. 3-3/4"	10	15	20	BEAUT "Taxi", approx. 3-3/4"	10	15	20

CONDITION CODE:

C6 - Good. Evident overall wear, well played with, but acceptable to many collectors

C8 - Very Good Minor wear overall, very clean

C10 - Mint (like new)

Note: Mint in Box commands a higher price. Condition below C6 brings considerable lower prices.

BEST TOY & NOVELTY FACTORY

by Fred Maxwell, Slushmold Contributing Editor and Margaret Rice
with the assistance of members of the Best family,
Perry Eichor, Kenneth Nudson and Ferd Zegel.

John M. Best, Sr., who founded Best Toy in Manhattan, Kansas, was an entrepreneur who stuck his neck out. Only senior citizens can understand how low our economy was in the 1930s, so starting a new business after watching other toy companies fail successively tells us something about John Best, and something about the perennial appeal of good toys. To Best, the molding of potmetal toys must have seemed a good risk for a second income as he was a printer who worked with metal alloys. And he probably had been following the ups and downs of "those TOYS with the NUMBERS" for he had lived in Clifton, the home of Kansas Toy Company.

It was started as a family hobby for his children, relatives, friends and neighbors according to Minnie Nelson, his daughter. Other employees we know of were John Best Jr. and his family, and Conrad Morsch, a molder. For a "hobby" it grew into a respectable business, supplying toy distributors and dime stores; for the toys are found in today's toy markets. After several years of operation it was sold to Ralstoy, a Ralston, Nebraska company, in 1939.

At this point we are not certain when Best started or what "number" in the series was his first molding. Although contradictory, evidence from family members suggests purchase of the assets of a Clifton Toy company occurred about 1933. Nor do we know whether he introduced any new patterns, although with his experience it is likely that he did. Regardless, it was an important chapter in the story of those wandering molds.(See history of Kansas Toy in this book).

Of great assistance was a donation from Dee Buchanan, Mrs. Nelson's granddaughter, of a faded copy of a Best Toy brochure. It appears to be a pre-publication printer's mockup, and undated; but its 42 illustrations (some shown here) were adequate to identify most of the Best and many of the Kansas toys in collections. With no paper trail to guide us previously, this was indeed a find. So with the publication of the 5th Edition much of the hearsay errors and confusion of this family of toys was eliminated. Many thanks to all who helped and continue to help.

(O'Brien: Dee Buchanan, great granddaughter of John Best Sr., also contributed a history in 1988 that may be of interest to readers: "About 55 years ago, John Milner Best Sr. and his wife Roseanna, purchased a company from Kansas Toy & Novelty Company located in Vining, Kansas - actually a suburb of Clifton. The Bests owned a newspaper, printing plant and book-bindery in Manhattan, Kansas. They moved the toy company to a building in back of their home at 530 Fremont Street, Manhattan. The family, in-laws and friends all worked making the lead cars produced by the toy company and were shipping them all over the world. There were also farm implements, tractors, airplanes, buses and trains as well as all types of cars. One of the Bests' grandchildren, Rosemary, remembers the Toy Factory well, as when she was about three years old and was playing about the factory she fell into one of the lead-melting pots head first. Very fortunately the lead was not hot - so she just had a bad bruise on her head; whereas if the lead had been hot and melted it would indeed have been a tragedy".)

Best Toy reproductions can usually be distinguished from those of earlier makes in the "numbers" dynasty if they have white rubber wheels and are embossed "Made in USA". However, some of their toys used the metal wheels (MW) of the Kansas Toy originals, or the later wood hubs with rubber tires (WHRT). It is also possible that Best modified or rebuilt his molds to create variations.

Best molded a great number of designs. In order to reduce redundancy in this book we list them here but will not describe them in detail if they are adequately covered in Kansas Toy or Ralstoy lists. The following numbered toys and some unnumbered duplicates were found: #6, 10, 14,17,20, 25, 26,27, 31, 32, 34, 35, 36, 37, 39, 40, 41, 42, 43, 45, 46, 47, 49, 51, 54, 55, 57, 58, 59, 60, 67, 70, 71, 72, 74, 76, 77, 78, 79, 80, 81, 85, 86, 87, 90, 91, 92, 93, 94, 95, 97, 99, 100, 101, 102.

BEST'S three different wheels, Top Row: BEV4, BEV7, BEV9a; Middle Row: BEV1, BEV8; Bottom Row: BEV11, BEV14. Courtesy of Fred Maxwell.

Box from a BEST TOYS Farm Set. All the Toys illustrated are from molds believed to have originated with Kansas Toys. Photo by Perry Eichor. Courtesy Fred Maxwell.

	C6	C8	C10
BEV1 Racer, "85", Record car w/large square fin, driver, HO, VG,12 exhaust ports, WHRT, 4"	10	15	20
BEV2 Sedan, "86", Lincoln ? 2 dr. fastback, slant grille w/grid pattern, HL, divided w/s, red wheel shirts, 4"	No Price Found		
BEV3 Sedan, "87", Brewster?	No Price Found		
BEV4 Sedan, "90", 2 dr. airflow, hood reaches front bumper w/no grille, 4 OW, hard rubber wheels, 3-1/2"	No Price Found		
BEV5 Sedan, "91", Cadillac ? 2 dr. airflow, high style vee grille, faired front fenders, 3-1/2"	No Price Found		
BEV6 Coupe, "92", Dodge?, chopped top, Brewster-like heart shaped grille, HO, long streamlined front fenders, 3-3/4"	No Price Found		

	C6	C8	C10
BEV7 Coupe "93", Cadillac ?, Streamlined, hood similar to #91, grid pattern grille, 2 OW, hard rubber wheels.(see illustration of #96),3-5/8"	16	24	32
BEV8 Large Sedan, "94", 2 dr. airflow, similar to #90, 4 OW, taxi lamp on roof, 4-1/2"	No Price Found		
BEV9a Sedan, "95", 2 dr. airflow similar to #94, w/3 headlamps, 4 OW, trunk, hard rubber wheels, Chrysler-Briggs show car?, 3 1/2"	No Price Found		
BEV9b Sedan, "95", Same as above with "Police Dept." shield on doors. Centered headlamp may be a siren. Other version have "Police" painted on roof, 3-1/2"	10	15	20
BEV10 Coupe, "96", Apparently same car as #93, Were both produced? 3-1/2"	No Price Found		
BEV11 Larger Racer, "97", Bluebird record car, driver, large fin, 12 exhaust ports, hard rubber wheels, faired, 4-1/2"	10	15	20
BEV12 Coupe, "98"	No Price Found		
BEV13 Coupe, "99", Pontiac?, streamlined, HO, rearmount, 4"	No Price Found		

Box from a BEST TOYS Set. The drawings on the boxtop offer good representations of BEST vehicles and cannon. All or most of the toys shown appear to have originated with Kansas Toy & Novelty. Courtesy Margaret Rice & Fred Maxwell.

BEST TOY Tanker: BEV15, BEV16. Photo courtesy of Perry Eichor.

34

(BEV 14) No. 100 - 4" long

(BEV 13) No. 99 - 4" long

(BEV 2) No. 86 - 4" long

(BEV 10) No. 96 - 3½" long

(BEV 5) No. 91 - 3½" long

(BEV 9a) No. 95 - 3½" long

(BEV 6) No. 92 - 3¾" long

(BEV 4) No. 90 - 3½" long

(BEV 11) No. 97 - 4½" long

(BEV 1) No. 85 - 4" long

No. 81 - 4½" long

No. 26 - 4" long

No. 76 - 4¼" long

No. 10 - Medium Racer

	C6	C8	C10
BEV14 Sedan, "100", Pontiac, streamlined, 2 dr., HO,HG, 4 OW, trunk, 4" long		No Price Found	
BEV15 Cab Unit, "101", International? sleeper cab, slanted grille, HO, 2 OW, 3-1/4"		No Price Found	
BEV16 Oil Transport,"102", Streamlined "Gasoline" semi-trailer to #101, 4 tanks, 4 storage compartments. Total length of cab-trailer 6 3/4", 4"	47	70	95
BEV17 ?Sedan, no #, DeSoto? Airflow 2 dr., HO,VG, HL, 4 OW, divided			

	C6	C8	C10
open windshield, bottom pan, Best? 3-7/8"		No Price Found	
Big Bang Army Tank No. ST, cast iron, 8-1/8"	35	50	100
Big Bang Motor Tank No. ST, cast iron, 9-1/2"	75	250	500
Big Boy: See Kelmet			
Boattail Speedster, cast iron, blue with nickel wheels, driver, circa 1920s 5" long	100	150	200
Brinks Truck Bank, lead alloy, 9" long.	175	263	350

BUDDY "L"

Buddy "L" toys were first manufactured by the Moline Pressed Steel Company, Moline, Illinois, in 1921, and were named after the son of the owner, Fred Lundahl. Lundahl had started the company about eight years earlier, manufacturing auto and truck parts (fenders, etc.). The toys were originally made as special items for his son, but as Buddy Lundahl's playmates began to clamor for similar toys of their own and their fathers began asking Lundahl senior to make duplicate toys for their sons, Lundahl went into the toy business. Buddy "L" toys were large, typically 21 to 24 or more inches long for trucks and fire engines. Construction was of very heavy steel, strong enough to support a man's weight. These were made until the early 1930s, when the line was modified and lighter weight materials were employed.

Following is a list of pre-1932 Buddy "L" toys compiled by Thomas W. Sefton.

Before this time, Fred Lundahl had died, having already lost control of the company. The company has changed names several times, being know as the Buddy "L" Corp., Buddy "L" Toy Co., etc., in recent years dropping the quotes around the L. Continuing to make toys till the present day, the company even put out a few wooden toys during World War II, when its main plant made nothing but war-related items. The early Buddy "L" trains are also popular, and tend to be worth even more than the vehicles. Buddy "L" material from the pre-1932 period is almost indestructible and as a consequence, 50% of the pieces found are either very rusty or have been repainted at some point. The basic metal seems to hold up forever, but repainting and rust drops the price well below "good".

Large Trucks	C6	C8	C10
Buddy L 200 Express Truck 1921-31	2000	4000	6000
Buddy L 201 Dump Truck (Ratchet) 1921-30	490	735	980
Buddy L 201A Hydraulic Dump Truck 1926-31	650	1100	1600
Buddy L 202 Coal Truck 1926-31	1800	2900	4000
Buddy L 202A Sand & Gravel Truck 1926-31	1800	3000	4500
Buddy L 203 Stake Truck 1921-24 1926-28	600	950	1400
Buddy L 203A Lumber Truck 1925-30	800	1400	2000
Buddy L 203B Baggage Truck 1929-31	850	1500	2100
Buddy L 204 Moving Van 1924-30	700	1100	1700
Buddy L 204A Railway Express 1926-31	900	1700	2250

	C6	C8	C10
Buddy L 206, 206B Street Sprinkler Truck 1924-31	100	1700	2400
Buddy L 206A Oil Truck 1925-30	800	1400	2000
Buddy L 207 Ice Truck 1926-31	550	875	1350
Buddy L 208 Coach 1928-31 (Lt. Green Motorbus)	1900	3100	4600
Buddy L 209 Auto Wrecker 1928-31 (Tow Truck)	1800	2900	4000
Fire Trucks			
Buddy L 205 Hook & ladder 1924-31	800	1400	1860
Buddy L 205A Pumper 1925-30	800	1450	1900
Buddy L 205AB (Working) Pumper 1930-31	475	825	1450
Buddy L 205B Aerial Ladder 1926-30	1200	2000	2875
Buddy L 205C Insurance Patrol 1925-30	650	1000	1350
Buddy L 205D Water Tower Truck (Working) 1930-31	1300	2200	3100
Model T Series			
Buddy L 210 Flivver Truck 1925-30	500	800	1180

BUDDY L, No.205AB, Pumping Fire Engine.

BUDDY L., Model T 210A, Flivver Roadster. Courtesy Wilkinson Collection, Detroit Antique Toy Museum.

	C6	C8	C10
Buddy L 210A Flivver Roadster 1925-27	650	1000	1450
Buddy L 210B Flivver Coupe 1925-30.	550	800	1200
Buddy L 211 Ford Dump Cart 1926-30.	800	1400	2000
Buddy L 211A Ford Dump Truck 1926-30	1000	1500	2000
Buddy L 212 Ford Express Truck 1929-30	500	800	1100
Buddy L 212A One-Ton Ford Delivery Truck 1929-30	1200	2000	3200

Contruction Equipment

	C6	C8	C10
Buddy L 220 Steam Shovel 1921-31	250	375	500
Buddy L 220A Heavy Steam Shovel 1929-30	850	1450	1850
Buddy L 220AB Heavy Shovel (on Treads) 1929-30	2500	4000	7000
Buddy L 230 Sand Loader 1925-31	500	800	1100
Buddy L 240 Small Derrick 1922-31	187	280	375
Buddy L 241 Large Derrick 1922-31	275	363	550
Buddy L 250 Overhead Crane 1924-27.	700	1100	1600
Buddy L 250A Traveling Crane 1928-30	1200	1800	2500
Buddy L 260 Pile Driver 1926-28	500	750	1000
Buddy L 270 Dredge (Clamshell) 1926-30	1000	2000	3000
Buddy L 270A Tractor Dredge (on Treads) 1929-30	3000	5000	7500
Buddy L 280 Concrete Mixer 1926-30..	400	600	800
Buddy L 280A Mixer (on Treads) 1929-31	1000	1500	2000
Buddy L 290 Road Roller 1929-31	200	2100	3600
Buddy L 300 Sand Screener 1929-30	700	1100	1700

	C6	C8	C10
Buddy L 350 Holsting Tower 1929-31	750	1125	1500
Buddy L 360 Aerial Tramway 1929-30	2000	3000	4500
Buddy L 400 Trencher 1928-31	1800	2700	4200

End listing by Thomas W. Sefton

Buddy L 1932 on

	C6	C8	C10
Buddy L "Allied Van Lines" Moving Van No. 366, 31" long	362	543	725
Buddy L "Army Signal Corps" Truck, 9141-42, 12" long	120	175	260
Buddy L Army Tank, wood, 1943, 13" long	85	130	175

BUDDY L, No. 205, Hook & Ladder. Courtesy Mapes Auctioneers.

	C6	C8	C10
Buddy L Army Transport, with towed cannon, 6-spoke wheels, 27" long.....	130	195	260
Buddy L "Army Truck 21", circa 1940, cloth top..................................	120	180	240
Buddy L Army Truck No. 506, 20-1/2" long..	125	188	250
Buddy L Army Truck, wood...................	100	150	200
Buddy L Automatic Tail-Gate Loader with steering handle...........................	240	360	480
Buddy L Baggage Truck No.11, 1933, 26-1/2" long............................	250	375	500
Buddy L Baggage Truck No. 41...........	65	98	130
Buddy L "Big Show Circus" Truck, wood, 1947, No. 484, 25-1/2" long.......	800	1300	1900
Buddy L City Baggage Dray No. 439, 1934, 19" long.................................	250	375	500
Buddy L City Baggage Dray No. 839, 1939, 20-3/4" long..............................	125	188	250
Buddy L Coca Cola Truck, wooden, circa WWII, only 3 known, worth $4200 in mint 1984, 19" long			
Buddy L Coca Cola Truck, post WWII 15" long..	117	175	235
Buddy L Concrete Mixer withTruck No. 54, 1937, 34-1/2" long.................	100	150	200
Buddy L Concrete Mixer No. 832, 1950-51, with motor sound, 10-3/4" long.........	275	363	550
Buddy L CountrySquire Station Wagon, 15" long..................................	90	135	180
Buddy L Curtiss Candy Truck................	550	825	1250
Buddy L Dairy Truck No. 2002 (Junior Line)1930-32, 24" long.........	275	363	550
Buddy L Dandy Digger No. 33...............	120	180	240
Buddy L Delivery Truck, Deluxe Rider No.803, 1945-48,22 3/4" long.	60	100	145
Buddy L Double Hydraulic Self-Loader-N-Dump Truck No. 5892...................	100	150	200

BUDDY L, No. 204A, Railway Express Truck.

BUDDY L, No. 205, Fire Truck.

BUDDY L, No. 300, Sand Screener.

BUDDY L, No. 205B, Hydraulic Aerial Truck.

BUDDY L, No. 483, Fire Chief's Car with Siren, wood, 1947. Photo by William G. Floyd.

BUDDY L, No. 280 Concrete Mixer, Courtesy Thomas G. Nefos, Federal Shipping Network.

38

BUDDY L, No. 5429, Merry-Go-Round. Courtesy Thomas G. Nefos, Federal Shipping Network.

	C6	C8	C10
Buddy L Dump Truck No.434, 1936	175	262	350
Buddy L Dump Truck No. 634, 20-1/2" long	140	210	280
Buddy L Emergency Auto Wrecker No. 3317	130	195	260
Buddy L Engine No. 29, 1933-34, 25-1/2" long	225	338	450
Buddy L Excavator Truck and Shovel Set No. 948, 1940, 27-1/2" long	300	450	600
Buddy L Express Trailer Truck No. 35, 1934	500	800	1200
Buddy L Fast Delivery Truck No.3313	75	112	150
Buddy L "Fast Freight", 20" long	225	338	450
Buddy L Fire Chief's Car with Siren No. 483, wood, 1947, 19-1/2" long	475	713	950
Buddy L Fire Ladder Truck, semi, rounded trailer fenders, 1960	70	105	140
Buddy L Greyhound Bus, winds up 16" long	280	420	560
Buddy L Greyhound Bus with Bell No. 481, wooden 18-1/2" long	450	675	900
Buddy L Hose Truck No. 38, 1933, 21-3/4" long	162	243	325
Buddy L Hook and Ladder Truck No. 859, wooden, 21-1/2" long	800	1300	1800
Buddy L Hydraulic Aerial Truck No. 27, 1933-34, w/ladders down 40" long	550	850	1200
Buddy L Hydraulic Dump Truck No. 10 1933-34, 24-3/4" long	700	110	1600
Buddy L Ice Truck No. 12, 1933-34, 26-1/2" long	230	345	460
Buddy L International Delivery Truck No. 51, 1935, 24-1/2" long	200	300	300
Buddy L Merry-Go-Round Truck No.5429	70	105	140
Buddy L Mister Buddy Ice Cream Van	70	105	140

	C6	C8	C10
Buddy L "Railway Express" Truck No. 480, wooden, 1947, 16-1/4" long	350	525	700
Buddy L Repair-It, 24" long	100	150	200
Buddy L Ride-N-Dump Truck	100	150	200
Buddy L "Riding Academy" No. 5455 Truck, with 3 horses	60	90	120
Buddy L Robotoy Dump Truck with driver, operates on remote control	600	925	1250
Buddy L Sand & Gravel Truck No.3312	130	195	260
Buddy L Scarab No. 211, no wind-up mechanism	250	375	500
Buddy L Scarab No. 711, winds up	219	328	438
Buddy L Service Truck, 1953	120	180	240
Buddy L "Shell" Truck, 13 1/2" long	240	360	480
Buddy L Siren Pull-n-Ride	120	180	240
Buddy L Steam Shovel and International Truck No. 16, 1937, 29 1/2" long 13 1/2" high	110	165	225
Buddy L Steam Shovel, mechanical, No. 30, 1935, 17-1/2" long, 13-1/2" high	225	338	450
Buddy L Steam Shovel on Treads (Junior Line)No. 2005, 1930-32 24" long	200	300	400
Buddy L Tank Truck No. 438, 1935, 19-1/4" long	450	675	900
Buddy L Tank Truck No. 938, 1941, 21 1/2" long	225	338	450
Buddy L "Texaco" Tanker, promo sold at gas stations, 25" long	100	150	200
Buddy L Traveling Zoo, Post WWII	50	75	100
Buddy L Utility Delivery Truck No. 946, 1941-42, 25" long	90	135	180
Buddy L Victory Jeep and Cannon, wood	100	150	200
Buddy L Water Tower No. 28, 1936	1500	2500	3500
Buddy L Wrecker No. 13, 1933,31" long	1000	1700	3000
Buddy L Wrecker. No. 37, 1933,24" long	200	300	400
Buddy L Wrecker No. W37, 1939, 25-1/4" long	100	150	200
Buddy L Wrecker No. 437, 1934,24" long	225	338	450
Buddy L Wrecker No. 503, 1940, 1941-42, 19-1/4" long	112	168	225
Buddy L No.647, 1949, 26-1/4" long	100	150	200
Buddy L Wrecker No. 813, 1938, 32" long	100	150	200
Buddy L Wrecker, Emergency Towing Rider No. 903, 1949, 33" long	75	112	150
Buddy L Wrecker No. 903, 1950, "Buddy L Emergency Towing" 33" long	100	160	225

BUDDY L, No. 484, "Big Show Circus" truck, wood, 1947. Photo by William G. Floyd.

	C6	C8	C10
Buddy L Wrecker No. 937, 1939, 25-1/4" long	130	180	285
Buddy L Wrecker No. 937, 1941-42 version, 25" long	50	95	135
Buddy L "Wrigley's Spearmint" Railway Express Truck. No. 835, 1938, 25" long	400	700	1000
Buddy L "Wrigley's Spearmint" Railway Express Truck, 1935, headlights light up, 23-1/8" long	450	675	900

BUDDY L, "Repair-It" (1953). Courtesy Mapes Auctioneers.

BUDDY L, No. 803, Deluxe Rider Delivery Truck. Courtesy Joe and Sharon Freed.

	C6	C8	C10
Buddy L "Wrigley's Spearmint Railway Express Agency" Truck No. 953, 1940	800	1350	1850

BUDDY L, No. 5892, Double Hydraulic Self-Loader-N-Dump Truck. Courtesy Thomas G. Nefos, Federal Shipping Network.

BUDDY L, No. 711, "Scarab". Courtesy Heinz Mueller, Continental Hobby House. (Bumpers missing in photo.)

BUDDY L, "Wrigley's Spearmint" Railway Express Truck, 1935. Courtesy Rodney A. Heesacker.

	C6	C8	C10
Buffalo Toys Silver Bullet Racer, 26" long	350	525	700
Buick, 1947, plastic, 5-3/8" long	5	8	10
Bus, 1930s, aluminum, 15-1/2" long	1800	3300	5500
Bus, late 1920s, six side windows, 23-1/2" long	150	225	300
Bus, cast iron, A.C. Williams? approx. 3-1/2" long	20	30	40
Bus, cast iron, 4" long	20	30	40
Bus, cast iron, five side windows, circa 1928, 4-1/2" long	100	150	200
Bus, cast iron, circa 1920s, 4-3/4" long	100	150	200
Bus, cast iron, with driver, rubber tires, 13" long	500	750	1000
Bus, Double-Decker, cast iron, four figures, 8" long	200	300	400
Bus, cast iron, double-decker, 9-1/2" long	400	600	800

BUS, 1930's 15-1/2" long, aluminum. Courtesy James S. Maxwell/ Virginia Caputo. Photo by Virginia Caputo.

C. A. W. NOVELTY COMPANY
Another Kansas Slushmolder Revealed

By Fred Maxwell, Slushmold Contributing Editor and Ferd Zegel
With the assistance of the Clay Center Historical Society, Gary Franson, Arlan and Gerry Conrad.

It is remarkable indeed that collectors had not found this fine company until 1990. Charles A. Wood not only ran a substantial operation but he made some of the finest replica toys in the slushmold industry. Ironically, Wood had one of the longest histories of the slushmold industry. Founded about 1925, his company was active until about 1940 when lead casting came to a halt with WWII.

All of Wood's output showed artistry, ingenuity and meticuluous craftmanship. All his toys are smooth, crisp, detailed moldings; with extra touches such as open windshields and 2 or 3 colors per toy. The early production had metal disk wheels with painted black "tires", or metal-spoked. When you find open, V-shaped, divided windshields, drivers inside cabs and trimotored aircraft with the outboard engines mounted on the landing gear struts you wonder how he did it for the 5¢ price. Perhaps Wood explained it, for he once told a reporter that it sometimes took 3 or 4 years to make a mold. The molds are also works of art-of the machinists art. This tells us something about his pride in his work; and also that toy-making was not his primary occupation at the time.

Charles Wood was born about 1891. He had lived and worked in Topeka and in nearby Clifton before coming to Clay Center. He was perhaps better known for his civic boosterism and good works. After he had helped establish the local airport he built and operated his own aircraft maintenance hangar. A master machinist, he made all his toy molds, production tools and toy parts, even plastic wheels.

Although researching this slush industry for 20 years, I had only heard rumors of a "small molder in Clay Center,

Kansas". Then, a few years ago, I found a small monoplane with initials "CAW" under a tailplane. I put the pressure on my Kansas friends with the happy result that eventually I saw a mint collection owned by a relative of Wood's and also a few pieces and some paper memorabilia in their Historical Society Museum. What a pleasant surprise!

Although we do not yet have a complete list, we have identified some of those "orphans" and some never heard of. Wood made airplanes, autos, novelties and trucks. Some of these have been well known to collectors, although unidentified. Clearly, this company and its toys deserve to be more fully known.

Note: The C & H Mfg. Co. was formed in 1940 by Rod Hemphill, the last C.A.W. employee, and Howard Clevenger. According to Mrs. Hemphill they only used original C.A.W. molds. Apparently this brave effort at revival managed to reproduce some toys before folding. These are heavier than C.A.W.'s and have black rubber wheels. Their claim to fame is in publication of the accompanying partial flyer which allowed us to solve the paternity of those handsome orphans. However, judging from the catalog numbers and our incomplete list below there must be several orphans out there. Can any of you collectors help?

Note: A C.A.W. trademark, seldom found (too costly?), were unique, lead blind hubs fitted over a wire axle. Sometimes found with ordinary nail axles piercing the hubs.

TOYS THAT SELL THEMSELVES

Modern Metal Toys that Sell the Year Around, Realistic in Every
Detail. Finished in Bright Colors with the Best of Lacquers

No. 25   AIR DRIVE COACH
Length 3⅞ in. He'ght 1⅜ in. Weight per
gro. 33 lbs. Retails for 10c.

Price per doz. ....

No. 32.   DE SOTO SEDAN
Length 3⅞ in. Height 1⅜ in. Weight per
gro. 32 lbs. Retails for 10c.
Price per doz. ....

No. 30   STREAMLINE COUPE
Length 3 in. Height 1 in. Weight per gro.
19 lbs. Retails at 5c.

Price per doz. ....

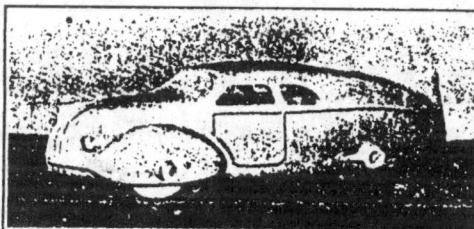

No. 33   WONDER SPECIAL
Length 3⅜ in. Height 1 in. Weight per gro
19 lbs. Retails for 5c.

Price per doz. ....

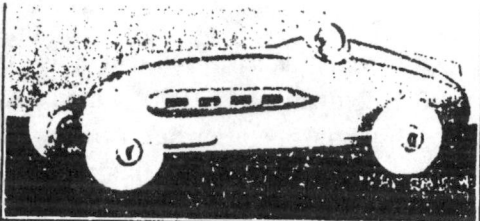

No. 31.   MARVEL RACER
Length 3⅝ in. Height 1 3-16 in. Weight
per gro. 20 lbs. Retails at 5c.

Price per doz. ....

No. 38   NEW DESIGN RACER
Length 3⅜ in. Height 1¼ in. Weight per
gro. 20 lbs. Retails for 5c.

No. 39
TRANSPARENT WINDSHIELD RACER
Length 3 in. Height 1 in. Weight per gro.
15 lbs. Retails for 5c.

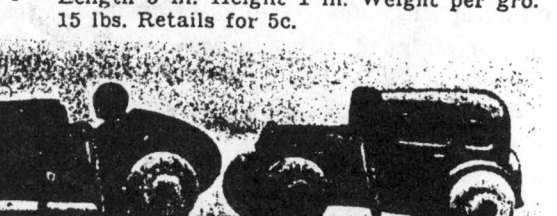

No. 40   THREE PIECE AUTO SET
Three toys on card. Length 6⅜ in. Height 1 in. Weight per gro. 40 lbs. Retails for 10c
per card.

Price per doz. ....

Each number packed one dozen
to box.

Colors: On all Airplanes 6 silver
4 red, 2 green, to dozen. On all
Autos 6 red, 2 blue, 2 green, 2
silver to dozen.

Rubber Wheels on All Autos
Plastic Wheels on Airplanes Except No. 29

TERMS: 2% Ten Days, Net 30
Days. Prices are f. o. b. St. Louis,
Mo.

C & H Mfg. Co.

1610 So. Florissant Rd.
ST. LOUIS, MO.

C.A. W. Toys later sold circa 1940 - early 1942 by C & H. Courtesy Fred Maxwell

C.A.W. CWV12b. Courtesy Gary Franson.

Left to Right: C.A.W. CWV4, CWV1. Courtesy Fred Maxwell.

C.A.W., CWV12c. Courtesy Gary Franson.

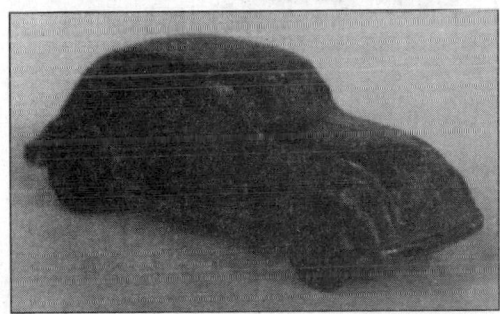

C.A.W., CWV9. Courtesy Gary Franson.

C.A.W., CWV5b (no rear propellor). Courtesy of Gary Franson.

C.A.W., CWV3. Courtesy Gary Franson.

C.A.W., CWV6. Courtesy of Gary Franson.

C.A.W., CWV12a. Courtesy of Gary Franson.

C.A.W., CWV2. Courtesy Gary Franson.

C.A.W., CWV8. Courtesy Gary Franson.

C.A.W., CWV13. Courtesy Gary Franson.

C.A.W., CWV11b. Courtesy Gary Franson.

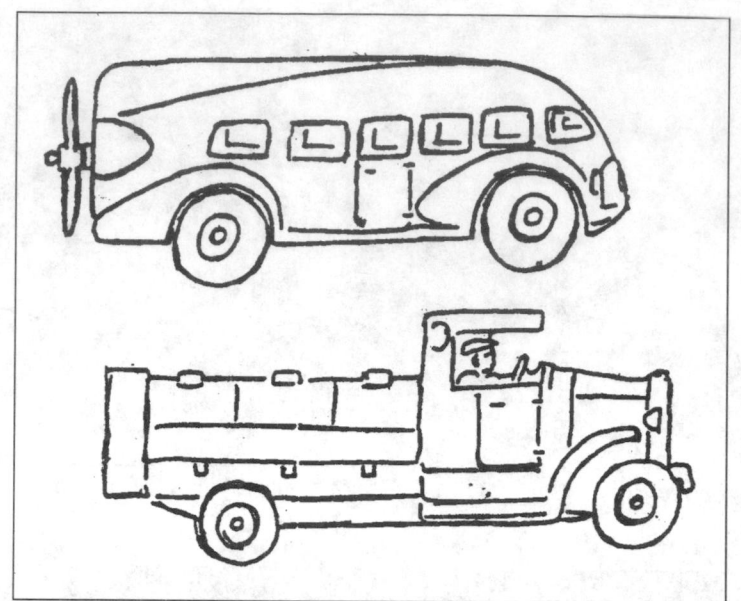

Line art C.A.W. toys: Top to Bottom: CWV5, CWV4. Drawings by Deb Eccles.

	C6	C8	C10
CWV1 Sport Roadster, no #, Open Packard, driver w/cap (gilt or silver), no windshield(w/s), horizontal grille (hg), vertical louvers (vl), no headlamps, rear-mount (rm), metal disk wheels (mdw), 3-1/2" long	20	30	40
CWV2 Sport Roadster, no #, similar to above, Buick?, no w/s, plain grille, vl, rm, right sidemount (sm) mdw, also spoked version (msw) 3-1/2" long	22	33	44
CWV3 Overland Bus, no #, Fageol? Yellow Line? tour bus, hg, no head-lamps, 12 windows, shallow "observer deck", mdw, left sm, 3-3/4" long			No Price Found
CWV4 Fuel Tanker, no #, Ford? Truck, cab w/driver inside, no w/s, hg, 3 tanks, hose compart., msw, 3-3/4" long	20	30	40

CWV5 Air Drive Coach, #25, Blimp-like bus w/fin and rear propeller drive. (b. Also a version molded w/o prop.) 12 open windows (ow), white

	C6	C8	C10
rubber wheels (wrw) with unique fitted hubs which cab hidden axles (see text note) 3-7/8" long			No Price Found
CWV6 Streamline Coupe, #30, Airflow, V-pattern grille, hood ornament (ho), 4 ow, small rear fin, small winged design on rear-wheel skirts, mdw also wrw. Bottom pan goes over rear axle, not under, 3" long	16	24	32
CWV7 Wonder Special, #33, Airflow coupe, 3 wheeled companion to #30 above, vg, 4 ow, wrw, front wheel skirts, pan goes over front axle, 3-3/8" long	16	24	32
CWV8 Marvel Racer, #31, streamlined FWD Indy type, driver, torpedo tail with very small fin, V-grille pattern, 8 exhaust ports, alum. wheels. Also found in a modern bubblepack, w/lucent hard plastic wheels, "Woodchuck Industries Metal Toys, Clay Center, Ks.". This name may have been a new idea, part of a recent market test, 3-5/8"			No Price Found
CWV9 DeSoto Sedan, #32, Airflow, divided windshield, b ow, hl, vg, ho, wrw, 3-7/8" long			No Price Found
CWV10 New Design Racer #38, stream-lined coupe, rounded tail, 2 oval open window shows driver, hood ornament loop (stringpull?), wrw w/hubs, 3-3/8" long			No Price Found

CWV11 Transparent Windshield Racer, #39, Indy FWD 2 man racer, v-shaped

C.A.W., CWV14. Courtesy Gary Farnson.

C.A.W., CWV7. Courtesy Gary Farnson.

C.A.W., CWV10. Courtesy Gary Farnson.

	C6	C8	C10
vg, dual exhausts, boattail, unique hub-tires as in #25 (also wrw). (Not complete if divided plastic wind-shield is missing (fragile), 3".............			No Price Found
CWV12 Three Piece Auto Set, #40 as follows:			
a. Midget Coupe Racer, no #, Hg, hl, divided open w/s, 2 ow, 2 colored body, mdw, headlamps and cowl ventilators!, 2-1/16"............	10	15	20
b. Midget Racer, no #, gilt driver, vl, hg, mdw.(easily confused w/Barclay #53), 2-1/8".......	10	15	20
c. Austin Bantam, no #, 2 dr. sedanette, 5 ow, hl, plain grille, rm, mdw. (easily confused with other makers' Bantams), 2".................	10	15	20
CWV 13 Dump Truck, no #, Ford?,			

	C6	C8	C10
hinged dump body, divided open w/s, 2 ow,hg, mdw, 3-1/8"........			No Price Found
CWV14 Tank Truck, no #, Ford?, 3 fuel tanks, otherwise matching above. Unusual 2 pc. body connected by rear axle, 3-3/16".........			No Price Found
"C2 to C Co." semi-trailer, cast iron steel wheels, small..............	30	45	60
Cabriolet with rumble seat, cast iron, circa 1920s..........................	200	300	400
Cadillac, plastic, 8" long.......................	20	30	40
"Cannonball Express" child's pedal car, red painted, 37" long...................	500	750	1000
Car, cast iron, 4" long...........................	75	112	150
Car, cast iron, with people, 3" long.........	35	52	70
Caterpillar Tractor, cast iron, red, with driver, chain treads.....................	150	225	300
Century of Progress cast iron Greyhound Bus, detachable trailer, 11"................	175	262	350

CHAMPION

The Champion Hardware Co., though in business from 1883-1954, produced toys only from 1930-36, as a Depression stopgap. As might be expected from a hardware firm, its toys were cast iron. During its toy years the Geneva, Ohio outfit was headed by C. I. Chamberlin.

	C6	C8	C10
Champion Coupe, Reo type,7-1/2" long....	212	318	425
Champion Gas and Motor Oil Truck, cast iron, circa 1930s, 8" long............	317	470	635
Champion four-casting nickeled radiator car, approx. 4" long...............	175	262	350
Champion Mack Dump, circa 1930s 7" long...	195	292	390
Champion Mack Stake Truck, circa 1930, 4-1/2" long.................................	90	135	180
Champion Mack Stake Truck,7-1/2" long..	237	355	475
"Champion" Motocycle and Rider, 4-1/2" long......................................	125	188	250
Champion Motorcycle, 7-1/4" long........	240	360	480
Champion Panel Delivery, 7-3/4" long...	425	638	850

CHAMPION, Mack Dump, 7" long. Courtesy Wilkinson Collection, Detroit Antique Toy Museum.

"CHAMPION", Policeman on Motorcycle. Courtesy Mapes Auctioneer & Appraisers.

CHEIN Mack Tanker Truck, 19" long, circa 1928. Courtesy Phillips New York.

	C6	C8	C10
Champion Policeman on Motorcycle, rubber tires, 7" long	500	750	1000
Champion Race Car, 2 riders, 5-1/2"	125	188	250
Champion Race Car, cast iron, detachable driver, 6" long	150	225	300
Champion Race Car, circa 1930s 9" long	363	543	725
Champion Sedan, 5-1/4" long	112	188	225
"Champion" Wrecker, cast iron, 7-1/2" long	265	400	530
Chein Army Truck, cannon on back, tin, early, 8-1/2" long	135	202	270
Chein Army Truck, open bed, tin, early, 8-1/2" long	135	202	270
Chein Hercules Mack Dump Truck tin, 20" long	490	675	900
Chein Hercules Motor Express, tin litho, Mack, 19-1/2" long	450	675	900
Chein Hercules Roadster	350	550	900
Chein Hercules Wrecker Truck, 20" long	500	750	1200
Chein "Junior Oil Tank" Truck, 1920s 8-1/2" long	62	93	125
Chein Mack Tanker Truck, circa 1928, Hercules, 19" long	500	750	1200
Chein Roadster, tin litho, circa 1925, 8 1/2" long	315	472	630
Chein "Royal Blue Line Coast to Coast Service"	800	1400	1800
Chein Touring Car, tin litho, 7" long	250	375	500
Chrysler Airflow, heavy sheet metal w/ wind-up motor. Tin grille, headlights and bumper, wooden wheels, 4" long	150	225	300

CHEIN Roadster, tin litho, circa 1925, 8 1/2" long. Courtesy Mapes Auctioneers & Appraisers.

CHEIN Hercules Motor Express. Courtesy Wilkinson Collection, Detroit Antique Toy Musuem.

	C6	C8	C10
Chrysler Airflow, cast iron, 1930s, 4-1/2" long	40	60	80
Chrysler Airflow, pressed steel, circa 1937 6" long	50	75	100
Circus Band Wagon, plays record and moves, comic musicians on top, circa 1922, 17" long	1000	1500	2000

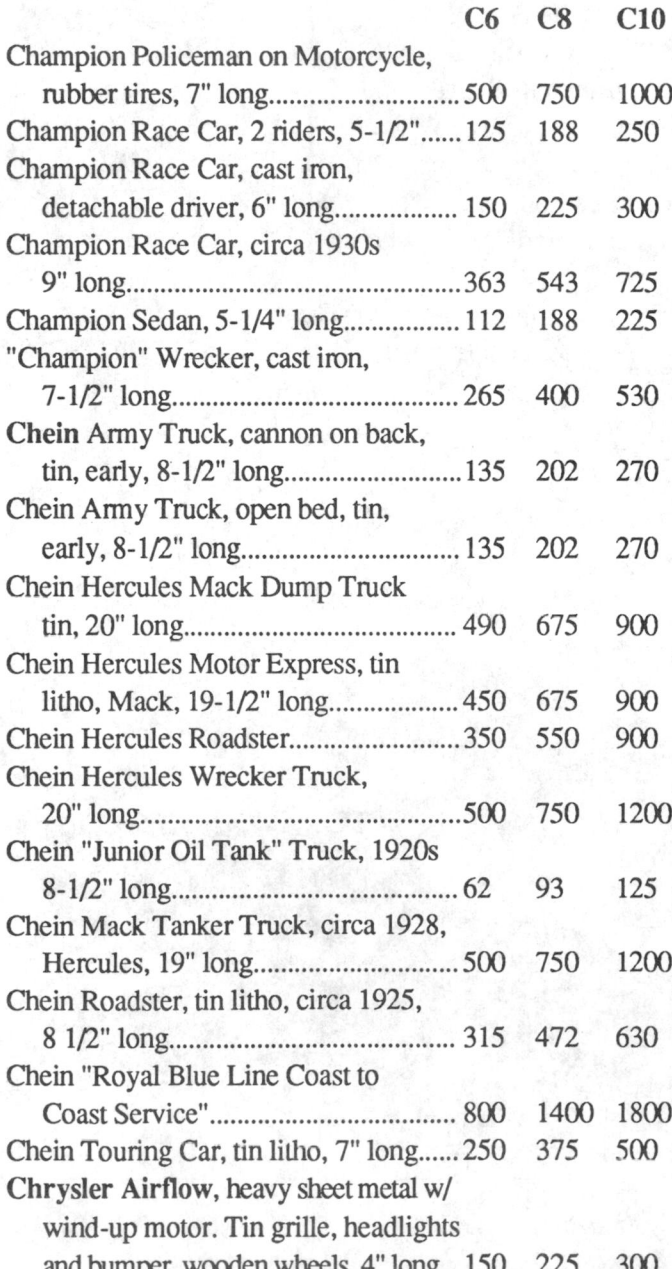

	C6	C8	C10
"City Fire Dept. Truck", 1930, pressed steel, rubber tires, 26" long	450	675	900
Clark friction auto, circa 1894, wood, iron and tin, 10-1/2" long	800	1300	2000
Clark friction auto, circa 1901, wood body covered with steel	700	1200	1500
Cleveland Toy Racer, aluminum, steel wheels, circa 1935, 13"long	175	262	350
Converse Auto with fringe on top, 3-seat, 1905, painted, pressed steel, clockwork, rubber tires	600	900	1200
Converse Fire Engine Ladder Truck, bell, wooden headlight, 1915, 10" long	1250	1875	2500
Converse Pick-up Truck, very early, open cab	500	750	1000
Converse Roadster, 1908, wind-up, open cab, 15-1/2" long	1100	1600	3000

	C6	C8	C10
Converse Touring Auto, 1910, pressed steel, canvas roof	900	1400	2300
Converse Transitional Taxi, clockwork, 10-1/2" long	525	770	1050
Cor-Cor Airflow windup, electric lights	700	1100	1700
Cor-Cor Bus, 23" long	500	750	1050
Cor-Cor Dump Truck, dumps back or side to side, 23" long	223	338	450
Cor-Cor Graham Paige Sedan, electric, 20" long	600	950	1300
Cor-Cor Van, painted metal, circa 1928, 23" long	200	300	400
Coupe, tin friction, 17-1/2" long	40	60	80
Coupe with rumble seat, tin, 1920s, 5" long	50	75	100

CLARK Friction Auto, circa 1894, 10-1/2" long, wood, iron and tin. Photo by Joe and Sharon Freed.

CONVERSE Transitional Taxi, 10-1/2" long. Courtesy Sotheby's New York.

CLEVELAND TOY racer, aluminum, 13" long. Courtesy Mapes Auctioneers & Appraisers.

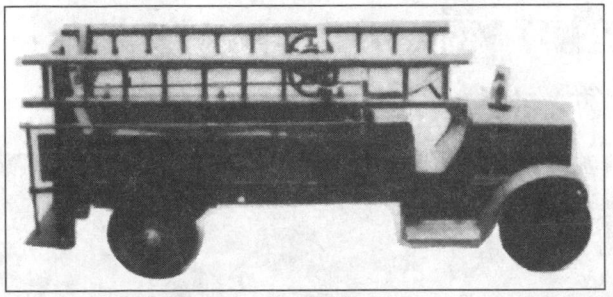

"City Fire Dept. Truck", 1930, 26" long. Courtesy Lloyd W. Ralston Auctions.

COURTLAND (WALT REACH)
NON-POWERED VEHICLES

List by Joe and Sharon Freed

	C6	C8	C10
600 Courtland Open Van Tractor-Trailer, 1946, retail price 49¢, L 13", W 3", H 3-1/4"	75	100	125
610 Courtland Side Dump Tractor-Trailer, 1946, retail prce 49¢, L 13", W 3", H 3-1/4"	50	75	100
620 Courtland Log Truck Tractor-Trailer, 1946, retail price 59¢, L 13", W 3", H 3-1/4"	75	100	125
700 Courtland Side Dump Tractor-Trailer, 1946, retail price 49¢, L 13", W 3", H 3-1/4"	50	75	100
900 Courtland Ice Cream Truck, 1946 retail price 39¢, L 9", W 3", H 2-3/4"	100	150	200
900 Courtland Moving and Storage Truck, 1946, retail price 39¢, L 9", W 3", H 2-3/4"	100	150	200

	C6	C8	C10
900 Courtland Fire Patrol No.2 Truck, 1946, retail price 39¢, L 9", W 3", H 2-3/4"	100	150	200
900 Courtland Express and Hauling Truck, retail price 39¢, 1946, L 9", W 3", H 2-3/4"	125	175	225
1050 Courtland Logging Camp Train Set, 1946 retail price $1.79, L 26-3/4", W 3", H 3-1/4"	No Price Found		
1060 Courtland Trailer Truck Parade, 1946, retail price $1.79, L 13", W 3", H 3-1/4"	No Price Found		
1070 Courtland Big 4 Truck Parade, 1946 retail price $1.79, The four 900 L 9-1/2", W 3-1/4", H-3"	No Price Found		
1200 Courtland Side Dump Tractor-Trailer, L 13", W 3", H 3-1/4"	100	150	200
Courtland Tractor-Trailer. Same tractor as No.2000 except marked, "Loft-Fresh Candies"	150	250	350

COURTLAND Non-Powered Vehicle Tractor-Trailer. Same tractor as No.2000 except marked "Loft-Fresh Candies". Photo courtesy Joe and Sharon Freed.

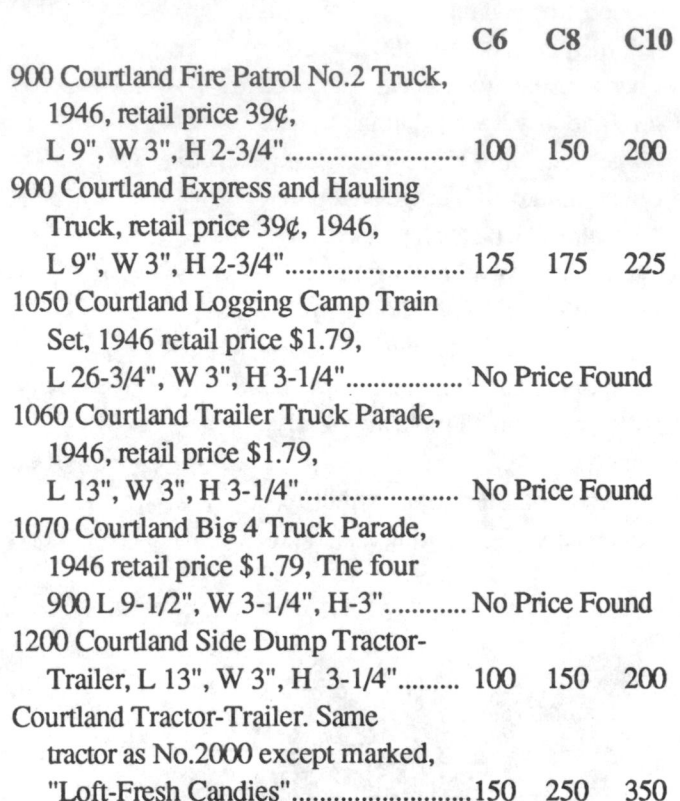

COURTLAND Friction-Powered Vehicle No.4000, Fire Chief Car, red & white, with red plastic bubble on hood. Photo courtesy Joe and Sharon Freed.

COURTLAND (WALT REACH)
FRICTION-POWERED VEHICLES

List by Joe and Sharon Feed

	C6	C8	C10
3875 Courtland Mechanical "Gulf" Gasoline Tractor-Trailer L 13", W 3", H 3-1/4"	175	250	325
4000 Courtland Woody Sedan, red & tan, L 7-1/4", W 3-1/4", H 2-3/4"	75	100	125

COURTLAND Non-Powered Vehicle No. 620 Log Truck. Photo courtesy Joe and Sharon Freed.

COURTLAND Friction-Powered Vehicle No.3875. Photo courtesy Mapes Auctioneers.

COURTLAND Friction-Powered Vehicle No.XXXX, Mechanical Military Gun Car, variation with litho gun shield. Photo courtesy Joe and Sharon Freed.

COURTLAND Friction-Powered Vehicle No.XXXX, "Pop-up" Ladder Fire Truck. Photo courtesy Joe and Sharon Freed.

COURTLAND Friction-Powered Vehicle No.XXXX, Dump Truck with dual rear wheels. Photo courtesy Joe and Sharon Freed.

	C6	C8	C10
4000 Courtland Woody Sedan, blue & tan,			
Note: This is one of only four Courtland styled toys stamped "A Walt Reach Toy by Courtland Toy co. Phila.,Pa. Made in U.S.A.". The only known Courtland-styled toys marked with the Courtland Toy Company, Philadelphia stamping is this No.4000 sedan,a non-powered "Fire Chief" car, a private garage similar to No. 9075 and a mechanical parking meter bank,			
L 7-1/4", W 3-1/4", H 2-3/4"	75	100	125
4060 Courtland Space Rocket Patrol Car, 1952 retail price 98¢,			
L 7-1/4", W 3-1/4", H 2-3/4"	150	225	300
7500 Courtland Mechanical State Police Car with siren,			
L 7-1/4", W 3-1/4", H 2-3/4"	125	175	225
7500 Courtland Mechanical Fire Chief Car with siren,			
L 7-1/4", W 3-1/4", H 3-1/4"	125	175	225
XXXX Courthland Dump Truck w/dual rear wheels,			
L 10-1/2", W 3", H 3-3/8"	125	200	275

	C6	C8	C10
7600 Courtland FBI Riot Squad Car			
L 7-1/4", W 3-1/4", H 2-3/4"	150	200	250
XXXX Courtland "Pop-Up" Ladder Fire Truck, L 13", W 3", H 3-1/4"	100	175	250
XXXX Courtland Mechanical Military Gun Car, painted gun shield,			
L 7-1/2", W 3-1/4", H 2-1/2"	125	200	275
XXXX Variation of above, lithographed gunshield	150	225	300

CRAFTOYS

By Fred Maxwell and Ron Eccles

Craftoy, a small Omaha, Nebraska firm, had a brief career casting slushmold vehicles before the War's need for lead brought the potmetal era to a long halt. We have discovered little more about the company than the accompanying sales sheet. It acquired some of the molds when Ralstoy was reorganizing about 1940.

For those readers accustomed to identifying by "those numbers", **Note**: #92 sedan has the same number as a Best Toy coupe but they are not the same car, #100 racer is obviously not the same as Best #100 sedan. Older molds were also used for #78 mixer, #81 racer and #102 gasoline semi-tanker, #101 fire truck, #103 speed car, #104 oil truck and #105 station wagon possibly come from Ralstoy. The ancestry of Kansas toy is evident in #17 tractor and the freight train set. The designs of the RR coal car, stockcar and tank car are recent or new. Thus we come to the end of the line as "those toys with the numbers" roll into history. These catalog numbers may or may not be found on the toys.

Black rubber wheels are seen to be characteristic of this line, but they are not exclusive with Craftoy.

	C6	C8	C10
Craftoy Tractor, "17", "Fordson", "Made in USA", farm tractor, driver, rear wheels larger, visible engine, 2-1/2"	8	12	16
Craftoy Fright Train, "3600", 16-1/2" Locomotive, 0-6-4, 4-1/2", "KT&N RR", cars 3-1/4", caboose 2-3/4", "Made in USA", value of indiv. cars	6	9	12
Craftoy Cement Mixer, "78", 2 open windows, "Made in USA", 3-3/4"	8	12	16
Craftoy Racer, "81", Miller FWD Indy racer, "Made in USA", 4-1/2"	10	15	20
Craftoy Sedan, #92, streamlined 2 door sedan, 4 open windows, screen pattern grille, 4" long	No Price Found		
Craftoy Racer #100, Indy type, driver, removable tin hood, rounded nose available in repros., 4-1/4" long	No Price Found		
Craftoy ? Racer, no #, Indy type, driver, removable tin hood, slanted nose, available in repros, 3-3/4" long	No Price Found		
Craftoy Fire Truck, #101, Hose Truck or Insurance Patrol, 4 open windows, 4-1/2" long	No Price Found		

Craftoy, Top #100. Bottom, Craftoy? Racer, No. #, Indy type, driver, removable tin hood. Photo by Fred Maxwell.

	C6	C8	C10
Craftoy Tanker, "102", 1938, International K-Line?, "Gasoline", semi-trailer, 2 open windows, See Ralstoy, 6-3/4" long	No Price Found		
Craftoy Speed Car, #103, streamlined closed racer, body trimmed in fantasy streamlines, 4-1/4" long, available in repros	No Price Found		
Craftoy Oil Truck, #104, 1938 International?, COE, "Gas","Oil" tanker, 2 open windows, 3-3/4"	No Price Found		
Craftoy Station Wagon, #105 streamlined, 4 open windows, 3-3/4"	No Price Found		

DAYTON FRICTION WORKS

Dayton was owned by D.P. Clark of Dayton, Ohio. Clark's wood and metal "Hill Climber" friction toys were his best known. Clark was in business from 1898, and his company was one of the first to use a friction motor, which is activated by moving the toy by hand against a surface and then releasing it. William Schieble, who joined the com-pany in the early 1900s, left in 1909 and formed the Schieble Toy and Novelty Company, using the "Hill Climber" name, which he felt was legally his, while Clark continued to use it, despite Schieble's lawsuits. Thus the parentage of some "Hill Climbers" is uncertain.

	C6	C8	C10
Dayton Coal and Ice Truck, tin, friction, circa 1920	200	300	400
Dayton Coupe, 1928, pressed steel,12"	260	390	520
Dayton Coupe, circa 1920, 12-1/2" long	600	900	1200
Dayton "Dayton Friction",pressed steel, rubber tires, 1920s, 14-1/4" long	250	375	500
Dayton Dump Truck	375	563	750
Dayton Fire Ladder Truck, 18" long	185	278	370
Dayton Fire Pumper, 1920	500	750	1000
Dayton Ladder Truck, 1920s	200	300	400

	C6	C8	C10
Dayton open Touring Car, dated 1909, friction motor, driver	250	375	500
Dayton Touring Car, friction motor, 13-1/2" long	500	750	1000
Dayton Touring Car, unpowered 13-1/2" long	350	525	700
Delivery Truck, cast iron, 3 1/2" long	60	90	120
Delivery Truck with driver, friction 10-1/2" long	100	150	200
Delivery Truck, Packard,steel, 28"long	400	600	800

DENT HARDWARE COMPANY

Dent, of Fullerton, Pennsylvania, was in business from 1895-1973. Henry H. Dent, with four partners, was the owner. Cast iron toys seem to have first emerged in 1898. Dent is known for particularly fine castings in its vehicles.

It was also one of the first manufacturers to try (with little success) aluminum toys (in the 1920s). Toys seem to have been phased out during the hard time of the Depression.

	C6	C8	C10
Dent "American Oil Co.", cast iron truck, approx. 10-1/2" long	800	1200	1600
Dent Bus, cast iron, 6-1/4" long	375	563	750
Dent "Bus Line", 9" long	387	580	775
Dent Bus, 10-1/2" long	500	800	1200
Dent Coast to Coast Bus, 7-1/2" long	125	187	250
Dent "Coast to Coast" Bus, 10" long	450	675	900
Dent "Coast to Coast" Bus, circa 1925, 15" long	750	1000	1500
Dent "Contractors" Mack Dump, open cab, 10-1/2" long	1200	2000	3000
Dent Coupe, 5" long	125	188	250
Dent "Express J & B" Stakebed Truck, 1915, driver, 14-1/2" long	500	800	1100
Dent Fire Truck, cast iron, 7" long	150	225	300
Dent Fire Ladder Truck with driver 8-1/2" long	450	675	900
Dent Fire Truck with ladder and men, cast iron, 18" long	900	1350	1800
Dent "Freeman's Dairy" Truck, sliding doors, milkman, 6" long	700	1100	1550
Dent Hose Reeler with men, cast iron, large	500	750	1000
Dent "Interurban" Bus, cast iron,9" long	425	638	850
Dent LaSalle, approx. 4" long	200	300	400
Dent Ladder Truck, two drivers, 10" long	250	375	500
Dent Mack Dump Truck, circa 1925, iron wheels, 4-1/2" long	55	82	110

	C6	C8	C10
Dent Model T two door sedan, iron wheels, circa 1925	125	187	250
Dent "Patrol",circa 1920s,6-1/2" long	125	187	250
Dent "Police Patrol", 8-3/4" long	750	1125	1500
Dent "Public Service" Bus, circa 1926, 13-1/2" long	2500	4000	5800
Dent Sedan, spare tire, has stop and go light, full bumpers on front, 7-1/2"	900	1350	1800
Dent Steam Roller, cast iron, 6" long	45	68	90
Dent Touring Car, driver & passenger, 12" long	450	675	900
Dent "Valley View Dairy", 8" long	700	1200	1700
Dent Yellow Cab, approx. 7-3/4" long	450	675	900
"Dept. of Street Cleaning" Dump Truck, circa 1935, 10-1/2" long	105	158	210

DENT "Police Patrol", approx. 8-3/4" long. Courtesy Phillips New York.

DINKY

Dinky toys were first made in England in 1932 under the name "Modeled Miniatures", later "Meccano Miniatures", and in 1934, "Dinky", which in England means "fetching"

	C6	C8	C10
Dinky 14c Coventry Fork Lift	27	41	55
Dinky 23h Ferrari Racer	17	26	35
Dinky 25c Flat Truck	75	112	150
Dinky 27f 1948 Plymouth Station Wagon	60	90	120
Dinky 29c Double Decker Bus	65	98	130
Dinky 30r Fordson Truck	17	26	35
Dinky 32c/576 Panhard Esso	100	150	200
Dinky 34 Royal Mail Van	45	68	90
Dinky 36b Bentley	40	60	80
Dinky 36c Humber, 1936	30	45	60
Dinky 36d Rover	62	93	125
Dinky 38c Lagonda	30	45	60
Dinky 38d Alvis	30	45	60
Dinky 39c Lincoln Zephyr	150	225	300
Dinky 40a Riley 4DS	29	43	58
Dinky 45 Vauxhall Victor	15	22	30
Dinky 97 Euclid Truck	11	16	22
Dinky 106 Thunderbird 2 space	45	68	90
Dinky 112 Triumph Purdey	17	26	35
Dinky 130 Ford Corsair	22	33	45
Dinky 134 Triumph Vitesse	22	33	45
Dinky 135 Triumph 2000	25	38	50
Dinky 137 Plymouth, 1963	45	68	90
Dinky 151 Austin Devon	17	26	35
Dinky 154 Ford Taurus	17	26	35
Dinky 157 Jaguar XK 120	55	82	110
Dinky 168 Ford Escort	17	26	35
Dinky 172 Studebaker Land Cruiser	70	105	140
Dinky 174 Hudson Hornet Sedan	62	93	135
Dinky 181 Volkswagen MBD	40	60	80
Dinky 200 Matra 630	17	26	35
Dinky 201 Plymouth Rally, 1976	17	26	35
Dinky 207 Triumph TR7 Leyland	17	26	35
Dinky 227 Beach Buggy	17	26	35
Dinky 241 Austin Taxi	17	26	35
Dinky 252 1968 Pontiac	22	33	45
Dinky 254 Taxi	21	31	42
Dinky 261 Telephone Van	37	55	75
Dinky 267 Dodge Fire Rescue	27	41	55
Dinky 267 Bedford Dump	9	13	18
Dinky 308 Leyland Tractor	25	38	50
Dinky 344 Estate Car	42	63	85

DINKY, Left to Right: 157 Jaguar KX120 Coupe, 334 Estate Car. Courtesy Phillips, New York.

DINKY, Left to Right: 174 Hudson Hornet Sedan, 172 Studebaker Land Cruiser. Courtesy Phillips New York.

DOEPKE "MODEL TOYS"

By Ray Funk

(See also Miscellaneous)

RAY FUNK is a leading collector and authority on trains and other toys, as well as a collector and authority on comic books and western literature.

Doepke "Model Toys" advertised their toys as outlasting all others 3 to 1. The company's full title was the "Charles Wm. Doepke Mfg. Co., Inc." of Rossmoyne, Ohio. Each toy was an authorized replica of the actual thing and the decals and coloring were exactly as upon the real equipment or trucks, with the exceptions of the manufacturer having his own, in this case "Model Toys."

At the end of the Second World War, the Doepke Corp. hit the market with five models, first in a line of heavy duty metal operating replicas, employing metal tread or authentic miniature tires, either Goodyear or Firestone, with authentic tread and name and tire sizes, exactly as on the real tires. This, to the best of my knowledge, has never been done so perfectly, even in the model kits of today.

These toys all had rubber smoke stacks, and received the approval of Parents Magazine, P.T.A., Boy's Life Magazine, and all other experts and advocates of good toys at that period. The first five numbers were 2000, 2001, 2002, 2006, 2007. Why not 3, 4, and 5, I cannot say. Perhaps Doepke had toys planned for these numbers that fell through. Following is a list of the Doepke vehicles.

No. 2000, Wooldridge H.D. Earth hauler, bright yellow, four huge tires, 25" long, and weighing 10 lbs. The actual manufacturer's address is listed as Sunnyvale, Calif. I'm sure most of you have seen the John Wayne movie, "The Fighting Seabee", which used several of these, along with caterpillar bulldozers and road graders. These Wooldridge's caught my eye with their maneuvering ability, and could traverse the roughest terrain easily. Two long doors, the length of the bottom of the dirt-hauling area, could be released to deposit a load. Price was $14.75 new in 1945.

No. 2001, Barber-Greene high-capacity bucket loader, 13" high, 10 lbs., dark green, all steel and rolling on steel tread, was designed as a toy to load earth haulers. Hand crank operated, operated exactly as the real thing. Price $14.75.

No. 2002, Jaeger Concrete Mixer, bright yellow, 15" long, 8 lbs. on four wheels, steerable via draw bar (all model toys steered exactly like the real thing), though perhaps the best-detailed, was the poorest selling toy, as although you could, it wasn't feasible to really mix concrete in them, due to

small amount received versus cleaning time. This toy was priced at $10.75 to $13.75.

No. 2006, Adams Diesel Roadgrader, dark orange, 26" long, 14 lbs., all six wheels, three axles, and blade adjustable to all angles, exactly like the real thing, steerable via steering wheel, priced at $14.75.

No. 2007, Unit Mobile Crane, dark orange, 11 1/2" long, 19 1/2" boom, 8 lbs. 8 oz., adjustable side jacks, steered via a drawbar, with block and tackle, and removable operating clam shell as standard accessory. Priced at $14.75.

No number 2008, as the next year, No. 2009 was released and No. 2000 dropped. **No. 2009** was a Euclid Earth-Hauler Truck, with uncoupling four-wheel tractor to use to tow other toys, 27" long, 11 lbs., Euclid green, or light roadgrader orange, the trailer dumped in the same way as the Wooldridge. Priced $14.75.

No. 2010, American-LaFrance Pumper Fire Truck, 18" long, 7 lbs., bright red with chrome trim, ladder, bell, fire extinguisher, hoses and nozzle, a reservoir that held water for hand-operated pressure pump. A beautiful toy at $16.75.

No. 2011, Heiliner Earth Scraper, 29" long, 13 lbs., bright dark red, loaded and dumped and operated on four wheels as the Wooldridge did. Priced at $16.75.

No. 2012, Caterpillar D6 Tractor and Bulldozer, caterpillar yellow, 15" long, 7 lbs., with real bulldozer treads for sharp realistic turning (removable only by using punch and hammer to remove connecting pin from between two of the pads) and adjustable bulldozer blade, plus heavy draw bar. Truly a beautiful toy at $13.75. Diesel motor was cast metal.

No. 2013 eliminated and replaced No. 2001, No. 2013, Barber-Green mobile high-capacity bucket loader, 22" long, 12" high, 10 lbs., buckets on chains and rubber conveyor belt, adjustable and steered by steering wheel, priced at $19.75.

No. 2014, American LaFrance Aerial Ladder Truck, 23" long, 42" extended ladder height, 11 lbs., bright red and chrome, bell, red light, adjustable side jacks, single unit truck steered by steering wheel, priced at $20.75.

Doepke "Model Toys" were doomed to extinction by lower-priced, lighter-constructed imitators of lesser quality, some of which were started in the 1920s, and others that came into being in the 1950s, several of which are still around today, but none ever containing, before or after, the heavy-duty constructed realism and operating qualities as had the one and only "Model Toys".

Of the Doepke Model Toys that were mass produced, several had variations in their basic construction from time to time. Usually these changes were an elimination of the more intricate operating procedures, and had little or no effect on the toy's overall outward appearance.

In Antique Toy World, Philip Sayer wrote a two part article on the Doepke Co., and featured pictures of nearly all toys manufactured by the firm. The ones that were produced in such limited numbers (only one to a few), are mentioned and often times described. Also listed are nearly all of the slight changes in the mass produced toys, though I could not find (perhaps overlooked it) mention of the change in the D6 Caterpillar. The first models to hit the market have the front axles held tightly forward by springs, so when being pushed forward and they strike a solid object to climb over, there is some give to absorb the shock and protect the tract pads. Later models eliminated this and opted for simple axle wells as in the rear wheels. Had I not had both types, this slight change would have easily gone unnoticed.

It would seem that the Doepke Co. would accept orders to make model toys of the real thing for the actual producers, and the toys with the most allure, playability, and feasible mass production design, and greatest entertainment provided to the child that received one, would be mass produced. Of the others that would not withstand rough handling by young hands, or because of cost and time required to produce them, there were only one to a few produced as previously mentioned. This is no doubt the explanation for the number gaps between the marketed items.

Among the scarcer articles produced, were even a few automobiles, avidly sought after by collectors that have delved into this company's past history to any depth. Of these, perhaps there were catalogs or brochures about them, though all I have seen are the ones dealing with the mass produced toys I have listed.

DOEPKE Catalog illustration of Model No. 2012. Photo by Bill Kaufman. Courtesy Ray Funk.

An ad for DOEPKE Model Toys. Photo by Bill Kaufman. Courtesy Ray Funk.

DOEPKE No. 2000 Wooldridge. Courtesy Ray Funk.

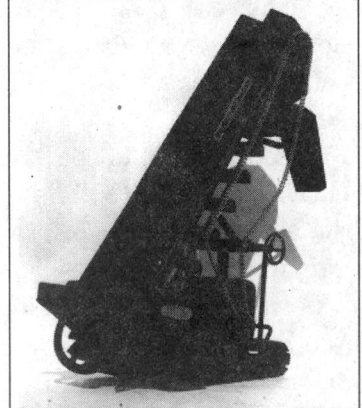

DOEPKE No. 2001, Barber-Greene high capacity bucket loader. Courtesy Ray Funk.

DOEPKE No. 2018 Jaguar. Courtesy Ray Funk.

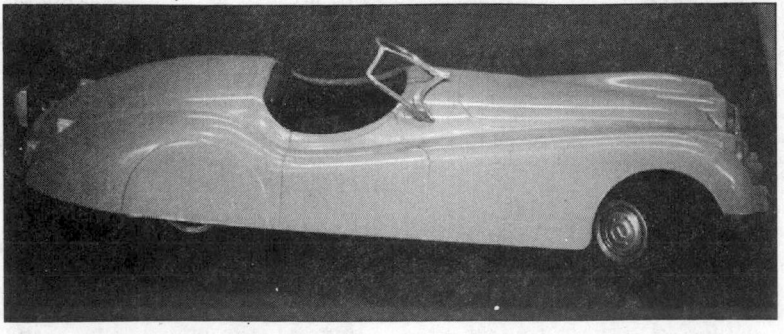

Dump Truck, steel wind-up, 4 1/2 long, Courtesy James S. Maxwell/Virgina Caputo. Photo by Virginia Caputo.

DOEPKE No. 2012, Caterpillar D6's. Courtesy Ray Funk.

DOEPKE No. 2007, Unit Mobile Crane. Courtesy Ray Funk.

	C6	C8	C10
Doepke No. 2000 Wooldridge H.D. Earth Hauler, 25" long	130	195	260
Doepke No. 2001 Barber-Greene high capacity bucket loader, tracks, 13" high	225	338	450
Doepke No. 2002 Jaeger Concrete Mixer, 15" long	180	270	360
Docpkc No. 2006 Adams Diesel Road Grader, 26" long	125	188	250
Doepke No. 2007 Unit Mobile Crane, 11-1/2" long	115	172	330
Doepke No. 2008 American LaFrance Aerial Ladder Truck	220	330	440
Doepke No. 2009 Euclid Earth Hauler Truck, 27" long	137	205	275
Doepke No. 2020 American LaFrance Pumper Fire Truck, 18" long	150	225	275
Doepke No. 2011 Heiliner Earth Scraper, 29" long	135	202	270
Doepke No. 2012 Caterpillar D6 Tractor and Bulldozer, 15" long	232	348	465
Doepke No. 2013 Barber-Greene Mobile high-capacity Bucket Loader, wheels, 22" long	212	318	425
Doepke No. 2014 American LaFrance Aerial Ladder Fire Truck, 23" long	175	262	350
Doepke No. 2015 Clark Airport Tractor and Baggage Trailers	230	345	460

	C6	C8	C10
Doepke No. 2015 MG, 1954, 15" long	225	338	450
Doepke No. 2018 Jaguar, 1955	325	487	650
Doepke No. 2023 Searchlight Truck 1955	550	850	1300
Druge Bros. "Hyster" lumber carrier	150	225	300
Dump Truck, cast iron "2205", 4-1/2" long	90	135	180
Dump Truck, tin, wooden wheels, 5-3/4" long	20	30	40
Dump Truck pressed steel, circa 1939, 6" long	50	75	100
Dump Truck, cast iron, driver, 7" long	90	135	180
Dump Truck (Beck), steers via horn on top of cab, late 1940s, large	60	90	120
Dump Truck, steel windup, 4-1/2" long	5	8	10

DUNWELL

Dunwell was the trade name given to its toys by Metal Products Co. of Clifton, New Jersey. Its trucks seem to have been sold circa 1953 - 1958. Their line resembles Tonka's rather closely, and is rare.

	C6	C8	C10
Dunwell Auto Transport	162	243	325
Dunwell Cattle Semi	90	135	180
Dunwell "Grain Hauler"	50	75	100
Dunwell Log Truck	115	172	230
Dunwell "Red Star Express Lines" Truck	300	450	650
Dunwell "Snowcrop" Refrigerator Semi	190	285	380
Dunwell "Steel Carrier Co." Semi	200	300	400
Dunwell Wrecker	175	263	350

DYNA-MODEL PRODUCTS COMPANY
(Dyna-Mo)
by Fred Maxwell

Dyna-Model Products Co., 93 South Street, Oyster Bay, Long Island, New York, may have pioneered the scale models industry dominating today's markets with their "Dyna-Mo" brand of HO toys to be used in train layouts. They are rather high quality pot-metal toys, identified by their method of assembling body parts, clamping axles between small posts and the standardized appearance of the undersides of the whole line.

Probably produced in the 1930's, and perhaps in the post-war era, the toys were made by a coarse diecasting process. The earlier vintage cars were made into two to five parts, exclusive of wheels and axles, to be pinned, clamped or glued together: body, frame, steering wheel, top and windshield. Some were packaged as kits, with instructions printed on the box: "Pinch ends of axel (their spelling) after installing wheels" (R-26). The toys were factory painted in as many as 4 colors per toy.

	C6	C8	C10
D1 Dyna "R-26 HO Surrey, 35c": Horseless carriage, tiller steering, 3 colors, 3 pc. body, kit, 1-3/4"	4	6	8
D2 Dyna Touring Car: Antique Stanley Steamer, open tonneau, rt. hand steering, 4 colors, 4 pc., 2"	4	6	8
D3 Dyna Speedster: Antique Mercer, rt. hand steering, 4 colors, 3 pc. 2"	4	6	8
D4 Dyna Roadster: Antique Buick?, open, rt. hand steering, 4 pcs., 3 colors, 1-7/8"	4	6	8
D5 Dyna Touring Car: Antique, realistic folded top attachable w/hinge pins, left hand steering, 5 pcs., 2 colors, 1-7/8"	4	6	8
D6 Dyna "R-61 HO Model T Ford 1914 touring with top 60c": one piece body, top up, 3 colors. "cut plastic windshield to fit, darken edges with ink or paint and glue top and windshield in place, in slots provided", 1-5/8"	4	6	8
D7 Dyna Touring Car: 1914 Ford, top down cast in one-piece body, glued windshield, 3 colors, 1-3/4"	4	6	8
D8 Dyna Roadster: 1920's Packard convertible, top down, rumble seat, one piece body, glued windshield, spoked wheels, 3 colors, 2"	6	9	12
D9 Dyna Roadster: Packard, same as above, top up, 3 colors, 2"	6	9	12
D10 Dyna Touring: Packard, same as above, top down, 3 colors, 2"	6	9	12
D11 Dyna Roadster: Model A Ford? top down, open rumble seat, disc wheels, one piece body, unpainted, 2"	2	3	4
D12 Dyna Sedan: Buick Sedan, 1930's, open windshield and windows, 2 colors, 2"	4	6	8
D13 Dyna "R-68 HO Buick Convertible 55c": late 1930s, open, 2 dr. sedan, top down, one piece body, solid cast windshield, disc wheels, 2-3/8"	6	9	12
D14 Dyna Sedan: Buick 2 dr. airflow, open windshield and windows 2-3/8"	6	9	12
D15 Dyna Taxi: Buick Sedan, late 1930's, open windshield and windows, 2 colors, 2-3/8"	6	9	12
D16 Dyna Convertible, Cadillac 2 dr. Sedan, late 1930's, 2-3/8"	6	9	12
D17 Dyna Sedan: Cadillac 2 dr. Sedan, open windshield and windows, incl. rear, late 1930's, 2-3/8"	6	9	12
D18 Dyna Taxi: Cadillac Sedan, late 1930's, open windshield and windows including rear, 2 colors, 2-3/8"	6	9	12
D19 Dyna Sedan: Pontiac 4 dr. airflow, open windshield and windows incl. rear, 2-3/8"	6	9	12
D20 Dyna Limousine: Cadillac, late 1930's, open windows as above, 2-1/2"	6	9	12
D21 Dyna Delivery Van: Pontiac, late 1930's, open windshield and door windows, 2-3/8"	4	6	8
D22 Dyna Pickup Truck: GMC?, late 1930's, open windows, spoked wheels, 2 pcs, 3 colors, 2-1/2"	4	6	8

	C6	C8	C10
D23 Dyna Wrecker: GMC?, late 1930's, open windows, 3 piece, 4 colors, 2-3/4"	6	9	12
D24 Dyna Dump Truck: Open windows, hinged body with realistic load of coal, 3 peices, 2 colors, dual rear wheels, 2-3/4"	8	12	16
D25 Dyna Pickup Truck: GMC?, 1930's,			

	C6	C8	C10
one piece, open windows, one color, 2"	4	6	9
D26 Dyna Pickup Truck: Mack?, "US Army", Air Corps star decals, late 1930's, 2 pc. body, 2 colors, 2"	4	6	8
D27 Dyna Truck: Mack? same chassis as above, but tarpaulin covered, 2 pc. body, 2"	4	6	8

DYNA-MODEL, Top, Left to Right: D1, Ford T Roadster, 1-7/8", D7, D3, Franklin Steam Touring 2 -1/8". Middle, Left to Right: D5, D6, D9, D10, D8. Bottom, Left to Right: D11, Cadillac Sedan 2", D23, D16. Photo by Fred Maxwell.

DYNA-MODEL, Top, Left to Right: D14, D20?, D12, Cadillac 2-door sedan, 2-3/8". Middle, Left to Right: D15, D18, D21. Bottom, Left to Right: D22, D23, D24. Photo by Fred Maxwell.

	C6	C8	C10
Eldon Corvette, 14" long	40	60	80
Eldon Road Race slot car set, 1965	32	48	65
Eldon Rocket-Firing Tank, 8" long	19	28	38
Eldon Tow Truck, plastic, 18" long	42	63	85

ERIE
(Parker White Metal)
Listing by Dave Leopard

According to James Apthorpe, Erie toys were made by Parker White Metal Company, which apparently began in Erie, Pennsylvania, but moved to Fairview (West of Erie), Pa. in the early 1960s. However, according to company officials he contacted, the firm made toys only prior to World War II. It printed no catalogs.

ERIE Sedan, two-door. Photo by James Apthorpe.

	C6	C8	C10
EV01 Lincoln Zephyr Sedan, 1936 painted, 5-1/2" long	40	50	60

	C6	C8	C10
EV02 Lincoln Zephyr Sedan, 1936, plated, 5-1/2" long	45	55	65
EV03 Lincoln Zephyr Sedan, 1936, painted, 3-1/2" long	25	30	35
EV04 Lincoln Zephyr Sedan, 1936, plated, 3-1/2" long	30	35	40
EV05 Packard Roadster, 1936, painted, 6" long	40	50	60
EV06 Packard Roadster, 1936 plated, 6" long	45	55	65
EV07 Packard Roadster, 1936, painted, 3-1/2" long	25	30	35
EV08 Packard Roadster, 1936, plated, 3-1/2" long	30	35	40
EV09 Ford Pickup Truck, 1935, low sides, painted, 5" long	40	50	60
EV10 Ford Pickup Truck, 1935, low sides, plated, 5" long	45	55	65
EV11 Ford Pickup Truck, 1935, high sides, large rear window, 5" long	40	50	60
EV12 Ford Pickup Truck, 1935, high sides, small rear window, 5" long	40	50	60
EV13 Ford Ice Truck, 1935, "Pure Ice Co.", 5" long	50	60	70
EV14 Ford Tow Truck, 1935, "Servel Body", 5" long	50	60	70

	C6	C8	C10
EV15 Cabover Truck, c. 1937, no tail gate, 3-1/4"................20		25	30
EV16 Cabover Truck, c 1937, tailgate, updated, 3-1/4" long..........20		25	30
EV17 Tow Truck, c. 1939, no chassis, 4-1/4" long..........30		35	40
EV18 Sedan, c. 1939, futuristic, fin on trunk, no chassis, 4-1/4" long.........30		35	40
EV19 Coupe, c. 1939, futuristic, no chassis, 4-1/4" long.........30		35	40
EV20 Sedan, c. 1939, sharknose, no chassis, 4-1/4" long.........30		35	40

Ertl

Ertl was begun by Fred Ertl Sr. in 1945, working out of his Dubuque, Iowa home. As business expanded, the firm moved to Dyersville. Ertl had learned about using sand molds in his native Germany, and very early in the company's history began working directly from the original blueprints to make his toy tractors, trucks and other wheeled toys. Ertl's specialty is farm toys, with rights obtained from such manufacturers as International Harvester and John Deere. Today Ertl is the largest manufacturer of toy farm equipment in the world, and in addition makes a number of other toys, such as cars, trucks and airplanes.

	C6	C8	C10
Ertl Allis-Chalmers B-112 Tractor.........70		110	165
Ertl Conoco Tanker.................75		120	175
Ertl Fleetstar Hi-Side Dump Truck, red/white...............85		135	195
Ertl Fleetstar Tilt Bed, green..........70		120	180
Ertl Fleetstar 10-wheel Dump Truck, red...............70		120	180
Ertl Ford 8000 Tractor, early..........25		40	60
Ertl GE Truck, white............15		22	30
Ertl Gleaner C-280 w/corn picker..........25		45	60
Ertl Grain Hopper, early............22		34	48
Ertl IHC Farmal 806, square fender........100		175	230
Ertl International Fleetstar Gravity Feed Truck..............150		250	350
Ertl International Scout, maroon, or blue...............85		135	195
Ertl John Deere 500 Bulldozer w/blade..............40		70	100
Ertl John Deere 6600 Combine..............60		100	140
Ertl Loadstar Box Van, lavender, white..............200		375	575
Ertl Lordstar Concrete Truck, red/wht... 225		400	600

	C6	C8	C10
Ertl Loadstar Dump Truck.................140		250	325
Ertl Loadstar Grain/Cattle Stake Truck.. 120		200	270
Ertl Loadstar Straight Cab & Chassis only...............55		85	125
Ertl Loadstar Tilt Bed, green/gray..........125		175	260
Ertl Loadstar Tow Truck, white/red.......200		375	575
Ertl Mary Kay Cosmetics Trailer Truck.....65		115	150
Ertl Mobile Tanker..................40		65	88
Ertl Picker..................25		40	60
Ertl Texaco Tanker No. 2......................150		250	350
Ertl "Van Lines" Pup Trailer only, white..............100		150	225
Ertl White Cabover Dump Truck, white/red.............165		265	400
Fallows Toys, Frederick & Henry Horseless Carriage with driver, cast iron and tin, circa 1905, 8".........350		525	700

FALLOWS TOYS, Frederick & Henry, Horseless Carriage with driver, 8" long. Courtesy Wilkinson Collection, Detroit Antique Toy Museum.

	C6	C8	C10
Fire Pumper, cast iron, circa 1935 5" long...............75		112	150
Fire Pumper, cast iron, approx. 6-1/2" long.......................100		150	200
Fire Pumper, cast iron, 11" long............125		187	250

FIRESTONE FA03 (both) with original box. Photo by Ron Smith.

Fire Pumper, cast iron, 5" long, circa 1935. Courtesy Mapes Auctioneers & Appraisers.

FIRESTONE

The following list, with its codings, was compiled by Dave Leopard.

	C6	C8	C10
FA01 '39 Mercury fastback 4 door sedan, 4-3/4" long	60	90	120
FA02 '35 Ford 2 door humpback sedan, 4-7/8" long	70	105	140
FA03 '36 Ford 2 door humpback sedan, 4-7/8" long	75	112	150
Ford coupe, 1924, 4" long	80	120	160
Ford coupe, blue, chrome wheels, 5" long	80	120	160
Ford coupe, cast iron, black, chrome wheels, circa 1920s, 5" long	80	120	160

GIFTCRAFT, TA01. Photo by Dave Leopard.

	C6	C8	C10
"Fordson" Tractor w/driver, cast iron, 5-3/4" long	140	210	280
Fordson Tractor with hay rake, cast iron, 1930s	150	225	300

Freidag

(pronounced "Friday"), circa 1920-22, Freeport, Illinois

	C6	C8	C10
Freidag Bus, cast iron 6-3/4" long	225	338	450
Freidag Coupe, cast iron, 5-3/4" long	290	435	580
Freidag Racer, driver & passenger 6-1/2" long	400	600	800
Gibbs "Gibbs No. 701" Truck	150	250	350
Giftcraft (possibly only the distributor) TA01 Fastback Sedan, circa 1946, Nash, solid rubber, 4" long	15	22	30

Fire Pumper, cast iron, 11" long. Photo by Bill Kaufman. Courtesy Good Old Days Store.

GIRARD Fire Chief Siren Coupe. Photo By Bill Kaufman.

GREY IRON "Midget" Vehicles, approx. 1-1/2" long. Photo by Stan Alekna.

New to most collectors, and perhaps all, is that Grey Iron made this Ford Coupe. It came in two sizes, 8-3/8" long and 5-5/8" long. It appears in a recently-discovered No. 24 Grey Iron catalog, suggesting it may have been sold in 1924. It came with a driver, as shown.

GIRARD Touring Bus. Courtesy Mapes Auctioneers & Appraisers.

GIRARD

	C6	C8	C10
Girard Coupe, battery operated headlights, 14" long	292	438	585
Girard Fire Chief Car, 15" long	250	375	500
Girard "Fire Chief Siren Coupe" 14-1/2" long	350	525	700
Girard Fire Truck, 1920s, 12" long	125	188	250
Girard Pump Truck, battery operated, headlights, 10" long	100	150	200
Girard Roadster, electrified, 14-1/2" long	195	292	390
Girard Side Dump, 11-1/2" long	97	145	195
Girard Stake Truck, electric, headlights, 10" long	150	225	300
Girard Tank Truck, wood wheels, 11-1/2" long	70	105	140
Girard Touring Bus, painted tin, circa 1920, 12" long	125	188	250
Girard Truck with Trailer, 1930s, 17" long	107	160	215
Goodee Cadillac Convertible, 1957?, 3" long	9	13	18

GREY IRON

	C6	C8	C10
Grey Iron, Convertible Midget, 1-1/2"	20	30	40
Grey Iron, Coupe Midget, 1-1/2" long	20	30	40
Grey Iron, Delivery Truck, Midget, 1-1/2" long	20	30	40
Grey Iron, Racer, Midget, 1-1/2" long	20	30	40

	C6	C8	C10
Grey Iron, Sedan, Airflow Type, Midget, 1-1/2" long	20	30	40
Grey Iron, Sedan, older, Midget, 1-1/2" long	20	30	40
Grey Iron, Sedan, 1927, 9" long	1000	1500	2000
"Guided Missile Unit No. 10" Truck, tin litho, circa 1960	60	90	120
Hafner "Auto Express Co." Truck, steel clockwork, 8-1/2" long	450	675	900
Hafner Curved Dash Olds, circa 1903, pressed steel, clockwork, 10"long	500	750	1000
Hafner Roundabout with upholstered drivers seat, steel clockwork, 7"	450	675	900
Hafner Touring Car, pressed steel, clockwork, 10" long	750	1125	1500
Happy Sam driving wood truck, circa 1920s, 8" long	80	120	160

HAFNER curved dash Olds, circa 1903. Courtesy Sotheby's New York.

HAFNER, Left to Right: "Auto Express Co.", Roundabout with upholstered driver's seat. Courtesy Sotheby's New York.

HILLCLIMBER Horseless Carriage, woman driver, 7" long. Courtesy Mapes Acutioneers & Appraisers.

HAFNER Touring Car, 10" long. Courtesy Sotheby's New York.

HESS
by Thomas G. Nefos

Promotional vehicles, all of them plastic, are turned out annually for Hess Service Stations in limited editions available to the public through the Christmas season. Hess headquarters are in Woodbridge, NJ, under the name Amerada Hess. Virtually all collector sales are mint in the box, thus the pricing here.

	MIB
1964 B-Model Mack Tanker	1895
1967 Split Window, Velvet Bottom Box	2200
1968 Tanker Truck	550
1969 Amerade Hess Truck	2600
1970 Pumper Fire Truck	600
1972 Split Window Tanker	295
1975 Box Trailer	310
1976 Box Trailer w/Barrels	300
1977 Tank Truck - Large Label	165
1978 Tank Truck - Small Label	175
1980 Training Van	295
1982 "First Hess Truck"	75
1983 "First Hess Truck", Bank	85
1984 Tank Truck Bank	80
1986 Ladder, Fire Truck, red	85
1987 "19 Wheeler" Truck w/Barrels	60
1988 Race Car Transporter	65

	MIB
1989 Ladder Fire Truck w/Siren, white	50
1990 Tanker Truck w/Horn	38
1991 Semi Tanker Truck	50
1992 Like 1991 but remote control	20

	C6	C8	C10
Hillclimber "Ambulance", very early, 10-1/2" long	500	800	1100
Hillclimber Armored Truck, pressed steel friction, 11" long	500	800	1100
Hillclimber Auto, woman driver, friction, very early, 6" long	500	750	1000
Hillclimber Hook and Ladder Wagon, painted pressed steel friction, driver, 20" long	500	750	100
Hillclimber Horseless Carriage, woman driver, cast iron and wood, very early, 7" long	400	600	800
Hillclimber Racer with track, 7-1/2" long	375	525	750
Hillclimber Touring Car, 11" long	375	562	750
Hiller Comet Race Car,"3", fuel-powered, circa 1940-42	1000	1500	2000
Hoge Fire Chief Car, 15" long	350	525	700
"Holmes Coal Co." pressed steel delivery truck, 17-1/2" long	400	600	800
Hook and Ladder, aluminum, with driver, 13" long	100	150	200
Hook and Ladder, tin friction, 21"long	100	150	200
Hose Wagon, 1897, two riders, friction toy	125	187	250

HESS 1970 Red Pumper Fire Truck. Courtesy Thomas G. Nefos, Federal Shipping Network.

"Holmes Coal Co.". Courtesy Sotheby's New York.

HESS 1976 Box Trailer. Courtesy Thomas G. Nefos, Federal Shipping Network.

HESS 1982 "First Hess Truck". Courtesy Thomas G. Nefos, Federal Shipping Network.

HESS 1989 Ladder Fire Truck. Courtesy Thomas G. Nefos, Federal Shipping Network.

HILLER, Comet Race Car "3". Photo by William G. Floyd.

HUBLEY

The Hubley manufacturing company was founded at least as early as 1892 by John Hubley, and made iron toys from the start at its plant in Lancaster, Pennsylvania. All toys at the beginning were cast iron, and some early toys included coal ranges, circus wagons and mechanical banks. Hubley's cast iron toys were popular almost from the start, and have long been collector's items, as they were well-made and attractive. By 1940, however, the cast iron toy, due to the increased cost of freight and foreign competition, was slowly becoming a thing of the past. At this time, when Hubley was the largest producer of cast iron toys and cap pistols in the world, it began to introduce die cast zinc alloy toys. During the Second World War, Hubley was 98% engaged in war production, turning out over five million M-74 bomb fuses, which the Hubley engineers played a large part in developing. Since the war, Hubley manufactures die cast toys and plastic toys exclusively. In 1952,

Hubley manufactured 9,763,610 toys and 11,184,878 cap pistols, about ten times the amount of toys and pistols they produced in 1930, but with a line of toys 80% smaller than in 1930. Hubley was acquired by Gabriel Industries in late 1965, and puts out holster sets, cap pistols, vehicles, hobby kits and a number of other toys.

HUBLEY, Dump Truck, Mack, 1930s, 6 tires, 10-3/4" long. Driver missing in photo. Courtesy James S. Maxwell/Virginia Caputo. Photo by Virgina Caputo.

	C6	C8	C10
Hubley Air Compress Truck, circa 1950s, 7" long	50	75	100
Hubley Army Motor Truck No. 807 with driver, 15" long	1100	1700	2500
Hubley Auto, 6-1/2" long	80	120	160
Hubley Auto, 1922, Chevy?, 9" long	400	600	800
Hubley Auto Carrier, w/three cars and one pickup truck, circa 1939, 10" long	432	648	865
Hubley Auto Express, cast iron, 9"	1500	2700	3800
Hubley Auto, circa 1950s, black plastic wheels, die cast	12	18	25
Hubley Avery Tractor, very early, 4-3/4" long	120	180	240
Hubley Bell Telephone Truck, 3-3/4" long	138	207	275
Hubley Bell Telephone, 5-1/4" long	230	345	460
Hubley Bell Telephone, 7" long	500	800	1100
Hubley Bell Telephone, tools and ladders, 8-1/4" long	425	638	850
Hubley Bell Telephone, with tools, 12" long	400	600	800
Hubley Bell Telephone Truck, 1940s, 12-1/2" long	45	68	90
Hubley Bell Telephone Truck, 1931, with derrick and windlass, auger, trailer with 10" pole, three digging tools, and two loose ladders, 10"	700	1000	1400
Hubley Bell Telephone, just ladders as equipment, 13" long	250	375	500

	C6	C8	C10
Hubley Bell Telephone Truck, implements, 9" long	600	1000	1350
Hubley Bell Telephone, post WWII, 24" long	87	130	175
Hubley Black & White Cab, 1920s	1200	2000	3000
Hubley "Borden's Milk Cream", deluxe version, rubber tires, clicker, 7-1/2"	2000	3500	5500
Hubley "Borden's Milk Cream", standard version, 6" long	650	1100	1500
Hubley Bulldozer, die-cast, front scoop, circa 1950, rubber treads, 10-1/4"	62	93	125
Hubley Bus, (futuristic type), circa 1935, 3-1/2" long	50	75	100
Hubley Bus, circa 1938, rubber wheels, 5-1/2" long	50	75	100
Hubley Bus, 1930s, 8" long	60	90	120
Hubley, die-cast, circa 1950s, 9" long	20	30	40
Hubley Cadillac, die-cast, 7" long	40	60	80
Hubley 2278 Car and 2279 House Trailer, circa 1939	150	225	300
Hubley Caterpillar Tractor, driver in cab, 3-1/4" long	200	300	400
Hubley Caterpillar Tractor, 9" long	62	93	125
Hubley Cattle Truck, post war	85	128	170
Hubley Cement Mixer, 18" long	400	600	800
Hubley Champion Stake Truck, 1930s, white rubber tires, 8-1/2" long	140	210	280

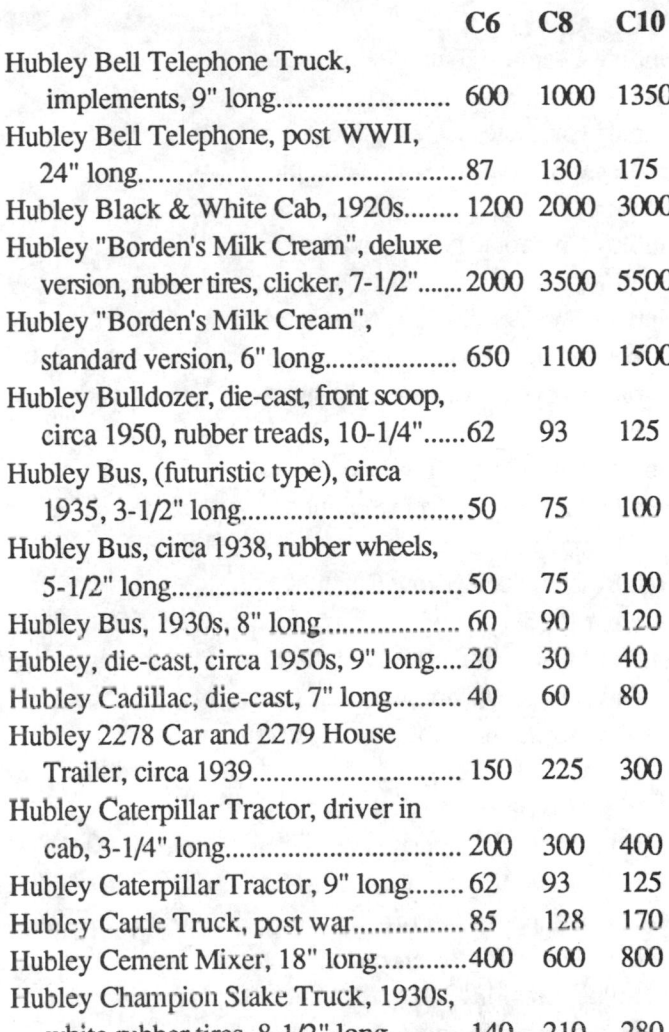

HUBLEY, Caterpillar, 3-1/4" long. Courtesy Mapes Auctioneers & Appraisers.

HUBLEY, Bell Telephone, 24" long, postwar. Courtesy Thomas G. Nefos, Federal Shipping Network.

HUBLEY, 5 Ton Truck. Courtesy Sotheby's New York.

	C6	C8	C10
Hubley Chemical Truck with ladders 13" long	200	300	400
Hubley Chevrolet 1932 Coupe, kit	25	38	50
Hubley Chevrolet 1932 Phaeton kit, 1960s	25	38	50
Hubley Chevrolet 1932 Roadster kit, 1960s	22	33	45
Hubley Chrysler Airflow, take-apart body, 4-1/2" long	125	188	250
Hubley Chrysler Airflow, take-apart body, 6-3/4" long	350	525	700
Hubley Chrysler Airflow, electrified, white rubber tires on wood hubs, 8" long	1200	2000	3300
Hubley Chrysler Airflow Racing Car, circa 1938	100	150	200
Hubley "Coal" Truck, circa 1922, cast iron, 9-1/2" long	650	1050	1500
Hubley Coal Truck, cast iron, with driver 16-3/4" long	1200	1800	2500
Hubley "Coast to Coast" Bus, cast iron, 1927, 13" long	1000	1600	2200
Hubley Corvette	220	330	440
Hubley Coupe, 1933 Ford	140	210	280
Hubley Coupe Roadster, rumble seat, rubber tires, 11" long	212	318	425
Hubley Crash Car, three wheel motorcycle, chrome wheels, 11-1/2"long	2500	4500	7200
Hubley Crash Car, circa 1937, white rubber tires, 4-3/4" long	50	75	125
Hubley Digger, Mack, General,10" long	450	700	1000
Hubley Duesenberg Town Car, build-it model, 9" long	24	36	48
Hubley Dump Truck, 5-1/2" long	87	130	175
Hubley Dump Truck, circa 1938, 7-1/2" long	295	442	590
Hubley Dump Truck, Mack, 1930s, 6 tires, 10-3/4" long	650	1000	1500
Hubley "Elgin, The" Street Sweeper, cast iron, 1931, 8" long	1500	2700	4200
Hubley Fire Engine Pumper, circa 1920, cast iron, black rubber tires, driver, boiler-tender, 12-1/2" long	350	525	700
Hubley Fire Engine Pumper, early, No. 504	350	525	700
Hubley Fire Engine No. 526, circa 1936, 10-1/2" long	175	263	350
Hubley Fire Engine, die cast, white rubber tires with wooden rims, circa 1941	112	168	225

	C6	C8	C10
Hubley Fire Ladder Truck, early, 8-1/2"	350	525	700
Hubley Fire Ladder Truck, circa 1920, 2 wood ladders, 15-1/2" long	300	450	600
Hubley Fire Ladder Truck, 19-1/2" long	600	950	1450
Hubley Fire Truck w/searchlight, white rubber tires with wooden rims	55	82	110
Hubley Fire Truck, 5" long	87	130	175
Hubley "5 Ton Truck", 8 wooden barrels, circa 1920, 17" long	600	900	1400
Hubley Ford Coupe, 1936	40	60	80
Hubley Ford Model A Coupe kit, 1960s	19	28	38
Hubley Ford Model A Phaeton Kit, 1960s	25	38	50
Hubley Ford Model A Pickup kit, 1960s	30	45	60
Hubley Ford Model A Station Wagon Kit, 1960s	45	68	90
Hubley Ford Model A Town Car kit, 1960s	29	44	58
Hubley Ford Model A Victoria kit, 1960s	22	33	45
Hubley Fordson Front-End Loader, cast iron, circa early 1930s	1200	2000	2800
Hubley Hook & Ladder No. 463	28	42	56
Hubley Hook & Ladder Truck, cast iron, 19-1/2" long	200	300	400
Hubley Road Roller, 4-1/2" long	110	165	220
Hubley Huber Road Roller, 8" long	400	600	800
Hubley Huber Road Roller, tractor-like, 7-3/4" long	300	450	600
Hubley Huber Road Roller, 13" long	2200	3300	5000
Hubley Huber Road Roller, 15" long	2500	3700	6000
Hubley "Jaeger" Cement Mixer	250	375	500
Hubley Jaguar Roadster, 1950s, 9"	85	127	170
Hubley Kiddietoy No. 432 MGTD Roadster, 6" long	110	165	220
Hubley Kiddietoy No. 510 series Dump Truck	125	188	250
Hubley Kiddietoy No. 457 Racer, diecast, rubber tires, 6-1/2" long	27	41	55
Hubley Kiddietoy "Patrol" Stake Truck, circa 1937	27	41	55
Hubley Ladder Truck circa late 1930s, 5" long	45	68	90
Hubley Ladder Truck, terraplane front, 1930s, 6" long	312	468	625
Hubley Ladder Truck, 1930s, 10" long	110	165	225
Hubley Ladder Truck, circa 1940, 13-1/2" long	400	600	800

HUBLEY Motorcycle, Harley-Davidson, w/ policeman, 1930's, approx. 6-1/2" long, swivel head, wheels and color variation. Courtesy Wilkinson Collection, Detroit Antique Toy Museum.

HUBLEY, Motorcycle, Parcel Post Delivery. Courtesy Sotheby's New York.

	C6	C8	C10
Hubley Life Saver Truck, circa 1930, hole in rear is large enough to hold packs of Life Savers, 4-1/4" long......	700	1100	1700
Hubley Life Saver Truck, small hole in rear, can't hold Life Savers.............	400	600	800
Hubley Limousine, six-door, 1920s, 7" long.............	150	225	300
Hubley Lincoln Zephyr, 7-1/4" long......	230	345	460
Hubley Lincoln Zephyr and House Trailer, cast iron, 14" overall.............	1000	1800	2600
Hubley Log Truck No. 469....................	42	63	85
Hubley Log Truck with five chained logs, black rubber tires, die-cast, approx. 19" long.................	84	130	175
Hubley Low Boy Truck, trailer, tractor....	200	300	400
Hubley Mack Dump Truck, with driver, 11-1/2" long.............	550	900	1300
Hubley Mack Truck Steam Shovel-Digger, circa 1920, nickel wheels and scoop, 7" long.............	1300	2200	3200
Hubley "Merchants Delivery", 1920s, approx. 6" long.................	375	562	750
Hubley MG, 8-3/4" long.................	65	98	130

	C6	C8	C10
Hubley MG 5-3/4" long.........................	24	36	48
Hubley "Milk Cream" Truck, 1930s, cast iron, white rubber tires, 3-1/2"....	160	240	320
Hubley Model T Coupe, 4" long.............	100	150	200
Hubley Monarch Tractor, 5-1/2" long....	600	900	1200
Hubley Motor Express Tractor and Trailer, black rubber tires, 500 series, approx. 19" long....................	162	243	325
Hubley 2287 "Motor Express" Truck and Trailer, 8" long.................	162	243	325
Hubley Motorcycle, Armored, w/side car and removable riders, 9" long......	900	1500	2100
Hubley Motorcycle, early, w/side car, 2 civilian riders, 4" long....................	160	240	320
Hubley Motorcycle, has light in front and place for battery, 6" long............	330	495	660
Hubley Motorcycle and rider, 4" long....	100	150	200
Hubley Motorcycle, "Harley-Davidson", civilian rider, 6" long.................	500	750	1000
Hubley Motorcycle, Harley-Davidson, w/policeman, 1930s, swivel head, small wheels near feet, 6-1/2" long....	500	800	1100
Hubley Motorcycle, Harley-Davidson, w/policeman, white rubber wheels 6" long.................	280	420	560

HUBLEY, Huber Road Roller, 8" long. Courtesy Mapes Auctioneers & Appraisers.

HUBLEY, Motorcycle, "U.S. Air Mail". Courtesy Sotheby's New York.

HUBLEY Motorcycle w/side car, battery-operated headlight, cop driver, passenger. Courtesy Sotheby's New York.

HUBLEY Motorcycle, Harley-Davidson w/side car and rider. Courtesy Sotheby's New York.

HUBLEY, Motorcycle w/side car. Courtesy Sotheby's New York.

	C6	C8	C10
Hubley Motorcycle, Harley-Davidson, Police, w/side car and rider, 5-1/4" long	460	690	920
Hubley Motorcycle Hill Climber, 1936, No. 649, 6-3/4" long	415	622	830
Hubley Motorcycle, Indian, policeman rider, nickel-plated cylinder, 9-1/2" long	850	1450	1850
Hubley Motorcycle, Kiddietoy, plastic, 5" long	15	22	30
Hubley Motorcycle policeman with side-car, 1920s, 4" long	125	188	250
Hubley Motorcycle with detachable cop, cast iron, "Made USA", circa, mid 1930s, 4-1/4" long	50	75	100
Hubley Motorcycle w/sidecar, battery operated headlight, cop driver, passenger, 8" long	700	1150	1750
Hubley Motorcycle with side car, No. 46-F, two demountable policemen, 8-1/2" long	800	1300	1800
Hubley Motorcycle, two-cylinder Indian, w/side car, no riders	600	900	1200
Hubley Motorcycle "Traffic Car", four cylinder Indian w/stake sides on two wheel cart, 8-1/2" long	1500	2500	4000

	C6	C8	C10
Hubley Motorcycle, Parcel Post Delivery, w/two-wheel cart, 9-1/4" long	1500	2500	3500
Hubley Motorcycle, "U.S. Air Mail", 9" long	900	1400	2400
Hubley Motorized Steam Pumper, circa 1930s, 4" long	50	75	100
Hubley Nite Coach, metal wheels, went on "Nu-Car" carrier, 1930s 3-1/2" long	30	45	60
Hubley "Nucar Transport" w/trailer 4 cars, 17" long	700	1250	1800
Hubley Packard, 15 parts, 1929,11" long, auctioned 1994, excellent, minor repairs, for $16,000			
Hubley Packard, 1930 "Phaeton" kit	30	45	60

HUBLEY Motorcycle, 6", has light in front and place for battery. Courtesy Sotheby's New York.

Left to Right: HUBLEY, "Merchants Delivery", ARCADE, ambulance, "City Ambulance", 6" long. Courtesy Chic Gast.

	C6	C8	C10
Hubley Packard Roadster Kit..................	40	60	80
Hubley "Panama" Digger, (hard to find), approx. 3-1/2" long..............	300	450	600
Hubley "Panama" Digger, 9-1/2" long...	600	950	1400
Hubley "Panama" Digger, Mack, 13" long................................	800	1400	2100
Hubley Parcel Post Motorcycle and sidecar, Harley-Davidson, 10"...........	1200	2000	3300
Hubley "Patrol", driver, policeman, 15-1/2" long................................	1400	2100	2800
Hubley Pipe Truck No. 803, circa 1950s, 9-1/2" long..............................	35	52	70
Hubley Power Shovel, 14"................	87	130	175
Hubley Pumper, circa late 1930s............	115	172	230
Hubley Pumper, terraplane front, 1930s, 6-1/4" long............................	150	225	300
Hubley Racer, "1790", approx. 5"..........	100	150	200
Hubley Racer ,1930s, 2 passengers, 5-1/2" long..............................	130	195	260
Hubley Racer, plastic, 6-1/2" long..........	44	66	88
Hubley Racer, driver, large tail fin, 7" long..............................	242	363	485
Hubley Racer, 2241, 1930s, 7-1/2" long.....	45	68	90
Hubley Racer No. 5, early wheels..........	1200	2000	2700
Hubley Racer No.5, painted and nickeled iron and aluminum, raise hood-see motor, 9-1/2" long............................	1200	2000	2700

	C6	C8	C10
Hubley Racer 629, 1936, 6-3/4" long.....	180	270	360
Hubley Racer "No.1", 8" long................	350	525	700
Hubley Racer, driver, rubber tires, 8".....	125	188	250
Hubley Racer, die-cast, black rubber tires, 4" long....................................	80	120	160
Hubley Racer, animated exhaust stacks, driver, 8" long..............................	500	800	1100
Hublely "Railway Express" Truck, rubber tires, 5" long............................	100	150	200
Hubley Road Grader, 12" long..............	60	90	120
Hubley Road Roller, late 1920s, driver, 8" long..............................	287	430	575
Hubley Road Scraper No. 481................	60	90	120
Hubley "Say it with Flowers" 10-1/2" long, auctioned 1994, excellent, for $18,000			
Hubley Sedan, 1920, cast iron, 7" long..	100	150	200
Hubley Sedan, 1928, cast iron, 7" long..	150	225	300
Hubley Sedan, circa 1938, 2-door, looks like Ford, rubber wheels, 3-1/2"........	60	90	120
Hubley Service Car, 4-1/4" long............	60	90	120
Hubley Service Car, cast iron, including wheels, 5" long................................	200	300	400
Hubley 726 Shovel Truck, circa 1930, 10" long..............................			No Price Found

HUBLEY "Elgin, The" Street Sweeper, 8" long. Courtesy Chic Gast.

HUBLEY, Motorcycle "Traffic Car". Courtesy Continental Hobby House.

HUBLEY, Stake Bed Truck, 7" long. Courtesy Mapes Auctioneers & Appraisers.

HUBLEY, Racer "1790". Photo by Bill Kaufman.

	C6	C8	C10
Hubley Sport Car No. 485	70	105	140
Hubley Stake Truck, circa late 1930s	150	225	300
Hubley No. 614 Stake Truck, circa 1930s	75	112	150
Hubley Stake Bed Truck, cast iron, 3-1/2" long	25	38	50
Hubley Stake Bed Truck, 7" long	77	125	155
Hubley Stake Truck w/trailer, No. 927, two pcs, 21" long	100	150	200
Hubley No.452 Stake-type Truck, black rubber tires, circa post WWII	80	120	160
Hubley Station Wagon, circa 1940s, 1950s, 8-1/2" long	75	112	150
Hubley Steam Roller, 5" long	150	225	300
Hubley Steam Shovel, "General", 7" long	375	562	750
Hubley Steam Shovel, "General", rubber tires on hubs, 9" long	500	750	1000
Hubley Steam Shovel, "General", 15" long	450	700	1000
Hubley Studebaker Roadster, frame and body separate	300	450	600
Hubley Studebaker Touring Car, cast iron	325	518	650
Hubley Telephone Truck, plastic	25	38	50
Hubley Touring Auto, 1915, cast iron, chauffeur and rider, 9-1/2" long	375	562	750

HUBLEY "Railway Express" Truck, 5" long. Courtesy Mapes Auctioneers & Appraisers.

HUBLEY, Nite Coach, 3-1/2" long, metal wheels, went on "Nu-Car" carrier, 1930's. Courtesy Chic Gast.

	C6	C8	C10
Hubley Tow Truck, cast iron, circa 1930s, 8-3/4" long	180	270	360
Hubley T-Bird	120	180	240
Hubley Tractor No. 472	30	45	60
Hubley Tractor, Ford 6000	150	225	300
Hubley Tractor, steam boiler in front, circa early 1920s, 4-3/4" long	125	188	250
Hubley Tractor, 1930s, 5" long	250	480	600
Hubley Tractor Loader No. 501, 1950s, 11" long	100	150	200
Hubley Tractor Trailer and Road Scraper No. 506	100	150	200
Hubley Trailer Truck, circa 1936-38	100	150	200
Hubley Transitional Fire Patrol, cast iron, driver, firemen, 1920, 12"	800	1300	2000
"Hubley U.S.A." Airflow type, circa 1937, approx. 3-1/2" long	20	30	40
Hubley Wrecker, chrome wheels, service car	45	68	90
Hubley Wrecker, 3-1/2"	42	63	85
Hubley Wrecker, rubber wheels, 1930, 4-1/2" long	65	100	135
Hubley Wrecker, 4-3/4" long	70	105	140
Hubley Wrecker, circa 1940, white wheels on large hubs, 6" long	165	248	330
Hubley Wrecking Truck, 1930, cast iron, rubber tires, 7-1/2" long	150	225	300
Hubley Yellow Cab, circa 1939, 8" long	500	750	1000

HUBLEY, "Panama" Digger, 13" long. Courtesy Joe and Sharon Freed.

	C6	C8	C10
Ideal American LaFrance Fire Truck.... 72		108	145
Ideal Barracuda Coupe, 1964, plastic, 4" long...................... 15		22	30
Ideal Cadillac, four door, 1948, plastic, 4" long...................... 25		38	50
Ideal Car Trailer, circa 1945, plastic, 3" long...................... 20		30	40
Ideal Car Trailer, 4 cars, plastic, 27" long...................... 40		60	80
Ideal Corvette............................ 50		75	100
Ideal Fix-it Convertible.................. 60		90	120
Ideal Mercedes Sedan, plastic, 9" long.. 35		52	70
Ideal Pickup Truck, American, 1948, plastic, 4" long...................... 20		30	40
Ideal Pickup Truck, Ford, 1940, plastic, 4" long...................... 20		30	40
Ideal Semi, 12" long...................... 26		39	52
Ideal "Television Repair" Truck............ 70		105	140
Ideal Tow Truck, plastic and metal, 17" long...................... 48		70	95
Ideal Tractor, 1948, plastic, 4" long........ 20		30	40
Irwin Dream Car Convertible, metal, 16" long...................... 200		300	400
Irwin Ford Sunliner, plastic friction, 9". 47		70	95
Irwin Ice Cream Truck, plastic............ 50		75	100
Irwin Jaguar Roadster, 6" long............ 35		52	70
Ives horseless carriage runabout, 6-1/2" long, 6" high to the top of jockey cap on driver...................... 2500		3750	5000
Ives steamer, cast iron, two drivers, 19-1/2" long........................ 500		750	1000
Jaeger Cement Mixer, cast iron............ 475		712	950

JAEGER Cement Mixer. Courtesy Mapes Auctioneers & Appraisers.

JANE FRANCIS TOYS

(Information and listing from Dave Leopard.)

These toys seem to have been made in Pittsburgh, Pa. during the early post-WWII period. All of their vehicles were diecast.

	C6	C8	C10
JF01 Pickup Truck, 6-1/2" long............ 30		40	50
JF02 Pickup Truck, No. 347, 5" long..... 20		25	30
JF03 Pickup Truck, No. 447, 5" long..... 20		25	30
JF04 Tow Truck, No. 447, 5" long........ 30		35	40
JF05 Gulf Truck, tin cover, No. 447, 5" long............................ 35		52	70
JF06 Sedan, fastback, futuristic, 6-1/2" long............................ 42		63	85
JF07 Sedan, fastback, futuristic, with windup motor, 6-1/2" long................. 70		105	140
Jane Francis "Gulf" Service Station, 8 pieces............................ 375		562	750
Jeep, glass candy container, 4" long...... 20		30	40
"Jeepster", rubber tires, 14-1/4" long... 20		30	40
Jones & Bixler, "Express J & B" Truck 15-1/2" long...................... 1000		1800	2500

JONES & BIXLER, "Express J&B" Truck. Courtesy Sotheby's New York.

THE JUDY COMPANY

History and listing by Dave Leopard

The Judy Company of Minneapolis, Minnesota made educational toys, including a farm set called Happy's Farm Family (patented in 1945), which included a solid rubber car, pickup truck, and tractor, along with human and animal figures.

	C6	C8	C10
JA01 Sedan, 2 dimensional, (part of set), solid rubber, 5-1/4" long............. 15		20	25
JT01 Pickup Truck, 2 dimensional (part of set), solid rubber, 5-1/4" long........ 15		20	25
JF01 Farm Tractor, 2 dimensional (part of set), solid rubber, 3-1/2" long........ 15		20	25

KANSAS TOY & NOVELTY COMPANY

By Fred Maxwell, Slushmold Contributing Editor and Bob Condray
with the assistance of Lorene Sorell, L.D. Morgison
& the Clifton Historical Society.

Although neither the first nor the last Kansas Toy has been firmly identified, we have made enough progress to have confidence in this listing. We found that those "toys with numbers" was more collector gossip than a good rule. Some slushmolds with numbers are not K.T.&N. and many K.T.&N. were not numbered. Numbers on racers and railroad cars seem appropriate, but on some others they are so disfiguring as to suggest a commercial need. Being unlabeled, unboxed bin-toys, the number may have been a convenience to certain wholesale buyers.

Arthur L. Haynes, an auto mechanic, started molding toys in his Clifton, Kansas shed for local stores in 1923. With clever hands and an artist's eye, he charmed his friends and local townspeople with his bright-colored toys. He made his patterns from advertising pictures, from local vehicles and probably from other makes of toys such as Tootsietoy. He made his own production tools. His range was diverse.

This was a town enterprise from the beginning. Jess Foster, the News editor, helped with alloy mixtures; Mr. Hadsell, the Union Pacific agent (see #38, an early promotional?), suggested they send samples to Woolworth's in New York. Clayton D. Young, a traveling salesman, saw the toys, joined the company and built a profitable business with the chain stores, including Kress, Kresge and Sears-Roebuck; and became a partner. At its peak of international sales in the late 1920s they employed as many as 65 in two shifts during the Xmas order season.

They were young people who had grown up together, a happy gang who joked and sang at their work. This informality was reflected in the local name, "the Hoopie Factory". Two or three of their early toys, and #26 and #33 were stripdowns - hoopies - probably raced locally. Whether "Whoopee", tractor toy #48, was a local spelling of this or whether it celebrated a fat, cheering order is not known. Certainly a lot of happy "Whoopee-e-e-s" must have floated from hoopie-land.

Teamwork there must have been, for a molder, according to Ernes Istas, could produce 2000 toys a day. Helen Istas was the secretary; Bill Haynes was another molder, showing the family nature of the work force, with its clippers (trimmers), painters, clampers (axles) and boxers. "Butch" Morgison, one of our sources, was each of these during his long career with the company. Haynes believed that he invented hollow-casting of metal toys, so he must have started with solid toys. One day he dropped his full mold,

spilling its hot metal. To his delight he had a perfect, hollow auto toy, with promise of savings of metal and shipping costs.

Because K.T.&N. founded a dynasty of several reproducers using original molds, many of which are in use today, collectors and dealers may be confused. To reduce this confusion I am including pertinent design details.

Metal wheels of several sizes and styles (disc, simulated wire and spoked), were characteristic of early K.T.& N. Rubber tires on wood hubs (popularized by Tootsietoy Grahams) were introduced on #75 in 1932. These were followed by white soft-rubber wheels (simulating balloon tires) and realistic white hard-rubber disc wheels sometimes painted with black "tires". Rubber wheels were used industry-wide, so are not good clues. Several Kansas Toys were made in 2 or 3 sizes (5¢, 10¢, 15¢). Bottom-pans were not cast until high numbers (#76). Many were made with string-pull loops or knobs in the handcrank position. All colors were used including gold, silver and pink; a few found with two-colored bodies may have been sales samples. Many early toys were finished in Egyptian lacquer, a japanning applied thinly so the bright metal showed through with a glittery look. A mint toy with this finish has a modern look. Later toys were enameled. "Made in USA" embossed on the bodies is a sure clue to reproductions for this copyright law went into effect in the late 1930s; as is black rubber wheels.

We found that Clayton Stevenson, a toymaker in his own right (see Lincoln White Metal Works and Midwest Toy), as a subcontractor had been furnishing some molds and some patterns since the mid-1920s, continued this support and must have originated those handsome designs from 3-

Fred Maxwell, collector and occasional author, has been collecting antique aircraft and vehicle toys for 25 years. This retirement hobby was started from scratch, for his lead soldiers were missing when he returned home from college. He founded Capital Miniature Auto Collectors Club 20 years ago to promote interest in the Central Atlantic states. He felt challenged by the lack of public knowledge and the ambiguity of that orphan category: Pot Metal or Slushmold Toys.

piece molds, such as #8, #58, #60, #80 and #91 with their intricate, realistic front ends. Some higher numbers have Stevenson-type patterned pans. These features slowed production and added to costs; but while blurring the difference between Kansas and Lincoln toys, made for rarity.

During its good years K. T. & N. produced more toys than any in the industry save Barclay. Mr. Young left the company in the late 1920s; whether it was the loss of his talents and assets or the onset of the Great Depression, the company was in trouble by 1930. George Hoeffer reorganized the company and moved it across town, but this effort lasted only a few months. Although K. T. & N. continued until 1935 a happy era was coming to an end for Clifton.

Among its many designs we were not surprised to find toys reflecting familiar vehicles (hoopies, stripdowns, midget racers, trucks, tractors and farm implements), but K. T. & N. also made miniatures of record-setting aircraft, and landspeed record cars (#6, #32, #46 and #97). All in all, remarkable from a shed in a small farming center!

NOTE: For additional photos and different views refer to Best Toy and Novelty Co., Craftoy and Ralstoy, all of whom reproduced from original K.T.& N. molds up to #102.

The following abbreviations are for the details and variations useful in identification of these wheeled toys:

HG	horizontal grille pattern			**UV**	unnumbered version
HL	horizontal hood louvers	**MSW**	metal open spoke wheels	**VG**	vertical grille pattern
HO	hood cap, Motometer or ornament	**MWW**	metal simulated "wire" wheels	**VL**	vertical hood louvers
L	lacquer finish	**OW**	open windows	**WS**	windshield
LI	landau irons on convertibles	**RM**	rearmount spare tire/wheel	**WV**	windshield visor
MDW	metal disc wheels	**SM**	sidemounted spare	**WHRT**	wooden hubs, rubber tires
MDSW	metal disc solid "spokes"	**SP**	stringpull knob in handcrank area	**WRDW**	white hard rubber disc wheels
MDWBT	wheels with black painted "tires"	**T**	external trunk	**WRW**	white soft rubber wheels (balloon tires)

	C6	C8	C10
KTV0 Large Coupe, no #, crude, high-bodied "Ford", HO, HG, no headlamps, SP,VL,5 windows, door handles. wheel type unknown because only a reproduction has been found, 3-1/4"............	No Price Found		
KTV1 Midget Racer, no #, no driver, torpedo tail, HO,SP,VL,HG, 5/8" MDW w/simulated lug nuts,lacquer finish. Some say this was their first toy; some say first had non-moveable wheels or was a large racer, 3" long......	20	30	40
KTV2 Midget Racer, no#, same as above, w/driver, plain MDW, lacquer. Easily confused with another maker's copy. See #31 and #67, 3" long...................	70	105	140
KTV3 Large Indy Racer, no#, driver, boattail, HO, MDW, lacquer, 6" long..............	No Price Found		
KTV4 Coupe, no#, crude, slant roof, shallow rear body, no fenders, hood similar to first racer above, lacquer. First "hoopie" or stripdown made?, 3-1/8" long...............	No Price Found		

KANSAS TOY Bus, KTV12. Photo courtesy Fred Maxwell.

	C6	C8	C10
KTV5 Sedan, no #, crude limousine or stretch taxi, 6 windows, louvered rear quarters, HO,VL,HG,T,SP, large MDW, lacquer, 3-3/8" long......	No Price Found		
KTV6 Coupe, no #, Convertible, LI, VL, HG,WV, SP, MDSW, lacquer, 2-7/8"..	30	45	60
KTV7 Coupe, "8", Convertible, LI, VL,HG, WV, SP, RM, MWW, no HO, no headlamps, enamel finish, also UVs with "Chrysler", headlamps and HO; or with MDSW, 3-1/8" long..	20	30	40

KANSAS TOY Racers, Left to Right, Top Row: KTV1, KTV2; Middle Row: KTV14, KTV24, KTV52; Bottom Row: KTV35, KTV25. Photo courtesy Fred Maxwell

	C6	C8	C10
KTV8 Coupe, "8", trunk convertible, T, HO, VG, SM, MDW, 3 1/8"			No Price Found

Note: #8 is the lowest numbered vehicle found. Its realistic, high quality signals the ending of a novice toymakers's experimental phase. The five coupes above have the same 1924 Chrysler hood and nice details like landau irons and kickplates, but not all had headlamps. The basic body expanded into this series of coupes, #14 roadsters, and sedans (all (?) unnumbered), lacquered or enameled, with 3 types of wheels: MDW, MDSW, and MWW. They were unnamed or named: Chrysler, Cadillac, Chevrolet. Any Fords out there? The large coupe, KTV9, is a scale-up of #8. Only 3 of these large pieces are known: the racer KTV3, John Deere tractor KTV19, and a mail-plane.

	C6	C8	C10
KTV9 Large Coupe, no #, Chrysler convertible, MWW and 2 golf club doors, larger version of #8, 5"			No Price Found
KTV10 Sedan, no#, "Chevrolet", 6 windows, LI, WV, VL, SP, RM, MWW, 2-7/8" long	16	24	32
KTV11 Sedan, no #, "Chevrolet", as above, HG, HO, MSW, 3-1/4"			No Price Found
KTV12 Overland Bus, "9", "Fageol", solid windows, 3-1/2" long	42	63	85
KTV13 Overland Bus, no #, "Fageol", 9 male passengers, driver and "baggage" cast on windows, HG, RM, MDW, also an UV w/various family passengers on windows, also w/comic characters (Kansas Toy?) 3-1/2"	26	39	52
KTV14 Indy Racer, "10", driver, boattail, exhaust right, VL, HG, HO, SP, MSW or MWW, also UV, 3-1/8"	6	9	12
KTV15 Roadster, "14" open "Chrysler", solid W/S, plain grille, HO, VL, SP, RM, MDSW, 3-1/8" long	18	27	36
KTV16 Roadster, no #, same as above, HG, 2 golf club doors, 3-1/8"			No Price Found
KTV17 Farm Tractor, "17", "Fordson". driver, HG, crank, no tow hook,			

	C6	C8	C10
large 1 1/4" and 3/4" MDW with 4 holes in discs, also found with same size 6 spoke wheels, See #57 2-7/8" long	35	52	70
KTV18 Farm Tractor, no#, same basic body as above, "Fordson" on radiator and crankcase, VG and tow hook, with smaller, plain MDW, 2-5/8"			No Price Found
KTV19 Large Farm Tractor, no #, Deere Model D, a finely crafted replica in 2 colors, steering shaft, fly wheel, belt drive wheel, rear fenders, large 2" and 1" 12-spoke wheels, 4-7/8"			No Price Found
KTV20 Truck, "20", Ford?, solid w/s, 2 OW, 3 tanks, VL, HG, rear faucet, MWW, versions w/and w/o driver, also an UV, 3-1/8" long	16	24	32

KANSAS TOY Autos, Left to Right, Top Row: KTV4, KTV5: Middle Row: KTV7, KTV7: Bottom Row: KTV26, KTV26, KTV43. Photo courtesy Fred Maxwell.

	C6	C8	C10

KTV21 Steam Tractor, "25", "Case",
crew of 2, tow loop, large front,
small rear MSW and flywheel.See
#71,also an UV w/no name, 3".......... 35 52 70

KTV22 Racer, "26", "Bearcat",
stripdown, long hood, motometer,
3 intakes, driver, open frame, left
exhaust, See #33, 4" long................. No Price Found

KTV23 Separator-Thresher, "27", tow
hook, auto-type MSW (not tractor
rims), lacquer or enamel, also
UV, see #72, 3" long......................... 35 52 70

KTV24 Midget Racer, "31", driver,
torpedo tail, VL, HG, HO, MWW,
lacquer, also UV, see #67, 2-1/8"...... 12 15 18

KTV25 Racer, "33", "Bearcat", stripdown, smaller version of #26
above, 3" long.................................. No Price Found

KTV26 Coupe, "35", Convertible, LI,
VL, HG, HO, RM, MWW, also
an UV, 2-1/4" long............................ No Price Found

KTV27 Locomotive-Tender, "36",
"KT & N RR", 6 MSW, 4
MDW, 0-6-4, 4-3/8" long.................. 7 10 14

KTV28 "Pullman" Car, "37",
"KT & N RR", 4 MDW, 3-1/2"......... No Price Found

KTV29 Box Car "38", Union Pacific
shield (an early promotional?),
"KT & N RR", 4 MDW, 3-1/4"......... No Price Found

KTV30 Tank Car, "39", ladder, filler,
"KT & N RR", MDW, 3-1/8" long....No Price Found

KANSAS TOY Vehicles; Left to Right, Top row: KTV16, KTV15; Second row: KTV14, KTV25; Third row: KTV33, KTV35. Bottom row: KTV36, KTV58. Photo courtesy Fred Maxwell.

	C6	C8	C10

KTV31 Caboose, "40", "KT & N RR",
stack, brakeman's cab, MDS, 2-3/4"..... No Price Found

KTV32 Stock Car, "41", "KT & N RR",
MDW...................................... No Price Found

KTV33 Dump Truck, "42", Ford?, driver,
no cab, diamond emblem on hinged
body, LV, HG, SP, MWW, 3-1/2"... 35 52 70

KTV34 Steam Road Roller, "43", driver,
SP, boiler, wooden rollers, 3-1/4"......10 15 20

KTV35 Racer, "46",1929 Golden Arrow
record car, driver, large tail fin,
MWW, 2-7/8" long........................... 12 18 24

KANSAS TOY Farm Vehicles: Left to Right, Top row: KTV17, KTV17; Middle row,: KTV23, KTV21; Bottom row: KTV23, KTV17. Photo courtesy Fred Maxwell.

KANSAS TOY Commercial Vehicles; Left to Right, Top Row: KTV20, KTV33; Middle row: KTV34, KTV36; Bottom row: KTV38, KTV41. Photo courtesy Fred Maxwell.

	C6	C8	C10

KTV36 Warehouse Tractor, "48",
"Caterpillar","Whoopee", driver,VL,
HG, HO, SP, tow loop, MWW,
also an UV, 3" long............................ 18   27   36

KTV37 Tour Bus, "49", 1928 Pickwick
COE "Nite Coach", HG, SP, MDW
duals,also an UV. See #59, 2-3/8"..... No Price Found

KTV38 Pickup Truck, "51", Ford w/cab,
VL,HG, tow loop, MDW, lacquer,
also an UV, 2-3/4" long..................... No Price Found

KTV39 Roadster, "54", Buick, driver
w/cap, rumble seat, T, plain hood
and grille, no headlamps, SM, MWW,
also an UV, see #77, 2-3/8" long....... 10   15   20

KTV40 Roadster, "54", same as above,
no trunk, 2-1/4" long......................... No Price Found

KTV41 Truck-Semi, "55", Ford, stake
trailer, VL, HG, MDW, 4" long........ No Price Found

KTV42 Farm Tractor, "57", Fordson,
driver, SP, MDW rear, MSW
front. Smaller version of #17,
also an UV, 1-3/4" long..................... No Price Found

KTV43 Sedanette, "58", Austin Bantam,
unique fighting cock on door panels,
4 OW, HL, VG, RM, MWW, 2-1/4"....No Price Found

KTV44 Tour Bus, "59", 1928 Pickwick
COE double-deck night-coach,
screen grille, larger version of
#49 above, also an UV with dual
wheels, 3-3/8" long............................ No Price Found

KTV45 Sedan, "60", 1930 Reo Royale?
or Chrysler 2 dr Brougham, plain
hood, vee-VG, square rear deck,
MDW, MDWSM, also an UV with
MWW and MWWSM, 3-1/2".......... 24   36   48

*Note: the following is a unique towed farm set with several
hinged or moving parts, each a different color and large
1-1/4" spoked tractor wheels.*

KTV46 Planter, "KTN No. 61",V-blade
plough with seed hopper, 4 piece
incl. wheels and 3 colors, 4" long...... 40   60   80

KTV47 Disc Harrow, "62", 8 discs on
same 1-5/8" wide frame as #61,
13 pieces, incl. discs and wheels,
4 colors, 4" long............................... 35   52   70

KTV48 Plough, "63", single blade
on same shaft as #61, 4" long............ 35   52   70

KTV49 Dirt Tumble, "64", adjustable
dumping scoop, 1-1/2" wide on
same frame as #62, 6 pieces,
4 colors, 4" long............................... 20   30   40

KTV50 Dirt Scraper, "65", blade
1-7/8", adjustable, on same
frame as #62, 3-5/8" long...................No Price Found

KTV51 Coupe, "66", streamlined
3-wheeler, 6 OW, MWW,
lacquer, 3-1/2" long...........................No Price Found

KTV52 Midget Racer, "67", driver,
torpedo-tail, VL,HG,HO,MDW,
smaller version of #31, also an UV
1-1/2" long......................................44   66   88

KTV53 Fire Engine, "70", Seagrave?
pumper, driver, VL, HG, MDW,
2-1/4" long...................................... No Price Found

KTV54 Steam Tractor, "71", crew of
2, tow-loop, small version of #25,
2-1/2" long...................................... 10   15   20

KTV55 Separator-Thresher, "72",
tow hook for #71, 2+"........................ No Price Found

KTV56 Army Tank, "74", "US Army",
WWI type, high turret, large front,
small rear wheels, OD color,
2-1/4" long...................................... No Price Found

KTV57 Racer, no#, miniature solid-cast
version of #10, moving wheels,
charm loop on nose, 1" long.............. No Price Found

*KANSAS TOY, Left to Right:
KTV22, mid 1930's, KTV25,
1920's. Photo by Perry Eichor.*

KANSAS TOY AND NOVELTY, KTV34. Photo by R.F. Sapita.

KANSAS TOY Vehicles with Wood Hubs; Left to Right, Top Row:KTTV64, KTTV65; Bottom Row:KTTV66, KT & N? #85. Photo courtesy Fred Maxwell.

KANSAS TOY TRANSITIONAL VEHICLES

	C6	C8	C10
KTTV58 Tractor, "48", "Caterpillar", "Whoopee" same as KTV36 except 3/4" grooved metal wheels with rubber track, 3" long	35	52	70
KTTV59 Tour Bus, no #, Pickwick COE, a more streamlined version of #59 above, with 8 open windows, 3 3/8" long			No Price Found
KTTV60? Fire Engine, no #, pumper, 2 firemen w/old style helmets, hose reel, HG, MDW, Kansas? 3-1/4" long	12	18	24
KTTV61 Army Tank, "74", "US Army", 2 gun turret, OD color, a different tank than #74 above, 2-1/4" long			No Price Found
KTTV62 Coupe, "75", Graham like (Tootsietoy), VG, SM, T, WHRT, 1933 issue, 4-1/4" long			No Price Found
KTTV63 Racer, "76", Auburn speedster, low driver, headrest fairing, SP, HG, slanted louvers, large oval fin, kickplates, HWRW or WHRT, 4-1/4"	20	30	40
KTTV64 Roadster, "77", open sport Duesenberg, W/S down, driver, VG, slanted louvers, SM, T, WHRT, 4" long	16	24	32
KTTV65 Concrete Mixer, "78", Truck w/water tank & mixing barrel, VG, HL, WHRT, found both with and w/o a bottom pan, sometimes called a fuel tanker, 3-3/4" long			No Price Found
KTTV66 Sedan, "79", 2 door, Graham like, 4 OW, VG, HL, RM, WHRT w/5 removable tires, found both with and w/o bottom pan, 4-1/4"			No Price Found
KTTV67 Coupe, "80", Convertible, top up, LI, 2 OW, VG, T, MWW w/MWW SM, 3-1/2" long	20	30	40
KTTV68 Coupe, "80", same as above except HRDW w/MDW SM. (a different casting re sidemounts) 3-1/2" long			No Price Found
KTTV69 Racer, "81", Miller, FWD, driver, 8 cyl., right exhaust, HG, WHRT, 1933 issue, 4-3/8" long			No Price Found
KTTV70 Sedan, "82", Pierce Arrow Silver Arrow fastback, 6 OW, HRDW, also an UV, 4" long			No Price Found
KTTV71 Indy Racer, "83", FWD type driver, VG, HL, right exhaust, WHRT, 4-5/8" long			No Price Found

KANSAS TOY, Left to Right: KTV17, KTV47, KTV46. Photo by Chic Gast.

KANSAS TOY Towed Implements; Left to Right, Top Row: KTV46, KTV49; Bottom Row: KTV47, KTV50. Photo Courtesy Fred Maxwell.

KANSAS TOY, KTV64. Photo by Craig A. Clark.

KANSAS TOY Autos with Hard Rubber Wheels; Left to Right,Top Row: KTTV59, KTV45; Middle Row: KTTV63; Bottom Row: KTTV67, KTTV72. Photo courtesy Fred Maxwell.

KELMET, No. 501, White Dump Truck, "Big Boy". Courtesy Joe and Sharon Freed.

	C6	C8	C10
KTTV72 Sedan "84", DeSoto?, airflow, 4 OW, HO, HG, HL, HRDW. 1934 issue, 3-5/8" long	20	30	40

Note: Although not yet certain when the hobo molds changed hands, the higher numbers are described and illustrated under Best Toy and Ralstoy.

	C6	C8	C10
Kelmet Aerial Ladder Truck	900	1450	2200
Kelmet No. 501, White Dump Truck, 25" long	875	1400	2150
Kelmet Tanker	1200	2100	3000
Kelmet White Fire Truck (ladder)	1000	2000	3000

KENTON

KENTON "Army Motor Truck 807", incorrect driver in photo. Courtesy Sotheby's New York.

KENTON Ambulance, 7"long, cast iron, driver incorrect. Courtesy Sotheby's New York.

KENTON "Jaeger" Cement Mixer Truck, 8" long. Courtesy HAKE'S Americana & Collectibles.

KENTON Steam Shovel. Courtesy Mapes Auctioneers & Appraisers.

	C6	C8	C10
Kenton Ambulance, cast iron, 7" long....	750	1300	1700
Kenton "Army Motortruck 807", cast iron, 14" long.....................................	600	950	1300
Kenton Auto, cast iron, early, 6" long....	250	375	500
Kenton Boattail Cut-Down Speedster, 1910, 7" long	120	180	240
Kenton Buckeye Ditcher..........................	500	850	1200
Kenton Bus, Double-Decker, 1920s 6" long..	500	850	1250
Kenton Bus, Double-Decker, 1920, 7-1/4" long..	1100	1650	2200
Kenton Bus, Double-Decker 9-1/2"........	500	800	1100
Kenton Bus, cast iron, 8" long................	175	262	350
Kenton Bus, 1920s, 10-3/4" long...........	375	525	750
Kenton Cattle Truck, cast iron, circa 1938, 8" long............................	150	225	300
Kenton Cement Mixer..............................	400	600	800
Kenton Circus Truck, 10" long...............	1500	2500	3900
Kenton "Coal" Dump Truck, 8-1/2 long............................	462	693	925
Kenton "Coast-to-Coast" Bus.................	350	525	700
Kenton "Contractors" Dump Wagon, cast iron , 9-3/4" long.......................	500	750	1050
Kenton Coupe, 5" long..........................	230	345	460

	C6	C8	C10
Kenton Dump Truck, 6" long...................	150	225	300
Kenton Emergency Truck, circa 1930s, black rubber tires, takes batteries for headlights and spotlight................	180	270	360
Kenton Fire Apparatus Truck.................	400	600	800
Kenton Fire Pump Truck, early with driver, approx. 10" long......................	375	562	750
Kenton Fire Pumper, 1920s, 14-1/2" long..	550	850	1320
Kenton Fire Pumper, circa 1920s, has gong, 18" long.............................	350	525	700
Kenton Fire Truck, w/pumper, 15" long...	1200	2000	2800
Kenton Franklin, air-cooled, 8-1/2"........	1300	1950	2600
Kenton "Hose" Truck, open cab, circa 1920s, green, driver, rider, hose, ladders, approx. 6-3/4" long..............	350	525	700
Kenton "Hose" Truck, 9" long.................	500	750	1050
Kenton Ice Truck, tongs and glass ice, 7-1/2" long..	362	545	725
Kenton Jaeger Cement Mixer, smaller size, iron wheels.................................	350	525	700
Kenton Jaeger Cement Mixer, 8" long...	1000	1500	2000

KENTON Buckeye Ditcher, 12-1/2" long. Courtesy Sotheby's New York.

KENTON Bus, Double-Decker 1920s, 7-1/4" long. Courtesy Lloyd W. Ralston Auctions.

KENTON Bus, Double-Decker, 9-1/2" long. Courtesy Phillips New York.

KENTON Touring Car, open, driver and passenger, 8-1/2" long (air-cooled Franklin). Courtesy Sotheby's New York.

	C6	C8	C10
Kenton Jaeger "Mixer", cast iron cement truck, 9" long	1200	2000	2700
Kenton Ladder Truck, cast iron, approx. 7-1/2" long	310	465	620
Kenton Ladder Truck, pressed steel ladders, 16" long	325	488	650
Kenton Ladder Truck, 17-1/4" long	750	1200	1700
Kenton "Merchant Delivery"	450	675	900
Kenton Overland Circus Cage Truck w/driver, 7-1/2" long	650	1000	1500
Kenton Overland Circus w/lion, 9" long	900	1350	1800
Kenton Patrol Wagon, marked "Patrol" on side, circa 1920s-30s, 9" long	500	800	1150
Kenton Phaeton Touring Car, 12"long	350	562	700
Kenton "Pickwick Nite Coach", cast iron, 14" long	1500	2500	3800
Kenton Pontiac, approx. 4" long	150	225	300
Kenton Racer, early, 7-1/2" long	350	550	750
Kenton Racer, early, cast iron, 9" long	600	1000	1400
Kenton Red Devil w/driver, 6" long	250	375	500
Kenton Road Grader, cast iron, rubber tires, nickel-plated moveable blade, 7-1/2" long	250	375	500
Kenton Roadster, driver, circa 1908, 6" long	300	450	600
Kenton Runabout Auto, 1900, 5" long	170	255	340

	C6	C8	C10
Kenton Runabout Auto, cast iron, resembles a 1910 Franklin, has driver, 7" long	600	1000	1400
Kenton Sedan, 4" long	110	165	225
Kenton Sedan, late 1930s, rubber tires, take apart body, 7" long	1200	2000	2800
Kenton "Speed" Stake Truck, circa 1927, 5-1/2" long	342	513	685
Kenton Sprinkler Truck, early, 8"	425	638	850
Kenton Stake Truck, 6" long	235	352	470
Kenton Steam Roller, "Galion Master" 6-1/2" long	225	338	450

KENTON Fire Pumper, 18" long, has gong. Courtesy Mapes Auctioneers & Appraisers.

KENTON Ladder Truck, pressed steel ladders, 16" long. Courtesy Lloyd W. Ralston Auctions.

KENTON Sedan, 7" long, late 30s. Courtesy Lloyd W. Ralston Auctioneers.

KENTON, boattail, cut-down speedster, 1910, 7" long. Courtesy Lloyd W. Ralston Auctions.

KENTON Tow Auto, 1920s, 9-1/2" long. Courtesy Lloyd W. Ralston Auctions.

	C6	C8	C10
Kenton Steam Shovel, Marion, 7-1/4"...	600	900	1200
Kenton Tank, cast iron 2-1/2" long.........	80	120	160

	C6	C8	C10
Kenton Touring Car, open, driver and passenger, 8-1/2" long........................	650	975	1300
Kenton Tow Auto, 1920s, 9-1/2"long....	1100	1800	2700
Kenton Yellow Cab, 1950s, 6-3/8"long.	470	705	940

KEYSTONE

Keystone, of Boston, Massachusetts, had an odd assortment of products; movie projectors, steel trucks, wooden boats and pressed wood forts and garages. Founded in June, 1922 or 1923 by Chester Rimmer and Arthur Jackson, it was first located in a small shop in Malden, Mass. under the name Jacrim, using parts of the partners' last names. Rimmer retired in 1958 and sold out to various companies. Address in Boston was 288 A Street. All numbers and descriptions in bold type are Keystone's own.

KEYSTONE No. 51, Police Patrol. Photo by Calvin L. Chaussee.

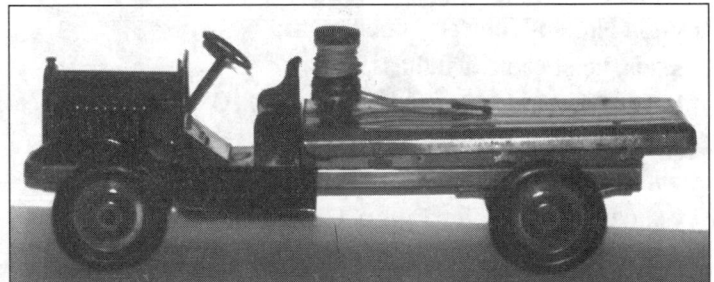

KEYSTONE No.55. Courtesy Joe and Sharon Freed.

	C6	C8	C10
Keystone No.? "Dugan Brothers" "ride'm" Truck......................	1200	2000	2800
Keystone No. 41 Dump Truck, 26-1/2" long..........................	425	638	850
Keystone No. 43 American Railway Express, 26" long........................	1300	2200	3150
Keystone No. 44 Truck Loader, 17-3/4" high..........................	175	263	350

	C6	C8	C10
Keystone No. 45 U.S. Mail Truck, 26" long................................	838	657	1675
Keystone No. 46 Steam Shovel, when arm is extended 26" long...................	200	300	400
Keystone No. 47 Steam Shovel, when arm is extended 34-1/2" long...........	250	375	500
Keystone No. 48 U.S. Army Truck 26" long................................	500	750	1000

KEYSTONE No. ??, "Dugan Brothers" "ridem" truck. Courtesy Joe and Sharon Freed.

KEYSTONE "Moving Van Long Distance Hauling". Courtesy Mapes Auctioneers & Appraisers.

KEYSTONE Packard Dump Truck, 26" long. Courtesy PB Eight-Four, New York.

KEYSTONE No. 43. American Railway Express.

	C6	C8	C10
Keystone No.49 Fire Truck, 27-1/2"long.	600	1000	1500
Keystone No.51 Police Patrol, 27-1/2" long	800	1400	1900
Keystone No. 52 Fire Truck, 27-1/2" long	650	1100	1500
Keystone No. 53 Sprinkler Truck, tank 12" long	650	1050	1450
Keyston No. 54 Koaster Truck, with skids, hoist cable, windlass, 26" long when skids retracted	800	1300	1800
Keystone No. 55 Koaster Truck, without skids and windlass	287	430	575
Keystone No. 56 Water Pump Tower, 29" long	500	800	1200
Keystone No. 57 Chemical Pump Engine, 27-1/2" long	700	1200	1600
Keystone No. 58 Moving Van, 26" long..	700	1200	1600
Keystone No. 60 Riding Steam Roller...	225	338	450
Keystone No.62 Hydraulic Dump Truck, 26" long	500	800	1200
Keystone No. 73 Ambulance, military, 27" long	800	1350	2000
Keystone No. 78 Wrecking Car,27" long.	600	1000	1300
Keystone 79 Aerial Ladder, 30-1/2"long.	600	1050	1350
Keystone No.??Greyhound Bus windup..	650	1100	1400
Keystone No.??Ladder Truck, 24" long..	475	700	950
Keystone No.??Plastic Sedan, c. 1950,			

	C6	C8	C10
hood lifts, gas tank fills & drains 4-1/2" long	14	21	28
Keystone No.??Steam Roller, red and black, air pressure whistle, brass bell, 20" long	340	510	680
Keystone No.??"World's Greatest Circus" Truck, circa 1930s, 26" long	1500	2700	4000

KEYSTONE No. 49 Fire Truck. Photo by Calvin L. Chaussee.

KEYSTONE No. 58, Moving Van. Courtesy Joe and Sharon Freed.

KILGORE

Kilgore, of Westerville, Ohio, appears to have begun toymaking in the 1920s. Its toys were cast iron and low-priced, with cap pistols its most popular line. But it also did well with a number of attractive trucks, fire engines and cars, as well as scattered aircraft and ships. Some subsidiary manufacturing was done in Lancaster, Pennsylvania and Canada. In 1937 Kilgore began making plastic cars, trucks, planes and buses, and later added plastic cap pistols, placing it among the first (if not the first) companies to produce plastic toys. Kilgore remained in business until at least 1978. The first owner, a Mr. Kilgore, sold out in 1921.

KILGORE "Fire Chief" Sedan, plastic. Photo by Dave Leopard.

KILGORE Pontiac, 10" long. Courtesy Sotheby's New York.

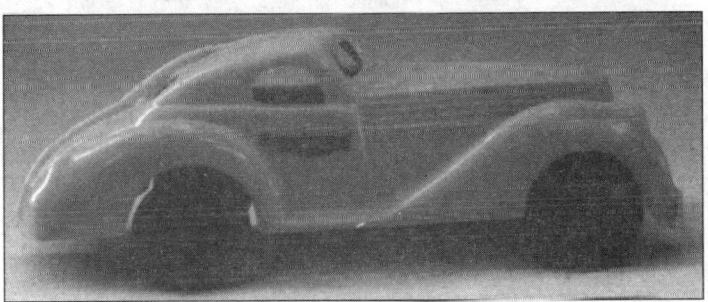
KILGORE Coupe, streamlined, plastic. Photo by Dave Leopard.

KILGORE Artic Ice Cream Truck.

	C6	C8	C10
Kilgore Arctic Ice Cream Truck, 8"long	800	1300	1800
Kilgore "Artic Ice Cream" Truck, 9"	500	750	1000
Kilgore Auto,"LF 1300A",w/driver	180	270	360
Kilgore Bus, plastic, advertised in 1937, 4" long	20	25	30
Kilgore Convertible w/Rumble seat, early 1930s, w/driver, 7" long	160	240	320
Kilgore Coupe, streamlined, plastic, advertised in 1937, 4" long	15	20	25
Kilgore Double-Decker Bus, circa 1930, 6" long	450	675	900
Kilgore Dump Truck, cast iron, circa 1934, 5-3/4" long	160	240	320
Kilgore Dump Truck, 1930s, 7"long	180	270	360
Kigore Dump Truck, cast iron, circa 1934, 8-1/2" long	362	445	725
Kigore "Express" Truck, plastic, advertised in 1937, 4" long	15	20	25
Kilgore "Fire Chief" Sedan, plastic, advertised in 1937, 4" long	15	20	25

	C6	C8	C10
Kilgore Fire Truck w/ladders	450	675	900
Kilgore Livestock Truck, 1930s, 7" long	275	365	550
Kilgore Livestock Truck, 9" long	500	800	1200
Kilgore Motorcycle, single rider, 4"	110	165	220
Kilgore Packard Luxury Sedan, take-apart body, 8-1/4" long	700	1300	1600
Kilgore Pierce-Arrow Roadster, take-apart body, 6-1/8" long	250	375	500
Kilgore Police Car, plastic, 1937, 4"	15	20	25
Kilgore Pontiac, cast iron, 1930, 10"	1200	2000	3000
Kilgore Roadster, driver, rumble seat, 6" long	262	395	525
Kilgore Sedan, 3-1/4" long	70	105	140
Kilgore "Special Delivery" Motorcycle	250	375	500
Kilgore Stutz Roadster, 13 parts	1100	1500	2500
Kilgore "Taxi", plastic, advertised in 1937, 4" long	15	20	25
Kilgore "Toy Town Delivery" Truck, 6-1/8" long	450	675	900

KINGSBURY

Kingsbury had its origins in 1886 in Keene, New Hampshire. Its owner was Harry T. Kingsbury, who bought the Wilkins Toy Company, apparently not changing that firm's name till after World War One. Steel and spring motors characterize Kingsbury's toys with cars, fire engines, farm equipment and racing cars its primary output. Kingsbury is still in business, but seems to have given up toy production in 1942.

KINGSBURY Golden Arrow Racer, 20" long. Courtesy Wilkinson Collection, Detroit Antique Toy Museum.

KINGSBURY Phaeton Auto, 1900, 9-12" long. Courtesy Lloyd W. Ralston Auctions.

	C6	C8	C10
Kingsbury Aerial Ladder Truck, pressed steel windup, circa 1941, ladder rises automatically to height of 38" when the truck runs into any obstruction, fireman on ladder climbs up and down by turning crank at base of ladder,early version new in 1905, 24" long	180	270	360
Kingsbury earlier version of Aerial Ladder Truck	500	800	1100
Kingsbury Airflow, circa 1934, pressed steel, rubber tires, 14" long	238	357	475
Kingsbury Airflow, clockwork,14" long	500	850	1200
Kingsbury Auto, very early, steel windup, 9-3/4" long	250	375	500
Kingsbury Bluebird Racer	1000	1700	2400
Kingsbury Brougham Sedan, pressed steel windup, 13" long	450	800	1200
Kingsbury Bus, pressed steel, 18" long	1500	2500	3500
Kingsbury Cannon Truck, very early, clockwork, 11" long	135	205	270
Kingsbury Cannon Truck, circa 1939, windup, 15" long	212	318	425
Kingsbury Caterpillar, windup, 8-1/2"	225	338	450
Kingsbury Cattle Truck, 1930s, 19" long	212	318	425
Kingsbury DeSoto, pressed steel windup, circa 1938, 14-1/2" long	275	363	550
Kingsbury Dump Truck, tin, driver 10" long	225	338	450

	C6	C8	C10
Kingsbury Dump Truck, early 30s, clockwork, 16" long	350	525	700
Kingsbury "Fire Chief" Coupe, 1930s 14" long	325	438	65
Kingsbury Fire Pumper, very early, clockwork iron and steel, 11" long	250	375	500
Kingsbury Fire Pumper, 1920s, 23" long	225	338	450
Kingsbury Fire Truck, 18" long	250	375	500
Kingsbury Ford Sedan & House Trailer, 1937, pressed steel, 23" long	287	430	575
Kingsbury Golden Arrow Racer, pressed steel windup, 20" long	600	900	1200
Kingsbury Greyhound Bus, windup	225	338	450
Kingsbury Ladder Truck, steel, driver, 22" long	187	280	375
Kingsbury Ladder Truck, circa 1930 35" long	1200	2100	3100
Kingsbury Ladder Wagon Fire Truck, tin, rubber tires, 23-1/2" long	90	135	180
Kingsbury Phaeton Auto, 1900, rubber slip tires, 9-1/2" long	500	800	1100
Kingsbury Rack Truck, pressed steel windup, 16" long	350	525	700
Kingsbury Roadster, electric head-lights, spring motor, luggage rack, 13" long	600	1000	1500

KINGSBURY Ladder Truck, 35" long. Courtesy Christie's East.

KNAPP "Electric Automobile", circa 1903. Courtesy Sotheby's New York.

	C6	C8	C10
Kingsbury Sedan, two door w/trailer, 1930s, clockwork, 22-1/2" long	438	657	875
Kingsbury Sunbeam Racer, sheetmetal, red w/rubber tires on steel wheels, clockwork motor, 19" long	600	950	1350
Kingsbury Tractor, mechanical w/driver, 8" long	250	375	500
Kingsbury Tractor and Cart, tin, w/iron driver, white rubber wheels circa 1930s	110	165	220
Kingsbury Transit Truck, 1930s, 19" long	238	358	475
Kingsbury Truck w/C Cap, tin, 10" long	175	262	350
Kingsbury Windup Car, curved dash, driver, 9" long	225	338	450
Kingsbury Wrecker, pressed steel windup, 13" long	250	375	500

	C6	C8	C10
Kingston Producers, Kokomo, Indiana, Electricar, the Red Arrow, 1930s, 15" long	150	225	300
Kingston Producers, Kokomo, Duesenberg, electric with transformer and steel track, 12" long	1200	2500	3700
Knapp "Electric Automobile", circa 1903, pressed steel, battery-activated, 11" long	1100	1750	2600
Ladder Truck, driver front and rear, cast iron, 5" long	45	68	90
Laketoy "John Wanamaker" Delivery Van, wooden, 10-1/2" long	180	270	360

LANSING SLIK-TOYS
(Listing and History by Dave Leopard)

Lansing Slik-Toys were made in Lansing, Iowa and sometimes bear the name "Kipp", in addition to the "Lansing" and "Slik-Toy" trademarks. Most Slik-Toys are made of aluminum in a single casting but some were made of hard plastic. The company made many farm and construction toys but the list below is confined to cars and trucks. All Slik-Toys I have seen bear a 4 digit number beginning with "9". If a toy bears such a number, even if it has no other markings, it is almost surely a Slik-Toy.

LAPIN Sedan, 6 side windows. Photo by Dave Leopard.

LAPIN Coupe, plastic 1939 Hudson? Photo by Dave Leopard.

	C6	C8	C10
Stakebody Truck, No. 9500, 11" long....	40	50	60
Sedan, Fastback, No. 9600, 7" long........	25	30	40
Sedan, Fastback, No. 9600, taxi version, 7" long..................................	30	40	45
Pickup Truck, No.9601, 7"long..............	25	30	40
Open Stake Truck, No. 9602, 7" long.....	25	30	40
Tank Truck, No. 9603, 7" long................	25	30	40
Sedan ,4 door, No. 9604, 6" long............	20	25	35
Pickup Truck, No. 9605, 6" long............	25	30	40
Firetruck, No. 9606, 6" long...................	20	25	35
Tank Truck, No. 9607, 6" long...............	20	25	35
Tractor/Trailer rig (milk tanker), No. 9610, 8" long..............................	30	35	45
Tractor/Trailer rig (grain trailer), No. 9611, 8" long..............................	25	30	40
Tractor/Trailer rig (flatbed trailer), No. 9613, 8" long..............................	25	30	40
Tractor/Trailer rig (log trailer),			

	C6	C8	C10
No. unknown, 8" long........................	25	30	40
Wrecker, No. 9617, 5" long....................	85	128	170
Firetruck, No. 9700, 3-1/2" long.............	20	25	35
Roadster, No. 9701, 3-1/2" long.............	20	25	35
Pickup Truck, plastic, No. 9703, 4" long..	20	25	35
End Slik-Toy			
Lapin Cadillac, 1948, 4 doors, 6" long..	10	15	20
Lapin Coupe, plastic, 1939 Hudson?......	10	15	20
Lapin Sedan, six side windows, plastic, 1939 Hudson?.................................	10	15	20
Lapin Stake Truck, Chevrolet, plastic, 1947, 4" long..................................	10	15	20
Lincoln Toys (Windsor, Ontario, Canada) Dump Truck, 7" long..........	55	82	110
Lincoln Toys "Dunlop Tires Tow Truck" wrecker.................................	77	115	155
Lincoln Toys "Sand Truck", dump, 14" long...	55	82	110

LINCOLN WHITE METAL WORKS

By Fred Maxwell, Slushmold Contributing Editor, Perry Eichor and Ferd Zegel

This Lincoln, Nebraska firm is now recognized as the maker of many of those high-quality pre-war slushmold "orphan toys". This long obscurity is all the more surprising because Clayton E. Stevenson, the founder, was a many-talented personage in the Dime Store Toy industry: an artist, a skilled craftsman and salesman with world-wide contacts. He had made toys at home since the early 1920s (see Mid-West Metal Novelty Co.); as a salesman for Western Diecasting Co. he furnished some molds to Kansas Toy Co. and may have furnished some to Tip Top Toy Co. and others. He may also have invented 3-piece molds, which were his specialty. The third piece was used to cast those uniquely realistic reentrant front-ends (grille, headlamps, fenders) but had to be pulled away in order to open the mold and dump the hot toy. These molds and the even more complex molds for those beautiful tri-motored aircraft (Lincoln's Fokker and C.A.W.'s Fords) were surprising in this competitive industry because it slowed production and added to costs. For us collectors it created rarity.

His was a remarkably long toy-making career, about 15 years, through the Great Depression. What we know came from a Xmas story in the Nebraska State Journal of November 20, 1931, a fine article in the Antique Toy World of January 1984, and from biographical information, photos and toys saved by his daughter, Marian.

Stevenson, an auto mechanic, was born in 1896 and raised in Axtell, Kansas. He, and his wife, Esther, moved to Lincoln in 1931 and started marketing toys in his name at 1250 Dakota St. For a new business, he had a rapid rise. In his first season he made "800,000 toys in three months". He was manager, purchaser, worker and salesman.

As his business grew - "30,000 toys a day and 27 to 30 laborers" at one time - he moved to a larger facility at 2204 Y Street. In 1935 he was listed at 3433 J Street. The toys were sold to Woolworth, Kress, Kresge and Schwartz Paper Co. stores, as well as all over the country, especially California and New York, and even abroad.

The factory was sold in 1940, after 9 (?) years of production, due to shortages of lead and rubber and the rising costs of labor - all due to expansion of war production. (We were not told who bought what, although a few clues point to nearby Ralstoy. Although 1940 is the date given by a family member, I did not find the business listed in Lincoln directories after 1937.)

A variety of toys were made, "tiny airplanes, midget racers, larger speed cars - about 6" long - brilliant sedans, small coupes, tri-motor plane models and miniature sawmills. They range in size from 3 to 7" (?) in length". "Mr. Stevenson, who does the modeling, uses pictures of planes and cars shown in magazines. For his midget racer he used a picture of a Miller special. His sedan is a replica of the front-drive Cord. His coupe is a Nash model. His trimotor plane is taken from a photo of a Ford product". This in 1931; other patterns were issued later. Early toys used metal wheels and tin propellers and had neat patterned bottom-pans we use as clues. Later toys had rubber wheels. This list below is incomplete; we were dependent on the few toys we have found. Can any of you collectors of rare Slush add to this history? Have you seen a Cord sedan? Could Stevenson have patterned or produced the "Cord" sold by Tommy Toy Co.? Have you seen a Nash coupe? Others from 3-piece molds?

LINCOLN WHITE METAL, LWV1, mid 1930s, LWV28, mid 1930s. Photo by Perry Eichor.

LINCOLN WHITE METAL, Top: LWV2, Bottom: LWV3. Photo by Perry Eichor.

	C6	C8	C10
LWV1 Indy Racer, Miller FWD Special, driver, rounded grille, horizontal cooling fins alongside hood, torpedo tail, 5-1/8" long...........		No Price Found	
LWV2 Speed Car, Bluebird record car, driver, V-8 engine with intake ports, triangular fin with wing design embossed, 6" long....................		No Price Found	
LWV3 Speed Car, Bluebird, smaller version of above, 4" long..................		No Price Found	
LWV4? Speed Car, A V-12 version of Bluebird with triangular fin, Lincoln?, 4-5/8" long........................		No Price Found	
LWV5 Sedan, Pierce-Arrow Silver Arrow, vertical vee-grille, head-lamps and front fenders faired, 6 open windows (OW), divided windshield (W/S), plain pan, 3-1/2" long......................................		No Price Found	
LWV6 Sedan, 2 door Chrysler or DeSoto airflow, hood ornament (HO),divided open W/S, horizontal louvers (HL), plain pan, 3-3/4"...........		No Price Found	
LWV7 Sedan, 2 door Pontiac, HO, grid pattern grille, HL, 4 OW, trunk, 3-7/8" long..............................		No Price Found	
LWV8 "Wrecker", high style with chopped top, Graham-like grille, 2 OW, fenders faired bumper to bumper, solid crane with grid			

	C6	C8	C10
pattern and hook, patterned pan "Made in USA", 3 1/2" long.............		No Price Found	
LWV9 Fire Engine Pumper with fire-man on rear step. Graham-like grille, fenders faired bumper to bumper, patterned pan "Made in USA", 3-3/4" long...........................		No Price Found	
LWV10 Tanker Truck, COE, 2 OW, 6 tanks, 8 compartments, patterned pan, "Made in USA", 3-3/4"..............		No Price Found	
LWV11 Railcar, Streamlined "UNION PACIFIC" and shield symbol, 2 OW in cab, 18 OW in passenger section, hidden rubber wheels, patterned pan, "Made in USA", 4-1/2" long..............		No Price Found	
LWV12 Fire Engine, steam pumper, 2 man crew, hose reel compartment, HO, HG, 3-1/4" long.........................		No Price Found	
LWV13 Speed Car, Bluebird, w/crossed flags on fin, V12, horizontal trim, patterned pan, 4-1/8" long.................		No Price Found	
LWV14 Coupe, streamlined Pontiac, HO,VG, HL, 2 OW, H trim on front fenders, embossed folded "trunk rack", patterned pan, 3-3/8"....		No Price Found	
LWV15 Coupe, Graham? slanted vee-grille, divided WS, 2 OW, SM, T, from 3-piece mold, 3-3/8" long.........		No Price Found	

LINCOLN WHITE METAL, LWV8. Photo by Perry Eichor.

LINCOLN WHITE METAL, Top: LWV10, Bottom: LWV11. Photo by Perry Eichor.

	C6	C8	C10
LWV16 Coupe, Oldsmobile, streamlined, slanted vee-grille, HO, HL, divided WS, 2 OW, RM, patterned pan, 4" long			No Price Found
LWV17 Coupe, streamlined Lincoln?, slanted vee-grille, divided WS, 2 OW, patterned pan, 3-1/2" long			No Price Found
LWV18 Coupe, Graham?, VG, SM, 2 OW, LI, T, from 3-piece mold 3-1/2"			No Price Found
LWV19 Coupe, slanted hood, rear-mount hub for rubber tire, (see Tootsie Graham)			No Price Found
LWV20 Coupe, vertical hood, wrap-around?, rear window, T			No Price Found
LWV21 Brougham, Graham?, vertical vee-grille, SM, 4 OW,T, from 3-piece mold, 3-1/2" long			No Price Found
LWV22 Stake Truck, slanted HG, divided WS, 2 OW, open stakes, rounded pan, 3-1/2" long			No Price Found
LWV23 Limosine, Graham? VG, MDWSM, 4 OW, LI, T, from 3-piece mold, 3-1/4" long			No Price Found
LWV24 Limosine, Nash?, VG, VL, MWWSM, 4 OW, T, from 3-piece mold, 2-1/2" long			No Price Found
LWV25 Indy Racer, small, 2-man, FWD, rounded hood, 4 cyl., exhaust left side			No Price Found
LWV26 Tractor, small Fordson			No Price Found
LWV27 Bus, Overland, HO, HG, VL,10 OW, 3-1/2" long			No Price Found
LWV28 Indy Racer, large, driver, slanted vee-grille, horizontal cooling fins, torpedo tail			No Price Found

	C6	C8	C10
LWV29 Indy Racer, large, driver, unusual grille design			No Price Found
LWV30 Indy Racer, large, different version of above			No Price Found
LWV31 Sedan, Lincoln Auto Co.?			No Price Found
LWV32 Sedan, Ford V-8			No Price Found

Note: Some of the above are so rare that they may not have been put into production.

Lincoln used several types of wheels: metal disc and metal "wire" with black painted "tires"; white rubber "balloon tires" then standard in the industry.

Abbreviations used above same as used for Kansas Toy Co.

Many of the above list came from private collections or photographs.

I have not seen realized prices for several years. The asking prices seen have been so volatile as to be not helpful as guides. Collectors of rare, quality slushmold toys should expect to pay above-average prices.

LINCOLN WHITE METAL, Top To Bottom: LWV24; LWV23; LWV15. Photo by Fred Maxwell.

LINCOLN WHITE METAL, Top To Bottom: LWV14, LWV18, LWV21. Photo by Fred Maxwell.

	C6	C8	C10
Lionel Electric Racing Automobile set	1000	1700	2400
Log Truck (Beck), steers via horn on top of cab, late 1940s, large	No Price Found		
Lumar: See Marx			
Lupor Ambulance	72	108	145
Lupor Fire Chief Car	42	63	85
Lupor Police Car, 1949 Ford	27	41	55

M & L TOY CO. INC.

M&L was incorporated October 21, 1947. It was located on Paterson Plank Road in Union City, New Jersey and got its name from the father & son who owned it, Morris and Louis (last name unknown). The company may have begun in 1946, and lasted till at least 1948. It made vehicles, trains, "jeweled swords, water guns, mechanical toys, and plastic horns. Most or all of its vehicles seem to have been sold unpainted and with plastic wheels. The alloy used in the vehicles was more than 99% zinc, with a smidgen of aluminum added. Most or all of their toys were copies. There were about thirty employees. By 1948 it was located at 123-33rd Street, Union City, New Jersey.

	C6	C8	C10
M&L (1) Racer, 2-3/4" long	10	15	20
M&L (2) Cabin Racer	12	18	25
Mack Dump Truck, cast iron, 12" long	650	1100	1600
Mack Dump Truck, cast iron, 1930s 8-1/2" long	275	362	550
"Mack" Ladder Truck, cast iron, 18" long	300	450	600
Mack Stake Truck, cast iron, 7" long	70	105	140

LINDSTROM

The Lindstrom Tool & Toy Company made windups of light pressed steel as well as tin. It was located in Bridgeport, Ct., and began making toy cars about 1913. It seems to have ceased production sometime in the 1940s.

	C6	C8	C10
Lindstrom Lumber Truck no. 160, steerable front wheels, tin, with driver, 10" long	125	187	250
Lindstrom Steam Roller no. 181, mechanical, 12" long	50	75	100

LINCOLN WHITE METAL, LWV31. Photo by Fred Maxwell.

LIONEL Electric Racing Automobile set. Courtesy Sotheby's New York.

M & L (1) Racer. Photo by Craig A. Clark.

M & L (2) Top: Cabin Racer, cast headlamps: Bottom Barclay Prototype, rhinestone headlamps missing. Photo by Perry Eichor.

MACK Dump Truck, cast iron, 1930s. Courtesy Mapes Auctioneers & Appraisers.

MACK Stake Truck, cast iron, 7" long. Courtesy Mapes Auctioneers & Appraisers.

MANOIL

List compiled by Terry Sells, numbers and words in bold are Manoil's own description. 701-706 began production in 1934.

	C6	C8	C10
Manoil **700 Sedan**, futuristic	57	85	115
Manoil **701 Sedan**, futuristic	50	75	100
Manoil **702 Coupe**, futuristic	67	100	135
Manoil **703 Wrecker**, futuristic	75	112	150
Manoil **704 Roadster**, futuristic, Pat. No. 95791	54	81	108
Manoil **705 Sedan**, futuristic, Pat. No. 95792	67	100	135
Manoil **706 Rocket**, futuristic bus-like vehicle, Pat. No. 95793	50	75	100
Manoil **70 Soup Kitchen**, large number	7	11	15
Manoil **70A Soup Kitchen**, small number	9	13	18
Manoil **71 Shell Carrier with Soldier on Shell Box**, has loop	12	18	24
Manoil **71A** same as above, no loop	8	12	17
Manoil **72 Water Wagon**, large number	11	16	22
Manoil **72A** same as above, small number	9	13	18
Manoil **72B** No number	10	15	20

	C6	C8	C10
Manoil **73 Tractor**, loop front	13	19	26
Manoil **73A Tractor**, plain front	11	16	23
Manoil **74 Armored Car with Anti-Tank Gun**	20	30	41
Manoil **75 Armored Car with Anti-Aircraft Gun**	27	41	55
Manoil **75A Armored Car with Siren**, siren cast separately	25	38	50

MANOIL Top left to right: 713, 716, P-7 and Bottom left to right: 714, P-10, P-11, P-9. Courtesy Marjorie and Peter Ruben.

	C6	C8	C10
Manoil **75A** Armored Car with Siren, siren cast with vehicle	34	51	68
Manoil **95** Tank	10	15	20
Manoil **96** Large Shell on Truck	11	16	22
Manoil **97** Pontoon on Wheels	17	26	35
Manoil **98** Torpedo on Wheels	9	14	19
Manoil **103** Gasoline Truck	11	16	22
Manoil **104** Chemical Truck	11	16	23
Manoil **105** Five Barrel Gun on Wheels	12	18	24
Manoil **(MC5)** Tank, composition	12	18	25

Manoil Post War Vehicles

	C6	C8	C10
Manoil **707** Sedan	25	38	51
Manoil **708** Roadster, horizontal radiator	28	42	57
Manoil **708A** Roadster, vertical radiator	37	56	75
Manoil **709** Fire Engine	17	26	35
Manoil **710** Oil Tanker	15	22	30
Manoil **711** Aerial Ladder	200	300	400
Manoil **712** Pumper	200	300	400
Manoil **713** Bus	12	18	24
Manoil **714** Towing Truck	10	15	20
Manoil **715** Commercial Truck	10	15	20
Manoil **716** Sedan	10	15	20
Manoil **717** Hard Top convertible	12	18	24

	C6	C8	C10
Manoil **718** Convertible	10	15	20
Manoil **719** Sport Car	10	15	20
Manoil **720** Ranch Wagon	10	15	20

Manoil Plastic Vehicles

	C6	C8	C10
Manoil **P-7** Roadster	8	12	16
Manoil **P-8** Sedan	8	12	16
Manoil **P-9** Pick-Up	8	12	16
Manoil **P-10** Towing Truck	8	12	16
Manoil **P-11** Road Scraper	8	12	16
Manoil **P-12** Tractor	8	12	16
Manoil **P-13** Dump Cart	8	12	16

End Manoil

MANOIL Vehicles and "Metal Action Cannon" No. 200, Left to Right; Top: 95, 96, 97, 98; Bottom: 103, 104, 105, 200. Photo by Ed Poole.

MANOIL, Left to Right, Top: 705, 708 early, 708 later; Bottom: 707, 710, 709. Courtesy Marjorie and Peter Ruben. Photo by Norbert Schachter.

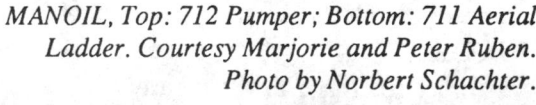

MANOIL, Top: 712 Pumper; Bottom: 711 Aerial Ladder. Courtesy Marjorie and Peter Ruben. Photo by Norbert Schachter.

MANOIL 69 Cannon, metal wheels, wood wheels, wood wheels variant. MANOIL Vehicles, Left to Right; Top: 70, 71; Middle: 71 with variant on wheel support, 72, 73 with front tow loop, 74; Bottom: 75, 75A with siren cast separately, 75A siren cast integrally. Photo by Ed Poole

MARX

	C6	C8	C10
Marx Air Force Truck, "Air Defense Group", ride'm toy, No. 3290, 32"....	125	188	250
Marx Air Force Truck, canvas top, 20"..	105	158	210
Marx Ambulance, No. 8500, 1930s, approx. 14" long..............................	250	375	500
Marx Ambulance, No. 8600, 1930s, approx. 14" long...........................	240	360	480
Marx "American Railroad Express Agency Inc." early 1930s, open cab, 7" long..	120	180	240
Marx American Truck Co. No. 65 moving truck, friction...........................	65	98	130
Marx Army Corps of Engineers, canvas top, 20" long........................	125	188	250
Marx Army Jeep w/Searchlight Trailer, steel..	87	130	175
Marx Army Staff Car, plastic friction,9"...	125	188	250
Marx Auto Transport, 1950s, w/tin litho cars (2 of them), 34" long..........	150	225	300
Marx "Auto Transwalk" No.T-50447B, 1930s truck w/three cars....................	200	300	400
Marx Big Boss Car Carrier, 42" long.....	80	120	160
Marx "Big Shot" Cannon Truck, plastic, fires cap-loaded missile, 22" long......	75	112	150
Marx "Chief-Fire Dept. No.1", "Friction Drive", circa 1948.............................	45	68	90
Marx "Cities Service" Wrecker...............	175	262	350
Marx "City Sanitation Dept. Help Keep Your City Clean", c. 1940, 12-3/4" long.	117	175	235
Marx Coal Truck, electric motor & lights, early..	280	420	564
Marx "Cloverdale Farms" Milk Truck...	110	165	220
Marx Coca Cola Truck, Linemar, tin friction, 3" long.................................	50	75	100
Marx Coca Cola Truck, Sprite decal, stamped steel, late 1940s to early 1950s, 20" long..................................	162	243	325
Marx Convertible Roadster, 1930s, nickel plated tin, 11" long.................	200	300	400
Marx Cord Convertible, 11" long..........	250	375	500
Marx Corvette Coupe, plastic friction, 8".	42	63	85
Marx "Deluxe Delivery" Truck..............	110	165	220
Marx Dump Truck, No. 695B,17" long..	100	150	200
Marx Dump Truck, 2-color,No.T751, c. 1930s	45	68	90
Marx No. 1084 Dump Truck..................	30	45	60
Marx Easter Stake Truck, 1938, 10-1/2" long......................................	190	275	380
Marx "Electrically Lighted Truck and Trailer Set" No. T-5715, c.1930s, 15"..	150	225	300

	C6	C8	C10
Marx Falcon w/plastic bubble top, black rubber tires................................	127	190	255
Marx "Fanny Farmer" Candy Truck, plastic...	100	150	200
Marx Fire Truck, friction, 25" long........	225	338	450
Marx Fix-All Convertible & Wrecker (set).	125	188	250
Marx Fix-It Jaguar, plastic, 12" long......	115	172	230
Marx G-man Pursuit Car, No. 7000, 1930s, 15" long...................................	250	375	500
Marx Gang Buster Car, No. 7200, 1930s, approx. 14" long.....................	550	825	1100
Marx "Gravel" Truck, 13" long..............	140	210	280
Marx "Gravel" Truck, 9"long..................	77	115	155
Marx Grocery Truck, 1950s, 14-1/2".....	62	93	125
Marx Guided Missile Truck No.4488....	220	330	440
Marx "Heavy Gauge Tractor" No. 926..	100	150	200
Marx "High-Boy Climbing Tractor" No. 950, 10-1/2" long........................	75	112	150
Marx Hi-Way Express Truck..................	112	168	225
Marx Hydraulic Dump.........................	115	172	230
Marx Ice Truck w/Tongs & Ice..............	150	225	300
Marx Jeep, 11" long.............................	37	56	75
Marx Lazy-Dazy Dairy Farm Pick-Up Truck and Trailer, 22" long...............	110	165	220
Marx Livestock Truck............................	85	128	170
Marx Lonesome Pine Trailer and Convertible Sedan, 1930s, 19"long.......	482	723	965
Marx "Lumar Contractors" 962 Dump Truck..	480	720	960
Marx "Lumar Contractors" Steam Shovel..	132	198	265
Marx "Lumar Contactors" Crane...........	120	180	240
Marx Lumar Power Grader....................	52	78	105
Marx Lumar Scoop-A-Dump................	62	93	125
Marx M.D. War Dept. Ambulance,1930s.	650	975	1300
Marx No. 1016 Machinery MovingTruck	262	395	525
Marx "Mammoth Truck Train", No. T-50-12345, c. 1930s, truck w/5 trailers.	175	262	350
Marx Marcrest Dairy Stake Truck..........	95	128	190
Marx "Motor Market".............................	80	120	160
Marx Mystery Taxi, circa 1930s, press down to operate.........................	80	120	165
Marx Navy Jeep No. 1078.....................	65	97	130
Marx Navy Jeep w/Searchlight Trailer..	100	150	200
Marx Nutty Mad Cars, friction, circa 1965, each, 4" long....................	70	105	140
Marx Panel Wagon................................	40	60	80
Marx Pepsi-Cola Truck, 1950s,11" long..	35	52	70
Marx "Pet Shop Delivery", 1950s,10"...	80	120	160
Marx Pickup Truck...............................	100	150	200

MARX "City Sanitation Dept. Help Keep Your City Clean". Photo by Calvin L. Chaussee.

MARX Tricky Taxi. Photo by William G. Floyd.

MARX Coca-Cola Truck, 20" long. Courtesy Richard MacNary.

MARX "Deluxe Delivery" Truck. Courtesy Thomas G. Nefos, Federal Shipping Network.

	C6	C8	C10
Marx "Power Grader" No. 1759, black or white wheels, 17-1/2" long	70	105	140
Marx Pure Milk Dairy Truck w/glass bottles, pressed steel, tin wheels, c.1940.	100	150	200
Marx REA Express Truck No. 1021	220	330	440
Marx Road Grader, Heavy-duty	50	75	100
Marx Rocker Dump No. 1752, 17-1/2"	60	90	120
Marx "Sand & Gravel" Dump Truck, 1940s, 10" long	62	93	125
Marx Searchlight Truck	92	138	185
Marx "Sinclair" Fuel Truck, steel	165	248	330
Marx Side Dump Truck, 4-color, No. T-475, circa 1940	105	158	210
Marx Side Dump Truck and Trailer, No. T-4045, circa 1930s	100	150	200
Marx "Siren Fire Chief", circa 1930, "F.D. 1st Batt.", 15" long	330	495	660
Marx Siren Police Car, No. 8300, 1930s, approx. 14" long	200	300	400
Marx " Sparkling Hot Rod Racer", 1950s plastic windup, 8" long	37	52	75
Marx Sports Coupe, 1930s, 15" long	200	300	400
Marx Stake-type Truck, 3-color, No. E-271, circa 1941	62	93	125
Marx Stake Truck, circa 1941, 15" long	75	112	150

	C6	C8	C10
Marx "Tricky Taxi", friction, 4 1/2"	60	90	120
Marx "U.S. Army Truck w/Searchlight Trailer", 1950s, 27" total length	150	225	300
Marx "U.S. Mail" Truck, 14" long	75	112	150
Marx "USA 41573147" Army Truck, circa 1952, 13-3/4" long	100	150	200
Marx "U.S. Navy Jeep w/Searchlight Trailer", 1950s, 21" total length	100	150	200
Marx Willys Jeep, steel, c. 1938, hood opens, windshield folds down, 12"	107	145	215
Marx Willys Jeep and Trailer, c. 1940s	37	56	75
Marx Willys Jeepster, plastic, windup	75	112	150
Marx Wrecker Truck No. T-16, c.1930s	150	225	300
Marx Wrecker Truck, 1920s, 10" long	100	150	200
Mattel Hot Wheels Chapparal 2G No. 6256	6	9	13
Mattel Hot Wheels Daredevil Loop pak. 1968	4	6	9
Mattel Hot Wheels Ford Coupe, No. 6253	10	15	20
Mattel Hot Wheels Jetthreat 11, No. 8235	15	22	30
Mattel Hot Wheels Poison Pinto, No. 9240	7	10	14
Mattel Hot Wheels Silhouette, No. 6209	8	12	16
Mattel Hot Wheels Trestle Aces Pak, 1968	4	6	9

METAL CAST PRODUCTS COMPANY

By Fred Maxwell, Slushmold Contributing Editor

Metal Cast Products, a reorganization circa 1925 of a venerable toy soldier and novelty company, S. Sachs, made hand-operated slushcasting molds for small businesses and hobbyists, what some have called the home casting industry. Since identical molds were sold to many franchisees we cannot identify the actual makers unless they engraved their names on their products. One who did was Fred Green Toys, whose name is found prominently on their toys. Metal Cast offered full support services to its franchisees, including marketing, printing, publishing and parts.

A variety of wheels may be found on its vehicles: metal disk wheels, metal spoke wheels, wood wheels w/rubber tires, and white or black rubber wheels.

We see many home cast lead soldiers and novelties, but the production of toy vehicles has not left much of a mark. Perhaps it was the Great Depression, perhaps it was the lack of identity; demand today seems weak. However, collectors of the unusual should find many collectibles; most of those I have seen were well designed and professionally finished.

	C6	C8	C10
Metal Cast Van Truck, #01-02, COE, cab, semi-trailer moving van. Trailer also found in a "FRED GREEN" VERSION, 6"	No Price Found		
Metal Cast Tank Truck, #01-03, same COE cab, semi-fuel tanker. My version is 5-3/4", "FRED GREEN TOYS","Made in U.S.A.", 6"	4	6	8
Metal Cast Open Rack Truck, #01-04, COE cab, stake semi-trailer, 6"	8	12	16
Metal Cast War Tank, #08, early heavy Sherman Tank, 4"	33	49	66
Metal Cast Cadillac Sedan, #40, 2 door, 5-1/4" long	No Price Found		
Metal Cast Packard Convertible, #41, 2 door, top down, 5-1/4"	10	15	20
Metal Cast Dump Truck, #43, COE chassis, dump body w/activating mechanism, 5-1/4"	No Price Found		
Metal Cast Streamline Sedan, #60, DeSoto? Airflow, 8 open windows, spoke wheels, rubber tires, 4"	10	15	20
Metal Cast Fire Engine, #61, hook and ladder truck, crew of 2, 4-1/2"	6	10	14
Metal Cast Racer, #62, Bluebird type record car, driver, 4-1/2"	No Price Found		
Metal Cast Coupe #63, convertible, 2 open windows, sidemounts, trunk	No Price Found		
Metal Cast Truck, #64, Dodge?, stake-body, 1920s, 2 OW, 4-1/4"	No Price Found		
Metal Cast Fire Engine, #65, Steam pumper w/watercannon, driver, 4"	No Price Found		
Metal Cast Fire Engine, no #, similar to #65 w/o watercannon, 3-7/8"	6	10	14
Metal Cast Racer, #92, large, no driver	No Price Found		

METAL CAST PRODUCTS, Top: Greyhound Bus, MCP #62; Middle: Limousine, MCP #40, MCP #60; Bottom: MCP #64. Photo by Perry Eichor.

METAL CAST PRODUCTS, Top: MCP #01-02; Middle: MCP #01-03; Bottom: MCP #40. Photo by Perry Eichor.

METAL CAST PRODUCTS, Tank. Photo by Ed Poole,

METAL MASTERS

listing by Dave Leopard

	C6	C8	C10
MM01 Roadster, c. 1938, 7" long...........20	30	40
MM02 Bus, c. 1938, 7-1/4" long............ 23	35	47
MM03 Pickup Truck, c. 1938, 7" long.... 20	30	40
MM04 Fire Truck version of pickup, c. 1938, 7" long................. 30	40	50
MM05 Tow Truck version of pickup, c. 1938, 7" long.................. 30	40	50
MM06 Jeep, c. 1947, 5-1/2" long........... 9	13	18
MM07 Station Wagon, c. 1940, 8-1/2"....40	55	65
MM08 Station Wagon, c. 1940, windup motor, 8-1/2"........................ 45	55	70

	C6	C8	C10
MM09 Station Wagon, c. 1940, ambulance version, 8-1/2" long......... 45	55	70
MM10 Tow Truck, c. 1940, "ABC Towing Service", 10" long................40	50	65
MM11 Tow Truck, c. 1940, wind-up motor, 10" long.............................19	28	38
MM12 Fire Truck, c. 1940, removable ladders, 10" long.............................. 30	45	60
MM13 Fire Truck, c. 1940, ladders, windup motors, 10" long...................50	65	80

METALCRAFT

Metalcraft, of St. Louis, Missouri, began producing its pressed steel trucks in 1931. About a million were sold, most as "advertising toys". In 1937, defeated by the Depression, Metalcraft shuttered.

	C6	C8	C10
Metalcraft "Bordens Milk" Truck...........225	338	450
Metalcraft "Bunte Candies" Truck, 12" long...175	262	350
Metalcraft Coca Cola Truck, pressed steel, rubber tires, circa late 20s-early 30s, 10 bottles in rack, "Every Bottle Sterilized", 11" long....675	1000	1350
Metalcraft Coca Cola Truck, 10 bottles, 1930s, 10-1/2" long............... 450	675	900
Metalcraft Coca Cola Truck, 10 bottles, late 1930s, long nose, stamped metal, 12" long................................. 450	675	900
Metalcraft Coca Cola Truck, circa 1928, w/bottles in racks......................500	800	1100
Metalcraft CW Coffee Dump Truck, 10-3/4" long..................................... 225	338	450

	C6	C8	C10
Metalcraft CW Coffee Wrecker..............267	400	535
Metalcraft Delivery Truck Van, steel, 11" long.. 215	322	430
Metalcraft "Goodrich Silvertone Tires" wrecker, w/3 spare tires......................300	450	600
Metalcraft "Heinz" Truck, circa 1932, "Baked Beans", "Bottled Vinegar", "Rice Flakes", 12" long......................325	488	650

METALCRAFT Coca-Cola Truck, 11" long. Courtesy Wilkinson Collection, Detroit Antique Toy Museum.

METALCRAFT Coca-Cola Truck, late 1930s, 12"long. Courtesy Richard L. MacNary.

METALCRAFT, Left to Right: Coca-Cola Truck, "Heinz" Truck. Courtesy Phillips New York.

	C6	C8	C10
Metalcraft "Kroger Food Express", 11" long	425	638	850
Metalcraft "Krug Bakery" Truck	450	675	935
Metalcraft "Machinery Hauling"	500	850	1200
Metalcraft "Meadow Gold Butter" Truck, battery lights, 13" long	500	750	1000
Metalcraft "Plee-Zing Quality Products"	275	362	550
Metalcraft "Pure" Oil Truck	360	540	720
Metalcraft "Shell Motor Oil" Truck	350	525	700
Metalcraft "St. Louis" Truck, circa			

	C6	C8	C10
1930, 11" long	250	375	500
Metalcraft Steam Shovel	85	128	170
Metalcraft "Sunshine Biscuits" Truck	175	262	350
Metalcraft "Towing & Repairs"	275	410	550
Metalcraft "Toy Town Grocery"	275	410	550
Metalcraft "Werks Tag Soap" Truck	275	362	550
Metalcraft "Weston's Biscuits"	215	322	430
Metalcraft "White King Delivery" Truck, 12" long	350	525	700

MIDGETOY
(A & E Tool & Gage Co., Inc.)
Rockford, IL.
By Thomas G. Nefos

The original owners of the Midgetoy factory were engaged in precision instrument production during WWII. In 1946 they decided to branch out into the die cast toy business and MIDGETOY was born. Their toys included everything from military vehicles to sports cars, jeeps and racers. In only 20 years (1966) they became the second largest producers of die cast toys in the nation (Tootsietoy was first). At their peak, Midgetoy produced over 20,000 toys per day. Some of the ideas that were implemented by Midgetoy (making several toys off the same mold at one time instead of only one & blister packaging of toys for point of sale) were quickly to be copied by the competition.

Each toy was given four coats of "lead free" paint with all materials being purchased locally (no foreign materials were ever used). It was not uncommon for the owners to employ elderly folks in nursing homes etc. to do some of the toy painting. Midgetoy would actually take the unfinished product to the elderly for final painting and decaling; thus giving them the opportunity to make some money and pass the time.

Midgetoy produced die cast toys from 1946 to 1981 when the original owners became too old and the factory was shut down.

MIDGETOY 6" Oil Tank Truck, 1957. Photo by Thomas G. Nefos, National Toy Connection.

MIDGETOY Scenic Cruiser Bus-Midgetoy Bus Lines, 1955. Photo by Thomas G. Nefos, National Toy Connection.

	G	V6	M
Midgetoy Oil Tank Truck, "Midgetoy Oil Co.", 1957, 6" long	17	26	35
Midgetoy Cadillac Ambulance, 1971, red/white, 3" long	7	11	15
Midgetoy Indy Car and Towing Trailer, late 40s, car 2", trailer 2-1/2"	10	15	20
Midgetoy Jeep, 1950s, red, 1-1/2"	5	8	10
Midgetoy Boat and Trailer, 1949, 2-3/4"	7	10	15
Midgetoy Scenic Cruiser Bus-Midgetoy Bus Lines, 1955, blue, 3-1/2"	9	13	18

	G	V6	M
Midgetoy Ford Torino Police Car, 1971 white, 2-1/2"	7	10	14
Midgetoy Ford Torino "Fire Chief", 1971, red, 2-1/2"	7	10	14
Midgetoy Ford Torino, 1971, green, 2-1/2"	7	10	14
Midgetoy Ford Mustang w/tow hook, 1970, orange, 2-1/2"	7	11	15
Midgetoy Sunbeam Racer-Utah Salt Flats, 1950, 3-1/2"	10	15	20

MIDGETOY 9" Semi-Auto Transporter (unlisted) with MG & Mustang, 1962. Value in mint $60. Photo by Thomas G. Nefos, National Toy Connection.

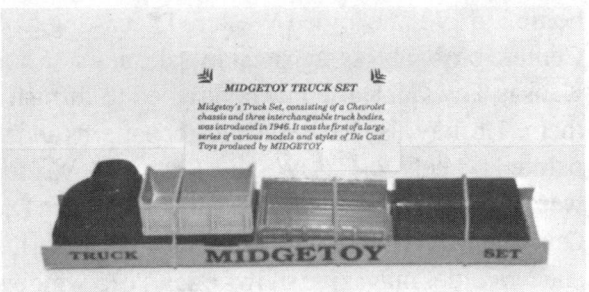

MIDGETOY Truck Set, Chevrolet chassis with 3 interchangeable bodies. 1946. Value in mint $45. Photo by Thomas G. Nefos, National Toy Connection.

MIDGETOY 6" Self-Propelled Artillery. Photo by Thomas G. Nefos, National Toy Connection.

MIDGETOY 9" Semi-Tanker (unlisted), 1963. Value in mint $30. Photo by Thomas G. Nefos, National Toy Connection.

	G	V6	M
Midgetoy Cadillac Convertible, 1949, green, 3-1/2"	10	15	20
Midgetoy Ford Mark IV, 1971, blue, 2-1/2"	7	11	15
Army Vehicles - O.D.			
Midgetoy Sherman Tank, late 40s, 4"	14	21	28
Midgetoy Self-Propelled Artillery, late 40s, 4"	12	18	25
Midgetoy Half Track, late 40s, 4-3/4"	12	18	25
Midgetoy Self-Propelled Artillery, 1957, 6"	14	21	28
Midgetoy Fuel Tank Truck, 1954, 4-1/2"	11	16	22
Midgetoy U.S.A. Jeep, 1950, 2-3/4"	7	11	15

MIDGETOY 6" American LaFrance Fire Truck, 1957. Mint value $32. Photo by Thomas G. Nefos, National Toy Connection

	G	V6	M
Midgetoy U.S.A. Jeep, 1950, 1-1/2"	5	8	10
Midgetoy Howitzer, late 40s, 3"	7	11	15
Midgetoy Staff Car, 1950s, 4-1/2"	12	18	25
Midgetoy Utility Trailer, 40s, 1-1/2"	6	9	12
Midgetoy Army Bus, 50s, 3-1/2"	10	15	20

MID-WEST METAL NOVELTY MANUFACTURING COMPANY
Another "Orphan" Dime Store Toy Maker is found.
By Fred Maxwell, Slushmold Contributing Editor, assisted by Ferd Zegel and John West.

In the late Twenties the U.S. auto industry, led by Ford, was not only booming but dominating global production; and auto toys were keeping up with their prototypes. We focus on three companies which had developed a thriving slushmold toy business: C.A.W. Novelty Co., Mid-West Metal Novelty Co. and Kansas Toy and Novelty Co. These were in small northern Kansas towns, Clay Center and Clifton, only a few miles apart. These toy makers had other things in common; they loved racers, they all used metal disc wheels with black-painted "tires", they tended to follow the lead of Tootsietoy and they left almost no paper trail. This last accounts for the difficulty toy historians have had identifying some excellent models and toys.

The above clues suggest that Mid-West was C.E. Stevenson's business title. Stevenson, an active business man, was at the center of all this. In 1923 he started casting toys at home. In 1925 he joined Western Diecasting Co., of Clay Center, probably as an outside salesman. Shortly after Kansas Toy Co. started he contracted to furnish molds to them. He may also have sold master patterns and those pre-painted wheels to C.A.W. and Kansas Toy, for all these were probably made in the foundry of Western Diecasting. Our sole surviving newsclip on Mid-West in a 1929 Toys and Novelties magazine shows a deluxe (5 window) coupe, a fairly exact copy of the Tootsie Buick, but with those Kansas black-painted "tires".

But what else did Mid-West make? Over the years we have found a group of auto toys with a family resemblance:

	C6	C8	C10
MW1 Large Coupe, no lamps, large diecast?, 5 "grooved" solid windows, disc wheels w/"lug bolts", HG, HO, VL, 3-1/2"			No Price Found
MW2 Yellow Taxicab, no lamps, door handles, 7 "grooved" solid windows, MDW w/rims but no bolts, HG, HO, VL, 2-3/4" long			No Price Found
MW3 Buick Coupe, no lamps, disc wheels, 5 "grooved" solid windows, HG, HO, VL, sidemounts, 3 variations 4 open windows; 5 smooth windows; MDW w/ "lug bolts", 3"			No Price Found
MW4 Midget Racer, driver crouched & hunched over steering wheel, torpedo tail, small disc wheels w/"lug bolts", HG, HO, VL, variation: narrower body and large wheels (the postwar "M & L" reproduction is more often found), 2-3/4"			No Price Found
MW5 Large Racer, basically similar to above but boattailed w/medium sized disc wheels, 3-5/8"			No Price Found
MW6 Truck, closed body, AC Mack, gas tank ahead of windshield, VG, screen louvers, stake-side body.			

Tootsie copies or look-a-likes; Tootsie wheels including those distinctive lug boltheads; metal disc wheels with a suggested rim between wheel and tire (see photos MV3, MV4), but most important - several versions of that Buick coupe seen in Toys and Novelties. The most likely maker was Stevenson, before he moved on to a larger city in 1931 and founded Lincoln (Nebraska) White Metal Works with which he thrived for years in spite of the Great Depression. (See earlier this book)

These Mid-West? toys are rarely seen today. If found, they should be low-priced.

The only known mention of Mid-West, as shown in the August, 1929 Toys & Novelties magazine.

	C6	C8	C10
Unique slushmold design w/solid pan and body open in rear (for pouring alloy), 3-1/4"			No Price Found

MIDWEST, two versions of MW3. Photo by Fred Maxwell.

MIDWEST, L to R: MW2; MW1. Photo by Fred Maxwell.

MIDWEST, Top to Bottom: two versions of MW4; MW5. Photo by Fred Maxwell.

MIDWEST, Left to Right: MW9, MW8. Photo by Fred Maxwell.

MIDWEST, Top: MW7, Bottom, Left to Right: MW7, MW11. Photo by Fred Maxwell.

C6   C8   C10

MW7 Large Roadster, Buick or Packard, long hood, top up, HG, HO, VL, door handles & hinges, RM, rear bumper. Variation: 2 colors, 3 solid windows, different, painted disc wheels, 3-5/8"............................ No Price Found

MW8 Touring Car, Ford T, driver & lady passenger w/muff, top down, no lamps, plain grille, HO, VL, door handles, disc wheels, 3-1/8"................No Price Found

MIDWEST, Left to Right: Unlisted; MW13. Photo by Fred Maxwell.

C6   C8   C10

MW9 Touring Car, top up, no seats, HG, HO, VL, RM, side lamps, door handles, disc wheels, 3-1/8"...... No Price Found

MW10 Bus, Yellow Coach?, high, school-bus body, no doors, 13 solid grooved windows, HG, RM, painted disc wheels, 3-3/4"................. No Price Found

MW11 Town Car, chauffeur, long hood, HG, HO, VL, L/I, 3 colors, 5 solid windows, grooved, door handles & hinges, disc wheels, 3-5/8"................ No Price Found

MW12 Bus, overland/safety, no lamps, no doors, no spares, HG, HO, 10 open windows, disc wheels. (same bus later reissued by Stevenson at Lincoln White Metal Works) 3-1/2"................................. No Price Found

MW13 Sedan, 2 door, Ford A, finely detailed screen grille, headlamps and fenders, (made with a 3-piece mold, a Stevenson specialty), VL, WSV, 4 open windows, door handles & hinges, painted disc wheels, 2-3/4"... No Price Found

MINIATURE VEHICLE CASTINGS, INC. cars. Courtesy Robert E. Wagner.

	C6	C8	C10
MW14 Sedan ?, Buick, same finely detailed front-end as above, "B" cast on grille, HO, VL, side lamps, WSV, 6 open windows, door-hinges, RM, painted wheels. (a similar car has been attributed to Barclay Mfg.), 3-1/16"...................... No Price Found			

MINIATURE VEHICLE CASTINGS INC.

Though these appear to be toys from the 1930s, they were first produced in 1985. The models were carved and cast by owner Robert E. Wagner. Made of die cast lead from silicone molds, they were sold for $21 apiece, and at least 3500 have been sold. Some are beginning to appear at toy shops and on dealer lists. 21 different types were made, amoung them a 1937 Ford Sedan, a 1937 Studebaker coupe and a 1936 Plymouth Sedan. The average length is about 4 1/2", and the New Jersey firm's name is visible (sometimes dimly) on a piece of tin soldered to the bottom. The toys today seem to sell at about double their original price.

	C6	C8	C10
Model T Ford, tin..	100	150	200
Motorcycle "Cop", cast iron 3-3/4" long..	80	120	160
Motorcycle, cast iron, white rubber tires, 3" long..	85	128	170
Motorcycle, Harley-Davidson, rider, 6" long...	275	410	550

"Moxie" Horse Car. Courtesy Sotheby's New York.

	C6	C8	C10
Motorcycle, Harley-Davidson, cast iron, cop rider, 9" long......................	400	600	800
Motorcycle w/sidecar, policeman rider, cast iron, 4" long......................	120	180	240
"Moxie" Horse Car(based on the actual promotional vehicle) tin litho, 8" long...	750	1125	1500

NEFF-MOON TOY COMPANY

Neff-Moon, of Sandusky, Ohio was owned by William Moon and Charles Neff. Production of their pressed steel toys began in 1923, with the firm, which seems to have been located above a grocery, apparently an early victim of the Depression.

	C6	C8	C10
Neff-Moon Groceries Van.......................	175	262	350
Neff-Moon Taxi, 12" long......................	350	525	700
Neff-Moon Tow Truck, circa 1925 16" long..	200	300	400
Nonpareil Ambulance.............................	30	45	60
Nonpareil Dry Goods...............................	30	45	60
Nonpareil Police Patrol............................	30	45	60
Nonpareil Toyville Express.....................	30	45	60

NORTH & JUDD

Research by collector C. B. C. Lee suggests that this company, located at the time in New Britain, Connecticut, made cast iron toys for only one year, probably 1930, for S.H. Kress. Their original designs appear to have been marked with the company's name, but their copies for the most part are unmarked. The company is still in business, making quality hardware.

	C6	C8	C10
Austin Convertible, open top, marked "North & Judd"................................. No Price Found			
Austin Sedan, 2 door, marked "North & Judd"................................. No Price Found			
Bus, looks like Dent, 4.667" long.......... No Price Found			

	C6	C8	C10
Ford Model A Coupe, looks like Arcade, length of left cab 1.528", has driver in window, trunk at rear.....................	No Price Found		
Ford Model T Stake Truck, like Arcade, but marked "Anchor Truck Co." (an anchor is North & Judd's trademark)	1000	2000	3000
Motorcycle Cop, like Hubley's "Cop",			

	C6	C8	C10
separate nickeled driver is held by mushrooms at front of handle-bars and on driver's feet....................	No Price Found		
Semi-Trailer Stake Truck, marked "North & Judd", 5-5/8" long..............	500	800	1100
Tractor, looks like Arcade, but has nickeled driver, 2.988" long..............	No Price Found		

NYLINT

The Nylint Toy and Manufacturing Company was formed in 1937 by Bernard C. Klint and David Nyberg (thus its name) in Rockford, Illinois. Toy production began in the spring of 1946. Since 1950, the firm has concentated on the production of heavy duty scale reproductions, in steel, of earth-moving equipement and over-the-road trucks. Part of the following list was provided by Jeffrey L. Hubbard.

NYLINT No. 2200 Michigan Shovel. Courtesy Continental Hobby House.

NYLINT No.1600 Payloader. Courtesy Continental Hobby House.

	C6	C8	C10
Nylint No. 600 Amazing Car, 1946-49, windup, 13-3/4" long...........................	138	178	275
Nylint No. 700 Lift Truck (fork lift), 1947- 49, windup...............................	110	165	220
Nylint No. 800 Scootcycle, 1948-50, windup, 7-1/4" long...........................	200	300	400
Nylint No. 1000 Deliverall, 1948-51, windup, 10" long............................	300	450	600
Nylint No. 1100 Elgin Street Sweeper, 1950-52,windup, 8-1/4" long.............	122	183	245
Nylint No. 1200 Pumpmobile, 1950-52, windup, 8-5/8" long...........................	120	180	240
Nylint No. 1300 Tournarocker, 1951-52, open tractor w/driver, 18" long..........	80	120	160
Nylint No. 1300 Tournarocker, 1953-57, closed cab, no driver, 18" long..........	55	82	110
Nylint No. 1400 Road Grader, 1951, small wheels, 19-1/4" long..................	80	120	160
Nylint No. 1400 Road Grader, 1952-58, larger wheels.....................................	50	75	
100Nylint No.1500 Tournahopper, 1951-56, 22-1/2" long...	117	185	235

	C6	C8	C10
Nylint No. 1600 Payloader, 1951, tan colored, 18" long.........................	120	180	240
Nylint No.1600 Payloader, 1952-55 red...	85	128	170
Nylint No. 1600 Payloader, 1956-57 light green..	85	128	170
Nylint No. 1600 Payloader, 1958, dark green and before year was out yellow (add 20% to yellow price)..	85	128	170
Nylint No. 1700 Tournahauler, 1953-56 30-1/4" long..	80	120	160
Nylint No. 1800 Traveloader, 1953-55 30" long..	120	180	240
Nylint No. 1900 Tournatractor, 1954-55, 14-3/4" long..	115	172	235
Nylint No. 2000 Speed Swing, 1955-58, 19" long..	100	150	200
Nylint No. 2100 Tournadozer, 1956-59 20" long..	70	105	140
Nylint No. 2200 Michigan Shovel, 1955-65, 31-1/2" long..................................	70	105	140

NYLINT 1960-61, No. 4100, U-Haul Truck. Courtesy Thomas G. Nefos, Federal Shipping Network.

	C6	C8	C10
Nylint No. 2300 Elgin Street Sweeper, 1956-57, Battery-operated version, closed cab	125	188	250
Nylint No. 2400 Electronic Cannon, 1956 has no radar antenna, 1957-60 has radar antenna, 22-1/2" long	95	140	190
Nylint No. 2500 Telescoping Crane, 1957-60, 27" long	180	270	360
Nylint No. 2600 Missile Launcher, 1957-60, 31-1/2" long	150	225	300
Nylint No. 2700 Uranium Hauler, 1958-59 22-1/2" long	175	262	350
Nylint No.2800 Guided Missile Carrier, first version (1958), nose cone of missile doesn't fire, 15-1/2" long	125	188	250
Nylint No. 2800 Guided Missile Carrier, later (through 1960), cone of missile fires	100	150	200
Nylint No. 2900 Jack Hammer, 1958-60 19-1/2" long	75	112	150
Nylint No. 3000 Grader-Loader, 1959-61, 23-3/4" long	70	105	140
Nylint No. 3100 Payloader Tractor-Shovel, 1959-61, 17-5/8" long	120	180	240

NYLINT No. 1300 Tournarocker. Courtesy Thomas G. Nefos, Federal Shipping Network.

	C6	C8	C10
Nylint No. 3200 Power & Light Lineman Truck, 1959-61, 35-3/4" long	155	232	310
Nylint No. 3300 Power & Light Posthole Digger, 1959-61, 35-3/4" long	175	262	350
Nylint No. 3400 Highway Emergency Unit, 1959-63, 18-5/8" long	70	105	140
Nylint No. 3500 Countdown Rocket Launcher, 1959-61, 21" long	75	112	150
Nylint No. 3600 Ford Rapid Delivery 18-1/4" long	180	270	360
Nylint No 3700 Street Sprinkler Truck, 18" long	140	210	280
Nylint No. 3800 Ford Sales & Service, 13-5/8" long	70	105	140
Nylint No. 3900 Ford Platform Tilt Truck, 15-3/4" long	87	131	175
Nylint No. 4000 Ford Speedway Truck w/Racer, 24-3/4" long	150	225	300
Nylint No. 4100 Ford Pickup & U-Haul Box Trailer	125	188	250
Nylint No. 4200 Bulldozer, 14" long	90	135	180
Nylint No. 4300 Ford U-Haul Rental Fleet	175	262	350
Nylint No. 4400 Camper on Pickup 13-1/2" long	85	128	170
Nylint No. 4600 Construction 4-Wheel Platform Dump, 15-3/4" long	122	183	225
Nylint No. 4700 Happy Acres Truck w/horses, 14" long	100	150	200
Nylint No. 48-4900 2-U-Haul Trailers 3-piece set, 33-1/14" long	100	150	200
Nylint No. 5000 Dump Truck w/Cement Mixer, 20-1/2" long	35	52	70
Nylint No. 5100 Dump Truck, 13-1/2"	37	56	75
Nylint No. 5200 Pickup Truck (Econoline), 11-1/4" long	80	120	160
Nylint No. 5300 Custom Camper on above, 12-1/2" long	55	82	110
Nylint No. 5400 Custom Camper on above w/boat, 23-1/2" long	120	180	240
Nylint No. 5500 Pepsi Truck, 16-1/2"	145	168	290
Nylint No. 5800 Ford Econoline Van, 12" long	85	128	170
Nylint No. 6000 American Oil Emergency Truck, 11-1/4" long	75	112	150
Nylint No. 6200 Kennel Truck w/dogs, 11-1/2" long	75	112	150
Nylint No. 6300 Horse Van, 23-1/2"	100	150	200
Nylint No. 6600 Mobile Home, Semi type, 30" long	142	213	285

	C6	C8	C10
Nylint No. 6700 Ambulance, 12" long...	138	208	275
Nylint No. 6800 Jalopy, 9-5/8" long.......	32	48	65
Nylint No. 6900 Airport Courtesy Van, 12" long....................	275	362	550
Nylint No. 7100 Fun on Farm Econoline Truck, 29 pcs.,11-1/4" long...............	87	130	175
Nylint No. 7300 Army Ambulance, 12" long.............................	66	99	132
Nylint No. 7900 Road Grader, 15" long.	36	54	72
Nylint No. 8000 Pony Farm Van, 7 pcs set, 11-1/4" long........................	135	198	270
Nylint No. 8100 Suburban Fire Pumper 12-1/2" long.............................	85	128	170
Nylint No. 8200 Bronco, 12-1/2" long...	67	100	135
Nylint No. 8300 Texaco Service Van, 12" long.............................	150	225	300
Nylint No. 8410 U-Haul Truck & Trailer, 1975, 22" long.....................	100	150	200

OHIO Fire Truck, 19-1/2" long, 1910. Courtesy Lloyd. W. Ralston Auctions.

OHIO Armored Car, c. WWI, 7-1/4" long Courtesy Lloyd W. Ralston Auctions.

	C6	C8	C10
Ohio Armored Car, circa WWI, friction, 7-1/4" long...........................	225	337	450
Ohio Coupe, 2-door, pressed steel, 17" long........................	150	225	300
Ohio Delivery Truck, 1920s, painted pressed steel, friction, 12" long..........	300	450	600

	C6	C8	C10
Ohio Fire Ladder Truck, 1920s, 13-1/2" long........................	200	300	400
Ohio Fire Patrol, pressed steel, cast iron, wood, very early, 9-3/4"............	500	750	1000
Ohio Fire Truck, pressed steel, cast iron, wood, very early 10-1/2"..........	1200	1800	2400
Ohio Fire Truck, friction, 19-1/2"...........	250	375	500
Ohio Pickup Truck, 1920s, friction, 13" long..............................	238	358	475
Ohio Roadster, cast iron and wood, friction, very early, 7-1/2" long..........	350	525	700
Ohio Roadster, 1920s, 13" long..............	175	262	350
Ohio Roadster, 1920s, friction, pressed steel, 18" long......................	312	468	625
Ohio Touring Auto, friction....................	100	150	200
Ohio Truck, "1909", friction, 10-1/2" long..............................	450	675	900
Ohlsson & Rice, midget race car, aluminum body, rubber tires, circa 1940s...................................	240	360	480
Oil and Gas Truck, cast iron, 8"............	200	300	400
Oil Truck, circa 1936, pressed steel, 10-3/4" long..............................	100	150	200
"Patrol" Motorcycle and rider, circa 1940, cast iron, 6-1/4" long................	100	150	200
"Patrol" Stake Truck, Wyandotte?, pressed steel, 4-7/8" long..................	40	60	80

OHIO Delivery Truck, 1920s, 12" long. Courtesy Lloyd W. Ralson Auctions

OHIO Roadster, 18" long, 1920s. Courtesy Lloyd W. Ralston Auctions.

"Patrol" Motorcycle and rider, circa 1940, 6-1/4" long, cast iron.

PEDAL CAR, "Ford". Courtesy Mapes Auctioneers & Appraisers.

	C6	C8	C10
Pedal Car, American National "Big Boy" Dump Truck	6000	10,000	22,000
Pedal Car, "American National Company Toledo Ohio, USA", sheet metal and wooden, dashboard with dials, rubber tread on wheels 46" long	1000	1500	2000
Pedal Car, "AMF", Hook and Ladder, late 1970s	200	300	400
Pedal Car, Boycraft, 1925, open coupe	2000	3500	6000
Pedal Car, circa 1905, chain driver, wooden spoke wheels	1250	1875	2500
Pedal Car, Cadillac, circa 1915, Toledo Metal Wheel Co. lithographed dashboard	500	750	1000
Pedal Car, Cadillac, early, 40-1/2"	800	1200	1600
Pedal Car, Chrysler Airflow	500	750	1000
Pedal Car, DeSoto, 1939	1250	1875	2500
Pedal Car, Essex, 1927	1100	1650	2200
Pedal Car, Fire Truck, Mack, SteelCraft	2500	4000	7000
Pedal Car, "Ford, 1896", Tubular frame w/wire wheels, sheet metal seat w/wooden back rest and steering lever, plate under seat has diagram of motor, 39" long	1000	1500	2000
Pedal Car, "Ford", 1937, painted steel	750	1125	1500
Pedal Car, Garton "Hot Rod"	410	615	825
Pedal Car, Gendron Lincoln	1500	2500	4000
Pedal Car, Gendron "Skippy", 1940	1200	2200	3500
Pedal Car, Hudson, wood and steel, folding windshield, tilt-up steering wheel	400	600	800
Pedal Car, Kidillac, circa 1950s	600	950	1400
Pedal Car, Lincoln 1921, Toledo	2500	5000	7500
Pedal Car Lincoln, 1937	1500	2400	3500
Pedal Car, Mercer Raceabout, 1920	2000	3000	4000

	C6	C8	C10
Pedal Car, Nash Sideway, 1920s, 34" long	1000	1500	2000
Pedal Car, Murray "Earth Mover"	500	800	1100
Pedal Car, Murray "Champion", 1955	500	800	1100
Pedal Car, open Coupe, 1920s or early 1930s, Gendron, 36" long	1200	1800	2400
Pedal Car, Packard Dual Cowl Phaeton, American National, 6' long	3000	4500	6000
Pedal Car, Packard Roadster, 1920s, American National, 45" long	3000	5500	8000
Pedal Car, "Packard", early, wire wheels	300	450	600
Pedal Car, "Pioneer" Race Car, metal and wood	700	1050	1400
Pedal Car, "Pioneer Lines", Gendron 36" long	1800	3000	5000
Pedal Car, Steelcraft Auburn streamliner	3000	5500	8000
Pedal Car, Steelcraft Buick, late 1920s, 36" long	4000	7000	12,000
Pedal Car, Steelcraft Chrysler Airflow	2500	3800	6500
Pedal Car, Steelcraft Jewett open coupe, 55" long	2500	5000	7500

PEDAL CAR, Cadillac, early, 40-1/4" long. Courtesy James S. Maxwell/Virginia Caputo. Photo by Virginia Caputo.

	C6	C8	C10
Pedal Car, Steelcraft 1939 Lincoln Zephyr	1700	2600	4000
Pedal Car, Terraplane, 1934	1500	2250	3000
Pedal Car, Winner, circa 1906	1000	1500	2000
Perfect Rubber Co. '35 Pontiac Slantback Sedan, 3-3/4" long	35	52	70
Playboy Dump Truck, tan, 22" long	150	225	300
Playby "Intercity Bus", cream color, 23-1/2" long	300	450	600

PYRO

Pyron began in 1939 in Pyro Park, Union City, New Jersey. The owner was William Lester. At its height, the company had 400 employees.

	C6	C8	C10
Pyro Race Car, 4" long	12	18	25
Pyro Range Patrol Truck	10	15	20
Pyro Road Roller	12	18	25
Pyro "U.S. Army" Truck	10	15	20
Pyro "U.S.M.C." Truck	10	15	20
Pyro "U.S. Navy" Truck	10	15	20
Race Car, cast iron, 9" long	235	352	470
Racer "Parker Special", simple body of heavy steel with steel wheels, 11"	75	112	150
Race Car, friction, w/driver, c. 1925	150	225	300
Race Car, circa 1918, 8" long	150	225	300
Racer, pressed steel w/driver, white rubber tires, rubberband and gear powered, 7-1/2" long	17	26	35
Racing Car, cast iron, w/figure, 51/2"	150	225	300
Racing Car, cast iron, w/driver, full figure, spiked wheels, early 1920s	75	112	150

Racing Car, cast iron, 5-1/2" long, with figure. Courtesy Wilkinson Collection, Detroit Antique Toy Museum.

	C6	C8	C10
Racing Car, cast iron, 7-1/4" long	260	390	520
Racing Set, 1930s, 3 tin racing cars, small tin garage	125	187	250
"Railway Express" Truck, cast iron early 1930s, 5" long	110	165	220

RAINBOW

The following list, with its codings, was compiled by Dave Leopard. Vehicles are broken down by types.

	C6	C8	C10
RA01 '35 Oldsmobile Coupe, 3-3/4"	30	45	60
RA02 '35 Oldsmobile 4 door Sedan, 3 1/4" long	29	45	58
RA03 '35 Oldsmobile 4 door Sedan, 5" long	41	62	82
RT01 '35 Studebaker (?) stake side pickup, 5-1/4" long	41	62	82
RR01 Open Racer, tapered tail, 4" long	25	38	50
RR02 Open Racer, tapered tail, 5" long	No Price Found		

RALSTOY

(Ralston Toy and Novelty Company)
*By Fred Maxwell, Slushmold Contributing Editor and Ferd Zegel
with Assistance of Alice Shooter and the Ralston Archives*

Ralston Toy & Novelty Co. was founded in July 1939 to manufacture slushmold toys and novelties. It was formed by Dr. Felix Despecher, former Mayor of Ralston, Nebraska, A.M. Erickson and Henry C. Nestor to acquire the assets of Best Toy Co. of Manhattan, Kansas and the surviving molds of Kansas Toy Co. of Clifton, Kansas. These assets included the temporary services of John M. Best, his molder Conrad Morsch and about 140 molds from these pioneering slushmold vehicle toy companies. The new enterprise was located in a building formerly occupied by the American Legion at 7632 Burlington St. This continued a low-cost toy line familiar to collectors since Kansas Toy was founded in 1923.

With the death of its founder, Dr. Despecher, about a year later the young company was forced into reorganization. Paul Massey, a lawyer, reorganized the company but had to give up production of potmetals soon thereafter due to the war's need for lead. To survive he turned to making wooden toys, including a replica of the famous Army Jeep of which about 2 million copies were sold through the Dime Stores, mainly Woolworth and Kresge. Other wooden toys included an Army tank, a Navy PT boat and a (rumored)

DUKW amphibious landing craft. These toys were completely made in Ralston except for Jeep wheels which were made in Omaha by the blind. When war-time labor became short handicapped workers were hired.

After the war the company turned to diecasting toys and novelties. As the business expanded it moved to 5707 So. 77th St., where it is today producing a well-know line of promotional trucks under Art Massey. But the post-war history is for other researchers.

By now the history of those migrating molds "with the numbers" is getting confusing. Although market values will depend on other factors than the actual makers we will mention some clues to assist collectors. Ralstoy did label a few of its toys. They liked bottom pans, introduced by Best to increase rigidity of these fragile toys; this provided a surface to emboss "Ralstoy" and "Made in USA". Military olive drab colors reflected the growing war consciousness. Wheels are not a good clue, even when the latest fad, black rubber wheels, were used.

Ralstoy probably reproduced many pieces from their acquired molds, but there is no practical way to know who made them when they are not labeled. (See Best Toy Co. and Kansas Toy Co. in this book.) The toys described below are mostly new issues.

RALSTOY, RAV11. Photo by Ed Poole.

RALSTOY, Sedan RAV12. Photo by Fred Maxwell.

	C6	C8	C10
RAV1 Dump Truck, "42", International ? COE, 2 open windows (OW), hinged tin dump body, different casting than Kansas Toy dump truck #42, 3-3/8"..No Price Found			
RAV2 Tractor, "48", "Caterpillar" tractor, "Whoopee", driver in different color, grooved wood 3/4" wheels w/rubber tracks on Kansas Toy body, 3".......... No Price Found			
RAV3 Army tank, "74", "US Army", 2 gun turret, entirely different tank than Kansas Toy #74, 2-1/4"......................	13	20	26
RAV4 Tanker Truck, "No. 102", "Ralstoy" International? sleeper cab, 3 3/8", 2 OW, vertical grille w/"Gasoline" semi-trailer, "No. 102", 4 tanks, storage compartments, 6-3/4"...	14	21	28
RAV5 Large Transporter, "Ralstoy" cab unit in RAV4 above, steel semi-trailer w/#74 tank, #34 muzzle loading cannon and #32 aircraft, olive drab color, not known if Ralstoy issued them as a set. (some stamped No. 108, some No. 101), 9"................................	20	45	60
RAV6 Large Gun Truck, "US Army Anti-Aircraft Unit", 3 axle carrier, AA gun, searchlight and crew of 3, 5-5/8"...	28	42	56

	C6	C8	C10
RAV7 Army Tank, "107", "US Army", wood grooved 3/4" track-laying wheels, 2 gun turret, larger version of #74 above, also version w/black rubber wheels, 3-1/8".........................	13	20	26
RAV8 Railway ? Gun, "108", version of #23 muzzle-loading cannon on wheeled platform w/hook and loop			

RALSTOY, Left to Right; Top: RAV5-Transporter w/tank #74, Cannon #34, Aircraft #32?; Middle: RAV6-Anti-Aircraft Unit, RAV8-Railway? cannon; Bottom: RAV7-Tank #107, cannon. Photo by Ed Poole.

RALSTOY, Left to Right, Top: RAV4; Middle: RAV2a, RAV2b, metal wheels; Bottom: Ralstoy Field Gun. Photo courtesy of Perry Eichor.

	C6	C8	C10
connectors,perhaps addition to #3600 toy train, 3-1/4"................................ 12	18	25
RAV10 Army Jeep, wooden, WWII issue. 20	30	40
RAV11 Army Tank, wooden, "USA W356", "Ralstoy" on bottom, WWII issue... 30	45	60
RAV12 Large Sedan, "2R", diecast, Cadillac?, "Ralstoy","Made in USA", 4 open vent windows, divided open wind- shield, 3 open rear windows, long fenders, rear wheel skirts,bumper guard, black rubber wheels, early postwar issue?, 5-5/8"..................................... 37	56	75
Ralstoy Ford Tractor, 1948, w/trailer, overall 9" long.................................... 30	45	60
Ralstoy Mayflower Moving Van............ 30	45	60
Rehrberger "David" Moving Van, circa 1924, 7-1/4" long...................... 1800	3000	4800
Remco Bulldog Tank............................ 46	69	92
Remco Flying Dutchman Antique Car.. 60	90	120

RENWAL

The Renwal Manufacturing Company, founded in 1939 by either Irving Rosemblum or Irving Lawner (accounts vary), seems to have begun as a manufacturer of a glass knife. A plastic knife replaced it, and probably led to the manufacture of plastic toys. Toy production began about 1945. When the firm went out of business circa the 1970s, the tooling was sold to Chein, which in turn sold it to Revell.

	C6	C8	C10
Renwal Cadillac Hardtop Convertible,5-1/2" 22	33	45
Renwal Cement Truck, 1940s, 6-1/2".... 50	75	100
Renwal Fire Ladder Truck plastic...........70	105	140
Renwal Gasoline Truck No.49, plastic... 30	45	60

	C6	C8	C10
Renwal Hardtop Convertible, 1940s, 6-1/2".22	33	45
Renwal Pickup Truck, diecast, black rubber tires, approx. 7" long...............12	18	25
Renwal Racer No. 173, w/driver, 9-1/2"....85	128	170
Renwal Speed King Racer, 6-1/2" long..18	27	36
Renwal TV Truck No. 260, w/camera, mike, working spotlight, 18"long...... 75	112	150
Renwal Visible Auto Chassis................. 225	338	450
Republic Roadster, 1920s, 10" long........175	262	350
Republic Taxi Cab w/driver, sheet- metal, friction motor, circa 1926........287	430	575
Reuhl Caterpiller D-7............................312	468	625
Reuhl Cedar Rapids Rock Crusher......... 600	900	1230
Revell Plumber's Truck, plastic 10" long...35	52	70
Richmond Dump Truck 107	160	215
Road Grader, cast iron, rubber wheels, 7-1/2" long............................100	150	200
Roadster, cast iron, early, driver 7" long.. 325	488	650
Roadster Tow Truck, cast iron, 5" long...60	90	120
"Rocket Launcher" Truck, "U.S.A.F.", friction, pressed steel and plastic, circa 1960...60	90	120

RUBBER VEHICLES

Unknown Manufacturers

The following list, with its codings, some since identified and placed elsewhere, was compiled by Dave Leopard. Vehicles are broken down by types.

	C6	C8	C10
UA06 '35 DeSoto 4 door Airflow Sedan, 5" long................................... No Price Found		
UA07 Chrysler 4 door Airflow Sedan, rear spare, ad on roof, 4-3/4" long.... No Price Found		
UA08 '35 Chrysler 2 door Airflow Sedan, 5-1/8" long............................50	75	100
UA09 '36 Plymouth 4 door Trunkback Sedan, 4-7/8" long............................ 75	112	150
UA10 '37 Plymouth 4 door Trunkback Sedan, 4-7/8" long............................ 75	112	150

RUBBER VEHICLES UA11. Photo by Dave Leopard.

	C6	C8	C10
UA11 '46 Nash, 2 door Fastback Sedan, hollow, molded tires, 4" long	12	18	25
UT04 '34 Dodge Rack Truck, 4-7/8"	No Price Found		
UR01 Open Racer, left side Header pipes, solid rubber, 3-1/2" long	No Price Found		
UR02 Open Racer, V-8, solid, large			

	C6	C8	C10
tires on wood hubs, 4" long	No Price Found		
UR03 Open Racer, solid, rubber tires on wood hubs, 6" long	No Price Found		
Saunders Fire Truck, siren, 13" long	50	75	100
Saunders Police Car	27	41	55
Saunders Sedan	32	48	65

SAVOYE PEWTER TOY COMPANY

Savoye was incorporated August 1930. In 1931 Savoye Pewter Toy Co., manufacturer of "pewter toys" (pewter was often the word used for lead alloy or potmetal) was listed in a directory at 69 Paterson Plank Road in North Bergen, New Jersey, with six male and three female employees. The names of the owners may have been Selma and Joseph Wigh. In 1934 at the same address the workforce was seven males and two females. Slushmold toys were probably their only product. Savoye was in the 1936 phonebook, and out of the February, 1937 directory. Collectors identify vehicle toys as Savoye if they have a somewhat coarse appearance, heavy slushmold body and white rubber tires on oversized red wooden hubs that are smooth on the outside surface (no axle showing); but whether this is simply lore is not known at present. The son of the one of the owners of Tommy Toy Co. thinks some Savoye-looking vehicles were made by Tommy Toy. If so, it's possible Savoye sold its molds to nearby Tommy toy. The following was contributed by Fred Maxwell, one of our principal slushmold researchers:

Those big red hubs and rubber tires are consistent with industry styles of the early 1930s, but the style of some of the vehicles is from an earlier era (see SA17 & SA19 whose metal wheels suggest an earlier beginning of the Savoye-Tommy Toy-Barclay dynasty).

SAVOYE, SA22. Photo by Perry R. Eichor.

	C6	C8	C10
SA1 Roadster, driver, open rumble seat, silver vertical grille, (VG, reminiscent of Tootsietoy Graham), vertical louvers (VL), 3-1/2" long	No Price Found		
SA2 Roadster, similar to above, different casting, 3-1/2" long	No Price Found		
SA3 Coupe, 2 open windows (OW), silver VG, (Graham like), VL, 3-3/8" long	20	30	40
SA4? Coupe, similar to above (Savoye or copy?), slanted louvers, fantasy grille and large black rubber wheels (original?), 3-3/8" long	14	21	28
SA5 Van, "Milk Grade A", 2 OW, sidemounts (SM), 3-1/4" long	20	30	40
SA6 Van, "Police Patrol", policeman on rear step, 6 OW, gilt trim, SM, 4" long	24	36	48

	C6	C8	C10
SA7 Bus, Heavy 5th Ave. Sight-Seeing bus, open overhanging upper deck, 12 OW, gilt or silver trim, 4-3/4"	54	71	108
SA8 Bus, Cross-Country Bus, partial upper deck, 12 OW, rearmount spare, 3-3/8"	20	30	40

SAVOYE, Left to Right, Top: SA10, SA15; Middle: SA7, SA6; Bottom: SA14, SA12. Photo by Fred Maxwell.

	C6	C8	C10

SA9 Bus, Tour Bus; Mack cab, 3-1/2"
2 OW, "Motor Coach", 5-1/4",
dual-axle semi-trailer, 12 OW, gilt
trim, 7-1/2" long................................. No Price Found

SA10 Truck, Heavy "Beer Truck", 6
wood barrels set in cast depressions
4-3/8" long.............................. 40   60   80

SA11 Truck, stake body, 4-1/2" long..... 12   18   24

SA12 Truck, stake body, hinged tail-
gate w/chains, 5-3/4" long.................No Price Found

SA13 Truck, Tow Truck, SA3- like
coupe cab, chain & hook on crane
4" long...................................... No Price Found

SA14 Truck, Heavy Tow Truck, over-
sized crane, wire hook, 5-3/4"........... No Price Found

SA15 Fire Truck, driver and steersman
w/high style gilt helmets, bell on
hood, 2 ladders (glued on), over-
sized wheel wells, oversized tires,
4-1/4" long............................... No Price Found

SA16 Fire Truck, driver & fireman w/
high style gilt helmets, 2 detachable
ladders on high rack, oversized wheel
wells, oversized tires, 3-3/4" long......No Price Found

SA17? Fire Engine, steam pumper,
driver & fireman w/high style gilt
helmets, large 10-spoke metal wheels,
an early Savoye? in the style of the
fire trucks above; large wheels would
explain over-sized wheel wells in
SA15 & SA16 above, 3-3/4"............. No Price Found

SA18 Tractor, Caterpillar? tractor
w/stack, 2-3/4" long............................10   15   20

SA19? Tractor, same as above w/large
10-spoke metal wheels, an early
Savoye? (same casting as Tommy
Toy but longer wheelbase than
Barclay #7), 3" long...................... No Price Found

SA20 Tank Car Set, tow cab shorter
version of SA13, 3-1/4"; 2 tank
cars 3-1/2", "Oil""Cap. 80000"
(RR type), not known whether
Savoye sold these as a set; no
known Savoye train, either, 10-1/4"..40   60   80

SA21 Gun Truck, Army, driver &
gunner, (angular rear deck distin-
guishes it from similar gun trucks)
3 1/4"....................................No Price Found

SA22 Pickup Truck............................... 20   30   40

(See the Aircraft Section for a blimp and a monoplane. Since we

SAVOYE, Left to Right, Top: SA1, SA2; Middle: SA7, SA3; Bottom: SA9. Photo by Fred Maxwell.

are still finding additions to our 6th Edition list, this list is probably still incomplete. Any help will be appreciated.)

SCHIEBLE TOY AND NOVELTY

Schieble, located in Dayton, Ohio, was formed in 1909 when William Schieble, former partner with D.P. Clark in the firm of that name, bought it out (Clark then formed the Dayton Friction Works, continuing to use Schieble's patents as well as the Hillclimber name, and protracted lawsuits followed).

	C6	C8	C10
Schieble Racer, team, circa 1910, steel windup. 12" long	450	675	900
Schieble Roadster, spare tire on back, 18-1/4" long	362	543	725
Schieble Sedan, 17" long	305	458	610
Schieble Touring Car, Circa 1909, 14" long	300	450	600
Schoenhut "Every Boy Auto Build 5 in 1 Toy" wood set to build, boxed	45	67	90

SEIBERLING RUBBER

Compiled by Dave Leopard

	C6	C8	C10
GA01 '35 Ford 2 door slantback sedan, 5" long	32	48	65
GA02 '35 Ford 2 door slantback sedan, 4" long	27	41	55
Slik-Toys - See Lansing			

SEIBERLING GA01. Photo by Dave Leopard.

SCHIEBLE Racer team, 12" long. Courtesy Wilkinson Collection, Detroit Toy Museum.

SCHIEBLE Roadster, 18 1/4" long. Courtesy Joe and Sharon Freed.

SMITTY TOYS

By Ray Funk

A line of large cast metal and aluminum toy trucks hit the market in 1945, the Smith-Miller "Smitty Toys", "Famous Trucks in Miniature", produced in Santa Monica, California. These trucks were doomed from the beginning as they were entering a highly competitive market, one that had toy producers of trucks dating back to the 30s and earlier, such as Buddy "L", Structo, Marx, Hubley, and in 46 Ny-Lint, Tonka in early 50s, and in the mid-1950s, Eldon plastics. However, despite the heavy competition, they fought to stay on the market for a full ten years, into 1955, outclassing virtually all toy trucks before and after, by far, although the last year they changed their profile from Mack Trucks to Auto-Car diesels, with opening doors and steering wheels that actually steered like the real thing. Their first trucks had two different classes, expensive replicas, of a smaller type of truck of no name that looked to be a half-breed Ford. I will list the cheaper line first.

No. 401 Tow Truck, 15" long, No. 402 Dump Truck 11 1/2" long, No. 403 Scoop Dump, 14" long (same dump with scoop), all complete cast, cast wheels and rubber tires.

The larger scale models were cast and aluminum, such as No. 404 Lumber Truck (six wheels), 19" long, $10.75; No. 404T Lumber Trailer, 17" long, $6.95; No.405 Silver Streak, 28" long (14 wheels) six wheel tractor and eight wheel bogey'd heavy duty grain trailer, $15.95; No. 406 Bekins Van, 29" long, six wheel tractor and four wheel trailer (single axle); No. 407 Searchlight Truck, long (six wheel) based frame 18 1/2" long with platform that has diesel motor (to hold batteries) and huge searchlight, at $16.95; No. 408 Blue Diamond ten wheel huge dump truck, last double set of duals bogey'd, 18 1/2" long, $17.95; No. 409 Pacific Intermountain Express (P.I.E.) six wheel trac-

tor semi with eight wheel bogey'd aluminum trailer, 29" long, $19.75, No. 410 Aerial Ladder semi, six wheel tractor and four wheel single axle trailer, 36" long, ladder extends to 48" high, $27.95. By 1950 some mid-West stores had the Aerial Ladder priced at $37.50, and various of the others higher-priced.

Later, various modifications were produced, one a straight Box Bed Truck, using the Searchlight Truck with metal box and rear double doors. Then yet another variation was the Box Truck employing the eight wheel bogey set-up, and the log trailer base with a same box to make a ten wheel straight truck and eight wheel trailer, as there were many on the California highways. Then the long base tractor (ten-wheeler) with bogey or rear eight wheels, hooked to Silver Streak and P.I.E. trailers, and yet other variations such as the P.I.E. eight wheel trailer minus top and raising rear door, as high-side grain hauler, and finally a long refrigeration trailer with small side door, all using ten-wheel tractors.

At the same time the company was putting the smaller wheels on the P.I.E. and Silver Streak trailers, and using the small six-wheeled cast "Half-Breeds" tractors, priced at lower competitive prices.

Their first Mack trucks were of the older 1940s types with running boards, old-type fenders and raised separate headlights, and all had fuel tanks, the later Mack trucks being 1954 Macks with air horn on top. (These were produced for just one year.)

The final year saw a complete change, Smith dropping out and Ironson coming in, changing the name to M.I.C. Toys, Miller-Ironson Corporation, and to the best of my knowledge they produced only four different, all cast trucks, and though no truck company name, definitely Auto-Car diesels. One was a heavy-duty tow truck as tows large semis, a flat bed with removable side racks, and turndown hydraulically lowering tailgate (up and down), door handles that worked to open doors, seat, steering wheel and front wheel which were steered like on the "model toy" fire trucks and others of the "model toy" line, the last, fire truck #410 with Mack tractor, I cannot say, as I only have the cab and no catalog or advertisement of this toy.

Honorable mention must be made, before closing, that one company in Minnesota, owned by Teamsters President Beck's son (in the late 1940s) put out a huge cast metal truck, mostly loggers and dumpers, which steered via a horn on top of the cab, and two, Wyandotte put out in 1950, a very realistic cab over semi six wheel tractor of cast and eight wheel bogey'd long aluminum trailer, with beautifully realistic cast center replica wheels and rubber tires. The fifth wheel on the tractor was operational to couple and uncouple from the trailer, and though of no name, the cast tractor was finely detailed, fuel tanks and all. The Wyandotte sold at $10 while the aforementioned, name unknown, and very short-lived trucks, sold at $20 each, a much too high price for the 1940s. All are now gone, but live on in the minds of those who played with them. There were a few minor variations of the Smith-Miller which I did not mention, and no doubt possibly some on all items that I do not know about, nor have catalogs depicting. Any added information would be appreciated.

Evidence via photographs, etc., has unearthed the fact that there are more in this toy truck line than I had listed.

An early Smitty truck is an all potmetal truck, mostly painted as an armored bank truck with square box and locking doors.

I received a picture of a tanker, using the small bastard six wheel tractor, and trailer having the dual-tandem setup. As by the pictures there did not seem to be any spare room in the wheel wells, I must assume that this was only produced with the small wheels and tractor. It is bright yellow, and has "SHELL" on the trailer.

Still yet another produced in the early years, a cattle hauling truck. This one was large as the largest S.M. and had the large early Mack with long frame. I have found this truck, minus wheels, so I can only assume that it was produced as many others with similar tractor frames as an 18 and also 14 wheeler. The enclosed trailer features double doors on the rear with latch, slotted vented sides and truck was same yellow as tanker, other than frame and fenders (all actually one piece on the early 'Macks') were gloss black, making an eye catching toy, colorwise.

How many different trucks, or variations Smitty produced. I have no idea, as I begin to suspect that like Doepke, at times they too made up a one, or few of a kind.

*(**NOTE**: New versions of SMITTY vehicles, using original and new parts, are currently being produced - See Leading Collectors and Dealers)*

	C6	C8	C10
Smitty (Smith-Miller) No. 201-L Lumber Truck, 60 boards, 6 wheels, 14" long	350	525	700
Smitty No. 202-M Material Truck, 3 barrels, 3 cases, 18 boards, 4 wheels, 14" long	450	675	900
Smitty No. 203-H Heinz Grocery Truck, 6 wheels, 14" long	317	475	635
Smitty No. 204-A Arden Milk Truck, 12 milk cans, 4 cases, 4 wheels, 14" long	300	450	600
Smitty No. 205-P Oil Truck, 4 drums, 6 wheels, 14" long	225	338	450
Smitty No. 206-C Coca-Cola Truck, 16 Coca-Cola cases, 4 wheels, 14" long	500	800	1175

SMITTY Catalog illustrations of Models 402, 401. Photo by Bill Kaufman. Courtesy Ray Funk.

SMITTY Catalog illustrations of Models 406, 405. Photo by Bill Kaufman. Courtesy Ray Funk.

SMITTY "Bank of America" Armored Truck. Courtesy Good Old Days Store.

SMITTY GMC Coca-Cola Truck. Courtesy R.L. MacNary.

	C6	C8	C10
Smitty No. 208-B Bekins Vanliner, 14 wheels, 22-1/2" long	650	1050	1600
Smitty No. 209-T Timber Giant, 3 logs, 14 wheels, 23-1/2" long	162	243	325
Smitty No. 210-S Stake Truck, 14 wheels, 23-1/2" long	250	375	500
Smitty No. 211-L Sunkist Special, 14 wheels, 23-1/2" long	150	250	375
Smitty No. 212-R Red Ball, 14 wheels, 23-1/2" long	150	250	375
Smitty No. 301-W GMC Wrecker, 4 wheeler	170	255	340
Smitty No. 302-M GMC Materials Truck, 4 barrels, 3 timbers	200	300	400
Smitty No. 303-R GMC Rack Truck, 6 wheels	140	210	280
Smitty No. 304-K GMC Kraft Foods, 4 wheels	350	525	700
Smitty No. 305-T GMC Triton Oil, 3 drums	175	263	350
Smitty No. 306-C GMC Coca-Cola, 4 wheels, 16 Coke cases	350	525	700
Smitty No. 307-L GMC Redwood Logger Tractor-Trailer, 3 logs	225	338	450

	C6	C8	C10
Smitty No. 308-V GMC Lyon Van Tractor-Trailer, 14 wheels	275	410	550
Smitty No. 309-S GMC Super Cargo Tractor-Trailer, 14 wheels, 10 barrels	200	300	400
Smitty No. 310-H GMC Hi-Way Freighter Tractor-Trailer, 14 wheels	150	225	310
Smitty No. 311-E GMC Silver Streak Express Tractor-Trailer, 14 wheels	200	300	400
Smitty No. 312-P GMC Pacific Inter-Mountain Express ("P.I.E.") Tractor-Trailer	250	375	500
Smitty No. 401 Tow Truck, 15" long	125	188	250
Smitty No. 402 Dump Truck, 11-1/2"	175	263	350
Smitty No. 403 Scoop Dump, 14" long	275	410	550
Smitty No. 404 Lumber Truck, 19"	300	450	600
Smitty No. 404T Lumber Trailer, 17"	175	263	350
Smitty No. 405 Silver Streak, 6-wheel tractor, 28" long	125	188	250
Smitty No. 406 Bekins Van, 6-wheel tractor and 4-wheel trailer, 29" long	338	528	675
Smitty No. 407 Searchlight Truck, "Hollywood Filmad" 18-1/2" long	450	675	900
Smitty No. 408 Blue Diamond,10-wheel dump truck, 18-1/2" long	500	800	1150
Smitty No. 409 Pacific Intermountain Express (P.I.E.), 6-wheel tractor semi w/8-wheel aluminum trailer, 29" long	330	495	660
Smitty No. 410 Aerial Ladder Semi, 6-wheel tractor and 4-wheel trailer, "SMFD", 36" long	420	630	840
Smitty No. 401-W GMC Wrecker, 6 wheels	85	128	170

SMITTY MIC Tow Truck, "Official Tow Car". Photo by Ray Funk.

Smitty "L" Mack Merchandise Van & Trailer, 12 wheels.
Photo by Bob Smith

Smitty "L" Mack Army Materials Truck, 7-piece cargo load, 10 wheel.
Photo by Bob Smith

Smitty MIC Aerial Ladder
Courtesy Ray Funk

A—House Trailer & Car. Die-cast extruded aluminum trailer has open-close doors and a removable top. Interior is luxuriously furnished. Car is a replica of a popular make modern hard-top convertible. 15" long and finished in smooth ivory and chrome. Overall length 42". $29.95*.

B—Liftomatic. Automatic lift tail gate is activated by a hydraulic cylinder and closes at top to protect load of barrels (included). Cab has full 45-degree steering ability. Doors open and close. 19¾" long. $17.95*. (Also recommended: Tow Truck, $14.95; Hydraulic Dump, $17.95*; Freuhauf, $19.95*.)

* Prices Approximate—See Page Six

MILLER-IRONSON TOYS are designed and built to exemplify perfection. Their unusual play features give them distinction which is positively unique.

Smitty MIC Lift Gate Truck, 6 wheels.
Photo by Bob Smith

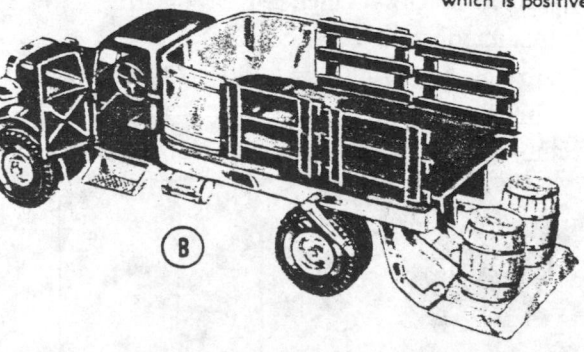

Smitty, Top: MIC House Trailer and MIC Lincoln Capri. Bottom: MIC Lift Gate Truck (Liftomatic).
From The Toy Yearbook, 1953-54

Tootsietoy vehicles, from a 1933 company catalog.

Smitty "L" Mack Army Personnel Carrier, 10 wheels.
Photo by Bob Smith

	C6	C8	C10
Smitty No. 402-M GMC Material Truck, 4 barrels, 2 timbers	200	300	400
Smitty No. 403-R GMC Rack Truck, 6 wheels	175	262	350
Smitty No. 404-B GMC Bank of America, lock and key, 4-wheels	230	345	460
Smitty No. 405-T GMC Triton Oil, 6 wheels, 3 drums	188	282	375
Smitty No. 406-L GMC Lumber Tractor-Trailer, 14 wheels, 8 timbers	162	245	325
Smitty No. 407-V GMC Lyon Van Tractor-Trailer, 10 wheels	100	300	400
Smitty No. 408-H GMC Machinery Hauler, 13 wheels	220	330	440
Smitty No. 409-G GMC Mobilgas Tanker, 14 wheels, 2 hoses	215	322	430
Smitty No. 410-F GMC Transcontinental Tractor-Trailer, 14 wheels	165	255	370
Smitty No. 411-E GMC Silver Streak Tractor-Trailer, 14 wheels	219	328	438
Smitty No. 412-P GMC P.I.E.,14 wheels	220	330	440
Smitty "B" Mack "Associated Truck Lines", 14 wheels	No Price Found		
Smitty "B" Mack Jr. Fire Truck, warning light, battery-operated,4 wheels	495	742	990
Smitty "B" Mack Orange Dump, 10 wheels	800	1400	2000
Smitty "B" Mack P.I.E.,18 wheels	450	675	900
Smitty Chevy Bekins Van, 14 wheels, plain tires, hubcaps, '45-46	180	300	400
Smitty Chevy Coca-Cola, 4 wheels, plain tires, early, '45-46	325	488	650
Smitty Chevy Flatbed Tractor-Trailer, 14 wheels, unpainted wood trailer, plain tires, hub caps, early, '45	120	180	240
Smitty Chevy Milk Truck, 4 wheels, plain tires, hub caps, early, '45-46	200	300	400

SMITTY Box Truck w /Box Trailer, 10 wheeler. Courtesy Ray Funk.

	C6	C8	C10
Smitty Ford Bekins Van, 14 wheeler, plain tires, hub, earliest Smitty?,'44	200	300	400
Smitty Ford Coca-Cola, 4 wheels, wood soda cases, early, '44	300	450	600
Smitty GMC Be Mac 14 wheel T-Trailer, 1949	185	278	370
Smitty GMC Coca-Cola Truck, 24 plastic bottles in 6 cases, 4 wheels 1954-55	262	393	525
Smitty GMC "Drive-O" Steerable Dump, 6 wheels, cable w/hand control, 1946	250	375	500
Smitty GMC "Furniture Mart" Pickup, 4 wheels	155	232	310
Smitty GMC Heinz Grocery Truck	200	300	400
Smitty GMC Machinery Hauler, 10 wheels	300	450	600
Smitty GMC Marshall Field & Company Tractor-Trailer, 10 wheel T-Trailer	500	750	1000
Smitty GMC Peoples First National Bank and Trust Company armored Truck, lock and key, 1951	262	393	525
Smitty GMC Rexall Drug, 4wheels	225	338	450

SMITTY Catalog illustrations of models, 407, 403, 409. Photo by Bill Kaufman. Courtesy Ray Funk.

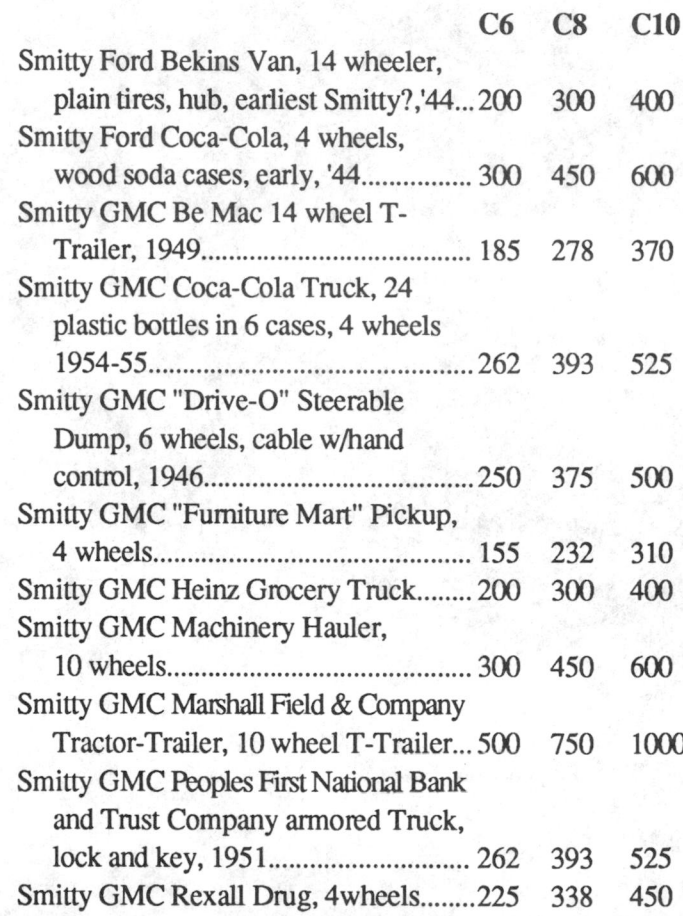

SMITTY Catalog illustration of model 410. Photo by Bill Kaufman. Courtesy Ray Funk.

"Star Brand Shoes Are Better" racing car. Courtesy Sotheby's New York.

	C6	C8	C10
Smitty GMC Searchlight Truck, "Hollywood Film Ad" w/trailer, 1953	525	638	1050
Smitty GMC U.S. Treasury Truck, armored truck, w/lock and key, 1952	250	375	500
Smitty "L" Mack Aerial Ladder, "SMFD", 8 wheels	350	525	700
Smitty "L" Mack Army Materials Truck, 3 barrels, 2 boards, 1 large crate, 1 small crate, 10 wheels	425	638	850
Smitty "L" Mack Army Personnel Carrier, 10 wheels	312	468	625
Smitty "L" Mack Bekins Van, all white, 10 wheels	800	1350	1950
Smitty "L" Mack Blue Diamond Dump, 10 wheels	600	900	1400
Smitty "L" Mack International Paper Co., 10 wheels	500	800	1100
Smitty "L" Mack Lyon Van, 6 wheels	550	850	1300
Smitty "L" Mack Material Truck, 2 barrels, 6 timbers, 6 wheels	500	750	1000
Smitty "L" Mack Merchandise Van, 6 wheels	375	562	750
Smitty "L" Mack Merchandise Van & Trailer, 12 wheels	275	410	550

	C6	C8	C10
Smitty "L" Mack Mobil Tandem Tanker, 12 wheels	675	1012	1350
Smitty "L" Mack Orange Hydraulic Dump, 10 wheels	350	550	800
Smitty "L" Mack Orange Material Truck, 3 barrels, 2 boards, 1 large crate, 1 small, 10 wheels	500	750	1000
Smitty "L" Mack P.I.E., 14 wheels	400	600	800
Smitty "L" Mack "Sibley's" Van, 6 wheels (rare)	450	675	900
Smitty "L" Mack Tandem Timber, 18 or 24 timbers (varies), 6 wheels	420	630	840
Smitty "L" Mack Telephone Truck, 6 wheels	700	1150	1600
Smitty "L" Mack West Coast Transport, 6 wheels	500	750	1000
Smitty MIC Aerial Ladder	400	600	800
Smitty MIC "Fruehauf Road Star" Tractor-Trailer, 14 wheels	500	750	1000
Smitty MIC House Trailer	400	600	800
Smitty MIC Hydraulic Dump, 10 wheels	600	1000	1300
Smitty MIC Lift-O-Matic, 2 barrels, 6 wheels	500	800	1100
Smitty MIC Lincoln Capri (for MIC House Trailer), steerable	425	638	850
Smitty MIC Lumber Truck, 9 timbers, 6 wheels	487	730	975
Smitty MIC P.I.E. Tractor-Trailer, 14 wheels	500	800	1100
Smitty MIC "Teamsters" Hydraulic Dump, 10 wheels	650	1000	1500
Smitty MIC "Teamsters" Tow Truck, 6 wheels	No Price Found		
Smitty MIC "Teamsters" Tractor-Trailer, 14 wheels	600	950	1400
Smitty MIC Tow Truck, "Official Tow Car", 6 wheels	500	750	1000
Smitty MIC Tow Truck, unpainted, polished, 6 wheels	475	700	950
Smitty MIC Tractor-Trailer, polished aluminum trailer, no decals, 14 wheels	450	675	900
Sonny Army Truck "U.S.A. 1120"	410	615	820
Sonny Dump Truck, 26" long	350	575	800
Sonny Moving Van	600	950	1300
Sonny Parcel Post Van	650	1000	1400
Sonny "USA 1120" Anti-Aircraft Truck	300	450	600

SONNY "US 1120" Artillery Truck, 26" long. Courtesy Joe Freed.

SONNY "USA 1120" Anti-Aircraft Truck, 24" long. Courtesy Joe and Sharon Freed.

STEELCRAFT Fire Truck, approx. 25" long.

STEELCRAFT Steam Shovel.

STEELCRAFT "U.S." Mail. Photo by Calvin L. Chaussee.

	C6	C8	C10
Sonny "US 1120" Artillery Truck, 26" long	350	525	700
"Star Brand Shoes Are Better", racing car, "The Winner", tin litho, 8-1/2" long	1200	1900	2800
Steam Pumper, "Boston," with lamp, cast iron wheels, 15-1/2" long	2500	3750	5000
Steam Pumper Fire Truck, cast iron, 5"	45	68	90
Steam Pumper Truck, cast iron, hard rubber wheels, driver, 12" long	150	225	300
Steam Pumper, tin and wooden chain, friction drive w/driver, "National", 10" long	200	300	400
Steam Pumper, tin and wooden friction drive, 11" long	70	105	140
Steam Roller, steam-engine powered	200	300	450
Steam Roller, cast iron, circa early 1930s, 4-3/4" long	75	112	150
Steam Shovel, "Sand Digger", 28"	150	225	300
Steelcraft Army Truck, Mack, circa 1930, 22" long	650	1000	1450
Steelcraft "City Delivery" Truck	390	685	780
Steelcraft "City Milk Co.", 18" long	300	450	600
Steelcraft Coca-Cola Truck, 12 bottles on side	400	600	800
Steelcraft "Cream Crest" Truck	450	675	900

	C6	C8	C10
Steelcraft Dump Truck, Airflow	2000	3500	5000
Steelcraft Dump Truck, Mack	500	750	1000
Steelcraft Fire Truck, 25" long	500	750	1000
Steelcraft "Fro-Joy" Ice Cream Truck, circa 1930s	350	525	700
Steelcraft GMC Scissor Dump Truck	500	800	1250
Steelcraft Inter City Bus, 24" long	330	495	660
Steelcraft Little Jim Fire Truck	500	850	1200
Steelcraft "Marion" Steam Shovel	187	280	375
Steelcraft Model T Roadster pedal car, Lic. #65-287, 50" long	325	488	650
Steelcraft Railway Express Truck, 26" long	1100	1600	2600
Steelcraft Road Roller, 16" long	150	225	300
Steelcraft "Sheffield Farms" Truck 1930s	263	393	525
Steelcraft Shell Motor Oil Truck w/oil barrels	300	450	600
Steelcraft Steam Shovel	225	338	450
Steelcraft Tank Truck, sheet metal, 25-1/2" long	1000	1700	2350
Steelcraft "U.S. Mail" circa 1928, 27-1/4" long	800	1300	1800

STRUCTO

Structo, of Freeport, Illinois, was founded in 1908 by three men: brothers Louis and Edward Strohacker and C.C. Thompson. They initially manufactured Erector Construction Kits, and about 1919 they started making toy vehicles.

In 1935 J.G. Cokey bought a majority of the business, and when he died in 1975, the toy patents and designs were taken over by the Ertl Company. (Numbered Structos are found at the end of this listing.)

	C6	C8	C10
Structo Army Ambulance No. 416, 17" long	175	263	350
Structo Army Truck w/canvas top, 21" long	150	225	300
Structo Army Van, pressed steel and canvas, No. 415, 17-1/2" long	170	255	340
Structo Bearcat Racer, clockwork, 12-1/4" long	325	490	650
Structo Camper w/cloth top, 12" long	25	38	50
Structo Cement Mixer, circa 1950s, 20" long	80	120	160
Structo Coupe, convertible, c. 1920s	550	850	1200
Structo Caterpillar Tractor w/trailer, heavy spring clockwork motor, steel treads, No. 46	250	375	500
Structo Communications Center Truck, 21" long	70	105	140
Structo Delivery Truck, tin, electric lights	150	225	300
Structo Dump Truck, early, Mack type	312	468	625

	C6	C8	C10
Structo Fire Dept. Emergency Patrol Truck, red bubble light, 1950s, 12" long	70	105	140
Structo Garbage Truck, 21" long	50	75	100
Structo Gasoline Truck, No. 912, 1950s, 13" long	75	112	150
Structo Guided Missile Launcher, No. 906 w/plastic launcher, missiles of wood and vinyl, 13" long	70	105	140

STRUCTO Dump Truck, early, Mack type. Courtesy Joe and Sharon Freed.

	C6	C8	C10
Structo Guided Missile Launching Truck, truck metal, missiles, etc., plastic, rubber tires	50	75	100
Structo Ladder Truck, 1950s	116	174	232
Structo Machinery Hauler	85	128	170
Structo Moving Van, open cab, circa 1920, No. 427, 16" long	238	358	475
Structo Packard Dump Truck, No. 405, circa 1930, 18" long	600	950	1400
Structo Pickup Truck, 13" long	150	225	300
Structo Pile Driver, 13" high	175	262	350
Structo Police Patrol Truck, No. 426, 17" long	400	600	800
Structo Renault Tank, clockwork, green w/red turret	225	338	450
Structo Roadster, 1920s, clockwork, 16" long	1000	1700	2400
Structo Sand Loader, circa 1928, 12" high	17	26	35
Structo "Sanitation Dept." Garbage Truck	50	75	100
Structo Searchlight Truck, truck, metal, light and generator plastic, uses batteries, has rubber tires	62	93	125
Structo Stake Truck, lights work, 1930s, 21" long	212	318	425
Structo Steam Shovel, 14" x 11"	162	243	325
Structo Steam Shovel, 16"	57	87	115
Structo Steam Shovel, 21" x 18"	50	75	100
Structo "Structo Telephone Co.", circa 1948, 12" long	80	120	160
Structo Tank, #48, 11" long	225	338	450
Structo Tank, olive drab w/orange turret, 10 metal wheels, 12-1/2"	150	225	300
Structo "Toyland Garage" Wrecker	80	120	160
Structo Toyland Oil Co.	175	262	350
Structo Tractor w/cast iron driver, early, caterpillar type, 8-1/2" long	200	300	400
Structo Truck Assortment No. 317: Dump Truck, blue, Stake Truck, Lumber Truck, each 9" long, 3-1/2" wide, 3 1/2" tall, heavy gauge metal, rubber wheels, original box folds to form garage, 1920s, price per set	75	112	150
Structo U.S. Mail Delivery Truck, No. 428, 17" long	187	280	375
Structo Whippet Tank, heavy spring clockwork motor enameled green, red and black, may read "Patented 1920", on sale in 1929, No.48, 12"	200	300	400

	C6	C8	C10
Structo No. 601 Motor Express Stake Truck, early 1950s	105	158	210
Structo No. 603 Package Delivery, early 1950s	80	120	160
Structo No. 605 Shovel Dump, early 1950s	150	225	300
Structo No. 607 Machinery Truck, early 1950s	170	255	340
Structo No. 609 Barrel Truck, early 1950s	140	210	280
Structo No. 700 Transport Trailer, early 1950s	115	172	230
Structo No. 702 Steel Cargo Trailer, early to mid-1950s	125	188	250
Structo No. 704 Overland Freight Trailer, early 1950s	75	112	150
Structo No. 704 Grain Trailer, early and mid-1950s (replaced Freight Trailer)	100	150	200
Structo No. 706 Auto Transport Trailer, sold 1953-54, w/cars	72	108	145
Structo No. 708 Cattle Trailer	100	150	200
Structo No. 811 Barrel Truck, windup, early-mid 1950s	85	128	170
Structo No. 822 Wrecker Truck, windup, early-mid 1950s	70	105	140
Structo No. 844 Hi-Lift Dump, windup, early 1950s	85	128	170
Structo No. 866 Gasoline Truck, windup, early 1950s	212	318	225
Sturdi Built Logging Truck	325	510	650
Sturditoy Ambulance, open cab, circa 1929, 26" long	2000	3500	5000
Sturditoy American Railway Express Truck, circa 1920s	1000	1500	2200
Sturditoy Coal Dump Truck, 1920s	700	1200	1700
Sturditoy Dump Truck, 1920s, 25"long	800	1300	1900
Sturditoy Dump Truck, 1920s, 26-1/2"	700	1100	1500
Sturditoy Pumper, c. 1930, 26"long	1200	2200	3600
Sturditoy "Struditoy Oil Company" Truck, circa 1929, 27" long	800	1300	1800
Sturditoy Traveling Store	800	1300	2000
Sturditoy "U.S. Mail" Truck	No Price Found		

SUN SA04. Photo by Dave Leopard.

	C6	C8	C10
Sturditoy U.S. Mail Screenside Truck...	800	1300	2000
Sturditoy Water Tower.........................	850	1350	2150
Sturditoy "Wells Fargo" Armored Truck, circa 1927, 24" long..........................	1000	1600	2700

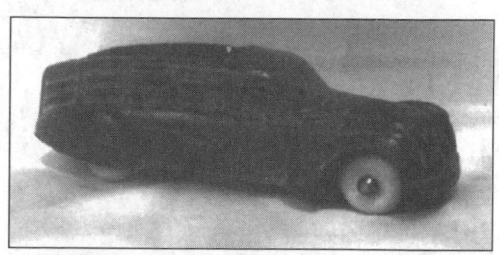

SUN ST01. Photo by Dave Leopard.

SUN RUBBER

Sun Rubber of Barberton, Ohio was founded in 1923. Toymaking started in 1924 and autos were introduced in April, 1935. Owner was Tom W. Smith Jr.

SUN ST03. Photo by Dave Leopard.

SUN ST02. Photo by Dave Leopard.

	C6	C8	C10
SA01 Coupe, external exhaust pipes, from 1936, No. 515, 4" long..............	20	30	40
SA02 '34 DeSoto Airflow, 4 door sedan, No. 500, 4" long......................	20	30	40
SA03 '40 Dodge, 4 door sedan, No. 12001, 4-1/2" long......................	20	30	40
SA04 "Teardrop" Sedan, circa 1936 No. 1010 (1936), 5-1/2" long.............	22	33	45
SA05 Art Deco Housetrailer, fits SA04, No. 1025, 4-3/8" long............	42	63	85

SUN ST07. Photo by Dave Leopard.

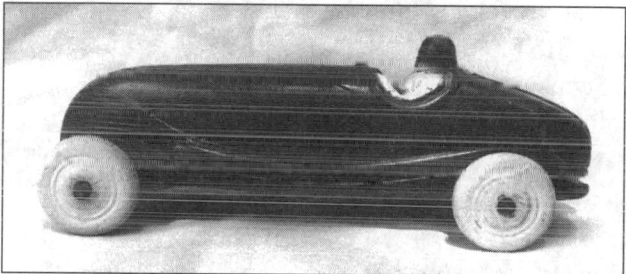

SUN SR03. Photo by Dave Leopard.

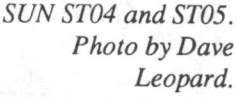

SUN SA07. Photo by Dave Leopard.

SUN ST04 and ST05. Photo by Dave Leopard.

SUN both SR01. Photo by Dave Leopard.

SUN ST08. Photo by Dave Leopard.

	C6	C8	C10
SA06 Town Car, Brewster type limo, exposed driver, No. 1015, 5-3/8".......27		41	55
SA07 Station Wagon, Woody, mid-30s, No. 12007, 3-3/4" long.....................20		30	40
ST01 Pickup Truck, stake sides, streamlined, No. 510, 4-1/2" long................22		33	45
ST02 Open Truck, stake sides, streamlined (White?), No. 1005, 5-1/4".......25		38	50
ST03 Tractor/Trailer, 1 piece, 3 axles, futuristic, No. 12013, 5-1/8" long......20		30	40
ST04 Open Truck, futuristic, No. 12003, 4-1/2" long...........................20		30	40
ST05 Open "Master" Truck, futuristic, No. 12111, 5-5/8" long.......................22		33	45
ST07 '36 White Bus, streamlined, No. 520 (1936), 4-1/4" long...............20		30	40
ST08 Ambulance, circa late 1930s, No. 12006, 3-3/4" long...................20		30	40
SR01 Open Racer, 2 drivers, No. 505 (1936), 4-3/8" long.............................20		30	40
SR02 Open Racer, full fenders on rear, No. 1000 (1936), 6-1/2" long.............27		41	55
SR03 Open Racer, boattail, "Super" racer, No. 12012, 6-3/4" long............ 25		38	50
SM01 Tank, revolving turret and gunner, No. 12015 (1946), 6" long................. 52		78	105
SM02 Scout Car, 4 gunners, No.12014 (1946), 6" long...................................40		60	80
Ted Toys Racer, wood, 2 riders, pull toy... 125		188	250
Texaco Tank Truck, 24" long.................35		52	70
Thimble Drome Racer, pusher.............. 125		188	250

THOMAS TOYS No. 457 Jet Car. Courtesy Islyn Thomas.

Thomas Toys

Thomas Toys was founded by Islyn Thomas in 1944. Located from first to last at 80 Clinton Street, Newark, New Jersey, at its peak it had 350 employees. The company's first toys were plastic jeeps, planes and vinyl dolls. In 1960 Thomas sold the firm to Banner.

	C6	C8	C10
Thomas Toys No. 133 Buick Torpedo Sedan, plastic, 11" long.......................20		30	40
Thomas Toys Harley-Davidson with removable rider, 3" long.................... 20		25	30
Thomas Toys Jet Car, No. 457.............No Price Found			
Thomas Toys No. 140 Loudspeaker Van, plastic, 4" long.......................... 20		25	30
Thomas Toys Wrecker, 4-1/2" long....... 12		18	24

TIP TOP TOY CO.

The Tip Top Toy Co. was located in San Francisco, and produced slush cast vehicles through most of the 1920s and 30s. The firm embossed its name inside some of its toys, but not all. (List by C.B.C. Lee and Craig A Clark)

These are a rare make of toys, evidently manufactured through most of the twenties and thirties in San Francisco by the Tip Top Toy Co. Photo by C.B.C. Lee.

	C6	C8	C10
Tip Top Coupe, 1923 Dodge, 3-1/8"...... 16		24	32
Tip Top Tanker, marked "Gasoline", 3-1/2" long............ No Price Found			
Tip Top Tow Truck, 3-5/16" long.......... 16		24	32
w/trailer, 5-1/4" overall...................... No Price Found			
Tip Top Pickup Truck w/tailgate, 3-3/16" long......................... No Price Found			
Tip Top Bus, 3-3/8" long.........................No Price Found			
Tip Top Coupe, 3-3/16" long.................. No Price Found			
Tip Top Coupe, 1935 Hupmobile 3-1/4" long............................ No Price Found			
w/trailer... No Price Found			
Tip Top Small Tanker, 2-11/16" long.... No Price Found			

	C6	C8	C10
Tip Top Small Tanker w/bumpers.........	No Price Found		
Tip Top "Parcel Delivery" Panel Truck, 2-1/8" long..	No Price Found		
Tip Top Small Coupe, 2-1/8" long.........	No Price Found		
Tip Top Studebaker Sedan, 1935, 2-9/16" long...................................	No Price Found		
Tip Top Stake Truck, 4 or 6 wheels, 5-5/16" long...	No Price Found		
Tip Top Airflow, smaller........................	No Price Found		
Tip Top Airflow, larger..........................	No Price Found		

TOLEDO METAL WHEEL COMPANY
("Blue Streak")

The Toledo Metal Wheel Company was located in Toledo, Ohio during at least the early and late 1920s. It manufactured a large range of pedal cars as well as toy trucks. Its trade name for its products was "Blue Streak."

	C6	C8	C10
Toledo No. 45 "Bull Dog" Truck, open cab, 26" long............................	500	1000	1500
Toledo No. 46 "Bull Dog" Dump Truck, 26-1/2" long......................	600	1000	1475
Toledo No. 47 "Bull Dog" Sprinkler Truck, 27-1/2" long......................	600	1100	1510
Toledo No. 48 "Bull Dog" Moving Van, 26" long..................................	550	1050	1550
Toledo No. 50 "Bull Dog" Coal Truck, 25" long.................................	800	1350	1875
Toledo Fire Pumper Pedal Car, red painted, 59" long..................	1250	1875	2500

TOMMY TOY

The following vehicles have been identified by Charles E. Weldon Jr., son of one of the owners of Tommy Toy. He is sure these are Tommy Toy, but admits there is always a chance he could be mistaken on some. Certainly the Cannon Truck, aside from the hubs, looks just like Barclay's, which was produced in the same years. Some others resemble Metal Cast, Savoye and other companies' vehicles.

However, since slush molds did tend to change hands, production of a vehicle by one company would not preclude later manufacture of the same toy by another company. American Alloy is known to have produced copies of Tommy Toy's soldiers using new molds. The only vehicle known to bear the Tommy Toy trademark is the 810 Cord.

TOMMY TOY, Left to Right, Top: TTV27, TTV28; Bottom: TTV2, TTV30, TTV32. Photo by Bill Kaufman. Courtesy Charles E. Weldon Jr.

TOMMY TOY, Left to Right, Top: TTV18, TTV17, TTV14, TTV16; Bottom: TTV10, TTV11, TTV12. Photo by Bill Kaufman. Courtesy Charles E. Weldon Jr.

	C6	C8	C10
TTV1 Aerial Ladder Truck (like Savoye), late 20s type.....................	20	30	40
TTV2 Airflow type Auto (like Kansas Toy), circa 1935..............................	32	48	65
TTV3 "Ambulance", late 20s-early 30s type................................	16	24	32
TTV4 "Beer Truck" w/wooden barrels, late 1930s.............................	14	21	28

	C6	C8	C10
TTV5 Cannon Truck, mid-30s(like Barclay; Barclay's had wooden hubs)...	17	25	34
TTV6 Convertible, no driver, mid-late 30s..	8	12	16
TTV7 Convertible w/driver, mid-late 30s, 1935 Oldsmobile........................	10	15	20
TTV8 Cord, 810 (1935)......................	40	60	80
TTV9 "Delivery Deluxe" Delivery Truck (like Savoye), late 30s.............	18	27	36

TOMMY TOY TTV8. Courtesy C.B.C. Lee.

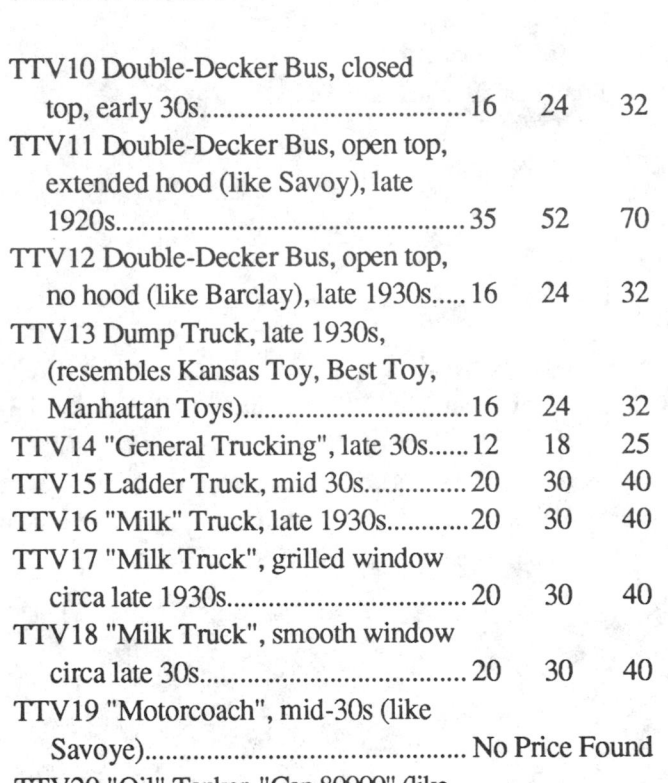

TOMMY TOY, Left to Right, Top: TTV20, TTV5, TTV7, TTV21; Bottom: TTV4, TTV18, TTV6. Photo by Bill Kaufman. Courtesy Charles E. Weldon Jr.

TTV10 Double-Decker Bus, closed
  top, early 30s.............................16 24 32
TTV11 Double-Decker Bus, open top,
  extended hood (like Savoy), late
  1920s......................................35 52 70
TTV12 Double-Decker Bus, open top,
  no hood (like Barclay), late 1930s.....16 24 32
TTV13 Dump Truck, late 1930s,
  (resembles Kansas Toy, Best Toy,
  Manhattan Toys)...........................16 24 32
TTV14 "General Trucking", late 30s......12 18 25
TTV15 Ladder Truck, mid 30s...........20 30 40
TTV16 "Milk" Truck, late 1930s............20 30 40
TTV17 "Milk Truck", grilled window
  circa late 1930s.........................20 30 40
TTV18 "Milk Truck", smooth window
  circa late 30s...........................20 30 40
TTV19 "Motorcoach", mid-30s (like
  Savoye)................................ No Price Found
TTV20 "Oil" Tanker, "Cap 80000" (like
  Metal Cast, which has different capacity
  number), 1930s, attaches to Tommy Toy
  Towing Car Coupe.........................8 12 16
TTV21 "Packard", Coupe, mid-30s........17 26 35
TTV22 "Police Patrol", open windows,
  late 20s-early 30s type.................40 60 80

	C6	C8	C10
TTV23 "Police Patrol", solid windows, late 20s-early 30s type	35	52	70
TTV24 Pumper, mid 1930s	12	18	25
TTV25 Pumper, large, red hubs, late 30s	11	16	22
TTV26 Pumper, small, late 30s	8	12	16
TTV27 Racing Car, large, circa mid-30s	16	24	32
TTV28 Racing Car, small, circa mid-30s	12	18	25
TTV29 Sedan, 4 door, circa 1935	17	26	35
TTV30 Sedan towing "Tourist" trailer, circa 1936-37	20	30	40
TTV31 Towing Car Coupe (like Savoye), early 30s type	16	24	32
TTV32 Tractor	12	18	25
TTV33 Wrecker, late 1930s	10	15	20

TOMMY TOY, Left to Right, Top: TTV31, TTV33, TTV13; Bottom: TTV9, TTV29, TTV30. Photo by Bill Kaufman. Courtesy Charles E. Weldon Jr.

TONKA

Tonka was incoporated in Mound, Minnesota, in September, 1946. The firm had secured the tooling for a steam shovel and crane and clam from Streator Industries, which had unsuccessfully introduced those toys at the Toy Fair in February, 1946. Tonka, which means "great" in Sioux-French, was located on the banks of Lake Minnetonka (and is now situated in Minnetonka itself). In 1948, Tonka introduced a fork lift with trailer, and in 1949 premiered its line of trucks, including a dump and wrecker. The firm had originally been incorporated as Mound Metal Crafts, with a line of tie racks and garden tools.

	C6	C8	C10
1947			
Tonka No. 50 Steam Shovel, 20-3/4" long	135	202	270
Tonka No. 150 Crane and Clam, 24" long	88	132	175
1948			
Tonka No. 200 Lift Truck and Cart	100	150	300
1949			
Tonka No. 100 Steam Shovel Deluxe, 22" long	100	150	200
Tonka No. 120 Tractor and Carry-All Trailer w/No. 50 Steam Shovel	155	280	350
Tonka No. 125 Tractor and Carry-All Trailer w/No. 100 Steam Shovel	150	250	350
Tonka No. 130 Tractor and Carry-All Trailer, 30-1/2" long	100	150	250
Tonka No. 140 "Tonka Toy Transport Van", 22-1/4" long	150	225	300
Tonka No. 170 Tractor and Carry-All Trailer w/No. 150 Crane and Clam	200	300	400
Tonka No. 180 Dump Truck, 12" long	100	150	240
Tonka No. 190 Loading Tractor, 10-1/2" long	No Price Found		
Tonka No. 250 Wrecker Truck, 12-1/2" long	100	150	250
1951			

(1950 almost identical to 1949 line with minor color and decal changes).

	C6	C8	C10
Tonka No. 145 Street Carrier Semi, 22" long	125	188	250
Tonka No. 175 Utility Hauler, 12" long	100	150	200
Tonka No. 400 Allied Van Lines Semi, 23-1/2" long	175	260	350

TONKA 1954 Steel Carrier Truck. Courtesy Continental Hobby House.

TONKA 1956 No. 950 Pumper. Photo by Calvin L. Chaussee.

	C6	C8	C10
1952			
Tonka No. 500 Livestock Hauler Semi, 22-1/4" long	90	135	180
Tonka No. 550 Grain Hauler Semi, 22-1/4" long	125	188	250
1953			
Tonka No. 575 Logger Semi, 22-1/4"	125	188	250
Tonka No. 575 Logger Semi, wood flat bed	125	150	250
Tonka No. 600 Road Grader, 17" long	50	75	100
Tonka No. 650 Green Giant Transport Semi, 22-1/4" long	150	225	350
Tonka Wrecker	110	150	250
Tonka No. 675 Trailer Fleet Set, 2 tractors (5 interchangeable trailers), per set	350	580	775
1954			

(Newer Style Trucks - Rounded Fenders)

	C6	C8	C10
Tonka No. 580 Pickup Truck	75	125	250
Tonka No. 700 Aerial Ladder Semi Fire Truck, 32-1/2" long	175	260	350
Tonka No. 725 Minute Maid Delivery Van, 14-1/2" long	250	350	550
Tonka No. 725 Star Kist Van, 14-1/2"	250	375	550
Tonka No. 750 Carnation Milk Step Van, 11-3/4" long	200	300	400
Tonka No. 750 Parcel Delivery Van, 11-3/4" long	200	300	400

	C6	C8	C10
Tonka Steel Carrier Truck	90	135	180
Tonka Wrecker	90	135	250
Tonka Utility Truck	112	168	225
Tonka No. 775 Road Builder Set - 5pc. set - Road Grader (semi T&T crane and dump truck)	350	525	700

TONKA 1954 No. 750. Photo by Mark McManus.

1955

	C6	C8	C10
Tonka No. 725 Minute Maid Orange Juice Van	275	350	550
Tonka No. 750 Carnation Milk Delivery Van	150	225	300
Tonka No. 880 Pickup Truck	125	180	250
Tonka No. 0850 Lumber Truck, 6 wheels	175	263	350
Tonka No.0860 Stake Truck, 6 wheels	80	120	160
Tonka Allied Van Lines	85	128	170
Tonka Dump	70	105	140
Tonka Freighter	90	135	180
Tonka Hook & Ladder	100	200	300
Tonka Livestock Truck	110	165	220
Tonka Loboy & Shovel	150	225	300
Tonka Rescue Van	100	200	300
Tonka Wrecker	100	150	200
Tonka No. 65 Trailer, Stake side	30	45	60
Tonka No. 600 Grader	40	80	100

1956

	C6	C8	C10
Tonka No. 120 Shovel & Carry-All (Loboy), 33" long total	188	282	375
Tonka No. 180 Dump Truck, 13" long	60	90	120
Tonka No. 600 Road Grader, 17" long	45	80	100
Tonka No. 700 Aerial Ladder, 32-1/2" long	100	200	350
Tonka No. 880 Pickup Truck, 13-3/4"	100	250	400
Tonka No. 950 Pumper, 17" long	150	225	300
Tonka No. 980 Hi-Way Dump Truck, 13" long	130	180	265
Tonka No. 990 Suburban Pumper, 17"	200	300	400

	C6	C8	C10
Tonka No. 991 Farm Stake Truck, 13" long	80	120	160
Tonka No. 992 Aerial Sand Loader Set, Loader and Dump Truck	175	260	350
Tonka No. 994 Sand Loader Set, Loader and Dump Truck	125	188	250
Tonka No. 996 Wrecker (white color), (AAA), 12" long	200	300	400
Tonka No. 998 Lumber Truck, 18-3/4" long	80	120	160
Tonka Rescue Squad Van, 11-3/4"	115	173	230
Tonka Green Giant Semi Reefer	155	250	400

TONKA, 1956, No. 994, Sand Loader. Courtesy Thomas G. Nefos, Federal Shipping Network.

1957

	C6	C8	C10
Tonka Aerial Ladder Truck	200	300	400
Tonka Big Mike Dual Hydraulic Dump Truck, 14" long	325	488	650
Tonka Farms Stake Truck	190	275	380
Tonka Gasoline Truck, 15" long	350	525	700
Tonka Hook & Ladder	150	225	300
Tonka Parcel Delivery Van, 12" long	200	300	400
Tonka Pickup w/Stake Trailer, 20-1/2" long	100	150	300
Stake Trailer alone	30	45	75
Tonka Stock Rack Truck w/Animals, 16-1/4" long	175	263	350
Tonka 3 in 1 Hi-Way Service Truck, w/2 snowblades, 13" long	200	300	400
Tonka Thunderbird Express Semi, 24" long	150	250	350
Tonka Wrecker	100	150	250

1958 Next Generation Cars

	C6	C8	C10
Tonka No. 02 Pickup Truck	60	90	120
Tonka No. 03 Utility Truck	92	138	185

	C6	C8	C10
Tonka No. 04 Farm Stake Truck	65	98	130
Tonka No. 05 Sportsman Pickup w/topper, 12-3/4" long	70	125	200
Tonka No. 06 Dump Truck	80	120	160
Tonka No. 12 Road Grader	75	112	150
Tonka No. 18 Wrecker Truck	100	150	200
Tonka No. 20 Hydraulic Dump Truck	132	198	265
Tonka No. 28 Pickup w/Stake Trailer & Animal	100	150	200
Tonka No. Sportsman Truck w/Box Trailer	150	225	300
Tonka No. 32 Stock Rack Truck	112	168	225
Tonka No. 33 "Gasoline" Truck, hinged back door, hose & nozzle	250	300	450
Tonka No. 34 Deluxe Sportsman w/Boat Trailer, 22-3/4" long	150	225	300
Tonka No. 35 Farm Stake w/2 Horse Trailer, 21-3/4" long	125	188	250
Tonka No. 36 Livestock Van	175	263	350
Tonka No. 37 Thunderbird Express	150	250	350
Tonka No. 39 Nationwide Moving Van, 24-1/2" long	250	375	500
Tonka No. 41 Hi-Way Service Truck	70	105	140
Tonka No. 43 Shovel & Carry-All Trailer	190	275	380
Tonka No. 45 Big Mike Dual Hydraulic Dump Truck w/snow plow	275	375	550
Tonka No. 46 Surburban Pumper	175	260	350
Tonka No. 48 Hydraulic Aerial Ladder	100	150	250

1959

	C6	C8	C10
Tonka No. 01 Service Truck, 12-3/4"	75	112	150

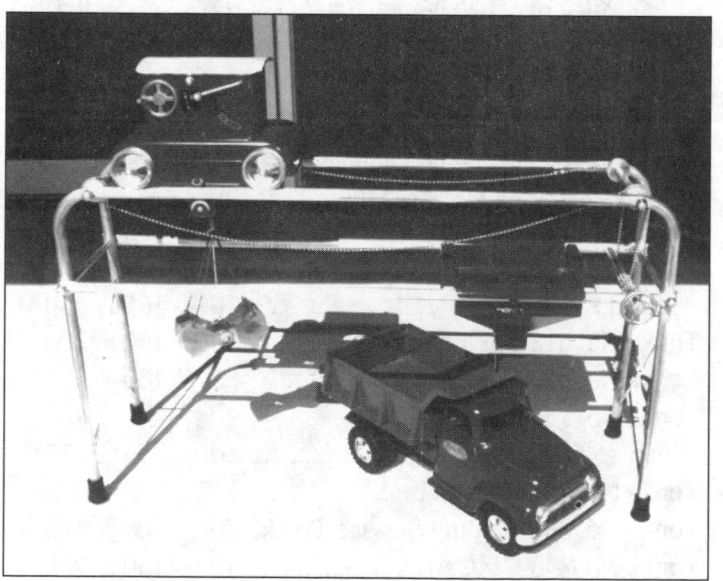

TONKA, 1956, No. 992 Aerial Sand Loader Set. Courtesy Thomas G. Nefos, Federal Shipping Network.

	C6	C8	C10
Tonka No. 05 Sportsman	40	60	80
Tonka No. 14 Dragline, 20" long	75	112	150
Tonka No. 16 Air Express	150	225	300
Tonka No. 22 Deluxe Sportsman	150	225	300

	C6	C8	C10
Tonka No. 30 Tandem Platform Stake, 28-1/4" long	140	210	280
Tonka No. 36 Tandem Air Express, w/trailer, 24-3/4" long	225	338	450
Tonka No. 40 Car Carrier	44	66	88
Tonka No. 41 Boat Transport, 38"	150	250	350
Tonka No. 42 Hydraulic Land Rover, 15" long	350	525	700
Tonka No. 44 Dragline & Trailer, 26-1/4" long	112	168	225
Tonka Sanitary Truck (square back)	250	350	500

1960

(Two Center Ribs on Truck Cabs Replaced by One Rib)

	C6	C8	C10
Tonka No. 01 Service Truck	75	112	150
Tonka No. 02 Pickup	60	100	175
Tonka No. 04 Farm Stake Truck	50	75	125
Tonka No. 05 Sportsman	75	112	150
Tonka No. 06 Dump Truck	55	82	110

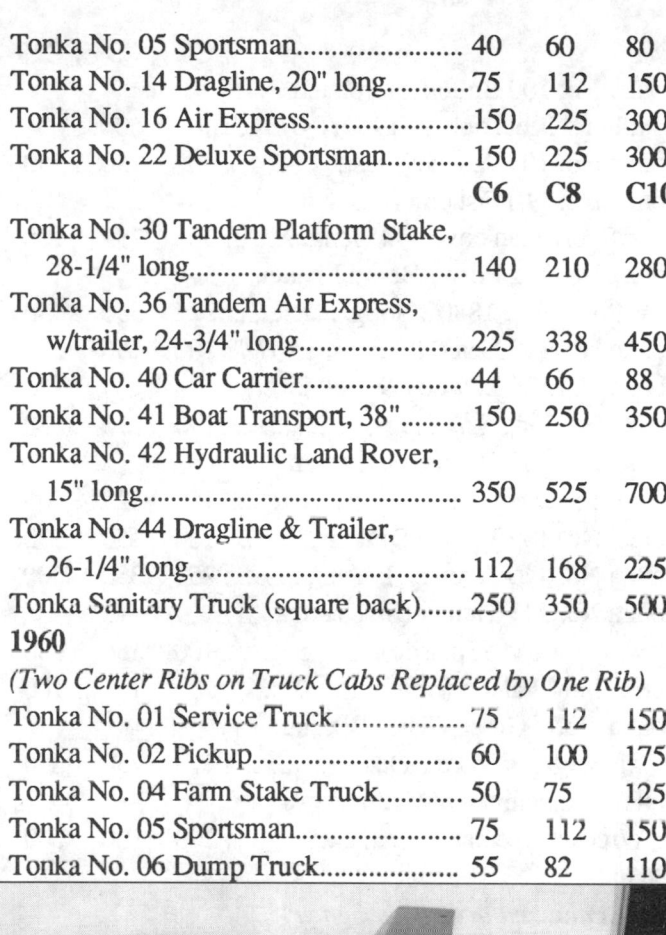

TONKA, 1960 No. 06 Dump Truck. Courtesy Thomas G. Nefos, Federal Shipping Network.

	C6	C8	C10
Tonka No. 08 Logger	150	225	300
Tonka No. 18 Wrecker, white sidewalls	85	128	170
Tonka No. 20 Hydraulic Dump	45	75	100
Tonka No. 22 Deluxe Sportsman	70	105	140
Tonka No. 28 Pickup & Trailer	100	150	200
Tonka No. 35 Farm Stake & Horse Trailer	125	188	250
Tonka No. 37 Thunderbird Express	150	250	350
Tonka No. 40 Car Carrier	75	125	250
Tonka No. 41 Boat Transport, 38" long	150	250	350
Tonka No. 46 Suburban Pumper	100	150	200
Tonka No. 48 Aerial Ladder	125	188	250

	C6	C8	C10
Tonka No. 100 Bulldozer, (plated roller wheels only in 1960) 8-7/8"....	40	60	80
Tonka No. 105 Rescue Squad, 13-3/4"..	90	150	250
Tonka No. 110 Fisherman Pickup w/Sportsman cover, 14" long............	50	75	100
Tonka No. 115 Power Boom Loader (1960 only), 18-1/2" long.................	225	350	450
Tonka No. 120 Cement Mixer, 15-1/2".	100	150	200
Tonka No. 125 Lowboy & Bulldozer, 26-1/4" long.........................	190	275	380
Tonka No. 130 Deluxe Fisherman (also new boat & trailer)....................	150	225	300
Tonka No. 135 Mobile Dragline............	100	150	250
Tonka No. 140 Sanitary Truck...............	250	350	500
Tonka No. 145 Tanker (first Tonka w/major use of plastic), 28" long.......	100	150	250
Tonka Ford Falcon (from set).................	50	75	100
Tonka "Jolly Green Giant" Special, white, green stake racks....................	175	250	350
Tonka "Standard" Oil Company Wrecker Special...............................	200	300	500

1961

("T" Eliminated in Grille's Center)

	C6	C8	C10
Tonka No. 02 Pickup.........................	60	90	120
Tonka No. 04 Farm Stake........................	35	52	70
Tonka No. 05 Sportsman.........................	65	98	130
Tonka No. 06 Dump...........................	55	82	110
Tonka No. 12 Road Grader, yellow........	50	75	100
Tonka No. 14 Dragline, yellow...............	62	93	125
Tonka No. 18 Wrecker........................	100	150	200
Tonka No. 20 Hydraulic Dump..............	75	112	150
Tonka No. 22 Deluxe Sportsman...........	No Price Found		
Tonka No. 35 Farm Stake Truck & Horse Trailer.................................	70	105	140
Tonka No. 39 Allied Van........................	112	168	225
Tonka No. 40 Car Carrier......................	100	150	250
Tonka No. 41 Boat Transport Truck.....	150	250	350
Tonka No. 48 Aerial Ladder..................	125	188	250
Tonka No. 116 Dump Truck w/Sand-loader, 23-1/4" long total..................	80	120	160
Tonka No. 117 Boat Service Truck (1961 only).....................................	75	150	250
Tonka No. 118 Giant Dozer, 12-1/2".....	50	75	100
Tonka No. 120 Cement Mixer.................	100	150	200
Tonka No. 130 Deluxe Fisherman..........	100	150	250
Tonka No. 134 Grading Service Truck, Trailer & Bulldozer, 25-1/2" long.....	100	150	250
Tonka No. 135 Mobile Dragline.............	100	150	250
Tonka No. 136 Houseboat Set, 29" long total.................................	200	300	400

	C6	C8	C10
Tonka No. 140 Sanitary Truck...............	(never made)		
Tonka No. 142 Mobile Clam, 27-1/4" long..................................	100	150	200
Tonka No. 145 Tanker.........................	100	150	250

1962

(New Tonka logo; Tonka above wavy line, Mound, Minnesota below)

	C6	C8	C10
Tonka No. 200 Jeep Dispatcher, 9-3/4"..	40	60	80
Tonka No. 201 "Serv-I-Care" 9-1/8"......	50	75	100
Tonka No. 249 Jeep Universal................	25	50	75
Tonka No. 250 Tractor, 8-5/8" long........	50	75	100
Tonka No. 300 Bulldozer........................	50	75	100
Tonka No. 301 Utility Dump, (revised Golf Club Tractor, 1961 only) 12-1/2".	100	150	200
Tonka No. 302 Pickup...........................	35	50	100
Tonka No. 308 Stake Pickup, 12-5/8".....	50	75	100
Tonka No. 350 Jeep Survey, fringe top, 10-1/2" long...........................	50	75	100
Tonka No. 402 "Loader", yellow & green..	40	60	80
Tonka No. 404 Farm Stake Truck..........	50	75	100
Tonka No. 405 Sportsman.......................	55	82	110
Tonka No. 406 Dump Truck...................	60	90	120
Tonka No. 410 "Jet Delivery" Truck, (1962 only), 14" long......................	100	150	250
Tonka No. 420 Airlines Luggage Service, 16-5/8" long......................	100	150	200
Tonka No. 512 Road Grader..................	45	68	90
Tonka No. 514 Dragline.........................	150	225	300
Tonka No. 516 Jeep Runabout, Trailer, Boat, 25-5/8" long total.........	75	112	150
Tonka No. 518 Wrecker.........................	45	75	125
Tonka No. 520 Hydraulic Dump............	60	90	120
Tonka No. 524 Dozer Packer, Packer has 11 tires, sold only in 1962, total 18-1/4" long....................................	75	150	200
Tonka No. 528 Pickup & Trailer............	50	75	100
Tonka No. 530 Camper, 14" long..........	50	100	150
Tonka No. 616 Dump Truck & Sand Loader..................................	70	105	140
Tonka No. 618 Giant Dozer...................	100	150	200
Tonka No. 620 Cement Mixer...............	85	150	200
Tonka No. 735 Farm Stake & Horse Trailer.................................	50	75	125
Tonka No. 739 Allied Van......................	112	168	225
Tonka No. 834 Grading Service Truck..	70	100	150
Tonka No. 840 Car Carrier....................	100	150	200
Tonka No. 926 Pumper Truck...............	100	150	200
Tonka No. 942 Mobile Clam.................	80	150	220

	C6	C8	C10
Tonka No. 1348 Aerial ladder	100	150	250

1963

(Faceted Headlights introduced)

	C6	C8	C10
Tonka No. 50 Mini-Tonka Jeep Pickup, 9-1/4" long	35	52	70
Tonka No. 56 Mini-Tonka Stake Truck, 9-1/4" long	35	52	70
Tonka No. 60 Mini-Tonka Dump 9-3/4" long	75	112	150
Tonka No. 68 Mini-Tonka Wrecker, 9-1/2" long	30	45	60
Tonka No. 70 Mini-Tonka Camper, 9-5/8" long	75	112	150
Tonka No. 200 Jeep Dispatcher	No Price Found		
Tonka No. 201 "Servi-I-Car"	55	82	110
Tonka No. 250 Tractor, yellow w/red seat	75	112	150
Tonka No. 251 Military Jeep Universal, 10-1/2" long	25	38	50
Tonka No. 300 Bulldozer	55	82	110
Tonka No. 302 Pickup	35	52	70
Tonka No. 308 Stake Pickup	35	52	70
Tonka No. 350 Jeep Surrey	50	75	100
Tonka No. 352 Loader	40	60	80
Tonka No. 354 Style-Side Pickup, 14" long	40	60	80
Tonka No. 404 Farm Stake Truck	60	90	120
Tonka No. 406 Dump Truck	45	68	90
Tonka No. 422 Back Hoe, 17-1/8"	65	98	130
Tonka No. 425 Jeep Pumper 10-3/4"	80	120	160
Tonka No. 512 Road Grader, red clearance lights	No Price Found		
Tonka No. 514 Dragline	60	90	120
Tonka No. 516 Jeep Runabout, Trailer & Boat	60	90	120
Tonka No. 518 Wrecker	25	38	50
Tonka No. 520 Hydraulic Dump Truck	45	68	90
Tonka No. 522 Style-Side Pickup & Stake Trailer, 22-3/4" long total	No Price Found		
Tonka No. 524 Dozer Packer, yellow	200	300	400
Tonak No. 530 Camper	25	38	50
Tonka No. 534 Trencher, 18-1/4"	32	48	65
Tonka No. 536 Giant Dozer	112	168	225
Tonka No. 616 Dump Truck & Sand Loader, yellow	67	100	135
Tonka No. 620 Cement Mixer	75	112	150
Tonka No. 625 Stake Pickup & Horse Trailer, 21-3/4" long overall	100	150	200
Tonka No. 640 Ramp Hoist, red & white, 19-1/4" long	175	263	350

	C6	C8	C10
Tonka No. 720 Terminal Train, 15 suitcases, 33-5/8" long total	105	158	210
Tonka No. 739 Allied Van	118	175	235
Tonka No. 840 Car Carrier	42	63	85
Tonka No. 926 Pumper	60	90	120
Tonka No. 942 Mobile Clam	75	112	150
Tonka No. 1001 Trencher & Loboy, 28-1/2" long total	75	112	150
Tonka No. 1348 Aerial Ladder Truck	100	150	200
Tonka No. 2100 Airport Service Set	150	225	300

1964

(Futuristic Cab introduced)

	C6	C8	C10
Tonka No. 77 Mini-Tonka Mixer, 9"	50	75	100
Tonka No. 86 Mini-Tonka Van, 16"	36	54	72
Tonka No. 90 Mini-Tonka Livestock Van, 16" long	50	75	100
Tonka No. 96 Mini-Tonka Car Carrier, 2 cars, 18-1/2" long	50	75	150
Tonka No. 250 Military Tractor, black seat	55	70	100
Tonka No. 251 Military Jeep Universal	35	55	75
Tonka No. 304 Jeep Commander, cavas top, 10-1/2" long	30	45	60
Tonka No. 315 Dump Truck, 13-1/2"	40	60	90
Tonka No. 375 Jeep Wrecker, 11"	50	75	150
Tonka No. 380 Troop Carrier, 14"	70	120	175
Tonka No. 384 Military Jeep & Box Trailer, 19-3/8" overall	50	75	150
Tonka No. 404 Stake Truck, red	70	120	170
Tonka No. 425 Jeep Pumper, black steering wheel	100	150	250
Tonka No. 504 Stake Pickup & Trailer, 21-5/8" long	50	75	100
Tonka No. 525 Jeep & Horse Trailer, 2 horses, 19-1/4" long total	45	68	90
Tonka No. 526 Shovel, 20" long	No Price Found		
Tonka No. 616 Dump Truck & Sand-loader, orange & yellow	75	125	175
Tonka No. 640 Ramp Hoist, park green & white, very rare	200	350	600
Tonka No. 739 Allied Van Lines, black knob on door	75	125	175
Tonka No. 900 Mighty Tonka Dump Truck (most popular Tonka of all: 9,655,000 sold between 1964-1983).	65	98	130
Tonka No. 942 Mobile Clam, yellow	50	75	100
Tonka No. 998 Aerial Ladder, 2 auxillary ladders	50	75	100

TOOTSIETOY
Compiled by John Gibson

TOOTSIETOY No.4638.
Courtesy Philips New York.

TOOTSIETOY Funnies No. 5101, 5106. Courtesy Christie's East.

	C6	C8	C10
Prewar			
Tootsietoy 4528 Limousine	16	24	32
Tootsietoy 4570 Ford Model T, Open Tourer	33	50	65
Tootsietoy 4610 Ford Model T, Pickup Truck	30	50	70
Tootsietoy 4629 Yellow Cab Sedan	15	23	30
Tootsietoy 4630 Federal "Grocery" Delivery Van	38	57	75
Tootsietoy 4631 Federal "Bakery" Delivery Van	50	80	105

TOOTSIETOY No. 4630 "Store Name" Federal Delivery Van (1924). Emil Kraus, State at 18th, an Erie, PA store. Collection & Photo John Gibson.

	C6	C8	C10
Tootsietoy 4632 Federal "Market" Delivery Van	35	60	75
Tootsietoy 4633 Federal "Laundry" Delivery Van	35	60	75
Tootsietoy 4634 Federal "Milk" Delivery Van	28	41	55
Tootsietoy 4635 Federal "Florist" Delivery Van	105	155	210
Tootsietoy 4636 Buick Coupe	23	34	45
Tootsietoy 4638 Mack Stake Truck	23	34	45
Tootsietoy 4639 Mack Coal Truck	23	34	45
Tootsietoy 4640 Mack Tank Truck*	23	34	45
Tootsietoy 4641 Buick Touring Car	28	42	55
Tootsietoy 4642 Long Range Cannon	13	18	25
Tootsietoy 4643 Mack Anti-Aircraft Gun	25	38	50
Tootsietoy 4644 Mack Searchlight Truck	27	41	55
Tootsietoy 4645 Mack "US Airmail Service" Truck	38	57	75
Tootsietoy 4646 Caterpiller Tractor, original treads only	27	41	55
Tootsietoy 4647 Renault Tank, original treads only	23	34	45
Tootsietoy 4648 Steamroller	65	95	125
Tootsietoy 4651 Fageol Safety Coach	27	41	44
Tootsietoy 4652 Fire Engine, Hook & Ladder	30	45	60

	C6	C8	C10
Tootsietoy 4653 Fire Engine, Water Tower	38	56	75
Tootsietoy 4654 Farm Tractor	35	53	70
Tootsietoy 4655 Ford Model A Coupe	20	30	40
Tootsietoy 4656 Buick Coupe in tin plate garage	60	90	150
Tootsietoy 4657 Buick Sedan in tin plate garage	60	90	150

TOOTSIETOY No. 4635 "Florist" Delivery Van, issued 1924. Collection & Photo John Gibson.

	C6	C8	C10
Tootsietoy 4658 Mack Insurance Patrol in tin plate garage	100	150	200
Tootsietoy 4665 Ford Model A Sedan	20	30	40
Tootsietoy 4666 Bluebird I Dayton Record Car	23	34	45
Tootsietoy 4670 Mack Tractor & 2 Semi-Trailers,"A&P" & "American Express"	115	170	225
Tootsietoy 4680 Overland Bus Lines	45	65	85
Tootsietoy 23 Racer w/Driver intact	45	68	90
Tootsietoy 190 Mack Auto Transport w/3 Buicks	75	115	150
Tootsietoy 190 Mack Auto Transport w/4 Buicks	115	170	225
Tootsietoy 191 Contractors' Tipper Set	90	130	175
Tootsietoy 5101 Andy Gump Roadster, standard	175	265	350
Tootsietoy 5101 Andy Gump Roadster, articulated	225	340	450
Tootsietoy 5102 Uncle Walt Roadster, standard	175	265	350
Tootsietoy 5102 Uncle Walt Roadster, articulated	225	340	450
Tootsietoy 5103 Smitty Motorcyle, standard	175	265	350
Tootsietoy 5103 Smitty Motorcyle, articulated	225	340	450

	C6	C8	C10
Tootsietoy 5104 Moon Mullins Police Wagon, standard	175	265	350
Tootsietoy 5104 Moon Mullins Police Wagon, articulated	225	340	450

TOOTSIETOY No. 4657 Tin plate Garage with No. 103 Buick Sedan. Collection & Photo John Gibson

	C6	C8	C10
Tootsietoy 5105 Kayo Ice Wagon, standard	150	225	300
Tootsietoy 5105 Kayo Ice Wagon, articulated	185	285	375
Tootsietoy 5106 Uncle Willie Row-boat, standard	135	210	275
Tootsietoy 5106 Uncle Willie Row-boat, articulated	175	265	350
Tootsietoy 6001 Buick Roadster, GM series	30	45	60
Tootsietoy 6002 Buick Coupe, GM series	28	41	55
Tootsietoy 6003 Buick Brougham, GM series	28	41	55
Tootsietoy 6004 Buick Sedan, GM series	28	41	55
Tootsietoy 6005 Buick Touring Car, GM series	50	75	100
Tootsietoy 6006 Buick Screenside Delivery Truck, GM series	35	53	70
Tootsietoy 6101 Cadillac Roadster, GM series	40	60	80
Tootsietoy 6102 Cadillac Coupe, GM series	40	60	80
Tootsietoy 6103 Cadillac Brougham, GM series	40	60	80
Tootsietoy 6104 Cadillac Sedan, GM series	40	60	80
Tootsietoy 6105 Cadillac Touring Car, GM series	60	90	120
Tootsietoy 6106 Cadillac Screenside Delivery Truck, GM series	48	71	95

Left to Right: TOOTSIETOY Herbie & Smitty Motorcycle and sidecar, TOOTSIETOY Andy Gump in Roadster. Courtesy PB Eight-Four, New York.

	C6	C8	C10
Tootsietoy 6201 Chevrolet Roadster, GM series	38	55	75
Tootsietoy 6202 Chevrolet Coupe, GM series	33	50	65
Tootsietoy 6203 Chevrolet Brougham, GM series	33	50	65
Tootsietoy 6204 Chevrolet Sedan, GM series	33	50	65
Tootsietoy 6205 Chevrolet Touring Car, GM series	55	83	110
Tootsietoy 6206 Chevrolet Screenside Delivery Truck, GM series	35	53	70
Tootsietoy 6301 Oldsmobile Roadster, GM series	38	55	75
Tootsietoy 6302 Oldsmobile Coupe GM series	35	53	70
Tootsietoy 6303 Oldsmobile Brougham, GM series	35	53	70
Tootsietoy 6304 Oldsmobile Sedan, GM series	35	53	70
Tootsietoy 6305 Oldsmobile Touring Car, GM series	55	83	110
Tootsietoy 6306 Oldsmobile Screenside Delivery Truck, GM series	45	68	90

TOOTSIETOY No. 6105 Cadillac Touring Car from Tootsietoy GM series (1927). Collection & Photo John Gibson.

TOOTSIETOY No. 5104 Moon Mullins Police Wagon (non-articulated) from the 1932 Funnies series. Collection & Photo John Gibson.

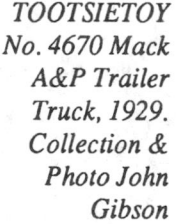

TOOTSIETOY No. 4670 Mack A&P Trailer Truck, 1929. Collection & Photo John Gibson

	C6	C8	C10
Tootsietoy 6-01 "No Name" Roadster GM series	55	83	110
Tootsietoy 6-02 "No Name" Coupe, GM series	55	83	110

TOOTSIETOY No. 4680 "Overland Bus", issued 1929 (later Diesteel wheels). Collection & Photo by John Gibson.

TOOTSIETOY, Left to Right: 4670, 4680, 4651, 4634. Courtesy Phillips New York.

	C6	C8	C10
Tootsietoy 6-03 "No Name" Brougham, GM series	55	83	110
Tootsietoy 6-04 "No Name" Sedan, GM series	55	83	110
Tootsietoy 6-05 "No Name" Touring Car, GM series	75	113	150
Tootsietoy 6-06 "No Name" Screenside Delivery Truck, GM series	65	95	125
Tootsietoy -- Ford Model A Van, "US Mail", sold in sets only	38	56	75

TOOTSIETOY No.6-06 "No Name" Delivery Truck (1933), often called "Screenside" (GM series). Collection & Photo John Gibson.

TOOTSIETOY No.6-05 "No Name" Touring Car (1933), GM series. Collection & Photo John Gibson.

	C6	C8	C10
Tootsietoy 4654 Farm Tractor for Army Field Battery Set #5071	58	86	115
Tootsietoy -- Box Trailer & Roadscraper Raker, sold only in boxed set, Farm Tractor No. 7003	135	205	275
Tootsietoy 6665 Ford Model A Sedan	25	38	50
Tootsietoy 101 Buick Coupe	10	15	20
Tootsietoy 102 Buick Roadster	13	19	25
Tootsietoy 103 Buick Sedan	10	15	20
Tootsietoy 104 Mack Insurance Patrol	23	34	45
Tootsietoy 105 Mack Tank Truck	28	41	55
Tootsietoy 108 Caterpillar Tractor, original treads only	23	34	45
Tootsietoy 109 Ford Pickup Truck	20	30	40
Tootsietoy 110 Bluebird I Daytona Record Car	28	41	55
Tootsietoy 0192 Mack Tootsietoy Dairy, 1 pc. cab, 3 trailers	75	113	150
Tootsietoy 0192 Mack Tootsietoy Dairy, 2 pc. cab, 3 trailers	115	165	225
Tootsietoy 0198 Mack Auto Transport, 1 pc. cab, 3 '35 Fords	150	225	300
Tootsietoy 0198 Mac Auto Transport, 2 pc. cab, 3 '34 Fords	215	320	425
Tootsietoy 0801 Mack "Express" Stake Semi-Trailer, 1 pc. cab	55	80	105

	C6	C8	C10
Tootsietoy 0801 Mack "Express" Stake Semi-Trailer, 2 pc. cab	63	95	125
Tootsictoy 0802 Mack "Domaco" Tank Semi-Trailer, 1 pc. cab	60	90	120
Tootsietoy 0802 Mack "Domaco" Tank Semi-Trailer, 2 pc. cab	65	98	130
Tootsietoy 0803 Mack "Long Distance Hauling" Semi-Trailer	87	130	175
Tootsietoy 0804 Mack "City Fuel" Coal Truck, 10 wheels	80	120	155
Tootsictoy 0804 Mack "City Fuel" Coal Truck, 4 wheels	125	187	250
Tootsietoy 0805 Mack "Tootsietoy Dairy" Semi-Trailer Truck	70	105	140
Tootsietoy 0806 Graham Wrecker	75	113	150
Tootsie 0807 Delivery Motorcycle adapted from 5103	175	260	350
Tootsietoy 0808 Graham "Tootsietoy Dairy"	75	113	150
Tootsietoy 0809 Graham Ambulance	75	113	150
Tootsietoy -- Graham "Commercial Tire & Supply"	112	168	225
Tootsietoy 0810 Mack "Railway Express Co." Truck w/"Wrigleys Gum" ad (1 pc. cab)	70	105	140
Tootsietoy 0810 Mack "Railway Express Co." Truck w/"Wrigleys Gum" ad (2 pc. cab)	75	115	150
Tootsietoy 0511 Graham Roadster 5 wheels	83	125	165
Tootsietoy 0512 Graham Coupe, 5 wheels	72	110	145
Tootsietoy 0513 Graham Sedan, 5 wheels	72	110	145
Tootsietoy 0514 Graham Convertible Coupe, 5 wheels	80	120	160

TOOTSIETOY, Left to Right;
4665, 5655, unnumbered "U.S.
Mail" (sold only in sets), 0716
"Doodlebug". Courtesy Phillips
New York.

	C6	C8	C10
Tootsietoy 0515 Graham Convertible Sedan, 5 wheels	80	120	160
Tootsietoy 0516 Graham Towncar, 5 wheels	88	130	175
Tootsietoy 0611 Graham Roadster, 6 wheels	83	125	165
Tootsietoy 0612 Graham Coupe, 6 wheels	72	110	145
Tootsietoy 0613 Graham Sedan, 6 wheels	72	110	145
Tootsietoy 0614 Graham Convertible Coupe, 6 wheels	80	120	160
Tootsietoy 0615 Graham Convertible Sedan, 6 wheels	80	120	160
Tootsietoy 0616 Graham Towncar, 6 wheels	75	113	150
Tootsietoy -- Graham Roadster, 4 wheels, Bild-A-Car	88	130	175
Tootsietoy -- Graham Coupe, 4 wheels, Bild-A-Car	65	98	130
Tootsietoy -- Graham Sedan, 4 wheels, Bild-A-Car	65	98	130
Tootsietoy 0712 LaSalle Coupe	133	200	265
Tootsietoy 0713 LaSalle Sedan	133	200	265
Tootsietoy 0714 LaSalle Convertible Coupe	143	214	285
Tootsietoy 0715 LaSalle Convertible Sedan	143	214	285
Tootsietoy 0716 Briggs Lincoln prototype, "Doodlebug"	60	90	125
Tootsietoy 6015 Lincoln Zephyr (plain version)	165	245	325
Tootsietoy 6015 Lincoln Zephyr (windup)	240	365	485
Tootsietoy 6016 Lincoln Wrecker (plain version)	275	415	550

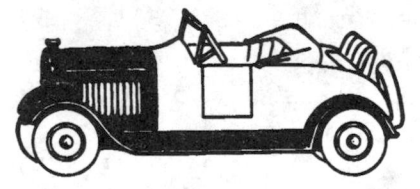

6-01 ROADSTER

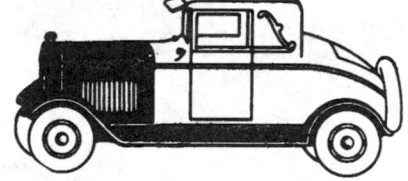

6-02 COUPE

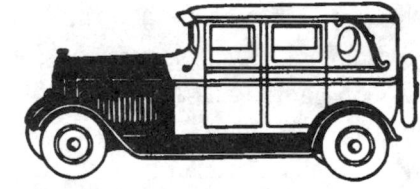

6-03 BROUGHAM

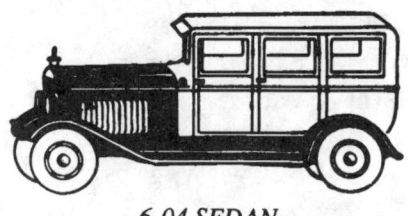

6-04 SEDAN

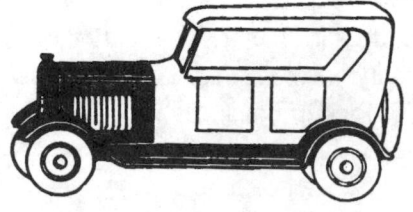

6-05 TOURING CAR

6-06 DELIVERY TRUCK

No. 4652 HOOK & LADDER

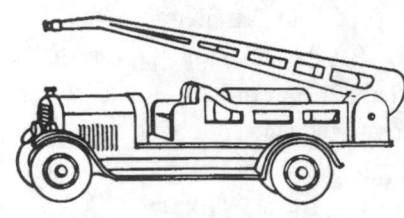

No.4652 WATER TOWER

	C6	C8	C10
Tootsietoy 6016 Lincoln Wrecker (windup)	350	525	700
Tootsietoy 0111 1934 Ford V8 Sedan	30	45	60
Tootsietoy 0111 1935 Ford V8 Sedan	15	23	30
Tootsietoy 0112 1934 Ford V8 Coupe	33	49	65
Tootsietoy 0112 1935 Ford V8 Coupe	18	26	35
Tootsietoy 0113 1934 Ford V8 Wrecker	38	56	75
Tootsietoy 0113 1935 Ford V8 Wrecker	33	49	65
Tootsietoy 0114 1934 Ford V8 Convertible Coupe	40	60	80
Tootsietoy 0114 1935 Ford V8 Convertible Coupe	30	45	60
Tootsietoy 0115 1934 Ford V8 Convertible Sedan	40	60	80
Tootsietoy 0115 1935 Ford V8 Convertible Sedan	30	45	60
Tootsietoy 0116 1935 Ford V8 Roadster	23	34	45
Tootsietoy -- 1935 Ford V8 Roadster Firechief's Car	50	75	100
Tootsietoy 0117 Zephyr Railcar	38	56	75
Tootsietoy 0118 DeSoto Airflow Sedan	23	34	45
Tootsietoy 120 Oil Tank Truck	23	34	45
Tootsietoy 0121 Ford Pickup Truck	18	26	35
Tootsietoy 0123 Ford "Special Delivery", "Camelback Van"	25	38	50
Tootsietoy 0123 Ford "Wieboldt's" Camelback Van	145	215	285
Tootsietoy 0123 Ford "Lewis's" Camelback Van	135	205	275

TOOTSIETOY No. 801 Mack Stake Truck, 1933. Collection & Photo John Gibson.

TOOTSIETOY No. 802 Mack "Domaco" Oil Trailer (1933). Collection & Photo John Gibson.

	C6	C8	C10
Tootsietoy 0123 Ford "Miller & Rhoads" Camelback Van	145	215	285
Tootsietoy 0123 Ford "McLeans" Camelback Van	145	215	285
Tootsietoy 0123 Ford "Shepards" Camelback Van	145	215	285

TOOTSIETOY 0805. Photo by Bill Kaufman. Courtesy Good Old Days Store.

TOOTSIETOY 0802. Photo by Bill Kaufman. Courtesy Good Old Days Store.

TOOTSIETOY No. 804 Mack "City Fuel Company" Truck, 10 wheel version issued 1933. Collection & Photo John Gibson.

TOOTSIETOY 0192. Courtesy Phillips New York.

TOOTSIE 0806. Courtesy Phillips New York.

TOOTSIETOY No. 804 Mack City Fuel Truck, rarer 4 wheel version made 1936-38. Collection & Photo John Gibson.

TOOTSIETOY NO. 805 Dairy Trailer, 1933. Collection & Photo John Gibson.

TOOTSIETOY unnumbered Graham "Commercial Tire & Supply Co." Van, issued 1935. Collection & Photo John Gibson.

TOOTSIETOY No. 716 Doodlebug, issued 1935 and patterned after Briggs prototype sedan. Collection & Photo John Gibson

	C6	C8	C10
Tootsietoy 180 Lincoln Zephyr & Roamer House Trailer w/o windup motor	435	655	875
Tootsietoy 180 Lincoln Zephyr & Roamer House Trailer w/windup motor	515	775	1035
Tootsietoy 187 Mack Auto Transport w/uptilted trailer & 3 vehicles	275	415	550
Tootsietoy 4634 Army Supply Truck	33	49	65
Tootsietoy 4635 Armored Car	33	49	65
Tootsietoy 1006 "Standard" Oil Truck	55	80	110
Tootsietoy 1007 "Sinclair" Oil Truck	55	80	110
Tootsietoy 1008 "Texaco" Oil Truck	55	80	110
Tootsietoy 1009 "Shell" Oil Truck	60	90	120
Tootsietoy 1010 "Wrigley" Box Van	55	80	110
Tootsietoy 1011 "Massey-Ferguson" Farm Tractor	200	300	400
Tootsietoy 1016 Auburn Roadster, jumbo torpedo-single color	23	34	45
Tootsietoy 1016 Auburn Roadster, jumbo torpedo-two tone	25	38	50
Tootsietoy 1017 Coupe, jumbo torpedo-single color	20	30	40
Tootsietoy 1017 Coupe, jumbo torpedo-two tone	23	34	45

	C6	C8	C10
Tootsietoy 1018 Sedan, jumbo torpedo-single color	20	30	40
Tootsietoy 1019 Pickup Truck, jumbo torpedo-single color	20	30	40
Tootsietoy 1019 Pickup Truck, jumbo torpedo-two tone	23	34	45
Tootsietoy 1026 Cross Country Bus, jumbo torpedo-fully skirted	30	45	60
Tootsietoy 1027 Wrecker, jumbo torpedo-single color	23	34	45
Tootsietoy 1027 Wrecker, jumbo torpedo-two tone	25	38	50
Tootsietoy 1040 Fire Engine, Hook & Ladder	35	50	70
Tootsietoy 1041 Fire Engine, Hose Car	35	55	75
Tootsietoy 1042 Fire Engine, Insurance Patrol, open end	30	45	60
Tootsietoy 1042 Fire Engine, Insurance Partol w/single ladder & rear fireman	38	56	75
Tootsietoy 1043 No. 111 Ford Sedan & small House Trailer	35	53	70

TOOTSIETOY No. 6015 Lincoln Zephyr (1937). This was a revised version of the #716 Doodlebug, and issued with or without a windup motor. Collection & Photo John Gibson.

TOOTSIETOY No. 113 Ford Wrecker (1935). Collection & Photo John Gibson

TOOTSIETOY No. 0123 "Lewis's Light Delivery Truck, store promotional version issued 1937. Frequently called "Camelback Van" by collectors. Collection & Photo John Gibson.

	C6	C8	C10
Tootsietoy 1044 Roamer House Trailer w/door & tin bottom	275	415	550
Tootsietoy 1045 Greyhound Deluxe Bus-open front fenders & tin bottom	55	83	110
Tootsietoy 1045 Greyhound Deluxe Bus-open front fenders	35	50	70
Tootsietoy -- TransAmerica Bus (sold only in sets)	90	130	175
Tootsietoy 1046 Station Wagon	43	64	85
Tootsietoy 230 LaSalle Sedan	15	20	30
Tootsietoy 231 Coupe	15	20	30
Tootsietoy 232 Open Touring Coupe	15	20	30
Tootsietoy 233 Boattail Roadster	15	20	30
Tootsietoy 234 Box Van	15	20	30
Tootsietoy 235 Oil Tank Truck	13	18	25
Tootsietoy 236 Fire Engine, Hook & Ladder	20	30	40
Tootsietoy 237 Fire Engine, Insurance Patrol	15	25	35
Tootsietoy 238 Fire Engine, Hose Wagon	20	30	40
Tootsietoy 239 Station Wagon	20	30	40

	C6	C8	C10
Miniature Vehicles			
Tootsietoy 510 Midget Assortment Boxed Set (8 pc)	75	100	150
Tootsietoy 510 Midget Assortment Boxed Set (10 pc)	90	130	175
Tootsietoy 610 Midget Assortment Boxed Set (12 pc)	100	150	200
Tootsietoy 1628 Bus	6	9	12
Tootsietoy 1629 Wrecker	7	10	14
Tootsietoy 1630 Racer	5	7	10
Tootsietoy 1631 DeSoto Airflow Sedan	5	7	10
Tootsietoy 1632 Zephyr Railcar	7	10	14
Tootsietoy 1634 Firetruck	7	10	14
Tootsietoy 1635 Delivery Van	6	9	12
Tootsietoy 1635 Delivery Van (Ambulance)	7	10	14
Tootsietoy 1666 Army Tank	4	6	8
Tootsietoy 1667 Armored Car	5	7	10
Postwar			
Tootsietoy 1954 American LaFrance Pumper, 3" long	10	15	20
Tootsietoy -- Atomic Cannon/155mm Howitzer, 5-1/4" long	100	150	200
Tootsietoy 1956 Austin Healy 100-6 4 passenger roadster, 6" long	20	30	40
Tootsietoy 1955 Austin Healy 100-6 unassembled kit, 6" long	150	225	300
Tootsietoy 1954 Buick Century Estate Wagon, 6 " long	18	26	35
Tootsietoy 1951 Buick LeSabre Experimental Roadster, 6" long	23	34	45
Tootsietoy 1949 Buick Roadmaster 4 door Sedan, 6" long	25	38	50

TOOTSIETOY Dodge D100 Panel Truck from 1956 and a No.1008 Texaco Oil Truck (1939-41). Courtesy Mapes Auctioneers.

	C6	C8	C10
Tootsietoy 1956 Caterpillar Roadscraper, 6" long	18	26	35
Tootsietoy 1950 Chevrolet Ambulance, 4" long	13	19	25
Tootsietoy 1955 Chevrolet BelAir, 4 door Sedan, 3" long	10	15	20
Tootsietoy 1956 Chevrolet Cameo Pickup, 4" long	13	19	25
Tootsietoy 1947 Chevrolet Coupe, 4" long	13	19	25
Tootsietoy 1950 Chevrolet Deluxe Panel Truck, 4" long	13	19	25
Tootsietoy 1950 Chevrolet Deluxe Panel Truck, 3" long	10	15	20
Tootsietoy 1960 Chevrolet El Camino w/camper/boat, 6" long	50	75	100
Tootsietoy 1960 Chevrolet El Camino, 6" long	18	26	35
Tootsietoy 1950 Chevrolet Fleetline 2 door Fastback Sedan, 3" long	10	15	20

	C6	C8	C10
Tootsietoy 1959 Chevrolet Semi Cab only	63	94	125
w/"Mobile" Trailer *	80	120	160
w/Hook & Ladder *	93	139	185
w/Log Trailer *	75	113	150
w/3 Boat Trailer *	78	116	155
w/3 Car Transport *	78	116	155
w/Army Flatbed *	80	120	160
w/"Dean Van Lines" *	75	113	150
Tootsietoy 1953 Chrysler New Yorker, 4 door Sedan, 6" long	18	26	35
Tootsietoy 1942 Chrysler Thunderbolt Experimental Roadster, 6" long	23	34	45
Tootsieboy 1941 Chrysler Windsor Convertible, 4" long	14	21	28
Tootsietoy 1950 Chrysler Windsor Convertible, 6" long	50	75	100
Tootsietoy 1960 Chrysler Windsor Convertible 4" long	13	19	25

TOOTSIETOY No. 1009 "Shell" Oil Tanker, issued 1938. Collection & Photo John Gibson.

TOOTSIETOY Firetrucks resembling Macks, Left to Right: No. 237 Insurance Patrol, No. 238 Hose Car, No. 236 Hook & Ladder (all issued 1940 and reissued postwar w/black tires). Collection & Photo John Gibson.

TOOTSIETOY No. 1044 Roamer Trailer (1937). Collection & Photo John Gibson.

	C6	C8	C10
w/"Mobile" Trailer *	80	120	160
w/Hook & Ladder *	93	139	185
w/Log Trailer *	75	113	150
w/3 Boat Trailer *	78	116	155
w/3 Car Transport *	78	116	155
w/Army Flatbed *	80	120	160
w/"Dean Van Lines" *	75	113	150
Tootsietoy 1953 Chrysler New Yorker, 4 door Sedan, 6" long	18	26	35
Tootsietoy 1942 Chrysler Thunderbolt Experimental Roadster, 6" long	23	34	45
Tootsieboy 1941 Chrysler Windsor Convertible, 4" long	14	21	28
Tootsietoy 1950 Chrysler Windsor Convertible, 6" long	50	75	100
Tootsietoy 1960 Chrysler Windsor Convertible 4" long	13	19	25
Tootsietoy 1954-55 Corvette Roadster, 4" long	13	19	25
Tootsietoy 1956 Dodge D100 Panel Truck, 6" long	20	30	40
Tootsietoy 1950 Dodge Pickup Truck, 4" long	13	19	25
Tottsietoy 1956 Ferrari Racer, 6" long	28	41	55
Tootsietoy 1931 Ford B Hot Rod, 3"	8	11	15
Tootsietoy 1956 Ford C600 Oil Tanker, 3" long	9	14	18
Tootsietoy 1962 Ford C600 Truck, 6"	18	26	35
Tootsietoy 1959 Ford Country Sedan Station Wagon, 6" long	18	26	35
Tootsietoy 1962 Ford Country Sedan Station Wagon, 6" long	13	19	25

	C6	C8	C10
Tootsietoy 1949 Ford Custom Convertible, 3" long	11	16	22
Tootsietoy 1949 Ford Custom 4 door Sedan, 3" long	11	16	22
Tootsietoy 1955 Ford Customline V8 2 door Sedan, 3" long	11	16	22
Tootsietoy 1962 Ford Econoline Pickup, 6" long	15	23	30
Tootsietoy 1949 Ford F1 Pickup, 3"	8	11	15
Tootsietoy 1949 Ford F6 Oil Tanker, 6" long	30	45	60
Tootsietoy 1949 Ford F6 Oil Tanker, 4" long	10	15	20
Tootsietoy 1949 Ford F6 Stake Truck (Pickup), 4" long	13	19	25
Tootsietoy 1957 Ford F100 Styleside Pickup w/rear window, 3" long	8	11	15
Tootsietoy 1957 Ford F100 Styleside Pickup w/o rear window, 3" long	8	11	15
Tootsietoy 1956 Ford F600 Army Gun Truck, 6" long	18	26	35
Tootsietoy 1955 Ford F600 Stake Truck w/tin cover, 6" long	60	90	120
Tootsietoy 1957 Ford Fairlane 500			

TOOTSIETOY 1948 Buick Super Estate Wagon - open grille (postwar). Collection & Photo John Gibson.

	C6	C8	C10
Convertible, 3" long........................	8	11	15
Tootsietoy 1960 Ford Falcon 2 door			
Sedan, 3" long............................	8	11	15
Tootsietoy 1956 Ford Farm Tractor, 6".....	25	38	50
Tootsietoy 1960 Ford LTD 2 door			
Hardtop, 4" long.........................	13	19	25
Tootsietoy 1952 Ford Mainline			
4 door Sedan, 3" long.....................	8	11	15
Tootsietoy 1954 Ford Ranch Wagon, 4"...	13	19	25
Tootsietoy 1954 Ford Ranch Wagon, 3"...	8	11	15
Tootsietoy 1940 Ford Special Deluxe			
Convertible, 6" long......................	28	41	55
Tootsietoy 1940 Ford V8 Hot Rod, 6"...	18	26	35
Tootsietoy 1948 GMC 3751 Greyhound			
Bus, 6" long................................	23	34	45
Tootsietoy 1957 Greyhound Sceni-			
Cruiser Bus, 6" long.....................	23	34	45
Tootsietoy 1040 Hook & Ladder, 4"......	18	26	35
Tootsietoy 1041 Hose Car, 4" long........	18	26	35
Tootsietoy 1941 International K1 Panel			
Truck, 4" long............................	20	30	40
Tootsietoy 1946 International K11 Oil			
Tanker, 6" long...........................	18	26	35
Tootsietoy 1960 International Metro			
Step Van, 6" long.........................	88	131	175
Totsietoy 1955 International RC180,			
6" long			
w/Rocket Launcher, Army version....	60	90	120
w/Grain Trailer.................................	30	50	65
w/Oil Tanker, no decals.................	30	50	65
w/Moving Van..............................	30	50	65
w/Boat Transport..........................	30	45	60
w/Car Transport............................	30	45	60
w/Gooseneck Trailer......................	25	38	50
Tootsietoy 1957 Jaguar type D, 3"..........	8	11	15
Tootsietoy 1954 Jaguar XK120			
Roadster, 3" long..........................	10	15	20
Tootsietoy 1956 Jaguar XK140 Coupe,			
6" long.....................................	18	26	35
Tootsietoy 1950 Jeep CJ3, Army			
version, 3" long...........................	8	11	15
Tootsietoy 1950 Jeep CJ3, Civilian			
version, 3" long...........................	8	11	15
Tootsietoy 1950 Jeep CJ3, Army			
version, 4" long............................	13	19	25
Tootsietoy 1950 Jeep CJ3, Civilian			
version, 4" long............................	13	19	25
Tootsietoy 1960 Jeep CJ5, Civilian			
version, 6" long............................	18	26	35
Tootsietoy 1960 Jeep CJ5, Army			

	C6	C8	C10
version, 6" long...........................	18	26	35
Tootsietoy 1960 Jeep CJ5, Snowplow			
version, 6" long...........................	38	56	75
Tootsietoy 1947 Jeepster, 3" long...........	9	14	18
Tootsietoy 1947 Kaiser Sedan, 6" long..	20	30	40
Tootsietoy 1956 Lancia Racer, 6" long..	38	56	75
Tootsietoy 1952 Lincoln Capri 2 door			
Hardtop, 6" long..........................	18	26	35
Tootsietoy 1955 Mack B Line Cement			
Mixer, 6" long............................	20	30	40
Tootsietoy 1955 Mack B Line Hook &			
Ladder, 6" long...........................	38	56	75
Tootsietoy 1955 Mack B Line Moving			
Van (w/o doors), 6" long.................	43	64	85
Tootsietoy 1955 Mack B Line Moving			
Van (w/doors), 6" long..................	60	90	120
Tootsietoy 1955 Mack B Line Log			
Trailer, 6" long...........................	43	64	85
Tootsietoy 1955 Mack B Line Oil			
Tanker, 6" long...........................	23	34	45
Tootsietoy 1955 Mack B Line Open			
Stake Truck, 6" long.....................	63	94	125
Tootsietoy 1947 Mack L Line Dump			
Truck, 6" long............................	18	26	35
Tootsietoy 1947 Mack L Line Fire			
Pumper, 6" long..........................	43	64	85
Tootsietoy 1947 Mack L Line Fire			
(ladder) Trailer, 6" long.................	43	64	85
Tootsietoy 1947 Mack L Line Log			
Truck, 6" long............................	43	64	85
Tootsietoy 1947 Mack L Line Moving			
Van, 6" long..............................	25	38	50
Tootsietoy 1947 Mack L Line Closed			
Side Stake, 6" long.......................	20	30	40
Tootsietoy 1947 Mack L Line Stake			
Trailer, 6" long...........................	63	94	125
Tootsietoy 1947 Mack L Line			
"Tootsietoys Coast to Coast", 6"........	43	64	85
Tootsietoy 1947 Mack L Line Tow			
Truck, 6" long............................	20	30	40
Tootsietoy 1956 Mercedes 190SL, 6"....	18	26	35
Tootsietoy 1955 Mercedes 300SL			
Gullwing (doors intact), 9" long........	150	225	300
Tootsietoy 1952 Mercury Custom			
Sedan, 4 door, 4" long..................	13	19	25
Tootsietoy 1949 Mercury Fire Chief			
Car, 4" long..............................	14	21	28
Tootsietoy 1949 Mercury Sedan			
4 door, 4" long...........................	13	19	25

*TOOTSIETOY Jeep CJ3, 3", 1950.
Photo by Ed Poole.*

	C6	C8	C10
Tootsietoy -- Metro Van, HO Series	8	11	15
Tootsietoy 1954 MG TF Roadster, 6"	21	32	42
Tootsietoy 1954 MG TF Roadster, 3"	10	15	20
Tootsietoy 1954 Nash Metropolitan Convertible, 3" long	30	45	60
Tootsietoy 1947 Offenhauser Hill Climber Racer, 3" long	9	13	18
Tootsietoy 1949 Oldsmobile 88 Convertible, 4" long	15	23	30
Tootsietoy 1959 Oldsmobile Dynamic 88 Convertible, 6" long	13	19	25
Tootsietoy 1955 Oldsmobile 98 Holiday 2 door hardtop, 4" long	13	19	25
Tootsietoy 1955 Oldsmobile 98 Holiday 4 door hardtop, Army version, 4"	13	19	25
Tootsietoy 1956 Packard Patrician 4 door Sedan, 6" long	18	26	35
Tootsietoy 1957 Plymouth Belvedere 2 door hardtop, 3" long	8	11	15
Tootsietoy 1950 Plymouth Special Deluxe 4 door Sedan, 3" long	8	11	15
Tootsietoy 1950 Pontiac Chieftan Deluxe Coupe Sedan, 4" long	13	19	25
Tootsietoy 1950 Pontiac Chieftan Fire Chief Coupe Sedan, 4" long	18	26	35
Tootsietoy 1955 Pontiac Safari Station Wagon, (#895), 9" long	100	150	200
Tootsietoy 1959 Pontiac Star Chief 4 door Sedan, 4" long	13	19	25
Tootsietoy 1956 Porsche Spyder Roadster, 6" long	18	26	35
Tootsietoy 1960 Rambler Super Cross Country Station Wagon, 4" long	15	23	30
Tootsietoy -- School Bus, HO series	10	15	20
Tootsietoy 1947 Studebaker Champion 5 window Coupe, 3" long	25	38	50
Tootsietoy 1960 Studebaker Lark Convertible, 3" long	8	11	15

	C6	C8	C10
Tootsietoy 1955 Thunderbird Coupe, 4" long	11	17	22
Tootsietoy 1955 Thunderbird Coupe, 3" long	8	11	15
Tootsietoy 1956 Triumph TR3 Roadster, 3" long	9	14	18
Tootsietoy 1950 Twin Coach Bus, 3"	23	34	45
Tootsietoy 1960 Volkswagen Beetle, 6" long	18	26	35
Tootsietoy 1960 Volkswagen Beetle, 3" long	5	8	10
Tootsietoy 1941 White Army Half Track, 4" long	18	26	35
Tow Truck, cast iron, 6" long	70	105	140
Tow Truck, cast iron, rubber wheels, 7 1/2" long	125	187	250
Trailer Truck "C to C C Co.", circa 1929, approx. 6-3/4" long	45	67	90
Traveleer Land Coach Traveler, Trailer Co., L.A., 1927	180	270	360
Truck, open back, cast iron, wheels marked "Hamilton Corhart", 4-1/4"	35	52	70
Truck, cab w/interchangeable flat bed and tank, sheet metal w/wooden wheels, 10-3/4" long	16	24	32
Turner Bulldog Mack, closed cab dump truck, red and green steel, 23" long	400	600	800
Turner Car Hauler	175	262	350
Turner Dump Truck, friction, circa early 1930s, 15-1/2" long	240	360	480
Turner Dump Truck, C-cab, 22" long	387	580	775
Turner Dump Truck, 26" long	450	675	900
Turner Fire Engine Pumper, 15"long	500	800	1100
Turner Hook and Ladder, circa 1930s, 15" long	170	255	340
Turner Lincoln Sedan, 26" long	3000	5000	7500
Turner "Overland Bus", pressed steel	No Price Found		
Turner Packard Roadster, 1920s, 16-1/2" long	800	1300	1900
Turner Packard (?) Roadster, friction, 26" long	900	1500	2200
Turner Speedster, circa late 1920s, early 1930s, 17" long	500	750	1000
Turner Steam Shovel	105	158	210

TOW TRUCK, cast iron, 6" long. Courtesy Mapes Auctioneers & Appraisers.

	C6	C8	C10
Wannatoy Cadillac, plastic, 9" long	7	11	15
Wannatoy Convertible, 6" long	7	11	14
Wannatoy Delivery Truck, 4" long	3	4	6
Wannatoy Tank Truck, 5" long	7	11	14
Weeden Auto, live steam, early, 8-3/4".	1500	3000	4500
Weeden Steam Fire Pumper	1300	2200	3500
Weeden Steam Road Roller, 1920s, brass, tin, cast iron, steam toy fired by alcohol, 7" long	250	375	500
Weeden Steam Tractor, 9" long	250	375	500

WEEDEN Auto, live steam, early. Courtesy Sotheby's New York.

	C6	C8	C10
Turner Tow Truck	250	375	500
Turner Water Truck w/Copper Tank	150	225	300
"U.S. Army Shooting Tank", wood, pre WWII, metal action, 6" long	22	33	45
U.S.A.W. No.60118 Half-Track, black wooden wheels, die cast, approx.4-3/4".	10	15	20
Vindex Coast to Coast Bus, cast iron, circa 1929, Salesman's sample, 12" long, mint, auctioned 1994 for $18,000			
Vindex Hay Loader, Case, 9" long	2000	3500	5600
Vindex "P&H" power shovel, cast iron, wheels in caterpillar base, handle revolves rig, 12" (17" extended)	2700	4100	8000
Vindex Pickup Truck, cast iron, 7-1/2"	300	450	600
Vindex Racer, cast iron, "2", circa 1920s, 11-1/2" long	1000	1600	2500

VINDEX MOTORCYCLES

list by Kent M. Comstock

	C6	C8	C10
(VM1) Motorcycle w/detachable cop, "Henderson", red or green, 9"	1000	1500	2500
(VM2) Motorcycle w/sidecar, 2 detachable cops, "Henderson", red or green, 9" long	1200	1800	3000
(VM3) Motorcycle w/package truck, "Henderson PDQ Delivery", w/ detachable blue rider, red or green, 9" long	1800	2500	3500

	C6	C8	C10
Wilkins Aerial Ladder Truck, 1910, windup. 18" long	500	750	1000
Wilkins Dray, driver, barrels, tiller	400	600	800
Wilkins Fire Engine, circa 1900 w/driver, steam boiler	462	693	925
Wilkins Hook and Ladder open truck, steel, windup motor, 9-1/4" long	238	360	475
Wilkins, Olds, 1904, curved dash, windup, 10"	400	600	800
Wilkins Truck, open cab, very early, clockwork, 11" long	450	675	900

WILKINS Hook & Ladder open truck, steel, windup motor, 9-3/4" long. Courtesy Phillips New York.

Choicer small cast iron pieces include: Top Row; A.C.Williams 1934 Ford (series included coupe and sedan); A.C.W. 1936 Ford (series includes coupe, sedan, roadster and panel truck and in a simpler single-piece casting only three, omitting the roadster); A.C.W. generic take-apart (series included coupe, sedan and take truck). Bottom row shows Arcade 1933 Nash (coupe and sedan); Arcade 1935 Ford (sedan and stake truck); Dent 1935 LaSalle (sedan, coupe, roadster, pickup truck, wrecker and panel truck). Photo by C.B.C. Lee.

A.C. WILLIAMS

A.C. Williams was founded in 1886 when Adam Clark Williams (1/22/1848-6/15/32) bought the J.W. Williams Company from his father. After a fire the firm was moved in 1893 from Chagrin Falls, Ohio to Ravenna. Toy production began about this time. Small cast iron toys were Williams' specialty, with banks, cars and aircraft predominant. A.C. Williams retired in 1919, but the firm continued to make toys until 1938, after which it continued in business in a non-toys capacity. Williams marked few, if any, of its toys. Two clues to an A.C. Williams toy are turned steel hubs and starred axle peens.

	C6	C8	C10
Williams "C to C Co." Stake Truck, 2 pcs, 7" long	242	363	485
Williams Car Carrier, w/3 Austins, 1920, 12-1/2" long	500	750	1000
Williams "Coast to Coast Cartage Co.", 8-1/2" long	150	225	300
Williams Coupe, 2-piece body, 1936, 3" long	90	135	180
Williams Coupe, rumble seat, side mounts, 1930, cast iron, rubber tires, 6-3/4" long	167	250	35
Williams Delivery Van, 8" long	350	525	700
Williams Dump Truck, 6-1/4" long	195	292	390
Williams 4-casting nickeled radiator car, approx. 4" long	75	112	150
Williams Laundry Truck, 8" long	400	600	800
Williams Lincoln Touring Car, 7" long	217	325	435
Williams Mack Gas Tank Truck, 3-3/4" long	115	172	230
Williams Mack Gas Tank Truck, 5-1/8" long	95	140	190
Williams Mack Gas Tank Truck, 7-1/4" long	345	517	690
Williams Mack Stake Truck, 3-1/2"	45	68	90
Williams Mack Stake Truck, 4-1/4"	80	120	160

	C6	C8	C10
Williams Mack Stake Truck, 5-1/8"	112	170	225
Williams Mack Stake Truck, 7" long	150	225	300
Williams Mack Stake Truck, 8-1/2"	200	300	400
Williams Mack Truck, 3-1/2" long	45	68	90
Williams Mack Truck, 4-3/4" long	95	140	190
Williams Mack Truck, 6-3/4" long	100	150	200
Williams Model T Coupe, 6" long	180	270	360
Williams "Moving & Storage Truck, 3-1/2" long	112	168	225
Williams Racer, boattailed, 6-1/2" long	225	338	450
Williams Sedan, 5" long	112	168	225
Williams Sedan, circa 1930, cast iron, streamlined rear fender, 6-1/2" long	250	375	500
Williams Sedan, circa 1931, cast iron, interchangeable body, 6-3/4" long	350	525	700
Williams Steam Roller, 1930s, 5-1/2"	55	82	110
Williams Studebaker, circa 1933-34, 2-tone sedan, approx. 4" long	110	165	220
Williams Tank, 4" long	67	101	135
Williams Taxi, 5-3/4" long	115	172	330
Williams Touring Car, cast iron, 9-1/2" long	475	712	950
Williams Touring Car w/driver, 5"	100	150	200

WILLIAMS Sedan, 6-1/2" long. Courtesy Philips New York.

	C6	C8	C10
Williams Wrecker, 6-1/2" long...............250		375	500
Willys Knight, cast iron, 1920s, w/driver, 8" long...............120		180	240
Wolverine Car & Trailer, press down to operate, 27" long...............235		352	470
Wolverine "Mystery Car", press down to make car move, circa 1938...............130		195	260
Wolverine Speeding Bus "5 Via Main St.", tin litho, driver and occupants, "19302", press down on rear to move, 14" long...............85		128	170
Wolverine Taxi, tin, 13" long...............82		123	165
Wolverine "White Mustang" dump truck, 14" long...............60		90	120
Wood Commodities Corp, Army Jeep and Cannon, 23" long...............62		93	125

WYANDOTTE LaSalle Sedan w/trailer. Photo by Calvin L. Chaussee.

WYANDOTTE
(ALL METAL PRODUCTS COMPANY)

Wyandotte seems to have been formed in the early 1920s, with pistols and rifles its main product. But by 1935 the Wyandotte, Michigan firm became best known for its simply built, streamlined, art deco steel cars and trucks, almost all of them employing wooden wheels. During WWII it made clips for the M-1 rifle, and after the war moved to Piqua, Ohio. In an attempt to diversify, it bought the Hafner trains line, but went out of business in 1956. Wyandotte's heavy gauge steel toys with baked enamel finish also included aircraft, doll buggies, musical toys, wagons and games.

	C6	C8	C10
Wyandotte Ambulance, swinging rear door, No. 340, 11-1/4" long...............75		112	150
Wyandotte Army Truck, steel w/wood wheels, 10" long...............75		112	150
Wyandotte Army Truck, 22" long...............100		150	200
Wyandotte Auto Transport, circa 1950s...............70		105	140

	C6	C8	C10
Wyandotte Bank Truck, 6-1/2" long.......37		56	75
Wyandotte Boattail Racer, steel, red w/white rubber tires, electric headlamps, 8-1/2" long...............62		93	125
Wyandotte Car Carrier, early 1930s.......125		188	250
Wyandotte Car Carrier, late, 22" long....150		225	300
Wyandotte Circus Truck, 10-3/4" long...250		375	500

WYANDOTTE Circus Truck, 10-3/4".

	C6	C8	C10
Wyandotte Circus Truck, No. 503 11" long...............250		375	500
Wyandotte Circus Truck w/Trailer, 19" long...............550		850	1300
Wyandotte City Delivery Truck, circa 1940...............225		338	450
Wyandotte Coffin Nose Cord, pressed steel, rubber tires, 13" long...............287		430	575
Wyandotte Coffin Nose Cord, Fire Dept. version, red...............365		548	730
Wyandotte Convertible (open) Roadster, 1930s, 10" long...............112		166	225
Wyandotte Coupe, 2 door, about 1930, 6" long...............45		68	90
Wyandotte Coupe, circa 1940, 6" long...............50		75	100
Wyandotte Coupe, circa 1930s, 7-1/2"...107		160	215
Wyandotte Coupe w/rumble seat, early 1930s, 8" long...............100		150	200
Wyandotte Coupe, circa 1935, red w/white rubber tires, electric headlight, 8-1/2" long...............100		150	200
Wyandotte Dairy Truck, 1930s, 12".......95		142	190
Wyandotte "Deluxe Delivery" Truck, circa 1936, 11" long...............50		75	100
Wyandotte Dump Truck No. 122...........45		68	90
Wyandotte Dump Truck No. 124...........50		75	100

WYANDOTTE Oil Tanker, 1930s. Photo by Calvin L. Chaussee.

WYANDOTTE Side Dump, 1930s, 20" long. Photo by Calvin L. Chaussee.

	C6	C8	C10
Wyandotte Dump Truck No. 326, 1931	112	168	225
Wyandotte Dump Truck, 1930s, 6"	150	225	300
Wyandotte Dump Truck, pressed steel, circa 1940, approx. 6-1/2" long	75	112	150
Wyandotte Dump Truck, steel, circa 1937, 7" long	40	60	80
Wyandotte Dump Truck, 12" long	37	56	75
Wyandotte Dump Truck, circa mid-1930s, white rubber tires, 15" long	67	100	135
Wyandotte Dump Truck, 1930s, 12-1/2"	57	85	115
Wyandotte Dump w/Sand Loader, circa 1941	300	450	600
Wyandotte Dump w/Scoop, post war	60	90	120
Wyandotte "Express" Trailer Truck, tin wheels	130	195	260
Wyandotte Fire Truck w/ladder, ringing bell, 1939, 12" long	120	180	240
Wyandotte "Grey Van", late, 24" long	155	232	310
Wyandotte Hydraulic Dump Truck, rear and side tip, 20" long	90	135	180
Wyandotte Ice Truck, marked "ICE" in sides, circa 1940, No. 348	250	375	500
Wyandotte LaSalle Sedan, 1930s	270	405	540
Wyandotte LaSalle Sedan w/trailer, 1930s, 25-1/2" long	440	660	880
Wyandotte "Medical Corps" open truck, circa 1939, 12" long	100	150	200

	C6	C8	C10
Wyandotte Motor Express Trailer Truck, circa 1950s	67	100	135
Wyandotte "Official AAA Service Car" 1930s, 12" long	150	225	300
Wyandotte Oil Tanker, 1930s	105	158	210
Wyandotte Pickup Truck, circa late 1930s, 6" long	30	45	60
Wyandotte "Pickway Pastures" Livestock Truck	45	68	90
Wyandotte Race Car, pressed steel, rubber tires, circa 1937, 8-1/2" long	122	183	245
Wyandotte Railway Express Truck, circa 1939, 12" long	165	247	330
Wyandotte School Bus, 1930s, 24"	100	150	200
Wyandotte Sedan, circa 1940, 4" long	35	52	70
Wyandotte Sedan, circa 1940, 6" long	55	82	110
Wyandotte Semi, Grey Lines, cast wheels	120	180	240
Wyandotte Semi-Trailer Stake Truck "Valley Farms Livestock Produce", 2-piece, 1940s, 8-1/2" long	52	78	105
Wyandotte Side Dump, 1930s, 20"	90	135	180
Wyandotte Stake Truck, rubber wheels, 5-1/2" long	55	82	110

WYANDOTTE Woody Convertible, top goes up and down. Photo by Calvin L. Chaussee.

WYANDOTTE Stake Truck, 10" long, battery-operated headlights. Courtesy Mapes Auctioneers & Appraisers.

	C6	C8	C10
Wyandotte Stake Truck about 1930, 6-3/4" long	60	90	120
Wyandotte Stake Truck 1930s, white rubber wheels, 7-1/2" long	37	56	75
Wyandotte Stake Truck, 1931, No. 325, 9-3/4" long	134	200	268
Wyandotte Stake Truck, battery-operated headlights, 10" long	150	225	300
Wyandotte Stake Truck, circa 1930s, 12" long	100	150	200
Wyandotte Stake Truck, 1930s, 15"	65	98	130
Wyandotte Stake Truck, 20" long	142	213	285
Wyandotte Station Wagon, Cadillac, 1941, Woody model, No. 1007, metal, 21" long	170	255	340
Wyandotte Steam Shovel, 16" long	65	98	130
Wyandotte Sunshine Dairy Truck, 12"	60	90	120
Wyandotte Tow Truck, late	100	150	200
Wyandotte Town & Country Chrysler Convertible, 1940s, 12" long	112	168	225
Wyandotte "Toytown Delivery", 1941, 21" long	150	225	300
Wyandotte "Toytown Estate" Station Wagon	125	188	250

	C6	C8	C10
Wyandotte "Toytown Ice Co.", circa 1941	60	90	120
Wyandotte Trailer Truck, plastic cab	65	98	130
Wyandotte Trailer Truck, 1950, extruded aluminum trailer	100	150	200
Wyandotte "Valley Farms", 8 1/2"	52	78	105
Wyandotte Woody Convertible, top converts, 12" long	162	243	325
Wyandotte Wrecker, 1930s, wooden wheels, 10" long	75	112	150
Wyandotte "Wyandotte Truck Lines" Stake Van	130	195	260
Wyandotte "Wyandottey", pressed steel, 2 door sedan, sweeping long fenders, circa WWII black plastic wheels	30	45	60

WYANDOTTE "Wyandotte Truck Lines" Stake Van. Photo by Calvin L. Chaussee.

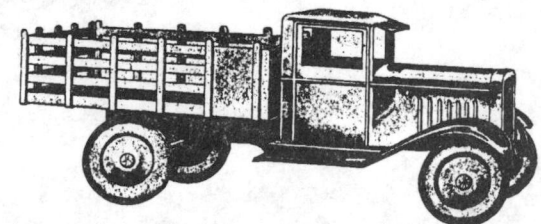

A Wyandotte ad from December, 1931, in Toys and Novelties Magazine.

MATCHBOX

by Mark McManus

(The average mint price of these toys was $20.13 in the last edition, rising to $29.93 in this, an increase of 49%.)

Matchbox Toys grew out of a company begun in 1947 by two former unrelated Navy friends, Leslie Smith and Rodney Smith. Manufacturing toys was not even planned at this point. On June 19, 1947, the two partners combined portions of their first names, and the name Lesney was born. In 1948, Lesney Products produced their first toy, a 4 1/2-inch Aveling Barford Road Roller. Encouraged by the brisk sales, three other toys were produced that year: a 4 1/2-inch Caterpillar Bulldozer, a 3 1/8-inch Caterpillar Tractor, and a 3 3/4-inch Cement Mixer. Value on these rare early Lesney toys today ranges up to $1000. It was decided to package the toys in a matchbox type box, and thereafter the toys would be known as "Matchbox". These small vehicles quickly became very popular, and all other toy lines were discontinued. These first small vehicles had metal wheels, but these were quickly changed to plastic. These type wheels are now know to collectors as "Regular" wheels, not to be confused with the "Superfast" wheels that were introduced in 1969. It is not uncommon to find slight color and style variations for the same vehicle. These variations were often due to paint or part shortages, and these variations are now highly sought after by collectors. 1956 saw the introduction of the "Models of Yesteryear" line. The king-size line was first developed and marketed

Mark B. McManus lives in Boonville, NY with his wife Suzanne and son Turner. Mark and Suzanne own and operate an AmeriSpec Home Inspection Service franchise in Northern New York. Mark is an avid miniature vehicle collector specializing in Matchbox vehicles. He currently owns several hundred Matchbox vehicles. He also owns numerous Tonka vehicles, several GI Joes and their accessories; as well as many miscellaneous items.

in 1957 and was known as Major Packs. Matchbox toys were first marketed in the United Sates in 1958, and by the early 1960's had become a household standard. 1993 marked the 40th anniversary of Matchbox toys, and these small vehicles are rapidly gaining popularity and value among collectors. Listed in the following pages are all of the basic models and some important variations. The C10 prices are for <u>unboxed</u> Matchbox.

	C6	C8	C10
No. 2 Hot Rod Jeep, 1971	5	7	10
No. 2 Hovercraft, 1976	5	7	10
No. 3 Cement Mixer, 1953	20	30	40
No. 3 Bedford Ton Tipper, 1961	6	10	14
No. 3 Mercedes Benz Ambulance, 1968	5	9	13
No. 3 Monteverdi Hai, 1973	5	7	9
No. 3 Porsche Turbo, 1978	4	7	10
No. 4 Tractor, 1954	28	40	54

Different versions of MATCHBOX boxes. Courtesy Gary Linden .

	C6	C8	C10
No. 1 Diesel Road Roller, 1953	15	27	35
No. 1 Aveling Barford Road Roller, 1964	15	21	30
No. 1 Mercedes Benz Lorry, 1968	5	8	12
No. 1 Mod Rod, 1971	7	10	15
No. 1 Dodge Challenger, 1976	4	6	8
No. 2 Dumper, 1953	20	34	40
No. 2 Muir-Hill Dumper, 1962	8	12	20
No. 2. Mercedes Trailer, 1968	4	6	10

MATCHBOX No.7 Horse-drawn Milk Cart. Courtesy Gary Linden.

MATCHBOX No. 12 Land Rover. Courtesy Gary Linden.

MATCHBOX No. 14 Bedford Lomas Ambulance. Courtesy Gary Linden.

	C 6	C8	C10
No. 4 Triumph Motorcycle & sidecar 1959	18	30	42
No. 4 Stake Truck, 1967	4	6	10
No. 4 Gruesome Twosome, 1971	3	5	8
No. 4 Pontiac Firebird, 1976	3	5	8
No. 4 '57 Chevy, 1981	3	5	8
No. 5 London Bus, 1954	20	30	40
No. 5 Lotus Europa Sports Car, 1969	10	18	25
No. 5 Seafire, 1976	3	5	8
No. 5 U.S. Mail Truck, 1981	4	6	10
No. 6 Quarry Truck, 1955	15	20	30
No. 6 Euclid 10 Wheel Quarry,1964	15	22	30
No. 6 Ford Pickup, 1969	8	12	18
No. 6 Mercedes Tourer, 1974	5	7	10
No. 7 Horse Drawn Milk Cart, 1955	40	60	80

	C6	C8	C10
No. 7 Ford Anglia, 1961	12	20	28
No. 7 Ford Refuse Truck,1967	6	8	12
No. 7 Hairy Hustler, 1971	5	7	10
No. 7 VW Golf, 1976	4	6	9
No. 8 Caterpillar Tractor, 1955	22	35	50
No. 8 Ford Mustang Fastback, 1966	7	10	15
No. 8 Wildcat Dragster, 1971	7	10	13
No. 8 De Tomaso Pantera, 1975	15	20	35
No. 9 Dennis Fire Engine, 1955	30	45	60
No. 9 Merryweather Marquis Fire Engine, 1959	12	18	24
No. 9 Boat & Trailer, 1967	5	7	9
No. 9 Javelin, 1972	5	7	9

MATCHBOX "Home Stores" building 3"long. Courtesy Gary Linden.

MATCHBOX No. 9 Merryweather Marquis Fire Truck. Courtesy Gary Linden.

	C6	C8	C10
No. 9 Ford Escort RS2000, 1978.............	3	5	7
No. 10 Mechanical Horse & Trailer, 1955.............	30	45	60
No. 10 Sugar Container Truck, 1961......	25	37	50
No. 10 Pipe Truck, 1967.........................	10	15	20
No. 10 Piston Popper, 1973....................	5	8	12
No. 10 Plymouth "Gran Fury" Police Car, 1980.............	3	4	5
No. 11 Petrol Tanker (Esso decal), 1955..	20	30	40
No. 11 Petrol Tanker, green body, no number on bottom.............................	125	175	275
No. 11 Jumbo Crane (Taylor), 1964.......	6	10	15
No. 11 Scaffolding Truck (Mercedes),1969	5	8	12
No. 11 Flying Bug, 1972...........................	5	8	11
No. 11 Car Transporter, 1977.................	5	8	10
No. 12 Land Rover, 1953......................	15	20	30
No. 12 Safari Land Rover, 1965.............	10	15	25
No. 12 Setra Coach, 1971.......................	8	12	15
No. 12 Big Bull, 1975.............................	5	8	10
No. 12 Citroen CX, 1981.......................	5	7	12
No. 13 Bedford Wreck Truck, 1955.......	20	35	50
No. 13 Thames Wreck Truck (MB Garages), 1959....................................	20	30	40
No. 13 Dodge Wreck Truck (BP Label), 1961, yellow cab, green body.............	15	20	25
No. 13 Dodge Wreck Truck, green cab, yellow body (rare).............................	275	450	600
No. 13 Baja Buggy, 1971........................	4	6	9
No. 13 Snorkel Fire Engine, 1977...........	4	5	6
No. 14 Daimler Ambulance, 1955...........	15	22	35
No. 14 Bedford Lomas Ambulance,........	20	30	40
No. 14 Iso Grifo Sports Car, 1968...........	5	8	12
No. 14 Mini Ha Ha, 1975.......................	6	9	12
No. 15 Prime Mover, 1955.......................	25	35	45
No. 15 Dennis Refuse Truck, 1963.........	12	18	24
No. 15 Volkswagen 1500 Saloon,1968..	8	15	22
No. 15 Fork Lift Truck, 1972.................	5	7	9
No. 16 Low-Loading Trailer, 6 wheels, 1955....................................	16	23	30
No. 16 Low-Loading Trailer, 8 wheels, 1955....................................	16	23	30
No. 16 Scammel Mountaineer Dump w/plow, 1961....................................	10	15	20
No. 16 Case Tractor Bulldozer, 1969.....	5	10	15
No. 16 Badger, 1974.............................	5	8	12
No. 16 Pontiac, 1981.........................	2	4	6
No. 17 Bedford Removal Van, 1955......	30	55	80
No. 17 Austin Taxi, 1960........................	25	40	55
No. 17 8 Wheel Tipper "Hoveringham", 1964....................................	7	12	15

MATCHBOX No. 19 MGA Sports Car. Courtesy Gary Linden.

	C6	C8	C10
No. 17 Horse Box "Ergomatic Cab", 1969.....................................	5	8	11
No. 17 Londoner, 1973...........................	8	12	16
No. 18 Caterpillar Bulldozer, 1955.........	15	23	30
No. 18 Field Car, 1969..............................	6	9	12
No. 18 Field Car, green plastic tires (rare).....................................	50	125	150
No. 18 Hondarora, 1975...........................	5	9	14
No. 19 MG Midget Sports Car, 1955.....	23	34	42
No. 19 MGA Sports Car, 1959.................	25	40	60
No. 19 Aston-Martin F.I., 1961.........	20	30	40
No. 19 Lotus Racing Car, 1965.............	5	7	9
No. 19 Road Dragster, 1971...................	4	6	8
No. 19 Cement Truck, 1976..................	5	7	9

MATCHBOX No. 25 Bedford "Dunlop" Van. Courtesy Gary Linden.

	C6	C8	C10
No. 20 E.R.F. Lorry Truck, 1955	25	40	55
No. 20 Taxi Cab (Chevrolet Impala), 1965	13	22	30
No. 20 Lamborghini Marzel, 1969	7	10	13
No. 20 Police Patrol, 1975	4	6	8
No. 21 Long Distance Coach "London to Glasgow", 1955	20	33	45
No. 21 Commer Milk Truck, 1961	20	32	44
No. 21 Foden Concrete Truck, 1969	6	10	15
No. 21 Road Roller, 1973	6	8	12
No. 22 Vauxhall Cresta, 1955	25	30	40
No. 22 Pontiac "Grand Prix" Sports Coupe, 1964	8	12	16
No. 22 Freeman Inter City Commuter, 1970	5	8	12
No. 22 Blaze Buster, 1975	4	6	8
No. 23 Caravan Trailer, 1956	4	7	10
No. 23 House Trailer Caravan, 1967	12	21	29
No. 23 Volkswagen Camper, 1970	5	7	10
No. 23 Atlas, 1975	5	7	11
No. 24 Excavator, 1956	14	20	27
No. 24 Rolls Royce Silver Shadow, 1967	7	8	12
No. 24 Team "Matchbox", 1973	8	12	17
No. 24 Diesel Shunter, 1979	3	5	7
No. 25 Bedford "Dunlop" Van, 1956	25	40	55
No. 25 Volkswagen 1200 Sedan, 1958	25	40	54
No. 25 B.P. Tanker, 1960	16	24	35
No. 25 Ford Cortina G.T., 1968	4	6	8
No. 25 Mod Tractor, 1972	9	12	17
No. 25 Flat Car & Container, 1979	3	5	7
No. 26 Ready Mix Concrete Truck, 1956	15	22	30
No. 26 GMC Tipper Truck, 1968	6	8	10
No. 26 Big Banger, 1972	4	6	8
No. 26 Site Dumper, 1976	3	5	7
No. 27 Bedford Low-Loader, 1956	25	35	50
No. 27 Bedford Low-Loader, metal wheels (rare)	150	225	300
No. 27 Cadillac Sedan, 1960	35	50	70
No. 27 Mercedes Benz, 230SL, 1965	5	7	10
No. 27 Lamborghini Countach, 1974	5	7	9
No. 28 Bedford Compressor Truck, 1956	20	30	40
No. 28 Thames Compressor Truck, 1959	15	20	25
No. 28 Mark Ten Jaguar, 1964	30	45	60
No. 28 Mack Dump Truck, 1968	6	9	13
No. 28 Stoat, 1974	7	12	17
No. 28 Lincoln Continental, 1980	8	12	15
No. 29 Bedford Milk Delivery Van, 1956	15	23	30
No. 29 Austin A55 Cambridge, 1961	15	25	33

MATCHBOX No. 28 Bedford Compressor Truck. Courtesy Gary Linden.

	C6	C8	C10
No. 29 Fire Pumper Truck, 1965	8	10	14
No. 29 Racing Mini, 1971	4	6	8
No. 29 Shovel Nose Tractor, 1976	5	8	11
No. 30 Ford Prefect w/towbar, 1956	25	38	50
No. 30 German Crane Truck, 1961	20	30	40
No. 30 Favin Crane, 8 wheel, 1965	10	15	20
No. 30 Beach Buggy, 1971	4	6	8
No. 30 Swamp Rat, 1977	4	6	8
No. 30 Articulated Truck, 1981	4	6	8
No. 31 Ford Customline Station Wagon, 1956	22	34	45
No. 31 Ford Fairlane Station Wagon, 1959	20	35	50
No. 31 Lincoln Continental, 1964	7	11	15
No. 31 Volks Dragon, 1971	5	7	9

MATCHBOX No. 36 Lambretta Motorcycle w/sidecar. Courtesy Gary Linden.

MATCHBOX No. 37 Coca-Cola Truck. Courtesy Gary Linden.

	C6	C8	C10
No. 31 Caravan, 1977	4	6	8
No. 32 Jaguar XK 140 Coupe, 1956	25	35	45
No. 32 Leyland Tanker, 1968	15	22	31
No. 32 Excavator, 1981	10	18	24
No. 33 Ford Zodiac MKII, 1956	20	33	45
No. 33 Ford Zephyr 6 MKIII, 1963	17	25	35
No. 33 Lamborghini Muira P400, 1969	9	14	20
No. 33 Datsun 126X, 1973	5	8	11
No. 33 Police Motorcyclist, 1977	4	6	8
No. 34 Volkswagen Microvan "Matchbox" Express, 1956	26	38	50
No. 34 Volkswagen Camper, 1961	13	19	25
No. 34 Formula 1 Racing Car, 1971	7	10	13
No. 34 Vantastic, 1976	4	7	11
No. 34 Chevy Pro Stocker, 1981	2	4	6
No. 35 Marschall Horse Box, 1956	35	60	75
No. 35 Sno-Trac Tractor, 1961	12	18	26

	C6	C8	C10
No. 35 Merryweather Marquis Fire Engine, 1970	5	9	13
No. 35 Fandango, 1975	5	7	9
No. 36 Austin A50 w/towbar, 1956	15	25	34
No. 36 Lambretta & Sidecar, 1960	33	49	65
No. 36 Opel Diplomant, 1966	8	12	17
No. 36 Hot Rod Draguar, 1971	5	8	17
No. 36 Formula 5000, 1975	4	6	8
No. 36 Refuse Truck, 1981	3	5	8
No. 37 Coca-Cola Truck, 1956	34	47	63
No. 37 Cattle Truck (Dodge), 1967	6	8	10
No. 37 Soopa Coopa, 1973	5	7	10
No. 37 Skip Truck, 1976	4	6	8
No. 38 Darrier Refuse Collector	18	26	34
No. 38 Vauxhall Estate, 1963	10	18	24
No. 38 Honda Motorcycle w/Trailer, 1968	10	14	20
No. 38 Stingeroo, 1973	6	8	10
No. 38 Armored Jeep, 1976	5	9	13
No. 38 Camper, 1981	3	5	7
No. 39 Ford Zodiac Convertible, 1956	24	36	48
No. 39 Pontiac Convertible, 1962	32	47	61
No. 39 Ford Tractor, 1967	5	9	14
No. 39 Clipper, 1973	6	8	11
No. 39 Rolls-Royce Silver Shadow MKII	4	6	8
No. 40 Bedford 7-Ton Tipper, 1956	20	29	41
No. 40 Hay Trailer, 1967	4	7	10
No. 40 Leyland "Royal Tiger" Coach/Long Distance, 1961	10	16	22
No. 40 Guildsman, 1971	5	8	11
No. 40 Horse Box, 1977	4	6	8
No. 41 "D" Type Jaguar Racing Car, 1956	75	110	145
No. 41 Ford G.T. 40 (Sports Racer), 1965	13	19	27

MATCHBOX No. 38 Darrier Refuse Collector. Courtesy Gary Linden.

MATCHBOX No. 46 Morris Minor 1000. Courtesy Gary Linden.

	C6	C8	C10
No. 41 Siva Spyder, 1972	6	9	12
No. 41 Ambulance, 1978	4	6	8
No. 42 Bedford "Evening News" Van, 1956	25	37	49
No. 42 Studebaker Lark Wagonaire, 1965	11	17	23
No. 42 Iron Fairy Crane, 1969	7	11	16
No. 42 Iron Fairy Crane, 1970 (spoke wheels)	25	35	45
No. 42 Tyre Fryer, 1972	4	7	10
No. 42 Container Truck, 1977	4	6	8
No. 43 Hillman Minx, 1957	25	40	55
No. 43 Aveling-Barford Shovel, 1962	10	17	24
No. 43 Pony Trailer, 1968	8	12	16
No. 43 Dragon Wheels, 1972	5	7	9
No. 43 Steam Loco, 1978	4	6	8
No. 44 Rolls-Royce Silver Cloud, 1957	16	22	31
No. 44 Refrigerator Truck, GMC, 1967	7	11	15
No. 44 Boss Mustang, 1972	3	5	7
No. 44 Passenger Coach, 1978	3	5	7
No. 45 Vauxhall Victor, 1957	12	20	28
No. 45 Ford Corsair w/green boat, 1959	9	13	17
No. 45 Ford Group Six, 1970	6	8	10
No. 45 BMW, 1976	5	8	11
No. 46 Morris Minor 1000, 1957	25	42	56
No. 46 Pickfords Removal Van, 1960	15	27	39
No. 46 Mercedes-Benz 300SE, 1968	6	10	14
No. 46 Stretcha Fetcha, 1972	5	9	13
No. 46 Ford Tractor, 1978	5	7	9
No. 47 Trojan "Brooke Bond" Van, 1957	26	40	52

MATCHBOX No. 49 Army Half Track MKIII. Courtesy Gary Linden.

	C6	C8	C10
No. 47 Beach Hopper, 1973	5	7	9
No. 47 Pannier Loco, 1980	3	5	7
No. 48 Sports Boat & Trailer, 1957	23	34	46
No. 48 Dodge Dumper Truck, 1967	9	14	19
No. 48 Pi-Eyed Piper, 1973	4	6	8
No. 48 Sambron Jack Lift, 1977	4	6	8
No. 49 Army Half Track MKIII, 1958	16	26	35
No. 49 Mercedes Unimog Truck, 1967	10	16	21
No. 49 Chop Suey, 1973	5	7	9
No. 49 Crane Truck, 1976	3	5	7
No. 50 Commer Pickup Truck, 1958	22	31	41
No. 50 John Deere-Lanz Tractor, 1963	13	20	29
No. 50 Ford Kennel Truck, 1969	9	14	18
No. 50 Articulated Truck, 1973	6	10	14

MATCHBOX No. 47 Trojan "Brooke Bond Tea" Van. Courtesy Gary Linden.

	C6	C8	C10
No. 47 Neilson Ice Cream Van, 1963	25	50	75
No. 47 Daf Tipper Container Truck, 1968	8	12	16

MATCHBOX No. 54 Army Saracen Personnel Carrier.

MATCHBOX No. 55 Ford Police Car.

	C6	C8	C10
No. 50 Harley Davidson Motorcycle, 1981	2	3	5
No. 51 Albion Truck "Portland Cement", 1958	14	20	28
No. 51 Tipping Farm Trailer, 1963	7	9	11
No. 51 8 Wheel Tipper Truck, 1969	6	9	12
No. 51 Citroen SM, 1972	5	7	9
No. 51 Combine Harvester, 1979	4	6	8
No. 52 Maserati 4 CLT, 1958	29	38	52
No. 52 BRM Racing Car, 1965	8	12	16
No. 52 Dodge Charger MKIII, 1970	4	7	10
No. 52 Police Launch, 1976	2	4	6
No. 53 Aston-Martin DB2/4, 1959	16	22	30
No. 53 Mercedes-Benz 220SE, 1968	15	22	31
No. 53 Ford Zodiac MKIV, 1968	9	12	16
No. 53 Tanzara, 1972	3	6	9
No. 53 C.J. 6 Jeep, 1977	4	6	8
No. 54 Army Saracen Personnel Carrier, 1959	12	17	25
No. 54 Cadillac Ambulance, 1965	15	23	30

MATCHBOX No. 56 Fiat 1500.

MATCHBOX No. 59 Ford "Singer" Van. Courtesy Gary Linden.

	C6	C8	C10
No. 54 Ford Capri, 1971	4	6	8
No. 54 Personnel Carrier, 1976	5	7	9
No. 54 Mobile Home, 1981	3	5	7
No. 55 D.U.K.W. (Army Amphibian), 1959	21	29	40
No. 55 Ford Police Car, 1963	50	73	100
No. 55 Mercury Parkland Police Car, 1969	12	18	24
No. 55 Mercury Police Car (Station Wagon), 1970	5	9	13
No. 55 Hell Raiser, 1975	3	5	7
No. 55 Ford Cortina, 1980	5	9	11
No. 56 London Trolley Bus, 1959	30	45	65
No. 56 Fiat 1500, 1965	8	11	15
No. 56 BMC 1800 Pininfarina, 1970	6	9	12
No. 56 Hi Trailer, 1975	4	6	8
No. 56 Mercedes 450SEL, 1980	4	6	8
No. 57 Wolseley 1500, 1959	17	24	31
No. 57 Chevrolet Impala, 1966	20	28	36
No. 57 Eccles Caravan, 1970	5	8	13
No. 57 Wild Life Truck, 1973	6	8	10
No. 58 British European Airways Coach, 1959	14	20	28
No. 58 Drott Excavator, 1963	23	35	47
No. 58 Daf Grider Truck, 1968	8	11	14
No. 58 Woosh-N-Push, 1972	6	9	12
No. 58 Faun Dumper, 1976	5	9	14
No. 59 Ford "Singer", Van, 1959	40	55	75
No. 59 Ford Fairlane Fire Car, 1964	25	40	65
No. 59 Fire Chief Car, 1966	70	95	130
No. 59 Planet Scout, 1975	12	17	24
No. 59 Porsche 928, 1981	5	7	9

MATCHBOX No. 60 Morris Omnitruck J-2 Pick-up. Courtesy Gary Linden.

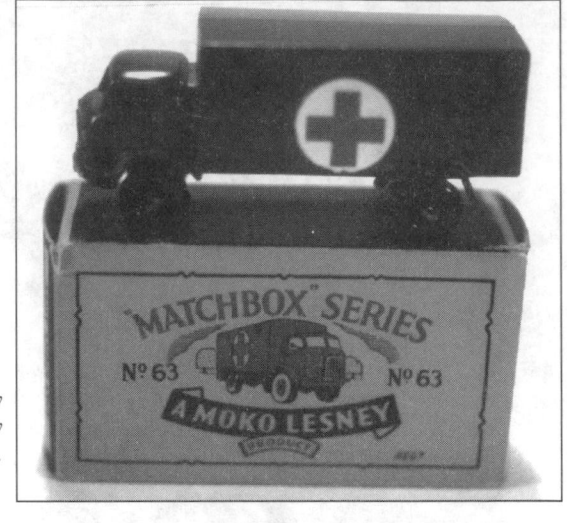

MATCHBOX No. 63 Army Ambulance. Courtesy Gary Linden.

MATCHBOX Garage, 3" long, metal, with early tow truck. Courtesy Gary Linden.

MATCHBOX No. 64 Scammell Army Wreck Truck. Courtesy Gary Linden.

MATCHBOX No. 68 Army Austin MK II Radio Truck. Courtesy Gary Linden.

MATCHBOX No. 69 Commer 30 CWT. Van "Nestle's". Courtesy Gary Linden.

	C6	C8	C10
No. 60 Morris Omnitruck J2 Pickup	15	24	32
No. 60 Truck w/Site Office, 1967	7	10	13
No. 60 Lotus Super Seven, 1971	6	8	10
No. 60 Holden Pickup, 1977	8	11	14
No. 61 Military Scout Car (Ferret), 1959	14	21	29
No. 61 Alvis Stalwart, 1967	18	27	40
No. 61 Blue Shark, 1971	4	6	8
No. 61 Wreck Truck, 1978	3	5	7
No. 62 General Army Lorry,1959	15	20	25
No. 62 TV Service Van, 1964	20	30	40
No. 62 Mercury Cougar, 1969	7	9	12
No. 62 Rat Rod Dragster, 1971	4	6	10
No. 62 Renault 17 TL, 1974	5	7	9
No. 62 Chevrolet Corvette, 1980	2	4	6
No. 63 Army Ambulance, 1959	23	34	44
No. 63 Airport Fire Fighting Crash Tender, 1964	15	21	29
No. 63 Dodge Crane Truck, 1968	9	13	18
No. 63 Freeway Gas Tanker, 1973	9	13	17
No. 64 Scammell Army Wreck Truck, 1959	16	27	35
No. 64 MG 1100, 1966	7	11	15
No. 64 Slingshot Dragster, 1971	5	8	13
No. 64 Fire Chief Car, 1976	3	5	7
No. 64 Caterpillar Tractor, 1981	3	5	7
No. 65 Jaguar 3.4 Litre Saloon, 1959	10	14	17
No. 65 Claas Combine Harvester, 1968	7	10	14
No. 65 Saab Sonnet, 1973	5	7	9
No. 65 Airport Coach, 1977	6	9	13

	C6	C8	C10
No. 66 Citroen DS19, 1959	16	20	27
No. 66 Harley Davidson Motorcycle & Sidecar, 1963	40	60	75
No. 66 Greyhound Bus, 1967	20	26	34
No. 66 Mazda RX500, 1972	5	7	9
No. 66 Ford Transit, 1977	5	9	14
No. 67 "Saladin" Armored Car, 1959	18	27	36
No. 67 Volkswagen 1600 T.L., 1968	7	9	11
No. 67 Hot Rocker, 1973	4	6	8
No. 67 Datsun 260Z, 1978	4	6	8
No. 68 Army Austin MKII Radio Truck, 1959	11	15	20
No. 68 Mercedes Coach, 1965	17	25	33
No. 68 Porsche 910, 1970	7	9	11
No. 68 Cosmobile, 1975	14	21	27
No. 69 Chevrolet Van, 1980	12	18	24
No. 69 Commer 30 Cwt. Van "Nestle's", 1959	25	35	45
No. 69 Hatra Tractor Shovel, 1965	12	16	22
No. 69 Rolls-Royce Silver Shadow, 1970	10	17	24
No. 69 Turbo Fury, 1973	6	8	11
No. 69 Wells Fargo security, 1978	5	9	14
No. 70 Ford Thames Estate Car, 1959	18	26	33
No. 70 Atkinson Grit-Spreading Truck, 1965	7	10	14
No. 70 Dodge Dragster, 1971	7	11	15
No. 70 S.P. Gun, 1977	3	6	9
No. 70 Ferrari, 1981	2	3	6
No. 71 Army Water Truck, 1959	14	22	30
No. 71 Jeep Pickup Truck, 1964	14	22	33
No. 71 Ford Heavy Wreck Truck, 1968	8	13	19
No. 71 Ford Heavy Wreck Truck, amber windows, light and white bumper	50	75	100
No. 71 Jumbo Jet, 1973	3	5	7
No. 71 Cattle Truck, 1976	4	6	8
No. 72 Fordson Tractor (Power Major), 1959	20	29	41
No. 72 Standard Jeep, 1967	8	12	16
No. 72 Hovercraft SRN6, 1972	7	11	17
No. 72 Bomag Road Roller, 1980	4	6	8
No. 73 RAF 10 Ton Pressure Refueler Tanker, 1959	20	29	41
No. 73 Ferrari Racing Car, 1963	14	25	33
No. 73 Mercury Station Wagon (Commuter), 1969	8	12	16
No. 73 Weasel, 1974	2	4	6
No. 73 Model "A" Ford, 1981	2	4	6

MATCHBOX No. 73 R.A.F. 10 Ton Pressure Refueler Tanker. Courtesy Gary Linden.

MATCHBOX Y-5 Talbot Van. Courtesy Gary Linden.

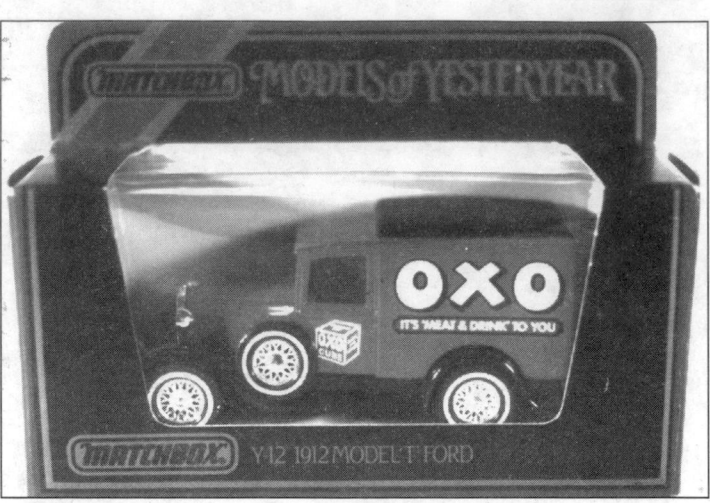

MATCHBOX Y-12 1912 Model T Ford. Courtesy Gary Linden.

MATCHBOX Y-6 1913 Cadillac. Courtesy Gary Linden.

MATCHBOX Y-14 1931 Stutz Bearcat. Courtesy Gary Linden.

	C6	C8	C10
No. 74 Mobile Refreshment Bar			
(Canteen), 1959	20	34	47
No. 74 Daimler Bus, 1966	12	17	25
No. 74 Toe Joe, 1972	4	6	8
No. 74 Cougar Villager, 1978	4	6	8
No. 75 Ford Thunderbird, 1959	44	65	87
No. 75 Ferrari Berlinetta, 1965	10	15	20
No. 75 Alfa Carabo, 1971	6	9	12
No. 75 Helicopter, 1976	4	6	8

Matchbox 'Models of Yesteryear'
(With Year of Introduction)

	C6	C8	C10
Y-1 1925 Allchin 7 N.H.P. Traction			
Engine, 1955	35	50	70
Y-1 1911 Model "T" Ford, 1964	13	20	27
Y-1 1936 Jaguar SS100, 1977	14	20	29
Y-2 1911 "B" Type London Bus, 1955	45	70	95
Y-2 1911 Renault 2-seater, 1963	10	18	28
Y-2 Prince Henry Vauxhall, 1970	10	15	20
Y-3 1907 London "E" Class Tramcar,			
1955	50	79	105

	C6	C8	C10
Y-3 1910 Benz Limousine, 1965	12	20	26
Y-3 1934 Riley MPH, 1972	10	14	19
Y-4 Sentinel Steam Wagon, 1955	49	67	90
Y-4 1905 Shank-Mason Horse-Drawn			
Fire Engine, 1960	95	135	185
Y-4 1909 Opel Coupe, 1966	15	25	40
Y-4 1930 Dusenberg Model J, 1976	15	25	35
Y-5 1929 LeMans Bentley, 1955	45	60	80
Y-5 1929 Supercharged 4:1/2 Litre			
Bentley, 1960	15	23	30
Y-5 1907 Peugeot, 1968	17	26	33
Y-5 1927 Talbot Van, 1978	20	28	39
Y-6 1916 A.E.C. "Y" type Lorry			
Truck, 1955	30	40	50
Y-6 1926 Type "35" Bugatti, 1961	20	30	40
Y-6 1913 Cadillac, 1967	27	40	54
Y-6 1920 Rolls-Royce Fire Engine, 1978	18	29	40
Y-7 1914 4-Ton Leyland, 1955	35	50	68
Y-7 1913 Mercer Raceabout Sportcar,			
1961	26	40	52
Y-7 1912 Rolls-Royce, 1967	25	36	44
Y-8 1926 Morris Cowley "Bullnose",			
1955	60	85	110
Y-8 1914 Sunbeam Motorcycle			
w/sidecar, 1962	23	34	48

	C6	C8	C10
Y-8 1914 Stutz Roadster, 1968	12	19	27
Y-8 1945 MC TC Sports Car, 1978	7	11	15
Y-9 1924 Fowler "Big Lion" Showman Engine, 1955	53	71	94
Y-9 1912 Simplex, 1967	25	38	51
Y-10 1908 Grand Prix Mercedes Racing Car, 1957	37	54	73
Y-10 1928 Mercedes-Benz 36/220, 1963	22	35	46
Y-10 1906 Rolls-Royce Silver Cloud, 1968	12	16	23
Y-11 1920 Aveling & Porter Steam Roller, 1957	36	52	69
Y-11 1912 Packard Landaulet, 1963	17	26	34
Y-11 1938 Lagonda Drophead Coupe, 1972	15	20	30
Y-12 1899 Horse-Bus (London), 1957	74	103	137
Y-12 1909 Thomas Flyabout, 1967	20	29	40

	C6	C8	C10
Y-12 1912 Model "T" Ford, 1979	12	19	25
Y-13 1862 American 4-4-0 Locomotive	30	45	60
Y-13 1911 Daimler, 1965	16	24	30
Y-13 1918 Crossley Truck, 1972	20	30	40
Y-14 1903 "Duke of Connaught" Locomotive, 1957	78	111	145
Y-14 1911 Maxwell Roadster, 1965	23	35	50
Y-14 1931 Stutz Bearcat, 1972	10	14	19
Y-15 1907 Rolls-Royce "Silver Ghost", 1960	19	30	40
Y-15 1930 Packard Victoria, 1969	10	15	20
Y-16 1904 Spyker Veteran Auto., 1961	26	39	53
Y-16 1928 Mercedes SS, 1971	10	15	20
Y-17 1938 Hispano Suiza, 1972	11	16	24
Y-18 1937 Cord 812, 1979	8	10	12
Y-19 1935 Auburn 851, 1980	5	8	11
Y-20 1938 Mercedes 540K, 1981	6	8	10
Y-21 1929 Woody Wagon, 1981	7	11	15

MATCHBOX Accessory Pack A-1 BP Gas Pump and BP sign, w/box. Courtesy Gary Linden.

Box Cover for MATCHBOX Service Station. Courtesy Gary Linden.

JAPANESE (ETC.) TIN CARS

By Ron Smith

(The average mint price of these toys was $335.98 in the last edition, rising to $359.12 in this, an increase of 7%.)

Tin toy cars have been manufactured since the first horseless carriages roamed the streets of the United States and Europe. They ranged in size and price from the tiny one-inch penny toy to the 28" Eldorado which sold at the ten dollar mark. Although there are German, Spanish and French toy cars listed here, our concentration will be the 1950's Golden Era of Japanese tin toy cars. These examples enjoy much popularity today and prices have been raised by the limitlessness of some people's insanity. Keep one thing foremost in your mind when trying to sell a toy at the mint listed price; the person who paid that price already has one.

Ron Smith has always loved toy cars and planes. He can still show you his first DinkyToy bought for him in 1940 by his aunt in Fred Harvey's Toy Store inside Cleveland's Terminal Tower Building. Born and raised in Shaker Heights, Ohio, Ron served in the United States Navy and attended John Carroll University. He has collected die cast cars, trucks and planes, cast iron toys, plastic promotional cars and, for the last 10 years, specialized in tin plate cars and planes. Ron lives in Solon, Ohio with his wife Joan and their two cats, Trouble and Bogart.

J1

J2

J5

J6

J7

J8

No.	Year	Model	Manufacturer	Power	Size	C6	C8	C10
J1	1960s	Aston-Martin DB5 (James Bond)	Gilbert	Friction	11-1/2"	50	100	200
J2	1960s	Aston-Martin DB6	Asahi Toy Co.	Friction	11"	100	400	800
J2A	1959	Austin Healey 100 Six Coupe	Bandai	Friction	8"	60	100	180
J2B	1959	Austin Healey 100 Six Convertible	Bandai	Friction	8	60	100	180
J3	1953	Buick	Marusan	Friction	7"	75	125	250
J4	1954	Buick Station Wagon	Unknown	Battery	8"	75	150	200
J5	1955	Buick Roadmaster	Yoshiya	Friction	11"	125	175	400

J13

J18

J20

All Photos by Ron Smith

No.	Year	Model	Manufacturer	Power	Size	C6	C8	C10
J6	1958	Buick Century	Yonezawa	Friction	12"	400	600	1000
J7	1958	Buick Century	Bandai	Friction	8"	80	110	130
J8	1959	Buick	T.N.	Friction	11"	90	150	300
J9	1959	Buick	Ichiko	Friction	12"	100	275	350
J10	1960	Buick	Ichiko	Friction	17-1/2"	150	250	600
J11	1961	Buick	T.N.	Friction	11"	50	100	175
J12	1961	Buick Emergency Car	T.N.	Friction	14"	50	95	125
J13	1963	Buick Wildcat	Ichiko	Friction	15"	200	400	800
J14	1966	Buick LeSabre	Asahi Toy Co.	Friction	19"	100	150	275
J15	1968	Buick Sportswagon	Asakusa	Friction	15"	150	180	250
J16	1950	BMW 600 Isetta	Bandai	Friction	9"	150	200	250
J17	1950	BMW Isetta (three wheels)	Bandai	Friction	6-1/2"	75	125	150
J18	1950	Cadillac	Marusan	Friction	11"	400	600	800
J19	1950	Cadillac	Marusan	Battery	11"	500	700	1000
J20	1952	Cadillac	Alps	Friction	11-1/2"	200	300	600
J21	1952	Cadillac	T.N.	Battery	13"	100	200	400
J22	1954	Cadillac	Gama	Friction	12"	200	300	500
J23	1954	Cadillac	Joustra	Battery	12"	200	300	500
J24	1959	Cadillac Sedan	Bandai	Friction	12"	75	100	200
J25	1959	Cadillac Convertible	Bandai	Friction	12"	75	100	200
J26	1960s	Cadillac	Bandai	Priction	17"	125	175	375
J27	1960	Cadillac	Yonezawa	Friction	18"	100	150	300
J28	1961	Cadillac 60	Unknown	Friction	9"	95	125	150
J29	1961	Cadillac Fleetwood	SSS	Friction	17-1/2"	150	300	500
J30	1962	Cadillac	Yonezawa	Friction	22"	100	250	350
J31	1963	Cadillac	Bandai	Friction	17"	125	200	350
J32	1965	Cadillac	Asahi Toy Co.	Friction	17"	125	250	400
J33	1965	Cadillac	Ichiko	Friction	22"	300	400	600
J34	1967	Cadillac	K.O.	Friction	10-1/2"	100	150	300
J35	1967	Cadillac	Unknown	Friction	10-3/4"	75	100	125
J36	1967	Cadillac El Dorado	Ichiko	Friction	28"	200	400	800
J37	1953	Chevrolet Corvette	Bandai	Friction	7"	75	100	150

J24

J25

J29

J34

J37

All Photos by Ron Smith.

J41

J38

J42

J46

No.	Year	Model	Manufacturer	Power	Size	C6	C8	C10
J38	1958	Chevrolet Corvette	Yonezawa	Friction	9-1/2"	200	300	600
J39	1962	Chevrolet Corvette	Bandai	Friction	8"	50	75	100
J40	1965	Chevrolet Corvette	Bandai	Friction	8"	65	90	125
J41	1964	Chevrolet Corvette	Ichida	Battery	12"	150	225	350
J42	1968	Chevrolet Corvette	Taiyo	Battery	9-1/2"	35	50	75
J43	1960s	Chevrolet Corvair	Bandai	Friction	8"	40	60	80
J44	1963	Chevrolet Corvair	Ichiko	Friction	9"	50	65	95
J45	1967	Chevrolet Camaro	Taiyo	Friction	9-1/2"	10	20	30
J46	1967	Chevrolet Camaro	T.N.	Friction	14"	150	250	400
J47	1967	Chevrolet Camaro	Modern Toys	Friction	11"	25	50	75
J48	1971	Chevrolet Camaro Rusher	Taiyo	Battery	9-1/2"	10	20	30
J49	1954	Chevrolet	Marusan	Friction	11"	300	400	800
J50	1955	Chevrolet	Marusan	Battery	10-3/4"	300	500	800
J51	1956	Chevrolet Station Wagon	Bandai	Friction	9-1/2"	75	125	175
J52	1956	Chevrolet Pickup	Bandai	Friction	9-1/2"	75	125	175
J53	1956	Chevrolet Convertible	Bandai	Friction	9-1/2"	100	150	225
J54	1958	Chevrolet Red Cross Ambulance	Bandai	Friction	8"	20	30	50
J55	1958	Chevrolet Pickup Truck	Bandai	Friction	8"	50	65	90
J56	1958	Chevrolet Convertible	Bandai	Friction	8"	60	90	125
J57	1958	Chevrolet Station Wagon	Bandai	Friction	8"	50	60	85
J58	1958	Chevrolet Sedan	Bandai	Friction	8"	75	100	125
J59	1959	Chevrolet Sedan/Convertible	SY	Friction	11-1/2"	200	300	600

J48

J49

J50
Photo Abensur.

J57

J59

J60

J62

All Photos unless marked otherwise, are by Ron Smith.

No.	Year	Model	Manufacturer	Power	Size	C6	C8	C10
J60	1960	Chevrolet	Marusan	Friction	11-1/2"	200	300	600
J61	1959	Chevrolet Wagon	SY	Friction	12"	60	90	120
J62	1961	Chevrolet Impala Sedan	Bandai	Friction	11"	100	200	400
J63	1961	Chevrolet Impala Convertible	Bandai	Friction	11"	100	200	400
J64	1962	Chevrolet Secret Agent	Unknown	Battery	14"	50	75	125
J65	1962	Chevrolet	Unknown	Friction	11"	125	250	350
J66	1963	Chevrolet Impala	Unknown	Friction	18"	200	300	400
J67	1960	Citroen DS 19 Convertible	Bandai	Friction	12"	300	600	900
J68	1960	Citroen DS 19 Sedan	Bandai	Friction	12"	300	600	900
J69	1960	Citroen ID 19 Station Wagon	Bandai	Friction	12"	300	600	900
J70	1950	Chrysler	Guntherman	Friction	11"	100	200	500
J71	1955	Chrysler	Yonezawa	Friction	8"	100	200	300
J72	1957	Chrysler New Yorker	Alps	Friction	14"	500	700	1000+
J73	1958	Chrysler	Unknown	Battery	13"	300	400	800
J74	1959	Chrysler Imperial Convertible	Bandai	Friction	8"	75	90	125
J75	1959	Chrysler Imperial Sedan	Bandai	Friction	8"	75	90	125
J76	1960	Chrysler Valiant	Bandai	Friction	8"	20	45	65
J77	1962	Chrysler Imperial	Asahi Toy Co.	Friction	16"	500	700	1000+

J63   J64   J65   *All Photos by Ron Smith.*

No.	Year	Model	Manufacturer	Power	Size	C6	C8	C10
J78	1960	DKW 1000 Convertible	Bandai	Friction	8"	90	125	200
J79	1960s	Datsun Bluebird 1200	Bandai	Friction	8"	60	75	125
J80	1950s	Divco Dugans Bakery Truck	Unknown, Japan	Friction	7-1/2"	300	400	600
J81	1930s	DeSoto	Masudaya	Friction	8"	300	400	800
J82	1958	Dodge Sedan	T.N.	Friction	11"	300	400	800
J83	1959	Dodge Truck	Unknown	Friction	24"	350	500	800
J84	1959	Dodge Pickup	Unknown	Friction	18-1/2"	350	500	800
J85	1968	Dodge Yellow Cab	T.N.	Friction	12"	90	125	175
J86	1958	Edsel Convertible/Sedan	Haji	Friction	10-1/2"	300	400	800
J87	1958	Edsel Wagon	Haji	Friction	10-1/2"	200	300	400
J88	1958	Edsel Ambulance	Haji	Friction	11"	200	250	300
J89	1958	Edsel Station Wagon	T.N.	Friction	11"	150	200	300
J90	1958	Edsel H.T.	Asahi	Friction	10-3/4"	300	400	600
J91	1958	Edsel H.T.	Toy Nomura	Friction	8-1/2"	100	150	250
J92	1958	Edsel	Yonezawa	Friction	10-1/2"	300	400	600
J93	1949	Ford Sedan	Guntherman	Wind Up	11"	150	300	400
J94	1951	Ford Sedan	Guntherman	Wind Up	11"	150	300	400
J95	1950	Ford Good Humor Ice Cream Truck	KTS, Japan	Friction	10-3/4"	100	150	300
J96	1955	Ford Pickup	Bandai	Friction	12"	150	250	300
J97	1955	Ford Station Wagon	Bandai	Friction	12"	150	250	300
J98	1955	Ford Ambulance	Bandai	Friction	12"	150	250	300
J99	1955	Ford Panel Truck	Bandai	Friction	12"	200	400	600
J100	1955	Ford Convertible	Bandai	Friction	12"	200	400	600
J101	1956	Ford H.T.	Yonezawa	Friction	12"	300	500	800
J102	1956	Ford Convertible	Haji	Friction	11-1/2"	400	600	1000+
J103	1956	Ford Sedan	Marusan	Friction	13"	500	800	1000+
J104	1956	Ford Wagon	Nomura	Friction	10-1/2"	100	150	300
J105	1957	Ford Fairlane Sedan	Ichiko	Friction	10"	100	200	300
J106	1957	Ford H. T.	T.N.	Friction	12"	100	200	300
J107	1957	Ford Sedan/Conv./Wagon/Pickup	Joustra	Friction	12"	200	250	300
J108	1957	Ford Sedan/Conv./Wagon/Pickup	Bandai	Friction	12"	200	250	300
J109	1957	Ford Station Wagon	Nomura	Friction	7-1/2"	60	80	100
J110	1958	Ford Retractable Top	K. Japan	Friction	10"	80	100	165
J111	1958	Ford Retractable Top	T.N.	Battery	11"	80	100	165
J112	1958	Ford Country Squire Station Wagon	Bandai	Friction	8"	60	80	100
J113	1958	Ford Fairlane H.T./Conv.	Bandai	Friction	8"	60	80	100
J114	1958	Ford Fairlane H.T./Conv.	Sankei Gangu	Friction	9"	90	115	125
J115	1959	Ford Fairlane Skyliner	Sankei Gangu	Friction	9"	90	115	125
J116	1950	Ford Station Wagon	T.N.	Friction	12"	100	150	200
J117	1959	Ford Retractable	T.N.	Friction	11"	80	100	165
J118	1960s	Ford Falcon	Bandai	Friction	8"	20	30	50
J119	1960	Ford	Haji	Friction	11"	125	150	300

J72 *Photo Bruce Sterling.*

J71

J73

J77

J86

J86

All Photos, unless marked otherwise, are by Ron Smith.

J87

J93

J96

J99

J100

J103 *Photo Bruce Sterling.*

J102   J106   J107   *All Photos by Ron Smith.*

No.	Year	Model	Manufacturer	Power	Size	C6	C8	C10
J120	1961	Ford Country Sedan	Bandai	Friction	10-1/2"	125	150	250
J121	1962	Ford Country Sedan	Asahi	Friction	12"	200	250	400
J122	1964	Ford H.T.	Ichiko	Friction	13"	125	150	200
J123	1964	Ford H.T.	Rico	Friction	17"	200	400	600
J124	1964	Ford Convertible	Rico	Friction	17"	200	400	600
J125	1965	Ford Galaxie H.T.	MT	Friction	11"	125	150	250
J126	1968	Ford Torino	S.T.	Friction	16"	200	300	500
J127	1956	Ford Thunderbird	T.N.	Friction	11"	300	400	600
J128	1956	Ford Thunderbird H.T. Clear Top	T.N.	Friction	11"	300	400	600
J129	1956	Ford Thunderbird	T.N.	Battery	11"	275	350	400
J130	1959	Ford Thunderbird Sedan	Bandai	Friction	8"	50	60	80
J131	1959	Ford Thunderbird Convertible	Bandai	Friction	8"	50	60	80
J132	1961	Ford Thunderbird Retractable	Yonezawa	Battery	11"	80	120	175
J133	1962	Ford Thunderbird Retractable	Yonezawa	Battery	11"	80	120	175
J134	1963	Ford Thunderbird Retractable	Yonezawa	Battery	11"	80	120	175
J135	1964	Ford Thunderbird Convertible	Asahi	Friction	12-1/2"	150	200	400
J136	1964	Ford Thunderbird H.T.	Asahi	Friction	12"	150	200	400
J137	1964	Ford Thunderbird	Ichiko	Friction	16"	100	200	400
J138	1965	Ford Thunderbird H.T.	Bandai	Friction	10-3/4"	60	85	125
J139	1965	Ford Mustang F.B.	Bandai	Friction	11"	45	65	90
J140	1965	Ford Mustang H.T./Conv.	Bandai	Fric/Bat	11"	75	125	150
J141	1965	Ford Mustang (FBI)	Bandai	Friction	11"	75	100	125
J142	1965	Ford Mustang Convertible	Yonezawa	Battery	13-1/2"	90	125	200
J143	1966	Ford Mustang F.B.	T.N.	Friction	17"	120	200	325
J144	1967	Ford Mustang	Bandai	Battery	13"	45	65	100
J145	1960s	Ford Taunus 17M Convertible	Bandai	Friction	8"	30	40	60
J146	1960s	Ford GT	Bandai	Battery	10"	65	85	125
J147	1957	Ferrari 250 G. Convertible	A.T.C.	Friction	9-1/2"	150	300	700
J148	1958	Ferrari	Bandai	Battery	11"	90	150	300
J149	1960	Ferrari Super America Coupe	Bandai	Friction	12"	100	200	300
J150	1960s	Ferrari Super America Convertible	Bandai	Friction	12"	100	200	300
J151	1960s	Fiat 600 Sedan	Bandai	Friction	8"	50	65	95
J152	1950s	International Cement Mixer	SSS	Friction	19"	300	600	800
J153	1950s	International Grain Hauler	SSS	Friction	23"	300	600	800
J154	1960	Jaguar XK150 H.T. Conv.	Bandai	Friction	9-1/2"	75	125	200
J155	1960s	Jaguar XKE Convertible	T.T.	Friction	10-1/2"	95	125	175
J156	1960s	Jaguar XKE Coupe	Lendolet Auto	Friction	10-1/2"	75	100	125
J157	1960s	Jaguar XK140	Bandai	Friction	9-1/2"	40	60	90
J158	1960s	Jaguar XKE	Bandai	Battery	10"	90	125	200
J159	1960s	Jaguar 3.4 Sedan	Bandai	Friction	8"	50	60	100
J160	1960s	Jaguar 3.4 Convertible	Bandai	Friction	8"	50	60	100
J161	1965	Jaguar XKE120	Alps	Friction	6-1/2"	90	150	350

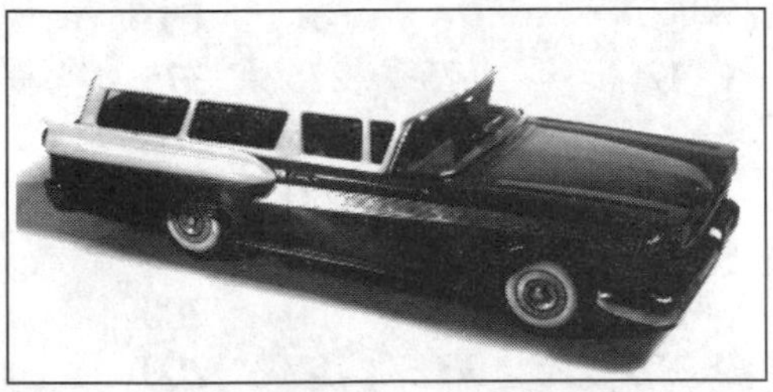

J116

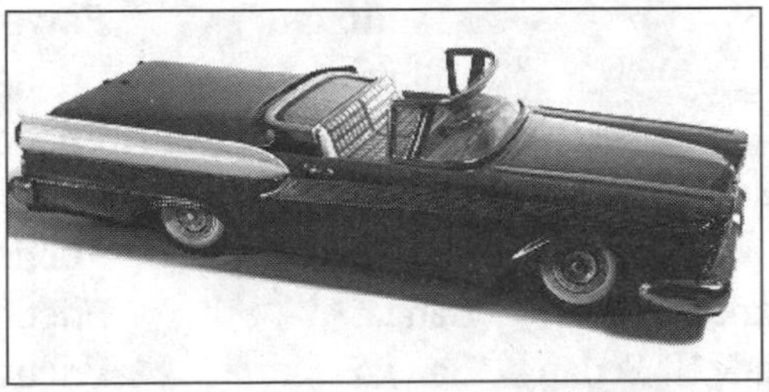

J117

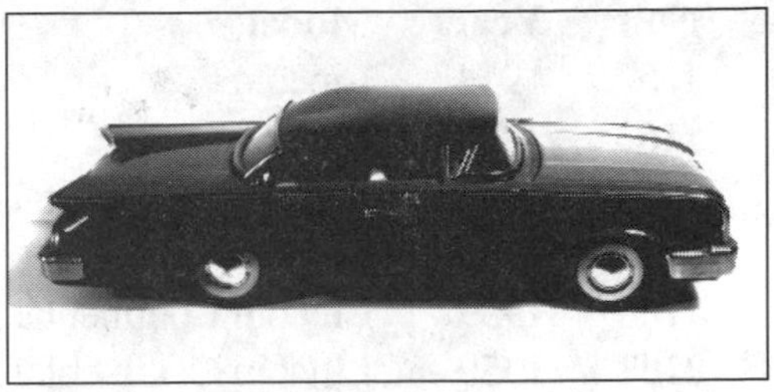

J119

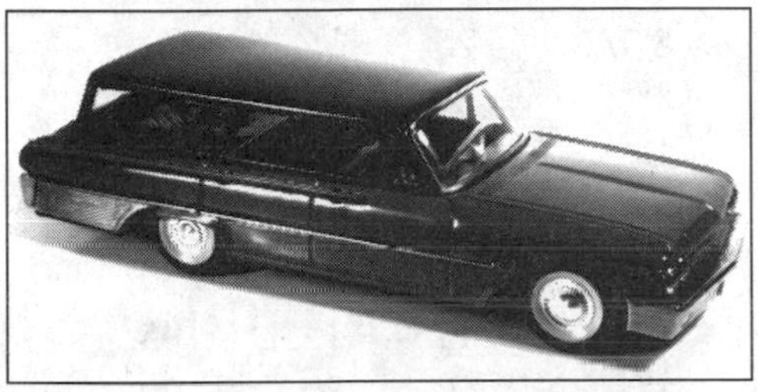

J120

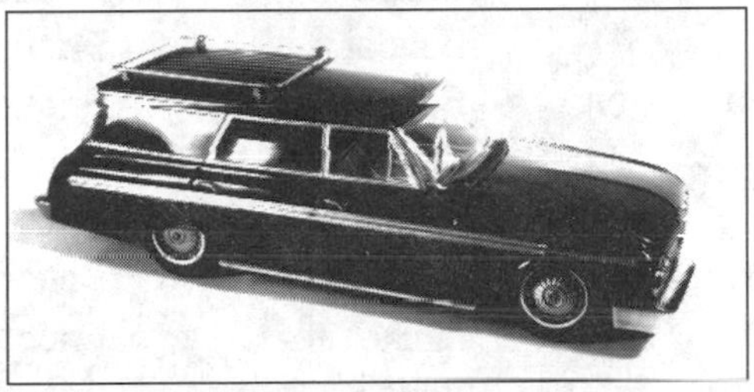

J121

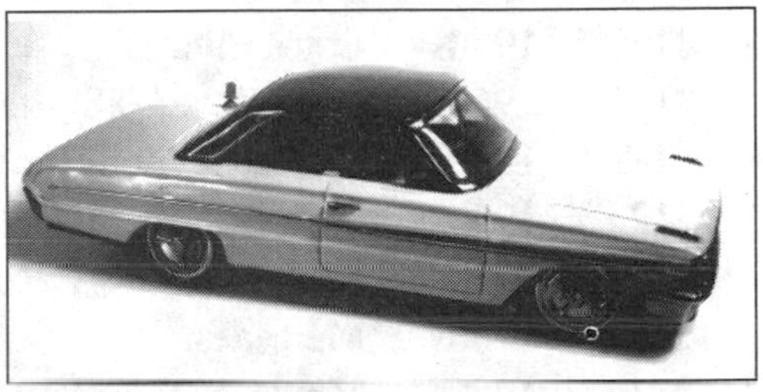

J122

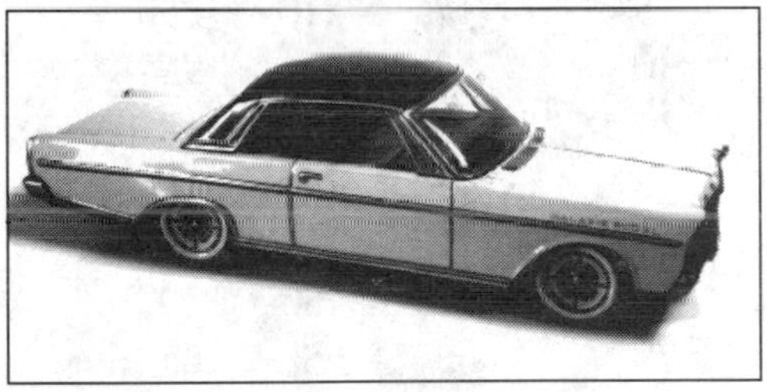

J125

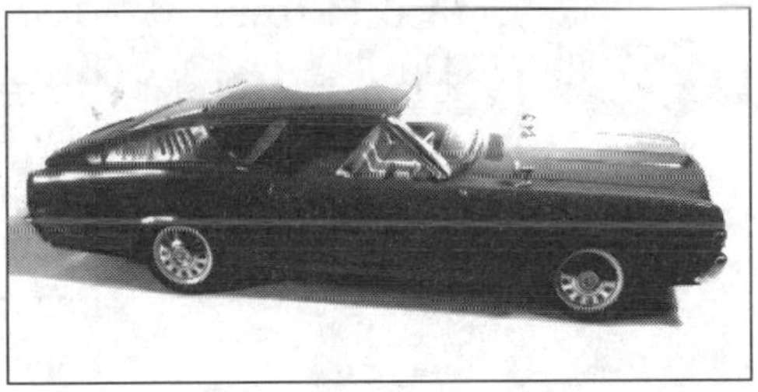

J126

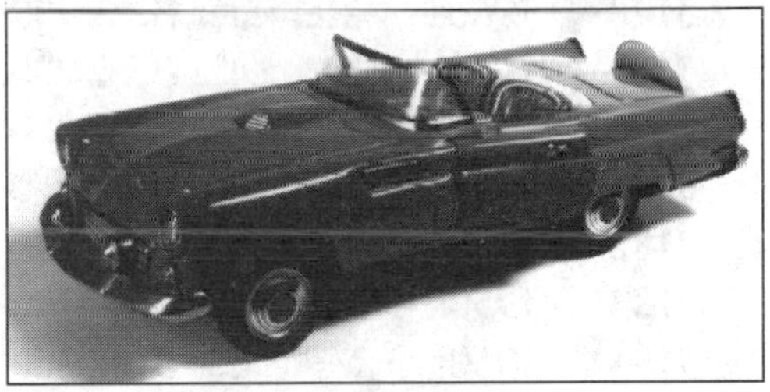

J129

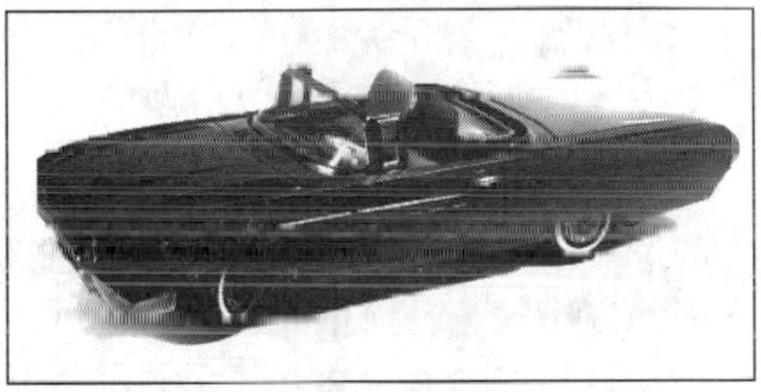

J134

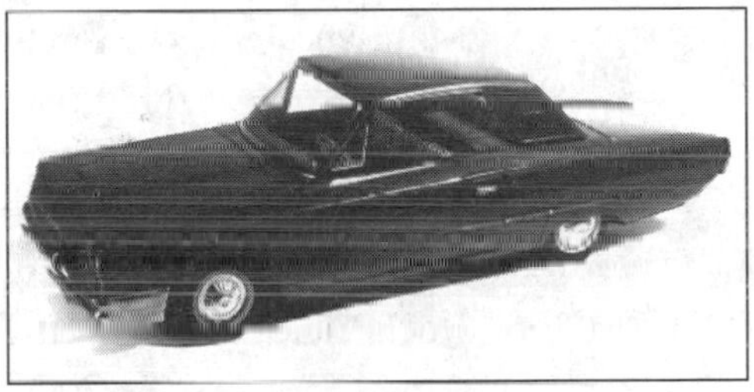

J136

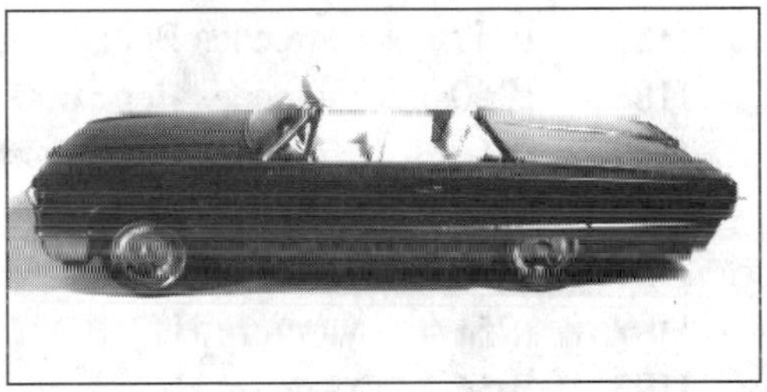

J137

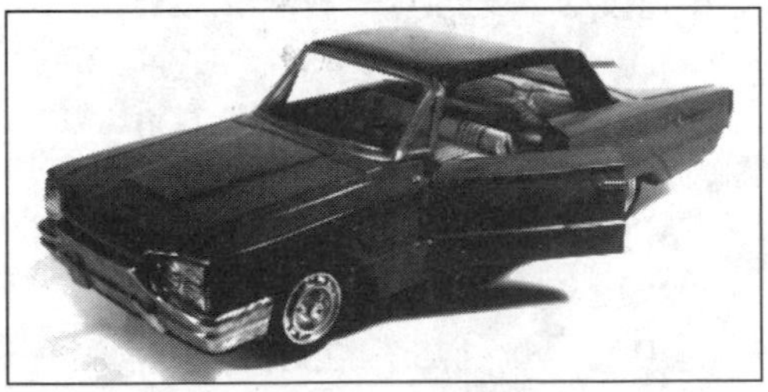

J138

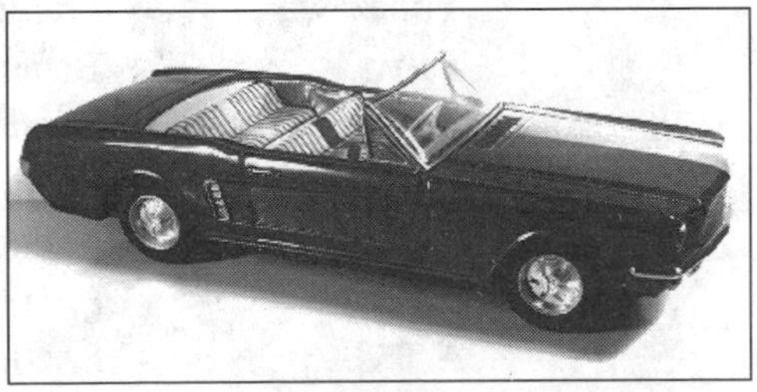

J140

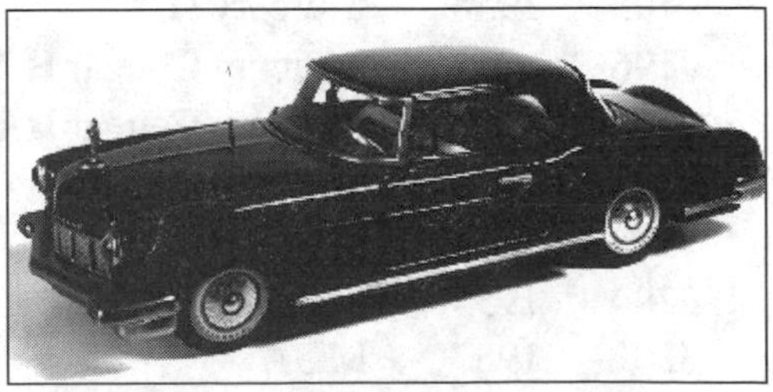

J164

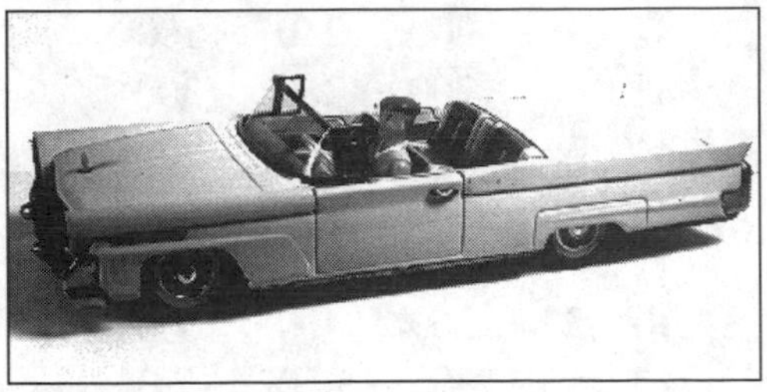

J166

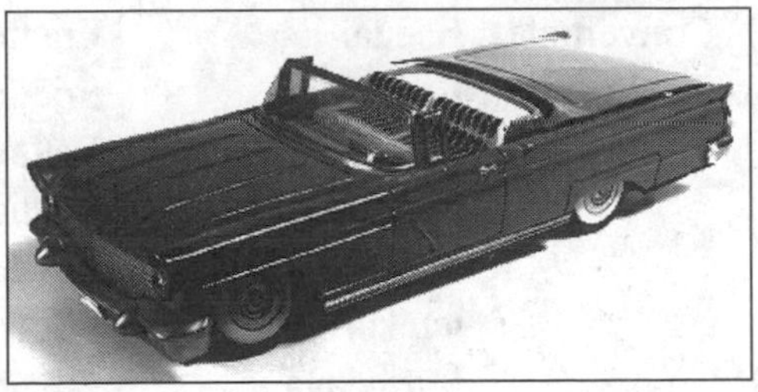

J168

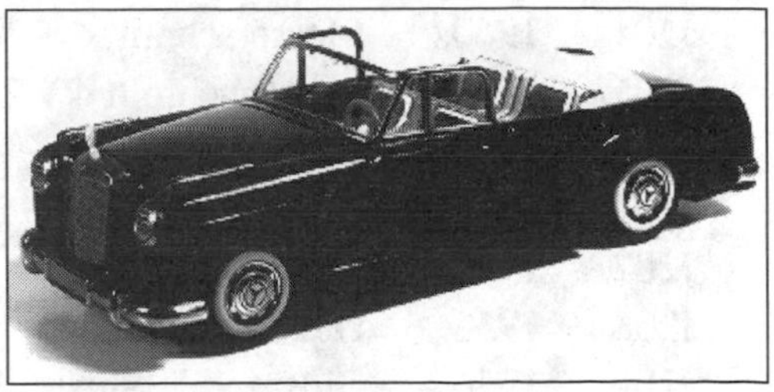

J177

All Photos by Ron Smith.

No.	Year	Model	Manufacturer	Power	Size	C6	C8	C10
J162	1954	Lincoln	Unknown	Friction	12"	175	275	375
J163	1955	Lincoln Sedan	Yonezawa	Friction	12"	250	325	500
J164	1956	Lincoln Continental Mark II	Linemar	Friction	12"	400	600	1000
J165	1956	Lincoln	Ichiko	Friction	16-1/2"	150	250	375
J166	1959	Lincoln Continental Mark III Conv.	Bandai	Friction	12"	90	150	200
J167	1959	Lincoln Continental Mark III Sedan	Bandai	Friction	12"	90	150	200
J168	1960	Lincoln H.T./Convertible	Yonezawa	Friction	11"	100	150	300
J169	1964	Lincoln	Unknown	Friction	10-1/2"	90	175	275
J170	1950s	Lotus Elite	Bandai	Friction	8-1/2"	25	35	45
J171	1960s	Land Rover "88" Station Wagon	Bandai	Friction	8"	30	40	60
J172	1950s	Mercedes Limousine	Tipp & Co.	Friction	14"	500	800	1000
J173	1950s	Mercedes Benz Racer	Line Mar	Friction	9-1/2"	95	150	185
J174	1950s	Mercedes Benz Racer W196	Marusan	Battery	10"	150	200	250
J175	1960s	Mercedes	Ichiko	Friction	12-1/2"	115	155	185
J176	1960s	Mercedes Benz 219 Sedan	Bandai	Friction	8"	50	80	100
J177	1960s	Mercedes Benz 219 Convertible	Bandai	Friction	8"	50	80	100
J178	1960s	Mercedes Benz 230 SL	Modern Toys	Battery	15"	175	210	250
J179	1960s	Mercedes Benz 230 SL	Alps	Battery	10"	65	75	95
J180	1960s	Mercedes Benz 230 SL	Yanoman	Battery	14-1/2"	125	155	185
J181	1960s	Mercedes Benz 250 SE	Ichiko	Battery	13"	110	140	185
J182	1960s	Mercedes Benz 250 S	Daiya	Friction	14"	110	155	175
J183	1950s	Mercedes Benz 300 SL	T.N.	Battery	11"	125	150	200
J184	1950s	Mercedes Benz 300 SL	KS	Battery	7"	45	65	85
J185	1950s	Mercedes Benz 300 SL	Dist. Cragstan	Battery	9"	65	95	125
J186	1950s	Mercedes Benz 300 SL	Bandai	Friction	8"	65	95	125
J187	1957	Mercedes Benz 300 SL	Marusan	Friction	8-1/2"	200	300	400
J188	1960s	Mercedes Benz 600	Unknown	Friction	10"	95	125	175
J189	1960s	Mercedes Benz Taxi	Bandai	Battery	10"	75	100	125
J190	1962	Mercedes Benz	SSS	Battery	12"	200	250	350
J191	1970	Mercedes Benz	Ichiko	Friction	24"	125	150	200
J192	1954	Mercury H.T.	Rock Valley Toys	Battery	9-1/2"	100	125	150
J193	1956	Mercury H.T.	Alps	Friction	9-1/2"	600	800	1000+
J194	1958	Mercury Station Wagon	Bandai	Friction	8"	60	80	100
J195	1958	Mercury H.T.	Yonezawa	Friction	11-1/2"	250	325	400
J196	1967	Mercury Cougar H.T.	Taiyo	Battery	10"	25	45	65
J197	1967	Mercury Cougar H.T.	Asakusa Toys	Friction	15"	200	400	600
J198	1952	MG TF	Unknown	Ftiction	8-1/2"	50	75	95
J199	1954	MG TD	SSS	Friction	6-1/2"	35	65	85
J200	1955	MG TF	Bandai	Friction	8"	95	125	150
J201	1957	MGA	A.T.C.	Friction	10"	175	250	400
J202	1960s	MG Magnette Mark III Sedan	Bandai	Friction	8"	95	125	150
J203	1960s	MG Magnette Mark III Convertible	Bandai	Friction	8"	95	125	150
J204	1960s	Messerschmitt 4 Wheels Convertible	Bandai	Friction	8"	200	250	300
J205	1960s	Messerschmitt 4 Wheels Sedan	Bandai	Friction	8"	200	250	300
J206	1950s	Nash	MSK	Battery	8"	40	70	90
J207	1956	Nash Ambassador	Sankei Gangu	Friction	8"	100	125	150
J207A	1952	Oldsmobile	Y	Friction	11"	150	350	500
J208	1956	Oldsmobile Sedan	Ichiko/Kanto	Friction	10-1/2"	200	400	600
J209	1956	Oldsmobile Super 88 Sedan	Masudaya	Friction	16"	300	400	600
J210	1958	Oldsmobile Sedan	A.T.C.	Friction	12"	200	300	400

J193

J195

J197

J208

J209

J210

J207A

J218A

All Photos by Ron Smith.

J215

J219

J222

J223

J224

J225

J227

J232

J235

J236

J237

J240

J242

J243

J252

J260

J265

J276

J278A

J265A

All Photos by Ron Smith.

No.	Year	Model	Manufacturer	Power	Size	C6	C8	C10
J211	1958	Oldsmobile Super 88 Sedan	A.T.C.	Friction	13"	250	325	425
J212	1958	Oldsmobile Sedan	Y	Friction	16"	300	400	700
J213	1959	Oldsmobile Sedan	Ichiko	Friction	12-1/2"	75	125	175
J214	1961	Oldsmobile Convertible	Yonezawa	Friction	12"	75	125	175
J215	1966	Oldsmobile Toronado	Bandai	Battery	11"	65	110	150
J216	1968	Oldsmobile Toronado	Ichiko	Friction	17-1/2"	300	400	500
J217	1950s	Opel Sedan	Yonezawa	Battery	11-1/2"	70	90	125
J218	1954	Pontiac Star Chief	Asahi	Friction	11"	250	350	600
J218A	1954	Pontiac	Minister	Friction	11"	NewIssue		20
J219	1967	Pontiac Firebird	Akasura	Friction	15-1/2"	90	150	275
J220	1967	Pontiac Firebird	Bandai	Friction	10"	30	55	75
J221	1967	Pontiac Firebird (w/wipers)	Bandai	Battery	9-1/2"	40	55	75
J222	1953	Packard Convertible/Sedan	Alps	Friction	16"	500	800	1500
J223	1957	Packard Hawk Convertible	Schuco	Battery	10-3/4"	300	400	800
J224	1956	Plymouth H.T.	Unknown	Friction	8-1/2"	200	400	600
J225	1956	Plymouth H.T.	Alps	Battery	12"	300	400	600
J226	1957	Plymouth Fury H.T.	Y	Friction	11-1/2"	300	400	600
J227	1958	Plymouth Fury	Bandai	Friction	8"	75	90	150
J228	1959	Plymouth Hardtop	A.T.C.	Friction	10-1/2"	200	400	600
J229	1959	Plymouth Convertible	A.T.C.	Friction	10-1/2"	250	400	600
J230	1961	Plymouth Sedan	Ichiko	Friction	12"	125	250	350
J231	1961	Plymouth Station Wagon	Ichiko	Friction	12"	125	165	195
J232	1961	Plymouth T.V. Car	Ichiko	Battery	12"	125	175	250
J233	1964	Plymouth Fury II.T.	Kusama	Friction	10"	60	80	100
J234	1960	Porsche 911	Bandai	Battery	10"	65	95	125
J235	1950s	Porsche Speedster	Distler	Battery	10-1/2"	200	300	500
J236	1960	Rolls Royce "Silver Coupe" Conv.	Bandai	Friction	12"	100	150	300
J237	1960s	Rolls Royce "Silver Coupe" Sedan	Bandai	Friction	12"	100	150	250
J238	1960s	Rolls Royce (with electric lights)	Bandai	Battery	12"	150	300	600
J239	1960	Rolls Royce	T.N.	Friction	10-1/2"	200	300	500
J240	1960s	Rambler Rebel Station Wagon	Bandai	Friction	12"	50	85	125
J241	1960	Renault	Bandai	Friction	7-1/2"	95	150	200
J242	1960s	Studebaker Avanti	Bandai	Friction	8"	125	175	300
J243	1954	Studebaker	Yoshiya	Friction	9"	150	200	300
J244	1960s	Saab 93B	Bandai	Friction	7"	50	70	90
J245	1960s	Subaru 360	Bandai	Friction	7"	75	100	125
J246	1960s	Triumph TR-3 Convertible	Bandai	Friction	8"	50	75	150
J247	1960s	Triumph TR-3 Coupe	Bandai	Friction	8"	50	75	150
J248	1960s	Toyopet Crown	Bandai	Friction	9"	40	50	75
J249	1960s	Toyota	Ichiko	Friction	16"	150	275	325
J250	1967	Toyota 2000 GT	A.T.C.	Friction	15"	150	275	325
J251	1960s	Vespa	Bandai	Friction	9"	50	75	125
J252	1960	VW Karmanna-Ghia	Bandai	Friction	7"	100	150	250
J253	1960s	Volkswagen Bus	A.T.C.	Friction	12"	125	175	350
J254	1960s	Volkswagen Pickup Truck	Bandai	Friction	8"	50	60	75
J255	1960s	Volkswagen Bus	Bandai	Friction	8"	50	60	75
J256	1960s	Volkswagen Bus	Bandai	Bat/Fric	9-1/2"	75	125	175
J257	1950s	Volkswagen Bus	Tipp & Co	Battery	9"	250	375	450
J258	1950s	Volkswagen Convertible	T.N.	Friction	9-1/2"	100	150	225
J259	1960s	Volkswagen Convertible	Bandai	Battery	7-1/2"	50	70	90

J284

J287

J286

J289

J290

J291

J288

All Photos by Ron Smith.

No.	Year	Model	Manufacturer	Power	Size	C6	C8	C10
J260	1960s	Volkswagen Convertible	Bandai	Battery	11"	110	145	185
J261	1960s	Volkswagen Convertible	Taiyo	Battery	10-1/2"	25	45	90
J262	1960s	Volkswagen	Bandai	Friction	8"	25	45	60
J263	1960s	Volkswagen	Bandai	Battery	10-1/2"	25	50	75
J264	1960s	Volkswagen	Bandai	Battery	11"	25	50	75
J265	1960s	Volkswagen w/wo Sun Roof	Bandai	Friction	15"	60	90	125
J265A	1950s	Volvo	Sweden	Windup	11"	600	700	1800
J266	1960s	Willys Jeep FC-150 Pickup	T.N. Toy Nomura	Friction	11"	50	75	95
J267	1950s	Zuendapp Janus	Bandai	Friction	8"	125	150	200
J268	1950s	Mazda Auto Tricycle K360	Bandai	Friction	6"	75	100	200
J269	1950	Daihatsu Midget	Kokyu Shokai	Friction	5"	75	100	200
J270	1950s	Daihatsu Midget	Yonezawa	Friction	7"	75	100	200
J271	1950s	Mitsubishi Auto Tricycle Leo	Bandai	Friction	5"	75	100	200
J272	1950s	Mitsubishi Auto Tricycle	Bandai	Friction	11"	100	150	300
J273	1950s	Orient Auto Tricycle	Yonezawa	Friction	9"	75	100	200
J274	1950s	Mazda Auto Tricycle	Bandai	Friction	8"	75	100	200
J275	1950s	Daihatsu Auto Tricycle	Nomura	Friction	11"	100	150	300
J276	1950s	Buick Futuristic LeSabre	Yonezawa	Friction	7-1/2"	200	300	600
J277	1963	Corvair Bertone	Bandai	Battery	12"	75	150	200
J278	1950s	Dream Car Buick Phantom	Tipp & Co.	Friction	12"	300	400	800
J278A	--	Dream Car	Y	Friction	17"	600	800	1500
J279	1960s	Dream Car Firebird III	Alps	Friction	11"	100	200	400
J280	1960	Ford Gyron	Ichida	Battery	11"	75	100	150
J281	1956	GM's Gas Turbine Powered Firebird III	Ashahi	Friction	8-1/2"	100	200	500
J282	1950s	Pontiac Dream Car	Mitsubishi	Friction	10"	100	200	500
J283	1950s	Atom Jet Car	Y	Friction	30"	300	500	1000
J284	1950s	Atom Car	Yonezawa	Friction	17"	200	400	800
J285	1950s	Record Racer NSU	Bandai	Friction	18"	100	150	200
J286	1950s	Agajanian Racer No. 98	Y	Friction	18"	500	800	2000+
J287	1950s	Champion's Racer No. 98	Y	Friction	18"	500	800	1200
J288	1950	Champion Racer No. 42	Gem	Friction	18"	500	750	1200
J289	1950	Champion Racer No. 15	German	Friction	18"	500	750	1200
J290	--	Electrospecial #21	Y	Battery	10"	300	500	800
J291	--	Midget Special #6	Y	Friction	7"	300	500	800

JAPANESE TIN AIRPLANES

By Ron Smith

The average mint price of these toys was $441.93 in the last edition,
rising to $497.50 in this, edition an increase of 13%.

No.	Type	Manufacturer	Power	Wingspan	C6	C8	C10
A1	Cessna	T.N.	Friction	25"	100	200	400
A2	Jenny Biplane	S & E	Friction	14-1/2"	75	125	150
A3	Jenny Biplane	S & E	Friction	14-1/2"	75	125	150
A4	Bristol Bulldog	S & E	Friction	14-1/2"	80	150	225
A5	Cessna	W. German	Friction	12"	50	80	150
A6	Ford	T.N.	Friction	15"	60	90	175
A7	Jenny Biplane	Haji	Friction	11-1/2"	20	40	80
A8	Ryan Spirit of St. Louis	HTC	Friction	12"	100	300	500
A9	U.N. Hospital Plane	HTC	Friction	12"	70	120	210

No.	Type	Manufacturer	Power	Wingspan	C6	C8	C10
A10	WWII Fighter	Japan	Friction	14-1/2"	80	150	250
A11	Constellation	Ingap	Friction	15"	100	200	400
A12	F3F Biplane	Cragstan	Battery	11-1/2"	150	300	600
A13	Bluebird Seaplane	S & E	Friction	13"	50	80	150
A14	B50	Bandai	Friction	7-1/2"	40	60	90
A15	Sky Bird "Spirit of St. Louis"	Bandai	Friction	9"	50	80	120
A16	Spitfire	HTC	Friction	10"	80	150	200
A17	P-51 Mustang	HTC	Friction	10"	90	160	250
A18	P-47 Thunderbolt	HTC	Friction	10"	80	150	200
A19	Zero	Japan	Friction	15-1/2"	New Issue		125
A20	De Havilland Comet	Rico	Windup	13"	100	150	350
A21	WWII Fighter	Spain	Windup	8-1/2"	100	200	300
A22	F-80	Bandai	Friction	7-1/2"	40	70	100
A23	Disney Comic Plane	Linemar	Friction	10"	100	150	400
A24	WWII Fighter	Spain	Windup	9"	100	150	300
A25	WWII Tri-Motor	Spain	Windup	9"	100	150	300
A26	Hospital Plane	Tekno	---	14"	300	600	1000

A1

A2

A3

A4

All Photos by Ron Smith.

A5

A6

A7

A8

A9

A10

A11

All Photos by Ron Smith.

169

A12

A13

A14

A15

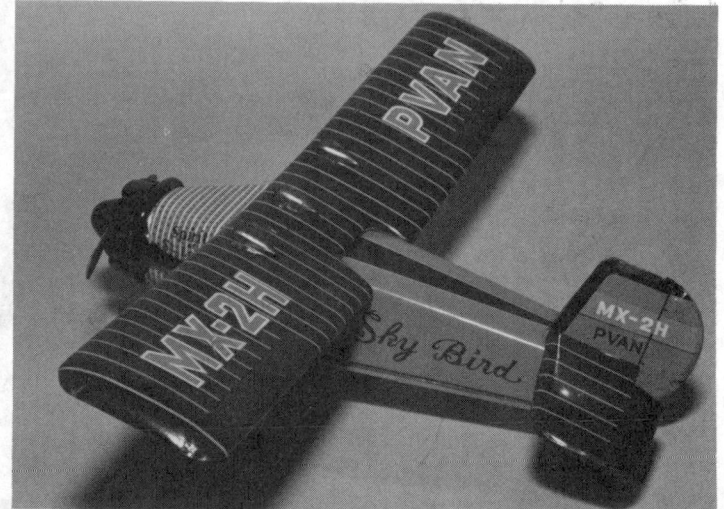

A18

A17

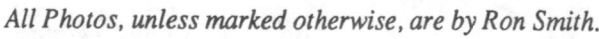

All Photos, unless marked otherwise, are by Ron Smith.

A22

A20

A23

A24

A21

A25

All Photos, unless marked otherwise, are by Ron Smith.

No.	Type	Manufacturer	Power	Wingspan	C6	C8	C10
A27	German Biplane	Tipp	Bat/WU	20"	500	1000	3000
A28	Construction	England?	---	22"	125	175	400
A29	30s German	Tipp	Windup	16"	700	1500	3200
A30	Fiat CR-42	Ingap	Windup	10'	500	700	1500
A31	Stuka	Dux	---	12"	200	400	800
A32	Hein	Banda	Friction	14"	200	350	500
A33	Zero	Nomura	Friction	14"	150	275	350
A34	Zero	Nomura	Friction	14"	150	275	350
A35	Lockheed Sirus	Japan	Friction	13"	400	800	1000
A36	Farman	Japan	Friction	10"	400	600	1000
A37	American Airlines DC-7	Japan	Battery	24"	200	400	600
A38	American Airlines Electra	Linemar	Battery	20"	200	400	500
A39	American Airlines Boing 727	Y	Battery	16"	125	175	225
A40	Boeing 707	Japan	Battery	18"	200	300	400
A41	Boeing Stratocruiser	T.N.	Friction	20"	300	400	600
A42	Comet Jetliner	Y	Friction	19"	200	300	400
A43	Eastern Constellation	MSK	Friction	7-1/2"	100	150	200
A44	Eastern Constellation	Hadson	Friction	12"	200	350	450
A45	Eastern DC-7	Bandai	Friction	17-1/2"	300	400	600
A46	Presidents Plane	Japan	Battery	20"	275	350	500
A47	Pan Am DC-7	T.N.	Friction	17"	300	600	800
A48	Pan Am Stato Clipper	Japan	Friction	14"	225	300	450
A49	Pan Am Jet Clipper	Linemar	Battery	18"	200	300	425
A50	Northwest DC-7	Y	Friction	10"	100	150	225
A51	Northwest Orient	Y	Battery	24"	300	500	650
A52	Northwest DC-7	Asahi	Friction	19"	300	600	900
A53	TWA Constellation	Y	Friction	12"	200	300	400
A54	TWA DC-4	Linemar	Friction	19"	150	350	475
A55	TWA DC-2	Japan	Windup	10"	175	300	425
A56	United DC-7 Mainliner	T.N.	Battery	19"	150	275	350
A57	United DC-7	Japan	Friction	23"	125	250	400
A58	B-29	Y	Friction	19"	150	300	475
A59	B-36	Y	Friction	26"	300	600	900
A60	B-45 Tornado	Bandai	Friction	16"	100	150	250
A61	B-47 USAF	Daiya	Friction	12"	150	225	325
A62	B-50 USAF	Y	Battery	19"	200	300	400

A26

A27

A28

A29

A32 Photo Tanaka.

A33 Photo Tanaka.

A34 Photo Tanaka.

A35 Photo Tanaka.

A36 Courtesy Sotheby's.

No.	Type	Manufacturer	Power	Wingspan	C6	C8	C10
A63	B-50 Superfortress	TCP	Friction	15"	200	300	400
A64	C-120 Pack Plane	Japan	Friction	16"	250	500	800
A65	C-124 Globemaster	Y	Friction	20"	250	600	800
A66	F-84 Airforce	Linemar	Battery	13"	100	150	200
A67	F-86 Airforce	J	Friction	10"	75	125	175
A68	F-94C Starfire	Y	Friction	18"	150	300	450
A69	F-102 USAF	HTS	Friction	11"	125	150	225
A70	F-104 Lockheed	Y	Friction	16"	125	150	175

ANIMAL-DRAWN

The average mint price in this section in the last edition was $1332.82
with the average mint price in this edition $1498.78, an increase of 12%.
(Left out of this averaging is the price paid for the George Brown "Charles".)

In this category, the toys generally commanding the highest prices are horse-drawn cast iron pieces. One reason for the eye-opening prices is that horse-drawn cast iron toys have considerable value apart from their lure as toys. There is an air of genuine Americana about them and they are likely to attract the interest of many who otherwise pay no attention to toys (decorators figure largely in this area.).

Since prices are often so high, reproductions, whether honest or dishonest, can be a problem. Things to look for when a reproduction is suspected include a rougher surface than an old toy would have (recastings are invariably rougher), uneven fit of pieces, a blurring of details, and "aging" that doesn't have the patina of age. Since at least one company, John Wright (formerly Grey Iron), is still manufacturing turn-of-the-century horse-drawn vehicles, some of them from the original molds, it is wise to become familiar with the field before investing heavily.

ALTHOF, BERGMANN "Express" Wagon, 26" long. Courtesy Sotheby's New York. Courtesy Ed Hyers Antique Toys.

ALL-NU Trotter. Photo by Bill Kaufman. Courtesy Evelyn Besser.

ALTHOF, BERGMANN "Fruits and Vegetables". Courtesy Ed Hyers Antique Toys.

	C6	C8	C10
"Alderney Dairy" Milk Truck, 2-horse wood and lithographed paper, possibly Schoenhut	175	263	350
All-Nu Trotter, lead alloy, 1941, approx. 4" long	22	34	45

ALTHOF, BERGMANN

Althof, Bergmann began in 1867, when L. Althof teamed with the brothers Bergmann, forming a jobbing firm (the brothers were already jobbers). In 1874 the New York company received two patents, one for a bell toy with three soldiers. In addition to bell and animal-drawn toys, they made (or jobbed out) toy furniture, banks, hoop and clockwork toys.

	C6	C8	C10
Althof, Bergmann "Express" Wagon pull toy, tin w/iron wheels, 26"	3000	5000	8000
Althof, Bergmann "Fruits and Vegetables", 17-1/2" long	5000	7500	10,000
Althof, Bergmann Milk Cart, "Pure Milk", c. 1880, 14" long	500	750	1000

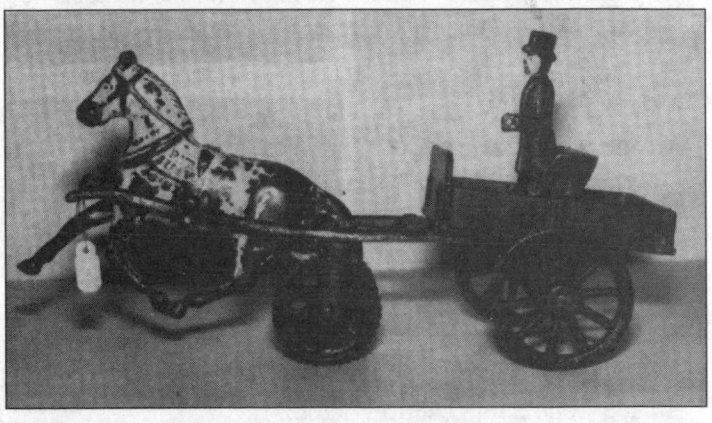

Carpenter Doctor's Cart. Courtesy Ed Hyers Antique Toys.

ALTHOF, BERGMANN "Milk Wagon", 13" long, tin. Courtesy Sotheby's New York.

	C6	C8	C10
Althof, Bergmann "Milk Wagon", tin, 13" long	600	900	1200

ARCADE
(ALL ARCADE TOYS ARE CAST IRON)

Circus Wagon

Every day is Circus Day for the child who has one of these toys. It is one of the most attractive items in our line. It fulfills the requirement of "a lot for the money."

The horses are black. The wagon is decorated in three brilliant colors. The driver wears the regulation circus uniform.

The extreme length of the toy including the horses is 14 inches.

The height, including driver is 9¾ inches.

No. 1 Circus Wagon includes the Animal.

No. 2 Circus Wagon is without the Animal.

Nos. 1 and 2 can also be supplied with four or six horse teams at a small additional cost.

PACKING

Packed each in a paper box, 3 dozen in a case.

No. 1. Case weight, net 145 pounds, gross 170 pounds.
Case measurements, 56x20½x17 inches.

No. 2. Case weight, net 125 pounds, gross 150 pounds.
Case measurements, 56x20½x17 inches.

A page from Arcade Catalog No. 26, with the hand-stamp "Received March 19, 1917" on it.

	C6	C8	C10
Arcade Bakery Wagon, 13" long	300	450	600
Arcade "Big Six Circus & Wild West" Wagon, (see Movies-"Tom Mix Big Six Circus", appears to be the same except for name), 14-1/2" long	425	638	850
Aracde Cart, wicker, horse, driver, cast iron	100	150	200
Arcade Coal Car w/Horse	150	225	300
Arcade Contractors Dump Wagon, horse team, driver, 14" long	250	375	500

Toy Hansom Cab

A very good idea of the design of this toy can be formed from the illustration, but the decoration which we use is one of its strong selling points. The cab itself is finished in brightly colored enamels. The driver wears a snappy uniform.

Altogether this is one of the most attractive toys that we have.
Extreme length 13½ inches. Extreme height 6½ inches.

PACKING

Each in a paper box, ¼ gross in a case.
Case weight, net 82 pounds, gross 100 pounds.
Case measurements, 32x22x12 inches.

Toy Ice Wagon

Every toy dealer should carry a large stock of these toy ice wagons as they are one of the largest sellers that we have.

It seems that an ice wagon is particularly attractive to children and this toy is correspondingly so.

We have made this of very heavy castings to stand rough handling and have decorated it with bright enamels.
Extreme length 12 inches. Extreme height 5½ inches.

PACKING

Each in a paper box, ¼ gross in a case.
Case weight, net 121 pounds, gross 153 pounds.
Case measurements, 26x22x17 inches.

167

	C6	C8	C10
Arcade "Contractors Dump Wagon", 2 horse, driver, 1930s, 13-1/4"	187	280	375
Arcade Farm Wagon, 2-horse, driver, 10-3/4" long	350	525	700
Arcade McCormick Deering Plow	175	263	350
Arcade McCormick Deering Farm Wagon, 2-horse	400	600	800
Arcade McCormick Deering Manure Spreader, w/team of horses	450	675	900
Arcade Sulky Plow, 1-horse, 10-1/2"	150	250	350
Bakery Wagon, 1-horse, cast iron, 13" long	100	200	300
Barclay "Animal Cage" Circus Wagon, circa 1930s, lead and tin, slush lead, approx. 9-7/8"	30	45	60

ARCADE "Contractors Dump Wagon". Courtesy Mapes Auctioneers & Appraisers.

Toy Transfer Wagon

A page from Arcade Catalog No. 26, with the hand-stamp "Received March 19, 1917" on it.

This is one of our most popular toys.
The body of the wagon is made of stamped steel, the other parts of cast iron.
The color scheme used adds greatly to the selling qualities of the toy.
  No. 1.   Without seat and figure.
  No. 2.   Complete as illustrated.

PACKING
  No. 1.   ½ dozen in a paper box, ¼ gross in a case.
    Case weight, net 54 pounds, gross 70 pounds.
    Case measurements, 26x13x12 inches.
  No. 2.   Each in a paper box, ¼ gross in a case.
    Case weight, net 63 pounds, gross 84 pounds.
    Case measurements, 25x16x13 inches.

Heavy Toy Dray

This is a strong, substantial toy made of the best grade of cast iron. It will stand very hard use.
The dray is finished in attractive enamels and helps to make it sell.
Extreme length 13½ inches.   Extreme height 7½ inches.

PACKING
Each one packed in a paper box. 3 dozen in a case.
Case weight, net 120 pounds, gross 154 pounds.
Case measurements, 26x19x17 inches.

168

	C6	C8	C10
Barclay Coach and Four, slush lead, circa 1930s, approx. 10-1/4"	30	45	60
Barclay Coach and Two, driver, no outrider	30	45	60
Barclay Covered Wagon w/Oxen, 1930s, "1849", 7" long	27	38	55
"Barnum and Bailey" Circus Cage, elephant drawn, 1930, painted, stained and litho wood, 35" long	400	600	800

"Barnum and Bailey" Circus Cage, 35" long. Courtesy Lloyd W. Ralston Auctions.

BLISS

Bliss was founded about 1832 by Rufus Bliss. Toymaking may not have begun till the late 1860s or early 1870s in its Rehoboth, Mass., plant. But by 1871 its toys were being advertised. Most were made of wood and the range was wide; from dollhouses to trains, Noah's arks and ships. In 1883 Bliss

ARCADE McCormick Deering Spreader.

BARCLAY Coach and Four, approx. 10-1/4" long. Photo by Bill Kaufman. Courtesy Evelyn Besser.

BARCLAY Coach and 2 horses, driver, no outrider. Photo by K. Warren Mitchell.

made what maight have been the first toy telephone set. The brilliant color lithography of Bliss's toys has made many of them prime collectibles.

	C6	C8	C10
Bliss Cinderella coach, 1890, paper litho on wood, 2 horses, 4 coachmen, lift off roof, blocks inside tell Cinderella story, 26" long	1000	3500	5500
Bliss Fire Hook and Ladder, 2 firemen, 2 horses, 29" long	2000	3000	4000
Bliss Fire Hook and Ladder, paper litho on wood, 31" long	1500	2500	4000
Bliss Pansy 4-Horse Stagecoach, 1890, paper litho on wood, 31"	1000	1500	2500
Bliss "Rough and Ready" Fire Engine, 2 horses, 30" long	1600	2700	4000
"Borden's Farm Products", wood, horse-drawn wagon pull-toy with articulated legs	1000	1500	2000
Bread Wagon "Bread and Cakes" w/driver, tin horse, 12-1/2" long	350	525	700
Brewery Wagon, cast iron and pressed steel, 2-horse w/driver, 20-1/2"	350	525	700
Brownie on Elephant-drawn Cart, cast iron	400	700	1000

BLISS "Rough and Ready" Fire Engine (missing rear fireman). Courtesy Christie's East.

BLISS Pansy 4-horse Stagecoach, 1890. Courtesy Lloyd W. Ralston Auctions.

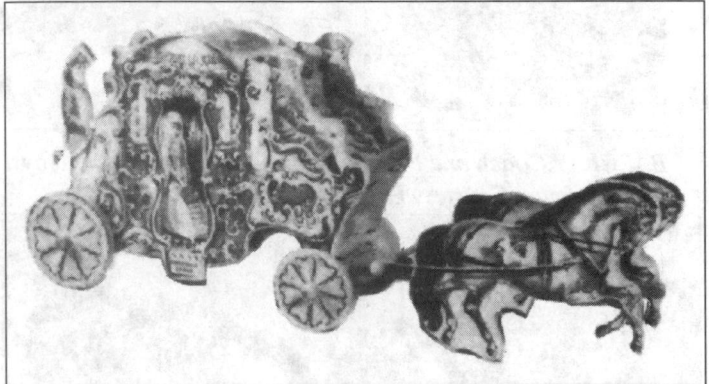

BLISS Cinderella Coach. 1890. Courtesy Lloyd W. Ralston Auctions.

BLISS Fire Hook & Ladder, 2-horse, approx. 30" long. Courtesy Wilkinson Collection, Detroit Antique Toy Museum.

	C6	C8	C10
Buckboard, cast iron, 1-horse and driver, 14" long	200	300	400
Buggy and Horse, tin	300	450	600
Buggy, pressed steel, cast iron wheels and horse	40	60	80
Buggy w/driver, cast iron, 6-1/2"	70	105	140

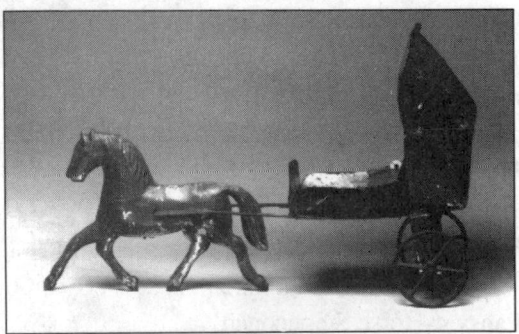

Buggy and Horse, tin. Courtesy Sotheby's New York.

CARPENTER

Carpenter (Francis W.) of Harrison and Port Chester, New York, was in business from 1844-1925. Malleable iron was its trademark; malleable iron being a type that has a bit of give, making it less fragile. Its two predominant lines were horse-drawn toys and trains.

	C6	C8	C10
Carpenter Cart, animated, c. 1902, cast iron, 10-1/2" long	450	675	900

	C6	C8	C10
Carpenter Cart, 2-horse, 12" long	250	375	500
Carpenter Cart, 2-wheel, 1-horse, no driver, pat. 1882	250	400	500
Carpenter Coal Cart, iron	2000	3000	4000
Carpenter Delivery Wagon, pat. 1881, 12" long	200	300	400
Carpenter Doctor's Cart	400	600	800
Carpenter Dump Cart, 1-horse, 12"	400	600	800
Carpenter Dump Cart, 2-horse	350	600	800
Carpenter Fire Patrol, cast iron, 2-horse, driver and 3 figures, 1885, 16-1/2" long	900	1400	1900
Carpenter Fire Wagon, 1-horse, 1-fireman	350	500	750
Carpenter Hook and Ladder, 2-horse, 2 firemen in standard helmets, early	800	1200	1600
Carpenter Hook and Ladder, cast iron, 2-horse w/driver and rear man, ladders circa 1883-1890, 26-1/2"	700	1050	1400
Carpenter Horse and Carriage, 1880, painted, cast iron, 14" long	750	1000	1500
Carpenter Horse Cart, cast iron, c. 1880, 1-horse, 2 men, 14-1/2" long	800	1200	1600
Carpenter Ox Cart, 2 oxen, cast iron, circa 1880-1903, 11" long	400	600	800
Carpenter Pumper, 2-horse, No. 33, 18" long	1000	1700	2600

CARPENTER, Left to Right: Cart, two-horse, 12" long, Dump Cart, one-horse, 12" long (driver not correct in photo). Courtesy Sotheby's New York.

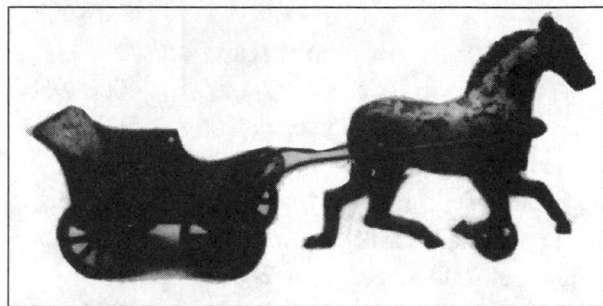

CARPENTER Horse and Carriage, 1880, 14" long. Courtesy Lloyd W. Ralston Auctions.

CARPENTER "Tally-Ho", approx, 27½" long. Courtesy Sotheby's New York.

CARPENTER Fire Patrol, cast iron, 2-horse (one figure in photo missing). Courtesy Sotheby's New York.

Cart one Horse, tin 15" long. Courtesy Lloyd W. Ralston Auctions.

CARPENTER Wagon, two-horse, 16" long (driver in photo replaced). Courtesy Sotheby's New York.

DENT Hook and Ladder, 1915, 14" long. Courtesy Lloyd W. Ralston Auctions.

Chariot with Clown, Camel-Drawn. Courtesy James S. Maxwell/Virginia Caputo. Photo by Virginia Caputo.

DENT Hose Reel, three-horse. Courtesy Sotheby's New York.

DENT Pumper, 1915, 14½" long. Courtesy Lloyd W. Ralston Auctions.

	C6	C8	C10
Carpenter Tally-Ho, 4-horse, cast iron, 7 festive riders in coach, 27-1/2"........	4000	9500	12,000
Carpenter Wagon, 2-horse, 10" long.....	550	850	1300
Carriage, metal and wood, 1-horse, malleable iron horse w/articulated legs and tail, carriage made of wood....	300	450	600
Cart, bull-pulled, cast iron, 2-wheeled cart......................	100	150	200
Cart, cast iron lion, 2 wheels, 8"long.....	125	188	250
Cart, 1-horse, cast iron, 9" long.............	50	75	100
Cart, 1-horse, early tin, 8" long.............	200	300	400
Cart, 1-horse, painted tin, 1890, 15" long......................	250	500	750
Cart w/driver and buffalo, cast iron, 7-1/2" long......................	400	600	800
Cart w/woman and prancing horse, cast iron, 10-1/4" long......................	500	750	1200
Cart w/elephant, cast iron, 7" long.........	125	188	250
Cart, stake sides, 1-horse, early cast iron, 7" long......................	150	225	300
Chariot drawn by tin horse, highly decorated, 13-1/2" long......................	125	187	250
Chariot w/clown, camel-drawn, cast iron......................	1000	1600	2400
Chein "Dispatch" Wagon, 1-horse, 11-1/2" long......................	90	135	180
Chief's Wagon, cast iron "Chief", 1-horse, c. 1915-1920, 12" long........	150	225	300
"Chief" Fire Chief Wagon, cast iron, 1-horse, 15-1/2" long......................	200	300	400
Circus Wagon, iron and tin, 2 horses, lion cage, 9" long......................	200	300	400
Circus Wagon, cast iron and wood, containing carved wood bear, 13" long......................	250	337	500
"City Sprinkler" cast iron, 8-1/4"........ No Price Found			
Coal Wagon, cast iron, small.................	50	75	100
"Coal" Wagon, cast iron w/driver and coal shovel, 9-1/4".............	137	202	275

	C6	C8	C10
Conestoga Wagon, cast iron,w/cloth cover and 2-horese, 12-1/2" long......	50	75	100
Conestoga Wagon, litho walking horses, iron wheels, 18" long............	140	210	280
Confectionary Wagon, early, 1-horse..	500	750	1000
Converse "Delivery" Wagon, wood seat, 1-horse, circa 1915.............	350	525	700
Courtland Circus Parade No. 300, "Monkeys" on side.............	150	250	350
Courtland Circus Parade No. 400, "African Lions" on side.............	150	250	350
Courtland Circus Parade No. 500, "Circus Band" on side (all Circus Parades 11-5/8" long).............	200	300	400
Courtland Easter Rabbit Pulling Van, No. 200, 11-5/8" long.............	75	100	150
Covered Wagon, cast iron, cloth top, 1-horse, driver, 13" long.............	170	255	340
Covered Wagon, tin, driver and horse, Indian head litho on side.............	40	60	80
Dent Buckboard, rider, 1-horse, very early, primitive looking.............	125	188	250
Dent Cart, horse and driver, 10" long....	125	188	250
Dent Cart, lady driver, horse, 11" long..	150	225	300
Dent Cart, mule, driver.............	250	375	500
Dent Contractors Dump Wagon, 2 horses, 15" long.............	150	225	300
Dent Coupe, 1-horse, driver, 9-3/4".......	125	188	250
Dent Dray, 2-horse, driver.............	550	9800	1300
Dent Dump Cart, black man, mule........	300	450	600
Dent Fire Engine Pumper, silver w/white horses, 2 horses, 21" long.............	400	750	1000
Dent Fire Engine Steam Pumper, 3 horses, 21" long.............	1000	1700	2400
Dent Fire Hook & Ladder, 27" long......	1000	1700	2400
Dent Fire Patrol, 3 horses, firemen figures, 15-1/2" long.............	400	1000	2000
Dent Fire "Patrol", c. 1905, 3-horse, cast iron, driver, 6 riders, 22" long...	1200	2000	2800
Dent Fire Pumper, c. 1908, 3-horse, driver, paint and nickel plate, 15-1/2"..	500	800	1100
Dent Fire Snorkle Wagon, 3-horse, driver.............	500	750	1000

Doctor's Cart, cast iron, 11" long. Courtesy Sotheby's New York.

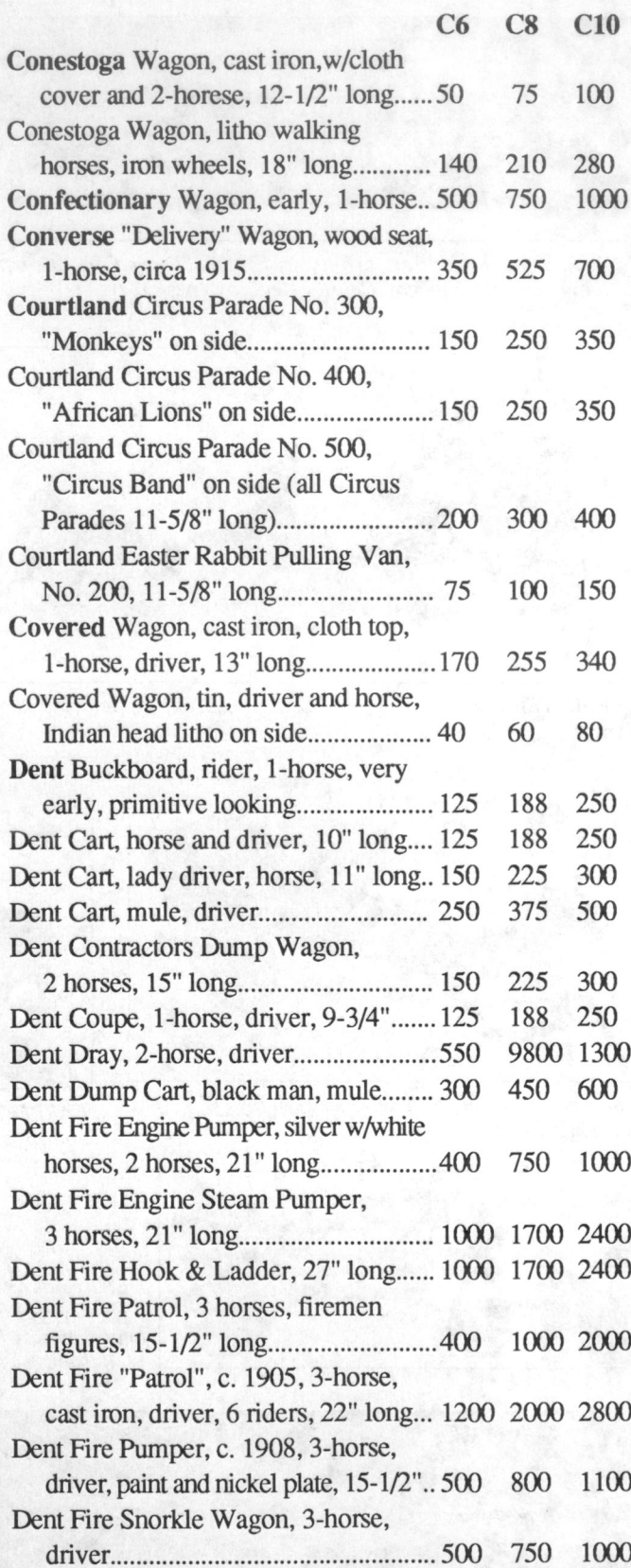

DENT Water Tower, c.1910 (driver missing). Courtesy Christie's East.

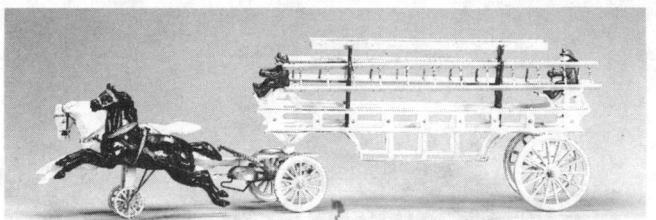

DENT Fire Hook & Ladder, 27" long. Courtesy Christie's East.

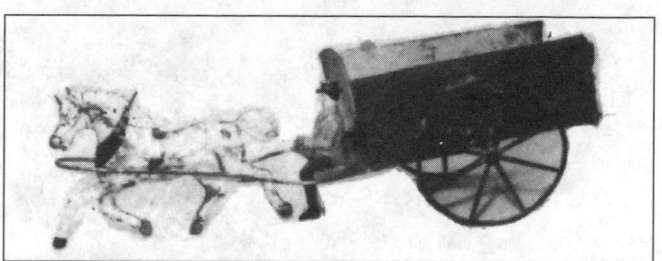

Dump Cart, "Hard and Soft Coal - Coke and Kindlings". Courtesy Lloyd W. Ralston Auctions.

	C6	C8	C10
Dent Hansom Cab, cast iron, c. 1905, lady passenger, driver, 14" long	700	1150	1600
Dent No. 57 Hansom Cab, 2-wheeled, 1-horse	175	262	350
Dent Hook and Ladder, 3-horse, extra large	500	1000	1500
Dent Hook and Ladder, painted cast iron, 1915, mechanized horses, 14" long	250	400	800
Dent Hose Reel, 3-horse, figures, 24", 10" horse	1200	2000	2900
Dent Horse and Cart, cart is tin	150	225	300
Dent Horse and Cart, low sides, all cast iron	125	188	250
Dent "Ice" Wagon, 2-horse, 12"	100	200	300
Dent "Ice" Wagon, 1-horse, 14" long	300	500	750
Dent "Ice" Wagon, cast iron, black horse pulling yellow and orange ice wagon, w/driver, c. 1910, 15-1/2"	675	1000	1350
Dent Ladder Wagon, 1890, 4-horse, may be longest cast iron toy made, 43-1/2"	3000	4500	6500
Dent Ox Wagon, 2 oxen, driver, cast iron, 16" long	250	500	600
Dent Ox Cart, stake sides, 1 ox	125	188	250
Dent Police Patrol, 3 horses, driver and 4 patrolmen, 21" long	500	1000	1500
Dent Pony Cart No. 20, has driver, team of horses, stake sides on cart	125	187	250
Dent Pumper, painted cast iron, 1915, moving horses, 14-1/2" long	650	1000	1500
Dent Road Car, 1-horse, driver in top hat, 2 seats, 16" long	450	675	900
Dent Sleigh, 1-horse, c. 1905, 16-1/4"	650	1000	1500
Dent Small Truck Wagon, stake sides	200	300	400
Dent 1-horse Truck Wagon, stake sides, w/driver, 16" long	200	300	400
Dent Sulky w/Jockey	150	225	300
Dent Surrey, horse has wheel attached to one leg	200	300	400
Dent Transfer Wagon, 2-horse, driver 26" long	650	1000	1650

	C6	C8	C10
Dent Water Tower, c. 1910, 2-horse, 31" long	900	1500	2200
Doctors Cart, cast iron, 11" long	850	1450	2000
Dog Cart (baby carriage), black cloth top, tin, 5-1/2" long	75	112	150
Dog Cart, circa 1875, tin, 10" long	400	600	800
Donkey and Cart, cast iron, w/driver	237	350	475
Donkey and Cart, tin, iron star wheels, 8" long	300	350	600
Donkey and Cart, tin, 8-1/2" long	250	375	500
Dray, cast iron, 1-horse, black horse pulling dray, 14" long	150	225	300
Dray Wagon, cast iron, driver and 2 horses, 18" long	250	375	500
"Dry Goods" cloth and wood 2-horse drawn wagon pull-toy, circa 1860, 26" long	400	600	800
Dump Cart, "Hard and Soft Coal-Coke and Kindlings", tin, 19"long	500	750	1000
"Dump Cart", horse pulling cart pull toy, 7-3/4" long	80	120	160
Dump Truck, cast iron and tin, 1-horse	200	300	400

JAMES FALLOWS

James Fallows was a foreman at the very early American tin toy company, Francis, Field and Francis. In 1874 he formed James Fallows & Company in Philadelphia. His toys were often marked "IXL" which may have stood for "I excel". Most of Fallows' toys were tine, though often with cast iron wheels. Papier mache was another prime material, in a toy line that was made up of over 200 items.

FALLOWS Horse and Carriage, 1890, 12-1/2" long. Courtesy Lloyd W. Ralston Auctions.

FALLOWS Streetcar, "4th Avenue". Courtesy Ed Hyers Antique Toys.

FALLOWS Covered Wagon, 12" long. Courtesy Lloyd W. Ralston Auctions.

FALLOWS "Pure Milk" Wagon, 12-1/2" long. Courtesy Lloyd W. Ralston Auctions.

	C6	C8	C10
Fallows Cart, tin, 12" long	500	750	1000
Fallows Cart and Horse, painted tin, 1870, 8-1/2" long	100	200	400
Fallows Covered Wagon, painted tin, litho paper scenes on sides, 12"	800	1000	1500
Fallows "Dump Cart", 1-horse, tin, circa 1890, 16" long	600	1000	1200
Fallows "Fancy Goods and Toys", 21" long	1750	2625	3500
Fallows "Fine Groceries" Delivery Wagon, 7-1/2" long	1250	1875	2500
Fallows Fire Pumper, 2-horse, very early, 18" long	5000	8500	10,000
Fallows Fire Pumper, tin, very early 24" long	5000	10,000	15,000
Fallows Horse and Carriage, 1890, American painted and stenciled tin, 12-1/2" long	500	750	1000
Fallows "Pure Milk" Wagon, 1895, painted and stenciled tin, 12-1/2"	800	1200	2000
Fallows Streetcar, "4th Avenue", 1-horse, tin	500	750	1000
Fallows Streetcar, 9" long	400	600	900
Fallows Streetcar, 2 horses, 10" long	350	500	800
Fallows Wagon and Donkey, cast iron, 10-1/2" long	175	263	350
Farm Wagon, cast iron, 2-horse, 10"	200	300	400

	C6	C8	C10
Farm Wagon, cast iron, 2 unusual horses, w/driver, 14" long	250	375	500
Farm Wagon, cast iron, large heavy horses, body wood, 25-1/2" long	300	450	600
Farm Wagon, tin, w/horse, 10-1/2"	40	60	80
"Fine Groceries", tin wagon, 2 horses, 14" long	400	600	800
Fire Hose Reel, cast iron, horse-drawn, 6" long	150	225	300
"Fire Patrol", cast iron, 3 horses, wagon contains 2 firemen and driver, 17" long	900	1350	1800
"Fire Patrol", 3 horses, driver, riders, 18-3/4" long	1000	1500	2000
"Fire Patrol" cast iron, 2 horses, 3 firemen, driver, c. 1910, 19"	1250	1875	2500
"Fire Patrol", cast iron, 2 horses, 3 firemen, 1 driver, circa 1890, 20-1/2" long	600	950	1300
Fire Pumper, cast iron, 3 horses, 11-1/4"	500	750	1000
Fire Pumper, cast iron, 2-horse w/driver, 13" long	600	900	1200
Fire Pumper, cast iron, 3 horses, 14-1/2"	650	1050	1500

"Fire Patrol", cast iron, 2-horse, 3 firemen and driver, 20-1/2" long, circa 1890. Courtesy Phillips New York.

	C6	C8	C10
Fire Pumper, cast iron, 2 horses, driver, 19-3/4" long	500	750	1000
Fire Pumper, circa 1910, cast iron, 3 horses, 17-1/2" long	500	750	1000
Fire Pumper, cast iron, 3 horses w/driver, fireman, circa 1910, 18-1/4" long	600	900	1200
Francis, Field and Francis Doctor's Buggy, 1-horse, tin, c. 1860, 14"		No Price Found	
"Friendship 1774" Fire Pumper, cast iron, rubber hose, 16" long	500	850	1200

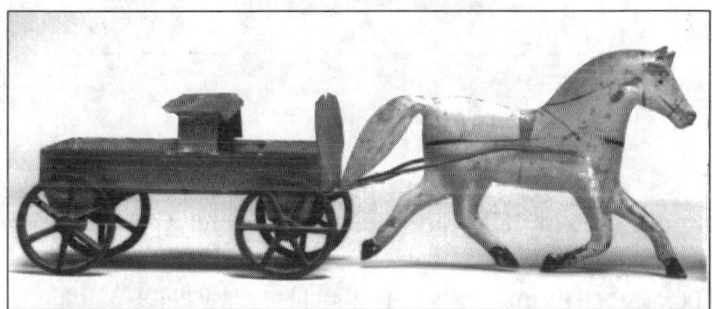

"Friendship 1774" Fire Pumper, 16" long. Courtesy Christie's East.

GEORGE BROWN

In 1856, George W. Brown, with Chauncey Goodrich, founded George W. Brown and Company, toymakers. Brown, an innovator, introduced the American clockwork toy (he'd spent 11 years in the clockmaking business). He invented many of his toys' mechanisms and may also have designed all or most of his toys. Brown worked primarily in tin, jobbing some of the work out to companies like Clinton, Connecticut's Union Manufacturing Company. Necessarily simple because of the material and manufacturing techniques employed, Brown's toys made up for it with brilliant hand-painted color and stenciling. Tops, rattles, flutes, wagons, fire engines, swords, trains and toy buckets were among the many items put out by the firm. The company merged with Stevens in 1868 and was dissolved in 1880.

	C6	C8	C10
George Brown Cab, driver, 1-horse, 8 1/2"long	560	840	1120
George Brown Cart and Horse, 1880, painted and stenciled tin, 7-1/2" long	200	300	500
George Brown "Charles" Hose Reel, circa 1870, tin, 15" long, auctioned in 1991 for $231,000			
George Brown Delivery Cart, 12"	1100	1800	2600

	C6	C8	C10
George Brown Doctor's Buggy, tin, cast iron, 14" long	650	975	1300
George Brown Dog Cart, c. 1870	400	700	1000
George Brown Dump Cart, painted tin, 1885, 8-1/4" long	100	150	200
George Brown Dump Cart, 1880, tin, back gate lifts out for dumping, 13"	200	300	400
George Brown "Eagle Chariot", painted tin, 1870, 11" long	500	1000	2500
George Brown "Express" Wagon, tin w/iron wheels, 10-1/2" long	300	450	600

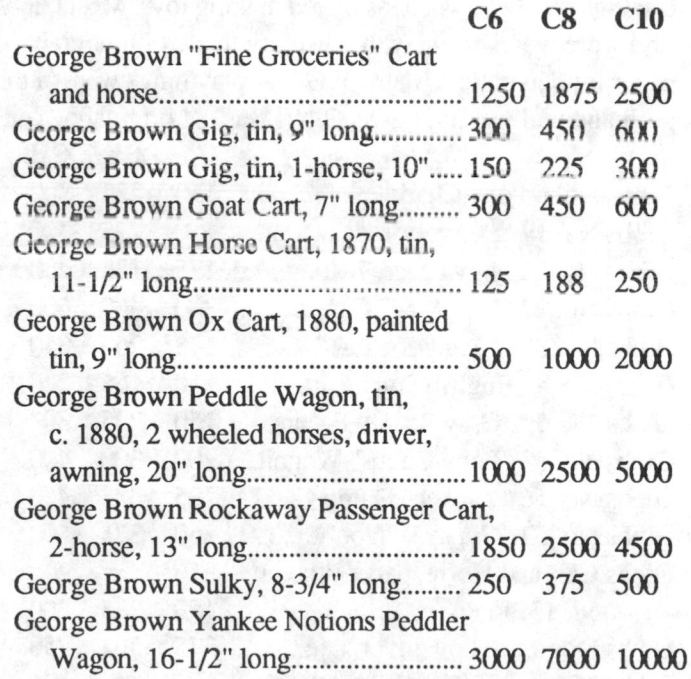

GEORGE BROWN "Express" Wagon, 10-1/2" long. Courtesy Sotheby's New York.

	C6	C8	C10
George Brown "Fine Groceries" Cart and horse	1250	1875	2500
George Brown Gig, tin, 9" long	300	450	600
George Brown Gig, tin, 1-horse, 10"	150	225	300
George Brown Goat Cart, 7" long	300	450	600
George Brown Horse Cart, 1870, tin, 11-1/2" long	125	188	250
George Brown Ox Cart, 1880, painted tin, 9" long	500	1000	2000
George Brown Peddle Wagon, tin, c. 1880, 2 wheeled horses, driver, awning, 20" long	1000	2500	5000
George Brown Rockaway Passenger Cart, 2-horse, 13" long	1850	2500	4500
George Brown Sulky, 8-3/4" long	250	375	500
George Brown Yankee Notions Peddler Wagon, 16-1/2" long	3000	7000	10000

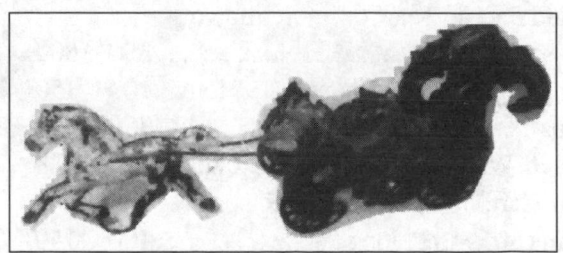

GEORGE BROWN Eagle Chariot. Courtes Lloyd W. Ralston Auctions.

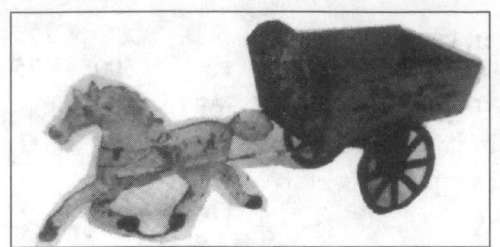

GEORGE BROWN Cart and Horse, 1880, 7-1/2" long. Courtesy Lloyd W. Ralston Auctions.

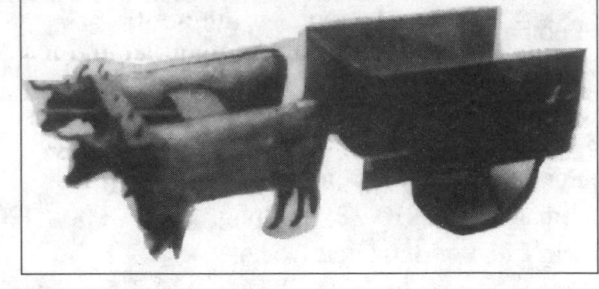

GEORGE BROWN Ox Cart, 9" long. Courtesy LLoyd W. Ralston Auctions.

GIBBS No. 50 "Gray Beauty Pacer". Courtesy Lloyd W. Ralston Auction.

GIBBS

Gibbs Manufacturing Company of Canton, Ohio began turning out toys in 1896 (after previously, from about 1830, manufacturing wooden barrels and tubs and metal plows). The company's first toy was a political giveaway for William McKinley. (McKinley was from Canton) It was a spring-operated top, and variations of it remained in the firm's catalogs till 1969, when it stopped making toys. Most Gibbs toys were wood or tin, with much use made of lithographed paper for decoration. Many of Gibbs' playthings were of the push and pull variety. Lewis Gibbs was the original owner.

GEORGE BROWN Dump Cart, 1885, 8-1/4" long. Courtesy Lloyd W. Ralston Auctions.

	C6	C8	C10
Gibbs No. 6 Pony Chariot	150	225	300
Gibbs No. 14 "Delivery 14"	150	225	300
Gibbs No. 15 Pony Pacer, 7" long	125	188	250
Gibbs No. 27 "U.S. Mail" Cart	300	450	600
Gibbs No. 35 "Pacing Joe"	175	263	350
Gibbs No. 40 English Pony Cart	110	165	220
Gibbs No. 50 "Gray Beauty Pacers"	150	225	300
Gibbs No. 53 "Pony Circus" Wagon	200	300	400
Gibbs No. 56 "Yankee" Dump Cart	225	338	450
Gibbs No. 57 "Gypsy Wagon"	250	375	500
Gibbs Cart and Horse, paper litho on wood, 13" long	150	225	300
Gibbs Dog Cart, boy driver	375	562	750
Gibbs "Groceries The Great Atlantic and Pacific Tea Co." mule-drawn cart, 12" long	350	500	1000
Gibbs Hay Wagon, 2 horses, 19" long	100	150	200
Gibbs Tea Co. Mule Cart	350	500	1000
Girard Wagon, 2 tin horses, stake sides	125	188	250
Goat Cart, iron goat and wheels, tin cart, 7-1/2" long	100	150	200
Goat Cart, tin early, 10-1/2" long	150	225	300

"Golden Pasture Farm Products, Milk and Cream". Courtesy Lloyd W. Ralston Auctions.

GIBBS "U.S.Mail" No. 27, 12" long. Courtesy Wilkinson Collection, Detroit Antique Toy Museum.

GIBBS TOYS

The best selling and most attractive toys on the market. Children cannot resist them. You have only to put Gibbs Toys on your counters and they sell themselves. All jobbers carry Gibbs Toys.

TO RETAIL AT 5c., 10c., 25c., 50c.

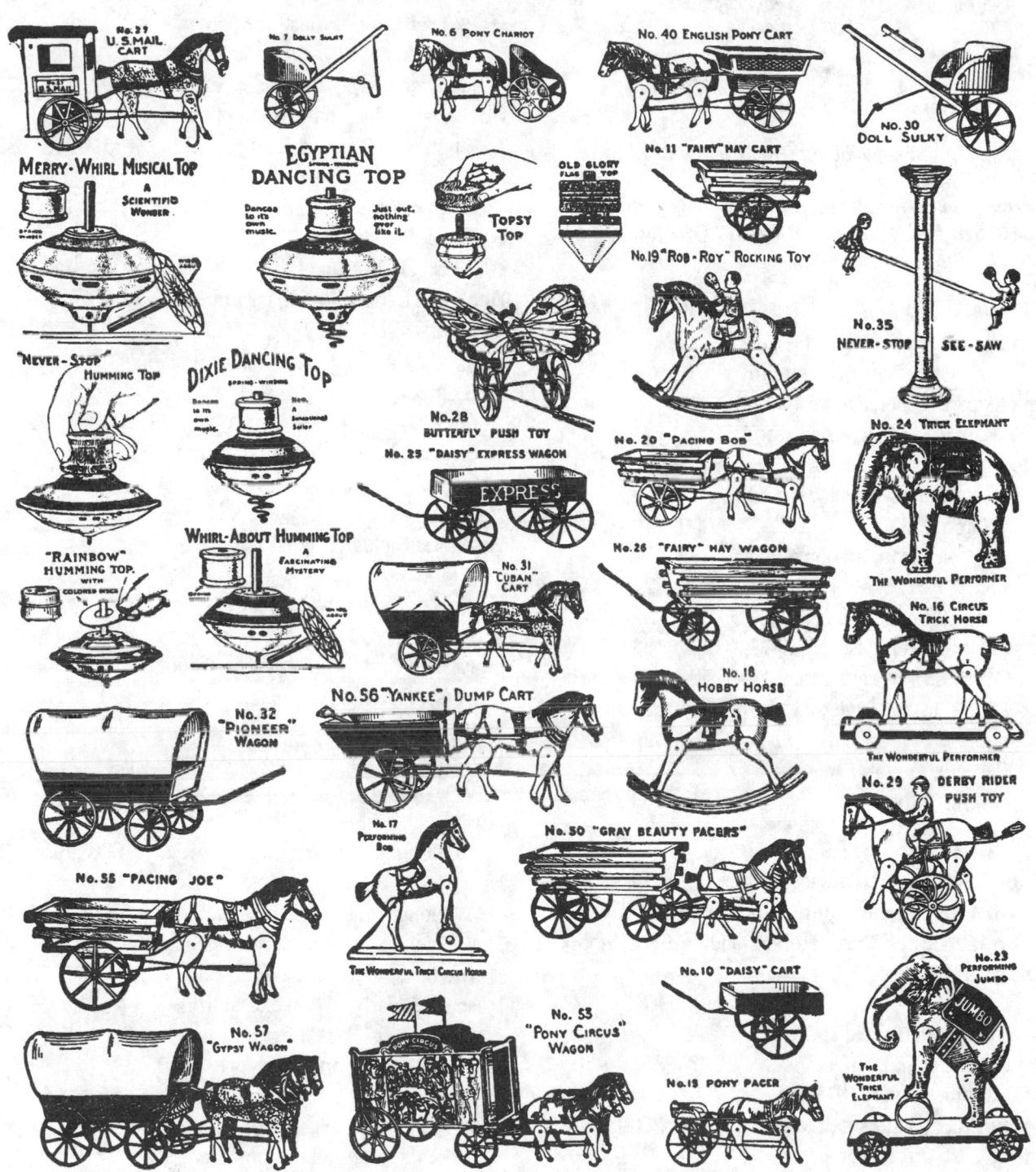

Gibbs Toys are always on display at our New York Agents

THE GIBBS MFG. CO. CANTON OHIO

NEW YORK AGENTS
The Owens-Kreiser Co.
The Strobel & Wilken Co.
Geo. Borgfeldt & Co.
Baker & Bennett Co.

An April, 1914 Gibbs ad.

No. 830.

Little, if anything, is known about Grey Iron's animal-drawn toys. This "Ice" wagon appears in a 1920s catalog. Probably the toy originated earlier. It seems to have come in three sizes: No. 825 at 10-1/4" long; No. 830 at 12-1/2" long; No. 845 at 14-5/8" long.

	C6	C8	C10
"**Golden** Pasture Farm Products, Milk & Cream", 1915, horse-drawn milk wagon, steering mechanism for child to ride, painted and stenciled wood, 30" long	500	750	100
Grass Cutter, 2 horses, driver, 2-wheeled cart, cast iron	1000	1500	2000
Hansom Cab, cast iron, no horse or figures	1500	2250	3000
Hansom Cab, 8" long	150	225	300
Hansom Cab w/driver, cast iron, 9-1/2"	120	188	250
Hansom Cab w/driver, cast iron, 9-3/4"	250	375	500
Hansom Cab, 1-horse, driver, cast iron, 10" long	285	426	570
Hansom Cab, tin, movable legs on horse, 15-1/2" long	175	263	350

HARRIS

Harris Toy Company of Toledo, Ohio seems to have begun production of cast iron toys during the late 1880s. The firm, which also jobbed for Dent, Hubley and Wilkins, stopped making toys in 1913.

	C6	C8	C10
Harris Brownie Shell Cart, 1903, cast iron	225	338	450
Harris Cart, mule driver, 10" long	250	500	750
Harris City Truck, 1-horse, driver	1200	2000	2700
Harris Dog Cart, girl driver, cast iron, 7" long	275	363	550
Harris Goat Cart, shell-type, cast iron, driver, 5" long	100	250	350
Harris Goat Cart, 2 goats, cast iron, driver	1000	2500	3000
Harris Hook and Ladder, 3-horse, cast iron, 19" long	140	210	280

	C6	C8	C10
Harris Transfer Wagon, 1903, 3 horses, 18-1/2" long	400	650	850
Harris Wagon, mule, 12" long	300	450	600
"**Hood's** Milk", Rich Toys, wood and tin, horse-drawn wagon pull-toy	37	56	75
Hook and Ladder, cast iron, tin and wood, 2 horses w/driver and three ladders, 16-1/2" long	150	225	300
Hook and Ladder, cast iron and tin, 3 horses, 2 firemen, ladders, 21"	175	263	350
Hook and Ladder, cast iron, 2 horses, 22-3/4" long	1000	1650	2000
Hook and Ladder cast iron, 3 horses w/driver, 25" long	500	750	1000
Hook and Ladder Truck, cast iron, 3 horses, 25-1/2" long	600	900	1200
Hook and Ladder Truck, cast iron, 3 horses, 2 drivers, 4 ladders, circa 1910-1914, 31-1/4" long	1000	1500	2000
Hook and Ladder, pressed steel and iron, figures, ladders, unusual hanging horses	250	375	500
Hook and Ladder, 3 horses, driver, 27-1/2" long	750	1125	1500
Hook and Ladder, wood ladder w/figurines, 3 horses, 29-1/2" long	750	1125	1500
Horse and Cart, litho paper on wooden horse, tin cart	150	225	300
Horse pulling 2-wheel cart, tin	450	675	900
Horse w/open carriage and driver in top hat, tin, 5-1/2" long	150	225	300
Hose Reel, cast iron, 1-horse w/driver, 11" long	1000	1650	2500
Hose Reel, cast iron, 1 horse w/driver, 12" long	1000	1650	2500
Hose Reel, cast iron w/driver and cord fire hose, 1-horse, 12-1/2" long	500	750	1000
Hose Reel, early, 2-horse, cast iron, w/figure, 14-1/2" long	500	750	1000
Hose Reel, cast iron, 3 horses, c. 1910, 19" long	600	900	1200
Hose Reel, Wagon, cast iron, driver, 2 horses, man standing on rear bumper, 21" long	750	1125	1500
Hose Reel, cast iron, c. 1910-1914, 3 horses w/driver and fireman, 21"	1000	1500	2000
Hose Reel, early, cast iron, unusual horse	500	750	1000
Hose Wagon, cast iron, 2 firemen, 3 horses and bell, 21-1/2" long	750	1125	1500

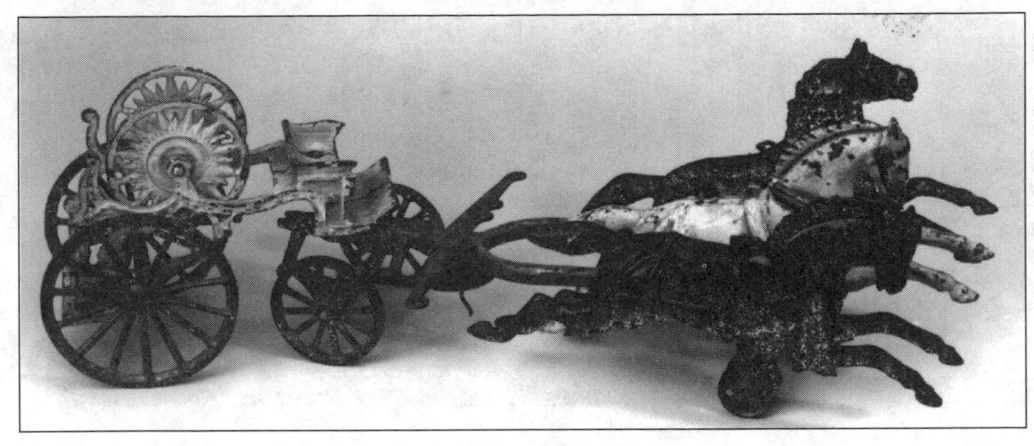

HOSE REEL, cast iron, 3 horses, 19" long. Courtesy Mapes Auctioneers & Appraisers.

	C6	C8	C10
Hubley Brake, 4-seated, 4 horses, 8 articulated passengers, 28"	5000	10,000	12,000
Hubley Brake, 3-seated, 2 plumed horses, cast iron, 18" long	3000	8500	10,000
Hubley Brake, 2-seat, driver, 3 women passengers, 16-1/2" long	2500	5000	75000
Hubley Brake, 2-seat, 16" long	1600	2700	4000
Hubley Brougham, cast iron and nickeled, horse and driver, 16" long	300	1000	1500
Hubley Brougham, top-hatted driver, 1-horse, 17" long	300	900	1500

	C6	C8	C10
Hubley Cab, 14" long	300	500	700
Hubley Cane Wagon, 15" long	600	900	1200
Hubley Cart, driver, 5-1/2" long	150	225	300
Hubley Cart, horse and driver, 8" long	155	232	310
Hubley Cart, wood, iron wheels, iron horse, 1910, 10-1/2" long	175	263	350
Hubley Chariot, cast iron, 8-3/4" long	500	750	1000
Hubley Chariot, 2-horse, driver, 9-1/2"	600	900	1200
Hubley Chariot w/clown, early, cast iron, 3 horses, 12-1/2" long	800	1200	1600
Hubley Chariot, Roman, w/driver, 3 horses	350	550	800
Hubley Coal Wagon, 2-horse, 16"	350	550	800
Hubley Coal Wagon, mule, 9" long	250	375	500
Hubley "Dray", 22" long	750	1100	1650

	C6	C8	C10
Hubley Dray Barrel Wagon w/barrels, barrel ramp, driver, 2 horses	1000	1600	2400
Hubley Eagle Milk Wagon, 12" long	300	750	1000
Hubley Essex Trap, 1890, cast iron, driver and horse, 13" long	500	1500	2500
Hubley Expandable Wagon w/wood bed, cast iron, 2 horses, driver, 26"	750	1125	1500
Hubley Farm Wagon, 1-horse, c. 1915, cast iron, 12-1/2" long	400	600	800
Hubley Fire Patrol, driver, 4 riders, all in standard helmets, 13" long	500	750	1000
Hubley Fire Patrol, driver, 4 firemen, prancing horse team, 21" long	700	1100	1500
Hubley Fire Pumper, cast iron, 2-horse w/driver, circa 1910, 14" long	200	400	600
Hubley Fire Pumper, cast iron, 2-horse, white-painted, circa 1906-1910, 19" long	750	1200	1700
Hubley Fire Pumper, 2-horse, cast iron, w/driver and 2 firemen, 20" long	750	1125	1500
Hubley Fire Pumper, 3 horses, w/driver, circa 1906-1910, 20-1/2" long	800	1200	1600

HUBLEY Brake, 4-seated, 4 horses, 8 articulated passengers. Courtesy Sotheby's New York.

HUBLEY Brake, 2-seat, 16" long. Courtesy Sotheby's New York.

HUBLEY Cab, 14" long. Courtesy Sotheby's New York.

HUBLEY Coal Wagon, 16" long, two-horse. Courtesy Sotheby's New York.

HUBLEY Chariot with clown, early, cast iron, three-horse, 12½" long. Courtesy Ed Hyers Antique Toys.

HUBLEY "Royal Circus" Calliope, 12¾" (medium). Courtesy Ed Hyers Antique Toys.

HUBLEY "Dray", 22" long (driver and horses in photo wrong). Courtesy Sotheby's New York.

HUBLEY Hose Tower Wagon, circa 1915, 28" long. Courtesy Sotheby's New York.

HUBLEY "Ice" Wagon, one-horse, 15" long. Courtesy Sotheby's New York.

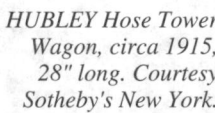

HUBLEY "Ice" Wagon, 9½" long, 1920's. Courtesy Lloyd W. Ralston Auctions.

	C6	C8	C10
Hubley Fire Pumper, 2 horses, cast iron, w/American Eagle, circa 1905-1910, 21" long	500	1000	1500
Hubley Gig, lady driver, horse drawn, 15" long	350	650	950
Hubley Hansom Cab, driver cast in window, horse	300	500	750
Hubley Hook and Ladder, 3 horses, 2 firemen, 2 wooden ladders, circa 1906-1910, 27-3/4" long	550	850	1300
Hubley Hook and Ladder, 2-horse, cast iron, 28" long	700	1200	1650
Hubley Hook and Ladder Wagon, 3 horses, w/eagle on shield on side 33" long	1200	2000	3000
Hubley Hose Reel, cast iron, 3 horses w/driver, circa 1906, 19" long	750	1200	1700
Hubley Hose Tower Wagon, c. 1915, 28" long	800	1300	1800
Hubley "Ice Wagon", 1920s, 9-1/2"	175	263	350
Hubley "Ice Wagon", 1910, cast iron, driver, horse, paint and nickel plate,14"	400	850	1200
Hubley "Ice" Wagon, 1 horse, 15"	800	1300	2000
Hubley "Ice" Wagon, 2-horse, cast iron 15" long	550	900	1300
Hubley "Ice" Wagon, 2-horse, cast iron, black horses pulling green wagon, w/driver, circa 1906, 15-1/2" long	800	1300	2000
Hubley "Ice" Wagon, driver, 2-horse, 16-1/2" long	1000	1650	2200
Hubley Landau Carriage, 1905, painted cast iron, 16-1/2" long	1400	2100	2800
Hubley Log Wagon, 2 oxen, driver, circa 1905, 15" long	600	1000	1300
Hubley Log Wagon, horse, 19" long	400	600	800
Hubley Milk Cart, 12-1/2" long	425	638	850
Hubley Milk Wagon, 5" long	140	210	280
Hubley Monkey Trapeze Circus Mirror Van, 12-1/2" long	500	800	1300
Hubley Phaeton, 1 horse	1200	2000	3000
Hubley "Police Patrol", driver, early, 3 riders, 13" long	500	750	1000
Hubley "Police Patrol, driver, 6 cops, 21" long	1000	1600	2200
Hubley Revolving Monkey Cage auctioned for $30,000 in 1988			
Hubley Roman Chariot, 3 small horses	425	637	850
Hubley Roman Chariot, 3 large horses	600	900	1200
Hubley Royal Circus, animals, driver, 2 horses, 15" long	500	1000	1200
Hubley Royal Circus Band Wagon, cast iron, 4 horses, 7 riders, 22"	1000	2000	3000
Hubley Royal Circus Band Wagon, c.1920, cast iron, 2 horses, 7 riders, 22-1/2"	1800	2900	4000
Hubley "Royal Circus" Bandwagon, 8 musicians and driver, 1920, 30"	1500	2250	3000
Hubley Royal Circus Bear Wagon, cast iron, 15" long	450	675	900
Hubley "Royal Circus" Calliope, 12-3/4" long (medium)	1400	2400	3400
Hubley "Royal Circus" Clown on Trapeze Van, 1920, oval-mirrored sides, 16-1/2"	1500	2500	3500
Hubley "Royal Circus" Farmer Van, 1920, head revolves and disappears in top of wagon as toy pulled, 16" long	2000	4000	6000
Hubley "Royal Circus" Giraffe Cage w/large and small giraffes, driver, 1920, 27" long	4200	7700	12,500
Hubley Royal Circus Lion Cage, 9"	300	500	750
Hubley "Royal Circus" Lion Wagon, w/rare grey horses and wagon, 15-3/4"	900	1350	1800
Hubley Royal Circus Polar Bear Cage, 1920s, 11-3/4" long	550	850	1450
Hubley Royal Circus Rhino Wagon, 16" long	1000	2000	3000
Hubley "Royal Circus" Tiger Wagon Cage, 1920, driver, 2 tigers, 16" long	350	750	1000
Hubley Santa Claus Sleigh, early, 1 reindeer, 15" long	800	1300	1800
Hubley Santa Claus Sleigh, 1910, cast iron, 2 reindeer, 16" long	600	1000	1500
Hubley Santa Claus Sleigh, early, 17" long	500	1000	1500
Hubley Shell Cart and Horse, 1905, 7" long	250	375	500
Hubley Sleigh, 1 horse, painted, cast iron, 1910, 14-1/2" long	500	800	1200
Hubley Sleigh, 1-horse, woman, w/ movable arms, early, 14-3/4" long	900	1400	2050
Hubley Sleigh, 1 horse, 1900, painted cast iron, nickel plated, 15" long	250	375	500
Hubley Sleigh, 2-horse, 1910, painted, nickel plated, cast iron, 15" long	250	375	500
Hubley Spring Wagon, horse, driver cast iron	200	300	400
Hubley Stanhope Gig, cast iron, 11-1/2"	200	300	400
Hubley Sulky, 8-1/2" long	187	280	375
Hubley Surrey, clockwork, 1894, cast iron, brass works, 5 colors, 9" long	500	1000	1500

HUBLEY Landau Carriage, 1905, 16-1/2" long. Courtesy Lloyd W. Ralston Auctions.

HUBLEY Log Wagon, 15" long, two oxen, driver. Courtesy Ed Hyers Antique Toys.

HUBLEY "Police Patrol", 21" long. Courtesy Sotheby's New York.

HUBLEY Sleigh, one horse, 15" long. Courtesy Lloyd W. Ralston Auctions.

HUBLEY Sleigh, two horses, 15" long. Courtesy Lloyd W. Ralston Auctions.

HUBLEY "Royal Circus" Lion Wagon, 15-3/4" long with rare grey horses and wagon. Courtesy Ed Hyers Antique Toys.

HUBLEY Sleigh, one horse, 14-1/4" long. Courtesy Lloyd W. Ralston Auctions.

HUBLEY Brake, Left to Right: 2-seated and 3-seated. Courtesy Sotheby's New York.

HUBLEY Royal Circus Bear Wagon, 15" long. Courtesy Sotheby's New York.

HUBLEY Left to Right: Royal Circus Band Wagon, 30" long, Revolving Monkey Cage (extremely rare). Courtesy Sotheby's New York.

HUBLEY "Royal Circus" Rhino Wagon. Courtesy James S. Maxwell/Virginia Caputo. Photo by Virginia Caputo.

HUBLEY "Royal Circus" Farmer Van. Courtesy James S. Maxwell/Virginia Caputo. Photo by Virginia Caputo.

HUBLEY Stanhope Gig. Courtesy Sotheby's New York.

HUBLEY Santa Claus Sleigh, 16" long. Courtesy Sotheby's New York.

HUBLEY "Royal Circus", Left to Right: Rhino Wagon, Tiger Wagon. Courtesy Sotheby's New York.

HUBLEY Monkey Trapeze Circus Van, 12-1/2" long. Courtesy Christie's East.

Hubley "Royal Circus" Band Wagon, 22" long, 4-horse, 7 riders (driver in photo incorrect). Courtesy Sotheby's New York.

	C6	C8	C10
Hubley Surrey, 2-horse, driver, rider, circa 1900, 12" long	240	360	480
Hubley Surrey, 2-horse, woman driver, 13-3/4" long	750	1125	1500
Hubley Surrey, 2-horse, driver, 18"	400	600	800
Hubley Surrey, tin and cast iron, 2-seat w/driver and woman passenger, 2-horse	600	900	1200
Hubley Surrey, 2-seat, driver, woman passenger, 2-horse, 13-3/4" long	600	900	1200
Hubley Trotter, 1900, cast iron, horse and driver, 8-3/4" long	200	300	400
Hubley Trotter Gig, lady driver, 11"	150	225	300
Hubley Wagon, horse, cast iron, 12"	150	225	300
Hull & Stafford Dump Cart	700	1000	1600
Hull & Stafford Express Wagon	350	550	750

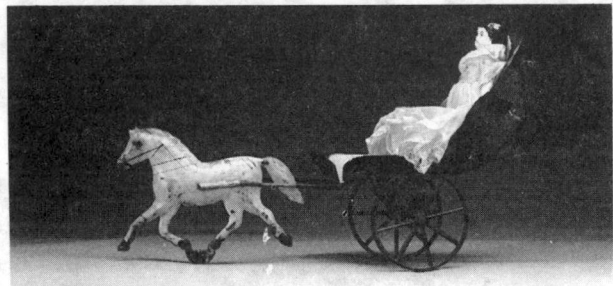

HULL & STAFFORD Gig, China Doll. Courtesy Christie's East.

	C6	C8	C10
Hull & Stafford Gig, China doll, circa 1885, 12" long	650	1150	1500
Hull & Stafford Liberty Hose Reel, c. 1870, 15-3/8", auctioned in touched-up condition in 1993 for $22,000			
Hull & Stafford "Prospect Park" Omnibus, c. 1880, 2-horse, driver, 16-1/2"	5000	10,000	15,000
Hull & Stafford Wagon, 9" long	800	1400	2000
Ice Cart, tin horse-drawn	200	300	400
"Ice" Wagon, 1 horse, cast iron, 12"	500	750	1000
Ice Wagon, cast iron, 2-horse, 12"	600	900	1200
Ideal Fire Pumper, 2 horses, cast iron, 2 riders, 20-1/2" long	250	500	750

IDEAL "Patrol", cast iron Fire Patrol, 21" long. Courtesy Sotheby's New York.

	C6	C8	C10
"Ideal Fire Department", 3 horses, cast iron, 30" long	500	1000	1500
Ideal "Patrol" cast iron fire patrol, 21" long	1000	1700	2500

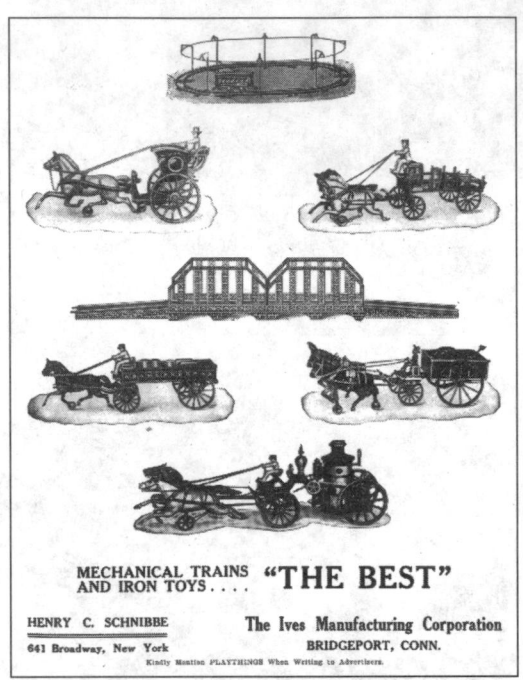

IVES toys from November, 1908. Courtesy Playthings Magazine.

IVES

Ives is one of the fabled companies in American toy history. It was founded by Riley Ives as a metal stamping shop by at least the late 1850s. About 1865 the company made tin whistles for New York Rubber's squeak toys. This seems to have led to Ives' first true toys, hot air playthings, which were put in motion by the hot air from stoves, laterns, etc. These were first sold in 1868. Son Edward Ives joined about 1860. Edward's son, Harry, took over the reins in1895. He was ousted in 1929, and the firm was dissolved in 1932. During its heyday, which lasted about 40 years, the firm put out a deluge of toys of every type, with quality its watchword. Toymaking was carried on from about 1870 till the end in Bridgeport, Connecticut.

	C6	C8	C10
Ives "Adams Express", 2-horse, 21"	700	1200	1700
Ives Bandwagon, 9-passenger, cast iron, 31-1/2" long	2500	4000	6000
Ives Caisson, driver, cannon, rider, 2 horses, 21" long	1700	3000	4000
Ives "Chief Fire Dept.", 14-1/2" long	400	700	1000
Ives Coal Dump Cart, donkey, black driver	500	750	1000
Ives Coal Dump Wagon, donkey, black driver	375	562	750

	C6	C8	C10
Ives Doctor's Cart, 2 wheels, 10-1/4"......	400	600	1000
Ives Dog Pulling Stake Cart...................	200	300	400
Ives Donkey Cart, 1 of 4 walking animal toys by Ives, circa 1890, cast iron 15" long..	750	1500	2500
Ives Dray Wagon, stake sides................	300	500	700
Ives "Fast Mail" Wagon, cast iron, walking horses, 17" long....................	750	2000	3500
Ives "Fire Patrol", circa 1890, 1 horse, 5 riders, driver, 19" long....................	1100	1700	2550
Ives Fire Patrol, 2-horse, driver, cast iron, 6 firemen, c. 1880-1910, 20-1/2".	800	1600	3000
Ives Fire Pumper, 2-horse, 13" long......	400	650	900
Ives Gig, 1890s, driver w/top hat, 5-1/2" long...	500	750	1000
Ives Hansom Cab w/walking horse, oversized..	4500	6500	10,000
Ives Hook and Ladder, Phoenix, circa 1890, 28" long...........................	1500	2400	3600
Ives Hook and Ladder, No. 45, c. 1885, ladders, pails, 28" long......................	900	1500	2100
Ives Hook and Ladder, c. 1890, cast iron, 2-horse, 2 riders, 29" long........	1000	1700	2500
Ives Hook and Ladder, cast iron, driver, 2-horse, 34" long..............................	1200	2000	2800
Ives Horse Cart, 1870, tin, 10" long......	600	950	1400
Ives Horse Cart, 1883, 2-horse,17-1/2".	750	1200	2500
Ives Hose Reel, cast iron, 1-horse, driver, "Phoenix", c. 1880-1910, 15" long...	1600	2400	3200

IVES Hook and Ladder No. 45. Courtesy Christie's East.

IVES Bandwagon, 31-1/2" long, 5 figures missing in photo. Courtesy James S. Maxwell/Virginia Caputo. Photo by Virginia Caputo.

IVES "Fire Patrol", 20-1/2" long. Courtesy Sotheby's New York.

IVES Dray Wagon, stake sides, 17" long. Courtesy Sotheby's New York.

IVES Coal Dump Wagon. Courtesy Sotheby's New York.

IVES "Chief Fire Dept.", 14-1/2" long (driver in photo incorrect). Courtesy Sotheby's New York.

	C6	C8	C10
Ives Hose Reel Wagon, 1-horse, driver, 16" long	750	1125	1500
Ives Ice Wagon w/mules, 1896	600	950	1400
Ives Ox Cart, 2 oxen	800	1300	1800
Ives "Patrol" Fire Wagon, 22" long	750	1125	1500
Ives Phoenix Pumper, c. 1890, cast iron, rarest of Ives pumpers (clockwork), 19" long	1500	2400	3800
Ives Police Patrol Wagon, 1890s, 6 patrolmen, driver, 20-1/2" long	1000	2000	3000
Ives Pumper, 23" long	2000	3200	4500
Ives Stake Wagon, 2 donkeys, 15-1/2"	400	600	800

	C6	C8	C10
Ives Steam Pumper, 2-horse, 20-1/2"	4000	6000	8000
Ives Walking Horse, pull toy, late 19th century, horse which walks by means of wheel mechanism under it, pulling a 2-wheeled cart	1800	2800	4000
Ives and Blakeslee Fire Pumper, 1893, cast iron, largest cast iron pumper made by Ives, 25" long	1500	3000	5500
Jones & Bixler Uncle Sam Chariot, cast iron, 11-1/2" long	750	1200	1800

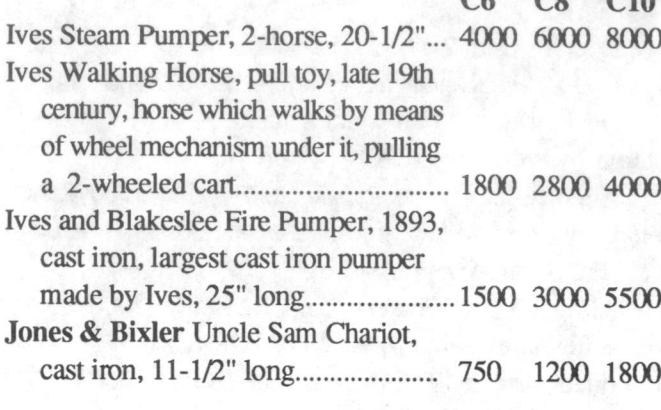

IVES Stake Wagon, 2 donkeys, 15-1/2" long. Courtesy Sotheby's New York.

IVES Hook and Ladder, 34" long. Courtesy Sotheby's New York.

IVES Hose Reel Wagon, 1 horse, driver, 16" long. Courtesy Sotheby's New York.

IVES Phoenix Pumper (clockwork). Courtesy Sotheby's New York.

IVES "Patrol" Fire Wagon, 22" long. Courtesy Sotheby's New York.

IVES Hook and Ladder, circa 1890, 29" long. Courtesy Sotheby's New York.

IVES Hook and Ladder, Phoenix. Courtesy Sotheby's New York.

JONES & BIXLER Uncle Sam Chariot. Courtesy Sotheby's New York.

KENTON

Kenton Lock Manufacturing Co. was incorporated in May, 1890, in Kenton, Ohio. In November of 1894, it became the Kenton Hardware Manufacturing Company, and around this period, began producing toys. It ceased production of horse-drawn toys in the early 1920s (except for a 1930s beer wagon), but in 1939 introduced a completely new line of horse-drawn pieces, running through 1954.

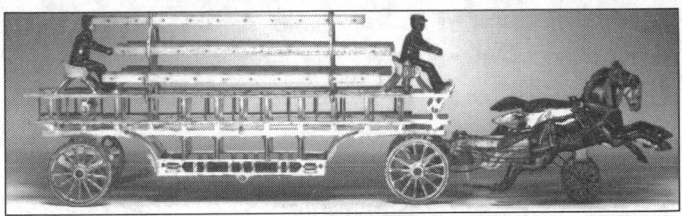

KENTON Hook and Ladder, 30" long. Courtesy Sotheby's New York.

KENTON Log Wagon, 15" long. Courtesy Sotheby's New York.

	C6	C8	C10
Kenton Aerial Fire Tower, 3 horses, driver, 30" long	800	1400	1900
Kenton Bakery Wagon, marked "Bakery", 1941	325	500	650
Kenton Band Wagon, musicians, driver, rider on horse	150	225	300
Kenton Boar Cart, circa 1910, cast iron, Egyptian driver, 8" long	350	500	750
Kenton Cabriolet, painted cast iron, 2nd series made into 1950s, 15"	162	243	325
Kenton Cement Mixer, driver, horse, 14" long	350	750	1000
Kenton Chariot, cast iron, 6" long	150	225	300
Kenton Chariot, w/comic driver, 1910, cast iron, 7-1/2" long	250	375	500
Kenton Chariot, 3-horse, cast iron	600	900	1200

	C6	C8	C10
Kenton "Chief" Wagon, 1-horse, driver, 12-1/4" long	500	800	1500
Kenton Circus Cage Wagon, 2 horses, 2 riders, driver, animal in cage	350	700	1000
Kenton "Coal" Cart, donkey pulling, black driver	365	550	725
Kenton Contractor's Wagon, w/black driver 15-1/2" long	400	600	800
Kenton Covered Wagon, cast iron, 2-horse	500	750	1000
Kenton "Cupid in Slipper", 1-horse cart, cast iron, 8-1/2" long	450	800	1100

KENTON "Milk" Wagon. Courtesy Sotheby's New York.

KENTON Overland Circus, Left to Right: Band Wagon, Bear Wagon. Courtesy Sotheby's New York.

KENTON "Overland Circus" Calliope Wagon. Courtesy Sotheby's New York.

KENTON Spider Phaeton, 11-1/2" long. Courtesy Sotheby's New York.

195

	C6	C8	C10
Kenton "Cupid" in horse-drawn slipper, 1-horse, 10-1/2" long	250	375	500
Kinton Delivery Cart, donkey, cast iron	150	225	300
Kenton Delivery Wagon No. 5 w/driver and 2 horses	400	600	800
Kenton Dog Cart, greyhound pulling dog riding, 7" long	250	375	500
Kenton Dray, 13-1/4" long	100	150	200
Kenton Dray, cast iron, 2 horses, black and white horses pulling green dray, w/driver, 13-1/2"	300	450	600
Kenton Dray No. 5, painted cast iron, 1930, 14-1/2" long	175	263	350
Kenton Dray Wagon w/horse and driver, cast iron, 14-3/4"	437	655	875
Kenton Dray, cast iron, 2 horses, pulling a green cart w/driver, late 1940s, 14-3/4" long	250	375	500
Kenton Dump Cart, mule	125	187	250
Kenton Dump Wagon, early 1900s, 10-1/4" long	150	225	300
Kenton Dump Wagon, 2 horses, lever releases bottom wagon	250	375	500
Kenton Egyptian Cart, elephant drawn	300	450	600
Kenton English Trap, 2-horse, woman, dog, c. 1895, 14" long	1600	2700	4000
Kenton Express Wagon, horse, driver cast iron	225	337	450

	C6	C8	C10
Kenton Express Wagon, 11" long	225	337	450
Kenton Farm Cart, mule, black driver, 10-1/2" long	375	562	750
Kenton Farm Wagon, driver, 1 horse, 14" long	300	500	700
Kenton Farm Wagon, 2-horse, cast iron, w/figure, 14-1/2" long	500	750	1100
Kenton Farm Wagon, driver, early, 1 horse, 15" long	300	450	600
Kenton Farm Wagon, 2-horse w/driver, 15" long	500	750	1000
Kenton Fire Ladder Wagon, front driver only, 12" long	150	225	300
Kenton Fire Ladder Wagon, horse drawn, drivers front/rear, 17" long	135	202	270
Kenton Fire Pumper, 2 horses, driver, 20" long	175	262	350
Kenton Fire Pumper, cast iron, 26-1/2" long, horses 11" long,	250	375	500
Kenton Fire Wagon, 2-horse, driver, equipment, bell, wagon nickel-plated, 23" long	200	300	400
Kenton Goat Cart, figure w/large cars, 7" long	250	375	500
Kenton Gravel Wagon, with 2 horses, 13" long	150	225	300

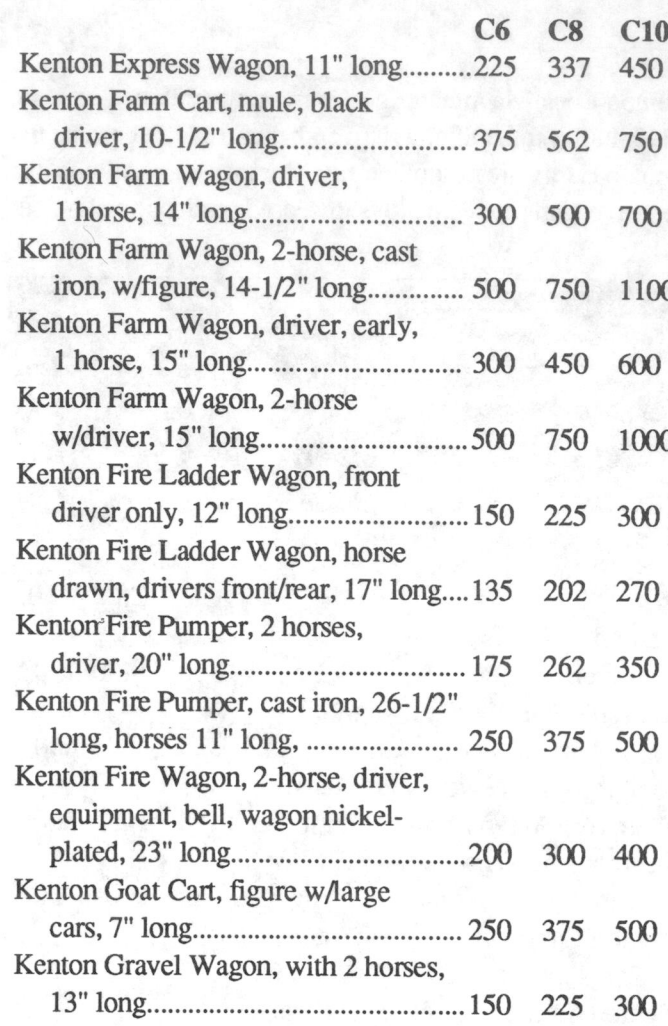

KENTON Plantation Cart, 1910. Courtesy Mapes Auctioneers & Appraisers.

KENTON Hose Reel, 1920, 13-1/2" long. Courtesy Lloyd W. Ralston Auctions.

KENTON Hook & Ladder, 1915, 26" long. Courtesy Lloyd W. Ralston Auctions.

KENTON Dray No. 5, 14-1/2" long. Courtesy Lloyd W. Ralston Auctions.

	C6	C8	C10
Kenton Hansom Cab, lady rider, driver in top hat, cast iron	700	1050	1400
Kenton Hansom Cab, top-hatted driver, 8" long	150	225	300
Kenton Hansom Cab, 1-horse, top-hatted driver, 10" long	1000	1500	2000
Kenton Hansom Cab, 12" long	500	750	1000
Kenton Hansom Cab, figures, horse, 15-1/2" long	300	500	700
Kenton Hook and Ladder Wagon, 2 horses, driver, 20" long	250	375	500
Kenton Hook and Ladder Wagon, nickel-plated, 2 horses, driver, 20" long	200	300	400
Kenton Hook and Ladder, 3 horses, cast iron, 16" long	300	450	650
Kenton Hook and Ladder, wagon, 3 horses, 17" long	250	375	500
Kenton Hook and Ladder, cast iron, 3 horses, circa 1910, 19" long	150	225	300
Kenton Hook and Ladder, 1915, painted cast iron, ladders, 26" long	600	1000	1400
Kenton Hook and Ladder, 30" long	1400	2200	3200
Kenton Hose Reel, 1920, painted cast iron, 13-1/2" long	500	750	1000
Kenton Hose Reel, cast iron, c. 1905, 2 horses, 14-1/2" long	600	900	1200
Kenton "Ice " Wagon, 2 horses, driver, 1920s, cast iron, 15" long	250	375	500
Kenton Landau, cast iron, white horse pulling green carriage w/driver, circa 1910, 15" long	600	900	1200
Kenton Log Wagon, 1-horse w/driver, 14-1/2" long	450	675	900
Kenton Log Wagon, black man, 2 oxen, early 1900s, cast iron, 15" long	500	800	1100
Kenton "Milk" Wagon, w/horse and driver	225	338	450
Kenton Overland Circus Band Wagon, 6 musicians and driver, 15-3/4"	445	682	910
Kenton "Overland Circus" Bear Wagon, cast iron, 2 horses w/driver, cage containing cast iron bears, 1940s, 13"	316	474	632
Kenton "Overland Circus" Calliope Wagon, 14-1/2" long	300	500	700
Kenton "Overland Circus", cast iron, 2 horses w/driver, cage containing cloth bear, 14" long	310	465	620
Kenton Ox Cart, cast iron, 5" long	100	150	200
Kenton Ox Cart, 7" long	110	165	220
Kenton Ox Cart, 12-1/2" long	150	225	300
Kenton Ox Wagon, 2 oxen, 18" long	400	600	800
Kenton "Patrol" No. 526, 2 horses, driver, riders, 17" long	650	1100	1500
Kenton Plantation Cart, 1910, black driver, mule, 10" long	225	337	450
Kenton "Polar Ice" Wagon, 2-donkey	500	750	1000
Kenton Police Patrol w/mule team, 16"	500	750	1000
Kenton Pumper, 3 horses, 18" long	400	600	800
Kenton Rabbit, pulling cart w/2 wheels and seat, cast iron, 5" long	200	300	500
Kenton Rhino Cart, 8" long	100	200	300
Kenton Sand and Gravel Dump Wagon, driver, 2 horses, 15" long	147	230	295
Kenton "Sand and Gravel" Dump Wagon, driver, 2 horses, 10" long	210	315	420
Kenton Spider Phaeton, cast iron, 11-1/2" long	850	1350	2000
Kenton Stake Wagon, 2 horses, driver w/reins, 15" long	225	338	450
Kenton Sulky, driver cast to sulky, 6" long	75	112	150
Kenton Sulky, 2-wheel race cart w/jockey and horse, 6" long	75	112	150
Kenton Sulky and driver, cast iron 7" long	250	375	500
Kenton Surrey, 2 horses, cast iron w/driver and passenger, 12-1/2"	150	225	300
Kenton Surrey w/fringe top, driver and passenger, 2 horses (c.1943?) 13" long	145	218	290
Kenton Surrey, 1-horse, approx. 1940, 16" long	150	225	300
Kenton Team of Horses w/log and black driver	500	750	1000
Kenton Transfer Wagon, 2 horses, driver.	650	975	1300
Kenton 3.2 Beer Delivery Wagon, cast iron, 1930s, 2 horses, driver, 10 wooden kegs, 14-1/2" long	350	525	700
Kenton Victoria Cab and horse, cast iron w/driver and woman, 15-1/2" long	150	225	300
Kenton No. 3, 1-horse Wagon, w/driver, 15" long	125	187	250
Kenton No. 5 Wagon, 1-horse, 15"	125	187	250
Kenton Wagon, 2 horses, 15" long	90	135	180
Kenton Wagon w/driver, 2 horses, 10-1/4"	100	150	200
Kingsbury Dray, 2-horse, cast iron, 20-1/4" long	300	450	600
Kingsbury Hook and Ladder, 3 horses, 2 riders, rubber covers on wheels, cast iron and pressed steel, 25-1/2"	400	600	800

	C6	C8	C10
Kingsbury Hook and Ladder, 2 horses, driver, 3 ladders, 27" long	600	900	1200
Kingsbury Ladder Truck, 1900, cast iron, tin and wood, 13" long	300	450	600
"The Klondike Ice Co., New York", tin ice wagon, 2 horses, 17-1/2"	350	525	700
Kyser & Rex Santa Claus in sleigh, cast iron and steel, auctioned in 1990 for $2,970.			
Ladder Wagon, cast iron, 2 ladders and 3 galloping horses, 13-1/2"	150	225	300
Ladder Wagon, cast iron, w/2 horses, 3 sections of ladder, bell, 25-1/2"	250	375	500
Ladder Wagon, cast iron w/2 drivers, 4 sections of ladder and 3 horses, Dart type, 30-1/2" long	200	300	400
Lancaster Hook and Ladder, 2 horses, cast iron, 25" long	150	225	300
Lancaster Hook and Ladder, 2 horses, 2 drivers, cast iron, 28" long	200	300	400
Lancaster Hook and Ladder, cast iron, 3 horses, 2 drivers, 28" long	250	375	500
Lancaster Hubley No. 58 Surrey, no driver	75	112	150
Lancaster Hubley No. 174 Surrey, w/1 seat, driver, horse	150	225	300
Landau, 4 horses w/driver, 24" long	300	450	600
Lehmann "Africa" tin friction toy, ostrich pulling cart	387	590	775

LEHMANN "Africa". Courtesy Sotheby's New York.

	C6	C8	C10
Lehmann "Duo" Rooster pulling egg cast w/a rabbit perched on top, tin friction	800	1200	1600
Lincoln Logs No. 30 Covered Wagon Set	62.50	93.75	125
Log Wagon, cast iron w/driver and 2 oxen, 15-1/4" long	450	675	900
Mail Cart, tin, horse-drawn	140	210	280
Marx Cart and Horse	90	135	180
Marx Covered Wagon, tin litho, friction, 9" long	60	90	120

	C6	C8	C10
Marx Toyland Milk & Cream Wagon, 1930s, 10-1/2" long	160	240	320
Marx Parcel Wagon w/2-horse team	55	83	110

MASON & PARKER Buckboard, 1-horse, 31" long. Courtesy Lloyd W. Ralston Auctions.

MASON & PARKER Cart and Horse, 13" long. Courtesy Lloyd W. Ralston Auctions.

	C6	C8	C10
Mason & Parker, Buckboard, 1-horse, 1910, pressed painted steel, 31"	500	750	1000
Mason & Parker Cart & Horse, 1910, painted pressed steel, mechanical action from axle, 13" long	500	750	1000
Mason & Parker Sleigh, 1-horse, 31"	600	1000	1400
McCormick Deering Farm Wagon, 2 horses, cast iron, 12-1/2" long	125	187	250
Merriam, Cab and Horse, 1880, painted and stenciled tin, 8-1/2" long	1000	1500	2000
Merriam Wagon and Horse, American painted & stenciled tin, 1890, 19-1/2" long	2500	3375	5000

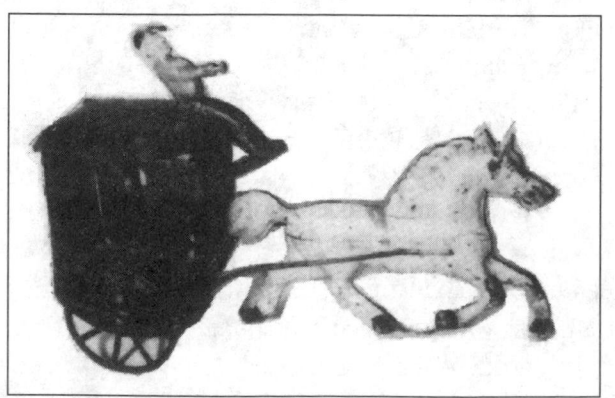

MERRIAM Cab and Horse, 1880, 8-1/2" long, Courtesy Lloyd W. Ralston Auctions.

MERRIAM Wagon & Horse, 1890, 19-1/2" long. Courtesy Lloyd W. Ralston Auctions.

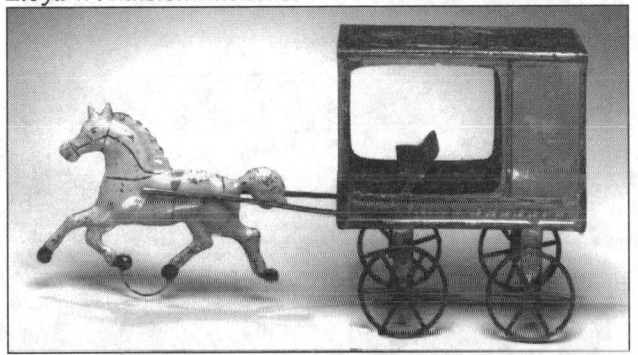

Milk Wagon, tin, 13" long (MERRIAM?). Courtesy Sotheby's New York.

	C6	C8	C10
Mess Cart, WWI-type, tin, 2-horse drawn, painted	100	150	200
Milk Wagon, goat-drawn, possibly George Brown, painted tin, 6"	150	225	300
"Milk" Wagon, driver and 1-horse, 12-3/4" long	100	150	200
Milk Wagon, tin, Merriam?, 13" long	500	800	1200
Mower, 2 horses and driver, cast iron, 10" long	150	225	300
"National Express" Wagon, tin litho, horse, 15" long	250	375	500
Omnibus, "People's" tin, w/2 horses, driver, c. 1880s-1890s	4000	6000	8000
Ox Cart, cast iron, w/ox, 5" long	120	180	240
Ox Cart, cast iron, 11-1/2" long	300	450	600
"Pansy" Stage Coach, Reed, 4 horses, driver, litho alphabet blocks, 28"	1000	1500	2000
Phaeton, 1-horse w/driver, 16" long	450	700	1000
Plow, 1-horse, cast iron, 10-3/4" long	150	225	300
Police Patrol Wagon, cast iron, figures and driver, 1-horse, 11-1/2" long	100	150	200
"Police Patrol", cast iron, 1-horse, 12"	150	225	300
"Police Patrol" Wagon, cast iron, w/driver and 5 policemen and 2 horses, 15"	1700	2800	4000

PRATT & LETCHWORTH

Pratt and Letchworth was in business from about 1880 into the 1890s. The Buffalo, New York firm sold its toys under the name Buffalo Toy Works. Iron and steel were its main materials, and all of its most prominent toys seem to have been horse-drawn.

	C6	C8	C10
Pratt & Letchworth Artillery, c. 1890, cast iron, hand painted, 4-horse caisson, cannon, 4 riders, 34", one auctioned in late 1990 for $19,250			
"Pratt & Letchworth" Cart, 10" long	150	225	300
Pratt & Letchworth Chemical Wagon, 3-horse, driver	3000	6000	9000
Pratt & Letchworth Chief's Wagon	1100	1650	2200
Pratt & Letchworth City Delivery Wagon, c. 1885, driver, barrels, horse	1100	1700	2500
Pratt & Letchworth Doctor's Cart, 1-horse, driver	500	800	1100
Pratt & Letchworth Double Surrey, 15" long	450	750	1100
Pratt & Letchworth Dray, 1-horse, cast iron and wood, 1890, 12" long	250	500	750
Pratt & Letchworth Fire Chief's Wagon, c. 1885, figure, 1-horse, 12" long	700	1100	1500
Pratt & Letchworth 4-seat Brake, 4 horses, driver, 7 passengers, 28" long	4000	7000	11,000
Pratt & Letchworth Gig, cast iron and pressed steel, 7 colors, 1 horse, 1 rider, 10-1/2" long	400	600	800
Pratt & Letchworth Hansom Cab, circa 1892, cast iron, 13" long	1200	1900	2800
Pratt & Letchworth Hay Cart, 10-1/2"	500	750	1000
Pratt & Letchworth Hose Reel, small, 1-horse, driver in standard helmet	900	1350	1800
Pratt & Letchworth Hose Reel, 1-horse, 14-1/4" long	900	1350	1800
Pratt & Letchworth Pumper, 2 horses	1750	2625	3500
Pratt & Letchworth Sulky, 8-1/2" long	400	650	900
Pratt & Letchworth Sulky, 15" long	500	750	1000
Pratt & Letchworth Surrey, rear seat, c. 1890, 1-horse, 15-1/2" long	500	850	1100
Pratt & Letchworth-Welker & Crosby Dray, 1-horse, driver, 14-1/2" long	500	850	1500

PRATT & LETCHWORTH Artillery. Courtesy Sotheby's New York.

PRATT & LETCHWORTH 4-seat Brake, 28" long.
Courtesy Sotheby's New York.

PRATT & LETCHWORTH Surrey, 15" long.
Courtesy Sotheby's New York.

	C6	C8	C10
Produce Wagon, painted tin, 1-horse, George Brown?, 12-1/2" long	350	525	700
Pull Toy, tin, horse and cart, iron wheels, 11" long	250	375	500
Pull Toy, horse and covered Delivery Wagon, tin, 5-1/4" long	150	225	300
Pull Toy, horse and wagon, 2 wheels, tin, 9-1/4" long	125	187	250
Pull Toy, horse-drawn carriage, tin, 12"	150	225	300
Pull Toy, horse pulling water wagon, tin, iron wheels, 6-3/4" long	350	525	700
Pull Toy, horse pulling water wagon, tin, iron wheels, 7-1/4" long	125	187	250
Pumper, driver part of casting, 2 horses, early, 15-1/2" long	200	300	400
Pumper, cast iron w/driver and 2 horses	325	500	750
Pumper, cast iron, 3 horses w/figure, 13" long	120	180	240
Reed "Band Chariot", 14 bandsmen, 28-1/2" long	800	1200	2000
Reed "Cinderella Coach" 26" long, auctioned in 1994 for $2,760			
Reed "Mammoth Show Circus Wagon", 3 animals, 2 trainers, c. 1890, paper on wood, 14" long	1100	1700	2500
Reed "Polar Bear" this was auctioned in 1994 for $7,475			
Reed Trolley, "Bowery & Central Park", paper on wood, 2 horses, 28"long	1500	2300	3500

PRATT & LETCHWORTH, Top to Bottom: Hansom Cab, circa 1892; Double Surrey, 15" long. Courtesy Sotheby's New York.

	C6	C8	C10
Rich Toys "Borden's Golden Crest", wooden dairy cart, 18" long	250	375	500
Rich Toys "Budweiser" Beer Wagon	300	500	800
Rich Toys "Rich's City Dairy"	125	188	250
Rich Toys Streetcar No. 59, 2 horses, c. 1925, 20" long	600	900	1200

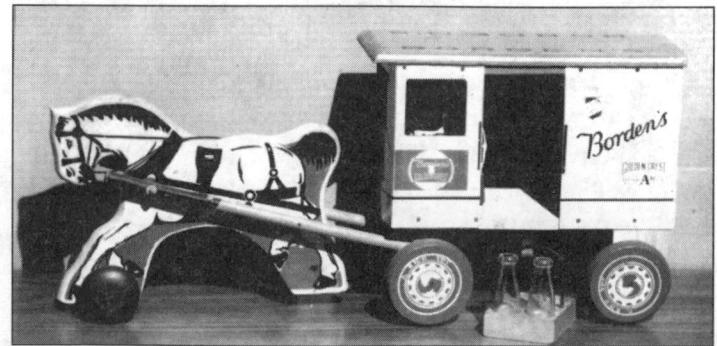

RICH TOYS "Borden's Golden Crest" wooden dairy cart.
Courtesy Joe and Sharon Freed.

PRODUCE Wagon, painted tin, 1-horse (George Brown?). Courtesy Sotheby's New York.

REED "Band Chariot". Courtesy Christie's East.

REED "Polar Bear"
Courtesy Christie's East.

REED "Cinderella Coach"
Courtesy Christie's East.

"**Sand and Gravel**" wagon w/driver,
   cast iron, 9-1/2" long...................... 150   225   300
Sand and Gravel Wagon, cast iron,
   2 horses, 10" long............................. 150   225   300
Sand and Gravel Wagon, 1-horse
   w/driver, cast iron, 10-1/2" long....... 175   262   350
"Sand and Gravel" Wagon, cast iron,
   driver, 2 horses, 14-3/4" long........... 100   150   200
"Sand and Gravel" Wagon w/driver
   and 2 horses, cast iron, 15" long....... 150   225   300
Santa and Sleigh, cast iron, 16" x 7".....500   750 1000
Santa Claus in wooden sleigh pulled
   by reindeer, Santa composition,
   reindeer plush w/cast pewter antlers,
   early, 25" long..................................1500 2250 300

	C6	C8	C10
Santa Claus, reindeer pulling sled, 2 reindeer pulling white sled containing black-painted Santa Claus	500	800	1200
Sheep, cast iron, pulling 2-wheeled tin wagon, 8" long	125	200	300
"**Sheffield Farms Company**", wooden horse-drawn milk wagon, horse has articulated legs, 21" long	250	400	650
Shimer "Choice Family Groceries Tea, Coffee & Spices", 12-1/2" long	500	800	1200
Shimer "Patrol", animated, cast iron, black prisoner, 5 cops, 21" long	3500	6500	9000
Shimer Surrey, woman driver	375	562	750
Smith, S.A., wood wagon, horse, c. 1910, 23" long	500	750	1000
Spring Wagon, cast iron w/driver, horse, 11" long	150	225	300
Spring Wagon, cast iron, driver, 1-horse, 14-1/2" long	150	250	350

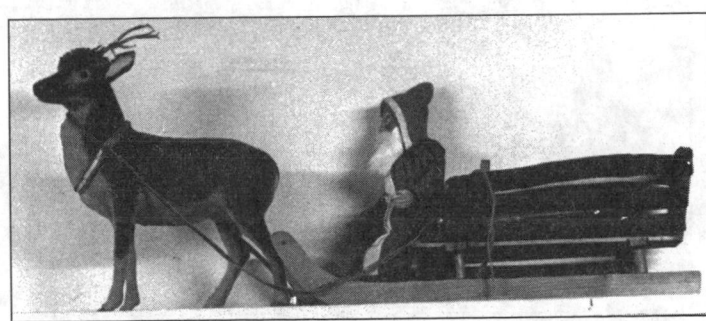

Santa Claus in wooden sleigh pulled by reindeer, 25" long.
Photo courtesy Garth's Auction Inc.

RICH TOYS No. 59 Streetcar, 2 horses, 20" long.
Courtesy Wilkinson Collection, Detroit Antique Toy
Museum.

SHIMER "Choice Family Groceries Tea, Coffee & Spices". Courtesy Sotheby's New York.

SHIMER "Patrol", animated, black prisoner. Courtesy James S. Maxwell/Virginia Caputo. Photo by Virginia Caputo.

	C6	C8	C10
Spring Wagon, driver and 2 horses, cast iron, 14-1/2" long	150	275	400
Spring Wagon, driver and 2 horses, miniature pick, shovel, sledge-hammer, cast iron, 14-1/4" long	600	900	1200
Spring Wagon, cast iron, 2 horses, 15"	150	225	300
Stagecoach w/cowboy driver and 2 horses, cast iron, 11" long	130	195	260
Stagecoach, 6 horses, cast iron, 27" long	60	90	120
Stake Bed Wagon, cast iron, 1 horse, 14-3/4" long	400	700	1000
Stanley Hay Wagon, 11" long	125	188	250
"Stanley" Surrey w/driver, lady passenger, 2 horses, 14-3/4" long	100	150	200
Steam Pumper w/stationary driver, 2 horses, cast iron, 9-1/4" long	100	150	250
Steam Pumper w/stationary driver, 3 horses, cast iron, 10-1/2" long	150	225	300
Steam Pumper w/stationary driver, 2 horses, cast iron, 15" long	500	750	1000
Steam Pumper w/stationary driver, 2 horses, cast iron, 15-1/4" long	800	1350	2000
Steam Pumper, cast iron, driver, 3 horses, bell, 17-1/2" long	600	900	1200

	C6	C8	C10
Steam Pumper, 2 horses, cast iron w/driver, 18" long	600	1000	1500
Steam Pumper, cast iron, driver and 2 horses, 20-1/2" long	800	1300	2000
Steam Pumper, cast iron, 3 horses and bell, 21-1/2" high	500	750	1000
Steamer w/driver, 2 horses, 17" long	600	900	1500
Stevens Black Man in cart whipping mule, painted cast iron, mechanical, 1890, 9" long	400	600	900
Stevens Donkey Cart, cast iron, 8"	300	500	700
Sulky, cast iron, horse and rider, cart mounted w/4 bells, 6-1/2" long	200	300	400
Sulky, cast iron, w/driver, 7-1/4" long	150	225	300
Sulky, cast iron w/driver, circa 1890s, 8-1/2" long	250	400	550
Sulky Rig, horse and driver pull toy, comic style, 10" long, 8" high, 1-1/4" thick	100	150	200
Surrey, cast iron, 2 horses, 13" long	150	225	300
"Teddy Bear" enclosed cart, painted litho tin, 1915, 9" long	600	900	1200

STEVENS Donkey Cart. Courtesy Sotheby's New York.

STEVENS Black Man in cart whipping mule, 9" long. Courtesy Lloyd W. Ralston Auctions.

Uncle Sam Eagle Head Chariot, 2 horses. Courtesy James S. Maxwell/Virginia Caputo. Photo by Virginia Caputo.

WILKINS TOY COMPANY

Wilkins, of Keene, New Hampshire, was begun by James S. Wilkins as the Triumph Wringer Company. But the tiny model Wilkins produced to promote his product proved so intriguing to prospective customers and their children that requests for them poured in. The real thing was quickly forgotten as Wilkins turned to toymaking. Its toys were generally cast iron and steel. The firm was acquired in 1894 by Kingsbury, which is still in business, though now as a tool and die maker.

	C6	C8	C10
Transfer Wagon, cast iron, 2 horses, driver	400	600	800
"Transfer Wagon", 3 horses and driver, cast iron, wagon bolted to team, 19"	500	850	1200
"Transfer" Wagon, cast iron, driver and 2 horses, 19-1/2" long	400	600	800
"Trotter, Jockey and Horse", cast iron, 6" long	150	225	300
Uncle Sam Eagle Head Chariot, 2 horses, cast iron, Jones & Bixler?	3000	5000	8000
"United States Transfer Co. No. 7", wood wagon w/cast iron wheels, 2 stuffed horses, 31" long	300	450	600
U.S. Mail Wagon, tin, 2 horses, 17"	175	262	350
Vindex John Deere Farm Wagon, 2 horses, 7-1/2" long	800	1300	1900
Wagon, 2-wheeled, w/driver, cast iron, 7-1/4" long	100	150	200
Wagon, cast iron, mule, driver, 2-wheeled wagon, 9-1/2" long	350	525	700
Wagon, 2-seater, cast iron, 1-horse	150	225	300
Walking Horse and Sulky Cart, horse of wood, moving legs and cart of tin, wheels cast iron, 7" long	250	375	500
Water Tower w/3 horses, cast iron and pressed steel, 43" long, horse 11" long	1000	1500	2000
Welker & Crosby Hose Reel 13-1/2"	1200	2000	2900
Welker & Crosby Ox Cart, 2 oxen, black driver	600	900	1200

	C6	C8	C10
Wilkins Aerial Fire Wagon, cast iron, 3 horses, driver, 43" long	1200	1800	2400
Wilkins Artillery, circa 1895, 2 horses, rider on caisson, seat top lifts off, cannon, 10" long	1000	1500	2000
Wilkins Buckboard, cast iron	120	180	240
Wilkins Caisson, horse-drawn, 18"	650	1000	1500
Wilkins Cane Wagon, mule, driver, 11" long	300	450	600
Wilkins Carriage, driver in derby, 1 horse, passenger	1000	1500	2000
Wilkins Cart, animated, 6" long	250	375	500
Wilkins Cart and Horse, 10" long	450	700	1000
Wilkins Car and Horse, driver, 12"	750	1200	1600
Wilkins Chariot, 4 horses, 7" long	180	270	360
Wilkins (?) Chariot, woman driver, 3 horses, cast iron, 10-1/2" long	400	600	800
Wilkins "City Truck" cast iron, 2 horses w/driver	1000	1500	2000
Wilkins "Coal and Wood" Wagon	750	1125	1500
Wilkins Delivery Wagon, driver, prancing horse team, 21" long	600	900	1200
Wilkins Doctor's Cart, circa 1900, 10-1/2" long	375	562	750
Wilkins Dog Cart, 1890, cast iron, 7-1/2" long	150	225	300
Wilkins Dog Cart, circa 1890, cast iron, large St. Bernard type dog, rider in cap, 10-1/2" long	600	950	1400
Wilkins Donkey Cart, 11" long	237	355	475
Wilkins Donkey Cart, 13-1/4" long	350	525	700
Wilkins Dray, cast iron, 15" long	300	450	600
Wilkins Dray, 2-horse, cast iron, 16" long	325	500	700
Wilkins Dray, 2 mules, driver, 17-1/2" long	600	900	1250

	C6	C8	C10
Wilkins Dray, cast iron and tin barrel, drawn by 2 horses, driver in derby hat, circa 1910, 20-1/2" long	900	1350	2200
Wilkins Fire Chief Buggy, 1 horse w/rider, 12" long	650	1050	1500
Wilkins Fire Chief Engine Pumper, 2 horses, 19" long	500	750	1000
Wilkins Fire Hose Reel, 10-1/2" long	350	550	750
Wilkins Fire Ladder Truck, cast iron, 3 horses, c. 1910, 2 firemen, 20"	415	622	830
Wilkins Fire Patrol, 6 firemen, 3 horses, 20" long	1700	2700	3650
Wilkins Fire Patrol Wagon, 4 firemen in wagon, 12" long	500	750	1000
Wilkins Fire Patrol, 2 horses, 2 men, cast iron	200	300	400
Wilkins Fire Pumper, 2 horses, 18"	1700	2800	4000
Wilkins Fire Pumper, horizontal chemical tank, 2 horses, 19 1/2" long	1700	2800	4000
Wilkins Fire Pumper, 2 horses, driver, 20" long	600	900	1200
Wilkins Fire Pumper, 3 horses, driver	700	1200	1600
Wilkins Gentleman's Cart, 1900, gentleman driver, white horse, 10"	300	450	600
Wilkins Gig, fancy, and driver, 10"	150	225	300
Wilkins Goat Cart, driver, circa 1900, 9-1/2" long	900	1350	2200
Wilkins "Groceries" Wagon, 1 horse, circa 1900, 13-1/2" long	200	300	400

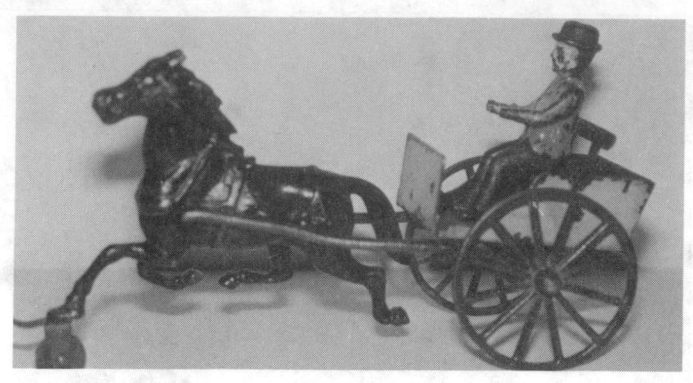

WILKINS Doctor's Cart, 10-1/2" long. Courtesy Christie's East.

	C6	C8	C10
Wilkins Hansom Cab, cast iron	150	225	300
Wilkins Hook and Ladder, 24" long	700	1100	1700
Wilkins Hook and Ladder, prancing team, cast iron, 27" long	750	1125	1500
Wilkins Hook and Ladder, 2 horses, horses sit on pegs, has ladders, figures	1000	1500	2000
Wilkins Hook and Ladder, 2 horses, 2 firemen	1000	1500	2000
Wilkins Hose Reel, 2 horses, 2 firemen in standard helmets, 16" long	1500	2500	3500
Wilkins Hose Reel, circa 1890, cast iron, 1 horse, 18" long	800	1300	1900
Wilkins Huckster's Wagon, 2 horses, driver	900	1350	1800
Wilkins Ice Wagon, horse, tin and cast iron, 10" long	150	225	300

WILKINS (?) Chariot, woman driver. Courtesy Sotheby's New York.

WILKINS Ox Cart, cast iron. Courtesy Sotheby's New York.

WILKINS Dray, cast iron and tin barrel. Courtesy Sotheby's New York.

WILKINS Hose Reel, 2 horses, 2 firemen in standard helmets. Courtesy Ed Hyers Antique Toys.

WILKINS Pumper, 2 horses, 2 firemen. Courtesy Ed Hyers Antique Toys.

	C6	C8	C10
Wilkins Landau	2000	3000	4000
Wilkins "Panama" Earth Mover, driver, 2 horses, 1903, 20" long	700	1100	1700
Wilkins Ox Cart, cast iron	300	500	700
Wilkins Phaeton, driver in top hat, gray pony	450	750	1100
Wilkins Phaeton, woman driver, late 1800s, 16" long	1000	2500	4000
Wilkins Plantation Cart, 1910, cast iron and pressed steel, tilt dump, 11"	500	750	1000

	C6	C8	C10
Wilkins Plow, 1 horse, driver, 10-1/2"	1300	2100	3100
Wilkins Police Patrol, driver, 2 horses, 6 policemen, 1911, 20" long	1700	2700	3700
Wilkins Pony Cart, 1-horse, driver, 7-1/2" long	400	600	800
Wilkins Pony Cart, 1-horse, driver, 9-1/2" long	500	800	1100
Wilkins Pumper, 2 horses, 2 firemen	1100	1650	2200
Wilkins Spring Wagon, driver, horses	300	450	600
Wilkins Stake Wagon, 1907	625	937	1250
Wilkins Steam Engine, 2 horses w/driver, 17" long	600	900	1300
Wilkins Streetcar, "Broadway Car Line 75", horse-drawn	1300	2000	3000
Wilkins Streetcar, "Consolidated Street RR712", cast iron, 14" long	1200	1900	2800
Wilkins Transfer Wagon, tin and cast iron, 15" long	500	850	1200
Wilkins Wagon, driver, mule, 9"long	300	450	600
Wilkins "Worlds Fair Street RR 372", 1-horse, 6 passenger, cast iron, 15"	500	850	1200
Williams Sulky, circa 1920, cast iron, 8" long	150	225	300
Wolverine Sulky Racer, plastic	38	53	75

WILKINS Fire Ladder Truck, cast iron, 3 horses, 20" long, circa 1910. Courtesy Mapes Auctioneers & Appraisers.

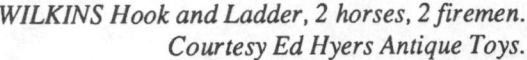

WILKINS Hook and Ladder, 2 horses, 2 firemen. Courtesy Ed Hyers Antique Toys.

WILKINS Streetcar, "Broadway Car Line 75", horse-drawn. Courtesy Mapes Auctioneers and Appraisers.

WILKINS Aerial Fire Wagon, cast iron, 43" long. Circa 1895 and believed to be the largest cast iron toy made during the 19th century. Courtesy Phillips New. York.

Top: Wilkins Fire Pumper, 19-1/2" long, horizontal chemical tank.
Bottom: L to R: Wilkins Fire Pumper, 18" long, 2 horses; Wilkins Hose Reel, 16" long, 2 horses, 2 firemen. Courtesy Christie's East.

WILKINS Phaeton, woman driver. Courtesy Christie's East.

WILKINS, Top to Bottom: "World's Fair Street R.R. 372", Transfer Wagon,
tin and cast iron, both 15" long. Courtesy Sotheby's New York.

WILKINS Streetcar, "Consolidated Street R.R. 712".
Courtesy Wilkinson Collection, Detroit Antique Toy Museum.

MECHANICAL BANKS

by Bill S. Bertoia

The average mint price in this category in the last edition was $8185.41 and in this edition it is $8813.03, an increase of 8%.

After trains, Mechanical Banks are perhaps the most avidly pursued of all the toys cataloged in this book, and the most collectible remain those which were produced in cast iron from around 1870 to 1908, over three hundred different types being produced during that period. One factor that adds to their interest is that many were manufactured with an eye to adult trade as well as to that of children (the "Tammany" bank, for instance). As a result, prices are high, and have been so long before any of the other toys in this book were thought of as collector's items. With prices of this sort, the problem of counterfeiting arises, and care is urged in the purchase of any high-priced bank. Briefly, counterfeits tend to be rougher, to fit together less smoothly, and to not have the patina or "look" of age.

Bill S. Bertoia is a recognized authority in the field of antique toys and banks. As an avid toy and bank collector, he is a member of the Antique Toy Club of America, the Mechanical Bank Collectors of America and the Still Bank Collectors of America. As an active Antiques Dealer Specialist in the field, he handled and appraised the largest collections to have been offered for sale including the Perelman Antique Toy Museum, The Atlanta Toy Museum, The Hegarty Mechanical Bank Collection, The Barenholtz Toy Collection and most recently the largest toy collection ever sold: The Acevedo Toy Collection. He is married to Jeanne Bertoia, the author of the Doorstop book. They have two young children who are starting to share their interest in collecting. They reside in Vineland, New Jersey.

	C6	C8	C10
Acrobat Bank, 5" high	1500	3500	6000
Alligator in Trough, patented 1867	10,000	20,000	35,000
Always Did Despise A Mule, black jockey on mule, 1879, 10" long	450	1000	2000
Always Did Despise A Mule, black on bench being kicked by mule, 1897	700	1500	2400
American Bank sewing machine	3000	6000	10,000
Artillery Bank, Union Officer w/mortar, firing at fort, 1877	650	1100	2100
Astronaut's Bank-gold moon w/rocket on stand, has rings showing orbit of space capsule, ring has astronauts' names: "Shepard, Grissom, Glenn, Carpenter, Schirra, Cooper", little plane up side of rocket shoots money into moon, pot metal, 11" high	25	38	50
Atlas Bank	1000	1750	3000
Bad Accident, mule and black on 2-wheeled car, 1887	850	1500	2500
Bear Hugging Tree	150	400	600
Bill E. Grin	400	1200	2000
Bird on Roof	500	1200	2500
Book of Knowledge Reproduction of Original Banks, c. 1950; Artillery Bank; Bulldog Bank; Creedmore; Eagle and Eagles; Jonah & Whale; Magician; Man and Pig; Man milking Cow; Teddy and the Bear; Trick Dog; Trick Pony, Tree Trunk and Buffalo. *(Note-original markings sometimes filed away from bottom and sold as originals).* Price per each	60	90	125

	C6	C8	C10
Boy on Trapeze	850	2000	3500
Boy Robbing Nest	850	2500	4000
Boy Scout	3000	4500	8000
Boys Stealing Watermelons	750	1500	2500
Bread Winner	8000	12,000	20,000
Bull & Bear, brass model	1000	1750	2500
Bulldog Savings Bank	1750	2500	3500
Bulldog, c. 1887, Judd	300	450	600
"Butting" Buffalo	1500	3500	6000
Butting Goat In Tree Stump, c. 1887, Judd	600	900	1200
Calamity, pat. August 29, 1905, J& E Stevens Co., 3 football players,	3500	8000	15,000
Called Out, 3 known	auctioned in 1993 for $14,300		
Cat and Mouse Bank	750	2000	3500
Charlie McCarthy, sitting w/legs crossed on top of trunk, drop coin in back and mouth moves, pot metal, copyright 1938, 5 3/4" high	75	125	200
Chein Monkey, seated, tips hat when coin dropped in, tin litho, 5" high	25	37	50
Chief Big Moon, Indian in teepee, 1899	750	1250	2250
Chimpanzee	1500	2200	3500
Chinese Reclining, 1882	1800	2800	4000
Circus Bank	auctioned in 1994 for $14,950		
Circus Ticket Taker	500	1000	1500
Clown & Harlequin	auctioned in 1988 for $90,000		
Clown on Bar	auctioned in 1993 for $70,000		
Clown on Globe, 1873	750	1700	2500
Columbus	200	400	600
Confectionery	3500	7000	12,000

ALWAYS DID DESPISE A MULE. Courtesy PB Eighty-Four, New York.

ALWAYS DID DESPISE A MULE. Courtesy Sotheby's New York.

ARTILLERY. Courtesy Sotheby's New York.

ALLIGATOR IN TROUGH. Courtesy Sotheby's New York.

ACROBAT. Courtesy PB Eighty-Four, NY.

BIRD ON ROOF. Courtesy Sotheby's New York.

BOY ON TRAPEZE. Courtesy Sotheby's New York.

CREEDMORE. Courtesy Sotheby's New York.

BULLDOG SAVINGS. Courtesy PB Eighty-Four, NY.

BUFFALO, BUCKING. Courtesy Sotheby's New York.

BOY SCOUT. Courtesy Sotheby's New York.

BREAD WINNER. Courtesy Sotheby's New York.

BULLDOG, dog swallows coin. Courtesy Sotheby's New York.

PICTURE GALLERY. Courtesy Sotheby's New York.

TEDDY AND THE BEAR. Courtesy PB Eighty-Four, NY.

WILLIAM TELL. Courtesy PB Eighty-Four, NY.

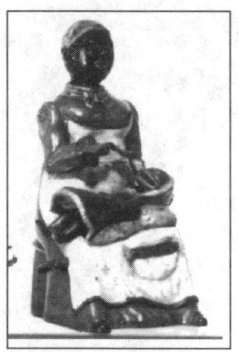

MAMMY FEEDING CHILD. Courtesy Sotheby's New York.

GIRL SKIPPING ROPE. Courtesy PB Eighty-Four, NY.

STUMP SPEAKER. Courtesy PB Eighty-Four, NY.

TRICK PONY. Courtesy PB Eighty-Four, NY.

ROLLER SKATING. Courtesy Sotheby's New York.

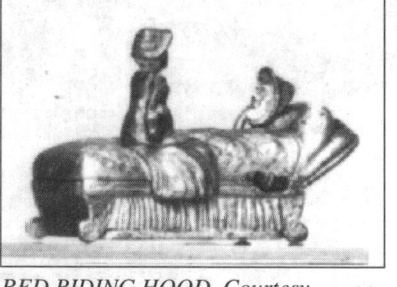

RED RIDING HOOD. Courtesy Sotheby's New York.

PADDY AND HIS PIG. Courtesy Garth's Auctions Inc.

ZOO. Courtesy Sotheby's New York.

FROG ON LATTICE. Courtesy PB Eighty-Four, NY.

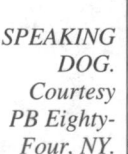

SPEAKING DOG. Courtesy PB Eighty-Four, NY.

	C6	C8	C10
Cow Kicking, cow kicks over boy.......	3500	6000	12,000
Creedmore Bank, man firing into tree, 1877, 10" long.................	200	500	750
Crowing Rooster..................	500	750	1000
Dapper Dan..................	200	400	600
Darktown Battery, black pitcher and catcher, 1888.............	1000	2500	5000
Darky Football............auctioned in 1988 for $245,000			
Darky and Cabin, 1885.................	300	600	1000
Dentist Bank, white dentist working on black patient, 1880.............	3500	6000	11,000
Dinah, bust of black woman, 6-1/2"....	150	350	500
Dog charges Boy, bronze finish...........	400	700	1000
Dog on Turntable, Judd Mfg. Co........	150	300	450
Dog Standing.................	150	350	500
Eagle and Eaglets, 1883..................	300	600	900
Elephant, late cast iron, Hubley...........	100	175	250
Elephant, Three Star, cast iron, trunk flips up to catch coin, 5" high..........	150	300	450
Elephant and Clowns.................	700	1300	2000
Elephant Howdah, 1920.................	250	500	750
Elephant Howdah, c. 1934, Hubley........	375	563	750
Ferris Wheel, Hubley/Bauer.................	1000	2000	3000
Fortune Teller pat. February 19, 1901, safe, complete w/roll of fortunes.....	400	600	800
Forty-Niner, The, donkey moves ear and tail.................	100	225	400
Freedman.................auctioned in 1988 for $250,000.			
Frog and Snake In Pond, litho tin mechanical bank in the form of a snake striking at a frog which opens its mouth to receive the coin.....	3000	4500	6500
Frog, Goat and Old Man.................	1500	3500	6000
Frog on Arched Track.........auctioned in 1988 for $35,000.			
Frog on Lattice, Stevens, 1870s...........	150	350	600
Frog on Rock, Kilgore Mfg. Co............	200	350	550
Frog on Stump, 1872.................	200	400	600
Frogs, two, J & E Stevens.................	600	900	1200
Gem, Dog and Building.................	200	350	500
Giant, holding a club.................	10,000	15,000	20,000.
Girl Skipping Rope, w/key.................	12,000	17,000	25,000.
Globe Savings Fund Bank..................	250	375	500
Guessing Bank.................	1500	2500	3500
Hall's Excelsior Bank, monkey cashier.	100	350	500
Hall's Lilliput, 1875.................	300	500	800
Hen and Chick, c. 1901, Stevens..........	1500	2100	3500
Hindu, 1882, Kyser & Rex.................	1000	1500	2000
Home building w/2 pillars, teller at window, tin.................	100	200	300
Horse Race.................	6000	9000	15,000
Humpty Dumpty.................	600	1000	2000
Independence Hall.................	150	325	500
Indian Shooting Bear, 1888.................	850	1500	2500
Initiating Bank First Degree.................	3500	6500	10,000

	C6	C8	C10
Jolly Nigger, bust.................	100	250	400
Jolly Nigger, high hat, 8" high.............	150	350	600
Jolly Nigger, moves ears.................	75	112	150
Jonah and the Whale, cast iron (Jonah in boat).................	1200	1800	3000
Jonah and Whale (Jonah emerges)...	20,000	30,000	45,000
Jumbo on Platform.................	800	1150	1500
"Keeping 'Em Flying" dime register, tin..	25	37	50
Kick Inn, litho paper and wood mechanical bank, Presto, a mule standing in front of a small building.................	250	375	450
King Aqua.................auctioned in 1988 for $95,000			
Leap Frog Bank, 2 boys, tree, 1891.....	1000	2000	3500
Liberty Bell.................	200	350	500
Lighthouse Bank, 1891.................	800	1000	1500
Lion and Monkeys.................	200	400	650
Lion Hunter.................	3500	5000	8000
Little Jocko.................	500	1000	1500
Little Joe.................	150	225	300
Locomotive.................	300	600	900
Magic.................	400	900	1500
Magician Bank, 1882.................	1500	4000	6500
Mama Katzenjammer and the Kids, 5-3/4"	3200	5000	6500
Mammy Feeding Child.................	2000	3250	5500
Mason and Hod Carrier, 1887.............	2500	4000	6500
Merry-Go-Round, semi-mechanical....	100	175	250
Meyers No. 84, Jumbo Elephant..........	100	250	350
Money Box Bank, hand-carved on wood base, 10-1/4".................	800	1200	1600
Monkey and Coconut.................	800	1500	2500
Mosque.................	800	1500	2000
Mule Bucking, black man riding a mule..	500	750	1000
Mule Entering Barn.................	300	600	900
National Bank.................	2500	5000	8000
Naughty Girl Bank, modern.................	25	50	75
New Creedmore Meyer No. 54............	200	300	400
New Bank, cast iron, c. 1875, brass policeman in building, 4-1/2" long.	200	350	500
North Pole, J&E Stevens Co., Eskimos and dog sled.................	10,000	15,000	25,000
Novelty Bank, house-like bank, 1873....	500	1200	200
Organ Bank, monkey and revolving cat and dog, 7-1/4" high.................	250	500	750
Organ Bank, monkey only.................	150	250	400
Organ Boy And Girl, pat. June 13, 1882, monkey flanked by boy and girl holding tambourine.................	350	700	1000
Organ Grinder And Bear.................	2000	3000	5500
Organ Grinder And Monkey, 1929.....	250	400	600
Owl, slot in back, cast iron.................	225	337	450
Owl, slot in head.................	150	300	500
Owl, turns head, cast iron.................	250	400	1000
Paddy And His Pig.................	1000	1500	3500
Panorama, building.................	3000	6000	10,000

FROGS, Two. Courtesy Sotheby's New York.

GEM. Courtesy Sotheby's New York.

KICK INN. Courtesy Sotheby's New York.

OWL, turns head. Courtesy PB Eighty-Four, New York.

MAGIC. Courtesy Sotheyb's New York.

HUMPTY DUMPTY. Photo courtesy PB Eight-Four, New York.

LEAP-FROG BANK. Courtesy Sotheby's New York.

INDIAN SHOOTING BEAR. Courtesy Sotheby's New York.

MONKEY AND COCONUT. Courtesy Sotheby's New York.

MAGICIAN. Courtesy Sotheby's New York.

MULE BUCKING. Courtesy Sotheby's New York.

MULE ENTERING BARN. Courtesy Sotheby's New York.

LION AND MONKEYS. Courtesy Sotheby's New York.

	C6	C8	C10
Patronize the Blind Man and His Dog, pat. Feb.19, 1878, J&E Stevens Co....	2000	4500	7000
Pegleg Beggar....	500	1000	1500
Pelican, cast iron, "Boy thumbs nose"....	800	1250	2000
Perfection Registering....	4500	7000	10,000
Piano, circa 1900, E.M. Roche....	250	500	750
Picture Gallery....	6000	10,00	16,000
Pig, Bismarck....	1500	3000	4500
Pig in High Chair....	250	375	500
Preacher in Pulpit....	30,000	40,000	50,000
Presto, shape of building....	150	250	400
Presto-Mouse on Roof, litho paper on wood....	7500	12,000	17,500
Professor Pug Frog's Great Bicycle Feat....	3500	6000	10,000
Pump, Bucket....	300	700	1000
Punch & Judy, Shepherd Hardware, Buffalo, NY, circa 1890....	650	1400	2200
Rabbit, tall....	300	500	800
Rabbit, small, circular base....	200	400	600
Rabbit in Cabbage Patch....	175	300	450
Red Riding Hood....	15,000	20,000	35,000
Roller Skating....	20,000	30,000	45,000
Rooster....	200	300	450
Santa Claus at Chimney....	750	1000	2000
See Him Frisk....auctioned in 1988 for $55,000			
Shoot the Chute....	12,500	17,500	25,000
Speaking Dog Bank, J&E Stevens, pat. 1885....	800	1500	2500
Springing Cat, lead alloy....sold in 1991 for $23,100			
Squirrel and Tree Stump....	500	850	1200
Standing Bear....	100	165	220
Strato Bank, pot metal, rocket and planet, 1950s, 8" long....	10	15	25

	C6	C8	C10
Stump Speaker, cast iron....	1000	1300	3000
Tabby....	150	350	600
Tammany Bank, 1875, 5-3/4" high....	200	400	1000
Tank and Cannon, 1916....	200	300	400
Teddy And The Bear, man firing at bear in tree, 1907....	800	1250	2200
Telephone....	150	300	450
3-Star Elephant, brass....	150	300	450
Trick Dog, clown w/hoop, dog and barrel, 1888 version, has 6-part base..	500	900	1800
Trick Dog, clown w/hoop, dark dog and dark barrel, 1929....	150	225	300
Trick Pony....	400	650	900
Turtle Bank....auctioned in 1988 for $30,000			
Two Frogs....(see Frogs, Two)			
U.S. Building, c. 1878, boy and dog in windows, Stevens?....	3100	4650	6200
U. S. and Spain....	3000	4000	5000
Uncle Remus....	2500	3500	5500
Uncle Sam, bust....	300	450	600
Uncle Sam, has umbrella in left hand, 1886....	1200	2000	3000
Uncle Tom, w/lapels and 1 star....	200	350	500
Uncle Tom, w/lapels, 1 star, brass base..	600	900	1200
United States Bank, Stevens....	650	975	1300
Watchdog Safe....	150	300	450
Weeden's Plantation, tin....	800	1500	2200
William Tell, 1896....	300	500	1000
Wireless Bank, 1913....	100	250	450
Woodpecker....	1500	2800	4000
World's Fair....	500	650	850
Zoo....	400	700	950

NOVELTY. Courtesy Sotheby's New York.

*"Professor Pug Frog's Great Bicycle Feat".
Courtesy Sotheby's New York.*

PIANO. Courtesy Sotheby's New York.

NEW BANK. Courtesy Sotheby's New York.

HORSE RACE. Courtesy PB Eighty-Four, New York.

LION HUNTER. Courtesy PB Eighty-Four, New York.

PEGLEG BEGGAR. Courtesy Sotheby's New York.

ORGAN GRINDER AND MONKEY. Courtesy Sotheby's New York.

ORGAN BANK, Monkey only. Courtesy Sotheby's New York.

MASON AND HOD-CARRIER. Courtesy PB Eighty-Four, New York.

PIG IN HIGH CHAIR. Courtesy Sotheby's New York.

PRESTO. Courtesy Sotheby's New York.

TRICK DOG. Courtesy Sotheby's New York.

PUNCH AND JUDY. Courtesy PB Eighty-Four, New York.

UNCLE REMUS. Courtesy Sotheby's New York.

DARKTOWN BATTERY. Courtesy PB Eighty-Four, New York.

SANTA CLAUS AT THE CHIMNEY. Courtesy PB Eighty-Four, NY.

CAT AND MOUSE - CAT BALANCING. Courtesy Phillips New York.

COW KICKING. Courtesy Sotheby's New York.

DARKY AND CABIN. Courtesy Sotheby's New York.

DINAH. Courtesy Sotheby's New York.

DENTIST. Courtesy PB Eighty-Four, NY.

DOG ON TURNTABLE. Courtesy PB Eighty-Four, NY.

GIANT. Courtesy Sotheby's New York.

JONAH AND THE WHALE. Courtesy Garth's Auction Inc.

CLOWN ON GLOBE Courtesy PB Eighty-Four, New York.

CHIEF BIG MOON. Courtesy PB Eighty-Four, New York.

HOME. Courtesy Sotheby's New York.

FORTUNE TELLER. Courtesy PB Eighty-Four, New York.

ELEPHANT AND CLOWNS. Courtesy Sotheby's New York.

A Full-color ad card for the bank listed here as Eagle and Eaglets. This sold at auction in late 1990 for $200. Courtesy James S. Maxwell/Virginia Caputo. Photo by Virginia Caputo.

AMERICAN PAPER TOYS

by Barbara and Jonathan Newman

(The average mint price of paper toys in the last edition was $55.33. This edition it's $61.00, an increase of 10%.)

The prices of paper toys have been almost flat since the last edition reflecting the economy in general. The economy seems to be gaining strength but paper toys haven't taken off much yet. Celebrity paper dolls of the 40's and W.W.II military theme materials still continue to show better increases than other paper toys.

There is still a constant stream of new models from around the world and an increased availability of some interesting East European paper toys.

The subject of paper toys is so vast that individual types continue to receive only superficial treatment even in books devoted to just paper toys. Some brief introduction here, nevertheless, should be attempted. They have been called cut-outs, punch outs and press outs. By whatever name, forts, planes, trains, paper dolls and much much more have been produced in paper. What adult does not have some memories (usually fond, often frustrating) of crisp uncut booklets, shiny boxes, or just complicated printed sheets of paper and cardboard toys?

From the end of the last century to the period after World War II, paper was, if not king, certainly close to the throne. It was, in many ways, the plastic of its day. Almost every toy subject matter can be found in a paper or cardboard version.

No collector of military toys or toy soldiers can be unfamiliar with the whole world of paper soldiers, even though they were never quite as popular in this country as in Europe, where paper soldiers were born about 200 years ago. American companies by the turn of the last century were turning out paper toys by the thousands. The most popular was easily the McLoughlin Bros. Company which started out with paper toys in 1857 in New York City. It was eventually bought out by Milton Bradley and moved to Springfield, Massachusetts in 1920. Their products included beautifully lithographed covered boxed sets of cardboard figures on wooden stands, or for the child with less resources, over a hundred different sheets of American and foreign armies to be cut out and mounted on little wooden stands.

During this same general time period, centered around the 10 years from 1895 to 1905, almost every major newspaper in the country (at least those big city ones with large Sunday editions) had Sunday "Art Supplements" which varied their "give away" fare from Armies or Navies of the world to historical panoramas illustrating our history, political figures and personalities of the day to cut-out dolls of celebrities with vast wardrobes of clothes. Even the "Globe Quadruple Perfecting Press" itself, offered as a cut-out to construct a complete diorama, was the Boston Sunday Globe's offering of August 6, 1896.

Paper houses and villages, a great favorite with little girls of the day, were sold by several companies. The earlier ones included the ubiquitous McLoughlin Bros. and Milton Bradley (yes, they're still around) and more recent ones were World War II era giants in the field, Built-Rite and Megow.

While there was no shortage of paper toys in the 20's and 30's, it was the World War II era that is really the Golden Age of paper toys in this country. The lack of traditional material to make toys caused even the king of toy companies, Lionel, to produce as its only offering in the war, a complete train set in die-cut cardboard. Who would have thought such a poor substitute in 1943 would be a sought after and valuable rarity today? If you have one in mint condition you've a real gem in both the world of toy trains and paper toys.

During the war years every conceivable type of toy, usually given a wartime, patriotic theme, was available. Punchout cardboard sets of "Rap-A-Jap", "Sink The Axis", "Camouflage Defense Force", books of punch out Naval Craft by Rigby, etc. were the birthday, Christmas or other presents of the forties and early fifties. A whole range of Built-Rite forts, trenches, troops and doll houses are among our own found memories. Celebrity paper dolls were at their zenith and, except for some infantile awareness of the war and being constantly forced to go to school against our will, little Barbara and Jonathan were having a great time playing with paper toys.

The list and illustrations could go on and on and someday perhaps a reasonably definitive book will be written. For the meantime, just settle for a brief introduction in words and pictures to either jog your own memory or perhaps kindle an interest in a lifetime passion for paper toys.

For those of you that already have a passion there are now quite a few books on the subject of paper dolls, a good general book on paper toys and at least two real specialty books are expected out shortly; on Paper Soldiers by Edward Ryan and one on World War II era paper toys by John Matthews.

Barbara and Jonathan Newman have been toy collectors for over 30 years and dealers running a mail order paper toy business for most of that time from Clifton Park in historic Saratoga County, New York. Barbara has successfully managed a business, two children who are grown and have children of their own, and Jonathan. Jonathan is a retired Army officer and senior New York State government employee. Their major disappointments in life are that they carelessly shot the heads off of hundreds of Britain's soldiers in the 1940s and that they bought toys instead of McDonalds stock in the 60s.

ARMY NURSE AND DOCTOR PAPER DOLLS. *Photo by Jonathan Newman. Courtesy Barbara and Jonathan Newman.*

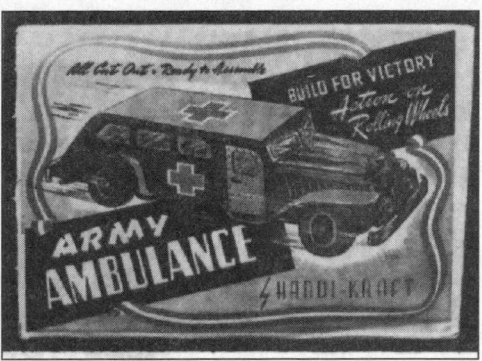

ARMY AMBULANCE BUILD FOR VICTORY ACTION ON ROLLING WHEELS. *Photo by Jonathan Newman. Courtesy Barbara and Jonathan Newman.*

ALL-NU Cardboard soldiers, No. 111, 109, 106, 108. *Photo by Jonathan Newman. Courtesy Barbara and Jonathan Newman.*

	C6	C8	C10
Air-Hostess, 1947, Saalfield 2546	30	40	50
Alice Faye, 1941, Merrill 4800	95	200	225
All-Nu decal sheet of soldiers, meant to be attached to heavy cardboard backing, c. 1942, by Frank Krupp	60	75	1000
All-Nu soldiers, circa 1942-3, 5" high on heavy cardboard			
100 Officer marching w/sabre	3.00	4.50	6.00
101 Marching, slope arms, WWI helmet	3.00	4.50	6.00
102 Bugler, campaign cap	3.00	4.50	6.00
103 Signalman, WW I helmet	3.00	4.50	6.00
104 Officer kneeling w/binoculars	3.00	4.50	600
105 Kneeling firing rifle w/WW I helmet	3.00	4.50	6.00
106 Throwing grenade, WW I helmet	3.00	4.50	6.00
107 Fixed bayonet, WW I helmet	3.00	4.50	6.00
108 Charging w/gas mask, WW I helmet	3.00	4.50	6.00
109 Charging w/rifle, port arms, WW I helmet	3.00	4.50	6.00
110 Seated machine gunner, WW I helmet	3.00	4.50	6.00
111 Flag-bearer, WW I helmet	3.00	4.50	6.00
112 General McArthur	10	12	14
113 Nurse	3.00	4.50	6.00
114 2 Men carrying wounded soldier on stretcher, WW II helmets	3.00	4.50	6.00
115 2 Men firing rifles from prone position, WW II helmets	3.00	4.50	6.00
116 Soldier on wireless radio	3.00	4.50	6.00
117 3 Soldiers w/rifles leaving boat, WW II helmets	3.00	4.50	6.00
118 2 Paratroopers, 1-w/tommy gun, WW II helmets	3.00	4.50	6.00

	C6	C8	C10
119 Ski Trooper	3.00	4.50	6.00
120 Soldier advancing w/rifle, WW II helmet	3.00	4.50	6.00
150 3 Men in jeep, WW I helmets	3.00	4.50	6.00
151 5 Man team w/cannon, WW I helmets	3.00	4.50	6.00
152 2 Men manning wheeled AA gun, WW I helmets	3.00	4.50	6.00
153 Tank w/3 men	3.00	4.50	6.00
154 Ambulance	3.00	4.50	6.00
155 Truck w/soldiers in rear, WW II helmets	3.00	4.50	6.00
All-Nu boxed set of 24 of the above soldiers	No Price Found		
American Beauties, Paper Dolls, c. 1942, Reuben Lilja & Co., No. 917	17	22	26
American Beauty Paper Dolls w/dresses worn by White House First Ladies 1789-1951, Merrill No.154815,1951	25	35	45
American Defense Battles Punch-out Book by George Trimmer, Merrill No. 3430, 1940	70	90	100
American Family Paper-Doll Book "Costumes for all the family from 1610 to now", Grinnel No.C1002	45	60	75
Amos & Andy-Cutout cardboard of just Andy, 8-1/2" high, stand-up	4	6	8
Animal Paper Dolls to Dress, 1950, Saalfield 2598, Bear, Monkey, Pig, Kitten	14	17	22
Animals to Paint, 1910, Saalfield	12	17	24
Ann Blythe, 1952 Merrill No. 2250-25	50	80	95

	C6	C8	C10
Army Air Forces Aircraft Identification Silhouette Model-Feb. 1943, 1/72 scale of Japanese fighter Najajima T-97, A.N.F. 7" x 11" envelope.......... 14	18	25	
Army Ambulance, c.1942, Handi-Kraft...27	38	45	
Army Cut-outs, 1937, Saalfield No.245...50	60	75	
Army Nurse and Doctor Paper Dolls, 1942, Merrill 3425.......... 40	50	75	
Around the World w/Bob and Barbara, 1946, Children's Press No.3000...... 10	15	20	
Assemble 9 Model Warplanes, 4 Model Tanks, 1941, Fawcett Publications, Lowe.......... 50	70	80	
Ava Gardner, 1949, 1952 Whitman No. 119215.......... 65	80	95	
Baby Brother by Queen Holden,1929, Whitman 920.......... 90	120	130	
Baby First Step, 1965 (Mattel), Whitman No. 1997.......... 8	12	15	
Babyland 1955, Merrill No. 3642.......... 45	55	70	
Baby Pat, 1963 Whitman No. 2072..... 8	10	12	
Babysitter Paper Dolls, Lowe No.945.... 32	40	45	
Barbara Britton Paper Dolls w/Magic Stay-on costumes, 1954, Saalfield 5190, boxed set.......... 50	60	65	
Barbie and Ken, 1962 Whitman No. 4797, 7" x 12" boxed set.......... 20	40	50	
Barbie and Skipper, 1964 Whitman No. 1957, Yachting outfits.......... 20	30	45	
Barbie Boutique, 1973, Whitman No. 1954 12	22	25	
Beautiful Paper Dolls by Betty Campbell, 1941, Saalfield No. 242, has some of same paper dolls as Little Miss America Paper Dolls.......... 50	60	75	
Belle of the Ball Paper Dolls, 1948, Saalfield 2702.......... 25	32	40	
Betsy McCall, 1971, Whitman No.4744. 12	18	22	
Betsy McCall around the world Paper dolls, circa 1962.......... 15	25	30	
Betsy McCall Dress 'N Play Paper Dolls, 1963, Standard/Toycraft/McCall No. 802, 12" x 18" boxed set.......... 16	25	30	
Betsy Ross and Her Friends-1963, Platt and Munk No. 224B, 7" x 11" boxed set.......... 15	25	30	
Betty and Joan, 1941, 1945, Whitman No. 1015, Joan also appears in Mary and Joan, Lois and Joan......... 30	45	55	
Betty Bonnett-Her Family and Friends by Sheila Young, George W. Jacobs & Co., Phila., 1915. Each series w/6 sheets & folder.			
First series.......... 125	150	180	
Second series.......... 100	145	175	

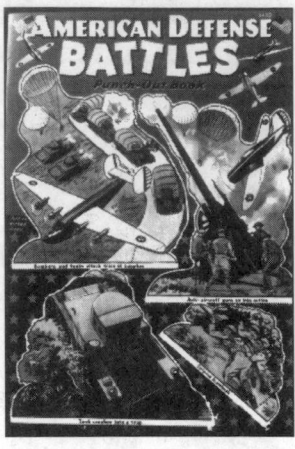

Left, ALICE FAYE. Right, AMERICAN DEFENSE BATTLES PUNCH-OUT BOOK. Photo by Jonathan A. Newman. Courtesy Barbara and Jonathan Newman.

	C6	C8	C10
Third series.......... 100	145	175	
Betty Grable, 1951, Merrill No.1558... 65	85	105	
Betty Sue-A Cut Out Doll, c. 1940, No. 1010.......... 18	25	30	
The Beverly Hillbillies - Jed, Jethro, Granny and Elly May, Whitman No. 1955, 1964.......... 25	35	40	
Big-Girl Paper Dolls, 1940, McLoughlin Bros., No. 707, actually Milton Bradley...18	25	35	
Big Invasion Punch-Out Book, 1964, Whitman No. 1936, punchout of beach landing.......... 18	30	45	
Bild-A-Set Construction Kit No. 85 boxed, Erector-type set of cardboard.... 18	25	30	
Binson-Freeman Pre Flight Trainer, cockpit and how to fly course.......... 75	113	150	
Birthday Party Stand-Up Cut-Out Dolls, 1944, National Syndicate Displays, Inc., 20 boys and girls..... 35	45	55	
Blue Bonnet Paper Dolls by Florence Salter, Merrill No. 3444, 1942.......... 30	40	45	
Blue Feather and Silver Cloud, 1940s, Abbott No. 1356, Indian dolls.......... 35	50	60	
Boarding School Dolls and Clothes, 1942, Merrill No. 3492.......... 40	55	60	
Bob Hope and Dorothy Lamour, 1942, Whitman No. 976.......... 190	225	240	
Bobby Socks Cut Out Dolls designed by Doris Lane Butler, 1945, Whitman, No. 988.......... 45	55	65	
Bombers by Schomburg, Whitman No. 961, 1943, B-17, B-25, B-24, Douglas A-20A, short "Stirling"..... 60	75	100	
Book of Airplanes, A. Whitman No. 923, 1930.......... 15	20	25	
Book of Paper Doll cut-outs, 1927, Saalfield, No. 2051.......... 40	60	75	

BOB HOPE & DOROTHY LAMOUR CUT-OUT BOOK. Photo by Jonathan Newman. Courtesy Barbara and Jonathan Newman.

BILD-A-SET CONSTRUCTOR KIT. Photo by Jonathan Newman. Courtesy Barbara and Jonathan Newman.

BETTY BONNET HER FAMILY AND FRIENDS (Second Series). Photo by Jonathan Newman. Courtesy Barbara and Jonathan Newman.

BIRTHDAY PARTY STAND-UP CUT-OUT DOLLS. Photo by Jonathan Newman. Courtesy Barbara and Jonathan Newman.

	C6	C8	C10
The Brady Bunch, 1973, Whitman No. 1976	12	20	25
Brenda Lee, 1964, No. 4360 De Journette, 6-1/2" x 10" boxed set, includes toy phonograph and records	45	60	75
Brenda Lee Teenage Celebrity, 1961, Lowe No. 2785	18	30	40

	C6	C8	C10
Bridal Party, 1950, Whitman No. 1187, five dolls	18	30	35
Bride and Groom, 1949, Merrill No. 3443	50	65	75
Bride and Groom, 1949, Merrill No. 1555	50	65	75
Bride and Groom Military Wedding Party, 1941, Merrill No. 3411, 16 dolls	80	90	100
Bride Doll Cut-Out Book, 1940s, Samuel Lowe No. 1043	25	45	55
Brother and Sister Statuette Dolls, 1950, Whitman 1182-15, 2 heavy cardboard 7-1/2" dolls	18	35	40
Buffy Paper Dolls ("Family Affair") 1968, Whitman No. 1955	18	25	30
Buffy and Jody, 1970, ("Family Affair"), Whitman 4764, two magic dolls w/stay-on wardrobes	18	25	30

BUILT-RITE

Built-Rite began in 1922 as a manufacturer of cardboard boxes. Somewhere along the line, at least as early as 1934, it began to produce cardboard construction toys. Judging by its catalogs, it sold its last fort (25A) in 1954. Its last few construction sets, three trains accessories sets, made their last appearance in the 1956 catalog until 1963-64 when the No. 1033 Doll House and No. 1027 Stock Farm appeared.

	C6	C8	C10
No. 1 Toy Soldiers, WW I helmets, per each	2	3	4
No. 2 Toy Trench	25	45	60
No. 7 Private Garage, brick	35	45	55
No. 7 Army Plane Hangar	45	55	65

All construction sets were out from 1967-68 on. In 1978 Built-Rite added plastic playsets No. 6002 Fort Laredo and No. 6001 Starship Counterforce Action Playset. It dropped the Built-Rite name for Warren in 1976, and continues to make card games, games and puzzles under that name. Its greatest period of success was probably enjoyed during and just prior to WWII.

	C6	C8	C10
No. 8 House, brick	65	80	90
No. 9 House, stucco and brick	65	80	90
No.10 House, 2-story, brick and shingle	65	80	90
No.14 "Front Line" Trench and Soldier set, w/trench, 6 WW II soldiers	40	55	60

BUILT-RITE, No. 20, Army Battery Set. Photo by Ed Poole.

BUILT-RITE, Airport No. 26. Photo by Jonathan A. Newman. Courtesy Barbara and Jonathan Newman.

BUILT-RITE, Fort No. 25 w/Barclay soldiers. Photo by Ed Poole.

	C6	C8	C10
No. 15 Commercial Garage	65	80	90
No. 16 Fort, no ramp	70	90	125
No. 17 Service Station	65	80	90
No. 18 Airport	65	75	85
No. 19 Railroad Station	60	70	80
No. 20 Railroad Tunnel	10	20	25
No. 20 Army Battery Set	90	125	145
No. 22 Army Outpost	45	65	75
No. 25 Fort, one ramp	85	115	125
No. 25A 26-piece Fort and Soldier Set same fort as 25, WW II soldiers, 2 sandbag foxholes and fiberboard pistol, sold through 1954	120	150	175
No. 26 United Airlines Airport Hangar	60	75	85
No. 27 Barn w/Animals	30	45	55
No. 28 Garage and Super Service Station	70	85	95
No. 29 Three Cart Set	25	40	45
No. 33 Lokdwood Dolls, late 1940s, paper dolls	20	30	45
No. 33 House, Tudor type	65	80	90
No. 34 House, two-story	65	80	90
No. 35 Modern Doll House	65	80	90
No. 36 House	65	80	90
No. 36F 3-Room Furnished Doll House	75	90	100
No. 37 Farm Machinery Set	30	45	55
No. 45 Living Room Furniture	45	55	65
No. 46 Dining Room Furniture	45	55	65
No. 47 Bedroom Furniture	45	55	65
No. 48 Bathroom Furniture	45	55	65
No. 49 Kitchen Furniture	45	55	65
No. 50 Army Raiders' Victory Unit, 28 pieces, truck, tank, AA gun, jeep, semi-track truck, 20 soldiers, WW II	70	85	95

	C6	C8	C10
No. 55 5 Miniature cardboard houses	30	55	60
No. 56 5 Miniature buildings, church, school, RR station, firehouse, drugstore	30	55	60
No. 57M 8-piece Farm Set	30	45	55
No. 60 Navy Battle Fleet and Coast Artillery Gun	30	55	70
No. 66 3-piece Kitchen	30	45	55
No. 75 Living Room Furniture	45	55	65
No. 76 Dining Room Furniture	45	55	65
No. 77 Bedroom Furniture	45	55	65
No. 77 American Ranger Fighters, 8 vehicles, WW II soldiers	75	85	95
No. 78 Kitchen Furniture	45	55	65
No. 83 Weapons Carrier	10	15	18
No. 84 Armored Car	10	15	18
No. 100A Fortress, c. 1938, 2 ramps	110	145	175
No. 105 Farm Set w/20 plastic animals	35	45	55
No. 111 Railroad Accessory Set	25	30	40
No. 112 American Fighters-includes 100A fortress w/soldiers, cannons, etc., 55-pieces, no flag on tower	110	145	175
No. 115 Doll House, Garage Set (w/car)	65	75	85
No. 119 Farm Set	40	60	70
No. 120 5-room Suburban Doll House	65	85	90
No. 127 Large Barn w/animals	30	45	50
No. 128 Miniature Village and Scenery Set	30	45	55
No. 148 Train Accessory Set	30	40	50
No. 156 Miniature Houses and Buildings	55	65	70
No. 178 Train Accessory Set	30	40	50
No. 201 26-piece Guardsman Set, 2 trenches, artillery base, cannon, pistol, WW II soldiers	70	90	120
No. 202 Train Scenery (28 pieces, Terminal, Scenery, etc.)	45	65	75
No. 204F Furnished Country Estate	60	80	90
No. 205 Medlee game, w/ships, cannon, etc.	No Price Found		
No. 210 Railroad Station and Acces	30	40	50

BUILT-RITE, No. 22, "Army Outpost". Courtesy John D. (Jack) Matthews.

BUILT-RITE, Fort No. 16. Courtesy John D. (Jack) Matthews.

	C6	C8	C10
No. 212 Station and Railroad Acces...	30	45	55
No. 245 Miniature Village	30	45	55
No. 252 Fort Set, 26 pcs, No. 25 Fort, post-war	100	145	175
No. 257 Fort Set, No. 25 Fort, 25 soldiers	No Price Found		
No. 298 Train Accessory Set	30	40	50
No. 300 Stock and Grain Elevator	25	35	45
No. 375 Station and Railroad Set	30	40	50
No. 415 House, c. 1943, 13" x 20" boxed set w/19" house and garage, 27 pcs of furniture, sedan, baby buggy, shrubbery, etc	80	100	125
No. 459 5 Rooms of Toy Furniture	45	55	65
No. 460 Pocket Size Series of Miniatures Paperdoll Set	15	20	24
No. 498 Train Accessory Set	25	35	45
No. 556 Miniature Village	No Price Found		
No. 566 Village	40	55	65
No. 1001 Modern Stock Farm	45	60	80
No. 1027 Stock Farm	45	60	80
No. 1033 Doll House	50	65	75
No. 1422 Fort and Soldiers (94 pcs, 2-ramp fort)	110	145	175
No. 1621 Army Camp: No. 16 Fort, trenches, tents, 108 soldiers	No Price Found		
No. 2011 Doll House & 88 pcs	No Price Found		
No. 2050 Country Estate, house, bushes, dog, cat, baby buggy	70	90	100
No. 2075 Colonial Cottage, 57 pcs	No Price Found		
Built-Rite Ranch, over 180 pieces	150	185	200
Camouflage Defense Force, airplanes, soldiers, anti-aircraft guns all hidden within farm buildings. Heavy cardboard. Jay Line Mfg. Co., 431, boxed, circa 1943	55	75	90
Career Girls w/Cloth-Like Clothes,1944, Whitman, No. 937 by Doris Lane Butler.	25	45	50

CAMOUFLAGE DEFENSE FORCE.

	C6	C8	C10
Charmin' Chatty, 1964, Whitman No. 1959	10	15	18
Charming Paper Dolls, circa 1960, Saalfield No. 1357	8	12	15
Cheerleader-Teenage Doll, 1950?, Stephens Publishing Co., No. 182, Mary & Elaine and 4 pages of clothes.	6	12	15
Children From Other Lands, 1961, Whitman, No. 2089, 8-cut-out dolls and native costumes	9	15	18
Children In The Shoe, 1949, Merril No. 1562	35	45	55
Cinderella Steps Out, Lowe No. 1242..	25	45	55
Circus Day-1946 by Art Tanchon, Stephens Printing No. 135, animals, clown, circus cages and wagons	15	20	25
Circus Paper Dolls, 1952, No. 2610, Saalfield	8	12	15
Claire McCardell-designer of the American look, 1956, Whitman No. 2067	45	55	65
Claudette Colbert, 1943, Saalfield No. 2451	150	190	225

CLAUDETTE COLBERT PAPER DOLLS.
Photo by Jonathan A. Newman. Courtesy
Barbara and Jonathan Newman.

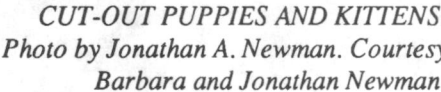

COLLEGE STYLE PAPER DOLLS.
Photo by Jonathan A. Newman. Courtesy
Barbara and Jonathan Newman.

CUT-OUT PUPPIES AND KITTENS.
Photo by Jonathan A. Newman. Courtesy
Barbara and Jonathan Newman.

	C6	C8	C10
Cloth-Like Clothes for 3 Cute Girls, 1949, Whitman No. 1178:15, flocked clothes	25	35	45
Clothes Make A Lady, 1941, Lowe No. 1029	25	35	45
Coke Crowd, The, 1946, Merrill No. 3445, 8 teens, costumes	50	65	75
College Style Paper Dolls, 1941, Merrill No. 3400	50	65	75
Colorgraphic Statue-ettes, 1943, 3-dimensional and stand-up paper dolls of Marine, Soldier, Sailor, Nurse, WAAC, WAVE, boxed	25	35	45
Comet Model Airplane Co. Die Cut Glider, 5-1/2" x 8" sheet containing die cut U.S. Army fighter printed in 1942 by the Comet Model Airplane Co	8	12	15
Commando Machine Gun 1940s, thin cardboard cut-out makes model over 25" long	15	20	25
Connie Francis, 1963, Whitman No. 1956	40	50	60
Coronation Cut-Out Model Book	50	60	65
Coronation Glitter Model Book	30	40	45
Coronation Paper Dolls and Coloring Book, 1953, Saalfield No. 4450, 10-1/2" x 15" book. Queen Elizabeth, Prince Philip, young Prince Charles, and Princess Ann	65	75	90
Cowboy and Cowgirl Cut-Outs, 1950, Merrill No. 3449	30	40	50

	C6	C8	C10
Cowboy Cutouts, c. 1930s, Platt and Munk	25	30	40
Cowboys and Indians Cut-outs, 1937, Saalfield	50	55	60
Cowgirl Jill and Cowboy Joe, Merrill, No. 3459	25	35	45

CUT AND STICK

222

CIRCUS DAY CUT-OUT BOOK. Photo by Jonathan A. Newman. Courtesy Barbara and Jonathan Newman.

DOUBLE WEDDING 15 PAPER DOLLS. Photo by Jonathan A. Newman. Courtesy Barbara and Jonathan Newman.

DENISON'S CREPE PAPER DOLL OUTFIT No. 36. Photo by Jonathan A. Newman. Courtesy Barbara and Jonathan Newman.

	C6	C8	C10
Cradle Crowd,The, 1948, 4 doll babies w/cloth-like clothes, Whitman No. 1173	45	55	65
Cut and Stick-Our Army and Navy in Action, Merrill No. 4835, 1942	30	40	50
Cut-Me Out Paper Dolls, 1940s, Abbott No. 1358	15	20	25
Cut-Out Dolls, Puppies and Kittens, Whitman No. 931, 1939	75	90	125
Cut-Out Dolls w/Paints and Clothes to Color, by Avis Mac, Whitman No. 983, c. 1930s, 11" x 18" book w/ 4 17" children and 16 pages of colthing and sheet of paints	50	70	75
Cyd Charisse,1956,Whitman No.2084	55	75	95
Dancing Dolls w/famous costumes, Merrill No. 3448, 1954, ballet dancers	40	50	60
Davy Crockett Punch Out Book, 1955, No. 1943	50	75	90
Deanna Durbin, 1940, Merrill No. 3480	175	200	225
Debs and Sub Debs Paper Doll Book, 1941, No. 2361, Saalfield, 20 punchouts	30	40	50
Decalco-Litho Co. Paper Dolls Sheets, c. 1920s, 8" x 10-1/2" sheets, 1. woman and girl and 9 outfits 2. woman and girl and 10 outfits 3. 2 women and 7 outfits. Price per sheet	10	15	20
Dennison's Crepe Paper Doll Outfit No. 36	70	90	125
Dennison's Dolls and Dresses No. 37, circa 1930	70	90	125
Diane and Daphne the Round About Dolls Book, 1937, No. 545 McLoughlin Bros., large cut-outs by Campbell	45	60	75

	C6	C8	C10
Diana Lynn Paper Dolls, 1953, Saalfield, 157910	45	55	65
Dick the Sailor, circa 1942, Samuel Lowe No. L1074	25	40	50
Disneyland Park Punch Out, 1960, No. 175	30	40	45
Dodie from My Three Sons TV series,1971, Artcraft No. 5115, Dodie and Dolly	20	25	35
Dolls from Storyland by Vivian Robbins,1948, Merrill 1554	30	45	55
Dolls that Walk-"They Walk-They Dance They Play", designed by Emily Sprague Wurl, Whitman No. 977, 1939, 2 identical girls and 2 identical boys	60	70	80
Donna Reed Paper Dolls, 1960, Saalfield/Artcraft No. 5197 9" x 12" boxed set	45	55	65
Doris Day, 1952, Whitman No. 210325	45	55	65
Dorothy Provine, 1962, Whitman No. 1964	40	50	65
Double Date Cut-out Dolls by Elinee Fon Vaughan, 1949, Whitman No. 962	35	40	50
Double Wedding, 1939, Merrill 3472	65	85	100
Down On The Farm, 1940s, Lowe 1056	18	25	30
Dr. Kildare and Nurse Susan, early 1960s, Lowe No. 2740	25	35	45
Dress-Up Doll Book, The, 1953, Treasure Books No. T-167	10	15	20
Dress-Up For the New York World's Fair by Judy and Barry Martin, Spertus No. 700, 1963	8	15	18
Dress-Up Paper Doll Cut-outs, 1947, Reuben Lilja & Co	15	20	25
8 Ages of Judy, The, by Fern Bisil Peat, 1941, Lowe L1025, Judy as baby and ages 1-7	60	75	85
Elizabeth Taylor,1950,Whitman No.973-10	65	85	100

FAIRY FOLK CUT-OUT PAPER DOLLS,
Little Bo-Peep. Photo by Jonathan A.
Newman. Courtesy Barbara and Jonathan
Newman.

GRACE KELLY 2 CUT-OUT DOLLS AND
CLOTHES. Photo by Jonathan A. Newman.
Courtesy Barbara and Jonathan Newman.

GLENN MILLER, MARION HUTTON
TURNABOUT DOLL BOOK. Photo by
Jonathan A. Newman. Courtesy Barbara
and Jonathan Newman.

	C6	C8	C10
Eskimo Cut-Outs by Milo Winter, 1939, Whitman 1054	25	35	45
Esther Williams, 1950, Merrill 1563, 3 dolls	75	85	95
Eve Arden Paper Dolls, 1953, Saalfield 158510	50	60	70
Evelyn Rudy-Little Star of Screen and Television, 1958, Saalfield No. 1745	30	40	45
Fabulous High Fashion Models, 1958, Bonnie Brooks/Child Craft No. 2776	8	12	15
Fairy Folk Cut-out Paper Dolls by Margaret Carlson, Still & Edwards Co., Inc. 1920s	15	30	35
Family Princess Paper Dolls, 1958, Merrill No. 1548	45	55	65
Family Affair,1968, Whitman No.4767	20	25	30
Family of Paper Dolls, 1947, Saalfield 2564	20	30	40
Family of Paper Dolls by Queen Holden, Whitman No. 991, mother, father, nurse, 6 kids	80	100	125
Farm Cut-outs by Milo Winter, 1938, Whitman No. 1054, 6-1/2" x 10-1/2", 6 pages of heavy paper cut-outs	25	35	45
The **Fashion** Book of the Round About Dolls, 1936, McLoughlin Bros.,over an 1" thick, 8 stand-up dolls plus scissors and pack of paper dolls clothes in package by Betty Campbell	50	70	80

	C6	C8	C10
Fashion Cut Outs w/Sturdibilt Dolls, 1940s, Lowe No. 1243	15	20	30
Fifteen ABC Blocks to Play and Learn, 1933, Whitman No. 976, book containing 15 die-cut blocks to put together. Illustrations of nursery rhymes, alphabet letters, animals and numbers on each block	15	25	35
Fire Fighters in Action, Saalfield, 1938	20	45	50
Fire House P-18 by Megow, 1945, brick firehouse, boxed set	30	45	55
Five Little Peppers, Little Women and Annie Lauries, 1941, Lowe L1030, 3-book set	50	60	75
The **Flying** Nun, 1968, 1969, Artcraft No. 4417	20	30	35
Four Sisters Paper Dolls, 1943, Saalfield No. 269	18	25	30
Fourteen Dogs To Cut Out and Stand Up, copyright 1930, Whitman, No. 935, 12 pages of dogs, cardboard punchouts	20	30	45
French Infantry-Milton Bradley?, c. 1915, approx. 6" high, single figure, each cardboard	2	4	5
Frontier Fort, 1952, Merrill No.257225	12	20	25
Fun Farm, Reed and Associates	6	12	15
Gene Autry Melody Ranch Cut-Out Dolls, 1950, Whitman No. 990-10	50	75	85
Gene Autry Ranch cut-out book, 1940 Merrill	65	80	90
Gene Autry Ranch cut-out book, 1953	50	70	80

HOUSE FOR SALE. Photo by Jonathan A. Newman. Courtesy Barbara and Jonathan Newman.

LITTLE MARY MIXUP AND HER FRIEND PEGGY. Photo by Jonathan A. Newman. Courtesy Barbara and Jonathan Newman.

	C6	C8	C10
Gigi Perreau Paper Dolls, 1951, Saalfield 1542	35	50	55
Gigi Perreau, 1951, Saalfield No. 2605	35	50	55
Girl Friend-Boy Friend Paper Dolls, 1955, Saalfield, No. 1605	15	20	22
Girl Friends paper dolls, 1944 Whitman No. 974	25	35	45
Girl Pilots of the Ferry Command, 1943, Merrill 4852	75	90	110
Girls in Uniform Paper Dolls Book, circa 1942, No. L1048	55	75	85
Glamour Parade Cut-out Dolls, Stephens Publishing Co., No. 184, 1950s?, 4 models and 4 pages of clothes	10	15	20
Glenn Miller, Marion Hutton Turn-about Doll Book, 1942, Lowe No. 21041	130	150	190
Gloria Jean Paper Doll Cut-outs, 1940, Saalfield No. 1661	70	85	100
Gone With The Wind, 1940, Merrill No. 3404, 18 dolls	325	350	400
Gone With The Wind, 1940, Merrill No. 3405, 5 dolls	300	350	400
Good Neighbor Paper dolls, 1944, Saalfield, No. 2487	12	20	25
Grace Kelly 2 Cut Out Dolls and Clothes No. 2049 Whitman, 1955	60	85	95
Grace Kelly, 1956, Whitman No. 2069	60	85	95
Gulliver's Travels No. 1261 cut-outs, 1939, Saalfield	55	65	75
Hair-Do Dolls by Queen Holden, 1948, Whitman 991	55	75	100

	C6	C8	C10
Harry the Soldier, 1941, Samuel Lowe, No. L1074	40	60	75
Hayley Mills, "The Moonspinners", 1964, Whitman No. 1960	40	45	50
Heavy Cruiser, "This is the Navy", circa 1943, Skyline Mfg. Co.	20	30	40
Hedy Lamarr Paper Dolls, Saalfield 1555	100	120	150
Hee Haw, 1971, Artcraft No. 5139	25	40	45
Heidi and Peter, circa 1970, Saalfield No. 1355	12	15	20
Here Comes the Bride, 1952, Whitman No. 118915	25	45	55
Here's the Bride, 1953, Whitman No. 2109	25	45	55
High School Girls, 1948, Merrill No. 1551	50	55	65
Historical Dolls To Cut Out and Dress, 1961, Platt & Munk No. 226B, 7" x 11" boxed set. Mother, Father, and 2 children of heavy cardboard, plus outfits	15	25	30
Holiday Paper dolls, 1950s, Saalfield No. 1742	10	15	20
Hollywood Fashion Dolls, 1939, Saalfield No. 397, 12 male and female dolls, clothes	35	45	55
Hollywood Fashions, 1949, Saalfield No. 1535	20	35	50
Hour of Charm Paper Dolls, 1943, women musicians, Saalfield No. 2481	70	90	115
House For Sale, 1962, Lowe No. 9042	30	40	45
House That Jack Built, c. 1895, Bliss, R.I. paper litho, house and story's characters w/stands	400	500	600
Howdy Doody Puppet Show Punchout Book, copyright 1952, Whitman No. 211129, punchout cardboard puppets may be controlled by strings. Includes Howdy, Bluster, Inspector, Dilly Dally, Clarabell, and Flubadub	50	55	65

JUNE BRIDE.

JAUNTY JUNIORS. Photo by Jonathan A. Newman. Courtesy Barbara and Jonathan Newman.

225

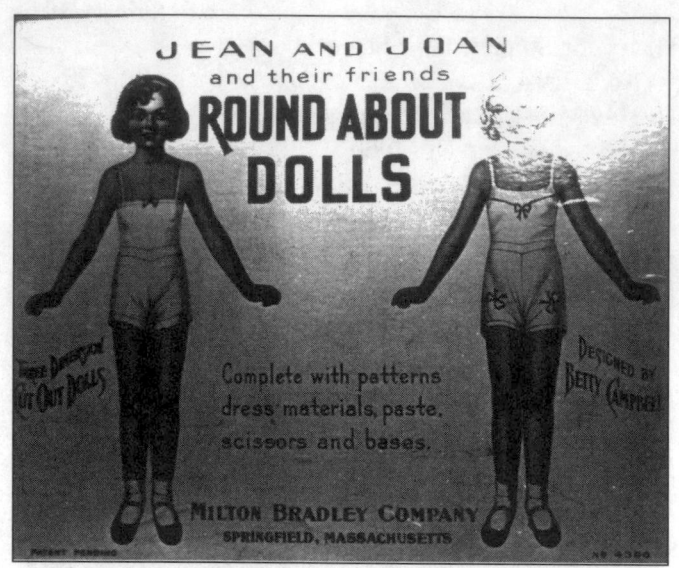

JEAN AND JOAN AND THEIR ROUND ABOUT DOLLS. Photo by Jonathan A. Newman. Courtesy Barbara and Jonathan Newman.

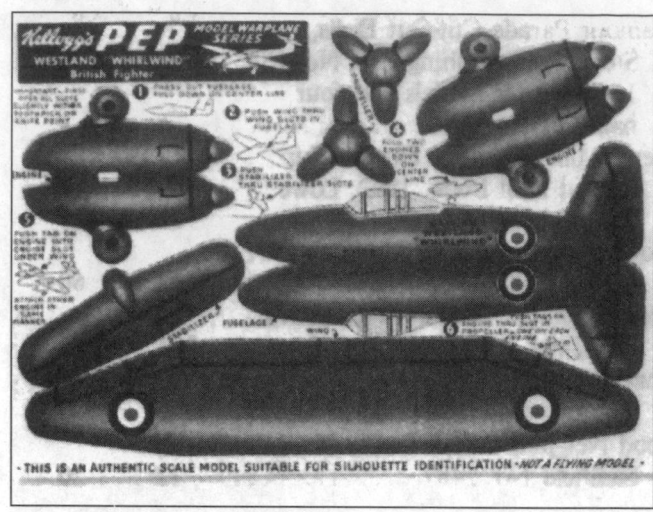

KELLOGG'S PEP WARPLANE, cardboard, circa 1944. Courtesy HAKE'S Americana & Collectibles.

	C6	C8	C10
Howdy Doody Sticker Fun, copyright 1951, Whitman No. 219525	25	35	38
Howdy Doody Sticker Fun, copyright 1953, Whitman No. 215825	25	35	38
Howdy Doody Sticker Fun Circus, copyright 1955, Whitman No. 2165	25	35	38
I Love Lucy-Lucille Ball and Desi Arnaz, 1953, Whitman No. 2101	55	75	85
Jack and Jill, 1962, Merrill No. 1561, 6 dolls and clothes from storyland	20	25	30
Jane Russell, 1955, Saalfield No. 2611.	45	75	85
Janet Leigh Cut-outs and Coloring Books, 1953, Merrill No. 2554	55	70	80
Janet Leigh, 1958, Abbott No. 1805	45	55	65
Jaunty Juniors, 1946, No. 903	20	30	35
Jean and Joan and their Friends, Roundabout Dolls designed by Betty Campbell, 1934, boxed set, Milton Bradley No. 4396	75	85	100
Jeanette MacDonald, 1941, Merrill 3640	175	200	225
Jimmy & Jane Visit Gene Autry at Melody Ranch, 1951, Whitman No. 118415	50	65	70
Joan's Wedding by Florence Sarah Winship, clothes designed by Ruth M. Ruhman, 1942, Whitman No. 990	40	55	65
Judy and Jack, Peg & Bill Cut-out Dolls by Pelagie Doane, 1940, Lowe No. L1024	45	65	80

	C6	C8	C10
"Julia"-Diahann Carroll, Julia, Corey, Marie and Earl J. Waggedorn, 1968, Artcraft No. 5140	25	35	40
Julia w/Julia, Earl J. Waggedorn and Corey, 1969, Saalfield	25	35	40
June Allyson, 1950, 1952, Whitman No. 119015	55	75	90
June Allyson, 1953, Whitman 1173:15	55	75	90
June Bride by Art Tanchon, 1946, Stephens No. 136	20	30	40
Junior Bombardier, 1953, Einson & Freeman Co. No. 202	20	35	40
Junior Prom by Newman, 1942, Lowe 1042	35	45	50
Karen Goes to College!, 1955, Merrill No. 1564	20	35	40
Kiddieland Village, c. 1935, Whitman No. 2004, 11-1/2" x 15" boxed set, 9 buildings and 65 cut-out figures	60	75	90
Kitty goes to Kindergarten, 1956, Merrill No. 1548	25	35	40
Lennon Sisters, 1957, Whitman No. 1979	30	45	55
Lennon Sisters, 1961, Whitman No. 1983	30	45	55
Lettie Lane Paper Family-Third Series, 1909, George W. Jacobs & Co., original house folder and 6 sheets	130	155	175
Liberty Belles Paper Doll Book, 1943, No. 3477, Merrill	45	60	65
Little Ballerina, 1953, Merrill No.154215	40	50	60

KIDDIELAND VILLAGE. Photo by Jonathan A. Newman. Courtesy Barbara and Jonathan Newman.

LITTLE FOLK'S FRIENDS. Photo by Jonathan A. Newman. Courtesy Barbara and Jonathan Newman.

LUCILLE BALL, DESI ARNAZ CUT-OUT DOLLS W/LITTLE RICKY. Photo by Jonathan A. Newman. Courtesy Barbara and Jonathan Newman.

THE LETTIE LANE PAPER FAMILY. Photo by Jonathan A. Newman. Courtesy Barbara and Jonathan Newman.

LITTLE FRIENDS FROM HISTORY. Photo by Jonathan A. Newman. Courtesy Barbara and Jonathan Newman.

LOTS OF LITTLE PAPER DOLLS. Photo by Jonathan A. Newman. Courtesy Barbara and Jonathan Newman.

	C6	C8	C10
Little Ballet Dancers, 1950s?, Saalfield No. 1743	10	15	18
Little Brothers and Sisters, 1953, Whitman No. 971:10, Tim, Kay Ann and Pete	15	20	25
Little Folks Friends, 1915, Saalfield No. 156	10	15	20
Little Friends from History by Muriel Wilhoite, Rand McNally No. 186, 1936	50	60	65
Little Friends Paper Dolls, 1950s, Saalfield No. 1746	10	15	18
Little Miss America Paper Doll Book, 1941, Saalfield No. 2358, 15 punchouts by Campbell	30	40	45
Little Nurse Cut-Out Book, early 1940s, Reuben H. Lilja and Co.,Inc., No. 909	18	25	30
Little Red School House Kindergarten, The, by Margo Voight, McLoughlin Bros., 1940, 2 teachers, 23 children	45	55	60

	C6	C8	C10
Little Women, circa 1970, Artcraft No. 5127	12	15	18
Lois and Joan Cut-out Dolls, 1941, 1945, Whitman No. 1015 (Joan also appears in Betty & Joan and Mary and Joan)	30	40	45
The **Lone** Ranger Rides Again Punch-out Set, DeJournette Mfg. Co., makes fences, figures of LR and Tonto, horses, campfire	30	40	50
Look-a-Like Cut-out Dolls, 1952, Whitman No. 97210, 2 mother and daughter pairs of dolls	15	20	25
Look Who I Am! 1952, Hart Publishing Co. by Doris Stelberg, 18" doll w/15 costumes, Spiral bound	12	18	22
Lori Martin in National Velvet 1962, Whitman No. 4612, 6" x 11-1/2" boxed set, paper dolls	18	30	35
Lost Horizon, 1973, Artcraft No. 5112	12	18	20
Lots of Little Paper Dolls by Angela Tuite Price, 1949, Saalfield No. 1537	20	30	35
Lucille Ball, Desi Arnaz Cut-out Dolls w/Little Ricky, 1953, Whitman 2116:25	60	75	90
Lucille Ball Paper Dolls, 1944, Saalfield 2475	60	75	90
Madame Hattie Fashions, 1940s, Reuben Lilja 908	30	40	45
Magic Mary, 1955, Milton Bradley No. 4010-1, 10-1/2" x 10-1/2" boxed set, complete w/magnetic doll and strips to put on clothes	10	15	20

	C6	C8	C10
Make Your Own Battle Set Mechanized Force, 1942, Electric Corporation of America	30	45	50
Margaret O'Brien Paper Dolls, Whitman 96410	100	120	150
Marge and Gower Champion, 1959, Whitman	55	75	90
Martha Hyer Paper Dolls, 1958, Saalfield 4423	40	50	55
Mary and Joan, 1941, 1945, Whitman No. 1015 (Joan also appears in Lois & Joan and Betty & Joan)	30	40	45
Mary Belle Cut-out Doll by Fern Bisel Peat, Saalfield No. 2100, 4 separate sheets, 17" doll w/3 sheets of clothes, 1934	50	60	70

	C6	C8	C10
Mary Jane-A Cut Out Doll, by Florence Winship, 1939, 1941, Whitman No. 1010 w/suitcase for accessories	40	45	50
Mary Lee-A Cut Out Doll, Whitman No. 1010, circa 1939	40	45	50
Mary Martin, 1942, Saalfield 2427	150	175	200
Mary of the WACS-A Young American, by Hilda Miloche and Wilma Kane, Whitman No. 1012, 1943	40	50	60
Mary Poppins, 1973, Whtiman No. 1977	20	30	35
Marybelle Mercer's Front and Back Dolls W/Wrap-Around Dresses by Queen Holden No. 978	75	90	100

MCLOUGHLIN BROS. OF BROOKLYN, NEW YORK

McLoughlin Brothers was the largest American producer of paper soldiers, and one of the earliest in the paper doll field. The firm, which traced its founding to 1828, began producing paper dolls at least as early as 1857. Among the other paper toys it sold were dollhouse furniture, toy theaters with actors and scenery, and blocks. The company was sold in 1920 to Milton Bradley.

	C6	C8	C10
McLoughlin Bros., circa 1884, mounted U.S.Cavalry, Hussar type, charging, several different poses. Price per figure	2.75	3	3.50
McLoughlin Bros. Infantry Soldiers, printed 1857, price per each $5, complete set $200-250			
McLoughlin Bros. Infantry, c. 1875, price per each	3	4	5
McLoughlin Bros., Zouaves, 1884, price per each	2.75	3.50	4.50
McLoughlin Bros. Brass Band, 1890, price per each	3.50	4.50	5.50
McLoughlin Bros. Grenadiers, 1890, price per each	3	3.50	4
McLoughlin Bros. Paper Dolls, 1860-1890, price per cut set $50 and up; uncut $100 and up, depending on title, date, etc.			
McLoughlin Bros. 100 Soldiers on Parade, circa 1898	300	350	400
McLoughlin Bros. 100 Soldiers on Parade, second set, c. 1898	300	350	400
McLoughlin Bros. 260 Series, circa 1889-1895;			
c. U.S. Regulars, spiked helmet, each	2.25	2.75	4.50
d. U.S. Infantry	2.25	2.75	3
e. Mounted U.S. Cavalry, Hussar type, charging	2.25	2.75	3

	C6	C8	C10
f. West Point Cadets	2.25	2.75	3
g. U.S. Regulars	2.25	2.75	3
h. U.S. Infantry	2.25	2.75	3
i. Bandsmen,various instruments, each	2.75	3	3.50
j. Navy - USS Boston	2.25	2.75	3
k. Grenadier Guards, each	2.25	2.75	3
l. Annapolis Cadets, each	2.25	2.75	3
McLoughlin Bros., printed 1898, sailor 5-1/4" high, landing party for USS Texas	4	5	6
McLoughlin Bros., U.S. Infantry from Spanish-American War, c. 1898, approx. 6" high on wooden blocks, price per figure	4	5	6
McLoughlin Bros., circa 1898, small glossy series, 4-1/2" high, West Point Cadets, price per figure	4	5	6
McLoughlin Bros., circa 1898, glossy series, U.S. Regulars, full dress, 5" high	4	5	6
McLoughlin Bros., c. 1898, British Infantry Red Coats, spiked helmets, 6" high on small wooden blocks, price per figure	4	5	6
McLoughlin Bros., c. 1898, U.S. Zouaves, Civil War era, blue coats, red baggy trousers, 6" high on small wooden blocks	4	5	6

McLOUGHLIN BROS. 100 SOLDIERS ON PARADE. Photo by Jonathan A. Newman. Courtesy Barbara and Jonathan Newman.

McLOUGHLIN BROS. THE NEW PRETTY VILLAGE. Photo by Jonathan A. Newman. Courtesy Barbara and Jonathan Newman.

McLOUGHLIN BROS., Building from New Pretty Village. Photo by Jonathan A. Newman. Courtesy Barbara and Jonathan Newman.

	C6	C8	C10
McLoughlin Bros. "02" Series, circa 1904-1910			
a. British Highlanders			
b. U.S. Zouaves			
c. U.S. Continentals			
d. U.S. Navy			
e. U.S. Infantry in Campaign Uniforms(Spanish-American War)			
h. American Indians, kneeling and standing			
i. West Point Cadets			
Price per figure	2	2.50	3
McLoughlin Bros., same as above g. West Point Cadets (round base) circa 1915	2	2.50	3
McLoughlin Bros. No. 0103 Dutch Paper doll, boy of the Village of Vollendam, c. 1910, 10-1/2" x 10-1/2" sheet	15	22	25

	C6	C8	C10
McLoughlin Bros., circa 1915, Boy Scout holding rifles across chests	4	5	6
McLoughlin Bros., Series No. 4026 10-1/2"x10-1/2" paper soldiers on sheet, 7 soldiers plus officer (5-1/2" high) in field uniform, c. 1916. 1. Belgium 2. France 3. Italy 4. Britain, price per sheet	20	30	40
McLoughlin Bros., New Folding Doll House, 1897, boxed set, cardboard w/litho paper	375	500	575
McLoughlin Bros., New Pretty Village Church Set, 1897	90	120	140
McLoughlin Bros., New Pretty Village School Set, 1897	90	120	140
McLoughlin Bros., New Pretty Village, individual bldgs	12	15	18
Me and Mimi, 1957, a Bonnie Story Book Doll, 6"x8" in the style of the Little Golden Books, a Doll and her Dolly Story Book, plus dolls and their dresses	12	20	25
Mexican Cut Outs by Milo Winter, 1938, Whitman 1054, 6 pages of people, animals, houses, etc	25	35	45
Mickey and Minnie Paper Dolls, 1930s 2 10" figures w/clothes	90	150	175
Model Airplanes, Samuel Lowe No. 1069, 1941, WWII airplanes, International	40	65	75
Model Battleship by Reed, circa 1945, 7" x 10"	15	20	25
Model Flat-top by Reed, c. 1945	15	20	25
Model Tanks, Lowe No. 1065, 1941	45	65	70
Model Tanks Construction Set, boxed set, 1942, Lowe No. 1267	45	65	70

ONE HUNDRED SOLDIERS PUNCH-OUT BOOK, 1943, Whitman 999. Courtesy John D. (Jack) Matthews

MODEL TANKS CONSTRUCTION KIT. Photo by Jonathan A. Newman. Courtesy Barbara and Jonathan Newman.

MODEL WAR PLANES CONSTRUCTION KIT. Photo by Jonathan A. Newman. Courtesy Barbara and Jonathan Newman.

MAYBELLE MERCER'S FRONT AND BACK DOLLS. Photo by Jonathan A. Newman. Courtesy Barbara and Jonathan Newman.

Make Your Own Battle Set Mechanized Force. Photo by Jonathan A. Newman. Courtesy Barbara and Jonathan Newman.

	C6	C8	C10
Model War Planes Construction Set, boxed set, 1942, Lowe No. 1266....	45	65	75
Modern Miss in Paper Dolls, 1942, by Van Swearingen, Saalfield 2397.....	30	40	45
Molly Bee, 1962, Whitman No. 2091...	20	35	45
Mommy and Me, 1954, Whitman No. 977:10.................	18	25	30
Mother and Daughter by Patrie Winston, Grinnel Lithographic No. C-1005, 15" mother, 11" daughter, 2 scotties, 1940........................	30	45	50
Mouseketeer Cut Outs, 1957, Whitman No. 1974................	40	50	55
Movie Starlets, 1946, Whitman No. 960, Gail Russell, Diana Lynn, Olga San Juan, Marjorie Reynolds, Joan Caulfield................	60	75	90

	C6	C8	C10
Movie Starlets Paper Dolls, c. 1949, Stephens Publishing Co. No. 178, 4 dolls Miss Premier, Miss Stardust, Miss Hollywood, Miss Preview and 4 pages of costumes...	20	25	30
Mrs. Beasley Paper doll Book, 1970, ("Family Affair" TV show) Whitman No. 1973................	12	15	20
My Fair Lady, 1965, Ottenheimer Publishers No. 2960-2, by Evon Hartman........	30	35	40
My Paper Doll's Sewing Kit, 1940, by Margot Voight, Grinnell C-1018....	22	45	48
My Twin Babies With Older Brother and Sister, 1940, Whitman 970.......	40	55	65
My Very First Paper Doll Book, 1957, a Bonnie Book No. 4732, Samuel Lowe..................	10	15	18
Nancy and Her Dolls w/7 Busy Days of Fun, 1944, Saalfield No. 2478................	20	40	45
Natalie Wood Paper Dolls, 1958, Whitman................	65	85	100
National Velvet, 1961, Whitman No. 1958................	25	38	45

ON GUARD A PUNCHOUT BOOK. Photo by Jonathan A. Newman. Courtesy Barbara and Jonathan Newman.

NEW SHIRLEY TEMPLE IN PAPER DOLLS. Photo by Jonathan A. Newman. Courtesy Barbara and Jonathan Newman.

OUR HAPPY FAMILY CUT-OUT SHEETS. Photo by Jonathan A. Newman. Courtesy Barbara and Jonathan Newman.

OUR SOLDIERS CUT-OUT ARMY UNIFORMS. Photo by Jonathan A. Newman. Courtesy Barabara and Jonathan Newman.

	C6	C8	C10
Navy Scouts Paper Doll Book, 1942, Merrill No. 3428	65	75	90
New Shirley Temple In Paper Dolls, The, 1942, Saalfield No. 2425	100	125	150
New York World's Fair Make A Model, 1963, by Ottenheimer, Spertus No. 600-50, includes Unisphere, Swiss Ride, N.Y. Port Authority, Heliport, etc.	18	25	30
Night Before Christmas W/Cut Outs, Whitman No. 948	18	25	30
19 Farmyard Animals To Cut Out and Stand Up, Copyright 1930, Whitman No. 935, 12 pages	30	35	40
Oklahoma w/Shirley Jones and Gordon MacRae, 1956, Whitman No. 1954	55	75	85
On Guard, 1942, Lowe No. L535	35	45	50
One Hundred Soldiers Punchout Book, 1943, Whitman 999	50	55	60
Our Happy Family Cut-Out Sheets, 1928, Sam'l Gabriel Sons Co. No. D141	65	75	90
Our New Home, 1930, story by Susan S. Popper, pictures by Helen E. Ohrenschall, Sam'l Gabriel Sons, hardcover book, 6 pages of rooms 6 gummed pages of people, furniture, etc.	80	100	125
Our Nurse Nancy - A Young American, by Hilda Miloche and Wilma Kane, 1943, cut-outs, Whitman No. 1012	45	50	55
Our Sailor Bob, 10" doll w/uniforms, Whitman, circa 1943	35	45	50
Our Soldier Jim, 1943, Whitman No. 3980, designed by Hilda Miloche and Wilma Kane, 10-1/2" standup doll w/uniforms	35	45	50

	C6	C8	C10
Our Soldiers Cut Out Army Uniforms by Nat Falk, Dell, 1941, 4 cut-out dolls and several uniforms	50	55	65
Our Wave Joan - A Young American by Hilda Miloche and Wilma Kane, 1943, Whitman No. 1012	40	45	50
Outdoor Paper Dolls, 1941, Saalfield No. 1958, 14 dolls and 4 pages of clothes	12	18	20
Over 80 Turn-About, Standup Sailors, 1943, Lowe No. 141	40	50	55
Over 80 Turn-About, Standup Soldiers, 1943, Lowe No. 140	40	50	55
Paper Doll Family And Their House by Florence and Margaret Hoopes, 1934, Saalfield No. 4125	60	70	75
Paper Doll Family And Their Trailer, Merrill No. 3436, 1938	70	80	90
Paper Doll "Joan" and Paper Doll "Bobby" by Queen Holden, 1928, Whitman 907	80	90	100
Paper Doll Outfit, American Toy Works No. 102, boxed set	50	60	75
Paper Doll Playmates, 1940 Saalfield No. 154, Nurse, 19 children, costumes, toys	40	50	55
Paper Dolls from Mother Goose, 1957, Saalfield No. 2758, Mary, Bo-Peep, Boy Blue, Bobbie Shaftoe, Miss Muffett, Jack Horner	15	20	25
Paper Dolls Julia and Marie by Angela Tuite Price, 1958, Saalfield No. 1530	18	20	23
Paper Dolls Of All Nations - New York World's Fair, 1939, Saalfield No. 227	45	50	60
Paper Dolls of Eve Arden, 1956, Saalfield 1706	50	65	75

PAPER DOLL FAMILY AND THEIR TRAILER. *Photo by Jonathan A. Newman. Courtesy Barbara and Jonathan Newman.*

PAPER DOLL OUTFIT DRESSES AND HATS. *Photo by Jonathan A. Newman. Courtesy Barbara and Jonathan Newman.*

PILOT AND STEWARDESS AIRLINER PAPER DOLLS.

PLAYHOUSE PAPER DOLLS *by Doris and Marion Henderson.*

Photos by Jonathan A. Newman. Courtesy Barbara and Jonathan Newman.

PAPER DOLLS TO CUT OUT AND PAINT.

PAPER DOLLS JULIA & MARIE

Photos by Jonathan A. Newman. Courtesy Barbara and Jonathan Newman.

	C6	C8	C10
Paper Dolls Peter and Peggy, 1935, Whitman No. 965, 64 pages by Dixon. Very large punchouts on front and back	40	50	55
Paper Dolls To Cut Out and Paint, 1920s, Saalfield No. 1180	55	65	75
Paper Dolls-United We Stand by Margot Voight, Saalfield No. 113, 6 children w/uniforms	45	60	70
The Partridge Family, 1971, Artcraft No. 5137	18	25	30
Partridge Family, 1972, Artcraft No. 5143	18	25	30
Pat Boone, 1959, Whitman No. 1968	40	45	50
Pat Crowley, 1955, Whitman No.2050	45	55	65
Patience and Prudence, 1958, Lowe No. 2736 (Popular singers of the 1950s)	15	20	25
Patsy, 1946, Children's Press, No. 30002, Patsy, dog, doghouse, etc.	25	30	35

PLAYHOUSE PAPER DOLLS. *Photo by Jonathan A. Newman. Courtesy Barbara and Jonathan Newman.*

PAPER DOLLS OF ALL NATIONS NEW YORK WORLD'S FAIR, 1939. *Photo by Jonathan A Newman. Courtesy Barbara and Jonathan Newman.*

	C6	C8	C10
Patsy A Wooden Doll W/Dresses (actually a 10" standup cardboard doll with wood backing), c. 1938, Whitman 3037	35	40	45
Patsy Ann and Her Trunk full of Clothes by Queen Holden, 1939, Whitman No. 992	80	90	100

	C6	C8	C10
Patti Page, 1958 book of paper dolls..	45	60	75
Patty's Party Paper Dolls, c. 1950, Stephens Publishing Co. No. 175....	12	18	20
Pert and Pretty, 1948, Merrill No. 1552...	40	45	50
Peter and Peggy, 1950, Whitman No. 99210.............	12	20	25
Peter and Peggy, Jerry and Joan Paper Dolls by Rachel Taft Dixon, 1935, Whitman No. 985......	55	65	75
Photo Fashions, 1953, Whitman No.973.	18	25	30
Pig Tails, 1949, Merrill No. 344410....	35	45	50
Pilot and Stewardess Paper Doll Book 1941, Merrill No. 3423..................	40	45	50
The **Pink** Wedding, 1952, Merrill No. 1559.................	50	55	65
Piper Laurie, 1953, Merrill No. 2551...	40	55	70
Playhouse Dolls, 1949, Stephens Publishing Co. No. 1965, 4 dolls and 4 pages of clothes..............	12	18	20
Playhouse Paper Dolls designed by Doris and Marion Henderson, Lowe No. 1028, 1941..............	25	35	40
Playhouse Paper Dolls, 1947, Saalfield No. 381.............	15	25	30
Playmates, 1952, Whitman No. 99510.	12	20	25
Playthings To Cut Out and Stand Up, circa 1935, Whitman No. 934, contains ventriloquist's dummy, floating ships, general's hat, lantern, animals, other moving toys..............	30	35	45
Play Time, 1952, Whitman 210525....	12	15	18
Playtime Pals, 1946, Lowe No. 1045..	12	18	20
Polly Patchwork and Her Friends by Pelagie Doane, 1941, Lowe No. 1024..	30	40	45

	C6	C8	C10
Polyanna Cut Out Dolls, 1941 Whitman No. 995.............	50	55	65
Popular Paper Dolls, 1942, Saalfield No. 1973.............	20	25	30
Portrait Girls W/Cloth-Like Clothes, 1947, designed by Hilda Miloche and Wilma Kane, Whitman No. 1170.	30	40	45
Power Models Cut Out Dolls Book, 1942, 6 dolls, Whitman No. 981......	55	90	120
Pressed Board Dolls and Their Dresses, boxed set, Lowe No. 1942.............	25	35	45
Pre-Teen Paper Dolls, c. 1960s, Saalfield No. 1366.............	8	12	15
Prince and Princess Paper Dolls, 1949, Saalfield No. 2706.............	20	30	35
Prom Time, 1962, Whitman No. 2084, 2 dolls and party clothes.......	15	20	25
Queen Holden! Betty and Bob, 1952, 12-1/2" high children, Whitman 99110....	50	55	60
Queen Holden! Hair-Do Dolls, 1948, 3 dolls, clothes and 31 different hair-dos, Whitman No. 991.............	40	55	75
Quiz Kids Paper Dolls, 1942, Saalfield 2430.............	90	100	125
Raggedy Ann and Andy, 1953, by Ethel Hays, Saalfield 2719.............	20	30	35
Raggedy Ann and Andy Paper Dolls, 1944, Saalfield No. 2719-15............	45	50	55
Raggedy Ann and Andy Paper Dolls, 1944, Saalfield No. 2741 by Ethel Hays.............	45	50	55
Raggedy Ann and Andy, 1968, Whitman No. 4740.............	15	20	25
"Rap-A-Jap", c. 1943, Woodburn Mfg. No. C1.............	50	60	70
Ready Cut Village, 1930s, no mfg. listed.............	55	70	80
Ricky Nelson paper dolls, 1959.........	35	45	50
Riders of the West Paper Dolls, 1950, Saalfield No. 2716-15............	15	20	25
Rigby's Book of Model Ships, 1953...	75	85	90
Rigby's Easy to Build Models of Fighting Planes.............	80	90	110
Rigby's Easier to Build Models of Naval Craft, 24 models of war-ships, 27 pages, 11-1/2" x 14", designed by Wallace Rigby, 1944, includes Battleship North Carolina, aircraft carrier, cruiser, destroyer,etc.....	90	110	135
Rigby Flying Models of Jet and Rocket Planes, 10 planes, 1949, Garden City Books.............	70	80	90

RIGBY'S Book of Model Ships. Courtesy Mapes Auctioneers & Appraisers.

"Rap-A-Jap". Courtesy Jack Matthews.

	C6	C8	C10
Rigby's Model Book of Flying Clippers, 11"x14" book designed by Wallace Rigby, 2 scale models of Douglas DC-Jet Clipper and Douglas DC-7C, 1947	60	70	80
Rigby's Model Sports Cars of the World, 1954, includes 18" "Sportsracer", Chevette, Jaguar, Mercedes-Benz, etc.	60	7	80
Robin Hood and Maid Marian, 1950s, Saalfield No. 1761, paper dolls	25	40	45
Rock Hudson Paper Dolls, 1957, Whitman No. 2087	35	45	55
Rosemary Clooney, Samuel Lowe No. 1256	40	45	55
Rosemary Clooney, 1958, Samuel Lowe No. 2487	45	60	70
Rowan & Martin's Laugh-In Punchout Paper Doll Book, 1969, Saalfield No. 1325, Rowan, Martin, Jo Ann Worley, Arte Johnson, Judy Carne and Goldie Hawn	25	35	40
Roy Rogers and Dale Evans, 1950, Whitman No. 1186	55	70	85
Roy Rogers and Dale Evans, 1954, Whitman No. 1950	55	70	85
Roy Rogers Cut Out Dolls, 1948, Whitman No. 995	60	90	125
Roy Rogers Sticker Fun Book, 1953, No. 2161	20	28	35
Royalty Cut Out Books: A Procession of the Knights of the Garter	55	65	70
Royalty Cut Out Books: Trooping The Colour	55	65	70
Ruth Newton's Cut-out Dolls and Animals "w/over 80 pieces to cut out and play with" 1934, 11" x 17"	55	65	75

	C6	C8	C10
Sally Ann A Cut Out Doll, circa 1940, Whitman No. 1010	30	40	45
Sally's Silver Skates, 1956 Merrill no. 1549	40	45	50
Sally the Standing Doll, 1940s, Lowe No. 1042	35	45	48
Sandra and Sue Statuette Dolls and Their Clothes, by Lee Lunzer, 1948, Whitman No. 1180	30	40	45
Sandra Dee, 1959, boxed, 2 dolls and 34 costume pieces, Saalfield No. 5511	40	50	55
Sandy and Sue, 1963, Whitman No. 1956	10	20	25
School Girl Paper Dolls, 1942, Saalfield No. 2400	30	40	45
Scissors Bird Paper Dolls, 1946, Stephens No. 137	15	20	25
Service Kit of America's Armed Forces-On Land-On Sea-In the Air, 1942, Lowe No. 265	40	50	55
6 Good Little Dolls, no date, Stephens Publishing co. No. 183	12	20	25
6 Movie Starlets, 1942, Anne Nagel, Peggy Moran, Jane Frazee, Anne Gwynne, Helen Parrish, Ann Gillis	135	150	175
Sharp Shooters, c.1915, Milton Bradley No. 4103, boxed set w/2 sets of 5 cardboard soldiers and 1 officer on stands	85	100	135
Skating Party Paper Doll Book, 1941, No. 2328, Saalfield, 17 punchouts	30	40	45
Skating Stars, 1954, Whitman No. 2105	20	30	40
Smart Paper Dolls, 1940, Saalfield No. 1935	30	45	50
Smash the Axis, 1943, Electric Corp. of America	35	50	55
Snow White and the Seven Dwarfs Paper Dolls, 1938, 12" x 17", Whitman No. 970	100	125	150
Snow White and the Seven Dwarfs, circa 1970, Whitman No. 1998	18	30	35
Soldiers, c. 1940, Concord Toy Co., boxed set contains 9 press-out soldiers, 3-1/2" each, wooden cannon and ammunition	50	60	75
Soldier Set by J. Pressman and Co., Inc., New York, No. 1551, c. 1940, contains 5 cardboard soldiers, 4-1/2" high and marbles	30	45	55
Soldiers, cardboard, approx. 6" high on wooden blocks, Navy, both officer and sailors, c. 1920, price per single figure	3	4	4.50

SERVICE KIT OF AMERICA'S ARMED FORCES ON LAND ON SEA AND IN THE AIR. Photo by Jonathan A. Newman. Courtesy Barbara and Jonathan Newman.

SOLDIERS FIVE WITH PISTOL. Photo by Jonathan A. Newman. Courtesy Barbara and Jonathan Newman.

SHARPSHOOTERS, box and contents. Photo by Jonathan A. Newman. Courtesy Barbara and Jonathan Newman.

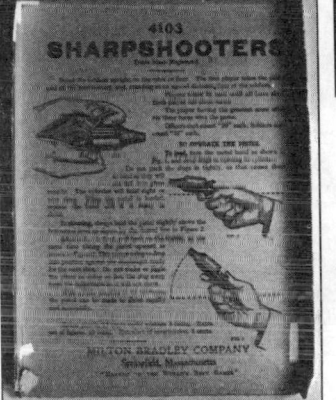

SOLDIERS by Concord. Photo by Jonathan A. Newman. Courtesy Barbara and Jonathan Newman.

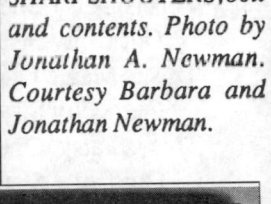

STREAMLINE FLYER. Photo by Jonathan A. Newman. Courtesy Barbara and Jonathan Newman.

	C6	C8	C10
Soldiers, cardboard, approx. 6" high on wooden blocks. Sailor, U.S.	3	4	4.50
Soldiers, cardboard, approx. 6" high on wooden blocks. U. S. Infantry in campaign hats, mounted. Price per single figure	3	4	4.50
Soldiers, cardboard approx. 6" high on wooden blocks, West Point Cadets.	3	4	4.50
Soldiers Five, c. 1920, boxed set, Milton Bradley No. 4395, 5-cardboard soldiers, pistol	80	100	125
Soldiers on Parade, early, Milton Bradley No. 4518, set of 10	50	80	90
Spaceport, U.S.A., 1953, Whitman	12	18	20
Sports Time, 1952, Whitman No. 210525	10	15	18
Square Dance Paper Dolls, 1950, Saalfield No. 2717	15	20	25

	C6	C8	C10
Square Dance Paper Dolls, By J. Voelz, Lowe 968-10	15	20	25
Stage Door Canteen, 1943, Saalfield 2468	60	75	90
Stand-Up Dolls, Honey and Bunny, Merrill No. 3403, 1936	60	75	90
Statuette Dolls, 1943, Whitman No. 992, 2 women	25	35	40
Statuette Dolls And Their Clothes, 1942, Whitman No. 998	30	40	50
Statuette Dolls And Their Clothes, 1946, Whitman No. 986, 2 girls and a boy	25	35	40
Stencils Large and Small by Roy Best, c. 1935, No. 954 (Whitman?) folder of 30 animals to punch out and use as stencils. Comes w/tiny box of crayons.	12	20	25

SALLY THE STANDING DOLL.

STATUETTE DOLLS AND THEIR CLOTHES.

Photos by Jonathan A. Newman. Courtesy Barbara and Jonathan Newman.

	C6	C8	C10
Stock Farm Set, circa 1944, Concern No. 123, boxed 1200 die-cut pcs. including house, barn, silo, chicken house, tractor, etc.	40	50	60
The Story of Cinderella, A Fold-A-Way Toy Book designed by Will Pente. Circa 1925, Reilly & Britton Co.	25	40	45
Streamline Flyer, 10-3/4"x13-1/2" boxed set, Concord Toy Co., No. 122, c. 1940, contains engine, station, crossing gates, crossing signal, baggage truck, baggage and people.	40	50	60
Style Shop Paper Dolls, 1943, Saalfield No. 1516.	20	30	35
Sub-Deb Paper Dolls by Irving Nurick, 1941, Merrill No. 3408, 12 teenage boy and girl dolls, clothes.	25	45	48
Sue and Tom Cut-Out Dolls Book, The, 1946, Lowe No. 149.	18	25	30
Sunbonnet Sue, 1951, Whitman No. 2062-29.	18	25	30
Sunshine Cut-Outs, Sports Series, Spring, by M&F Hoopes, 1926, 4-part foldout, Stroll & Edwards Co.	70	80	90
Susan Dey as Laurie ("Partridge Family" TV show), 1972, Artcraft, Fashions by Kate Greenaway.	18	25	30
Sweetheart Paper Dolls, 1943, Saalfield No. 2458.	30	40	45
Sweetie Pie Twins, 1949, Stephens Publishing Co. No. 166, Jane and Jean.	15	20	25
Swing-A-Plane by J.L.Schilling Co., Model of a Flying Tiger, 1944, flies on string.	10	15	18
Tammy, 1963, A Little Golden Story Book w/paper dolls to cut out and dress. Illustrated by Ada Salvi.	15	20	25

	C6	C8	C10
Tarzan of the Apes, 1933 figure set.	30	50	55
Teen Gal Cut Out Dolls, 1943, by Hilda Miloche and William Kane, Whitman No. 980.	40	50	55
Teen Town, 1949, Merrill No. 3443.	35	45	50
That Girl-Marlo Thomas, 1967, Saalfield No. 1351.	25	40	50
That Girl-Marlo Thomas, 1967, Saalfield No. 1379.	25	40	50
They Stand Up by Avis Mac, 1939, Whitman No. 932, 13" x 18" w/5 children.	65	75	90
30 Toy Soldiers, c. 1943, Whitman No. 2950.	35	50	60
This is Bunny One Of The Five Cut-Out Dolly Sisters,Whitman, 1939.	35	45	50
This is Dotty One Of The Five Cut-Out Dolly Sisters, Whitman, 1939.	35	45	50
This is Magic One Of The Five Cut-Out Dolly Sisters, Whitman, 1939.	35	45	50
This is Patsy, One Of The Five Cut-Out Dolly Sisters, Whitman, 1939.	35	45	50
This is Peggy One Of The Five Cut-Out Dolly Sisters, Whitman No. 1002, 1939.	35	45	50
This Is The Navy No. 500A Skyline Mfg., Destroyer and PT Boat, circa 1942.	20	30	35
This Is The Navy No. 501, circa 1942, Skyline Mfg., Heavy Cruiser.	20	30	35
Three Bears Cut Out Book, copyright 1939, Whitman No. 1020, Goldilock and 3 Bears.	40	55	60

STAND-UP DOLLS HONEY AND BUNNY.

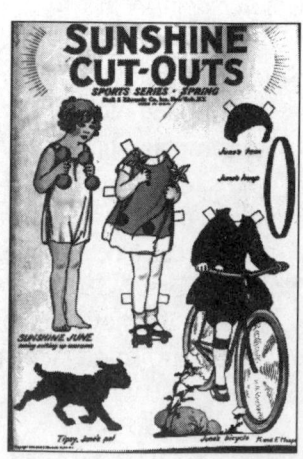

SUNSHINE CUT-OUTS SPORTS SERIES, SPRING.

Photos by Jonathan A. Newman. Courtesy Barbara and Jonathan Newman.

Left: THIS IS BUNNY, ONE OF THE FIVE CUT-OUT DOLLY SISTERS, Right: THIS IS PATSY, ONE OF THE FIVE CUT-OUT DOLLY SISTERS. Photo by Jonathan A. Newman. Courtesy Barbara and Jonathan Newman.

	C6	C8	C10
Three Flying Models of Famous Allied Fighting Planes by Judd Reed, 9"x12", contains Hell Cat, Spitfire and Stormovik planes, included is "American Ace Spotter", w/turning dial of 48 3-view silhouettes of 16 planes in little windows, 1944	30	40	45
Three Little Girls Who Grew And Grew And This Is How They Grew, 1945, Whitman No. 99410	30	45	50
Three Little Girls Who Grew And Grew And This Is How They Grew, w/cloth-like clothes, flocked, 1945, Whitman No. 1176	25	40	45
Three Little Pigs Cut Out Book, Copright 1939, Whitman No. 1020, Pigs and Big Bad Wolf	40	55	60
Three Sweet Baby Dolls To Cut Out And Dress, 1954, Whitman No. 975	15	20	25
Thrilltown Railroad, 1943, Reed, Pullman Passenger Set	60	80	90
Tiny Chatty Twins Paper Dolls, 1963, Whitman No. 1985	15	20	25
Toby Tyler Circus Playbook Punch Out, 1959, No. 1936	30	40	45
Tom Corbett Space Cadet Punch Out Book, 1952, Saalfield No. 4304, 14" long 10-1/2" wide	35	45	50
Tom the Aviator, circa 1942, Samuel Lowe No. L1074	20	30	40
Toni Hair-Do Cut-Out Dolls, Lowe No. 1284, 1950	35	48	55
Top Notch Paper Dolls, 1948, Saalfield No. 1504	20	28	35
Toy Models: Warplane and Tank Punch-out, 1941, Fawcett Publications, Lowe	45	50	65

	C6	C8	C10
Toy Town, 1916, series of 50 different buildings by American Color Type Co., boxed set	75	100	125
Transfer Pictures, Copyright 1939, Whitman No. 1085, 100 decalcomanias	10	15	18
Treasure Hour Puppet Book, No. 4, 1968, Murray Sales and Service, The Rustlers of Rocky Ranch, a play of cowboys and Indians in 5 scenes, cut-out section makes model theater	18	25	30
Tricia, 1969, Artcraft No. 4248	20	30	35
Tricia Paper Dolls, 1970, Saalfield No. 1248, White House tour game, White House stand-up doll of Tricia Nixon and costumes	20	30	35
Trudy Phillips and Her Crowd, 1954, Whitman No. 2104	22	30	40
Tuesday Weld Paper dolls, 1960, Saalfield No. 5112 boxed 2 dolls and 58 costume pieces	40	50	55
Turnabouts Dolls Book, The, 1940s, Lowe No. 1048, dolls printed front view on each side	35	45	48
TV Star Time Paper Dolls, c. 1950s, Abbott No. 1367	15	20	25
TV Tap Stars Paper Dolls, Lowe 99010	15	18	20
22 Animals To Cut Out and Stand Up, copyright 1930, Whitman, No. 935, rabbits, bears, owls, squirrels, etc.	30	40	50
Twiggy Paper Doll, 1967, Whitman No. 1999, w/"plastilon" Twiggy dress for small girls	25	30	35
Tyrone Power & Linda Darnell, 1941, Merrill No. 3438	155	180	200
Umbrella Girls, 1956, Merrill No. 2562, wrap-around dresses	45	50	55
Uncle Sam's Little Helpers Paper Dolls by Ann Kovach, 1943, Saalfield 2450	35	45	50
United States Soldiers, 1942, Samuel Lowe No. L1063	45	50	55
U.S. Commandos Book, 1943, Lowe No. 1089	40	50	60
U.S. Infantry-Spanish/American War, approx. 6" high soldier on small wooden block	3	4	4.50
Victory Girls-Arlene the Airline Hostess, circa 1940s, Lowe	45	55	60
Victory Punch-Out Tanks, Soldiers, Sailors, Planes, circa 1943, Lowe No. 848	45	55	60
Victory Volunteers, 1942 dolls w/ uniforms by Merlin, Merrill 3424	55	75	90

TONI HAIR-DO CUT-OUT DOLLS. Photo by Jonathan A. Newman. Courtesy Barbara and Jonathan Newman.

	C6	C8	C10
Virginia Mayo, 1957, Saalfield No. 4422	45	60	70
WACS and WAVES, 1943, Whitman No. 985	55	75	85
Walking Paper Doll Family No. 1074, Saalfield 1934	60	75	80
Walt Disney's Babes in Toyland, 1961, Golden Punch-Out Book No. 10363	25	40	45
Walt Disney's Jane and Michael from Mary Poppins, 1963, Watkins/Strathmore 1892-6	20	30	35
Walt Disney's Let's Build Disneyland, 1957, Whitman No. 1986, forms sets for Adventureland, Frontierland, Tomorrowland and Fantasyland	18	30	35
Walt Disney's Mary Poppins, 1964, Whitman No. 1982	25	30	35
Walt Disney Match and Patch Sticker Fun, 1953, Whitman, Mickey Mouse, Donald Duck, Pluto, Goofy, etc.	10	15	18
Walt Disney Presents Hayley Mills in "That Darn Cat", 1965, Whitman No. 1955	25	35	45
Walt Disney Sticker Fun Book, 1951, Whitman	8	12	15
Walt Disney Sticker Fun With Peter Pan, 1952, Whitman	10	12	15

	C6	C8	C10
War Between The States, 1959, Golden Press No. GF152	40	65	75
War Plane Cut Outs, 1943, heavy stock, 8 different scale models, 10" x 14"	30	35	40
Wedding Paper Dolls, 1970, Whitman No. 1970	12	15	20
We're A Family Cut-Out Dolls, 1954, Whitman No. 1181	25	40	45
White House Party Dresses, 1961, Merrill No. 1550	30	35	40
Whitman No. 1146, little paper doll books, 3-1/2" x 7-1/2", copyright 1939.			
a. Nancy and Tommy			
b. Ann and Arthur			
c. Kitty and Billy			
d. Muriel and David			
e. Cynthia and Bobby			
f. Judy and Dick	45	60	65
Whitman Paper Doll Book, 1933 No. 3059, 4 dolls, 10 sheets of clothes in folder	35	55	65
Winnie's New Wardrobe by Geraldine Cline, 1939, McLoughlin Bros. No. 555	25	30	35
Young Patriot Invasion Set, c. 1944, Colorgraphic No. 500, contains destroyer, amphibian tractor, tank, jeep, anti-tank gun, bomber and diver bomber, 10-1/2" x 13" boxed set	70	80	90
Young Patriot-Learn To Know Your Army, 1943, Colorgraphic No. 350, tank, howitzer, jeep, anti-tank gun, bomber, fighter and soldiers. Guns shoot, bombs drop, etc.	70	80	90
Young Patriot-Learn To Know Your Navy, 1943, Colorgraphic construction set No. 360, 10"x14" boxed set includes battleship, destroyer, aircraft carrier, mosquito boat, submarine, planes depth charges, etc., w/moveable parts	70	80	90
Ziegfeld Girl Paper Dolls, No. "1", 1941, Merrill No. 3466	170	190	225
Zoo Cut-outs by Milo Winter, 1938, Whitman No. 1054, 6 pages of heavy cut-out animals	25	35	45

TIN WINDUP

(See also Movie, Comic Character, Disney)

The average mint price for tin wind-ups in the last edition was $480.05, and in this volume averages $521.73, an increase of 9%.

Unlike most toys in this book, tin wind-ups do not "feel" particularly good in the hand, and depend more on the lure of motion and colorful lithography. Esthetically the most appealing, perhaps, are those of Lehmann, a Germany company which also patented a number of its toys in the United States, and which holds a strong attraction for a large number of collectors.

	C6	C8	C10
A.C. Gilbert Delivery Truck, open, circa 1915	210	320	425
A.C. Gilbert Racer, early	500	750	1050
A.C. Gilbert "U.S. Mail Parcel Post" Truck, circa 1915	425	638	950
Aircraft Carrier, circa post WW II, tin litho, Japan, approx. 15" long	90	135	180
"Aircraft Carrier X53", w/5 jet planes, tin litho, circa 1950s	75	112	150

ARNOLD Motorycle "Mac 700", getting on. Photo by Scott Smiles

ARNOLD Motorcycle "Mac 700", riding. Photo by Scott Smiles.

A.C.GILBERT "U.S. Mail Parcel Post" Truck. Courtesy Christie's East.

AUTOMATIC TOY COMPANY, Auto Speedway. Photo by Don Hulzman.

ANIMATE TOY CO.

In 1918 this firm was located at East 17th Street in New York City, and its president was L.T. Savage. By 1931 it had moved to 30 North 15th Street in East Orange, New Jersey, and employed ten men and forty women. In 1934 the president-vice president was George V. Turnbull and the secretary-treasurer was George H. Webb. Five men and eleven women made up the work force.

	C6	C8	C10
Animate Toy "U.S. Baby Tank". pat. 6/20/16, new in 1918, 2-1/2" long	40	60	80
Animate Toy "Climbing Tractor", 1929, 9" long	105	158	210
Arnold Motorcycle, "Mac 700", black version	625	938	1250
Arnold Motorcycle, "Mac 700", red version	750	1125	1500

	C6	C8	C10
Automatic Toy Co. "Auto Speedway", circa 1930	100	150	200
Automatic Toy Co. Cross-Over Trolley Set	90	135	180
Automatic Toy Co. "Dizzy Liz", No. 180, 1940s, 5" long	100	150	200
Automatic Toy Co. "Jungle Pete", No. 175, 15" long	90	135	180
Automatic Toy Co. "Mysterious Alpine Express", 1940s, 20" long, 14" wide, 2" high	72	108	145
Automatic Toy Co. "Operation Airlift", 1950s, 2 plastic planes	80	120	160
Automatic Toy Co. "Rocket Space Ship" No. 305, sparks, 1940s, 8-1/2" long	87	130	175

239

Bueschel, Fritz (Hackettstown, NJ) "George Washington Bridge". Courtesy Christie's East.

	C6	C8	C10
Automatic Toy Co. "Space Shooting Range", 1950s, 15" long	150	225	300
Automatic Toy Co. "Magic Crossroads" Track, 2 wind-up cars, circa 1950	130	195	260
Automatic Toy Co. Speedway, 1930s, w/2 race cars, garage	175	262	350
Baby L Racing Boat, 1930, Lindstrom, 11" long	110	165	220
"Barnum & Bailey", c. 1935, elephant pulling a 4-wheeled cart loaded with a collapsible cage containing a camel, a monkey, a lion and a giraffe, each mounted on 4 wheels	150	225	300

	C6	C8	C10
Biplane, very early, Wright Bros.- like paper propellor blades, 6" long	400	600	800
Bird in Cage, German, 3-1/2" high	225	338	450
Bird w/flapping wings, 1930s, German, 6-1/2" long	100	150	200
Black Boy eating watermelon w/dog biting his backside, 1920s, German	475	638	950
Boy on St. Bernard on rocker, 6-3/4"	600	900	1200
Bueschel, Fritz (Hackettstown, NJ) "George Washington Bridge"	650	975	1300
Buffalo Bill, hand-painted, hand-soldered, German, 1910	625	938	1250
Buffalo Toys, "Aero Speeders", 1920s, carousel w/3 planes, screw-rod spring drive, 10" tall	125	188	250
Buffalo Toys, "Aero-Zeps", 3 zeppelins fly on carousel, 9" high	150	225	300
Buffalo Toys, "Bumper Ride", 1930s, 10" long	100	150	200
Buffalo Toys, Dodgem Car, 1930s, 10" long	130	195	260
Buffalo Toys, "T-zer", 1925, (screw drive), 6" high	180	240	360
"The **Cackling** Hen of Paradise", turn side handle and hen cackles; patented, 8" long	80	120	160
"Cakewalk Dancers"**, short black man dancing w/tall, heavy black woman	400	600	800

Buffalo Toy Aero-Speeders. Courtesy Don Hultzman. Photo by Ron Chojnacki.

Baby L. Racing Boat, 11" long. Courtesy Lloyd W. Ralston Auctions.

Caterpillar Tractor, "1916". Photo by Bill Kaufman. Courtesy Good Old Days Store.

CHEIN Drummer Boy. Courtesy Scott Smiles. Photo by Mike Adams.

CHEIN Marine, hand on belt. Courtesy Scott Smiles. Photo by Mike Adams.

	C6	C8	C10
"Candy" Cart driven by monkey in cap, also marked "Candy", c. 1950s.......	100	150	200
Carousel w/4 biplanes and pilots, paper vanes, flag finial, 1920s, German, 17" high.............	1200	1800	2400+
Carousel w/4 double horse and riders that alternate w/ 4 women in cars, velvet top w/ball fringe, flag finial, 17" high..............	1600	2400	3200+
Carousel w/4 men in canoes, propellers w/paper vanes, 11" high..................	1400	2100	2800¹
Carter, Chinese pushes Cart, 1920s....	130	195	260
Carter, "Pan-Gee the Funny Dancer", 1920, 10" high................................	350	525	700
Cat pushing Cage w/2 mice, 8-1/4"....	300	450	600
Caterpillar Tractor, "1916", rubber treads, tin wind-up, probably by Woodhaven Metal Stamping Co., Brooklyn, NY......................	142	214	285

CHEIN

Chein (pronounced "Chain") was founded in 1903 by Julius Chein. The New Jersey company specialized in lithographed metal toys, the majority of them mechanical. In 1918 it was located at 310 Passaic Avenue, Harrison, New Jersey, with 250 employees. In 1934 it had 55 male and 92 female workers. In a 1946-47 directory it listed 148 male and 132 female employees. Chein made toys until 1979, and is still in business today in Burlington, New Jersey.

	C6	C8	C10
Chein Alligator w/native on its back....	150	225	300
Chein "Army Drummer", 1930s, plunger-activated, 7" high...............	130	195	260
Chein Barnacle Bill, looks like Popeye, 1930s...................................	225	338	450
Chein "Barnacle Bill in a Barrel", 1930s, 7" high..................	250	375	500

	C6	C8	C10
Chein "Barnacle Bill the Sailor", punching a bag, 7-1/2".....................	750	1125	1500
Chein Bass Drummer (like Chein Drummer Boy, but drum vertical)..	150	225	300
Chein Bear w/hat, pants, shirt, bow-tie, circa 1938.................................	50	75	100
Chein "Ski-Boy", 1930s, 8" long.........	150	225	300
Chein Cabin Cruiser, 1940s, 9" long...	50	75	100
Chein Chick, brightly colored clothes and polka dot bow-tie, 4" high........	30	45	60
Chein Chicken pulling wheelbarrow, 1930s, 6" x 3-1/2"............................	50	75	100
Chein "Clown in Barrel", 1930s, 8" high..	275	362	550

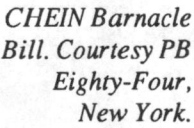

CHEIN Barnacle Bill. Courtesy PB Eighty-Four, New York.

CHEIN "Barnacle Bill in a Barrel". Courtesy PB Eighty-Four, New York.

CHEIN Bear w/Hat. Courtesy Scott Smiles.

CHEIN "Ferris Wheel", 1930s. Courtesy Scott Smiles.

CHEIN Duck. Coutresy Scott Smiles.

CHEIN Penguin. Courtesy Scott Smiles. Photo by Mike Adams.

CHEIN Mechanical Aquaplane, 7-1/2" wingspan. Courtesy Perry R. Eichor.

	C6	C8	C10
Chein Clown Puncher	375	562	750
Chein Clown w/umbrella	120	180	240
Chein "Dan-Dee Dump Truck"	200	300	400
Chein "Doughboy", 1920s, 6" high	200	300	400
Chein "Drummer Boy", w/shako, circa 1930s, 9" high	105	158	210
Chein Duck, waddles, 1930, 4" high	65	98	130
Chein Duck, long-beaked, in orange sailor suit, not Donald Duck, but similar, waddles, 6" high	100	150	200
Chein "Ferris Wheel", 6 compartments, ringing bell, 1930s, 16-1/2" high	225	338	450
Chein "Greyhound" Bus, 9" long	85	130	175
Chein Handstand Clown, 1940s, 6"high	70	105	140
Chein "Indian In Headdress", 1930s, 5-1/2" high	100	150	200
Chein "Jumping Rabbit", 1925, 5" long	120	180	240
Chein Marine, hand on belt, 1950s, 6" high	100	150	200
Chein "Mark I" Cabin Cruiser, 1957, 8-1/2" long	27	41	55
Chein "Mechanical Aquaplane", No.39, boat-like pontoons, 1932, no insignia, 8-1/2" long, 7-1/2" wingspan	125	188	250
Chein "Mechanical Aquaplane", post WW II insignia	187	280	375
Chein "Mechanical Aquaplane" pre-WW II insignia	220	330	440
Chein "Mechanical Fish", 1940s, 11"	40	60	80

CHEIN Handstand Clown. Courtesy Scott Smiles.

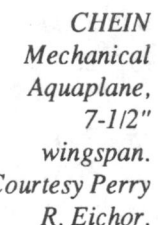

CHEIN PIG. Photo by Scott Smiles.

CHEIN Mechanical Frog Man. Photo by Don Hultzman.

CHEIN "Roller Coaster", 1930s. Courtesy Don Hultzman. Photo by Ron Chojnacki.

CHEIN "Roller Coaster", 1950s. Courtesy Don Hultzman. Photo by Ron Chojnacki.

	C6	C8	C10
Chein "Mechanical Frog Man", 1950s, 11" long	92	138	185
Chein "Mechanical Rocket Ride", No. 400, 1950s, 18" high	600	900	1200
Chein "Melody Player", No. 135, 1930s, 4 rolls, 6-3/4" high	100	150	200
Chein "Musical Aero Swing", 1940s, 10" high	287	430	575
Chein "Navy Frog Man" No. 122, 1950s, 12" long	100	150	200
Chein Pan-Am Clipper, 1930s, pontoons, 11" wingspan	387	582	775
Chein Peggy Jane Boat, 13" long	62	93	125
Chein Penguin in tuxedo type jacket, circa 1940	75	112	150
Chein Pig, 1940s, 4-1/2" high	42	63	85
Chein "Playland Merry-Go-Round", 1930s, 9-1/2" high	292	438	585
Chein "Playland Whip", No. 340, 4 bump cars, driver's head wobbles	450	675	900
Chein Rabbit in shirt and pants, c. 1938	45	68	90
Chein Rabbit pulling cart	20	30	40
Chein Rabbit w/wheelbarrow	75	112	150
Chein "Race Car No. 52", 1930s, 6-1/2" long	80	120	160
Chein "Racer #3", 1920s, 6-1/2" long	150	225	300
Chein "Ride-A-Rocket"	300	450	600
Chein "Rocket Ride" No. 400, 4 rockets, 18" high, base 11" diameter	487	730	975
Chein "Roller Coaster", circa 1938, includes 2 cars	250	375	500
Chein "Roller Coaster", 1950s, includes 2 cars	175	262	350
Chein "Santa Elf", 1920s, 6" high	250	375	500
Chein "Ski Boy" No. 157, 1940s, 7-3/4" long 5-1/4" tall	150	225	300
Chein "Skin Diver No. 122", 1950s, 12" long	80	120	160
Chein "Space Ride" No. 205, 1950s, 10" high	500	750	1000
Chein " Space Ride", 1940s, lever action, 9" high	600	900	1200
Chein "Spirit of St. Louis" Airplane, 1930s, 8" long, 8" wingspan	250	375	500
Chein Taxi, 1920s, 7" long	175	263	350
Chein Toy Town Helicopter, 1950s, 13" long	90	135	180
Chein Turtle w/Native on back	150	225	300
Chein "U.S. Army Sergeant" No.153, 1950s, 5-1/2" high	40	60	80
Chein "Walking Pelican", 1930s, 5" high	100	150	200
Circus-type Trainer, baton in hand, revolves, w/rooster on each side, musical, German, 3-1/2" long	200	300	400
Clown in Donkey Cart, 7-1/2" long	60	90	120
Clown in Hoop, Japan, 6-1/2" high	150	225	300
Clown Musicians, 4, on a pedestal, musical, 8" high	300	450	600
"Clown on Scooter", 1915, Tipp Co., 6" tall	200	300	400

COURTLAND MFG. CO.
WALT REACH

(History based on information from Joe and Sharon Freed)
Walter Reach, owner of Courtland, had a burning desire to be known as the second Louis Marx. Also functioning as designer, he began production in 1944 with two die-cut cardboard toys (a rabbit and cart and horse and cart). Reach turned to tin litho

toys after the war, a number of them non-wind-ups. At its height, Courtland, located first in Camden, New Jersey, and later in Philadelphia, had 600 workers and in 1947 its sales exceeded 1.5 million. But success was short-lived, and the firm lasted just seven years.

Courtland Toys Listing by Joe and Sharon Freed

	C6	C8	C10
No. 15 Mechanical Lawn Mower, 1950 retail price 79¢, 1951 retail-98¢, 8-1/4" wide, 24" high, 3" wheels	50	75	100
No. 20 Mechanical Lawn Mower, 1950 retail-$1.29; 1951 retail-$1.49, 11-1/4" wide, 29" high, 5" wheels	65	90	115
No. 21 Mechanical Lawn Mower, 1951 retail-$2.98, 12" wide, 29" high, 5" wheels	75	100	125
No. 25 Mechanical Power Lawn Mower, 1951 retail-$2.98, 12" wide, 29" high 5-3/4" wheels	85	110	135
No. 200 Easter Rabbit and Trailer, 1946 retail-49¢, 11-5/8" long, 3" wide, 3-1/2" high	75	100	150
No. 300 Circus Elephant & "Monkeys" Cart, 1946 retail-49¢, 11-5/8" long, 3" wide, 3-1/2" high	150	250	350
No. 400 Circus Elephant & "African Lions" Cart, 1946 retail-49¢, 11-5/8" long, 3" wide, 3-1/2" high	150	250	350
No. 500 Circus Elephant & "Circus Band" Cart, 1946 retail-49¢, 11-5/8" long, 3" wide, 3-1/2" high	200	300	400
No. 1070 Mechanical Big 4 Truck Parade, 1947 retail-$3.39, 9" long, 3" wide, 2-3/4" high	No Price Found		
No. 1200 Mechanical Trailer-Truck, 1947 retail-$1.00, 13" long, 3" wide, 3-1/4" high	125	175	225
No. 1300 Mechanical Ice Cream Truck, retail 79¢, 9" L, 3" W, 2-3/4" H	125	175	225
No. 1300 Mechanical Moving & Storage Truck, 1947 retail-79¢, 9" long, 3" wide, 2-3/4" high	125	175	225
Sames as above, w/No. 130 litho on the sides of the truck bed	150	200	250
No. 1300 Mechanical Fire Patrol No. 2 Truck, 1947 retail-79¢, 9" long, 3" wide, 2-3/4" high	125	175	225

	C6	C8	C10
No. 1300 Mechanical Express and Hauling Truck, 1947 retail-79¢ 9" long, 3" wide, 2-3/4" high	150	200	250
No. 1400 Mechanical "Automatic Ladder" Fire Truck, 1947 retail-$1.00, 9" long, 3" wide, 2-3/4" high	150	200	250
No. 1500 Mechanical Road Roller Truck, 9" long, 3" wide, 3-1/4" high	175	250	325
No. 1600 Mechanical Dump Truck, 7" long, 3" wide, 2-3/4" high	75	125	150
No. 2000 Mechanical "ESSO" Gasoline Tractor-Trailer, 13" L, 3" W, 3-1/4" H	200	250	300
No. 2000 Mechanical Gasoline Tractor-Trailer, 13" L, 3" W, 3-1/4" H	125	175	250
No. 2050 Mechanical Milk Tractor-Trailer, "American Dairies", 13" long, 3" wide, 3-1/4" High	175	225	275

NOTE: 1951 catalog shows Milk Trailer markings that read the same as above except 'Approved' is used in the place of the words 'Vitamin D'. This variation is not known to have been produced.

	C6	C8	C10
No. 2100 Mechanical Hook and Ladder Tractor-Trailer, 13"L, 3"W, 3-1/4" H	100	150	200
No. 2150 Mechanical Emergency Rescue Squad Tractor-Trailer, 13"long, 3"wide, 3/1/4" high	125	175	225
No. 2200 Mechanical Logging Tractor-Trailer, 13" L, 3" W, 3-1/4" H	100	150	200

COURTLAND Motor Guaranteed for Life No. 2000 Mechanical Gasoline Tractor-Trailer (packed in individual boxes all with motor guarantee certificate). Courtesy Joe and Sharon Freed.

COURTLAND *Motor Guaranteed for Life No. 2050 Mechanical Milk Tractor-Trailer. Courtesy Joe and Sharon Freed.*

COURTLAND *Motor Guaranteed for Life No. 2200 Mechanical Logging Tractor-Trailer. Courtesy Joe and Sharon Freed.*

	C6	C8	C10
No. 2300 Mechanical Open Van Tractor-Trailer, 13" L, 3" W, 3-1/4" H	100	150	200
No. 2350 Mechanical Open Van Tractor-Trailer, 13" L, 3" W, 3-1/4" H	100	150	200
No. 2375 Mechanical Heavy Duty Sand and Gravel Tractor-Trailer, 13" long, 3" wide, 3-1/4" high	100	150	200
No. 2400 Mechanical Trailer Tow Truck, 13" long, 3" wide, 3-1/4" high	100	150	200
No. 2600 Mechanical Freight Haulers Tractor-Trailer, 13" L, 3" H, 3-1/4" W	100	150	200
No. 2700 Mechanical Side Tipper Tractor-Trailer, 13" L, 3" H, 3-1/4" wide	125	175	225
No. 2800 Assortment consists of 2 No.2000 Gasoline Trucks, 2 No. 2050 Milk Trucks, 2 No. 2200 Log Trucks, 2 No. 2350 Open Van Trucks, 2 No.2600 Freight Hauler Trucks and 2 No. 2700 Side Tipper Trucks-Wholesale Assortment Only			No Price Found
No. 3000 Mechanical Road Roller Truck, 9" long, 3" wide, 3-1/4" high	200	300	400

	C6	C8	C10
No. 3100 Mechanical Dump Truck, 7" long, 3" wide, 3-1/4" high	125	200	275
No. 3200 Mechanical Stake Bed Truck, 7" L, 3" W, 3-1/4" H	100	150	200
No. 3800 Assortment consists of 6 No. 3200 Stake Bed Trucks and 6 No. 3100 Dump Trucks. Wholesale Assortment Only			No Price Found
No. 3900 Courtland Mechanical Side Tipper Tractor-Trailer, "Black Diamond Coal Company-340",13" L, 3" H, 3-1/4" W	175	225	300
No. 4000 City Meat Market Delivery Sedan, 7 1/4" L, 3 1/4" W, 2 3/4" H	75	100	150
No. 4000 Modern Bakery Delivery Sedan, 7-1/4" L, 3-1/4" W, 2-3/4"H	75	100	150
No. 4000 Fire Chief Car, red & white, 7-1/4" L, 3-1/4" W, 2-3/4" H	74	100	150
Same as above, all red	100	125	175
No. 4000 Checker Cab Car, green & yellow, 7-1/4" L, 3-1/4" W, 2-3/4"H	100	125	175
Same as above, green and white	125	150	200
No. 4500 Express Service Pickup, 7-1/4" L, 3-1/4" W, 2-3/4" H	75	100	125

COURTLAND *Motor Guaranteed for Life No. 2100 Mechanical Hook & Ladder Tractor-Trailer. Courtesy Joe and Sharon Freed.*

COURTLAND *Motor Guaranteed for Life No. 2150 Mechanical Emergency Rescue Squad. Courtesy Joe and Sharon Freed.*

COURTLAND No. 3000 Mechanical Road Roller Truck. Courtesy Joe and Sharon Freed.

COURTLAND No. 6050 Mechanical Farm Tractor. Courtesy Continental Hobby House.

COURTLAND "Motor Guaranteed For Life" No. 5100 "Black Diamond" Coal Truck. Courtesy Joe and Sharon Freed.

COURTLAND 5300. Photo by Joe Freed.

COURTLAND No. 4000 Checker Cab Car. Courtesy Joe and Sharon Freed.

COURTLAND No. 4000 City Meat Market Delivery Sedan. Courtesy Joe and Sharon Freed.

XXXX COURTLAND Mechanical Side Tipper Tractor-Trailer, "Black Diamond Coal Company 340". Courtesy Joe and Sharon Freed.

XXXX COURTLAND Motor Guaranteed For Life No. 6500 Mechanical Ice Cream Scooter. Courtesy Joe and Sharon Freed.

	C6	C8	C10
No. 4500 Country Produce Pickup, 7-1/4" L, 3-1/4" W, 2-3/4" H	75	100	125
No. 4500 Modern Decorators Pickup, 7-1/4" L, 3-1/4" W, 2-3/4" H	75	100	125
No. 5000 Mechanical Operation No. 51 Crane Truck, 13" long, 3-5/8" wide, 5" high	125	175	250
No. 5100 Mechanical "Black Diamond" Coal Truck, 10-1/2" long, 3" wide, 3-3/8" high	125	175	250
No. 5200 Mechanical No. 51 Steam Shovel, 15-1/2" long, 3-3/4" wide, 9-1/2" high	100	125	150
No. 5300 Mechanical Combination Steam Shovel carried by low-boy tractor-trailer, 15-1/2" L, 3-7/8" W, 10-1/2" H	150	200	300
No. 5800 Assortment consists of 3 No.2300 Aluminum Open Van Trucks, 3 No. 2150 Emergency Rescue Squad Trucks, 3 No. 2375 Sand &Gravel Trucks & 3 No. 2400 Towing Service Trucks Wholesale Assortment Only	No Price Found		
No. 6000 Mechanical Farm Tractor w/scraper, rear tires are large rubber and front are small rubber tires, 8-3/4" long, 4-3/4" wide, 4-1/2" high	75	100	150
No. 6050 Mechanical Farm Tractor w/o scraper, rear tires are large rubber and front are small rubber tires, 7-1/2" long, 4-3/4" wide, 4-1/2" high	55	75	100
No. 6075 Mechanical Farm Tractor w/o scraper, rear tires are large tin litho while the front are small rubber tires, 7-1/2" long, 4-3/4" wide, 4-1/2" high	125	175	225
No. 6100 Mechanical Caterpillar Tractor w/rubber treads, 6" long, 3" wide, 4-1/2" high	150	200	250
No. 6500 Mechanical Ice Cream Scooter, 6-1/2" long, 3" wide, 4-1/2" high	150	225	300
No. 7000 Mechanical Fire Chief Car w/siren, 7-1/4" long, 3-1/4" wide, 2-3/4" high	100	150	175
No. 7500 Mechanical State Police Car w/siren, 7-1/4" long, 3-1/4" wide, 2-3/4" high	100	150	200

No. 7500 Mechanical Parking Meter and Bank, base 6"x6", 24-1/2" high.

NOTE: This is one of only four Courtland toys stamped "A Walt Reach Toy by Courtland Toy Co., Phila. Pa. Made in U.S.A."The only known Courtland styled toys marked with the Courtland Toy Company, Philadelphia stamping is this mechanical parking meter bank, a No.4000 sedan, a non-power "Fire Chief" car, a private and a garage similar to

	C6	C8	C10
No. 9075	100	125	150
No. 8000 Mechanical "Rocking R Ranch" See-Saw, 17-3/4" long, 2-1/8" wide, 6" high	50	75	100
No. 8500 Mechanical Chromed Trimmed Tow Truck, tow boom shows detail, 8" long, 3-1/4" wide, 3-1/2" high	125	200	275
No. 8500 Mechanical Chromed Trimmed Tow Truck, tow boom is solid color, 8" long, 3-1/4" wide, 3-1/2" high	150	225	300

End Courtland

	C6	C8	C10
Dancing dogs, 2, and a boy w/whip	200	300	400
Dancing horse, 2 small bells on top of bridle, 7-1/2" high	100	150	200
Ferris Wheel carrying eight gondolas, the gondolas containing a total of 16 small bisque dolls, 33 1/2" high	1200	1800	2400
Ferris Wheel, carved w/figures and music box, 17"	400	600	800
Freight Cart pulled by man in cap, w/luggage on cart, circa 1940	60	90	120
Gama "Komical Walking Cat", circa 1929, 7" high	150	225	300

GIRARD

Girard Model Works was founded in Girard, Pennsylvania in 1906 by C. G. Wood. Originally it made patterns, models and special machinery, with Wood's son Frank joining the firm a few years after its inception. In 1918 they began making toys for "a large firm in New York" (otherwise unidentified), and in 1920 began making them under their own name, originally as "Wood's Mechanical Toys". By 1931 the firm had a thousand employees, with Louis Marx by then associated with Girard. During the Depression he took over the firm. The last Girard toys seem to have been produced in 1975, though the firm remained in business until 1980. Many of Marx's and Girard's toys are interchangeable.

GIRARD Monoplane, high wing, one engine, 1920. Courtesy Lloyd W. Ralston Auctions.

GIRARD Railroad Handcar. Courtesy Mapes Auctioneers & Appraisers.

	C6	C8	C10
Girard Air Mail Bi-plane, 3-engine	600	900	1200
Girard"Bi-Wing Monoplane", 1918, 12" long, 14" wingspan (Wood's)	150	225	300
Girard Bus w/driver, 12-1/2" long	187	280	375
Girard Coolie & Pushcart	140	210	280
Girard "Farm Boy Walking", 1920, (w/shovel and rake)(Wood's), 6"	450	675	900
Girard "Fire Chief" Siren Coupe, 1930s, 14" long	135	200	270
Girard "Flasho the Mechanical Grinder", 1920s	100	150	200
Girard "Goble, the Gobbling Goose"	120	180	240
Girard Man pushing wheelbarrow, 5-1/2".	200	300	400

GIRARD "Flasho the Mechanical Grinder". Courtesy Scott Smiles. Photo by Mike Adams.

	C6	C8	C10
Girard Monoplane, high wing, 1-engine, 1921-22, 13" long	350	525	700
Girard Pierce-Arrow Coupe, c. 1932, green, orange & cream, 14" long	350	525	700
Girard Race Car No. 2, 8" long	300	450	600
Girard Railroad Handcar	125	188	250
Girard "Spirit of St. Louis", 9" long	400	600	800
Girard "Tri-Motor Air Lines", 1920s	175	263	350
Girard "U.S. Marines" Monoplane	No Price Found		
"Ham and Sam", 1950s, Linemar, 4" x 5" base, 6" high	450	675	900
"Ham and Sam", maker unknown, piano player and dancer	450	675	900
Hansom Cab, horse moves backward and forward as wheels rotate, driver atop cab, 5-3/4" long	100	150	200
Hy Line Car, Ultra-Streamlined 2-door coupe type, circa 1938	100	150	200
Hy-Lo, Buffalo Toys Ferris Wheel, 14-1/2" high	150	225	300
Indian, like cigar store Indian, c. 1937	70	105	140
Ingap Mouse Car, Italian, eccentric wheels, arms extend, 6" long	1650	2475	3300
Ives "Destroyer""3009", 1923, painted, 9" long	400	600	800
Ives Submarine, 10-1/2" long	300	450	600

"Ham and Sam" maker unknown, piano player and dancer. Courtesy Ed Hyers Antique Toys.

IVES Tugboat "King". Courtesy PB Eight-Four, New York.

INGAP Mouse Car. Courtesy Christie's East.

	C6	C8	C10
Ives Tugboat "King"	150	225	300
Jantzen Bathing Suit Girl Scooter	400	600	800
Jep Seaplane (France), 13-1/2" long	1000	1600	2200
Katz Toys, "Coney Island", 1930s, 18" long-roller coaster w/8-passenger car and 4 monoplanes on pylon	400	600	800
Katz Toys NY, "The Question Mark" airplane, 18" wingspan, high-wing, 2-motors	250	375	500
Kellerman "Armored Vehicle", 1930s, 4" long	55	88	110
Kingsbury Ambulance, 7" long	200	300	400
Kingsbury Artillery Launcher	75	112	150
Kingsbury Biplane, c. 1925, single engine, rubber wheels, 16" long	437	655	875
Kingsbury "Bi-Wing Airplane", 1918, 16" long-17" wingspan (w/cast iron pilot)	600	900	1200
Kingsbury Borden's Milk Truck	250	375	500
Kingsbury Convertible w/rumble seat, electric headlamps, hard rubber wheels, 12-1/2" long	180	270	360
Kingsbury Fireman's Ladder Truck, hard rubber wheels, driver, 23-1/2" long	200	300	400

	C6	C8	C10
Kingsbury Monoplane, high wing, single engine, windup wheels and spins prop via rubber band, 1930s, 11" long	300	450	600
Kingsbury Roadster, electric headlamps, 12-1/2" long	250	375	500
Kingsbury Station Wagon, 1920s	150	225	300
Kingsbury "Streetcar", 1930s, No. 782, 9" long	200	300	400
Kingsbury "Transatlantic Air-Go-Round"	250	375	500
Lehmann "Adam the Porter", 1920s, 9" high	400	600	800
Lehmann "Aha" Delivery Van, 1920s, 5-1/2" long	600	900	1200
Lehmann "Ajax" Warrior w/2 clubs	1050	1575	2100
Lehmann "Alabama Coon Jigger"	600	900	1200
Lehmann "Also"	475	562	950

IVES Destroyer, "3009". Courtesy PB Eighty-Four, New York.

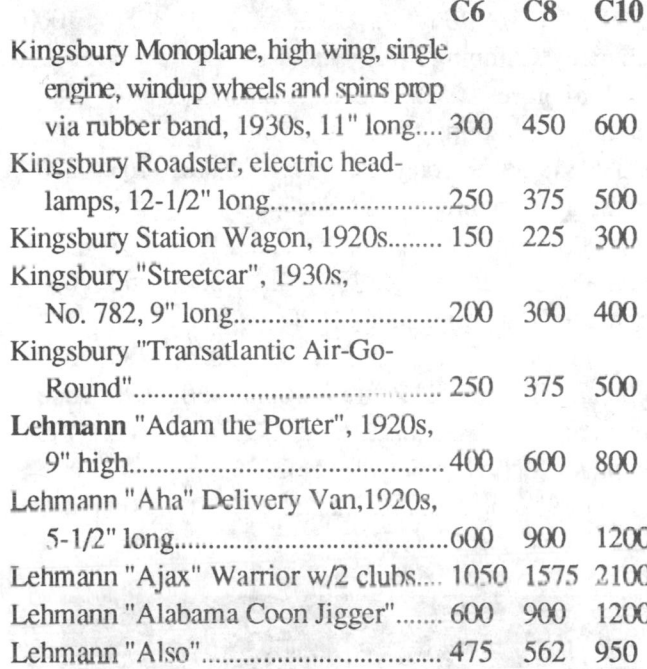

JEP Seaplane (France). Courtesy Christie's East.

	C6	C8	C10
Lehmann "Am Pol", Amundsen driving, figure behind w/umbrella, map of North Pole	1800	2700	3750
Lehmann "Anxious Bride", chauffeur on tricycle, woman in car	1000	1700	2500
Lehmann "Autin"	425	638	850
Lehmann Autobus	1200	2000	2800
Lehmann "Autohutte" Garage No. 771, 6" long	125	188	250
Lehmann Baker & Sweep	2500	3750	5000
Lehmann Balky Mule, 1930s, 7-1/2" long	350	525	700
Lehmann Berolina Car	1500	2400	3500
Lehmann "Bucking Bronco, Wild West", 6-1/2" long	500	750	1000
Lehmann "Climbing Miller", cardboard blades	340	510	680
Lehmann "Climbing Monkey", (Tom 385), 1920s, 9" long	110	165	220
Lehmann "Crawling Beetle, The", 1900s, 4" long	175	263	350
Lehmann Crocodile, circa 1905	300	450	600
Lehmann "Dancing Sailor", 1920s, 7-1/2" high	325	488	650
Lehmann "Daredevil" Zebra Cart	450	675	800
Lehmann "Duo"	700	1000	1400
Lehmann "Echo Motorcycle" No. 725, 1907, 9" long	1200	2000	2800

LEHMANN, Top to Bottom: "Uhu", "Lehmann's Autobus 590". Courtesy Sotheby's New York.

	C6	C8	C10
Lehmann "EHE & Co.", open bed	450	675	900
Lehmann EPL I dirigible	450	675	900
Lehmann EPL II dirigible	750	1125	1500
Lehmann "Express", porter pulling cart, circa 1927, 6" long	350	525	700
Lehmann Galop Racer No. 1 w/garage	800	1200	1600
Lehmann "Galop" Zebra Cart	225	338	450
Lehmann "Going to the Fair"	1100	1700	2700
Lehmann Heavy Swell, dude-it-up man	1000	1600	2200
Lehmann "Ito" Sedan, 1920s, 6-1/2"	600	1000	1400
Lehmann "Kadi", 2 Chinese carrying chest	600	950	1300
Lehmann Lana Auto	1200	2100	3200
Lehmann "Lehmann's Autobus 590"	1200	1800	2400
Lehmann "Li La", early car w/2 excited women passengers, driver in top hat and dog w/turning head, 5-1/2"	900	1500	2100
Lehmann "Lo Li", clown and ring master	5000	8000	12,000
Lehmann "Lo Lo", early car, driver	300	450	600
Lehmann "Lu-Lu" bird	100	150	200
Lehmann "Mandarin", 2 coolies carrying Chinese in sedan chair	1500	2500	400
Lehmann Mars Cycle	500	800	1200
Lehmann "Masuyama", coolie pulling rickshaw	1000	1500	2100
Lehmann Mensa Delivery Van	900	1500	2200
Lehmann "Mikado Family", 1920s, 6-1/2" long	1100	1700	2600
Lehmann Mixtum	1000	1600	2400
Lehmann "Motor Car Kutsche", 1897, 5-1/2" long	350	525	700
Lehmann "Motor Coach", 1920s, 5-1/2" long	250	385	525
Lehmann "Naughty Boy"	500	800	1100
Lehmann "Na-Ob", man driving horse cart, wheels marked w/elf, 6" long	370	505	740
Lehmann "New Century Cycle", 1907, 5" long	500	750	1000
Lehmann "Nu-Nu" No. 733, rickshaw w/puller and rider, circa 1913, 4-1/2" long	475	712	950
Lehmann "Oh My", 10" high	375	562	750
Lehmann "OHO" patented 1903	362	495	725
Lehmann "Onkel"	550	825	1100
Lehmann "Paak-Paak" ducklings in cart pulled by duck	300	450	600
Lehmann "Paddy Pig", circa 1912, 6" long	1200	2000	2700

LEHMANN Alabama Coon Jigger.

LEHMANN Dancing Sailor. Courtesy Christie's East.

LEHMANN, Left to Right: "Naughty Boy", "Quack-Quack", "Onkel". Courtesy Sotheby's New York.

LEHMANN, Left to Right: "Li La", "Zig Zag", "Tut Tut". Courtesy Sotheby's New York.

	C6	C8	C10
Lehmann "Pao Pao" peacock, 10" long...	250	375	500
Lehmann "Performing Sea Lion,The", 1900s, 7" long	175	263	350
Lehmann "Peter", 3-wheeled car	1200	1900	2700
Lehmann "Power Carriage"	360	540	720
Lehmann "Quack-Quack", mother duck pulling cart w/3 small ducks	300	450	600
Lehmann "Rad-Cycle", circa 1927, 5" long	800	1300	1750
Lehmann "Rollo Chair"	1000	1700	2400
Lehmann Stubborn Donkey, clown in donkey cart, 7-1/2" long	350	525	700
Lehmann "Taka" Battleship	600	950	1400
Lehmann Tap Tap, man pushing wheelborrow	375	562	750
Lehmann "Terra"	1100	1700	2500
Lehmann "Tom" climbing monkey 8" long	40	60	80
Lehmann "Tut-Tut", man in car w/horn, 6-3/4" long	650	1000	1500
Lehmann "Uhu" amphibious car	650	1000	1500

	C6	C8	C10
Lehmann "Walking down Broadway" strolling couple	2000	3000	4000
Lehman Walking Sailor, 7-1/2" high	525	775	1050
Lehmann Wild West	375	562	750
Lehmann "Zig Zag" patented 1903, 5" long	1000	1500	2000
Lehmann "Zikra" No. 752, 1920s, 7" long	900	1350	1800
Lehmann "Zulu", black man in cart pulled by ostrich	750	1125	1500
Lewco "See-Saw Circus", 1940s, 6-1/2"..	130	195	260
Limousine, license plate "N.Y. 1918" litho, approx. 6" long	200	300	400

LEHMANN "Kadi". Courtesy Sotheby's New York.

LEHMANN, Left to Right: "Express", "Paddy Pig". Courtesy Sotheby's New York.

LEHMANN "Ito". Courtesy Christie's East.

LEHMANN, Left to Right: Stubborn Donkey, EPL-II Dirigible, "Motor Coach", "Bucking Bronco, Wild West". Courtesy Sotheby's New York.

	C6	C8	C10
Lindstrom "American Railway Express" Truck & Trailer, 16" long	375	562	750
Lindstrom Bird	90	135	180
Lindstrom "Betty", 1930s, shako walker, 8" tall	100	150	200
Lindstrom Bumper Car, 6-1/2" long	200	300	400
Lindstrom Dancing Dutch Boy, 1930s, 8" high	125	188	250
Lindstrom "Dancing Lassie", shako, 1930s, 8" tall	100	150	200
Lindstrom "Delfine 7" Motorboat, circa 1930	175	263	350
Lindstrom "Johnny the Dancing Clown" No. 122, 1930s, 8" tall	200	300	400
Lindstrom "Katrinka", 1930s, 8" tall	100	150	200
Lindstrom "Lindstrom's Ferry Boat", litho, approx. 8-1/4"	100	150	200
Lindstrom "Lindstrom Flyer", 14"	100	150	200
Lindstrom, "Mammy", 1930s, shako walker, 8" tall	300	450	600
Lindstrom "Miss America" speedboat	120	180	240
Lindstrom "Parcel Post No.2" Truck	200	300	400
Lindstrom Racing Car, 1930s, 6"	162	243	325
Lindstrom "Skeeter Bug", 1930s, (bumper car), 9" long	120	180	240
Lindstrom Speedboat, 7" long	46	69	92
Lindstrom Speedboat, circa 1950, 18-1/2" long	150	225	300

	C6	C8	C10
Lindstrom "Sweeping Betty"	120	180	240
Lindstrom "Sweeping Mammy" No. 1750, 1930s, shako walker while sweeping, 8" tall	250	375	500
Lupor "City Cab"	67	100	135
Lupor Metal Products N.Y. Racer No. 8, 1930s	75	112	150

LINDSTROM toys 1930s, Sweeping Mammy, Betty, Mammy (Shakos). Courtesy Don Hultzan.

LEWCO See-Saw Circus with box. Courtesy Scott Smiles. Photo by Mike Adams.

LOUIS MARX

By the 1950s, Louis Marx was the largest manufacturer of toys in the world; six large factories in the U.S., and ownership of interest in factories in seven other countries. Marx, born in Brooklyn in 1896, was working for "Toy King" Ferdinand Strauss when he was in his teens, and by the age of twenty his energy and enterprise had made him a director of that company. A falling out with Strauss persuaded him to go into business for himself, and in 1921 he and his brother began making their own toys, including some adaptations of items by the now-defunct Strauss. Marx's watchword seems to have been quality at the lowest possible price, and he was such a favorite with toy buyers that he had virtualy no need for salesmen or advertising. Although Marx made virtually every type of toy with the exception of dolls, his tin windup toys are probably the most favored by toy collectors. Marx, in April, 1972, sold his company to the Quaker Oats Company, who in 1976 sold it to Europe's largest toy manufacturer, Dunbee-Combex-Marx. The company went into bankruptcy in 1980. Louis Marx died in 1982 at the age of 85. In 1982 American Plastics bought much of the Marx assets and in 1990 began producing toys from the original molds. In the first Marx break-up, certain rights and molds were retained in Mexico, and these continue.

MARX
Acrobatic
Marvel.
Photo by
Don Hultzman.

	C6	C8	C10
"Acrobatic Marvel", 1930s, monkey on 13" spring and 7-1/2" rocking base.....	115	172	230
Air Mail Biplane, 1930, 4-engine........	300	450	600
Air Mail Monoplane, 1930, 2-engine...	165	248	330
Airplane, U.S. Army No. 6, 2-engine, no guns, 18" wingspan.....................	175	262	350
Airplane No. 90, light fuselage............	100	150	200
Airplane No. 90, medium fuselage......	100	150	200
Alligator...	65	98	130
"Ambulance" w/siren, 1930s, 14-1/2"...	325	488	650

	C6	C8	C10
Ambulance, "M.D. War Dept.", 1930s....	450	675	900
"American Tractor" w/implements, 1920s, 10" long...............................	200	300	400
Armored Trucking Co..........................	110	165	220
"Army Dive Bomber" No. 482.............	137	205	275
Army Staff Car, 1930s, litho steel........	250	375	500
"Army Staff Car", W-601158, with flasher and siren, 1940s, 11" long...	115	172	230
Army Truck, cloth cover, 1930s, 10"..	290	435	580
Automatic Car Wash, windup car, 6"..	200	300	400
"Automatic Fire House", 1950s, Fire Chief Car, 7-1/2" long, Volunteer Fire Dept. Garage, 19" long...........	200	300	400
"Automatic Reversing Road Roller", 1925, 9" long..................................	200	300	400
Balky Mule, pre-war............................	115	172	230

MARX Balky Mule, post war, with box.
Courtesy Scott Smiles. Photo by Mike Adams.

	C6	C8	C10
"Balky Mule", 1950s, 8" long.............	60	90	120
"Bear Cyclist", 1930s, 6" long.............	150	225	300
"Beat It" The Komikal Kop, 1930s.....	300	450	600
"Be Bop-The Jivin' Jigger", 1948,10"..	200	300	400
"Bi-Wing Airplane", 1930s, 18" wingspan..	250	375	500
"Big Parade", moving vehicles, soldiers, tin airplane, etc., 1929, 24" long.....	172	258	345
"Big Silver", Mack Dump Truck..........	250	375	500
Big Three Aerial Acrobats, 1920.........	200	300	400
Big Lizzie Car, early 1930s, 7-1/4"......	150	225	300
Bomber, 4-engine, c. 1941, 18" wingspan.	200	300	400
Bomber, 4-engine, c. 1940, camouflaged,18" wingspan.............	200	300	400
Bomber, 2-engine, 18" wingspan.........	200	300	400
Boy on Trapeze...................................	100	150	200

MARX "Ambulance" with siren. Courtesy Mapes Auctioneers & Appraisers.

MARX "Big Silver" Mack Dump Truck. Courtesy Ed Hyers Antique Toys.

	C6	C8	C10
Bulldozer Climbing Tractor, caterpillar type, circa 1950s, 10 1/2" long	150	225	300
Bumper Auto, streamlined, circa 1939, large bumpers, front and rear	150	225	300
"Busy Bridge", vehicles on bridge,1935.	350	525	700
"Busy Delivery" (black Pinocchio), 1930s, 9" long, 8" high	675	1012	1350
"Busy Miners", 1930s, includes 2-1/4" tin litho miner's car, 16-1/2" long	150	225	300
"Busy Parking Station", 1930s, 17" long w/2" tin race car	200	300	400
"Butter & Egg Man", 1930s, 8" high	475	712	950
Cadillac Roadster, trunk w/ tools on luggage carrier, 1930, 13" long	200	300	400
Car Carrier, 3 racers, 22-3/4" long	1000	1600	2200
"Careful Johnnie",1950s, 5-1/2" long	100	150	200
Cat w/ball in front, 2 wheels in back, circa 1938, see "Roll Over Cat"			
Caterpiller Climbing Tractor, c. 1950s, 10" long	100	150	200
"Charleston Trio", 1 black adult, dog, black kid dancer, 1921	450	700	1000
Chicken Snatcher, black holding chicken, dog biting at the seat of his pants, circa 1927	900	1350	1850

	C6	C8	C10
Climbing Tractor, sparkling, 1960s, 8-1/2" long	100	150	200
"Climbing, Fighting Tank"	125	188	250
"Coast Defense", circular, w/3 cannon, revolving airplane, 1929	450	685	925
"Coast to Coast" Greyhound Bus,1930s	500	850	1200
"Coke Coal City Coal Co." Truck	500	800	1150
"Construction" Tractor	300	450	600
"Coo Coo Car", 1920s, 7-1/2" long	450	700	1000
"Cowboy Rider", c. 1941, cowboy w/lariat on dapple or black horse	150	225	300
Crazy Dora nodder head (also "Dan").	100	150	200
"Cross-Country Flyer", Zeppelin and Airplane, 1920, fly around 18" hangar tower.	400	600	800
"Dan Dipsy Car", 1950s, (plastic nodder), 5-1/2" long	175	262	350
"Dapper Dan Coon Jigger", 1910	450	675	900
Dare Devil Flyer, new in 1928	400	600	800
"Daredevil Motor Drome", 1930s, 2" windup car, 5-1/2" high, 9" diameter	100	150	200
"Deluxe Delivery Truck", 1950s, 11"	100	150	200
Deluxe Tractor, 6 wheels, four in treads	225	375	500
"Dipsy Doodle Bug" Dodgem cars (Dan or Dora), 6" high (pair)	250	375	500

MARX "Busy Bridge". Courtesy PB Eight-Four New York.

MARX Charleston Trio, one adult, child, dog.
Courtesy Ed Hyers Antique Toys.

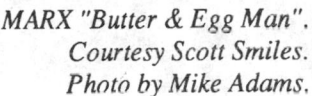

MARX Bulldozer Climbing
Tractor. Courtesy Continental
Hobby House.

MARX "Butter & Egg Man".
Courtesy Scott Smiles.
Photo by Mike Adams.

	C6	C8	C10
Donkey pulling cart, w/rider, 1950s, 10" long	110	165	220
"Dora Dipsy Car", 1950s, (plastic nodder), 5-1/2" long	150	225	300
"Dottie the Driver", 1950s, 6-1/2"	105	160	215
Doughboy Tank, no side turrets	92	138	185
Doughboy Tank, 2 side turrets, w/top turret, 1930, soldier w/gun pops out, 9-1/4" long	200	300	400
"Driver Training Car", 1950s, 6" long.	87	130	175
"Drive-UR-Self Car", 1950s, 11" long	250	375	500
Dump Truck, 13" long	250	375	500
"Fire Dept. Chief", c. 1950s, 11" long.	120	180	240
"Fireman Joe", ladder 24", 1930s, 8" tall	125	188	250
"1st Batt. F.D. Chief's Car", siren, battery headlights, 16"	200	300	400
"Firewater Boat", 1920, 9" long	350	525	700
"Flipo the Jumping Dog, See Me Jump", on hind legs, c. 1940, 3-1/2" x 4"	90	135	180
"Flying Fortress 2905" sparkling aeroplane, 1940s, 4 engines	225	338	450
"Funny Face", new in 1928	400	600	800
"Funny Flivver", circa 1925	400	600	800
G-Man Pursuit Car, 1930s	250	375	500
"George the Drummer Boy", 1930s, 9" tall w/moving eyes	120	180	240
"George the Drummer Boy", 1930s, 9" tall w/stationary eyes, No. 881	100	150	200
"Ghee Whiz" Auto Racer, 1930s, 4 2" long tin cars, 13" diameter	450	700	1000

	C6	C8	C10
"Giant King Racer", circa 1930s, "711"	150	225	300
Giant Reversing Tractor Truck w/tools, "Hauling", circa 1950s, 14" long	100	150	200
Golden Pecking Goose, dated July 8, 1924, hops along pecking at ground, 9-1/2" long	115	172	230
"Hauling" 6-wheel Tractor Truck	200	300	400
"Hee-Haw" balky mule, 1929, 6-color litho, goes backward, forward and rears, farmer and his dog on seat and 5 milk cans in cart, 10-3/4" long	170	225	340
"Helicopter Skyport", 1950s, 2 plastic copters, 9" x 11"	100	150	200
Highboy Climbing Tractor, circa 1950s, 10-1/2" long	75	112	150
Highboy Tractor, sparkles, circa 1950s, 10" long	67	100	135

MARX
Coo-Coo Car.
Photo by
Don
Hultzman.

255

MARX " *Flipo the Jumping Dog". Courtesy Mapes Auctioneers.*

MARX G-Man Pursuit Car. Courtesy Gary Linden.

MARX "Royal Van Co.". Courtesy Mapes Auctioneers & Apraisers.

	C6	C8	C10
"Honeymoon Cottage" RR	60	90	120
"Honeymoon Express", old-fashioned train on circular track, 1927	125	188	250
"Honeymoon Express", circa late 1930s	110	165	220
"Honeymoon Express", circa 1940, circling train and plane 9-3/8 diameter.	87	130	175
"Honeymoon Express", streamlined train on circular track, 1947, 9-3/8"	65	98	130
"Hoppo the Waltzing Monkey w/Cymbals", 1930s, 9-1/2" high	200	300	400
"Ice Man"	300	450	600
Jalopy Pickup Truck, 7"	80	120	160
"Jazzbo Jim", 1920s, 9" high	275	362	550
"Jolly Joe" Jeep, 1940s, plastic helmet, 6" long	200	300	400
"Joy-Rider" 1929, College Boy driver w/bag, wording on car "goes backward, forward, circles and rears" head moves, 8" long	300	450	600
Jumpin' Jeep, circa WW II, 6"	175	262	350
"King Racer" 1930s, 8-1/2" long	500	800	1100
"Let the Drummer Boy Play", 1930s, 8-1/2" high	400	600	800
Light Duty Climbing Tractor, 1930s	162	243	325
"Limping Lizzie" Car	200	300	400
"Looping Plane", No. 182	100	150	200
"Looping Plane", No. 382	100	150	200
Lucky Stunt Flyer	200	300	400
"Mack Dump Truck", 1930s, (City Coal Co.), 13" long	350	525	700

	C6	C8	C10
"Main Street", moving vehicles, traffic cop, etc., 1929	312	468	625
"Mammy's Boy", 1930s, 11" tall	400	600	800
"Mechanical Airplane", new in 1928	200	300	400
"Mechanical Roadster", 1950s, 11"	100	150	200
"Mechanical Speedway Racer"	100	150	200
Mechanical Station Wagon	135	188	250
"Mechanical Taxi Cab", 1950s, 11"	80	120	160
"Mechanical Tractor", c. 1930s, 6"	110	165	220
"Mechanical Tractor w/Earth Grader", circa 1950s, 21-1/2" long	107	160	215
Merrymakers, 4 mice, 3 in band, 1 a dancer, 1929, w/marquee	700	1050	1600
Same as above w/o marquee, has conductor with baton	450	675	900
Same as above w/o marquee, has violinist	550	825	1100
"Midget Climbing Fighting Tank", circa 1935, Pat. No. 1,334,539, approx. 5-1/2" long	72	108	145
Midget Climbing Tractor, circa 1950, 5-1/2" long	70	105	140
"Midget Racer", 1950s, plastic, 6"	50	75	100
"Midget Special", race car-driver in old headgear and goggles, No. 2 racer, 1930s, 5" long	65	98	130
"Midget Special", race car driver in old headgear and goggles, No. 7 racer, 1930s, 5" long	72	108	145

MARX "Merrymakers" without marquee. Courtesy Phillips New York.

MARX Piggy. Courtesy Scott smiles. Photo by Mike Adams.

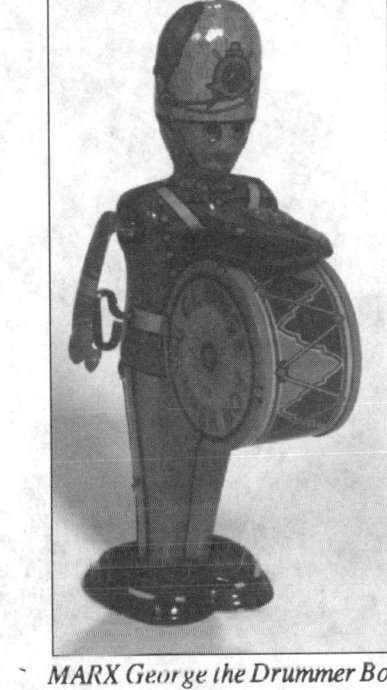

MARX George the Drummer Boy with moving eyes. Courtesy Scott Smiles. Photo by Mike Admas.

MARX "Honeymoon Express" circa late 1930s. Courtesy Phillips New York.

MARX Highboy Climbing Tractor. Photo by Don Hultzman.

MARX Fireman on Ladder. Courtesy Scott Smiles

MARX Mystic Motorcycle. Courtesy Scott Smiles. Photo by Mike Adams.

Marx "Midget Special". Courtes Scott Smiles.

MARX "Midget Climbing, Fighting Tank". courtesy K. Warren Mitchell.

MARX "Rex Race Car". Courtesy Thomas G. Nefos, Federal Shipping Network.

MARX "Old Jalopy" large and small. Courtesy Ed Hyers Antique Toys.

MARX "Rocket Fighter". Courtesy Don Hultzman. Photo by Ron Chojnacki.

MARX "P.D." Police motorcycle w/sidecar. Courtesy Gary Linden.

MARX Ride 'Em Cowboy. Photo by Don Hultzman.

MARX "Reversible Coupe, The Marvel Car". Courtesy Mapes Auctioneers & Appraisers.

MARX "Tom Tom Jungle Boy". Photo by Ed Hyers Antique Toys.

	C6	C8	C10
Minstrel Figure, 11" high..................	160	240	320
"Monkey Cyclist", 1930s....................	100	150	200
"Moon Creature", 1950s, (Japan)			
5-1/2" high.................................	90	135	180
"Motor Squad", sidecar........................	240	360	480
"Motorcycle Trooper", 1935...............	212	318	425
"Mountain Climber", 1960s (Japan),			
32" long, 4" car..............................	80	120	160
"Mysterious Kitty Kat", 1950s, 8".......	90	135	180
"Mystery Police Cycle", 1930s, 4-1/2"...	110	165	220
Mystery Tunnel......................................	60	90	120
"Mystic Motorcycle", circa 1930s........	115	172	230
"New Flivver", 1920s, 7" long.............	200	300	400
"New Rocket Racer", 1930s, 16".........	200	300	400
"New York", circular, w/train, new in			
1928, tin airplane, 9-1/2" diameter..	600	900	1200
Nodding Goose.....................................	70	105	140
"North American Van Lines Inc. Long			
Distance Moving" Truck..................	125	188	250
"Old Jalopy"..	120	180	240
"Old Jalopy", small, 1950s, Linemar...	75	112	150
"P.D." Motorcyclist, Pat. No.2001625,			
approx. 4" long................................	150	225	300
"P.D." Police motorcycle w/sidecar,			
wood wheels, on-off lever, 1930s,			
3-1/2" long.....................................	150	225	300
"Parade Drummer", 1930s, "Let the			
Drummer Boy Play While You			
Swing and Sway"............................	400	600	800
"Parcel Post U.S. Mail", early,			
8-1/2" long.....................................	225	338	450
Peter Rabbit, eccentric car....................	300	450	600
"Piggy", 4" high....................................	62	93	125
"Pike's Peak Mountain Climber",			
1930s, 3-1/2" tin car, 30" long........	300	450	600
"Pinched" Roadster, motorcycle cop			
in circular track, circa 1927,			
9-1/2" x 9-1/2".................................	450	675	900

MARX Rookie Pilot. Photo by Scott Smiles.

	C6	C8	C10
"Play-Away-Piano", 1930s, w/song-			
book, 9" x 9"...................................	60	90	120
"Police Patrol", motorcycle w/sidecar,			
1935..	150	225	300
Police Precinct Police Patrol armored			
truck, circa early 1930s, 10-1/2".....	2000	3000	4000
"Police Siren Motorcycle", 1930s,			
8" long..	300	450	600
"Police Squad", motorcycle cop			
w/sidecar..	240	360	480
"Power Snap Caterpillar Climbing			
Tractor", 1950s, 8" long..................	112	168	225
"Prone WW I Soldier", 1925, 8" long..	100	150	200
Racer No. 2, 1930s, 5" long..................	70	105	140
Racer No. 3, 1930s, 5" long..................	75	112	150
Racer No. 5, 1930s, 5" long..................	75	112	150
Racer No. 7, 1930s, 5" long..................	87	130	175
Racing Car, circa 1940, 2-man team,			
litho, 12"...	110	165	220
Racing Car, "12", circa 1950, plastic			
driver, litho....................................	162	248	325
Racing Car, "27", plastic driver, litho,			
circa 1950.......................................	150	225	300
"Range Rider", 1940s, 8-1/2" high.......	150	225	300
"Range Rider", 1940s, 10-1/2" high			
on rocker base.................................	175	262	350
"Red Cap" Porter.................................	500	750	1000
"Red Devil Stunt Auto", 1930s, 12"			
long ramp w/2 1/2" tin racer............	150	225	300

MARX Cat, with Ball. Courtesy Scott Smiles.
Photo by Mike Adams.

MARX Ring-A-Ling Circus. Photo by Scott Smiles.

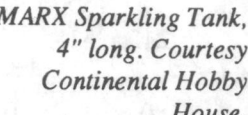

MARX Sparkling Tank, 4" long. Courtesy Continental Hobby House.

	C6	C8	C10
"Reversible Coupe", "The Marvel Car", circa 1938	245	368	490
Reversing Road Roller	135	202	270
Reversing Tank. 1930s	65	98	130
"Reversing Tractor"	275	412	550
"Rex" Race Car, 1920s	162	243	325
"Rex Mars Planet Patrol", 1950s, pastel colors, 9-1/2" long	185	277	370
"Ride 'Em Cowboy"	120	180	240
"Ring-A-Ling Circus", early ringmaster and circus animals, green base	600	900	1225
Same as above, pink base	750	1125	1500
Road Roller, circa 1930, has driver, 8-1/2" long	375	562	750
"Rocket Fighter" c. 1950s, complete w/tail fin and sparking mechanism.	300	450	600
Rocket Racer, 1930	250	375	500
"Rodeo Joe", 1933	175	262	350

	C6	C8	C10
"Rolover Plane", circa 1940	192	288	385
"Rolover Tank"	80	120	160
"Roll Over Cat"	65	98	130
"Roll Over Plane" circa 1920s	137	205	275
"Rookie Cop" w/siren, 1930s, 8-1/2"	300	450	600
Rookie Pilot, No. 77, c. 1940, 7" long.	250	375	500
Rooster Pulling Wagon, 1930s	60	90	120
Royal Bus Line, 10" long	175	262	350
"Royal Coupe", 1920s, 9" long	350	525	700
"Royal Van Co." "We Haul Anywhere", 9" long	350	525	700
"Running Scottie", 1940s, 5-1/2" long	150	225	300
"Sam, the Gardner", 1950s, 8" tall, (includes 6 plastic tools)	100	150	200
"Sand and Gravel Truck-Builders Supply Co.", 1920	100	150	200
Scenic Express Train Set, circa 1950s	90	135	180
"Sheriff Sam & His Whoopee Car", 1960s, 6" long	117	175	235
"Single Track Speedway", 1938, 8 track sections, 4" long windup car	70	105	140
"Sky Hawk" Airport Tower, No. 333, 2 planes, tower 7-1/2" high	180	270	360
Skybird Flyer, new circa 1927	187	280	375

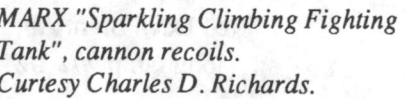

MARX "Sparkling Climbing Fighting Tank", cannon recoils. Curtesy Charles D. Richards.

MARX "Speed Boy Delivery". Courtesy Don Hultzman. Photo by Ron Chojnacki.

MARX Sparkling Soldier Motorcycle (Tin Wind-up).
Courtesy Don Hultzman. Photo by Ron Chojnacki.

MARX Toyland's Farm Products.

	C6	C8	C10
"Skyscraper Go-Round", 1930s, mono plane, Zeppelin, 13-1/2" high	400	600	800
Smoky Joe, The Climbing Fireman, 1930s	200	300	400
Smoky Sam, The Wild Fireman	112	168	225
"Soap Box Derby Racer", marked #3, 5-1/2" long	100	150	200
Soldier, prone, firing rifle, WW I helmet	90	135	180
"Space Mobile", 1960s (Japan), 32" long, 3 sections, 4" long car	120	180	240
"Space Satellite w/Launching Station", 1950s, 9" x 12" base and plastic accessories	70	105	140
Sparkling Climbing Bulldozer Tractor, later	187	280	375

	C6	C8	C10
"Sparkling Climbing Fighting Tank", cannon recoils	142	213	285
"Sparkling Climbing Tank", 1939	85	128	170
Sparkling Climbing Tractor, 1940s	75	112	150
Sparkling Climbing Tractor, c. 1950s, 8-1/2" long	162	243	325
"Sparkling Climbing Tractor and Trailer", circa 1950s, 16" long	130	195	260
Sparkling Heavy Duty Bulldog Tractor w/Road Scraper, c. 1950s, 11"	140	210	280
"Sparkling Luxury Liner", 1950s, 14" long	100	150	200
"Sparkling Mountain Climber Train Set", 1950s, tin loco & car, 9" long	100	150	200
Sparkling Soldier Motorcycle, c. 1940	300	450	600
Sparkling Rocket Ship	350	525	700
Sparkling Space Tank	187	280	375
Sparkling Super Power Tank, c. 1950s, 9-1/2" long	110	165	230

MARX "Subway Express", Chein "Boy Skier".
Courtesy Don Hultzman. Photo by Ron Chojnacki.

MARX Turnover Tank No. 3. Photo by Max Heiss.

	C6	C8	C10
Sparkling Tank, 4" long	65	98	130
"Sparkling Tractor", tractor w/plow blade, 1939	140	210	280
Sparkling Tractor and Trailer Set "Marbrook Farms", circa 1950s, 21" long	100	150	200
Sparkling Turn Over Tank	50	75	100
Sparkling Warship, (same as U.S.S. Washington), 14" long	75	112	150
"Speed Boy Delivery", (motorcycle delivery), 1930s, battery operated lights, 9-3/4" long	300	450	600
Same as above, no lights	230	345	460
"Speed King" Racer, 1930s, 16" long	425	638	850
Speedway Coupe, battery to be inserted for headlights, 8" long	312	468	625
"Spic and Span, the Hams What Am", drummer and dancer, 1924	800	1250	1800
"Spic Coon Drummer", 1924, 8-1/2" high	900	1400	2000
"Streamline Speedway", 1938 (tin figure 8 track, 2-windup cars), 31" long	112	168	225
Streamlined Coupe	225	338	450
"Subway Express" w/plastic tunnel 1950s, 9-3/8" diameter	100	150	200
"Super Streamline Racer", 1950s, 17" long	138	207	275
"Tidy Tim" Streetcleaner, pushing wagon, 1933, 7-1/2" H, 8-1/2" L	500	800	1100

MARX Trombone Player, Linemar. Photo by Scott Smiles.

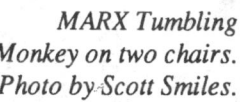

MARX Tumbling Monkey on two chairs. Photo by Scott Smiles.

MARX "Whoopee Car". "Yale-Princeton" pennants on wheels. Courtesy Mapes Auctioneers and Appraisers.

MARX Zippo the Climbing Monkey. Photo by Ron Chojnacki. Courtesy Don Hultzman.

	C6	C8	C10
"Tom Tom Jungle Boy"	125	188	250
"Toto Acrobat"	100	150	200
"Tower Aeroplane", 1940s, two 3" tin airplanes, 7-1/2" high	200	300	400
"Toyland Farm Products", 1930s, milk wagon, 10-1/2" long	450	675	900
"Toy Town Dairy", horsedrawn cart, 1930s, 10-1/2" long	150	225	300
Tractor, early 1940s	119	177	238
Tractor and Trailer Set, 1930s, similar to climbing tractor set, but w/rounded and radiator front and copper finish metal. Tin plow attaches to front, silver metal trailer attaches to rear, has tin, copper finish and "balloon" tires	150	225	300
Tractor and Trailer, circa 1950s, 16-1/2" long	150	225	300
"Trans-Atlantic Zeppelin", 1930s, rear propeller, 10" long	250	375	500
"Tricky Fire Chief", 1925, 4" car on 6" x 10" base	200	300	400
"Tricky Motorcycle", 1930s, non-fail action, 4-1/4" long	138	207	275
"Tricky Taxi", 1940s, 4-1/2" long	150	225	300
Tricky Taxi On A Busy Street	150	225	300
Trolley, headlight, bell, 9" long	170	225	340
"Tumbling Monkey", 1930s, on two chairs, 5" high	110	165	220

	C6	C8	C10
"Tumbling Monkey on Trapeze", 1920s, 6" high	100	150	200
Turn Over Tank No. 3	100	150	200
"TWA-U.S. Mail-990", c. 1941, 5"	125	188	250
"U.S. Army" bomber, post-War, 1940s, 2-engine	162	243	325
"U.S. Army Fighter Plane", 1940, 8" wingspan	200	300	400
"U.S. Mail" Truck, 9-1/2" long	450	680	975
"U.S. Mail - TWA Biplane", 1930s, 15" long, 18" wingspan	400	600	800
"U.S.S. Washington" Battleship	120	180	240
"Uncle Wiggily, He Goes A Ridin' ", 1935	*See Comic Character*		
Vacationland Express	62	93	125
Wacky Taxi	75	112	150
Walking Clancy	400	600	800
Walking Drummer Boy, "Let The Drummer Boy Play While You Swing and Sway", circa 1939	350	525	700
Wee Scottie, 5" long	150	225	300
Whoopee Car, laughing cows on wheels, driver looks like cowboy, 1929	190	285	380
Whoopee Car, "Yale-Princeton" pennants on wheels	312	468	625
"Whoopee Car w/Flappers", 7-1/2" long	375	562	750
"Wonder Cyclist", 1930s, 9" high	200	300	400
Xyophonist, 5"	100	150	200
"Yellow Cab-LMN 52", 1940s, 6-1/2" long	170	255	340
Zeppelin, 10" long	162	243	325
"Zeppelin", 1925, (propeller on front), 11" long	200	300	400
Zeppelin, 1930s, 27" long	200	300	400
Zeppelin TransAtlantic, 10" long	162	243	325
"Zippo, The Climbing Monkey", 1930s, 9-1/2" long	110	165	220

End Marx

MARX "U.S. Mail" Truck, 9-1/2" long. Courtesy Phillips New York.

OHIO ART Automatic Airport. Photo by Ron Chojnacki. Courtesy Don Hultzman.

SCHUCO Motodrill Clown 1007. Photo by Don Hultzman.

SCHUCO Examico 4001. Photo by Ron Chojnacki. Courtesy Don Hultzman.

SCHUCO Micro Racer 1040. Photo by Don Hultzman.

	C6	C8	C10
"**Mike** Mallard The Climbing Fireman", 1950s, Linemar Co., 13-3/4" high (ladder), w/4 1/2" long tin duck	200	300	400
Mohawk Toys Checker Cab, c. 1920s, 6-3/8" long	130	195	260
Mohawk Toys Yellow Taxi, c.1920s, 6-3/8" long	117	175	235
"**Movie** Man" Touring Car, rare	2000	3000	4000
Newsboy "Extra" w/cab and bell, circa 1940s, Japan	150	225	300
"**Nifty** Bus"	1100	1750	2500
Nifty "N.Y. to Paris" PNX211 plane, 7" wingspan	400	600	800

OHIO ART

	C6	C8	C10
Ohio Art "Automatic Airport", 1940s 9" high	90	135	180
Ohio Art Boat, 14" long	80	120	160
Ohio Art Cabin Cruiser, 15" long	70	105	140
Ohio Art "Circus Shooting Gallery", 1950s, 12" high, 17" long	60	90	120

OHIO ART Giant Ride Ferris Wheel. Photo by Don Hultzman.

	C6	C8	C10
Ohio Art "Coast Guard Seaplane", 1950s, 10" wingspan	100	150	200
Ohio Art "Commando Joe", 1950s, 8" long	90	135	180
Ohio Art "Giant Ride Ferris Wheel", 1950s, 16" high	150	225	300
Ohio Art Hot Job Floatplane	100	150	200
Ohio Art "Injun Chief", 1950s, 8" long	60	90	120
Ohio Art "Jungle Eyes Shooting Gallery", 1950s, 18" L, 14" H	90	135	180
Ohio Art "Mechanical Sea Plane"	100	150	200
Ohio Art "Sea Patrol" Seaplane, 10" wingspan	62	93	125
Ohio Art "Switch and Dump Train", 1950s, 28" long	100	150	200
Ohio Art "Traffic Control", 1950s, tin windup cars, 3-1/2" long, base 19" x 13"	60	90	120
Ori-O Tailspin 4" puppy	10	15	20
Orkin Coast Guard Cutter, 25" long	350	525	700
Pecking Bird, 1927, 5-1/2" long	45	68	90
Pecking Chicken, 1927, 5-1/2" high	40	60	80
"**PT 10**", tin litho PT boat, c. 1941	60	90	120

	C6	C8	C10
Ranger Steel Products, Roslyn Heights, NY Billiard Table, 2 players, No. 850, 1950s, 14" long	175	262	350
Ranger Steel Products Cross Country Turnpike, 26" x 14"	90	135	180
Roadster, orange and green	120	180	240
Santa Claus in red cloth suit and holding Christmas tree, 5-1/2" H, (Occupied Japan)	200	300	400
Santa Claus w/green sleigh, Christmas tree, presents and white celluloid reindeer, bell, sleigh on 3 wheels, (Occupied Japan), 8-1/2" long	220	330	440

SCHUCO

by Don Hultzman

Schuco was founded in 1912 by Heinrich Muller and Herr Schreyer which was later called Schreyer and Co. and adopted the name "Schuco" as its trademark. Schuco toys are noted for their ingenious mechanisms, and were produced in the 1930s-1950s, and marked either "Germany" or " U.S. Zone-Germany". Other markings are reissues.

	C6	C8	C10
"Akustico 2002", 1940s, 5-1/2" long	112	168	225
"Anno 2000", 1940s, 5-1/2" long	80	120	160
"Buick" No. 5311, 9" long	200	300	400
"Cadillac DeVille Convertible 5505", 1960s, plastic, 11" long	90	135	180
"Charly 1005", 1950s, motorcycle w/driver, 3-1/2" long	300	450	600
"Combinatio 4003", 1950s, w/windup horn, 7-1/2" long	175	263	350
"Curvo 1000", 1950s, 5" long	138	200	275
"Dalli 1011", 1950s, tin car & plastic driver, 6-1/2" long	80	120	160
"Electro Radiant 5600", 1950s, battery operated, 16" long, 19" wingspan	400	600	800
"Electro Record 5555", 1950s, battery operated, plastic, 11" long	50	75	100
"Electro Submarine" No. 5552, 1950s, 13" long	90	135	180
"Elektro Ingenico 5311", 1950s, remote control, 8-1/2" long	250	375	500
"Examico 4001", 1950s, 5-speed BMW, 6" long	112	168	225
"Fex 1111", 1950s, 6" long	100	150	200
"Gas Station 3054", 1950s, 8" long	60	90	120
"Grand Prix Racer 1070", 1950s, 6"	100	150	200
"Hegi-Fipsi 110", 1950, airplane kit (glider)	70	105	140
"Hopsa", 1950s, 4" high	120	180	240

	C6	C8	C10
Ingenico No. 5335	275	412	550
"Jaguar 1250", 1940s, 5-1/2" long	160	240	320
"Kommando Anno 2000", 1940s, 5-1/2" long	100	150	200
"Lasto 3042", 1950s, truck, 4-1/2"	60	90	120
"Magico Auto 2008", 1950s, responds to blowing, 5-1/2" long	150	225	300
"Magico Car and Garage", 1950s, 6"	120	180	240
"Mercedes 190SL, 2095", 1950s, 8"	225	338	450
"Mercedes TYP SSK 1928", 1950s, 4" long	100	150	200
"Mercer Auto 1225", 1950s, 7-1/2"	90	135	180
"Micro-Jet 1030"-Thunderjet, 1950s, 5" wingspan, 5-1/2" long	80	120	160
"Micro-Jet 1031"-Magister 170R, 1950s, 5" wingspan, 5-1/2" long	80	120	160
"Micro-Jet 1032"-Super Sabre F 100, 1950s, 5" wingspan, 5-1/2" long	90	135	180
"Micro-Jet 1033"-Douglas F4 D-1, 1950s, 5" wingspan, 5-1/2" long	80	120	160
"Micro Racer 101", 1950s, Porsche style, 3-1/2" long	90	135	180
"Micro Racer 102", 1950s, Indy style, 3-1/2" long	90	135	180
"Micro Racer 104", 1950s, Indy style, 3-1/2" long	90	13	180
"Micro Racer 1036", 1950s, 4-1/2"	100	150	200
"Micro Racer 1040", 1950s, 4" long	100	150	200
"Micro Racer 1041", 1950s, 4" long	60	90	120
"Micro Racer 1042", 1950s, 4" long	100	150	200
"Micro Racer 1043", 1950s, 4" long	70	105	140
"Micro Racer '57 Ford 1045", 1950s, 4" long	100	150	200
"Micro Racer Apha Romeo 1048", 1950s, 4" long	90	135	180
"Micro Racer Go Kart 1035", 1950s, 4" long	100	150	200
"Micro Racer Hot Rod 1036", 1950s, 4" long	90	135	180
"Micro Racer-Mercedes Benz 1038", 1950s, 4" long	100	150	200
"Micro Racer-Mercedes Benz 1044", 1950s, 4" long	110	165	220
"Micro Racer Mercer 1036/1", 1950s, 4" long	100	150	200
"Micro Racer Porsche 1047", 1950s, 4" long	110	165	220
"Micro Racer Rally 1034", 1950s, 10' 6" long 8 three lane tracks	60	90	120

SCHUCO, Left to Right" Solisto Monkey Drummer, Monkey Lifter, Monkey Fiddler. Photo by Don Hultzman.

SCHUCO, Left to Right: Solisto Clown Drummer, Clown Juggler, Clown Fiddler. Photo by Don Hultzman.

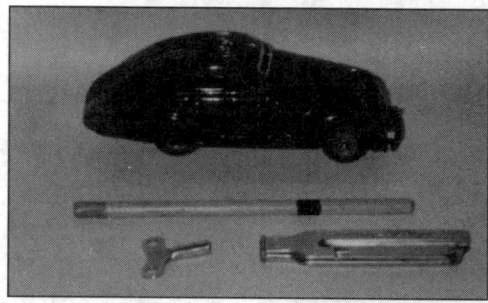

SCHUCO Magico Auto 2008. Photo by Don Hultzman.

SCHUCO Studio Racer 1050. Photo by Don Hultzman.

	C6	C8	C10
"Micro Racer Stake Truck 1049", 1950s, 4" long	90	135	180
"Micro Racer Volkswagen 1046", 1950s, 4" long	90	135	180
"Micro Racer Volkswagen Polizei 1039", 1950s, 4" long	100	150	200
"Mikifex 922", 1950s, non-fall action mouse, 3-1/2" long	40	60	80
"Mirakocar 1001", 1950s, non-fall action, 4-1/2" long	72	108	145
"Mirakomot 1012", 1950s, non-fall action, 5-1/4" long	300	450	600
"Monkey Car", 1930s, orange-black, smiling monkey, 6" long	1400	2100	2800
"Motodrill 1006", 1950s, circular action, 5" long	300	450	600
"Motodrill Clown 1007", 1950s, composition head, 5" long	400	600	800
"Mystery Car 1010", 1950s, non-fall action, 5-1/2" long	90	135	180
"PanAm Clipper", 533S, 19" wingspan	300	450	600
"Porsche Formel II-1037", 1950s, 4-1/2" long	80	120	160
"Racing Boat 1015", 1950s, non-fall action, 5" long	90	135	180
"Radio 4012", 1950s, musical car, 6"	200	300	400
"Solisto", Clown Drummer, 1950s, 4-1/4" tall	100	150	200
"Solisto", Clown Fiddler, 1950s, 4-1/4" tall	100	150	200
"Solisto", Clown Flutist, 1950s, 4-1/4" tall	130	195	260
"Solisto", Clown Juggler, 1950s, 4-1/2" tall	200	300	400
"Solisto", Monkey Drummer, 1950s, 4-1/2" tall	140	210	280
"Solisto", Monkey Fiddler, 1950s, 4-1/2" tall	125	188	250

	C6	C8	C10
"Solisto", Monkey Flutist, 1950s, 4-1/2" tall	120	180	240
"Solisto", Monkey Lifter, 1950s, lifts pig or bear, 4-1/2" tall	150	225	300
"Sonny 2005", 1950s, mouse w/balloon in BMW, 5-1/4" long	200	300	400
"Station Car 3118", 1950s, 4-1/2" long	60	90	120
"Studio Racer 1050", 1950s, includes tools, 5-1/2" long	110	165	220
"Submarine 3007", 1950s, tin and plastic, 12" long	70	105	140
"Synchromatic 5700", 1950s, resembles Packard Hawk, 11" long	500	750	1000
"Telesteering 3000 Limo", 1950s, 4" long	50	75	100
"Varianto 3010", 1950s, tin cars are 4-1/2" long, 2-car playset	100	150	200
"Varianto 3010 Super", 1950s, service station w/2 4-1/2" tin cars	170	225	340
"Varianto 3010/0", 1950s, truck and garage, 4-1/2" long	50	75	100
"Varianto 3041 Limo", 1950s, 4" long	50	75	100

"Skidoodle", Nifty. Photo courtesy PB Eighty-Four.

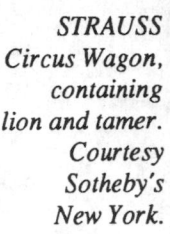

STRAUSS Circus Wagon, containing lion and tamer. Courtesy Sotheby's New York.

	C6	C8	C10
"Varianto 3064", 1950s, all plastic, 8" long	30	45	60
"Varianto Box 3010/30", (tin garage and 3041 Limo), 1950s, 4-1/2" long	110	165	220
"Varianto Bus 3044", 1950s, 4" long	60	90	120
"Varianto Electro 3112", 1950s, truck, 4" long	60	90	120
"Varianto Electro 3112u", 1950s, truck, 4-1/2" long	60	90	120

End Schuco

	C6	C8	C10
Selrite, "Home Run King", 1930s, 4" x 6" base w/5" tall hitter	437	655	875
"Skidoodle", Nifty, circa 1920, family in odd-looking car	1700	2550	3400
Speedboat, "G.E. 200", tin litho, circa 1930	80	120	160
Spinning Globe, tin litho, 2 tin planes circling it, circa 1930	200	300	400
"Spirit of America" Airplane PNX211, NY to Paris, litho on wings	200	300	400
Steam Roller, circa 1925	100	150	200

STRAUSS Hooligans Hack. Courtesy Mapes Auctioneers & Appraisers.

STRAUSS

Ferdinand Strauss was an immigrant from Alsace. He began as a toy importer in the early 1900s, and by 1914 had four New York toy shops. When war disrupted imports of toys, he began manufacturing them. In 1918 he was located in East Rutherford, New Jersey, with fifty employees. Eventually Strauss was known as "The Founder of the Mechanical Toy Industry in America." Strauss seems to have been wholly or partially out of business in the late 1920s, and then resumed turning out wind-ups and other toys until at least 1941-42. He is also famous for having given employment to the very young Louis Marx.

	C6	C8	C10
"Air Devil" monoplane	300	450	600
"Alabama Coon Jigger", 9-3/4"	410	615	820
"Alabama Coon Jigger-Tombo", 1918, 10-1/2" high, 3" x 5" base	370	555	740
"Aluminum Flying Airship"-LA 1017, 1930s, 9" long	275	362	550
"Big Show Circus Truck"	1200	2200	3000
"Big-Trixo", climbing monkey, 10" long	150	225	300
Billiards Player	300	450	600
Black Porter pulling wheelbarrow, 6-1/4"	180	270	360

STRAUSS "Alabama Coon Jigger". Courtesy Mapes Auctioneers & Appraisers.

STRAUSS, Top Left: Jackee the Hornpipe, Top Right: Leaping
Lena, Middle Right: Knockout Prize Fighters, Bottom: Billiards
Player. Courtesy PB Eight-Four, New York.

STRAUSS Interstate Double-Decker Bus, 10-1/2" long.
Courtesy Lloyd W. Ralston Auctions.

STRAUSS "Jenny the Balky Mule".
Courtesy Scott Smiles.

	C6	C8	C10
"Bus Deluxe", 1920s, 12" long	425	638	850
"Check-A-Cab", 8 1/2" long	625	938	1250
"Chicago Zeppelin", 1930s, 9" long	400	600	800
Circus Wagon, containing lion and tamer, no engine compartment, 8-1/2" long	420	630	840
Circus Wagon, has engine compartment, 10" long	1100	1700	2500
"Dandy Jim", copyright 1921	250	375	500
"Dizzie Lizzie"	150	225	300
Flying Airship dirigible	285	428	570
"Ham and Sam The Minstrel Team", piano player and banjoist, 1921, 6-1/2" long	500	750	1000
"Haul Away Truck", No. 22, dump body	240	360	480
Hooligans Hack	300	450	600
Interstate Double Decker Bus, 1920	437	655	850
"Jackee The Horn Pipe Dancer", No. 51, 8-1/2" long	500	750	1000
"Jazzbo Jim The Dancer on the Roof", 1910, 10" high	300	450	600
"Jenny the Balky Mule", 6-color litho, goes backward, forward and rears, farmer holding extended tin grain pail from his seat in front of mule's			

	C6	C8	C10
face to keep him moving, vegetables in cart, No. 55, 10" long	225	338	450
"Jocko the Golfer"	337	506	675
Knock-Out Prize Fighters, c. 1910, No. 52, 7" high	450	675	900
"Kraka Jack Car", 1920s, 5-1/2" long	150	225	300
"Leaping Lena"	325	488	650
"Long Haulage Truck"	350	525	700
"Mailplane"	225	338	450

STRAUSS Rollo Chair.

STRAUSS "Santee Claus". Courtesy Sotheby's New York.

	C6	C8	C10
"Miami Sea Sled", 1920s, w/4" dinghy attached, 10" long	250	375	500
Monkey driving 3-wheel cart pulled by bulldog, 1930s, 4-1/2" high	280	420	560
"Old Jalopy, The", 4 college kids	100	150	200
"Play Golf", 1920s, 7" x 12" base w/5" high golfer	275	412	550
"Red-Cap Porter", porter pushing a large trunk	300	450	600
"Red Star Van"	400	600	800
Rollo Chair, black man pushing boardwalk chair, "Stock, DRGM, December 6, 1921"	500	750	1000
"Santee Claus", 1921, in sleigh, 2 reindeer, 6" high	950	1425	1900
"Speedwagon"	200	300	400
"Standard Oil", Truck, "73"	325	488	650
"Tip Tip" man w/wheelbarrow	500	750	1000
"Tip Top Dump Truck"	500	750	1050
"Tip Top Porter", No. 40, 1920s, 6" long	245	368	490
Tippy Canoe	167	250	335
"Tom Twist", 1920s, 8-1/2" tall	300	450	600
"Travel Chiks", chickens on railroad car	362	543	725
"Trikauto", No. 53	185	278	370
"Water Sprinkle" Truck	450	675	900
"What's It?" Car, No. 53, 1925, 9-1/2" long	600	900	1200
"Yell-O Taxi", 8-1/2" long	450	675	900

End Strauss

	C6	C8	C10
Structo red and black painted tin windup automobile, 15" long	90	135	180

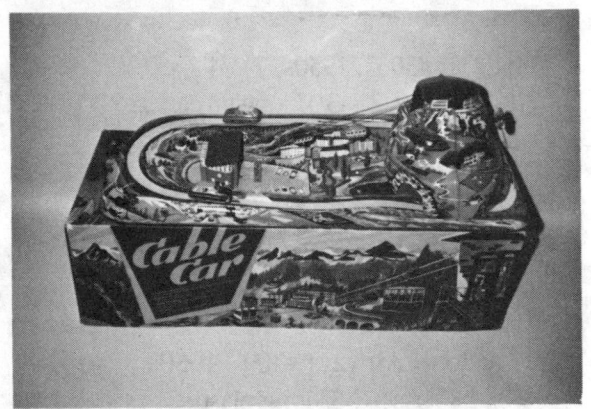

TECHNOFIX "Cable Car" on box. Photo by Don Hultzman.

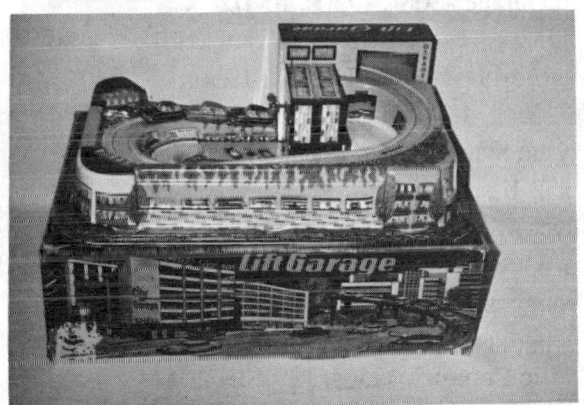

TECHNOFIX "Lift Garage" on box. Photo by Don Hultzman.

	C6	C8	C10
Structo Racer, early 1920s	150	225	300
Structo Steam Shovel, large size, rubber wheels, early	80	120	160
Structo Toyland Garage Truck	120	180	240
"Super Rocket Racer", tin litho, 1940s?	200	300	400
Sweetie Pie Boat, Lindstrom, 1920s	100	150	200

TECHNOFIX
by Don Hultzman

The Technofix Co., founded in Nuremberg, Germany by Gebruder Einfalt, was engaged in German military technology during WW II. After the war, Technofix diverted its expertise to toy manufacturing. It was noted for its quality, detailed mechanical toys. Among these were impressively large, 3-dimensional, platform toys. These colorful toys were made from stamped tin blanks and highlighted with delicate relief features that duplicated realistic outdoor-recreational themes. In the late 50's, vacu-form plastic took the place of tin; quality declined; the toys less durable and sales dropped. Soon after many Technofix toys began to carry the Ohio Art trademark.

	C6	C8	C10
"Alpine Express #300", 1950s,(Ohio Art #614), 6-1/2" x 32" long extended, 2 3" tin cars	140	210	280

	C6	C8	C10
"Cable Car #303", 1950s, 7-3/4" x 18-1/2" long, 2 1-3/4" long tin cars	220	330	440
"Coney Island #290", 1950s, 14" x 21" long, 2 3" long tin cars	90	135	180
"Grand Prix", 1950s, 14" x 21" long, 3 3" tin cars	140	210	280
"Hoilday Camp #304", 1950s, 9" x 28-1/2" long, 2 3-1/2" cars	400	600	800
"International Airways #309", 1950s, 9" x 28" base, 1 5" long plastic jet airplane	300	450	600
"Lift Garage #308", 1950s, 10-1/2" x 15" long base, 3 1-3/4" tin cars	120	180	240
"Motorcycle & Sidecar #225", 1950s, 7" long, 4-3/4" high	180	270	360
"Mystic Station #306", 1950s, 17" x 8" base, tin car	70	105	140
"Silver Mine Express", 1950s, 23" x 6" base, w/3"-long tin car	90	135	180
"Toboggan #290", 1950s, 14" x 21" long base, 2 3-1/2" tin cars	150	225	300
"Traffic Control", 1950s, 13" x 19" long base, 3 3-1/2" tin cars	60	90	120
"Traffic Crossing w/Police Control", 1950s, 2 3" tin cars	100	150	200

End Technofix

	C6	C8	C10
"**Tip** Top Toy Airplane" high wing single engine, "Giant Flyer No. 200", 1930s, 23" long, 19 1/2" wingspan	500	750	1000
Tom Turkey, "B&S", turkey struts, tail spreads, then moves up and down, German, 6" long	180	270	360

TPS "Bear Playing Ball" with box. Photo by Don Hultzman.

T.P.S.

by Don Hultzman

"TPS" is the trademark of Toplay, Ltd., founded in 1956 and is noted for its most unusual and unique mechanical toys. A Japanese Company.

TPS. Pop Eye Pete and Comical Clara. Photo by Don Hultzman.

	C6	C8	C10
"Animal Barber Shop", 1950s, 5" H	200	300	400
"Animals Playland", 1950s, 9-1/4"	120	180	240
"Ball Playing Giraffe", 1950s 8-1/2" tall	100	150	200
"Basketball Monkey", 1950s, 7-1/2" tall	180	270	360
"Bear Golfer", 1950s, assembled 7-1/2" long	150	225	300
"Bear Playing Ball", 1950s, 19" long, 4" high	200	300	400
"Bo Bo the Strongman", 1950s, 6"	200	350	600
"Bouncing Doll Ball", 1950s, 5-1/4"	100	150	200
"Bunny Family Parade", 1950s, 13"	50	75	100
"Busy Choo Choo", 1950s, 5-1/2" x 9-1/4" base w/2 1/4" tin locomotive	90	135	180
"Busy Mouse", 1950s, 6" x 9" base w/3 1/4" tin mouse	90	135	180
"Calypso Joe", 1950s, 6" tall	300	450	600
"Candy Loving Canine", 1950s, 5-1/2" high	90	135	180
"Champ On Ice-Bear Skater Trio", rare, 9" long	400	600	800
"Circus Acrobatic Seal and Ball", 5" high	80	120	160
"Circus Bugler", 1950s, (w/trombone), 7" tall	300	450	600
"Circus Clown and Monkey", 1950s, 5" high	150	225	300
"Circus Clown on Ball" (?), 1950s, 5-1/2" high	150	225	300
"Circus Cyclist", 1950s, 6-1/2" tall	150	225	300
"Circus Parade", 1950s, 11-1/2" long	200	300	400
"Circus Seal", 1950s, (w/plastic ball on nose), 6-1/2" high	70	105	140

TPS Pango Pango with box. Photo by Scott Smiles.

TPS Cyclist-Gay 90s. Photo by Scott Smiles.

TPS Hockey Player with box. Photo by Don Hultzman.

	C6	C8	C10
"Cleo Clown-The Dogs", 1950s, 4-1/2" high	200	300	400
"Climbing Panda", 1970s, all plastic, 6" high	40	60	80
"Climbing Pirate", 1950s, (string climber), 6" long	120	180	240
"Climbo the Climbing Clown", 1950s, (string climber), 6" long	150	225	300
"Clown Jalopy Cycle", 1950s, friction, 9" long	200	300	400
"Clown Juggler", 1950s, 6" tall	200	300	400
"Clown Juggler w/Monkey", 1950s, 9 1/2" tall	600	900	1200
"Clown Making The Lion Jump Thru The Flaming Hoop", 1950s, 4-1/2"	180	270	360
"Clown on Rollerskates", 1950s, 5-3/4" tall	200	300	400
"Clown Trainer and His Acrobatic Dog", 1950s, 4-1/2" high	150	225	300
"Cock-A-Doodle", 1960s, 8" long	50	75	100
"Combat Tank On Battle Front", 1950s, 6-1/4" x 15" base, w/2 1/4" tin windup tank	120	180	240
"Comical Clara", 1950s, 5-1/2" tall	350	525	700
"Coney Island Scooter", 1950s, 10" square w/2 1/2" tin bumper car	100	150	200
"Dancing Couple", 1950s, 5-1/2" tall	90	135	180
"Dreamland Airport", 1950s, 6-1/2" x 12" base w/3 1/2" tin helicoper	90	135	180
"Drive Tester", 1950s, 7" x 10-1/2" base and 2 2" tin cars	80	120	160
"Educational Pet Pooch", 1950s, 4" high	100	150	200

	C6	C8	C10
"Fishing Bear", 1950s, 7-1/2" high	100	150	200
"Fishing Monkey on Whale", 1950s, 9" long	400	600	800
"Flying Birds w/voice", 1950s, (includes 2 tin birds), 4" diameter base	200	300	400
"Gay 90's Cyclist", 1950s, 7" high	150	225	300
"Girl Skipping Rope", 1950s, 12" long, 6" high	150	225	300
"Girl w/Chickens", 1950s, 6" tall, 5" long	100	150	200
"Happy Caterpillar", 1950s, 13" long	80	120	160
"Happy Hippo", 1950s, 5-1/2" long	350	525	700
"Happy Skaters" (bears), 1950s, 6-1/2" tall	250	375	500
"Happy Skaters" (monkey), 1950s, 5-1/2" tall	250	375	500
"Happy Skaters" (rabbit), 1950s, 5-1/2" tall	250	375	500
"Happy the Violinist", 1950s, 9" tall	150	225	300
"Hockey Player", 1950s, 6" tall	150	225	300
"Hungry Whale", 1950s, w/3" long small whale or fish, 5" long	40	60	80
"Joe-The Acrobat", (clown), 1950s, 5-1/2" high	150	225	200
"Juggling Clown", 1950s, 8-1/2" tall	200	300	400

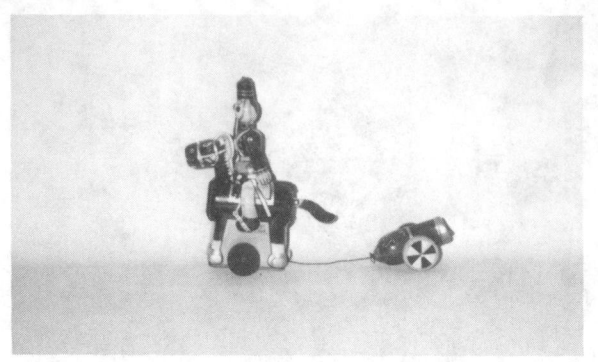

TPS Mounted Cavalryman with Cannon. Photo by Don Hultzman.

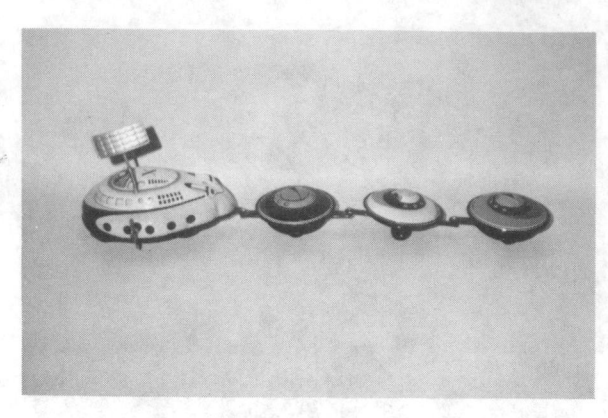

TPS Satellite Fleet. Photo by Don Hultzman.

	C6	C8	C10
"Ladder Truck", 1950s, 2" tin fire engine, 5-1/2" x 9-1/4" base	80	120	160
"Lady Bug Family Parade", 1950s, 12" long	80	120	160
"Lucky Monkey Playing Billiards", 1950s, (includes plastic balls), 6" long	150	225	300
"Magic Choo Choo", 1950s, 5-1/2" x 9-1/4" base w/2 1/4" tin locomotive	90	135	180
"Magic Circus", 1960s, (includes tin seal and monkey), 6" high	80	120	160
"Magic Cross Road", 1950s, 5-1/2" x 9-1/4" base w/2 1/4" tin locomotive	90	135	180
"Magic Tunnel", 1950s, 6" x 9" base w/2" tin "Dreamland Bus"	90	135	180
"Mailman with Geese", 1950s, 6" tall	150	225	300
"Mama Kangaroo w/Playful Baby In Her Pouch", 1950s, 6" tall	100	150	200
"Midget Lady Bug", 1950s, 7-1/2"tall	60	90	120
"Missle Robot", 1960s, 6" high	80	120	160
"Mr. Caterpillar", 1950s, 12" long	50	75	100
"Monkey Basketball Player", 1950s, 7" high	150	225	300
"Monkey Golfer", 1950s, assembled 7-1/2" long	150	225	300
"Monkey on Whale", 1950s, 4" long, 3-3/4" high	300	450	600
"Mountain Climber", 1950s, (string climber), 6-1/2" long	120	180	240
"Mounted Cavalryman w/Cannon", 1960s, 5-1/2" high w/2 1/2" long tin cannon	300	450	600
"Mouse Race Cat", 1950s, 10" x 10"	90	135	180
"Oscar the Seal", 1950s, 5" tall	80	120	160
"Pango Pango", 1950s, 6" tall	120	180	240
"Performing Seal and Monkey w/Fish", 1950s, 4-1/2" tall	300	450	600

	C6	C8	C10
"Playland Scooter", 1950s, 6" x 9" base w/2" long tin car	90	135	180
"Police Patrol", 1950s, 5-1/2"x 9-1/2" base and 2" tin police car	80	120	160
"Pop Eye Pete", 1950s, 5-1/2" tall	350	525	700
"Popeye and Oliveoyl", 1950s, 9-1/2"	1000	1500	2000
"Popeye Cyclist", 1950s, 6-1/2" high	400	600	800
"Popeye Skater", 1950s, (Linemar), 6-1/2" tall	500	750	1000
"Rabbit and Bear Playing Ball", 1950s, 19" long, 5" high	200	300	400
"Samson the Strongman", 1950s, 6" tall	250	375	500
"Satellite Fleet", 1960s, 12" long	150	225	300
"Seal and Monkey w/Fish", 1950s, rare, 5" high, 4" long	250	375	500
"Shuttle Zoo Train", 1950s, 5-1/2" x 9-1/4" base and 2 pc. tin train	80	120	160
"Skating Chef", 1950s, 6" tall	150	225	300
"Skating Chef", (Black), 1950s, 6"	250	375	500
"Skip Rope Animals", 1950s, 8" long	110	165	220
"Skippy the Tricky Cyclist", 1950s, 6" tall	150	225	300

UNIQUE Artie the Clown in his Crazy Car. Courtesy Don Hultzman. Photo Ron Chojnacki.

	C6	C8	C10
"Sports Car Race", 1960s, 8" x 14" base and 4 plastic racers	100	150	200
"Susie the Ostrich", 1950s, rare, 5-1/2" high	300	450	600
"Suzy Bouncing Ball", 1950s, 5 1/2" tall	90	135	180
"Take-off Airport", 1950s, 5-1/2" x 9-1/2" base w/3" tin airplane (fighter)	80	120	160
"Tippy Toy Train", 1960s, gravity action, 6" diameter, 4" high	60	90	120
"Touchdown Pete", 1950s, 5" tall	170	235	340
"Tricycle Tot", 1960s, 5-1/2" long	70	105	140
"Trombone Player", 1950s, (w/trombone), 5-1/4" tall	150	225	300
"Tumbling Chimp", 1950s, 4-1/2"	150	225	300
"Violin Player", 1950s, (w/violin), 5-1/4" tall	200	300	400
"Wagon Fantasyland", 1950s, 11" long	150	225	300

End TPS

	C6	C8	C10
Trolley, horse-drawn, German	150	225	300
Two rotating blimps and two cars, w/passengers, that spin and rotate, German, 11-1/2" high	600	900	1200
"**2001** Circus", 1930, 8" long	450	675	900
Train Set, 1930s, 3 pieces, wooden wheels, 20" long	150	225	300
"U.S.A. Army", D-105 Truck, 10-1/2" long	100	150	200

UNIQUE "Kiddy Cyclist". Courtesy Scott Smiles.

UNIQUE ART MFG. CO.

Unique Art Mfg. Co. was in business from 1916, when it introduced its Merry Juggler and Charlie Chaplin. In 1931 it was located at Waverly and Peshine Avenues in Newark, New Jersey. Its president was Wm. Marbe, and there were 28 male employees (no females listed). In 1934 employees numbered 110 male and 165 female (same address). In a 1946-47 directory the address was 200 Waverly Avenue, Newark and the president was Smuel Burger (this last name may be incorrect; the handwriting in my notes is hard to read). Employees were equally divided: 125 male and 125 female. Unique was still manufacturing toys, mainly windups, in 1952. Little else is known about the company, except that at some date, Louis Marx bought it.

	C6	C8	C10
Unique Artie the Clown in his Crazy Car	262	393	525
Unique "Bombo the Monk", 2 piece, tree 9-1/2" high, monkey 5-1/2" long, 1930s	112	180	225
Unique "Capitol Hill Racer", 1930s, 17-1/2" long w/2" tin racing car	120	180	240
Unique "Casey the Cop", early	600	900	1200
Unique "Dandy Jim" Dancer, 1921	475	712	950
Unique "Daredevil Motor Cop", 1940s, 8-1/2" long	200	300	400
Unique "Finnegan", 1930s, w/cardboard luggage, 14" long	150	225	300

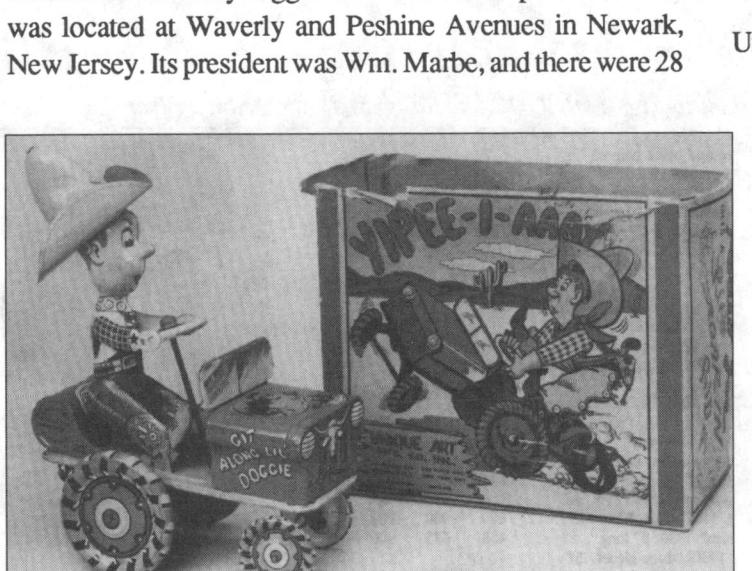

UNIQUE G.I. Joe and his Jouncing Jeep. Courtesy Scott Smiles. Photo by Mike Adams.

UNIQUE Rodeo Joe Crazy Car. Courtesy Mapes Auctioneers & Appraisers.

UNIQUE "Lincoln Tunnel". Courtesy Christie's East.

UNIQUE Flying Circus. Photo by Don Hultzman.

Walking Man, carring red top hat over his head, head revolves to reveal three different faces. Photo courtesy PB Eighty-Four.

Top: "2001" Circus. Bottom: UNIQUE Krazy Kar, 1940. Courtesy Lloyd W. Ralston Auctions.

UNIQUE "Jazzbo Jim- The Dancer on the Roof". Courtesy Sotheby's New. York.

Left to Right: UNIQUE Sky Rangers, Marx Skybird Flyer. Courtesy Phillips, New York.

UNIQUE "Bombo the Monk".
Courtesy Scott Smiles.

UNIQUE "G.I. Joe and K-9 Pups".
Courtesy Scott Smiles.

	C6	C8	C10
Unique Flying Circus, elephant supports flying plane and flying clown	900	1400	2000
Unique "G.I. Joe and His Jouncing Jeep", Post WW II, 7"	175	262	350
Unique "G.I. Joe and the K-9 Pups", circa 1941, 9" high	150	225	300
Unique "Gertie the Galloping Goose", 1930s, 9 1/2" long	142	213	285
Unique "Hee Haw" donkey pulling milk cart, 10" long	140	210	280
Unique "Hillbilly Express", 1930s, 3 pcs. and 3 1/4" tin locomotive, 18" long	150	225	300
Unique "Hobo Train", 1920s, dog biting pants of hobo atop train, 8-1/2".	300	450	600
Unique "Hott an' Tott" musical band, 1920s	650	975	1300
Unique "Jazzbo Jim" dancer, new in 1921	375	562	750
Unique "Jazzbo Jim-The Dancer on the Roof", 1920s, 10" high, base 5" x 3" x 3"	312	468	625
Unique "Kid-Go-Round" plastic horsemen and boat	125	188	250
Unique "Kiddy Cyclist", 1930s, steers figure 8 pattern and rings bell, 8-3/4" tall	200	300	400
Unique Krazy Kar, new in 1921	300	450	600
Unique "Lincoln Tunnel", moving vehicles, cop, 1935, 24" long	275	363	550

	C6	C8	C10
Unique "Motorcycle Cop", 1930s, 9" long	220	330	440
Unique Musical Sail-Way Carousel w/3 kids in spinning plastic boats, 9" tall	170	255	340
Unique "Pecking Goose", Witch and Cat	360	540	720
Unique "Rodeo Joe" Crazy Car	175	262	350
Unique "Rollover Motorcycle Cop", 1935	200	300	400
Unique "Sky Rangers" plane and Zeppelin revolving from tower, 1933	200	300	400

End Unique

	C6	C8	C10
Walking Man, carrying red top hat over his head, head revolves to reveal 3 different faces	450	675	900
Wilkins Roadster, early w/driver, 9" long	300	450	600
Wilkins Auto, early, woman driver, 9" long	290	425	580
Wolverine Acrobat	110	165	220
Wolverine "Acrobatic Monkeys", No. 810, 1930s, 10" diameter base	200	300	400
Wolverine "Autolift", 1930s, includes 2 1/2" tin car and 4 sections of track, 10-1/4" high	125	188	250

S.S. Wolverine Oceanliner.

	C6	C8	C10
Wolverine "Drummer Boy", 14" high....	130	195	260
Wolverine "Drum Major", No. 27, patent 1892546, 1930s, 13-1/4" tall on circular 4-1/4" base...............	170	225	340
Wolverine "Drum Major" No. 27, pat. 1892546, 1930s, 13-5/8" tall on rectangular 4-1/2"x 6-1/2" base.	200	30	400
Wolverine Farm Wagon, 1950s, plastic, 10" long..............................	25	38	50
Wolverine Jet Roller Coaster and small car, 21" long extended...........	130	195	260
Wolverine "Loop-A-Loop", 1930s, includes small car No. 30, 19"........	150	225	300
Wolverine Luxury Liner........................	90	135	180
Wolverine "Mechanical Man on the Flying Trapeze", 1930s, 8-1/2" high	100	150	200
Wolverine "Merry-Go-Round", 1930s, includes 4 tin-litho flags, No. 31, 11" diameter, 12" high....................	225	338	450
Wolverine, "Neck & Neck", 1940s, horse racing game, 36" long............	70	105	140
Wolverine Pontiac Mystery Car...........	100	150	200
Wolverine "S.S. Wolverine", 14-1/2" long....................................	100	150	200

	C6	C8	C10
Wolverine Sandy Andy Caterpillar Tractor, Trailer, 21" long.................	425	638	850
Wolverine "Sandy Andy Circus", dancing toy.....................	150	225	300
Wolverine "Sandy Andy" Tank, 14" long................................	90	135	180
Wolverine "Zilotone", w/6 interchangeable records, 1930s...............	500	750	1050
Woodhaven "Robot Bus w/the Mechanical Brain", 1940s, 13-1/2" long.......................................	100	150	200
Woodhaven Tractor, 1916.....................	40	60	80
World on base, windup plane circles it, German............................	100	150	200
Wyandotte Carnival, 16" x 11"..........	425	638	850
Wyandotte Carousel, 5-1/4" high.........	175	262	350
Wyandotte Chicken pulling Chick in Cart, 7-1/2" long.........................	60	90	120
Wyandotte Duck pulling tin Easter cart, litho, wooden wheels, 15" long..	75	112	150
Wyandotte "Hoky-Poky", handcar w/2 clowns.....................................	112	168	225
Wyandotte "Man On The Flying Trapeze", 1930s, 9" high.................	125	188	250
Wyandotte "Red Ranger Ride 'Em Cowboy", circa 1930s, rocker base, No. 515, 6-1/2" high........................	112	168	225
Yone Chef, Japanese, c. 1960s............	90	135	180
Yone Soldier, Japanese, c. 1960s.........	90	135	180
Yone Pirate, Japanese, c. 1960s............	115	172	230

BATTERY-OPERATED TOYS

by Don Hultzman

(The average mint price of these toys was $348.45 in the last edition, rising to $392.76 in this edition, an increase of 13%.)

"Made in Japan" are the words toy collectors look for in their pursuit of high-quality mechanical tin toys.

Before World War II, these words were synonymous with cheap, poor quality, drab-looking toys made from recycled materials and ideas. Most of the toys were people-animal oriented with less emphasis on vehicle, nautical, or aircraft-type toys. They were powered either by a spring or a flywheel and didn't last too long or do too much as far as play-value goes. These inexpensive, poor quality toys kept Japan a third-rate toy manufacturing nation until after World War II, when Japan's surrender resulted in economic chaos for this industrial nation.

In their quest for economic recovery and to compete in a toy market already dominated by Germany and America, the Japanese knew they had to come up with a new, different, and exciting type of toy that would make them more desirable than their competitors.

The Japanese toy designers concentrated their technology on a different type of toy operation. Not satisfied with the limited action and short duration of spring-driven or flywheel-propelled toys, the toy engineers developed a small electric motor, powered by flashlight batteries. This mini-motor took up less room than other mechanisms, had a longer-running duration, and enabled the toy to perform more functions. This development opened up an entirely new dimension in toy design and introduced the concept of the battery-operated toy!

The Toy designers integrated this new concept into hundreds of automaton-like toys, capable of as many as eight different type of actions all in one cycle. These unique toys were an instant hit with the foreign market, especially the USA. These clever, unusual and high-quality toys made Japan the dominant toy producer and exporter for the next 20-30 years.

Again, Japan flooded the market with these ingenious, well-made toys while quality control remained a high priority. These merits were not only apparent in their figural toys, but also in their vehicle line. Here, the Japanese toy makers concentrated on very fine detail and quality especially in their scale-model passenger cars, with the ultimate goal of making them look like the "real thing" and they succeeded. Their workmanship carried over into their other vehicle lines, such as motorcycles, emergency and construction vehicles as well as their novelty (silly) and comic character cars, trucks, and space toys.

No other nation was able to equal or surpass the impetus & determination of the Japanese toy makers until Japan relinquished its domination by re-aligning its economy in the electronic-automotive field.

Now that they are approaching middle age, it is no wonder that these fine toys remain in great demand today and often very pricey!

Don Hultzman confesses he has always been a collector of toys, but didn't really get serious about the hobby until ten or so years ago, not only collecting but also repairing them. Born and raised in Cleveland, Ohio, he received a masters degree in Guidance and Administration at Kent State, and is currently employed by the Panama City School System as a school Counselor. He does free-lance writing as a science consultant to the encyclopedia department of World Publishing Co. and lives in Brunswick Hills, Ohio. Many of his tin wind up toys can be seen in the 1983 MGM movie "A Christmas Story", and 1994's "It Runs In The Family".

CONDITION OF A TOY AND ITS RELATION TO PRICE

The value of a battery operated toy depends not only on its desirability, rarity and complexity, but very much on its condition. A toy in "mint" condition is generally worth twice as much as a toy in "good" condition. A toy in "very good" condition will be equally priced between "good" and "mint".

C-10- "Mint", means just that - the condition in which the toy was originally issued - **perfect** - regardless of age. It will also be in perfect mechanical condition, complete with all accessory parts when applicable, and will look "brand new". The cloth or fur (plush) covering on some battery toys may reveal some discoloration (yellowing) due to age, but this should not affect its value as a "mint" toy as long as it is clean. All toys in this category must be in perfect working condition. The original box in mint condition will significantly enhance the value of any "mint" toy.

C-8- "Very Good", indicates the condition of a battery toy that has seen some use and is starting to show its age. It will still be in perfect working order and have all its accessory parts where applicable. It will have some age-soiling, but will have no rust or corrosion. Overall, it will have an appearance of "freshness" and still be highly desirable to the fussy collector.

C-6- "Good", applies to a battery toy that has seen considerable use, wear and tear, some age soiling, but still in perfect working condition with no missing parts of accessories. The "wet" toys may show some slight surface rust that can be easily removed. A toy in "good" condition is still a welcome addition to any toy collection, but will be targeted for upgrading by a piece in better condition.

Any battery toy below the condition of "good" will reflect a drastic reduction in value. Toys in good shape, but missing accessory parts, will not lose as much value as those that are severely rusted, corroded, painted over, have parts broken off and are totally inoperable. These "poor" toys are usually collected for their "scrap value" by the toy repairer and seldom are they worth more than $10.00.

The key to grading is to use common sense and avoid wishful thinking. Since grading the condition of a toy may be difficult at times, consulting with an expert in the field, if possible, could clear up any lingering doubts. (See back section of this guide for references of toy collectors.)

GUIDELINES FOR THE CARE AND REPAIR OF YOUR BATTERY-OPERATED TOY

by Don Hultzman

Your prized battery toy needs T.L.C. and when it stops working, you now have a frustrating disaster on your hands. To avoid this, the following suggestions should be of some help:

Battery toys, like other mechanical toys, should be operated periodically to keep them loosened up. A lightweight spray lubrication now and then will help considerably if the mechanism is accessible. Do not over-lubricate as the excess may stain any cloth or fur covering on some battery toys.

A good quality car wax or polish will keep the lithographed and bare metal parts looking like new - especially on the "wet" toys. Always test an obscure lithographed area to make sure the polish doesn't soften or dissolve the paint. Care should be exercised when polishing metal parts adjoining any cloth or plush covering, as the substance may stain the coverings. Light surface rust usually disappears with a careful polishing. Nothing can be done for deep rust or corrosion without ruining the value of the toy. Repainting will only further reduce the value and is not recommended.

Should your battery toy fail to operate, the following steps might be helpful:

1. Make sure it is not gunked-up and that no moving parts are binding.
2. Make sure the battery contacts are not dirty or corroded - if so then clean them with crocus cloth. ALWAYS USE FRESH BATTERIES!
3. Lightly tap the toy with your finger or **lightly** nudge one of the moving parts while the switch is "on".

If none of the above steps work, then your toy needs "major surgery". This means the toy must be completely torn down, repaired and reassembled. Most battery toys are repairable as long as they have not been destructively tampered with and no parts are missing or corroded beyond repair. This job is best left to an expert in toy repair and should never be attempted by one who doesn't know what he is doing. Expert repairs will not affect the value of a battery toy so long as the repair is **undetectable** and the toy looks and functions **exactly** as if did before the repair. Such repairs are acceptable in toy collecting circles. Expert repairs are also expensive but well worth the investment if it means the difference between a "mint" (and prized toy) and one below the grade of "good", since an inoperable toy is practically worthless, regardless of condition

	C6	C8	C10
"A-B-C Fairy Train," 1950s, M-T Co., 14½" long, one pc., four actions	80	120	160
"Accordion Bear," 1950s, "Y" Co., 10½" tall, six actions	220	330	440
"Accordion Bear," 1950s, MST Co. (Flare Toy), 9¼" high, five actions	140	210	280
"Accordion Player Bunny," 1950s, Alps Co., 12" tall, 9" long, six actions	200	300	400
"Accordion Player Hobo With Baby Monkey Playing Cymbals," 1950s, Alps Co., six actions	250	375	500
"Acrobat Clown," 1960s, 9" tall, Y-M Co., minor toy	60	90	120
"Acro Chimp Porter," 1960s, Y-M Co., 8½" tall, minor toy	50	75	100
"Acrobat Robot," 1970s, S-H Co., 4½" tall, three actions	50	75	100
"Air Cargo Prop-Jct Airplane - Seaboard World Airlines," 1960's, Marx Co., 12" long, 14½" wingspan, five actions	200	300	400
"Air Control Tower," 1960s, Bandai Co., 11" high, 37" span (extended), four actions (includes detachable airplane and helicopter	200	300	400
"Air Defense Pom-Pom Gun," 1950s, Linemar Co., 14" long, five actions	130	195	260
"Air Taxi Helicopter" 1960s, Haji Co., three actions	50	75	100
"Aircraft Carrier" - with multi-actions, 1950's, Marx Co., six actions, 20" long	300	450	600
"Aircraft Carrier - Forrestal, 1950's, Linemar, 13¾" long, three actions, (includes detachable plastic airplane)	200	300	400
"Aircraft Carrier," 1950s, Marx Co., 20" long, eight actions	200	300	400
"Airport Saucer," 1960s, MT Co., 8" diameter, four actions	90	135	180
"Airport Saucer", 1960's, S-T Co., four actions , 9" diameter	100	150	200
"All Stars Mr. Baseball Jr.", 1950's, K Co., three actions, RARE, (includes 8 plastic balls)	500	750	1000
"Alley - The Exciting New Roaring Stalking Alligator," 1960s, Marx Co., 17½" long, five actions	150	225	300
"American Airlines - 4 Prop Airliner," 1960s, Waco Co., 12" long, 16½" wingspan, four actions	120	180	240
"American Airlines DC-7" (with automatic turnover propellers), ca.1950s, Linemar, 7 action, 19" wingspan	200	300	400
"American Airlines Airliner DC-7," Multiaction," 1960s, Yonezawa Co., 21" long 23½" wingspan, seven actions	195	285	380
"American Airlines Airliner DC-7," 1960s, Linemar Co., 17½" long, 19" wingspan, seven actions	200	300	400
"American Airlines Electra," 1950s, Linemar Co., 18" long, 19½" wingspan	200	300	400
"American Airlines Flagship Caroline" 1950s, Linemar Co., 18" long, 19½" wingspan, three actions	190	285	380
"American Circus Television Truck" 1950's, Exelo Co., 9¼" long, six actions, RARE, (includes detachable metal antenna)	600	900	1200
"Amphibian Navy Patrol Plane" with Flashing Lights, 1950s, Alps Co., 13" long - 15" wingspan, five actions, RARE	900	1350	1800
"Amtrak Locomotive" 1960s, ST Co., 16" long, minor toy	60	90	120
"Andy Gard - Brink's Armored Car-Bank," 1950s, General Molds & Plastics Corp. 6¾" long, minor toy	40	60	80
"Andy Gard Combat Knight No. 143," 1960s, General Molds & Plastic Corp., 10-1/4" high, three actions (includes lance, stanchion 3 plastic rings and helmet plume)	50	75	100
"Animated Santa on Rotating Globe," 1950s, HTC Co., 15" high, five actions	400	600	800
"Animated Squirrel," 1950s, S&E Co., 8½" tall, eight actions, rare	100	150	200
"Answer Game Machine" robot, 1960s, Ichida Co., 14½" tall, educational toy, eight actions	400	600	800
"Anti-Aircraft Jeep," 1950s, "K" Co., 9½" long, five actions	100	150	200
"Anti-Aircraft Jeep", 1950s, T-N Co., 11" long, six actions, (includes detachable tin radar antenna)	250	375	500
"Anti-Aircraft Unit No. 1," 1950s, Linemar Co., 12½" long, three electrical actions and three manual actions	150	225	300
"Antique Gooney Car," 1960s, Alps Co., 9" long, four actions	70	105	140

Accordion Bear. Photo by Don Hultzman.

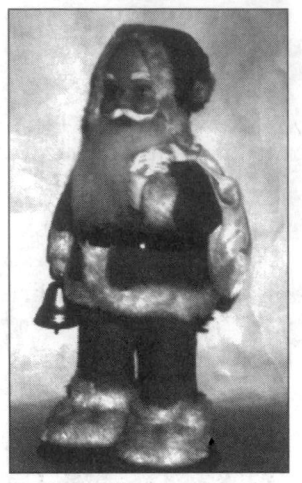

Automated Santa. Photo by Don Hultzman.

Air Defense Pom-Pom Gun. Photo by Don Hultzman.

Antique Gooney Car. Photo by Don Hultzman.

American Airlines Electra.. Photo by Don Hultzman.

Arthur A-Go-Go. Photo by Don Hultzman.

Accordion Player Hobo with Baby Monkey Playing Cymbals. Photo by Don Hultzman.

American Circus Television Truck. Photo by Don Hultzman.

Acrobat Robot. Photo by Don Hultzman.

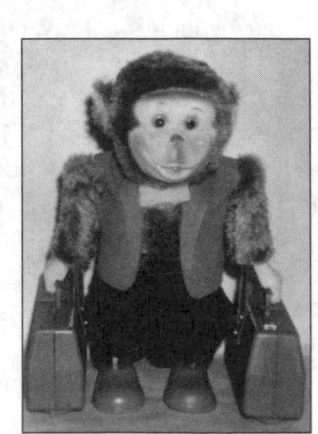

Acro Chimp Porter. Photo by Don Hultzman.

Air Control Tower. Photo by Don Hultzman.

280

	C6	C8	C10
"Apollo II-American Eagle Lunar Module", 1960s, DSK Co., 10" high, seven actions, (includes detachable plastic antenna)	200	300	400
"Apollo Lunar Module," 1970s, DSK Co., 6" high, four actions, mostly plastic	170	205	240
"Apollo Spacecraft", 1960s, M-T Co., 10" long, four actions, (includes detachable astronaut)	200	300	400
"Apollo Space Ship USA-NASA", 1960s, M-T Co., 9" long, four actions	70	105	140
"Apollo Super Space Capsule," 1960s, S H Co., 9" high, five actions	100	150	200
"Apollo-X Moon challenger," rocket, 1960s, T-N Co., 16" long, six actions	120	180	240
"Armored Attack Set," 1960s, Marx Co., jeep 6¼" long and tank 5¼" long, (plus 15 2" plastic figures)	150	225	300
"Army Radio Jeep - J1490," 1950s, Linemar Co, 7¼" long, four actions	100	150	200
"Army Helicopter" - Huey by Bell, 1960s, T-N Co., six actions, 10½" long	90	135	180
"Arthur A-Go-Go," 1960s, Alps Co., 10" high, six actions, (includes detachable cymbals and drum set)	200	300	400
"Astro Captain", 1960s, Daiya Co., 6½" tall, three actions, RARE	300	450	600
"Astro Dog," 1960s, "Y" Co., 11" high, 2 cycles, five actions (looks like Snoopy)	100	150	200
"Astro Dog," 1960s, Y-M Co., 11" tall, three actions	90	135	180
"Astrobase" (motorized), 1960s, Ideal Co., 20" high, six actions	140	210	280
"Atom Motorcycle", 1950s, M-T Co., five actions, 11¾" long	450	675	900
"Atom Rocket 7", vehicle with fins, 1950s, M-T Co., 9½" long, four actions	120	180	240
"Atomic Boat", 1950s, Famus Co., minor toy, 15" long	150	225	300
"Atomic Fighter" robot, 1950s, S-H Co., 11" tall, five actions	100	150	200
"Atomic Rocket X-1800", 1960s, M-T Co., three actions, 9" long	150	225	300
"Attacking Martian Robot," 1950s, S-H Co., 11½" tall, 7 actions - two cycles	120	180	240

	C6	C8	C10
"Auto-Top Ferrari Convertible", 1960s, Bandai Co., three actions, 11" long	450	675	900
"Automatic Toll Gate", 1955, Sears, 16"x17" base, six actions, (includes 8" tin Valiant)	150	225	300
"Automated Santa," ca. 1960s, Santa Creations Co., 3 actions, 10¼" tall	100	150	200
"B-58 Hustler Jet", 1950s, Marx Co., four actions, 21" long, 12" wing-span	450	675	900
"Baby Carriage", 1950s, T-N Co., 11¾" long, 7" high, minor toy (includes plastic baby bottle to activate switch)	60	90	120
"Ball Blowing Clown," 1950s, T-N Co., 11" tall, three actions (with ball)	180	270	360
"Ball Playing Bear," 1940s, no marking, 10-1/2" tall, six actions (includes five celluloid balls and one umbrella), rare	200	300	400
"Ball Playing Dog," 1950s, Linemar Co., 9" high, three actions	120	180	240
"Balloon Blowing Monkey," 1950s, Alps Co., 11⅛" tall, five actions with balloon	100	150	200
"Balloon Blowing Teddy Bear," 1950s, Alps Co., 11⅛" tall, six actions with balloon	100	150	200
"Balloon Vendor," 1960s, Y Co., 12" tall, four actions (includes four plastic balloons and tin tray)	130	195	260
"Baragon", 1960s, Bullmark Co., three actions, 10" tall	290	435	580
"Barber Bear," 1950s, T-N Co., (Linemar) 9½" tall, five actions	300	450	600
"Barking Boxer Dog," 1950s, Marx, 7" long, minor toy	50	75	100
"Barking Dog," 1950s, STS Co., 7" long, 7" high, four actions, two cycles	50	75	100
"Barking Spaniel Dog," 1950s, Marx, 7" long, minor toy	50	75	100
"Barney Bear Drummer," 1950s, Alps Co., 11" tall, five actions, resembles "Steiff" bear	130	195	260
"Barnyard Rooster," 1950s, Marx, 10" high, five actions	100	150	200
"Bartender," 1960s, T-N Co., 11½" tall, six actions	40	60	80
"Batmobile," 1972 National Periodical Publications, ASC Co., 12" long, three actions	180	270	360

Aircraft Carrier. Photo by Don Hultzman.

Aircraft Carrier - Forrestal. Photo by Don Hultzman.

Alley ... Alligator. Photo by Don Hultzman.

Amphibian Navy Patrol Plane. Photo by Ron Chojnacki. Courtesy Don Hultzman.

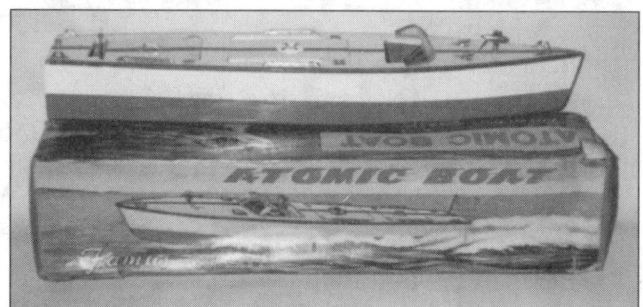

Atomic Boat. Photo by Don Hultzman.

Astro Dog. Photo by Don Hultzman.

Atom Motorcycle. Photo by Don Hultzman.

Armored Attack Set. Photo by Don Hultzman.

282

Anti-Aircraft Jeep. Photo by Don Hultzman.

Bartender. Photo by Bill Kaufman. Courtesy Good Old Days.

Big Wheel Coca-Cola Truck. Photo by Don Hultzman.

Bubble Blowing Popeye. Photo by Don Hultzman.

Busy Secretary. Photo by Don Hultzman.

Barking Spaniel Dog, Sleeping Baby Bear, Barking Boxer Dog, Pap Bear - Smoking.

Ball Blowing Clown, Sammy Wong-the Tea Totaler, Nutty Nibs.

Ball Playing Dog. Photo by Don Hultzman.

Baragon. Photo by Don Hultzman.

Frankie the Rollerskating Monkey, Buttons - Puppy with a Brain, Jocko - the Drinking Monkey, Blushing Willie. Courtesy Don Hultzman. Photo by Ron Chojnacki.

Barber Bear. Photo by Don Hultzman.

Bear Target Game. Photo by Don Hultzman.

Big John - The Indian Chief. Photo by Don Hultzman.

Batmobile. Photo by Don Hultzman.

Bongo Player. Photo by Don Hultzman.

Bowling Bank. Photo by Don Hultzman.

Bubble Blowing Musician. Photo by Don Hultzman.

Bubble Blowing Kangaroo. Photo by Don Hultzman.

Brewster the Rooster. Photo by Don Hultzman.

Black Smithy Bear. Photo by Ron Chojnacki. Courtesy Don Hultzman.

	C6	C8	C10
"Battery Locomotive No. 123," 1950s, T-N Co., 10" long, three actions	30	45	60
"Bear Chef" (Cutey Cook), 1960s, "Y" Co., 9½" tall, five actions, (includes chef hat and tin litho egg)	150	225	300
"Bear Target Game," 1950s, M-T Co., 8¾" high and 4"x5" base (includes gun, rubber tipped darts, detachable drum), four actions	200	300	400
"Bear - the Cashier," 1950s, M-T Co., 7½" high, five actions	190	285	380
"Bear the Magician", 1950s, MTS Co., nine actions, 12½" tall, RARE	1000	1500	2000
"Beauty Parlor Bear," 1950s, S&E Co., 9½" high, seven actions, rare	600	900	1200
"Begging Puppy," 1960s, "Y" Co., 9" long, six actions	40	60	80
"Bengali - The Exciting New Growling, Prowling Tiger," 1961, Marx Co., Linemar Div., 18½" long from nose to end of tail, 2 cycles, three actions	100	150	200
"Betty Bruin - Cashier," 1950s, Linemar, 9" tall, six actions	*See Suzy-Cashier Bear*		
"Big Dipper", 1960s, Technofix Co., minor toy, 21" long - 11" high, (includes three tin cars)	100	150	200
"Big Hunter - Automatic Gun," 1950s, Tada Co., 21" long - extended, three actions	50	75	100
"Big John," 1960s, Alps Co., 12" high, three actions	60	90	120
"Big John - The Indian Chief," ca. 1960s, T-N Co., 5 actions, 12½" tall	90	135	180
"Big Loo - Your Friend From The Moon," 1960s, Marx Co., 38" tall, twelve actions (includes balls, darts, compass, etc.)	1000	1500	2000
"Big Max Robot," 1958, Remco Co., 8" long, 7" tall, four actions	100	150	200
"Big Ring Circus Truck," 1950s, M-T Co., 13" long, three actions	140	210	280
"Big Shot Cadillac," 1950s, T-N Co., 10" long, four actions, Rare	200	300	400
"Big Wheel Coca Cola Truck," 1970s, Taiyo Co., three actions	80	120	160
"Big Wheel Family Camper," 1970s, 10" long, three actions	60	90	120
"Big Wheel Ice Cream Truck", 1970's 10" long, three actions	60	90	120
"Biller Train No. 573", 1950s, T-N Co., 13" long (includes rubber cable track and two hopper cars), a minor toy - Rare	70	105	140

	C6	C8	C10
"Billy Blastoff Space Scout," Eldon Co., 1960s, 4 actions, 16" long	90	135	180
"Billy the Kid Sheriff," 1950s, "Y" Co., 10½" tall, 2 cycles, four actions	180	270	360
"Bimbo the Clown," 1950s, Alps Co., 9¼" tall, three actions, (includes detachable hat)	300	450	600
"Bingo Clown," 1950s, T-N Co., 13" tall, three actions	200	300	400
"Blacksmith Bear," 1950s, A-1 Co., 9½" tall, six actions	180	270	360
"Black Smithy Bear," 1950s, T-N Co., 9" high, four actions, RARE	200	300	400
"Blink-A-Gear-Robot," 1960s, S-H Co., 14½" tall, five actions	400	600	800
"Blinky-the-Clown," 1950s, no marking, 10-1/2" tall, five actions (includes multicolor paper hat)	300	450	600
"Blow-Up-Ball Locomotive," 1950s, M-T Co., 9-1/2" long, minor toy, (includes celluloid ball)	80	120	160
"Blushing Willie," 1960s, Y Co., 10" tall, four actions	60	90	120
"Bobby Drinking Bear," 1950s, Y Co., 10" tall, six actions	200	300	400
"Bobby the Drumming Bear," 1950s, Alps Co., 10" tall, four actions	210	315	420
"Boeing 727 Jet Liner," 1960s, Y Co., 17½" long, 16¼" wingspan, three actions	140	210	280
"Boeing 727 Jet Plane," 1960s, M-T Co., 12½" long, 10⅜" wingspan, three actions	150	225	300
"Bomber Pilot," 1960s, K-O Co., 10½" long, 9" wingspan, six actions	190	285	380
"Bongo, Drumming Monkey," 1960s, Alps Co., 9½" high, three actions, includes plastic hat	80	120	160
"Bongo Player," 1960s, Alps Co., 10" tall, four actions	80	120	160
"Bowling Bank," 1960s, M.B. Daniel & Co., 10" long, three actions	90	135	180
"Brave Eagle," 1950s, T-N Co., 5 actions, 11" tall	90	135	180
"Breakfast Chef," 1960s, K Co., 8¼" tall, minor toy (includes plastic egg and coffee maker)	70	105	140
"Brewster the Rooster," 1950s, Marx Co., 9½" high, five actions	120	180	240
"Bristol Bulldog Airplane," T-360, S&E Co., lights, prop spins, stop & go, noise, 4 actions, 12" long, 14½" wingspan	160	240	320

Cabin Cruiser with Outboard Motor. Photo by Don Hultzman.

Caterpillar Tank M-1. Photo by Don Hultzman.

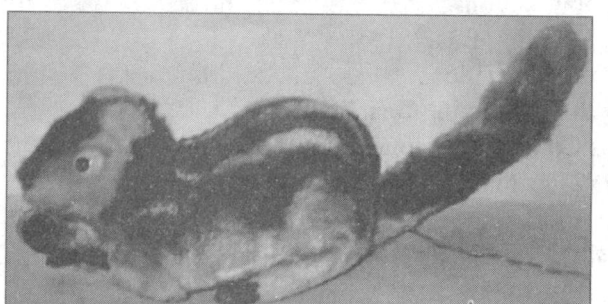

Chippy the Chipmunk. Photo by Don Hultzman.

Circus Jet. Photo by Don Hultzman.

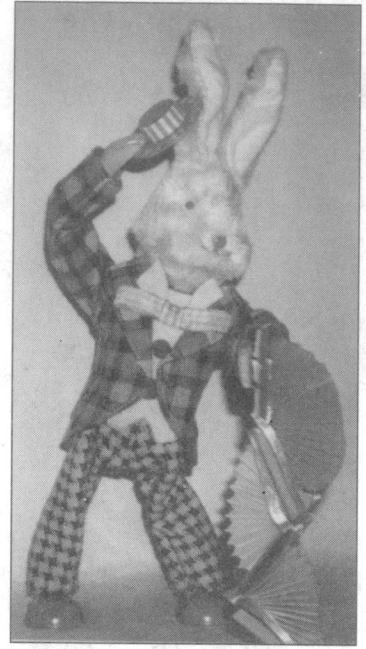

Bunny - The Magician. Photo by Don Hultzman.

Captain Blushwell. Photo by Don Hultzman.

Clown & Monkey Car. Photo by Don Hultzman.

Clancy the Great, Ideal. Photo by Ron Chojnacki. Courtesy Don Hultzman.

Cragstan Astronaut. Photo by Don Hultzman.

Clown & Lion. Photo by Don Hultzman.

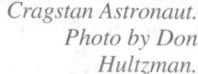

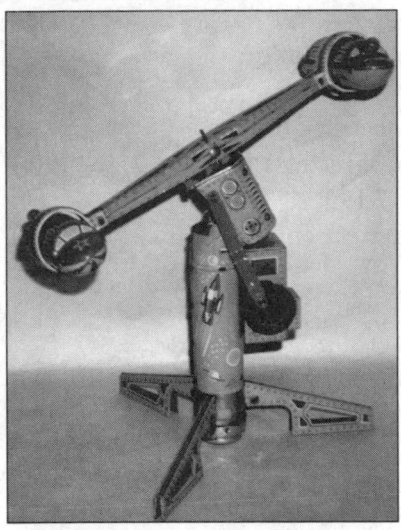

Coney Island Rocket Ride. Photo by Don Hultzman.

Cragstan Roulette - A Gambling Man. Photo by Don Hultzman.

Drinking Dog. Photo by Don Hultzman.

Coca Cola Dispenser Bank. Photo by Don Hultzman.

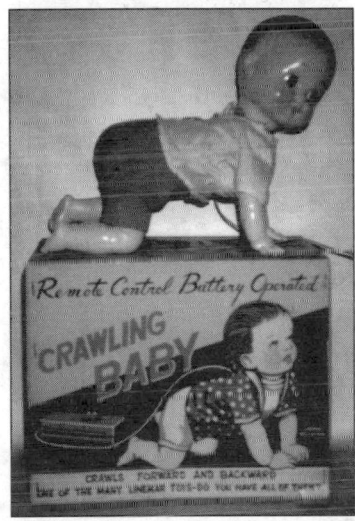

Crawling Baby. Photo by Don Hultzman.

Drum Monkey. Photo by Don Hultzman.

Electro Train Transcontinental. Photo by Don Hultzman.

Electric Vibraphone. Photo by Don Hultzman.

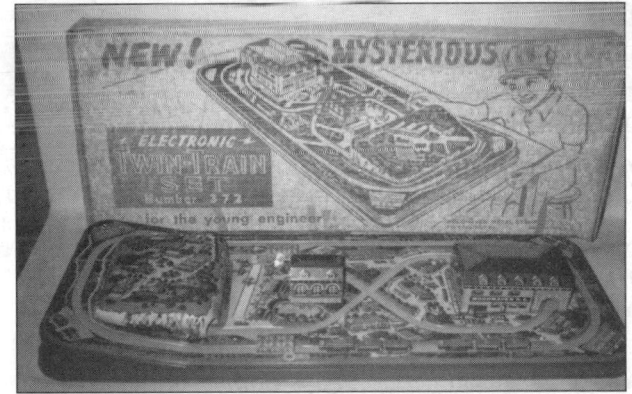

Electronic Twin Train Set - Woodhaven Co.. Photo by Don Hultzman.

Crazy Car. Photo by Don Hultzman.

Electronic Periscope (Nautilus) Firing Range. Photo by Don Hultzman

287

	C6	C8	C10
"**Broadway** Trolley," 1950s, M-T Co., 10½" long, four actions - two cycles..*See "Tinkling Trolley"*			
"**Bruno** the Accordion Bear," 1950s, "Y" Co., 10½" tall, five actions	140	210	280
"**Bubble** Blowing Bear," 1950s, M-T Co., 9½" high, 4"x5" base, four actions	140	210	280
"Bubble Blowing Boil Over Car," 1950s, M-T Co., three actions, 10" long	90	135	180
"Bubble Blowing Boy," 1950s, "Y" Co., 7" high, four actions	100	200	300
"Bubble Blowing Bunny," 1950s, "Y" Co., 7" high, four actions	100	150	200
"Bubble Blowing Dog," 1950s, "Y" Co., 8" high, three actions	100	150	200
"Bubble Blowing Kangaroo," 1950s, M-T Co., 9" high (base to tip of ears), three actions - RARE	200	300	400
"Bubble Blowing Lion," 1950s, M-T Co., 7½" high, 3½"x 7" base, four actions	100	150	200
"Bubble Blowing Musician," 1950s, "Y" Co., 11" tall, three actions	200	300	400
"Bubble Blowing Monkey," 1950s, Alps Co., 10" tall, four actions, includes plastic bowl for bubble solution	100	150	200
"Bubble Blowing Popeye," 1950s, Linemar Co., 11¾" tall, five actions	1000	1500	2000
"Bubble Blowing Washing Bear," 1950s, Y Co., 8" high, three actions, (includes plastic washtub)	170	255	340
"Bubbling Bull," 1950s, Linemar Co., 6½" long, 8" high, five actions (Plastic bowl)	90	135	180
"**Bulldozer**," 1950s, T-N Co., 7½" long, five actions	60	80	120
"Bulldozer," 1950s, M-T Co., 11" long, six actions	70	105	140
"**Bunny** The Cashier," 1950s, M-T Co., five actions, 7½" high	150	225	300
"Bunny The Magician," 1950s, Alps Co., 14½" tall, five actions, (includes card-ribbon apparatus for card trick)	200	300	400
"**Burger** Chef," 1950s, "Y" Co., 9" tall, eight actions (includes chef's hat and tin-litho hamburger)	100	150	200
"**Busy** Bizzy Friendly Bug," 1950s, M-T Co., 6¼" long, three actions	60	90	120
"Busy Housekeeper, The," 1950s, Alps Co., 8½" tall, four actions	160	240	320
"Busy Housekeeper, The" (bunny) 1950s, Alps Co., 10" tall, four actions	150	225	300
"Busy Cart Robot", ca.1960s, S-H Co.,			
4 actions, (includes plastic wheelbarrow), 11" high	200	300	400
"Busy Secretary," 1950s, Linemar Co., 7½" high, 7¼" long, seven actions	150	225	300
"Busy Shoe Shining Bear," 1950s, Alps Co., 10" high, five actions	140	210	280
"**Butt** Stompin' Ashtray," 1977, Poynter Prod., 7¼" high, four actions (includes tin manhole cover, ashtray insert and 4½" high plastic shoe)	40	60	80
"**Buttons**-Puppy With A Brain," also called "Buttons The Push Button Pup," 1960s, Marx, 12" high, 8 actions	200	300	400
"**B-Z** Porter" Baggage truck, 1950s, M-T Co., 7½" long, 6½" high, minor toy, includes three pcs. of luggage (tin)	140	210	280
"B-Z Rabbit," ca. 1950s, M-T Co., 4 actions, 7" long	60	90	120
"B-Z Vendor" - ice cream cart, 1950s, M-T Co., three actions, 7½" long, RARE	450	675	900
"**Cabin** Cruiser," ca. 1950s, SGK Co., 3 actions, 21½" long	150	225	300
"Cabin Cruiser With Outboard Motor," 1950s, Linemar Co., 12" long, minor toy	100	150	200
"Cable Train," 1940s, T-N Co., 12" long, four pc. set, minor toy	80	120	160
"**Cadillac**" car, 1949, Ashai Toy Co., 10" long, three actions	140	210	280
"**Calypso** Joe," 1950s, Linemar, 11" tall, four actions - RARE	300	450	600
"**Camera** Shooting Bear", 1950s, Linemar Co., 11" tall, five actions (includes plastic worms), also called Cine-Bear	450	675	900
"**Candy** Vending Machine Bank," 1950s, Wonderful Toy Co., 9" high, five actions - RARE	600	900	1200
"**Capitol** Airlines Viscount 321," 1950s, Linemar, 11" long, 14" wingspan, four actions	160	240	320
"**Cappy** the Baggage Porter Dog," 1960s, Alps Co., 12" high, 11" long, four actions	100	150	200
"**Captain** Blushwell," 1960s, "Y" Co., 11" tall, six actions	80	120	160
"Captain Hook," 1950s, Marusan Co., 10¾" high, three actions, (includes tin sword and felt hat) RARE	800	1200	1600
"**Caterpillar**," 1950s, Alps Co., 16" long, three actions	90	135	180

	C6	C8	C10
"Caterpillar Tank M-1", 1950s, M-T Co., five actions, 8½" long, 11" long with barrel extended	150	225	300
"Central Choo Choo," 1960s, M-T Co., 15" long, three actions	40	60	80
"Champion Weight Lifter," 1960s, Y-M Co., 10" tall, five actions	100	150	200
"Chaparral 2F," car, 1960s, Alps Co., 11" long, five actions	80	120	160
"Charlie the Drumming Clown," 1950s, Alps Co., six actions (includes detachable drum and cymbals), 9½" tall	150	225	300
"Charlie Weaver," 1962, T-N Co., 12" tall, six actions	40	60	80
"Change Man Robot"-Astronaut, 1960s, S H Co., four actions 13¼" tall, RARE	4000	6000	8000
"Charm the Cobra," 1960s, Alps Co., 6" high, three actions	150	225	300
"Chee Chee Chihuahua," 1960s, Mego Co., 8" high, five actions	30	45	60
"Chef Cook," 1960s, Y Co., 11½" tall with hat on, five actions (includes tin litho egg and hat)	150	225	300
"Chemical Fire Engine," 1950s, HTC Co., 10" long, four actions	100	150	200
"Chief Robotman," 1950s, K.O. Co., 12" tall, four actions	450	675	900
"Chimp and Pup Rail Car," 1950s, T-N Co., 8" high, four actions	90	135	180
"Chimp With Xylophone," 1970s, Y Co., 12" long, 8" high, minor toy (includes 4 records and hammer)	100	150	200
"Chimpy the Drumming Monkey," 1950s, Alps Co., 9" high, six actions, includes detachable drum and cymbals	70	105	140
"Chippy the Chipmunk," 1950s, Alps Co., 12" long, (nosetip to tail tip), four actions	90	135	180
"Christmas Time," 1950s Murusan Co., 10" high, 7" base diameter, three actions - RARE	400	600	800
"Cindy the Meowing Cat," 1950s, Tomiyama Co., 12" high, (nosetip to tail tip), 2 cycles, four actions	50	75	100
"Cine Bear", See "Camera Shooting Bear"			
"Circus Elephant With Blowing Ball and Parasol," 1950s, T-N Co., 9¾" high, three actions (includes celluloid ball and tin litho umbrella), rare	150	225	300
"Circus Fire Engine," 1960s, M-T Co., 11" long, four actions	130	195	260
"Circus Jet," 1950s, T-N Co., three actions, 9" high assembled, Jet 6¼" long	90	135	180
"Circus Lion," 1950s, Rock Valley Toy Co., (Via), 11" high, four actions, includes whip and flannel carpet with levers (2 cycles)	300	450	600
"Clancy The Great," 1960s, Ideal Toy Co., three actions, 19½" tall without hat, (includes plastic hat and test coin)	100	150	200
"Climbing Donald Duck On His Friction Fire Engine," 1950s, Linemar Co., four actions, 12" long	450	675	900
"Climbing Fireman," 1950s, TPS Co., 24" high assembled, five actions (includes 3 tin ladder sections)	200	300	400
"Climbing Linesman," 1950s, T.P.S. Co., 24" high when assembled, three actions, (includes 3 tin pole sections) Rare	250	375	500
"Clown Circus Car," 1960s, M-T Co., 8½" long, 9" high, five actions	140	210	280
"Clown and Lion", 1960s, M-T Co., four actions, 11¾" high from base to top of tree	240	360	480
"Clown on Unicycle," 1960s, M-T Co., 10½" high, three actions	210	315	420
"Clown with Lion," 1950s, T-N Co., 12" high, four actions (includes spiral apparatus)	200	300	400
"Clowns Bank, The," 1940s, unmarked, 10" high, minor toy (all plastic)	80	120	160
"Clown-The-Magician No. 40244," 1950s, Alps Co., 12" tall, six actions includes card-ribbon apparatus for card trick	200	300	400
"Coca-Cola Dispenser - Bank," 1950s, Linemar Co., minor toy, 9½" tall, (includes four plastic Coke glasses and rubber stopper)	450	675	900
"Cock-A-Doodle-Doo Rooster," 1950s, Mikuni Co., 8" high, four actions	80	120	160
"Colonel Hap Hazard" Robot, 1968, Marx Co., 11¼" tall, four actions	350	525	700
"Combi-O-Mixer," 1950s, Excelo Co., (mixer-blender), 9" long, 9" high, minor toy	30	45	60
"Comic Hungry Bug," VW auto, 1970s, Tora (S-T) Co., 7¾" long, five actions	40	60	80
"Comic Musical Car," 1960s, T-N Co., four actions, 6" long, 8½" tall	70	105	140

	C6	C8	C10
"Comic Road Grader," 1950s, Bandai Co., 9" long, four actions	70	105	140
"Comic Road Roller," 1960s, Bandai Co., four actions, 9" long	70	105	140
"Coney Island Penny Machine," 1950s, Remco Co., 13" high, minor toy, (includes plastic prizes)	120	180	240
"Coney Island Rocket Ride," 1950s, Alps Co., 13½" high, four actions	400	600	800
"Continental Blue Locomotive," 1960s, M-T Co., 12½" long, 4 actions	30	45	60
"Corvair Bertone," 1970s, Bandai Co., four actions, 12" long	50	75	100
"Cowboy Riding Horse," 1950s, T-N Co., 7" high, three actions	70	105	140
"Cragstan Astronaut," 1950s, Daiya Co., 14" tall, four actions	400	600	800
"Cragstan Beep Beep Greyhound Bus," 1950s, Cragstan Co., 20" long, three actions	110	165	220
"Cragstan Biplane," 7F7, U.S. Navy, 1950s, T-N Co., 9½" long, 11½" wingspan, four actions	200	300	400
"Cragstan Biplane-7F18," 1950s, T-N Co., 12" long, 14⅜" wingspan, five actions	220	330	440
"Cragstan Crapshooter," 1950s, Y Co., 9½" tall, four actions, includes pair of small dice	100	150	200
"Cragstan Crapshooting Monkey," 1950s, Alps Co., 9" tall, three actions, includes pair of small dice	70	105	140
"Cragstan Dishwasher - Automatic," 1960s, Alps Co., 9" high, (includes 24 pc. dish sct, 2 dish baskets and metal tray), minor toy	50	75	100
"Cragstan Firebird III", 1950s, Alps Co., three actions, 11½" long	400	600	800
"Cragstan Flying Plane - With Pylon Tower," 1950s, minor toy, plane 8" long, 9½" wingspan, tower 26" high	120	180	240
"Cragstan Great Astronaut, 1960s, Alps Co., 14" tall, five actions	500	750	1000
"Cragstan's Mr. Robot," 1960s, Y Co., 10½" tall, four actions	350	525	700
"Cragstan Mother Goose," 1960s, Y Co., 8¼" high, six actions	90	135	180
"Cragstan One-Arm Bandit," 1960s, Y Co., 6¼" high, three actions, includes 3"x3¼" sign	100	150	200
"Cragstan Peanut Vendor," 1950s, T-N Co., 8" tall, five actions (includes felt hat)	180	270	360
"Cragstan Playboy," 1960s, Cragstan Co., 13" high, five actions	100	150	200
"Cragstan Roulette - A Gambling Man," 1960s, Y Co., 9" tall, five actions, (includes steel ball, chips, tin table, game sheet)	140	210	280
"Cragstan Satellite," 1950s, Cragstan Co., 8" diameter, 5½" high	90	135	180
"Cragstan Smoking Jet Plane - U.S.A.F." 1950s, T-N Co., 11½" long, 7½" wingspan, four actions	120	180	240
"Cragstan Talking Robot," 1960s, Y Co., 10½" tall, three actions	320	480	720
"Cragstan Telly Bear," 1950s, S&E Co., 8" high, six actions	240	360	480
"Cragstan Tootin'-Chuggin' Locomotive," 1950s, Cragstan Co., 24" long, three actions (longest single piece battery toy made)	70	105	140
"Cragstan Tugboat," 1950s, San Co., 12¾" long, three actions	140	210	280
"Cragstan Vertol 1107 Helicopter," 1950s, T-N Co., 13½" long, four actions, includes rotors	120	180	240
"Cragstan Western Locomotive," 1950s, Cragstan Co., 12" long, four actions	60	90	120
"Cragstan's Two Gun Sheriff," 1950s, Y Co., 9½" tall, five actions (includes tin hat)	130	195	260
"Crane Tractor," 1950s, SKK Co., 7½" long, 11½" high extended	70	105	140
"Crawling Baby," 1940s, Linemar Co., 11" long, 8½" high, minor toy	50	75	100
"Crazy Car," 1950s, Marusan Co., five actions, 9" long	60	90	120
"Cycling Daddy," 1960s, Bandai Co., 10" high, four actions	110	165	220
"Cyclist Clown," 1950s, K Co., seven actions, 7" high	200	300	400
"Cyclist Clown," 1950s, M-T Co., 6½" high, six actions	200	300	400
"Cyclist Clown," 1950s, Alps Co., 9" high, five actions	200	300	400
"Cymbal Playing Turnover Monkey, 1960s, T-N Co., 8" tall, three actions	50	75	100

Cragstan "Tootin-Chuggin Locomotive", Greyhound Bus Scenicruiser.

Fire Command Car. Photo by Don Hultzman.

Dynamic Fighter Robot. Photo by Don Hultzman.

Fighter Airplane. Photo by Don Hultzman.

Cragstan Biplane 7F18. Photo by Don Hultzman.

Flashy Jim Robot. Photo by Don Hultzman.

Excavator Robot. Photo by Don Hultzman.

Charlie Weaver. Photo by Bill Kaufman. Courtesy Good Old Days.

Farm Truck. Photo by Don Hultzman.

Farm Truck. Photo by Don Hultzman.

Fighter Jet. Photo by Don Hultzman.

291

	C6	C8	C10
"Daisy - The Jolly Drumming Duck," 1950s, Alps Co., 9" high, seven actions, (includes detachable drum and cymbals, rare	140	210	280
"Dalmation One-Man Band No. 90262," 1950s, Alps Co., 9" high, six actions, includes cymbals and stand	120	180	240
"Dancing Merry Chimp," 1960s, Kuramochi Co., (C-K), 11" tall, five actions	100	150	200
"Dancing Sweethearts," 1950s, T-N Co., 7" tall, minor toy	90	135	180
"Dandy-The Happy Drumming Pup," 1950s, Alps Co., 8½" high, six actions, (includes detachable drum and cymbals)	100	150	200
"Dapper Jigger Dancer," 1950s, Haji Co., 12" tall, minor toy	140	210	280
"Dennis The Menace" (Playing London Bridge), 1950s, Rosko, 9" high, 3 actions, includes xylophone	100	150	200
"Dentist Bear," 1950s, S&E Co., 9½" tall, 6¾"x4¼" base, seven actions, includes detachable head	300	450	600
"Desert Patrol Jeep," 1960s, M-T Co., 11" long, four actions, includes turret gunner	90	135	180
"Destroyer 206" boat, 1950s, Y Co., 14" long, six actions, includes detachable antenna and five depth charges	110	165	220
"Diesel Locomotive," 1950s, Cragstan Co., minor toy, 16½" long	30	45	60
"Dino Robot," 1960s, S-H Co., 11" tall, five actions	500	750	1000
"Disney Acrobats" (Mickey, Donald & Pluto), 1950s, Linemar Co., 9" high, minor toys	400	600	800
"Disney Fire Engine", 1950s, Linemar Co., 11" long, four actions	440	660	880
"Disneyland Fire Engine," 1950s, Linemar Co., 18" long, five actions	350	525	700
"Docking Rocket," 1960s, Daiya Co., 16" long, 24" extended, six actions, (includes plastic radar antenna)	100	150	200
"Dog Family", 1960s, Alps Co., 11" long, four actions	30	45	60
"Dog Sled," T-N Co., 14" long, four actions - RARE, 1950s	300	450	600
"Dolly Dressmaker," 1950s, T-N Co., 7" high, ten actions, includes cloth sample ("Dolly Seamstress" on box) Rare	150	225	300
"Donald Duck," 1960s, Linemar Co., 8" tall, four actions	200	300	400
"Donald Duck Locomotive," 1970s, M-T Co., three actions, 9" long	150	225	300
"Donald Duck Trolley," 1960s, M-T Co., 11" high, three actions	160	240	320
"Douglas C-124 Globe Master," ca. 1950s, Yonezawa Co., 8 actions, 20½" wingspan, 18" long	300	450	600
"Douglas DC-9TWA Jet Plane" 1960s, T-N Co., four actions, 14" long, 17" wingspan	100	150	200
"Doxie The Dog," 1950s, Linemar Co., 9" long, five actions	30	45	60
"Dozo-The-Steaming Clown," 1960s, T-N Co., Rosko toys, 10" tall, five actions	200	300	400
"Dream Boat Hot Rod", ca.1950s, T-N Co., 4 actions, 7" long	140	210	280
"Drill," 1950s, Linemar Co., 6" long, includes attachments, minor toy	20	30	40
"Drinker's Savings Bank," 1960s, Illfelder Co., 9" high, minor toy	90	135	180
"Drinking Captain," 1960s, S&E Co., 12" tall, six actions	100	150	200
"Drinking Dog," 1950s, Y Co., four actions	90	135	180
"Drinking-Licking Cat," 1950s, T-N Co., 10" high, 4"x4" base, six actions	120	180	240
"Drum Bear," ca. 1950s, Alps Co., 5 actions, walks, lights, beats drum, noise, 7¾" tall	150	225	300
"Drum Monkey," 1970s, Yada Co., 8" high, three actions	40	60	80
"Drummer Bear," 1950s, Alps Co., 10" tall, six actions	140	210	280
"Drumming Mickey Mouse," 1950s, Linemar, 10" tall, four actions, Rare	700	1050	1400
"Drumming Polar Bear," 1960s, Alps Co., 12" tall, three actions	100	150	200
"Ducky Duckling," 1960s, Alps Co., 8" high, four actions	50	75	100
"Dump Truck No. 7343," 1960s, T-N Co., 10¼" long, seven actions	60	90	120
"Dynamic Fighter Robot," 1960s, Junior Toy Co., 10" tall, five actions	70	105	140
"Earthman-Astronaut", 1950s, T-N Co., five actions, 9½" tall, RARE	900	1300	1800
"El Toro-Cragstan Bullfighter," 1950s, T-N Co., 9½" long, four actions, includes detachable tin matador	100	150	200

	C6	C8	C10
"Electric Powered TV and Radio Station," 1950s, Marx, 30" long, three actions	80	120	160
"Electric Remote Control Robot," 1950s, M-T Co., 7½" tall, four actions, Rare	500	750	1000
"Electric Robot," 1950s, Marx, 14½" tall, five actions	300	450	600
"Electric School Bus," 1950s, M-T Co., 9½" long, minor toy	70	105	140
"Electric Vibraphone," 1950s, T-N Co., 7½" long, 5½" high, three actions	70	105	140
"Electro Special Racer," 1950s, Yonezawa Co., 10" long, three actions	500	750	1000
"Electro Train Transcontinental," 1950s, "M" Co., 20½" long, (3 pcs.) three actions	90	135	180
"Electronic Countdown," 1959, Ideal Toy Co., 24" long, six actions	60	90	120
"Electronic Fighter Jet 4800," 1950s, 19" long, eleven actions	120	180	240
"Electronic Fire House," 1940s, Banner Co., 7" square, minor toy (includes plastic fire engine)	70	105	140
"Electronic Periscope (Nautilus) Firing Range," 1950s, Cragstan, 11" high on tripod, three actions	100	150	200
"Electronic Twin Train Set #372," 1950s, Woodhaven Metal Stamping Co., minor toy, 28" long - 11" wide, (include two 3 pc. trains)	100	150	200
"Engine Robot," 1960s, S-H Co., 9½" tall, four actions	100	150	200
"Excavator Robot," 1960s, S-H Co., 10" tall, four actions	200	300	400
"Expert Motor Cyclist," 1950s, MT Co., 12" long, five actions, Rare	600	900	1200
"F-14-A Navy Jet Fighter," 1960s, T-N Co., six actions, 13" long, 13" wingspan	200	300	400
"F-101A Voodoo Fighter," 1960s, K-O Co., minor toy, 15" long, 14" wingspan	100	150	200
"FS-059-Fighter Plane", (Jet with prop), 1950s, T-N Co., five actions, 11" long, 13" wingspan	170	255	340
"Fairyland Loco," (Locomotive), 1950s, Daiya Co., 9" long, four actions	60	90	120
"Farm Truck", 1960s, Alps Co., 11" long, three actions	120	180	240
"Farm Truck," 1950s, T-N Co., five actions, 9" long	120	180	240
"F.D. Fire Engine," 1960s, Y-M Co., 10" long, 12" high when ladder is extended, four actions	110	165	220
"Feeding Bird Watcher," 1950s, Linemar, 9" high, five action, (includes detachable tin branch and bird), Rare	300	450	600
"Ferris Wheel Truck," ca. 1950s, Linemar Co. (?) 4 actions, 11" long	400	600	800
"Fido - The Xylophone Player," ca. 1950s, Alps Co., body sways, head turns, arms activate lights, sound, 6 actions, 8¾" high, includes detachable xylophone	150	225	300
"Fighter," (airplane), 1960s, K-O Co., 10½" long, 9" wingspan, six actions	160	240	320
"Fighter Airplane," ca. 1960s, Marx Co., 4 actions, 7" wingspan	60	90	120
"Fighter Jet" ca. 1960s, Marx Co., 4 actions, 7" wingspan	60	90	120
"Fighting Bull," 1960s, Alps Co., 9½" long, five actions	70	105	140
"Fighting Bull," 1970s, Rock Valley Tech Co., 12" long, nose to tail tip, four actions, two cycles	100	150	200
"Fighting Robot," 1970s, S-H Co., four actions, 10" tall, (all plastic)	70	105	140
"Fighting Spaceman," 1960s S-H Co., 12" tall, five actions	150	225	300
"Fire Boat," 1950s, M-T Co., 15" long, five actions	150	225	300
"Fire Chief No. 8 Car," 1960s, Y Co., 11¼" long, three actions	90	135	180
"Fire Chief Mystery Action Car," 1960s, T-N Co., 9¾" long, four actions	130	195	260
"Fire Command Car," 1950s, T-N Co., five actions	170	255	340
"Fire Engine," 1950s, Marusan Co., four actions, 9" long	120	180	240
"Fire Engine," 1950s, T-N Co., (Electro Toy), three actions, 9" long - ladder extends 13"	150	225	300
"Fire Engine," 1950s, Y Co., 12" long, ladder extends 16", six actions	100	150	200
"Fire Engine," ca. 1950s, S-H Co., 3 actions, 8" long	100	150	200
"Fire Patrol Boat," 1950s, KKS Co., 12" long, three actions	110	165	220
"Firebird Racer," 1950s, Tomiyama Co., four actions, 14¼" long	300	450	600

"Mod Monster, Blushing Frankenstein", Hootin' Haunted House, Frankenstein Monster.

Flintstone Yacht. Photo by Don Hultzman.

B-Z Porter, Cragstan "Tugboat", Goodtime Charlie, Picnic Bunny.

The Floating Satellite Target Game. Photo by Don Hultzman.

Maxwell Coffee Loving Bear, Bird WatchingBear, Cragstan Peanut Vendor.

Fork Lift Truck. Photo by Don Hultzman.

Gear Robot. Photo by Don Hultzman.

Go-Kart, M-T Co.. Photo by Don Hultzman.

Bulldozer, Shaking Old-Timer Car, Tractor.

Foto Finish. Photo by Don Hultzman.

Fruit Juice Counter. Photo by Don Hultzman.

294

Treasure Chest Bank, Santa Bank, Hole-In-One Bank, Poverty Pup Bank.

Drinking Captain, Hi Jinks of the Circus, Cragstan "Playboy"

Flower Watering Pup, Rock 'N Roll Monkey, Barney Bear Drummer.

Silver Mountain Express, Spirit of 1776.

Chimpy, Drumming Monkey, Happy Santa One-Man Band, Fred Flintstone's Bedrock Band, Dalmation One-Man Band.

Greyhound Bus.

Hamburger Chef.

Happy Singing Bird in Cage, Cragstan-One Arm Bandit, Comic Hungry Bug, Mag-oo.

Grandpa Bear.

Happy 'N Sad Magic Face Clown.

Courtesy Don Hultzman. Photos by Don Hultzman and Ron Chojnacki unless marked otherwise.

Green Caterpillar.

295

	C6	C8	C10

"**Fire** Tricycle," 1950s, T-N Co., 9½" long, four actions ...... 180 / 270 / 360

"**Fishing** Bear," (also Fishing Panda Bear, Polar Bear, Forest Bear), 1950s, Alps Co., 10" high, six actions, (includes detachable pond, tin fish) ...... 160 / 240 / 320

"**Fishing** Bears-Bank," 1950s, Wonderful Toy Co., 9½" tall, six actions, Rare ...... 500 / 750 / 1000

"**Flashing** Jet-FC-657 Airplane-U.S.A.F. 7452," 1950s, Marx Co., 7" long, 6" wingspan, four actions ...... 100 / 150 / 200

"**Flashy** Jim" 1950's, S.N.K. Co. (Ace), Minor toy, 7¾" tall, RARE ...... 1100 / 1650 / 2200

"**Flashy** Ray Space Gun," 1950's, T-N Co., 18½" long, minor toy ...... 50 / 75 / 100

"**Flintstone** Yacht", 1961 Remco Co., 17" long ...... 100 / 150 / 200

"**Floating** Satellite Target Game," 1960's, 8½" high, (includes tin gun, rubber tipped darts & celluloid ball) ...... 100 / 150 / 200

"**Flutter** Birds," 1950s, Alps Co., 26½" high when assembled, six actions, includes detachable pulley assembly, Rare ...... 300 / 450 / 600

"**Flying** Dutchman-PH-KLM Airliner," 1950s, T-N co., 11" long,, 14" wingspan, five actions ...... 100 / 150 / 200

"**Flying** Jet Plane-Boeing 747P,'" 1960s, J Toy Co., 13" long, 12" wingspan, five actions ...... 90 / 135 / 180

"**Flying** Platform", 1950's, Cragstan Co., four actions, 5½" diameter-9" high, (includes detachable tin soldier) -RARE ...... 200 / 300 / 400

"**Flying** Tiger Airplane," 1960s, Marx Co., 7" long, 7" wingspan, four actions (remote control) ...... 60 / 90 / 120

"**Ford** Model T," 1950s, Nihonkogei Co., 10¼" long, four actions (includes detachable tin roof) ...... 60 / 90 / 120

"**Ford** Mustang 2"x 2," 1960s, Wenmac-AMF Co., four actions, 16" long ...... 60 / 90 / 120

"**Ford** Skyliner" 1950s, T-N Co., four actions, 9" long ...... 100 / 150 / 200

"**4** Prop Airplane," 1960s, Waco Co., 17" long, 16¼" wingspan, four actions ...... 140 / 210 / 280

"**Fork** Lift Truck," 1960s, M-T Co., 10¼" high, Minor Toy ...... 80 / 120 / 160

"**Foto** Finish"-Racehorse, 1950's, M-T Co., minor toy, 12" long ...... 120 / 180 / 240

"**Frankenstein**" (tin), 1950s, Marx Co., (Japan), 12" tall, five actions (remote control) ...... 600 / 900 / 1200

"**Frankenstein** Monster," 1960s, T-N Co., 14" tall, six actions ...... 140 / 210 / 280

"**Frankie**-The Rollerskating Monkey," 1950s, Alps Co., 12" tall ...... 130 / 195 / 260

"**Fred** Flintstone on Dino", 1961, Marx Co., (Japan) eight actions, 22" long ...... 350 / 525 / 700

"**Fred** Flintstone Bedrock Band," 1962, Alps Co., 9½" high, four actions ...... 400 / 600 / 800

""**Friendly** Jocko-My Favorite Pet," 1950s, Alps Co., 8" high, five actions (includes detachable cymbals, plastic cup) ...... 150 / 225 / 300

"**Fruit** Juice Counter," 1960s, "K" Co., 8" long, 8" high, three actions (includes plastic barrel, lid, glasses and tin tray) ...... 90 / 135 / 180

"**Funland** Cup Ride," 1960s, Sonsco Co., 7" tall, 6"x 6" base, three actions, includes 6" umbrella ...... 100 / 150 / 200

Galloping Cowboy Savings Bank," 1950s, Y Co., (Cragstan), 8" high, 6½" long, minor toy. Rare ...... 450 / 675 / 900

"**Gama** Mercedes Benx 220 SE Sedan," 1960s, Mignon Co., 9" long, three actions ...... 140 / 210 / 280

"**Gear** Robot" 1960s, "Y" Co., 10" tall, four actions ...... 250 / 375 / 500

"**Gino**-Neapolitan Ballon Blower," 1960s, Tomiyama Co., (Rosko), 10" tall, five actions, includes bubble solution plastic tray ...... 110 / 165 / 220

"**Girl** With Baby Carriage," 1960s, T-N Co., 8" high, three actions ...... 90 / 135 / 180

"**Go-Go** Girl," (bar toy), 1969 Poynter Prod. Co., 15¼" tall, minor toy (risque toy - PG rated) ...... 40 / 60 / 80

"**Go** Kart," 1960s, M-T Co., 6½" long, minor toy (includes control wire with steering key) ...... 90 / 135 / 180

"**Go** Kart," 1950s, Rosko Co., 10" long, three actions, includes detachable head ...... 90 / 135 / 180

"**Godzilla**," 1960s, Bullmark Co., five actions, 10½" tall ...... 300 / 450 / 600

"**Godzilla** Monster," 1970s, Marusan Co., 11½" tall, three actions ...... 200 / 300 / 400

Puzzled Puppy, Shutter Bug, Popcorn Vendor.

Military Police Car, Desert Patrol Jeep.

Teddy the Rhythmical Drummer, Major Tooty, McGregor, Cycling Duddy.

Happy Naughty Chimp. Photo by Don Hultzman.

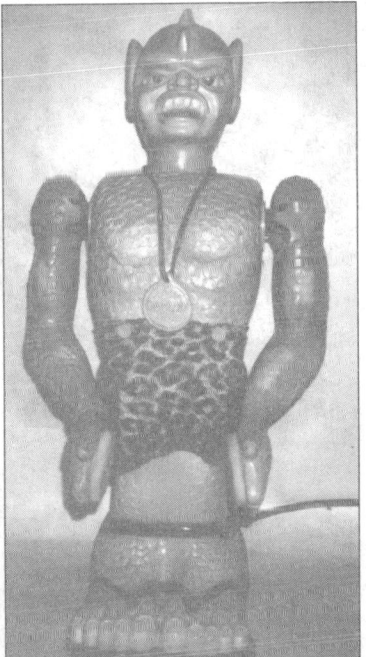

The Great Garloo.

Fighting Spaceman.

Fishing Bear, three variations

Courtesy Don Hultzman. Photos by Don Hultzman and Ron Chojnacki unless marked otherwise.

Fighter. Photo by Don Hultzman.

Highway Skill Driving.

297

Highway Drive.

Roaring Gorilla, Mighty Kong, Dancing Merry Chimp.

Heavy Machine Gun.

Railroad Handcar, Winner-25-Rocket, Biller Train No.573.

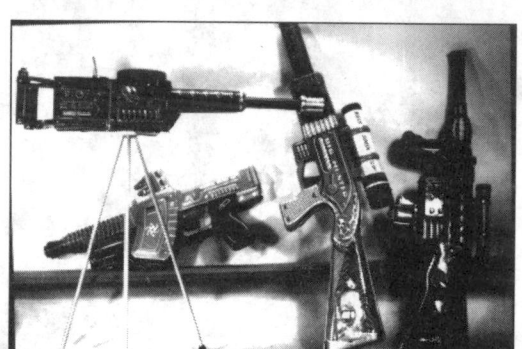

Ray Gun, Universal Machine Gun, Big Hunter Automatic Gun, Flashy-Ray Gun.

Balloon Vendor, Miss Friday, Sam the Shaving Man, Gino the Neapolitan Balloon Blower.

Hoop Zing Girl.

Hy-Que Monkey.

Jolly Bear the Drummer Boy.

Jolly Daddy.

Jolly Bambino.

Hiller Hornet Helicopter

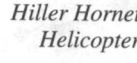

Courtesy Don Hultzman. Photos by Don Hultzman and Ron Chojnacki unless marked otherwise.

298

	C6	C8	C10
"**Golden** Locomotive," 1950s, Nihonkogei Co., 10½" long, minor toy	40	60	80
"**Golden** Gear Robot", 1960's, S-H Co., five actions, 9" tall	300	450	600
"**Golden** Roto Robot," 1960s, S-H Co., 8½" tall, five actions	100	150	200
"**Gomora** Monster", 1960's Bullmark Co., four actions, 8" tall, (includes plastic missles)	150	225	300
"**Gorilla**", 1950s T-N Co., five actions 9¼" tall (white or brown)	200	300	400
"**Go-Stop Benz Racer**", 1950s, Marusan Co., three actions, 11" long	150	225	300
"**Good** Time Charlie," 1960s M-T Co., 12" tall, seven actions	100	150	200
"**Grace** Ocean Liner", 1950s, M-T Co., three actions, 15"long	250	375	500
"**Grandpa** Bear," (rocking chair),1950s, Alps co., 9" tall, five actions	150	225	300
"**Grand-Pa** Car," 1950s, Y Co., 9" long, four actions	50	75	100
"**Grandpa** Panda Bear", 1950's, M-T Co., five actions, 9" tall	140	210	280
"**Great** Garloo, The", 1960s, Marx Co., 23" tall, seven actions, (includes chain and medallion)	300	450	600
"**Green** Caterpillar", 1950's Daiva Co., three actions, 19½" long	150	225	300
"**Greyhound** Bus", 1950s, KKK. Co., minor toy, 7¼" long	90	135	180
"**Greyhound** Bus-Scenicruiser," 1950s, I.Y. Metal Toy Co., 16" long, three actions	90	135	180
"**Greyhound** Bus with Headlights," 1950s, Linemar co., 10¼" long, three actions	100	150	200
"**Grumman** F9F Navy Jet"-Cougar, 1950's, K Co., three actions, 11½" long, 10¼"wingspan	150	225	300
"**Guided** Missile Launcher," 1950s, Irco Co., 8" long, 3" tall, 5" wide, three actions (includes plastic missiles)	110	165	220
"**Gypsy** Fortune Teller", 1950's, Ichida Co., five actions,12" high with hat, 5¾"x 7" base, (includes: 20 fortune cards)RARE	700	1050	1400
"**H-O** Gauge Electric Train set wtih Real Smoke", 1960's, Amico Co., 23" long- total length, 17 pc. set	70	105	140
"**Hamburger** Chef," 1960s, K Co., 8" long, 8" high, three actions, (includes tin frying pan, hamburger, plastic bottles)	110	165	220
"**Handy** Hank Mystery Tractor," 1950s, T-N Co., 9" long, four actions	50	75	100
"**Happy** Band Trios," 1970s, M-T Co., 12" high, seven actions ...Rare	400	600	800
"**Happy** Clown Car," 1960s, Y Co., 6½" long, three actions	100	150	200
"**Happy** Clown Theater," (with Pinocchio-like puppet), 1950s, Y Co., 10" tall, three actions	190	285	380
"**Happy** Fiddler Clown, The"1950s, Alps Co., 9½" high, four actions, includes tin litho violin,	230	345	460
"**Happy** Miner," 1960s, Bandai Co., 11" tall, three actions	110	165	220
"**Happy** Naughty Chimp," 1960s, Daishin Co., 9½" high, assembled, four actions	50	75	100
"**Happy**'n Sad Magic Face Clown," 1960s Y Co., 10" tall, five actions	150	225	300
"**Happy**'N' Sad Face Cymbal Clown," 1960s, Y Co., 10"tall, five actions	200	300	400
"**Happy** Plane", 1960s, TPS Co., three actions, 9"long, 10½" wingspan	100	150	200
"**Happy** Santa", 1960s, "Z" Co., 11" tall, three actions	100	150	200
"**Happy** Santa" (Walking), 1950s, Alps Co., 11" tall, five actions	150	225	300
"**Happy** Santa-One Man Band," 1950s, Alps Co., 9" high, six actions, includes cymbals and stand	140	210	280
"**Happy** Singing Bird," 1950s, M-T Co., 9" high, bird 3" long, 5⅝" dia. base, three actions	60	90	120
"**Happy** the Clown Puppet Show", (with Pinocchio-like puppet), 1960's, Y Co., 10" tall, three actions	190	285	380
"**Happy** Tractor," 1960s, Daiya Co., 8" long, four actions	40	60	80
"**Harbor**-Queen Boat", 1950's, M-T Co., 12" long, minor toy	150	225	300
"**Hasty** Chimp," 1960s Y Co., 9" high, four actions	50	75	100
"**Haunted** House Mystery Bank", 1960s, (Disneyland promotion), Brumberger Co., 7⅝" high, four actions,	250	375	500
"**Heavy** Machine Gun," 1950s, T-N Co., 24" long, 13" high on tripod, four actions (includes detachable tripod and plastic ammo belt)	100	150	200

	C6	C8	C10
"Hi Bouncer Moon Scout" robot, 1968, Marx Co., 11¼" tall, five actions, includes five plastic balls, Rare	450	675	900
"High Jinks of the Circus," 1950s, T-N Co., 14" high, extends to 29", six actions	200	300	400
"Highway Drive," 1950s, T-N Co., 15½" long, three actions (includes tin magnetic car)	70	105	140
"Highway Patrol Police Special, 1960's, Y Co., five actions, 11½" long	100	150	200
"Highway Patrol Jeep," 1950s, Daiya Co., 10" long, four actions	70	105	140
"Highway Skill Driving," 1960s, K Co., 13" long, three actions	70	105	140
"Hiller Hornet Helicopter," 1950s, Alps Co., 12¼" long, 15" 2-pc. metal rotor, four actions	120	180	240
"Hippo Chef" (Cuty Cook) 1960s, Y Co., 10" tall, five actions (includes chef hat and tin litho egg)	150	225	300
"Hobo Clown With Accordion" (with cymbal playing monkey), 1950's, Alps Co., six actions, 10½" high	200	300	400
"Hole-In-One Bank," 1960s, no marking, 8½" long x 3½" wide, minor toy, includes marked test coin and golfer	70	105	140
"Holiday Sink-Stove Combination," 1950s, T-N Co., 9" high, minor toy includes 3 pc. pan set	40	60	80
"Hoop Zing Girl," 1950s, Linemar Co., 11½" tall, minor toy	150	225	300
"Hoopy-the Fishing Duck," 1950s, Alps Co., 10" high, seven actions (includes magnetic fish and detachable 'pond')	180	270	360
"Hootin' Hollow Haunted House," 1960s, Marx, 11" high, eight actions	500	750	1000
"Hooty the Happy Owl," 1960s, Alps Co., 9" tall, six actions	90	135	180
"Hot Rod" car, 1950s, T-N Co., 10" long, minor toy	160	240	320
"Hot Rod Custom 'T' Ford", 1960s, Alps Co., four actions, 10½" long	180	270	360
"Hot Rod Limousine", 1960's Alps Co., four actions, 10½" long	180	270	360
"Hungry Baby Bear", 1950s, "Y" Co., 9½" tall, six actions	180	270	360
"Hungry Cat," 1960s, Linemar Co., 9" high, seven actions (includes tin tray and plastic fish)	300	450	600
"Hungry Hound Dog," 1950s, Y Co., 9½" high, six actions	190	285	380
"Hungry Sheep," 1950s, M-T Co., 9" long, three actions, 2 cycles	100	150	200
"Hy Que Monkey," 1960s, T-N Co., 17" tall, six actions	150	225	300
"Hysterical Robot, The," (a.k.a. 'Hysterical Harry and Happy Harry'), 1960s, S-H Co., 13½" tall, seven actions	150	225	300
"Ice Cream Loving Bear" (?), 1950s, M-T Co., 9½" high, three actions, rare	200	300	400
"Ice Cream Truck," 1960s, Bandai Co., 10½" long, five actions	100	150	200
"Indian Joe," 1960s, Alps Co., 12" tall, four actions	80	120	160
"Indian Signal Choo Choo," 1960s, Kanto Toys Co., 9½" long, four actions	80	120	160
"Interceptor," target game, 1950s, S&E Co., 13" high, 16" wingspan, four actions	150	225	300
"Interplanetary Rocket", 1960s, Y Co., 14¾" tall, five actions	120	180	240
"JDN 7673 Sedan-4 door", 1920's, Distler Co., minor toy and one of the earliest battery operated toys, 14" long, Rare	400	600	800
"James Bond's Aston-Martin"......see "007 Aston Martin"			
"James Bond-007 Car-M101," 1960s, Daiya Co., 11" long, seven actions, includes ejectable driver......see "M101 Aston Martin"			
"Jeep-USA," 1950s, TKK Co., 12½" long, a minor toy	70	105	140
"Jeep No. 10560," 1950s, Cragstan, 5½" long, a minor action toy	70	105	140
"Jet Airport with 4 Jet Airplanes," 1960s, Turnpike Lines (Sears), 12½" long, seven actions	150	225	300
"Jet Plane Base," 1950's, Y Co., 7¼" x 11" base, plane 9" long, 7" wingspan, seven actions (includes crank) RARE	450	675	900
"Jig-Saw-Matic," 1950s, Z Co., 7¼" high, 4½"x 8½", a minor action toy	40	60	80

Jolly Pianist

Tank (M-4), Tank (X-3), Tank (M-103).

Jolly Santa on Snow.

Jumbo - The Bubble Blowing Elephant.

King Size Fire Engine

Kissing Couple

Lambo

Leo - The Growling Pet Lion with Magic Face Change.

Knight In Armor Target game.

*Courtesy Don Hultzman.
Photos by Don Hultzman and Ron Chojnacki unless marked otherwise.*

Lion.

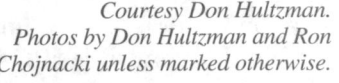

James Bond's Aston-Martin.

301

	C6	C8	C10

"**Jo**-Jo the Flipping Monkey", 1970s, T-N Co., (Illfelder), 10" high, minor toy 50   75   100

"**Jocko** the Drinking Monkey," 1950s, Linemar, 11" tall, four actions, includes top hat 90   135   180

"**John's** Farm Truck," 1950s, T-N Co., 9" long, seven actions 100   150   200

"**Jolly** Bambino," 1950s, Alps Co., 9" high, five actions, includes candy pieces, ... 300   450   600

"**Jolly** Bear Peanut Vendor, The" 1950s, T-N Co., five actions, 8" high (includes: felt hat) 200   300   400

"**Jolly** Bear the Drummer Boy," 1950s, K Co., 7" tall, five actions 100   150   200

"**Jolly** Bear With Robin", 1950s, M-T Co., 10" high, three actions, RARE 400   600   800

"**Jolly** Daddy", 1950's, Marusan Co., four actions, 8¾" tall 160   240   320

"**Jolly** Drummer Chimpy," 1950s, Alps Co., 9" high, 6 actions, includes cymbals and stand 80   120   160

"**Jolly** Drumming Bear," 1950s, T-N Co., 7" tall, four actions 70   105   140

"**Jolly** Penguin," 1950's, T-N Co., 7" tall, five actions 100   150   200

"**Jolly** Pianist," 1950s, Marusan Co., 8" high, five actions 100   150   200

"**Jolly** Santa on Snow," 1950s, Alps Co., 12½" tall, four actions, two cycles (includes tin skis) 150   225   300

"**Josie** The Walking Cow," 1950s, Daiya Co., 14" long, 8½″ high, seven actions, two cycles 120   180   240

"**Journey** Pup," ca. 1950s, S&E Co., Four actions, remote control, 7½" long 50   75   100

"**Jumbo** The Bubble Blowing Elephant," 1950s Y Co., 7¼" high, three actions, includes plastic bowl for bubble solution 80   120   160

"**Jungle** Jumbo", 1950s, B.C. Co., 10" high, six actions, two cycles, hunter resembles Teddy Roosevelt 200   300   400

"**Jungle** Trio," 1950s, Linemar, 8" high, eight actions, includes tin litho whistle, ... 450   675   900

"**Jupiter** Robot," 1950s, Yonezawa Co., 12¾" tall, four actions 150   225   300

"**Jupiter** Rocket Launching Pad," 1960s, T-N Co., 8½" long, 7" high 190   285   380

"**K-55** Electric Tractor", ca. 1950s, M-T Co., 3 actions, 7" long 70   105   140

"**King** Flying Saucer," 1960s, K.O. Co., 7½" diameter, three actions 70   105   140

"**King** Size Fire Engine", 1960's, Bandai Co., three actions, 12½" long 150   225   300

"**Kissing** Couple," 1950s, Ichida Co., 10¾" long, five actions 150   225   300

"**Kitchen-ette** Stove and Sink," 1940s, no marking, 6½" long x 6¾" high, a minor toy, includes kitchen utensils and side tray and stoppers 50   75   100

"**Knight** In Armor", 1950's, M-T Co., five actions, 10" tall, RARE 1100   1650   2200

"**Knight** in Armor Target Game," 1950s, M-T Co., 12" tall, three actions (includes crossbow and rubber tipped darts) 200   300   400

"**Knitting** Grandma," 1950s, T-N Co., 8½" tall, three actions 140   210   280

"**Kooky**-Spooky Whistling Tree," 1950s, Marx Co., 14¼" tall, six actions, (two color schemes) 500   750   1000

"**Ladder** Fire Engine", 1950s, Linemar Co., five actions, 13" long 170   255   340

"**Lady** Pup Tending Her Garden," 1950s, Cragstan Co., 8" high, five actions 170   255   340

"**Lambo**" - With Magnetic Trunk and Light, 1950s, Alps Co., seven actions, 16" long with trailer, (includes two tin logs and trailer), Rare 250   375   500

"**Laughing** Clown, The" 1960s, S-H Co., 14" tall, seven actions 160   240   320

"**Lectric** Revolver," 1950s, Daisy Mfg. Co., 11½" long, three actions 40   60   80

"**Leo**-The Growling Pet Lion With Magic Face-Change," 1970s, Toyiyama Co., 9" long, 2 cycles, three actions 100   150   200

"**Light** House," 1950s, Alps Co., 8½" high, 6¾" x 6¾" base, five actions (includes detachable spin-ball tower) Rare 600   900   1200

Bongo Monkey, Chef Cook, Cola Drinking Bear.

Happy Fiddler Clown, Roarin' Jungle Lion, Mama Dog Feeding Hungry Baby Dog.

Patrol Helicopter, Cragstan Biplane, T360 Monoplane.

Western Badman-Red Gulch Bar, Drinker's Savings Bank.

Happy the Clown Puppet Show Drummer Mickey Mouse, Clown the Magician.

Jet Plane Base

Smoking Grandpa in Rocking Chair, Rocking Chair Bear, Mama Bear & Hungry Baby Bear, Pop Drinking Bear.

Linemar Music Hall

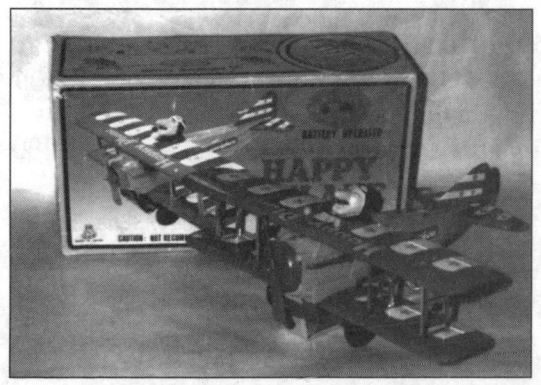

Happy Plane T.P.S. Co., 3 actions.

Jungle Trio.

Loop the Loop Clown.

Courtesy Don Hultzman. Photos by Don Hultzman and Ron Chojnacki unless marked otherwise.

	C6	C8	C10
"**Lighted** Freight Train," 1950s, Y Co., four actions, 25½" long, five pcs., 8 section track	70	105	140
"**Lighted** Space Vehicle wtih Floating Satellite," 1960s, M-T Co., 8½" long, three actions (includes cell ball)	150	225	300
"**Linda** Lee Laundromat," washing machine, 1940s, T-N Co., 6½" high, a minor toy	30	45	60
"**Linemar** Music Hall", 1950's, Linemar Co., four actions, 8" high-7¾"x 5½" base	150	225	300
"**Lion**," 1950s, Linemar, 9" long, four actions	70	105	140
"**Lion** Target Game," 1950s, M-T Co., 7½" high, four actions (includes dart gun and darts)	120	180	240
"**Locomotive**-Continental Blue," 1970s, 13" long, four actions, M-T Co.	40	60	80
"**Loop** The Loop Clown", 1960s, T-N Co., minor toy, 10" high	80	120	160
"**Looping** Airplane", ca. 1960s, "Y" Co., Sears (distributor), minor toy, 14-1/2" high, airplane 5" long	40	60	80
"**Looping** Space Tank", 1960's, Daiya Co., five actions, 8" long	300	450	600
"**Los** Walky-Son" 1960s, Geyper Co., 11½" high, 15" wide, includes detachable rifles and baton	120	180	240
"**Lost** in Space Robot," 1966, Remco Co., 13" tall, three actions	200	300	400
"**Love**-Beetle-Volks," 1960s, K.O. Co., 10" long, three actions	60	90	120
"**Lucky** Crane," 1950s, M-T Co., 8½" high, five actions (includes tin prizes) RARE	400	600	800
"**Lucky** Locomotive," 1950s, Marusan Co., four actions, 8" long	40	60	80
"**Lucky** Seven -Dice Throwing Monkey," 1960s, Alps Co., 11½" tall, five actions (includes plastic straw hat, five dice, two game sheets, twenty chips)	100	150	200
"**Lufthansa** Jet Airplane," 1960s, GAMA Co., 19½" long, 18½" wingspan, three actions	110	165	220
"**Lunar** Captain", 1960's, T-N Co., 13½" long extended, five actions	110	165	220
"**Lunar** Loop/Swing and Orbiting Action," 1960s, Daiya Co., 14" high, 12" diameter hoop, three actions	100	150	200
"**M-101** Aston Martin Secret Ejector Car," 1960s, Daiya Co., 11" long, six actions, (includes ejectable passenger)	200	300	400
"**Mac** the Turtle," 1960's , "Y" Co., 8" high, five actions	100	150	200
"**Magic** Action Bulldozer," 1950's, T-N Co., 9½" long, three actions	100	150	200
"**Magic** Color Moon Express," 1960s, S-H Co., 13" long, four actions	90	135	180
"**Magic** Man Clown", 1950s, Marusan Co., five actions, 11" tall	260	390	520
"**Magic** Snowman," 1950's, M-T Co., (Santa Creations) 11¼" tall, four actions, (includes detachable tin broom, plastic pipe and styro ball)	150	225	300
"**Magnet** Rail Moon Orbiter," 1960s, "Y" Co., 14" high, 12" diameter, minor toy	70	105	140
"**Mainstreet**", 1950s, Linemar Co., three actions, 19½" long, Rare	250	375	500
"**Major** Tooty," 1960s, Alps Co., (R.F.), 14" tall, three actions, includes drum and hat	100	150	200
"**Make** Up Bear", 1960s, M-T Co., four actions, 9" high, Rare	500	750	1000
"**Mambo**-the Jolly Drumming Elephant," 1950s, Alps Co., 9½" high, six actions, includes cymbals and stand	100	150	200
"**Man** in Space - Astronaut," 1960s, Alps Co., 6" tall, a minor action toy	100	150	200
"**Mars** Explorer," Robot, 1950s, S-H Co., 9½" tall, seven actions	200	300	400
"**Mars** Explorer"-Astronaut, 1960's, S-H Co., six actions 10" tall	250	375	500
"**Mars** King Robot No. 12101," 1960s, S-H Co., 9½" tall, four actions	210	315	420
"**Marshall** Wild Bill," 1950s, Y Co., 10½" tall, four actions, 2 cycles, includes tin cowboy hat	180	270	360
"**Martian** Robot," 1970s, SJM Co., 12" tall, four actions	60	90	120
"**Marvelous** Car", T-Bird, 1956, T-N Co., three Actions, 11" long	250	375	500
"**Marvelous** Fire Engine, 1960s, "Y" Co., 11" long, four actions	100	150	200
"**Marvelous** Mike," 1950s, Saunders Co., 17" long, four actions	150	225	300
"**Maxwell** Coffee-Loving Bear," 1960s, T-N Co., 10" tall, five actions	120	180	240
"**McGregor**," 1960s, T-N Co., 12" tall when standing, six actions	100	150	200
"**Mechanic Robot**", 1960s, S-T Co., 12" tall, five actions	150	225	300

Lucky Seven - Dice Throwing Monkey.

Magic Man Clown.

Mechanized Robot (Robbie).

Mainstreet.

Marshal Wild Bill.

Marvelous Mike.

Marvelous Fire Engine.

Mickey Mouse Locomotive.

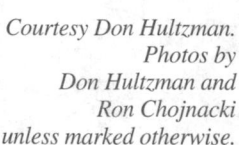

Mighty Mike, the Barbell lifter.

Mischievous Monkey.

Military Command Car.

Courtesy Don Hultzman. Photos by Don Hultzman and Ron Chojnacki unless marked otherwise.

	C6	C8	C10
"**Mechanized Robot, The**," ('Robby') 1950's, T-N Co., 13½" tall, fouractions, Rare	600	900	1200
"**Mercury** Explorer," 1960's, T.P.S. Co., 8" long, five actions	120	180	240
"**Mercury X-1 Space Saucer**," 1960s, "Y" Co., 8" diameter, four actions	70	105	140
"**Merry** Christmas"-Santa In His Rockin' Chair, 1950s, Alps Co., three actions, 21" tall assembled, (includes detachable tree and stocking) RARE	500	750	1000
"**Merry Ice Cream Truck**", 1960s, Bandai Co., 10½" long, five actions	90	135	180
"**Mexicali** Pete-Drum Player," 1960s, Alps Co., 10½" high, three actions	60	90	120
"**Mickey** Mouse and Donald Duck Fire Engine," 1960s, M-T Co., 16" long, three actions	300	450	600
"**Mickey Mouse Locomotive**," 1960's, M-T Co., six actions, 9" long	200	300	400
"**Mickey Mouse Melody Railroad**," 1960's, Frankonia Co., minor toy, 6¾" long (handcar), (includes 4 circular rails with xylophone bars), RARE	800	1200	1600
"**Mickey Mouse on Handcar**," 1960s, M-T Co., 9¾" long, 7¾" high, three actions	300	450	600
"**Mickey Mouse Sand Buggy**," 1960s, M-T Co., 11" long, four actions	150	225	300
"**Mickey Mouse Trolley**," 1960s, M-T Co., 11" high, three actions	150	225	300
"Mickey the Magician", 1960s, Linemar, 10" tall, four actions, includes tin rabbit	900	1350	1800
"**Mighty** Mike the Barbell Lifter Bear," 1950s, "K" Co., 10½" tall, four actions	150	225	300
"**Mighty Kong**," 1950s, Marx, 11" tall, five actions	250	375	500
"**Mighty Robot**," 1960s, K-O Co., 11½" tall, four actions	900	1350	1800
"**Military** Air Defense Truck", 1950's, Linemar Co., four actions, 15¼" long	100	150	200
"**Military Command Car**", 1950's, T-N Co., five actions, 11" long	150	225	300
"**Military Jet Plane**," 1960s, Marx Co., 16" long, 14" wingspan, three actions	100	150	200
"**Military Police Car**," 1950s, Linemar, 8½" long, six actions	100	150	200
"**Million** Bus", 1950s, KKK Co., three actions, 12" long, RARE	1250	1875	2500
"**Mimi** Poodle with Bone," 1950s, T-N Co., 11" long, 10" high, five actions, two cycles, (includes plastic bone)	50	75	100
"**Mischievous** Monkey," 1950s, M-T Co., 18" tall, six actions, includes tree and monkey	300	450	600
Mischievous Monkey with Bulldog," 1950s, T-N Co., 12" high, four actions	220	330	440
"**Miss** Friday- The Typist," 1950s, T-N Co., 8" tall, six actions, removable head	150	225	300
"**Missile** Robot-Mr. 45," M-T Co., 17½" tall, five actions	100	150	200
"**Mr.** Atom - The Electronic Walking Robot," 1950s, Advance Doll & Toy Co., 17" tall, six actions	400	600	800
"Mr. Atomic" robot, 1950s, Cragstan, 11" tall, three actions, rare	2500	3750	5000
"Mr. Baseball Junior", 1950s, T-N Co., 7" high, three actions (with game box)	450	675	900
"Mr. Chief" Robot, 1950s, K-O Co., 12" tall, four actions	450	675	900
"Mr. Fox, the Magician - With the Magical Disappearing Rabbit," 1960s, Y Co., 9" tall, five actions, includes plastic rabbit	400	600	800
"Mr. Hustler Robot," 1960s, Taiyo Co., 11" tall, six actions	200	300	400
"Mr. MacPooch"-Taking A Walk And Smoking His Pipe, 1950's, SAN Co., four actions, 8" tall	130	195	260
"Mr. Magoo Car," 1961, Hubley Co., 9" long, five actions, includes cloth roof top	200	300	400
"Mr. Mercury" Type I (all tin), 1960s, Marx Co., 13" tall, seven actions	400	600	800
"Mr. Mercury" Type II (lighted), 1960s, Marx Co., seven actions	400	600	800
"Mr. Robot" - The Mechanical Brain, 1950s, Alps Co., three actions, 8" tall, RARE	600	900	1200
"Mr. Strong Pup - Weight Lifting Dog", 1950s, "K" Co., 9" tall, five actions	130	195	260
Mr. Traffic Policeman," 1950s, A-I Co., 14" tall, 6"x6" base, four actions	250	375	500
"Mr. Zerox," 1960s, S-H Co., 9½" tall, four actions	150	225	300
"**Mix-ette** Mixer," 1940s, KDP Co., 9" high when assembled, a minor toy, includes mixer stand and bowl	30	45	60

Light House.

Lucky Crane with Box.

Magic Snowman.

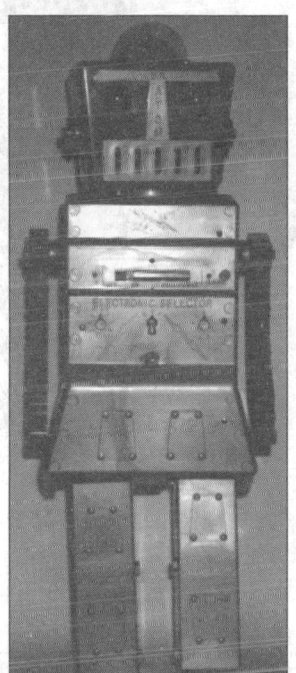

Mr. Atom - Robot.

M-101 Aston-Martin Secret Ejector Car.

Based on the exciting CBS TV Series

LOST iN Space

REMCO

ROBOT

MOVES FORWARD
WORKING ARMS
LIGHTS BLINK
BODY TURNS

MOTORIZED

"Lost in Space" Robot.

Mickey Mouse on Handcar.

Mr. Robot

Mobile Satellite Tracking System.

Moon Patrol Space Rover.

Courtesy Don Hultzman. Photos by Don Hultzman and
Ron Chojnacki unless marked otherwise.

Moon Globe Orbiter.

Musical Showboat.

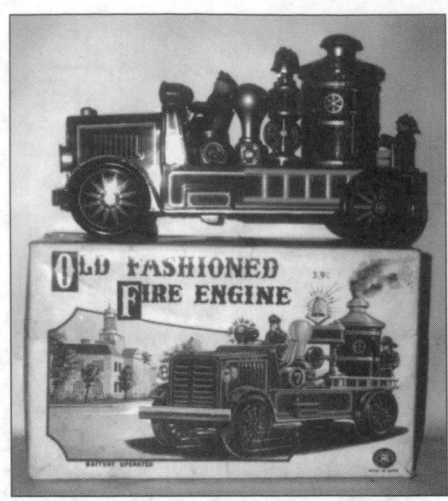

Old Fashioned Fire Engine.

"Ol' MacDonald's Farm Truck". Courtesy
Mapes Auctioneers & Appraisers.

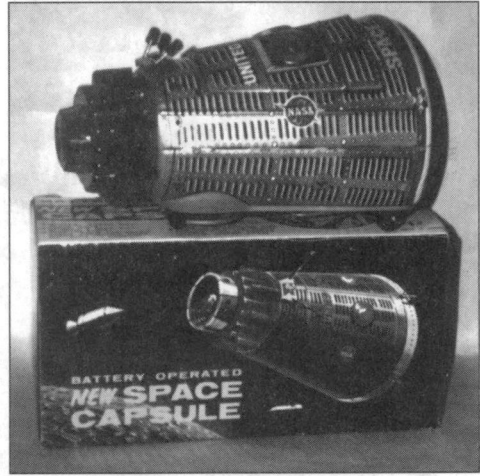

New Space Capsule.

Mystery Police Car.

Papa Bear - Reading & Drinking
In his Old Rocking Chair.

Warpath Indian, Nutty Mad Indian, Indian Joe.

Tank (M-81), Tank (M-35), Tank (M-56), Tank (M-197).

Monkee-
Mobile

Nautilus SSN 571 Submarine.

Courtesy Don Hultzman. Photos by Don Hultzman and
Ron Chojnacki unless marked otherwise.

308

	C6	C8	C10

"**Mobile** Satellite Tracking Station", 1960's, Y Co., six actions, 9" long, (includes detachable antenna............................ 400 600 800

"**Mobile** Space T.V. Unit With Trailer," 1960's T-N Co., six actions, RARE ..500 750 1000

"**Mod** Monster - Blushing Frankenstein," 1960s, T-N Co., 13¼" tall, five actions............................150 225 300

Modern Robot," 1950s, Yoshiya Co., four actions, 12" tall, RARE ..450 675 900

"**Monkee**-Mobile," 1967, ASC Co. (Aoshin Co.) minor toy, 12" long ..300 450 600

"**Monkey** Handcar," 1950s, T-N Co., 7" high, three actions 70 105 140

"**Monkey** On A Picnic," 1950s, Alps Co., 9½" high seven actions 150 225 300

"**Monorail** Rocket Ship," 1950s, Linemar Co., 10" long with supports and rail rods, minor toy.........140 210 280

"**Monster** Robot," 1970s, S-H Co., three actions, 10" tall 70 105 140

"**Moon** Astronaut," 1950s, Daiya Co., 9" tall, four actions...........................500 750 1000

"**Moon** Explorer" Robot, 1960s, Bandai Co., 17½" tall (feet to antenna top), five actions, rare..............................600 900 1200

"**Moon** Explorer," Vehicle, 1960s, Gakken Co., five actions, 11" long 150 225 300

"**Moon** Express," Magic Color, 1950's, TPS Co., 12" long, three actions......120 180 240

"**Moon** Globe Orbiter," ca. 1960s, "Y" Co., (Mego) 3 actions, rocket orbits globe, noise, lights, 10½" high ...100 150 200

"**Moon** Orbiter," 1960s, Y Co., minor toy, 4" long, includes 6 sections of track and trestles 120 180 240

"**Moon** Patrol Space Rover," 1960s, Gakken Toy Co., 11½" long, five actions........140 210 280

"**Moon** Rocket," 1950s, Y Co., 15¼" long, three actions. Rare.......400 600 800

"**Moon** Traveler - Apollo Z," 1960s, T-N Co., 12" long, 15" extended, five actions.....................................120 180 240

"**Mother** Bear-Sitting and Knitting In Her Old Rocking Chair," 1950s, M-T Co., 9½" high, four actions.......................170 255 340

"**Motorcycle** Cop", 1950s, Daiya Co., 10½" long, 8¼" high, five actions 300 450 600

"**Mountain** Cable Car," 1950s, Cragstan Co., 9" long, minor toy, includes cable 60 90 120

"**Movieland** Drive-In Theater," 1959, Remco Co., 14" long, minor toy (includes 6 small cars ad cards, filmstrips)................................60 90 120

"**Multi** Action Electra Jet - KLM Royal Dutch Airlines PH-DSF," 1960's T-N Co., 14" long, 17" wingspan, three actions.................. 110 165 220

"**Mumbo** Jumbo," (Hawaiian drummer,) 1960s, Alps Co., 9¾" high, three actions 100 150 200

"**Musical** Bank Organ Grinder & Monkey," 1950s, HTC Co., 8" tall, four actions, includes test coin and detachable celluloid monkey, Rare 500 750 1000

"**Musical** Bear" (Drum and cymbals), 1950s, Linemar Co., 10" tall, six actions (including detachable tin horn).......................................200 300 400

"Musical Bulldog Playing Piano," 1950s, SAN Co., 8½" tall, 6"x 9" base, four actions. 600 900 1200

"Musical Cadillac Car", 1950s, Irco Co., 9" long, minor toy...........200 300 400

"**Musical** Clown" (New Adventures of Clown), 1960s, T-N Co., 9" tall, three actions 150 225 300

"**Musical** Comic Jumping Jeep", 1970s, Alps Co., 12" long, six actions 70 105 140

"**Musical** Drummer Robot," 1950s, T-N Co., 8¼" tall, three actions, RARE..............................4000 6000 8000

"Musical Jackal," 1950s, Linemar Co., 10" tall, six actions.RARE........... 250 375 500

"Musical Jolly Chimp," 1960s, C-K Co., 10½"high, five actions, two cycles 50 75 100

"**Musical** Marching Bear," 1950s, Alps Co., four actions, 11" tall, (includes detachable tin horn) 200 300 400

"**Musical** Showboat," 1960s, Gakken Toy Co., 13" long, minor toy, (Includes two detachable smokestacks)............................100 150 200

"**My** Fair Dancer," 1950s, Haji Co., 10½" tall, minor toy......................100 150 200

"**Mystery** Fire Chief Car No. 81", 1950s, Sanshin Co., 9¼" long, three actions 100 150 200

309

	C6	C8	C10
"Mystery Plane," 1950s, T-N Co., four actions, 10" long, 10½"wingspan	120	180	240
"Mystery Police Car," 1960s, T-N Co., 9¾" long, 6" wide, 4" high, three actions	100	150	200
"NAR Television Truck," 1950s, Linemar Co., 12" long, four actions (includes six strip film inserts)	300	450	600
"NBC Television Truck", 1950s, Linemar Co., five actions, 9" long	300	450	600
"Neptune Tugboat," 1950s, M-T Co., 15" long, 7" high, four actions	90	135	180
"New Astronaut" Robot, 1970s, S-H Co., 9½" tall, six actions	80	120	160
"New Bell Ringer Choo Choo", locomotive, 1960s, M-T Co., 10" long, three actions	50	75	100
"New Space Capsule", 1960s, S-H Co., six actions, 9" long	120	180	240
"News Service Car," 1960s, TPS Co., 10" long, four actions	150	225	300
"Non-Stop Robot," 1960s, M-T Co., 15" tall, three actions, Rare	600	900	1200
"Nutty Mad Indian," 1960s, Marx, 12" tall, four actions	90	135	180
"Nutty Mads Car" (Drincar), 1960s, Marx Co., 9¼"long, three actions	140	210	280
"Nutty Nibs," 1950s, Linemar, 11½" tall, a minor action toy, includes litho bowl of nuts and steel ball, Rare	550	825	1100
"007 Aston Martin," 1966, Gilbert Co., 11½" long, eight actions, (includes ejectable passenger)	210	315	420
"007 Secret Agent's Car," (Impala), 1960s, Spesco Co., (Joy Toy), 15" long, five actions	170	255	340
"Ol' Macdonald's Farm Truck", 1960's, Frankonia, four actions (includes plastic pig, cow and chicken)	100	150	200
"Ol' Sleepy Head Rip," 1950s, "Y" Co., 9" long, seven actions,	150	225	300
"Old Fashioned Fire Engine," 1950's, M-T Co., four actions, 12½" long	120	180	240
"Old Fashioned Car," 1950s, S-H Co., 10" long, four actions	50	75	100
"Old Fashioned Telephone Bear," (?) 1950s, M-T Co., 9½" high, four actions	100	150	200

	C6	C8	C10
"Old Ford Touring Car," 1950s, Z Co., 10" long, four actions	40	60	80
"Old Time Automobile," 1950s, "Y" Co., 8¾" long, three actions (includes detachable tin litho driver and steering wheel)	80	120	160
"Old Timer," Car, 1950s, Cragstan Co., 9" long-three actions	90	135	180
"Oldtimer Automoball," 1950s, M-T Co., 10" long, three actions, includes celluloid ball	90	135	180
"Oldtimer Sunday Driver," 1960's, Daiya Co., 9" long, four actions	70	105	140
"Overland Choo Choo Express" locomotive, 1950s, M-T Co., 14" long, a minor action toy	30	45	60
"Overland Stage Coach," 1960s, Ichida Co., 18" long, four actions	100	150	200
"P-51 Mustang Shooting Fighter Plane", 1950's, T-N Co., minor toy, 9" long, 9" wingspan	90	135	180
"Pacific Piping Express Locomotive," 1960s, Kanto Toy Co., 14" long, four actions	40	60	80
"Pan Am Sky Taxi-Helicopter," 1960s, Haji Co., 3 actions, 11" long	70	105	140
"Pan American World Airways 'Seven Seas' DC-7," 1950s, T-N Co., 15" long, 19" wingspan, five actions	140	210	280
"Panda Bear," 1970s, M-T Co., (Masudaya Co.), 10" long, four actions, mostly plastic	30	45	60
"Papa Bear - Reading & Drinking in his Old Rocking Chair," 1950s, M-T Co., four actions, 10" high	150	225	300
"Passenger Bus," 1950s, "Y" Co.,16" long, four actions	230	345	460
"Pat O'Neill," 1960s, T-N Co., 12" tall, standing, six actions	150	225	300
"Pat The Dog", 1950s, NGS Co., 9½" long, five actions, two cycles	30	45	60
"Pat the Roaring Elephant," 1950s, "Y" Co., 9" long with attached baby elephant, four actions	150	225	300
"Patrol Auto-Tricycle," 1960s, T-N Co., 19" long, 7½" high, four actions	200	300	400
"Patrol Helicopter No. 7", 1960s, Bandai Co., 11" long, four actions	70	105	140
"P.D. No. 5 - Police Patrol Car," (Buick),1960s, Asakusa Toy Co., 11½" long, three actions	80	120	160

	C6	C8	C10
"**Penguin** on Tricycle," 1950s, T-N Co., 6½" high, three actions	100	150	200
"**Pepi**-Tumbling Monkey," 1960s, Yanoman Toy Co., 9½" high, minor toy	40	60	80
"**Peppermint** Twist Doll," 1950s, Haji Co., 12" tall, minor toy	150	225	300
"**Peppy** Puppy," 1950s, "Y" Co., 8" long, 6½" high, seven actions, two cycles, (includes tin litho bone)	50	75	100
"**Pet** Turtle," 1960s, Alps Co., 7" long, four actions, two cycles	70	105	140
"**Pete** the Space Man," 1960's, Bandai Co., 5" tall, minor action (Walking Mate Series)	60	90	120
"**Peter** The Drumming Rabbit," 1950s, Alps Co., (VIA-Cragstan), 13" tall, five actions	150	225	300
"**Phillips** '66' Power Yacht, 1950's, unmarked, minor toy, 18" long, (includes plastic parts for yacht and dock)	70	105	140
"**Pick-Up** Truck," T-N Co., 10" long, four actions	100	150	200
"**Picnic** Bear," 1950s, (with Coke, Pepsi and generic logo) Alps Co., 10" high, five actions	90	135	180
"**Picnic** Bunny," 1950s, Alps Co., 10" tall, four actions	100	150	200
"**Picnic** Monkey," 1950s, Alps Co., 4 actions, 10" high	70	105	140
"**Picnic** Poodle," 1950s, STS Co., 7" long, 7" high, four actions, two cycles	30	45	60
"**Pierrot** Monkey Cycle", 1950s, M-T Co., 8" long, 10½" high, five actions	300	450	600
"**Piggy** Barbecue," 1950s, Y Co., 9½" tall, five actions, includes chef's hat and tin litho fried egg	150	225	300
"**Piggy** Cook," 1950s, Y Co., 9½" tall, 4"x 6" base, five actions, includes chef's hat and tin litho fried egg	140	210	280
"**Pinkee** the Farmer," 1950s, M-T Co., 9½" long, seven actions	100	150	200
"**Pinky** The Clown," 1950s, Rock Valley Toy Co., (Via) 10¼" tall, five actions, (includes tin litho propeller-ball on nose) Rare	200	300	400
"**Pinocchio** Playing London Bridge," 1962, T-N Co., (Rosko), 10" tall, three actions, includes xylophone	150	225	300

	C6	C8	C10
"**Pioneer** Covered Wagon," 1960s, Ichida Co., 14½" long, four actions (includes detachable canopy and driver)	120	180	240
"**Pipie** the Whale," 1950s, Alps Co., 12" long, minor toy	70	105	140
"**Piston** Action Bulldozer," 1960s, Linemar Co., 7½" long, two cycles	90	135	180
"**Piston** Action Robot", 1950's, T-N Co., three actions, 8¼" tall, resembles "Robbie"	900	1350	1800
"**Piston** Head Robot", 1960's, S-H Co., three actions, 10" tall	150	225	300
"**Piston** Robot," 1960s, S-H Co., 10½" tall, four action	110	165	220
"**Pistol** Pete," 1950s, Marusan Co., 5 actions, 10¼" high, includes tin hat	200	300	400
"**Planet** Explorer," 1950's, S-H Co., four actions, 9" long	150	225	300
"**Planet** Rover," wheeled tank, 1960s, J Co., 9" long, 6½" high, six actions	140	210	280
"**Planet** 'Y' Space Station," 1960's, T-N Co., three actions, 9" diameter	140	210	280
"**Playful** Pup in Shoe," 1960s, "Y" Co., 10" long, three actions	40	60	80
"**Playful** Puppy," 1950s, M-T Co., 7⅜" long, 5" high, four actions	100	150	200
"**Pluto**," 1960s, Linemar Co., 10" long, five actions	200	300	400
"**Polar** Bear," 1970s, Alps Co., 8" long, three actions	50	75	100
"**Police** Auto Cycle," 1960s, (motorcycle and plastic driver), Bandai Co., five actions. Remote Control	150	225	300
"**Police** Motorcycle," 1950s, M-T Co., 11¾" long, seven actions	180	270	360
"**Police** No. 5" Police Car, 1950's, T-N Co., four actions, 9½" long	90	135	180
"**Police** Patrol Jeep," 1960's T-N Co., 4 actions, lights, bump & go, noise, smoke, 9¼" long	100	150	200
"**Pom Pom** Tank", 1950's, S&E Co., 12" long, five actions	160	240	320
"**Popcorn** Eating Bear," 1950s, M-T Co., 9" high, five actions	100	150	200
"**Popcorn** Vendor," No. 4035, 1960s, S&E Co., 8" high, 7" long, six actions, includes litho umbrella	200	300	400

311

Pat O'Neill.

"Old Timer" Car, Cragstan. Courtesy Mapes Actioneers & Appraisers.

Pistol Pete.

Peppermint Twist Doll.

Cragstan "Crapshooter", Tumbles the Bear, Overland Stage Coach.

Piston Robot.

Piston Action Robot (Robbie).

Pioneer Covered Wagon.

Pinky The Clown, Circus Elephant, Tom & Jerry Handcar (Tom).

Puffy Morris, Piggy Cook, Cragstan "Crapshooting Monkey".

Courtesy Don Hultzman. Photos by Don Hultzman and Ron Chojnacki unless marked otherwise.

312

	C6	C8	C10
"Popcorn Vendor Truck," 1960s, T-N Co., 9" long, three actions	150	225	300
"Popeye and Rowboat With Moving Oars", 1950's, Linemar Co., three actions, 10" long RARE	5000	75000	10000+
"Porsche With Visible Engine," 1964, Bandai Co., 10" long, three actions	90	135	180
"Poverty Pup," bank, 1966, Poynter Products Co., 6" long, 4¼" high, three actions	60	90	120
"Power Shovel," 1950s, Alps Co., 15" long, extended, six actions	90	135	180
"Pretty Peggy Parrot," 1950s, T-N Co., 11" long, six actions	250	375	500
"Princess the French Poodle," 1950s, no markings, 9" long, 8" high, five actions	40	60	80
"Professor Owl," 1950s, E-T Co., 8" high, five actions, includes two discs	200	300	400
"Project Yankee Doodle," 1959, Remco Co., 15" long, six actions (includes plastic missiles, rockets & accessories)	60	90	120
"Puffy Morris," 1960s, Y Co., 10" tall, five actions, uses real cigarette	100	150	200
"Puzzled Puppy," 1950s, M-T Co., 7½" long, 5" high, five actions	100	150	200
"Queen of the Sea," 1950's, M-T Co., four actions, 21½" long (includes detachable antenna and flag)	300	450	600
"RCA-NBC Mobile Color T.V. Truck," 1950s, Yonezawa Co., 9" long, four actions	300	450	600
"R.R. Line Locomotive," 1950's, Marx, 6½" long, four actions	40	60	80
"R-35 Robot," 1950's, M-T Co., 7½" tall, five actions	300	450	600
"Racecar #25", 1950's, Alps Co., three actions, 9" long, RARE	800	1200	1600
"Radar Jeep", 1950's, T-N Co., 11" long, four actions	150	225	300
"Radar Robot," 1960s, T-N Co., 9" tall, three actions, remote robot-face control box	600	900	1200
"Radar Robot", 1970s, S-H Co., 12" tall five actions	70	105	140
"Radar Scope Space Scout", 1960s, S-H Co., three actions, 9¼" tall	140	210	280
"Radio Rex," 1920's, Elmwood Button Co., 5"x7" dog house, minor toy (includes cell. dog)	70	105	140

	C6	C8	C10
"Railroad Hand Car," 1950's, KDP Co., 8" long, a minor toy, includes rubber track	90	135	180
"Railway Yard - Shuttle Train," 1950's, ATC Co., 8" long, track 28" long, three actions, includes locomotive boxcar and track	100	150	200
"Ranger Robot," 1950's Daiya Co., six actions, 11" tall	400	600	800
"Ray Gun," machine gun, 1950s, T-N Co., 17½" long, three actions, includes tripod	50	75	100
"Reading Bear," 1950's, Alps Co., 9" tall, five actions	100	150	200
Rembrandt - Monkey Artist, 1950s, Alps Co., 8" high, five actions	200	300	400
"Reversible Diesel Electric Tractor," 1950s, Marx Co., minor toy	50	75	100
"Ricki- The Begging Poodle," 1950s, Rock Valley Toys (VIA), 9" long, 8" high, 5 actions	30	45	60
"Riverboat," 1950s, Marusan Co., 12¾" long, three actions (includes detachable tin smokestack	130	195	260
"River Queen Sidewheeler," 1950s, M-T Co., 13½" long, three actions	140	210	280
"Road Construction Roller," 1950s, Daiya Co., 8½" long, four actions	60	90	120
"Road Grader," 1960s, T-N Co., 12" long, three actions	50	75	100
"Road Roller," 1950s, M-T Co., 9" long, four actions	60	90	120
"Roaring Gorilla," (white gorilla),1950s, T-N Co., 9¼" tall, five actions .... see "Gorilla"			
"Roaring Gorilla Shooting Gallery," 1950s, M-T Co., 9½" tall, three actions (includes fold-out target box, tin gun, plastic darts)	200	300	400
"Roarin' Jungle Lion," (?) 1950s, Marx Co., 16" long, nose to tail tip, four actions, 2 cycles	140	210	280
"Robbie Robot," 1950s, Yonezawa Co., 13" tall, five actions ....see "Mechanized Robot"			
"Robby Space Patrol", 1950's, T-N Co., 12-1/2" long, five actions, RARE	2000	3000	4000+
"Robert the Robot," 1950s, Ideal Toy Co., 14" tall, three actions	120	180	240
"Robert the Robot Mechanical Bulldozer," 1950's, Ideal Toy Co., 9" long, four actions, RARE	300	450	600
"Robot", 1950's, Y Co., minor toy, 6" tall, RARE	600	900	1200

	C6	C8	C10
"Robot," 1960s, Y Co., 10½" tall, three actions	400	600	800
"Robot 2500," 1970s, Durham Industries, 10½" tall, four actions	60	90	120
"**Robotank** TR-2", 1960s, T-N Co., four actions, 5" high	140	210	280
"Robotank-Z Space Robot," 1960s, T-N Co., 10¼" high, five actions	300	450	600
"Rock 'N' Roll Hotrod", (Dreamboat), 1950s, T-N Co., three actions, 7" long	140	210	280
"**Rock** 'N' Roll Monkey, 1950s, Rosko Co., 13" tall, five actions, includes plastic hat (3 variations)	160	240	320
"**Rocket** Express"-Rocket Ship Monorail, 1950s, Linemar Co., three actions, 10" long (20 pc. rail & girder set)	100	150	200
"Rocket Launching Pad," 1950s, "Y" Co., 8½" high, five actions (includes tin litho satellite and rocket)	160	240	320
"**Rocking** Chair Bear," (?) 1950s, M-T Co., 10" high, five actions	100	150	200
"Rocking Santa," 1950s, Alps Co., 10" high, four actions, Rare	300	450	600
"**Roller** Skater," 1950s, Alps Co., minor toy, 12" tall	90	135	180
"**Rollerskating** Clown," 1950s, T.P.S. Co., 6" tall, minor toy, RARE	500	750	1000
"**Romance** Car M-841," 1950s, "M" Co., 8" long, three actions	90	135	180
"**Rootbeer** Counter," 1960s, "K" Co., 8" long, 8" high, three actions (includes plastic barrel & glasses & tin tray)	100	150	200
"**Rosko** Robot", 1950s, Rosko Co., five actions, 13" tall	500	750	1000
"**Rotate**-O-Matic Super Astronaut," 1960's, S-H Co., 11½" tall, six actions, two cycles	100	150	200
"**Rover** The Poodle Bell Ringer," 1960's, Alps Co., three actions-2 cycles, 10½" tall	60	90	120
"**Roy** Roger Western Telephone," Ideal Co., 1950s, 3 actions, 9" high	90	135	180
"**Royal** Cub In Buggy," (pushed by Mama Bear), 1940s, S&E Co., 8" long, 8" high, six actions	140	210	280
"**Rudy** the Robot," 1968, Remco Co., 16¼" tall, four actions	110	165	220
"**SSN-571** Submarine"-Nautilus, 1950s, Marusan Co., minor toy, 16" long, (rudder extended)	120	180	240
"SSN-571 Submarine", Skate, 1950s, Marusan Co., minor toy, 16" long (rudder extended)	120	180	240

	C6	C8	C10
"**Sam** the Shaving Man," 1960s, Plaything Toy Co., 11½" tall, seven actions, includes metal mirror	150	225	300
"**Sammy** Wong- The Tea Totaler," 1950s, T-N Co., 10" tall, four actions	160	240	320
"**Santa** Bank," 1960, HTC Co., (Trim a Tree), 11" high, four actions	150	225	300
"Santa Claus - Bellringer," 1950s, Santa Creations Co., 13" tall, five actions	90	135	180
"Santa Claus," No. M-750 (Sitting on House), 1950's, H.T.C. Co., 8" high, four actions	100	150	200
"Santa Claus on Handcar," 1960s, M-T Co., 10" high, three actions	120	180	240
"Santa Claus on Scooter," 1960s, M-T Co., 10" high, four actions	120	180	240
"Santa Claus - Stands & Sits," 1960s, T-N Co., 10" tall, six actions	150	225	300
"Santa Copter," 1960s, M-T Co., 8½" long, three actions	70	105	140
"Santa in Rocker," 1950s, Alps Co., 21" high, from base to tree top, four actions (includes detachable tree and stocking) rare	*see "Merry Christmas"*		
"Santa Claus Phone Bank," 1950s, S&E Co., 7 actions, 8" high, includes remote 4¾" high payphone	400	600	800
"Santa Sled", 1950s, T-N Co., 14" long, four actions, Rare	300	450	600
"Santa the Bellringer," 1950s, Chase Import Co., 7" high, minor toy (electro-magnet activated & Blinker bulb)	100	150	200
"Santa Fe Diesel"-Battery Cable Train With Headlight, 1950s, T-N Co., minor toy, 13½" long, (2 pc. hookup)	80	120	160
"**Satellite** Interceptor"-Target set, 1950s, Linemar Co., minor toy (2 pc. set with 6½" long gun-telescope, 5" high blower and 2 plastic darts and styro ball)	200	300	400
"Satellite Target Game," 1960s, S-H Co., 8" high, 10½" wide, minor toy (includes celluloid ball and special gun)	100	150	200
"**Saxophone** Playing Monkey," 1950s, Alps Co., 9½" high, four actions	200	300	400
"**School** Bus," 1950s, Cragstan, 20½" long, a minor toy	70	105	140
"**Sea** Bear #7 Racing Boat," 1950's, Bandai Co., minor toy 10" long	60	90	120

Circus Lion.

Peter the Drummer Rabbit, Picnic Bear, Bunny the Magician.

Police Auto Cycle.

Cragstan "Schoolbus", Cragstan "Western Locomotive", New Bell Ringer Choo-Choo.

Police No. 5.

Pretty Peggy Parrot.

Mickey The Magician.

Mr. Fox the Magician-blowing magic bubbles, Professor Owl, Mr. Fox the Magician with the Magical Disappearing Rabbit.

Bubble Lion, Wild West Rodeo, Cragstan "Bullfighter".

Courtesy Don Hultzman. Photos by Don Hultzman and Ron Chojnacki unless marked otherwise.

Queen of the Sea.

Trumpet Playing Monkey, Monkey On A Picnic, Busy Housekeeper.

"Nutty Mads Car"

Power Shovel.

Police Motorcycle.

"Ol' Sleepy Head Rip", 1950's.

New Astronaut.

Musical Bulldog.

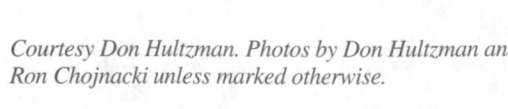

Playful Puppy.

Funland Cup Ride, Big Shot Cadillac.

Animated Squirrel, Cock-A-Doodle-Doo Rooster, Josie-the-Cow, Sparky-the-Seal.

Old Fashioned Telephone Bear, Cragstan Telly Bear, V.I.P. the Busy Boss, Telephone Bear.

Broadway Trolley, Battery Locomotive No. 123, A-B-C Fairy Train, Smoking Pop Locomotive-the General.

Roaring Gorilla Shooting Gallery.

Tom & Jerry Choo-Choo, Old Timer Automoball.

River Boat.

Root Beer Counter.

Robert The Robot Mechanical Bulldozer, Rare, Value $400 in mint.

Royal Cub in Buggy, Cry-Baby-In-Buggy.

Courtesy Don Hultzman. Photos by Don Hultzman and Ron Chojnacki unless marked otherwise.

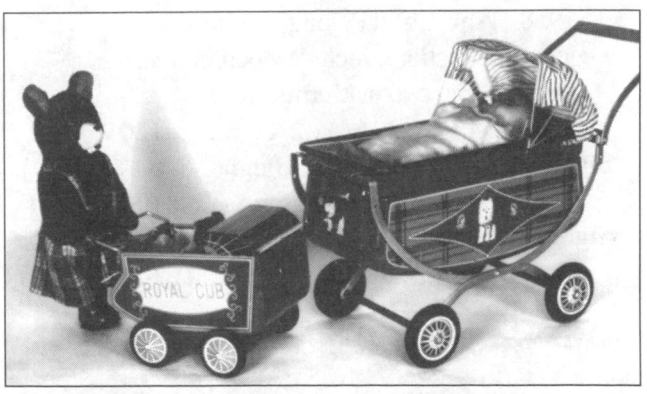

317

	C6	C8	C10
"**Seascape** Tugboat," 1950's, Marx Co., three actions, 6½" long	50	75	100
"**Secret** Service Action Car," (Green Hornet" motif), 1960s, ASC Co., 11" long, four actions, rare	400	600	800
"**Serpent** Charmer," 1950s, Linemar Co., 7" high, four actions	250	375	500
"**Shaggy** The Friendly Pup," 1960s, Alps Co., 8" long, three actions	40	60	80
"**Shaking** Classic Car," 1960s, T-N Co. 7" long, four actions	50	75	100
"**Shaking** Old-Timer Car No. 2511-1", 1960s, T-N Co., 9" long, four actions, includes plastic driver	60	90	120
"**Shark**-U-Control Racing Car," 1961, Remco Ind. Inc., 19" long, all plastic, minor toy	80	120	160
"**Sheriff** Car," 1950's, T-N Co., four actions, 10" long	80	120	160
"**Shoe** Maker Bear," 1960s, T-N Co., 8½" high, three actions	140	210	280
"**Shoe**-Shaking Dog," 1950s, M-T Co., 8" long, 6" tall, five actions	40	60	80
"**Shoe** Shine Bear," 1950s, T-N Co., 9" tall, five actions	130	195	260
"**Shoe** Shine Joe," 1950s, Alps Co., 11" high, six actions	140	210	280
"**Shoe** Shine Monkey," 1950s, T-N Co., 9" high, five actions	140	210	280
"**Shooting** Bear," 1950s, SAN Co., 10" tall, six actions	160	240	320
"**Shooting** Gorilla", 1950s, M-T Co., 12" high, four actions (includes tin gun and darts)	160	240	320
"**Shutterbug**," photographer, 1950s, T-N Co., 9" tall, five actions	400	600	800
"**Shuttling** Freight Train," 1950's, Cragstan Co., six actions, 51" long-assembled (includes locomotive, lumber car, 4pc. of track, platform, logs)	110	165	220
"Shuttling Train and Freight Yard," 1950s, Alps Co., 11" long, track 51" long, four actions, includes locomotive, baggage car, two platforms, litho luggage	120	180	240
"**Sight** Seeing Bus," 1960s, Bandai Co., 14½" long, four actions	100	150	200
"Sight Seeing Bus", 1950s, Yonezawza Co., minor toy, 9" long	140	210	280
"**Sikorsky** Rescue Army Helicopter," 1950's, Alps Co., four actions, 11" long	90	135	180
"**Silver** Bell Choo Choo," 1950s, Kanto Co., 12" long, three actions	40	60	80
"**Silver** Mountain Express Locomotive," 1960's, M-T Co., four actions, 15¾" long	40	60	80
"**Silver** Mountain Locomotive," 1950s, M-T Co., 16" long, three actions	40	60	80
"Silver Ray Secret Weapon Space Scout", 1960's, S-H Co., six actions, 9" tall, RARE	750	1075	1500+
"**Silver** Streak Locomotive No. 6682," 1950s, M-T Co., 16" long, four actions	40	60	80
"**Singing** Bird In Cage," 1950s, T-N Co., 9" high, 4"x 6" rectangular base., four actions	100	150	200
"**Siren** Fire Car," 1950's, M-T Co., 9" long, four actions	130	195	260
"**Siren** Patrol Car," 1960's, M-T Co., four actions, 12½" long	90	135	180
"**Siren** Patrol Motorcycle," 1960's, M-T Co., three actions, 12" long	200	300	400
"**Skating** Circus Clown," 1950's, TPS Co., minor toy, 6" tall, RARE	500	750	1000
"**Skiing** Santa," 1960s, M-T Co., 12" tall, four actions, (includes tin skis)	150	225	300
"**Skipping** Monkey," 1960s, T-N Co., 9½" tall, minor toy	40	60	80
"**Sky** Patrol Flying Saucer," 1950s, K-O Co., 7½" diameter, seven actions, includes detachable antenna	100	150	200
"**Sky** Patrol"-Space Cruiser, 1950's, T-N Co., five actions, 13" long	150	225	300
"Sky Taxi-Panam-Boeing Vertol 107" 1970s, Haji Co., 12¾" long, three actions, includes 2 detachable rotors	120	180	240
"**Slalom** Game," 1960's, T-N Co., minor toy, 15¼" long (includes plastic skier)	100	150	200
"**Sleeping** Baby Bear," 1950s, Linemar, 9" long, six actions, includes detachable Alarm Clock	240	360	480
"**Sleeping** Pup," 1960s, Alps Co., 9" long, five actions	60	90	120
"**Slurpy** Pup," 1960s, T-N Co., 6½" long, 4" high, four actions	50	75	100

R-35 Robot.

Radar Scope Space Scout.

Santa Pay-Phone Bank.

Radio Rex. Unlike listing, this was made by John Hugo Co. of New Haven, Conn., with a last patent date of 1922. Auctioned with box in generally fine condition in late 1990 for $198. Courtesy James S. Maxwell/Virginia Caputo. Photo by Virginia Caputo.

Rocket Express -, Monorail.

Rabbits And The Carriage.

"Rotate-O-Matic Super Astronaut, with box. Courtesy James S. Maxwell/ Virginia Caputo. Photo by Virginia Caputo.

"Radar Robot"", 1960's, T-N Co. Courtesy James S. Maxwell/ Virginia Caputo. Photo by Virginia Caputo.

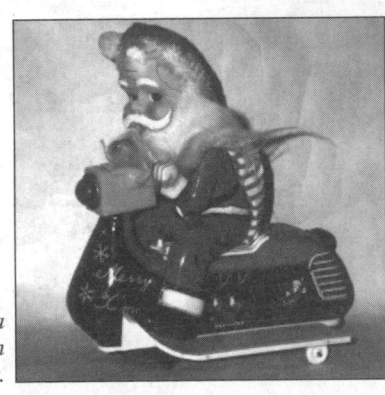

Santa Claus on Scooter.

Sneezing Bear.

Courtesy Don Hultzman. Photos by Don Hultzman and Ron Chojnacki unless marked otherwise.

	C6	C8	C10
"**Smilex** Deluxe Coffee Set," 1950s, Y Co., 12" high assembled, minor toy includes four sets of cups, saucers and spoons-plastic 60		90	120
"**Smoky** Bear," 1950's, SAN Co., four actions, 9" tall (includes detachable tin hat-Pioneer) 220		330	440
"**Smoky Bill on Old Fashioned Car**," 1960s, T-N Co., 9" long, four actions 120		180	240
"**Smokey the Bear Jeep**," 1950s, M-T Co., 10" long, four actions 220		330	440
"**Smoking** Bulldozer," 1960s, WKC Co., 9" long, four actions 90		135	180
"**Smoking Bunny**," 1950s, SAN Co., 10½" tall, four actions 100		150	200
"**Smoking Elephant**," 1950s, Marusan Co., 8¾" tall, four actions 130		195	260
"**Smoking Grandpa**," (in Rocking Chair,) 1950s, SAN Co., 8" tall, four actions (Type I-eyes open) 150		225	300
"**Smoking Grandpa**," (in Rocking Chair) 1950s, SAN Co., 8" tall, four actions (Type II-eyes closed) 160		240	320
"**Smoking Jet Plane**," 1950s, T-N Co., 12" long, 11" wingspan, four actions 150		225	300
"**Smoking Pop Locomotive-the General**," 1950s, SAN Co., 10¼" long, four actions 70		105	140
"**Smoking Popeye**," 1950s, Linemar, 9" tall, five actions, rare 800		1200	1600
"**Smoking Robot**," 1960s, M-T Co., 10" tall, four actions (all plastic) ... 90		135	180
"**Smoking Spaceman**," 1950s, Linemar Co., 12" tall, six actions. 800		1200	1600
"**Smoking U.S.A.F Jet**," 1950s, T-N Co., 13" long, 12" wingspan, four actions 150		225	300
"**Smoking Volkswagen**," 1960s, Aoshin Co., 10½" long, four actions.............60		90	120
"**Smoking PaPa Bear**," 1950s, SAN Co., 8" tall, four actions 110		165	220
"**Smoky** Joe-Fancy Mobile," 1960s, T-N Co., 4 actions, smokes, lights, bump & go, noise, 9" long 100		150	200
"**Snake** Charmer (And Casey the Trained Cobra)" 1950s, Linemar Co., 8" high, four actions 250		375	500
"**Snappy** the Dragon," 1960s, T-N Co., 30" long, six actions, rare......2000		3000	4000+

	C6	C8	C10
"**Sneezing** Bear," 1950s, Linemar Co., 9" high, five actions 200		300	400
"**Snoopie** the Non-Fall Dog," 1960s, Amico Co., 8" long, three actions. 50		75	100
"**Snoopy** Sniffer," 1960's, M-T Co., four actions, 8" long.....................50		75	100
"**Somersaulting** Pup With Bark,"1960's, T-N Co., four actions, 2 cycles, 9" long...50		75	100
"**Sonicon** Space Rocket," 1960's, M-T Co., minor toy, 13" long 250		375	500
"**Space** Capsule," 1960s, M-T Co., 10" long, four actions, includes styrofoam saucer and astronaut..... 100		150	200
"**Space Capsule-5**", 1960's, M-T Co., four actions, 10½" long 150		225	300
"**Space Commando-Spaceman**," 1960s, M-T Co., 7¾" tall, four actions 500		750	1000
"**Space Commando**"-Space Station , 1960s, T-N Co., 10" diameter, four actions 150		225	300
"**Space Explorer #1041**, 1960s, Yonezawa Co., 7¾" high, extends to 11½" high, six actions, rare 600		900	1200
"**Space Explorer Ship**" 1950s, M-T Co., six actions, 11" diameter, (saucer) ..80		120	160
"**Space Fighter**," Robot, 1970s, S-H Co., 9"tall, six actions 70		105	140
"**Space Frontier Saturn 5 Rocket**," 1960s, K-Y co., (Yoskino Toy Co.,) 18" long, six actions.............100		150	200
"**Space Patrol Car**," 1950s, T-N Co., four actions, 9½" long 300		450	600
"**Space Patrol Car**,"-With Lighting guns-1950s, Linemar Co., 9" long, three actions 450		675	900
"**Space Patrol Robot**," 1950s, S-H Co., 11" tall, six actions........................140		210	280
"**Space Patrol Rocket**," 1970s, M-T Co., 11" long, three actions............70		105	140
"**Space Patrol- Snoopy**," 1960s, M-T Co., 11" long, four actions 100		150	200
"**Space Patrol Tank**," 1950's, Cragstan Co., five actions, 9" long (includes detachable tin jet plane) 150		225	300
"**Space Patrol 3 Saucer**," 1950s, K-O Co., 7½" diameter, five actions 100		150	200
"**Space Patrol Vehicle**," 1950s, K Co., 9" long, four actions........................130		195	260
"**Space Patrol Vehicle**," 1960s, M-T Co., 9½" long, three actions 100		150	200
"**Space Pioneer**"-Vehicle, 1960's, M-T Co., three actions, 12" long ...100		200	300

Teddy-Go-Cart, Mambo-the Jolly Drumming Elephant.

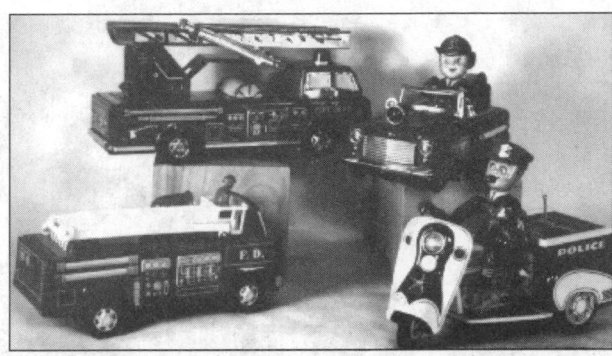

F.D. Fire Engine, Fire Engine, Fire Chief Mystery Action Car, Police Motorcycle Cop.

"Talking Parrot"

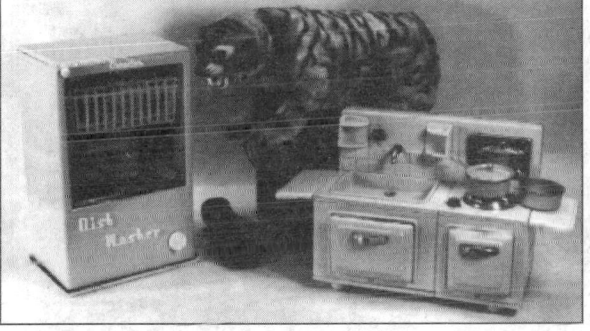

Cragstan Automatic Dishwasher, Bengali Tiger, Holiday Sink/Stove Combination.

The Big Parade.

Champion Weight Lifter.

Tom and Jerry Car.

Smoking Robot.

"Susie the Cashier Bear".

"Talking Robot".

Courtesy Don Hultzman. Photos by Don Hultzman and Ron Chojnacki unless marked otherwise.

Santa Claus - Bellringer.

Santa Fe Diesel.

Shooting Bear.

U.S. Air Force Smoking Jet.

Trumpet Playing Bunny

Shoe Shine Joe.

Satellite Interceptor

Musical Jolly Chimp, Grand-Pa Car, Circus Fire Engine.

Mix-ette Mixer, Wash-O-Matic Washing Machine, Jig-Saw-Matic Jigsaw, Kitchen Stove & Sink.

Courtesy Don Hultzman. Photos by Don Hultzman and Ron Chojnacki unless marked otherwise.

Sikorsky Rescue Army Helicopter.

322

	C6	C8	C10
"Space Robot Trooper," 1950s, K-O Co., 7½" tall, three actions, Rare	500	750	1000
"Space Robot (X-70)", 1960s, T-N Co., 12" tall, five actions,	500	750	1000
"Space Robot Car," 1950s, Yonezawza Co., six actions, 9¼" long, Rare	1000	1500	2000
"Space Rocket-Blue Eagle," 1950s, Masuya Toy Co., 15" long, (tail to probe tip)	120	180	240
"Space Rocket-Solar X," 1960s T-N Co., 15½" tall, five actions	150	225	300
"Space Scooter," 1960s,, M-T Co., 10½" high, 8" long, three actions	100	150	200
"Space Scooter," -Snoopy or Astro-Dog, 1960s, M-T Co., three actions, 8" long	80	120	160
"Space Ship," 1950s, I.Y. Co., 9½" diameter, four actions	180	270	360
"Space Ship," 1970s, M-T Co., 9" long, three actions	90	135	180
"Space Ship X-5," 1970s, M-T Co., 8" diameter, four actions	60	90	120
"Space Ship X-8," 1960s, Tada Co., 8" long, four actions	100	150	200
"Space Station," 1950s, T-N Co., 9" diameter, four actions	100	150	200
"Space Station," 1950s, S-H Co., 11¾" diameter, five actions	500	750	1000
"Space Tank," 1960s, K-O Co., 6" long, four actions" Robbie Type"	2000	3000	4000+
"Space Tank," 1950s, Daiya Co., 8" long, four actions	120	180	240
"Space Tank-M41," 1950s, M-T Co., 9" long, four actions (includes detachable plastic antenna)	100	150	200
"Spaceman," Robot, 1950s, Linemar, 7½" tall, three actions	350	525	700
"Spaceman," Robot, 1950s, T-N Co., 9¼" tall, four actions	400	600	800
"Spad XIII S-7 Stunt Biplane," 1960s, T.P.S. Co., 9" long, 10⅜" wingspan, three actions	130	195	260
"Spanking Bear," 1950s, Linemar Co., 9" high, six actions	150	225	300
"Sparking Burp Gun," 1950's, Mark Co., three actions, 24" long	40	60	80
"Sparkling Mike The Robot," 1950s, Ace Co., 7½" tall, three actions, rare	1000	1500	2000
"Sparky Savings Bank", 1930s, Byron Co., 4" long, 4½" high doghouse, minor toy (electro-magnet action includes 4" long compo dog)	60	90	120

	C6	C8	C10
"Sparky the Seal," 1950s, M-T Co., 6" high, 7" long, four actions, two cycles, includes celluoid ball	80	120	160
"Spirit of 1776," locomotive No. 4406, 1976, M-T Co., 15¾" long, five actions	40	60	80
"Sports Car Race Set," 1960's, TPS Co., Minor toy, 8"X14" base, includes 4 plastic racecars	80	120	160
"Star Strider" Robot, 1980s, S-H Co., six actions, 12" tall	110	165	220
"Steam Roller (Road Roller), 1950s, T-N Co., (Rosko), 12" long with trailer, four actions	90	135	180
"Steam Roller," 1950s, "Y" Co., 8" long, four actions (includes tin trailer)	100	150	200
"Steerable Tank," 1950s, Linemar Co., 9" long, 5 actions	60	90	120
"Strange Explorer," 1960s, DSK Co., 7½" long, four actions	300	450	600
"Strato Jct U.S.A.F.," 1950s, T-N Co., 13" long, 14" wingspan, three actions	120	180	240
"Strutting My Fair Dancer," (Dancing Sailor Girl), 1950s, Haji Co., 12" tall, (two pieces) a minor toy	100	150	200
"Struttin' Sam," 1950s, Haji Co., 10½" tall, minor jigger toy	200	300	400
"Sunbcam Jeep No. 1", 1940s, 10" long, Marusan Co., three actions	100	150	200
"Sunday Driver," 1950s, M-T Co., 10" long, four actions (includes detachable driver)	70	105	140
"Super Astronaut," Robot, 1960s, S-H Co., 11½" tall, five actions, two cycles	110	165	220
"Super Astronaut Robot," 1960s, SJM Co., 12" tall, four actions	150	225	300
"Super Giant Robot, 1960s, S-H Co., 15½" tall, six actions	200	300	400
"Super Jet," 1950s, T-N Co., three actions, 12" long, 8" wingspan	250	375	500
"Super Space Capsule," 1960s, S-H Co., 9" high, four actions	100	150	200
"Super Space Commander," 1960s, S-H Co., 10" tall, three actions	70	105	140
"Superman Tank," 1950s, Linemar Co., 10¼" long, three actions rare	600	900	1200+
"Surrey Jeep," 1960s, T-N Co., 11" long, three actions	90	135	180
"Susie the Cashier Bear," 1950s, Linemar Co., 9" high, six actions	300	450	600

Sky Patrol.

Slalom Game.

Smoking Popeye.

Space Patrol 3 Saucer.

Space Capsule - 5.

Somersaulting Pup.

Smoky Bear.

Thunder Jet Boat.

Space ExplorerShip X-7.

Star Strider.

Space Pioneer.

Courtesy Don Hultzman. Photos by Don Hultzman and Ron Chojnacki unless marked otherwise.

Teddy Bear Swing.

Strutting Sam.

The Playing Monkey.

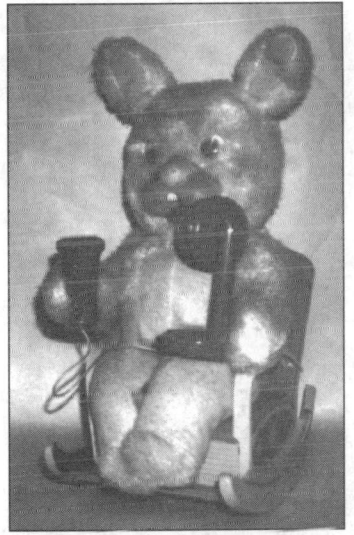

Telephone Bunny - Ringing And Talking in his Old Rocking Chair.

Television Spaceman.

The Loser.

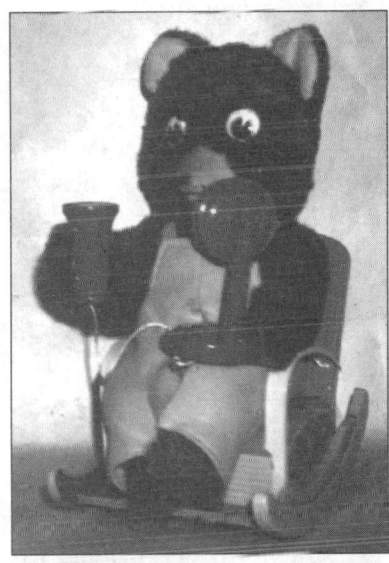

Telephone Bear - Ringing and Talking In His Old Rocking Chair.

Tom and Jerry Handcars.

Sunday Driver.

Tric-Cycling Clown.

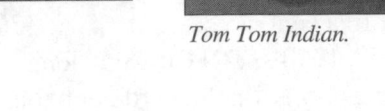

Tom Tom Indian.

Courtesy Don Hultzman. Photos by Don Hultzman and Ron Chojnacki unless marked otherwise.

	C6	C8	C10
"Suzy-Q Automatic Ironer," 1950s, GW Co., 7" high, four actions	90	135	180
"Suzette the Eating Monkey," 1950s, Linemar Co., 8¾" high, 7"x 5" base, five actions (includes tin litho steak) RARE	300	450	600
"Swingtail Airplane Flying Tigers," 1960s, Marx Co., 19½" long, 21" wingspan, seven actions	300	450	600
"Swing Tail Cargo Plane-Flying Tiger," 1960s, T-N Co., five actions, 14" long-14" wingspan	300	450	600
"Switchboard Operator" 1950s, Linemar, 7½" high, four actions, rare	350	525	700
"Swivel-O-Matic Astronaut" robot, 1960s, S-H Co., 11½"tall, five actions, 2 cycles	80	120	160
"T 360 Monoplane," 1950s, S&E Co., 12" long, 14½" wingspan, four actions ...... *see "Bristol Bulldog Airplane"*			
Talking Parrot," 1950s, T-N Co., 18" high, six actions (called "Pete")	200	300	400
"Talking Police Car-Mystery Action," 1960s, Y Co., 14" long, three actions	70	105	140
"Talking Robot," 1960s, Yonezawa Co., three actions, 10¾" tall, rare	600	900	1200
"Tank M-4 Combat Tank," 1960s, Taiyo Co., 11½" long, 13" with gun barrel extended, five actions	80	120	160
"Tank M-35," 1950s, HTC Co., 8" long, three actions	100	150	200
"Tank M-41," 1970s, J Co., 8¼" long, four actions	100	150	200
"Tank M-48-T," 1960s, T-N Co., 8¼" long, four actions	90	135	180
"Tank M-56," 1940s, M-T Co., 7½" long, wheel drive, seven actions	100	150	200
"Tank M-81," 1960s, M-T Co., 8½" long, seven actions	100	150	200
"Tank M-103," 1950s, M-T Co., 7" long, three actions	90	135	180
"Tank M-107-US Army," 1950s, Y Co., 6" long, 4 actions (includes four missiles)	120	180	240
"Tank M-X," 1950s, T-N Co., 8½" long, five actions	70	105	140
"Tank T-5," 1950's, T-N Co., 8½" long, three actions (includes detachable radar antenna)	110	165	220

	C6	C8	C10
"Tank 392-U.S. Tank Division," 1950's, Marx Co., three actions, 9½" long	70	105	140
"Tank X-3" (explorer defense), 1950s, Cragstan Co., 7¾"long, five actions, (includes six cartridge shells)	130	195	260
"Tank X-75," 1950's, M-T Co., 9" long, three actions (includes tin gun and darts)	110	165	220
"Tank-Daisymatic No 64 Rapid Fire Tank," 1960s , Daisy Mfg. Co., 8" long, four actions	120	180	240
"Tank-Daisy-Matic No. 80," 1965, Daisy Mfg. Co., 8½" long, five actions (includes darts)	100	150	200
"Tank Robot," 1960s, S-H Co., five actions, 10" tall	300	450	600
"Tarzan," 1966, Marusan Co., (Banner), four actions, 13" tall,	500	750	1000
"Taxi," (yellow cab), 1950s, Linemar Co., 7½" long, five actions	100	150	200
"Taxi Cab," 1950s, "Y" Co., 8½" long, five actions	90	135	180
"Taxi Cab," 1960's, Y Co., four actions, 9" long	90	135	180
"Teddy Bear Circus Acrobat," 1950's, Tomiyana Co., three actions, 15" high (includes detachable bear flyer). Rare.	500	750	1000
"Teddy Bear Swing," 1950s, T-N Co.,three actions, two cycles, 17" high, (includes four wire supports and tin sign)	250	375	500
"Teddy-Go-Kart," 1960s, Alps Co., 10½" long, four actions	100	150	200
"Teddy the Artist," 1950's, Y Co., 8½" high, 5¼"x 7" base, 3 actions, includes removable tray and 9 patterns	300	450	600
"Teddy the Boxing Bear," 1950s, "Y" Co., 9" tall, five actions	150	225	300
"Teddy the Rhythmical Drummer," 1960s, Alps Co., 11" tall, three actions	100	150	200
"Telephone Bear," 1950s, Linemar, 7½" high, six actions	160	240	320
"Telephone Bear - Ringing and Talking In His Old Rocking Chair," 1950s, M-T Co., 10" high, four actions	200	300	400
"Telephone Bunny-Ringing and Talking In His Old Rocking Chair," 1950s, M-T Co., 10" high, four actions	170	255	340
"Television Spaceman," 1960s, Alps Co., 14½" high to tip of antenna, six actions	400	600	800
"Television Truck," 1950s, Linemar Co., 11" long, three actions	250	375	500

Turn-O-Matic Gun Jeep.

Twin Coupled Tramcars.

U.S. Army Machine Gunner. Photo by Don Hultzman. Collection of Beau Cassity.

Walking Bear with Xylophone.

Two Stage Rocket Launching Pad.

Worried Mother Duck & Baby.

Winner of the West.

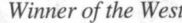

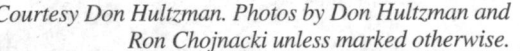

Twin Racing Cars.

Courtesy Don Hultzman. Photos by Don Hultzman and Ron Chojnacki unless marked otherwise.

	C6	C8	C10

"The Big Parade," 1963, Marx Co., 11½" tall, 15" wide, four actions (includes detachable gun and baton)................120 180 240

"The Loser," (Bar Toy), ca. 1971, Poynter Prod. Co., 3 actions, 13" high 40 60 80

"The Rabbits and Carriage," 1950's, S&E Co., four actions, 10" tall (should have tin Butterfly).............150 225 300

"The Playing Monkey", 1950s, S&E Co(Ahi Brand), six actions, 10" tall, includes detachable hat and tin yo yo............................200 300 400

"Thunder Jet Boat," 1950s, Bandai Co., 9¾" long, three actions 130 195 260

"Tin Man" Robot, 1960s, Remco Industries, Inc., 21" tall, all plastic, four actions 100 150 200

"Tinkling Trolley," 1950's, M-T Co., four actions, two cycle, 10½" long, includes two plastic cowcatchers...110 165 220

"Tiny Jeep," 1950's, WACO Co., 4¼" long, minor action............................30 45 60

"Tiny Tank," 1950's WACO Co., 4¼" long, minor action 30 45 60

"Tom and Jerry Car," 1960s, Rico Co., (Spain) 13" long, three actions, rare ..400 600 800

"Tom and Jerry Choo Choo," 1960s, M-T Co., 10¼" long, five actions..120 180 240

"Tom and Jerry Handcar- Jerry," 1960s, M-T Co., 7¾" high, 7¾" long, three actions 130 195 260

"Tom and Jerry Handcar- Tom," 1960s, M-T Co., 9¾" high, 7¾" long, three actions 130 195 260

"Tom and Jerry Helicopter," 1960s, M-T Co., 9½" long, three actions ..110 165 220

"Tom and Jerry Highway Patrol," 1960s, M-T Co., 8" long, three actions 120 180 240

"Tom and Jerry Jumping Jeep," 1960s, M-T Co., 9" long, three actions 120 180 240

"Tom-Tom Indian," 1961, Y Co., 10½" tall, four actions 80 120 160

"Topo Gigio Playing the Xylophone," 1960s, T-N Co., three actions.........300 450 600

"Torpedo Boat-PT 107," 1950s, Linemar 11½" long, three actions...................110 165 220

"Tractor", 1950s, Showa Co., 7-1/2" long, four actions (includes litho tin driver)..60 90 120

"Tractor," 1960s, Y Co., 6" long, three actions 50 75 100

"Tractor On Platform," 1950's, T-N Co., tractor 9" long, trailer 7" long, minor toy 80 120 160

"Train Robot," 1950's, M-T Co., four actions, 15½" tall, rare ....1500 2250 3000+

"Traveler Bear," 1950s, Linemar Co., 8" high, three actions 80 120 160

"Treasure Chest" Bank, 1960s, Illfelder Co., 11" tall, five actions, two cycles, risque toy- pg rated 90 135 180

"Tric-cycling Clown," 1960s, M-T Co., five actions, 12" high 300 450 600

"Tricky Dog House," No. 673, 1960s, Y Co., 6¾" high, 7¼" long, 6¾" wide, four actions............................60 90 120

"Trumpet Playing Bunny," 1950s, Alps Co., 10" high, four actions 150 225 300

"Trumpet Playing Monkey," 1950s, Alps Co., 9" high, four actions, includes tin horn...............................170 255 340

"Tubby the Turtle," 1950s, Y Co., 7" long, three actions 50 75 100

"Tugboat," 1950s, Marx, 6½" long, a minor toy...50 75 100

"Tugboat," 1950s, Marusan Co., 3 actions, 13½" long 110 165 220

"Tumbles the Bear," 1960s, Y-M Co., (Yanoman), 8½" tall, minor toy, includes porter's hat.......................80 120 160

"Turn Signal Robot," 1960s, T-N Co., 11" tall, five actions (Auto Accessory)..160 240 320

"Turn-O-Matic Gun Jeep," 1960s, T-N Co., 10" long, five Actions 100 150 200

"Turntable Xylophone Melody Train," 1960s, Cragstan Co., 29½" long assembled, three actions 50 75 100

"TWA Multiaction DC-7C Airliner," 1960s, Yonezawa Co., 22½" long, 23¼" wingspan, seven actions.......200 300 400

"Twin Coupled Tram Cars," 1950s, K Co., minor toy, 11½" long (two cars).......100 150 200

"Twin Racing Cars," 1950s, Alps Co., three actions, 7" long-10" long with coupling rod)..................400 600 800

"Twirly Whirly," 1950's, Alps Co., four actions, 13½" high..................350 525 700

"Twist Dancer" (Let's Twist), 1960s, no mfr. mark, minor toy, 15" high .100 150 200

"Two Stage Rocket Launching Pad," 1950s, T-N Co., 7" long, 4" wide, 8" high, three actions (includes 2 plastic-rubber rockets) 250 375 500

	C6	C8	C10

"UFO-X05," 1970s, M-T Co., 7½"
    diameter, three actions 50   75   100

"**Union** Mountain Cable Lines," Monorail
    set, 1950s, T-N Co., car 8" long, 16 pc.
    oval track, 22"x 32", minor toy..........80   120   160

"**United** DC7 Mainliner," 1950s, Yonezawa
    Co., 14" wingspan, five actions 200   300   400

"**United** Mainliner Stratocruiser,"
    1950s, Linemar, 19½" long, 13"
    wingspan, four actions 190   285   380

"**United** States Ocean Liner," 1950s, Linemar
    Co., 14" long, three actions 200   300   400

"**United** States Ocean Liner," 1950s,
    Y Co., three actions, 18½" long.....300   450   600

"**Universal** Machine Gun," 1950s, T-N
    Co., 14¾" long, three actions 70   105   140

"**USA**-NASA Apollo Space Ship, 1960s,
    M-T Co., 9" long, four actions..........150   225   300

"Usa-NASA Gemini Space Capsule,"
    1960s, M-T Co., 9"long, four actions
    (includes detachable astronaut).......120   180   240

"U.S. Army Machine Gunner," 1960s,
    unmarked, 10" long, 4 actions 100   150   200

"U.S. Air Force Military Airlift
    Command Jet," 1960s, T-N Co.,
    14" wingspan, 4 actions 130   195   260

"U.S. Air Force Smoking Jet No.
    75029," 1950s, (rare) T-N Co.,
    12" wingspan, 3 actions, smokes,
    engine noise, bump & go 200   300   400

"U.S. Navy Pom Pom Gun," 1950s,
    Remco Co., 20" long, four actions. 80   120   160

"U.S. Royal Tire-Mechanical Toy" (Ferris
    Wheel) souvenir for 1964-65 N.Y.
    World's Fair (now permanently
    located at Uniroyal Co. on rt.. 94, west
    of Detroit), includes plastic figures,
    minor toy, 10" high, Ideal.................100   150   200

"Video Robot," 1960s, S-H Co., 10"
    tall, three actions 90   135   180

"V.I.P the Busy Boss," 1950s, S&E
    Co., 8" high, six actions 220   330   440

"Visible Ford Mustang," 1960s, Ban-
    dai Co., 10" long, four actions 80   120   160

"Vision Robot," 1960s, S-H Co.,
    11¾" tall, five actions 150   225   300

"Voice Control Astronaut Base,"
    1969, Remco Co., 19" long, four
    actions (includes plastic missiles
    and phonograph records) 90   135   180

"Volkswagen Convertible," 1950's,
    T-N Co., three actions, 9¾" long ...250   375   500

"Volkswagen-Elektrik," 1950s, Mignon
    Co., 8½" long, three actions 70   105   140

"Volkswagen No. 7653," 1960s, Ban-
    dai Co., 10" long, three actions......90   135   180

"Volkswagen With Visible Engine," 1960s,
    K.O. Co., 7" long, three actions.......80   120   160

"Volkswagen with Visible Engine No.
    4049," 1960s, Bandai Co., 8" long,
    three actions 90   135   180

"Wagon Master," 1960s, M-T Co.,
    18" long, four actions.....................120   180   240

"Walking Bear with Xylophone," 1950s,
    Linemar Co., 10" high, seven actions . 200   300   400

"Walking Elephant," 1950s, Linemar
    Co., 8½" long, three actions 90   135   180

"Walking 'Esso' Tiger," 1950s, Marx
    Co., 11½" tall, four actions 250   375   500

"Walking Itchy Dog," 1950s, Alps
    Co., 9" long, five actions 60   90   120

"Walky-Son" (Los), 1960s, rare, Geyper
    Co., 4 actions, 11½" high, includes
    detachable guns and baton ...._see "Los Walky Son"_

"Warpath Indian," 1950s, Alps Co.,
    12" tall, three actions....................80   120   160

"Wash-O -Matic" washing machine,
    1940s, T-N Co., 5¾" high, 4¼"
    diameter, a minor toy, includes lid..30   45   60

"Water Spouting Whale with Flopping
    Tail," 1950s, KKS Co., 13" long,
    minor toy.....................................100   150   200

"Western Badman", (Red Gulch Bar),
    1960s, M-T Co., 9-3/4" high, eight
    actions, includes 3 plastic bottles
    and 2 plastic glasses........................ 300   450   600

"Western Express," Locomotive, 1960s,
    Kanto Toy Co., 14" long, four actions .50   75   100

"Western Locomotive," 1950s, M-T
    Co., 10½" long, four actions...........50   75   100

"Western Special Locomotive," 1950s,
    M-T Co., 12" long, five actions 50   75   100

"Wheel-A-Gear" Robot, 1960s, Taiyo
    Co., 14" tall, five actions 250   375   500

"WHOH-Skyway Patrol Helicopter," 1950s,
    M-T Co., 18" long, four actions...........100   150   200

"Whirlybird Helicopter," 1960s, Remco
    Co., 25" long, three actions 80   120   160

"Whistling Showboat," 1950s, M-T
    Co., 14" long, three actions............120   180   240

"Wild West Rodeo," 1950s, Linemar, 6½"
    long, 8" high, five actions, includes
    plastic bowl for bubble solution.........100   150   200

	C6	C8	C10
"Windy the Elephant" 1950s, T-N Co., 9¾" high, 3 actions, includes celluloid ball and tin litho umbrella	140	210	280
"Winner-23," Rocket, 1950s, KDP Co., (Excelo), 5½" long, minor action, includes rubber track	150	225	300
"Winner of the West"-Overland Stagecoach with Four Galloping Horses, 1950s, Alps Co., four actions, 18" long	200	300	400
"Winston the Barking Bulldog," 1950s, Tomiyama Co., three actions, two cycles, 10" long	70	105	140
"Worried Mother Duck and Baby", 1950s, T-N Co., 11" long, 7" high, three actions	100	150	200
"X-7 Space Explorer Ship," 1960s, M-T Co., 7" diameter, four actions	90	135	180
"X-70 Robot," 1960s, T-N Co., 12¼" tall, five actions, Rare	500	750	1000+
"X-1800 Space Vehicle," 1960s, M-T Co., 9" long, five actions (includes detachable plastic antenna)	140	210	280
"X-F 160 Jet Airplane," 1960s, K-O Co., 8" wingspan	80	120	160
"Yeti the Abominable Snowman," 1960s, Marx, 12" tall, four actions	300	450	600
"Yo-Yo Clown," 1960s, Alps Co., 9" high, three actions (includes plastic yo-yo)	170	255	340
"Yo-Yo Monkey," 1960s, Alps Co., 9" tall, three actions (includes plastic yo-yo)	140	210	280
"Yo-Yo Monkey," 1960s, Y-M Co., 12" tall, spring extension to 32", minor	100	150	200
"Yummy Yum Kitty", 1950s, Alps Co., 9½" high, 5 actions	200	300	400
"Zero Fighter Plane," 1950s, Bandai Co., 12½" long, 15" wingspan, three actions	160	240	320
"Zoom Motorboat," 1950s, K Co., 12" long, three actions	90	135	180
"Zoomer the Robot," 1950s, T-N Co., 8" tall, three actions	250	375	500

Smoking Popeye. Courtesy Christie's East.

Superman Tank, Linemar. Courtesy Christie's East.

Mechanized Robot. Courtesy Christie's East.

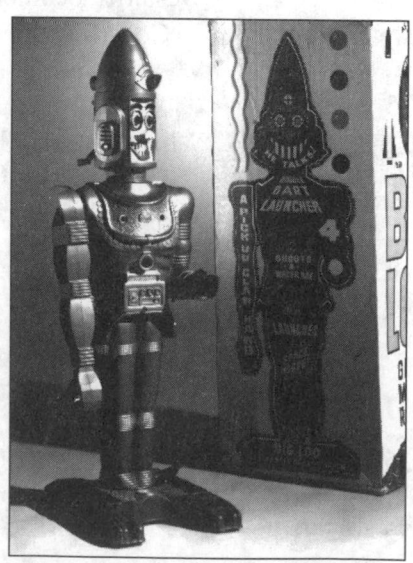

Big Loo. Courtesy Christie's East.

"Mechanized Robot" (Robby). This toy was auctioned, with box, in late 1990 in near-mint condition for $27,830. Courtesy James S. Maxwell/Virginia Caputo. Photo by Virginia caputo.

SOLDIERS

The average price in the last edition of American dimestore soldiers listed here was $45.29 and in this edition it is $50.74, an increase of 12%.

CONDITION OF A TOY SOLDIER AND ITS RELATION TO PRICE

The price of a toy soldier depends not only on its desirability, but on its condition. "Mint" means just that; the condition in which it was originally issued - perfect, regardless of age, not the slightest blemish. Needless to say this is a fairly rare state of affairs, but enough soldiers exist in mint condition to make it an employable term. Many people, hoping to dispose of toys, are tempted to term them "mint" when they are really "near mint", "very good" or sometimes even just "good". Inevitably this can result in unhappiness all around, and not infrequently, in a canceled sale.

"Very Good" indicates a soldier which has obviously seen use; with signs of wear and aging, but with most of its paint remaining and in general having a freshness to its appearance that makes it seem attractive and collectible to all but the most discriminating.

"Good" signals a soldier that has seen considerable wear, but has at least one half to one third of its original paint, and is basically sound. A collector will collect it, but will often not be wholly satisfied with it as an example of

his collection, and thus prices are well below that which the same item in mint can command.

Condition below good results in another drastic drop in price, and figures with missing parts, although otherwise in excellent condition, will usually fall into this lower-priced category. At present, a BARCLAY soldier minus its tin helmet (signaled by a large round hole in the top of its head) is worth about half of what it would otherwise bring. Rust, even small spots of it on the cast iron soldiers, can seriously lower their price, as can repainting of any of the soldiers. "Near-Mint," "Fine," "Very Fine" and similar terms often found in sellers' descriptions, denote conditions between Mint and Very Good, and are priced accordingly.

The key to grading is to avoid wishful thinking. Grading can sometimes be a problem for the uninitiated, but common sense will usually prevail, and when possible a consultation with an expert in the field can often clear up lingering doubts. A toy in its original box is worth up to 10 to 20% more if the box is in mint condition, with the price dropping as condition lessens.

BARCLAY

(See Vehicles, Animal-Drawn, Aircraft and Miscellaneous)

Barclay Mfg. Co. was the largest manufacturer of toy soldiers in the U.S. prior to World War II, selling millions of figures annually. The company, named after Barclay Street in West Hoboken, New Jersey, (now 10th Street in Union City) began in 1924 or late 1923, owned by an elderly Frenchman, Leon Donze (1865-66-1950) and by Michael Levy (c. 1895-10/9/64), who became affiliated by buying a partnership. Levy eventually took over the company (around 1929) and it was he who turned it into a major one. From five employees in 1924, the company expanded to a pre-War peak of 400 workers, and moved several times as it was forced to expand. Barclay's soldiers came in four styles prior to World War II. The first, which were probably produced almost from Barclay's beginning, were small, with the mounted figures having moving arms. The second, approximately 3-1/4" high, with a separate tin helmet, seem to have begun production in 1935, and were designed and sculpted by Barclay employee Frank Krupp. This figure (the tin helmet was subcontracted) was rather stiff and is known by collectors as "short stride" because its marching figures' feet were close together. The third style, again by Krupp, also had a separate tin helmet, was more realistic, and is known as "long stride." These were on sale as early as 1936. In 1937 or 1938, a clip was designed to hold on the tin helmets, as the formerly glued-on helmets

frequently came off, and drew complaints from the chain stores such as Woolworth's, which sold Barclay toys. The fourth style, introduced about 1939-1940, when Barclay moved from slush casting to die casting its soldiers, was by free-lance artist Olive Kooken (1904-1964), and is known as "cast helmet", as the soldiers featured helmets that were an integral part of the figure. Barclay's soldiers were made of antimonial lead, consisting of about 13% antimony and the rest lead. When slush-molding was done, only one mold was made of each single figure. The lead would be poured into the mold, rocked, and immediately poured out, those providing a hollow figure. Later, the die-cast molds produced a number of the same figures at the same time. During the Second World War Barclay laid off all but four of its employees, and did sub-contract work. It was never as successful after the war, and finally closed down in 1971, by this time employing only 50-75 people. Although Barclay assigned numbers to its figures from the beginning for its own records, many of the soldiers themselves bore no numbers. Figures listed with a question mark after the number are based on the memory of longtime Barclay employee George Fall, whose memory, judged against known Barclay numbers, is quite accurate, but not infallible. All short stride Barclays have separate helmets.

Top left to right: Ba, Baa, Bb, Bba, Bc
Bottom left to right: Be, Bfa, Bg, Bh

Left to right: Bi, Bj, Bk

L to R: Bl, Bm

Pre - 1934
*(All **bold words** and numbers are **Barclay's Own Description**)*

	C6	C8	C10
(Ba) **87?** Mounted Officer, moving arm holding sword, on rearing horse	26	39	52
(Baa) **87?** Same as above on cantering horse..................	26	39	52
(Bb) **87?** Mounted Officer, moving arm holding bugle, on rearing horse	26	39	52
(Bba) **87?** Same as above, on cantering horse...............	26	39	52
(Bc) **87?** Mounted Officer, moving arm holding pistol on cantering horse....	32	48	64
(Bd) **88?** Mounted Cowboy with lasso....	No Price Found		
(Be) **89?** Mounted Indian, moving arm holding rifle.....................	40	60	80
(BeA) Same as above, holding pistol	40	60	80
(Bf) **90?** Mounted Cowboy with pistol..	40	60	80
(BfA) **90?** Mounted Cowboy with moving arm, holding rifle (horse's tail missing in photo)	35	53	70
(Bfa) Indian Chief on foot, 54mm high, blue and red-striped headdress, may look like Ideal I-14...........................	No Price Found		
(Bfb) Indian brave on foot, 54 mm high, carrying rifle across stomach ...	No Price Found		
(Bg) **186?** Cavalryman mounted, 2¾" high, no moving parts, modeled on French toy soldier, circa late 1920s-early 30s	11	16	22
(Bh) **486 Cavalryman**, approx. 2¼" high, circa early 30s, no moving parts	10	15	21
(Bi) Baseball fielder, approx. 1⅞" high, circa 1920s	42	63	85
(Bj) Baseball pitcher, circa 1920s	42	63	85
(Bk) Baseball batter, circa 1920s..........	42	63	85
(Bl) Mounted Indian on rearing horse ...	15	23	30
(Bm) **200 Jockey on Horse**	17	25	34
(Bn) **No. 87 Officer on Horse**, smaller size, circa 1931 (4 known)	125	188	250

Bn
Courtesy Bill O'Brien

1934 and After

	C6	C8	C10
(BA) Paint Your Own Army Set No. 2003, circa 1934, boxed.................	120	180	240
(BAa) Paint Your Own Army Set No. 2003, larger size than above, same toys, with compartment for one more toy. Only 1 known	No Price Found		
(BAC) **89 Indian on Horse** (on catalog sheet with Ethiopians).....................	23	35	46
(BAD) **90 Cowboy on Horse** (on catalog sheet with Ethiopians)	22	33	45
(B1) **89 Indian on Horse**	13	19	26
(B1-A) As above, Indian's head turned to his right........................	22	33	44
(B1a) **89 Indian on Horse** two feathers (earlier)...............................	22	33	44
(B2) **90 Cowboy on Horse**	14	21	28

Top L to R: BAC, BAD, B1, B1a
Bottom L to R: B2, B2A, B2AA

L to R: B2C, B3

L to R: B3A. B4

Top L to R: B5, B6, B7, B9, B10, B11
Bottom L to R: B12, B13, B14, B15, B16

L to R: B12, B12A
Photo by K. Warren Mitchell

	C6	C8	C10
(B2A) **90 Cowboy on Horse** variation, thinner bullets in gunbelt, saddle not as long	14	21	29
(B2AA) **90 Cowboy on Horse**, variation, no bullets in gunbelt	50	75	100
(B2AAA) **100 Masked Rider on Horse** (may not have been produced; in the order sheet the figure faces forward)	No Price Found		
(B2B) **100? "Masked Rider With Lasso"**, horse's tail down	22	33	44
(B2C) **100? "Masked Rider With Lasso"**, horse's tail up	18	27	36
(B3) 87? Mounted, in grey cap, intermediate size	37	53	75
(B3A) **87 Officer on Horse**, in cap, khaki or grey, larger black, grey or brown horse	17	26	35
(B4) 87? Mounted in colored jacket and cap, may be Chinese or Japanese (horse's tail missing in photo)	24	36	48
(B5) **701 Flagbearer**, tin helmet, short stride	12	18	25
(B6) **701 Flagbearer**, tin helmet, long stride	10	15	20
(B7) **701 Flagbearer**, cast helmet	9	14	19
(B8) **701** Flagbearer, Cuban flag variation painted for 10 Woolworth's in Cuba, cast helmet or pot helmet	No Price Found		

	C6	C8	C10
(B9) **701 Machine-Gunner**, kneeling, short stride	8	12	16
(B10) **702 Machine-Gunner**, kneeling, long stride	10	15	20
(B11) **702** Machine-Gunner, kneeling, cast helmet	10	15	20
(B12) **703 Sniper**, kneeling, firing short stride	8	12	16
(B12A) 703 Sniper, kneeling, firing, short stride, shorter rifle, in front of fingers fat portion of gun and thin portion of barrel about equal length	10	15	20
(B13) **703 Sniper**, kneeling, firing, long stride, tin helmet	10	15	20

Top L to R: B17, B18, B18a, B19, B20, B21

Bottom L to R: B22, B23, B24, B25, B25a, B25b, B26, B27, B28

B18a Courtesy Don Pielin

Top L to R: B29, B30, B31, B32, B33, B34

Bottom L to R: B35, B36, B37, B37a, B38, B39, B40

	C6	C8	C10
(B14) **704 Soldier on Parade**, shoulder arms, short stride	8	12	16
(B15) **704 Soldier on Parade**, shoulder arms, long stride, tin helmet	9	13	18
(B16) **705 Soldier at Attention** (actually port arms)	11	16	21
(B17) **705** Soldier at Attention (actually port arms), cast helmet	10	15	21
(B18) **706 Soldier**, charging, short stride	9	14	19
(B18a) Same as above, with shorter rifle, sling around hand, two known.	425	638	850
(B19) **706** Tall, tin helmet, solid puttees	300	450	600
(B20) **706** Soldier, charging, tin helmet, long stride	55	82	110
(B21) **706** Soldier, charging, cast helmet	13	19	26
(B22) **707** At Attention, cast helmet	10	15	21
(B23) **708 Officer** with sword, short stride	12	18	25
(B24) **723 Marine Officer**, same as above, in blue	16	24	33
(B25) **708 Officer**, with sword, tin helmet, long stride	8	12	17
(B25a) 708 Officer with sword, tin helmet, long stride, no chest strap	60	90	120
(B25b) 723 Marine Officer with sword, tin helmet, long stride, no chest strap, in blue	60	90	120
(B26) **723 Marine Officer**, with sword, tin helmet, long stride	12	18	25

	C6	C8	C10
(B27) **708** Officer with sword, cast helmet	32	48	65
(B28) **708** Marine Officer with sword, cast helmet	27	40	55
(B29) **709 Bugler**, short stride	11	16	22
(B30) **709 Bugler**, long stride, tin helmet	8	12	17
(B31) **710 Drummer** short stride	11	16	22
(B32) **710 Drummer** long stride, tin helmet	11	16	22
(B33) **711 Drum Major**, short stride	12	18	25
(B34) **711** Drum Major, long stride, tin helmet	12	18	25
(B35) **743 West Point Officer**, short stride	7	11	15

334

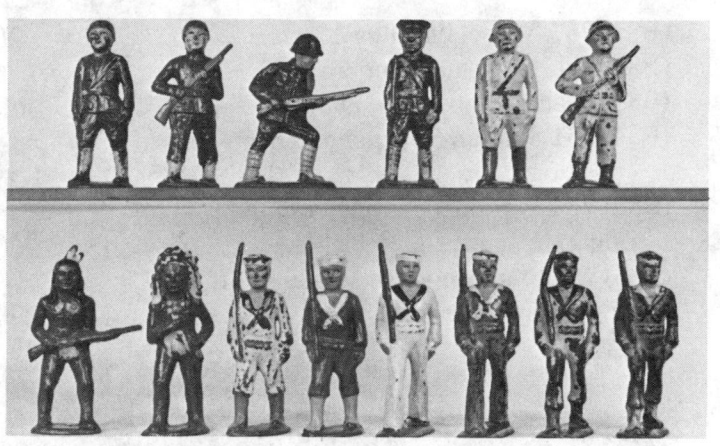

Top L to R: B41, B42, B43, B44, B45, B46
Bottom L to R: B47, B48, B49, B50, B51, B51a, B52, B52a

Top L to R: B53, B54, B55, B55a, B56, B57, B58
Bottom L to R: B59, B59a, B60, B61

	C6	C8	C10
(B36) **718 West Point Cadet**, with rifle, short stride	10	15	20
(B37) Same as above but painted as wooden soldier, only 4 known	300	450	600
((B37a) Same as B36, with line-and-dot eyes, white pants, white gloves	10	15	20
(B38) **718 West Point Cadet**, long stride	8	12	16
(B39) **724 Ethiopian Soldier**, circa 1935-36	100	150	205
(B40) **725 Ethiopian Officer**, circa 1935-36	109	164	218
(B41) **727 Italian Officer**, circa 1935-36	90	135	180
(B42) **726 Italian Soldier**, circa 1935-36	100	150	200
(B43) Japanese, charging with rifle, circa 1937	60	90	120
(B44) Japanese Officer, circa 1937 (this is the original Ethiopian officer, painted as a Japanese)	110	165	220
(B45) Chinese or Mongolian Officer in steel helmet, circa 1937	112	168	225

	C6	C8	C10
(B46) Chinese or Mongolian Rifleman circa 1937, pronounced right breast pocket	82	123	165
(B46a) Same as above, narrower face, faint right breast pocket	82	123	165
(B47) **717 Indian Brave**, rifle across waist	7	11	14
(B48) **716 Indian Chief**	7	11	15
(B49) **719 Sailor White Uniform**, marching, short stride	9	13	18
(B50) **720 Sailor Blue Uniform**, like above.	11	16	23
(B51) **719** Sailor White Uniform, long stride, bell bottoms	7	11	15
(B51a) 720 Sailor in Blue Uniform, long stride, bell bottoms	12	18	25
(B52) **719 Sailor in White Uniform**, in puttees	8	12	16
(B52a) **720 Sailor Blue Uniform**, in puttees	9	13	18
(B53) **756 Sailor, Flagbearer**, long stride	15	22	30
(B54) **721 Naval Officer**, short stride, tin top to cap	45	68	90
(B54a) Same as above, in blue	50	75	100
(B55) **721 Naval Officer**, short stride	11	17	23
(B55a) 721 Naval Officer, same as above, in blue	100	150	200
(B56) **721 Naval Officer**, long stride	11	16	23
(B57) **722 Marine**, short stride, tin top to cap	45	68	90
(B58) **722 Marine**, short stride	11	16	22
(B59) 722 Marine, long stride	10	15	20
(B59a) 722 Marine, long stride, white cap (probably post-War)	11	16	22
(B60) **757 Sailor with Signal Flags**	13	19	27
(B60a) **757 Sailor with Signal Flags**, flat underbase, minor variations in cap	13	19	27
(B61) **728 Machine Gunner Lying Flat**	9	13	18
(B62) **728 Machine Gunner Lying Flat**, cast helmet	10	15	21
(B63) **728 Machine Gunner Lying Flat**, cast helmet, lip of base extends under gun barrel	11	16	22
(B64) **750 Soldier, Crawling**	10	15	20
(B65) **730 Soldier Signal Man with Flag**	10	15	21
(B66) **731 Soldier Pigeon Dispatcher**	11	16	22
(B67) **732 Soldier Telephone Operator**	8	12	16
(B68) **733 Soldier Bullet Feeder** (actually a shell)	8	12	17
(B69) **734 Soldier Ammunition Carrier**	9	13	18
(B70) **735 Soldier Range Finder**	9	13	18
(B71) **736 Soldier Sentry**	9	13	19

Top L to R: B62, B63, B64, B65
Bottom L to R: B66, B67, B68, B69, B70, B71

Top L to R: B72, B73, B74, B75, B76, B77
Bottom L to R: B78, B79, B79a, B80, B81, B81a, B82, B83

	C6	C8	C10
(B72) **737 Soldier Charging Machine Gunner**, tin helmet	8	12	17
(B73) **737** Soldier Charging Machine gunner, cast helmet	15	22	31
(B74) **738 Soldier Bomb Thrower**	10	15	21
(B75) **738** Soldier Bomb Thrower, tall, tin helmet, solid puttees	300	450	600
(B76) **738** Soldier Bomb Thrower, rifle off ground, tin helmet	12	18	25
(B77) **738** Soldier Bomb Thrower, rifle off ground, cast helmet	16	24	32
(B78) **739 Soldier Fifer**	11	16	22
(B79) **740 Soldier French Horn**	10	15	20
(B79a) Machine Gunner, seated, cast helmet, bandage-type puttees	16	24	33
(B80) **741 Aviator**	8	12	17
(B81) **745 Navy Doctor,** in white, flat underbase	9	13	19
(B81a) **746 Army Doctor,** in brown, flat underbase	11	16	22
(B81A&B) **746** Doctor, as above, inverted base	8	12	16

	C6	C8	C10
(B82) **767 Nurse,** kneeling	10	15	20
(B83) **744 Nurse,** hand on hip	8	12	17
(B83a) Same as above in blue	50	75	100
(B84) **751 Soldier, Sharpshooter,** prone position	10	15	21
(B85) **762 Wounded,** sitting, arm in sling	10	15	20
(B86) **707 Sharpshooter,** standing, firing, short stride	10	15	20

Top L to R: B84, B85, B86, B87, B88
Bottom L to R: B89, B90, B91, B92

	C6	C8	C10
(B87) **747 Sharpshooter,** standing, firing, long stride	10	15	20
(B88) **747** Sharpshooter, standing, firing cast helmet	9	13	19
(B89) **748 Soldier, Running** with rifle, tin helmet	10	15	20
(B90) **748** Soldier, Running, with rifle, cast helmet	13	19	27
(B91) **749 Soldier, Gas Mask,** charging with rifle	10	15	20
(B92) **749** Soldier, Gas Mask, charging with rifle cast helmet	13	19	27
(B93) 310 Army Motorcyclist	20	30	40
(B93a) **310 Cop** on motorcycle	23	35	46
(B93b) 310 Motorcyclist, head higher	20	30	40
(B93c) 310 Cop on motorcycle, head lower	20	30	40
(B93d) 310 Motorcyclist, larger, markings on cycle, like B93A and B93B, but cruder	25	38	50
(B93A) **310** Army Motorcyclist, post-War, dot eyes or none at all, larger, motor variation	25	38	50
(B93B) **310** Cop on Motorcycle, post-War, dot eyes, or none at all, larger, Motor variation	22	33	45
(B94) **715 Cowboy** with tin hat brim	9	13	18
(B94A) Same as above, badge, stripes, painted on vest		No Price Found	

Top Row, Left to Right: B93, B93b, B93c.
Bottom Row, Left to Right: B93d, B93A, B93B

Top L to R: B94, B95, B95A, B95a, B96
Bottom L to R: B97, B97a, B98, B99, B100

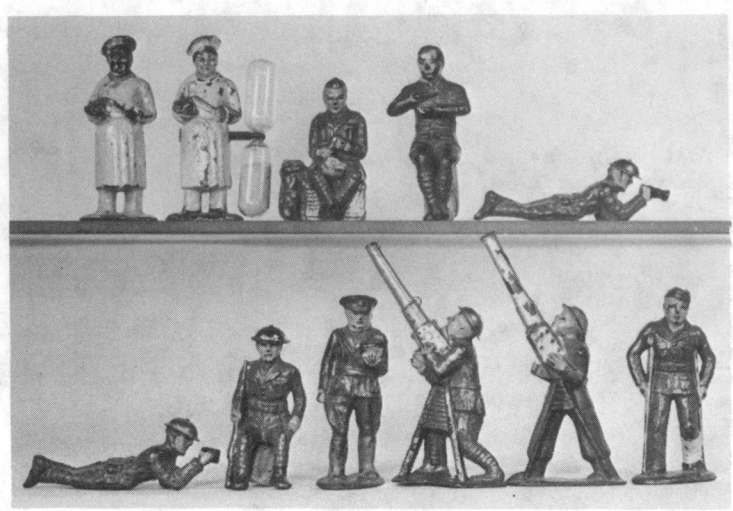

Top L to R: B110, B110a, B111, B112, B113
Bottom L to R: B114, B115, B116, B117, B118, B119

	C6	C8	C10
(B95) **752 Cowboy with lasso**	8	12	16
(B95A) 752 Masked Cowboy with lasso	8	12	16
(B95a) 752 Cowboy with lasso, Post-WW II version, lasso goes directly through hands	8	12	16
(B96) **753 Cowboy With Two Guns,** pointing one	8	12	17
(B97) **754 Indian Chief,** tomahawk and shield	8	12	17
(B97a) Same as above, flat base, some with fatter legs	5	8	11
(B98) **755 Indian, Bow and Arrow**	6	9	13
(B99) **756 Indian Chief,** long headdress, may only have been produced post-WW II	43	66	86
(B100) **757 Indian Brave,** standing with bow and arrow, may only have been produced post WW II	14	21	28

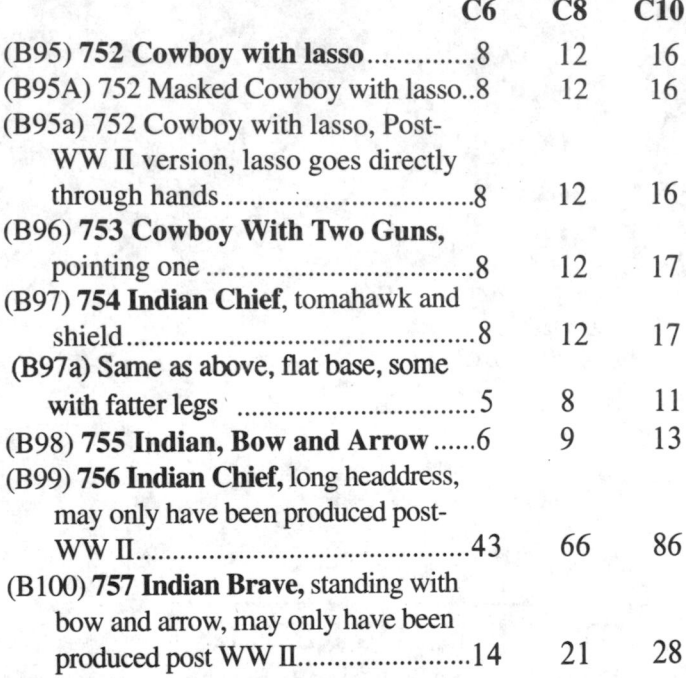

Top L to R: B101, B102, B102a, B103, B104
Bottom L to R: B105, B106, B107, B107a, B108, B109

	C6	C8	C10
(B101) **758 Camera Man,** kneeling, tin helmet	17	25	34
(B102) **759 Soldier, Stretcher Bearer,** open hand	36	54	72
(B102a) **759** Soldier, Stretcher Bearer, closed hand	9	13	19
(B103) **760 Surgeon,** with stethoscope	11	16	23
(B104) **761** Lying wounded, tin helmet	7	11	14
(B105) **763 Raiding,** in crouch, in helmet	11	16	22
(B106) **767 Advance,** raised rifle, tin helmet	13	19	26
(B107) **765 Bayoneting,** although no bayonet, thrusting with gun muzzle; tin helmet	21	32	43
(B107a) **756** Bayoneting, same as above, no bayonet, cast helmet	80	120	160
(B108) **766 Clubbing** with rifle, tin helmet	27	41	54
(B109) **766** Clubbing with rifle, cast helmet	45	68	90
(B110) **769 Cook** holding roast	14	21	29
(B110a) 769 Cook egg-timer	35	52	70
(B111) **771 Peeling Potatoes**	12	18	24
(B112) Soldier eating	18	27	36
(B113) 729 Soldier with Binoculars, long binoculars	12	18	25
(B114) **729 Soldier with Binoculars,** short binoculars	46	69	93
(B115) **760 Soldier Sitting Position**	15	22	31
(B116) **776 Officer Reading Orders**	9	13	19
(B117) **774** Soldier with AA gun, tin helmet	10	15	20
(B118) **774** Soldier with AA gun, cast helmet	8	12	17
(B119) **775** Wounded on crutches	11	16	22

Top L to R: B101, B102, B102a, B103, B104
Bottom L to R: B105, B106, B107, B107a, B108, B109

L to R: B120, B120a, B121

	C6	C8	C10
(B120) **776** Standing at searchlight, smooth lens, elevation wheel 50		75	100
(B120a) **776** Standing at searchlight, smooth lens, no elevation wheel 55		82	110
(B121) **776** Standing at searchlight, ridges along base (this and following have ridged lenses) 14		21	29

L to R: B122, B123, B124, B125

	C6	C8	C10
(B122) **776** Standing at searchlight, smooth base connected to searchlight, no elevation wheel 14		21	29
(B123) **776** Standing at searchlight, low seat, not connected to searchlight 12		18	24
(B124) **776** Standing at searchlight, high seat, two rivets in front of left foot 18		27	36
(B125) **776** Standing at searchlight, high seat, no rivets in front of left foot.......15		22	30

L to R: B126, B127, B128, B129, B130

	C6	C8	C10
(B126) **777** Marching with pack, tin helmet......................................10		15	21
(B127) **777** Marching with pack, cast helmet. 9		13	18
(B128) **778** Officer with gas mask, cast helmet......................................10		15	21
(B129) **779** Firing from behind wall, cast helmet 32		48	64
(B130) **780** Falling with rifle, cast helmet .18		27	36

L to R: B131, B132, B133, B134, B135

L to R: B136, B137, B139, B140, B141

L to R: B142, B143, B144, B145

	C6	C8	C10
(B131) **781** Digging, cast helmet 22		33	45
(B132) **782** Leaning out, with field phone, antenna, cast helmet 34		51	68
(B133) **783** Crouching with binoculars, cast helmet 18		27	37
(B134) **784** Parachutist landing.............12		18	25
(B135) **785** Skier in white, cast helmet, 1940, with separate metal skis. (Meant to be Finn) No left breast pocket 22		33	45
(B135a) as above, has left breast pocket. Same value as above			
(B136) **785** Skier in white, no skis 11		16	22
(B137) **785** Skier in brown, no skis.......26		39	52
(B138) **785** Skier in red, meant to be Russian, may not have been produced (listing based on memory) ......No Price Found			
(B139) **787** Diver with axe 350		525	700
(B140) **788** Marching with slung rifle, cast helmet 10		15	20
(B141) **789** Soldier with AA gun, cast helmet, sitting............................. 11		16	22
(B142) **790** Two soldiers on raft, cast helmet...32		48	65
(B143) **791** Two-man rocket team........13		19	26
(B144) **792** Mechanic with airplane engine, prop spins, brace on back of engine bulges 22		33	44

L to R: B146, B147, B148, B149, B150

L to R: B160, B161, B162, B163, B164, B165, B166

	C6	C8	C10
(B144a) Same as above, brace on back of engine doesn't bulge) 22	33	44
(B145) Soldier kneeling with anti-tank gun, cast helmet 12	18	25
(B146) **960 Surgeon and Soldier** 46	69	92
(B147) **951 Soldier Wireless Operator** .. 16	24	33
(B148) **952 Soldier, Dispatcher with Dog** 29	44	59
(B149) **953** American Legionnaire in overseas cap, tall, made for 1937 Legion convention in New York, 12 known color combinations 150	225	300
(B150) 954? American Legionnaire flag-bearer, tall, cloth flag, made in 1937, as above, five known 300	450	600

	C6	C8	C10
(B160) **613 Porter,** with whisk broom ... 7	11	15
(B161) **612 Conductor** 7	11	15
(B162) **615 Engineer** 7	10	14
(B163) **616 Boy** 5	8	11
(B164) **617 Girl** 5	8	10
(B165) **618 Elderly Woman** 6	9	13
(B166) **619 Old Man** 7	11	14

L to R: B151, B151A, B152, B153

L to R: B167, B168, B169, B170, B171, B171a, B172

	C6	C8	C10
(B167) **620** Minister walking 21	32	43
(B168) **621** Minister holding hat 9	13	18
(B169) **621** Newsboy 6	9	13
(B170) **622** Shoeshine boy 14	21	28
(B171) **623** Detective with pistol 55	82	110
(B172) **624** Burglar 60	90	120

L to R: B154, B155, B156, B157, B158, B159

L to R: B173, B174, B175, B176, B177, B178, B179

	C6	C8	C10
(B151) **961 At Typewriter,** with typewriter and table 32	48	64
(B151A) **770 At Mess,** typist alone, apparently meant to sit at mess table 7	11	15
(B152) **374 Army Motorcycle,** with side-car 37	56	75
(B153) **45** "Machine Gunner and Driver" 26	39	52
(B154) **714 Pirate** 9	13	18
(B155) **713 Knigh**t with pennant 8	12	17
(B156) **712 Knight** with shield 7	11	15
(B157) **610 Woman Passenger,** with dog .. 5	8	11
(B158) **611 Man Passenger,** overcoat over arm 6	9	12
(B159) **614 Red Cap** with bags 8	12	16

	C6	C8	C10
(B173) **625 Bride** 10	15	20
(B174) **626 Groom** 9	13	18
(B175) **627 Girl in Rocker** 9	13	18
(B176) **628 Boy Skater** 6	9	12
(B177) **629 Girl Skater** 6	9	12
(B178) **630 1/2 Man and Woman on Park Bench** 16	24	33
(B179) Seated man and woman in winter coats 15	22	31
(B180) **635 Man Speed Skater** 7	11	15
(B181) **636 Girl Figure Skater** 7	11	15
(B182) **801 Boy Scout Hiking** 32	48	65
(B183) **802 Boy Scout Saluting** 14	21	29
(B184) **803 Boy Scout Signaling** 17	26	35
(B185) **804 Boy Scout Cooking** 22	33	44
(B186) **850 Policeman,** arm raised 7	11	15

B198

L to R: B199, B200

Top L to R: B180, B181, B182, B183, B184, B185
Bottom L to R: B186, B186a, B187, B187a, B188, B189

	C6	C8	C10
(B186a) 850 Policeman, figure eight base..	11	16	23
(B187) **851 Fireman,** with axe	11	16	23
(187a) Fireman with axe, flat under-base..	12	19	25
(B188) **852 Fireman** (with hose)..........	13	19	26
(B189) **853 "Postman"**	7	11	15

	C6	C8	C10
(B198) **510 One Horse Open Sleigh**			
(Sleigh, horse, seated man and woman).	44	66	88
(B199) **530 Man Pulling Children on Sled.**	23	35	47
(B200) **535 Young Man putting**			
Skates on Girl Sitting on Bench...	50	75	100

Post World War II

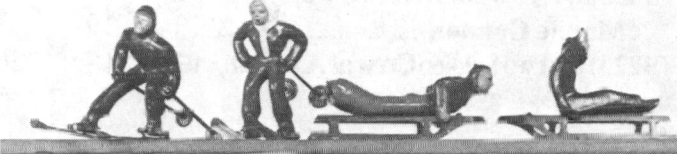

L to R: B190, B191, B192, B193

	C6	C8	C10
(B190) **495 Man on skis**	11	16	22
(B191) **496 Girl on skis**	11	16	22
(B192) **497 Man on Sled**	9	13	19
(B193) **498 Girl on Sled**	9	13	18

L to R: B194, B195, B196, B197

	C6	C8	C10
(B194) **499 Santa Claus on Sled**..........	20	30	40
(B195) **500 Santa Claus on Skis**..........	26	39	52
(B195a) **500 Santa Claus on Skis,** no skis			
or poles and no holes for them..........	29	44	59
(B196) Santa Claus with holly sprig	35	52	70
(B197) Santa Claus seated, bag of toys			
at side, made to ride in sleigh	100	150	200

Top L to R: B201, B202, B203, B204, B205
Bottom L to R: B206, B207, B208, B209

	C6	C8	C10
(B201) **701** Flagbearer, pot helmet........	11	16	23
(B202) **703?** Kneeling, firing rifle.........	20	30	40
(B203) **705** Port Arms	11	16	23
(B204) **707** Order Arms	11	16	23
(B205) 708 Officer with Sword.............	11	16	23
(B206) **728** Prone Machine Gunner	11	16	22
(B207) 737 Tommy-gunner...................	10	15	21
(B208) **747** Standing Firing Rifle..........	11	16	22
(B209) 774 AA Gunner..........................	8	12	17

341

L to R: B210, B211, B212, B212a, B213

L to R: B214, B215, B216, B217, B218, B218a

L to R: B215, B215a
Courtesy Charles Breslow

Top L to R: B219, B220, B221
Bottom L to R: B222, B223

	C6	C8	C10
(B219) **81 Two soldier Crew at Radar Equipment**	13	19	26
(B220) **82 Three Soldier Crew at Range Finder**	14	21	28
(B221) **83 Two Soldier Crew at Searchlight**	12	18	24
(B222) **84 Two soldier Crew at Mobile Cannon**	13	19	27
(B223) **85 Two Soldier Crew at A.A. Gun**	13	18	26

	C6	C8	C10
(B210) 777 Marching at Slope	10	15	20
(B211) **788** Marching, rifle slung	10	15	20
(B212) **789** AA gunner	11	16	23
(B212a) Cowboy, two pistols, one in air	22	33	45
(B213) Drum Major	31	46	62
(B214) Drummer	25	38	50
(B215) Bugler	22	33	44
(B215A) Bugler, buttons run down front of uniform	22	34	45
(B216) Clarinetist	26	39	52
(B217) Tubist	28	42	56
(B218) Sailor, white	17	25	34
(B218a) **720 Blue Sailor**	17	26	35

Top L to R: B224, B225, B226
Bottom L to R: B227, B228, B229, B230, B231

	C6	C8	C10
(B224) **187 Officer on Horse** (pot helmet)	42	63	85
(B225) **188 Cowboy on Horse** (lasso)	11	16	22
(B226) **189 Indian on Horse**	11	16	23
(B227) **190 Cowboy with Pistol on Horse**	15	22	30
(B228) **800 Black Knight w/Sword & Shield**	9	13	19

Top L to R: B232, B233, B233a, B234
Bottom L to R: B235, B23A, B235B, B236, B237, B238

Top L to R: B239, B240, B240a, B241
Bottom L to R: B242, B242a, B243, B243a, B244, B244a

Top L to R: B245, B246, B247, B248, B249
Bottom L to R: B250, B251, B252, B253, B254

	C6	C8	C10
(B229) **801 Knight w/Red & Blue Shield & Sword**	12	18	25
(B230) **802 Knight w/Orange & Black Shield & Sword**	9	13	18
(B231) **803 Knight w/Red & Green Shield & Sword**	9	13	19
(B232) **901 Soldier Flag Bearer**	9	13	19
(B232A) Same as above, in red (probably never made)			
(B233) **903 Soldier Sniper** (kneeling)	7	11	14
(B233A) 903 same as above, in red (not shown)	45	68	90
(B234) **906 Soldier Charging**	7	11	15
(B234A) Same as above, in red (not shown)	52	78	105
(B235) **908 Soldier Officer**	7	11	14
(B235A) Same as above, in blue	32	48	64
(B235B) Same as above, in red	50	75	100
(B236) **909 Soldier Bugler**	7	11	14
(B236A) Same as above, in red (not shown)	52	78	105
(B237) **919 Sailor White Uniform**	7	11	14
(B238) **920 Sailor Blue Uniform**	8	12	17
(B239) **922 Marine**	7	11	15
(B240) **928 Soldier Machine Gunner Lying Flat**	7	11	14
(B240A) Same as above, in red	45	68	90
(B241) **929 Soldier w/Pistol, Crawling**	15	22	31
B(241A) Same as above, in red	55	82	110
(B242) **937 Soldier, Charging Machine Gunner** (holding tommy gun)	7	10	14
(B242A) Same as above, in red	50	75	100
(B243) **938 Soldier Bomb Thrower**	7	10	14
(B243A) Same as above,, in red	62	93	125
(B244) **941 Aviator**	7	10	14
(B244A) Same as above, in red	62	93	125

	C6	C8	C10
(B245) **947 Soldier Marksman**	7	10	15
(B245A) Same as above, in red	52	78	105
(B246) **948 Soldier Running**	7	11	15
(B246A) Same as above, in red	52	75	105
(B247) **950 Cowboy w/Pistol Shooting**	12	18	25
(B248) **951 Cowboy w/Rifle**	8	12	16
(B249) **952 Cowboy w/Lasso**	6	9	13
(B250) **953 Cowboy w/Pistol** (upraised)	6	9	13
(B251) **954 Indian w/Shield & Tomahawk**	5	8	11
(B252) **955 Indian w/Rifle**	6	9	12
(B253) **956 Indian w/Knife & Spear**	6	9	12
(B254) **957 Indian w/Bow & Arrow**	6	9	12
(B255) **960 Soldier, Wounded, w/Crutches**	14	21	28
(B255A) Same as above, in red	62	93	125
(B256) **961 Soldier, Wounded Head & Arm**	12	18	24
(B256A) Same as above, in red (not shown)	62	93	125
(B257) **962 Nurse**	17	26	34

343

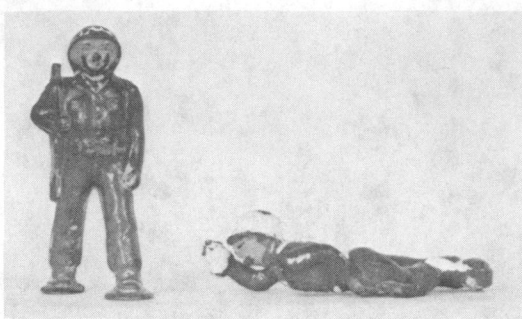

L to R: B260a, B241a

Top L to R: B270, B269, B267, B268, B265
Bottom L to R: B270a, B263, B264, B266
Courtesy John Schmidt

Top L to R: B255, B256, B257, B258, B258a, B259
Bottom L to R: B260, B261, B261a, B262, B262a

L to R: B271, B272, B273, B274
Photo by Don Pielin

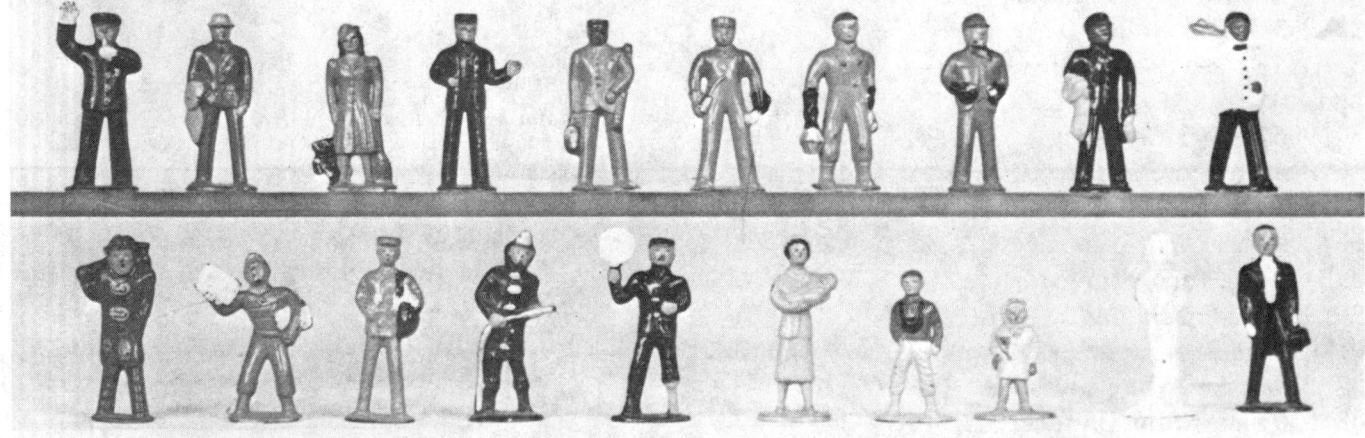

Top L to R: 350, 351, B295, 353, 354, 355, 356, 357, 358, 359
Bottom L to R: 360, 361, 362, 363, 366, 369, 370, 371, 372, 373

	C6	C8	C10
(B258) **974 Soldier, Anti-Aircraft Gunner**	7	10	14
(B258A) Same as above, in red	45	68	90
(B259) **977 Soldier Under Marching Orders** (marching)	5	8	10
(B259A) Same as above, in red (not shown)	45	68	90
(B260) **988 Soldier, Marching w/Gun on Back** (Gun slung over shoulder)	6	9	13
(B260A) Same as above, in red	50	75	100

	C6	C8	C10
(B261) **990 Soldier w/Bazooka**	7	11	15
(B261A) Same as above, in red	52	78	105
(B262) **991 Soldier Flame Thrower**	7	11	15
(B262A) 991, same as above, in red	50	75	100
"Midi" Size (Smaller Than Pod Foot)			
(B263) **200** Flame Thrower	40	60	80
(B264) Bugler	32	48	65
(B265) Officer with binoculars	40	60	80
(B266) Talking on Field Phone	31	46	62

A Schoenhut
Humpty-Dumpty Circus
Box for set No.2036,
circa 1925.
Courtesy Christie's East.

Schoenhut bisque-headed circus performers, *(L to R)* Hoop,
paper-covered; Lion Tamer (C6); Lady Rider (C6); Lady.
Courtesy Jim & Patsy Carlson.

Clark Friction Auto, circa 1894?, 10 1/2" long. *Courtesy
Joe and Sharon Freed.*

German
Civilian Composition
Figures, Photo 2.
*Photo by James L.
Theobald.*

Sturditoy Coal Dump Truck, 1920's.
Photo by Tim Oei.

Tonka No.120 Tractor and Carry-All Trailer
with No.50 Steam Shovel (very early type
with rubber tracks in large set box).
Photo by Tim Oei.

Wyandotte Coffin Nose Cord
with wind-up motor.
Photo by Tim Oei.

Buddy L Delivery
Truck, Deluxe Rider
No.803.
*Courtesy Joe and
Sharon Freed.*

The top layer of a Midgetoy
salesman's sample box.
*Courtesy Thomas G. Nefos,
National Toy Connection.*

Smitty GMC Searchlight Truck, "Hollywood
Film-Ad". *Photo by Bob Smith.*

Tootsietoy No.803
1933 World's Fair issue
Mack Van Trailer Truck.
John Gibson Collection.

Tootsietoy No. 5105 Kayo Ice Wagon (articulated version)
from 1932 Tootsietoy Funnies Series (Vehicles).
John Gibson Collection. Photo by John Gibson.

Top to Bottom: Cor-Cor Graham Paige Sedan,
Sturditoy "Sturditoy Oil Company" truck, Buddy-L Ice
Truck. *Courtesy Christie's East.*

Structo Tank, olive drab with
orange turret, ten metal wheels,
12 1/2" long.
Courtesy Joe and Sharon Freed.

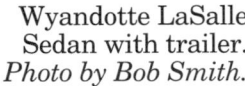

Wyandotte LaSalle
Sedan with trailer.
Photo by Bob Smith.

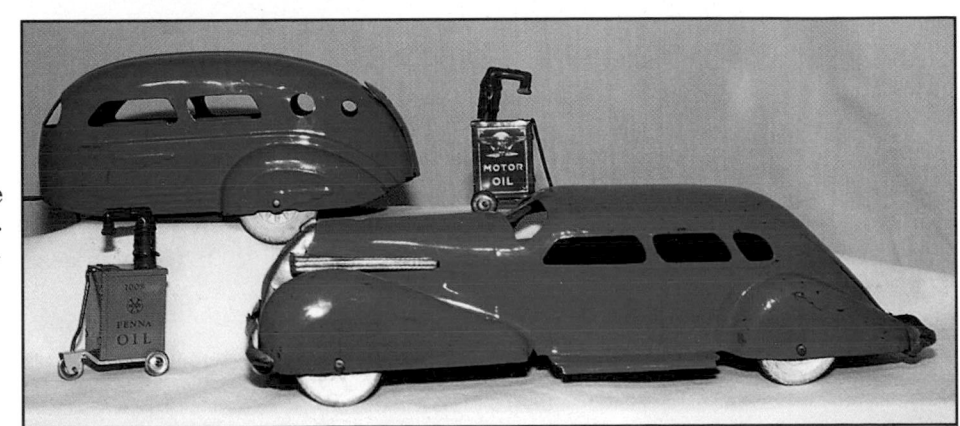

Arcade AR219. *Courtesy Thomas G. Nefos, National Toy Connection.*

Arcade AR170. *Photo by Bob Smith.*

Nylint No.4300 (Ford) U-Haul Rental Fleet. *Courtesy Thomas G. Nefos, National Toy Connection.*

Tootsietoy No. 1040 Hook & Ladder. *Courtesy The Graham Werkes.*

Unique Daredevil Motor Cop, tin windup. *Photo by Kent M. Comstock.*

Kenton "Overland Circus" Calliope Wagon, circa 1940. *Courtesy Christie's East.*

Hubley "Royal Circus" Tiger Wagon, 15 3/4" long with rare grey horses. *Courtesy Christie's East.*

Reed Trolley, "Bowery & Central Park," circa 1895. *Courtesy Christie's East.*

Pratt & Letchworth Four-Seat Brake, 28" long. *Courtesy Christie's East.*

Reed Cinderella Twin Horse-Drawn Coach. *Courtesy Christie's East.*

Hull & Stafford "Prospect Park" Omnibus, circa 1880. *Courtesy Christie's East.*

Bliss "Rough & Ready" fire engine (missing rear fireman), circa 1895. *Courtesy Christie's East.*

TPS Football Player, tin windup.
Photo Scott Smiles.

Babes In Toyland Soldier,
Linemar (Disney).
Photo Scott Smiles.

Wyandotte Hoky Poky Handcar, tin windup.
Photo Scott Smiles.

Chein Rabbit, tin windup.
Photo Scott Smiles.

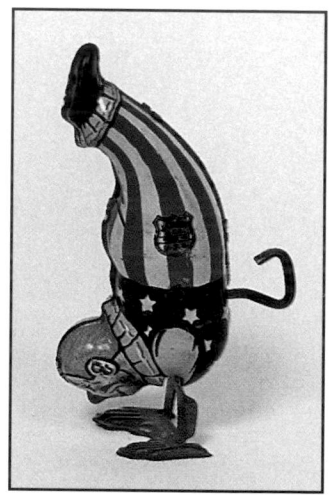

Chein Handstand Clown,
tin windup.
Photo Scott Smiles.

Yone, *L to R:* Soldier, Chef, Pirate, tin windup.
Photo Scott Smiles.

TPS Circus Parade, tin windup. *Photo Scott Smiles.*

Chein Indian in Headdress, tin windup.
Photo Scott Smiles.

Five versions of Marx's "Wee Scottie," also identified on its boxes as "Running Scottie". *Photo Scott Smiles.*

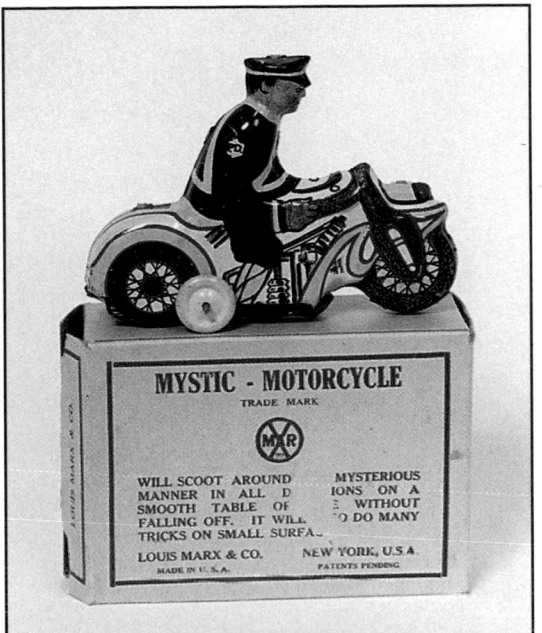

Marx Mystic Motorcycle, tin windup. *Photo Scott Smiles.*

Strauss Jenny the Balky Mule, tin windup. *Photo Scott Smiles.*

TPS Pango Pango, with box, tin windup. *Photo Scott Smiles.*

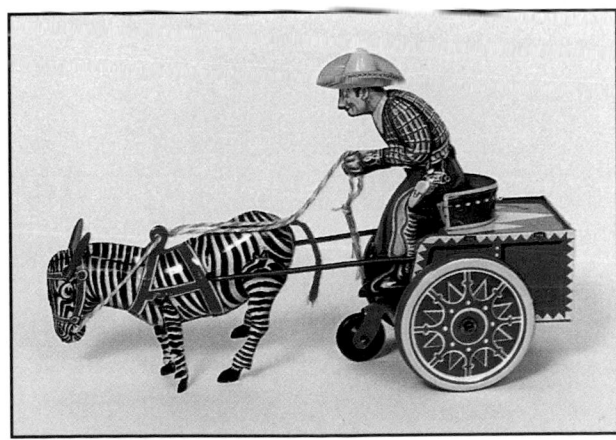

Lehmann Galop, tin windup. *Photo Scott Smiles.*

Marx Dagwood the Driver (Comic Character). *Photo Scott Smiles.*

Pull Toy, Elephant, tin, 8 1/2" long, circa 1890 (Miscellaneous).
Courtesy Christie's East.

Ramp Walkers, large plastic, Popeye and
Wimpy. *Photo by Randy Welch.*

"Gypsy Fortune Teller" (Battery-Operated).
Courtesy Don Hultzman.

"Beauty Parlor Bear" (Battery-
Operated). *Courtesy Don Hultzman.*

"Jungle Jumbo" (Battery-Operated).
Courtesy Don Hultzman.

Renwal Viking Ship No.245, with box. *Photo by Tim Oei.*

A Number 42 Weeden National Playthings steam engine, circa 1940. Value $100 - $125. *Photo by Richard Leach.*

A boxed set of Grey Iron's Clever Clowns (Miscellaneous). *Photo by Harold Haseley*

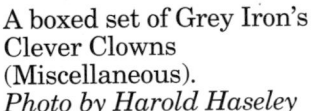

Bell Toy, Stevens, "Evening News Baby Quieter," 1890s (Miscellaneous). *Courtesy Christie's East.*

GI Joe Action Sailor No.8050 Official Sea Sled and Frogman (box). *Photo by Barry Goodman.*

Circa 1931, Chicago's J. Edward Jones produced this 3" high hollowcast metal soldier. Later adapted and modified (in a 3 1/4" height) by the Windy City's American Metal Toys, Inc. (see AM13.) Very rare, it is probably worth at least $300 in mint condition.
Courtesy Ed Laucus.

The boxtop and contents of the super-rare Buck Rogers Figures by M.T. (Comic Character).
Photos by Barry Goodman.

Cardboard candy containers produced circa 1939-1942 by New York's American Mint Corporation are valuable to both gum card-candy wrapper buffs and toy soldier collectors. 2-9/16" high, they can run in value, depending on rarity and general desirability, from $100 to more than $200 apiece.
Ted Bruce collection.

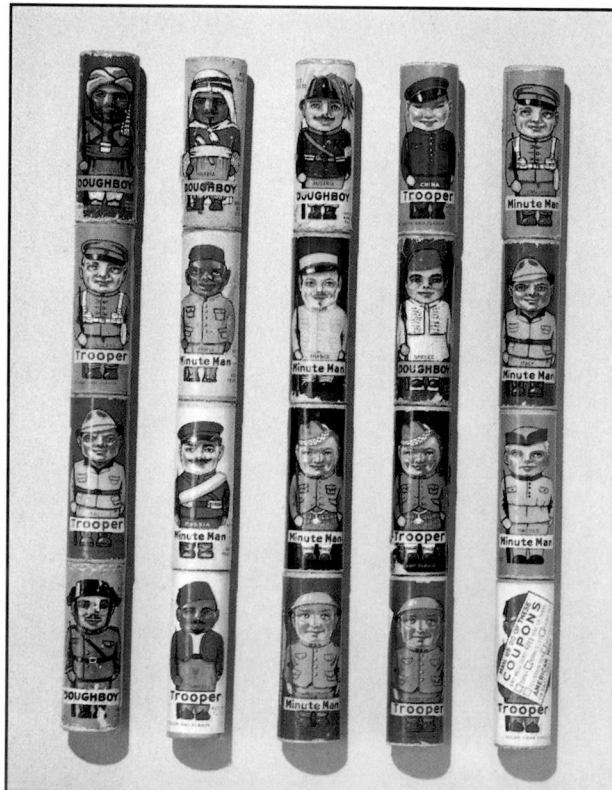

Circa 1947, New Jersey's H.B. Toys produced unauthorized versions of Captain Marvel and Captain Marvel, Jr., calling them Robe Man and Robe Boy. Extremely rare, they even come in a variation in Captain Marvel, Jr., and presumably with Captain Marvel. At left, with a lightning bolt on chest, and at right without, the latter presumably to avoid complications with Fawcett Publications, which owned the Marvel copyrights. (Comic Character). *Photo by Don Patman, courtesy Bob Emmons.*

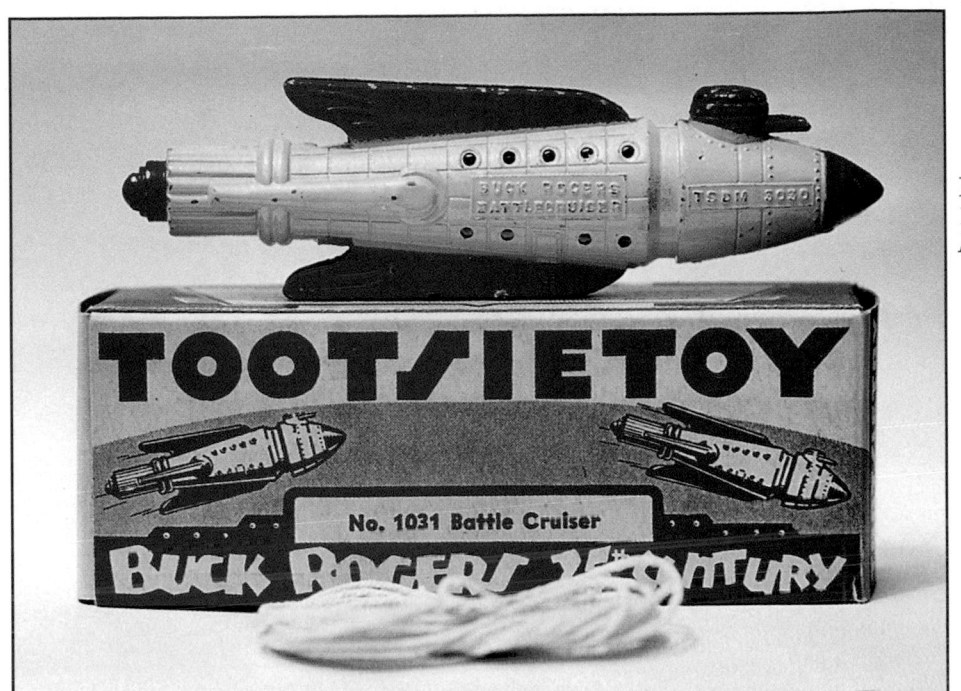

Buck Rogers Battle Cruiser, 1937. John Gibson Collection. *Photo by John Gibson.*

Tootsietoy No. 1812 Sky Fleet Miniature planes. *John Gibson Collection. Photo by John Gibson.*

Buck Rogers Flash Blast Attack Ship, 1937 (Comic Character). *John Gibson Collection. Photo by John Gibson.*

Wyandotte Rocket Racer #319 (Aircraft). *Photo by Brian Seligman.*

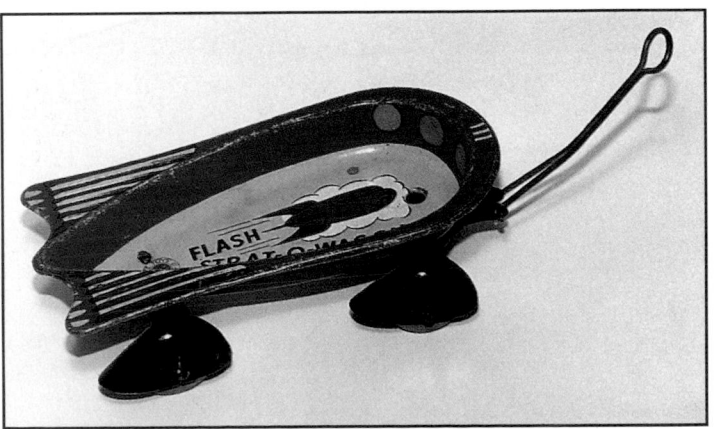

Wyandotte "Flash Strat-O-Wagon" (Miscellaneous). *Photo by Brian Seligman.*

Wyandotte Mystery Plane No.101.
John Gibson Collection. Photo by John Gibson.

Tootsietoy 722 Military DC-4, 1941.
John Gibson Collection. Photo by John Gibson.

Jep Seaplane, 13 1/2" (Tin Windup).
Courtesy Christie's East.

Hubley H21.
Photo Perry Eichor.

Steelcraft
"Graf Zeppelin",
30 1/2" long.
*Restored and
photographed by
Tim Oei.*

A12 F3F Biplane
(Japanese Tin Airplanes).
Photo by Ron Smith.

Early Tootsietoy Airplanes,
L to R: No.4482 Bleriot without
loop; unnumbered "Spirit of
St. Louis" (not SR of France);
No.4482 Bleriot with Loop.
John Gibson Collection.
Photo by John Gibson.

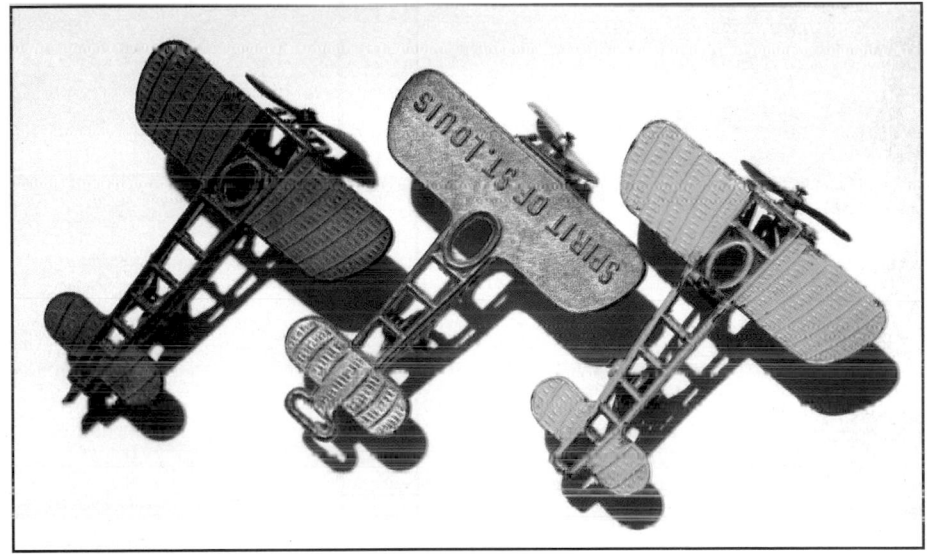

A9 U.N. Hospital Plane
(Japanese Tin Airplanes).
Photo by Ron Smith.

Bliss "St. Louis," circa 1895.
Courtesy Christie's East.

Marklin "Columbus,"
circa 1920.
Courtesy Christie's East.

Marklin
"Priscilla" Steam
Yacht, circa 1900.
*Courtesy
Christie's East.*

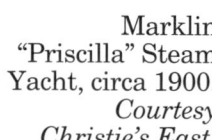

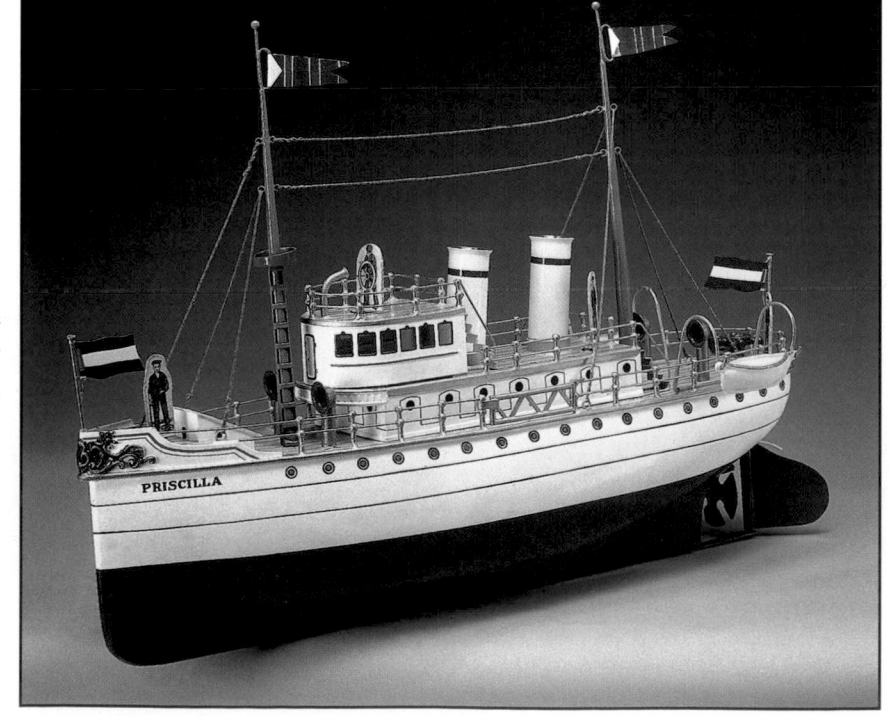

Ives "Old Mammy Washing Clothes"
(Miscellaneous). *Courtesy Christie's East.*

Marx Ring-A-Ling Circus, tin windup.
Photo Scott Smiles.

Selrite Home Run King, tin windup.
Photo Scott Smiles.

Circus Bank, mechanical bank. *Courtesy Christie's East.*

Mechanical Banks:
(Top) Dentist, *(Bottom, Left to Right)* Calamity, Clown on Globe.
Courtesy Christie's East.

Girl Skipping Rope mechanical bank.
Courtesy Christie's East.

Mechanical Banks:
(Top) Magician,
(Bottom, Left to Right)
Cat & Mouse, Cat Balancing
and Mason.
Courtesy Christie's East.

Darktown Battery mechanical bank.
Courtesy Christie's East.

	C6	C8	C10		C6	C8	C10
(B267) Advancing with Rifle	30	45	60	(B280) **355 Oiler**	4	7	9
(B268) Marching, slung rifle	37	56	75	(B281) **356 Brakeman**	4	7	9
(B269) Firing Bazooka	30	45	60	(B282) **357 Engineer**	5	8	10
(B270) Firing Tommygun	30	45	60	(B283) **358 Porter**	4	7	9
(B270A) Walking Forward, rifle at side, pointing down	30	45	60	(B284) **359 Dining Steward**	5	8	10
(B271) Cowboy with Rifle	7	11	15	(B285) **360 Hobo**	5	8	10
(B272) Cowboy with Pistol	7	11	15	(B286) **361 Newsboy**	4	6	8
(B273) Indian with Hatchet	7	11	15	(B287) **362 Mailman**	4	7	9
(B274) Indian with Rifle	7	11	15	(B288) **363 Fireman**	4	7	9
(B275) **350 Policeman**	4	7	9	(B289) **366 Peg Legged Gateman**	6	9	12
(B276) **351 Man**	4	7	9	(B290) **369 Woman Carrying Baby**	5	8	10
(B277) **352 Woman**	5	8	10	(B291) **370 Little Boy**	4	7	9
(B278) **353 Conductor**	4	7	9	(B292) **371 Little Girl**	3	5	7
(B279) **354 Redcap**	4	7	9	(B293) **372 Bride**	9	13	18
				(B294) **373 Groom**	7	11	15
				(B295) Woman with dog	7	10	14

MANOIL

(See also Vehicles, Aircraft, Ships and Miscellaneous)

Manoil began production of toy soldiers in 1935. It was in business as early as 1927 under the name Jack Manoil, turning out metal lamps and novelties at 34 West Houston Street in New York City. The company changed its name to Man-O-Lamp Corporation on July 11, 1928, and was owned by Maurice Manoil (12/4/1893-9/15/74) and Jack Manoil (1/29/02 9/1/55), two brothers who had emigrated from Rumania in the early 1900s. The final name-change to Manoil Manufacturing Co., Inc. took place on July 7, 1934.

The two brothers were essentially partners, with Maurice handling the business end of the operation and Jack, who oversaw the creative area, working closely with Walter Baetz (1894-1978), who sculpted all the company's toys.

Manoil advanced firmly into toy-making in 1934, with seven vehicles, and moved to other addresses as it grew, leaving Manhattan in 1937 for Brooklyn, and then in June, 1940, moving to Waverly, New York (which afforded excellent shipping by rail), employing 225 people at its peak.

With the onset of World War II, Manoil shut down, but then resumed production of soldiers in a fine-grained composition form (employing sulfur) in January, 1944. Brittle, the pieces were ultimately unsuccessful, and their manufacture ended by the end of the year.

After the Second World War, the company introduced several new lines of soldiers, (also containing some of its pre-War soldiers and its appealing Happy Farm series), but they were no longer distributed as widely.

Manoil's soldiers have a distinctive jauntiness to them, at times veering on caricature, the latter trait becoming more pronounced as the years wore on. In 1953 the firm moved to a smaller location in Waverly, changing its name to Jack Manoil Specialty Company, but went out of business shortly after Jack's death. Baetz and Jack Manoil were both keenly interested in the company's soldiers and would work late into the night as they collaborated on ideas for them. One of Baetz's continuing concerns was to design the molds so that there was no structural weakness in the soldiers as a result of air bubbles. For this reason, many of Manoil's soldiers were redesigned a number of times, sometimes with subtle and sometimes with broad variations.

Unlike Barclay, Manoil also produced plastic toys, selling millions of vehicles and airplanes in its later years. Models of Manoil and Barclay soldiers are being reproduced (see Leading Collectors and Dealers), hollow-cast from the original molds. **All bold words and numbers are Manoil's own description.**

Top L to R: M1, M2, M3, M4, M5, M6, M7, M8
Bottom L to R: M9, M10, M11, M12, M13, M14, M15

	C6	C8	C10		C6	C8	C10
(M1) **7 Flag Bearer,** hollow base version.	40	60	80	(M18) **12 Machine Gunner** (Prone), spaces under body	25	38	50
(M2) **7 Flag Bearer,** second version	11	16	22	(M19) **12 Machine Gunner** (Prone), no aperture between hands and gun	12	18	24
(M3) **7 Flag Bearer**	11	16	22	(M20) **12 Machine Gunner** (Prone), no aperture, pack on back	10	15	20
(M4) **8 Parade,** hollow base version	21	31	42	(M21) **13 Cadet,** hollow base, no buckle on belt	24	36	48
(M5) **8 Parade,** stocky version	8	12	17	(M22) **13 Cadet,** second version	10	15	20
(M6) **8 Parade,** campaign cap straight on head	20	30	40	(M23) **14 Sailor,** hollow base	27	41	55
(M7) **8 Parade,** number on back	32	48	64	(M23a) Same as above, in blue	30	45	60
(M8) **8 Parade,** fifth version	10	15	20	(M24) **Sailor,** second version	10	15	20
(M9) **9 Officer,** hollow base version	38	57	76	(M25) **15 Marine,** hollow base	33	50	66
(M10) **9 Officer,** second version	10	15	20	(M26) **15 Marine,** second version	9	14	19
(M11) **10 Bugler,** hollow base version	31	46	62	(M27) **16 Ensign**	10	15	20
(M12) **10 Bugler,** second version	10	15	20	(M27a) **16 Ensign,** hollow base	30	45	60
(M13) **11 Drummer,** hollow base version	34	51	68				
(M14) **11 Drummer,** stocky version	13	19	26				
(M15) **11 Drummer,** vertical drum	19	28	38				

L to R: M16, M17, M18

(M16) **12 Machine Gunner** (Prone), grass on base	13	19	26	(M28) **17 Signal Man,** hollow base version	21	32	43
(M17) **12 Machine Gunner** (Prone), flat base, no grass	12	18	25	(M29) **17 Signal Man,** second version	19	28	39

Top L to R: M19, M20
Bottom L to R: M21, M22, M23, M23a, M24, M25, M26

L to R: M27a, M27, M28, M29

L to R: M30, M31, M32, M34, M35, M36, M36a

	C6	C8	C10
(M30) **18 Cowboy,** hollow base version	21	32	42
(M31) **18 Cowboy,** second version	10	15	21
(M32) **18A Cowboy With Hands Up**	12	18	24
(M33) **18A Cowboy With Hands Up** (subtle variation)	12	18	24
(M34) **20 Doctor** (same as 20K, but in white)	11	16	23
(M35) **20K Doctor** (khaki)	15	22	30
(M36) **21 Nurse**	8	12	17
(M36a) **21 Nurse,** no hem in skirt, shorter, etc.	14	21	28
(M37) **Indian** with hatchet	75	112	150
(M38) **22 Indian** with knives	11	16	22

L to R: M37, M38, M38aa, M38a, M38b, M39

L to R: M40, M41, M42

	C6	C8	C10
(M38aa) **22 Indian,** with knives, same as above, minor difference in hairline may be casting flaw	No Price Found		
(M38a) **22 Indian,** with knives, right toes off base	11	16	23
(M38b) **22 Indian,** with knives, sarong-like garment, only three known	No Price Found		
(M39) **23 Machine Gunner Sitting,** seated on four pillows, bullets feed from ammo box	12	18	25
(M40) **23 Machine Gunner Sitting,** markings under base	11	16	22
(M41) **Machine Gunner Sitting,** squarer-looking, markings near right leg	11	16	22
(M42) **24 Cannon Loader**	8	12	16

Top L to R: M43, M44, M45, M46
Bottom L to R: M47, M48, M48a, M49, M50

	C6	C8	C10
(M43) **25 Sniper (kneeling)** hollow base, **not Manoil,** probably Paul Paragine	40	60	80
(M44) **25 Sniper (kneeling)** folding rifle	150	225	300
(M45) **25 Sniper (kneeling)** short thin rifle	10	15	20

	C6	C8	C10
(M46) **25 Sniper (kneeling)** longer, thicker rifle	10	15	21
(M47) **26 Sniper,** folding rifle	130	195	260
(M48) **26 Sniper**	9	14	19
(M48a) **26 Sniper,** shorter rifle, angle different on underside of rifle	10	15	20
(M49) **27 Tommy Gunner,** bloated version	15	22	31
(M50) **27 Tommy Gunner,** second version	10	15	20

Top L to R: M51, M52, M53, M54
Bottom L to R: M55, M56, M57, M58, M58a

	C6	C8	C10
(M51) **28 Observer**	10	15	21
(M52) **29 Wounded Soldier (Walking)**	11	16	22
(M53) **30 Wounded Soldier (Lying)**	9	14	18
(M54) **30 Wounded Soldier (Lying)** number on back, shorter head	9	14	18
(M55) **31 Bomb Thrower,** three grenades in pouch	12	18	24
(M56) **31 Bomb Thrower,** two grenades in pouch	11	16	22
(M57) **32 Stretcher Carrier,** no medical kit	10	15	20
(M58) **32 Stretcher Carrier,** medical kit	10	15	21
(M58a) **32 Stretcher Carrier,** medical kit, number on back, buttons on uniform, different pockets and collar from above	45	68	90
(M59) **33 Sitting Soldier**	20	30	40
(M60) **34 Aviator**	11	16	23
(M61) **35 Hostess,** in white	36	54	72
As above, in green	32	48	65
(M61a) **35 Hostess in Khaki**	150	225	300
(M62) **36 Soldier With Bayonet Charging**	21	31	42
(M63) **37 Soldier with Gun Charging**	23	34	46
(M64) **38 Soldier With Gun Butting**	27	41	55
(M65) **39 Soldier With Bayonet Jabbing**	28	42	57

Top L to R: M59, M60, M61, M61, M61a, M62
Bottom L to R: M63. M64. M65. M66

L to R: M67, M68, M69

	C6	C8	C10
(M66) **40 Soldier (Kneeling With Bayonet)**	30	45	60
(M67) **41 Soldier (Crouching With Hand Grenade)**	27	41	54
(M68) **42 Field Doctor (Crawling)**	39	58	78
(M69) **43 Officer (Lying Down - Shooting Revolver)**	27	41	55
(M70) **44 Crawling Scout With Gun,** left leg high when right leg on ground (only three known)	90	135	180
(M71) **44 Crawling Scout With Gun,** left leg lower	26	39	52
(M72) **45 Observer (With Periscope)**	16	24	32
(M73) **46 Anti-Aircraft Gunner,** barrel of gun drops below arm	9	13	19
(M74) **46 Anti-Aircraft Gunner,** barrel of gun ends at arm	10	15	21
(M75) **47 Anti-Aircraft Searchlight**	12	18	24
(M75a) **47** like above, with tin lens	55	83	110
(M75b) **47** like M75, number on back, helmet looks as if it was adapted to look like WW II helmet	10	15	21
(M76) **48 Navy Gunner**	12	18	25
(M77) **49 Policeman**	9	13	19
(M78) **49 Policeman,** slightly larger	9	13	19
(M79) **50 Bicycle Dispatch Rider**	15	22	30
(M80) **51 Motorized Machine Gunner**	28	42	57

L to R: M70, M71, M72

Top L to R: M73, M74, M75, M75a, M75b
Bottom L to R: M76, M77, M78, M79

Top L to R: M87, M88, M89, M89a
Bottom L to R: M90, M91, M92, M92a, M93, M94

Top L to R: M80, M81, M81a
Bottom L to R: M82, M83, M84, M85, M86

	C6	C8	C10
(M81) **52 Motorcycle Rider,** number over rear wheel, grass base	16	24	33
(M81a) **52** Same as above, motor variation	No Price Found		
(M82) **52 Motorcycle Rider**	20	30	40
(M83) **53 Sitting Soldier Without Gun**	16	24	33
(M84) **54 Sitting Soldier Eating**	24	36	48
(M85) **55 Sitting Soldier At Table With Phone & Map**	16	24	32
(M86) **56 Paymaster**	84	126	168
(M87) **57 Camouflage Sharpshooter Lying Down**	13	19	27

	C6	C8	C10
(M88) **58 Parachute Jumper**	12	18	25
(M89) **59 Soldier Writing Letter**	32	49	65
(M89a) Same as M89, foot not curled up, pencil is flat, helmet rounder, fuller	37	56	75
(M90) **60 Cook's Helper With Ladle,** normal helmet	22	33	45
(M91) **60 Cook's Helper with Ladle,** helmet looks as if it was adapted to look like WW II helmet	60	90	120
(M92) **61 Soldier With Camera**	32	48	64
(M92a) **Soldier With Camera,** thinner arm	33	49	66
(M93) **62 Soldier With Gas Mask & Gun**	13	19	26
(M94) **63 Soldier With Gas Mask With Flare Pistol**	12	18	24
(M95) **64 Soldier Playing Banjo**	55	82	110
(M96) **65 Deep Sea Diver**	10	15	20
(M96a) As above, painted gray	13	19	26
(M97) **65 Deep Sea Diver** with "65" on chest	10	15	20
(M98) **66 Soldier With Gun on Parade with Overseas Cap**	30	45	60
(M99) **67 Soldier With Gun and Pack Marching**	9	13	19
(M100) **68 Soldier Boxing**	37	55	74

Top L to R: M95, M96, M97, M98, M99, M100, M101
Bottom L to R: M102, M103, M104, M105, M106

Top L to R: M107, M108, M109, M110, M111
Bottom L to R: M112, M112a, M113, M114, M115, M115a

Top L to R: M116, M117, M118, M119, M120
Bottom L to R: M121, M121a, M122, M123, M124

	C6	C8	C10
(M109) **82 Anti-Aircraft With Range Finder** 14		21	28
(M110) **83 Soldier Trench Mortar**......14		21	29
(M111) **84 Soldier With Shell** 17		26	35
(M112) **85 Aviator Holding Bomb**......13		19	27
(M112a) **Aviator Holding Bomb,** hand variation.................................13		19	26
(M113) **86 Aviator Mechanic With Propeller,** away from head 250		375	500
(M114) **86 Aviator Mechanic With Propeller,** orange prop, flat lower hand................................52		78	105
(M114a) **86** Silver prop.........................60		90	120
(M114b) **86** Orange prop, curved lower hand.....................................44		66	88
(M115) **87** Aviator carrying bomb sight20		30	40
(M115a) **87** Aviator carrying bomb sight, smaller base ....No Price Found			
(M116) **88 Radio Operator Standing** .29		45	59
(M117) **89 Radio Operator (Lying Down)** 17		26	35
(M118) **90 Soldier Digging Trench** 26		39	52
(M119) **91 Soldier With Barbed Wire,** wide-faced version 22		33	45
(M120) **91 Soldier With Barbed Wire** ..18		27	36
(M121) **92 Fire Fighter** in white..........51		76	102
(M121a) **92 Fire Fighter** in gray..........90		135	180
(M122) **93 Soldier on Guard Duty** 42		63	85

	C6	C8	C10
(M101) **77 Lineman & Telephone Pole,** pole comes with two different-shaped bases, oval or diagonal..45		68	90
(M102) **78 Anti-Tank Gun,** round shield, 4 variations based on Vickers 2.95 mountain gun 15		22	31
(M103) **78 Anti-Tank Gun,** squared shield..17		26	35
(M103a) **78 Anti-Tank Gun,** angled shield..No Price Found			
(M104) **78 Anti-Tank Gun,** wooden wheels...27		41	55
(M105) **79** Soldier marching with gun slung at angle 87		130	175
(M106) **80 Anti-Aircraft Machine Gunner.** 11		16	23
(M107) **81 Machine Gunner and Helper,** aperture between hand and machine gun 14		21	29
(M108) **81 Machine Gunner and Helper,** no aperture 14		21	29

L to R: M123a, M123

	C6	C8	C10
(M123) **94 Soldier Running With Cannon** marked "Manoil USA," "1" cannon slants to right when looked at from above 17	26	35	
(M123a) **94 Soldier Running With Cannon,** no markings, cannon straight from above, face narrower 19	28	38	
(M124) **94 Soldier Running With Cannon,** wood wheels, thin face 28	42	56	

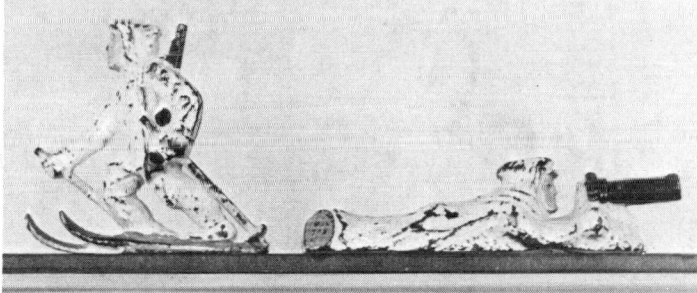

Top L to R: M125, M126
Bottom L to R: M127, M128

(M125) **99 Finn with Skis**....................35	52	71	
(M126) **100 Finn Machine Gunner** 27	41	55	
(M127) **101 Soldier Jumping With Chute** 52	77	105	
(M127a) **101 Soldier Jumping With Chute,** foot variation, number in different place......................No Price Found			
(M128) **102 Soldier Jumping With Machine Gun** 41	62	82	

HAPPY FARM SERIES

According to the late Peter Ruben, a great number of color varieties and shades in this series exist, many of which can be related to the women who did the detail painting, and the season, as represented by 41/2 with long and short sleeve dresses. A number of Happy Farm figures were produced circa 1960 for the Smithsonian Museum, solid-cast with a patina or black finish.

Top L to R: M129-M131, M132, M133, M134, M135
Bottom L to R: M136, M137, M138, M139, M140

	C6	C8	C10
(M129) **41/1 Bench**..............................5	8	10	
(M130) **41/2 Girl** 5	8	10	
(M131) **41/3 Young Man** 5	8	10	
(M132) **41/4 Man Carrying Sack on Back** 13	19	26	
(M133) **41/5 Farmer Pitching Sheaves** 13	19	26	
(M134) **41/6 Farmer Sharpening Scythe**....11	16	23	
(M135) **41/7 Blacksmith Making Horseshoes** 13	19	27	
(M136) **41/8 Farmer Cutting WithScythe**.13	19	26	
(M137) **41/9 Farmer Cutting Corn** 12	18	25	
(M138) **41/10 Farmer Sowing Grain** .10	15	21	
(M139) **41/11 Man Carrying Sheaves Under Arm**......................................13	19	27	
(M140) **41/12 Scarecrow With Top Hat**..12	18	25	
(M141) **41/13 Farmer Carrying Pumpkin**...11	16	22	
(M142) **41/12 Darky Eating Watermelon** .40	60	80	
(M143) **41/15 Scarecrow With Straw Hat** 12	18	25	
(M144) **41/16 Watchman Blowing Out Lantern**...13	19	26	
(M145) **41/17 Hod Carrier With Bricks** ...15	22	30	
(M146) **41/18 Man Chopping Wood** ..12	18	25	
(M147) **41/19 Mason Laying Bricks**...16	24	32	

Top L to R: M141, M142, M143, M144, M145, M146
Bottom L to R: M147, M148, M149, M150, M151

M156

M157

M158

	C6	C8	C10
(M148) **41/20 Man Dumping Wheel Barrow**	13	19	26
(M149) **41/21 Old Man Fixing Shoe**	15	22	30
(M150) **41/22 Blacksmith With Wheel**	12	18	25
(M151) **41/23 Carpenter Carrying Door**	26	39	52

M160

M153

M152

M159

M161

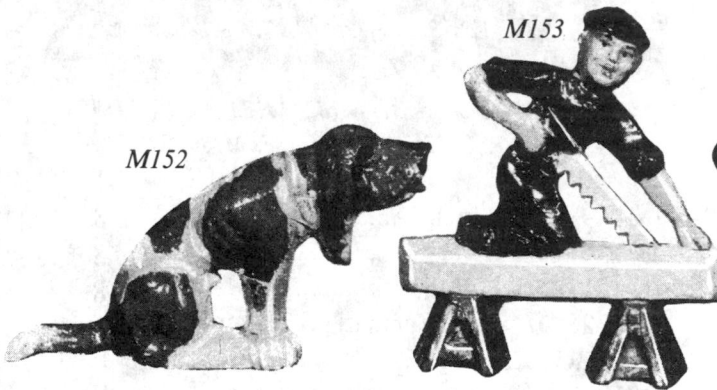

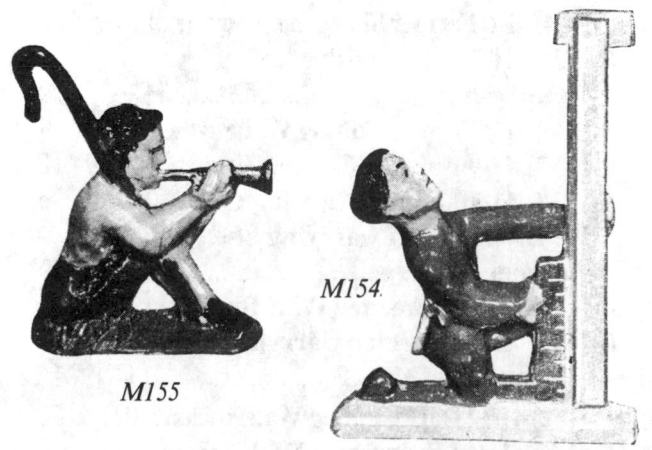

M155

M154

	C6	C8	C10
(M156) **41/28 Lady With Pie**	13	19	27
(M157) **41/29 Lady With Child**	16	24	32
(M158) **41/30 School Teacher**	22	33	44
(M159) **41/31 Girl Watering Flowers**	11	16	23
(M160) **41/32 Woman Lifting Hen From Nest**	13	19	26
(M161) **41/33 Woman With Butter Churn**	12	18	24
(M162) **41/34 Woman Laying Out Wash On Grass**	14	21	29
(M163) **41/35 Woman Sweeping With Broom**	12	18	25
(M164) **41/36 Man Juggling Barrel**	21	32	43
(M164a) As above, in khaki	31	46	62
(M165) **41/37 Man Planting Tree**	22	33	44
(M166) **41/38 Girl Picking Berries**	21	31	43
(M167) **41/39 Farmer At Water Pump**	11	16	22
(M168) **41/40 Boy Carrying Wood**	13	19	26
(M169) **41/41 Stacks of Sheaves**	9	14	19

	C6	C8	C10
(M152) **41/24 Hound**	14	21	28
(M153) **41/25 Carpenter Sawing Lumber**	13	19	26
(M154) **41/26 Carpenter With Square**	32	48	64
(M155) **41/27 Shepherd With Flute**	30	45	60

Top L to R: M162, M163, M164, M164a, M165
Bottom L to R: M166, M167, M168, M169

	C6	C8	C10
(M169) **41/41/ Haystack** is a rare variant, easily distinguished by the bottle and jug by its side ....No Price Found			
(M169a) Boxed Happy Farm Set (10 pieces) mint with box, no standard contents 180	180	275	360

End Happy Farm Listing

MANOIL COMPOSITION

Top L to R: MC1, MC2. Bottom L to R: MC3,
MC3a, MC4. Courtesy Marjorie and the late Peter Ruben.

(MC1) Prone machine-gunner	25	37	50
(MC2) Seated machine-gunner	24	36	48
(MC3) Motorcyclist	24	36	48
(MC3A) Motorcyclist, mirror variation of above...	24	36	48
(MC4) Firing camouflaged AA gun	24	36	48

POST-WAR

M170 through M176 were the first new Post WWII series, and were produced only for a limited time. On a trial basis early production was also sold unpainted.

Top L to R: M170, M171, M172, M173
Bottom L to R: M174, M175, M176

	C6	C8	C10
(M170) Flag Bearer (thin), circa late 1945..12	12	18	25
(M171) **46-A Parade** (thin), circa late 1945.. 18	18	27	36
(M172) Tommy Gunner (thin, circa late 1945).. 13	13	19	27
(M173) Machine Gunner Sitting (thin), circa late 1945 31	31	47	63
(M174) Machine Gunner Lying (thin), circa late 1945 50	50	75	100
(M175) Sniper (thin), circa late 1945....27	27	41	54
(M176) **45/6** Parade (thin), circa late 1945.16	16	24	32

Top L to R: M177, M178, M179, M180, M181, M182
Bottom L to R: M183, M184, M185, M186

L to R: M187, M188, M189, M190, M191, M192, M193

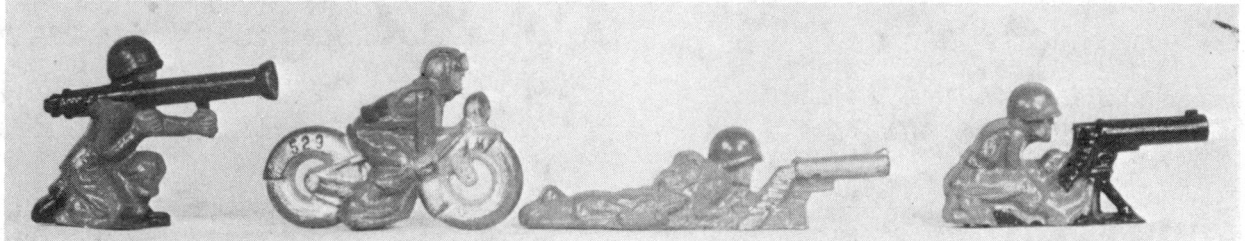

L to R: M194, M195, M196, M197

L to R: M198, M199, M200, M201, M202

L to R: M203, M204, M205, M206

	C6	C8	C10		C6	C8	C10
(M177) **45/7 Flag Bearer**	17	25	34	(M184) **45/14 Soldier With Shell For Bazooka** (some marked "46/14")	16	24	32
(M178) **45/8 Parade**	11	18	23	(M185) **45/15 General** (some "46/15")	85	127	170
(M179) **45/9 Combat**	14	21	28	(M186) **45/16 Mine Detector** (some "46/16")	18	27	37
(M180) **45/10 At Attention** (present arms)	16	24	32	(M187) **521** Flag Bearer, all 500s, circa 1950	14	21	29
(M181) **45/11 Sniper**	17	25	34	(M188) **522** Parade	14	21	29
(M182) **45/12 Tommy Gunner**	12	18	25	(M189) **523** Soldier in poncho	19	28	38
(M183) **45/13 Soldier With Bazooka Cannon** (some marked "45/18")	16	24	33				

(M190) **524** Combat...............................15   23   31
(M191) **525** Aviator Holding Bomb......17   25   34
(M192) **526** Observer............................17   26   35
(M193) **527** Aircraft Spotter 21   31   43
(M194) **528** Soldier with bazooka 14   21   28
(M195) **529** Motorcycle rider 28   42   56
(M196) **530** Machine gunner (lying) 17   26   35
(M197) **531** Machine gunner sitting 15   23   30
(M198) **532** Sniper (Kneeling) 18   27   36
(M199) **533** Soldier with gas mask
   with flare pistol 19   29   38
(M200) **534** Sniper.............................16   24   33
(M201) **535** Soldier throwing hand grenade.16   24   32
(M202) **536** Anti-Aircraft gunner 19   28   38
(M203) **537** Soldier with tommy gun ...18   27   36
(M204) **538** Soldier firing up 18   27   36
(M205) **539** Stretcher bearer 55   83   110
(M206) **540** Wounded Soldier (lying)...57   86   115

MY RANCH CORRAL SERIES

Top L to R: M215, M216, M217, M218
Bottom L to R: M219, M220, M221, M222

L to R: M207, M208, M209, M210

(M207) **C-23 Cowboy Rider** 7   11   15
(M208) **C-24 Cowgirl Rider**...............7   11   15
(M209) **C-29 Mounted Cowboy**..........29   44   58
(M210) **C-30 Mounted Cowboy
   Shooting**...............................27   41   55
(M211 C2 Ranch fence, gate.................29   43   59
(M212) C12 Blanket over Fence
   Section....................................21   31   42
(M213) C18 Small Calf 7   10   14
(M214) C20 Bull, head turned 8   12   16
(M215) C19 Cow feeding 7   10   15
(M216) C28 Short Cactus 8   12   16
(M217) C14 Brahma Bull 9   13   18
(M218) C26 Large Cactus....................13   20   26
(M219) C1 Fence 5   8   11
(M220) C25 Small Horse......................10   15   20
(M221) Horse for Mounted Cowboy 15   22   30
(M222) Horse for Mounted Cowgirl.....15   22   30
(M223) Small Gate 15   22   30
(M224) Large Gate...............................14   21   28

M211

L to R: M212, M213, M214

GREY IRON

Grey Iron made the only 3¼" cast iron soldiers. The company began in 1840 as the Brady Machine Shop in Mount Joy, Pennsylvania, where it has remained to this day, and in 1881 was organized as the Grey Iron Casting Company, Limited. As early as 1903 it was manufacturing toy banks and stoves, cap pistols, wheeled toys and trains, as well as a number of non-toy items. On August 14, 1917, the company was granted two patents for their 40 mm solid cast iron Grey Klip Armies, which they then manufactured through 1941, the last of the series emerging in 1938 as "Uncle Sam's Defenders", painted khaki rather than nickel-plated, as the earlier versions had been. The soldiers were not successful at first, but with the advent of a new distributor, the company was swamped with orders, and in January, 1933, introduced a new line of thirty-five different cast iron soldiers, in an approximately 3" size (four Revolutionary War soldiers; an infantryman, a foot officer, a flagbearer and a mounted officer, may have been introduced earlier, as they are numbered lower, but were not part of the 1933 announcement).

The figures tended to be slight, and while apparently successful, were superseded in July 1936 by Grey's "Iron Men" series, a slightly larger, more robust model, which continued to be sold until World War II ended all toy production. Designers for the soldiers were at least two; Edward Musser and Samuel S. Schmidt. The soldiers were hand-poured and then painted on an assembly-line basis, and at least initially were sold for a dime, while their competitors charged a nickel. Grey is still in business today as the John Wright division of Donsco, and has recently been producing, on an erratic basis, some unpainted soldiers from its old molds. Some years ago, the author saw, at a Pennsylvania flea market, some crude, cast iron Continental Soldiers, about 2½" high, which he believes may be early Grey Iron, but none have surfaced since, and there is no evidence that Grey made them. However, they would be valuable to serious collectors, and in mint would probably bring about $40 apiece. **All bold words and numbers are Grey Iron's own description.**

GREYKLIP ARMIES

GREY IRON (GA) Set 1, Company A. Courtesy Karl Zipple.

GREY IRON (GB) Set 2, Company B. Courtesy Karl Zipple.

GREY IRON (GC) Set 3, Company C. Courtesy Karl Zipple.

	C6	C8	C10
(GA) **Set 1/Company A,** at attention, consists of bugler, officer, flagbearer, drummer, rifleman, price per each......	3	4.50	6
(GB) **Set 2/Company B,** marching, consists of bugler, officer, flagbearer, drummer, rifleman, price per each...................	3	4.50	6
(GC) **Set 3/Company C,** charging, consists of bugler, officer, flag-bearer, drummer, rifleman, price per each..	3	4.50	6
(GD) **Set 4/Troop D,** consists of four mounted troopers, one mounted officer, troopers all look alike, price per each...............................	4.50	6.75	9
(GE) **Set 5/Battery E,** two-piece set, led by officer from Troop D, second piece is a gun limber with four horses, several attached soldiers, price for second piece.......	9	13	19

GREY IRON (GD) Set 4, Troop D. Courtesy Karl Zipple.

GREY IRON (GE) Set 5 Battery E
Courtesy Don Pielin

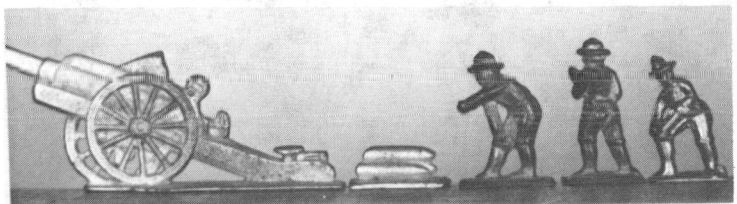

GREY IRON (GF) Set 6, Battery F
Courtesy Don Pielin

GREY IRON (GG) Set 5 Aviation Corps (Above two photos)
Courtesy the late Karl Zipple

	C6	C8	C10
(GF) Set 6/Battery F, consists of shell stack, loader bending, loader standing, gunner, cannon, price per each, shells double	3.50	5.25	7
(GG) Set 5/Aviator Corps, consists of pilot (two of the same figure in set) and plane with detachable wing. Price for set	70	105	140
(GH) Uncle Sam's Defenders, consists of charging rifleman, machine gunner, charging officer, rifleman at attention, flagbearer, officer saluting, price per each (double the price on saluting officer and flagbearer)	3	4.50	6

End Greyklip Armies

GREY IRON (GH) Uncle Sam's Defenders.

L to R: G1, G2, G3, G3a, G4
Photo by Ed Poole

L to R: G10, G10A

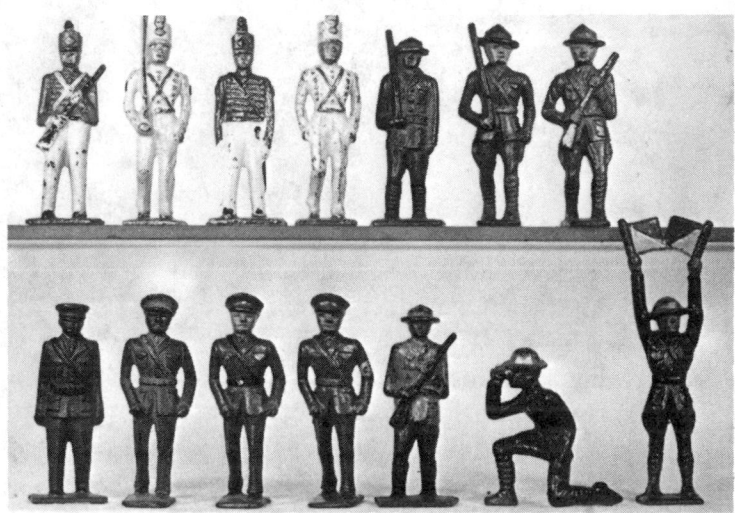

Top L to R: G5, G6, G7, G8, G9, G10, G11
Bottom L to R: G12, G13, G14, G15, G16, G17, G18

Top L to R: G19, G20, G21, G22, G23
Bottom L to R: G24, G25, G26, G27, G28, G29, G30

	C6	C8	C10
(G1) **1 Colonial Soldier** 14		21	28
(G2) **1A Colonial Foot Officer**.............12		18	25
(G3) **1B Colonial Color-Bearer** 175		263	350
(G3a) 1B Colonial Color-Bearer, 1950s version, with rifle barrel drilled out for flag......................................25		38	50
(G4) **1MA Colonial Mounted Officer**..22		33	45
(G5) **2 Cadet,** early version 8		12	17
(G6) **2 Cadet**.....................................11		16	23
(G7) **2A Cadet Officer,** early 8		12	17
(G8) **2A Cadet Officer**........................15		22	31
(G9) **3 U.S. Infantry, Shoulder Arms,** early..7		11	14
(G10) **3 U.S. Infantry, Shoulder Arms** 7		11	14
(G10a) Same as above, no tie..................No Price Found			
(G11) **3/1 U.S. Infantry, Port Arms**....10		15	20
(G12) **3A U.S. Infantry Officer,** early 7		11	15
(G13) **3A U.S. Infantry Officer** 8		12	16
(G14) **3AP Traffic Officer** (same as above, in blue)................................10		15	21
(G15) **3AR Red Cross Officer** (same as above, with armband) 15		22	30

	C6	C8	C10
(G16) **4 U.S. Infantry, Port Arms,** early ..7		11	15
(G17) **4A U.S. Doughboy Officer With Field Glasses** 12		18	25
(G18) **4/1 U.S. Doughboy Signaling** ...14		21	29
(G19) **4/2 U.S. Doughboy Combat Trooper**...13		19	26
(G20) **4/3 U.S. Doughboy With Range Finder** 40		60	80
(G21) **4/4 U.S. Doughboy Ammunition Carrier**..42		63	85
(G22) **4/5 U.S. Doughboy Sharpshooter** .13		19	26
(G23) **4/6 U.S. Doughboy With Bayonet**...15		22	31
(G24) **5 U.S. Infantry, Charging,** early 8		12	16
(G25) **6 U.S. Doughboy, Port Arms,** early..10		15	20
(G26) **6 U.S. Doughboy, Shoulder Arms** 7		11	15
(G27) **6A U.S. Doughboy Officer,** early..9		13	18
(G28) **6A U.S. Doughboy Officer** 8		12	17
(G29) **6/1 U.S .Doughboy Charging** ...7		10	14
(G30) **6/2 U.S. Doughboy Sentry** 9		13	18

Top L to R: G31, G32, G33, G34
Bottom L to R: G35, G37, G38

Top L to R: G39, G40, G41, G42, G43, G44
Bottom L to R: G45, G46, G47, G48, G49

Top L to R: G50, G51, G52, G53, G54
Bottom L to R: G55, G56, G57, G58, G59

	C6	C8	C10
(G31) 6/3 U.S. Doughboy Bomber, crawling	10	15	20
(G32) 6/4 U.S. Doughboy Grenade Thrower	17	25	34
(G33) 7 U.S. Doughboy Charging, early	9	13	18
(G34) 8M U.S. Cavalryman, early	18	27	36
(G35) 8M U.S. Cavalryman	18	27	36
(G36) 8M U.S. Cavalry Color Bearer With Silk Flag (not shown, same as G34)	No Price Found		
(G37) 8MA U.S. Cavalry Officer, early	20	30	40
(G38) 8MA U.S. Cavalry Officer	20	30	40
(G39) 9 U.S. Marine, early	7	11	15
(G40) 9 U.S. Marine	9	13	18
(G41) 10 Royal Canadian Police, early	12	18	24
(G42) 10 Royal Canadian Police	16	24	32
(G43) 10M Royal Canadian Mounted Police (same as G34)	21	31	43
(G44) 10M Royal Canadian Mounted Police (same as G35)	26	39	52

	C6	C8	C10
(G45) 11 Indian, with hatchet, early	7	11	14
(G46) 11 Indian Chief, with knife	7	11	15
(G47) 11/1 Indian Brave, shielding eyes	12	18	24
(G48) 11/2 Chief Attacking, upraised tomahawk	50	75	100
(G49) 11M Indian Mounted, early	18	27	37
(G50) 11M Indian Mounted, lying on horse	34	51	68
(G51) 11/1M Indian Scout, Mounted, firing pistol rearward	112	168	225
(G52) 12 Cowboy, early	7	11	15
(G53) 12 Cowboy	7	11	15
(G54) 12/1/Hold-Up Man	12	18	25
(G55) 12/2 Cowboy With Lasso, with lasso price is 55.00 in mint	19	27	39
(G56) 12/3 Bandit, surrendering	54	81	108
(G57) 12M Cowboy Mounted, early	23	39	46
(G58) 12M Cowboy Mounted	28	42	56
(G59) 12/1M Masked Cowboy Mounted	162	243	325

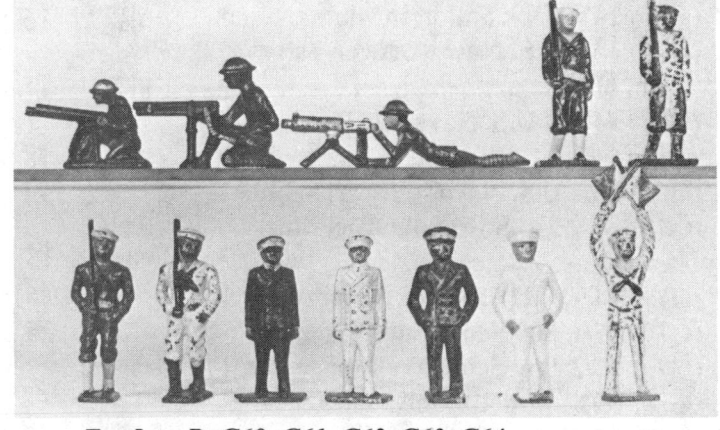

Top L to R: G60, G61, G62, G63, G64
Bottom L to R: G65, G66, G67, G68, G69, G70, G71

	C6	C8	C10
(G60) 13 U.S. Machine Gunner, early	9	13	18
(G61) 13 U.S. Machine Gunner	7	11	15
(G62) 13/1 U.S. Machine Gunner	9	13	19

	C6	C8	C10
(G75) **16/2 Pirate Chief**	10	15	20
(G76) **16/3 Pirate With Dagger**	12	18	24
(G77) **16/4 Pirate With Hook**	11	16	23
(G78) **16/5 Pirate With Sword**	10	15	20
(G79) **17/1 Legion Drum Major,** early	25	38	50
(G80) **17/1 Legion Drum Major**	11	16	22
(G81) **17/2 Legion Bugler,** early	9	13	19
(G82) **17/2 Legion Bugler**	10	15	20
(G83) **17/3 Legion Drummer,** early	9	14	18
(G84) **17/3 Legion Drummer**	9	14	18
(G85) **17/4 Legion Color Bearer**	11	16	23
(G86) **18/1 Ethiopian Tribesman,** circa 1936	29	43	58
(G87) **18/2 Ethiopian Chief**	37	55	74
(G88) **18/3 Ethiopian Soldier, Shoulder Arms**	26	39	53
(G89) **18/3A Ethiopian Officer**	38	57	76
(G90) **18/5 Ethiopian Soldier, Charging**	29	44	59
(G91) **Italian or English Desert Infantryman**	95	142	190
(G92) **Italian or English Desert Officer**	80	120	160
(G93) **19 Knight In Armor**	8	12	16
(G94) **20 Red Cross Doctor**	15	22	31
(G95) **21 Stretcher Bearer**	20	30	40
(G96) **22 Stretcher With Patient**	15	22	31
(G97) **22/1/Wounded Sitting**	45	68	90

Top L to R: G72, G73, G74, G75, G76, G77, G78
Bottom L to R: G79, G80, G81, G82, G83, G84, G85

Top L to R: G86, G87, G88, G89, G90, G91, G92
Bottom L to R: G93, G94, G95, G96, G97

	C6	C8	C10
(G63) **14 U.S. Sailor,** in blue, early	8	12	17
(G64) **14 U.S. Sailor,** in white, early	8	12	16
(G65) **14 U.S. Sailor,** in blue	8	12	17
(G66) **14W U.S. Sailor,** in white	8	12	16
(G67) **14A U.S. Naval Officer,** early, in blue	8	12	17
(G68) **14AW U.S. Naval Officer,** early, in white	9	13	18
(G69) **14A U.S. Naval Officer,** in blue	7	10	14
(G70) **14AW U.S. Naval Officer** in white	7	11	15
(G71) **14/1W U.S. Sailor Signalman**	13	19	26
(G72) **15/1 Boy Scout Saluting,** early	12	18	25
(G73) **15/2 Boy Scout Walking,** early	11	16	23
(G74) **16/1 Pirate Boy** (all pirates circa 1935, were also sold as a Treasure Island set, with either tent or treasure chest included, pirates meant to represent Jim, Captain Flint, Long John, Blind Pew, Billie Bones)	13	19	26

Top L to R: G98, G99, G100, G101, G102
Bottom L to R: G103, G104, G105

	C6	C8	C10
(G98) **22/2 Wounded On Crutches**	20	30	40
(G99) **23 Red Cross Nurse**	12	18	24
(G100) **25 Aviator** (24 is non-soldier)	22	33	44
(G101) **Ski Trooper,** circa 1940, with skis four times the noted price	13	19	26
(G102) **Greek Evzone**	55	82	110
(G103) **75 Radio Set, Operator and Aerial**	75	113	150
(G103A) **75 Radio Set, Operator only**	44	66	88
(G104) **D26 Nurse and Wounded Soldier**	100	150	200
(G105) **D27 Doughboy Supporting Wounded Soldier**	130	195	260

L to R: G107, G106
Photo by K. Warren Mitchell

*(G106) U.S. Cavalryman, probably
Grey Iron, like G34, but horses's
head and left leg up 70   105   140
*(G107) U.S. Cavalry Officer, Probably
Grey Iron, like G87, but horse's
head and left leg up 60   90   120
*These may not have been produced by Grey Iron, but instead by
Distinctive Products, Inc.

Top L to R: G108, G109, G110, G111
Bottom L to R: G112, G113, G114

(G108) **6AF Foreign Legion Officer** . 15   22   30
(G109) **6F Foreign Legion - Shoulder
Arms** 15   22   30
(G110) **6/1F Foreign Legion Charging** .17   25   34
(G111) **6/3 Foreign Legion Bomber** ...40   60   80
(G112) **13F Foreign Legion Machine
Gunner** 13   19   27
(G113) **8A/F Foreign Legion Cavalry
Officer** 27   41   55
(G114) **8/F Foreign Legion
Cavalryman** 34   51   68
(G115) Foreign Legion Stretcher Bearer,
only one known ....No   Price   Found

AMERICAN FAMILY SERIES
(approximately 2-1/4" high)

Top L to R: T1, T2, T3, T4, T5, T6, T7
Bottom L to R: T8, T9, T10, T11, T12-T13

The American Family Travels
T-1 **Man in traveling suit** 5   8   11
T-2 **Woman in traveling costume** 5   8   10
T-3 **Boy in traveling suit** 4   6   9
T-4 **Girl in traveling suit** 6   9   13
T-5 **Conductor** 6   9   12
T-6 **Engineer** 6   9   12
T-7 **Porter** 6   9   13
T-8 **Policeman** 6   9   12
T-9 **Postman** 5   8   11
T-10 **Newsboy** 8   12   16
T-11 **Preacher** 7   11   15
T-12 **Old Colored Man - sitting** 8   12   16
T-13 **Seat** 4   6   8

Top L to R: F1, F2, F3, F4, F5
Bottom L to R: F6, F7, F8, F9

The American Family on the Farm
F-1 **Farmer** 5   8   10
F-2 **Farmer's Wife** 6   9   13
F-3 **Girl** 5   8   11
F-4 **Hired Man digging** 6   9   12
F-5 **Horse** 7   10   14
F-6 **Cow** 3   5   7

Top L to R: F10, F11, F12
Bottom L to R: F13, F14

	C6	C8	C10
F-7 Calf	3	5	7
F-8 Pig	3	5	7
F-9 Sheep	4	6	9
F-10 Goat	4	6	8
F-11 Goose	3	5	7
F-12 Dog	3	5	7
F-13 Gate with Post	10	15	20
F-14 Fence	7	11	14

Top L to R: H1, H2, H3, H4, H5, H6 on H13
Bottom L to R: H7, H8, H9, H10, H11, H12

THE AMERICAN FAMILY AT HOME

	C6	C8	C10
H-1 Man with watering can	6	9	13
H-2 Woman with basket	7	11	15
H-3 Boy flying kite	7	10	14
H-4 Girl skipping rope	10	15	21
H-5 Old man sitting	4	6	8
H-6 Old woman sitting	4	6	8
H-7 Colored cook	11	16	22
H-8 Colored man digging	18	27	37
H-9 Garageman	8	12	16

	C6	C8	C10
H-10 Delivery Boy	6	9	13
H-11 Milkman	6	9	12
H-12 Dog	4	6	9
H-13 Lawn Seat	4	6	9

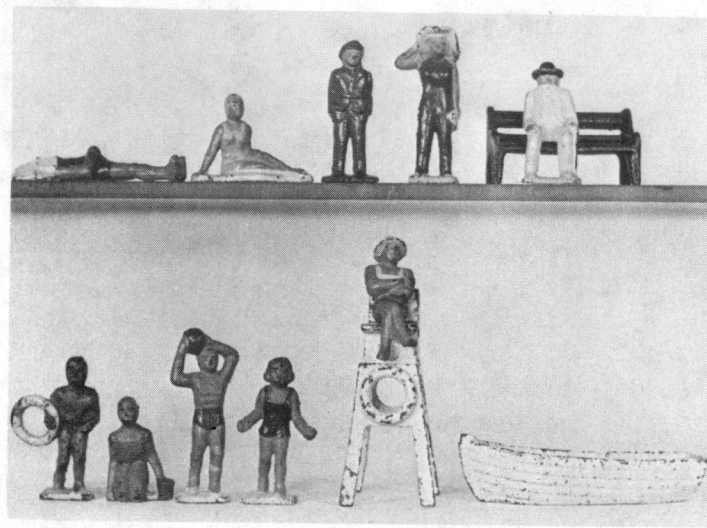

Top L to R: B1, B2, B3, B4, B5 on B13
Bottom L to R: B6, B7, B8, B9, B10, B11, B12

THE AMERICAN FAMILY ON THE BEACH

B-1 Man in bathing suit	10	15	20
B-2 Woman in bathing suit	10	15	20
B-3 Boy in summer suit	6	9	12
B-4 Girl in slacks	9	13.50	18
B-5 Old Man Sitting	3	5	7
B-6 Boy with Life Preserver	9	13	18
B-7 Girl with Sand Pail	9	13	18
B-8 Boy with Ball	9	13	18
B-9 Girl Catching Ball	8	12	16
B-10 Life Guard	11	16	22
B-11 Life Guard's Chair	12	18	24
B-12 Life Boat	12	18	24
B-13 Bench	4	6	8
B-14 Cabana	No Price Found		

Top L to R: R1, R2-R8, R3, R4, R5, R6-R9
Bottom L to R: R10, R11, R15, R16

THE AMERICAN FAMILY ON THE RANCH

R-1 Cowboy with lasso	9	14	18
R-2 Cowboy Rider	19	28	38

	C6	C8	C10
R-3 Cowboy squatting	8	12	16
R-4 Boy in CowboySuit	8	12	16
R-5 Girl in Riding Suit	7	11	15
R-6 Cowgirl Rider	11	16	22
R-7 Stallion	8	12	16
R-8 Bucking Bronco	10	15	20
R-9 Colt	6	9	12
R-10 Burro	7	11	15
R-11 Calf	5	8	11
R-15 Rooster and Chickens	4	6	8
R-16 Three Ducks	5	8	10

THE CHAMPIONS ON THE DIAMOND

	C6	C8	C10
M69 Fielder in Position, appox 1½" high	17	26	35

AUBURN RUBBER

Although AUBURN (also Aub-Rub'r) was founded in 1913, in Auburn, Indiana, as the Double Fabric Tire Corporation, making auto tubes and tires for Model T Fords, etc., it didn't produce its first toy until 1935, with five soldiers. The prototype was a Palace Guard, which AUBURN President and chief stockholder A.L. Murray had obtained in England. The model was taken to a local pattern-maker who made patterns from it, and then the company made the original molds from lead and molded sample toys for Murray. These samples were next taken to an artist and decorated per Murray's instructions. Presented to buyers, they immediately caught on. The soldiers were molded in 24" rubber presses, each containing forty to sixty soldiers, with cure time approximately 6-12 minutes. The soldiers, once trimmed, were dipped in a base laquer (advertised as "pure vegetable dyes") and then sent down a decorating conveyor, where as many as 24 women, using small camel hair brushes, added finishing touches, painting the faces, shoes, belts, buttons, medals, and finally eyes. After drying,each was wrapped individually in waxed paper and packed three dozen to a chip-board carton and twelve dozen to a corrugated carton for shipment. Design of the soldiers was credited to Edward McCandlish, a free-lance artist. The soldiers sold well from the beginning, with approximately 200 of the 400 AUBURN employees (AUBURN consistently made non-toy products as well) involved in them and other toys on a two-shift basis. Shortly after the first soldiers were introduced, animals and wheeled vehicles, the first a Cord automobile, were marketed, all successfully. AUBURN produced no soldiers during the war, and few after, though it continued to make toys in great quantity (70,000 wheeled items a day in 1962, for example). In 1960 the toys portion of AUBURN was purchased by the town of Deming, New Mexico, where it remained until it went out of business in 1969. AUBURN'S soldiers, all approximately the standard 3¼" length, went through three stages. The first were frail-looking, with long, thin bodies; the second, which emerged as early as September, 1938 , were stockier and larger-headed, and the third, introduced in 1941, were more well-proportioned and realistic. Unlike its competitors, AUBURN produced no cowboys, Indians, sailors or civilians, except for baseball and football players and two farm workers. AUBURN's infantry came in colors other than brown. The blue were meant to represent U.S. Marines. The white also were sold as Marines. It is thought that some Auburn Ethiopians remain to be discovered. Still elusive is the A35 running pilot, known to have been sold, but with none currently known to be in any collection.

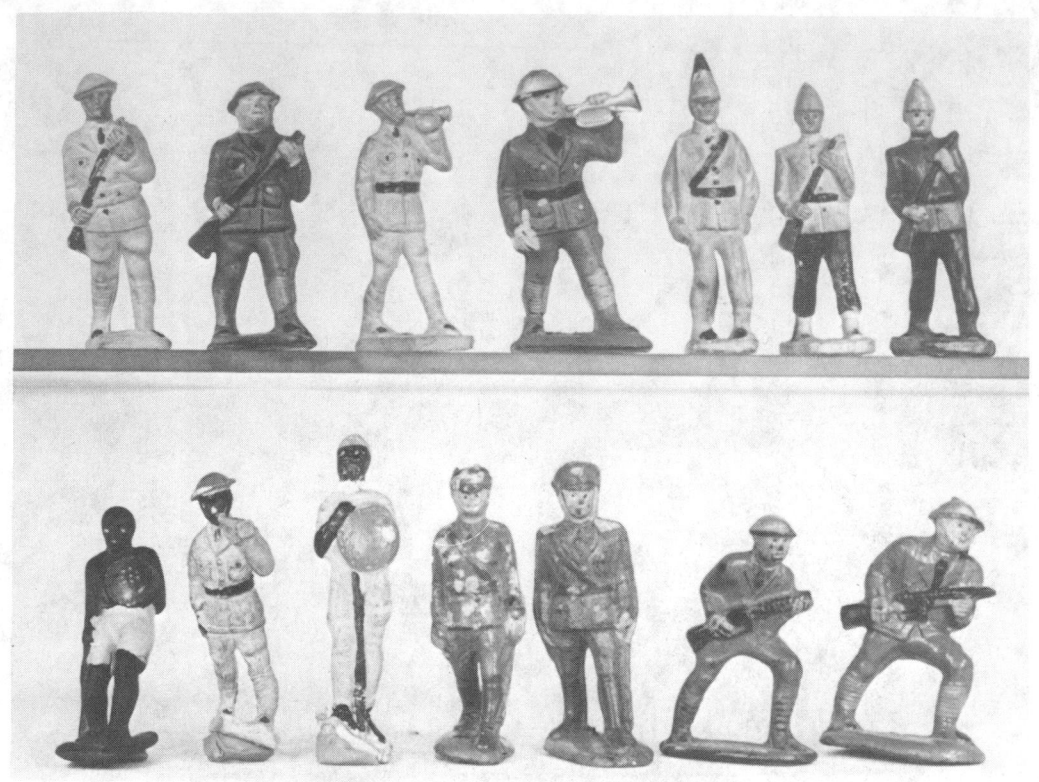

Top L to R: A1, A2, A3, A4, A5, A6, A6a
Bottom L to R: A7, A7a, A7b, A8, A9, A10, A11

A14a
Courtesy Ron Steiner

*(All **bold words** and numbers are **Auburn's own descrition**)*

	C6	C8	C10
(A1) **1200 Infantry Private**	8	12	16
(A2) **200 U.S. Infantry Private**	7	11	15
(A3) **1202 Infantry Bugler**	8	12	17
(A4) **202 Bugler, U.S. Infantry**	10	15	20
(A5) **Foreign Legion**, also **White Guard** officer, **No. 220**	11	16	22
(A6) **214 & 218 Foreign Legion Private**	10	15	20
(A7) Ethiopian with shield and rifle	60	90	120
(A7a) Ethiopian bugler	No Price Found		
(A7b) Ethiopian with rifle and shield, in robes	50	75	100
(A8) Officer, early	10	15	20
(A9) **204 U.S. Infantry Officer**	7	11	15
(A10) **1238 Charging Soldier**	22	33	45
(A11) **238 Charging Soldier** with tommy gun	9	13	18
(A12) **232 Officer on Horse**	18	27	37
(A13) **230 Machine Gunner**	10	15	21
(A14) **224 Red Cross Doctor**	17	26	35
(A14a) Army Doctor, Khaki uniform	No Price Found		
(A15) **226 Red Cross Nurse** white or khaki uniform	18	27	36
(A16) **206 Stretcher Bearer**	17	25	34
(A17) **208 Wounded Soldier**	18	27	37

	C6	C8	C10
(A18) **216 Observer With Binoculars**	8	12	16
(A19) **236 Signalman**	30	45	60
(A19a) **Signalman**, early smaller size, only three known	100	150	200
(A20) **222 Sniper**, crawling, rifle over shoulder	32	48	65
(A21) **234 Bomb Thrower**	12	18	25
(A22) **242 Anti-Aircraft Gun**	16	24	33
(A23) **1546 Motorcycle Cop**, blue or khaki as soldier	25	38	50

Top L to R: A12, A13, A14, A15, A16
Bottom L to R: A17, A18, A19, A20

364

Top L to R: A21, A22, A23, A24
Bottom L to R: A25, A26, A27, A28, A29

Top L to R: A30, A31, A32, A33
Bottom L to R: A34, A36, A37, A38, A39

Top L to R: A40, A41, A42, A43
Bottom L to R: A44, A45, A46

A35

Rough sketch from memory going back 40 years of A35. Note no box in hand, head tilted up toward left, left hand forward. None known.

	C6	C8	C10
(A24) **240 Motorcycle Soldiers,** with sidecar	25	38	50
(A25) **Aircraft Defender**	15	22	30
(A26) **Color Bearer**	22	33	44
(A27) **Marching Soldier**	12	18	25
(A28) **Firing Soldier**	22	33	44
(A29) **272 Plane Shooter**	18	27	36
(A30) **Sound Detector**	18	27	36
(A31) **Searchlight**	18	27	36
(A32) **296 Trench Mortar**	17	25	34
(A33) **Tank Defender**	25	36	48
(A34) **Tank Soldier,** running with box	16	24	32
(A35) Pilot running, looking skyward, in pilot helmet and goggles	No Price Found		
(A36) **Motor Scout**	20	30	40
(A37) **258 Baserunner**	15	22	31
(A38) **252 Batter**	20	30	41
(A39) **256 Fielder or Baseman**	18	27	37
(A40) **250 Pitcher**	26	39	52
(A41) **254 Catcher**	17	25	34
(A42) **268 Carrier** football player	17	25	34
(A43) **264 Center** football player	16	24	32
(A44) **262 Backfieldman,** football player	20	30	40
(A45) **260 Lineman,** football player	16	24	33
(A46) **266 Passer,** football player	21	32	42
(A47) Motorcycle Cop, large 5" high	25	38	50
(A48) Cowboy, large, on wheeled horse	33	50	66

365

AMERICAN METAL TOYS

Until recently, these 3-1/4"-high dimestore soldiers were attributed to Chicago toy soldier-maker J. Edward Jones. Though Jones did make many other figures, research by the author has established the following group were produced by American Metal Toys, Inc., also of Chicago. The president of the firm was Royce Reyff (1898-1986) and his partner was C. Raymond Pierson. The address was 215 No. Racine. Although the company formally incorporated October 24, 1939,

it begain in 1937 and seems to have gone out of business in April, 1942, when its supply of metal was cut off by the demands of World War Two. Sculpting and diemaking were by Henry Kasselowki, who had also worked for Jones. Four of the soldiers sold by American Metal Toys (AM1, AM2, AM26, AM43) were originally produced by Jones (all four are in a range below 3-1/4"), but whether Kasselowski used Jones' old molds or made new ones isn't as yet known.

For American Metal Soldiers in gray, increase the price by 40%.

L to R: AM1, AM1a
Courtesy K. Warren Mitchell

Top L to R: AM9, AM10, AM10a, AM11
Bottom L to R: AM12, AM13, AM14, AM15

	C6	C8	C10
(AM4) Observer w/binoculars and rifle...	35	52	70
(AM5) Wire-cutter, prone......................	225	338	450
(AM6) Soldier with rifle, gassed or shot in neck......................................	170	255	340
(AM7) Stretcher-bearer.........................	50	75	100
(AM8) Kneeling with AA Gun............	44	66	88
(AM9) Charging, port arms..................	125	188	250
(AM10) Firing machine gun on stump.	35	52	70
(AM10a) Same as above, No. 1 on pocket..	100	150	200
(AM11) Grenade thrower, no weapons..	55	83	110
(AM12) Seated with rifle........................	40	60	80
(AM13) Officer in greatcoat, pointing, holding pistol....................................	105	158	210
(AM14) Prone with rifle, trunk upraised.	65	98	130
(AM15) Prone, firing double-barreled machine gun....................................	62	93	125

Top L to R: AM1, AM2, AM3, AM4
Bottom L to R: AM5, AM6, AM7, AM8

	C6	C8	C10
(AM1) German, Kneeling with rifle.....	105	158	210
(AM1a) Same as above, short rifle.......	110	165	220
(AM2) German, charging with rifle......	107	160	215
(AM3) German, prone machine gunner..	70	105	140

Top L to R: AM16, AM17, AM18, AM19
Bottom L to R: AM20, AM21,.AM22, AM23, AM23a

	C6	C8	C10
(AM16) Kneeling, firing anti-tank gun.	40	60	80
(AM16a) Same as above with barrel brace, "23" on wheel	50	75	100
(AM17) Cook w/chef's hat, frying pan.	57	85	115
(AM18) Ammunition Carrier	200	300	400
(AM19) Motorcyclist with machine gun mounted on motorcycle	70	105	140
(ΛM20) Flagbearer (similar to Barclay B7)	112	168	225
(AM21) Kneeling with searchlight	40	60	80
(AM21a) Kneeling with searchlight, "27", "Made in USA" on sides of stanchion	55	82	110

Top L to R: AM24, AM25, AM26, AM27
Bottom L to R: AM28, AM28a, AM29, AM30, AM31

	C6	C8	C10
(AM22) Seated with phone	48	72	96
(AM23) Kneeling, firing rifle, no stand	67	100	135
(AM23a) Same as above, shorter rifle	75	112	150

	C6	C8	C10
AM24) Prone, body arched, firing machine gun	60	90	120
(AM25) Bugler	82	123	165
(AM26) Soldier with gas mask, plunging rifle down, slightly smaller in size	107	160	215
(AM27) Nurse w/bag, like Barclay B82.	45	68	90
(AM28) Doctor with bag, like Barclay B81 (in khaki, add $45 in mint)	40	60	80
(AM29) Standing, firing rifle	47	70	95
(AM30) Wounded supine, like Manoil M53	44	66	88
(AM31) Cowboy on rearing horse, firing backward	130	195	260
(AM32) Marching with rifle	74	110	148
(AM33) Cowboy kneeling	30	45	60
(AM33A) Cowboy kneeling, with base, rare	No Price Found		
(AM34) Indian on rearing horse	50	75	100
(AM35) Indian with bow (copy of Beton's)	No Price Found		

AM35a

Top L to R: AM32, AM33, AM34
Bottom L to R: AM36, AM37, AM38

AM39
Courtesy Don Pielin

L to R: AM40, AM41
Courtesy Don Pielin

	C6	C8	C10
(AM35a) Indian kneeling-shooting	24	36	48
(AM36) Tramp	9	13	18
(AM37) Farmer	6	9	13
(AM38) Farmer's Wife	7	10	14
(AM39) Cowboy on Prancing Horse, similar to Barclay B2			No Price Found
(AM40) Knight w/shield, flat underbase.			No Price Found
(AM41) Knight with pennant, flat underbase	64	95	128
(AM42) Kneeling Nurse, <u>probably</u> American Metal, copy of Barclay's but shorter, squatter			No Price Found
(AM43) Cowboy shooting (on foot)	15	22	30

Barclay kneeling nurse at left, AM42 at right.
Photo by Barry S. Josephs

AM43
Courtesy Don Pielin - Old Toy Soldier

MARX PLAYSETS

by Barry Goodman

One of the most successful toy lines in the history of plastic toys was the playset. Although the history of the playset spans from the late 1940's to the present, its heyday was from the mid 1950's to the late 1960's. A playset is a toy containing figures and varied accessories designed to be played with. The most common themes are those involving military campaigns throughout the ages. These include Prehistoric Scenes, Vikings and Romans, The Civil War, Western Adventures and World War II. Those containing either an important historical figure (Johnny Ringo) or an event (i.e. Custer's Last Stand), are the most desirable. Prices have steadily increased in the past few years. Literally hundreds of sets were made by the Marx company. The sets come in different sizes, and variations upon the same theme are common. The only constant was the child's imagination in creating a new adventure each and every time the playset was set up and played with!

Atomic Cape Canaveral Missile Base, value mint in box $250. Photo by Barry Goodman

Battle of the Blue & Gray. Mint in box value $700

Alamo Play Set, Mint in box value $750. Photo by Barry Goodman

Battleground Play Set, Mint in box value $300. Photo by Barry Goodman

Arctic Explorer, Series 2000. Mint in box value $500. Photo by Barry Goodman

Beachhead Assault Set, Mint in box value $100. Photo by Barry Goodman

369

Beach-Head Landing Set, Mint in box value $500.
Photo by Barry Goodman

Construction Camp, value mint in box $250.
Photo by Barry Goodman

Ben-Hur, Mint in box value $800
Photo by Barry Goodman

Cape Canaveral, value mint in box $300.
Photo by Barry Goodman

Blue and Gray Armies, value in Mint $250.
Photo by Barry Goodman

Construction Camp, value mint in box $400.
Photo by Barry Goodman

Blue and Gray, Sears Heritage Play Set, value Mint in box $125.
Photo by Barry Goodman

Daniel Boone Frontier Play Set, value mint in box $250.
Photo by Barry Goodman

Fort Apache, Sears Heritage, value Mint in box $150
Photo by Barry Goodman

Desert Fox, value mint in box $350.
Photo by Barry Goodman

Fort Dearborn, value Mint in box $350.
Photo by Barry Goodman

Fort Apache Set, Series 1000, value mint in box $250.
Photo by Barry Goodman

Gallant Men Army Play Set, value Mint in box $500
Photo by Barry Goodman

Gunsmoke Dodge City, value Mint in box $1000.
Photo by Barry Goodman

Knights & Vikings, value Mint in box $250.
Photo by Barry Goodman

Jungle Animal Playset, value Mint in box $700.

Military Academy, value Mint in box $350.
Photo by Barry Goodman

Knights & Castle Miniature Playset, value Mint in box $150
Photo by Barry Goodman

Modern Colonial Doll House, series 750, value mint in box $150.
Photo by Barry Goodman

Modern Farm Set, value Mint in box $200.
Photo by Barry Goodman

Modern Farm Set, value Mint in box $150.
Photo by Barry Goodman

Rhine River Battle, value Mint in box $200.
Photo by Barry Goodman

Modern Service Station, value Mint in box $300.
Photo by Barry Goodman

Robin Hood Castle Set, value Mint in box $350.
Photo by Barry Goodman

Prehistoric Times, Series 1000, value Mint in box $300.
Photo by Barry Goodman

Service Station, value Mint in box $250.
Photo by Barry Goodman

Sons of Liberty, Sears Heritage, value Mint in box $150.
Photo by Barry Goodman

U.S. Armed Forces Training Center, Series 1000, value Mint in box $350.
Photo by Barry Goodman

Tales of Wells Fargo, value Mint in box $500.
Photo by Barry Goodman

U.S. Army Training Center, value Mint in box $200.
Photo by Barry Goodman

Troll Village, Miniature Play Set, value Mint in box $125.
Photo by Barry Goodman

Western Town, value Mint in box $500.
Photo by Barry Goodman

Untouchables, value Mint in box $1200.
Photo by Barry Goodman

ACTION FIGURES

Though there had previously been similar toys, it was Hasbro's G.I. Joe which truly created the category of the Action Figure.

Don Levine, the Director of Development for Hasbro, conceived the idea of G.I. Joe while standing outside a Manhattan art supply shop in February, 1963. A licensing agent had suggested a military toy based on a t.v. series, "The Lieutenant." Levine had discarded the idea of a tie-in because the series was for adults, but the thought was in his mind as he looked at an artist's manikin in the shop window. The idea of a boy's soldier with movable parts came to him.

Sam Speers, who worked under Levine, came up with the engineering for G.I. Joe, both the mechanical and esthetic inventions (for which he received many patents), which included devising a way that enabled the toy to stand on its own (unlike artists' manikins) in various positions and while holding weapons or bearing equipment. Speers also thought of the added touch of the facial scar (the 11½" height was because the Barbie doll was that tall and a great success).

Noted artist Phil Kraczkowski sculpted the head, which was **not** a composite of 23 Medal of Honor winners, despite ad claims to that effect, and though Speers designed the parts and how they should go together, Walter Hansen and Norman Jacques did the sculpting of the body. It wasn't an easy sell to the Hasbro executives for Levine and Speers, but after the first year's enormous success, Levine was upped to Vice President and Speers moved up to Levine's job as Director of Development.

(Note: after the Hasbro-G.I. Joe listing, all Action Figures are listed alphabetically by company.)

(Mint prices for G.I. Joe toys in the last edition average $102.26, and in this edition $102.64, for an increase of just .004%.)

ADDITIONAL G.I. JOE INFORMATION
by Barry Goodman

G.I. Joe first entered the U.S. market in 1964. The 11½" doll would undergo several changes during its eleven-year life span, 1964-75. The first dolls, 1964-69, had painted hair and were based primarily upon military uniforms of World War II. In 1965, Hasbro added six foreigners to the series (Japanese, German, French, Australian, Russian, British). These were distinctly different in appearance. An easy way of knowing if you have a foreigner is that the scar found on the GI is not present.

In 1965, Hasbro introduced a black G.I. Joe, which today is one of the most sought-after.

In 1967, Hasbro introduced its "Vietnam series" outfits, which were pulled off the market very quickly due to the negative response to the Vietnam war raging in southeast Asia. Thus these uniforms (green and tan airborne M.P., Air Security set and Marine Jungle Fighter) are the most sought after and scarcest. This was the year that also produced the extremely scarce nurse doll.

Protests about the war continued, so in 1969 Hasbro dropped the military line and substituted the "adventurer series". G.I. Joe was transformed from a military doll to an adventure doll. In 1970 G.I. Joe received flock hair and then a flocked moustache and beard. Furthermore, the "adventurer" line was dropped and the "Adventure Team" line substituted. The theme of this line was that G.I. Joe would fight nature and the elements, rather than other men.

In 1972, G.I. Joe was given a "kung-fu" grip. The same year, the oil embargo created havoc because oil-based plastic became prohibitively expensive. Because of this, in 1973 Hasbro changed the basic composition of the plastic, which created a much more fragile doll that by 1975 children had totally lost interest in.

Most collectors concentrate on the 1964-9 dolls. Hasbro consulted military manuals to create the most realistic and authentic boys' doll ever made.

Barry James Goodman is a Leading collector and authority on G.I. Joe dolls and 1960s character figures. As an active toy dealer, he has been able to amass one of the largest collections of G.I. Joes.

ACTION SOLDIER (Revised listings by Barry Goodman)	C6	C8	C10
7000 - GI Joe 5 Star Jeep, 106mm Rocket Launcher, ¼ ton trailer, tripod mounted searchlight and four 106mm shells	50	125	175
7100 - "Let's Go Joe" board game	15	22	40
7500 - GI Joe Action Soldier	35	55	75
7501 - Combat Set A Field jacket	5	10	15

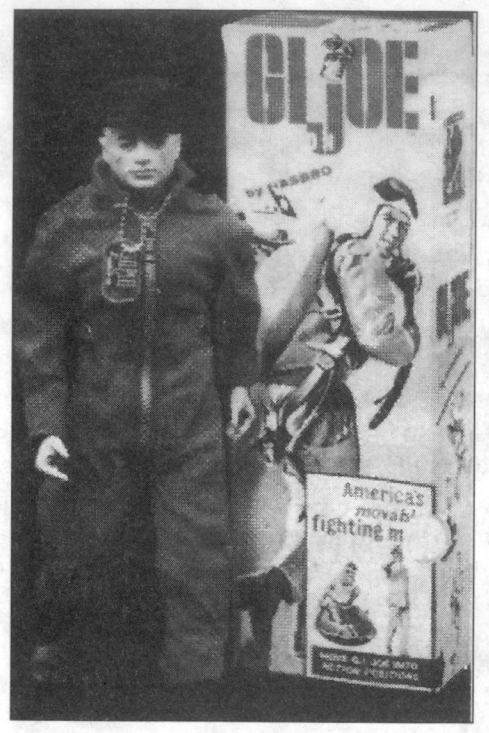  

1965 Catalog Illustrations.

	C6	C8	C10
M-1 rifle	5	10	15
Bayonet	5	10	15
Cartridge belt	5	10	15
Six hand grenades	5	10	15
Price for 7501 Set	35	50	60
7502 - Combat Set B - back pack, canteen and cover, entrenching tool and cover, mess kit, utensils and single pouch cartridge belt, each individually	5	10	15
Price for 7502 Set	35	50	60
7503 - Combat Fatigue Shirt	5	8	12
7504 - Combat Fatigue Pants	5	8	12
7505 - Combat Field Jacket	8	15	20
7506 - Combat Field Pack - entrenching tool and cover	10	20	30
7507 - Combat Helmet, camouflage netting and foliage	10	20	25
7508 - Army Sandbags Set	5	10	12.50
7509 - Canteen with cover and mess kit, utensils	5	10	15
7510 - M-1 Rifle with bayonet and cartridge belt with six grenades	20	40	50
7511 - Camouflage Netting with poles and foliage	5	10	15
7512 - Bivouac Set A - zipped sleeping bag, M-1 Rifle, bayonet, cartridge belt, canteen with cover, and mess kit with utensils, individually	5	10	15
7513 - Bivouac Set B - tent, stakes, poles, foliage, camouflage netting, entrenching tool with cover	10	20	35

	C6	C8	C10
7514 - 30 cal. tripod mounted machine gun, ammo box	10	15	25
7515 - Zippered Sleeping Bag	10	15	25
7517 - Command Post Set - Rain Poncho, .45 pistol w/belt and holster, field radio, field phone, wire roll, map and map case, individually	5	10	15
7518 - .45 Pistol, holster, belt	5	10	15
ammo pouch	5	10	15
six grenades	5	10	15
cloth hat	5	10	15
Price for 7518 Set	25	45	80
7519 Rain Poncho	5	10	15
7520 - Field Phone, Field Radio, Wire Spool, Map Case and map, individually	5	10	15
7521 - Military Police Set - "Ike" Jacket, trousers, ascot, white belt, nightstick, .45 pistol, holster, armband and duffel bag, stem gun	35	50	60
7522 - Jungle Fighter Set - belt, entrenching tool, mess kit, utensils, canteen, cover, machete, sheath and Jungle knife	35	50	70
7523 - Duffel bag	5	10	15
7524 - MP Uniform	250	350	500
7524 - "Ike" Jacket, ascot and MP armband	15	25	35
7525 - "Ike" Trousers	5	10	15
7526 - MP Helmet, black	50	100	150

	C6	C8	C10
7526 - MP Helmet, white belt, .45 pistol, holster and nightstick	20	30	40
7527 - Ski patrol helmet, winter white cartridge belt, winter white M-1 rifle and six grenades	20	30	40
7528 - Bazooka and two shells	10	20	30
7529 - Snow Shoes, pick axe, climbing rope and sun goggles	15	20	35
7530 - Mountain Troops Set - Snow shoes, winter white belt, winter white field pack, pick axe, climbing rope and four grenades	20	30	40
7531 - Ski Patrol Set - two-piece white parka, gloves, boots, skis, poles and sun goggles	20	50	75
7532 - Special Forces Set - uniform, beret, bazooka, two shells and four grenades	25	75	125
7533 - Beret, M-16 rifle and field radio	25	50	75
7536 - Green Beret Set - G.I. Joe action soldier dressed in special forces uniform, M-16 rifle, .45 pistol, belt, holster, six grenades and field radio	75	200	275
7537 - West Point Cadet Set - parade uniform, cap, feather, sword, scabbard, M-1 rifle and dress shoes	75	200	275
7538 - Heavy Weapons Set - 81 mm mortar, 3 shells, M-60 machine gun, tripod, ammo belt, bullet proof vest, bullet belt and 2 grenades	40	100	125
7590 - GI Joe talking action soldier	75	125	150
8000 - Official GI Joe footlocker	10	15	30

GI Joe 8030 Desert Patrol Jeep box.   Photo by Barry Goodman

	C6	C8	C10
8030 - GI Joe desert patrol jeep w/.50 cal. tripod mounted machine gun, radio antenna and GI Joe desert trooper	300	600	900

ACTION SAILOR

	C6	C8	C10
7600 - GI Joe Action Sailor	50	75	90
7601 - Sea Rescue Set A - inflatable raft, oar, sea anchor, tow line, flare gun, knife, scabbard and first aid kit, individually	5	10	15
7602 - Frogman Set - three pc. black scuba set, swim fins, face mask, oxygen tanks, depth gauge, knife, scabbard and depth charges	50	125	175
7603 - Black scuba suit jacket and hood	15	50	100

Sears' G.I. Joe Forward Observer Set. Photo by Barry Goodman.

G.I. Joe Astronaut. C6: 30. C8: 50. C10: 70. Mint in box add 70%. Photo by Barry Goodman.

G.I. Joe Vietnam Marine Jungle Fighter. Photo by Barry Goodman.

G.I. Joe Russian. Photo by Barry Goodman.

G.I. Joe Nurse. Photo by Barry Goodman.

G.I. Joe Tan Airborne M.P., 1967. Photo by Barry Goodman.

G.I. Joe Japanese. Photo by Barry Goodman.

G.I. Joe Australian. Photo by Barry Goodman.

G.I. Joe German. Photo by Barry Goodman.

G.I. Joe 5 Star Jeep. C6: 50. C8: 80. C10: 150. Mint in Box add 70%. Photo by Barry Goodman.

	C6	C8	C10
7604 - Black scuba suit pants 7.50	25	35
7605 - Swim fins, face mask, knife,			
scabbard and depth gauge 20	30	50
7606 - Oxygen tanks.........................5	10	15
7607 - Navy Attack Set - life jacket,			
semaphore flags, hand held search-			
light and binoculars, individually ... 5	10	25
7610 - Navy attack helmet, hand held			
searchlight and binoculars 15	30	40
7611 - Life jacket.............................5	10	15
7612 - Shore Patrol - jumper,			
neckerchief, trousers, white belt,			
.45 pistol, holster, nightstick, arm-			
band, sailors cap and duffel bag..... 35	75	90
7613 - Shore Patrol Jumper Set.............15	30	40
7614 - Shore Patrol Pants 5	10	15
7615 - USN duffel bag 5	10	15
7616 - Shore Patrol w/stripe.................100	200	350
7616 - Shore Patrol helmet, white			
belt, .45 pistol, holster and			
nightstick.............................10	25	30
7618 - .30 cal tripod mounted			
machine gun and ammo box 20	30	45
7619 - Dress Parade M-1 rifle,			
bayonet, white cartridge belt and			
white billyclub 15	45	60
7620 - Deep Sea Diver Set - divers'			
suit, gloves, helmet, breastplate,			
air pump, hoses, weighted belt,			
weighted shoes, signal float, line,			
knife, scabbard and sledge hammer ...20	50	75
7621 - Landing Signal Officer Set -			
safety striped jumpsuit, cloth			
helmet with headphones, goggles,			
binoculars, signal paddles, clip-			
board, pad, pencil and flare gun......30	50	100
7622 - Sea Rescue Set B - same as Sea			
Rescue Set A also includes life			
jackets 10	30	40
7623 - Deep Freeze Set - fur parka,			
pants, boots, snow sled, flare gun			
and ice pick 25	50	70
7624 - Annapolis Cadet Set - dress			
parade jacket, cap, pants, belt,			
shoes, sword, scabbard and white			
M-1 rifle 80	200	275
7625 - Breeches Buoy Set - buoy,			
pulley, slicker jacket, pants, flare			
gun and hand held searchlight 75	150	225
7626 - LSO helmet w/headphones,			
signal paddles, flare gun, clip-			
board, pad and pencil 25	50	75
7627 - USN Life ring.........................10	25	30

	C6	C8	C10
7628 - White sailor's cap, boots and			
GI Joe dogtags 15	25	35
7690 - GI Joe talking action sailor 75	150	175
8050 - Official GI Joe Sea Sled - w/GI			
Joe frogman..................................100	225	275

ACTION MARINE

GI Joe Action Marine equipment box.
Photo by Barry Goodman

	C6	C8	C10
7700 - GI Joe Action Marine.................30	55	65
7701 - Communications Set - M-1 car-			
bine, camouflage poncho, field			
phone, field radio, wire spool,			
binoculars, map and map case,			
individually 5	10	15
7702 - Camouflage poncho 5	10	15
7703 - Field radio, field phone, wire			
spool, map and map case 5	10	15
7704 - Flag Set - Old Glory, Army			
flag, Navy flag, Marine Corps flag			
and Air Force flag 30	60	100
7705 - Paratrooper Set - parachute			
pack, M-1 carbine, six grenades,			
knife, scabbard, belt, ammo			
pouch, canteen and cover,			
individually 5	15	25
7706 - M-1 carbine, six grenades,			
knife, scabbard, belt, ammo			
pouch, canteen and cover,			
individually 5	10	15
7707 - Camouflage helmet, foliage and			
helmet cover................................10	25	30
7708 - Camouflage netting, foliage,			
poles and securing line....................5	10	15
7709 - Parachute Pack......................... 15	20	25
7710 - Dress Parade Set - traditional			
Marine "dress blues", cap and			
white M-1 rifle 20	40	60

G.I. Joe Polar Explorer. C6: 100. C8: 200. C10: 250. Mint in box add 70%. Photo by Barry Goodman.

	C6	C8	C10
7711 - Beachhead Set A - flame thrower, camouflage tent, poles, stakes, belt, ammo pouch, mess kit and utensils, individually	5	10	15
7712 - Beachhead Set B - M-1 rifle, cartridge belt, six grenades, field pack, bayonet, entrenching tool, cover, canteen and cover, individually	5	10	15
7713 - Field pack, entrenching tool and cover	10	30	40
7714 - Camouflage fatigue shirt	5	8	12
7715 - Camouflage fatigue pants	5	8	12
7716 - Mess Kit, utensils, canteen and cover	5	10	15
7717 - M-1 Rifle, bayonet, cartridge belt and six grenades	20	30	40
7718 - Flame thrower	10	15	20
7719 - Medic Set - stretcher, crutch, satchel, stethoscope, plasma bottle, IV tube, splints, bandage rolls, armbands and hospital flag, cloth bag	50	100	125
7720 crutch, stethoscope, plasma bottle, I.V. tube, splints and bandage rolls	10	25	35
7721 - Medic's helmet, satchel and two armbands	15	30	50
7722 - Fatigue cap, boots and G.I. Joe dog tags	20	25	35
7723 - G.I. bunk bed	15	25	35
7727 - Weapons Rack with rack, M-1 rifle, M-1 carbine, M-16 rifle and 40 mm grenade launcher	30	50	60
7731 - Tank Commander Set - leather jacket, tanker's helmet, belt, .30 cal. M-60 machine gun, tripod, ammo box, radio and tripod	75	100	150

	C6	C8	C10
7732 - Jungle Fighter Set - green fatigue shirt, pants, campaign hat, AR-15 rifle, belt, knife, machete, sheath, canteen, cover, flame thrower and field phone	200	350	500
7790 - G.I. Joe talking action Marine	95	150	200

ACTION PILOT

	C6	C8	C10
7800 - G.I. Joe action pilot	30	55	75
7801 - Survival Set - inflatable raft, sea anchor, tow line, oar, knife, scabbard, flare gun, first aid kit and inflatable USAF life vest	50	75	100
7802 - Inflatable raft, sea anchor, tow line and oar	10	25	30
7803 - Dress Uniform - jacket, shirt, tie, pants, garrison cap, wings and captain's bars	20	40	60
7804 - Dress Jacket	10	15	20
7805 - Dress Pants	10	15	20
7806 - Dress Shirt and Cap	10	15	20
7807 - Scramble Set - gray flight suit, inflatable life vest, .45 pistol, holster, belt, clipboard, pad and pencil	25	40	75
7808 - Gray flight suit	5	10	15
7809 - Inflatable life vest, flare gun, knife, scabbard and first aid kit	10	20	30
7810 - Crash helmet w/oxygen mask	20	40	50
7811 - Parachute pack	10	15	25
7812 - Communications Set - field radio binoculars, map, map case, clipboard, pad and pencil	20	30	60
7813 - Marine Jungle Fighter (Vietnam)	200	300	450
7813 - A.P. Helmet Set	10	30	40
7820 - Crash Crew Set - metallic heat suit, hood, gloves, boots, tool belt and CO_2 fire extinguisher	35	65	90
7822 - Colorado Air Cadet Set - uniform, sash, cap, dress shoes, M-1 rifle, sword and scabbard	75	125	150
7823 - Fighter Pilot Set - G-suit, boots, "Mae West" life jacket, helmet, oxygen mask, flashlight and working parachute	75	200	375
7824 - Air Sea Rescue Set - three pc. orange scuba suit, mask, swim fins, air tanks, flare gun, first aid kit, rescue life ring and marker-buoy	25	60	100
7890 - G.I. Joe talking action pilot	75	200	275
7900 - G.I. Joe Action Soldier Colored (sic)	100	200	300

Left to Right: 8200, 8201, 8202, 8203, 8204, 8205. Courtesy of Sam Speers.
(The figures in this photo are not those actually sold in foreign uniforms.)

	C6	C8	C10
8020 - Official G.I. Joe Space Capsule - space suit, boots, gloves, helmet and recording of mercury control communications	80	150	260
8040 - Deluxe Crash Crew Set - fire truck, working water pump, working siren, blinking red light, fire axe, metallic heat suit, boots, gloves and hood, white stretcher	200	350	450
G.I. Jane (1965) Army Nurse	500	800	1000

"ACTION SOLDIERS OF THE WORLD"

	C6	C8	C10
8100 - German Storm Trooper - w/cartridge belt, luger pistol, holster, field pack, "Potato Masher" grenades, 9 mm Schmeisser machine gun and iron cross medal.	140	275	325
8101 Japanese Imperial Soldier w/field pack, Nambu pistol, holster, cartridge belt, Arisaka rifle, bayonet and Order of the Kite medal	150	350	400
8102 - Russian Infantryman - W/D.P. light machine gun, bi-pod, field glasses, case, anti-tank grenades, ammo box and order of Lenin medal	140	275	350
8103 French Resistance Fighter - w/ Lebel revolver, shoulder holster, knife, grenades, radio set, 7.65mm Mas submachine gun and Croix de Guerre medal	140	225	275

	C6	C8	C10
8104 - British Commando w/gas mask, case, canteen, cover, sten mark 25 submachine gun and Victoria Cross medal	150	300	350
8105 - Australian Jungle Fighter - w/ grenades, flame thrower, jungle knife, entrenching tool, bush machete, sheath and Victoria Cross medal	140	225	275
8200 - German storm trooper	120	200	250
8201 - Imperial Japanese soldier	140	200	275
8202 - Russian Infantryman	120	200	225
8203 French Resistance Fighter	120	200	225
8204 - British Commando	120	200	225
8205 Australian Jungle Fighter	120	200	225
8300 - Equipment For German Storm Trooper - field pack, Luger pistol, holster, cartridge belt, 9mm Schmeisser machine gun, "Potato Masher" hand grenades and Iron Cross medal	30	75	100
8301 - Equipment For Japanese Imperial Soldier - cartridge belt, field pack, Arisaka rifle, bayonet, Nambu pistol, holster and order of Kite medal	30	90	150
8302 - Equipment For Russian Infantryman - field glasses, case, D.P. light machine gun, bi-pod, belt, ammo box, anti-tank grenades and order of Lenin medal	30	75	125

	C6	C8	C10
8303 - Equipment For French Resistance Fighter - shoulder holster, Lebel revolver, 7.65 Mas submachine gun, grenades, radio, knife and Croix de Guerre medal....	15	30	45
8304 - British Commando Equipment - canteen, case, cartridge belt, gas mask, case, stern mark 2-S sub-machine gun and Victoria Cross medal...	30	90	125
8305 - Australian Jungle Fighter Equipment - flame thrower, jungle knife, grenades, bush machete, sheath, entrenching tool and Victoria Cross medal	15	20	30

	C6	C8	C10
NOTE: The **Irwin Company** made the following vehicles and planes for G.I. Joe under license from Hasbro: an Armored Car, a Half Track, two motorcycles, a Duck, three airplanes, a German staff car, a Mine Sweeper and a Racing Car. The boxes are very desirable, and add 70% to the price of each toy. All sell in the following range	200	350	500
Mego also made a crash crew fire truck for GI Joe	100	250	350

Photo Boxes run $400 - $500 in Mint.

G.I. Joe Photo Boxes, worth $400 each in mint. Photo by Barry Goodman.

G.I. Joe Cadet Photo Boxes, each worth $500 in mint. Photo by Barry Goodman.

G.I. Joe Irwin German Staff Car. Photo by Barry Goodman.

G.I. Joe Irwin Amphibious Duck. Photo by Barry Goodman.

*GI Joe Adventurers:
Talking Adventure Team
Commander, life-like hair,
beard box.*

Photo by Barry Goodman

*GI Joe Adventurers:
Sea Adventurer box.
Photo by Barry Goodman*

	C6	C8	C10
4200 - 4255			
4200 Mess Kit & Canteen Set (45) . 15		20	30
4205 Machete & Scabbard Set (55) . 20		30	40
4210 Pistol & Helmet Set (45) 15		20	30
4211 Pistol Belt & Holster (45) 15		20	30
4215 Walkie Talkie (35) 10		15	25
4219 Morse Code Set (40) 15		20	30
4221 Flame Thrower Water Gun (50) 20		30	40
4226 Flare Gun Flashlight (45) 20		25	30
4230 Combat Boots (90) 15		20	30
4245 Poncho (35) 10		20	25
4250 Pup Tent (55) 20		30	40
4255 Combat Jacket Set (65) 15		30	45
4256 M.P. Set (60) 20		30	40

End G.I. Joe

	C6	C8	C10
G.I. JOE ADVENTURERS			
7782 Air Adventurer 20		45	55
7280 Land Adventurer 20		45	55
7281 Sea Adventurer 20		45	55
7283 Talking Man of Action 50		75	100
7284 Man of Action, likelike hair . . 25		40	55
7290 Talking Adventure Team Commander 35		50	65
7291 Talking Adventure Team Commander Black 80		150	225
7292 Talking Adventure Team Commander, likelike hair, beard 35		60	75
Astronaut and Space Capsule Set With Equipment 80		140	200
Secret of the Mummy's Tomb Set with figure, vehicle, equipment 40		80	120
Adventure Team Helicopter 20		50	75
Adventure Team Training Tower 20		45	85
Adventure Team Headquarters 25		40	60
Adventure Team Outfit, pants, flare gun 8		12	16
Adventure Team Outfit, trenchcoat, walkie-talkie 8		12	16
Adventure Team Outfit, camouflage clothes, gun, holster 8		12	16

	C6	C8	C10
Hasbro Charlie's Angels, Cheryl Ladd, 8" high 6		12	18
Hasbro Charlie's Angels, Farrah Fawcett-Majors, 8" high 6		12	18
Hasbro Charlie's Angels, Jaclyn Smith, 8" high 6		12	18
Hasbro Charlie's Angels, Kate Jackson, 8" high 6		12	18
Hasbro Charlie's Angels Outfits, each . . . 4		8	12

COLORFORMS *(List by Jim Main)*

Prices in parentheses are mint on card or in Box.

OUTER SPACE MEN

	C6	C8	C10
Colossus Rex ($150.00) 35		50	125
Cmdr. Comet ($150.00) 35		50	135
Astro-Nautilus ($150.00) 35		50	150
Xodiac ($150.00) 35		50	125
Orbitron ($150.00) 35		50	90
Electron ($150.00) 35		50	85
Alpha ($150.00) 35		50	80

	C6	C8	C10
Gabriel The Lone Ranger No. 23620, 9½" high, fully-jointed, cloth clothes 10		30	45
Gabriel Tonto No. 23621, 9½" high, fully-jointed, cloth clothes 15		35	55
Gabriel Scout No. 23626, jointed 9		20	25
Gabriel Silver plus 8-Way Action Saddle No. 27625, jointed....................9		20	25
Gabriel Tonto and Scout No. 28691, cloth clothes 25		50	75

	C6	C8	C10
Gabriel The Lone Ranger and Silver No. 28675, with 8-way trick Action Saddle, cloth clothes 30		65	85
Gabriel Silver No. 31635, with removable saddle, bridle 8		15	25
Gabriel Scout No. 31636 for 3¾" Tonto, includes removable saddle and bridle . 8		20	30
Gabriel Butch Cavendish No. 31632, 3¾" high, jointed, new in 1981, with pistol. 8		15	25
Gabriel Smoke No. 31637 (Butch Cavendish stallion), with removable saddle and bridle 8		15	25
Gabriel The Lone Ranger No. 31630 (Legend of the Lone Ranger), 3¾" high, jointed, new in 1981 5		15	25
Gabriel Tonto No. 31631, 3¾" high, with pistol and knife, new in 1981..5		15	25
Gabriel General George Custer No. 31633, 3¾" high, with pistol 5		15	25

	C6	C8	C10
Gabriel Buffalo Bill Cody No. 31634, 3¾" high, jointed, comes with carbine..5		15	25
Gabriel Figure Assortment No. 31601, 3¾" high, Lone Ranger, Tonto, Butch Cavendish, General Custer, Buffalo Bill, each individually........5		15	25
Gabriel House Assortment No. 31602, includes Silver, Scout, Smoke (for 3¾" figures), each individually 5		15	25

GALOOB *(list by Jim Main)*

Prices in parentheses are mint on card or in box.

DEFENDERS OF THE EARTH - 5½" tall

	C6	C8	C10
Flash Gordon ($15.00) 5		7	9
Garax ($25.00)..9		11	13
The Phantom ($20.00) 7		9	11
Ming ($15.00)...5		7	9
Mongor ($35.00) 10		14	18
Mandrake ($20.00) 7		9	11
Lothar ($15.00).......................................5		7	9
Flash's Swordship ($40.00) 15		18	21
Garax's Swordship ($40.00)..................15		18	21
Gilbert Honey West, 12" high, 1965 40		65	90
Gilbert James Bond, 12" high 40		55	95
Gilbert (James Bond) Odd Job, 1960's..100		150	200
Gilbert James Bond Action Toy Set No. 1, 1965 - figures of 007 as scuba diver, Domino and Largo with Disco Volante's yacht, display box 30		75	90
Gilbert James Bond Action Playset No. 2 - Bond, Goldfinger, Odd Job and spin-top pool table, display box 30		40	60
Gilbert James Bond Action Toy Set No. 3 in display box, 1965, - figures of 007 on Laser Table, Goldfinger, Odd Job and Dr. No. 30		40	60
Gilbert James Bond Action Playset No. 4 - Dr. No, Bond, Domino and firespitting Dragon Tank, display box 30		40	60
Gilbert James Bond Action Playset No. 5 - Bond with Beretta, Money Penny, M, and M's secret desk, display box 30		40	60
Gilbert James Bond No. 1, 3½" high, with Beretta pistol...........................10		15	20

*GILBERT James Bond
3½" figures 1 - 10.
Courtesy Bill Nutting.*

	C6	C8	C10
Gilbert James Bond No. 2 with rifle, 3½" tall, 1965 10		15	20
Gilbert James Bond No. 3 in Scuba Suit with Spear Gun, 3½" tall, 1965 10		15	20
Gilbert James Bond No. 4 Odd Job, 3½" tall, 1965 8		12	15
Gilbert James Bond No. 5 M, Bond's boss 8		12	15
Gilbert James Bond No. 6 Goldfinger 8		12	15
Gilbert James Bond No. 7 Miss Moneypenny 8		12	15
Gilbert James Bond No. 8 Largo, 3½" tall, 1965 8		12	15
Gilbert James Bond No. 9 Domino, 3½" tall, 1965 8		12	15

	C6	C8	C10
Gilbert James Bond No. 10 Dr. No with poison vial................................8		12	15
Gilbert Man From Uncle Ilya Kurayakin, 12" high........................40		60	80
Gilbert Man From Uncle Napoleon Solo 40		50	75

GILBERT MOON McDARE *(Listing by Jim Main)*

	C6	C8	C10
Moon McDare 12" figure ($125.00) 25		35	45
Space Suit outfit ($60.00).....................15		20	25
Space Mutt set ($80.00)........................15		30	45
Space Gun Set ($35.00).........................10		14	18
Moon Explorer Set ($60.00)..................15		20	25
Action Communication Set ($60.00).....15		20	25
Space Accessory Pack ($35.00) 10		14	18

HARTLAND PLASTIC ACTION FIGURES

by Gary J. Linden

Hartland Plastics, Inc. is located in southern Wisconsin and has been producing plastic figures and other plastic products since the 1950's. In 1953 The Lone Ranger, Tonto, Roy Rogers, Dale Evans and Bullet were produced. The production of these and other western figures lasted for about 10 years. The figures were molded in Acetate plastic and then painted. Most of these figures came with removable accessories, which included hats, hand guns, rifles, saddles and reins. Some of the figures had an accessory item unique to himself. Josh Randle's mares leg (rifle), Custer's Saber and Wyatt Earp's Bunt line special (long barrel revolver) to name a few. The reason for the vast price range in these western figures is that most of the common ones (C10 price of $150.00) had over 200,000 cast. The rarer figures, Col. Mackenzie for example, had only about 5,000 cast. The figures were molded in two

halves, front and back for people, and left and right for the animals (horses and Bullet). A few things to keep in mind are that there were two different Lone Ranger figures. The older one, which is wearing chaps and is more of a generic figure, and the newer figure that looks more like Clayton Moore. Also there were three different Lone Ranger horses (Silver). The generic Lone Ranger's horse has a chain for reins. The newer Lone Ranger (Clayton Moore type) has both a standing horse and a rearing horse. The # 804 Sgt. Preston and the # 804 Sgt. Lance O'Rourke appear to be the same figure with a different name on the box. The #817 Jim Bowie and his horse Blaze are the same horse and the figure used for Davy Crockett and his horse Streak, the only difference being the hats. Crockett has a Coonskin cap and Bowie has a cowboy-type hat. The boxes that all these figures came in were one of three types. The box was either plain cardboard with some printing on it or some colored art work on it, and others had a full color photo on the outside. The gunfighters who had moveable arms came in either an artwork box or a box with a see-thru front. The 8" western wranglers came in a window box and the 5½" western horse and riders came on a blister card. Some of the accessory parts (hats, guns and saddles) are being reproduced today.

Hartland also produced sport figures. There were 30 different football figures, an offensive and a defensive player from each of the 14 different teams of the time and two different personage figures, Johnny Unitas being the most sought-after. Also the figures of the Redskins and the Cowboys are the most wanted out of the 28 non-personage players. There were 18 different personage baseball players produced, along with a bat boy. The rarest of the baseball figures is Dick Groat. In 1989 it was the 25TH anniversary of the baseball figures and the Hartland Company reissued all 18 players and the bat boy. These figures have a 25 in a circle on their back just below the belt.

C10 Is a figure that is mint in the box with all paper work and paper tag

C8 Is a mint figure that does not have the box or paper work or paper tag

C6 Is a figure that has been played with and shows some wear. Also a few accessory parts are missing and there is no box, paper work or paper tag

HARTLAND WESTERN & HISTORICAL FIGURES

(List by Gary J. Linden)

9½ " TALL FIGURES	C6	C8	C10
801 - Lone Ranger (old/chaps)	50	90	150
801 - The Lone Ranger (newer)	50	90	150
801P - Western Champ	50	90	150
801P - Western Champ (extra large)	50	90	200
802 - Dale Evans	50	90	150
804 - Sgt. Preston	75	140	250
804 - Sgt. Lance O'Rourke	75	140	250
805 - Tonto	50	90	150
806 - Roy Rogers	60	100	225
808 - General Robert E. Lee	50	90	150
809 - Wyatt Earp	50	90	150
812 - Brave Eagle	75	140	300
813 - Chief Thunder Cloud	50	90	150
814 - General Custer	60	100	175
815 - General George Washington	50	90	150
816 - Cochise	50	90	150
817 - Jim Bowie	75	140	250
818 - Cheyenne	50	90	150
819 - Buffalo Bill	75	140	300
821 - Tom Jeffords	75	140	250
822 - Matt Dillon	50	90	150
823 - Annie Oakley	75	140	250
824 - Major Seth Adams	50	90	200
825 - Hoby Gilman	75	140	250
826 - Lucas McCain	75	140	250

	C6	C8	C10
827 - Bill Longly	100	240	400
828 - Josh Randle	120	290	480
829 - Colonel Randal Mackenzie	150	400	800
864 - Jim Hardie	50	90	150
866 - Paladin	50	90	150
? Davy Crockett	75	140	250
? Gil Favor	100	240	400
? Bret Maverick	60	100	175
? Johnny Yuma	120	325	600
? Turfking & Jockey	60	100	175
700 - Bullet	25	45	75

FAMOUS GUNFIGHTER SERIES

	C6	C8	C10
709 - Marhsall Wyatt Earp	50	120	200
761 - Chris Colt	50	120	200
762 - Bret Maverick	50	120	200
763 - Clay Holister	50	120	200
764 - Jim Hardie	50	120	200
765 - Vint Bonner	75	175	300
766 - Paladin	50	120	200
767 - Dan Troop	75	175	300
768 - Johnny McKay	100	240	400
769 - Bat Masterson	65	135	225

8" WESTERN WRANGLERS (Riders Are Removable)

	C6	C8	C10
611 - Alkali Ike	35	75	125
612 - Cactus Pete	35	75	125
613 - Comanche Kid	35	75	125

5½" WESTERN HORSE & RIDERS (Hats & Riders Are Removable)

C10 Mint on blister card..50

C8, Mint, Complete, off card............................30

C6 Played with, off card, Missing Hat 15

Cheyenne, Gil Favor, Johnny Yuma, Wyatt Earp, Matt Dillon, The Lone Ranger, Tonto, Bret Maverick, Roy Rogers, Jim Hardie, Lucas McCain, Paladin

HARTLAND No. 805 and No. 801 Lone Ranger (newer). Courtesy Rex and Richard Gray.

HARTLAND No. 801 Lone Ranger (old chaps). Photo by Gary J. Linden.

HARTLAND No. 802 Dale Evans. Photo by Gary J. Linden.

HARTLAND No. 804 Sgt. Lance O'Rourke. Photo by Gary J. Linden.

HARTLAND No. 806 Roy Rogers. Photo by Gary J. Linden.

HARTLAND No. 809 Wyatt Earp. Photo by Gary J. Linden.

HARTLAND No. 864 Jim Hardie. Photo by Gary J. Linden.

HARTLAND No. 828 Josh Randle. Photo by Gary J. Linden.

HARTLAND No. 816 Cochise. Photo by Gary J. Linden.

HARTLAND No. 817 Jim Bowie. Photo by Gary J. Linden.

HARTLAND No. 819 Buffalo Bill. Photo by Gary J. Linden.

HARTLAND No. 821 Tom Jeffords. Photo by Gary J. Linden.

HARTLAND No. 822 Matt Dillon. Photo by Gary J. Linden.

HARTLAND No. 826 Lucas McCain. Photo by Gary J. Linden.

HARTLAND No. 769 Bat Masterson. Photo by Gary J. Linden.

HARTLAND No. 700 Bullet. Photo by Gary J. Linden.

388

HARTLAND No. 761. Photo by Gary J. Linden.

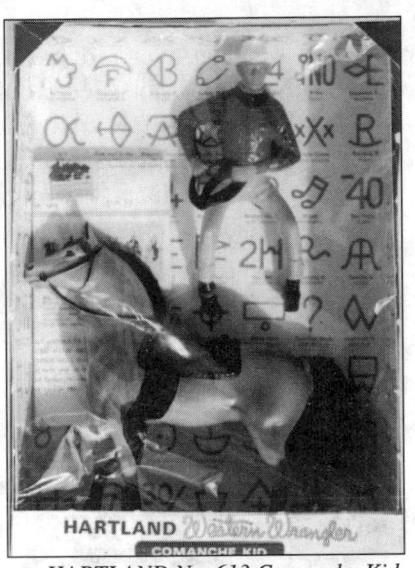

HARTLAND No. 613 Comanche Kid. Photo by Gary J. Linden.

	C6	C8	C10
Ideal Captain Action No. 3400-9 - costumed figure, Lightning Sword, scabbard, gun, gun belt, 12" high ...75	125	200
Ideal Action Boy 3420-7, new in 1967, 9" high, costumed, Panther, Space Helmet, utility belt, ray gun knife 125	200	250
Ideal Dr. Evil No. 3465-2, new in 1968, 12" high, costumed with laser gun ...125	200	250
Ideal Batgirl, 12" high, 1967 250	350	400
Ideal Mera (Aquaman's wife), 1967, 12" high 250	350	400
Ideal Supergirl, 12" high, 1967 250	350	400
Ideal Wonder Woman, 1967, 12" high .250	350	400
Ideal Aqua Lad Outfit No. 3423-1 - costume, octopus, boots, belt with sea horse knife, sea shell axe, no figure included in outfits 200	300	600
Ideal Aquaman Outfit No. 3408-2 - costume, swordfish sword, conch horns, fins, trident spear, knife with sheath, Aquaman face mask ..110	165	220
Ideal Bat Girl - helmet, cape, batarang, boots, bat gloves, halter dress for alter ego Barbara Gordon..................250	350	500
Ideal Batman Outfit No. 3402 -5 - costume, emblem , cape, boots, utility belt with 2-way radio buckle, flashlight, Batarang, laser-beam, Batrope, reel with grappling hook, hood, Batman face mask......125	250	400
Ideal Buck Rogers Outfit No. 3416-5 face mask, space belt, twin jet packs, space helmet, space gun, space light, space boots, canteen ..140	165	200

	C6	C8	C10
Ideal Captain America Outfit No. 3409-0 - uniform, belt with holster, ultrasonic pistol, laser-beam gun, boots, shield, Captain America face mask 160	225	275
Ideal Flash Gordon Outfit No. 3403-3 - silver astro-suit, space helmet, silver boots, space belt with holster and ray pistol, oxygen guidance "Zot" gun, Flash Gordon face mask................................100	125	165
Ideal Green Hornet Outfit No. 3413-2 - face mask, watch message receiver, gas pistol, hornet sting, TV scanner with phone, shoulder holster, gas mask, shoes, costume .250	400	650
Ideal Lone Ranger Outfit No. 3406-6 - Wild West cowboy outfit, gun belt, two holsters, two pistols, boots with spurs, Winchester rifle, cowboy hat, Lone Ranger face mask, blue shirt version 175	200	250
Red shirt version..............................200	275	350
Ideal The Phantom Outfit No. 3407-4 - costume, rifle with scope, belt, holster, pistol, knife, boots, Phantom face mask................................90	135	175
Ideal Robin Outfit No. 3421-5 - 2 suction grips, Bat-a-Rang Launcher, Bat-a-Rang, 2 Bat grenades...........145	195	250
Ideal Sgt. Fury Outfit............................125	175	225
Ideal Spiderman Outfit No. 3414-0 - spray tank with hose, utility belt, spider hook with rope and handle, mask, light, boots...........................225	275	350
Ideal Steve Canyon Outfit No. 3405-8 - uniform, 50 mission hat, parachute pack, garrison belt, holster, .45 automatic, helmet with oxygen mask, knife, boots, Steve Canyon face mask................100	175	250
Ideal Super Girl - cape, costume, boots, Krypto dog, halter dress for alter ego Linda Lee Danvers..........250	350	450
Ideal Superboy Outfit No. 3422-3 - uniform, belt, boots, cape, telepathic scrambler, interspace language translator, chem lab 200	275	350
Ideal Superman Outfit No.3401-7 - costume, super shield, belt, flying cape, boots, arm shackles, block of Kryptonite, Superman face mask, Krypto the dog..............................130	175	200

	C6	C8	C10

Ideal Tonto Outfit No. 3415-7 - face
   mask, gun belt, head band, pistol,
   knife, bow, quiver, 4 arrows, moc-
   casins, eagle.....................150   225   275

Ideal Communicator Kit No.3454-6 -
   Solar Power Pack, Rotating
   Antenna dome, Beam Projectors,
   Secret Sound Horn.......................150   275   350

Ideal Directional Communicator Set
   No. 3454-6 - Solar Power Pack,

Rotating Antenna dome, power plugs,
   beam projectors, Secret Sound Horn..150   250   300

Ideal Dr. Evil Gift Set No. 3466-0 -
   Dr. Evil, lab coat, 2 disguise
   masks, Reducer, Hypnotic Eye,
   Ionized Hypo, Laser Ray Gun,
   Thought Control Helmet 250   400   700

Ideal Dr. Evil Sanctuary No. 8701-5 -
   "space age" carrycase, storage
   bins, Dr. Evil figure 350   600   800

Captain Action and Action Boy

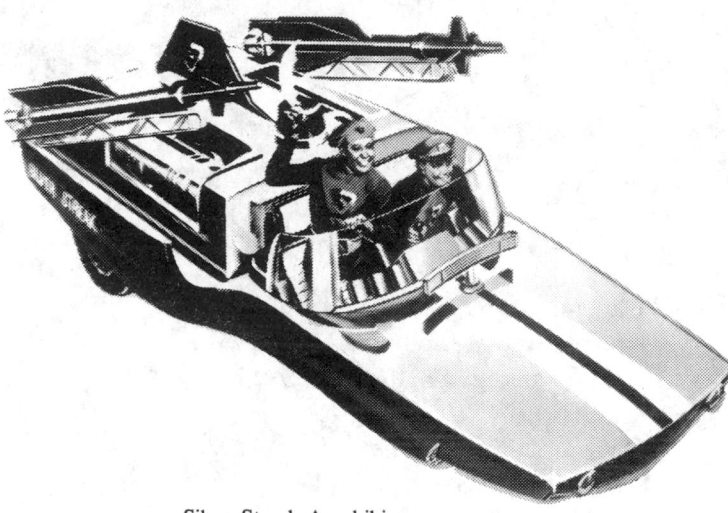

Silver Streak Amphibian

Top, Left to Right: Flash Gordon Outfit, Spiderman Outfit, Steve Canyon Outfit, Green Hornet Outfit, Lone Ranger Outfit, Tonto Outfit. Bottom, Left to Right: The Phantom Outfit, Batman Outfit, Captain America Outfit, Aquaman Outfit, Buck Rogers Outfit, Superman Outfit.

IDEAL Directional Communicator Set No. 3454-6 - Solar Power Pack, Rotating Antenna dome, power plugs, beam projectors, Secret Sound Horn

IDEAL Parachute Pack No. 3453-B - Parachute with Body Harness and Back Pack, Crash Helmet, jump boots

	C6	C8	C10
Ideal Jet Mortar No. 3452-0 - Mortar with Blaster Tripod, Radar Scanner, Ammo Carrier, two mortar missiles	90	175	250
Ideal Parachute Pack No. 3453-B - Parachute with Body Harness and Back Pack, Crash Helmet, jump boots	100	150	250
Ideal Power Pack No. 3455-3 - Thrust Ejector, Cosmic Boots, Cosmic Gloves, Flight Helmet	90	135	175
Ideal Silver Streak Amphibian No. 3449-6, 21¼" long	200	600	900

	C6	C8	C10
Ideal Survival Vest No. 3450-4 Utility Vest with Fishing Kit, Mirror, First Aid Kit, Folding Spade, 3 pc. Extension Claw Hook, Machete, Utility Belt with Flare Pistol and holster, Flares, Dagger, Ammo and Hatchet	175	300	400
Ideal Weapons Arsenal No. 3451-2 - Electronic Rifle, 2 Revolvers, Carbine, Automatic, 2 Grenades, Combat Knife, All - Purpose Knife, Ray Gun, Storage Rack	175	250	325

KENNER

Kenner was formed in 1947 on Kenner Street in Cincinnati by three brothers; Al, Phil and Joe Steiner. In 1967 General Mills took it over. The "Star Wars" toys have probably been its most notable success, and follow Kenner's other action figures and toys in this listing. **Because figures that are mint on the card or in the box are so important in this category, their prices are shown in parentheses immediately following the listing.**

	C6	C8	C10
Alien, 18" high, new in 1980, "Alien" movie. Fully articulated jaws, tail moves, head glows in dark	75	150	225

Raiders of the Lost Ark (Listing by Jim Main):
3¾" figures:

	C6	C8	C10
Indiana Jones ($75.00)	10	15	25
Marion Ravenwood ($150.00)	20	30	40
Toht ($10.00)	4	5	6
German Mechanic ($35.00)	6	8	10
Indiana Jones in German Uniform ($75.00)	10	15	20
Belloq ($45.00)	10	20	30
Belloq (mail in figure) ($25.00)	6	8	10
Cairo Swordsman ($20.00)	4	5	6
Arabian Horse ($35.00)	5	10	15

	C6	C8	C10
Streets of Cairo playset ($50.00)	10	12	15
Well of Souls playset ($75.00)	15	20	25
Map Room playset ($30.00)	5	10	15
Desert Convoy Truck ($30.00)	8	12	15
Indiana Jones 12" figure ($250.00)	60	80	125

Six Million Dollar Man (Listing by Jim Main)
12" Figures:

	C6	C8	C10
Steve Austin ($50.00)	15	20	25
Bionic Woman, Jamie Summers ($50.00)	15	20	25
Oscar Goldman ($50.00)	15	20	25
Fembot ($75)	20	25	30
Maskatron ($75)	20	25	30
Bionic Bigfoot ($75)	20	25	30
Bionic Beauty Salon ($60)	20	25	30
Bionic Mission Vehicle ($45)	15	18	21
Mission Control Playset ($125)	25	35	45

	C6	C8	C10
Venus Space Probe ($75.00)	20	30	40
Transport Repair ($30.00)	8	12	16
O.S.I. Headquarters ($75.00)	20	30	40
Test Flight at 75,000 Ft. ($35.00)	9	13	17
O.S.I. Undercover ($35.00)	9	13	17
Mission to Mars ($35.00)	9	13	17
Critical Assignment Arms ($25.00)	7	10	12

SUPER POWERS FIGURES (listing by Jim Main):

	C6	C8	C10
Aquaman ($35.00)	10	15	20
Flash ($10.00)	4	5	6
Batman ($40.00)	15	20	25
Superman ($15.00)	5	7	9
Green Lantern ($45)	10	12	14
Hawkman ($40.00)	10	15	20
DeSaad (20.00)	6	8	10
Robin ($25.00)	5	10	15
Braniac ($20.00)	6	8	10
Luthor ($10.00)	4	5	6
Penguin ($25)	10	15	20
Joker ($35.00)	10	15	20
Wonder Woman ($15.00)	5	7	9
Mr. Freeze ($25.00)	5	10	15
Tyr ($25.00)	5	10	15
Plastic Man ($75)	10	15	20
Golden Pharoah ($125)	25	35	45
Orion ($25.00)	12	15	18
Steppenwolf ($10.00)	4	5	6
Clark Kent ($45)	10	15	20
Parademon ($20.00)	6	8	10

	C6	C8	C10
Cyborg (150)	50	75	100
Mantis ($20.00)	6	8	10
Kalibak ($20.00)	6	8	10
Samurai ($125)	30	40	50
Mr. Miracle ($135)	35	50	65
Captain Marvel (Shazam) ($40)	11	13	15
Firestorm ($35.00)	12	15	18
Darkseid ($15.00)	6	7	8
Red Tornado ($25.00)	12	15	18
Green Arrow ($75)	10	15	25
Martian Manhunter ($25.00)	12	15	18
Dr. Fate ($20.00)	8	10	12
Cyclotron ($75.00)	30	40	50

Vehicles/accessories (listing by Jim Main):

	C6	C8	C10
Batmobile ($75)	20	25	30
Supermobile ($25.00)	10	13	16
Batcopter ($75)	20	25	30
Delta Probe One ($20.00)	10	12	14
Justice Jogger ($20.00)	10	12	14
Lex-Soar 7 ($20.00)	10	12	14
Kalibak Boulder Bomber ($20.00)	10	12	14
Darkseid Destroyer ($30.00)	10	15	20
Hall of Justice playset ($125)	30	45	60
All Terrain Trapper ($85)	20	40	60

STEVE SCOUT

	C6	C8	C10
Steve Scout figure ($40.00)	15	20	30

KENNER STAR WARS ACTION FIGURES
By Whit Alexander and Neal Bates

The first set of 12 figures was introduced in 1977 and by 1984 over 80 different action figures were offered.

Over the 7 year marketing period attention given to detail and variation of accessories increased.

STAR WARS ACTION FIGURES (SW-A)

The first set of action figures all read 1977 on their legs and included SW-A1, SW-A3, SW-A4, SW-A5, SW-A6, SW-A10, SW-A11, SW-A12, SW-A15, SW-A17, SW-A18, and SW-A20. The next set read 1978 and included the 5 cantina figures (SW-A8, SW-A9, SW-A19A, SW-A19B, SW-A21), plus 4 more (SW-A13, SW-A14, SW-A15, SW-A16 and SW-A7). Bobba Fett (SW-A2) was the only figure issued in 1979.

	C6	C8	C10
SW-A1 Ben (Obi-Wan) Knobi: 3¼" high, rust with removable brown cape and retractable blue light-saber, 1977 ($80.00)	4	8	12
SW-A2 Boba Fett: 3¾" high, blue-gray with backpack and laser pistol (Weapon No. 1). Originally			

offered only through special mail order and was the only Empire Strikes Back character to be offered a year prior to the movie's release date. 1979.. ($225.00) .... 4 | 8 | 12

	C6	C8	C10
SW-A3 Chewbacca: 4¼" high, brown with silver bandolier and laser rifle (Weapon No. 6). 1977. ($80.00)	4	8	12
SW-A4 C-3PO: 3¾" high, metallic gold with no accessories. 1977 ($100.00)	4	8	12
SW-A5 Darth Vader: 4¼" high, black with removable black cape and retractable red light-saber. 1977. ($125.00)	4	8	12

Left to Right: SW-A15, SW-A12, SW-A1, SW-A5.

Left to Right: SW-A3, SW-A17, SW-A4, SW-A10.

Left to Right: SW-A20, SW-A11, SW-A18, SW-A6.

Left to Right: SW-A9, SW-A19B, SW-A19A, SW-A21, SW-A8.

Photos Courtesy Whit Alexander and Neal Bates.

	C6	C8	C10
SW-A6 Death Squad Commander (Star Destroyer Commander); 3¼" high, gray with black helmet and Laser pistol (Weapon No. 1). 1977. ($150)	4	8	12
SW-A7 Death Star Droid: 3¾" high, metallic silver with no accessories. 1978. ($70.00)	4	8	12
SW-A8 Greedo: 3¾" high, green with laser pistol (Weapon No. 2). 1978 ($50)	4	8	12
SW-A9 Hammerhead: 4" high, brown with blue suit and laser pistol (Weapon No. 1), 1978 ($50)	4	8	12
SW-A10 Han Solo: 3¾" high, white shirt with black vest and pants. Equipped with laser pistol (Weapon No. 2). 1977. ($225)	4	8	12
SW-A11 Jawa: 2¼" high, brown with brown cloth cape and laser rifle (Weapon No. 4) 1977. ($80)	3	6	10
SW-A12 Luke Skywalker: 3¾" high; white shirt with beige pants. Equipped with retractable light-saber. 1977 ($200)	3	6	10
SW-A13 Luke Skywalker X-Wing Pilot: 3¼" high, orange with white helmet and laser pistol (Weapon No. 2). 1978 ($25.00)	3	6	10
SW-A14 Power Droid: 2¼" high, blue TV set shape with clicking legs. No accessories. 1978. ($55.00)	2	4	8
SW-A15 Princess Leia Organa: 3½" high, white with removable white cape and laser pistol (Weapon No. 3). 1977. ($150)	4	8	12
SW-A16 R5-D4: 2½" high, white trash-can shape with red detail. No Accessories. 1978. ($75.00)	5	10	15
SW-A17 R2-D2: 2¼" high, white with blue detail and chrome-dome head which clicks when turned. No accessories. 1978. ($75.00)	5	10	15
SW-A18 Sand People: 3¾" high, tan with removable tan cape and Gaffic Stick (Weapon No. 5). 1977. ($75.00)	5	10	15
SW-A19A Snaggletooth: 3¾" high, blue with silver boots and laser pistol (Weapon No. 1). Offered only with Cardboard Cantina. 1978. ($65.00)	4	8	12

	C6	C8	C10

SW-A19B Snaggletooth: 2⅞" high, red
with laser pistol (Weapon No. 1).
1978. ($55.00)......................4 8 12

SW-A20A Stormtrooper: 3¾" high,
white with white helmet and laser
pistol (Weapon No. 1). 1977. ($125) .4 8 12

SW-A21 Walrus Man: 3¾" high, blue
with orange suit and green head.
Equipped with laser pistol
(Weapon No. 1). 1978. ($50) 3 7 11

The Empire Strikes Back Action Figures

ESB-A1 AT-AT Commander: 3¾" high,
gray with gray hat and laser pistol
(Weapon No. 1). 1980. ($30) 3 6 10

ESB-A2 AT-AT Driver: 3¾" high, light
gray with white helmet and laser
pistol (Weapon No. 7). 1980. ($17.00).3 6 9

ESB-A3A Bespin Security Guard: 3⅞"
high, black man has navy uniform
and laser pistol (Weapon No. 1).
1981 ($20) 3 7 11

ESB-A3B Bespin Security Guard: 4"
high, white man has navy uniform
and laser pistol (Weapon No. 1).
1980 ($25) 3 7 11

ESB-A4 Bossk: 4" high, yellow with
olive head and laser rifle (Weapon
No. 6), 1980 ($20) 3 7 11

ESB-A5 C-3PO: 4" high, metallic gold
with removable limbs and papoose.
(Acc. No. 13), 1980 ($90) 3 6 10

ESB-A6 Cloud-Car Pilot: 3¾" high,
white with orange and yellow
helmet, with laser pistol (Weapon
No. 9a) and walkie-talkie (Acc.
No. 9b), 1981, ($40) 3 6 10

ESB-A7 Dengar: 3⅝" high, white and
brown with backpack and head
wrap. Equipped with laser rifle
(Weapon No. 2), 1980, ($20) 2 4 6

ESB-A8 FX-7: 3⅜" high with head down,
silver with 9 movable arms and retract-
able head, no accessories, 1980,
($40)......................2 4 8

ESB-A9 4-LOM: 3⅝" high, tan with
removable tan cape and brown
removable backpack. Equipped
with laser pistol (Weapon No. 11).
1981. ($40) 2 4 8

ESB-A10 Han Solo (Bespin outfit): 4"
high, navy vest with brown pants
and laser pistol (Weapon No. 3).
1980 ($45) 3 6 10

Left to Right: SW-A7, SW-A16, SW-A14, SW-A2, SW-A13.

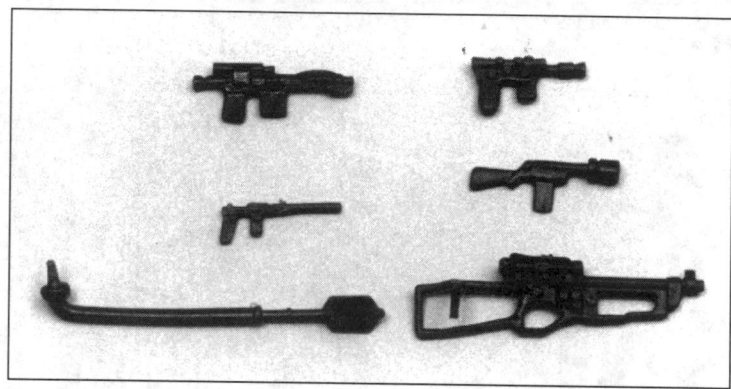

Star Wars Action Figures Weapons and Accessories. Left to Right, Top row: 1,2; Middle row: 3,4; Bottom row: 5, 6.

Photo Courtesy Whit Alexander and Neal Bates.

	C6	C8	C10

ESB-A11 Han Solo (Hoth outfit): 4"
high, blue fur-lined parka with
brown boots and laser pistol
(Weapon No. 3), 1980, ($30) 3 6 10

ESB-A12 IG-88: 4⅝" high, gray with
black bandolier and laser guns
(Weapons No. 1 & 16). 1980.
($20)......................3 6 10

ESB-A13 Imperial Commander: 3⅞"
high, black hat and laser pistol
(Weapon No. 14), 1980, ($20) ...2 4 8

ESB-A14 Imperial Stormtrooper (Hoth
Battle Gear): 3⅞" high, white with
white veil and removable white
skirt. Equipped with laser rifle
(Weapon No. 2), 1980 ($20).....3 5 9

ESB-A15 Imperial Tie-Fighter Pilot:
3¾" high, black with gray boots
and gloves and laser pistol
(Weapon No. 9a), 1982 ($20)....2 4 8

ESB-A16 Lando Calrissian: 4" high,
light blue with dark blue pants
and removable cape. Equipped
with laser pistol (Weapon No. 1).
1980 ($20) 2 4 8

ESB-A17 Lobot: 3⅝" high, gray-brown
with yellow sleeves and computerized

	C6	C8	C10

head band. Equipped
with laser pistol (Weapon No. 1).
1980 ($20) 2   4   8

ESB-A18 Luke Skywalker (Bespin
Fatigues): 3⅞" high, tan with
brown boots. Equipped with laser
pistol and light-saber (Weapons
No. 3 & 5). 1980 ($45) 3   7   11

ESB-A19 Luke Skywalker (Hoth Battle Gear): 3¾" high, white with
brown vest and scarf and laser
rifle (Weapon No. 17). 1981.
($35) 3   6   10

ESB-A20 Princess Leia Organa (Bespin
Gown): 3½" high, brick red with
pink cape and laser pistol
(Weapon No. 4). 1980. ($45) 3   7   11

ESB-A21 Princess Leia Organa (Hot
Outfit): 3¾" high, white with tan
vest and laser pistol (Weapon No.
4). 1980 ($45) 3   6   10

ESB-A22 R2-D2 (With Sensorscope):
2½" high, white with blue detail.
One head panel extends into
radar. No accessories. Bottom

reads "1977" but new head was
added circa 1980. ($30) 2   4   6

ESB-A23 Rebel Commander: 3⅞"
high, white with brown scarf and
laser rifle (Weapon No. 7). 1980.
($20) 3   6   10

ESB-A24 Rebel Soldier: 3⅞" high,
white with brown vest and white
hat. Equipped with laser pistol.
(Weapon No. 1). 1980. ($30) 3   6   10

ESB-A25 2-1B: 3¾" high, blue with
transparent middle and gas mask.
Has medical stick. (Acc. No. 12).
1980. ($30) 3   7   11

ESB-A26 Ugnaught: 2¾" high, gray
with blue apron and tool-purse
(Acc. No. 8). 1980. ($30) 3   6   10

ESB-A27 Yoda: 2" high, brown with
light green head, has cloth tan
robe, removable belt, orange snake
and brown stick (Acc. Nos. 10a &
10b). 1980. ($20)   3   6   10

ESB-A28 Zuckuss: 3¾" high, gray
with blue fly-eyes and laser rifle
(Weapon No. 15), 1982.($35) 3   6   10

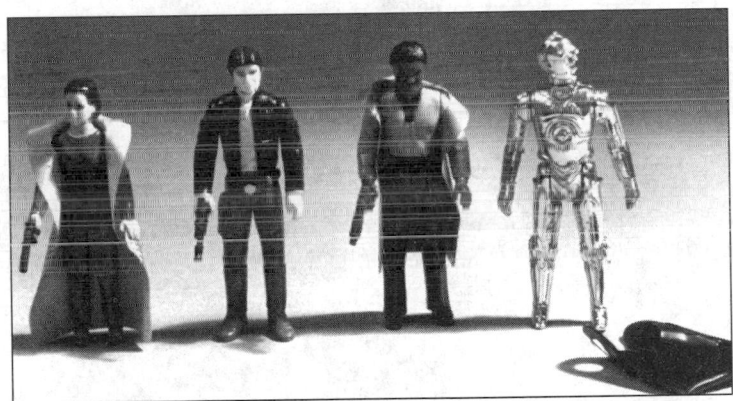

Left to Right: ESB-A21, ESB-A10, ESB-A16, ESB-A5.

Left to Right: ESB-A25, ESB-A21, ESB-A8.

Left to Right: ESB-A18, ESB-A22, ESB-A27.

Left to Right: ESB-A19, ESB-A11, ESB-A23, ESB-A24.

Photos Courtesy Whit Alexander and Neal Bates.

Left to Right: ESB-A14, ESB-A2, ESB-A15, ESB-A13, ESB-A1.

Left to Right: ESB-A17, ESB-A6, ESB-A3B, ESB-A26, ESB-A3A.

Left to Right: ESB-A7, ESB-A28, ESB-A9, ESB-A12, ESB-A4.

THE RETURN OF THE JEDI ACTION FIGURES

	C6	C8	C10
RJ-A1 Admiral Ackbar: 3⅞" high, white with tan vest and rust "lobster" head, black stick (Acc. No. 1). 1983 ($15)	1	2	3
RJ-A2 AT-ST Driver: 3⅞ high, light gray with dark gray helmet and laser pistol (Weapon No. 2). 1984 ($15)	2	3	4
RJ-A3 B-Wing Pilot: 3⅞" high, red with silver and brown helmet and laser pistol (Weapon No. 2). 1984 ($15)	1	2	3

	C6	C8	C10
RJ-A4 Bib Fortuna: 4⅛" high, blue with removable beige cape and removable gray chestplate. Has wrap-around horn and staff (Acc. No. 6). 1983 ($15)	1	2	3
RJ-A5 Biker Scout: 4" high, black with white armor and laser pistol (Weapon No. 4). 1983 ($15)	2	3	4
RJ-A6 Boushh: 3⅝" high, beige and brown with silver armor. Has silver and orange removable helmet and laser stick. (Weapon No. 7). 1983. ($20)	1	2	3
RJ-A7 Chief Chirpa: 3" high with removable brown hood and staff (Acc. No. 21). 1983 ($15)	1	2	3
RJ-A8 8D8: White droid with silver and brown detail. No accessories. 1983 ($15)	1	2	3
RJ-A9 Emperor's Royal Guard: Brick red and crimson cape and tunic with staff (Weapon No. 8). 1983 ($15)	2	3	4

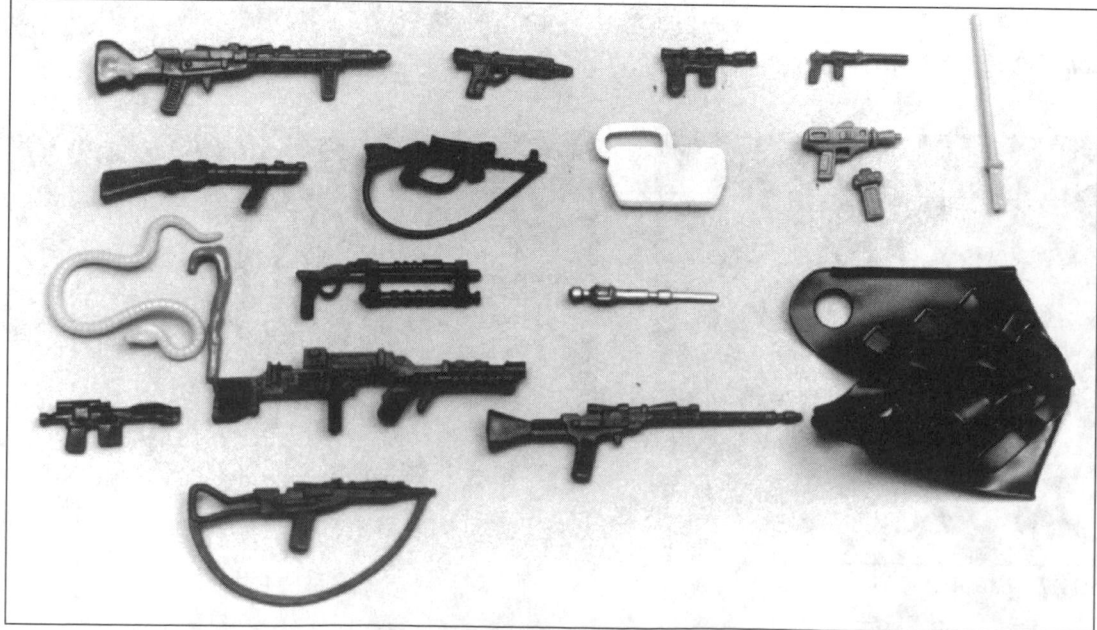

The Empire Strikes Back Action Figures Weapons and Accessories. Top row, Left to Right: 2, 1, 3, 4, 5. Second row: 6, 7, 8, 9a, 9b. Third row: 10a, 10b, 11, 12, 13. Fourth row: 14, 15, 16. Bottom: 17. Photos Courtesy Whit Alexander and Neal Bates.

Left to Right: RJ-A28, RJ-A7, RJ-A15, RJ-A25.

Left to Right: RJ-A13A, RJ-A13B, RJ-A8, RJ-A18.

Left to Right: RJ-A3, RJ-A11, RJ-A1, RJ-A17.

Left to Right: RJ-A5, RJ-A22, RJ-A19.

Photos Courtesy Whit Alexander and Neal Bates.

	C6	C8	C10
RJ-A10 Gamorrean Guard: 3⅞" high, olive with brown garment and battle axe (Weapon No. 3). 1983 ($15)	1	2	3
RJ-A11 General Madine: 4" high, light gray with black boots and gloves and blue sleeves and white wand (Acc. No. 16). 1983. ($15)	1	2	3
RJ-A12 Han Solo (Trench Coat): 4" high, dark gray pants with light gray shirt and removable camouflage cape and laser pistol (Weapon No. 22). 1984. ($20)	2	3	4
RJ-A13A Klaatu: 4" high, dark green with gray shirt and silver helmet. Has animal pelt skirt and skiff stick (Weapon No. 9). 1983 ($15)	1	2	3
RJ-A13B Klaatu (Skiff Guard Outfit): 3⅞" high, dark green with off white garment and brown helmet with laser stick (Weapon No. 10). 1983. ($15)	1	2	3
RJ-A14 Lando Calrissian (Skiff Guard Disguise): 3⅞" high, brown vest with armor. Has removable brown helmet and skiff stick (Weapon No. 9). 1982. ($15)	1	2	3
RJ-A15 Luke Skywalker (Jedi Knight Outfit): 3⅞" high, black with removable olive cape. Has laser pistol and light-saber (Weapons No. 5a and 5b) 1983. ($25)	1	2	3
RJ-A16 Logray: 3⅝" high, cream and brown striped with removable black hood, medicine bag and staff (Acc. No. 18). 1983. ($15)	1	2	3
RJ-A17 Nien Nunb: 3⅞" high, red with navy vest, dark gray helmet and laser pistol (Weapon No. 17). 1983 ($15)	1	2	3
RJ-A18 Nikto: White shirt with ice-blue vest and gray pants. Has brown head wrap and laser stick (Weapon No. 11). 1983 ($15)	1	2	3
RJ-A19 Princess Leia Organa (Combat Poncho): 3⅝" high, gray with removable helmet and combat poncho. Has removable belt and laser pistol (Weapon No. 2). 1984 ($20)	1	2	3
RJ-A20 Prune Face: 3⅞" high, lime green pants with cream shirt and			

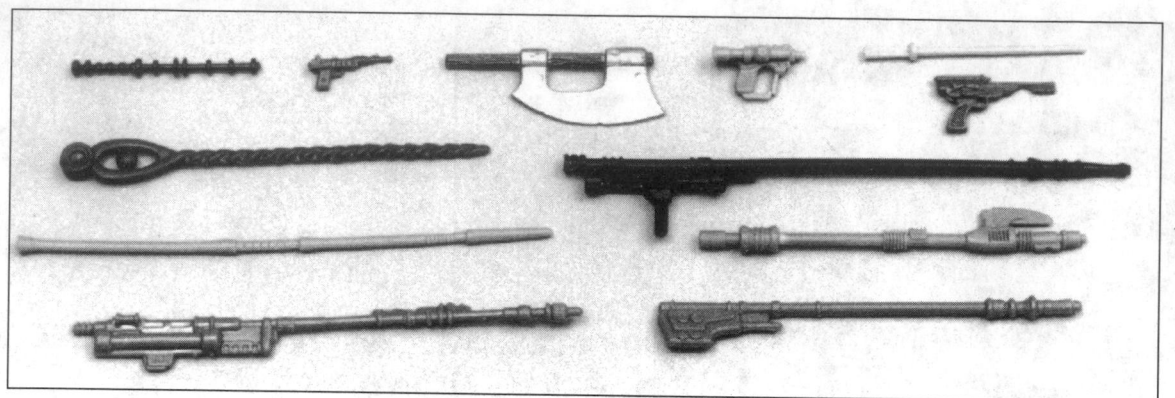

The Return of the Jedi Action Figures Weapons and Accessories, Top row, Left to Right: 1, 2, 3, 4, 5a, 5b. Second row: 6, 7. Third row: 8, 9. Bottom row: 10, 11. Photo Courtesy Whit Alexander and Neal Bates.

Top row, Let to Right: 12, 13, 14, 15. Second row: 17, 18, 19, 20, 21, 16. Bottom row: 22, 23, 24. Photo Courtesy Whit Alexander and Neal Bates.

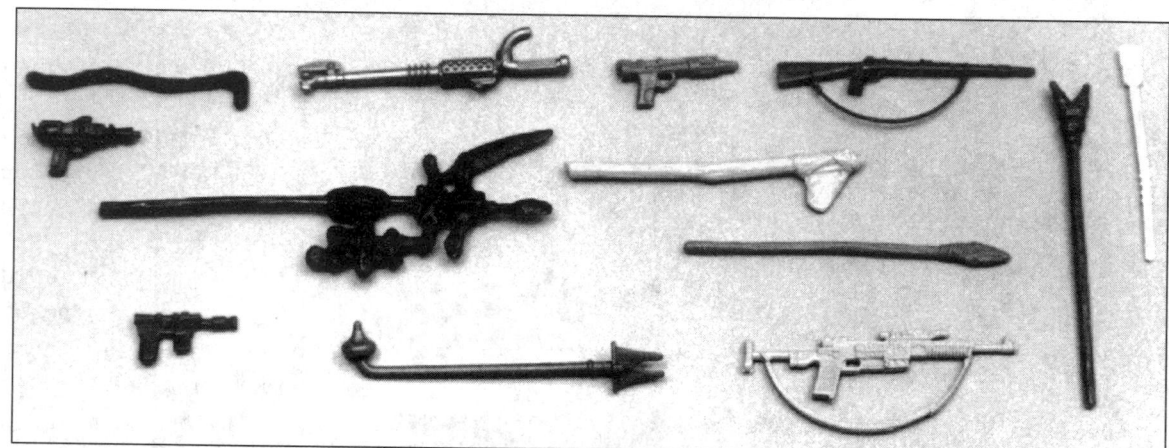

	C6	C8	C10
removable tan cape. Has eyepatch and laser rifle. (Weapon No. 15) 1984 ($15)	1	2	3
RJ-A21 Rancor Keeper: 4" high, olive pants with no shirt. Has removable hood and stick (Acc. No. 23). 1984 ($15)	1	2	3
RJ-A22 Rebel Commando: 4" high, olive uniform with green helmet, brown backpack and laser rifle (Weapon No. 24). 1983 ($15)	1	2	3
RJ-A23 Ree-Yees: 3⅝" high, peach with three eyes and brick red garment and laser rifle. (Weapon No. 13). 1983. ($15)	1	2	3
RJ-A24 Squid Head: 4" high, white with white skirt, has removable belt and olive cape; head has 4 tentacles, has laser pistol. (Weapon No. 14). 1983 ($15)	1	2	3
RJ-A25 Teebo: 3⅞" high, light and dark gray striped. Has removable hood and horn on sling. Also has axe (Acc. No. 19) 1984 ($15)	1	2	3
RJ-A26 The Emperor: 4" high, dark gray with staff (Acc. No. 12). 1984 ($15)	1	2	3
RJ-A27 Weequay: 3⅞" high, ice blue shirt with beige pants and brown			

	C6	C8	C10
vest, gray ponytail and skiff stick (Weapon No. 9). 1983 ($15)	1	2	3
RJ-A28 Wickett W. Warrick: 2" high, brown with creme belly, removable hood and spear (Weapon No. 20). 1984. ($20)	1	2	3

VEHICLES

These vehicles are intended for use with the action figures and many are battery operated (B/O).

STAR WARS VEHICLES (SW-V)

	C6	C8	C10
SW-V1 Darth Vader Tie-Fighter (B/O), 9¾" long x 11¾" wide, dark gray with spherical cockpit and removable wing panels, red laser lights up and emits a whirring sound. 1978 ($65.00)	12	18	25
SW-V2 Imperial troop Transport: (B/O), 10¼" long x 5¼" wide, gray with red stripes, has rear and 6 side compartments, dual cockpit and rotating laser cannons and radar, 2 prisoner holsters, 6 red buttons play a variety of recordings ($65)	10	15	20
SW-V3 Jawa Sandcrawler: 14½" long x 5⅝" wide, rust brown with			

SW-V6, Tie-Fighter. Figure not included. Photo Courtesy Whit Alexander and Neal Bates.

SW-V7, X-Wing Fighter. Figure not included.

Photos Courtesy Whit Alexander and Neal Bates.

SW-V1, Darth Vader Tie-Fighter. Figure not included.

SW-V4, Landspeeder. Figure not included.

SW-V2, Imperial Troop Transport. Figures not included.

	C6	C8	C10
wireless remote control. 1979. ($350)	60	90	120
SW-V4 Landspeeder: 9½" long x 6" wide, brown with chrome grills, 3 jets and windshield, wheels can be lowered by shifter in cockpit. 1978. ($75)	10	15	20
SW-V5 Millenium Falcon: (B/O) 20½" long x 16½" wide, off-white with gray laser cannon. Main compartment has chessboard, laser ball, floor panel and revolving laser cannon. Emits whirring sound when side button is pressed. 1979. ($120)	15	22	30
SW-V6 Tie Fighter (B/O) 7⅛" long, 10¼"			

	C6	C8	C10
wide, white with spherical cockpit and removable black wing panels, red laser lights up and emits whirring sound. 1978. ($65.00)	8	12	16
SW-V7 X-Wing Fighter (B/O), 13¾" long, 11½" wide, white with red and yellow stripes and 4 laser cannons. Wings open into "X" position, red laser lights up and emits whirring sound. 1978 ($55)	8	12	16

SW-V5, Millenium Falcon. Figures not included.
Photo Courtesy Whit Alexander and Neal Bates.

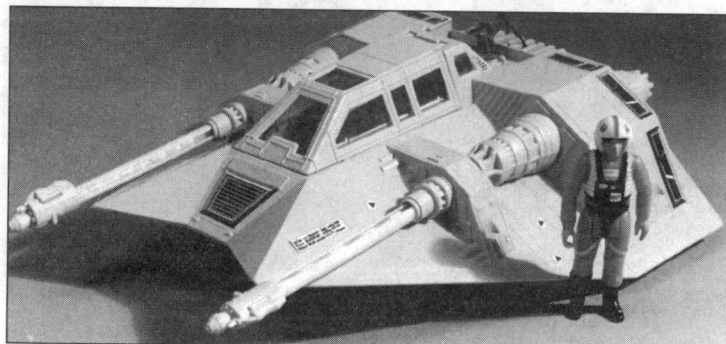

ESB-V6, Snowspeeder. Figure not included.

ESB-V7, Twin-Pod Cloud Car. Figure not included.

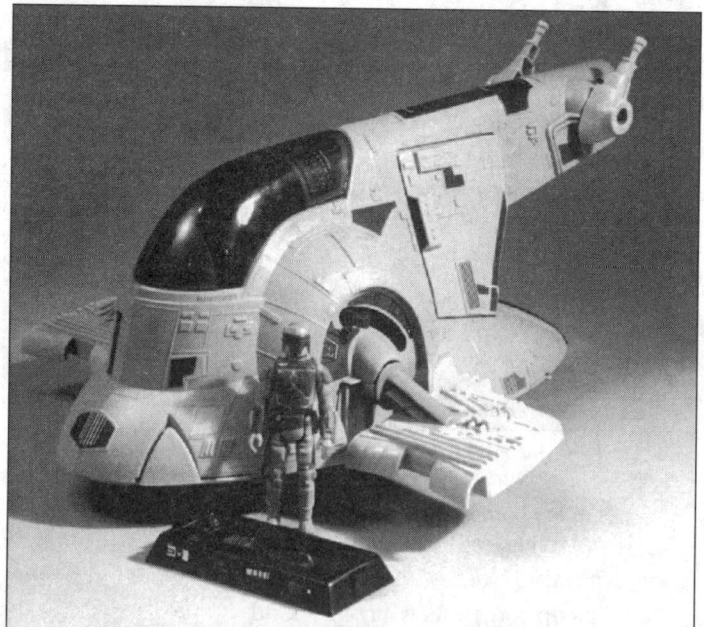

ESB-V5, Slave-1. Boba Fett not included.

Photos Courtesy Whit Alexander and Neal Bates.

ESB-V2, AT-ST (Scout Walker). Figures not included.

THE EMPIRE STRIKES BACK VEHICLES (ESB-V)

	C6	C8	C10
ESB-V1 AT-AT: (B/O), 17½" high, 22" long, light gray with black detail, 4 moveable legs and swiveling cockpit, 2 laser cannons light up and pulsate. 1981 ($150)	15	22	32
ESB-V2 AT-ST (Scout Walker): 11¼" high, light gray, button on back moves legs. 1982. ($50)	8	12	16
ESB-V3 Imperial Star Destroyer, swiveling laser cannon on bow and meditation chamber. 1981. ($100)	16	24	32
ESB-V4A MCL-3: light gray with tank treads and dome top. 1981. ($25)	4	6	8
ESB-V4B MTV-7: light gray with spring-loaded steamroller legs. 1981. ($25)	4	6	8
ESB-V5 Slave 1: 15" long, 12¾" wide, gray with blue windshield, 2 swiveling wing flaps, black cargo door, gray side door, revolving laser cannons on tail. Han Solo in Carbonite. 1981. ($90)	9	13	18
ESB-V6 Snowspeeder (B/O) 12¼" long, 12¾" wide, light gray with 2 light up laser cannons, rear harpoon gun with harpoon on string. 1980. ($50)	8	12	16
ESB-V7 Twin-Pod Cloud Car: 10½" wide, 8¾" long, rust orange with dual pod cockpit. 1980. ($75)	10	15	20

THE RETURN OF THE JEDI VEHICLES (RJ-V)

	C6	C8	C10
RJ-V1 B-Wing Fighter: light gray, cockpit on right side with fin-wing extending to the left. Circa 1985. ($65)	15	22	30
RJ-V1 A Battle-Damaged Imperial Tie-Fighter ($45)	10	15	20
RJ-V2 Ewok Combat Glider: brown with harness for one action figure and 2 stone-bombs. c.1984 ($75)	25	35	45
RJ-V3 Imperial Shuttle: light gray, stationary center fin and side wings that fold up. Circa 1984. ($150)	20	30	40
RJ-V4 Speeder Bike: 8¾" long, light brown with black engine and detail. Bike "explodes" when pack is pressed. 1983. ($20)	2	3	5

	C6	C8	C10
RJ-V5 Y-Wing Fighter: light gray with twin hollow engines, 3 retractable landing skids. Circa 1984. ($65)	7	12	15

STAR WARS PLAYSETS (SW-P)

	C6	C8	C10
SW-P1 Action Figure Display Stand: 20" long, **5-1/2"** wide, gray base with moving discs for 12 action figures. Front has decal with the names of the 12 original action figures. Cardboard backdrop depicts a spaceship dogfight. Available through special mail order only. 1978. ($125.00)			
SW-P2 Cardboard Cantina: 18" long, 7" high, tan base has 11 action figure pegs. Backdrop has scene from Mos Eiseley city street. Available only with Cantina figure set which included SW-A8, SW-A9, SW-A19A, and SW-A21. 1978. Sears exclusive ($325)	30	45	60
SW-P3 Collector's Case: 2 trays hold a total of 24 action figures. Case depicts scenes from Star Wars. ($75)			
SW-P4 Creature Cantina: 13¾" long, 7¾" wide, tan orange base has bar and table, 2 action levers and floor button which opens the doors. Also has cardboard backdrop depicting cantina scene. 1979 ($125)			

ESB-P9, Taun-Taun. Figure not included. Photo Courtesy Whit Alexander and Neal Bates.

	C6	C8	C10

SW-P5 Death Star Space Station: 22¼" high, gray and black, 3 floors and basement trash compactor. Compactor has foam trash and green monster. Floors have drawbridge, grappling hook swing, "exploding" laser cannon and catwalk. Main tower has elevator and 2nd and 3rd floors have cardboard surface panels. 1977. ($150)

SW-P6 Droid Factory: 13" x11", tan-orange base holds 38 interchangeable droid parts and crane with hook. 1979 ($125) 22 33 45

SW-P7 Land of the Jawas: 13½" long, 8¼" wide. Tan base has sand cave and action lever. Escape pod fits into crater. Cardboard backdrop depicts sandcrawler and has moving elevator. 1979. ($175)

SW-P8 Patrol Dewback: 10½" long, green and white lizard has 4 posable limbs and trap door in back. Tail and head move together. Also has brown saddle and harness. 1979. ($30) 5 8 10

EMPIRE STRIKES BACK PLAYSETS (ESB-P)

ESB-P1 Cardboard Bespin Set: 9" high, 11¾" wide, cardboard base has 6 action figure pegs. Backdrop depicts Cloud City scene and has protruding Carbonite Chamber. Available only with action figures ESB-A7, ESB-A10, ESB-A17 and ESB-A26. 1980. Sears Exclusive ($150)

ESB-P2 Collector's Case: 2 trays hold a total of 24 action figures. Case depicts scenes from The Empire Strikes Back ($22.00)

ESB-P3 Dagobah Playset: gray with brown tree stump, 3 action levers, mud puddle and 2 storage containers. 1981. ($45.00)

ESB-P4 Darth Vader Collector Case: 14½" high, 16" wide, black with room for 31 action figures and accessories. Circa 1980. ($22.00)....4 6 8

ESB-P5 Hoth Ice Planet: 13½" long, 8¼" wide, white base has snow cave and action lever. Tank-radar sits in crater. Cardboard backdrop depicts AT-AT with moving elevator. 1981. ($150) 15 23 35

	C6	C8	C10

ESB-P6 Hoth Wampa: 6" high, white with 4 posable limbs. Circa 1981. ($20) 4 6 8

ESB-P7 Imperial Attack Base: 17¼" long, 10" wide, white with revolving laser cannon and gray control room, 3 action levers make 2 part snowbridge fall, control room "explode" and action figure fall ($75) 10 15 20

ESB-P8 Probot and Turret: 15½" long, 9¼" wide, white base has action lever and post for gray probot. Turret has door and revolving laser platform. 1979. ($125) 20 30 40

ESB-P9 Taun-Taun: 9¾" from head to tail, gray and white with brown horns, trap door in back and 4 posable limbs, brown saddle and harness. 1980. Split Belly ($25.00)..6 9 12

ESB-P10 Taun-Taun as above, 1981, Closed Belly. ($30) 5 7 10

RETURN OF THE JEDI PLAYSETS (RJ-P)

RJ-P1 C-3PO Collector Case: metallic gold with room for 31 action figures and accessories. Circa 1983. ($30) 5 8 10

RJ-P2 Chewbacca Bandolier Strap: black, holds 10 action figures and accessories. Circa 1983. ($11.00) 2 3 4

RJ-P3 Ewok Assault Catapult: brown logs with rotating winch and 2 gray boulders. Circa 1983. ($20) .3 5 7

RJ-P4 Jabba the Hutt Playset: 11" long, 5¼" wide, grayish-brown platform with 2 doors, with Jabba, Salacious Crumb and a long-armed green monster. 1983. ($40) 9 13 18

RJ-P5 Land of the Ewoks: 22" high, 16" long, tan platform supported by 3 trees, spit over the firering, stool, moving elevator, net and litter for carrying action figures. 1983. ($50) 15 22 30

RJ-P6 Rancor Monster: 10" high, tan with 4 posable limbs. 1983. ($30) 6 9 12

RJ-P7 The Jabba The Hutt Dungeon: 13" x 11", gray base, crane with hood and branding iron. Complete with action figures RJ-A13B, RJ-A18 and RJ-A8. 1983 ($55) 10 15 20

	C6	C8	C10
RJ-P8 Sy Snootles and the Max Rebo Band: complete with blue keyboardist and keyboard, spotted singer and microphone, pink clarinet player and microphone. Circa 1983. ($40) 10	15	20

LARGE FIGURES AND DOLLS

	C6	C8	C10
Ben (Obi-Wan) Knobi, 12" high, light-saber, removable cape ($250) 60	90	120
Boba Fett, 13¼" high, laser rifle, molded backpack ($250.00)..........50	75	100
C-3PO, 12" high ($125) 32	48	65
Chewbacca, 18" high, stuffed ($60.00).20	30	40
Chewbacca, 15" high, with laser crossbow ($120.00)..........25	38	50
Chewbacca, 8" high, furry ($80.00).......8	12	15
Darth Vader, 15" high, light-saber and removable cape ($150.00).........40	60	80
Han Solo, 12" high, laser rifle ($450.00).100	150	225
IG-88, 15" high, laser weapons ($500.00)..........100	150	200
Jawa, 8¼" high, hooded cape and laser rifle ($150) 30	50	75
Luke Skywalker, 11¾" high, lever-like arm and grappling hook ($225.00).....75	112	150
Princess Leia Organa, 11½" high, combable hair ($140.00) 30	50	75
RS-D2, 7½" high, head clicks when turned ($85.00)..........30	45	60
R2-D2, radio controlled ($110.00).......20	32	45
Stormtrooper, 12" high, has laser rifle ($200) 45	65	90

DIE CAST VEHICLES

Kenner Series 1

	C6	C8	C10
Darth Vader Tie Fighter ($65.00)..........15	25	35
X-Wing Fighter ($55.00) 13	20	30
Land Speeder ($55.00)..........13	20	35
Tie Fighter ($50.00) 12	18	25

Kenner Series II

	C6	C8	C10
Millenium Falcoln ($120.00) 35	50	70
Darth Vader's Star Ship Destroyer ($120) 20	30	40
Princess Leia's Command Ship ($120).20	30	40
Tie Bomber ($750.00)..........200	350	500
Y-Wing Fighter ($100.00)..........30	45	60

Kenner Series III

	C6	C8	C10
Snow Speeder ($95.00)..........22	35	50
Slave I Space Ship ($45.00)..........10	15	25

	C6	C8	C10
Twin-Pod Cloud Car ($45.00)..........10	15	25

End Star Wars

	C6	C8	C10
LJN "V" Action Figures (TV Series)....8	12	16

MARX *(Listing by Jim Main)*

8 to 12" Figures:

	C6	C8	C10
Johnny Apollo Astronaut ($75) 40	50	60
Johnny and Jane Apollo Deluxe Set w/vehicles ($450.00)..........125	150	175
Stoney Smith ($80.00) 35	45	55
Sir Gordon, The Golden Knight ($125).........35	45	55

Marx Bravo, The Golden Knight's Horse, box.
Photo by Barry Goodman

	C6	C8	C10
Bravo, The Golden Knight's Horse ($75)..........20	25	30
Sir Stuart, The Silver Knight ($125) ..35	45	55
Valor, The Silver Knight's Horse ($75)..........20	25	30
Mike Hazzard, Double Agent ($250.00)..........60	90	120
Girl From UNCLE (Marx British issue) ($500) 90	120	150
Eric the Viking ($145) 15	30	75
Odin the Viking Chieftain ($145).......... 15	30	75

Marx Sir Stuart, the Silver Knight.
Photo by Barry Goodman

Marx Erik the Viking, box.
Photo by Barry Goodman

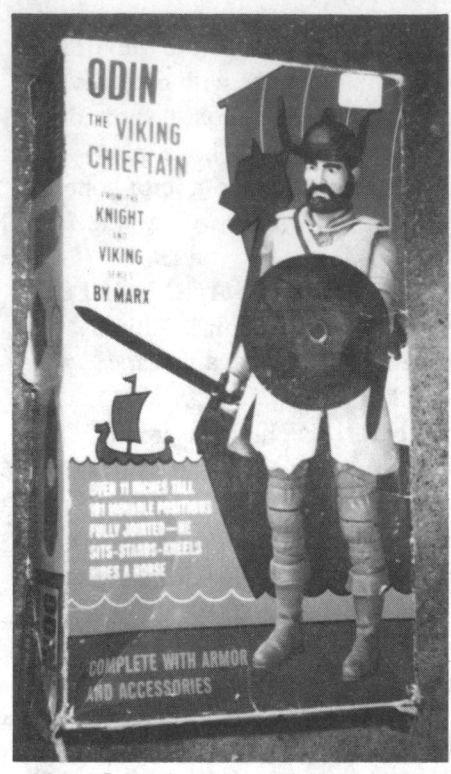

Marx Odin the Viking Chieftain, box.
Photo by Barry Goodman

Marx Valor, the Silver Knight's Horse, box.
Photo by Barry Goodman

Best Of The West:	C6	C8	C10
Johnny West ($50.00)	30	40	50
Jay West ($50.00)	15	20	25
Janice West ($50.00)	15	20	25
Josie West ($45)	10	15	25
Jane West ($60.00)	20	25	30
Brave Eagle ($125)	25	35	75
Chief Cherokee ($65)	10	18	30
Daniel Boone ($145)	15	30	75
Jamie West ($40.00)	15	20	25
Thundercolt ($75)	10	12	15
Thunderbolt ($40.00)	15	20	25
Sheriff Garret ($125)	15	20	50
Sam Cobra ($75.00)	25	30	35
Pancho ($35.00)	10	12	15
Flack ($35)	8	10	12
Flick (($25.00)	8	10	12
Flame ($40)	8	10	12
Flame w/ Corral set ($75)	20	25	30
Jane West Set ($140.00) (w/corral and horses)	50	60	70
Johnny West Set w/horse and Jeep ($200.00)	75	90	115
Johnny West w/ Wild Mustangs set ($125.00)	45	60	75
Princess Wild Flower ($90)	20	25	60
Buffalo ($200)	15	20	25

	C6	C8	C10
Chief Cherokee w/ Teepee set ($150.00)	50	65	80
Circle X Ranch Playset ($225.00)	80	110	140
Commanche ($45.00)	15	20	25
Buckboard and Horse ($600)	60	70	80

*Marx Best of the West Chief Cherokee.
Photo by Barry Goodman*

*Marx Best of the West Johnny West,
box.*   *Photo by Barry Goodman*

*Marx Best of the West
Josie West
Photo by Barry Goodman*

*Marx Best of the West Jane West, box.
Photo by Barry Goodman*

*Marx Best of the West Daniel Boone.
Photo by Barry Goodman*

*Marx Best of the West Princess
Wild Flower.
Courtesy Barry Goodman*

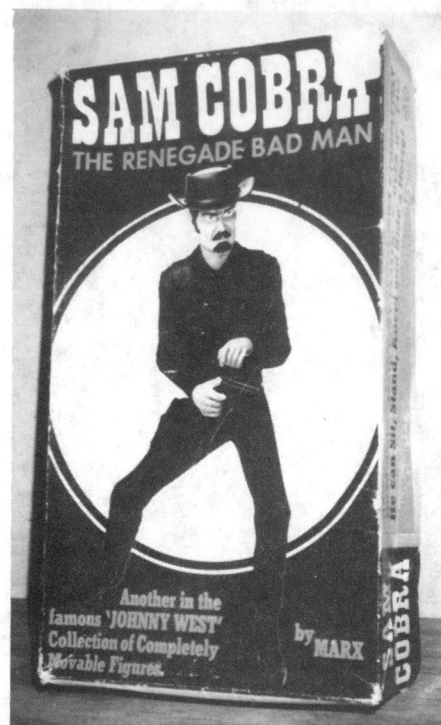

Marx Best of the West Sam Cobra, box.
Courtesy Barry Goodman

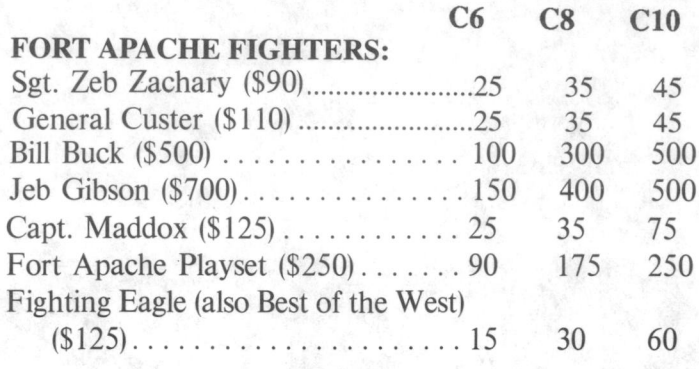

	C6	C8	C10
FORT APACHE FIGHTERS:			
Sgt. Zeb Zachary ($90)	25	35	45
General Custer ($110)	25	35	45
Bill Buck ($500)	100	300	500
Jeb Gibson ($700)	150	400	500
Capt. Maddox ($125)	25	35	75
Fort Apache Playset ($250)	90	175	250
Fighting Eagle (also Best of the West) ($125)	15	30	60

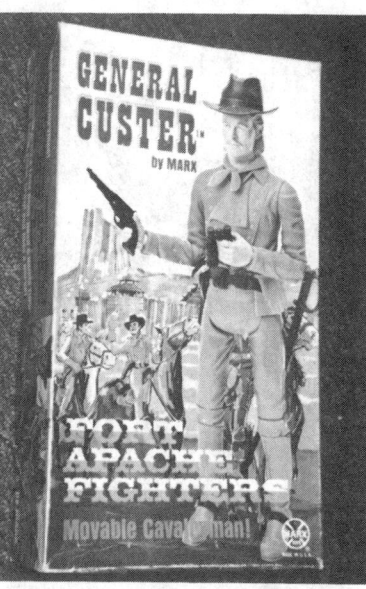

Marx Fort Apache Fighters:
Sgt. Zeb Zachary, box.
Photo by Barry Goodman

Marx Fort Apache Fighters:
General Custer.
Photo by Barry Goodman

Marx Best of the West Buffalo
Photo by Barry Goodman

Marx Best of the West Buckboard and Horse (Thunderbolt).
Photo by Barry Goodman

Marx Fort Apache Fighters:
Capt. Maddox, box.
Photo by Barry Goodman

Marx Fort Apache Fighters:
Fighting Eagle.
Photo by Barry Goodman

MATTEL

Mattel was founded in 1945 by Harold Mattson and Ruth and Elliot Handler (the "Matt" in Mattson and "El" in Elliott formed the firm's name). The business, created to make picture frames, began in a Los Angeles garage, with Mattson bowing out early due to poor health. Toys were made almost from the beginning, furniture fashioned from the plastic and wood scraps left over from the frames. Its most famous toy is the Barbie doll.

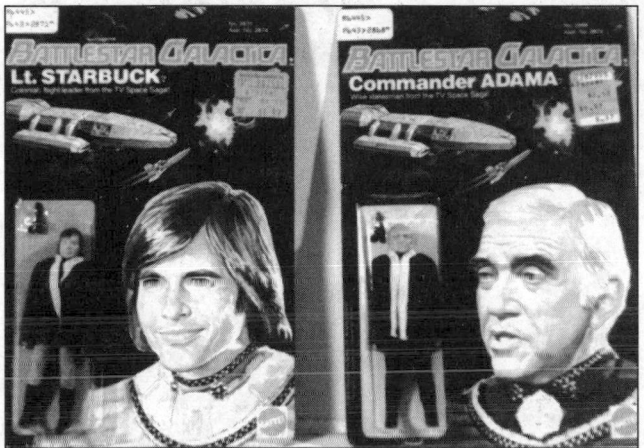

MATTEL Battlestar Galactica figures, Left to Right: Lt. Starbuck, Commander Adama. Courtesy Rex and Richard Gray.

	C6	C8	C10
Construction/Machine Gunner adv. ($25.00)	10	12	14
High Explosive Miner adv. ($25.00)	10	12	14
Karate outfit ($25.00)	10	12	14
Photographer/Secret Agent adv. ($25.00)	10	12	14
Policeman/SWAT adv. ($25.00)	10	12	14
Race Driver outfit ($25.00)	10	12	14
Sea Spy uniform ($25.00)	10	12	14

BATTLESTAR GALACTICA (List by Jim Main):

	C6	C8	C10
Starbuck ($15.00)	4	5	6
Cmdr. Adama ($20.00)	8	9	10
Apollo ($15.00)	4	5	6
Baltarr ($30)	4	5	6
Cylon ($35)	8	9	10
Gold Cylon ($75)	10	13	16
Boray ($20.00)	8	9	10
Ovion ($60)	10	13	16
Daggit ($20)	3	4	5
Lucifer ($40)	4	5	6
Imperious Leader ($20)	3	4	6

12" Figures

	C6	C8	C10
Cylon ($60)	15	20	25
Colonial Warrior ($60)	15	20	25

BIG JIM'S P.A.C.K. (List by Jim Main):

	C6	C8	C10
Big Jim ($60.00)	15	25	35
Double Trouble Big Jim ($50.00)	10	20	30
Double Trouble Zorak ($50.00)	10	20	30
Torpedo Fist ($75)	10	20	50
Warpath ($75)	10	20	50
Dr. Steel ($75)	10	20	50
The Whip ($75)	10	20	50

Accessories/vehicles/outfits:

	C6	C8	C10
Blitz Rig ($90.00)	30	45	60
The Howler ($35.00)	10	15	20
P.A.C.K. Dunebuggy ($30.00)	8	13	18
Lazervette ($50.00)	10	20	30
The Beast ($75.00)	20	30	40
Artic Uniform ($25.00)	10	12	14

MATTEL Major Matt Mason in flexible space suit with jet propulsion pack and space sled.

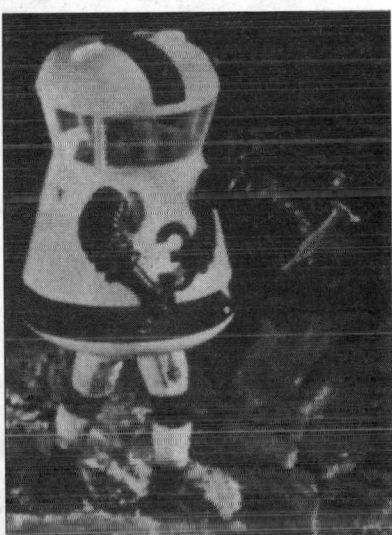

MATTEL Major Matt Mason with moon suit.

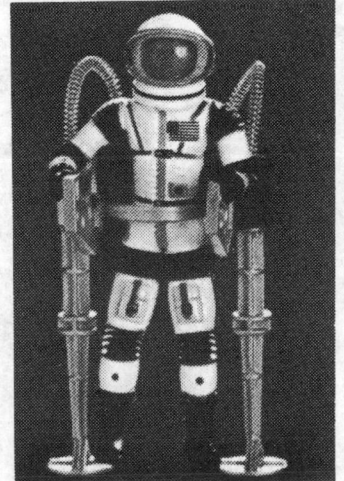

Famous spaceman with exclusive Voice Command Flight Pak. Says five things while "Flying on space cord". Removable VCF Pak may be used with all other Mattel Astronauts as well.

CLASH OF THE TITANS (List by Jim Main)

4" Figures:

	C6	C8	C10
Thallo ($20.00)	5	7	9
Calibos ($20.00)	5	7	9
Charon ($20.00)	5	7	9

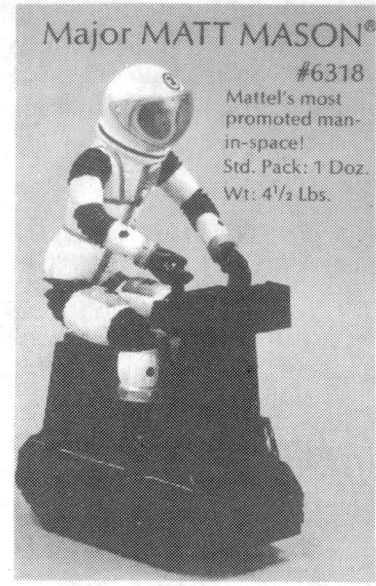

Major MATT MASON® #6318
Mattel's most promoted man-in-space!
Std. Pack: 1 Doz.
Wt: 4½ Lbs.

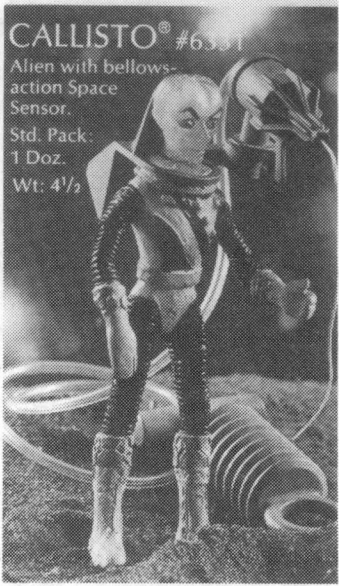

CALLISTO® #6331
Alien with bellows-action Space Sensor.
Std. Pack: 1 Doz.
Wt: 4½

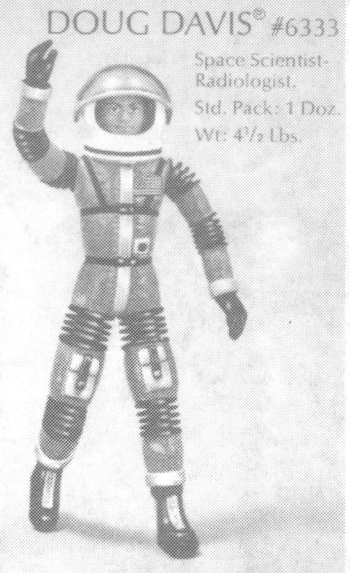

DOUG DAVIS® #6333
Space Scientist-Radiologist.
Std. Pack: 1 Doz.
Wt: 4½ Lbs.

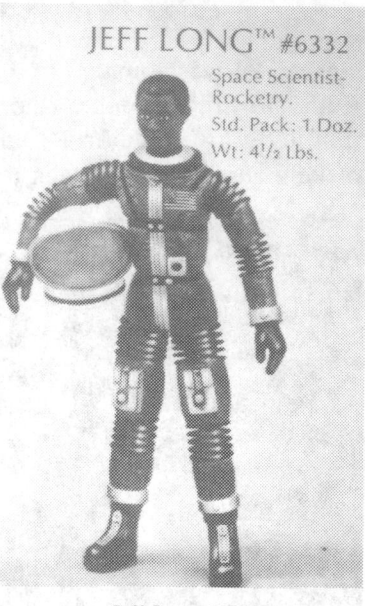

JEFF LONG™ #6332
Space Scientist-Rocketry.
Std. Pack: 1 Doz.
Wt: 4½ Lbs.

Major Mat Mason 6318   Callisto 6331   Doug Davis 6333   Jeff Long 6332

Reentry Glider 6360

Space Crawler 6304

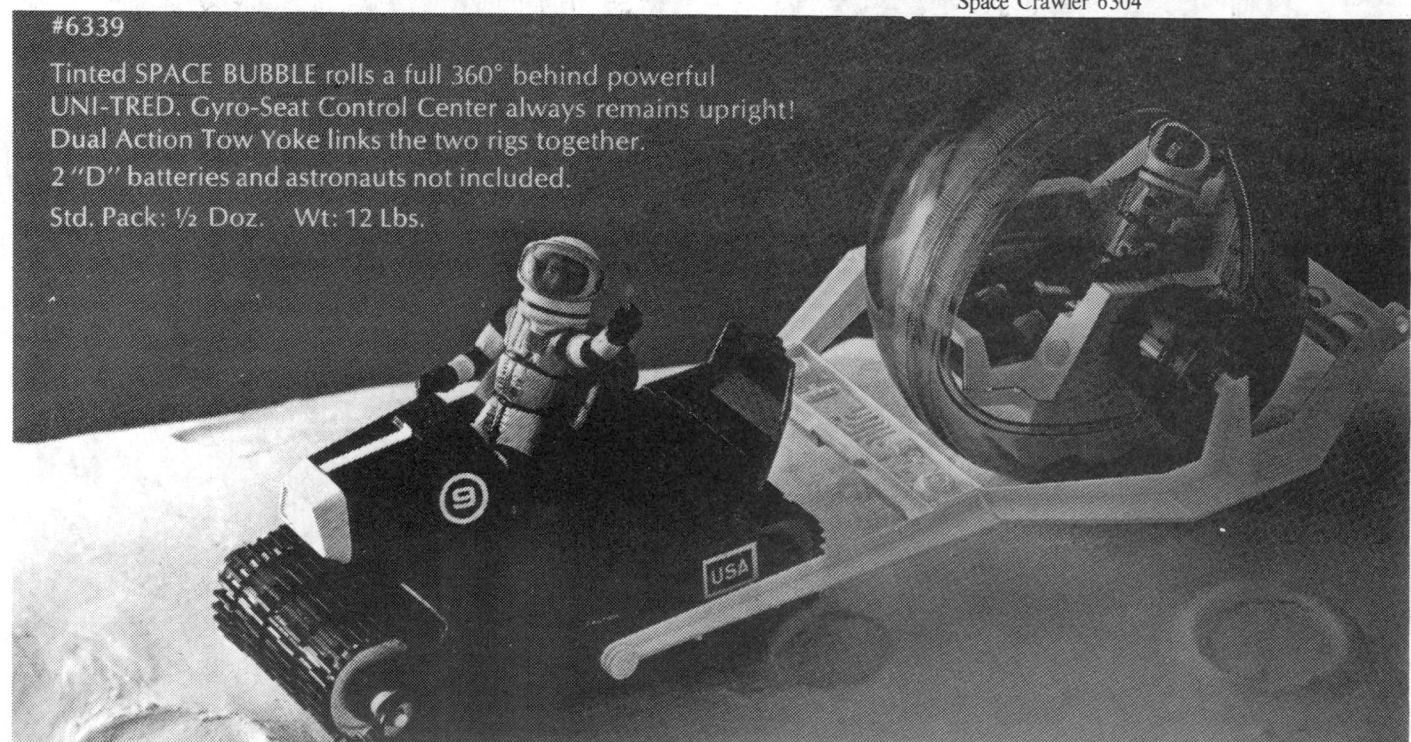

#6339
Tinted SPACE BUBBLE rolls a full 360° behind powerful UNI-TRED. Gyro-Seat Control Center always remains upright! Dual Action Tow Yoke links the two rigs together. 2 "D" batteries and astronauts not included.
Std. Pack: ½ Doz.   Wt: 12 Lbs.

	C6	C8	C10
Perseus ($20.00)...................5		7	9
Pegasus ($75) 10		14	18
Kraken ($135) 45		60	75
Perseus/Pegasus set ($50) 15		20	25

FLASH GORDON 4" set (List by Jim Main):

	C6	C8	C10
Flash Gordon ($25.00) 8		12	16
Thun ($25.00) 8		12	16
Ming ($35) 8		12	16
Lizard Woman ($45) 10		14	18
Beastman ($45) 8		12	16
Dr. Zarkov ($20.00) 7		9	11

MAJOR MATT MASON (List by Jim Main):

	C6	C8	C10
Callisto ($200.00) 35		40	45
Captain Lazer ($150.00) 40		60	80
XRG-1 Re-Entry Glider ($225.00) 60		80	100
Talking Major Matt Mason ($180.00)...50		75	100
Talking Command Console ($150.00)..40		60	80
Space Station ($200.00)............60		90	120
Space Station/Space Crawler Deluxe Action Set ($450.00)..........150		200	250
Star Seeker ($175.00).............60		90	120
Supernaut Power Limbs pak ($50.00) ..15		25	30
Unitred ($75.00)..............20		30	40
Unitred and Space Bubble set ($125.00)............40		60	80
Space Bubble ($50.00).........15		25	30
Astro Trac ($125.00)..............40		60	80
Space Shelter Pak ($45.00) 10		15	20
Space Probe Set ($45.00)........10		15	20
Space Power Suit Pak ($60.00).........20		30	40
Doug Davis w/ Lunar Trac ($300) ...30		45	150
Galaxy 3 playset ....No Price Found			
Firebolt Space Cannon ($150.00) 40		60	80
Space Mission Team w/MMM, JL, Calisto and DD ($500.00)..........100		150	200
Space Discovery Set w/DD, MMM and Calisto ($400.00)..........85		125	165
Sgt. Storm w/ Cat Trac ($150.00) 40		60	80
Sgt. Storm w/ Flight Set ($200.00) 50		75	100
Gamma Ray Gard ($60.00)............20		30	40
Jeff Long w/ Lunar Trac ($225.00).......60		80	100
Lunar Base Command Set ($375.00)...100		125	150
MMM Rocketship Case ($90.00) 40		50	60
Satellite Locker ($75.00) 30		40	50
Satellite Launch pak ($50.00) 15		25	30
MMM w/ Space Sled ($175.00)...........40		60	80
MMM w/ Moon Suit ($200.00) 50		70	90
MMM w/ Cat Trac ($150.00)...............40		60	80
Reconojet Pak ($50.00)...............15		20	25
Scorpio ($500) 75		100	300

PHOTO BOX Accessory Paks:

	C6	C8	C10
Supernaut Power Limbs ($175.00) 15		20	25
Space Shelter Pak ($175.00) 15		20	25
Gamma Ray Gard ($175.00) 15		20	25
Space Power Suit ($175.00)...............15		20	25
Super Power Equipment Set ($200.00)...............25		50	75

SPACE: 1999 (list by Jim Main):

	C6	C8	C10
Cmdr. Koenig ($50) 10		14	18
Dr. Russell ($45) 10		12	14
Prof. Bergman ($30.00) 10		14	18
Moonbase Alpha Playset ($150) 15		20	25
EAGLE 1 Spaceship (Not for 8" figures, but for figures w/ craft) ($150.00) ..25		50	75

MARVEL SUPER HEROES SECRET WARS (list by Jim Main):
4 - 1/4" Figures

	C6	C8	C10
Iron Man ($20.00) 6		8	10
Captain America ($25) 5		6	7
Wolverine ($35.00) 12		15	18
Spiderman (Black costume) ($35) ..10		12	14
Spiderman (Red costume) ($35) 10		12	14
Doctor Doom ($15.00)............5		6	7
Kang ($10.00) 5		6	7
Magneto ($15.00)............5		6	7
Baron Zemo ($35) 10		12	14
Daredevil ($25) 5		6	7
Falcon ($30.00) 10		14	18
Hobgoblin ($45) 10		14	18
Iceman ($70) 20		25	30
Constrictor ($40.00) 20		25	30
Electro ($40.00) 20		25	30

Accessories/vehicles:

	C6	C8	C10
Tower of Doom ($80.00) 30		40	50
Doom Roller ($25.00)...............8		12	16
Doom Chopper ($50.00)............15		20	25
Turbo Copter ($50.00) 15		20	25
Dark Star ($40.00) 12		16	20
Star Dart ($75.00) 20		30	40
Marvel Super Heroes Machine ($125) ..25		40	55
Marvel Super Villains Machine ($80.00)...............25		40	55
Turbo Cycle ($40.00) 12		16	20

End Mattel

MEGO

	C6	C8	C10
BLACK HOLE - 12" *(List by Jim Main)*			
Pizer ($45.00) 15	20	25
Dr. Durant ($50.00) 15	20	25
Captain Holland ($50.00) 15	20	25
Harry Booth ($45.00) 15	20	25
Dr. Reinhardt ($50.00) 15	20	25
Kate McCrae ($50.00) 15	20	25
3 ¾"			
V.I.N. cent ($35) 4	6	8
Pizer ($12.00) 3	5	7
Capt. Holland ($12.00) 3	5	7
Harry Booth ($12.00) 3	5	7
Kate McCrea ($25.00) 5	7	9
Old Bob ($40.00) 10	15	20
Humanoid ($70) 10	15	20
Dr. Durant ($12.00) 3	5	7
Maximillian ($45) 5	7	9
Starr ($85) 10	15	20
Dr. Reinhardt ($12.00) 3	5	7
BUCK ROGERS *(List by Jim Main)*			
12":			
Buck ($60) 15	20	25
Wilma ($75) 18	23	28
Dr. Huer ($40.00) 10	15	20
Killer Kane ($65) 12	14	16
Twiki ($45) 8	12	15
Draco ($50) 10	15	20
3¾":			
Buck ($20.00) 6	8	10
Ardella ($12.00) 3	5	7
Wilma ($15.00) 5	7	9
Dr. Huer ($10.00) 3	5	7
Tiger Man ($35) 5	8	11
Draco ($20) 3	5	7
Killer Kane ($10.00) 3	5	7
Twiki ($12.00) 3	5	7
Draconian Guard ($25) 5	8	11
Accessories:			
Laser Scope Fighter ($50) 10	16	22
Star Fighter ($60) 10	17	25
Draconian Marauder ($50) 10	16	22
Star Fighter Command Center ($40.00) 10	15	20
FLASH GORDON - 10" *(List by Jim Main)*			
Flash ($75) 20	25	30
Dale ($75) 20	25	30
Dr. Zarkov ($55) 20	22	25
Ming ($125) 25	30	35

	C6	C8	C10
KISS: 12" *(List by Jim Main)*			
Paul ($125.00) 35	40	60
Gene ($125.00) 35	45	50
Ace ($160.00) 45	55	75
Peter ($140.00) 40	45	50
MOONRAKER - JAMES BOND - 12" *(List by Jim Main)*			
Bond ($125.00) 30	35	40
Holly ($125.00) 30	35	40
Jaws ($175) 40	45	75
Hugo Drax ($100.00) 20	25	30
ONE MILLION YEARS B.C. - 8" *(List by Jim Main)*			
Mara ($60.00) 15	20	25
Grog ($50.00) 15	20	25
Orm ($50.00) 15	20	25
Trag ($50.00) 15	20	25
Planet of the Apes 8" figures *(List by Jim Main)*			
Zira ($40.00) 5	10	15
Cornelius ($40.00) 5	10	15
Astronaut ($75) 10	15	20
Burke ($60.00) 10	15	20
Verdon ($60.00) 10	15	20
Dr. Zaius ($40.00) 5	10	15
Gen. Urko ($50) 5	10	15
Ursus ($50) 5	10	15
Soldier Ape ($50) 5	10	15
Galen ($40.00) 5	10	15
Accessories:			
Battering Ram ($35.00) 10	15	20
Village Playset ($75.00) 15	25	35
Treehouse Playset ($75.00) 15	25	35
Fortress Playset ($75.00) 15	25	35
Forbidden Zone Trap ($60.00) ...20	30	40
Catapult and Wagon ($40.00) ...10	15	20
Dr. Zaius' Throne ($30.00) 8	12	16
Palamino ($30.00) 8	12	16
Jail ($35.00) 10	15	20
Bend N' Flex figures:			
Zira ($25.00) 4	7	10
Cornelius ($25.00) 4	7	10
Soldier Ape ($25.00) 8	12	15
Astronaut ($30.00) 8	12	15
Dr. Zaius ($25.00) 4	7	10
Galen ($25.00) 4	7	10
Star Trek TV Series 8" *(List by Jim Main):*			
Kirk ($40.00) 10	15	20
Spock ($40.00) 10	15	20
McCoy ($60.00) 15	25	35
Scotty ($45.00) 12	18	25

	C6	C8	C10
Lt. Uhura ($60.00)	15	25	35
Andorian ($160.00)	40	60	80
Cheron ($140.00)	35	45	55
Mugato ($350.00)	100	150	200
Talosian ($300.00)	90	110	130
Romulan ($300.00)	90	110	130
Gorn ($175.00)	45	65	85
Neptunian ($150.00)	50	60	70
Keeper ($125)	50	60	70

STAR TREK THE MOTION PICTURE - 12"

	C6	C8	C10
Kirk ($40)	10	15	20
Spock ($45)	10	15	20
Decker ($80)	20	25	30
Illia ($40)	10	15	20
Klingon ($60)	15	20	25
Arcturian ($125)	20	25	30

3¾"

	C6	C8	C10
Kirk ($10.00)	3	5	7
Spock ($12.00)	3	5	7
McCoy ($15.00)	4	6	8
Decker ($10.00)	3	5	7
Scotty ($15.00)	4	6	8
Klingon ($20.00)	8	10	12
Illia ($10.00)	3	5	7
Arcturian ($50)	10	12	50
Zaranite ($65)	10	12	50
Rigellian ($65)	12	14	50
Betelgeusian ($65)	12	14	50
Megarite ($65)	12	14	50

SUPERHEROES *(Lists by Jim Main):*
(Bx = Box, BP = Blister Pack):

	C6	C8	C10
Iron Man (Bx - $110.00)	25	35	45
Lizard (Bx - $175.00)	30	45	60
Kid Flash (BP - $300.00)	60	85	110
Speedy (BP - $400.00)	80	120	150
Wonder Girl (BP - $300.00)	60	85	110
Aqualad (BP - $300.00)	60	85	110
Aquaman (Bx - $140.00)	15	20	25
Batgirl (Bx - $300.00)	60	85	110
Batman (w/removable Mask (Bx - $325.00)	65	90	120
Batman (Bx - $125.00)	20	25	30
Batman (BP - $70.00)	20	25	30
Joker (Bx - $140.00)	25	35	40
Isis (Bx - $325.00)	20	40	60
Isis (BP - $125.00)	20	40	60
Conan (BP - $325.00)	80	120	150
Falcon (Bx - $100.00)	25	35	40
Thor (Bx - $425.00)	80	120	150
Tarzan (Bx - $75.00)	20	25	30
Supergirl (Bx - $375.00)	80	120	150
Spiderman (Bx - $90.00)	8	12	15

	C6	C8	C10
Spiderman (BP - $30.00)	8	12	15
Superman (Bx - $100.00)	10	15	20
Superman (BP - $65.00)	10	15	20
Catwoman (Bx - $175.00)	25	40	65
Captain America (Bx - $90.00)	20	30	40
Captain America (BP - $65.00)	20	30	40
Hulk (Bx - $60.00)	8	12	15
Hulk (BP - $35.00)	8	12	15
Mr. Fantastic (Bx - $75.00)	8	12	15
Mr. Fantastic (BP - $30.00)	8	12	15
Invisible Girl (Bx - $75.00)	8	12	15
Invisible Girl (BP - $30.00)	8	12	15
Human Torch (Bx - $75.00)	8	12	15
Human Torch (BP - $30.00)	8	12	15
Thing (Bx - $75.00)	8	12	15
Thing (BP -$30.00)	8	12	15
Riddler (Bx - $325.00)	25	45	65
Wonder Woman (Bx - $130.00)	20	40	60
Green Arrow (Bx - $175.00)	40	60	80
Penguin (Bx - $95.00)	15	25	35
Penguin (BP - $70.00)	15	25	35
Robin (Bx - $100.00)	10	15	20
Robin (BP - $60.00)	10	15	20
Robin w/removable mask ($425.00)	75	115	145

FIST FIGHTERS:

	C6	C8	C10
Robin ($225.00)	40	60	80
Batman ($250.00)	40	60	80
Joker ($300.00)	50	70	90
Riddler ($325.00)	50	70	90

ALTER EGO FIGURES:

	C6	C8	C10
Clark Kent ($400)	125	175	225
Peter Parker ($400)	125	175	225
Bruce Wayne ($400)	125	175	225
Dick Grayson ($400)	125	175	225

BENDIES:

	C6	C8	C10
Aquaman ($65.00)	15	20	25
Wonder Woman ($80.00)	20	25	30
Superman ($50.00)	10	15	20
Supergirl ($225.00)	60	75	90
Captain America ($60.00)	15	20	25
Batgirl ($225.00)	60	75	90
Tarzan ($50.00)	10	15	20
Penguin ($80.00)	20	25	30
Riddler ($125.00)	30	45	60
Joker ($100.00)	25	35	45
Mr. Mxyzptlk ($75.00)	20	25	30
Robin ($40.00)	8	13	18
Shazam ($50.00)	10	15	20
Spiderman ($50.00)	10	15	20
Catwoman ($175.00)	45	60	75
Batman ($90.00)	20	30	40

SUPERMAN - THE MOVIE - 12" figures	C6	C8	C10
Superman ($60.00)	15	20	25
General Zod ($50.00)	10	15	20
Jor-El ($50.00)	10	15	20
Luthor ($50.00)	10	15	20

WONDER WOMAN:

	C6	C8	C10
Wonder Woman w/ Diana Prince outfit ($150.00)	20	35	50
Wonder Woman w/o Lynda Carter pic ($65.00)	15	20	25
Nubia ($100.00)	25	35	45
Steve Trevor ($80.00)	20	25	30
Queen Hippolite ($100.00)	25	35	45

THE WALTONS: *(List by Jim Main)*
8"

	C6	C8	C10
John boy ($35.00)	6	9	12
Granpa ($35.00)	6	9	12
Granma ($35.00)	6	9	12
Ellen ($35.00)	6	9	12

Accessories/playsets for 8" figures:

	C6	C8	C10
Wayne Foundation Playset ($500)	150	225	300
Batcave Playset ($250.00)	75	90	105
Captain Americar ($150.00)	45	60	75
Green Arrowcar ($150.00)	45	60	75
Jokermobile ($125.00)	20	25	30
Batmobile ($125.00)	20	25	30
Hall of Justice Playset ($400.00)	100	150	200
Batcycle ($150.00)	25	40	55
Batcopter ($140.00)	35	45	55
Aquaman vs. the Great White Shark ($750.00)	175	250	325
Mobile Bat-Lab ($275.00)	60	80	100
Super Action SuperVator ($100.00)	30	40	50
Spider-Car ($100.00)	25	35	45

COMIC ACTION/POCKET SUPER HEROES *(List by Jim Main)*
3¾"

	C6	C8	C10
Captain America ($50.00)	10	15	20
Batman ($50.00)	10	15	20
Robin ($40.00)	8	12	15
Green Lantern ($60.00)	12	18	25
Superman ($40.00)	8	12	15
Shazam ($45.00)	10	15	20
Green Goblin ($60.00)	12	18	25
Joker ($50.00)	10	15	20
Hulk ($25.00)	8	10	12
Penguin ($35.00)	8	12	15
General Zod ($25.00)	8	10	12
Aquaman ($40.00)	8	12	15

	C6	C8	C10
Jor-El ($25.00)	8	10	12
Lex Luthor ($25.00)	8	10	12
Spiderman ($45.00)	10	15	20
Wonder Woman ($45.00)	10	15	20

Accessories/Playsets for above figures:

	C6	C8	C10
Batcave Playset ($150.00)	30	35	40
Fortress of Solitude Playset ($225.00)	75	90	125
Spider Car w/Spiderman and Green Goblin figures ($125.00)	20	30	40
Spider Car w/Spiderman and Hulk figures ($80.00)	20	25	30
Wonder Woman Collapsible Tower/ Invisible Plane Playset ($150.00)	50	65	80
Invisible Plane ($60.00)	15	20	25
Batmachine ($90.00)	20	25	30
Batmobile ($175.00)	30	40	50
The Mangler ($90.00)	20	25	30
Batman Collapsible Bridge Playset - w/ Batman and Robin ($200.00)	60	75	90
Batman Collapsible Bridge Playset - w/Batman, Robin, Joker and Penguin ($300.00)	90	105	120
Pressman Lone Ranger with his Horse, Silver, No. 7750 new in 1967, jointed, 40 accessories including working (cold) branding iron	*No Price Found*		
Pressman Tonto & his horse Scout No. 7751, new in 1967, jointed, 40 accessories including cold branding iron kit	*No Price Found*		
Remco Energized Green Goblin, battery-operated, 12"	37	56	75
Remco Energized Hulk, battery-operated, 12"	25	37	50
Remco Energized Superman, battery-operated	37	56	75

Pressman Tonto No. 7751.

Pressman Lone Ranger No. 7750.

TOPPER

	C6	C8	C10
THE TIGERS (*List by Jim Main*)			
Tex ($30.00)	10	15	20
Sarge ($30.00)	10	15	20
Big Ears ($30.00)	10	15	20
Bugle Ben ($30.00)	10	15	20
Combat Kid ($30.00)	10	15	20
Pretty Boy ($30.00)	10	15	20
Rock ($30.00)	10	15	20
Machine Gun Mike ($30.00)	10	15	20
The Tigers' Headquarters, Sears Exclusive ($100.00)	40	60	80

FIGURE KITS

by David Welch

(C10 prices for Figure Kits averaged $94.83 in the last edition and this time $145.96, an increase of 54%.)

In recent years, plastic model kits, in particular plastic figure kits, have become associated with the world of toys. Buyers of 1960s and 1970s movie, TV, and cartoon memorabilia find that figure kits fit rather nicely into their collections. The 1960s is considered the "Golden Age" for plastic kits with Aurora by far leading the way in diversity of product and current-day demand. Aurora's line-up of original and glow issue Universal Studios monsters are today's most sought-after figure kits.

CONDITION OF A KIT AND RELATION TO PRICE

Rating the condition of a figure kit can be difficult because factors such as (1) assembled parts, (2) painted parts, (3) missing pieces, (4) missing instructions, (5) box condition, and (6) country of origin drastically affect value. Mint in box [MIB] is the condition upon which the following values are based.

MIB SEALED: mint in box with box shrink wrap; most kits had factory wraps on boxes. Provided the boxes are not damaged. collectors may pay a 10-20% premium over MIB price. BEWARE of bogus re-sealing by dishonest individuals.

MIB: a complete, unused kit with an excellent box and instructions and no glue or paint on pieces. Most collectors insist that plastic "trees" that held pieces be present with pieces still attached. Again, the price listed is for a kit in this condition.

PARTIAL ASSEMBLY: a partially built kit with excellent box/instructions and no painting prices at 85% of MIB at best. The more assembly, the more price decreases. Old styrene glues actually "melted" pieces together. White glues (such as Elmers) do not decrease value as much as Styrene glues because they can be removed.

PARTIAL PAINTING: a complete, partially painted kit with excellent box/instruction and no gluing prices at 85% of MIB at best. Painting is not as serious as gluing because most experienced modelers know how to strip paint. Again, the more painting, the more price decreases because stripping takes time and is not always completely successful.

PARTIAL ASSEMBLY/PAINTING: together, these 2 factors can make pricing very difficult. A general guideline would be 70% of MIB with excellent box/instructions.

BUILT-UP: a fully assembled, complete kit with no box/instructions has a value of 15-45% of MIB. The more expensive the MIB kit, the more desirable the built-up. If a kit was issued several times, built-up value decreases. For example, Aurora's design of Frankenstein was issued four times (Aurora 1961, 1969, 1972, and Monogram 1983). Thus, its value is usually only 15% of MIB. Vehicles such as Batmobiles and UFOs go toward low percentages because of low visual appeal . Further,

without instructions, an inexperienced person will find it virtually impossible to determine if a built-up is complete. Except for very high-priced kits, incomplete built-ups have little value.

MISSING PIECES: one missing piece from a kit gives a big decrease in value regardless of all other combined factors. Even a MIB kit missing one piece is worth only 80% at best of a truly complete MIB kit! Some collectors will not buy a kit missing a piece at all.

INSTRUCTIONS: missing instructions deduct 5-10% of MIB price. 1960s instructions sheets alone sell at $5-$10. Sheets for rare, expensive kits such as Aurora's Gigantic Frankenstein can bring over $35!

BOXES: the market for empty figure kit boxes is almost exclusive to Aurora boxes. Generally, an excellent condition box has no split corners, tape, paint, glue, punctures, severe creases, or scuffs. Excellent boxes alone have maximum value of 40% MIB price. Aforementioned box defects decrease value on MIB kits by 20% or more.

FOREIGN ISSUE: Again, this factor is an issue primarily with Aurora kits. Aurora had branches in Canada, England, and Holland which issued boxes and instructions that sometimes had wording in other languages and plastic parts in colors other than what US issues had. Ninety percent of the kits you'll ever see will not be foreign issues, but just in case, some collectors (not all) devalue MIB foreign issue kits to about 75% of US MIB prices.

A WORD ABOUT PRICING: If you're more confused about how to price a kit now than you were before, don't feel badly! Even experienced dealers have a difficult time pricing kits when faced with missing pieces, painted parts, box wear, etc. These guidelines are just that-guidelines.

It should be noted that kit values vary widely due to region of the country and local collector demand. There is strong interest in American kits, for example, in Europe and Japan. American dealers have found some of these individuals willing to pay very highly relative to U.S. collectors. So, the values listed here are conservative, mid-range prices that are indicative of what most collectors would be willing to pay. Obviously, some collectors will pay more and some will pay less.

Special thanks to Greg Roccaro of Staten Island, New York, and to Mark Karpinski of Denver, Pennsylvania, for price information. Some kit numbers and dates were taken from <u>Science Fiction and Figure Kits</u> by John Burns of Edmond, Oklahoma. Though not a price guide, it serves as an excellent reference regarding all known kits of this genre.

David Welch is a nationally known dealer in cartoon, comic, and TV character items. He has been collecting and/or dealing since age 13. He has contributed information for various price guides including Tomart's Disneyana *(condensed edition),* Tomart's Space Adventure Collectibles, *and periodically* Overstreet's Comic Book Price Guide. *Aside from the world of collectibles, he enjoys spending time with his wife, Cynthia, and two boys, Jordan and Evan, as well as his alter-ego endeavors as a paper restorer, professional musician, and youth leader in the Church of Jesus Christ of Latter Day Saints.*

AURORA
By David Welch

Regarding the Aurora monster line-up, some information may be confusing. To clarify the Frankenstein listing, for example: Frankenstein was issued first in 1961 in a long, rectangular box. The Frightening Lighting 1969 issue was the same kit with duplicate glow parts that were optional. The box was the same shape with a lightning bolt added to the art. In 1969 and 1972, the optional glow format continued and square boxes with altered artwork were introduced. The 1969 glow boxes are thicker and sturdier than the 1972 glows. In many cases, the color of the plastic was different between the original and glow issues. The plastic kit itself will always carry the date of its original issue. The Monster Scenes and Monsters Of The Movies Frankensteins are completely different kits than the 1961, 1969, and 1972 issues.

For the Aurora line in general, dates listed may vary a year either way. It is the kit name and kit number that are most relevant. Please note, too, that different kits carried identical numbers (i.e. King Kong Glow 465 and Frankenstein's Flivver 465).

AURORA store display of its Monster Scenes, with Dr. Deadly, the Victim and Hanging Cage. Courtesy Toy Collector News. Photo by Rex Gray.

AURORA Phantom of the Opera and Napoleon Solo figure kits. Courtesy Toy Collector News. Photo by Rex Gray.

	C6	C8	C10
Addams Family House, 805, 1965			675
Alfred E. Neumann, 802, 1965			150
Allosaurus, 736, 1972			90
American Astronaut, 409, 1967			60
Ankylosourus, 744, 1974			85
Apache Warrior, 401, 1961			300
Aramis, K10, 1958			75
Archies Car, 582, 1969			50
Athos, K8, 1958			75
Babe Ruth, 862, 1965			300
Banana Splits Buggy, 832, 1969			200

	C6	C8	C10
Batboat, 811			425
Batcycle, 810, 1967			425
Batman, 467, 1964			250
Batman Comic Scenes, 187, 1974			60
Batmobile, 486, 1966			250
Batplane, 487, 1966			200
Black Beauty, (Green Hornet) 489, 1967			425
Black Knight, various issues			15
Blackbeard, 463, 1965			175
Blue Knight, various issues			12
Bride of Frankenstein, 482, 1964			600

Aurora King Kong No. 468 figure kit. Photo by Barry Goodman

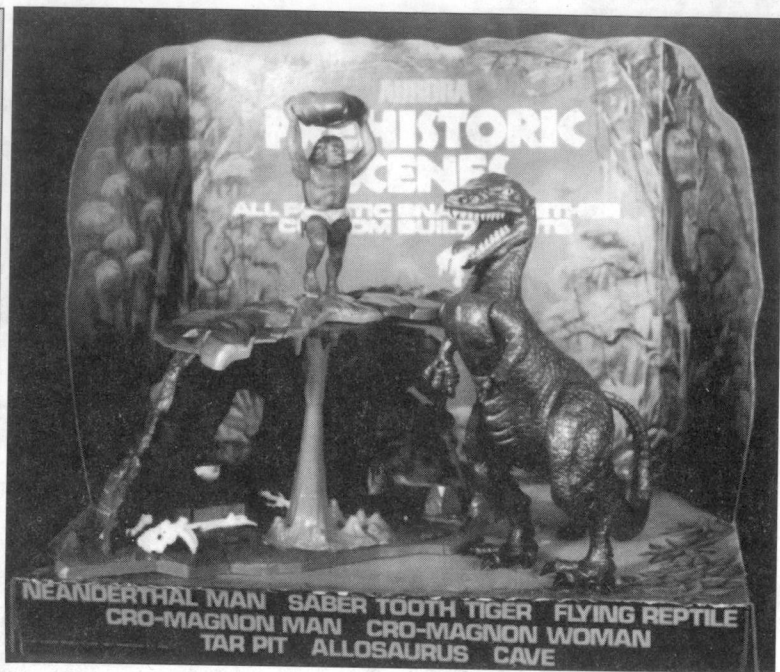

AURORA Store Display of its Prehistoric Scenes showing Cro-Magnon Man. Courtesy Toy Collector News. Photo by Rex Gray.

Aurora Godzilla's Go-Cart. Greg Roccaro Collection. Courtesy David Welch.

Aurora Gigantic Frankenstein ("Big Frankie"). Greg Roccaro Collection. Courtesy David Welch.

Aurora King Kong's Thronester. Greg Roccaro Collection. Courtesy David Welch.

	C6	C8	C10
Captain Action, 480, 1966			225
Captain America, 476, 1966			250
Captain America Comic Scenes, 192, 1974			80
Captain Kidd, 464, 1965			125
Cave, 732, 1972			30
Cave Bear, 738, 1972			50
Chinese Girl, 416, 1957			35
Chinese Mandarin, 415, 1957			35
Chitty Chitty Bang Bang, 828, 1968			60
Confederate Raider, 402, 1959			350
Crusader, K7, 1959			100
Creature From the Black Lagoon, 426, 1963			350
Creature From the Black Lagoon, Glow, 483, 1969/1972			150
Creature From the Black Lagoon, Monsters of the Movies, 654, 1975			150
Cro Magnon Man, 730, 1971			40
Cro Magnon Woman, 731, 1971			40
Customizing Monster Kit No. 1, 463, 1963			135
Customizing Monster Kit No. 2, 464, 1963			135
D'Artagnan, 410, 1966			90
Dempsey vs. Firpo, 861, 1965			65
Dick Tracy, 818, 1968			165
Dick Tracy Space Coupe, 819, 1968			135
Dimetrodon, 745, 1974			75
Dr. Deadly's Daughter, (The Victim), Monster Scenes, 632, 1971			90
Dr. Deadly, Monster Scenes, 631, 1971			120
Dr. Jekyll, 460, 1965			275
Dr. Jekyll, Glow, 482, 1969/1972			100
Dr. Jekyll, Monsters of the Movies, 654, 1975			50
Dracula, 424, 1962			300
Dracula's Dragster, 466, 1966			350
Dracula, Frightening Lightening, 424/454, 1969			350
Dracula, Glow, 454, 1969/1972			100
Dracula, Monsters of the Movies, 656, 1975			165
Dutch Boy, 413, 1957			35
Dutch Girl, 414, 1957			35
Flying Reptile, 734, 1974			70
Flying Saucer, 256, 1975			95
Flying Sub, 254, 1975			100
Flying Sub, 817, 1968			175
Forgotten Prisoner, 422, 1966 (Repros Say "1992 Tomy")			450
Forgotten Prisoner, Frightening Lightening, 422/453, 1969			500
Forgotten Prisoner, Glow, 453, 1969/1972			135
Frankenstein, 423, 1961			295
Frankenstein, Frightening Lightening, 423/449, 1969			325
Frankenstein, Glow, 449, 1969/1972			135
Frankenstein, Monster Scenes 633, 1971			175
Frankenstein, Monsters of the Movies, 651, 1975			175
Frankenstein's Flivver, 465, 1964			325
Frog, The 451, 1966			225
George Washington, 852, 1965			100
Ghidrah, Monsters of the Movies, 658, 1975			285
Giant Bird, 739, 1972			75
Giant Woolly Mammoth, 743, 1972			100
Gigantic Frankenstein ("Big Frankie") 470, 1964 with 3 bottles paint & brush			1000+
Gladiator, 405, 1959 with sword			175
Gladiator, 406, 1959 with trident			175
Godzilla, 469, 1964			500
Godzilla, Glow, 466, 1969/1972			150
Godzilla's Go-Cart, 485, 1966			1000+
Gold Knight on Horseback, K5,1957/475, 1965			200
Green Beret, 413, 1966			100
Gruesome Goodies, Monster Scenes, 634, 1971			100
Guillotine, 800, 1964			500
Hanging Cage, Monster Scenes, 637, 1971			100
Hercules, 481, 1965			250
Horned Dinosaur, 741, 1972			75
Hulk, 421, 1966			200
Hulk, Comic Scenes 184, 1974			75
Hunchback, 461, 1964			250
Hunchback of Notre Dame, 481, 1969/1972			100
Illya Kuryakin, 412, 1966			175
Indian Chief, 417, 1957			60
Indian Squaw, 418, 1957			60
James Bond, 414, 1966			250
Jerry West, 865, 1965			110
Jesse James, 408, 1966			200
Jimmy Brown, 863, 1965			90
John F. Kennedy, 851, 1964			110
Johnny Unitas, 864, 1965			90
Jungle Swamp, 740, 1972			100
King Kong, 468, 1964			500
King Kong's Thronester, 484, 1966			1000+
King Kong, Glow, 465, 1969/1972			100
Land of the Giants, Snake Scene, 816, 1968			350
Land of the Giants Spaceship, 830, 1968			400
Lone Ranger, 808, 1967			125
Lone Ranger, Comic Scenes, 188, 1974			35
Lost In Space, 419, 1966			700
Lost in Space, 420, 1966			950
Mad Barber, 455			1000+
Mexican Caballero, 421, 1957			45
Mexican Senorita, 422, 1957			45
Mod Squad Woodie, 583, 1970			100
Moon Bus, 829, 1968 (2001: A Space Odyssey)			210
Mr. Hyde, Monsters of the Movies, 655, 1975			35
Mummy, 427, 1963			250
Mummy's Chariot, 459, 1965			425
Mummy, Frightening Lightening, 427/452, 1969			300
Mummy, Glow, 452, 1969/1972			90
Munsters Family, 804, 1965			700
Napoleon Solo, 411, 1966			175
Neanderthal Man, 729, 1972			50

	C6	C8	C10
Nutty Nose Nipper, 806, 1965			175
Odd Job, 415, 1966			300
Orion, 252, 1975			95
Pain Parlor, 635, 1971			125
Pan Am Space Clipper, 148, 1968 (2001: A Space Odyssey)			150
Pendulum, The, Monster Scenes, 636, 1971			120
Penguin, 416, 1967			475
Phantom of the Opera, 428, 1963			275
Phantom of the Opera, 451, 1969/1972			90
Phantom of the Opera, Frightening Lightening, 428/451, 1969			350
Porthos, K9, 1958			75
Pushmi-Pullyu, (Dr. Doolittle) 814, 1968			75
Rat Patrol Diorama, 340, 1967			100
Red Knight, various issues			30
Robin, 488, 1966			80
Robin, Comic Scenes, 193, 1974			75
Robot, 418, 1968 (Lost in Space)			700
Rodan, Monsters of the Movies, 657, 1975			275
Sabre Tooth Tiger, 722, 1972			90
Scotch Lad, 419, 1957			40
Scotch Lassie, 420, 1957			40
Seaview, 707, 1966			250
Seaview, 253, 1975			100
Silver Knight, various issues			15
Spartacus, 405, 1965			180
Spiderman, 477, 1966			250
Spiderman, Comic Scenes, 182, 1974			100
Spiked Dinosaur, 742, 1972			90
Spindrift, 255, 1975			100
Steve Canyon, 404, 1966			125
Superboy, 478, 1965			250
Superboy, Comic Scenes, 186, 1974			95
Superman, 562, 1963			225
Superman, Comic Scenes, 185, 1974			65
Tar Pit, 735, 1971			100
Tarzan, 820, 1967			125
Tarzan, Comic Scenes, 181, 1974			24
Tonto, 809, 1967			135
Tonto, Comic Scenes, 183, 1974			20
Tyrannosaurus Rex, 746, 1974			200
U.S. Infantryman, 1956			75
U.S. Marine, 412, 1956			75
U.S. Marshall, 408, 1959			100
U.S. Sailor, 410, 1958			75
U.F.O., 813, 1968			200
Undertakers Dragster, 570			250
Vampire, 452, 1966			250
Vampirella, Monster Scenes, 638, 1971			175
Viking, K6, 1959			120
Voyager, 831, 1969 (Fantastic Voyage)			500
Wacky Back Whacker, 807, 1965			200
Willie Mays, 860, 1965			200

	C6	C8	C10
Witch, Glow, 470, 1969/1972			120
Witch, 483, 1965			250
Wolfman, 425, 1962			300
Wolfman's Wagon, 458, 1965			450
Wolfman, Frighting Lightening, 425/450, 1969			350
Wolfman, Glow, 450, 1969/1972			100
Wolfman, Monsters of the Movies, 652, 1975			175
Wonder Woman, 479, 1965			550
Zorro, 801, 1965			150

ADDAR

Caesar, Planet Of The Apes, 106, 1974	$25
Cornelius, Planet Of The Apes, 101, 1973	$25
Cornfield Roundup, Super Scenes, 216, 1975	$18
Dr. Zaius, Planet Of The Apes, 102, 1973	$25
Dr. Zira, Planet Of The Apes, 105, 1974	$25
General Aldo, Planet Of The Apes, 104, 1974	$25
General Ursus, Planet Of The Apes, 103, 1974	$25
Jail Wagon, Super Scenes, 217, 1975	$18
Soldier On Stallion, Planet Of The Apes, 107, 1975	$35
Spirit In A Bottle, Super Scenes, 227, 1975	$25
Tree House, Super Scenes, 215, 1975	$25

AMT

Bigfoot, 7701	$25
Dragula, Munsters TV Car, 905, 1964	$165
Exploration Set, 958, 1974	$75
Fred Flintstones Family Sedan, 496, 1974	$45
Fred Flintstones Rock Cruncher, 497, 1974	$45
Fred Flintstones Sports Car, 495, 1974	$45
Galileo 7, 959, 1974	$45
Klingon Cruiser, 922, 1967	$120
Klingon Cruiser, 952	$65
Klingon Cruiser, 971, 1979	$27.50
Klingon Cruiser, 6682, 1985	$12.50
K-7 Space Station, 955, 1975	$40
Mr. Spock With Snake, 956, 1975	$60
Mr. Spock Without Snake, 973, 1979	$30
Munsters Koach, Munsters TV, 1964	$175
Romulan Ship, 957, 1975	$45
Spaceship Set, 953, 1975	$60
Spaceship Set, 6677, 1984	$27.50
USS Enterprise With Lights, 931, 1967	$175
USS Enterprise Without Lights, 951, 1976	$50
USS Enterprise, 970, 1979	$27.50
USS Enterprise, 6676, 1983	$18
USS Enterprise, 6675, 1985	$18
USS Enterprise Bridge, 950, 1975	$27.50
Vulcan Shuttle, 5112, 1979	$24
Vulcan Shuttle, 972, 1980	$24
Vulcan Shuttle, 6679, 1985	$15

HAWK

Beach Bunny Catchin Rays, 542, 1964	65
Daddy The Swingin Suburbanite, 532, 1963	65

	C6	C8	C10
Davey The Psycho Cyclist, 531, 1963			65
Digger The Way Out Dragster, 530, 1963			65
Drag Hag, 536, 1963			65
Endsville Eddy, 537, 1963			65
Francis The Foul, 535, 1963			30
Frantic Banana Punishing Skins, 548, 1965			75
Frantic Cats, 549, 1965			75
Freddie Flameout, 533, 1963			75
Hodad Making The Scene, 543, 1964			75
Hot Dogger Hangin Ten, 541, 1964			75
Hot Dogger Hangin Ten, 164, 1970, Glow			45
Huey's Hut Rod, 538, 1963			75
Huey's Hut Rod, 163, 1969, Glow			45
Killer McBash, 539, 1963			75
Leaky Boat Louie, 534, 1963			75
Riding Tandem, 544, 1965			75
Sling Rave Curvette, 637, 1964			25
Steel Pluckers Havin A Bash, 547, 1965			75
Totally Fab, 550, 1965			75
Wade A. Minit, 636, 1964			75
Wierdsville Customizing Kit, 301, 1964			300
Woodie On A Surfari, 540, 1964			75
Woodie On A Surfari, 165, 1970			40

LINDBERG

	C6	C8	C10
Big Wheeler, 277, 1965			100
Blurp, 280, 1964			45
Creeping Crusher, 273, 1965			100
Glob, 281, 1964			45
Green Ghoul, 274, 1965			100
Krimson Terror, 272, 1965			150
Mad Maestro, 284, 1965			175
Mad Mangler, 275, 1965			100
Road Hog, 276, 1965			100
Satan's Crate, 279, 1965			200
Scuttle Bucket, 278, 1965			100
Voop, 283, 1964			45
Zopp, 282, 1964			45

MONOGRAM

	C6	C8	C10
Dracula, 6008, 1983, re-issue of Aurora kit			25
Flip Out, Fred Flypogger, 105, 1965			100
Frankenstein, 6007, Aurora re-issue			25
Godzilla, 6300, 1978 Aurora re-issue			40
Mummy, 6010, 1983, Aurora re-issue			25
Speed Shift, Fred Flypogger, 106, 1965			100
Super Fuzz, Fred Flypogger, 104, 1965			150
Superman, 6301, 1978, Aurora re-issue			15
Wolfman, 6009, 1983, Aurora re-issue			25

MPC

	C6	C8	C10
Alian, 1961, movie, 1979			95
Barnabas Collins, TV Dark Shadows, 1550, 1969			200
Barnabas Vampire Van, TV Dark Shadows, 1626, 1969			135
Batman, 1702, 1984, Aurora re-issue			20

	C6	C8	C10
C3PO, Star Wars, 1913, 1978-1980			15
C3PO, Star Wars, 1935, 1983			10
Condemned To Chains, 5003, 1973, Disney Pirates Of Caribbean			30
Curl's Girl, 103, 1965			75
Curl's Girl With Hot Shot, 103, 1965			75
Darth Vader, 1916, 1978/1980			20
Dead Man's Raft, 5005, 1973, Pirates Of Caribbean			65
Dead Men Tell No Tales, 5001, 1973, Disney Pirates of Caribbean			65
Escape From The Crypt, 5053, 1974, Disney Haunted Mansion			65
Fate Of the Mutineer, 5004, 1974, Disney Pirates Of Caribbean			65
Freed In The Nick Of Time, 5007, 1973, Pirates Of The Caribbean			65
Ghost Of America With Stroker McGurk, 104, 1964			110
Ghost Of The Treasure, 5006, 1973, Pirates Of Caribbean			65
Grave Robbers Reward, 5050, 1974, Disney Haunted Mansion			65
Hoist High The Jolly Roger, 5002, 1973, Pirates of Caribbean			65
Hot Curl, 101, 1965			75
Hot Shot With Hot Dog, 103, 1965			75
Incredible Hulk, 1932, 1979			20
Play It Again Sam, 5052, 1974, Disney Haunted Mansion			65
Raiders Coach, Paul Revere & Raiders, 1969, 0622			150
R2-D2, Star Wars, 1912, 1978 1980			20
R2-D2, Star Wars, 1934, 1983			10
Spiderman, 1931, 1978			20
Stroker McGurk And Surf Rod, 100, 1964			65
Superman, 1701, 1985, Aurora re-issue			20
Tall T With Stroker McGurk, 102, 1964			65
Vampire Midnight Madness, 5051, 1974, Disney Haunted Mansion			75
Werewolf, TV Dark Shadows, 1552, 1969			210
Yellow Submarine, Beatles, 617, 1968			225

MULTIPLE

	C6	C8	C10
Automatic Baby Feeder, 955, 1965			20
Back Scrubber and Hat Remover, 958, 1965			20
Disappearing Lady, 1257, 1966			45
Floating On Air, 1256, 1966			45
Iron Maiden, 981, 1966			120
Painless Tooth Extractor, 956, 1965			20
Saw The Lady In Half, 1258, 1966			45
Signal For Shipwrecked Sailor, 957, 1965			20
Torture Chair, 980, 1966			120
Torture Wheel, 979, 1966			120

PYRO

	C6	C8	C10
The Curler, 177, 1970			35
Der Baron, 166, 1970			35
Ghost Rider, 167, 1970			35

	C6	C8	C10
The Gladiator, 175, 1970			35
Lil Corporal, 168, 1970			35
Rawhide, 276, 1958			60
Restless Gun, 277, 1958			60
Surf's Up, 176, 1970			40
Wyatt Earp, 278, 1958			60

REMCO

	C6	C8	C10
Flintstones Sports Car, 450, 1961			125
Flintstones Yacht, 451, 1961			125
Flintstones Paddy Wagon, 452, 1961			125

REVELL

	C6	C8	C10
Angel Fink, 1307, 1965			150
Beatnik Bandit, 1279, 1963, Ed Roth			100
Birthday Bird, 2051, 1960 (Dr. Seuss)			150
Bonanza, 1931, 1966			120
Brother Rat Fink, 1304, 1964			50
Busby The Afghan Yak, 2006, 1959, (Dr. Seuss)			150
Cat In The Hat, 2000, 1958 (Dr. Seuss)			150
Cat In The Hat With Thing 1&2, 2050, 1960 (Dr. Seuss)			150
Dragnut, 1303, 1963, Ed Roth			95
Fink Eliminator, 1310,. 1965, Ed Roth			200
Flash Gordon and Martian, 1450, 1965			120

	C6	C8	C10
Flipper and Sandy, 1930, 1965			90
Game of the Yertle, 2100, 1960 (Dr. Seuss)			125
George Harrison, 1353, 1964			150
Gowdy The Dowdy Grackle, 2002, 1958 (Dr. Seuss)			150
Grickily The Gractus, 2005, 1959 (Dr. Seuss)			150
Grickily, Busby, and Rosco, 2081, 1060 (Dr. Seuss)			250
Horton The Elephant, 2052, 1960 (Dr. Seuss)			150
John Lennon, 1352, 1964			150
Mothers Worry, 1302, 1963, Ed Roth			100
Mr. Gasser, 1301, 1963, Ed Roth			100
Norval The Bashful Blinket, 2003, 1959 (Dr. Seuss)			150
Outlaw, Ed Roth			100
Paul McCartney, 1350, 1964			110
Phantom And Witch Doctor, 1451, 1965			120
Rat Fink, 1305, 1963			40
Ringo Starr, 1351, 1964			110
Robbin Hood Fink, 1270, 1965, Ed Roth			300
Roscoe The Many Footed Lion, 2004, 1959 (Dr.Seuss)			150
Scuz Fink, 1308, 1964			300
Superfink, 1308, 1964			300
Surfink, 1306, 1965			100
Tingo The Stroodle, 2001, 1958 (Dr. Seuss)			150
Tingo, Gowdy, And Norval, 2080, 1960, (Dr. Seuss)			300
Tweedy Pie With Boss Fink, 1271, 1965 Ed Roth			200

PEZ CANDY DISPENSERS

by David Welch

(Pez in C10 condition in the last edition averaged $64.67. In this, they 'average $142.19, an increase of 111%.)

Pez candy dispensers first became available in the US around 1950. The candy itself was produced in Austria as far back as the 1930s. It wasn't until the late 1940s that the "box" or dispenser became available with the candy. The very first dispenser had no head (the aspect most of us associate with Pez), making it resemble a Bic lighter. Soon thereafter, a Spacegun, full-bodied Santa and Robot, and many more appeared. Who can forget the fun of your favorite cartoon friends tilting their heads back to give you a piece of Pez candy?!

Over the years, Pez dispensers have been manufactured in Austria, Yugoslavia, Hong Kong and USA. Dispensers are usually marked with one of these four patent numbers: (a) 2,620,061; (b) 3,410,455; (c) 3,845,882; or (d) 3,942,683. It is virtually impossible to date a dispenser with any surety, although the patent number can sometimes be a vague indicator. Neither the country of origin, patent number, nor age are necessarily tied to value. The bottom line on value is which head is on the dispenser!

Since their introduction in the US, Pez dispensers have been continuously available to present day. As of January, 1991, there are approximately 250 different Pez dispensers known. This figure excludes color variation and other minor differences occurring on individual dispensers. Only the most valuable dispensers are currently listed here. Other companies such as Totems, Yummies, and Smarties copied the dispenser-with-head concept but none have approached the universal acceptance of Pez.

CONDITION

Prices given are for excellent or better condition dispensers. Defects such as missing pieces, melt marks, scuffs, excessive dirt, and cracks decrease the value by a minimum of 20%. The condition of the cartridge that holds the candy does not affect value as much as the condition of the head. Exceptions to this rule apply in the cases of Regulars, Die-Cuts, Guns, Zorro A, Psychedelics and other dispensers in which the cartridge itself is an important part of the identity or appearance. Missing head pieces and facial melt marks can render most dispensers virtually valueless. However, the heads alone are sometimes of value on the most expensive dispensers.

Pez Gun, B. Handgun. Courtesy Barry Koester.

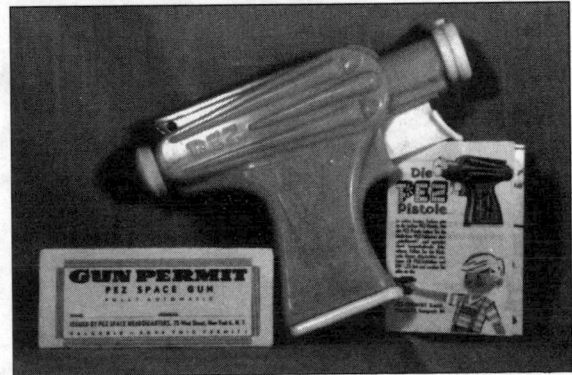

Pez Gun, A. Space 1950s. Courtesy Barry Koester.

	C10
Alpine, 1972 Olympics	450
Arithmetic	200
Astronaut	
A. White helmet	70
B. Blue helmet	70
C. Clear helmet	85
D. Clear helmet with "Cocoa Marsh" on side	100
E. Small helmet (silver or white)	200
Baseball Glove with ball	110
with home plate/bat	250
Batman with cape	90
Betsy Ross	45
Bozo	90
Bozo Die-Cut ("Bozo/Butch" on side)	110
Bride with white veil	400
Brutus (from Popeye)	110
Bullwinkle	115
Camel Whistle	10
Captain	75
Casper	80
Casper Die-Cut ("Casper" on side)	100
Chick in Egg (no hat)	70
Clown with "Pez" on hat (Peter Pez) No Feet	60
Cow with large nose, circular ears	70
Cowboy	175
Creature From the Black Lagoon	
A. With green cartridge/head	125
B. Darker green head/orange cartridge	95
C. Black head	115

Crocodile 45

Daniel Boone with coonskin cap 90

Doctor 45

Dog 40

Donald Duck Die-Cut (3 Duck nephews on side) ... 90

Dopey 100

Easter Bunny with thin/straight ears 120

Easter Bunny Die-Cut (bunny with eggs on side) 300

Football Player 75

Frankenstein 125

Giraffe 45

Green Hornet 185

Groom with black top hat and hat band 120

Gun

    A. Space 1950s 115

    B. Handgun (mail-order premium) 125

    C. Space 1980s 60

Indian Brave 100

Indian Chief 40

Indian Squaw 50

Joker, softhead (Batman) 60

Knight 100

Koala whistle 12

Lion's Club Lion, 1962 400

Make-A-Face (similar to Mr. Potato Head) with approxi-
    mately 24 face pieces .... 800 +

Mary Poppins 300

Mickey Mouse Die-Cut ("Minnie" on side) 90

Monsters, softheads, 6 different, each 70

Olive Oyl 120

Orange 65

Panther, blue head 45

Pear with visor 375

Penguin, softhead (from Batman) 60

Peter Pan 85

Pilgrim 65

Pineapple 400

Pinocchio, (old version) has eyes looking up, feather
    is part of hat 90

Popeye, (old version) hat cannot be removed 90

Psychedelic Eye, hand holding eyeball 250

Psychedelic Flower, eyeball in flower 300

Regular (no heads)

    A. Personalized, has paper label on side 125

    B. Witch, has pictures of witches on side .... 750+

    C. Golden Glow, with gold shiny finish 75

    D. US Zone Germany marking 120

    E. With none of the above markings 100

Rhino Whistle 12

Robot, full body (3 colors) 200

Sailor, full white beard with blue hat 70

Santa, full body 100

Santa, face and beard same color 70

Santa, small head with flesh face and white beard 80

Snow White 65

Snowman with Arms, 1976 Olympics 275

Stewardess 65

Thor (helmet with wings) 90

Tinkerbell 100

Uncle Sam 60

Witch, 1 piece orange head 110

Wolf, 1984 Olympics

    A. Ski hat 350

    B. Bobsled hat 350

    C. No hat 350

Wolfman 120

Wounded Soldier 90

Zorro

    A. Says "Zorro" on side 65

    B. Without "Zorro" on side 30

Pez Make-A-Face. Courtesy Barry Koester.

Pez, Left to Right: Mickey Mouse, Donald Duck, Easter Bunny, Casper, Bozo, all die cut. Courtesy Barry Koester.

Pez, Left to Right: Psychedelic Eye, Psychedelic Flower. Courtesy Barry Koester.

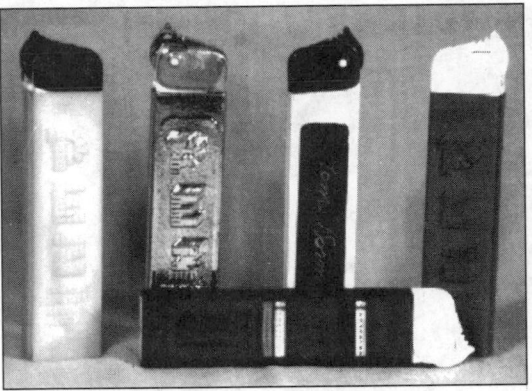

Pez, Left to Right: Regular E, C, A, E. Bottom: Arithmetic. Courtesy Barry Koester.

Pez, Left to Right: Santa Face and beard same, full body, flesh face. Courtesy Barry Koester.

Pez, Left to Right: Uncle Sam, Wounded Soldier, Betsy Ross, Captain, Daniel Boone (1976 Bicentennials). Courtesy Barry Koester.

Pez Wolf, 1984 Olympics, Left to Right: A, C, B, Snowman with Arms. Courtesy Barry Koester.

Pez, Left to Right: Regular B. Witch, Witch, 1 piece. Courtesy Barry Koester.

Pez, Left to Right: Wolfman, Creature from Black Lagoon, Frankenstein. Courtesy Barry Koester.

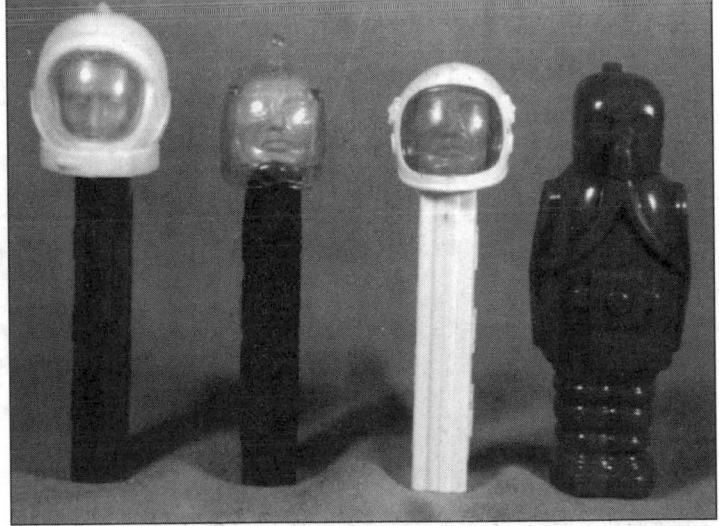

Pez Astronauts, Left to Right: A, C, E, Robot, full body. Courtesy Barry Koester.

Pez, Left to Right: Indian Squaw, Indian Chief, Indian Brave, Pilgrim (1976 Bicentennials). Courtesy Barry Koester.

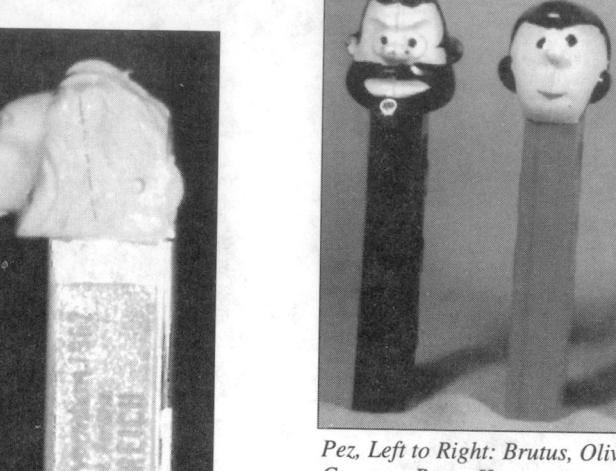

Pez, Left to Right: Brutus, Olive Oyl, Popeye. Courtesy Barry Koester.

Pez Lion's Club Lion. Courtesy Barry Koester.

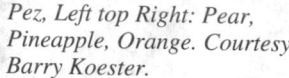

Pez, Left top Right: Pear, Pineapple, Orange. Courtesy Barry Koester.

Pez, Left to Right: Groom, Bride. Courtesy Mary Ann Kennedy.

Pez Monsters, Soft Heads, Left to Right: Spook, Air Spirit, Vamp, Zombie, Spook, Diabolic. Courtesy Barry Koester.

Pez, Left to Right: Dopey, Snow White, Peter Pan, unlisted, Tinkerbell. Courtesy Barry Koester.

PREMIUMS

The average mint price of premiums was $80.86 in the last edition,
rising to $109.34 in this, an increase of 35%.
(Not included in the pricing is the Superman Comics Magazine Ring.)

TOYS FREE AS THE AIR

By Jim Harmon

Many radio premiums were nearly as free as the wonderful radio shows that advertised them.

We did have to pay the electric bill (or our folks did) to run the radio, and to get the offered toys we did have to send in a box-top from the sponsor's product.

Sometimes it was only that, a proof of purchase (Orphan Annie and Captain Midnight were particularly generous in responding with gifts for inner labels or inner seals from Ovaltine drink mix) and other times, usually only a dime was required "to handle the cost of handling and mailing". (That's really all it did do - the cost of the premium itself came from the advertising budget.)

The lure of the premium to kids then and for grown-up kids who are now collectors is difficult to explain to those who never lived through the era themselves. The ring or badge was more than the toy itself; it was our tangible link to those magical friends on the other side of the speaker cloth.

Those voices were wonderful out there - The rumbling bass of Brace Beemer as the Lone Ranger; the slightly "country" sound of Curley Bradley as Tom Mix; Bret Morrison, whom we recognized even as children was "sophisticated" as Lamont Cranston, alias The Shadow - but they were bodiless and yes, a bit remote.

It was the premium they offered, the same as the one they were using in the story, that put us in touch with them.

There were historic precedents for radio premiums. There were pictures of famous actresses in cigarette packages around the turn of the century, and early radio personalities, such as bandleader Vincent Lopez, offered their autographed pictures. But such footnotes to history aside, radio premiums began with **Little Orphan Annie** in 1931. The plucky little waif from the Sunday comics first gave away sheet music of her theme song ("Who's that little chatterbox with the pretty auburn locks?") and her own photo, but very shortly, she offered a drinking mug that could be used to shake-up Ovaltine powder with milk to make something resembling a soda fountain milk shake. The first significant radio premium, it was the only successful one that encouraged further use of the sponsor's product.

Many different models of the shake-up mug were offered by Annie, and later by Captain Midnight (on both radio and TV). So successful were the offers, shake-up mugs are not rare or high in dollar value. (The most sought after is the orange and blue, embossed - not decaled - Midnight mug.)

It took two more years after Annie came to radio for the fledgling medium to develop its really classic adventure heroes. In 1933, there appeared the Lone Ranger, Tom Mix and Jack Armstrong. Unlike Annie, the two Westerners and the All-American Boy were still around until the 1950s, when television began driving out all radio drama. In those nearly twenty years, these shows offered hundreds of give-away toys, which inspired similar premiums on dozens of other shows.

Any small toy that could be manufactured inexpensively enough might turn up as a premium. Those concerned with the great outdoors were popular. We had compasses, pedometers, telescopes, flashlights, pocketknives, signal mirrors, portable telegraph sets.

The secret society of childhood had its emblems and tokens. So had secret decoders and secret manuals of every size and description. It is these and other **paper** items that have the greatest dollar value. They were the most easily lost or used up in the rush to adulthood. A Captain Midnight Secret Manual is worth more than the metallic decoder it accompanied.

The rarest paper item is the Lone Ranger Frontier Town offered about 1947. To complete this model of a Western village, one had to get four different envelopes by mail, then augment this by buying several packages of Cheerios to cut out the model buildings from the packs. The complete set has been known to sell for hundreds of dollars and today might bring $1,500.00, the highest dollar premium.

Perhaps the most popular single type of premium was the ring. Rings let the listener show his loyalty to the fraternity of his favorite hero, but in a less officious and more "grown-up" way than the badge (although they were also highly popular). Besides . . . the rings looked neat, and many of them could **do** things - some of them pretty incredible things.

As with radio premiums in general, the Tom Mix show (and Ralston cereal's premium manufacturer, the Robbins Company) blazed the trail with ingenious ring designs. In 1937, Tom Mix Straight Shooters could get a Signet Ring with their own initial on it. (Years later, Captain Midnight would offer a ring that would ink-stamp your initial.) By 1938, Tom had a ring that let you look in a peep-hole and see a magnified picture of himself and his horse, Tony. (Technology had progressed so much that by the fifties, Straight Arrow offered a similar ring that put your own photo, if supplied, alongside radio's great Indian hero.)

After World War II and the ease in metal rationing, Tom Mix offered a Magnet Ring (good for picking up paperclips - like the one on the stolen plans to the atomic bomb, in Tom's case). His spinning siren whistle ring was neat (but admittedly borrowed in design from Jack Armstrong's 1937 Egyptian Whistle Ring). Tom's Sliding Whistle Ring that played different musical notes (about 1948) was unique, however. His Look-Around Ring concealed an inner mirror that let you see behind you (sort of), a design rustled for a later Tennessee Jed ring.

The final Tom Mix ring looked attractive, sporting a glowing cat's-eye, but the Tiger-Eye Ring was only lightweight plastic in 1949, a far cry from the well-crafted metal rings of a decade earlier. But then, the decade was nearly over, and so was the era, fading in the light of another glowing eye in the living room.

The Shadow's own Glow-in-the-Dark Ring in 1939 has a band composed of two sculpted Shadow Figures holding up a jagged blue stone - a proxy lump of his sponsor's product, Blue Coal. One of the very few Shadow premiums and the best-looking, this ring has sold for $950.

One glowing plastic ring - the identical mold - was used for several different radio shows. The band had two crocodiles holding a setting in their mouths. The "stone" was **black** when it was Jack Armstrong's Dragon Eye Ring in 1940. It was **green** for "Terry and the Pirates" in the mid-forties, but it was **black** for Carey Salt's Shadow ring in 1947 (not the rare Blue Coal model). The setting was **red** for Buck Roger's Ring of Saturn in 1945. It is back to **black** in the slightly lumpy counterfeit being manufactured today, one of the handful of premiums of simple enough design to be faked for profit. The best way to authenticate these rings is by the accompanying paper instruction sheets, naming the famous character whose prize it is.

These rings, as are all radio premiums, are worth whatever you will pay to possess them. A fair average price is $60 with $300 a top price for very rare, complex and fragile items. Of course, many items are priced much higher. But nobody who is not familiar with the whole field should pay more. Even though $500 or more may be easier to come by today than a dime and a box-top were in those days of yesteryear.

There has been a radical change in the prices of radio and early TV premiums (and associated toys), beginning in 1992 and reaching a new status in 1994. For nearly twenty years, there had been no appreciable rise in premium prices. In fact, premium prices had not even kept up with inflation. You could have bought a Tom Mix Magnet Ring for $35 in 1967 and bought the Magnet Ring for the same $35 in 1987. But now there has come a radical change in premium pricing, especial-

ly for rings. The Magnet Ring generally brings $95 in 1994.

Part of the reason is the unnatural influence of "investor" types who have manipulated the market, much as they had the old comic book market for years. The results have been mixed. Prices have risen, but the number of premium collectors and the number of premium objects is far smaller than their counterparts in the comic book field. As a result, most premiums have virtually disappeared from the market. Now is the time to buy, if premiums can be found. They may never be cheaper, and they may never be seen again.

Despite rarity, **condition** is still very important. No matter how rare, a premium that is battered, defaced or broken is virtually worthless. Premiums with missing parts can be worth something, since the missing part might be matched up eventually.

New stores of premiums newly found in attics no longer seem to be turning up. But older collectors who have amassed collections are retiring from their occupations, and sadly, selling their collections for needed money. Some die, and survivors sell. These collectors and families know the value of collectibles and sell for top market value. The number of these "retiring" collectors is still fairly small and does not greatly affect the general state of rarity of premiums.

The items connected to once well-known characters, and those still famous, such as the Lone Ranger, Tom Mix, Buck Rogers, Buck Jones and Gene Autry, have the highest prices, prices still on the rise. Minor and nearly forgotten characters such as Scoop Ward and Speed Gibson are still not being given away. The knowledge of the dealer that these were once well-known characters will generally prevent a button from selling under $15, a badge for not less than $25, or a ring for not under $30.

Rings have a great appeal to many, and are the hottest ticket in the premium market - the rare ones are going up and up. The Shadow Blue Coal Ring, Green Hornet Seal Ring, and Captain Midnight Mystic Sun God Ring will probably go over the thousand dollar mark soon.

Cereal boxes of the sponsors who offered the premiums, especially with premium offers on the boxes, have become valuable. Near the top of the line are complete boxes of the nine Lone Ranger Frontier Town Cheerios packs (about two hundred dollars each; the backs off the boxes with unassembled model buildings can go for thirty-five). Tom Mix Ralston boxes (late '40's—50's) go for up to $400.

A few new authentic premiums have appeared in recent years: Boraxo offered a 20 Mule Team model in 1980 (similar to the Death Valley Days original of the '30s, '40s, and '50s); Cheerios offered a Lone Ranger Deputy Kit in 1981 styled after the movie of that year but similar to earlier offers with mask, badge, etc.

In 1982, Ralston began a limited Tom Mix revival with which the present author, Jim Harmon, was involved; offering a set of four Mix Ralston cereal bowls, a wind-up wrist watch, a Straight Shooters membership kit, a Tom Mix photo. a Mix in-box miniature comic book (edited by Harmon), and a Long Play recording with old Mix radio episodes and one 1983 episode featuring Curley Bradley and produced by Harmon. In 1993-94, Ralston again showcased Tom Mix on their boxes, but offered only a chance for the customer to write in their memories of Tom.

In 1987, Ovaltine resurrected their original formula in jars, and instituted new premiums of their character, Captain Midnight of the Secret Squadron, with a tee-shirt that year, with a Midnight digital watch in 1988, and armpatch in 1989 (apparently the last of the cur-rent revival). Dick Tracy premiums came with the new movie in 1990, such as the Quaker wrist radio. Superman continued his over fifty-year-long association with Kellogg's cereals in 1994, appearing on the box, and inside with a mini-comic book for Kellogg's Cinnamon Mini-Buns.

Prices on these are already comparable to older premiums, topped by the Tom Mix watch at $300. The biggest premium news of the early '90's was the sale of a Superman comic book premium ring for a record $18,000 and then resale for $43,000. But this event was really a part of the world of incredibly-priced Golden Age comic books. In effect, the ring was treated as another rare old comic book, not as the premium ring it was. This astonishing sale could only raise the value of a real radio premium, the Superman Crusaders Club ring, from $65 to a less than overwhelming $185. Real radio and TV premiums from broadcast series still have broken the $1,000 barrier only with the complete Lone Ranger Frontier Town, so far as can be documented.

JIM HARMON is a writer of non-fiction (The Great Radio Heroes) and science fiction (including the often-anthologized "The Place Where Chicago Was"), magazine editor (Monsters of the Movies) and has written virtually every category of fiction and non-fiction, writing for hardcovers, paperbacks, pulp magazines (Famous Western), slick magazines (TV Guide), providing scripts and action performances for movies, television and, jprobably more than any other person currently active, dramatized radio. After finding the legendary but reclusive Curley Bradley, Harmon produced first a new Western/mystery series of Curley Bradley's Trail of Mystery in 1975, and went on to produce and act in a new series of Curley Bradley's original role, Tom Mix, in 1982-83 for Hot Ralston cereal. During this period, Harmon also contributed to cereal box design, editorial and art supervision for a new comic book of Mix, a Mix dramatic LP album, and radio-TV appearances of Curley and himself. In 1992, Harmon's new book, Radio Mystery and Adventure appeared to reviews such as "more depth than any other book on radio". For 1995, he hopes to offer new audio productions of the "lost episodes" of Carlton E. Morse's I Love a Mystery. He lives in Burbank, CA with microbiologist wife, Barbara, and near daughter Dawn.

	C6	C8	C10
Admiral Television Studio Giveaway - 1953 paper punchout TV studio and characters, features Sky King, Flight to Mars, Walt Disney's Peter Pan and Three Little Pigs. 15"x16"	62	93	125
Amos & Andy Pepsodent Give-away- Amos' Wedding	42	63	85
Amos & Andy Puzzle	50	75	100
Archie Comics Club Button	5	8	10
Aunt Jemima Breakfast Club Badge, metal	12	18	25
Barney Baxter Junior Birdmen of America wings, metal, circa late 1930s	12	18	25
Bendix Radio - 5½" WW II military figures circa 1944. Color photos with stands. a. Lt. (jg) Navy; b. Marine 1st Lt. (dress uniform); c. Commander-Coast Guard; d. Army Air Force officer with parachute harness; e. 2nd Lt. with modern Mae West; f. Flier with flying suit; g. Capt. Army Air Force; h. Air officer with fur-lined jacket and helmet. Price per each	5	8	10
Betty Boop face mask - 1931 theatre premium	25	38	50
Betty Boop pin "Roxy Theatre, New York," large	17	26	35
Blondie & Dagwood Go To Leisureland, 1940, Westinghouse	10	15	20
Bobby Benson Code Rule 1935 cardboard decoder, Hecker H-O	42	72	95
Bobby Benson's Game Circus, 1934	37	53	75
Buck Jones Club Ring	37	53	75
Buck Jones Horseshoe Pin	37	53	75
Buck Jones Jr. Sheriff Badge	37	53	75
Buck Rogers Badge, enameled	75	112	150
Buck Rogers Birthstone and initial ring	175	263	350
Buck Rogers Chief Explorer Badge	62	93	125
Buck Rogers lead figures, solid, Cocomalt, Buck, Wilma, Killer Kane, per each	12	18	25
Buck Rogers Flight Commander Whistle Badge	75	112	150
Buck Rogers Girl's charm bracelet	75	112	150
Buck Rogers Helmet	175	263	350
Buck Rogers Knife	75	112	150
Buck Rogers Morton Salt Punch-o-Bag, 1930s	37	56	75
Buck Rogers Morton Salt Spaceship (came in envelope)	75	112	150

	C6	C8	C10
Buck Rogers Pendant	37	56	75
Buck Rogers Pinback button, circa 1935, Whitehead and Hoag, "Buck Rogers in the 25th Century"	37	56	75
Buck Rogers Repeller Ray Ring (seal ring)	172	263	350
Buck Rogers Ring of Saturn, glows in the dark, with red stone	150	225	300
Buck Rogers Ring of Saturn Instruction Sheet	37	56	75

BUCK ROGERS ring of Saturn. Courtesy Jim Harmon.

BUCK ROGERS Chemical laboratory. Courtesy HAKE'S Americana & Collectibles.

	C6	C8	C10
Buck Rogers Solar Scouts Badge, all brass color	50	75	100
Buck Rogers Solar Scouts Spaceship Commander Badge, 1936 Cream of Wheat premium	50	75	100
Buck Rogers Solar Scout Sweater Emblem	37	56	75
Buck Rogers Telescope	62	93	125
Buck Rogers items given away for Cream of Wheat green triangle (sold in stores also):			
Buck Rogers Films for projector	7.50	11	15
Buck Rogers Interplanetary Game	75	112	150
Buck Rogers lead figures, hollow lead, Buck, Wilma, Huer, Robot, Kane, Ardala, average price per each, Britains	200	300	400
Buck Rogers Lite Blaster Flashlight	32	48	65
Buck Rogers Movie Projector	100	150	200
Buck Rogers Printing Set (12 rubber stamps)	42	63	85

	C6	C8	C10
Buck Rogers Super Dreadnaught, balsa wood	50	75	100
Buck Rogers Uniform	225	338	450
Buffalo Bill Bamby Bread Horseshoe Badge, late 1930s	12	18	25
Buffalo Bill Jr. brass ring, Buffalo in relief on top, TV premium	22	33	45
Buster Brown Gang (Smilin' Ed) Ring	32	48	65
Buster Brown Gang tab pins, assorted, price per each	10	15	20
Butter-Nut Bread premium, "Sail-Me" glider with 4½" wingspan, c. 1930	7	11	15
Captain America Sentinel of Liberty Badge	125	188	250
Captain Franks Air Hawks Ring	32	48	65
Captain Franks Air Hawks Wings, circa late 1930s, Post's 40% Bran Flakes premium	32	48	65
Captain Gallant Medal, c. 1950 dated 1939-1945 with an animal on it	17	26	35
Captain Gallant Medal, 1950s, this one is a cross with GRI on it	17	26	35
Captain Hawk Sky Patrol Propeller Badge, circa late 1930s	22	33	45
Captain Marvel Club button	37	56	75
Captain Marvel's Magic Whistle c. 1943, American Seed Co. Has full color picture of Captain Marvel on both sides and American Seed Co. ad on the inside	25	38	50
Captain Midnight Aerial Torpedo Bomber (Airplane), 1941	57	85	115
Captain Midnight American Flag Loyalty Badge, 1940	37	56	75
Captain Midnight Flight Patrol Wings Badge, 1941	42	63	85
Captain Midnight Flight Patrol Wings Badge, 1942	42	63	85
Captain Midnight Code-O-Graph Decoder Pin, 1941, Eagle on top	75	112	150
Captain Midnight Code-O-Graph Badge, 1942, with photo of Captain Midnight	88	132	175
Captain Midnight Code-O-Graph, 1945, magnifier	75	112	150
Captain Midnight Code-O-Graph, 1946, Mirrormatic, (best looking, desirable)	100	150	200
Captain Midnight Code-O-Graph, 1947, works as a whistle	37	56	75
Captain Midnight Code-O-Graph, 1948, round, with mirror	62	93	125
Captain Midnight Code-O-Graph, 1949, Key-O-Matic (with key)	100	150	200

	C6	C8	C10
Captain Midnight Detect-O-Scope, 1941	50	75	100
Captain Midnight Flight Commander Commission, 1956	30	45	60
Captain Midnight Flight Commander Flying Cross, 1942	42	63	85
Captain Midnight Flight Commander Ring, 1941	125	188	250
Captain Midnight Flight Commander Signet Ring, 1957	138	205	275
Captain Midnight Flight Commander Ring, 1959	138	205	275

CAPTAIN MIDNIGHT Code-O-Graph Badge, 1942. Courtesy Jim Harmon.

CAPTAIN MIDNIGHT Medal, 1940. Courtesy Jim Harmon.

	C6	C8	C10
Captain Midnight Jumping Bean Target, 1939	17	26	35
Captain Midnight MJC-10 Plane Detector, 1942, distance-finder	62	93	125
Captain Midnight Magic Blackout Lite-Ups, 1942	37	56	75
Captain Midnight 1941 Manual for Decoder	75	112	150
Captain Midnight 1942 Manual for Decoder	125	188	250
Captain Midnight 1945 Manual for Code-O-Graph	50	75	100
Captain Midnight 1946 Manual for Code-O-Graph	47	70	95

	C6	C8	C10
Captain Midnight 1947 Manual for Code-O-Graph	47	70	95
Captain Midnight 1948 Manual for Code-O-Graph	47	70	95
Captain Midnight 1949 Manual for Code-O-Graph	47	70	95
Captain Midnight 1956 Manual for Decoder Badge	125	188	250
Captain Midnight 1957 Manual for Silver Dart decoder	125	188	250
Captain Midnight Marine Corps Ring, 1942	75	112	150
Captain Midnight medal, brass, pictures of cast, secret word, spinner, 1940	12	18	25
Captain Midnight Mystic Eye Detector Ring, 1942	88	132	175
Captain Midnight Mystic Sun God Ring, 1946	375	562	750
Captain Midnight Printing Ring, 1948	75	112	150
Captain Midnight Secret Squadron Decoder Badge, 1955	100	150	200
Captain Midnight Secret Squadron Decoder Badge, 1956	100	150	200
Captain Midnight Secret Squadron Insignia transfer, 1949	17	26	35
Captain Midnight Service Ribbon pin, 1944	37	56	75
Captain Midnight Silver Dart Decoder Badge, 1957	100	150	200
Captain Midnight Spy Scope, 1947	48	72	95
Captain Midnight Surprise Package, 1942	25	38	50
Captain Midnight 3-Way Mystic Dog Whistle, 1942	25	38	50
Captain Midnight Trick and Riddle Book, 1939 Skelly Oil Premium, 64 pages	17	25	35
Captain Midnight Weather Wings, 1940, predicts weather	37	56	75
Captain Midnight Whirlwind Whistling Ring, 1941	75	112	150
Capt. Tim Ivory Club Pin - Ivory Soap, circa 1936	10	15	20
Captain Video Flying Saucer Ring	75	112	150
Captain Video Rite-O-Lite	48	72	95
Captain Video Rocket Launcher and Ships, 1950s	100	150	200
Captain Video Secret Seal Ring, 1950s	88	132	175
Captain Video Space Fleet Ray Gun, 1952, TV premium - Powerhouse	125	188	250
Captain Video X-9 Rocket Balloon, 1950s	27	40	55

	C6	C8	C10
Chandu the Magician Galloping Coin Trick, 1930s	27	40	55
Chandu The Magician Hindu Cones, 1930s	27	40	55
Chandu Boxed Set of Tricks	325	488	650
Charlie McCarthy Puppet Doll - 21" high, cardboard, Chase & Sanborn mailer	37	56	75
Charlie McCarthy Radio Party Game - Giveaway by Standard Brands, 1938, 21 cardboard figures	42	63	85
Cinnamon Bear (annual Christmas show, circa 1940s) Silver Star	30	45	60
Cisco Kid Badge, western hat on chain, 1950s	17	26	35
Cisco Kid cardboard gun, 7" long, Harvest Bread giveaway, clicker sounds when handle squeezed	17	26	35
Cisco Kid and Pancho face masks, 1953, price per each	25	38	50
Cisco Kid Triple S Club Kit	25	38	50
Cisco Kid Picture Ring, 1950s	50	75	100
Coco Wheats Radio Club Badge shape of microphone	25	38	50

CRACKER JACK

Cracker Jack was first introduced in 1893 by the Ruckheim brothers, F.W. and Louis, at the Chicago World's Columbian Exposition. Toys first appeared in the boxes of popcorn and peanuts in 1912 and were bought from various manufacturers. Over 10,000 different have been produced over the years. From 1912 to 1930 they included whistles, tops, yo-yos, brooches and puzzles. From 1930 to 1940 the accent was on miniatures, such as irons, shoes, binoculars, trolley cars, trains, etc. 1940 to 1950 tended towards military items, with plastics being introduced in the late 1940s. Prices can range from $1.00 or less to $80.00. There are about thirty serious Cracker Jack collectors known in this country.

	C6	C8	C10
David Harding Counterspy, Junior Agent Badge	37	56	75
Davy Crockett goldplated ring	10	15	20
Dick Tracy Air Detective Ring	50	75	100
Dick Tracy Badge, "Capt."	40	60	80
Dick Tracy Badge, "Crime Stoppers"	12	18	25
Dick Tracy Badge, "Detective," picture of Tracy and Junior	17	26	35
Dick Tracy Badge, "Lt."	37	53	75
Dick Tracy Badge - Republic Pictures	37	53	75
Dick Tracy Badge - "Sgt."	30	45	60
Dick Tracy Decoder, green, 1948	22	33	45
Dick Tracy Decoder, red, 1948	22	33	45

	C6	C8	C10
Dick Tracy Detective Club Badge with secret money pouch in rear	37	53	75
Dick Tracy Glider Airplane, 1938	37	53	75
Dick Tracy Ring, in shape of Tracy's head	32	48	65
Dick Tracy Secret Compartment Ring	75	112	150

DICK TRACY Secret Service Patrol Member Pin. Courtesy Jim Harmon.

	C6	C8	C10
Dick Tracy Secret Service Patrol Member pinback, early 1940s	15	23	30
Dick Tracy Secret Service 2nd Year Member Pin	22	33	45
Dick Tracy's Secret Detective Methods & Magic Tricks, 1939 Quaker Oats, 68 pages	30	45	60
Dionne Quints "All Aboard for Shut-Eye Town" paper dolls, Palmolive Soap	17	26	35
Don Winslow Decoder Torpedo	45	68	90
Don Winslow Honor Badge	25	38	50
Don Winslow Magic Slate Secret Code Book	25	38	50
Don Winslow Ring	42	63	85
Don Winslow USN Secret Code Book, 1935, 16 page Oxydol giveaway, 7¾" x 4"	25	38	50
Donald Duck Punchout figure, circa late 1940s, Donald Duck Bread	30	45	60
Donald Duck Playboard, 1946, 9" high, Comics giveaway	25	38	50
Elsie The Cow, set of four figural buttons on color illustrated card, Borden 1949	12	18	25
Fighting Devil Dogs Ring, 1938, Republic Pictures serial ring, has bulldog head on top	62	93	125
Flash Gordon Ring, 1949 Post Toasties Corn Flakes	25	38	50
Fort Apache (Rin Tin Tin) plastic ring 1950s TV premium	15	22	30
Frank Buck Explorer's sun watch, post WW II (offered by Jack Armstrong)	48	72	95
Frank Buck Leopard Ring	125	188	250
G.E. Punchout Circus - 65 pieces	72	108	145
G.E. Rodeo Punchout - 65 pieces	72	108	145
G-Man Badge	10	15	20

FRANK BUCK Explorer's Sun Watch. Courtesy Jim Harmon.

	C6	C8	C10
G-Man Official Signet Ring, 1933-35, G-man radio program premium, metal	25	38	50
Gabby Hayes Antique Cars, 1950s, set for:	37	56	75
Gabby Hayes Quaker Cannon Ring, 1950s	50	75	100
Gabby Hayes Western Gun Collection, 6 weapons, 3 pistols, 3 rifles, solid non-working, 1950s	37	56	75
Gabby Scoops Junior Press Club Card, 1945 Crackajack Comics	10	15	20
Gabby Scoops 1940-41 Press Card, Crackajack Comics	10	15	20
Gangbusters Pin	25	38	50
Goofy Playboard, 1946, 9" high, comics giveaway	17	25	35
Green Hornet Secret Compartment Ring, hornet seal, glows in dark	275	310	550
Gun, cardboard - Giveaway from Theatorium in Lykens, Pa. Pat'd Dec. 1914 by Spots Spec. Co. Lexington, Ky. Swoop downward to produce bang. "The Bang Gun For Young America"	7	11	15
H.C.B. Club Kit, contains badge, etc., early Cream of Wheat	25	38	50
Hop Harrigan Para-Plane, cardboard plane from Grape Nut Flakes plus two code signal blinders. Also in tail of plane is a small parachute that drops a cardboard "water" canister	162	243	325
Hop Harrigan (unmarked) Sun Dial Ring	30	45	60
Hopalong Cassidy Bar 20 Compass ring	32	48	65
Hopalong Cassidy Face Ring	32	48	65
Hopalong Cassidy tin badge, Post Raisin Bran giveaway, circa 1950s	17	26	35
Howdy Doody Climber - cardboard, with string, Welch's Premium, 1950s	37	56	75
Howdy Doody Face Flashlight Ring, 1950s	32	48	65

	C6	C8	C10
Howdy Doody Flicker Key Chain - 3D picture of Howdy Doody flicks to Poll Parrot (Poll Parrot Shoes), 1950s	17	26	35
Howdy Doody Flicker Ring - Poll Parrot Premium, flicks from Howdy to Poll	22	33	45
Howdy Doody 8" Howdy Doody flexible cardboard figure - Wonder Bread	32	48	65
Howdy Doody puppet, Mars Candy, cardboard, 15" high, 1950s	37	56	75
Howdy Doody Princess dancing puppet, 13" high, joints moveable, 1950s Snickers premium	17	26	35
Howdy Doody, Princess Spring, etc. cardboard figure, 14" high	17	26	35
I Am A Spy Smasher button, 1940, Fawcett Comics	25	38	50
Indian Chief tin badge, Post Raisin Bran, circa 1950s	5	8	10
Indian Gum Chief's Head Ring - Goudey Gum card premium, 1930s, silver	10	15	20
Jack Armstrong Crocodile Ring, glows in the dark, green stone	88	132	175
Jack Armstrong Big 10 Football Game	45	68	90
Jack Armstrong Explorer's Telescope	17	25	35
Jack Armstrong Flashlight	15	23	30
Jack Armstrong Hike-O-Meter	22	33	45
Jack Armstrong Magic Answer Box	42	63	95
Jack Armstrong Ped-O-Meter (blue or silver models)	22	33	45
Jack Armstrong, Secret Norden Bomb Sight, circa WW II with three bombs, paper target ships	175	263	350
Jack Armstrong paper airplane models, many different, price per each	17	25	35

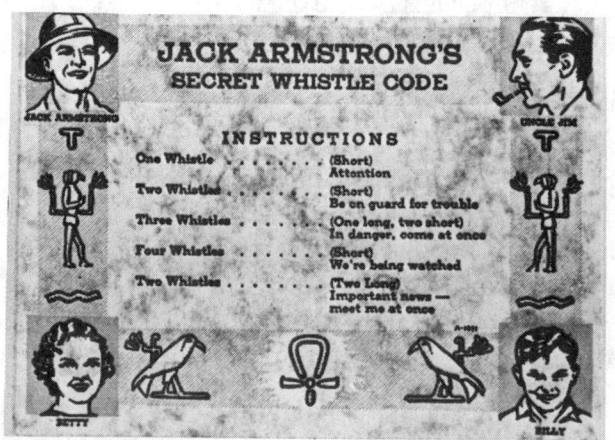

JACK ARMSTRONG Secret Whistle Code Card. Courtesy Jim Harmon.

JACK ARMSTRONG Ped-O-Meter. Courtesy Jim Harmon.

	C6	C8	C10
Reprints of above (identified as such)	5	7.50	10
Jack Armstrong Secret Whistle Code Card for Secret Egyptian Coder Siren ring	15	23	30
Jack Armstrong Secret Egyptian Coder Siren Ring, late 1930s, Wheaties	48	72	95
Jack Armstrong 3-D viewer, filmstrip	37	56	75
Jeff paper mask, 1933 Shell Oil	10	15	20
Jimmie Allen Colonial Gasoline Flying Cadet wings, late 1930s, bronze	17	26	35
Jimmie Allen High-Speed Gasoline Flying Cadet wings, late 1930s, bronze	20	30	40
Jimmie Allen Richfield Hi-Octane Flying Cadet wings, circa 1930s	20	30	40

JIMMIE ALLEN Richfield Hi-Octane Flying Cadet wings. Courtesy Jim Harmon.

	C6	C8	C10
Jimmie Allen Richfield Hi-Octane Pilot's Identification Bracelet, late 1930s, all metal	21	32	42
Jimmie Allen Skelly Oil Die-Cut Airplane cadet wings, late 1930s	15	23	30
Jimmie Allen Skelly Oil Flying Cadet Wings, late 1930s, bronze	15	23	30
Joe E. Brown pin	10	15	20
Junior G-Man Membership kit, circa mid-1930s	37	56	75

	C6	C8	C10
Junior G-Men of America, late 1930s, gold-plated tin badge	22	33	45
Junior Texas Ranger Badge, 1936 premium	17	26	35
Kellogg's Frogmen, 1950s, add baking soda and they swim underwater	10	15	20
Kellogg's Krumbles - Around-the-World paper dolls. Each cutout from box contains boy and girl, 10: Italy 11: Mexico 13: France 17: Czechoslovakia. Price per each	5	8	10
Kellogg's Nautilus Nuclear Submarine, 1950s	25	38	50
Kellogg's Pep Airplane Carrier, 6½"x10" cut-out sheet with airplane carrier, 5 planes with ¾" wingspan	37	56	75
Kellogg's Pep Warplanes circa 1945, balsa wood models, price per each	12	18	25
Kellogg's Pep Warplanes circa 1945, balsa, with Superman ad on envelope	12	18	25
Kellogg's Pep Warplanes - circa 1944, cardboard, price per each	7	11	15

"The Liberty Gun For Young American - McGarth's Big Store", 7" cardboard with photos of Charlie Chaplin. Courtesy HAKE'S Americana & Collectibles.

	C6	C8	C10
"The Liberty Gun For Young America - McGrath's Big Store," 7" cardboard with photos of Charlie Chaplin	20	30	40
Little Orphan Annie Necklace, circa 1936, metal enamel figure of LOA on metal chain	18	27	36
Little Orphan Annie pinback button, Little Orphan Annie, Member Funy Frosty's Club, mid-1930s	21	32	42
Lone Ranger, A Republic Serial - brass star badge	62	93	125
Lone Ranger Atom Bomb Ring (very common)	48	72	95

	C6	C8	C10
Lone Ranger Blackout Kit, 1942, Kix cereal glow in the dark material (two pieces), glow in the dark pledge to flag, glow in the dark Lone Ranger Volunteers armband, plus instruction	48	72	95
Lone Ranger Bond Bread Safety Club Badge, 1938	22	33	45
Lone Ranger Clicker Pistol, black, 1939 movie giveaway, Lone Ranger on one side and ruby on other, non-moveable silver cylinder	75	112	150
Lone Ranger Deputy Shield - brass with secret compartment	37	56	75
Lone Ranger Flashlight Ring	37	53	75

LONE RANGER Frontier Town, complete. Courtesy HAKE'S Americana & Collectibles.

	C6	C8	C10
Lone Ranger Frontier Town - full set	1000	1500	2000
Lone Ranger Glow-in-the-dark Belt, 1941	75	112	150
Lone Ranger Hiyo Silver Pin, 1938	17	26	35
Lone Ranger Kix Air Base with cereal box cut-outs, precursor of Frontier Town - complete $300			
Lone Ranger Lucky Piece - advertises 17th anniversary 1933-50	25	38	50
Lone Ranger Mask. About the last radio premium, c. 1953 or 1954, back of black mask promotes a personal appearance by "The Lone Ranger and Silver!"	25	38	50
Lone Ranger Movie Film ring, late 1940s Cheerios premium	47	70	95
Lone Ranger Pedometer, 1948 Cheerios	15	23	30
Lone Ranger Rubber Band Gun and 6 different targets, 1938 Morton Salt giveaway, cardboard	37	56	75
Lone Ranger Secret Compartment Ring, with picture of Lone Ranger and Silver	88	132	175
Lone Ranger Silver bullet, secret compartment compass	37	56	75

LONE RANGER Secret Compartment Ring. Courtesy Jim Harmon.

	C6	C8	C10
Lone Ranger Silver Saddle Film ring, late 1940s, Cheerios	62	93	125
Lone Ranger Chief Scout Badge, Silvercup Bread, early 1940s premium, red, blue and gold	75	112	150
Lone Ranger Safety Scout Badge, Silvercup Bread, 1935	22	33	45
Lone Ranger Silvercup Bread Safety Patrol, metal-silver and blue	22	33	45
Lone Ranger Six-Shooter Ring, gun ring with plastic and metal gun attached to top. Turn wheel and flint sparks	75	112	150
Lone Ranger Victory Corps Badge, 1942, Kix Cereal	32	48	65
Lone Ranger Weather Ring - color square stone on top with litmus paper. No markings to identify as Lone Ranger	32	48	65
Magic Show Kit, 1946 General Mills	15	22	30
Magician's Book of Cigarette Tricks, 1933, Camel Cigarettes	10	15	20
Major Bowes - Home Microphone	30	45	60
Maltex Health Club - pinback button	5	8	10
Melvin Purvis Junior G-Man Corps Badge, late 1930s	22	33	45
Melvin Purvis Junior G-Man Corps Roving Operative Badge, late 1930s	22	33	45
Melvin Purvis Law and Order Ring	37	56	75
Melvin Purvis Law & Order Patrol Lieutenant's Secret Operator Badge, mid-1930s	37	56	75
Melvin Purvis Law & Order Patrol Secret Operator Badge, late 1930s	37	56	75
Melvin Purvis Secret Operator, Girl's Division	30	45	60
Mickey and Donald's Race to Treasure Island, 1939, 12"x25" Standard Oil giveaway	88	132	175
Mickey and Donald's Race to Treasure Island, 1939, map of U.S. in full color 20"x27", Calco Gasoline giveaway, with stamps	300	450	600

	C6	C8	C10
Mickey Mouse Club Pinback button, "Copyright 1928-30 by W.E. Disney," 1¼"	50	75	100
Mickey Mouse Globe Trotters Map, 28"x20", NBC Bread, 1937	325	488	650
Mickey Mouse Globe Trotters Map, 28"x22", NBC Bread, with all pictures pasted on	325	488	650
Mickey Mouse Globe Trotters Map, 1930s, Pevely Milk premium	325	488	650
Mickey Mouse Official Money, 1930s Mickey Mouse Cones dollar bills Denomination is "1" (each)	10	15	20
Mickey Mouse Playboard, 1946, 9" high, comics giveaway	25	38	50
Morton Salt "Bat-O-Ball," 1939, features The Shadow (cartoon)	62	93	125
My-T-Fine Grocery Store folds into an 8"x3" full color grocery store with period products on the shelves, shoppers, workers, etc. Dated 1930	37	56	75
Nabisco Finger Puppet Rings, Slim Chants, horse Humbolt, gun, hand, Prairie Mary, Tagalong Boswell, Cold Deck Charlie, Sam Spiel, price per each figure	2	3	5
Nabisco Santa Fe Twin Unit Diesel Train, 1956, includes engine, train, tracks, ground, background	12	18	25
Nabisco Sound-Jet Glider	10	15	20
Nabisco Trailblazers of America cards, six cards make up horse-drawn van and open van, 1956	5	8	10
Nabisco Shredded Wheat Nabisco Flying Circus, 1948, designed by Wallace Rigby, 4"x7" cards, planes, once cut out, can glide. Series of 24. Price per each	5	8	10
The Nebbs - Detroit Times series No. 27544 (comic strip)	7	11	15
New York World's Fair Children's World G-Man Badge, giveaway, 3-color brass badge	25	38	50
Newsboy Brand Soups and Vegetables Official Booster Badge, late 1930s	5	8	10
Pep Pins - Little Orphan Annie	7	11	15
Pep Pins - Flash Gordon	15	22	30
Pep Pins - Felix the Cat	5	8	10
Pep Pins - The Phantom	7	11	15
Pep Pins - Popeye and Olive Oyl - each	7	11	15

	C6	C8	C10
Pep Pins - Superman	17	26	35
Pep Pins - Others, includes Smitty, Inspector, Harold Teen, Skeezix, Corky, Pop Jenks, Goofy, Spud, Andy Gump, Gravel Gertie, Punjab, Hans, Kayo, Smilin' Jack, Dagwood, B.O. Plenty, Mr. Bailey, Shadow, Moon Mullins, Flattop, Rip Winkle, Uncle Willie, Emma, Inspector, Chief Brandon, Vitamin Flintheart, Sandy, Uncle Bim, Sundown, Lillums, Tilda, Uncle Walt, Perry Winkle, Judy, Min Gump, Wilmer, Smoky Stover, Daisy, Ma Winkle, Tess Trueheart, Herbie, Mamie, Breezie, Pat Patton, Maggie, Barney Google, Fat Stuff, Chief Brandon, Toots, Nina, etc., average	5	8	10
Pep Rings - Jack Kramer, Dennis O'Keefe, Burt Lancaster, Sitting Bull, Pocahontas, Pan American Clipper, Douglas F-3D Sky Knight, Republic XF91 Thundercepter, each	10	15	20
Pepsodent's Moving Picture Machine shows Mickey Mouse, Donald Duck, Snow White and Seven Dwarfs in color	225	338	450
Pillsbury-Farina Complete Tel-A-Phone Set, 1938, two holders, mouthpieces, ear phones and 50 feet of line	25	38	50
Pinocchio Playboard, 1946, Disney Comics sub. giveaway	25	38	50
Popeye The Sailor Man Button, ¾" copyright 1935, theatre giveaway	15	22	30
Popsicle Movie Star coins - Aluminum coins circa early 1930s, includes Irene Dunne, Clark Gable, Marion Davies, Fredric March, Marie Dressler, Gary Cooper	5	8	10
Porcelain Enamel & Mfg. Co. 6" West Point Cadet on 3"x6" card with Pemco ad on back	2	3	5
Post Grape Nuts Flakes Playing-Filling Station, circa 1950s	5	8	10
Post Toasties 1939 Walt Disney cut-out figures on box, Mickey the Traffic Cop, two types of Pinocchio, etc. Price per each box	25	38	50

	C6	C8	C10
Post Toasties Corn Flakes Comic Rings 1949, Fritz, Hans, Tillie the Toiler, Toots, Casper, etc.	15	22	30
Post's Cereal Junior Detective Club Sergeant Badge, late 1930s	15	22	30
Post's Explorer Ring, 1947, includes compass, sun watch, sunset predictor and star finder, plastic dome	25	38	50
Post Cereal Rings - 1948, Perry Winkle, Winnie Winkle, Harold Teen, Skeezix, Lillums, Herbie, Smoky Stover, etc.	15	22	30
Post Cereal Rings - 1948 - Dick Tracy	15	22	30
Post Grape Nuts tin rings, Little King, Phantom, Skeezix, Lillums, Harold Teen	15	22	30
Post Raisin Bran Sheriff Badge	10	15	20
Radio Orphan Annie - Annie and Joe Corntassel button, 1931	15	22	30
Radio Orphan Annie - Associated Membership Pin, 1934	15	22	30
Radio Orphan Annie Bandanna, 1934	21	32	42
Radio Orphan Annie Birthstone Ring, 1935	75	112	150
Radio Orphan Annie Capt. Sparks Aviation Trainer	225	338	450
Radio Orphan Annie Circus Cut-Outs, 1935	150	225	300

Left to Right: RADIO ORPHAN ANNIE Decoder Badges, 1938 and 1939. Courtesy Jim Harmon.

RADIO ORPHAN ANNIE Decoder Badge 1936. Courtesy Jim Harmon.

	C6	C8	C10
Radio Orphan Annie Code Captain Belt and Buckle, 1940	48	72	96
Radio Orphan Annie Code Captain Pin, 1939	32	48	65
Radio Orphan Annie Manual, 1934	62	93	125
Radio Orphan Annie 1935 Decoder Manual	62	93	125
Radio Orphan Annie 1936 Decoder Manual	62	93	125
Radio Orphan Annie 1937 Decoder Manual	62	93	125
Radio Orphan Annie 1938 Decoder Manual	62	93	125
Radio Orphan Annie 1939 Decoder Manual	62	93	125
Radio Orphan Annie 1940 Decoder Manual	75	112	150
Radio Orphan Annie 1942 Decoder Manual and cardboard decoder	175	263	350
Radio Orphan Annie Decoder Pin, 1935	25	38	50
Radio Orphan Annie Decoder Badge, 1936	25	38	50
Radio Orphan Annie Decoder Badge, 1937	25	38	50
Radio Orphan Annie Decoder Badge, 1938	25	38	50
Radio Orphan Annie Decoder Badge, 1939	25	38	50
Radio Orphan Annie Decoder Badge, 1940	25	38	50
Radio Orphan Annie Foreign Coins, 1937	25	38	50
Radio Orphan Annie Goofy Circus, 1939	37	56	75
Radio Orphan Annie Identification Bracelet, 1934	37	56	75
Radio Orphan Annie Identification Bracelet, 1935	32	48	65
Radio Orphan Annie Identification Tag, 1939	32	48	65
Radio Orphan Annie Magic Transfer Pictures, 1935	32	48	65
Radio Orphan Annie Magic Transfer Picture, 1937	32	48	65
Radio Orphan Annie Mask, 1933	50	75	100
Radio Orphan Annie Mystic Eye Ring, 1939	62	93	125
Radio Orphan Annie Package, 1942, includes Whirl-O-Matic Decoder, Whistle Badge, booklet, and order blanks	175	263	350
Radio Orphan Annie Pin, 1937	17	26	35

	C6	C8	C10
Radio Orphan Annie Portrait Ring, 1934, ring has head of Annie embossed on top	48	72	95
Radio Orphan Annie Premium Manual, 1937	62	93	125
Radio Orphan Annie Premium Manual, 1938	62	93	125
Radio Orphan Annie Punchouts	120	180	240
Radio Orphan Annie Ring, 1934	48	72	95
Radio Orphan Annie Ring, 1935	48	72	95
Radio Orphan Annie Roller Skates, 1938	50	75	100
Radio Orphan Annie Secret Egyptian Compass and Sundial, 1938	48	72	95
Radio Orphan Annie Secret Society Pin, 1934	25	38	50
Radio Orphan Annie Signet Ring, 1937	62	93	125
Radio Orphan Annie Silver Star Pin, 1934	48	72	95
Radio Orphan Annie Silver Star Pin, 1935	48	72	95
Radio Orphan Annie Secret Society Silver Star Ring, 1936	48	72	95
Radio Orphan Annie Silver Star Ring, 1937	48	72	95
Radio Orphan Annie Silver Star Ring, 1938	48	72	95
Radio Orphan Annie School Pin, 1939	20	30	40
Radio Orphan Annie Secret Guard Clicker, 1942	25	38	50
Radio Orphan Annie Shake-Up Game, 1931	17	26	35
Radio Orphan Annie 3-Way Dog Whistle, 1940	30	45	60
Radio Orphan Annie Treasure Hunt Game, 1933	37	56	75
Radio Orphan Annie Treasure Hunt Game, 1935	37	56	75
Range Rider & Dick West button, Peter Pan bread, 1950s	37	56	75
Red Ryder Lucky Coin	7	11	15
Renfrew of the Mounted pin-back	7	11	15
Rin Tin Tin "Ball-in-the-hole" Games (sealed coin-size games of Rinty, Rip Masters, Fort Apache, etc.) each	9	13	18
Rin Tin Tin Ring, plastic, 1950s	17	26	35
Rin Tin Tin set of plastic dinosaurs (Radio-TV 1954)	48	72	95
Rin Tin Tin Wonderscope (Telescope-			

	C6	C8	C10
Microscope-Compass) Radio-TV 1954, has "Rin-Tin-Tin" on face (Same item, without name, recently, perhaps currently, on sale in stores for under $1.00) 30	45	60
Rip Masters (Rin Tin Tin) plastic rings, 1950s 17	26	35
Rocky Lane's Explorer's Sun Watch, 1951, Carnation Milk 22	33	45
Roy Rogers Branding Iron Ring 48	72	95
Roy Rogers Deputy Badge 10	15	20
Roy Rogers Microscope Ring, 1947, Quaker Oats 48	72	95
Roy Rogers Paint Set, 1950s 12	18	25
Roy Rogers Signal Badge with mirror, secret compartment and whistle 48	72	95
Roy Rogers Silver Hat Ring 30	45	60
Roy Rogers - Trigger's Lucky Horseshoe, full size, black rubber ... 12	18	25
Roy Rogers Tuck-A-Way Gun 12	18	25
Scoop Ward News of Youth Official Reporter Badge, late 1930s, Ward's Soft Bun Bread giveaway ... 10	15	20
Secret Three Badge, with manual of secret codes 10	15	20
Sgt. Preston Distance Finder 37	56	75
Sgt. Preston Firefighting Set 37	56	75
Sgt. Preston Flashlight - Signals, has two filters 37	56	75
Sgt. Preston Klondike Land Pouch 22	33	45
Sgt. Preston Klondike Movie Film Viewer 47	72	95
Sgt. Preston Pedometer 22	33	45
Sgt. Preston Police Whistle with nylon cord, brass, 1950 25	38	50
Sgt. Preston Skinning Knife 30	45	60
Sgt. Preston Totem Pole Set 50	75	100
Sgt. Preston Trail Kit, rare, (probably the most complex of all premiums) 250	375	500
Sgt. Preston Yukon Village 250	375	500
Shadow Ring, Glow in Dark, "blue coal" jewel on white ring 375	562	750
Shadow "Carey Salt" Ring (same as J. Armstrong Crocodile ring with black stone; this ring has been counterfeited; original is smoothly circular with clean-cut design 175	263	350
Shield G-Man Club Badge, 1942, Pep Comics premium, lithographed celluloid pinback 37	56	75
Skippy S.S.S.S. Captain, pinback button, all celluloid, 1930s 12	18	25

SKY KING Teleblinker Ring. Courtesy Jim Harmon.

	C6	C8	C10
Skippy Compass, 1930s? 10	15	20
Sky Birds Propeller Ring, brass and silver, 1930s, Goudey Gum premium 12	18	25
Sky King Aztec Indian Ring 88	132	175
Sky King Detecto Microscope 47	72	95
Sky King Detecto Writer 62	93	125
Sky King Electronic Television Ring 88	132	175
Sky King Magni-Glo Ring 88	132	175
Sky King Mystery Picture Ring (picture never works) 50	75	100
Sky King Navajo Indian Ring 88	132	175
Sky King - Small plastic statues of Sky King, Penny, Sky King's horse, Sky King's plane The Songbird, Nabisco giveaways in Wheat Honey and Rice Honey, 1950s, each 15	22	30
Sky King Signal Scope 62	93	125
Sky King Stamp Kit 42	63	85
Sky King Teleblinker Ring 88	132	175
Snow White Game, Tek Toothbrush 35	56	75
Space Patrol Binoculars, circa 1950s 100	150	200
Space Patrol Diplomatic Pouch, contains money, stamps, etc. 125	188	250
Space Patrol Goggles 47	72	95
Space Patrol 1951 Jet Glow Code Belt .. 125	188	250
Space Patrol Ring, with secret powder compartment, circa early 1950s 125	188	250
Space Patrol Smoke Gun, 1950s 137	205	275
Space Patrol Space Helmet, circa 1950s .. 162	243	325
Space Patrol 1952 Space-O-Phone 88	132	175
Space Patrol Space Ship, circa 1950s... 88	132	175
Speed Gibson's Flying Police Badge, Dreikorn's Bread 12	18	25
Straight Arrow Face Ring, circa early 1950s 48	72	95
Straight Arrow Magic Cave Ring, 1949 with original art 88	132	175

	C6	C8	C10
Straight Arrow Magic Cave Ring, reissued 1988 with new art and customer's photos (Discontinued)	20	30	40
Straight Arrow Puppets and props, 1949, Nabisco radio premium	30	45	60
Straight Arrow Target Game, lithographed tin target board, 10"x14" National Biscuit Company copyright on the edge	37	56	75
Straight Arrow Tom-Tom, circa early 1950s	25	38	50
Straight Arrow Wrist Bracelet with secret compartment - circa early 1950s	37	56	75
Sunbrite "Junior Nurse Corps" brass badge	5	8	10
Sunbrite "Junior Nurse Corps" pinback button, pictures of Dorothy Hart	4	6	8
Superman Comics Magazine Ring, reportedly sold for $42,000.			
Superman Crusader Ring	125	188	250
Superman Kellogg's Gy Rocket	48	72	95
Superman Kellogg's Silver Jet Airplane Ring, plane flies off	48	72	95
Superman Kellogg's Walkie-Talkie	37	56	75
Superman Pin, 1940s, "Read Superman Action Comics Magazine"	22	33	45
Superman Planes from Pep cereal, set of 8, 1948	30	45	60
Superman Premium Club Set - Certificate, Button and Decoder	112	168	225
Superman Tim Club Ring	175	263	350
Superman's Secret Code, circa 1939	24	36	48
Supermen of America button - 1939 version, 1⅜" pinback button	32	48	65
Tarzan Gift Statues, Foulds, 1930s, Tarzan, Jane, Kala, etc. Price per set	475	700	950
Tarzan Jungle Map and Treasure Hunt Weston Biscuit, 1933	60	90	120
Tennessee Jed Lariat	37	53	75
Tennessee Jed Look Around Ring, 1940s	30	45	60
Tennessee Jed Paper Gun, circa 1940s	21	32	42
Terry And The Pirates Glow in the Dark ring, crocodiles on sides	32	48	65
Terry And The Pirates Gold Detector ring	48	72	95
Texas Longhorn tin badge, Post Raisin Bran, circa 1950s	5	8	10
Tom Corbett Space Cadet Badge, early 1950s	32	48	65
Tom Corbett Space Cadet Belt Buckle Decoder, early 1950s	75	112	150

TOM MIX Look-Around Ring. Courtesy Jim Harmon.

TOM MIX Six Shooter. Courtesy Jim Harmon.

	C6	C8	C10
Tom Corbett Decoder, cardboard, 1950s	30	45	60
Tom Corbett Rings, Kellogg's, 1950-55, 12 different including: Space Cruiser, Rocket Scout, Space Academy, Space Suit, Space Helmet, Corbett-Space Cadet, Cadet Dress Uniform, Girl's Space Uniform, Parallo-Ray Gun, Strate-Telescope, Sound Ray Gun, per each	15	22	30
Tom Mix Airplane and Parachute	88	132	175
Tom Mix Arm Patch (TM bar on checkerboard design) 1933 - predominantly blue: 1947- predominantly red; 1983 - predominantly black (worth probably as much as older versions - only 1000 issued)	25	38	50
Tom Mix Badge - Ranch Box	37	56	75
Tom Mix Bag of Marbles	17	26	35
Tom Mix Bandanna, has TM Brand	50	75	100
Tom Mix Baseball	21	31	42
Tom Mix Baseball bat	21	31	42
Tom Mix Baseball cap	25	38	50

ANSWERS to TOM MIX mysteries!

THE TELEVISION MURDER: Photograph of Mint- ... ed own hands to fake marks on more (Frame 3) shows he needed thick ... someone had choked him, the little- glasses. Why didn't he have them on ... ould have been at the bottom was watching Television when shot? ... not at top. dow glass shows bullet was fired from ins ... room. Hole is always smaller on side wh ...

TOM MIX Compass-Magnifying Glass, 1937. Courtesy Jim Harmon.

ANSWERS to TOM MIX mysteries!

THE TELEVISION MURDER: Photograph of Mint- deror ... own hands to fake marks on more (Frame 3) shows he needed thick neck. If someone had choked him, the little- glasses. Why didn't he have them on if he finger mark would have been at the bottom was watching Television when shot? Win- of the neck . . . not at top. dow glass shows bullet was fired from inside room. Hole is always smaller on side wh ...

TOM MIX Compass Magnifying Glass, 1947. Courtesy Jim Harmon.

	C6	C8	C10
Tom Mix Belt Buckle with Secret Compartment, belt glows in the dark (offered only on cereal boxes after radio show ended)	62	93	125
Tom Mix Blowdart Game	48	72	95
Tom Mix Branding Iron, TM Brand	48	72	95
Tom Mix Bullet Flashlight	48	72	95
Tom Mix Bullet Telescope, bird-call device comes with it, approx. 4" long	30	45	60
Tom Mix Catalog of Straight Shooter Premiums, 8½"x11" b/w sheet with order form on reverse and descriptions and small pictures of premiums on the front. Includes sheepskin vest, rodeo rope, leather cuffs, wood gun, lucky spinner, etc.	17	26	35
Tom Mix Charm Bracelet with charm-steer head, gun, horseman, TM brand	47	71	95

	C6	C8	C10
Tom Mix coloring Book (Ralston, circa 1949)	17	26	35
Tom Mix Compass Magnifying Glass, 1947, silver color (Note: Originals have "Japan" written on the back. Imitations have the words "Comet-Japan" on the back)	40	60	80
Tom Mix Compass - Magnifying Glass, 1939, brass	62	93	125
Tom Mix Compass - Magnifying Glass, circa 1948, glows in the dark, plastic	62	93	125
Tom Mix Cowboy Shirt	125	188	250
Tom Mix Cowboy Vest	75	112	150
Tom Mix Cowgirl Skirt	125	188	250
Tom Mix Decoder Badge 1940 moveable 6-shooter points to symbols	88	132	175
Tom Mix Decoder Buttons Instruction Sheet, 1946, Ralston	12	18	24
Tom Mix Decoder Pins - Tom, Tony, Jane, Sheriff, Wash. Price per pin	12	18	24
Tom Mix Decoder Pin "Curley Bradley"	18	27	36
Tom Mix Deputy Ring, 1934, chewing gum premium	125	188	250
Tom Mix Glow-in-the-Dark Arrowhead, 1946, has compass and magnifying glass	48	72	95
Tom Mix Gold Ore Badge	37	56	75
Tom Mix Ore Charm, 1940, Ralston, contains genuine gold ore under plastic dome	37	56	75
Tom Mix "Good Luck" Spinner	25	38	50
Tom Mix Horseshoe nail ring, 1933 (can be verified only by accompanying papers)	30	45	60
Tom Mix Identification Bracelet	37	56	75
Tom Mix Initial Ring, 1935	88	132	175
Tom Mix Look-Around Ring, circa post 1945	48	72	95
Tom Mix Lucky Wrist Band, 1936, Ralston premium, metal, TM bar brand, with leather strap and buckle	45	68	90
Tom Mix Magnet Gun and Signal Arrowhead bracelet, gun and arrowhead glow in the dark	50	75	100
Tom Mix Magnet Ring, 1945	48	72	95
Tom Mix Makeup kit (two grease-paint model, plus five grease-paint model)	250	375	500
Tom Mix 1941 Manual	48	72	95
Tom Mix 1944 Manual	48	72	95

TOM MIX Decoder Badge
Courtesy Jim Harmon

TOM MIX Magnet Ring
Courtesy Jim Harmon

TOM MIX Brand Ring

TOM MIX Sharpshooters Medal
Courtesy Jim Harmon

TOM MIX Straightshooters Medal
Courtesy Jim Harmon

TOM MIX Mystery Picture Ring ad. Courtesy Jim Harmon.

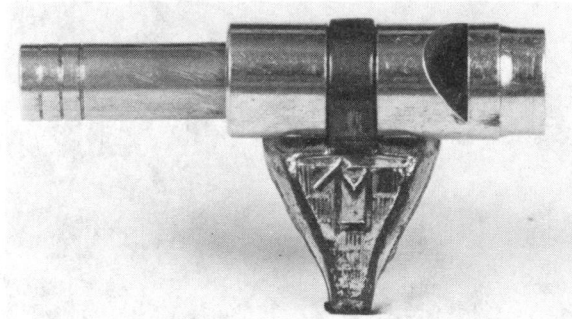

TOM MIX Whistle Ring
Courtesy Jim Harmon

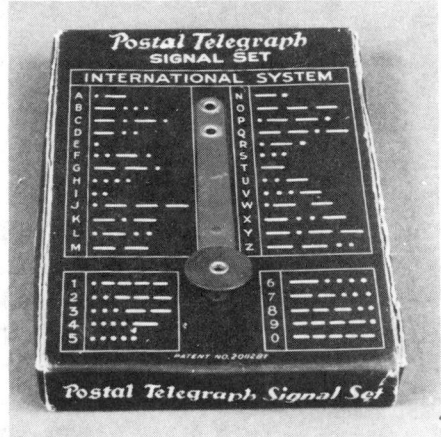

TOM MIX Postal
Telegraph Set. Courtesy
Jim Harmon.

	C6	C8	C10
Tom Mix 1946 Manual	37	56	75
Tom Mix Mask, cardboard	350	525	700
Tom Mix Mystery Picture Ring, 1939, with "look-in" picture of Tom Mix and Tony, viewed through one side of the ring	125	188	250
Tom Mix Parachute - 1936 Ralston premium	48	72	95
Tom Mix Periscope	48	72	95
Tom Mix Postal Telegraph Set - Blue, metal clicker, 1938	48	72	95
Tom Mix Premium Enclosures and Correspondence; Many picture postcards, letters on Straight Shooter stationery, etc. were sent out to listeners who wrote in to the radio show; these and various coupons, instruction sheets, contest entries are offered by dealers and collectors. Average value	18	27	36
Tom Mix Telegraph Set - red, uses batteries, 1940	120	180	240

	C6	C8	C10
Tom Mix Ralston Straight Shooters Pocket Knife, 1940	48	72	96
Tom Mix RCA TV set - shows photographs or comic strips (brown model or reddish model)	32	48	65
Tom Mix Secret Code Manual	37	56	75
Tom Mix Sharpshooters Medal, glows in the dark	75	112	150
Tom Mix Sheriff of Dobie County Siren Badge, 1946, Ralston	42	63	85

	C6	C8	C10
Tom Mix Signal Arrowhead, 1949 with magnifying glass and "whizzer" flute-type whistle, made of lucite	42	63	85
Tom Mix Signal Flashlight	42	63	85
Tom Mix Signature Ring, pre WW II	125	188	250
Tom Mix Siren Ring, 1945	48	72	95
Tom Mix Six-Shooter - wooden, barrel breaks and cartridge drum spins - 1933	100	150	200
Tom Mix Six Shooter - wooden, barrel spins, 1936	100	150	200
Tom Mix Six-Shooter - wooden, no moving parts, 1939	88	132	175
Tom Mix Spinning Rope, 1936, Ralston, hemp with wood handle	47	72	95
Tom Mix Spurs - metal, with plastic glow-in-the-dark rowels. Late	62	93	125
Tom Mix "Square and Fair" Spinner	32	48	65
Tom Mix Straight Shooters Campaign Medal, gold	37	56	75
Tom Mix Straight Shooters Campaign Medal, silver	37	56	75
Tom Mix Sundial Watch	50	75	100
Tom Mix Telephone Set	62	93	125
Tom Mix Telescope, TM brand on side	48	72	95
Tom Mix Tiger Eye Ring, 1949, Ralston	125	188	259
Tom Mix TM Brand ring, circa 1933	55	82	110
Tom Mix Tri-Color Flashlight	48	72	95

	C6	C8	C10
Tom Mix Wrangler Badge, 1936, Ralston	48	72	95
Toonerville Trolley cardboard village put out by Coca Cola	88	132	175
Trigger Button, ⅞", Post Grape Nut Flakes	3	5	7
Welch's Grape Juice Train, paper engine, box car, passenger car, caboose. Price for each	3	5	7
Complete Set above	12	18	25
Wheaties Jogometer	12	18	25
Wheaties Pedometer, circa late 1940s	10	15	20
Wild Bill Hickok Bunkhouse Set (cutout pin-ups of Bill, Jingles, guns, ropes, etc.)	25	38	50
Wild Bill Hickok Treasure Map & Guide, 1952, Kellogg's	48	72	95

Tom Mix Western Movie Viewer. Courtesy Jim Harmon.

	C6	C8	C10
Tom Mix Western Movie Viewer - shows scenes from Tom Mix films, 1935	75	112	150
Tom Mix Whistle Ring, 1945	48	72	95

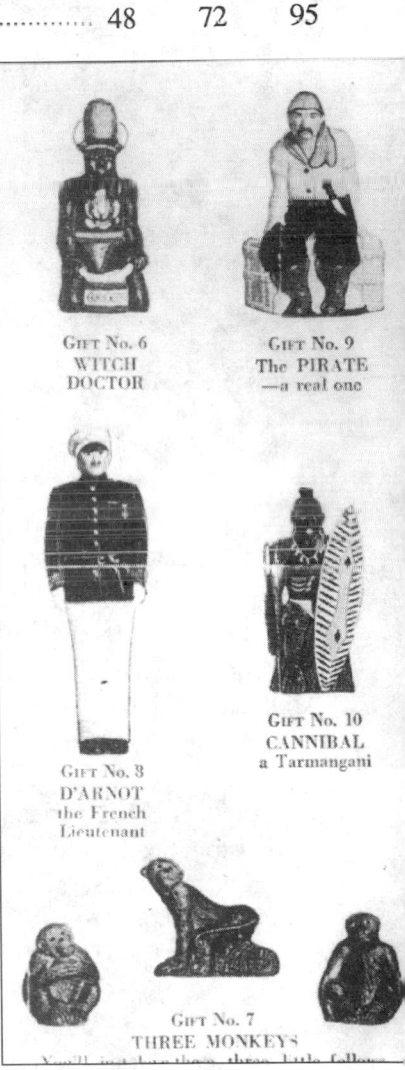

Tarzan Gift Statues, Foulds.

COMIC CHARACTER

(See also Movies, Battery-Operated, premiums, Paper, Mechanical Banks, Ramp Walkers, Vehicles - Tootsietoy)

Average mint price of these toys in the last edition was $671.96 and this year was $750.09 an increase of 12%.

Comic character toys are attractive to collectors as they are often colorful and eye-catching, as well as evocative of happy childhood memories. Popeye continues to be a magnet for collectors, with such as The Yellow Kid, Buck Rogers, Flash Gordon, Tarzan, Superman, Felix the Cat, Barney Google and Happy Hooligan also proving strong lures.

Alphonse, HUBLEY, two goats pulling wagon. Courtesy Kruse Auctioneers.

B.O. PLENTY holding SPARKLE PLENTY. Photo by Don Hultzman.

BARNEY GOOGLE cloth and wood doll, SHOENHUT. Courtesy Sotheby's New York.

	C6	C8	C10
Albert Alligator (Pogo) plastic, 1969, approx. 5" high ("Duz")	8	12	16
Alfred E. Neumann, Effanbee, 1960, vinyl	125	188	250
Alphonse, Hubley, in a goat-pulled cart, cast iron, 13¾" long, 7½" high, early 1900s, from comic strip team of Alphonse and Gaston, head-nodder, movable arms and hands	300	450	600
Alphonse in horse-drawn carriage, nodder toy, circa 1910, 10½" long	550	825	1100
Alphonse, Hubley, mule pulling wagon, 7" long, cast iron nodder	300	450	600
Alphonse, Hubley, two goats pulling wagon, cast iron, 13¾" long, 7½" high, early 1900s, head-nodder, movable arms and hands	200	300	400
Alphonse Nodder Figure	600	900	1200

	C6	C8	C10
Alphonse & Gaston animated car, cast iron, auctioned in 1990 for $15,000, $7840 and $12,650.			
Andy Gump Roadster, "348" Arcade, 7" long	1500	2400	3500
Same as above, deluxe version	2000	3100	4400
Andy Gump wooden dancing doll 9", tin legs	125	188	250
Archie & Veronica Jalopy, illos on side, 7" tin wind-up, Spanish	260	390	520
Archie Hand Puppet, 1973, Ideal, vinyl	25	38	50
B.O. Plenty holding Sparkle Plenty, circa mid-1940s, tin wind-up, Marx	170	255	340
Baby Snookums (The Newlyweds) fabric doll, 5½" high	150	225	300
Baby Sparkle Plenty paper dolls, Saalfield No. 1510	35	52	70
Barney Google, cloth and wood, Schoenhut			*See Schoenhut*
Barney Google Doll, 9" high, wood with composition head, movable arms and legs	200	300	400
Barney Google glass candy container	175	262	350
Barney Google Hand puppet, Gund	45	68	90
Barney Google and Sparkplug pulltoy, tin litho, Sparkplug in barn	1500	2250	3000
Barney Google and Sparkplug Scooter Race, 1920's, Nifty Toy Co., 8" long pull toy	3000	4800	6500
Barney Google riding Sparkplug, wooden			*See Schoenhut*
Barney Google riding Sparkplug, 3" metal paperweight	75	112	150
Barney Google tin wind-up circa 1923	500	750	1000
Barney Google and Sparkplug, tin wind-up by Nifty	1100	1600	2400
Batman Batchute, 1966	22	33	45
Batman Bat Ray, Remco, 1977	30	45	60
Batman Batmobile, Corgi No. 267	65	98	130

Alphonse, HUBLEY, mule pulling wagon. Courtesy Christie's East.

Alphonse & Gaston animated car, cast iron. Courtesy James S. Maxwell/Virginia Caputo. Photo by Virginia Caputo.

Andy Gump Roadster "348", ARCADE. Courtesy Christie's East.

BLONDIE, "Blondie's Jalopy". Courtesy Christie's East.

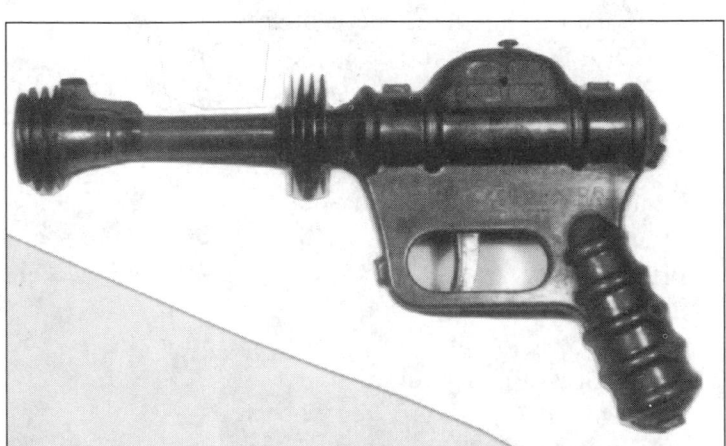

Buck Rogers Disintegrator Pistol. Courtesy James S. Maxwell/Virginia Caputo. Photo by Virginia Caputo.

Bluto (Popeye) Dippy Dumper. Courtesy Christie's East.

	C6	C8	C10
Batman "Batmobile-Batman Driver," 1966, Marx	65	98	130
Batman "Batmobile- Robin Driver," Marx, 4" long	65	98	130
Batman Bullhorn, 1966, Bayshore Ind, plastic	30	45	60
Batman candy container, Pez	*See Pez*		
Batman "Flying Batman", 1966 Ideal, 12" inflatable	10	15	20
Batman glasses, 1966	4	6	8
Batman Handpuppet, cloth body	28	42	56
Batman Handpuppet, vinyl, Ideal, 1965	30	45	60
Batman Helmet and cape, helmet fits over whole head, 1966, Ideal	50	75	100
Batman Hot Line Batphone, Marx	250	375	500
Batman Picture Pistol, Marx, 1966	225	338	450
Batman Playset, Ideal, 1966	1100	1700	2500
Batman Playset, Ideal, 1973	60	90	120
Batman Soaky	30	45	60
Batman Thingmaker set, 1960s	35	52	70
Batman Utility Belt, 1941, with belt-radio buckle	800	1300	1900
Batman Utility Belt Set, 1979, Remco	50	75	100
Beauregard (Pogo), plastic, 1969	10	15	20
Beetle Bailey Handpuppet, Gund	45	68	90
Beetle Bailey "Pop Up Beetle Bailey", Linemar tin litho	180	270	360
Beetle Bailey vinyl figure, 3"	8	12	16
Beetle Bailey's Camp Swampy Playset, MPC	115	172	230
Billy Batson (Capt. Marvel) Magic Box	50	75	100
Blondie "Blondie's Jalopy", 16" long	1200	2000	2800
Blondie Hingees Set, 1944	20	30	40
Blondie, 1940, Whitman 982, paper cut-outs	37	56	75
Blondie, 1947, Whitman 967, paper cut-outs	37	56	75
Bluto (Popeye) Dippy Dumper Truck, celluloid, tin, 9½"	500	750	1050
Bluto on Horse Cart, celluloid and tin windup, 7½"	400	600	800
Bonnie Braids (Dick Tracy), "Bonnie Braids Doll," Marx, 1950s, wind-up, 9" long	200	300	400
Bonnie Braids Paper Dolls - Dick Tracy's daughter and wife Tess, Saalfield No 2724, 1951, cut-outs	25	38	50

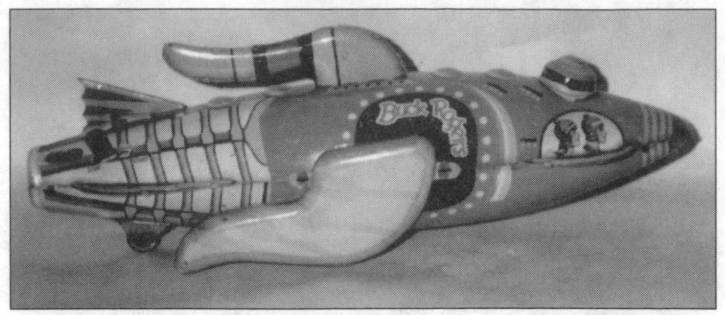

BUCK ROGERS Rocket Ship. Photo by Don Hultzman.

BUCK ROGERS Battlecruiser. Courtesy PB Eighty-Four.

BUCK ROGERS Rocket Police Patrol. Courtesy PB Eighty-Four.

Flash Attack Ship. Courtesy PB Eighty-Four.

Venus Duo Destroyer. Courtesy PB Eighty-Four.

	C6	C8	C10
Bonnie Braids Walker, Charmore Co., 1951, tin litho walker, nurse-maid pushes Bonnie, plastic	See Ramp Walkers		
Boob McNutt, 9" high	See Schoenhut		
Boob McNutt tin wind-up, Strauss	450	675	900
Boots and Her Buddies Paper Dolls, 1943, Saalfield 2460	27	41	55
Bringing Up Father, Hingees, 1944	20	30	40
Broom Hilda, 14" high, Knickerbocker, circa 1970	38	53	75
Brutus (Popeye) cardboard mask, 1940s	40	60	80
Brutus Soaky	22	33	44
Buck Rogers Atomic Pistol, 1946, U-235, sparks and pops, Daisy	130	195	260
Buck Rogers Battle Cruiser, Toot-sietoy, 1937, two grooved wheels on top to run on string	125	188	250
Buck Rogers Casting Set, 1930s, Junior Caster, Rapaport Bros	325	488	650
Buck Rogers Chemical Laboratory, Gropper Toys, 1937	1000	1500	2000

	C6	C8	C10
Buck Rogers Disintegrator pistol, 1936, Daisy	60	90	120
Buck Rogers figure, Tootsietoy, 1¾" high	38	56	75
Buck Rogers figures, boxed, by M.T., U.S.A., rubber, approx. 2-1/2" high, only one set known, sold in 1994 for $1300.			
Buck Rogers "Flash Blast" Attack Ship, Tootsietoy, 1937, two grooved wheels on top to run string, 4½" long	112	168	225
Buck Rogers Flying Saucer, 1940s, paper	75	112	150
Buck Rogers Helmet Daisy, 1933, leather	200	300	400
Buck Rogers lead figures - these are generally new, from early casting sets. Sell for $8.00 painted.			
Buck Rogers Liquid Helium water pistol, Daisy, 1936	500	750	1000
Buck Rogers "Pop" pistol, 1930s	120	180	240
Buck Rogers Rocket Pistol, XZ-31, 1934, Daisy, 9½" long	115	172	230
Buck Rogers Rocket Police Patrol, wind-up, Marx, 1939	600	900	1300
Buck Rogers Rocket Ship, Marx Wind-up, 12" long, 1934	800	1200	1650

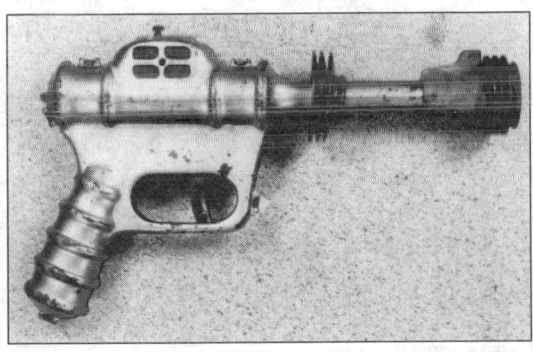

BUCK ROGERS Atomic Pistol. Courtesy HAKE'S Americana & Collectibles.

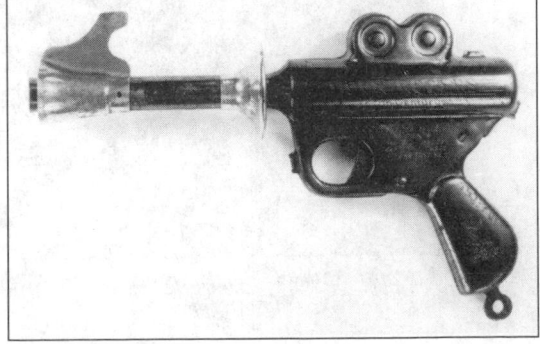

BUCK ROGERS Rocket Pistol. Courtesy HAKE'S Americana & Collectibles.

	C6	C8	C10
"Buck Rogers Rubber Band Gun," 5"x10" punchouts card, 1940	50	75	100
Buck Rogers Sonic Ray Gun, yellow plastic, uses bulb and battery, 1952	75	112	150
Buck Rogers Strato Kite, 1946	25	38	50
Buck Rogers Super-Scope, 1952, Norton-Honer Mfg. Co., 8½" long, adjustable plastic telescope	92	138	185
Buck Rogers Super Sonic Glasses (binoculars), 1953	50	75	100
Buck Rogers U-238 Atomic Pistol & Holster set, 1948	300	450	600
Buck Rogers U-238 Atomic Pistol & Holster set, with box, adventure book and coupon, 1948, Daisy	450	675	900
Buck Rogers "USN Los Angeles" Tootsietoy, 5" long dirigible	117	175	235
Buck Rogers Venus Duo Destroyer, Tootsietoy, two grooved wheels on top to run on string, 1937	125	188	250
Buck Rogers Walkie Talkie, 1950s	90	135	180
Buck Rogers "Wilma" pistol and holster set, 1930s, small version of Buck Rogers "Pop" pistol	212	318	425
Buster Brown cast iron, painted	130	195	260
Buster Brown in cart pulled by Tige, 7½" long, cast iron	135	200	270
Buster Brown & Tige paper dolls, J. Ottman Lith. Co., N.Y. Envelope, dolls, Tige, 4 suits, 4 hats, plus hat for Tige	60	90	120
Buster Brown & Tige ring, brass, 1930s	50	75	100
Buster Brown & Tige tin windup, circa early 1900s, streetlamp, bell	2000	3500	5000
Buster Brown Doll, 23" high, 1920s	110	165	220
Buster Brown figure, lead	10	15	20
Buster Brown, Lehmann tin windup, drives horseless carriage	1100	1650	2200
Buster Brown Rolly Dolly	*See Schoenhut*		
Buster Brown Secret Agent Periscope, c.1950, 20" long	12	18	25
Buster Brown Seesaw, Buster and Tige, 9½", German tin windup	1000	1500	2000
Buttercup (Toots & Casper) stuffed cloth doll, 18" high, jointed head, arms, legs, circa 1924	250	375	500
Buttercup, 14" high cloth doll	450	700	1000
Buttercup, crawls, 4¼", German, cloth and composition	50	75	100
Buttercup & Spareribs, Nifty, Buttercup beats Spareribs with broom, 1920s, 7½" long	800	1300	1800

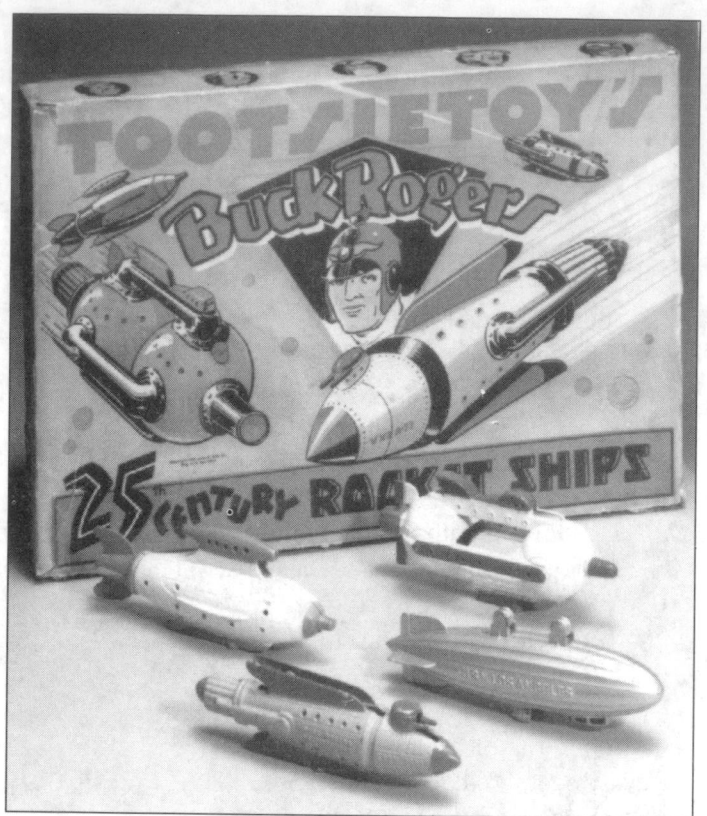

Buck Rogers Rocket Ships with box. Left to Right: Battlecruiser, Venus Duo Destroyer, Flash Attack Ship, "U.S.N. Los Angeles" (the latter listed in Aircraft). Courtesy Christie's East.

Buster Brown & Tige tin wind-up, circa early 1900s, streetlamp, bell. Courtesy Christie's East.

Buttercup & Spareribs, NIFTY. Courtesy Christie's East.

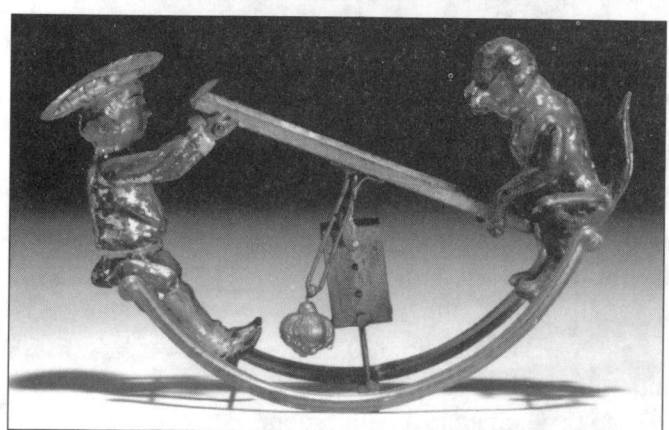

Buster Brown Seesaw, Buster and Tige. Courtesy Christie's East.

Captain Marvel Comic Hero Punch-Outs. Courtesy Bruce Bergstrom-Artman Originals.

446

Captain Marvel Buzz Bomb. Courtesy Continental Hobby House.

	C6	C8	C10
Captain America Handpuppet, 1966	90	135	180
Captain America Utility Set, Remco, 1977	15	22	30
Captain Marvel, hollow metal, c.1947, H.B. Toys, extremely rare	No Price Found		
Captain Marvel Buzz Bomb	22	33	45
Captain Marvel Comic Hero Punch-Outs, 1942, Samuel Lowe, has Captain Marvel (2), Capt. Marvel Jr., Bulletman, Bulletgirl, Spy Smasher, Ibis, Golden Arrow (2), Minute Man, Freddy Freeman, Mr. Scarlet, Commando Yank, Pinky, Bulletdog	200	300	400
Captain Marvel "Flying Captain Marvel", paper, 1944-47, Reed, 7 x 10"	17	26	35
Captain Marvel Gun, movie gun with film	175	263	350
Captain Marvel Magic Flute, copyright 1946, picture of Captain Marvel on side	60	90	120
"Captain Marvel Race Car No. 1", 1947, 4" long tin windup	90	135	180
"Captain Marvel Race Car No. 2", 1947, 4" long tin windup	80	120	160
"Captain Marvel Race Car No. 3", 1947, 4" long tin windup	70	135	140
"Captain Marvel Race Car No. 4", 1947, 4" long tin windup	70	135	140

Captain Marvel Race Cars, Complete set mint in box, value $1000. Courtesy Christie's East.

	C6	C8	C10
Captain Marvel Porsche Car, Corgi, 1979, No. 262	22	33	45
Captain Marvel Toss Bag	40	60	80
Captain Marvel Jr. Ski Jump, 7"x10", circa 1946, paper, Reed & Associates, Chicago	15	22	30
Captain Marvel's Magic Picture, circa 1944, Reed	40	60	80
Captain Marvel's Magic Eyes, circa 1945, Reed	30	45	60
Captain Marvel's Rocket Raider, circa 1944-47, Reed	50	75	100
Captain Marvel Jr., hollow metal, c.1947, H.B. Toys, approx. 3¼" high	1000	1500	2200
Charlie Brown composition bouncing head, 1950s, possibly first Peanuts toy	20	30	40
Charlie Brown, plastic jointed, "1952"	14	21	28

CHESTER GUMP Pony Cart. Courtesy PB Eighty-Four, New York.

	C6	C8	C10
Chester Gump 13" high oilcloth doll, circa 1920s, Livelong Toys	100	150	200
Chester Gump Cart, Arcade, 1920s, horse, open two-wheel cart, Chester driving	450	675	900

447

	C6	C8	C10
Comic Strip Rings, 1953, King Features, Phantom, Blondie, Barney Google, etc. 15	22	30
Comics Paper Doll Cut-out Book, Saalfield, 1935, page each of Popeye, Katzenjammers, Just Kids, Blondie, Dumb Dora, Annie Rooney, Polly and Her Pals........175	263	350
Churchy (Pogo) plastic, 1969, 4½" high....7	11	15
Dagwood Aeroplane, 1935, Marx "Dagwood's Solo Flight".........450	675	900
Dagwood "Dagwood the Driver" Crazy Car, 1935, Marx, 8" long... 500	750	1000
Dagwood Marionette, 15" wood body, plastic head, hands, feet, "Hazelle's," life-like hair, 1940s.....60	90	120
Daisy Mae Dogpatch Family Doll, Circa 1950s 125	188	250

DICK TRACY Squad Car No.1, MARX, 11" long. Courtesy Gary Linden.

DICK TRACY Squad Car No.1, MARX, 6¾" long. Courtesy Gary Linden.

DAISY MAE WITH LI'L ABNER IN PAPER DOLLS. Photo by Jonathan A. Newman. Courtesy Barbara and Jonathan Newman.

DICK TRACY Riot Car. Photo by Gary Linden.

	C6	C8	C10
Daisy Mae and Li'l Abner Paper Dolls with Mammy and Pappy Yokum, Saalfield No. 2360, 1941 45	68	90
Daisy Mae with Li'l Abner in Paper Dolls, Saalfield No. 280, 1942........45	68	90
Daisy Mae Stringless Marionette, 1940s, National Mask & Puppet Corp 70	105	140
Dan Dunn Det. Corps Secret Operative 28 tin badge, circa 1930s........30	45	60
Dennis the Menace, 7" high, Hall,1957........55	82	110
Dennis the Menace Squirt Gun Figure, 5½" high, 1954, plastic 31	47	62
Denny Dimwit (Winnie Winkle) 11" composition doll, 1940s 70	105	140
Dick Tracy, 13½" high, painted composition, mouth moves 275	413	550
Dick Tracy Air Detective Wings, circa late 1930s........20	30	40

	C6	C8	C10
Dick Tracy and Junior Knife with Crimestopper whistle and clue detector........40	60	80
Dick Tracy Automatic, Hubley, with picture of Eagles 65	98	130
Dick Tracy Click Pistol, Marx No. 36...37	56	75
"Dick Tracy Copmobile", Ideal, 1963, plastic 60	90	120
"Dick Tracy Crime Stoppers Lab", 1940s, Porter Chem Co., 10"x12" box........150	225	300
Dick Tracy Crimestoppers Set, badge, handcuffs, billy club, John Henry 32	48	65
Dick Tracy detective badge with secret compartment, late 1930s, large, metal, leather pouch on back........ 40	60	80
Dick Tracy Detective Fingerprint Set, 1933 40	60	80
"Dick Tracy Double Target Game", 1941, 9½" square with 8" tin gun and darts........100	150	200
Dick Tracy Electronic Wrist Radio, Remco 32	48	65
Dick Tracy G-Man windup gun, Marx 100	150	200
Dick Tracy Handpuppet, Ideal, 1961 ...22	33	45

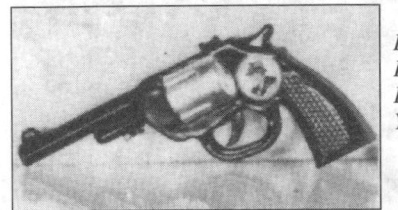

DICK TRACY Click Pistol. Courtesy PB Eighty-Four, New York.

DICK TRACY SIREN POLICE PISTOL
"PULL THE TRIGGER AND CALL ALL CARS"
A REAL NOISEMAKER

Here is something new in the way of a toy pistol. It is equipped with a loud siren which is operated merely by pulling the trigger of the gun. To work the pistol, hold it in the hand as shown in the illustration, and give the trigger a vigorous pull with the finger. This causes the mechanism of the siren to rotate at a tremendous speed. The more you pull the trigger the faster it rotates and the louder it sounds. You can keep it going as long as you like—it won't hurt the mechanism, for it is well and strongly made and will stand rough handling and hard usage. Any boy will be proud to own this pistol, for it is different than that used for cyclists it will serve the purpose of a bicycle horn or bell. The pistol is made entirely of heavy sheet metal with baked enamel finish. Its barrel is 3¼ inches, and the length of the pistol over all is 8½ inches and it weighs about 9 ounces. It has the DICK TRACY trade mark on the siren, as shown in the engraving above. Each pistol comes to you complete in a box with full color. The pistol is absolutely harmless, as it uses no caps, no cartridges or ammunition of any kind, hence you can give it to your child with perfect safety. It is a gift that any boy will appreciate. Though priced at 35c it is easily worth half a dollar of anyone's money.
DICK TRACY SIREN POLICE PISTOL. Price Postpaid....... **35c**

Ad for the Dick Tracy Siren Pistol by Marx, 1930s.

DICK TRACY "Police Station" with 7" long automatic siren car. Courtesy Don Hultzman. Photo by Ron Chojnacki.

	C6	C8	C10
Dick Tracy Hingee, paper figures, 1940s, set of six	20	30	40
Dick Tracy Inspector General badge	75	112	150
Dick Tracy Pen-Lite, 1940s?	30	45	60
Dick Tracy Playset, Ideal, 1973	36	54	72
Dick Tracy "Police Station" with 7" long automatic siren car, 1950s	175	262	350
Dick Tracy Power Jet Squad Gun, Mattel, 28" long, 1962	72	108	145
Dick Tracy Riot Car, circa 1946, Marx, heavy tin or sheetmetal litho, 7½" long, friction motor	150	225	300
Dick Tracy Siren Pistol, red with blue siren, circa late 1930s	35	52	70
Dick Tracy Siren Police Whistle No. 64, Marx, tin	40	60	80
Dick Tracy Soaky	20	30	40
Dick Tracy Space Coupe, 1966, Aurora	375	563	750
Dick Tracy Sparkling Pop Pistol, tin litho, Marx No. 96	100	150	200
Dick Tracy Squad Car, convertible, heavy tin or sheetmetal, 20" long, Marx, circa 1948, friction motor with siren and battery-powered flashing light, Dick Tracy and Sam Catchum in plastic	200	300	400
Dick Tracy Squad Car No. 1, Marx, 11" long, friction	162	243	325
Dick Tracy Squad Car No. 1, Marx, 6¾" long, friction	150	225	300
Dick Tracy Sub-Machine Gun, 1946, "Raider"	100	150	200
Dick Tracy Target Game, Marx, G25	100	150	200
Dick Tracy Target Game, Marx G34	100	150	200
Dick Tracy Telephone, Marx, 1967	37	56	75
Dick Tracy tin wind-up police car, 1949, 7" long	150	225	300
Dick Tracy viewer, 1940s, two films	80	120	160
Dick Tracy Jr. Click Pistol No. 78, Marx, aluminum	80	120	160
Dick Tracy's Handcuffs for Junior, circa 1946, John Henry Products No. 700	50	75	100
Dick Tracy Water Pistol, plastic, 1955	50	75	100

Dr. Pimm (little Nemo) Rolly Dolly. Courtesy Christie's East.

	C6	C8	C10
Dr. Pimm (Little Nemo) Rolly Dolly, 11½" high, Schoenhut	2000	3000	4000
Don Winslow Flashlight Gun	70	105	140

	C6	C8	C10
Ella Cinders 17" high cloth and com-position, 1925	100	150	200
Elmer Fudd Handpuppet, 1950s	20	30	40
Elmer Fudd Soaky, 10" high, 1960s	15	22	30
Favorite Funnies large size rubber print set, Dick Tracy, Orphan Annie, etc. 14 stamps, pad, booklet	32	48	64
Felix The Cat, 2" high, cast iron, 1923, Dent	145	218	290
Felix The Cat, 2" high, pot metal nodding head figure, copyright Pat Sullivan on bottom of feet	100	150	200
Felix The Cat, 2½" high, lead	300	450	600
Felix The Cat 2½" high, cast iron, with tin umbrella	200	300	400
Felix the Cat, 4" high, wooden	*See Schoenhut*		
Felix the Cat, 6" high, wood	*See Schoenhut*		
Felix the Cat, 6½" rubber squeeze toy, Eastern Moulded Products	115	172	230
Felix the Cat, 7 - 9", wood	*See Schoenhut*		

Felix the Cat "Speedy Felix" car and Felix the Cat, 2½" high, cast iron, with tin umbrella. Courtesy Christie's East.

Left to Right: Felix the Cat Walker, German, tin Wind-up, Felix the Cat Pull Toy, Felix chases mice. Courtesy Sotheby's New York.

FELIX THE CAT on scooter. Courtesy Phillips New York.

Felix the Cat, 13" high, composition. Courtesy Christie's East.

	C6	C8	C10
Felix The Cat, 9" high, 1940s, wood, jointed with rubber head	100	150	200
Felix The Cat 12" high, wood	300	450	600
Felix The Cat, 13" high, composition, circa 1930s	300	450	600
Felix The Cat Doll, 15" high, stuffed, Gund, hands molded rubber, the rest cloth, circa 1950	80	120	160
Felix The Cat, China Set	60	90	120
Felix The Cat on fire truck, gong bell pull toy	110	165	220
Felix The Cat on pole, Schoenhut, 9" high, wood	287	432	575
Felix The Cat on scooter, Nifty	550	900	1300

	C6	C8	C10
Felix The Cat on tricycle, gong bell pull toy	220	330	440
Felix The Cat Pull Car, 12" long, Borgfeldt, 1925	300	450	600
Felix the Cat Pull Toy, Felix chases mice	400	600	800
Felix the Cat pulled by Mule, c.1920s (Spain), auctioned for $14,850 in 1993.			
Felix the Cat Soaky	22	33	45
Felix The Cat "Speedy Felix" in car	500	800	1200

	C6	C8	C10
Felix The Cat Walker, German tin windup	430	645	860
Flash Gordon "Air Ray" pistol, 10" long, shoots blast of air using rubber diaphragm	125	188	250
Flash Gordon Arresting Ray, Marx, 1936?, picture of Flash on handle	130	195	260
Flash Gordon Automatic Disintegrator, Hubley	200	300	400
Flash Gordon belt, many illos, large plastic buckle showing rocket ship in flight, 1950s	40	60	80
Flash Gordon Casting Set, Home Foundry, 1934, boxed price	600	850	1000
Flash Gordon Click Ray Pistol, 1950s, 10" long, Marx	300	450	600
Flash Gordon jet-propelled kite	27	41	55
Flash Gordon playset, Tootsietoy, No. 1793, diecast, 1978	22	33	45
Flash Gordon Playsuit, Esquire Novelty, 1952	100	150	200
Flash Gordon Radio Repeater clicker pistol, No. 58, Marx, 1950s, 10" long	475	712	950
Flash Gordon Rocket Fighter, Marx wind-up, 12" long, 1939	450	675	900
Flash Gordon Signal Pistol, tin litho, Marx No. 74, 1940s	400	600	800
Flash Gordon Solar commando; three plastic space men and one ship, 1950s	60	90	120
Flash Gordon Space Cruiser, 1952	50	75	100

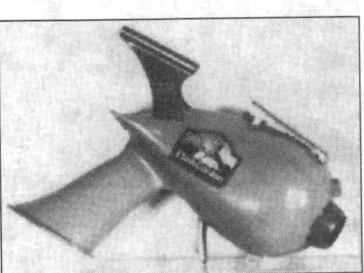

FLASH GORDON Signal Pistol. Courtesy PB Eighty-Four, New York.

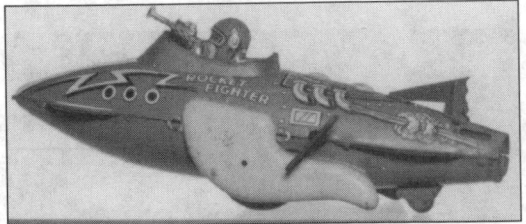

FLASH GORDON Rocket Fighter. Courtesy PB Eighty-Four, New York.

	C6	C8	C10
Flash Gordon Space Outfit, Esquire Novelty, 1952	100	150	200
Flash Gordon Space Target, metal, standup, Alex Raymond illustration, 12x14	80	120	160
Flash Gordon Sparkling Battle Rocket, 1969	40	60	80
Flash Gordon Strat-O-Wagon, 9" long, Wyandotte	120	180	240
Flash Gordon Two way telephone, Marx, circa 1940	100	150	200
Flash Gordon water gun, plastic, 1950s, Marx 7" long	150	225	300
Flip (Little Nemo) Bell Toy, 6½" long, cast iron	400	600	800

Flip (little Nemo) Bell Toy. Courtesy Christie's East

	C6	C8	C10
Foxy Grandpa, 17" high, cloth and composition	450	675	900
Foxy Grandpa Bell Toy, vehicle pulled by two boys, cast iron, 7" long	425	638	850
Foxy Grandpa clockwork figure, tin, German, 8¼" high	300	450	600
Foxy Grandpa Jack in the Box, papier mache and paper litho on wood, 1900, 4" square	160	240	320
Foxy Grandpa Nodder, papier mache, 1900 6" tall	120	180	240
Foxy Grandpa nodder, Hubley, circa 1910, cast iron, 6½", Grandpa large-headed in cart pulled by donkey	500	750	1000
Foxy Grandpa nodder, Harris, cast iron, in donkey cart, 7¼" long	225	338	450
Foxy Grandpa, composition, rides Donkey, 9" long platform pulltoy	450	675	900
Foxy Grandpa Roly Dolly *See Schoenhut*			
"Gasoline Alley Garage and Auto Racer," 1924, Girard, tin litho garage and "Bearcat Racer" car	400	600	800

Foxy Grandpa Roly-Dolly. Courtesy Lloyd W. Ralston Auctions.

Foxy Grandpa Jack in the Box. Courtesy PB 84 New York.

Happy Hooligan on a ladder. Courtesy PB Eighty-Four, New York.

Happy Hooligan, 9½" high, bisque face, dressed as clown. Courtesy Christie's East.

Happy Hooligan Roly-Poly. Courtesy Lloyd W. Ralston Auctions.

Happy Hooligan in cart, horse pulled.

Foxy Grandpa clockwork figure. Courtesy PB 84 New York.

Happy Hooligan in Car, Hill Brass. Courtesy Christie's East.

Gloomy Gus in horse cart, Harris. Courtesy Christie's East.

Happy Hooligan Police Patrol. Courtesy James S. Maxwell/Virginia Caputo. Photo by Virginia Caputo.

Left to Right: Foxy Grandpa nodder, Harris, Foxy Grandpa Bell Toy. Courtesy Christie's East.

Happy Hooligan in horse-drawn wagon with Gloomy Gus, Driver. Courtesy Christie's East.

Henry Trapeze. Courtesy Christie's East.

HI-WAY HENRY. Courtesy Phillips New York.

Jeep (Popeye) wood-jointed. Courtesy Christie's East.

HUMPHREYMOBILE. Courtesy Mapes Auctioneers & Appraisers.

"Jiggs Jazz Car", NIFTY. Courtesy Christie's East.

LI'L ABNER AND HIS DOGPATCH BAND, UNIQUE. Courtesy Phillips New York.

Hingees comic figures (listed in this book by character), circa 1944.

Jaymar wood-jointed toys, 5" high and shorter, Left to Right: Popeye, Olive Oyl, Wimpy, Moon Mullins, Kayo, Little Orphan Annie, Sandy. Photo by Blossom Abell.

453

	C6	C8	C10
"Gloomy Gus," (Happy Hooligan's brother), 1903, Harris Toy Co., cast iron, 5" tall	150	225	300
Gloomy Gus in goat cart, cast iron, 14" long	400	600	800
Gloomy Gus in horse cart, Harris, cast iron, 14" long	1600	2400	3200
Gloomy Gus in mule cart, Harris, cast iron	300	450	600
Green Hornet Aurora Slot Car	125	188	250
Gremlin (Gloom) T.E. Powers, in leather clothes, 1943	20	30	40
Happy Hooligan, 9½" high, bisque face, dressed as clown	550	825	1100
Happy Hooligan Cymbals Player	300	450	600
Happy Hooligan Donkey Cart, circa 1925, (possibly Wilkins), 10" long	240	360	480
Happy Hooligan Hand Puppet, cast iron and cloth, 9¼"	35	52	70
Happy Hooligan in car, 5¾", circa 1903, Hill Brass, cast iron	1800	2900	4000
Happy Hooligan in cart, Kenton, early 1900s, 10¼" long, 7½" high, horse-pulled, head nods, cast iron	600	1000	1400
Happy Hooligan in cart, windup, 1930s, European	1000	1500	2000
"Happy Hooligan In Donkey Cart", 1930s, Ingap Co., 6⅜" long	650	1050	1500
Happy Hooligan in Goat Cart, 7½" long, cast iron	200	300	400
Happy Hooligan in Horse Cart, Wilkins, cast iron, 17" long	500	750	1000
Happy Hooligan in horse-drawn wagon, with Gloomy Gus, driver, Harris, c. 1905, cast iron	1750	2650	3500
"Happy Hooligan Jigger," 1920s, Kiddee Metal Toys, 10" tall, Crank action	800	1200	1600
Happy Hooligan Jigger, Kiddies' Metal Toys Co., tin litho, dressed as clown, tap dances on drum, windup, 9"	650	975	1300
Happy Hooligan on a Ladder	200	300	400
Happy Hooligan on Donkey, celluloid	212	318	425
Happy Hooligan on Rabbit, Candy Container, composition, 7½"	900	1350	1800
Happy Hooligan Police Patrol, Kenton, 18" long, Happy hit by cop as Gloomy Gus drives	2200	3700	5000
Happy Hooligan Roly Poly	50	75	100
Happy Hooligan walking toy, Chein wind-up, 1932, 6" high	362	543	725
Happy Hooligan, wooden	*See Schoenhut*		

	C6	C8	C10
Harold Teen Ukulele, wood, 21", 1930s	100	150	200
Heckle, squeeze toy, 1950s	27	41	55
Henry, 9½" high rubber squeeze toy, 1950s	20	30	40
Henry and his Brother, celluloid wind-ups, Japanese, on wheels	950	1425	1900
Henry celluloid and tin wind-up, Japanese, Henry sits on elephant's trunk	1000	1500	2000
Henry "Henry and his Swan," celluloid mechanical	2150	3225	4300
Henry "Henry Eating Candy," 1950s, Linemar	300	450	600

Left to Right: Henry and his Brother, Henry's Mahout on Donkey, Henry on Trapeze. Courtesy Christie's East.

Henry celluloid and tin wind-up, Japanese, Henry sits on elephant's trunk. Courtesy Christie's East.

	C6	C8	C10
Henry On Trapeze, just Henry, celluloid windup	400	600	800
Henry Trapeze, Japan, windup, part celluloid, Henry, brother and mahout...................................	750	1250	1700
Henry's Mahout on donkey	350	525	715
Herby, 10" oilcloth doll	20	30	40
Herman (Harvey Comics Character) "Herman Nodder," 1950s, Linemar, 4½" high - Rare	300	450	600
Hi-Way Henry, wind-up, 1920s, jalopy with man, woman, laundry above roof ...	2200	3700	5800
Hoppy the Flying Marvel Bunny, circa 1944-47, Reed, paper	6	9	12
Howland Owl (Pogo), 1969, plastic, 4½" high ("Duz")...........................	6	9	12
Humphrey, 14½" high, Ideal, cloth and composition..........................	175	263	350
Humphrey Mobile (Joe Palooka) tin wind-up, circa mid-1940s, Wyandotte, 7½" high with smokestack...	425	638	850
Ignatz (Krazy Kat), 6" high	115	162	230
Jane Arden, 1942, Saalfield 2408, paper dolls.....................	30	45	60
Jean (Gasoline Alley), Livelong toys	25	38	50
Jeep (Popeye) wood-jointed, 1930s, 6" (rare)	425	638	850
As above, 7¼"	350	525	700
As above, 8" (rare)	500	750	1000
Jeff 6" composition doll, ball joints, felt clothes.........................	200	300	400
Jeff bendable figure, 1946	120	180	240
Jeff Stick Puppet, 12" high	40	60	80
Jiggs 3" high, hard plastic, 1960s...........	6	9	12
Jiggs 5" wood-jointed doll, Jaymar?	80	120	160
Jiggs 7" high, wood-jointed doll, Schoenhut........................ *See Schoenhut*			
Jiggs Bumper Car, 1920s, German, auctioned 1993 for $11,500			
"Jiggs Jazz Car," Nifty, 1920s windup, 6½" long........................	1100	3000	5500
Jiggs Stick Puppet, 12" high..................	80	120	160
Joan Palooka doll, Ideal.	85	128	170
Joe Palooka, 4" high, wood-jointed	35	52	70
Joe Palooka 5½" high wood-jointed doll..	50	75	100
Joe Palooka Championship belt buckle, circa early 50s, heavy gold-plated brass buckle shows Palooka with hands raised in victory	50	75	100
Joe Palooka Filmatic, 12 different comic strips.......................	50	75	100

KATZENJAMMER KIDS. Mama Spanking Kid, KENTON, 1911. Courtesy Ed Hyers Antique Toys.

KRAZY KAT platform toy, NIFTY, used Felix the Cat's head as a cost-cutting measure. It also made the Felix version. Courtesy Phillips New York.

	C6	C8	C10
Joe Palooka Punching Bag, ca. 1950....	50	75	100
Katzenjammer Kids, Hingees, 1945......	16	24	32
Katzenjammer Kids, Mama spanking Kid, other Kid standing, as Sailor drives mule cart, Kenton, 1911, 12" long.................................	1100	1800	3300
Katzenjammer Kids See-Saw Bell Toy, Kenton....................................	900	1350	1800
Kayo (Moon Mullins), 5" high, Jaymar, wood jointed	56	84	112
Kayo, 9¾" oilcloth doll	60	90	120
Kayo 10" high Sun Rubber circa 1937, head swivels	200	300	400
Komic Kamera - All metal viewer circa mid-1930s, used to view 35mm film strips. With set of five film strips	80	120	160
Komic Kamera, without film strips	24	36	48
Krazy Kat Platform Toy, tin wind-up, Nifty, 1920s, 7½" long.............	175	262	350
Krazy Kat Teacup & Saucer, 1930s, Chein.	20	30	40

LITTLE LULU doll. Courtesy Toy Collector News.

LITTLE MARY MIXUP AND HER FRIEND PEGGY. Photo by Jonathan Newman. Courtesy Barbara and Jonathan Newman.

LITTLE ORPHAN ANNIE STOVE, 4⅜" high. Courtesy James S. Maxwell/Virginia Caputo. Photo by Virginia Caputo.

Little Orphan Annie skipping rope. Courtesy Christie's East.

Little Lulu, 14" high, Georgene Novelties. Courtesy Christie's East.

Comic strip toys of the 1920s from LIVE LONG TOYS, of 221 W. Madison Street, Chicago, Ill.. The owners seem to have been William A. Benoliel and Eileen Benoliel. The stuffed oilcloth dolls shown here are from "Gasoline Alley". From left, Baby Skeezix, Uncle Walt, Pal, Rachel the Maid, Jean the Playmate, Auntie (Phyllis) Blossom, Skeezix as a boy. Photo by Blossom Abell.

456

	C6	C8	C10
Li'l Abner Dogpatch Family doll, circa 1950s	110	165	220
Li'l Abner Handpuppet, Baby Barry, 1957	42	63	85
Li'l Abner and His Dogpatch Band, 1945, Unique, wind-up	375	562	750
Li'l Abner stringless marionette, 1940s, National Mask & Puppet Corp	70	105	140
Little Beaver Archery Set, 1951	30	45	60
Little King Walker, plastic, circa 1956. *See Ramp Walkers*			
Little King, wooden pull toy, Jay-Mar, 1938, 4" high	80	120	160
Little Lulu 10" high felt doll	100	150	200
Little Lulu 14" high, Georgene Novelties, stuffed doll	365	545	730
Little Lulu, 14" high, doll with mask face, 1944, M.H. Buell	55	83	110
Little Lulu "Shape Book," 1971, Whitman No. 1970	10	15	20
"Little Max Speshul," (Joe Palooka), SALS metal tin windup	3500	5250	7000
Little Mary Mixup And Her Friend Peggy, 1922, Saalfield No. 294, paper dolls	40	60	80
Little Nemo and Mr. Flip bell toy	600	975	1300
Little Orphan Annie, 5" high, Jaymar, wood jointed	65	98	130
Little Orphan Annie 9½" printed fabric doll, 1930s	60	90	120
Little Orphan Annie 16¼" oilcloth doll, circa 1920s	100	150	200
Little Orphan Annie Hingees, 1944, Annie, Sandy, Daddy, Punjab, price per set	20	30	40
Little Orphan Annie Junior Commandos, 1943, Saalfield No. 299	30	45	60
Little Orphan Annie & Sandy Pulltoy, Wood, 1930s, 8"	130	195	260
Little Orphan Annie Skipping Rope, tin wind-up, 1930s, Marx, 5" high	350	525	700
Little Orphan Annie and Sandy, tin wind-up, Marx, 1930s, 2 pc. set, 4½" long	450	675	900
Little Orphan Annie Soaky	14	21	28
Little Orphan Annie stove, 8" high, circa 1930s	125	188	250
Little Orphan Annie stove, 4⅜" high	100	150	200
Little Orphan Annie Water Pistol	70	105	140
Lonesome Polecat (Li'l Abner), 1950s, rubber squeak toy, Reinert	50	75	100
Lucy 7¾" high squeeze toy, 1950s	12	18	24

	C6	C8	C10
Lucy plastic, joined, "1952"	14	21	28
Lucy 8¾" high, vinyl squeeze toy, 1950s	15	22	30
Maggie 3" hard plastic, 1960s	6	9	12
Maggie 9" high wood jointed doll		*See Schoenhut*	
Maggie & Jiggs, 1920s, Nifty, seated on 4-wheeled platform, 8" long	1000	1600	2200
Maggie & Jiggs tin litho squeeze toy, circa 1925, German, 8"	400	600	800
Maggie & Jiggs wind-up, Strauss, 1924, 7¼" long, German	800	1200	1600
Mammy Yokum, Dogpatch Family doll, 1957, Baby Barry Co.	105	158	210
Mammy Yokum Handpuppet, 1957, Baby Barry Co.	42	63	85
Mandrake the Magician Magic Kit, 1949, Transogram	32	48	65

Maggie & Jiggs tin litho squeeze toy. Courtesy Christie's East.

MAGGIE & JIGGS, 1920s, NIFTY. Courtesy PB Eighty-Four, New York.

MOON MULLINS and KAYO on Hand Car. Courtesy Phillips New York.

PAL Gasoline Alley, oilcloth, cotton stuffed.

457

	C6	C8	C10
Mighty Mouse, rubber, 9" high, no mfr. listed 44	66	85
Mighty Mouse, 15" high, vinyl 300	450	600
Mighty Mouse Soaky 12	18	25
Moon Maid's Daughter (Dick Tracy) 16½" doll with space helmet, Ideal, 1965 90	135	180
Moon Mullins, 5" high, Jaymar, wood jointed 55	83	110
Moon Mullins, 11½" high, Famous Artists Synd., 1930s, stuffed doll 50	75	100
Moon Mullins and Kayo on Hand Car, 1930s, 6" long, Marx tin wind-up 350	525	700
Moon Mullins and Mamie Face Masks, 1933, each 20	30	40
Movie Komics, reels of film for toy viewers, circa 1940s 14	21	28
Mrs. Blossom (Gasoline Alley) 17" high oilcloth, Livelong Toys 120	180	240
Mutt 8" high composition doll with ball joints, felt clothes 200	300	400
Mutt bendable figure, 1946 140	210	280
Mutt Wooden Dancing Doll 40	60	80
Nancy 14" high stuffed doll, Georgene Novelties 90	135	180
Olive Oyl, 2½" high, cast iron 175	263	350
Olive Oyl 11" Gund marionette 42	63	85
Olive Oyl "Ballet Dancer", Linemar tin mechanical 250	375	500
Olive Oyl Handpuppet, circa 1938, Gund 60	90	120
Olive Oyl Hingees No. 102, paper punchouts, Reed & Associates 12	18	24
Olive Oyl Mask, cardboard, 1940s 20	30	40
Olive Oyl Riding Tricycle, 4", Linemar 1400	2100	2800
Olive Oyl Rubber Squeeze Toy, 1950s 90	135	180
Olive Oyl approx. 5" high, Jaymar circa 1940s, jointed wood figure 92	137	185
Olive Oyl and Sweepea Hand Car, Marx, 1930s 240	360	480
Pal (Gasoline Alley) oilcloth doll, cotton-stuffed, 1923, Livelong Toys 90	135	180
Pappy Yokum Doll, Dogpatch Family Doll, 1957, Baby Barry Co... 100	150	200
Pappy Yokum Handpuppet, Baby Barry, 1957 42	63	85

	C6	C8	C10
Peanuts figures: Charlie Brown, Lucy, Linus, Schroeder, Snoopy, Avon, price per each 10	15	20
Pete (the Tramp?) 1930s composition doll, strung 130	195	260
Peter Rabbit Chickmobile 700	1100	1600
Pogo plastic, 1969, 4" high 7	11	15
Pogo Pogomobile 200	300	400

Popeye "Boom Boom Popeye". Courtesy Mapes Auctioneers & Appraisers.

Popeye, 10½" high, wood-jointed, circa 1932. Courtesy Christie's East.

Popeye, 14" high, composition. Courtesy Christie's East.

	C6	C8	C10
Popeye 3½" high, cast iron, circa 1930 175	263	350
Popeye 4" high, solid celluloid, 1930s 125	188	250
Popeye, 5" high, Jaymar, wood, jointed 60	90	120

Let to Right: Popeye & Olive Oyl jiggers, Popeye Express - MARX, overhead airplane.

POPEYE in a Barrel, CHEIN. Photo by Don Hultzman.

POPEYE, 8" high, celluloid, key-wind, head spins, foreign. Courtesy Phillips New York.

POPEYE Spinach Patrol. Photo by C.B.C. Lee.

Popeye in a Barrel, celluloid wind-up walker. Courtesy Christie's East.

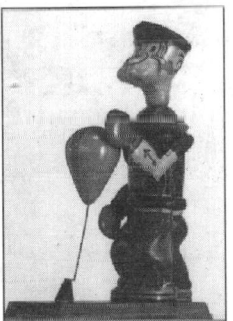

POPEYE Puncher. Courtesy Sotheby Parke Bernet.

Popeye Dippy Dumper. Courtesy Christie's East.

Popeye the Pilot. Courtesy Sotheby's New york.

POPEYE "POPEYE PATROL", HUBLEY, 8½" long. Courtesy Phillips New York.

POPEYE the Pilot. Photo by Don Hultzman.

	C6	C8	C10
Popeye, 6½" high, Chein tin windup walker	387	580	775
Popeye 7" high, hollow rubber, dated "1935" on back	100	150	200
Popeye, 8" high, wood body, jointed, composition head	325	488	650
Popeye, 8" high, celluloid, keywind, head spins, foreign, 1930s, Japan	300	450	600
Popeye, 9" high, celluloid wind-up, neck goes up and down, circa 1930	450	675	900
Popeye, 10" high cast iron doorstop	1500	2300	3400
Popeye, 10¼" high, wood-jointed, circa 1932	225	338	450
Popeye, 11" high, wood jointed, circa 1935	300	450	600
Popeye 11" high, Chein, circa 1935	320	480	640

459

	C6	C8	C10
Popeye 14" high, "Cameo" hard rubber, jointed at neck, hips, shoulders	115	172	230
Popeye 14" high, composition, "Popeye 1935 King Features Syn"	575	950	1250
Popeye 14" high, wood and composition, jointed arms and legs, "1935"	200	300	400
Popeye 15" high, composition, rolling up sleeve	100	150	200
Popeye, 17" high, Knickerbocker, stuffed cloth, 1930s	187	230	375
Popeye 20" high, rubber arms and head, stuffed body, Gund, circa 1950s	70	105	140
Popeye Acrobat, Marx, tin wind-up	2700	4050	5400
"Popeye and Mean Man" - Mechanical Fighters, 1950s, Linemar Co., 6" long - RARE	6000	9000	12000
"Popeye Basketball Player," Linemar tin wind-up	550	925	1200
Popeye "Bifbat" paddle toy, 1929	60	90	120
Popeye "Bo Lo Paddle," 1929	20	30	40
Popeye "Boom Boom Popeye," Fisher Price, drummer, 491	*see Fisher-Price*		
Popeye carrying parrots in cages, Marx wind-up, 1935, 7¾" high	300	450	600
Popeye "Dippy Dumper" truck, Marx	550	925	1200
Popeye Drummer, 7-1/8" high, Chein, thumb-worked	550	925	1200
Popeye "Eccentric Plane," 1940, Marx wind-up, 8" long	450	675	900
Popeye Express - Marx, overhead airplane, 1935, flies over train	500	750	1000
Popeye Express - Marx, Popeye pushing box with parrot, wind-up, 1935	487	730	975
Popeye Handcar, Marx, 1935, Popeye & Olive Oyl, composition, 6" long	700	1050	1400
Popeye Handpuppet, Gund	19	28	38
"Popeye Heavy Hitter," Chein, tin wind-up, 11½"	2500	3900	6000
Popeye Hingee paper figures, No. 102, Reed, 1940s	62	93	125
Popeye in a Barrel, celluloid windup walker, 5½" high, Japan	700	1100	1500
Popeye in a Barrel, Chein, 7" high	450	675	900
Popeye in a Horsecart, Marx, celluloid and tin, circa 1935, 7½"	1500	2400	3500
Popeye Jack-in-the-Box, Mattel Co., tin mechanical, Popeye pops out of spinach can	45	68	90

	C6	C8	C10
Popeye Knockout Bank	350	525	700
"Popeye Lantern Toy," 1950's, Linemar, 7½" high	325	488	650
Popeye "Popeye Jigger" (on rooftop), Marx wind-up, 9½" high	500	750	1000
Popeye mask, cardboard, 1940s	30	45	60
Popeye Moving Van, tin friction, Linemar	400	600	800
Popeye One-Man Band, pole with drum and cymbals, rubber Popeye head on top, 69" high, 1950s	100	150	200
Popeye Pirate, click pistol, Marx No. 68	175	263	350
Popeye the Pilot, 1930, Marx wind-up early version, 8" long	750	1300	1700
Popeye the Pilot, later version, 8" long	500	750	1000
Popeye "Popeye & Olive Oyl Slinky Handcar" 1950s pulltoy, Linemar	1100	1800	2500
Popeye on a Tricycle, Linemar, metal and celluloid	500	750	1000
Popeye "Popeye On A Unicycle," Linemar, 1950s, windup	600	900	1200
Popeye "Popeye Patrol," Hubley, 8½" long	2500	4000	5400
Popeye Puncher, Chein, 1930, tin and celluloid, floor bag	500	750	1000
Popeye Puncher, Chein, overhead bag	1600	2700	3500
Popeye Pushing wheelbarrow, plastic walker, Marx, circa 1950s	50	75	100
Popeye Rollerskating, Linemar	500	750	1050
Popeye Roly-Poly, 3½" celluloid, Japan	100	150	200
Popeye Roly Poly Target Game, Knickerbocker, 1958	95	143	190
Popeye in a Rowboat, 1935, Hoge	2500	4000	5500
Popeye rubber squeeze toy, 1950s	20	30	40
Popeye Sand Toy teeter-totter with Popeye, Sweepea, Olive Oyl, Jeep, tin litho	500	750	1000
"Popeye Shadow Boxer," 1930s, Chein, 7" tall	700	1150	1600
Popeye "Smoking Popeye", battery-operated, Linemar, 8½" high	1500	2250	3000
Popeye Soaky	22	33	45
Popeye "Sparkling Popeye," 1959, Chein Co., 5" long	150	225	300
Popeye on Sparkplug, 1930s	*See Fisher-Price*		
Popeye "Popeye Spinning Olive Oyl in a Chair," 1950s, Linemar, 9" high	1000	1700	2500
Popeye "Spinach Patrol" Hubley	850	1400	1900

POPEYE Basketball Player box. Courtesy Phillips New York.

POPEYE on a Unicycle, LINEMAR. Courtesy Phillips New York.

Popeye Turnover Tank, LINEMAR. Photo by Don Hultzman.

"Popeye & Olive Oyl Slinky Popeye Handcar." Courtesy Christie's East.

POPEYE Rollerskating. Courtesy PB Eighty-Four, New York.

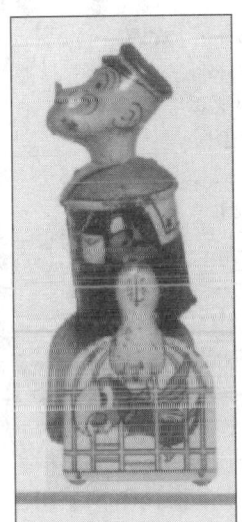

POPEYE carrying parrots in cages. Courtesy PB Eighty-Four, New York.

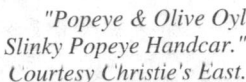

"Popeye The Champ", MARX. Courtesy Phillips New York.

"POPEYE EXPRESS". Photo Courtesy PB Eighty-Four.

Popeye in a Rowboat, 1935, HOGE. Courtesy Christie's East.

Popeye & Olive Oyl, Ball Toss. Courtesy Christie's East.

461

	C6	C8	C10
Popeye Spinach Wagon 3000	5000	7000
Popeye Squeeze Toy, Linemar 400	600	800
Popeye Strength Tester, Holgate, 14".. 65	98	130
Popeye Transit Co., Linemar, tin trailer truck 400	600	800
"Popeye" The Champ, Marx 1050	1700	2300
Popeye "Tumbling Popeye," Linemar, 5" high wind-up 450	675	900
Popeye Turnover Tank, Linemar tin wind-up, 1950s, 6" long................325	490	650
Popeye Walker, plastic, pushing cart.....20	30	40
Popeye Whistle Pipe, Northwest Products of St. Louis, 3½" long, cardboard bowl with illos of Popeye characters, metal stem with whistle at base.......................70	105	140
"Popeye Xylophone Player," 1957, American Preschool Co., 9" long ..250	375	500
Popeye Yazoo Pipe, Northwestern Productions, St. Louis, Mo, 1934 80	120	160
Popeye & Olive Oyl Ball Toss, circa 1950, 19" long, Linemar, tin wind-up 600	950	1300
Popeye & Olive Oyl Jiggers (Popeye dancing on roof, Olive Oyl playing concertina), Marx............650	1000	1400
Popeye & Olive Oyl Sand Toy, tin litho, T. Cohn, 8¼" high 450	675	900
Porky (Pogo) plastic, 1969 8	12	16
Porky Pig cowboy with lariat, Marx tin wind-up, 1949, 9" high.............400	600	800
Porky Pig squeeze toy, Sun Rubber, approx. 6" high, hollow with squeaker, has hands behind back, circa 1940......................... 30	45	60
Porky Pig hand puppet, 1950s, 8" high 30	45	60
Porky Pig Soaky, 9" high, 1960s...........10	15	20
Porky Pig tin litho wind-up, 1939, 8½" high, holding umbrella, Marx ..275	363	550
Porky Pig tin litho wind-up, holds umbrella, raises hat, Marx, 1939, 8".....400	600	800
Prince Valiant Castle Fort, Marx, boxed set with knights, etc.............250	375	500
Prince Valiant Crossbow Pistol Game 22	33	45
Prince Valiant Shield, tin litho..............30	45	60
Prince Valiant Sword and tin Scabbard, 1950s, Mattel 50	75	100
Rachel (Gasoline Alley) oilcloth doll, cotton-stuffed, 1923, Live long Toys.....................................120	180	240

Porky Pig, tin wind-up, with original box. Courtesy Wilkinson Collection, Detroit Antique Toy Museum.

	C6	C8	C10
Red Ryder BB guns . . . . See BB Guns
Red Ryder Molding Set, 1948 40	60	80
Red Ryder Target Game, 1939 34	51	68
Robin (Batman) Soaky 26	39	52
Roosevelt Bear on Bicycle, tin litho, 9" long, circa 1920.........................225	338	450
Rudy the Ostrich (Barney Google), 1924, tin, Nifty..............................550	950	1250
Sad Sack 15½" vinyl doll, 1950...........140	210	280
Sad Sack 20" high vinyl doll, cloth uniform, Sterling Doll Co., circa 1952 70	105	140
Sandy, 5" long, Jaymar, wood jointed ...60	90	120
Sandy 10½" long oilcloth doll, circa 1920s, Live Long Toys 140	210	280
Sandy (Orphan Annie's dog) with suitcase in mouth, tin wind-up.............350	525	700
Sandy (Orphan Annie) "Sandy Dog with Magic Tail," 1930s, Marx, 7" long 162	243	325
Sandy (Orphan Annie) "Sandy's Dog House" with wheeled Sandy, Marx...300	450	600
Schroeder (Peanuts) rubber squeeze toy, circa 1960............................10	15	20
Secret Agent X-9 Gun and Billy Club...12	18	24
Sergeant Snorkel (Beetle Bailey) Handpuppet 33	50	67
Shmoo (Li'l Abner) doll, vinyl inflatable, 15" high, 1940s................60	90	120

Rudy the Ostrich. Courtesy James S. Maxwell/Virginia Caputo. Photo by Virginia Caputo.

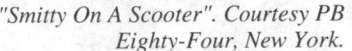

"Smitty On A Scooter". Courtesy PB Eighty-Four, New York.

Roosevelt Bear on Bicycle. Courtesy Wilkinson Collection, Detroit Antique Toy Museum.

SPARKPLUG, 1920s, SCHOENHUT. Courtesy PB Eighty-Four, New York.

Sandy (Orphan Annie) "Sandy's Dog House". Courtesy Christie's East.

Sandy with suitcase in mouth. Courtesy Christie's East.

	C6	C8	C10
"Sight Seeing Auto 899", cast iron, Kenton, circa 1910, has Mama Katzenjammer, Uncle Heine, Alphonse, Gloomy Gus, Happy Hooligan, 10½" long	3300	5100	7850
Skeezix oilcloth doll, cotton-stuffed, 1924 (Baby Skeezix), Live Long Toys	95	142	190
Skeezix oilcloth doll, cotton-stuffed, 1924 (as boy) Live Long Toys	100	150	200
Skeezix Radio Toy, circa 1924, 5" high, tin litho	1000	1500	2000
Skippy, celluloid, 5½" high	150	225	300
Skippy Oilcloth doll, 12" high, with hat	50	75	100
Smitty 9¾" oilcloth doll	100	150	200
"Smitty On A Scooter," tin wind-up, Marx, circa 1930, 8" high	1100	1700	2300

	C6	C8	C10
Smokey Stover, hard plastic, 3" high, 1960s	12	18	25
Smokey Stover, Hingees, 1944	8	13	17
Snoopy Astronaut, doll, 9½" high, 1969, vinyl	10	15	20
Snoopy Bus, 1960s, tin litho	16	24	32
Snoopy rubber squeeze toy, 1958	10	15	20
Snowflakes & Swipes platform toy, 7½" long, tin litho, circa 1929	1700	2700	4000
Snuffy Smith Handpuppet, cloth, with rubber head, Gund, "King Features"	35	52	70
Sparkle Plenty Paperdoll Set, 1948, Saalfield No. 5160	20	30	40
Sparkle Plenty Washing Machine, Kalon Radio Corp., litho tin, crank action, circa 1947, 13" tall	100	150	200

DAISY Superman Krypto-Raygun Ad.

"Sight Seeing Auto 899". Courtesy Christie's East.

Toonerville Trolley, "Crackerjack" size. Courtesy Wilkinson Collection Detroit Antique Toy Museum.

Snowflake & Swipes. Courtesy Christie's East.

THIMBLE THEATRE Mystery Playhouse figures, Olive Oyl, Popeye, Wimpy. Courtesy Mapes Auctioneers & Appraisers.

Superman Rollover Airplanes, Left to Right: Blue, Red, Bronze-tone or Gold. Courtesy Christie's East.

"Toonerville Trolley", NIFTY tin wind-up. Courtesy PB Eighty-Four, New York.

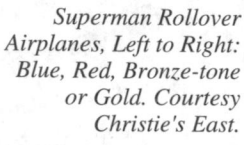

Toonerville Trolley, DENT. Photo by Don Hultzman.

Toonerville Trolley, lead, circa 1923. Courtesy PB Eighty-Four, New York.

464

	C6	C8	C10
Sparkplug, 1920s, Schoenhut jointed wood figure	*See Schoenhut*		
"Sparkplug" (Barney Google), on wheels, 3¼" high	300	450	600
Sparkplug (Barney Google) stuffed cloth	125	188	250
Sparkplug Candy Container	75	112	150
Spiderman Handpuppet, 1966, Ideal	42	63	85
Spiderman Webmaker, Chemtoy, 1977	22	33	45
Steve Canyon Glider Bomb Truck, Ideal	62	93	125
Steve Canyon Jet Helmet, 1959	42	63	85
Sunshine (Jockey) riding Sparkplug (Barney Google) platform toy, 9" long	1600	2400	3200
Superman, 5" high, Mego Bendy, 1973	22	33	45
Superman, 13" high, wood and composition, Ideal, 1940	575	875	1250
Superman Acme Movie Viewer, 1940	250	375	500
Superman Acme Movie viewer, 1947, with film	75	112	150
Superman Acme movie viewer, 1955, with film	45	68	90
Superman Acme movie viewer, 1965	17	25	34
Superman Cut-Out Adventure Book	60	90	120
"Superman Cut-Outs", Saalfield 177, 1940	500	750	1000
Superman Handpuppet, Ideal, 1965	26	39	52
Superman Holding Airplane, Marx tin wind-up, 1940	1100	1650	2200
Superman Krypto Ray Gun, Daisy No. 94, 1939, with seven film strips	225	338	450
Superman Krypton Rockets, circa 1939	160	240	320
Superman Kryptonite Rock	6	9	12
Superman Playset, Ideal, 1973	44	66	88
"Superman Rollover Airplane," 1940s, Marx Co., 6½" long, blue version	1100	1650	2200
"Superman Rollover Airplane," 1940s, Marx Co., 6½" long, bronze-tone version	700	1050	1400
"Superman Rollover Airplane," 1940s, Marx Co., 6½" long, red version	950	1600	2100
Superman Rollover Tank, 1940s, 4" long	400	600	800
"Superman Roll Over Tank" (silver version) Marx Co., 1940s, 4" long	5500	900	1250
Superman Soaky	17	26	35
"Superman Tank", Linemar, 12" long	*See Battery Operated*		
"Superman Tank", Linemar, 4" long	550	825	1100
Superman Tricky Trapeze, 1966, Kohner	12	18	25

	C6	C8	C10
Superman Water Pistol, shape of Superman flying, circa 1950s	35	52	70
Sweepea Hingees No. 102, 1944, paper punchouts, Reed	20	30	40
Sweepea Mask, cardboard, 1940s	10	15	20
Tarzan, Corgi Gift Set No. 36, figures and truck with cage trailer	40	60	80
Tarzan, mask of Akut the Ape, Northern Paper Mills, 1933	60	90	120
Tarzan, mask of Numa the Lion, paper, 1933 by Northern Paper Mills	60	90	120
Tarzan, mask of Tarzan, 1933, Northern Paper Mills, paper	70	105	140
Tarzan In The Jungle dart board game, 1935, large	130	195	260
Tarzan "Tarzan In The Jungle," 1935 battery-operated target game	140	210	280
Tarzan Thingmaker Kit, Mattel, 1966	32	48	65
Terry And The Pirates Hingees, 1944, set contains Terry, Flip Corkin, Pat Ryan, Burma, Taffy Tucker	22	33	45
Thimble Theatre Mystery Playhouse "Starring Popeye with Wimpy and Olive Oyl," copyright 1939, Harding Products, Philadelphia, 12x10x3", figures composition, with wooden "Shuffle" feet, individual figures sell for $325 in mint	1250	1875	2500
Three Flying Marvels (Captain, Jr., Mary), paper, circa 1944-47, Reed	22	33	45
Toonerville Trolley, lead, circa 1923	200	300	400
Toonerville Trolley, tin wind-up, "Copyright 1922 by Fontaine Fox," 7½" high, Skipper driving, Nifty	500	750	1080
Toonerville Trolley, 1921, Strauss wind-up, RARE	425	638	850
Toonerville Trolley, 1⅞" high, sometimes called Crackerjack size	450	675	900
Toonerville Trolley, Dent, aluminum	450	675	900
Toonerville Trolley - Dent, cast iron	500	750	1000
Toonerville Glass Candy Container, 3¼" long	425	638	850
Toonerville Trolley, "Powerful Katrinka," 6½" long, pushing boy in wheelbarrow, tin wind-up, Lehmann, 1925	1200	2200	3000
Toonerville Trolley, "The Powerful Katrinka," raises and lowers Jimmy in her hand, tin windup, 6¾" high, Nifty, 1925	1700	2500	4000

Left to Right: Toonerville Trolley "The Powerful Katrinka", 6½" long, pushing boy in wheelbarrow; "The Powerful Katrinka", raises and lowers boy in her hand. Courtesy Sotheby's New York.

Uncle Wiggily, MARX, Crazy Car. Courtesy Sotheby's New York.

Uncle Wiggily Crazy Car, DISTLER (Germany). Courtesy Wilkinson Collection, Detroit Antique Toy Museum.

RACHEL, Gasoline Alley, oilcloth, cotton stuffed.

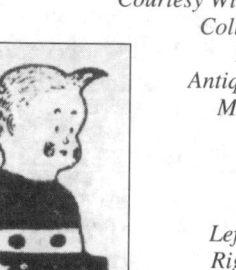

SKEEZIX, oilcloth, cotton stuffed.

Left to Right: Yellow Kid, 6½" high, cast iron, burlap gown, Yellow Kid in Goat Cart. Courtesy Christie's East.

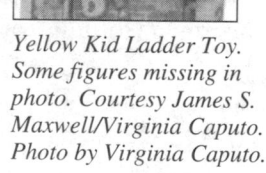

Yellow Kid Ladder Toy. Some figures missing in photo. Courtesy James S. Maxwell/Virginia Caputo. Photo by Virginia Caputo.

	C6	C8	C10
Toonerville Trolley, wood, 7" long, 6 people	125	188	250
Tweety Bird rubber squeeze toy, 1950s	15	22	30
Tweety Bird Soaky	12	18	24
Uncle Walt (Gasoline Alley), oilcloth, 26" high, Live Long Toys	80	120	160
Uncle Wiggily Crazy Car, Distler (Germany), circa 1922, 9½" long	1100	1700	2400
Uncle Wiggily, Marx, Crazy Car	500	750	1000
Walter Lantz ink stamp character set, 12 different rubber stamps	12	18	24
Western Thrills with Billy The Kid, character from Funny Animals Comics, circa 1944-47, Reed, paper toy	12	18	24
Willie The Worm and Sammy in Car Trouble, paper toy, Fawcett Comics characters, Reed, circa 1944-47	10	15	20

	C6	C8	C10
Willie The Worm and Sammy Flying Machine	12	18	25
Willie The Worm and Sammy Fish-n Fun	10	15	20
Wimpy 3" hard plastic figure, 1960s	12	18	24
Wimpy 3⅛" high, cast iron Hubley	175	262	350
Wimpy 4" high, wood-jointed, "by K.F.S."	100	150	200
Wimpy, 5" high, Jaymar, jointed wood figure	100	150	200
Wimpy 8" high rubber squeeze toy	75	112	150
Wimpy Dippy Dumper	550	825	1100
Wimpy Handpuppet, Gund	25	38	50
Wimpy mask, cardboard, 1940s	10	15	20
Wimpy Motorcyclist, Linemar	400	600	800
Wimpy Tricyclist, Linemar	500	750	1000
Wonder Woman String Puppet, Madison, 1977	34	51	68

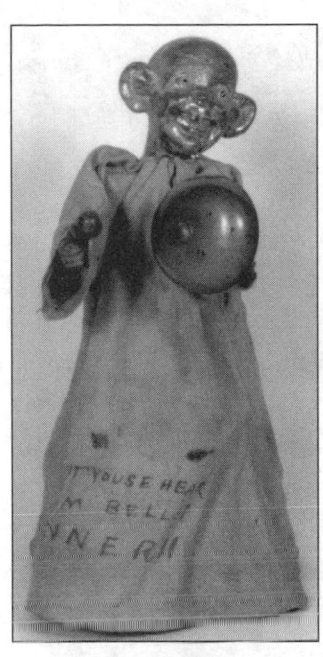

Yellow Kid Standing Bell Ringer. Courtesy James S. Maxwell/Virginia Caputo. Photo by Virginia Caputo.

WIMPY Tricyclist, LINEMAR. Courtesy Phillips New York.

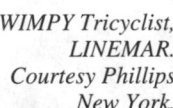

Yellow Kid Cap Bomb, 1½" high. Courtesy James S. Maxwell/Virginia Caputo. Photo by Virginia Caputo.

Yellow Kid Stuffed Doll, Arnold Print Works, 8" high.. Courtesy James S. Maxwell/Virginia Caputo. Photo by Virginia Caputo.

	C6	C8	C10
Woody Woodpecker Handpuppet, Mattel, 1962, "W. Lantz" rubber head, cloth body	29	43	58
Woody Woodpecker, 6½" high, rubber, "Walter Lantz"	10	15	20
Woody Woodpecker Soaky	10	15	21
Yellow Kid Cap Bomb, cast iron, 1½" high	107	160	215
Yellow Kid 6½" high, cast iron, burlap gown, movable arms	475	713	950
Yellow Kid, 8" high, Arnold Printworks, "Design copyrighted 1894 and 1896"	225	338	450
Yellow Kid in Cart, Kenton, early 1900s, 10" long, 6" high, pulled by mule, cast iron	800	1200	1600
Yellow Kid in Goat Cart, Kenton, 1890, painted cast iron, 7½" long	400	600	800
Yellow Kid Ladder Toy, 16½" high	600	900	1200
Yellow Kid papier mache and wood, 11" high, early 1900s	400	600	800
Zero (Beetle Bailey), hand puppet, Gund, 1960s, vinyl & cloth	40	60	80

CONDITION CODE:

C6 - Good. Evident overall wear, well played with, but acceptable to many collectors

C8 - Very Good Minor wear overall, very clean

C10 - Mint (like new)

Note: Mint in Box commands a higher price. Condition below C6 brings considerable lower prices.

MOVIES, RADIO, TELEVISION

(See also Paper, Premiums, Banks, Miscellaneous, Comic Character, Ramp Walkers, Marx Playsets, Action Figures, Figure Kits)

The average mint price in this category in the last edition was $349.10 and in this edition averages $374.16, an increase of 7%.

AMOS &ANDY tin wind-ups, 12" high, eyes move. Courtesy Lloyd W. Ralston Auctions.

AMOS &ANDY Fresh-Air Taxi, cast iron. Courtesy Christie's East.

AMOS & ANDY Fresh-Air Taxi. Courtesy Sotheby's New York.

	C6	C8	C10
Alien doll, Kenner, 1979 125	188	250
Alvin Chipmunk Soaky, 1963 9	13	18
Amos Sparkler 600	900	1200
Amos tin windup, 1930, Marx, 12" high, moving eyes 600	900	1200
Same as above, eyes don't move . . . 500	750	1000
Amos and Andy in car, glass, 4½" long 362	543	725
Amos and Andy wood jointed dolls, 6" high, price for pair, Jaymar 300	450	600
Amos and Andy Fresh-Air Taxi, cast iron, 6" Dent 600	950	1300
Amos & Andy Fresh-Air Taxi, tin wind-up, Marx, 8" long, 1930s 500	750	1050
Andy Tin Windup, 12" high Marx, 1930s, moving eyes 550	925	1200
Same as above, eyes don't move . . . 500	750	1000
Andy Panda, 14" high, Ideal, plush, 1950s 60	90	120
Augie Doggie Soaky 22	33	45
Babalooie Soaky 12	18	25
Babalooie, 14", rubber face 35	52	70
Baby Huey Hand Puppet 20	30	40
Baby Huey Hand Puppet, Gund, late 1950s 65	32	48
Baby Sandy Pull Toy, Gong Bell, 12½" long, Sandy & Goose . . . 150	225	300
Barney Rubble (Flintstones) 10" high vinyl doll, 1960 25	38	50
Bat Masterson Gun & Holster set with cane and vest, 1958, Carneli 150	225	300

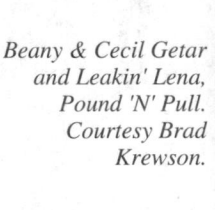

Beany & Cecil Getar and Leakin' Lena, Pound 'N' Pull. Courtesy Brad Krewson.

	C6	C8	C10
BEANY & CECIL *(list by Brad Krewson)*			
Beany Doll (doesn't talk), 15" high, Mattel, 1960 35	52	70
Beany Doll, Talks, 17" high, Mattel, 1960 55	82	110
Beany Halloween Costume, Ben Cooper 35	52	70
Beany Hat with Two Propellers 35	52	70
Beany & Cecil Colorforms set, 1961, with box 60	90	125
Beany & Cecil Getar, Cecil's eyes move, 1961, Mattel 24	36	48
Beany & Cecil Tea Set, 6 place settings, 1960, Worcester 36	54	72
Cecil Halloween Costume, Ben Cooper . 62	93	125
Cecil Disguise Kit, Mattel, 1962 37	56	75
Cecil Doll (doesn't talk), Mattel, 24" high, 1960 42	63	84

Beany & Cecil Leakin' Lena, plastic toy boat. Courtesy Brad Krewson.

Left to Right: Betty Boop, 12" high, jointed wood and composition, Betty Boop, 7" high, celluloid, Japanese. Courtesy Christie's East.

	C6	C8	C10
Cecil Doll, talks, Mattel, 29" high, 1960	92	137	185
Cecil Hand Puppet, talks, Mattel, 1961	35	52	70
Cecil Music Box, metal, plays show's theme song, Cecil pops up, 1961, Mattel	135	202	270
Dishonest John Handpuppet, talks, Mattel, 1961	65	98	130
Leakin' Lena plastic toy boat, Irwin Toy, 1962	75	112	150
Leakin' Lena wood toy ship, Pressman, 1960s	80	120	160
Leakin' Lena Pound & Pull, wooden, Pressman, 1961	85	127	170

End Beany & Cecil

	C6	C8	C10
Beatles, Ringo, John, Paul, George, 5" vinyl figures, 1964, Remco. Price per each	27	41	54
Beatles Soakies, each	75	112	150
Ben Casey Doll, 12" high, 1962	85	127	170
Ben Casey Play Hospital Set, Transogram	95	142	190
Ben Hur Sword, scabbard and shield, Marx, only produced in 1959, when movie was made	142	213	285
Betty Boop, approx. 3¾" high, "1931", wood-jointed, Jaymar	90	135	180
Betty Boop, 7" high, celluloid, Japanese, head shakes	600	900	1200
Betty Boop, 9½" tall, 1930s, jointed	240	360	480
Betty Boop, 12" high, jointed, wood and composition, c. 1930	500	750	1000
Betty Boop acrobat, celluloid and metal, Japanese, 1930s windup	350	550	750
Betty Boop and Bunny mechanical toy	150	225	300
Beverly Hillbillies car, Ideal, 1960s, windup	325	488	650

Beverly Hillbillies Car, IDEAL. Photo by Ron Chojnacki. Courtesy Don Hultzman.

	C6	C8	C10
Bob Burns Bazooka, brass kazoo-like toy, patterned after radio-movie comic Burns' famous musical invention (the Army weapon gets its name from it) metal sliding tube, M.M. Pochapia Toys, 13" long when not extended, 1930s	20	30	40
Bob Hope Handpuppet, c.1940s	25	38	50
"Bojangles Dances Again," tin litho and wood, 1930s, tap button on base and he dances	200	300	400

	C6	C8	C10
Bozo the Clown Bendem Doll, Knickerbocker	20	30	40
Bozo the Clown Handpuppet, Capital, 1962	15	22	30
Bozo the Clown Jumpkin, Kohner, 1960	13	19	26
Bozo the Clown Soaky	11	16	22
Bozo the Clown Squeeze Toy, 9"	60	90	120
Bozo the Clown talking handpuppet	30	45	60
Buck Jones Rangers chaps	90	135	180
Buffalo Bill Jr. belt and buckle (TV), 1950s	25	38	50
Bugs Bunny Handpuppet, early 1950s	40	60	80
Bugs Bunny Soaky, 10" high	17	26	35
Bugs Bunny & Porky Pig talking toy, 1940s, has record that talks	95	143	190
"Bullet" (Roy Rogers' dog) stuffed doll, circa 1955	40	60	80
Bullwinkle, 14" high, stuffed, 1970, Gund	35	52	70
Bullwinkle, Terrytoons, 15" high, 1961	50	75	100
Bullwinkle Flexie, Whamo	16	24	32
Bullwinkle Periscope, Lido, 1960s,	10	15	20
Bullwinkle Soaky, 11" high	25	38	50

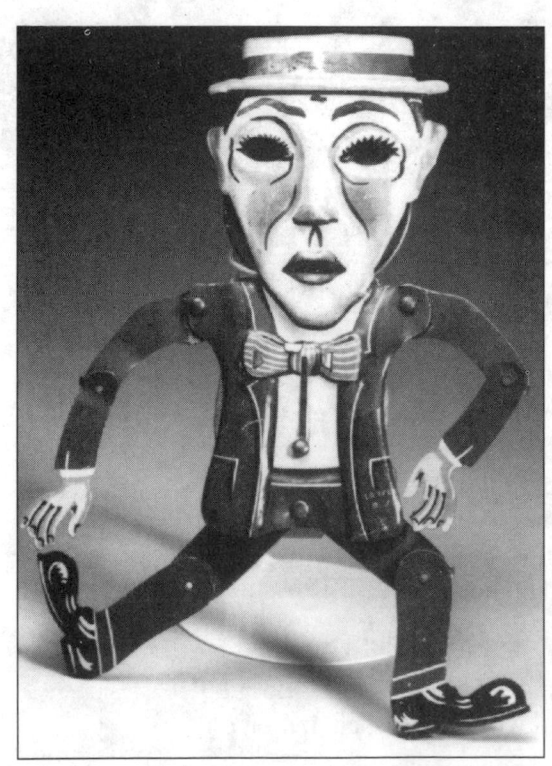

Buster Keaton Sparkler, Spanish, Courtesy Christie's East.

	C6	C8	C10
Buster Kenton Sparkler, Spanish, c. 1925, tin litho, 7" high, arms and legs move	1650	2475	3300

	C6	C8	C10
Captain Gallant Foreign Legion Holster outfit	80	120	160
Captain Gallant Marx Playset	400	600	800
Captain Kangaroo 20" talking doll, 1967	55	82	110
Captain Kangaroo badge, tin shield, 1960s	20	30	40
Casper The Friendly Ghost 11" stuffed doll, body is beanbag, 1960s	35	52	70
Casper The Friendly Ghost Hopper, 1950s, Linemar, 5" high	300	450	600
Casper the Friendly Ghost Squeak toy, 8"	31	47	62
Casper The Friendly Ghost Turnover Tank, Linemar tin wind-up	240	360	480
"Casper the Talking Ghost"	45	68	90
Cecil Sea Serpent	*See Benny & Cecil*		
Charlie Chaplin Bell Ringer squeeze toy, German, tin litho, metal bell, 7¼"	900	1350	1800
Charlie Chaplin Bell Toy, cast iron, circa 1912, 9¾"	300	450	600
Charlie Chaplin Bell Toy, metal, 3-wheeled, 5¼"	350	525	700
Charlie Chaplin Bicycle Rider String Toy, c.1920s	350	525	700
Charlie Chaplin, celluloid, 4" high	900	1350	1800
Charlie Chaplin "Charlie's Back" doll, 1971, Milton Bradley	45	68	90
Charlie Chaplin Cymbal-Player, tin litho, squeeze action, German-made, 6¾"	700	1050	1400
Charlie Chaplin "Dancing Charlie", cardboard	87	131	175
Charlie Chaplin Doll, Boucher, 7½" high, steel, lead and cloth, ball-jointed, movable arms, legs and feet	250	375	500
Charlie Chaplin Doll, Louis Amberg, 14" high, circa 1915, composition and cloth	75	113	150
Charlie Chaplin driving 3-wheel vehicle, tin windup, Paya (Spain)	2100	3150	4200
Charlie Chaplin, Ferguson Novelty Co., 9" high, windup, composition, cloth and metal walker	1100	1650	2200
Charlie Chaplin flat tin litho, tips hat when string is pulled	110	165	220
Charlie Chaplin, Mark Hampton Company, 9" high, composition, "CHAS. CHAPLIN" on base	350	525	700
Charlie Chaplin, Martin, 1920, clockwork, 7" high, papier mache, lead, wire cane, cloth clothes	500	750	1000

Charlie Chaplin, Left to Right: Charlie Chaplin Cymbal-Player, Charlie Chaplin wind-up, 7" high, French, Charlie Chaplin, Mark Hampton Co., Charlie Chaplin tin litho squeeze toy, Spanish, Charlie Chaplin Wind-up Walker, Charlie Chaplin Bell Toy, metal, 3-wheeled, Charlie Chaplin, Ferguson Novelty Co..Courtesy Christie's East.

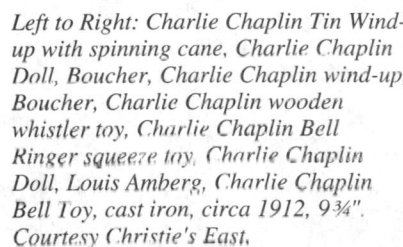

Left to Right: Charlie Chaplin Tin Wind-up with spinning cane, Charlie Chaplin Doll, Boucher, Charlie Chaplin wind-up, Boucher, Charlie Chaplin wooden whistler toy, Charlie Chaplin Bell Ringer squeeze toy, Charlie Chaplin Doll, Louis Amberg, Charlie Chaplin Bell Toy, cast iron, circa 1912, 9¾". Courtesy Christie's East.

	C6	C8	C10
Charlie Chaplin, Schuco tin wind-up, 1920s	400	600	800
Charlie Chaplin tin litho squeeze toy, Spanish, c. 1925, 7¾" high	900	1350	1800
Charlie Chaplin tin litho windup, 7" high, walks	1300	1950	2600
Charlie Chaplin Tin Windup, 8½" high, Nifty, 1920s	1100	1650	2200
Charlie Chaplin Tin Windup with spinning cane, 6¾" high (Unique Art?)	900	1350	1800
Charlie Chaplin Tricycle Rider tin windup, c. 1930, 3½"	900	1350	1800

Left to Right: Charlie Chaplin Tricycle Rider, Charlie Chaplin driving 3-wheel vehicle. Courtesy Christie's East.

471

	C6	C8	C10
Charlie Chaplin windup, Boucher, metal, tin and cloth, 8¼" high	1000	1500	2000
Charlie Chaplin windup, 7" high, French, composition, tin and cloth walker	450	675	900
Charlie Chaplin Windup Walker, composition, cloth and metal, 11½" high	200	300	400
Charlie Chaplin wooden whistler toy, circa 1920, whistles "How Dry I Am", 13¼" high	1250	1875	2500
Charlie McCarthy, 7½" high, celluloid	337	455	675
"Charlie McCarthy" written on top hat, standing erect, tin wind-up, circa 1938	330	495	660
Charlie McCarthy rubber doll, Effanbee	45	68	90

Charlie McCarthy Drummer Boy. Courtesy Christie's East.

Charlie McCarthy, approx. 20" high, Effanbee, mouth moves. Courtesy Christie's East.

Charlie McCarthy, 20" high, Effanbee, mouth moves, in tweed jacket. Courtesy Christie's East.

	C6	C8	C10
Charlie McCarthy, approx. 20" high, Effanbee, mouth moves	350	525	700
Charlie McCarthy, 20" high, Effanbee, Mouth moves, in tweed jacket	425	638	850
Charlie McCarthy, 20" high, Effanbee in summer suit, mouth moves	400	600	800
Charlie McCarthy in his Benzine Buggy, Marx	425	638	850
Charlie McCarthy Drummer Boy, 1938 Marx tin windup, 8" high	500	750	1000
Charlie McCarthy Facemask, molded gauze, complete with separate monocle	50	75	100
Charlie McCarthy Handpuppet, composition head, circa 1939	105	158	210
Charlie McCarthy paper money	3	4	5
Charlie McCarthy Tap Dancer, Marks Bros., 1938	100	150	200
Charlie McCarthy Ventriloquist doll, composition with cloth body, ring pull in back of head to activate lower jaw, 14½" tall	600	900	1200

Charlie McCarthy in his Benzine Buggy. Courtesy PB Eighty-Four, New York.

	C6	C8	C10
Charlie McCarthy 13" high, composition mouth moves, 1930s	120	180	240
Charlie McCarthy, 20" high 1950s cardboard puppet	45	68	90

CONDITION CODE:

C6 - Good. Evident overall wear, well played with, but acceptable to many collectors

C8 - Very Good Minor wear overall, very clean

C10 - Mint (like new)

Note: Mint in Box commands a higher price. Condition below C6 brings considerable lower prices.

Charlie McCarthy paper money. Courtesy Toy Collector News.

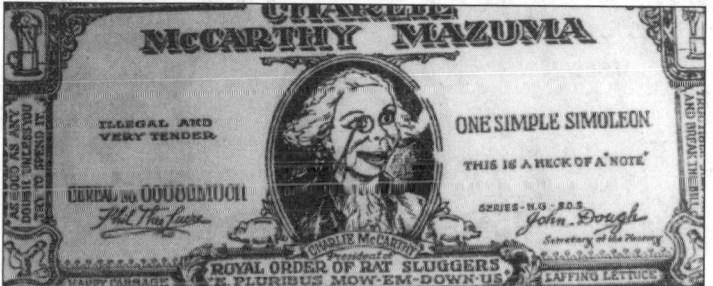

Charlie McCarthy paper money. Courtesy Rex and Richard Gray.

"Charlie McCarthy and Mortimer Snerd Private Car". Courtesy Phillips New York.

	C6	C8	C10
Charlie McCarthy Ventriloquist Doll, 18"	300	450	600
Charlie McCarthy Ventriloquist Doll, 33", Puppet Maker K&S	500	750	1000
Charlie McCarthy "Charlie McCarthy and Mortimer Snerd Private Car," Marx, two heads sticking out of top of car	1300	2000	2700
Charlie Weaver Nodder	94	141	188
CHIPS Motocycle, Mego	10	15	20
CHIPS Rescue Copter Fleet, 1979	9	13	18
Cisco Kid Broomstick Horse, 1950s, "Ride 'em Cisco Kid"	35	53	70
Cisco Kid Neckerchief with nickel sombrero slide	50	75	100
Cisco Kid Western Outfit, 1950s	60	90	120
Clyde Beatty Hingees Set, 1944	20	30	40
Cowardly Lion (Wizard of Oz) molded gauze facemask	40	60	80
Creature Soaky	50	75	100

	C6	C8	C10
Dale Evans holster outfit	90	135	180
Daniel Boone (Fess Parker) Canoe, vinyl, 18" long	10	15	20
Daniel Boone Cannon, Remco, 1964	80	120	160
Danny O'Day (Jimmy Nelson) ventriloquist doll	62	93	125
Deputy Dawg, 14" high stuffed doll, Ideal, 1961	45	68	90
Deputy Dawg Soaky	11	16	22
Dick Van Dyke doll from Chitty Chitty Bang Bang, 1967, talks, Mattel	40	60	80
Dr. Doolittle Pushimi Pullyu, 1965	20	30	40
Dr. Doolittle Music Box, Gee-Tar, Mattel, 1967	38	56	75
Dr. Doolittle Talking Handpuppet, 1967	40	60	80
Dragnet Crime Lab, 1955, flashlight, signal gun, badge, handcuffs, fingerprint kit, etc.	100	150	200
Dragnet Police Set, gun, handcuffs, badge	35	52	70
Dragnet Los Angeles Police No. 714 badge	12	18	25
Dragnet Shoulder Holster & Pistol, 1950s	62	93	125
Dragnet talking police car, Ideal Toys, circa 1954	105	158	210
Dragnet Water Pistol, circa 1955, 714 badge emblazoned on handle	20	30	40
Dragnet Whistle, black plastic	7	10	14
Dukes of Hazzard, 4 vehicles, Ertl set	12	18	25
Ed Wynn Fire Chief, ax in hand, jointed wood	80	120	160
Ed Wynn Fire Chief, litho on wood, pull toy, Schoenhut, 12" long	*See Schoenhut*		
Elmer Fudd Handpuppet early 1950s	46	69	92

CONDITION CODE:

C6 - Good. Evident overall wear, well played with, but acceptable to many collectors

C8 - Very Good Minor wear overall, very clean

C10 - Mint (like new)

Note: Mint in Box commands a higher price. Condition below C6 brings considerable lower prices.

Flintstone Pals on Dino, Fred and Barney riders, MARX.

FROGGIE THE GREMLIN. Courtesy Toy Collector News.

Fanny Brice (Baby Snooks), IDEAL. Courtesy Christie's East.

	C6	C8	C10
"Flintstone Flivver," 1962, Marx, (Japan), Friction, 6¾" long	375	562	750
Flintstone's Fred Flintstone, 5¾" high, hollow vinyl figure	22	33	44
Flintstones "Hopping Barney Rubble," 1962, Marx (Japan) windup, 4" high	200	300	400
Flintstones "Hopping Fred Flintstone," Linemar, 4" high	200	300	400
Flintstones "Hopping Dino," 1962, Linemar, 4" high	240	360	480
Flintstones Pebbles 7" jointed doll	37	56	75

	C6	C8	C10
Fanny Brice (Baby Snooks), Ideal, composition and wire doll, 12" high	110	165	220
Farfel (Jimmy Nelson) handpuppet, Juro	85	127	170
Farmer Alfalfa (Terrytoons) circa 1950, 17½" high, stuffed body, vinyl head, hands	30	45	60
Flintstones Bam Bam 12½" high, Ideal	27	40	55
Flintstones "The Flintstones Bedrock Express Handcar," 1962, Marx wind-up playset 22x26	225	338	450
Flintstones Choo Choo Train, Marx, "Bedrock Express," tin wind-up, Linemar Co., 13" long, 1950s	400	600	800
Flintstones "Dino On Tricycle," 1962, Linemar, 4" high	425	638	850
Flintstones "Dino the Dinosaur," 1961, Linemar, 9" long	300	450	600
Flintstones "Flintstone Friction Cars," (Fred, Barney, Wilma, etc.), 1962, Linemar, 4" long, price per each	150	225	300
Flintstones "Flintstone Pals" (Barney on Dino), Linemar, 1962, 8" long, windup	205	308	410
Flintstones "Flintstone Pals" (Fred on Dino), Linemar, 1962, 8" long, windup	225	338	450

Flintstones Playset, Marx.
Photo by Barry Goodman

	C6	C8	C10
Flintstones Playset, Marx	160	240	320
"Flintstones Mechanical Shooting Gallery," 1962, Marx, 13" long	150	225	300
Flintstones Motorized Yacht	375	562	750
Flintstones Paddy Wagon, Remco, 1961	100	150	200
Flintstones Tinykins, Marx	25	38	50
"Flintstone Tricycle", Wilma rider, Marx	240	360	480

	C6	C8	C10
Flintstones Turnover Tank, Linemar tin wind-up, 1950s, 4" long 275	363	550
Flip Wilson Geraldine talking doll, Shindana, 1970 30	45	60
Flub-A-Dub push puppet, plastic, felt, wood, 5" high 50	75	100
Flub-A-Dub (Howdy Doody) 3½" plastic figure 55	82	110
Frankenstein Soaky 37	56	75
Flying Nun, 4¾", Hasbro, 1960s . . 40	60	80
Flying Nun Flying Toy, Rayline, 1970.50	75	100
Frankenstein Soaky 57	85	115
Froggie the Gremlin hollow rubber doll, squeeze toy, 5" high, of the Buster Brown radio with TV show, squeeze and tongue sticks out, 1950s, Rempel 60	90	120
Froggie The Gremlin, 9¼" squeeze toy 200	300	400
Froggie The Gremlin, 10¾" squeeze toy 225	375	450
Gabby (Gulliver's Travels), 10½" high, Ideal, wood-jointed 300	450	600
Gangbusters Target Game, Marx . . 55	82	110
Gene Autry Marionette, 18" high, 1940s...140	210	280
Get Smart Spy Purse Kit, Miner Ind., 7" long...30	45	60
Gomez (Addams Family) handpuppet . 55	82	110
Green Horney Bendie, Lakeside, 1967 10	15	20
Green Hornet Car, Corgi 150	225	300
Green Hornet Handpuppet, Ideal..........200	300	400

	C6	C8	C10
Green Hornet Hat with Flipdown mask, Arlington Hat Co. 62	93	125
Green Hornet Raft 175	263	350
Green Hornet Signal Ray, Colorforms, 1966. 300	450	600
Green Hornet Walkie Talkies, Remco 200	300	400
Groucho Marx "Ventriloquist Play Pal," Goldberger 32	48	65
Gulliver's Travels Boat, wooden (Paramount)...110	165	220
Gulliver's Travels Drum, tin, Chein, 1939 25	38	50
Gulliver's Travels Musical Top, Chein .30	45	60
Gulliver's Travels Sandpail, tin, Chein....75	112	150
Gumby "Bendee" figure.........................12	18	25
Gumby "Gumby's Jeep", 12" metal, 1960s 125	188	250
Gumby Handpuppet, 1965, Lakeside....14	21	28
Gumby vinyl wind-up, dated 1966, approx. 4" high 37	56	75
Gunsmoke Handcuffs & Badge, c.1952 42	63	85
Harold Lloyd Bell Toy, German, 6½" high 275	362	550
Harold Lloyd Bumper Car, German, 1920s, auctioned 1993 for $17,600		
Harold Lloyd Donkey Cart, tin litho, Spanish, c. 1929, 9¼" long...........2200	3300	4500
Harold Lloyd "Funny Face," Marx wind-up walker, 1929 550	825	1100
Harold Lloyd Policeman, 12" high, tin wind-up...367	550	725
Harold Lloyd Sparkler, German tin litho...500	750	1000

Harold Lloyd, Left to Right: Harold Lloyd Bell Toy, Harold Lloyd "Funny Face", Harold Lloyd Sparkler. Courtesy Christie's East.

Harold Lloyd Donkey Cart. Courtesy Christie's East.

	C6	C8	C10
Henry Fonda Texas Ranger Sheriff Badge, The Deputy, 1951	20	30	40
Herman Munster Doll, Mattel	137	205	275
Herman Munster Hand puppet, vinyl, 1960s	44	66	88
Herman Munster Talking Puppet	75	112	150
Highway Patrol "Highway Patrol Car," Broderick Crawford litho, 8" long	65	98	130
"Highway Patrol Pistol Outfit," Halco, 1956, gun, holster, badge, handcuffs, ID, whistle, etc.	125	188	250
Hoot Gibson Cowboy Outfit, Wornova Clothes, 1935	70	105	140
Hoot Gibson lariat	40	60	80
Hoot Gibson Wornova Clothes (Squaw style), 1930s	60	90	120
"Hopalong Cassidy Automatic Television Set," 1950s, Automatic Toy Co., 5" cube	150	225	300
Hopalong Cassidy Badge, tin with inset photo	27	41	55
Hopalong Cassidy Binoculars, circa 1950, plastic	30	45	60
Hopalong Cassidy compass	105	158	210
Hopalong Cassidy Cowgirl's outfit	125	188	250
Hopalong Cassidy dart board, 14"x17", stagecoach holdup and target practice, 1950, Toy Ent.	65	98	130
Hopalong Cassidy Doll, 1930s-40s, 28" high	250	375	500
Hopalong Cassidy Field Glasses, 1940, metal	80	120	160
Hopalong Cassidy Flashlight Gun, plastic, 8" long, Hoppy's name on side	30	45	60
Hopalong Cassidy Handpuppet	60	90	120
Hopalong Cassidy "Hop-A-Long Cassidy," 1938 Marx 9½" high (on "Range Rider" rocker base)	375	562	750
Hopalong Cassidy knife, circa mid-1940s, 3½" long	90	135	180
Hopalong Cassidy Photo Ring, circa late 1940s	35	52	70
"Hopalong Cassidy Picture Gun and Theater", 1939, Stephens Co., 12" long - 8" high	200	300	400
Hopalong Cassidy Rocking Horse Cowboy, Marx	500	750	1000
"Hopalong Cassidy Shooting Gallery", 1950s, Automatic Toy Co., 18" long	200	300	400
Hopalong Cassidy Signet Ring, all metal, late 1940s	30	45	60
Hopalong Cassidy Spurs, leather and metal	60	90	120
Hopalong Cassidy Western Frontier set, with figures, stagecoach and buildings	300	450	600
Hopalong Cassidy Zoomerang Gun, shoots paper, Tigrett Enterprises, Chicago, 1950, 9" long	145	218	290
Howdy Doody 4" high plastic push-puppet, Kohner, has NBC mike	75	112	150
Howdy Doody 6" high, wall walker doll	31	46	62
Howdy Doody 7½" high, 1950s, plastic cloth clothes, eyes close, mouth opens	200	300	400
Howdy Doody 12" high, moveable jaws, Goldberger Dolls	35	52	70
Howdy Doody, 21" high, Ideal, 1950s	150	225	300
Howdy Doody 26" ventriloquist dummy	55	82	110
Howdy Doody Acrobat, Arnold, 1950s	200	300	400
"Howdy Doody Air-O-Doodle Circus Train," Kagran, 1950s, wind-up, 16" long	90	135	180
Howdy Doody and Bob Smith at the piano, tin wind-up, Unique	725	1088	1450
Howdy Doody "Clarabelle Clown," 1950s, Linemar, squeeze action cable, 6½" high	187	280	375
Howdy Doody "Clarabelle Clown," 1950s, Linemar, 5" high, Kagran Corp., wind-up	200	300	400
Howdy Doody "Clarabelle Hurdy Gurdy," 1950s, FBA Industries, Kagran, 8" long	200	300	400
Howdy Doody, Clarabelle's horn, 1950s	50	75	100
Howdy Doody Clarabelle Marionette, Peter Puppet Playthings, 1950s	125	188	250
Howdy Doody, Clarabelle Playsuit, Wonderland Costumes	62	93	125
Howdy Doody, Dilly-Dally Marionette, Peter Puppet Playthings, 1950s	260	390	520
Howdy Doody hand puppets, no date, no. mfr., rubber heads, cloth bodies	35	52	70
Howdy Doody Jeep, Marx windup	200	300	400

Howdy Doody Pumpmobile. Photo by Don Hultzman.

Jackie Coogan ("The Kid") tin wind-up walker.

Jackie Gleason "Away We Go" Bus. Courtesy Don Coviello.

Joe Penner tin wind-up. Courtesy Sotheby's New York.

HOOT GIBSON Cowboy outfit, WORNOVA CLOTHES, apparently new in 1935 and still on sale in 1939. Courtesy Heinz Mueller, Continental Hobby House.

Left to Right. Lone Ranger Doll, 20" high, Tonto, 20" high, both DOLLCRAFT. Courtesy Christie's East.

Harold Lloyd Bell Toy. Courtesy Sotheby's New York.

Jetsons Turnover Tank, LINEMAR. Photo by Don Hultzman.

HOWDY DOODY and BOB SMITH At The Piano. Courtesy PB Eighty-Four, New York.

JETSON EXPRESS Choo Choo Train. Photo by Don Hultzman.

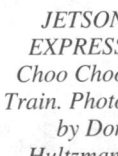

477

	C6	C8	C10
Howdy Doody Life Preserver, plastic, 1950s, show Howdy, Mr. Bluster, etc.	30	45	60
Howdy Doody Marionette, 17" high, wooden arms and legs, composition head	120	180	240
Howdy Doody Marionette, 16" high, composition head, hands and feet, handpainted features, 1950s	125	188	250
Howdy Doody Mask, rubber	12	18	24
Howdy Doody Piano, Howdy plays it	160	240	320
Howdy Doody plastic puppet toys, with levers in back of head to move mouths. Consists of Howdy, Bluster, Clarabelle, Princess, Dilly Dally, Tee-Vee Toys No. 549. Price for set	120	180	240
Howdy Doody plastic Ukulele, Emenee, 1950s	55	82	110
Howdy Doody Princess Summer-Fall Winter-Spring Puppet	75	112	150
Howdy Doody "Pump-Mobile," Nylint, unauthorized Howdy, rides cart, 8½" long, 7" high	275	363	550
Howdy Doody "Put-In-Head," similar to Mr. Potato Head, but with Howdy characters: Howdy, Bluster, Clarabelle, Princess. Price for set	50	75	100
Howdy Doody Sand Forms, 1952, molds of Howdy, Bluster, Flub-A-Dub, Clarabelle, plus shovel	20	30	40
Howdy Doody Squeeze Toy, 7" high	40	60	80
Howdy Doody TV Set with paper filmstrips, Lego, 1950s	42	63	85
Howdy Doody tin wind-up, circa 1950, Marx, 5" high, Howdy plays banjo and moves head	200	300	400
Howdy Doody tin wind-up circa 1950, Howdy does jig and Bob Smith sits at piano, Marx, 5½" high	550	825	1100
Howdy Doody wood-jointed doll, 13" high	175	263	350
Howdy Doody wood-jointed doll, 5½" high, holding NBC mike	200	300	400
Howdy Doody Zippy the Chimp Marionette, 1950s, Peter Puppet Playthings	550	800	1200
Huckleberry Hound, 18" stuffed doll, 1959, Knickerbocker	45	68	90
Huckleberry Hound as Fireman, rubber squeeze toy, 1960s, 9" high	27	41	55
Huckleberry Hound with top hat, Dell, rubber squeeze toy, 1960s, 6" high	15	22	30
Huckleberry Hound "Huckleberry Hound Car," 1962, Marx (Japan), wind-up, 4" long	130	195	260
Huckleberry Hound "Huckleberry Hound Hopper" 1962, Linemar, 4½" high	200	300	400
"Huckleberry Hound Tricycle," 1961, Linemar, 4" high	400	600	800
Hugh O'Brian-Wyatt Earp, Dodge City Western Town, Marx, 1950s	450	675	900
1 Spy Target Set	40	60	80
J. Fred Muggs (Today Show) hand puppet, 1954	41	62	82
J. Fred Muggs pull toy, Gong Bell	90	135	180
Jackie Coogan glass candy container, 5" high	800	1200	1600
Jackie Coogan 5½" high celluloid, 1920s	130	195	260
Jackie Coogan ("The Kid") tin wind-up walker, German, 7" high	800	1200	1600
Jackie Gleason "Away We Go" bus, 13"	450	675	900
Jackie Gleason costume (Kramden), money-change, etc	187	280	375
Jackie Gleason (Reggie Van Gleason) climbing toy	100	150	200
Jackie Gleason "Story Stage Theatre," Utopia Enterprises, copyright 1955	85	128	170
James Bond "Aston Martin" No. 271, Corgi, die-cast	50	75	100
James Bond "Aston Martin" No. 270, Corgi, die-cast	67	100	135
James Bond Aston-Martin...............*See Battery-Operated*			
James Bond 007 Attache Case, 11". Code Book, rifle, which converts to pistol, bullets, Code-O-Matic, billfold with money and James Bond business cards and instructions, circa 1965	175	262	350
James Bond Camera, shoots	125	188	250
James Bond Hand puppet, A.C. Gilbert, 1965	140	210	280

	C6	C8	C10
"James Bond-100 Shot Repeater Cap Pistol with Silencer," 1961, 9" long - total length - from "Goldfinger" - Lone Star Co.	162	243	325
Jerry Mahoney ventriloquist dummy	120	180	240
Jerry Lewis/Dean Martin two-sided handpuppet	125	188	250
Jetsons "Astro - the Jetsons' Dog," 1963 Marx wind-up (Japan), 5" high	212	318	425
Jetsons "George Jetson" 1963 Marx, (Japan) squeeze action cable, 4" high	150	225	300
Jetsons George Jetson circa 1965, Marx, tin wind-up, 4" high	190	275	380
Jetsons "Jetson Express Choo Choo Train," 1960s Marx (Japan), wind-up, 13" long	250	375	500
Jetsons Turnover Tank, Linemar tin wind-up	205	308	410
Joe Penner tin wind-up, Marx, circa 1930s, 8" high, tips hat, walks, "Wanna Buy a Duck?"	375	562	750
Jungle Jim Playset, Marx	500	800	1100
King Little (Gulliver's Travels), Ideal, 12" jointed composition	250	375	500
Kukla & Ollie Puppet Theatre, cardboard, 1962	50	75	100
Lambchop Shari Lewis Handpuppet	10	15	20
Lone Ranger Acme Moviescope Set, 1948, includes 4 films: No. 1 Superman, No. 2 Lone Ranger, No. 3 Lone Ranger, No. 4 Lone Ranger. With pop-up box including films and viewer	72	108	145
Lone Ranger and Silver composition figure, 1938, 4½" high	75	112	150
Lone Ranger Bendy, Lakeside, No. 8705, 6" high, 1967	16	24	32
Lone Ranger Chuck Wagon Lantern	75	112	150
Lone Ranger Deputy Badge, 1950s	16	24	32
Lone Ranger Doll, 20" high, 1938, very realistic composition head, hands, feet, Dollcraft	300	450	600
Lone Ranger Flashlight	80	120	160
Lone Ranger Handpuppet, vinyl head, c.1956	80	120	160
Lone Ranger Hand puppet, Ideal, 1966	20	30	40

LONE RANGER, "Hiyo Silver", the Lone Ranger. Courtesy PB Eighty-Four, New York.

LONE RANGER, Left to Right: 1938 MARX wind-up, litho version, 1938 MARX wind-up, chrome version. Photo by Don Hultzman.

	C6	C8	C10
Lone Ranger Harmonica, Magnus, 1950	40	60	80
Lone Ranger Hat, 1930s, official	37	56	75
Lone Ranger Hat, cowboy hat of white felt w/red trim. "Lone Ranger Hi! Yo! Silver!" inscribed, 1940s	22	33	45
Lone Ranger Official First Aid Kit with contents, 1938, tin litho	105	158	210
Lone Ranger "Official Outfit," 1939, mask, jail keys, badge, silver bullet, glow belt, Lone Ranger buckle, Lee Powell and Chief Thundercloud on belt	112	180	225
Lone Ranger "Lone Ranger Official Outfit," M.A. Henry Co., 1942 (belt, holster, guns, cuffs)	70	105	140
Lone Ranger 1938 Marx wind-up (on "Range Rider" rocker base), 10½" high	400	600	800
Lone Ranger 1938 Marx wind-up, chrome version, 8½" high from top of lariat	500	750	1000
Lone Ranger 1938 Marx wind-up, litho version, 8½" high from top of lariat	200	300	400
Lone Ranger Picture Printing Set, 1939, 8 rubber stamps	50	75	100
Lone Ranger Push Toy, Kohner, wood base, 1950s	55	82	110

Lone Ranger Ranch Set, series 500.
Photo by Barry Goodman

Milton Berle Car. Courtesy Mapes Auctioneers & Appraisers.

Mortimer Snerd band, MARX. Courtesy Christie's East.

Mortimer Snerd tin wind-up, MARX. Courtesy PB Eighty-Four, New York.

	C6	C8	C10
Lone Ranger, Ranch Set, series 500, Marx Playset	300	450	600
Lone Ranger Rides Again movie viewer, 1939	60	90	120
Lone Ranger Rodeo, Marx set with metal bldgs., plastic figures, etc., 1950s, No. 9392	200	300	400
Lone Ranger Signal Siren, Flashlight, 1950's, with silver bullet secret code, United States Electric Mfg. Co.	80	120	160
Lone Ranger Silver Bullet Knife, length 3" closed	92	138	185
Lone Ranger "Stringless Marionette" handpuppet, cloth and vinyl	120	180	240
Lone Ranger Strongbox (coinbank)	50	75	100
Lone Ranger Target Game, 1938, Marx	70	105	140
Lucy (Peanuts) 1950s, vinyl squeeze doll	15	22	30
Lurch (Addams Family), Remco	60	90	120
Magilla Gorilla Hand puppet, Ideal, 1960s	30	45	60
Magilla Gorilla, Ideal, 8" high	30	45	60
Magilla Gorilla, Ideal, 1960s, 19" high	130	195	260
Mary Poppins Hand puppet, Gund	47	77	95
Matt Dillon, U.S. Marshall badge (Gunsmoke)	15	22	30
Men Into Space space helmet, retractable visor, space mike, etc. From series starring William Lundigan as Col. McCaulety. Made of fortiflex	55	82	110
Milton Berle Car, two large wheels, two small, Marx, 1950s, "What the Hey," etc. written on car	250	375	500
Mortimer Snerd, 5" high, Celluloid	200	300	400

	C6	C8	C10
Mortimer Snerd, 13" high, Ideal, composition and wire	262	393	525
Mortimer Snerd Band, Marx, wind-up, 1935, "Hometown Band"	450	675	900
Mortimer Snerd, Jack In The Box, circa 1930s, 8" high	100	150	200
"Mortimer Snerd Teeth," plastic teeth and dental wax, circa 1950	15	22	30
Mortimer Snerd Tin Wind-up, Marx, circa 1939, Mortimer's hat tips as he walks	275	363	550
"Mortimer Snerd's Tricky Auto," 1939, Marx	400	600	800
Mr. Ed handpuppet, Mattel, 1962	35	57	70
Mr. Magoo Car, battery, tin litho...*See Battery Toys "MaGoo"*			
Mr. Magoo Doll, Ideal, 15" high	65	88	130
Mr. Magoo Handpuppet	25	38	50
Mr. Magoo Soaky, 11" high	15	22	30
Mummy Soaky	42	63	85
Munsters, Grandpa Hand puppet, vinyl, 1960s	56	84	112

	C6	C8	C10
Munsters, Herman ....See Herman Munster			
Munsters, Lily Munster handpuppet, 1960s...50		75	100
My Favorite Martian "Martian Magic Tricks," Gilbert, 1964, magic set 50		75	100
Oliver Hardy Bendem Doll, 1960, Knickerbocker 12		18	25
Oliver Hardy Doll, Dean 400		600	800
Oliver Hardy Handpuppet, Knickerbocker...35		52	70
Oliver Hardy Roly Poly, 10½" high, plastic 22		33	45
Oliver Hardy Sparkler, Isla, Spanish ...1000		1500	2000
Oliver Hardy windup, Lakeside, 5" high, 1960s...35		52	70
"Oswald, Universal Pictures, Irwin Prod." 18½" wind-up, wood and cardboard body with cloth clothes, stuffed arms and head, character created by Disney, early 800		1300	1800
Oswald Stuffed Toy, 20⅞" high 200		300	400
Our Gang Dolls and Clubhouse, Mego, 1975. 175		262	350
Pink Panther handpuppet, early, cloth body, Gund......................................15		22	30
Pinky Lee Pull Toy, Gong Bell.............100		150	200
Pinky Lee vinyl doll. Squeeze and his head pops up, 1950 140		210	280
Poky (Gumby) "Bendee" figure.............10		15	20
Poky Handpuppet, 1965, Lakeside........13		19	26
Poky "Jack In The Box", Lakeside, 1965 16		24	32
Poky vinyl windup, dated 1966, approx. 4" high 37		56	75
Quick Draw McGraw, 17½" Knickerbocker 105		158	210
Quick Draw McGraw, "Animal Airplane," 1960s, Linemar, 8½" long - 9½" wingspan (Yogi Bear and Huckleberry Hound's head also used) 400		600	800
Quick Draw McGraw "Quick Draw McGraw Hopper," 1962, Linemar, 4½" high 200		300	400
Ramar of the Jungle Playset 217		325	435
Rat Patrol Giant Action Battle Set 112		168	225
Rat Patrol Jeep, Marx 150		225	300
Ricochet Rabbit, Ideal 37		56	75
Rifleman (TV) Ranch, Marx 350		525	700
Rin Tin Tin and Rusty Knife, 1950s......60		90	120
Rin Tin Tin - Marx Fort Apache Stockade, 1950s, No. 3628 210		315	420

"Oswald" wind up, wood and cardboard body with cloth clothes (1932 ad).

Mortimer Snerd, 13" high, IDEAL. Courtesy Christie's East.

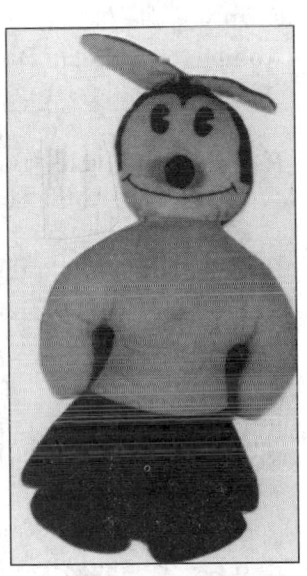

Oliver Hardy Sparkler, ISLA. Courtesy Christie's East.

Oswald stuffed toy, 20⅞" high. Courtesy James S. Maxwell/Virginia Caputo. Photo by Virginia Caputo

Rifleman Ranch, Marx. Photo by Barry Goodman

Rin Tin Tin Marx Fort Apache stockade playset.
Photo by Barry Goodman

ROY ROGERS "Stage Coach Wagon Train". Courtesy Continental Hobby House.

Roy Rogers "Roy Rogers Chuckwagon", Nellie Belle Jeep. Photo by Don Hultzman.

Scrappy (Columbia Pictures), 14½" high. Courtesy Christie's East.

Roy Rogers Signal Flashlight. Photo by Gary J. Linden.

	C6	C8	C10
Robin Hood Bow & Arrow Set, 1956, Richard Greene	6	9	12
Robin Hood Money Pouch, six foreign coins from Richard Greene TV series, 1953-54	20	30	40
Robin Hood Money Pouch, fifteen foreign coins, from Richard Greene TV series	20	30	40
Robin Hood Shield. Badge with embossed Robin Hood and gem stone, circa 1956	25	38	50
Rocky The Flying Squirrel Bendee figure, 1960s	12	18	25
Rocky the Flying Squirrel Hand puppet	25	38	50
Rocky The Flying Squirrel Soaky	15	22	30
Rootie Kazootie Marionette, 14" hard rubber head and hands, wooden shoes and body wearing clothes	90	135	180
Rootie Kazootie, 19", Effanbee	62	93	125
"Roy Rogers and Bullet Hobby Horse," No. 812, 1950s, N.N. Hill Brass Co., 19" long	200	300	400
Roy Rogers bandanna, large	32	48	65
Roy Rogers Bobbin' Head doll, 6" high, 1962	90	135	180
Roy Rogers Branding Iron Set	40	60	80
Roy Rogers Double R Bar Ranch, 1950s, tin litho ranch house, Marx	90	135	180
Roy Rogers Mineral City, town with hotel, music hall, cafe, bank, barber shop, trade goods, etc., tin	185	278	370
Roy Rogers Nellie Belle Jeep, metal	85	128	170
Roy Rogers pocket flashlight	40	60	80
Roy Rogers Quickshooter Hat with Secret Gun	90	135	180

	C6	C8	C10
Roy Rogers "Ranch Lantern," No. 90, metal, hurricane type with plastic chimney, 1950s, 7¾" tall	50	75	100
Roy Rogers Rodeo Ranch, Marx Playset.	100	150	200
Roy Rogers "Roy Rogers Buckboard," 1950s, Ideal, 16" long	65	98	130
Roy Rogers "Roy Rogers Chuck Wagon," Ideal, 1950s, 13" long	150	225	300
Roy Rogers "Roy Rogers Fix-it Stage Coach," 1950s, Ideal, 13" long	80	120	160

	C6	C8	C10
Roy Rogers "Roy Rogers Horse Trailer & Jeep," Ideal, 1950s, 15" long	175	263	350
Roy Rogers "Roy Rogers Stage Coach Wagon Train," wind-up, 14" long, plastic, 1950s	112	168	225
Roy Rogers Signal Flashlight	90	135	180
Roy Rogers Telescope	40	60	80
Roy Rogers and Trigger Pocket Knife	75	112	150
Roy Rogers Wagon Train, Marx	150	225	300
Roy Rogers Western Town Playset, Marx	260	390	520
Scarecrow (Wizard of Oz) molded gauze facemask	60	90	120
Scrappy (Columbia Pictures), 14½" high, circa 1935, E.D. & T.C. Co., cloth and composition	320	480	640
Scrappy & Margie wooden pull toy, 13½" long, he plays xylophone, she revolves	165	248	330
Sgt. Bilko Holster Set from the CBS TV series "You'll Never Get Rich," starring Phil Silvers. Photo illustrated box contains leather holster and belt with realistic Army .45 made of silvered die cast metal. Sgt.'s arm patch and Sgt. Bilko hat with Badge, Halco Brand, 1956	100	150	200
Shadow Crimefighter Detection Belt, with pistol, handcuffs, etc., 1978, Madison Ltd.	15	22	30
Shadow Felt Hat, early 1940s	187	280	375
Shirley Temple Playhouse	120	180	240
Small Fry Club Kit, 1949, button, etc., Dumont TV show (may be premium)	30	45	60
"Sneak" Facemask, molded gauze (Gulliver's Travels,) 1939	50	75	100
Soupy Sales doll, 1965, Sunshine Doll Co., 5" high	70	105	140
Soup Sales Marionette, Knickerbocker, 1966	52	78	105
Stan Laurel Bendem Doll, 1960, Knicker bocker	17	26	35
Stan Laurel Doll, Dean	400	600	800
Stan Laurel Handpuppet, Knickerbocker	40	60	80
Stan Laurel wind-up, Lakeside, 5" high, 1960s	35	52	70
Star Trek - Mr. Spock Vulcan Ears, 1976	5	8	10
Sylvester Hand puppet early 1950s	50	75	100

	C6	C8	C10
Sylvester, 1971, 15" high, cloth	30	45	60
Sylvester Soaky	13	20	27
Tales of the Texas Rangers Deputy Badge	12	18	24
Tarzan Bendy, Mago, 1972	25	38	50
Tennessee Tuxedo Soaky	24	36	48
Theodore (Chipmunk) Soaky	8	12	16
Three Stooges handpuppet, 1959, 9½" high, Moe, Curley and Larry, price per each	65	98	130
Tim Holt Litho Target with Dart Gun	70	105	140
Tinman Facemask (Wizard of Oz) molded gauze	60	90	120

Tom Corbett Space Academy Set, Marx
Photo by Barry Goodman

	C6	C8	C10
Tom Corbett Space Academy Set, Marx No. 7000	325	488	650
Tom Corbett, 7 different figures, same as above, price per set	28	42	56
Tom Corbett Cosmic Vision Space Helmet, one-way vision, plastic, early 1950s	250	375	500
Tom Corbett Space Cadet Molding and Coloring Set, Model Craft (All Tom Corbett toys 1950-55)	60	90	120
Tom Corbett Space Cadet Field Glasses, 3 power, Herald, 5½" long	12	18	25
Tom Corbett Space Cadet Flashlight with built-in signal siren, 7" long, metal, US Alite Corp	70	105	140
Tom Corbett Official Outfit, Yankiboy	275	362	550
Tom Corbett "Polaris" Rocket Ship, wind-up Marx, 1952, 12" long, Tom, Astro and Rogers looking out of cockpit	375	563	750
Tom Corbett Space Hat, Lee	40	60	80
Tom Corbett Space Cadet official Space Pistol, Marx No. 105	120	180	240

TOM CORBETT "Polaris" Rocket Ship. Photo by Don Hultzman.

	C6	C8	C10
Tom Corbett Space Cadet Rifle, Marx, No. 0239	125	188	250
Tom Corbett Space Station	325	488	650
Tom Corbett Space Cadet, 2-Way Space Phone, Zimmerman	80	120	160
Tom Corbett "Tom Corbett Space Cadet Atomic Rifle," Marx, 1950s, 24" long	150	225	300
Tom Corbett "Tom Corbett Space Cadet Official Space Pistol," 1950s, Rockhill, 9½" long	100	150	200

"Tom Mix Circus Wild West" by Arcade. The wagon is wood.

	C6	C8	C10
Tom Mix "Circus Wild West," Arcade circus wagon with driver, two horses, 14½" long, circa 1936, wagon is wood - (See Animal Drawn, Arcade "Big Six")	550	825	1100
Tom Mix metal and leather spurs, 1934 (not a premium)	150	225	300
Tom Mix on Tony, Arcor Rubber, 1930s	50	75	100
Tom Mix Rocking Horse, wooden, 1930s	225	338	450
Tom Mix Rodeorope, 1928, comes with box and instructions	100	150	200
Tonto (Lone Ranger) 20" high doll, 1938, very realistic, composition head, hands, feet, Dollcraft	500	750	1000

W.C. Fields, 19" high, Effanbee. Courtesy Christie's East.

Tom Corbett Space Cadet Flashlight with built-in signal siren. Photo by Gary J. Linden.

	C6	C8	C10
Tonto Hand puppet, mid 1950s, vinyl head	47	80	95
Tonto Hand puppet, Ideal, 1966	25	38	50
Topo Gigio (Ed Sullivan Show) Nodder	55	82	110
Topo Gigio Airplane, friction	75	112	150
Umbriago (Jimmy Durante) hand-puppet, 1945, American Merchandise	60	90	120
Uncle Fester Hand puppet, vinyl, 1960s	40	60	80
Underdog, small	40	60	80
Underdog, medium	50	75	100
Underdog, large	62	93	125
Untouchables Tommy Gun, 1950s, Marx, 23" long	48	72	96
W.C. Fields, 19" high, Effanbee, movable mouth	425	638	850
Waterfront (TV series) "Cheryl Ann" tug, 21", 1950s	100	150	200
Wendy (Casper) Soaky, 10" high	16	24	32
Wild Bill Hickock & Jingles holster set	50	75	100
Wild Bill Hickock & Jingles TV Show, 42 piece Western Bunkhouse	17	26	35
Wild Bill Hickock Marshal Star Badge with picture of Hickock and Jingles in center	16	24	32

	C6	C8	C10
Wizard of Oz masks, set of five, Einson-Freeman Co., Inc., 1939, "Par-T-Mask"	150	225	300
Wizard of Oz, Mattel, four-headed hand puppet, c.1967, talks	60	90	120
Wizard of Oz, Mego, Dorothy & Toto	22	33	45
Wizard of Oz, Mego, General	42	63	85
Wizard of Oz, Mego, Glinda, 8", 1972	22	33	45
Wizard of Oz, Mego, Lion, 1972, 15" long	30	45	60
Wizard of Oz, Mego, Mayor Munchkin	40	60	80
Wizard of Oz, Mego, Munchkins (4), per each	32	48	65
Wizard of Oz, Mego, Scarecrow, 1972, 8" high	22	33	45
Wizard of Oz, Mego, Tinman, 8" high, 1972	22	33	45
Wizard of Oz, Mego, Wicked Witch, 8", 1972	37	56	79
Wizard of Oz, Mego, Wizard, 8"	12	18	24
Wizard of Oz, Mego, Emerald City Playset	25	38	50
Wizard of Oz Munchkinland Playset	80	120	160
Wizard of Oz, Witch's Castle, Mego	175	262	350
Wolfman Soaky	50	75	100
Wyatt Earp U.S. Marshall Badge, Lone Star	18	27	36
Wyatt Earp U.S. Marshall Badge, 20th century, 1950s, Hugh O'Brian photo	20	30	40
Wyatt Earp U.S. Marshall's Outfit, Pla-Master	80	120	160
Yellow Submarine (Beatles), Corgo	125	188	250
Yogi Bear, 7½" high, stuffed, 1973, Knickerbocker	15	22	30
Yogi Bear Friction Car, Marx, 1962	100	150	200
Yogi Bear Go-Cart, Linemar	138	205	275
Yogi Bear Hand puppet, 1959	15	22	30
Yogi Bear "Jellystone National Park" Marx Playset	350	525	700
Yogi Bear Tricky Trapeze, 1967, 5" high	50	75	100
Yogi Bear "Yogi Bear Car," 1962 Marx (Japan), 4" long	100	150	200
Yogi Bear "Yogi Bear Hopper," 1962, Linemar, 4" high wind-up	300	450	600
Yosemite Sam, Dakin Squeak Toy, 1970, 4" high	10	15	20

DISNEY
(See also Paper, Premiums, Fisher-Price)

The average mint price of Disney toys in the last edition
was $586.47 and in this edition it is $663.41 an increase of 13%.

Although Walt Disney was involved in animation as early as 1920, his first really notable character was Oswald the Rabbit, introduced in 1927. However, Disney did not own the rights, which eventually fell into the hands of another animator, Walter Lantz. Mickey Mouse first appeared in the 1928 short "Plane Crazy", but the third Mickey cartoon, "Steamboat Willie", seems to have been the first released, on

November 18, 1928, and Mickey was a success from that point on. Minnie Mouse also appeared in the latter film, with Pluto emerging in 1930, though not called that till 1931, Goofy debuting in 1932, and Donald Duck in 1934. Mickey Mouse toys were first produced in 1930, and since then the stream of Disneyana has been unending, and apparently all of it deemed collectible.

DAVY CROCKETT Powder Horn, DAISY. Courtesy Toy Collector News.

	C6	C8	C10
Alice in Wonderland Marionette, Peter Puppet	92	138	185
Babes In Toyland, tin litho wind-up Indian on rollerskates, Linemar, 1950s, 6½" tall	200	300	400
"Babes In Toyland Soldier", 1950's, Linemar, 6½" tall, tin windup	120	180	240
Babes In Toyland Wood Officer on horseback, wheeled, Jaymar	175	263	350
Babes In Toyland Wood Soldier with cannon, Jaymar	210	315	420
Babes in Toyland Wood Soldier with rifle, Jaymar, 9" high	60	90	120
Bambi "Jumping Bambi", Linemar, 1950s, trigger action, 6" high	250	375	500
Bambi Soaky	13	19	26
Bashful 1½" lead figure, Britains	40	60	80
Bashful, 5¾" high, Seiberling Rubber	90	135	180
Bashful, approx. 7" high, Ideal	125	188	250
Bashful, approx. 12" high, 1938, Ideal	80	120	160
Bashful Party Mask, 1937	20	30	40
Bashful stuffed doll	60	90	120
"Big Bad Wolf and The Three Little Pigs", 1950s, Linemar, 4¼" tall, 4 pc. set	750	1125	1500
Big Bad Wolf Halloween costume, 4'high	60	90	120
Big Bad Wolf celluloid pinback, 1¼"	38	53	75

	C6	C8	C10
Big Bad Wolf Stuffed toy in tux, with carnation, glass eyes, 20" tall	450	675	900
Captain Hook Hand puppet, Gund, 1950	25	38	50
Captain Hook marionette, Peter Puppet Playthings	95	143	190
"Casey Jr. Disneyland Express", loco, 3 cars, tin & plastic, Marx	75	112	150
Cinderella Handpuppet, "1957"	22	33	45
Cinderella wind-up 4¾" high, Irwin, umbrella, spins and dances	58	87	116
Cinderella and Prince - Dancing, No. 7000, Irwin Co., 1950s, plastic wind-up, 5" high	90	135	180
Cleo facemask, (Pinocchio) by Gillette, 1939	20	30	40
Cleo The Goldfish (Pinocchio) Sun Rubber squeeze toy	22	33	44
Davy Crockett Auto-Magic Picture Gun	30	45	60
Davy Crockett Badge, 1950s, "Frontier Marshal"	27	41	55
Davy Crockett Coonskin Hat	20	30	40
Davy Crockett doll, 8" high, Fortune Toy, 1950s	60	90	120
Davy Crockett doll, 20" high, Gund, vinyl	60	90	120
Davy Crockett Flying Arrows, balsa wood figures to be made into flying arrows. Copyright 1955	10	15	20
Davy Crockett "Frontierland Davy Crockett Outfit", gun, coonskin hat, etc.	47	70	95
Davy Crockett hand-gun, pop-action, tin litho, 1950s	42	63	85
Davy Crockett Play Knife, 1950s	18	27	36
Dave Crockett Play Set	450	675	900
Davy Crockett Powder Horn, Daisy	20	30	40
Davy Crockett Prairie Wagon, 5" long	75	112	150
"Davy Crockett Wagon Train", 1950's, Marx (plastic) 14" long	150	225	300

	C6	C8	C10
Disney Showboat, 1960, large	62	93	125
"Disney Show Boat", 1981, Playworld Toys, plastic	4	6	8
Disneyland Concert Xylophone, Tudor, 18" long	30	45	60
Disney Ferris Wheel, circa late 1956, Chein, tin wind-up, 17" high	350	525	700
Disneykins, Marx, Set	100	150	205
"Disneyland Happy Birthday Carousel", 1950s, Ross Co., 6" high	100	150	200
"Disneyland Jeep", 1960s, Marx, 10" long push toy	250	375	500
"Disneyland Melody Player", 1950s, Chein, 7" cubic, 4 rolls	200	300	400
"Disneyland Melody Player" Extra paper rolls, different songs, 1950s, for Melody Player, each	10	15	20
Disneyland Playset, Marx	425	638	850
Disneyland Roller Coaster, Chein, 10" high, 2 tin cars, 1950s	382	575	765
Doc 1½" lead figure, Britains	60	90	120
Doc (Snow White), approx.7" high, Ideal	125	188	250
Doc, 9" composition with velvet clothes, Knickerbocker	100	150	200
Doc, 11½" high, stuffed molded oil-cloth face, Ideal	100	150	200
Doc Party Mask, 1937	14	21	28
Doc Seiberling Rubber, 1938	50	75	100
Donald Duck, 3½" high, celluloid walker, Japan wind-up	325	488	650
Donald Duck, 4" high tin wind-up, Linemar, with umbrella	300	450	600
"Donald Duck", 5" high, 1930s, long-billed celluloid, Borgfeldt (Japan)	750	1125	1500
Donald Duck, 6" high, 1930s, long billed, celluloid wind-up	450	675	900
"Donald Duck", 6" high, 1950s, Linemar squeeze action	140	210	280
"Donald Duck", 6" high, Schuco wind-up, German, "984"	275	362	550
Donald Duck, 6" high drummer, mechanical, Linemar	300	450	600
Donald Duck 6" high, Seiberling Rubber, long-billed, 1930s	250	375	500
"Donald Duck" 7" high, 1960s, Marx wind-up, hard plastic	67	100	135
Donald Duck, 9" high, composition and cloth, long billed, in Russian costume	1000	1500	2000

DISNEYLAND Ferris Wheel. Courtesy HAKE'S Americana & Collectibles.

DISNEYLAND Happy Birthday Carousel. Photo by Don Hultzman.

DISNEYLAND Roller Coaster, Chein. Courtesy Continental Hobby House.

	C6	C8	C10
Donald Duck, 9" high, 1930s, long-billed, composition, Knickerbocker	800	1300	1800
Donald Duck 10" high, Sun Rubber	100	150	200
Donald Duck 13" stuffed doll, long-billed, Knickerbocker, 1930s	150	225	300
Donald Duck, 13" high, celluloid, 1940s	135	198	270
Donald Duck, 13½" high, Gund, circa 1949	110	165	220
Donald Duck 13½" high, Character Novelty, 1940	110	165	220
Donald Duck 16" high, long bill, 1930s	75	112	150
Donald Duck Acrobat, Linemar, 1950s, 8½" high	230	345	460
"Donald Duck and His Nephews", 1950s, Marx, 11" long-plastic wind-up	250	375	500
"Donald Duck and Huey With Voice", 1950s, Linemar, 7" long (string pull toy)	500	750	1000

	C6	C8	C10
Donald Duck Captain, Kohner Push Puppet, 1950s, wood and plastic	100	150	200
Donald Duck "Choo Choo" No. 450	....See Fisher-Price		
"Donald Duck Climbing Fireman", 1950s Linemar, 13½'" wind-up	700	1200	1600
"Donald Duck Convertible", 1950s, Linemar, 5" long, tin, friction	400	600	800
Donald Duck Crawler, celluloid wind-up, 9¾" long	650	1100	1500
Donald Duck Delivery Tricycle, tin and plastic, 5", Marx	180	270	360
"Donald Duck Dipsy Car", 1950s, 5¼" long, Marx, tincar, (plastic Mickey or Donald)	287	430	575
Donald Duck "Dipsy Car - Donald Duck", 1950s, Linemar wind-up, 6" long	350	525	700
"Donald Duck Disney Flivver", 1950s, Linemar, 5½" long, push-down on head	300	450	600

Donald Duck Dipsy Car. Photo by Don Hultzman.

Donald Duck and Pluto in Roadster, SUN RUBBER. Photo by David Leopard.

Donald Duck Xylophone Player. Courtesy Lloyd W. Ralston Auctions.

DONALD DUCK, 6" high, Sieberling, rubber, long-billed. Courtesy HAKE'S Americana & Collectibles.

	C6	C8	C10
Donald Duck Doctor Kit	60	90	120
Donald Duck "Donald & His Nephew" 1950s, Linemar, pull string action, 5½" high	400	600	800
Donald Duck "Donald the Driver", 1950s Linemar friction car, 6½" long	250	375	500
Donald Duck "Donald the Drummer", 1950s, Marx wind-up, 9" tall	250	375	500
Donald Duck "Donald Race Car", celluloid wind-up, occupied Japan	275	363	550
"Donald Duck Drummer", 1950s, Linemar wind-up, 6" high walker	350	525	700
"Donald Duck Drummer", 1950s Linemar wind-up, 6" tall, rocker	300	450	600
Donald Duck Duet, small Donald, large Goofy, circa 1945, Marx tin wind-up	500	750	1000
"Donald Duck Dump Truck", 1950s, Linemar, 5" long	300	450	600
Donald Duck Fire Chief Crazy Car, Linemar wind-up, tin litho, rubber hat, extremely rare	700	1250	1700
"Donald Duck In His Convertible", 1950s, Linemar friction, 6" long	300	450	600
Donald Duck Jigger, 11" high, papier mache wind-up	800	1200	1600
Donald Duck Mousketeers Hat	15	22	30
Donald Duck on paddle, string-puller, long-billed	*See Fisher-Price*		

Donald Duck Duet. Courtesy Mapes Auctioneers & Appraisers.

Donald Duck on Rocking Horse. Courtesy James S. Maxwell/Virginia Caputo. Photo by Virginia Caputo.

	C6	C8	C10
Donald Duck on Pluto, celluloid wind-up	1400	2200	3200
Donald Duck on Rocking Horse, Japan, celluloid tin, wind-up, 3⅜" long	3000	4500	6000
"Donald Duck on Tractor", 1950s, Marx friction, 3½" long, plastic	120	180	240

Donald Duck and his Nephews. Photo by Don Hultzman.

Donald Duck, 9" high, composition and cloth, long billed, in Russian costume. Courtesy Christie's East.

DONALD DUCK Climbing Fireman. Photo by Don Hultzman.

Donald Duck Railroad Car. Courtesy Christie's East.

Donald Duck Rowboat, Chad Valley. Courtesy Christie's East.

	C6	C8	C10
"Donald Duck on Trapeze", 1930's, Borgfeldt, 9" high-Donald 4¾" long	275	362	550
Donald Duck pulled by Pluto, celluloid, with tin cart, Japan, 1930s, long billed	1750	2625	3500
Donald Duck pulltoy, baton-twirler, No. 400	*See Fisher-Price*		
Donald Duck pultoy, No. 765, plastic feet, 1950s	*See Fisher-Price*		
Donald Duck pulltoy, 6½" long, long-billed, on platform	*See Fisher-Price*		
Donald Duck pull toy, No. 400, 1940, 10" tall, 7½" long, wooden figure with movable arms and legs, composition head	*See Fisher-Price*		
Donald Duck pull toy - wagon, circa 1940, No. 544	*See Fisher-Price*		
Donald Duck pull toy, with Xylophone, circa 1938, No. 185	*See Fisher-Price*		
"Donald Duck Railroad Car" with Pluto, Doghouse, 10" long, Lionel No. 1107, 1930s	450	675	900
Donald Duck Riding Mule, long-billed celluloid wind-up, 7¾"	850	1275	1700
Donald Duck Roly Poly, 3¾", 1940s	187	280	375
Donald Duck Rowboat, Chad Valley (England), wood and paper litho, 12¼" long	300	450	600
Donald Duck Rubber Boat, Sun Rubber Co., circa 1940s	40	60	80
Donald Duck Skier, Linemar	300	450	600
Donald Duck Skier, Marx, 1940s, plastic Donald	150	225	300
Donald Duck Soaky	12	18	24
"Donald Duck Straight Shoooter", 1960s plastic wind-up, 6½" high	187	280	375

	C6	C8	C10
Donald Duck Swimmer, celluloid wind-up, 6½"	650	1000	1500
Donald Duck Teapot, Ohio Art	30	45	60
Donald Duck Tractor, Sun Rubber	112	188	225
Donald Duck Tricycle, 3½" long, Linemar, wind-up, 1950s	312	468	625
"Donald Duck Tricycle", (with twirling parasol), 1950s, MT Co., Japan, 7½" high	200	300	400
"Donald Duck Waddler", 1930s, K Co., Japan, long bill, tin and celluloid, 3¼" high	600	900	1200
"Donald Duck Waddler", 1930s, "K" Co., 3½" tall	600	900	1200
"Donald Duck Washing Machine", 1950s, MT Co., Japan, 7½" high	400	600	800
"Donald Duck with Whirling Tail", 1950s, Linemar, tin wind-up, 5¼" high	300	450	600
"Donald Duck with Whirling Tail", 1950s, Marx plastic wind-up, 6½" high	100	150	200
Donald Duck Zylophone, Tudor, 10" long	27	41	55
Donald Duck and Pluto in roadster, Sun Rubber, 1930s, about 6½" long	62	93	125
Donkey (Pinocchio), Knickerbocker, stuffed	95	142	190
Donkey (Pinocchio) rubber, Seiberling, 1940	70	105	140

DOPEY Tin Wind-up, MARX. Courtesy PB Eighty-Four, New York.

DONKEY (Pinoccho) rubber, 4" high. Courtesy HAKE'S Americana & Collectibles.

	C6	C8	C10
Dopey 1½" lead figure, Britains	40	60	80
Dopey, approx. 7" high, Ideal	125	188	250
Dopey Doll, 9" composition with velvet clothes, Knickerbocker	100	150	200
Dopey 10" rubber squeeze toy, 1950s	10	15	20
Dopey, approx. 12" high, Ideal, 1938	150	225	300
Dopey, Doc pull toy, 14" long	200	300	400
Dopey Doll, Madame Alexander, 1938	150	225	300
Dopey Hand Puppet, composition, 1938, Crown Toys, bell, buckling belt	140	210	280

	C6	C8	C10
Dopey Handpuppet, Gund, 1950s.......	21	31	42
Dopey Marionette, circa 1952, Peter Puppet Playthings	80	120	160
Dopey Party Mask, 1937.....................	20	30	40

FERDINAND & MATADOR. Photo by Don Hultzman.

DUMBO Tin Windup, MARX, Dumbo flips over. Photo by Don Hultzman.

	C6	C8	C10
Dopey Soaky	19	28	38
Dopey tin wind-up, Marx, 1938...........	315	472	630
Dumbo hand puppet, Gund, circa 1955, 10"	21	31	42
Dumbo tin wind-up, Marx, Dumbo flips over, 1941, 4" high	268	400	535
Elmer Elephant 5" celluloid and string figure, 1930s	120	180	240
Elmer Elephant pull toy, 1936................	*See Fisher-Price*		
Elmer Elephant, rubber, Seiberling, head moves	50	75	100
Ferdinand The Bull, Linemar..............	300	450	600
Ferdinand The Bull, copyright 1938, Marx, tail whirls, body shakes, wind-up.......	283	425	566
Ferdinand the Bull, handpuppet, 1938, Crown	55	82	110
Ferdinand The Bull pull toy, Hill, 8¾" long..	175	262	350
Ferdinand The Bull, late 1930s, Seiberling Latex Products, hard rubber, 6" long, 3½" high	53	80	106
Ferdinand The Bull, jointed, wood, 9"	125	188	250
Ferdinand and Matador, 1938, Marx tin wind-up	500	800	1100

ELMER ELEPHANT, rubber, SEIBERLING, head moves. Courtesy HAKE'S Americana & Collectibles.

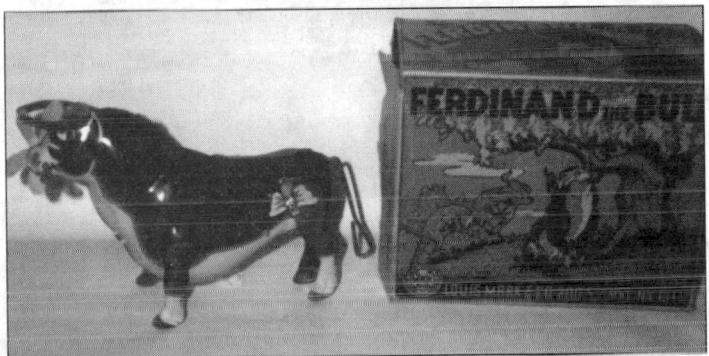

Ferdinand the Bull, Copyright 1938, MARX. Photo by Don Hultzman.

Goofy "Goofy the Walking Gardener". Courtesy Christie's East.

	C6	C8	C10
"Figaro", 1950s, Linemar, tin friction toy, 3" long	70	105	140
Figaro (Pinocchio) paper mask, 1939, Gillette	20	30	40
Figaro tin wind-up, Marx, 1940, 4¾" long	150	225	300
"Flower," 1950s, Linemar, 3" long friction, tin	115	172	230
Frontierland Logs, No. 915, Halsam	10	15	20
Gepetto facemask (Pinocchio) by Gillette 1939	22	33	45
Gepetto 5½" wood figure holding his chin, Multi Products, 1940	70	105	140
Goofy, 5¼" high tin wind-up, Linemar	300	450	600
Goofy "Goofy the Walking Gardener," Marx, tin wind-up	650	975	1400
Goofy on a unicycle, tin wind-up 5½" high	600	1000	1550
Goofy Soaky	10	15	20
Goofy 1930 tin figure	400	600	800
"Goofy Tricycle", 1950s, Linemar, 4" tall	550	850	1250
"Goofy With Whirling Tail", 1950s, Linemar, 5" tall	300	450	600
"Goofy with Whirling Tail," 1950s Marx plastic wind-up, 8" high	37	56	75
"Goofy's Disneyland Stock Car", 1950s, Linemar, 6" long	200	300	400
"Goofy's Stock Car", Linemar, 1950s, 6" long	175	262	350
Grumpy lead figure, 1½" high, Britains	40	60	80
Grumpy, approx. 7" high, Ideal	140	210	280
Grumpy 9" high, composition, velvet clothes, Knickerbocker	100	150	200
Grumpy Doll, stuffed, oilcloth face, velvet pants, 11" high, 1938	80	120	160
Grumpy, 11½" high, stuffed, molded oilcloth face, Ideal	90	135	180
Grumpy, Ideal, approx, 12" high, 1938	75	112	150
Grumpy Par-T Mask, 1937	7	11	15
Grumpy rubber squeeze toy, 1950s	10	15	20
"Gym Toys Acrobats," 1950s Linemar, 8½" high (Mickey, Donald, Minnie, etc.) each priced at	200	300	400
Happy 1½" lead figure, Britains	30	45	60
Happy 3¼" high, Seiberling Rubber, 1938	60	90	120
Happy, approx. 7" high, Ideal	130	195	260
Happy marionette, Madam Alexander, 9½" high, 1938	110	155	220

JIMINY CRICKET, LINEMAR tin litho wind-up. Photo by Don Hultzman.

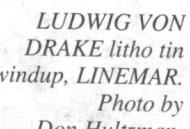

LUDWIG VON DRAKE litho tin windup, LINEMAR. Photo by Don Hultzman.

	C6	C8	C10
Happy party mask, 1937	40	60	80
Happy rubber squeeze toy, 1950s	10	15	20
Happy, approx. 12" high, Ideal, 1938	110	165	220
Horace Horsecollar hand puppet, Gund, circa 1960	17	25	34
"Huey - Louie - Dewey Locomotive," 1950s, Marx friction, 3½" long, plastic	50	75	100
"Jiminy Cricket" 6" high, 1950s Linemar squeeze cable hopper	200	300	400
Jiminy Cricket, 9" high, wood jointed, Ideal, 1940	225	368	450
Jiminy Cricket, 10" high, Knickerbocker, circa 1940	300	450	600
Jiminy Cricket 12" approx. rubber head, wooden feet, cloth body, Gund	22	33	45
Jiminy Cricket 13" high, latex head, hands and feet, cloth body	60	90	120
Jiminy Cricket 14" high, Crown Toy, felt and cloth	150	225	300
Jimmy Cricket 15½" high, Crown Toy, felt and cloth	150	225	300
Jiminy Cricket facemask (Pinocchio) 1939 from Gillette	25	38	50
Jiminy Cricket Handpuppet, vinyl and cloth, Gund	22	33	44
Jiminy Cricket, Linemar, tin litho wind-up, 1950s, 5½" tall	300	450	600
Jiminy Cricket pushing bass fiddle, Marx walkie	15	22	30
Jiminy Cricket Soaky	16	24	32
Johnny Tremain Flintlock cap pistol, Marx	60	90	120

	C6	C8	C10
Jungle Book Dancing Bear, Marx plastic wind-up	80	120	160
Ludwig Von Drake, 7" rubber squeeze toy, c.1960, Dell	37	56	75
Ludwig Von Drake, litho tin wind-up, Linemar, 1950s, 6" tall	300	450	600
Ludwig Von Drake Talking Doll	50	75	100
Ludwig Von Drake go-cart, friction, Marx, 1961	175	263	350
Mad Hatter puppet (Alice in Wonderland)	30	45	60
Mad Hatter, Gund	200	300	400
Mad Hatter's Taxi, Linemar, 5" long, 1950s	250	375	500
Mickey Mouse, first toy made by Borgfeldt of NY in 1930, wooden Mickey with jointed hands, arms, legs and wire tail, leather ears. "Copyright 1928-1930 by Walter E. Disney"	550	825	1100
Mickey Mouse larger-size squeeze toy with clothes, 1950, Sun Rubber	30	45	60

Mickey Mouse Tumbler, SCHUCO, atop Mickey Mouse Piano, MARKS BROS. Courtesy Christie's East.

	C6	C8	C10
Mickey Mouse with red shirt and yellow pants, squeeze toy, Sun Rubber, 1950	34	51	68
Mickey Mouse, 3½" high, Seiberling Rubber, 1930s	90	135	180
Mickey Mouse, 5" high celluloid, "fat head"	150	225	300
Mickey Mouse 5" high wood doll, Fun-E-Flex leather ears	250	375	500
Mickey Mouse, 5½" high, vibrates, Linemar tin wind-up, 1950s	300	450	600
Mickey Mouse, 6" high, rubber, circa 1935, Seiberling	160	240	320
Mickey Mouse, 7" high, wood jointed, early Borgfeldt	390	585	780

	C6	C8	C10
"Mickey Mouse," 7" high, 1960s Marx wind-up, hard plastic	130	195	260
Mickey Mouse, 8" high, Sun Rubber	60	90	120
Mickey Mouse, 8" high, wooden, jointed arms and legs, circa 1933	600	900	1200
Mickey Mouse, 9½" high, "Dell," rubber	40	60	80
Mickey Mouse, 10" high, Sun Rubber, 1940s	30	45	60
Mickey Mouse, 11" high, cloth "Walt Disney Mickey Mouse Geo. E. Borgfeldt & Company New York" on bottom of one foot	337	505	675
Mickey Mouse, 12" high, 1930s, Knickerbocker	325	488	650
Mickey Mouse, 12" high felt doll, early 1930s, Steiff	600	950	1280
Mickey Mouse, 12" high Bandleader, Knickerbocker, 1935	650	1100	1500
Mickey Mouse, 12" high, Borgfeldt	625	938	1250
Mickey Mouse, 12" high, "Cowboy Mickey", Knickerbocker, 1936	2000	4000	6200
Mickey Mouse, 13¾" high, stuffed, early (Dean Rag?)	400	600	800
Mickey Mouse, 16" high, stuffed, 1930s	650	975	1300
Mickey Mouse, 17", rubber, Lakeside Mfg. Co.	80	120	160
Mickey Mouse, 18" high, felt, Character Co., circa 1939-40	70	105	140
Mickey Mouse, 19½" high, circa 1935, Knickerbocker, in cowboy outfit	1400	2100	2800
Mickey Mouse, 21" high, circa 1933	350	525	700
Mickey Mouse, 31" high, all felt dressed, opening in back for storing things, black jacket with yellow buttons, red pants, bells on toes of yellow shoes, 1950s	120	180	240
Mickey Mouse, 1950s, Linemar, tin friction toy, 3" long	70	105	140
Mickey Mouse, 1930s, 4" long, pie-eyed tumbler, Schuco	150	225	300
Mickey Mouse, Acrobat, clockwork trapeze, celluloid Mickey, 1930s, Japan	500	850	1150
"Mickey Mouse Acrobat" 1950s, Linemar (Gym Toys), 9" high, Mickey 6" long	235	352	470
Mickey Mouse Airmail, rubber "Mickey's Airmail"	77	115	155
Mickey Mouse and Donald on boat, celluloid	1000	1600	2250

Mickey Mouse Bank, cast iron, 9" high, French-made. Courtesy James S. Maxwell/Virginia Caputo. Photo by Virginia Caputo.

MICKEY MOUSE, 7" high, wood-jointed, early, BORGFELDT. Courtesy HAKE'S Americana & Collectibles.

Mickey Mouse, 13¾" high, stuffed. Courtesy James S. Maxwell/Virginia Caputo. Photo by Virginia Caputo.

MICKEY MOUSE, 5" high wood doll, FUN-E-FLEX, leather ears. Courtesy HAKE'S Americana & Collectibles.

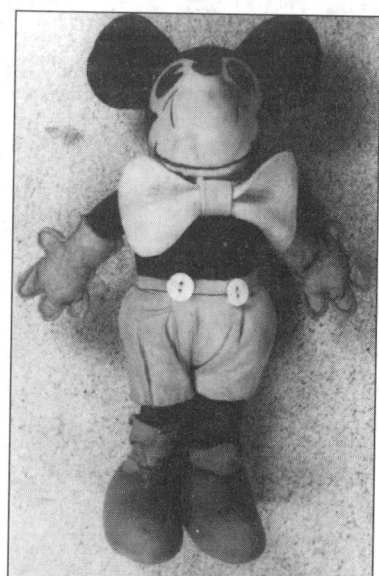

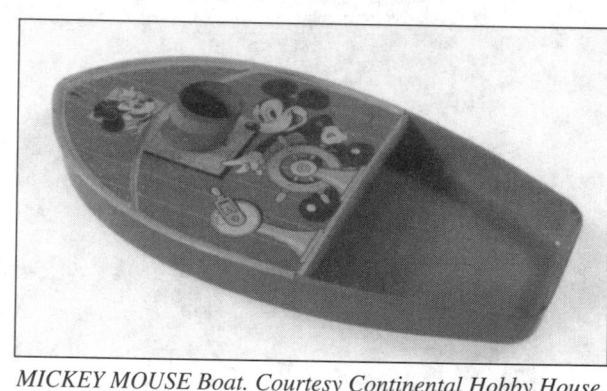

MICKEY MOUSE Boat. Courtesy Continental Hobby House.

MICKEY MOUSE, 11" high, cloth, "Walt Disney Mickey Mouse Geo. E. Borgfelt & Company, New York" on bottom of one foot. Courtesy HAKE'S Americana & Collectibles.

MICKEY MOUSE Mickey on Scooter, LINEMAR. Photo by Don Hultzman.

MICKEY'S TRACTOR, SUN RUBBER. Photo by Dave Leopard.

MICKEY MOUSE Felt Doll, STEIFF, 12" high. Courtesy Lloyd W. Ralston Auctions.

	C6	C8	C10
Mickey Mouse and Donald on back of alligator, Marx, 1950s, plastic walker..60	90	120
Mickey Mouse and Donald Handcar, windup, plastic, 1948, Marx 137	202	275
Mickey Mouse and Donald in fire truck, late 1930s, Sun Rubber, 6½" long 57	85	115
Mickey Mouse and Minnie Mouse Tea Set, circa 1935, 13 pieces 140	210	280
Mickey Mouse and Minnie Mouse Swing Toy, celluloid with red and green flag, 11½" tall 420	630	840
Mickey Mouse Bank, Cast iron, 9" high, France, "Depose," auctioned for $880 and $9504 in late 1990		
Same as above, aluminum, also France 550	850	1300
Mickey Mouse Banjo, 1930s, 17" long ...140	210	280
Mickey Mouse Beverages felt soda jerk hat, shows Mickey from shoulders up saying "have one on me," 5"x11", circa 1930 60	90	120
Mickey Mouse Boat, 13" 150	205	300
Mickey Mouse Bubble Buster Gun, metal Mickey standing at gun sight. Cast iron, Kilgore, 6" long...119	178	238
"Mickey Mouse Bus Lines - Walt Disney Stars", Gong Bell, circa 1960, 19½" long riding toy 150	225	300
Mickey Mouse cardboard mask, circa 1935 60	90	120
Mickey Mouse, celluloid on wood hobby horse, 4½", circa 1935.......1050	1700	2300
Mickey Mouse Circus, Geo. Borgfeldt 6/3785, 1931, two wood figures revolving on swinging mechanism, 11" long...............500	850	1200
Mickey Mouse Circus Train Set, Lionel No. 1536, Engine, tender, containing Mickey, three carriage cars, dining car, Mickey Mouse Circus, Mickey Mouse Band, composition Mickey and track.............. 1300	2200	3500
Mickey Mouse Circus Train, Mickey shoveling tender, three Disney Circus cars, wind-up train, red, circa 1931 900	1550	2200
Mickey Mouse Clicker, tin litho, circa 1930, Mickey showing teeth while playing violin................90	135	180
Mickey Mouse, "Climbing Mickey Mouse," 1930s, Dolly Toy Co., cardboard, 8" long 435	652	870

	C6	C8	C10
Mickey Mouse Club Auto-Magic Picture Gun, 1946, projects films ...35	52	70
Mickey Mouse Club Newsreel Projector 62	93	125
"Mickey Mouse Dipsy Car," 1950s, 5¼" long, Marx, tin car, plastic Mickey...........200	300	400
"Mickey Mouse Dipsy Car," 1950s, Linemar, 5¼" long, all tin 319	478	638
Mickey Mouse Drum, Ohio Art, 6" diameter, tin................55	82	110
Mickey Mouse Drum Set, tin and cardboard, circa 1940, Minnie watching while Mickey juggles.....240	360	480
Mickey Mouse Drummer, Kohner Push Puppet, 1950s 100	150	200
Mickey Mouse Explorer's Outfit 87	132	175
"Mickey Mouse Express," 1950s Marx, 9" diameter (Mickey in airplane)......200	300	400
Mickey Mouse Express tin litho train set, 14" long, base 21x13", Marx, 1950s 700	1100	1700
Mickey Mouse Hand Car, green base .700	1200	1700
Mickey Mouse Hand Car, red base 800	1300	2000
"Mickey Mouse Handcar", 1930s, Lionel Co., 7" long - with Minnie, orange housing 750	1250	1900
Mickey Mouse Hingees, 1944 30	45	60
Mickey Mouse holding flag, cast iron, 1930s 140	210	280
Mickey Mouse Hurdy Gurdy, auctioned in 1993 with reattached arm, possible repaint, for $18,700		
Mickey Mouse Jazz Drummer, finger-activated tin toy, Nifty 4¾" high ...700	1200	1800
"Mickey Mouse Jockey", 1935, M-T Co., 4½" long - celluloid Mickey on wooden hobby horse................1200	1800	2400
Mickey Mouse Kaleidoscope, 1950s 14	21	28
Mickey Mouse Knickerbocker doll, 1935, 22" high 500	750	1000
Mickey Mouse, lead, 2½" high, 1933, Allied Toys 70	105	140
Mickey Mouse Marionette, circa 1930, 9½" high, felt body stuffed with cotton 112	158	225
Mickey Mouse Marionette, Peter Puppet Playthings Co., 1952, 14" tall..100	150	200
"Mickey Mouse Meteor Five-Car Train, Walt Disney's" tin litho, Marx, 43" long 300	450	600
Mickey Mouse "Mickey-In-The-Box," 7" high jack-in-the-box.................260	390	520

Mickey Mouse, Left to Right, 18" high, 16" high, both stuffed. Courtesy Sotheby's New York.

Mickey Mouse 19½" high, circa 1935, Knickerbocker. Courtesy Christie's East.

MICKEY MOUSE "Mickey-In-The-Box". Photo PB Eighty-Four, New York.

MICKEY MOUSE Acrobat (1930s, Japan). Photo PB Eighty-Four, New York.

MICKEY MOUSE Drum, OHIO ART, 6" diameter, tin. Courtesy HAKE'S Americana & Collectibles.

"Mickey Mouse and Donald Duck Handcar". Photo by Don Hultzman.

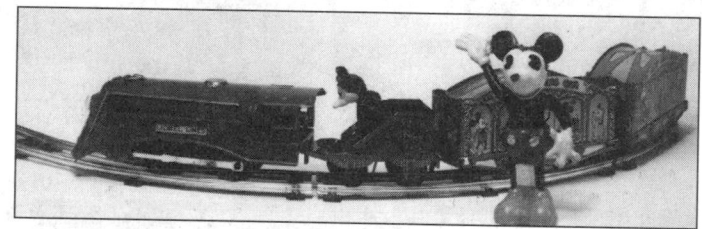

MICKEY MOUSE "Climbing Mickey Mouse", DOLLY TOY COMPANY. Courtesy Phillips New York.

MICKEY MOUSE Circus Train Set. Photo PB Eighty-Four, New York.

Mickey Mouse, "Mickey on Scooter", 1950s, LINEMAR. Courtesy Christie's East.

"Mickey Mouse Bus Lines - Walt Disney Stars." Courtesy Wilkinson Collection, Detroit Antique Toy Museum.

496

	C6	C8	C10
Mickey Mouse On Pluto, rocks, tin wind-up, Linemar, 1950s, 6½" long	1200	2000	3000
Mickey Mouse "Mickey on Scooter," 1950s, Linemar, 4½" high, all tin, Rare	1000	1700	2400
Mickey Mouse "Mickey on Unicycle," 1950s, Linemar, 5" high	500	750	1000
Mickey Mouse "Mickey Race Car," celluloid windup, occupied Japan	250	375	500
Mickey Mouse "Mickey the Driver," 1950s Marx (Japan), 6½" long friction	400	600	800
Mickey Mouse "Mickey the Magician," Linemar, 10", battery-operated	1200	1800	2400
Mickey Mouse "Mickey the Musician - I Play the Xylophone," 1950s Marx wind-up, 10" high	300	450	600
Mickey Mouse "Mickey's Delivery," Pluto on Tricycle-Cart, tin litho wind-up, celluloid head on Pluto, Linemar, 1950s, 5½" long	450	675	900
Mickey Mouse "Mickey's Mouse-kemovers" moving van, 13" long, 1950s, Linemar	375	562	750
Mickey Mouse "Mickey's Service Truck," 1950s Marx friction, 3½" long, plastic	50	75	100
Mickey Mouse "Mickey's Tractor," Sun Rubber, 1930s, Mickey's head turns, 4½" long	100	150	200
"Mickey Mouse Motorcycle," 1950s Linemar friction, 3" long	200	300	400
"Mickey Mouse Motorcycle", 1950s, Linemar, tin friction, 3½" long	300	450	600
"Mickey Mouse Movie Fun Optical Toy", 1950s, Mastercraft, 7"x7"x5"	150	220	300
Mickey Mouse Movie-Jecter, 1935	116	174	232
Mickey Mouse Movie Projector No. E-18, Keystone, 1930s, 10" high	225	375	450
"Mickey Mouse Newsreel," 1950s, Mattel, 9½" high, includes 3 records and 5 films	100	150	200
Mickey Mouse on Hand Car, Japan, 8" long, basket on back	138	208	275
Mickey Mouse Old Fashioned Sailing Vessel - See Mickey Mouse Pirate Ship			
Mickey Mouse Organ Grinder, Minnie Mouse dancing on organ pushed by much larger Mickey, German	1200	1800	2400

	C6	C8	C10
Mickey Mouse piano, wooden, grand, with decal showing Mickey playing, Minnie listening, circa 1935	200	300	400
Mickey Mouse Piano, Marks Bros., circa 1935, 10"	1250	1875	2500
Mickey Mouse Pirate Ship, Ideal	130	195	260
Mickey Mouse Pocket Knife, 1935	40	60	80
"Mickey Mouse Projector No. E-18" 1930s, Keystone Co. 7" long, 10" high, 9" wide	200	300	400
Mickey Mouse "Puddle Jumper," No. 310, circa 1950s	*See Fisher-Price*		
Mickey Mouse Puppet, approx. 10" high, "Gund"	11	16	22
Mickey Mouse Puppet, early 40s style, very large composition head, hands and feet, the rest of the body wood, cloth costume, felt ears	175	263	350
Mickey Mouse Puppet, Pelham 24" high, rubber legs and arms, wood body	175	263	350
"Mickey Mouse Race Car," 1930s, T.M. Co., 3" long	300	450	600
Mickey Mouse Racing Car, red lithographed tin wind-up car with Mickey at the wheel, 4" long, 1930s	400	600	800
"Mickey Mouse Rollerskater," 1950s, Linemar, 6" high	500	750	1000
Mickey Mouse Roly Poly, celluloid, early, 4" high	187	280	375
Mickey Mouse Rower, Fun E Flex, wooden, 10¾"	1700	2550	3400
Mickey Mouse "Running Mickey on Pluto," 1940s, M-T Co., 5½" long, celluloid, occupied Japan	2000	3500	6500
Mickey Mouse "Santa Car with Mickey Mouse and His Gift Pack" hand car, Lionel No. 1105, 1935	900	1350	1800
Mickey Mouse Saxophone Player, 1930s	800	1300	2000
Mickey Mouse "Scooter Jockey," Mavco Co., 1950s, all plastic, 6" high wind-up	160	240	320
Mickey Mouse Slate Dancer, c.1931, auctioned for $29,150 in 1993			
Mickey Mouse Soaky	8	12	16
Mickey Mouse Soldier Set, cardboard soldiers, gun	500	850	1200

Mickey Mouse, celluloid, on wood hobby horse. Courtesy Christie's East.

MICKEY MOUSE Racing Car. Photo PB Eighty-Four, New York.

Mickey Mouse Hand Car. Photo PB Eighty-Four, New York.

Mickey Mouse Circus. Photo PB Eighty-Four, New York.

Mickey Mouse Dipsy Car, MARX. Photo by Don Hultzman.

Mickey Mouse Express. Photo by Don Hultzman.

Mickey Mouse Tap Dancer, crank toy, German. Courtesy Christie's East.

Mickey Mouse "Mickey the Magician". Courtesy Christie's East.

Mickey Mouse Washer. Courtesy Phillips New York.

	C6	C8	C10
Mickey Mouse Sparkler Toy, 1930s, 5½" tall, Nifty	450	675	900
Mickey Mouse Tambourine, Noble & Cooley Co., 1936, 9" heavy paper head, Mickey juggling while Minnie watches	310	465	620
Mickey Mouse Tap Dancer, crank toy, German, sold for $17,600 in 1990.			
Mickey Mouse Tea Service, 24 piece, tin, Chein, 1930s	120	180	240
Mickey Mouse Tin Flute	40	60	80
Mickey Mouse Tin Washboard set, circa 1935, complete	80	120	160
Mickey Mouse Tool Chest, 1935, Hamilton Metal, complete	170	255	340
Mickey Mouse on Tricycle, tin litho, wind-up, celluloid Mickey, 1940s, 3½" long	450	675	900
"Mickey Mouse Tricycle", 1950s, Linemar, 4" tall	450	675	900
Mickey Mouse Trapeze, celluloid, 1930s, Bargfeldt	500	825	1100
Mickey Mouse Trapeze, wood, c.1930s	50	75	100
Mickey Mouse Tumbler, Schuco, 4" high	200	300	400
Mickey Mouse Tumbling, 1947, Marks Bros., 8" high	42	63	85
Mickey Mouse Viewer, with film of "Brave Little Tailor," 1946	60	90	120
Mickey Mouse Walker, plastic	20	30	40
Mickey Mouse Washer, 1932 or 33 Ohio Art Co., tin litho washing machine, 7" high, two scenes with Mickey, Minnie, Pluto	100	150	200
"Mickey Mouse with Twirling Tail," 1950s Linemar, 5½" high	450	675	900
Mickey Mouse Xylophone, tin wind-up, 1930s	400	600	800
Mickey Mouse Xylophone Player, Linemar, tin wind-up, 1950s, 6" high	500	825	1150
Mickey Mouse Club Bow and Arrow Set, circa 1955	20	30	40
Mickey Mouse Club Snap-on Ears, plastic, 1950s	10	15	20
"Mickey & Minnie Acrobats," 1934, Borgfeldt (Japan), 11" high	600	900	1275
Mickey & Minnie Barrel organ, English	112	168	225
Mickey & Minnie Mouse Car, Gong Bell, circa 1933, wood & metal, 10¾" long	1050	1575	2100
Mickey & Minnie on Elephant, celluloid, Japan, 1930s, auctioned in 1990 for $7150.			

	C6	C8	C10
Mickey & Minnie on Motorcycle, tin litho	4000	6000	8000
Mickey & Minnie Mouse Playland, celluloid, Japan	1800	2700	3600
Minnie Mouse, wooden, Fun-E-Flex	150	225	300
Minnie Mouse 3" high, wooden, jointed, 1940s	100	150	200
Minnie Mouse, 5" high, celluloid, 1930s, "Fat head"	225	338	450
Minnie Mouse, 5½" high, wooden, 1930s	187	286	375
Minnie Mouse, 6" high, celluloid, 1930s, string tail	425	638	850
Minnie Mouse, 7" high, Fun-E-Flex	300	450	600
"Minnie Mouse" 7" high, 1960s Marx wind-up, hard plastic	70	105	140

Mickey Mouse Rower, Fun-E-Flex. Courtesy Christie's East.

Mickey & Minnie Mouse Playland, 10¼".. Courtesy Christie's East.

	C6	C8	C10
Minnie Mouse 10½" high, Sun Rubber, 1940s	40	60	80
Minnie Mouse, 12" high, 1930, wearing dress, high heels, undies	225	338	450

499

Minnie Mouse carrying two suitcases. Courtesy Christie's East.

Mickey & Minnie on Elephant, celluloid, Japan. Courtesy Christie's East.

MINNIE MOUSE Knitter. Photo by Don Hultzman.

	C6	C8	C10
Minnie Mouse 14½" high, early cloth figure dressed in a red and white polka dot skirt, wearing composition heeled shoes	300	450	600
Minnie Mouse 16" high , cloth, early 1930s	650	975	1300
Minnie Mouse cardboard mask, circa 1935	40	60	80
Minnie Mouse Carrying Two Suitcases, tin wind-up, 6½" high, circa 1928, Spanish, auctioned for $12,100 (with replaced ears) in 1990.			
Minnie Mouse cowgirl, Knickerbocker, 18" high, 1936	470	705	940
Minnie Mouse Handpuppet, Peter Puppet Playthings, circa 1952	100	150	200
Minnie Mouse Knitter, tin litho wind-up, Linemar, 1950s, 7" high	375	562	750
Minnie Mouse Lead, 2½" high, 1933, Allied Toys	70	105	140
Minnie Mouse Marionette, circa 1930, 9½" high, felt body stuffed with cotton	112	168	225
Minnie Mouse Marionette, 13" wood and composition, 1950s	100	150	200
Minnie Mouse Puppet, Pelham, 24" high, rubber legs and arms, wood body	195	292	390

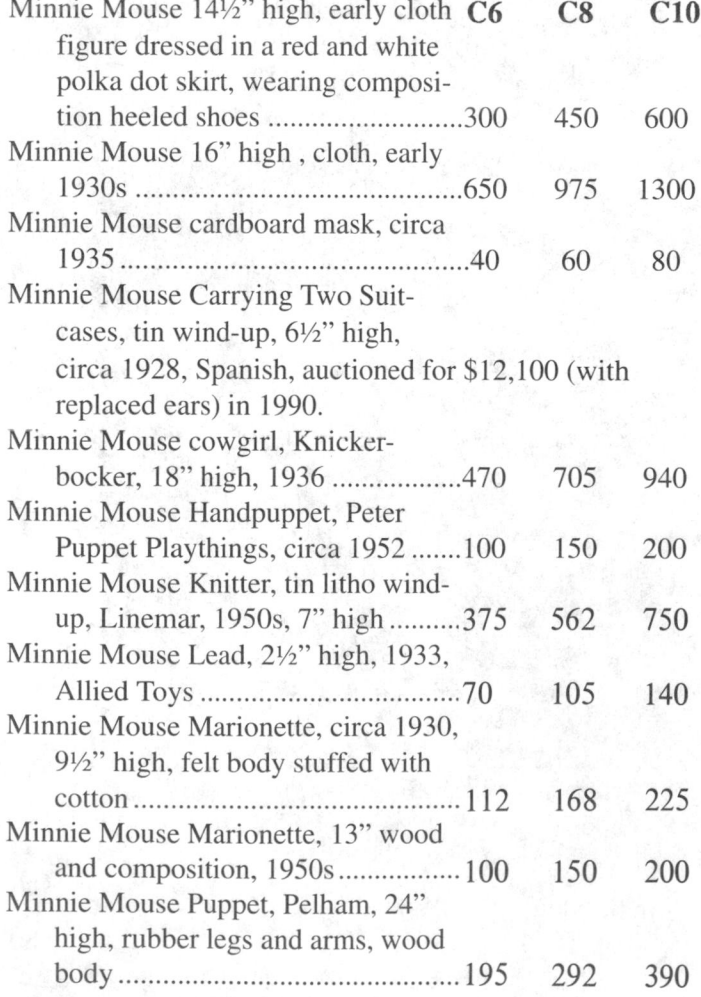

CONDITION CODE:

C6 - Good. Evident overall wear, well played with, but acceptable to many collectors

C8 - Very Good Minor wear overall, very clean

C10 - Mint (like new)

Note: Mint in Box commands a higher price. Condition below C6 brings considerable lower prices.

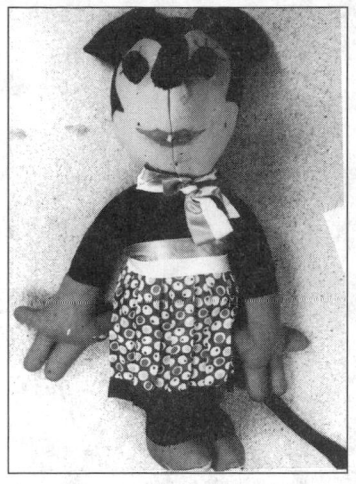

MINNIE MOUSE 16" high, cloth, early 30s. Courtesy HAKE'S Americana & Collectibles.

MICKEY MOUSE Xylophone Player, LINEMAR. Photo by Don Hultzman.

Left to Right; MINNIE MOUSE DOLL 14½" high, MICKEY MOUSE, 21" high. Photo PB Eighty-Four, New York.

	C6	C8	C10
Minnie Mouse Roly Poly, celluloid, 4"	60	90	120
Minnie Mouse Tricycle, 1950s, Linemar, 4"	300	450	600
Minnie Mouse Walker, plastic	20	30	40
Minnie Mouse Washing Machine, 1950, Precision Specialties, Inc.	100	150	200
"Mouseketeer Electric TV Story Teller, T. Cohn, late 1950s, tin litho TV set and record player, records and film reels	150	225	300
Mouseketeers Hat, 50% wool, 50% rayon, by Denayaluee, 1950s	30	45	60
Mouseketeers Play Outfit	75	112	150
Mouseketeers Soaky	14	21	28

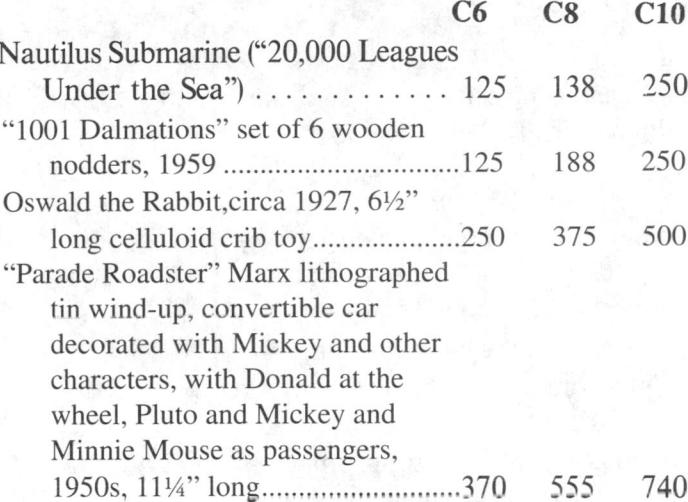

	C6	C8	C10
Nautilus Submarine ("20,000 Leagues Under the Sea")	125	138	250
"1001 Dalmations" set of 6 wooden nodders, 1959	125	188	250
Oswald the Rabbit, circa 1927, 6½" long celluloid crib toy	250	375	500
"Parade Roadster" Marx lithographed tin wind-up, convertible car decorated with Mickey and other characters, with Donald at the wheel, Pluto and Mickey and Minnie Mouse as passengers, 1950s, 11¼" long	370	555	740

PECOS BILL, MARX windup, plastic, 1950s. Photo by Don Hultzman.

	C6	C8	C10
Pecos Bill, Marx wind-up, plastic, 1950s	237	355	475
Peter Pan 9¾" high, Sun Rubber, circa 1952	16	24	32
Peter Pan Jolly Roger Pirate Ship	17	26	35
Peter Pan Marionette, circa 1952, Peter Puppet Playthings	100	150	200
Peter Pan Tea Set, circa 1953, 23 pieces	275	363	550
Peter Pan Train Car, 1977	22	33	45
Pinocchio cloth and jointed wood figure, Kreuger	160	240	320
Pinocchio 2½" high, molded wood fiber figure, Multi Products, 1940	100	150	200
Pinocchio 5" high, molded wood fiber figure, Multi Products, 1940	150	225	300
Pinocchio, 5½" high, rubber, Seiberling	27	41	55
Pinocchio 7½" high, jointed, circa 1940, Ideal	75	112	150
Pinocchio 8" high, Ideal	132	198	264

501

	C6	C8	C10
Pinocchio 10½" high, Ideal, wood and composition	250	375	500
Pinocchio 10½" high, wood and papier mache wind-up, George Borgfeldt, 1940	350	525	700
Pinocchio 11" high, jointed, circa 1940	200	300	400
Pinocchio 12" high, Ideal jointed wood and composition	300	450	600
Pinocchio 15" high, Knickerbocker, stuffed	92	138	185
Pinocchio, 18" high, soft cloth, c.1940s	125	188	250

PINOCCHIO, tin windup, MARX, "Walking Pinocchio". Courtesy Ed Hyers Antique Toys.

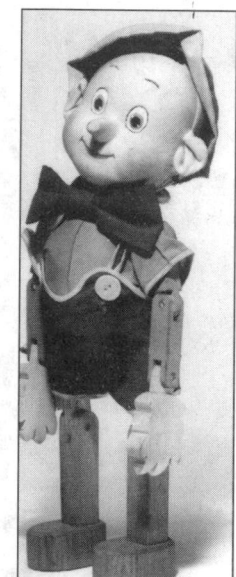

Pinocchio, cloth and jointed wood figure, KREUGER. Courtesy PB Eighty-Four, New York.

PINOCCHIO Doll, IDEAL, 8" high. Lloyd W. Ralston Auctions.

PINOCCHIO, tin litho windup, LINEMAR. Photo by Don Hultzman.

	C6	C8	C10
Pinocchio 19¾" high, jointed, circa 1940	400	600	800
"Pinocchio Delivery", Marx	325	488	650
Pinocchio Handpuppet, Gund, 1950s	15	22	30
Pinocchio Paper Mask, Gillette, 1939	12	18	24
Pinocchio Express, pull toy, 1940, 11" long	*See Fisher-Price*		
Pinocchio on Donkey, pull toy, 1940, bell-ringer	*See Fisher-Price*		
Pinocchio Soaky	6	9	13
Pinocchio The Acrobat, "Watch Him Go!" tin wind-up, 1939, Marx	250	375	500
Pinocchio tin wind-up, litho eyes, 8½" high, Marx, standing erect, circa 1940	300	450	600
Pinocchio tin wind-up, Marx, standing erect, moving eyes, 1939, 8½" high	360	540	720
Pinocchio, tin litho wind-up, Linemar Co., 1950s, 5½" tall	244	366	488
Pinocchio "Walking Pinocchio," Marx, plastic, 1950s	40	60	80
Pluto, 3", bendable legs, circa 1934, wooden	180	270	360
Pluto 4" long Seiberling Rubber, circa 1935	60	90	120
Pluto, 6" long, wood, Borgfeldt	175	263	350
Pluto, 7½" long, Seiberling Rubber	50	75	100
Pluto 9" long, wood jointed	250	375	500
"Pluto", 1950s, Linemar, tin friction toy, 3" long	105	158	210
"Pluto" Marx wind-up, 1960s plastic, 4½" high	60	90	120
Pluto Acrobat, Gym Toys, Linemar	250	375	500

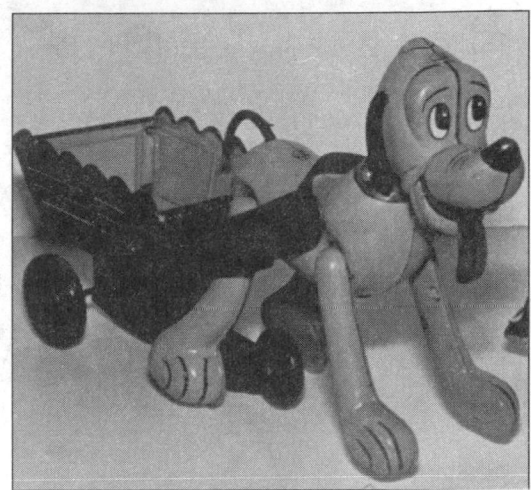

"Pluto - Pulling Cart", 1950s LINEMAR. Courtesy Ed Hyers Antique Toys.

GILLETTE, Free Pinocchio masks offer from 1940 (see Cleo, Figaro, Gepetto, Jiminy Cricket). Courtesy Rex and Richard Gray

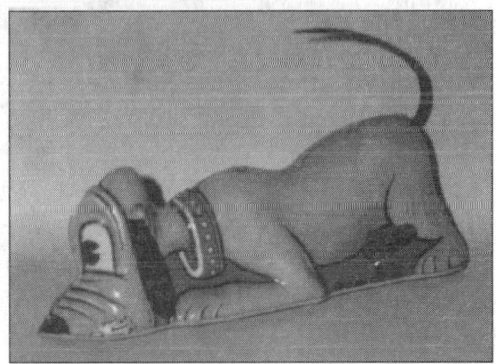

Pluto "Wise Pluto". Photo by Don Hultzman.

Pluto Mysterious Pluto, MARX. Photo by Don Hultzman.

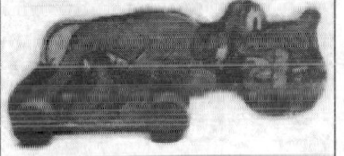

Pluto With Basket, 8" long. Courtesy Lloyd W. Ralston Auctions.

Pluto, plastic wind-up, MARX, metal tail spins.

PLUTO Drum Major. Photo by Don Hultzman.

PLUTO "Watch Me Roll Over," MARX.

PLUTO "Playful Pluto & Goofy". Photo by Don Hultzman.

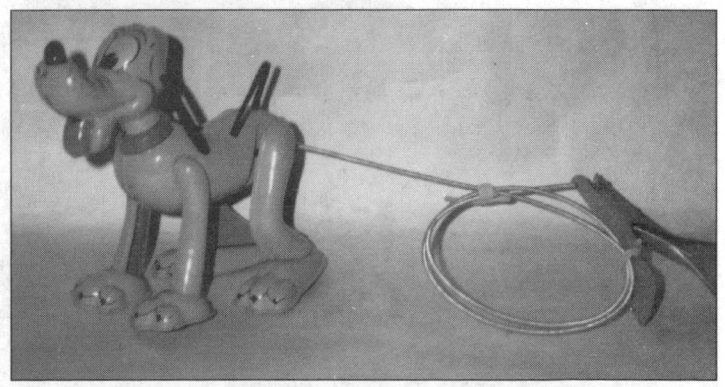

PLUTO tin litho squeeze-action with cable, LINEMAR. Photo by Don Hultzman.

	C6	C8	C10
Pluto "Begging Rollover Pluto," 1950s, Linemar, 6½" long	100	150	200
Pluto Drum Major, Marx tin windup, 1940s	175	263	350
Pluto "Drum Major" Linemar, 1950s, 6½" tall, tin litho wind-up	280	420	560
Pluto hand puppet, Gund, 1950s	16	24	36
"Pluto In His Sports Car," 1950s, 4" long, friction drive, all plastic	50	75	100
Pluto, lead, 2½" high, 1933 Allied Toys	52	78	105
"Pluto Motorcycle," 1950s, Linemar, tin friction toy, 3½" long	300	450	600
Pluto "Musical Pluto," 1960s, Marx, (Dog Race Type), 8"x8" base with 2½" Pluto-plastic	400	600	800
Pluto Mysterious Pluto, Marx	150	225	300
Pluto on Rockers, wooden, circa 1930s	150	225	300
Pluto, plastic wind-up, Marx, metal tail spins, 1950s	75	112	150
Pluto "Playful Pluto & Goofy" 1950s Linemar, 2 piece set, windups	800	1300	2000
"Pluto - Pulling Cart," 1950s Linemar friction, 8½" long	392	588	785
Pluto Pull-toy, wood, c.1940s, unmarked, looks un-Disney	65	98	130
Pluto, sitting position, rubber squeeze toy, 1960s	20	30	40
Pluto Soaky	10	15	20
Pluto Squeeze toy, Sun Rubber No. 11520, 1930s	45	68	90
Pluto, tin litho squeeze-action with cable, Linemar, 1950s, 4¼" tall	200	300	400
"Pluto Tricycle", 1950s, Linemar, 4" tall	225	338	450
Pluto "Watch Me Roll Over," Marx, 1939	180	270	360

	C6	C8	C10
Pluto, "Wise Pluto," 1939, Marx, 8" long, (like "Watch Me Roll Over")	212	318	425
Pluto With Basket paper litho on wood, 8" long	*See Fisher-Price*		
"Pluto with Whirling Tail," 1950s, Linemar wind-up, 4" high	185	278	370
Pluto, wooden, hand base, string-operated, many jointed, marionette-type, 1936	*See Fisher-Price*		
Practical Pig Doll, Gund	112	168	225
Practical Pig, tin litho windup, Linemar	260	390	520
"Professor Von Drake Go Mobile," 1950s, 6" long, Linemar windup	150	225	300
Sand Pail, 1938, Ohio Art tin litho, Mickey, Minnie and Goofy pictured	112	168	225
Seven Dwarfs, all, puppet-marionettes, Pelham	1500	2250	3000
Seven Dwarfs, all, Seiberling Rubber, 1938, 5½" high	350	525	700
Seven Dwarfs, approx. 8", vinyl squeeze, 1950s, each	30	45	60
Si-Am (Lady & Tramp) 16" high, stuffed, vinyl face, Gund, circa 1955	40	60	80
Sleeping Beauty Hand Puppet, Gund, 1950s	31	47	62
Sleeping Beauty squeeze toy, sitting with animals, 6½"	27	41	55
Sleepy 1½" lead figure, Britains	45	68	90
Sleepy, Ideal, approx. 7" high	125	188	250
Sleepy, Ideal approx. 12" high, 1938	120	180	240
Sleepy party mask, 1937	20	30	40
Sneezy, 1½" lead figure, Britains	45	68	90

SEVEN DWARFS, puppet-marionettes, PELHAM.

	C6	C8	C10
Sneezy, 3¼" high, Seiberling Rubber, 1938 60	90	120
Sneezy, Ideal, approx. 7" high 125	188	250
Sneezy, Ideal, approx. 12" high, 1938 120	180	240
Sneezy Party Mask, 1937 20	30	40
Sneezy rubber squeeze toy, 1950s 10	15	20
Snow Shovel, 26" long, shows Mickey and Pluto building snowman 90	135	180
Snow White and the Seven Dwarfs lead figures by Lincoln Logs, all ...500	750	1000
Snow White 2½" lead figure, Britains ..45	68	90
Snow White doll, Seiberling Rubber ...250	375	500
Snow White, 12" high, Knickerbocker, 1940s 187	280	375
Snow White 13" high, Madame Alexander, 1938 120	180	240
Snow White, Ideal, 15" high, 1938 150	225	300
Snow White Party Mask 20	30	40
Snow White Soaky 9	13	18
Snow White Washing Machine, circa 1950, Revell Plastics, 7½" high with wringer 80	120	160
Snow White and the Seven Dwarfs Blocks, 18 blocks, in box 175	263	350
Snow White and the Seven Dwarfs, 4½" dishes, china, with cups, creamer, sugar bowl, 6" plate 210	315	420
Snow White and the Seven Dwarfs drum, tin litho, 1930s 125	188	250
Snow White and the Seven Dwarfs musical top, Chein, 6½" across 110	165	220
Snow White and The Seven Dwarfs Sewing Set, Hasbro 20	30	40
Snow White Sink and Stove, Wolverine 40	60	80

	C6	C8	C10
Three Little Pigs Acrobats, Celluloid, Japan 700	1100	1700
Three Little Pigs clothes washer, Chein 102	153	205
"Three Little Pigs - Drummer," 1930s, 4½" tall, Schuco 262	393	525
"Three Little Pigs - Flutist", 1930s, 4½" tall, Schuco 275	362	550
Three Little Pigs Mask, 1933 Par-T-Mask 40	60	80
Three Little Pigs Sand Bucket, 3" tall ..30	45	60
"Three Little Pigs - Violinist," 1930s, 4½" tall, Schuco 283	425	566
Three Little Pigs wooden pig, circa 1933, Borgfeldt, fiber arms and legs, 3¼" high 120	180	240
"Thumper", 1950s, Linemar, tin friction toy, 3" long 70	105	140
Thumper Soaky 11	16	22
Thumper 6" friction, Marx, 1950s 100	150	200
Thumper 7" squeeze toy, Sun Rubber ...30	45	60
Thumper 14" high, Gund, 1950s 38	57	76
Thumper 17" high, Gund, early 1940s ..80	120	160
Timothy Mouse (Dumbo) stuffed, 17" high, Character Novelty, 1942 160	240	320
Tinkerbell Handpuppet, Gund 42	63	85

Seven Dwarfs, all, Seiberling Rubber, 1938, 5½" high. Photo by Stan Alekna.

Snow White and the Seven Dwarfs, IDEAL, Snow White approx. 15" high, the Dwarfs 7". Courtesy Christie's East.

	C6	C8	C10
"Tramp The Dog," 1960s, Linemar friction, 4" high	90	135	180
Tramp Handpuppet, Gund	22	33	44
Uncle Scrooge Handpuppet, 1960s? wearing high hat	20	30	40
Uncle Scrooge Limousine, "$" on back fender	110	165	220
Uncle Scrooge vinyl squeeze toy bank, 7" high, circa 1960	40	60	80
"Walt Disney Character Carousel," 1950s, Linemar Co., 7" high with 3" characters	300	450	600
"Walt Disney Character T.V. Set", 1950s, Automatic Toy Co., 5" cubic	150	225	300
"Walt Disney Stars" bus, 19" long, Gong Bell	450	675	900
Walt Disney Television Car, Marx, 1950s, 7½" long	238	347	475
"Walt Disney's Friction Delivery Wagon," 1950s, Linemar, 6" long, Mickey, Donald, Pluto, etc.	200	300	400

	C6	C8	C10
"Walt Disney's Friction Go-Mobile," 1960s Marx (Japan), 6" long, Mickey, Pluto, Donald, etc.	150	225	300
"Walt Disney's Mechanical Tricycle," 1950s Linemar, 4" high, Pluto, Mickey, Donald, etc.	200	300	400
"Walt Disney's Television Playhouse," Marx Playset, 39 characters	232	348	465
Wendy (Peter Pan), handpuppet, Gund	14	21	28
Wendy Marionette, 1950s	75	112	150
Witch (Snow White) party mask	20	30	40
Zorro Handpuppet, Gund	21	31	42
Zorro Hat with hideaway mask and gloves, 1950s	46	69	92
Zorro Flintlock Pistol, Marx	35	52	70
Zorro Playset, Marx	350	525	700
Zorro Ring, black top with Z and 'Zorro' name	32	48	64
Zorro Sword, 24" long, 1960s	5	8	10

RAMP WALKERS
by Randy Welch

Ramp Walkers date back to at least 1873 when Ives patented a cast iron elephant walker.

Wood and composite ramp walkers were made in Czechoslovakia and the USA from the 1920's through the 1940's. The most popular were made by John Wilson of Watsontown, Pennsylvania and were sold worldwide. These became known as "Wilson Walkies". Most are two legged and stand approximately 4-1/2" tall and utilize an empty cardboard thread cone for the body. Many have a patent number stamped on the bottom of one foot.

Plastic Ramp Walkers were primarily manufactured by the Louis Marx Co. and were made from the early 1950's through the mid 1960's. By far the majority were produced in Hong Kong, but some were made in the USA and sold under either the Marx logo or by the Charmore Co., a subsidiary of Marx.

Other manufacturers include Fun World (USA), Dolls Inc. (USA), Ohio Art (USA), Educational Toys subsidiary of Topper Corp. (USA), and Gantoy (England).

The three common sizes are: (A) Small premiums approx. 1-1/2" x 2", (B) the more common medium size approx. 2-3/4" x 3", and (C) large size approx. 4" x 5". Most of the smaller walkers were unpainted while the medium and larger sizes were hand and/or spray painted.

Colorful tin lithographed ramps were available for some of the Marx plastic walkers but most relied on homemade ramps or a weighted string hanging over the end of the table, which pulled the toy along.

There were some quite interesting variations on the use of walkers. A few are listed below:

*The Minnesota Electronics Corp. took the generic pig made by Marx and glued a small magnet in the back end. This was boxed with a plastic child's ring which also had a small magnet glued to the top. When the ring was placed near the pig's back end, the like polarities of the two magnets forced the pig to walk along a flat surface.

*Ohio Art produced a plastic farm set named the "Walker Farm". This included a barn with a ramp along with 7 walking people and animals pushing interchangeable parts such as: lawnmower, lawn roller, wheelbarrow & spreader.

*The "Colonial Action Target Game" by Marx includes a long lithographed tin ramp, a plastic bear ramp walker, a small working plastic rifle, and 5 wooden bullets. The box was placed behind the ramp as a backdrop. The child would shoot at the bear as it waddled down the ramp.

*In 1971, Educational Toys, (subsidiary of Topper Corp.) made a Sesame Street walking letter set named "Big Birds Blunder Proof Walking Letter Set". This set included 6 walking letters, 12 word keys and a plastic ramp A word key with a picture on it was inserted into the base of the ramp. The child would then attempt to spell the word for the picture on the key. The letters would march down the ramp and if the word was spelled correctly, Big Bird would pop up with a sign saying "OK!". If the word was misspelled, all the letters would fall down. Additional letters and a ramp extension were sold separately.

Because the value of walkers is significantly reduced when the paint is scratched or with cracks and breaks, I have decided to only list the prices for those in mint condition.

"I began collecting tin wind-up toys ten years ago while visiting a local auction house. I became interested in ramp walkers a few years later (for the second time) when I purchased a plastic Huckleberry Hound and Yogi Bear walker at a flea market for $5.00. I remember marching the walkers down the incline of my old wooden school desk top in the late 1950's. After finding that there was no reference material available, I began contacting dealers and collectors and have completed a list and photos of more than 300 known walkers. My other areas of interest include tin lithographed sparklers."

Randy Welch

PLASTIC

Big Bad Wolf & 3 Little Pigs (Disney)
Photo by Randy Welch

Donald & Goofy Riding A Go-Kart (Disney)
Photo by Randy Welch

Mickey w/Pluto Hunting (Disney)
Photo by Randy Welch

	C10
Donald & Goofy riding a go-cart, MARX	40
Fiddler & Fifer Pigs, MARX	40
Goofy riding a hippo, MARX	45
Jiminy Cricket w/cello, MARX	20
Mad Hatter & March Hare, MARX	50
Mickey & Minnie carrying a basket of food, MARX	40
Mickey pushing lawn roller, MARX	35
Minnie pushing baby stroller, MARX	35
Mickey & Donald riding on an alligator, MARX	40
Mickey w/Pluto hunting, MARX . .	40
Pluto, MARX	20

HANNA-BARBERA & KING FEATURES

Astro & Rosey (Hanna Barbera)
Photo by Randy Welch

Fred Riding Dino (Hanna Barbera)
Photo by Randy Welch

DISNEY

	C10
Big Bad Wolf & mason pig, MARX	40
Big Bad Wolf & 3 little pigs, MARX	125
Donald pushing a wheelbarrow, MARX	25
Donald pulling 3 nephews in a wagon, MARX	35

Astro, MARX	150
Astro & Rosey, MARX	95
Astro & George Jetson, MARX . . .	95
Fred Flintstone & Barney, MARX .	40
Fred & Wilma riding on dinosaur, MARX	60
Fred riding on green Dino, MARX	70

Little King & Guard (King Features)
Photo by Randy Welch

	C10
Little King & guard	75
Pebbles riding on purple Dino, MARX	70
Popeye pushing spinach can wheelbarrow, MARX	25
Top Cat & Benny, MARX	65
Yogi Bear & Huckleberry Hound, MARX	50

OTHER CHARACTERS

Figaro the Cat w/Ball (Other Characters)
Photo by Randy Welch

Chilly Willy penguin on sled pulled by parent, MARX	25
Figaro the cat w/ball, MARX	25
Hap & Hop soldiers, MARX	20
Mother Goose w/goose, MARX . . .	60
Santa w/white sack, ?	40
Santa w/yellow sack, MARX	35
Santa w/gold open sack, MARX . . .	45
Santa & Mrs. Claus (faces on both sides), FUN WORLD	40
Santa & Snowman (faces on both sides), FUN WORLD	40
Spark Plug the horse, MARX	175

MARX ANIMALS WITH RIDERS SERIES

	C10
Ankylosaurus w/clown, MARX . . .	25
Bison w/native, MARX	25
Brontosaurus w/monkey, MARX . .	25
Hippo w/native, MARX	25
Lion w/clown, MARX	25
Stegosaurus w/black caveman, MARX	25
Triceratops w/native, MARX	25
Zebra w/native, MARX	25

OTHER

	C10
Baseball player w/bat & ball, MARX	30
Bear, MARX	15
Boy & girl dancing, MARX	40
Bull, MARX	15
Bunnys carrying large carrot, ?	30
Bunny pushing cart, MARX	45

Bunny w/Carrot on back of Dog
Photo by Randy Welch

Bunny w/carrot on back of dog, MARX	60
Camel w/2 humps head bobs up & down, ?	20
Chicks carrying large Easter Egg, ?	30
Chinamen carrying a duck in a basket, MARX	30
Chipmunks in marching band playing drum & horn, MARX	30
Chipmunks carrying acorns, MARX	30
Dachshund dog, MARX	15
Dairy Cow, MARX	15
Duck Mama w/3 ducklings, MARX	25
Duck, MARX	15
Dutch boy & girl, MARX	30
Elephant, MARX	20
Farmer pushing wheelbarrow, MARX	20
Firemen, MARX	25

L to R: Frontiersman w/Dog; Indian Woman w/Baby on Travois
Photo by Randy Welch

	C10
Frontiersman w/dog, MARX	95
Goat, ?	20
Horse circus style, MARX	15
Indian woman pulling baby on travois, MARX	95
Kangaroo w/baby in pouch, MARX	25
Marty's Market lady pushing shopping cart, MARX	40
Monkeys carrying bananas, MARX	50
Nurse maid pushing baby stroller, MARX	15
Pig, MARX	15
Pigs two carrying third in basket, MARX	40
Poodle (made by Gantoy England), GANTOY	40

Tin Man Robot Pushing a Cart
Photo by Randy Welch

LONG JOHN SILVER PREMIUM
(1989 - with plastic coin weight)

	C10
Capt. Flint parrot (green), LJS	15
Flash turtle (green & Yellow), LJS .	15
Quinn penguin (black & white), LJS	15
Sylvia dinosaur (lavender & pink), LJS	15
Sydney dinosaur (yellow & purple), LJS	15

Pumpkin Head Man & Woman
Photo by Randy Welch

Pumpkin head man & woman faces on both sides, FUN WORLD	45
Reindeer, MARX	25
Sailors S.S. Shoreleave, MARX	20
Sheriff facing outlaw, MARX	50
Tin Man robot pushing a cart, MARX	125

FUNNY FACE KOOL-AID PREMIUM
(All with plastic coin weight)

Choo-Choo Cherry, PILLSBURY . .	60
Goofy Grape, PILLSBURY	60
Jolly Ollie Orange, PILLSBURY . .	60
Root'n Toot'n Raspberry, PILLSBURY	60

SMALL PLASTIC W/METAL LEGS

	C10
Cow, MARX	15
Cowboy on horse, ?	20
Donald Duck pushing wheelbarrow, MARX	30
Dog (Pluto-like), MARX	15
Elephant, ?	20
Mexican cowboy on horse, ?.....	20
Mickey & Minnie Mouse, MARX .	40
Pluto, MARX	30

LARGE PLASTIC

	C10
Baby Walk-a-Way baby, MARX...	40
Baby Teeny Toddler walking girl, DOLLS, INC.	40
Baby Walking baby w/moving eyes cloth dress, MARX	40
Baby Walking baby in Canadian Mountie uniform, MARX	50
Baby Walking baby in Pirate clothes, MARX	50
Cow Milking cow, MARX	40
Cow Wiz Walking Milking Cow Charmore, MARX	50

Double Walking Doll
Photo by Randy Welch

	C10
Double Walking Doll (boy behind girl), ?	45
Horse w/English rider, MARX	40
Horse, MARX	30
Horse w/rubber ears & string tail, MARX	30
Popeye & Wimpy w/heads on springs, MARX	65

CELLULOID

ERWIN

	C10
Popeye, ERWIN	60

CAST IRON

IVES

	C10
Elephant Pat 1873, 3½" long, lead legs, IVES	125

Ives cast iron Elephant, Pat. 1873
Photo by Randy Welch

WOOD & COMPOSITE

Wilson, L to R: Indian Chief, Black Mammy, Soldier
Photo by Randy Welch

WILSON

	C10
Black Mammy, WILSON	35
Clown, WILSON	30
Elephant on 4 legs, WILSON	30
Eskimo, WILSON	60
Indian Chief, WILSON	45
Little Red Riding Hood, WILSON .	35
Nurse, WILSON	30
Olive Oyl, WILSON	150
Penguin, WILSON	25
Pinocchio, WILSON	150
Popeye, WILSON..............	150
Rabbit, WILSON	40

Wilson, L to R: Little Red Riding Hood, Clown, Nurse
Photo by Randy Welch

	C10
Sailor, WILSON	30
Santa Claus, WILSON	60
Soldier, WILSON	25
Wimpy, WILSON	150

CZECHOSLOVAKIAN

Dog on 4 legs, CZECH	20
Man with carved wooden hat, CZECH	25
Monkey, CZECH	30
Pig, CZECH	20
Policeman, CZECH	35

RAMPS IN BOX

Circus Horse, MARX	60
Comical Action bear w/long ramp, including gun & bullets, MARX	125
Dick Tracy's Nursemaid takes Bonny Braids for stroll, MARX	100
Disney long ramp w/generic street scene, MARX	200
Felix wood ramp w/wood walker	1,400

L to R: Hap & Hop; Circus Horse (both tin litho)
Photo by Randy Welch

	C10
Hap & Hop the Dauntless Doughboys, MARX	80
"I Like Ike" elephant, MARX	125
Nora the Nursemaid, MARX	75
Plank ramp (generic) for cow, pig, ducks, bear etc..., MARX	50
S.S. Shoreleave sailors, MARX	75

A Marx Flier.

MAGIC MARXIE WORLD FAMOUS WALKING TOYS

© WALT DISNEY PRODUCTIONS

© KING FEATURES SYNDICATE, INC. 1962

© HANNA-BARBERA PRODUCTIONS INC. 1962 TRADE MARK OF SCREEN GEMS INC. LOUIS MARX & CO., INC. AUTHORIZED USER

LOUIS MARX & CO., INC.

START YOUR COLLECTION!

HERE ARE A FEW OF THE MANY WAYS WALKING TOYS CAN BE MADE TO WALK......AFTER DOING THESE, INVENT VARIATIONS OF YOUR OWN.

USE A BOOK, OR A SIMILAR OBJECT, TO MAKE A RAMP HEIGHT OF ABOUT 1 INCH IN 12 INCHES OF LENGTH.

TO MAKE TOY WALK ON A FLAT SURFACE, TIE A LENGTH OF THREAD ABOUT 36 INCHES LONG TO TOY. ATTACH A SMALL WEIGHT TO OTHER END OF THREAD. PLACE TOY ON TABLE WITH WEIGHT HANGING OVER EDGE. PULL BACK TO FULL LENGTH OF STRING, ROCK GENTLY AND RELEASE.

TO MAKE TOY WALK BACKWARDS—BRING THREAD BACK BETWEEN LEGS—FACE TOY AWAY FROM TABLE EDGE—ROCK GENTLY AND RELEASE.

A GENTLE PUSH WITH A PENCIL WILL MAKE TOY WALK ON A SMOOTH SURFACE.

TOY WALKS TO TABLE EDGE AND STOPS.

PRINTED IN HONG KONG

A Marx Flier

WHITE KNOB WINDUPS

By M. Aaron Roy

White Knob Windups (WKW) are small, plastic mechanical toys which came on the market around the mid-to-late 1970's. They get their name from the little white (sometimes colored on newer toys) ridged knob at the end of a metal rod which extends from the body and winds the motor when rotated.

Most WKWs offer a single basic movement or action. "Walkers", "hoppers", "climbers", "rollers", "flip-overs", or "pop-overs" perform on a flat surface while toys intended to be pinned on clothing may have eyes which move "up-and-down" or ears which wiggle "back-and-forth". "Swimmers" move in water. A few of the most desireable WKWs have multiple movements occuring at the same time or in sequence. White Knob Windups were (and are) typically sold loose or in bubble packaging. A few came boxed in sets with other figures or with accessories. Production originally was in Japan, Macao, Singapore and Taiwan, but more recently is centered in China.

WKWs come in a variety of themes: transportation, tools and utensils, sports, space, popular culture, novelty, musical, movies and television, holidays and seasons, foods, fast-food giveaways, fairy tales, Disney, cartoon and comic character, animals, and anatomical parts. Some White Knob Windups have been produced by well-known companies such as Tomy,® Galoob,® Russ,® and Mattel® while others seem to be sold by small companies or importers with no reference as to manufacturer.

The following list is only representative of the many hundreds of WKWs which have been produced. Color, structural, and decorating variations exist in many examples, while toys originally issued by one company (e.g., Tomy®) may be released later by another company (e.g., Playskool®). Prices quoted below reflect the original releases that are often marked as to manufacturer. As with other toys, WKWs in original packaging will be more valuable. Number 10 values reflect mint, working wind-ups with all accessories

Aaron Roy is a Professor of Psychology at Ashland University in Ashland, Ohio, and owner of the LAKE ERIE TOY MUSEUM on Kelleys Island near Marblehead, Ohio where his personal collection of toys from 1870 to 1980 is on display. He has collected a wide range of toys for about 30 years and is the author of numerous professional and hobby-related articles.

Tomy White Knob Windup Cabbage Patch Kids. Photo by M. Aaron Roy.

Tomy White Knob Windup Cabbage Patch Kids. Photo by M. Aaron Roy.

CHARACTERS

	C6	C8	C10
Barbie (Mattel, 1986 & Arco, 1988)			
Microwave Oven, Sewing Machine, Radio/Tape Deck, VCR, Camera Telephone, Computer, Mantel Clock, Stereo Mixer. Each	1	2	3
Cabbage Patch Kids (Tomy, 1985)			
Crawler: boy or girl, each	4	6	8
Girl in walker	4	6	8
Boy with basketball	6	9	12
Boy on stick horse	6	9	12

515

Tomy White Knob Windup Cabbage Patch Rocking Baby. Photo by M. Aaron Roy.

	C6	C8	C10
Girl Cheerleader	6	9	12
Girl baton twirler	6	9	12
Rocking Babies: Basinette, Swing, Rocking Horse, each	10	15	20
E.T. Walker (LJN, 1982)	6	9	12
Muppets (Tomy, 1983)			
Pop-Ups: Animal Drummer or Great Gonzo's Shark Escape, each	8	12	16
Pop-Overs: Miss Piggy or Great Gonzo, each	8	12	16
Flip-Floppers: Animal Jalopy or Miss Piggy Swinetrek, each	8	12	16
Swimmers: Kermit the Frog, Miss Piggy, Fozzie the Bear, each	7	10	14

Tomy White Knob Windup Pac Man. Photo by M. Aaron Roy.

	C6	C8	C10
Pac Man rollers (Tomy, 1982)			
Mr. or Mrs., each	6	9	12
Inky Ghost (Blue)	8	12	16

	C6	C8	C10
Blinky Ghost (Red)	8	12	16
Pink Panther (Bandai-America, 1981)			
Pink Panther Walker	8	12	16
Inspector Walker	6	8	12
Popeye (Durham, 1980)			
Popeye or Brutus Walker, each	10	15	20
Q*Bert Hopper (Kenner, 1983)	6	9	12

Tomy White Knob Windup smurfs. Photo by M. Aaron Roy.

	C6	C8	C10
Smurfs Walkers (Galoob, 1982)			
Musicians: trumpet, guitar, drum	4	6	8
Figures: Jokey holding present, Smurfette, Papa Smurf, Flying Smurf, Gargomel, each	4	6	8
Plain Walker (Blue Knob)	10	15	20
Smurf on Swing	6	9	12
Smurfs on Teeter Totter	6	9	12
Smurfs Jumping Rope	6	9	12
Smurf Fun House (Mushroom)	10	15	20
Snoopy (Aviva)			
Swimmer or walker	6	9	12
Walkers: Snoopy with Top Hat, Snoopy as Red Baron, Snoopy as Bull Fighter, Woodstock with flowers, each	3	5	7
Snorks (Tomy, 1984)			
Swimmers: 5 different, each	6	9	12
Walkers: 5 different, each	6	9	12
The Chipmunks Hoppers (Imperial, 1983)			
Alvin with harmonica	6	9	12
Simon with guitar	6	9	12
Theodoor with drums	6	9	12
Tom & Jerry Walkers (Multitoys, 1989)			
Tom or Jerry	4	6	8
Spike, Tyke, Droopy, Quacker, each	5	8	10

Tomy White Knob Windup Snorks. Photo by M. Aaron Roy.

	C6	C8	C10
Wizard of Oz Walkers (Multitoys, 1988)			
Scarecrow, Alice, Witch, each....	4	6	8

NON-CHARACTERS

	C6	C8	C10
Babies (Tomy, 1977)			
Crawler or Walker, each..............	10	15	20

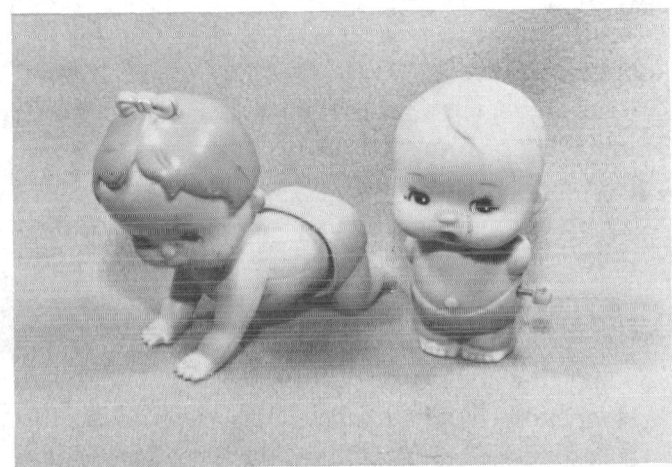

Tomy White Knob Windup Babies. Photo by M. Aaron Roy.

	C6	C8	C10
Bathtubbies (Tomy, 1983)			
Swimming Whale, Frog, Bear, Seal, Penquin, Turtle, Goldfish, and Duck, each............................	2	3	4
Box Pops (Tomy, 1981)			
Rolling box stops and "Wacky Clown", "Funny Face" or "Looney Bird" pops out of the top, each......................................	9	13	18
Bumbling Boxing Game (Tomy, 1982)			
Two walking boxers on ring........	8	12	16

	C6	C8	C10
Curious Critters (Tomy, 1984)			
Rollers that are directed by a magnetic wand			
Dogs: 2 different ones, each...	8	12	16
Cats: 2 different ones, each....	8	12	16
Flip Floppers (Tomy, 1983)			
Bus, Plane, Car, Racer, Space Ship, Helecopter, Train, Dune Buggy, each..............................	2	3	4
Get Along Gadgets Rollers (Tomy, 1983)			
Toaster, Clock, Phone, Coffee Pot, Record Player, each..............	4	6	8
Get Along Gang Rollers (Tomy, 1984)			
Zipper Cat or Dotty Dog on a handcar, each............................	6	9	12
Lamb or Moose on a raft, each....	6	9	12
Porcupine or Moose on a skateboard, each................................	6	9	12
Home Run Homer Game (Tomy, 1982)			
Baseball hopper on green playing field...	10	15	20

Tomy White Knob Home Run Homer Windup Game. Photo by M. Aaron Roy.

	C6	C8	C10
Hop-A-Long Hoopster Game (Tomy, 1982)			
Hopping basketball on court........	10	15	20
Hilarious Hats Walkers (Tomy, 1983)			
Cowboy, Football, Police, each...	6	10	14
Inch-A-Longs (Bandai-America, 1981)			
Dog, Crocodile, locomotive and truck crawling rollers, each..........	4	6	8
Lil' Big Toppers (Tomy, 1983)			
Elephant roller, multi-actions......	10	15	20
Clown in Car or Bear, each.........	5	8	10

517

	C6	C8	C10
Mad Balls Rollers (Spearhead, 1986) Screamin Meemie, Horn Head, Skull Face, Slobulus. Heads w/ moving tongues, each	2	3	4
Major League Baseballs (Russ, 1989) Baseball hoppers w/colors and logos of each team, each	4	6	8
Major League Football (Russ, 1989) Helmut hoppers w/colors and logos of each team, each	4	6	8
Mini-Appliances (Galoob, 1979) Floor Buffer, Stereo & Speakers, Sewing Machine, Blender, Mixer, Food Processor, each	3	5	7
Mini-Tools (Galoob, 1980) Circular Saw, Jigsaw, Sander, Drill, Chain Saw, each	4	6	8
Mini-Tools (Imperial, 1988) Chain Saw, Drill, Jigsaw and Circular Saw, each	2	3	4
Minimals (Tomy, 1982) Dog, Duck, Elephant, Hippopotomus, Horse, Giraffe rollers about 1-1/2 inch long w/exterior wheels and back hole "hook", each	11	16	22
Mity Machines (Galoob, 1984) Pile Driver, Pounder, Bulldozer and Backhoe, each	5	7	9
Pocket Pets Hoppers (Tomy, 1983) Goose, Squirrel, Penguin, Turtle, Frog, Toucan, Beetle, Rabbit, Dog, Owl, Duck, and Chicken, each	2	3	4
Prancing Ponys (Tomy, 1983) Pinto, Arabian Stallion, Palomino,			

Tomy White Knob Windup Rascal Robots. Photo by M. Aaron Roy.

	C6	C8	C10
Appaloosa w/accessories of a saddle, bridle, bucket and brush	8	12	16
Rascal Robots or Pocket 'Bots (Tomy, 1977) 3 different walkers	4	6	8
Robot Lion Force (LJN, 1984) Black, red, green, yellow robot	5	10	15
Scurry Furries (Tomy, 1982) Rabbit, Dog, Raccoon, Owl, and Green Dragon Hoppers or Rollers that are "fur" covered	7	10	14
Snow Funnies Rollers (Tomy, 1981) Bear or Rabbit on skis, each	2	4	6
Strolling Bowling Game (Tomy, 1982) Hopper bowling ball knocks pins over on lane	10	15	20
Ugh-A-Bugs Crawlers (Tomy, 1981) Stag Beetle, Tarantula, and Atlas Beetle, each	6	9	12

GUNS

(See also Premiums, Comic Character)

Average mint prices of guns in the fourth edition were $114.32 and in this edition
they average $172.86, an increase of 51%.

SOME THOUGHTS ON TOY GUN COLLECTING

By Charles W. Best

Amid all the various toys in the world, the toy gun stands out as the one type most distinctly American and native to the United States, and with good reason. From the earliest days of our history up through the late 19th century, firearms were the primary tool that enabled us to survive, settle, explore, and subdue this land. Firearms gave us our freedom in 1776 and were instrumental in preserving that freedom throughout our first hundred turbulent years. Those years, as we now know, were to become an era of "romantic" wars when boys and young men dreamed of attaining fame and glory on the battlefield or out on the Western Frontier. The War of 1812, the Mexican War, the Civil War, and numerous Indian conflicts were all fought, basically, with small arms, so it is small wonder then that when toys first began to be mass produced after the Civil War, toy guns were among the first to appear on the market. Their success was instantaneous and toy guns remained among our most popular selling toys until as recently as the 1960's.

Although toy guns were patented in the 1850's they were not manufactured in any quantity until a decade later due to the wartime shortages. These early toy guns were, for the most part, pea shooters and cork poppers and were usually made of wood with metal hardware although iron and lead types may occasionally be found among them. As you might suspect, these early examples are hard to find today and most are known only through their patent drawings. By 1870, inventors, trying to add realism to these toy guns, began using paper caps, a then new invention which had been developed just prior to the Civil War and was known as the Maynard Tape Primer. This tape primer was originally intended to detonate muzzle loading arms and closely resembled a roll of modern day paper caps. Now, for the first time, toy guns could make a loud noise yet still be relatively safe and harmless. Naturally, this spurred the demand for these new toys and designers worked overtime to create new and appealing guns. Their output was prolific and, today, the period from 1870 to 1900 is regarded as the "golden age" of the toy gun and especially the toy cap pistol, in America.

By 1880, the cast iron cap pistol had become the most popular type of toy gun by far and the various toy makers, primarily J. & E. Stevens and Ives, were competing among themselves to see who could produce the most unique and appealing designs. A glance at any collection of these early day toy pistols will show that, in those days, realism was secondary to artistic imagination. Many pistols from this period were literally covered with ornamentation and, is some cases, any resemblance to a real gun was purely coincidental. Leaf and scroll designs were the most popular but pistols can also be found with numerous other designs, including both two and three dimensional figures. Those guns with moving figures are known as "animated" pistols and even though not as rare as some, are worth much more to a collector than an ordinary-looking pistol from the same period.

Another very desirable pistol from this same era is now known as the "head" pistol and featured a head, either animal or human, which was placed at the breech end of the barrel with the mouth open to receive the cap. Over two dozen varieties of head and animated pistols are known to exist but are so much in demand that they are seldom offered for sale.

The most popular material used to make these early toy pistols was, of course, cast iron, which continued to be used heavily into the 20th century, until the demands of World War II cut off the supply. Many varieties of old toy guns were, however, made of other materials than iron. I have seen examples made from such diverse materials as paper, wood, steel, tin, lead, rubber, zinc, glass, and even wax. During the Second World War, to meet the heavy demand, toy guns were even made of molded sawdust mixed with glue. After the war a few cast iron pistols were produced and assembled, using both new and old parts, but the cost proved to be prohibitive, and makers soon turned to less expensive metals such as steel and die cast zinc. By 1950, most toy pistols were being made of the die cast material and also plastic, both of which continue to be used today.

From almost the very beginning, toy gun makers have felt the need to personalize their products and literally hundreds of different names can be found embossed on these little guns. Some examples that come to mind are: EXCELSIOR, VICTOR, AMERICAN BULLDOG, ACORN, SUN, BOOM, DARB, ACE, DAISY, COWBOY KING, POLO, TRIUMPH, TERROR, etc. Many names were used only once on one particular gun and then dropped while others have reappeared time and again on different guns over the years. This custom of naming toy guns still goes on today and a visit to any toy store will turn up names such as: COWHAND, TOP GUN JR., 007, etc. Many of these names seem to reflect current events or personalities while on others, the meaning has become obscure.

For the toy collector, or would-be collector, the collecting of toy guns and especially pistols, not only offers a large diversity of models and styles but, because of their tremendous popularity in the past, also the opportunity to find and acquire interesting and unusual examples at an affordable price. Guns from as far back as the 1920's and '30's can still be found at flea markets, garage sales, and second hand stores, often at a price that is only a fraction of what other toys from these same years will sell for.

NOTE: Measurements given, in general, are from one end of the gun to the other, rather than on a diagonal from grip to muzzle. Much of the information on manufacturers,

measurements, etc., comes from Charles W. Best's excellent book "Cast Iron Toy Pistols" (see bibliography). Dates of manufacturers can vary within five years, though most of the later dates are considerably more accurate.

CHARLES W. BEST is a leading authority on toy weapons, and has been collecting them in earnest since 1966. His collection is regarded as one of the finest and most comprehensive in existence, and has won many awards at various gun shows. In addition to writing a number of articles on the subject in such magazines as Gun Report and Antique Toy World, he is the Author of "Cast Iron Toy Pistols" (see Bibliography).

	C6	C8	C10
Ace cast iron cap pistol. Stevens, "Made in U.S.A." 5" long, 1930	27	41	55
Ace cast iron cap pistol, 5" long, 1935	22	33	45
Acme steel cap automatic, repeater, circa 1930	12	18	25

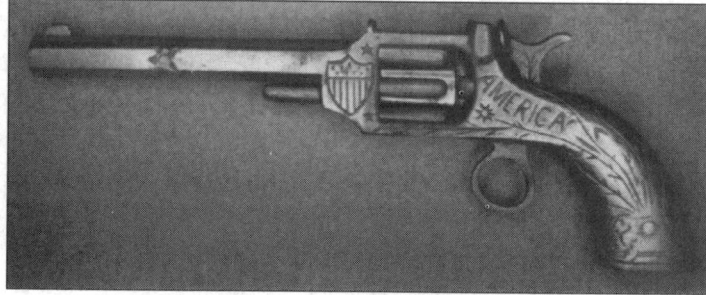

"America" by STEVENS. Photo by Charles W. Best.

American Bulldog, 1910. Courtesy Sotheby's New York.

	C6	C8	C10
Acorn cast iron pistol	75	100	150
Admiral Dewey cast iron cap bomb	50	75	100
Aeromatic Glider Gun, steel automatic, circa 1940, shoots balsa airplanes	48	72	95
Agitator, The, cast iron cap and torpedo shooter, 1908, John Fox, 8¼"	125	188	250
Aim To Save, circa 1909	150	225	300
Air Blaster, Wham-O, shoots burst of air, plastic	35	52	70
Air Raid Warning signal pistol	30	50	75
America cap pistol with shield, pat. 1873	150	225	300
America, 1880, Stevens, 8¾"	135	200	275
American cast iron cap pistol, Kilgore, 1940, 9⅝"	125	188	250
American Bulldog cast iron .22 cal. blank shooter, 1910, 4½" long, second trigger tips barrel to load, Kenton, handle projects outward	40	60	80

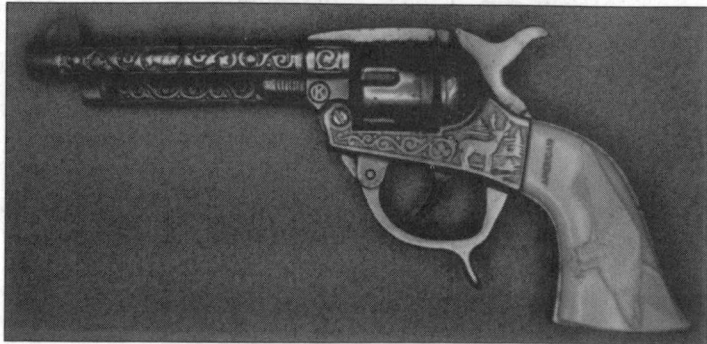

"American", by KILGORE. Photo by Charles W. Best.

Army 45. Photo by Charles W. Best.

	C6	C8	C10
American Bulldog cast iron .22 blank shooter, 1920, 4½" long, Kenton, second trigger tips barrel to load, handle curves inward 45	68	90
Army cast iron cap pistol, 1910............40	60	80
Army 45 cast iron cap automatic, Hubley 1940 "Made in U.S.A." 6⅝"......65	98	130
Army 45 diecast zinc cap automatic, Hubley, 1940, plastic grips, "Made in U.S.A." 6½" long......40	60	80
Army pistol with revolving cylinder, tin litho, Marx no. 625 17	25	35
Army sparkling pop gun, Marx No. 197 17	25	35
Atomic Disintegrator cap pistol, Hubley......135	200	270
Atomic Flash space gun, Chein ... 31	46	62
Auto Magic Picture Gun, projects film onto wall. 1936. comes with film and instructions, in box 75	112	150
Automatic die-cast cap pistol, Hubley No. 290, 6½"......54	81	108
Automatic Repeater Paper Pop Pistol No. 74, Marx, aluminum......15	20	25
Automatic Repeater, pressed steel, 7" long, 1920s, Wyandotte No. 40......20	25	30
Bang cast iron cap pistol, Kilgore, "Made in U.S.A.," 6" long......25	38	50
Bang-O cast iron cap pistol, Stevens, 1938, "Made in U.S.A.," 7" long....45	68	90
Banner, blank-shooting mechanical cast iron pistol, Ives, 5" 150	175	250

Left to Right. Top: BIG BILL, PLUCK, DICK. Middle: ATOMIC DISINTEGRATOR, SURE SHOT SAFETY. Bottom: TIGER, GENE AUTRY 44. Photo Courtesy Garth's Auctions Inc.

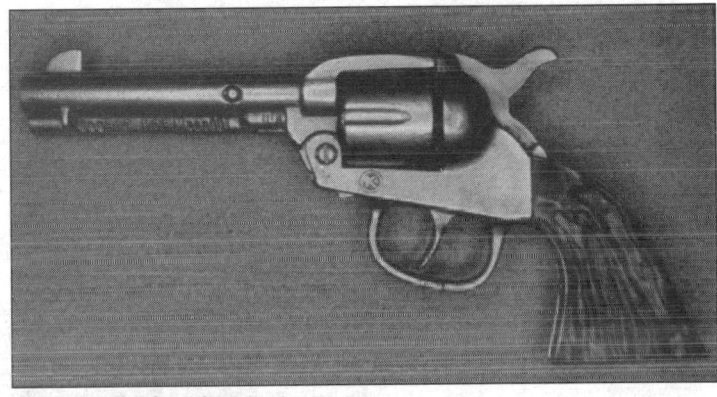

"Big Horn". Photo by Charles W. Best.

Banner. Courtesy Sotheby's New York.

	C6	C8	C10
Bell Pistol, Wyandotte......17	26	35
Benjamin Pump early BB gun, before 1910 75	112	150
Biff cast iron cap automatic, Kenton, 1935, "Made in U.S.A. Pat. Apld. For," 4½" 30	45	60
Biff Jr. cast iron cap automatic, Kenton 1935, "Made in U.S.A. Pat. Apld. For," 4⅛" long 30	45	60

	C6	C8	C10
Big Bang Pistol No. 6P, 7⅞" long .. 75	175	350
Big Bang Rifle No. 21-60, 21-3/16" long 750	2000	3500
Big Bill cast iron cap pistol, large hammer, "Made in U.S.A.," Kilgore 1935, 4⅞" 30	45	60
Big Bill cast iron cap pistol, Kilgore, 1925, 5½" long 30	45	60
Big Bill cast iron cap pistol, large hammer, "Made in U.S.A.," Kilgore 1930, 5¾" 50	75	100
Big Buster cast iron cap automatic, Kilgore 1915, "Patd Jul 2 1907, Made in U.S.A.," 5", two-piece trigger......75	112	150
Big Chief cast iron cap pistol, Kilgore, 1935, 6" long......25	38	50
Big Chief cast iron cap pistol, Kilgore, 1935, has star and "K", 6" 25	38	50

	C6	C8	C10
Big Chief cast iron cap pistol, early-looking, but made in 1930, 3½", Dent "Made in U.S.A."	22	33	45
Big Clip cast iron cap pistol, Stevens 1930, "Made in U.S.A.", 6¾"	25	38	50
Big Horn cast iron cap pistol, revolving cylinder, Kilgore, 1939, 8⅜"	150	225	300
Big Injun, hammerless	150	225	300
Big Scout, 1935	60	90	120
Big Scout, 1940 (engraved)	30	45	60
Bigger Bang large hammer cast iron cap pistol, Kilgore 1930, 6" long	32	48	65
Bill	35	52	70
Billy The Kid cast iron cap pistol, Kilgore 1930, 6¾"	125	188	250
Black Jack cast iron cap pistol, long barrel, Kenton 1930, "Pat. Sept. 11-23", 11"	125	188	250
Blaze Away Dart Pistol, Marx No. G23	15	22	30
Bob cast iron cap pistol, Kilgore, 1930, 5" long	25	38	50
Bobcat die-cast cap pistol, 1950s, Kilgore, 4¼"	19	28	38
Boom	150	225	300
Border Patrol cast iron cap automatic, Kilgore, 1930, 4¼" long	32	48	65
Border Patrol cast iron cap automatic, Kilgore, 1935, "Pat. Apld. For, Made in U.S.A.," 4½" long	50	75	100

	C6	C8	C10
Border Patrol, 1940	50	75	100
Boss cast iron mammoth cap pistol, 1925, Kenton, 6¼"	30	45	60
Boy's Delight Pat. June 1891, cast iron cap pistol	150	225	300
Boy's Police Automatic 8" cardboard pop gun, circa 1940s	8	12	15
Brat cast iron cap pistol	30	45	60
Bravo	75	112	150
Brevet Depose	300	450	600
Bronc cast iron cap pistol, Kenton 1935, "Kenton, Made in U.S.A.," 6"	30	45	60
Buc-A-Roo cast iron cap pistol, Kilgore 1940, 7¾"	50	75	100
Buck cast iron pistol, Hubley 1930, looks earlier, 3¼"	55	82	110
Buddy, 1930	25	38	50
Buddy, 1935	25	38	50
Buffalo Bill, 1890	200	300	400
Buffalo Bill cast iron cap pistol, Kenton, 1925, "Pat. Sept. 11-23," 11⅜", very long barrel	150	225	300
Buffalo Bill cast iron cap pistol, Kenton 1930, "Pat Sept. 11-23," 13½", perhaps the longest-barreled cap pistol	150	225	300
Buffalo Bill cast iron cap pistol, Stevens, 1940, "Made in U.S.A.", 7¾" long	40	60	80

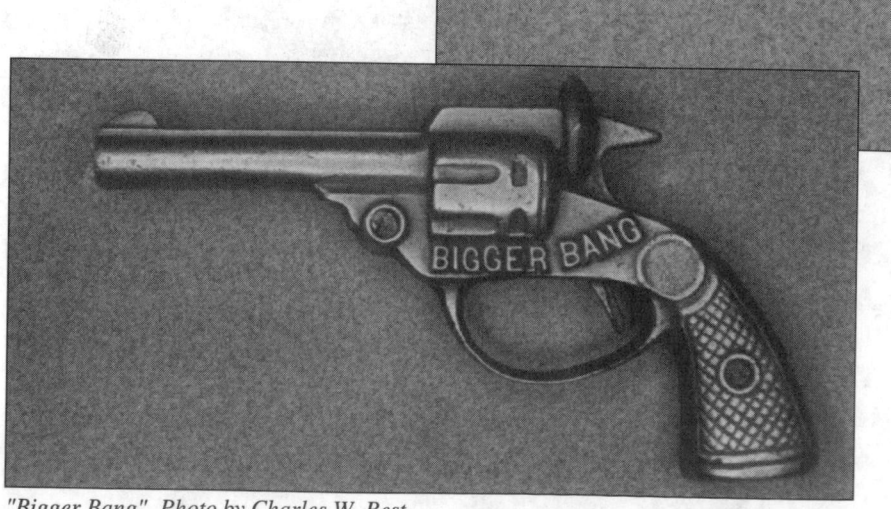

Bull's Eye Safety. Photo by Charles W. Best.

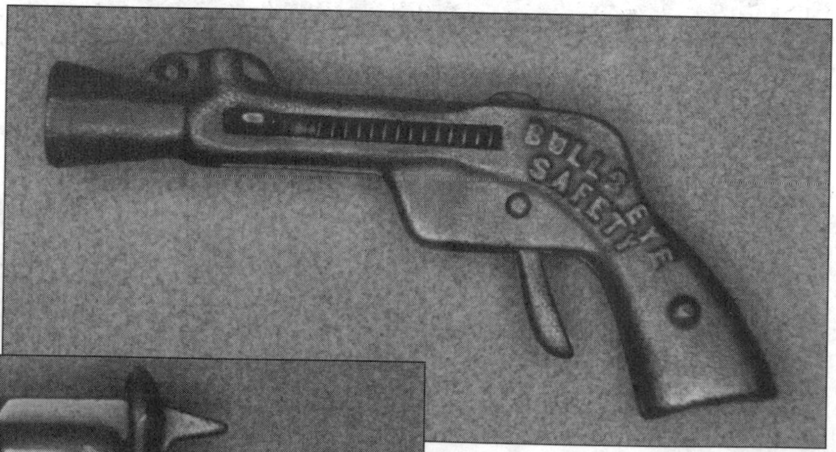

"Bigger Bang". Photo by Charles W. Best.

Border Patrol, 1940. Courtesy Sotheby's New York.

	C6	C8	C10
Bull cast iron cap pistol, Hubley, 1940, "Pat Appld. for Pat. Mch. 25, '24," 6¼"	25	38	50
Bulldog cast iron cast-iron cap pistol, Kenton, 1923, 5½"	55	82	110
Bull Dog cast iron cap pistol, Hubley, 1935, "Pat. 1,488,046," 6¼" long	27	41	55

"Buster", maker unknown, 1901, 6" long.

	C6	C8	C10
Bulldozer cast iron cap pistol, six-shooter, July 1874	150	225	300
Bull's Eye cast iron cap pistol, Kenton, 1940, "Gene Autry" signature on grips, 6½"	125	188	250
Bullseye Safety cast iron pistol, flare barrel, with spring	75	112	150
Bunker Hill cast iron cap pistol, National, 1925, 5¼" long	25	38	50
Burp Gun, Mattel, 1956, 13" long, aluminum, die cast, plastic	45	68	90
"Buster," maker unknown, 1901, 6"	62	93	125
Buster cast iron cap automatic, 1910, Kilgore, 5½"	45	68	90

	C6	C8	C10
Butting Match mechanical pistol, cast iron	250	375	500
Cadet, 1930	27	41	55
Cal, 1925	30	45	60
Cannon - Animated Cap Pistol	250	375	500
Cap Bomb, cast iron, head shape	75	112	150
Cap Bomb, dog's head	80	120	160
Cap Pistol, cast iron, ornate, 1878	65	98	130
Cap Pistol, cast iron, revolving cylinder, 1887	100	150	200
Cap Pistol, cast iron, six-shot, dated 1895	100	150	200
Cast iron pistol, ornate, six shot, 1895	100	150	200
Cast iron pistol, shoots caps, embossed	20	30	40
Cast iron pistol, shoots caps, plated barrel	17	26	35
Cap pistol, steel, repeating, red, Wyandotte, 8" long	15	22	30
Captain cast iron cap automatic, Kilgore, 1940, 4¼" long	35	52	70
Cat (animated)	450	675	900
Cavalier cast iron cap automatic, Kilgore, 1935, "Pat. Appld. For, Made in U.S.A.," 4½"	35	52	70
Challenge, 1890	150	225	300
Champ Automatic, 5", die cast, Hubley	22	33	45
Chief (1900-1910)	110	165	220
Chief cast iron .22 cal. blank shooter, Kenton, 1915, 6" long, second trigger tips up barrel to load	50	75	100
Chief cast iron cap pistol, Hubley 1930, "Pat 1,488,046," 6⅛"	30	45	60
Chief cap pistol, aluminum single shot, Hubley	30	45	60

Cannon. Courtesy Sotheby's New York.

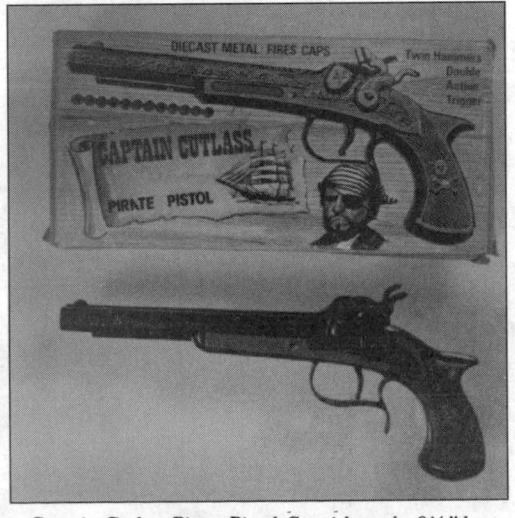

Champ". Photo by Charles W. Best.

Captain Cutlass Pirate Pistol, Spanish-made, 9½" long. Copy of Pirate by HUBLEY. Cast zinc. Photo by Charles W. Best. No Price Found.

Clown (on barrel). Photo by Charles W. Best.

	C6	C8	C10
Chieftain cast iron cap pistol, National, 1920, 11" long	75	112	150
Chinese Must Go mechanical cap pistol	300	450	600
"Click Pistol" Marx No. 32	15	22	30
Click Pistol, Marx, approx. 7¾" long, pressed steel, with box	15	22	30
Click Pistol, tin litho, Marx No. 36	15	22	30
Clicker Pistol, plain black, late 1930s, early 1940s	15	22	30
Clip Jr. cast iron cap pistol, Stevens, 1935, 5¼"	25	38	50
Clipper cast iron cap automatic, Kilgore, 1935, 4⅛"	55	82	110
Clown and mule animated pistol	500	750	1000
Clown (on a barrel)	350	525	700
Colt cast iron cap pistol, Stevens 1920, "Patented June 17, 1890, Made in U.S.A.," 5½"	35	52	70
Colt cast iron cap pistol, Stevens, 1935, 6½"	27	41	55
Colt .45 die cast Hubley	95	142	190
Columbia 1885 cast iron cap pistol	200	300	400
Columbia 1890 cast iron cap pistol, Stevens, 8¾"	200	300	400
Columbia cast iron cap pistol, pat. June 1891	200	300	400
Columbian Junior Early BB gun	250	375	500
Comet, 1885, 5½", Stevens	150	225	300
Comet, 1925, 7⅛", Stevens	40	60	80
Cop cast iron cap pistol Hubley 1930 "Pat 1,488,046" or "Pat. Mch. 25 '24," 5"	25	38	50
Cork-popper pistol, Wyandotte, spur trigger	15	22	30
Cork-shooting rifle, Marx No. 206	25	38	50
Corn Shooter cap pistol	55	82	110
Corporal, maker unknown, 1900, 8⅞"	62	93	125
Cowboy cast iron cap pistol, Ives, 1890, 7⅝"	125	188	250
Cowboy cast iron cap pistol, Stevens, 1935, "Made in U.S.A.," 3½"	27	41	55
Cowboy cast iron cap pistol, long barrel, Stevens, 1930, "Made in U.S.A."	175	263	350
Cowboy cast iron cap pistol, Hubley 1940 "Made in U.S.A.," 8"	75	112	150
Cowboy King, 1940	100	150	200
Coyote die cast Hubley	27	41	55
Crack, 1925, Stevens, 5"	40	60	80
Cupid, 1900, 5¼"	62	93	125
Dagger Derringer die cast Hubley	35	52	70

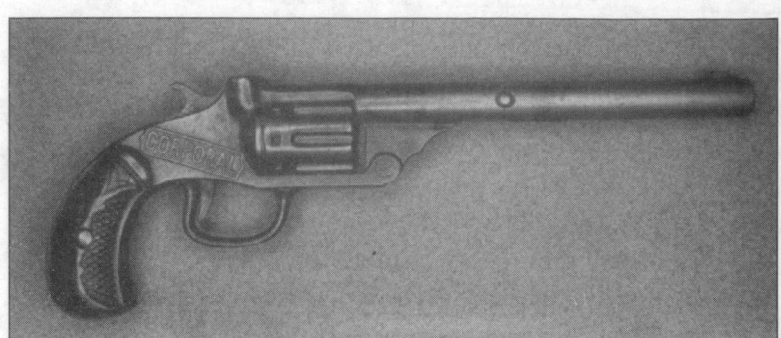

"Corporal". Photo by Charles W. Best.

"Columbia" by STEVENS, 1890. Photo by Charles W. Best.

Daniel Boone Wilderness Scout Derringer. Photo by Gary J. Linden.

"Dagger Derringer". Photo by Charles W. Best.

Dolphin. Courtesy Sotheby's New York.

"Doughboy". Courtesy Charles D. Richards.

Duck, Courtesy Sotheby's New York.

DRAGNET - Detective Special Reporting Revolver Cap Gun, circa 1955. Courtesy HAKE'S Americana & Collectibles.

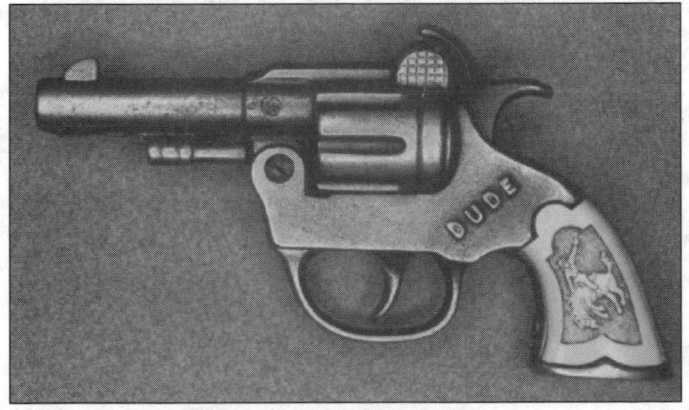

Dude cast iron cap. Photo by Charles W. Best.

	C6	C8	C10
Dandy cast iron cap pistol, Hubley, 1935, can have variety of markings, 5¾"	45	68	90
Daniel Boone Wilderness Scout Derringer, Marx, mint on card	25	38	50

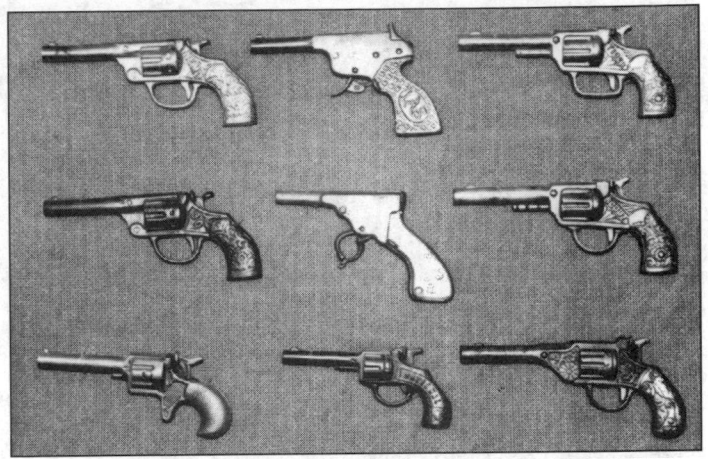

Typical Cast Iron Cap Pistols 1900-1910. Left to Right Top: NEMO, LAS, TIGER 1915. Middle: GO, BUSTER 1910, SCOUT 1890. Bottom: unmarked, NATIONAL, Stevens 1920, unmarked. Courtesy Charles W. Best.

	C6	C8	C10
Darb cast iron cap pistol, Kenton 1930 "Pat. Sept. 11-23," 5½" long	30	45	60
Dart Pistol, Wyandotte, colorful, fancy lithographing	11	16	22
David	40	60	80
Dead Shot, Stevens, 8¾"	125	188	250
Defence, 1896	75	112	150
Derby cast iron cap pistol, Hubley, 1930, 7"	30	45	60
Detroit cast iron cap pistol, 1910, 6⅝" long	65	98	130
Dick cast iron cap pistol, Hubley 1930, 6"	30	45	60
Dick cast iron cap automatic, Hubley 1940, "Made in U.S.A.," 4⅛"	30	45	60
DIK cast iron cap pistol, Kenton 1935, "Pat. Sept. 11-23," 4¾"	27	41	55
Dixie (1888-1890)	75	112	150
Dixie cast iron cap pistol, Kenton 1935, "Made in U.S.A. Pat. Appld. For," 6¼"	35	52	70
Doc cast iron cap piston, Kenton, 1926, "Pat. Sept. 11-23", 4-1/2"	55	82	110
Dolphin animated cap pistol (may actually be Sea Serpent)	400	600	800
Double-barrel cast iron cap pistol, dated 1880	125	188	250
Double-barrel pop gun-rifle, Marx No. 230	.50	75	100
Double-barrel cork gun rifle, Marx No. 232	50	75	100
Double-faced cap bomb, cast iron	60	90	120
Double-trigger cast iron match-shooting pistol, large, Stephens, PA 1873	125	188	250
Doughboy cast iron cap automatic, Kilgore 1920, "Made in U.S.A.," 5"	45	68	90
Dragnet Detective Special repeating revolver cap gun, circa 1955	27	41	55
Duck, animated cap pistol, cast iron, 3¾" long, 1884	2500	3000	5000

	C6	C8	C10
Dude cast iron cap pistol, Stevens, 1887, "Pat. Mar. 22 '87", 3-1/2".....	75	112	150
Dude cast iron cap pistol, plastic grips, 1941, Kenton, 6-1/2"........................	40	60	80
Eagle cast iron cap pistol, Stevens, 1895, "Pat. June 17,1890", 7-1/2"...	82	123	165
Eagle, circa 1940................................	40	60	80
Echo cap pistol, six-shooter, cast iron, 1881................................	150	225	300
Echo cast iron cap pistol, Stevens, 1920, 4-1/4"..	32	48	65
Echo cast iron cap pistol, Stevens, 1930, "Made in U.S.A.", 4-1/2"......	25	38	50
Excelsior cast iron cap pistol, Stevens, 1875, "Pat'd Apr. 22,'73", 5-1/4".....	125	188	250
Federal cast iron cap pistol, Kilgore, 1920, 5-1/2"..	25	38	50
Federal cast iron cap automatic, Kilgore 1940, has removable clip to hold caps, 4-7/8"...........................	37	56	75
Federal cast iron cap pistol, Kilgore, 1920,"Pat. Dec. 14; Made in U.S.A."	37	56	75
Federal-Kilgore No. 1, cast iron cap pistol, 1925, Kilgore, 5-1/4".............	25	38	50
Federal No. 2, cast iron cap pistol, Kilgore, 1925, 6-3/8"........................	60	90	120
Fido, 1910, 4"...	50	75	100
Firecracker pistol, filigree handle, cast iron...	100	150	200
First No. 1, 1920, 6-3/4"........................	135	190	270
Five-barrel Firecracker pistol, iron and brass, 1877................................	500	800	1200
5-Star steel dart pistol, Wyandotte.......	15	22	30
Flash cast iron cap pistol, Hubley, 1934, "Pat'd", 6-1/4"........................	37	55	75
Flintlock, die cast, Hubley....................	42	63	85
Flintlock Junior, die cast, Hubley........	13	19	26
Flintlock Midget, die cast, Hubley.......	15	22	30
Four Way, cast iron cap pistol, Kenton, 1930, "Pat. Appld. For", shoots pea or dart, rubber band and cap, all at same time...............................	150	225	300
49-ER, cast iron cap pistol, Stevens, 1940, 9"..	125	188	250
Fox, cast iron cap pistol, Hubley, 1935, 4-1/2"....................................	22	33	45
Frontier, cast iron cap pistol, Ives, 1890, "Pat.June 21, 1887 and June 17, 1890" Dog's head atop the barrel facing hammer................	200	300	400

Typical Cast Iron Cap Pistols, 1920-1930. Left to Right, Top: OH BOY 1922, BUNKER HILL, BIG BILL 1925; Middle; FEDERAL 1920, RANGER 1920, NEW 50 SHOT INVINCIBLE; Bottom: IMPERIAL, MASTER 1922, NATIONAL No. 380. Courtesy Charles W. Best.

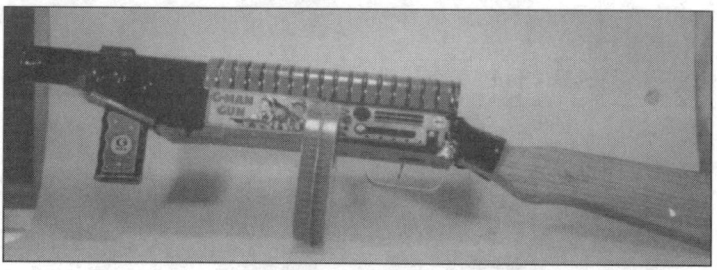

G-MAN GUN, MARX, tin litho with wood stock. Courtesy Gary Linden.

FEDERAL-KILGORE No. 1. Courtesy Sotheby's New York.

	C6	C8	C10
G-Man, cast iron cap automatic, Kilgore 1935, looks like German Luger, removable magazine holds caps, 6"..	67	100	135
G-Man, bakelite-framed cap automatic, Kilgore, 1940, 6"............................	42	63	85
G-Man, clicker pistol, tin, black..........	17	26	35
G-Man, wind-up steel spark pistol, painted finish.................................	20	30	40
G-Man, wind-up steel spark pistol, nickel finish with jewels on grip.....	22	33	45

"G-Man Automatic", Marx, sparkles

Top to Bottom: Flintlock, Flintlock Jr., Flintlock Midget. Photo by Charles W. Best.

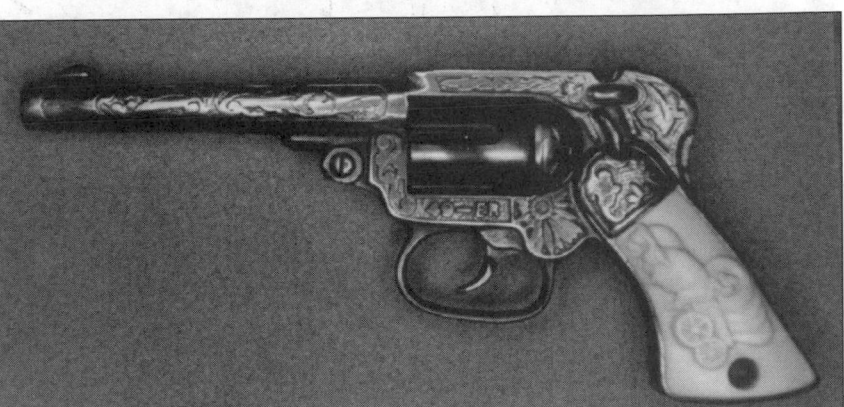

"49-ER". Photo by Charles W. Best.

Typical Cast Iron Cap Pistols, 1900-1910, Left to Right, Top: AMERICAN BULLDOG 1920, AGITATOR, THE HANSON-LINDSBORG K.S.; Middle: MAGIC 1900, unmarked .22 blank shooter, unmarked; Bottom: COWBOY 1890, BOSS 1925, STAR 1910. Courtesy Charles W. Best.

G-Man cast iron cap automatic, KIGORE, 1935. Photo by Charles W. Best.

	C6	C8	C10
when wound, 1930s	40	60	80
G-Man automatic sparkling pistol, Marx No. 43, aluminum	27	41	55
G-Man automatic sparkling pistol, Narx No. 44, tin	27	41	55
G-Man automatic sparkling pistol, Marx No. 85, tin	27	41	55
G-Man Gun, Marx, tin litho w/wood stock machine gun	165	250	330
G-Man Gun, Marx No 707	20	30	40
G-Man Silent Alarm Pistol, Marx No. 54, tin	17	26	35
G-Man Sparkling Sub-machine Gun, Marx, siren, tin, 26" long	60	90	120
G-Man Tin Windup Machine Gun, 1940s, miniature	20	30	40
Gang Busters full size Marx Sub-			

	C6	C8	C10
Machine Gun	125	188	250
Gem cast iron cap pistol, Stevens, 1900, 3"	27	41	55
Gem, 1925	27	41	55
Gene Autry cast iron cap pistol, Kenton, 1939, 8-3/8"	100	150	200
Gene Autry cast iron cap pistol, Kenton, 1939, "Made in U.S.A. Pat. Appl'd For", 6-1/2"	85	127	170
Gene Autry cast iron cap pistol, Kenton, 1940, "Made in U.S.A." red grips, 6-1/2"	82	123	165
Gene Autry cast iron pistol (doesn't fire caps), Kenton, 1940, "Made in U.S.A.", 6-1/2"	80	120	160
Gip, 1900	40	60	80
Go cast iron cap pistol, 1910, maker unknown, 6-3/4"	35	52	70
Go Bang	100	150	200
Guard cast iron cap pistol, Kilgore, 1935, "Made in U.S.A.", 6-1/4"	30	45	60

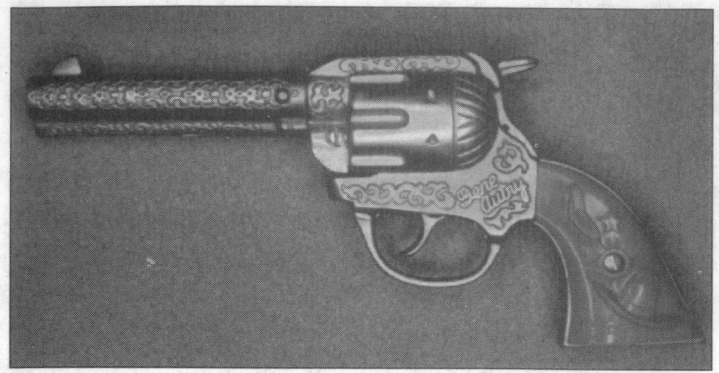

Gene Autry cast iron cap pistol, KENTON,1939, 8-3/8". Photo by Charles W. Best.

"Hopalong Cassidy". Photo by Charles W. Best.

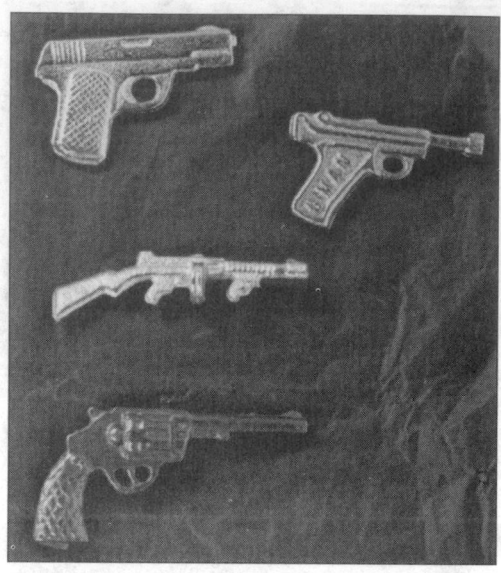

GREY IRON cast these solid cast iron weapons in the 1930s and early 1940s. John Wright casts them today. The Revolver is 2-1/2" long. Since there may be no way of telling old castings from new, the price averages about $1 each.

	C6	C8	C10
H-Bar-O cast iron cap pistol, Kilgore, 1925, "Made in U.S.A." 7-1/2"	45	68	90
Halt	40	60	80
Hammerless cast iron cap pistol, Stevens, 1892, "Pat. Appl'd For" four revolving triggers, hammer, concealed, 7-1/4"	150	225	300
Hanson-Lindsborg K.S. cast iron fire-cracker pistol, 1905, Hanson "Pat. Appl'd For", fires firecracker, 6-3/8"	65	98	130
Hero cast iron cap pistol, Stevens, 1937, 5-1/4"	30	45	60
Hero, 1940	15	22	30
Hero Auto cast iron cap automatic, 1920, Stevens, 4-3/4"	37	56	75
Hi-Ho cast iron cap pistol, Stevens, 1940, "Made in U.S.A.", 7"	37	56	75
Hi-Ho cast iron pistol, can fire caps, Stevens, 1940, "Made in U.S.A.", 7"	37	56	75
Hi-Ho cast iron cap pistol, Kilgore, 1940, 6-1/2"	37	56	75
Hi-Ho cast iron cap pistol, Kenton, 1940, "Pat. Sept.11-23", 5-1/8"	37	56	75
Hi-Ranger cast iron cap pistol, Stevens, 1940, 7-3/4"	40	60	80
Hopalong Cassidy 9" Revolver,			

	C6	C8	C10
Wyandotte, "Hopalong" on both sides of handle	162	243	325
Hopalong Cassidy 10" Revolver with bust of Hopalong, Schmidt	135	200	270
Hub cast iron cap pistol, Hubley, 1940, 6-1/4"	25	38	50
Hustler cast iron pistol	55	82	110
Ibex, 1895, Stevens, 4-1/2"	60	90	120
Ideal, tin dart-shooter	15	22	30
Imperial cast iron cap pistol, Kilgore, 1935, 5-1/4"	45	68	90
Indian cast iron cap pistol, Kenton, 1931, 8-1/8"	60	90	120
Invincible New 50 Shot, 1930	30	45	60
Invincible cast iron cap pistol, Kilgore, 1935, "Pat. Dec. 14", 5-1/4"	20	30	40
Jack Armstrong airplane gun, Daisy, 1936	35	52	70
Jax cast iron cap pistol, Kenton, 1930, "Pat. Sept. 11-23", 4"	22	33	45
Johnnie's Little Gunn	700	1100	1700
Joker	135	200	270
Jumbo cast iron cap pistol, "Pat. June 17, 1890: Made in U.S.A.", Stevens, 1895, 9-1/2"	110	165	220
Jr. Police Chief, cast iron cap automatic, Kenton, 1938, "Made in U.S.A.", 3-7/8"	30	45	60
Junior: Police 32 cast iron cap pistol, Hubley, 1940, "Hubley; Pat'd.			

Some classic Hubley die-cast cap pistols from the 1950s. Row 1: COLT .45, FLINTLOCK; Row 2: PIONEER, Padlock Pistol w/key, FLINTLOCK JR.; Row 3: COYOTE, FLINTLOCK MIDGET; Row 4: DAGGER DERRINGER, REMINTON .36; Row 5: ARMY .45 (automatic). Courtesy Charles W. Best.

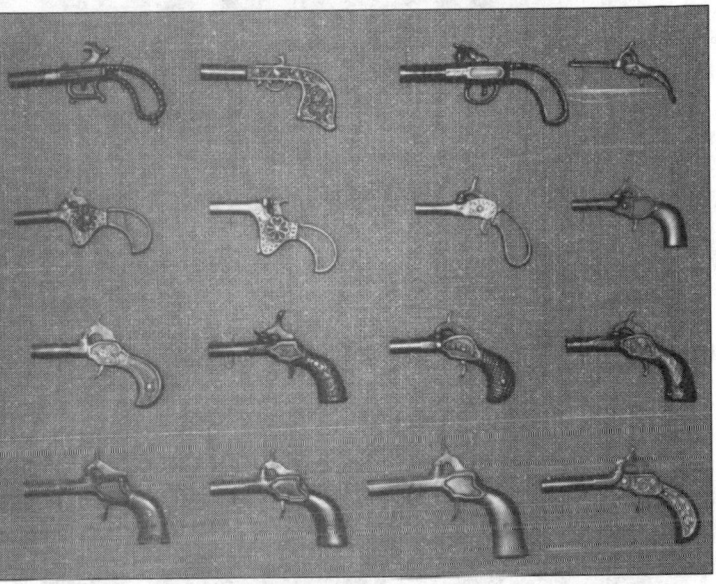

Typical Cast Iron Cap Pistols, 1880-1890. Left to Right, Top Row; FRONTIER, ECIIO, LION; Row 2: TERROR, BREVET DEPOSE, US NAVY; Row 3: HAMMERLESS, AMERICA; Row 4: Unmarked, TEXAS JACK. Photo courtesy Charles W. Best

	C6	C8	C10
2088891", 5-1/4"	30	45	60
Jr. Ranger .32 cal., 1925	25	38	50
Junior Six-Shooter cast iron cap pistol, Kilgore, 1935, 5-1/2"	30	45	60
"Just Out" cast iron animated cap pistol, 1880s	1700	2900	5000
Kid, 1930	27	41	55
Kido cast iron cap pistol, Kenton,1936, "Kenton, Made in U.S.A.", 5-3/8"	25	38	50
Kilgore cast iron cap pistol, Kilgore, 1910, 5"	30	45	60
Kilgore cast iron cap pistol, Kilgore, 1912, 5-1/4"	30	45	60
King cast iron cap pistol, Pat. Aug. 1879	100	150	200
King cast iron cap pistol, Stevens, 1925, "Made in U.S.A.", 4-3/4"	72	108	115
King, 1930	22	33	45
Kit Carson Cast iron cap pistol, Kenton, 1928, "Pat.Sept. 11-23", 9"	45	68	90
Korker	135	200	270
L.F. & Co.	75	112	150
Las cast iron cap pistol	80	120	160
Lasso 'Em Bill cast iron cap gun, red rubies in handle, cylinder turns, 1930, 9"	200	300	400
Lawmaker cast iron cap pistol, Kenton, 1941, 8-3/8"	100	150	200
Liberty 1875	162	243	325
Liberty, circa 1912, tin, ornate	35	52	70
Lightning Express, mechanical cap			

"Just Out". Courtesy Lloyd W. Ralston Auctions.

	C6	C8	C10
pistol, train slides forward along barrel to explode cap at end, 1913, Arcade or Kenton, 5"	300	450	600
Lion, Ives, 1887, 3-3/4"	300	450	600
Lion, 1890, Stevens, 5-1/4"	200	300	400
Lion 1920	37	56	75
Lion head cast iron cap pistol, Pat. 1890, Stevens, 5-1/4"	200	300	400
Little Bill cast iron cap pistol, Kilgore, 1925, 5"	22	33	45
Little Chief Firefighter, water squirt gun.	8	12	16
Lone Eagle cast iron cap pistol, Kilgore, 1929, 5-1/4"	50	75	100
Lone Ranger cast iron cap pistol, Kilgore, 1938, 8-1/2"	135	200	270
Lone Ranger click pistol, Marx	50	75	100

Invincible. Courtesy Sotheby's New York.

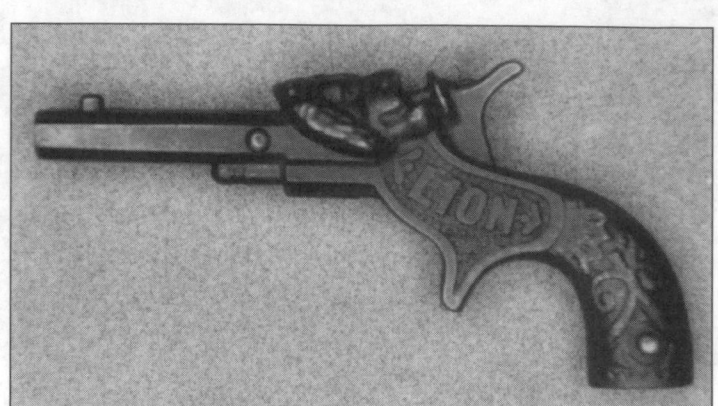

"Lion" by IVES, 1887. Photo by Charles W. Best.

Top to Bottom:
"Lone Eagle",
"Patrol".
Photo by
Charles W. Best.

Lightning Express. Courtesy Sotheby's New York.

	C6	C8	C10
Lone Ranger 45 Flasher Flashlight Pistol, Marx	30	45	60
Lone Ranger Smoking Click Pistol, Marx	20	30	40
Lone Ranger Sparkling Pop Pistol, tin litho, Marx No. 096	35	52	70
Lone Ranger tin pop gun, 1950s, picture of Lone Ranger on handles	30	45	60
Lone Ranger Western Gun Collection, c. 1939, six miniature guns mounted on card w/history of guns on back	60	90	120
Long Boy cast iron cap pistol, Kilgore, 1922, "Made in U.S.A.", 11"	80	120	160
Long Tom cast iron cap pistol, Kilgore, 1939, 10-3/8"	250	375	500
Look Out dog's head cast iron cap pistol	200	300	400
M&L water pistol, die-cast, rubber ball	10	15	20
Machine Gun, cast iron cap automatic, Kilgore, 1938, comes w/crank, which when turned, fires the caps rapidly, "Ra-Ta-Ta-Tat", 5"	85	127	170

	C6	C8	C10
Magazine, 1892	100	150	200
Magic cast iron .22 cal. blank pistol, Kenton, 1900, "Pat'd Oct. 17 '99", ornate, has second trigger to open barrel for loading, 6-1/4"	65	98	130
Major	37	56	75
Mars, 1920	45	68	90
Marx miniatures of Famous Guns: Civil War Revolver; Mare's Leg; Tommy Gun; Saddle Rifle, price for mint on card	55	82	110
Mascot cast iron cap automatic, Kilgore, 1936, 3-7/8"	25	38	50
Master cast iron cap automatic, 1922, Kilgore, 4-5/8"	27	41	55
Master cast iron cap automatic, Kilgore, 1930, 4-5/8"	27	41	55
Mauser, The, maker unkown(English?), 1915, 6-3/4"	250	375	500
Me and My Buddy, animated pistol w/figure, steel, Wyandotte	42	63	85
Medrick Repeater	75	112	150
Mick 1930	32	48	65
Minute Man cast iron cap rifle, Kilgore, 1936, "Pat. Appl'd For", "Made in U.S.A.", 20"	162	243	325
Model, Pat. 1890, cast iron, 5-3/8"	30	45	60
Model 1900	70	105	140

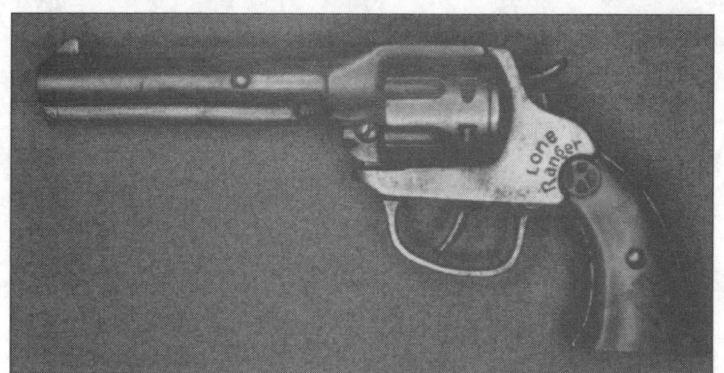

"Lone Ranger", 1940. Photo by Charles W. Best.

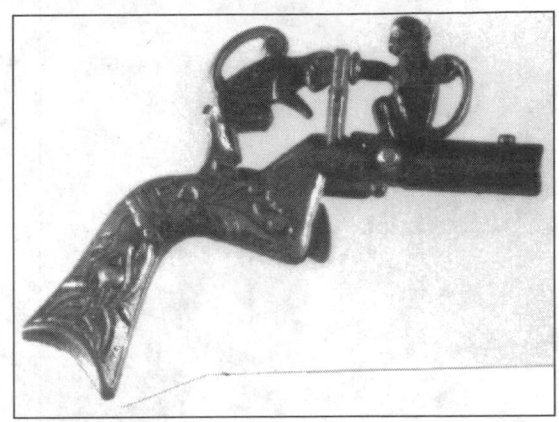

Monkey. Courtesy Sotheby's New York.

Typical cast iron cap pistols, 1910-1920. Left to Right. Top: HERO AUTO, REX 1914, TERROR 1915, NATIONAL 1915; Middle: KILGORE 1910, KILGORE 1912, FEDERAL 1920, NEW 50 SHOT INVINCIBLE; Bottom: NATIONAL 1911, NATIONAL 1909, BIG BUSTER. Courtesy Charles W. Best.

"Officer Pistol". Photo by Charles W. Best.

"The Mauser". Photo by Charles W. Best.

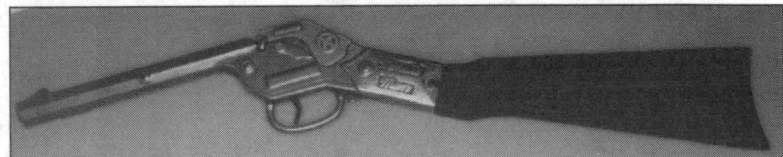

Minute Man cast iron cap rifle, KILGORE. Photo by Charles W. Best.

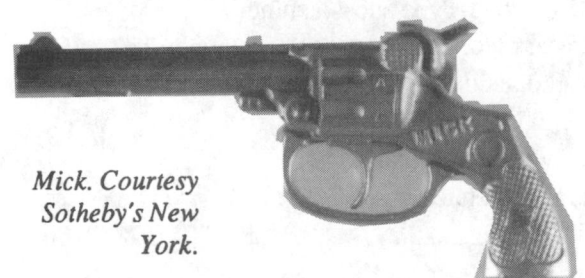

Mick. Courtesy Sotheby's New York.

531

Monkey and Coconut. Photo by Charles W. Best.

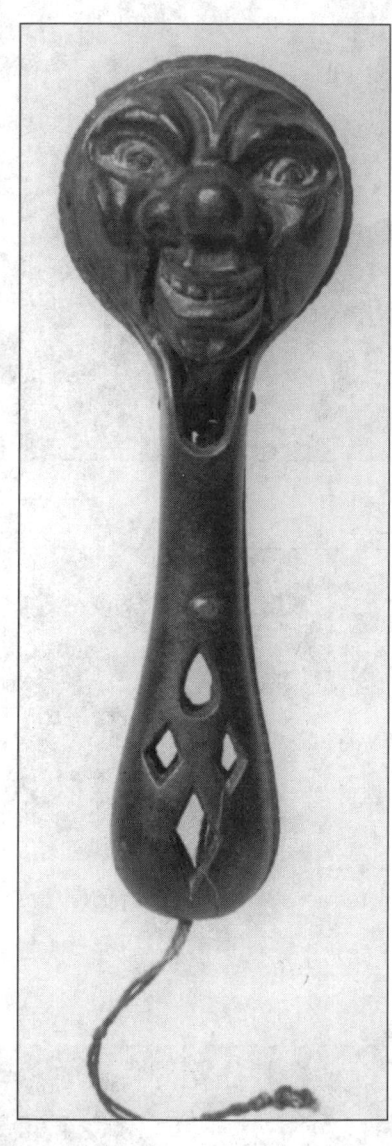

"Moonface". Photo by Charles W. Best.

	C6	C8	C10
Monkey and Coconut animated cap pistol, 1878, 1882, 4-1/4"...............	No Price Found		
Monkeys animated cap pistol, Lockwood, 1882, 4-1/4"................	550	825	1100
Moonface capshooter, Stevens, circa 1880................	500	750	1000

	C6	C8	C10
Mordt cast iron cap pistol, maker unknown, 1930, 8".........................	60	90	120
Mountie cap automatic, Kilgore No. 6, die cast, 6"......................	30	45	60
National, 1915.............................	37	56	75
National cast iron cap automatic, 1915, National, 3-3/4".....................	55	82	110
National cast iron cap pistol, National, 1909, 4-7/8".......................	37	56	75
National cast iron cap pistol, National, 1911, 5"......................................	62	93	125
National cast iron cap pistol, Stevens, 1920, 3-5/8"......................................	42	63	85
National cast iron cap automatic, National, 1925, "Made in U.S.A.", 5-1/4"......................................	45	68	90
National cast iron cap automatic, National, 1925, 4-1/4".....................	35	52	70
National No. 350, cast iron cap automatic, National, 1928, 5-1/2"..........	37	56	75
National No. 380 cast iron cap pistol, 1930s, National, 7".........................	35	52	70
National Liquid Pistol, Parker/Stearns, 1900, 4-7/8".....................................	55	82	110
Navy, 1878...	125	188	250
Navy, 1907...	75	112	150
Navy, 1925...	35	52	70
Navy cast iron cap pistol, Kenton, 1930, "Pat. Sept. 11-23", 5-1/2"......	37	56	75
Navy double barrel cap pistol..............	150	225	300
Nemo cast iron cap pistol, maker unknown, 1910, 6-5/8"....................	45	68	90
New 50 Shot Invincible cast iron cap pistol, 1930, Kilgore, 5-1/2"............	27	41	55
Nigger Head cap pistol, cast iron, Ives, 1887, 4-1/2"...........................	600	900	1200
No. 500 (like Luger), 1935..................	55	82	110
Novelty cast iron cap pistol, Stevens, 1885, "Pat. Appl'd For", 5".............	150	225	300
Nu-Matic Paper pop gun, 7".................	22	33	45
Officer Pistol, cast iron cap automatic, Kilgore, 1940, modeled after German Luger, 6"............................	62	93	125
Official Detective-Type sub-machine Gun, Marx No. 2146.......................	50	75	100
Oh Boy automatic cap, Kilgore, 1933, "Made in U.S.A.; Pat'd,. Aug. 8, 1933", works both as automatic and crank-operated rapid-fire gun, 4-1/8"...	85	128	170

"Mordt". Photo by Charles W. Best.

National cast iron cap automatic, National, 1925, 4-1/4". Courtesy Sotheby's New York.

	C6	C8	C10
Oh Boy cast iron cap pistol, National, 1922, 5-1/2"	35	52	70
Oh Boy iron cap pistol, Kenton, 1930, "Pat. Sept. 11-23", 5-1/8"	25	38	50
OK cast iron cap automatic, maker unknown, 1935, 3-3/4"	35	52	70
Old Ironsides cast iron cap pistol, 10-3/4"	65	98	130
101 Ranch	165	250	330
Our Army Forever	175	263	350
"P"	70	105	140
P-38 steel clicker pistol, circa 1945	17	26	35
Padlock cup pistol, and key, Hubley, 4-1/4"	60	90	120
Pal cast iron cap pistol, Kilgore, 1930, 4"	20	30	45
Pal cast iron cap automatic, Kilgore, 1930, 4"	30	45	60
Parole	40	60	80
Pat cast iron pistol, Kenton, 1935, "Pat. Sept. 11-23", 6-1/8"	22	33	45
Patrol cast iron cap pistol, Hubley, 1939, "Made in U.S.A.", 6"	32	48	65
Pawnee Bill, circa 1940	100	150	200
Pea Matic pea-shooting steel repeater	15	22	30
Pea Shooter	15	22	30
Pea shooter, pewter, highly embossed handle	35	52	70
Peacemaker cast iron cap pistol, Stevens, 1940, "Made in U.S.A.", 8-1/2"	100	150	200
Peerless, 1905, 5-1/2"	70	105	140
Persuader cast iron cap pistol, Kenton, 1939, "Made in U.S.A.", Pat. Appld. For", 6-3/8"	70	105	140
Pet, Hubley, diecast, 4-1/4"	12	18	25
Ping-Pong rifle	10	15	20
Pioneer diecast Hubley	92	138	185
Pirate cap pistol diecast zinc w/cast iron hammers and trigger, Hubley, 1941, two-barrel, two hammers that cock, 9-3/8"	50	75	100

	C6	C8	C10
"Pistol Packin' Mama", wood w/cardboard sides, c. 1944, four revolving triggers, shoots wooden pegs, 8-1/2"	20	30	40
Pluck cast iron cap pistol, at least 4 versions known, 1895 version	62	93	125
Pluck cast iron cap pistol, Stevens, 1930, "Made in U.S.A.", early-looking, 3-1/2"	19	28	38
Police large steel automatic cap pistol 8"	20	30	40
Police 1935 automatic	40	60	80
Police bakelite-framed cap automatic, Kilgore, 1940, 5-1/4"	35	52	70
Police Chief, 1935	30	45	60
Police Chief gun and leather shoulder holster set, c. late 1940s, Wyandotte	25	38	50
Polo, 1878, Ives, 6"	50	75	100
Polo, later, Ives, has trigger guard	50	75	100
Pono cast iron cap pistol, Kenton 1936, "Pat. Sept. 11-23", 5-1/8"	30	45	60
Powder keg cast iron cap bomb	85	128	170
Premier Safety, 1914	37	56	75
President, cast iron cap pistol, 1925, Kilgore, 8-3/4"	60	90	120

"National Liquid Pistol". Photo by Charles W. Best.

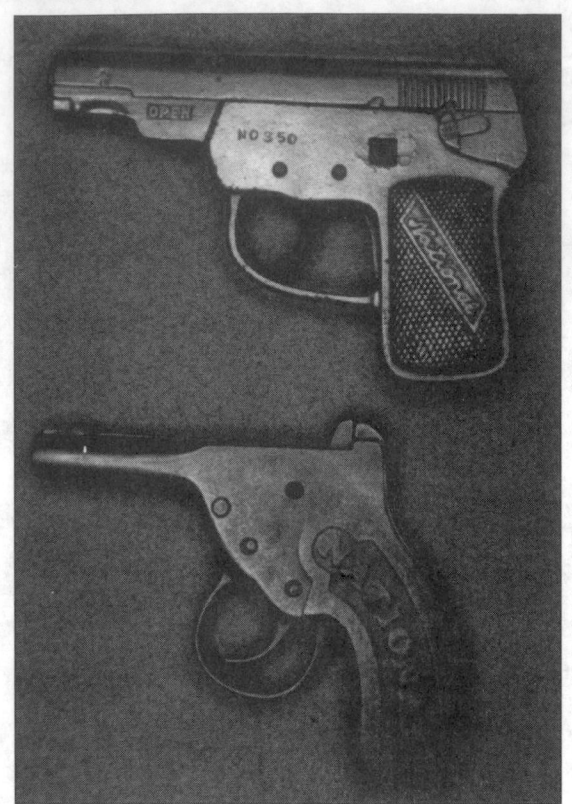

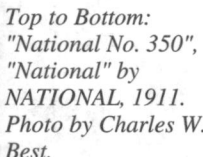

Top to Bottom: "National No. 350", "National" by NATIONAL, 1911. Photo by Charles W. Best.

Pirate, HUBLEY, 1941. Photo by Charles W. Best.

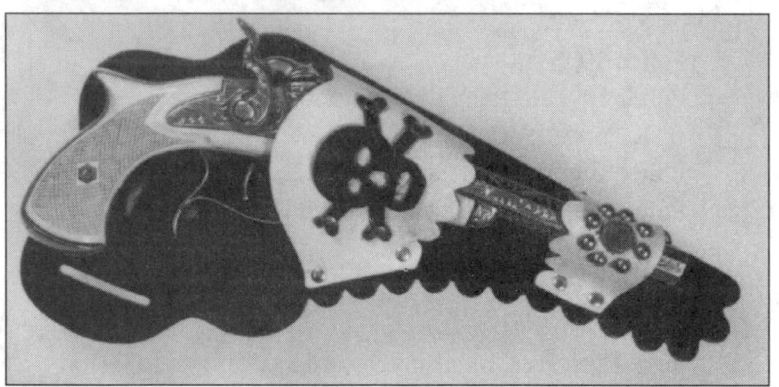

Pirate, HUBLEY, in rare original holster. Photo by Charles W. Best.

Pirate, HUBLEY, with original box. Rare colored stock and blue finish, probably post WWII. Photo by Charles W. Best.

Presto, with original box. Courtesy James S. Maxwell/Virginia Caputo. Photo by Virginia Caputo.

Top: Pluck, STEVENS, 1930. Bottom: Big Chief, 1930, DENT. Photo by Charles W. Best.

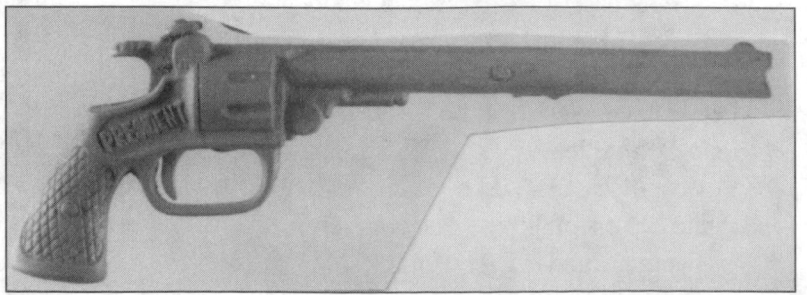

President. Courtesy Sotheby's New York.

Punch & Judy. Courtesy Sotheby's New York.

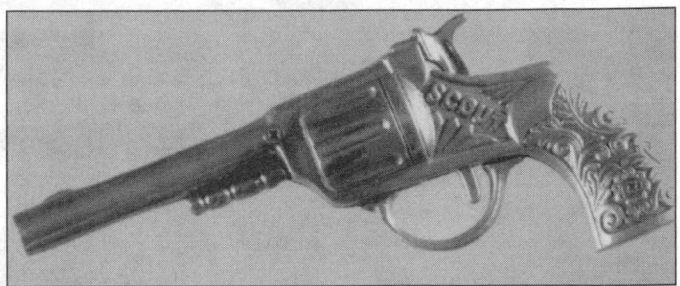

Scout cast iron cap pistol, STEVENS, 1890. Courtesy Sotheby's New York.

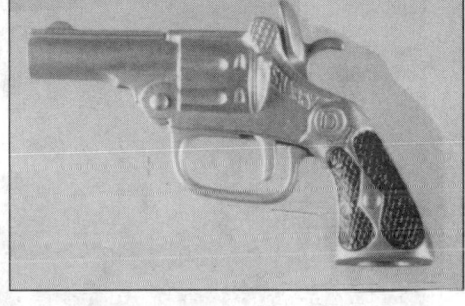

Snappy. Courtesy Sotheby's New York.

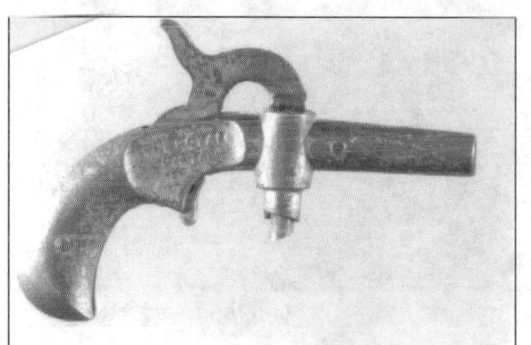

The Royal
Pistol. Courtesy
Sotheby's New
York.

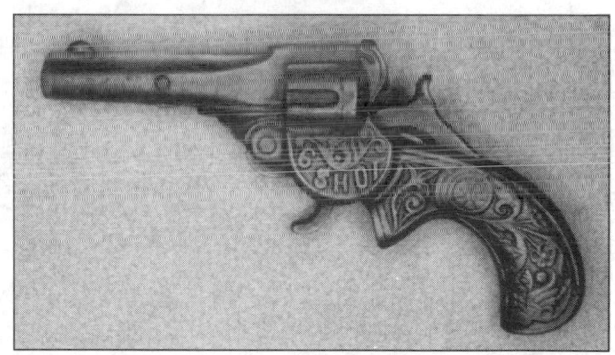

Sambo. Courtesy Sotheby's New York.

Sea Serpent. Photo by Charles W. Best.

6 Shot cast iron cap pistol, STEVENS, 1895. Photo by Charles W. Best.

Red Ranger Steel Clicker Pistol, WYANDOTTE. Courtesy Continental Hobby House.

"Sport" by Ives. Photo by Charles W. Best.

535

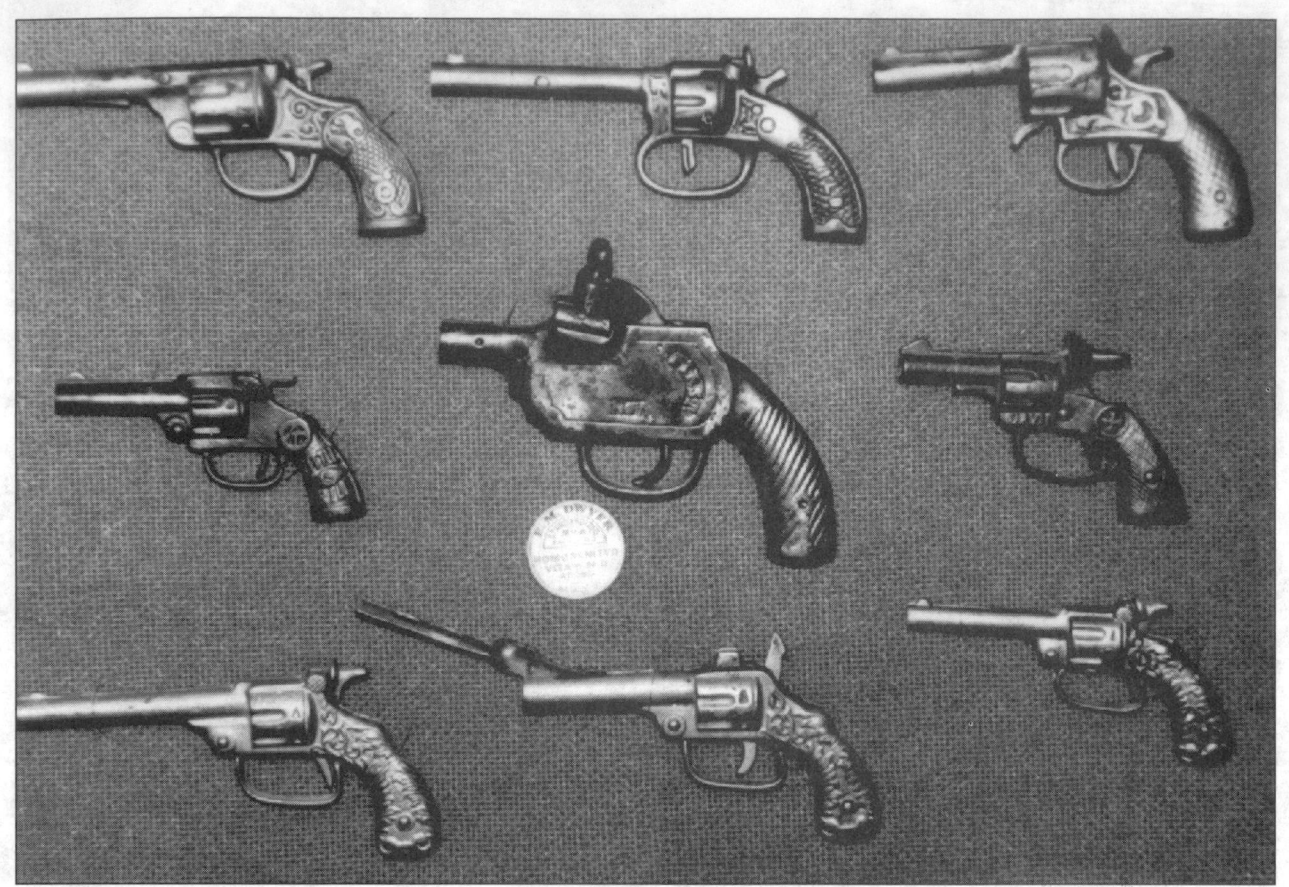

Typical Cast Iron Cap Pistols, 1910-1920. Left to Right. Top: DETROIT, WILD WEST, Unmarked; Middle: LITTLE BILL, FIRST NO.1, DAVID; Bottom: all unmarked with the middle a disk shooter. Courtesy Charles W. Best.

	C6	C8	C10
Presto cast iron cap automatic, Kilgore, 1940, 5-1/8"....................... 46		69	92
Punch & Judy cast iron animated cap pistol, 1880, "Patented", Ives, Punch explodes cap w/nose, on Judy's back, 5"....... 400		600	800
Pup, 1930..................................... 27		41	55
Ranger (1890-1900)............................. 80		120	160
Ranger cast iron cap pistol, Kilgore, 1920, 5-3/8".................................. 50		75	100
Ranger cast iron cap pistol, Kilgore, 1939, 8-1/2"................................. 85		127	170
Ranger cast iron cap pistol, Kilgore 1940, hammer protudes more than earlier version, 8-1/2"................. 85		127	170
Record...10		15	20
"Red Ranger", steel clicker pistol, Wyandotte, circa 1939, black, red "jewel", 8"................................. 17		26	35
"Red Ranger" steel clicker pistol, Wyandotte, circa 1941, 8".............. 15		22	30
Red Ranger steel click pistol, Wyandotte, 7-3/4"............................17		26	35
Red Ranger steel six shooter repeater w/plastic handles, Wyandotte,			

	C6	C8	C10
revolving cylinder............................37		56	75
Remington .36 die cast, Hubley........... 46		69	92
Repeater Space Gun, Wyandotte, 1930s... 35		52	70
Repeating Cap Pistol, Marx No. G375, die cast...................................... 20		30	40
Rex cast iron cap automatic, 1914, Dent, 4-1/8"..................................... 30		45	60
Rex cast iron cap automatic, Kilgore, 1939, 3-7/8"..................................... 35		52	70
Rex Mars Planet Patrol X-92 Gun....... 50		75	100
RIP, circa 1909.................................65		98	130
Rival, 1920... 50		75	100
Rob Roy, circa 1875........................... 150		225	300
Rocket Ship Space Pistol, late 1940s, Irwin.. 25		38	50
Rotor Fifty cast iron cap pistol, Kilgore, 1930, 6-1/8"...................... 42		63	85
Royal Pistol, The, 1878, cast iron cap mechanical pistol, fires spring-loaded top which is attached to bottom of the barrel, "Pat. Apr. 23, '78" approx. 5".. 400		600	800
S & S, 1880..................................... 100		150	200

	C6	C8	C10
Safety cast iron cap pistol, Hubley, 1924, "Pat. Mch. 25,'24", 5"	27	41	55
Safety First cast iron cap automatic, 1920, "Safe", maker unknown, 3-3/8"	30	45	60
Sambo cast iron cap pistol, hammer hits head, 1887, Ives, "Pat. June 21, 1887", 4-3/8"	175	263	350
Say I cast iron cap bomb	75	112	150
Scout cast iron cap pistol, Stevens, 1890, "Pat. June 17, 1890", 7"	72	108	145
Scout cast iron cap pistol, Stevens, 1935, "Made in U.S.A.", 6-3/4"	27	41	55
Scout cast iron cap pistol, Stevens, 1940, 6-1/8"	27	41	55
Scout cap pistol, tin, 1914, automatic	25	38	50
Scout Jr. cast iron cap pistol, Stevens, 1935, "Made in U.S.A.", 6"	32	48	65
Scoutmaster, Dent, 6-3/4"	65	98	130
Sea Serpent	*see Dolphin*		
Senator cast iron cap pistol, Kilgore, 1925, marked w/star and "K", 7"	50	75	100
1776-1876 cast iron cap pistol, Stevens, 1876, produced for America's (100th) centennial, 5-1/4"	150	225	300
Shoo Fly cast iron cap pistol	90	135	180
Shoot the Hat cast iron mechanical cap pistol	400	600	800
Shotgun, double-barreled, steel, wood stock, 28", both barrels break down, cock and shoot	35	52	70
Siren Signal Pistol, Marx, 1940s, tin	27	41	55
Siren Sparkling Airplane Pistol, tin litho, Marx No. 182	50	75	100
Siren Sparkling Pistol, tin litho, Marx No. 164	45	68	90
Six Shooter cast iron cap pistol, Kilgore, 1935, 6-1/2"	75	112	150
Six Shooter cast iron cap pistol with plastic-type grips, Kilgore, 1935, 6-1/2"	80	120	160
Six Shooter cast iron cap pistol, Kilgore, 1938, "Made in U.S.A." on hammer, 6-1/2"	32	48	65
Six Shooter cast iron cap pistol, Kilgore, 1938, "Made in U.S.A.", on hammer, plastic type grips, 6-1/2"	57	85	115
Six Shooter cast iron cap pistol, Kilgore, 1930, 7"	37	56	75
Six Shooter Automatic cast iron cap pistol (not an automatic), Kilgore, 1934, 6-1/2"	72	108	145
6 Shot cast iron cap pistol, Stevens, 1895, "Pat. U.S.A., Jan. 22, 1895", 6-3/4"	125	188	250
Sliko cast iron cap pistol, Kenton, 1930, "Pat. Sept. 11-23", 6-1/4"	27	41	55
Snap, 1890	35	52	70
Snappy, 1930, Dent, 5"	37	56	75
Snappy Jack, circa 1935, English	37	56	75
Space Gun, Remco	25	38	50
Sparkling Atom Buster, die cast, Marx No. 46	30	45	60
Sparkling G-Man Sub-Machine Gun, Marx No. 2308	62	93	125
Sparkling G-Man Sub-Machine Gun, Marx No. 2310	62	93	125
Sparkling Pop Gun, Marx No. 198	25	38	50
Sparkling Space Gun, Marx	45	68	90
Sparkling Sure Shot	17	26	35
Spitfire cast iron cap automatic, Stevens, 1940, "Made in U.S.A.", 4-5/8"	37	56	75
Sports Ives, 1875, 4"	175	263	350
Sport cast iron cap pistol, Kilgore, 1930, "Made in U.S.A.", 7-1/2"	50	75	100
Spud Gun, tin automatic, c. 1940	15	22	30
Spud Gun No. 504, B.J. Cossman, Hollywood, Calif., die cast	30	45	60
Spy cast iron cap pistol, Kilgore, 1936, "Made in U.S.A.", 4 1/4"	30	45	60
Star pot metal cap pistol, steer on handle	5	8	10
Star, circa 1878	125	188	250
Star cast iron cap pistol, 1910, Stevens, 6-1/4"	35	52	70
Stephans Pat., 1873, 5"	120	180	240
Stevens Repeater cast iron cap pistol, Stevens, 1930, "Mammoth Cap; Made in U.S.A.", 6-1/4"	70	105	140
Stevens 6 Shot, 1932, Stevens, 6-1/4"	35	52	70
Stevens 6-Shot Rapid Load cast iron cap pistol, 1932, Stevens, "Made in U.S.A.", 6-1/2"	30	45	60
Streamline Siren Sparkling Pistol, tin litho, Marx No. 155	35	52	50
Sun cast iron cap pistol	90	135	180
S & W cast iron cap gun, 6"	27	41	55
Super cast iron cap pistol, Kenton, 1930, "Pat. Sept. 11-23", 8-3/4"	35	52	70
Super Automatic Tom Gun, steel spark automatic	15	22	30
Super Nu-Matic Paper Buster Gun	30	45	60
Sure Shot 1870-1880	165	250	330
Sure Shot cast iron cap automatic, Hubley, 1940, 4-1/4"	27	41	55

Top, Left to Right: "Teddy", "Chief"; Middle: "Buffalo Bill";
Bottom, Left to Right: "25 Jr", "Pal", "Army 45". Courtesy
Mapes Auctioneers & Appraisers.

Texan, die cast, gold plated deluxe version,
HUBLEY, circa 1950. Value mint in box $250.
Photo by Charles W. Best.

STEVENS 6 Shot. Courtesy Sotheby's New York.

Texan, HUBLEY, late cast iron model. Early models have a rampant
colt instead of a star on the grips. The cylinder is die cast, circa 1940-
48. Photo by Charles W. Best.

	C6	C8	C10
Target cast iron cap pistol, Hubley, 1935, "Pat. 1,488,046", 8"	50	75	100
Teddy cast iron cap pistol, Hubley, 1938, 5-5/8"	25	38	50
Terror, 1888	250	375	500
Terror, cast iron cap automatic, Dent, 1915, "Pat. Jan 16 '15, 4-1/4"	35	52	70
Terror, 1925	30	45	60
Terror, people embossed, cast iron cap pistol, 1882	175	260	350
Texan cast iron cap pistol, Hubley, 1940, "Made in U.S.A.", 9-1/4"	125	188	250
Texan Jr. cast iron cap pistol, Hubley, 1941, "Made in U.S.A.", 8-1/8"	60	90	120
Texas cast iron cap pistol, Kenton, 1936, "Pat. No. 1993916", 5-3/4"	45	68	90
Texas cast iron cap pistol, Kenton, 1930, "Pat. Sept. 11-23", 6-5/8"	45	68	90

	C6	C8	C10
Texas Centennial, 1936, 11"	225	338	450
Texas Jack, 1886, Ives, 9-3/8"	150	225	300
The Big Noise, circa 1922	45	68	90
The Forty Five cast iron cap pistol, unusual shape, National, 1928, "Made in U.S.A.", 11-1/8"	110	165	220
The Sheriff cast iron cap pistol, Stevens, 1940, 8-1/2"	55	82	110
Tiger cast iron cap pistol, Stevens, 1915, 6-3/4"	32	48	65
Tiger cast iron cap pistol, Hubley, 1935, 6-7/8"	27	41	55
Tin Tin Gun, turn crank and it makes noise, Woodhaven Metal Stamping Co., 3 x 5"	15	22	30
Tip Top cast iron cap pistol, 1880, Stevens, 3-1/2"	125	188	250
Trainer	20	30	40

Typical cast iron cap pistols 1920-1930. Left to Right; Top Row: DANDY (Police .38), SIX SHOOTER; Second Row: ARMY .45, TEXAS CENTENNIAL 1936, G-MAN: Third Row: BULL DOG, MACHINE GUN, TARGET; Fourth Row: TEXAN JR., SIX SHOOTER; Fifth Row: LASSO 'EM BILL, LONE RANGER; Sixth Row: GENE AUTRY, AMERICAN; Bottom: GENE AUTRY, PAWNEE BILL. Courtesy Charles W. Best.

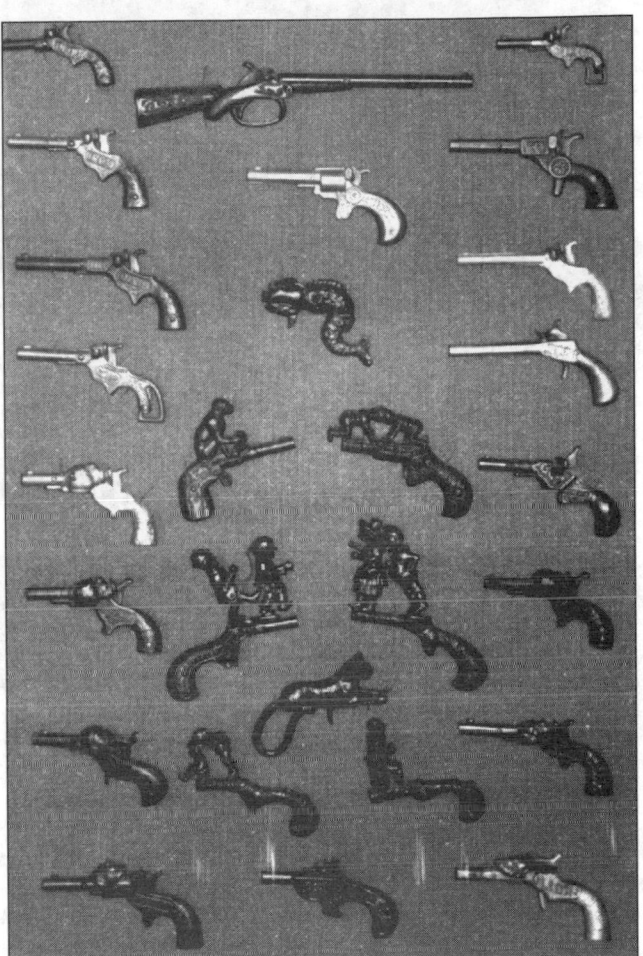

Typical cast iron cap pistols 1880-1890. Left to Right; Top Row: PLUCK, JOHNNIES'S LITTLE GUN (rifle), ACORN; Second Row: IBEX, 1776-1876, VICTOR; Third Row: DIXIE, Sea Serpent, CHIEF; Fourth Row: ZIP, VOLUNTEER; Fifth Row: LOOK OUT, Monkey with Coconut, BUTTING MATCH, NOVELTY; Sixth Row: BULL DOG, CHINESE MUST GO, PUNCH & JUDY, SAMBO; Seventh Row: CAT (animated); Eighth Row: NIGGER HEAD, SHOOT THE HAT, CLOWN (on barrel), LION; Bottom: FRONTIER, ECHO, LION. Courtesy Charles W. Best.

	C6	C8	C10
Trapper cast iron cap automatic, Kilgore, 1935, fires only single shot, but roll of caps can be carried in the grip, 4-1/2"..	45	68	90
Triumph, 1878, 5-1/8"..........................	125	188	250
Trooper, cast iron cap pistol, Hubley, 1938, 5-1/8"....................	20	30	40
Trooper die cast, Hubley, 6-1/2"..........	19	28	38
Trooper Safety, 1925......................	35	52	70
Trooper Safety cast iron cap pistol, Kilgore, 1930, "Pat. Pend; Made in U.S.A.", operates either as straight cap pistol or can be fired w/crank,10"..	85	128	170
Trooper Safety cast iron cap pistol, Kilgore, 1925, 10-1/4".....................	75	112	150
25 Jr. cast iron cap automatic, Stevens, 1930, Made in U.S.A., Patented, 4-1/8".	20	30	40
25-50 cast iron cap automatic, Stevens, 1928, "Pat. Appl'd. For; Made in U.S.A.", 4-1/2".............................	30	45	60

	C6	C8	C10
25-50, 1930..................................	30	45	60
25-50 cast iron cap automatic, Stevens, 1935, "Made in U.S.A.; Pat, Appld. For", 4-1/2"......................................	22	33	45
25-50 cast iron cap automatic, Stevens, 1935, "Oil Moving Parts; Made in U.S.A., Patented", 4-1/2"................	25	38	50
25-50 cast iron cap automatic, can be fired rapidly w/crank, hole near muzzle holds removable crank, Stevens, 1935, "Oil Moving Parts; Made in U.S.A., Patented".............	45	68	90
25-50 Target cast automatic w/"silencer" type barrel, Stevens,1935, "Oil Moving Parts, Made in U.S.A., Patented"....	100	150	200

Typical cast iron cap pistols 1900-1910. Left to Right; Top Row: STAR, Unmarked, "P", SNAP; Second Row: MODEL, MODEL, Unmarked; Third Row: GIP, WILDWEST, Unmarked; Bottom: MAJOR, CHIEF, RIVAL. Courtesy Charles W. Best.

Top to Bottom: "Tip Top", Unmarked, maker unknown, 1878, 3 3/4" long. Photo by Charles W. Best.

25-50 cast iron cap automatic, STEVENS, 1935, "Oil Moving Parts", with original box. Courtesy James S. Maxwell/Virginia Caputo. Photo by Virginia Caputo.

25 Jr. with original box. Courtesy James S. Maxwell/ Virginia Caputo. Photo by Virginia Caputo.

	C6	C8	C10
Two Dogs On Bench cap shooter (only two known, the one sold, condition unknown, sold for $3,400 in 1981, its last sale)			
"2 in 1" cast iron cap pistol, 9-1/4"	55	82	110
"2 Monkeys", 1882, cast iron animated cap pistol, maker unknown, monkey butts head against coconut held by another monkey, 4-1/2"	500	750	1000
Two Time cast iron cap and rubber band pistol, 1930, Kenton, "Pat. Appld. For", 9-1/4"	50	75	100
Unmarked, unknown maker, 1878, 3-3/4"	75	112	150
Unxld Steel cap automatic, nickel plated, 6-1/2"	30	45	60
Urica	10	15	20
U.S.A. Liquid Pistol cast iron water pistol, Parker-Stearns, 1896, Pat. June 30, 1896", 4-3/4"	55	82	110
U.S. Navy, 1885, 6-1/2"	65	98	130
Veteran 1935	45	68	90
Victor cast iron pistol	125	188	250
Villa cast iron cap pistol, Dent, 1934, Made in U.S.A.", 4-3/4"	37	52	75

	C6	C8	C10
Volunteer cast iron cap pistol Stevens, 1873, "Pat. April 22, '73"	125	188	250
W on one side, S on other, cast iron cap pistol, nickel-plated, normal size barrel	27	41	55
W on one side, S on other, snub nose, single shot, cast iron nickel-plated	27	41	55

Top to Bottom: "Wild West", "101 Ranch", "Victor", "Rodeo". Photo by Charles W. Best.

540

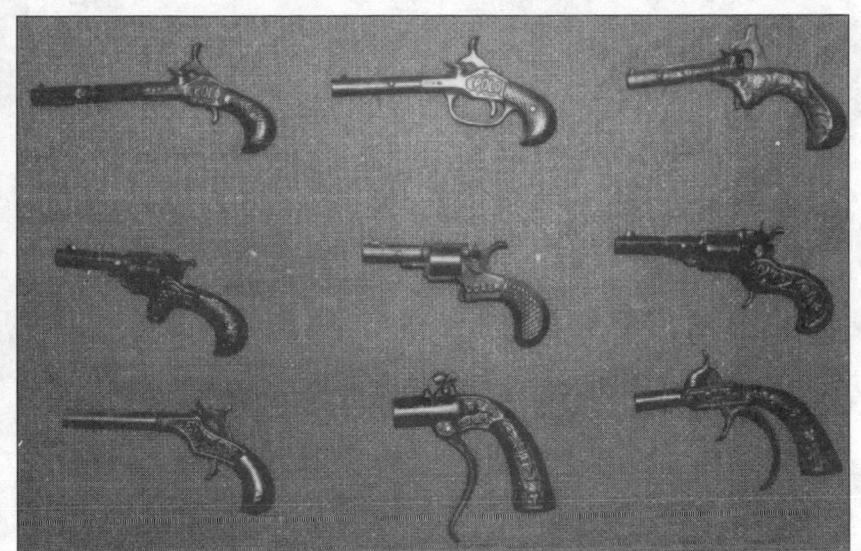

Tyical cast iron cap pistols 1870-1880. Left to Right: POLO, POLO, TRIUMPH; Second Row: BRAVO, JOKER, COMET; Bottom: EXCELSIOR, L.F. & C., STEPHANS PAT. Courtesy Charles W. Best.

Wyandotte guns, as shown in a January, 1925 ad. Courtesy Playthings Magazine.

Typical cast iron cap pistols 1920-1930. Left to Right; Top Row. PLUCK, BUCK, GEM, unmarked, unmarked; Second Row: DAISEY, BILL, VILLA; Third Row: ZIP, BILL, KING: Bottom Row: SAFETY, BULL, COP. Courtesy Charles W. Best.

	C6	C8	C10
War cast iron cap pistol, Kenton, 1930, "Pat. Sept, 11-23", 4-1/4"	35	52	70
Warrior cast iron cap pistol, maker unknown, 1926, "Pat. Appld. For, 1926", 9"	75	112	150
Water Pistol, Wyandotte No. 41	10	15	20
Water Pistol, Wyandotte, unmarked	10	15	20
Western cast iron cap pistol, Kenton, 1935, "Pat. Sept. 11-23", 7"	32	48	65
Western cast iron cap pistol, Kenton 1931, 7-1/4"	65	98	130
Western cast iron cap pistol, Kenton, 1939, "Made in U.S.A.", 7-1/2"	30	45	60
Westo cast iron cap pistol, Kenton, 1936, "Kenton", 7"	30	45	60
Westo cast iron pistol (doesn't fire			

	C6	C8	C10
caps), 1938, Kenton, "Kenton", 7"	27	41	55
Whoopie cast iron cap pistol, Kenton, 1932, 5-7/8"	37	56	75
Wild West cast iron cap pistol, National, 1930, "Made in U.S.A.", 6-1/2"	35	52	70
Winner cast iron cap automatic, Hubley, 1940, 4-3/8"	35	52	70
Wizard 1896	65	98	130
Woodsman cast iron cap automatic, Stevens, 1938, "Patented; Made in U.S.A.", 5-1/4"	55	82	110
Wyandotte double barrel shotgun, c. 1935, steel and wood, 25"	47	70	95
Xtra cast iron pistol, Kenton, 1936, "Made in U.S.A.", 5"	27	41	55
Yank cast iron cap pistol, 1880	125	188	250

Typical cast iron cap pistols 1890-1900. Left to Right; Top Row: Unmarked, S&S, Unmarked, FIDO; Second Row: HALT, COLT, RANGER; Third Row: CUPID, NAVY, ARMY; Bottom: 6-SHOT 1895, U.S.A. LIQUID PISTOL, STAR. Courtesy Charles W. Best.

Wyandotte Toys from 1935 ad.

Typical cast iron cap pistols 1910-1920. Left to Right; Top Row: ECHO, CRACK, CAL; Second Row: Unmarked, unmarked, PEERLESS; Third Row: "730", LION, LION, Unmarked Automatic; Fourth Row: PREMIER SAFETY, Unmarked, OK, PREMIER SAFETY; Bottom (small pistols): GEM, GEM. Courtesy Charles W. Best.

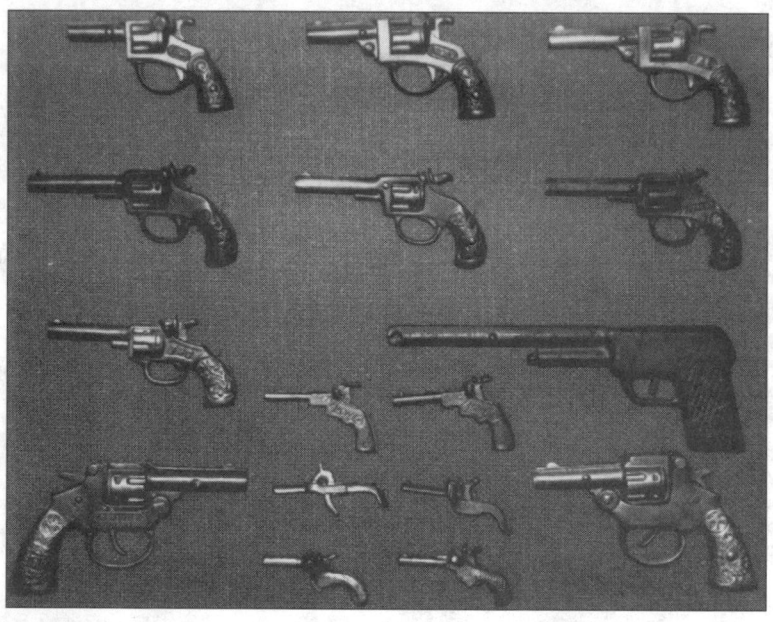

Typical cast iron cap pistols 1920-1930. Left to Right; Top Row: Unmarked, OK, Unmarked, Second Row: SAFETY FIRST, SCOUT MASTER, ARMY; Third row: WARRIOR, Unmarked, TWO TIME; Buttom: Unmarked blank shooters. Courtesy Charles W. Best.

	C6	C8	C10
Yankee cast iron cap pistol, Stevens, 1895, 5-1/2"	125	188	250
York cast iron cap pistol, Kenton, 1930, "Pat. Sept. 11-23", 7"	35	52	70
Young Sportsman, wood, circa 1868	75	112	150
Zip (1880-1890)	37	56	75
Zip cast iron cap pistol, Hubley, 1930, 5"	27	41	55
Zip cast iron cap pistol, Hubley 1938, 6"	27	41	55
Zulu cast iron cap pistol, marker unknown, 1890, has decoration of African warrior with spear pursuing bird, 6-5/8"	150	225	300

Western-Style Toy Guns
by James Schleyer

In the past few years, interest in toy guns has escalated tremendously as collectors realize their charm, beauty and scarcity. America's love affair with its childhood memories has pushed the demand for toy guns far beyond what is currently available in the marketplace. Virtually every child played with toy guns, and the countless battles, gunfights, and hunting expeditions have taken a heavy toll. Many toy guns were discarded, confiscated by teachers, lost or broken due to their fragile nature. The survival rate of many guns is extremely low, especially with the die cast guns.

Today's collector can specialize in single manufacturers such as: Hubley, Kenton, Kilgore, etc. They can collect various types such as: revolvers, derringers, automatics, rifles, etc. They might specialize in just pop guns, water pistols, clickers, dart guns, or cap shooters. There are niches like special finishes in gold, antique bronze, blue, black and nickel. A few only collect guns with revolving cylinders or those that accept fake bullets. Since there are thousands of toy gun varieties, every collector should be able to find a special favorite. For many years, collectors favored the older cast iron guns and they still have a dedicated following. However, the die cast toy guns from the 1940-1965 era are currently receiving more attention. The prices for these newer toys are escalating well beyond those of earlier guns.

The post-war era until 1965 witnessed an explosion of "western" movies, radio programs, TV shows, comic books, clothing, memorabilia and toy guns. The cowboy craze touched virtually every product, advertisement and person. Toy guns that resembled a Colt Peacemaker or Winchester rifle found a welcoming market. This was the era of glamorous finishes, sparkling metals, inventive mechanisms, fake bullets, gimmicks, colorful character names, imaginative plastic grips and fancy holster sets gleaming with metal studs and jewels! It was the era where Hoppy, Roy, Gene and the Lone Ranger were predominant heroes. It's fairly obvious why so many collectors want only western or cowboy-style toy guns.

The current rage of cowboy collectibles has driven the prices of even the most common items into oblivion. In my opinion the demand far out-weighs the supply and prices will continue to escalate. This section of the book will only address itself to western-styled toy guns. It primarily covers all the die cast, plastic and tin guns with a special section of older cast iron western favorites. Remember, the listing is to provide an approximate value guide for collectors and is not a price list. Toy guns were seldom pampered so only a minimal amount have survived in mint condition. For this reason I have listed the price for an average condition specimen with no broken or missing parts, most of its original finish and works properly. Obviously, particular guns demand a higher value based on their marketability and popularity with collectors. Rarity does not necessarily dictate a higher price. Generally, a Gene Autry or Hopalong Cassidy toy gun will bring a higher value than a generic cowboy gun, even if it is a seldom seen variety.

Mint condition or new guns are double the value quoted in the listing. Used guns, in below average condition, with broken or missing parts, cracks or loss of finish are valued at half, or less, of the price listed. The original boxes are worth approximately $25 to $150 each depending on the demand of the gun variety. Dummy models that cannot fire caps are quite rare and are worth about $25 additional. Even a complete set of bullets for guns that accept them are valued at $25 to $65. Gold, antique bronze and blued finishes are rarer and usually add $25 to $50 to the value of a mint gun. Replating and refinishing toy guns is becoming more common so be aware of ones that look too good. Many parts, particularly hammers, are being newly cast, so check that the color or finish of all parts looks similar. Counterfeit guns are beginning to appear as values rise, so exert some caution and purchase from reputable dealers.

Use caution when purchasing broken or damaged toy guns, as repairs, especially on die cast guns, can be expensive or nearly impossible. The western collectible craze has directly affected other toys such as: children's clothes, cuffs, spur sets, holsters, badges, rubber knives, gloves, hats, comic books, etc. The current vogue is fancy, leather holster sets with jewels and studs. All cowgirl or cowboy western outfits are a colorful addition to a toy gun collection and will generate many smiles from their inherent memories. Wrist cuffs and spurs are valued at $50 to $150 depending on the amount of decorative jewels and studs. Any with a known character name bring the highest value, especially if they match a holster set. Of interest is the fact that most collectors of authentic western memorabilia also add toy items and guns to their holdings, which adds to the scarcity of quality toy guns and holsters.

This new listing contains 120 additional toy guns not found in previous editions. Current values of most guns have risen 20% to 35% over the last two years.

Codes used in the listing.

Rep..........................Repeater
SS.............................Single Shot
Bul............................Accepts Bullets
RC..........................Revolving Cylinder
N...............................Nickel Finish
BK............................Black or Dark Finish
G..............................Gold Finish
AB............................Antique Bronze Finish
BE............................Blue Finish
LB............................Long Barrel
CW..........................Civil War Style-Dragoon
L-H..........................Leslie-Henry

Value Guide Notes

All prices quoted are for average condition guns that have no broken or missing parts, most of the original finish and work properly. Mint guns are double the quoted price and those with broken or missing parts and minimal finish are worth half or less than the price listed.

Clockwise from the arrow; Kilgore Champion Fast Draw, Mattel Shootin' Shell Fanner .45, Wild Bill Hickok Leslie-Henry 44, Gene Autry Bronze Leslie-Henry 44, Marx Thundergun, Hubley Cowboy with Turquoise grips, Nichols Stallion .45 Mark II, Hubley Ric-O-Shay .45, Hubley .44 Cal. Model 1860, Hubley .45 Colt, Nichols Stallion .45 1st Model, Leslie-Henry Maverick Long Barrel, Actoy Bronze Wyatt Earp, Hubley Wyatt Earp Long Barrel, Lone Star Apache, Classy Roy Rogers, Kilgore Roy Rogers, Leslie-Henry Gene Autry Long Barrel, Halco Marshal 6-7 Shot, Gold Hubley Cowboy Classic and in the center a rare Leslie-Henry Gene Autry in Antique Bronze.

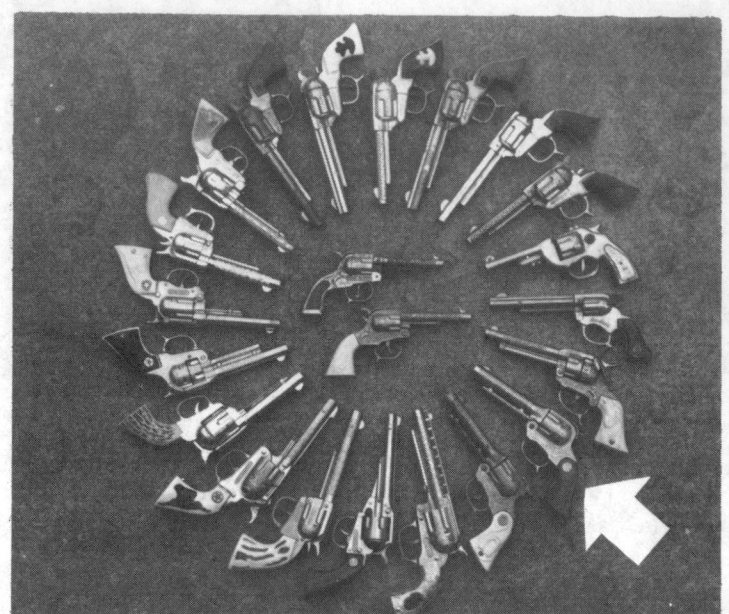

Clockwise from the arrow; Wyandotte Gold Hopalong Cassidy, Red Ranger by Wyandotte, Hubley Deputy, Hubley Remington .36 Long Barrel, Cowboy King by Stevens, Hubley Marshal, Mattel Shootin' Shell Fanner, Hubley Gold Texan Jr., Hubley Western, Stevens small Cowboy King, Kilgore Mustang, G. Schmidt Davy Crockett, Schmidt Hopalong Cassidy Long Barrel, G. Schmidt Engraved Hopalong Cassidy, G. Schmidt Dale Evans, G. Schmidt Polished Buckin' Bronc, G. Schmidt Engraved Roy Rogers with jewels, Lone Ranger clicker, G. Schmidt Dale Evans small frame, Leslie-Henry Gene Autry, and in the center; a Buzz Henry gold Gene Autry with insert grips and a Gene Autry with full size grips.

James Schleyer is a long-time collector and appraiser who has specialized in toy guns for many years. He has authored four other collector books, written numerous articles and several newsletters on collectibles. He is the former president of the Toy Gun Purveyors (TGP), an international organization that shared knowledge and memories of toy guns, and former editor of the TGP quarterly newsletter.

Die Cast, Tin, Plastic

Apache, 11 3/4", Lone Star, CW, N, G	$50
Apache, (Black finish in some Roy Rogers' holster sets)	$50
Gene Autry, 9" Leslie-Henry N, G	$85
Gene Autry, 9" Leslie-Henry, Antique Bronze (Rare)	$125
Gene Autry, 10 1/2" Leslie-Henry LB (Rare)	$135
Gene Autry, 7 1/2" Buzz Henry, Insert Grip, G, N	$65
Gene Autry, 7 1/2" Buzz Henry, Full Grip, G, N	$70
Gene Autry, 26" Dbl. Brl. "Pop" Empress H.- Marx-Britain	$175
Gene Autry, Wooden "Pop" Rifle-Hollywood Craft	$65
Gene Autry, 27" Flying "A" Ranch Rifle-Leslie-Henry-Lever	$100
Gene Autry, 10 1/2" Leslie-Henry Pop-up Cap Box-N, G	$175
Gene Autry, 11" Leslie-H 44, RC, N, AB, G	$100

Gene Autry, 11" Leslie-H 44, RC takes Bullets (Rare)	$125
Big Buck, 8 1/4", Kilgore, Single Shot	$25
Big Chief, 8", Stevens-Indian Head Grips N, G & AB	$40
Big Horn, 7 1/4", Kilgore, RC, Lanyard Ring on Some	$35
Billy The Kid, 8" Service Manufacturing Co., Rep., N	$35
Bonanza, 9", Leslie-Henry, N and Gray Metal	$75
Bonanza, 10 1/2", Leslie-Henry Long Barrel, N (Rare)	$100
Bonanza, 10", Hubley-Halco, Like Late Texan, Jr. (Rare)	$100
Bonanza, 11". Leslie-Henry 44, RC, N & AB	$85
Brave, 6", Nichols, Single Shot, N &BE	$35
Bronco, 9 1/4", Kilgore, RC, Tree Engraving, Horse grip	$50
Bronco, 8 1/2", Kilgore, RC, Horse Engraving, N, G & BE	$50
Buckeroo, 8", Actoy, Single Shot	$20
Buck, 6 1/2", Kilgore, Single Shot	$25
Buck, 7 1/4", Kilgore, Repeater	$35
Buckle Gun, 3", Mattel, Remington Style Derringer	$50
Buck'n Bronc, 8 1/2" Schmidt, Small Frame (Rare)	$50
Buck'n Bronc, 9", Schmidt, Eng., Horse-rider Grip, N & G	$90
Buck'n Bronc, 9", Schmidt, Metal Grips or Stag, N & G	$85
Buck'n Bronc, 9", Schmidt, Eng.,Hoppy Grips, N & G	$150
Buck'n Bronc, 10 1/2", Schmidt, Engraved, W/WO Rib	$90
Buck'n Bronc, 10 1/2", Schmidt, Plain, Long Barrel	$85
Buck'n Bronc, 10 1/2", Schmidt, Hoppy Cameo Grips (Rare)	$150
Buffalo Bill, 8", Stevens	$30
Buffalo Bill 45, 10 1/2", Balantyne Mfg. Co., RC, Steel	$85
Bunt-Line, 10 1/2", Lone Star, Notch-Bar Grips	$65

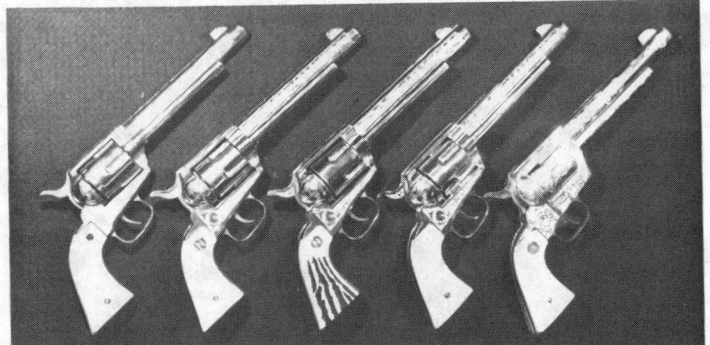

Nichols' Guns, L-R: Stallion .45 1st Model, Stallion .45 Mark II, same with stag grips, Kusan Stallion .45 with dummy bullets and transparent grips and a Mustang 500.

L-R: Lone Star Roy Rogers, L-H/Halco Marshal, Mattel Shootin' Shell Fanner, Nichols Stallion .38, Mattel Shootin' Shell .45 Fanner.

Kit Carson, 8 1/4', Kilgore, Rep., N & G.....................................$35
Kit Carson, 10', Kilgore, Rep. N & G..$45
Hopalong Cassidy, 7 1/2" Wyandotte, SS, N & G.................$100
Hopalong Cassidy, 9", Wyandotte, Rep, N & G....................$125
Hopalong Cassidy, 9", Schmidt, Eng. Hoppy Cameo, N.........$150
Hopalong Cassidy, 9", Schmidt, Eng. Cameo, Gold (Rare).....$250
Hopalong Cassidy, 9", Leslie-Henry, N (Very Rare)..............$200
Cavalry, 11 1/4", Leslie-H., CW Style, RC, AB, Stag Grips.....$45
Champion, 9", Leslie-Henry (Gene's Horse), N & G.................$85
Champion, 11", Kilgore, Fast Draw Timer in Grips, N.............$65
Cheyenne, 32", Daisy, Ricochet Lever Rifle...........................$65
Cheyenne, 10", Hamilton, Rep., N..$30
Cheyenne, 9", Kilgore, N, Transparent Stag Grips..................$65
Chief, 7", Hubley, Single Shot...$12
Cisco Kid, 8 1/2", Lone Star, Rep..$65
Colt Special, 7", Nichols, Rep..$40
Colt Revolving Cyl. Rifle, 31", Mattel "Shootin' Shell"..........$150
Colt .38, 10 3/4", Hubley, RC, Engraved, Bullets...................$100
Cowboy, 12", Hubley, RC, N, BK & BE, Rep.............................$75
Cowboy Classic, 12", Hubley, RC, Gold with Black Grips.....$100
Cowboy Jr., 9", Hubley, Rep., Lanyard Ring, N & G, RC...........$40
Cowboy King, 9 1/2", Stevens, Rep. Stag Grips.......................$40
Cowboy King, 9", Stevens, Rep. Pearl Grips, N & AB.............$40
Cowhand BB, 10 1/2", Schmidt, Eng. W/WO Jewel in Grip.....$75
Cowhand 250, 8 1/2", Nichols, N & BE....................................$35
Cowman, 8 1/2", Nichols N & BE..$35
Cowpoke, 9 1/4", Lone Star, Notch Bar Grips.........................$50
Cowpoke Jr., 8", Lone Star, Single Shot..................................$25
Cowpuncher, 8 7/8", Nichols, Single Shot, N & BE...................$30
Cowtyke, 7 5/8", Nichols, Rep., N & BE...................................$35
Coyote, 8 1/4", Hubley, CW Style, Rep....................................$35
Crackfire Winchester Rifle, 30", Mattel..................................$50
Dagger-Derringer, 7", Hubley, O/U, Eng., Push-out Knife.......$60
Davy Crockett, 9", Leslie-Henry, Rep. (Rare).........................$125
Davy Crockett, 10 1/4", Schmidt, Rep., Metal Stag, (Rare)....$125
Davy Crockett, 8" Marx, Tin Clicker..$30
Davy Crockett, 35" Daisy, Lever Pop Rifle...............................$85
Davy Crockett, 7 1/2", Buzz Henry, N & G, (Rare)................$100
Davy Crockett, 12", Schmidt, RC, Compass, Copper G., (Rare).$150
Davy Crockett, 8 1/2", Schmidt, Single Shot, (Rare)..............$100
Davy Crockett, 25" Hubley, Flintlock Buffalo Rifle.................$85
Deputy, 10 3/4", Hubley, Ribbed Barrel, All Metal, Rep..........$55
Deputy-BB, 8 1/2", Schmidt, Small Frame, Rep.......................$45

Deputy, 7 1/2", Kilgore, Rep., N & G......................................$45
Deputy Sheriff, 6 3/4", Kilgore, RC, Rep.................................$45
Derringer, 3", Lone Star, Single Shot, BE................................$10
Derringer, 4", Hamilton, SS, N & BE.......................................$10
Derringer, 4", Nichols, Rem.-O/U, Shoots Bul., N & BE..........$30
Derringer, 4", Nichols, Rem.-O/U, N & BE...............................$25
Derringer, 4", Kusan-Nichols, Rem.-O/U, N & BE...................$15
Matt Dillon 45, 11 1/2", Halco, Break-top, RC, Bul., (Rare)....$150
Double-Derringer, 4", Leslie-II., O/U Rotating Barrels............$15
Dyna-Mite, 3", Nichols, Derringer, Bul., N, G & BE.................$20
Eagle, 8", Kilgore, RC, N & G, Eagle Grips.............................$45
Johnny Eagle, 36", Topper, Red River Rifle, Bul.Firing............$50
Wyatt Earp, 9", Actoy, Rep., N & AB.......................................$50
Wyatt Earp, 11", Actoy, Buntline Special, N & AB...................$85
Wyatt Earp, 9", Hubley, N, Rep...$65
Wyatt Earp, 9", Leslie Henry, Rep., N.....................................$85
Wyatt Earp, 10 1/2", Leslie-Henry, Long Barrel, (Rare).......$135
Wyatt Earp, 11, Hubley, Long Barrel, Rep..............................$85
Wyatt Earp, 9", L.I. Die Cast Co.,Rep. (Identical to Hubley)....$75
Wyatt Earp, 11", Service Mfg. Co., (Identical to Hubley)..........$95
Wyatt Earp, 10 1/2", Schmidt, Plain, Rep., (Rare)................$100
Wyatt Earp, 10 1/2", Schmidt, Scroll Engraved, (Rare)..........$150
Wyatt Earp, 13 1/2", Lone Star, Buntline Special...................$85
Wyatt Earp, 18", Young Premium, Buntline Spec., Clicker.......$65
Dale Evans, 10 1/2", Schmidt, Engraved, Jewel Grip. (Rare)....$150
Dale Evans, 8 1/2", Schmidt, Small Frame. (Very Rare).........$175
Dale Evans, 7 1/2", Buzz Henry, Insert Grips, N & G (Rare)..$100
Fanner 50, 10 5/8", Mattel, No Bul., No RC, N & BK...............$45
Fanner 50, 10 5/8", Mattel, RC, Bul. N & BK...........................$50
Fanner, 9", Mattel "Shootin' Shell", RC, Bullets......................$75
Fanner 50, 10 5/8", Mattel Safari, Impala Grips N & AB..........$45
Fanner 38 Snubnose, 7", Mattel "Shootin' S.", Agent Zero........$85
Fanner 45, 11 1/4", Mattel "Shootin' S.", RC, Bul. (Rare)........$200
Flip, 10", Hubley, Rep...$45
Flip Special Rifleman, 32", Hubley Ring Lever.........................$85
41-40, 10 1/4", Nichols, RC, Bul. Engraved, N........................$135
Frontier, 9", Kilgore, Rep..$25
Frontier Rifle, 35 1/4", Hubley..$75
Frontier 45, 10 1/2", Lone Star, RC, Bul.,Indian Grips.............$85
44 Daisy, 10 1/2", Cap & Ball Type Like Nichols 61, (Rare)..$125
44 Cal. Model 1860, 14", Hubley RC, Bul., CW, (Rare)..........$135
45 Colt, 14", Hubley, RC, Bul. CW...$100
45 Texan, 14", Hubley, RC, Bul., CW, Rare............................$200

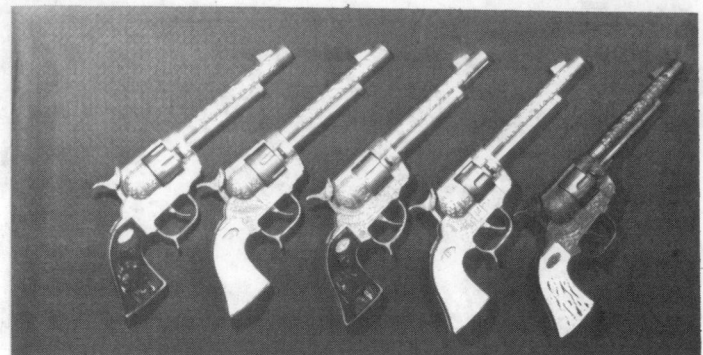

Leslie-Henry .44 Varieties L-R: Gene Autry-Gold, U.S. Marshal, Gene Autry-Nickel, Wild Bill Hickok and Wagontrain-A. Bronze.

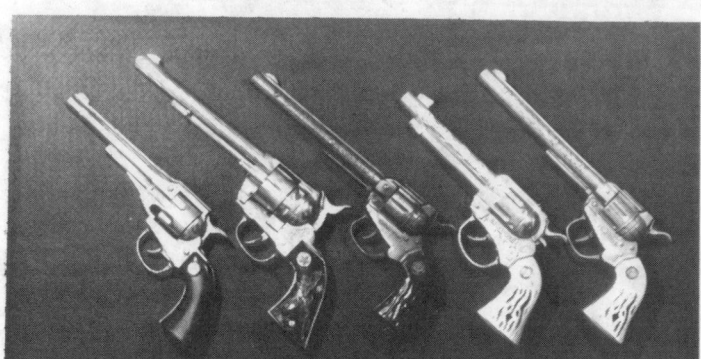

L-R: Hubley Remington .36 LB, Hubley Cowboy Classic-Gold, Actoy W. Earp Buntline-AB, Actoy Restless Gun and Actoy Wells Fargo.

45 Smoker, 10", Product Engineering Co....................................$45
45 Long Colt, 12", Hubley, Plastic & Metal Clicker.................$20
Gabriel, 8 3/4", Rep..$20
Gray Ghost, 9 1/4", Lone Star, Rep., Silver Grips, (Rare).........$100
Grizzley, 10 1/4", Kilgore, RC, Bear Grips, N & G..................$100
Gunfighter, 9 1/4", Lone Star, Rep., Horsehead Grips...............$45
Gunsmoke, 9", Leslie-Henry, Rep., Horsehead Grips...............$85
Gunsmoke, 9", Leslie-Henry, Rep., Bronze M. Dillon Grips...$125
Gunsmoke, 10 1/2" L-H Long Barrel, Bronze Grips, N & G........$135
Gunsmoke, 10", L-H, Pop-Up Cap Box, Bronze Grips.............$135
Haig Western, 13 1/2", Buntline, Plastic & Metal, BB & Cap...$50
Hide-A-Mite, 3", Canell, SS, Derringer....................................$30
Hide-A-Way, 3 1/2", Leslie-Henry Derringer, Bul.....................$30
Hide-A-Way, 3 1/2", Esquire Derringer, AB, N & G, Engraved....$35
High Chaparral, 34", Daisy 94 Rifle..$85
Indian Scout Rifle, 30", Mattel Shootin' S., Rolling Block.......$135
Jesse James, 9 1/4", Lone Star, Rep...$65
Johnny Ringo, 10 1/2", Marx, Fast Draw Lanyard, Rep.............$65
Kelly's Rifle, 32", Hubley, Rep., Lever Rifle............................$45
Alan Ladd, 10 1/4", George Schmidt, (Rare)............................$150
Laramie, 9", Leslie-Henry, Rep. N., (Rare)...............................$135
Lasso Em Bill, 10 1/4", George Schmidt, Stag Grips.................$85
Lawman, 34", Daisy, Winchester R., Smoke & Noise..............$100
Lone Ranger, 32" Marx, Deluxe Winchester Rifle, (Rare).......$125
Lone Ranger, 8", Marx, Tin Clicker Deluxe, Jewel & Decal.....$45
Lone Ranger, 8", Marx, Tin Clicker, L.R. Celluloid Insert Grip..$75
Lone Ranger, 10", Actoy, Rep., N & AB, (Rare).......................$100
Lone Ranger, 10", Actoy, Detachable Stock-Barrel Ext, (Rare)..$225
Lone Ranger .32, 8", Actoy, N., (Rare)......................................$100
Lone Ranger, 26", Marx Winchester Rifle, Silver Color............$75
Lone Ranger, 7 1/4", Victory "V", Composition Material..........$85

Lone Rider, 8", Buzz Henry, SS, Block Letters, N & BK.........$50
Lone Rider, 8", Buzz Henry, SS, Script Letters, N & BK.........$60
Lone Rider, 8", Leslie-Henry, Gold, Black Insert Grips, Rep....$75
Longhorn, 10 1/2", Leslie-Henry, Pop-up Cap Box, N.............$100
Mares Laig, 14" Marx, "Wanted Dead or Alive", Lever-Pstl..$100
Mares Laig, 14", Actoy, Pony Boy Rifle-Gun, Ejects Bul.......$125
Marshal BB, 10 1/4", George Schmidt.......................................$65
Marshal, 10", Hubley, Rep...$35
Marshal, 10 1/2", Leslie-Henry/ Halco, RC, Bul, N & AB........$85
Marshal, 10 1/2", L-H/Halco "6-7 Shot" Extra Shot Barrel, Rare..$150
Marshal, 10", L-H, Pop-up Cap Box, N.....................................$85
Marshal, 8 1/2", Halco-Gabriel, Rep, N.....................................$25
Marshal, 8 1/2", Halco, Rep, N, Trans. Amber Grips................$30
Bat Masterson, 9", Carnell, RC, N, (Rare)................................$100
Bat Masterson, 9", Lone Star, Notch Bar Grips, N, (Rare)........$100
Bat Masterson, 9 1/2", Lone Star, Stag Grips, N, (Rare)............$125
Maverick, 3 1/4", Leslie-Henry, Derringer, Bul........................$30
Maverick, 10", L-H, Pop-Up Cap Box, N, (Rare).....................$125
Maverick, 10 1/2", G. Schmidt, Scroll Engr, Steerhead Grip...$200
Maverick, 9", Leslie-Henry, Rep, N...$75
Maverick, 10 1/2" Leslie-Henry, N, Long Barrel, (Rare)...........$125
Maverick 45, 11", Halco, Break Top, RC, Bul, (Rare).............$200
Maverick, 8 3/4", Lone Star, Notch Bar Grips...........................$75
Maverick Rifle, 26", Lever Action Winchester...........................$85
Me & My Buddy, 8", Marx, Action Cowboy Tin Clicker.........$65
Model 61, 10 1/2", Nichols, RC, CW Style, N & BE, (Rare)....$185
Model 61, 10 1/2", Daisy-Kusan, Similar to Nichols, (Rare)....$185
Model 94 Winchester, 27", Nichols, Lever Action.................$100
Model 95 Winchester, 36", Nichols, Lever, Bullets, (Rare).....$150
Mustang, 9 1/4", Kilgore, Rep, G & N $35
Mustang 500, 12 1/4", Nichols, Rep., N & BE.........................$125

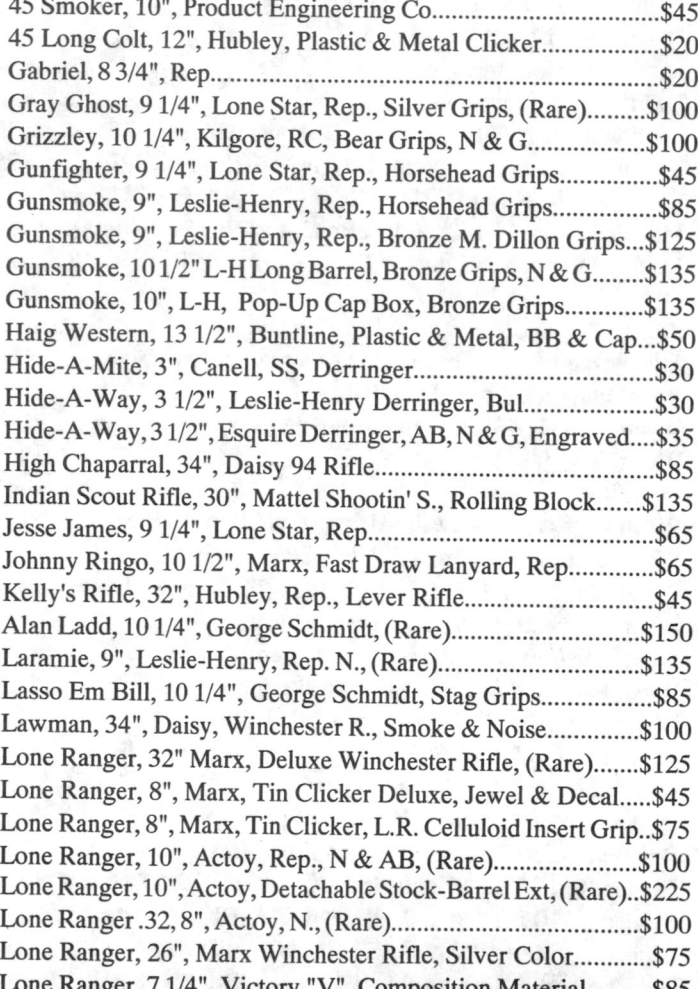

George Schmidt Guns L-R: Hopalong Cassidy, Dale Evans, Lasso 'em Bill, Roy Rogers with jewels, Buckin' Bronc, engraved Maverick.

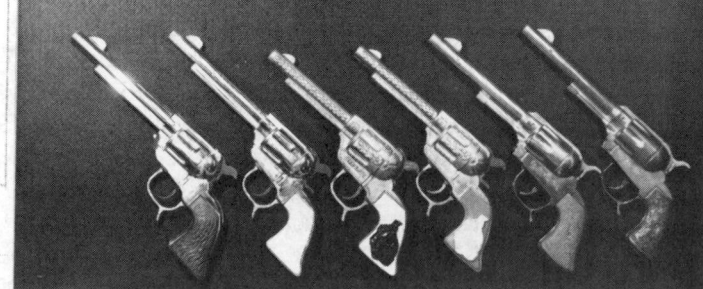

George Schmidt Guns L-R: Alan Ladd-Shane, Cowhand, Buckin' Bronc SB, same red grips, Classy Roy Rogers and Latco Ruf Rider.

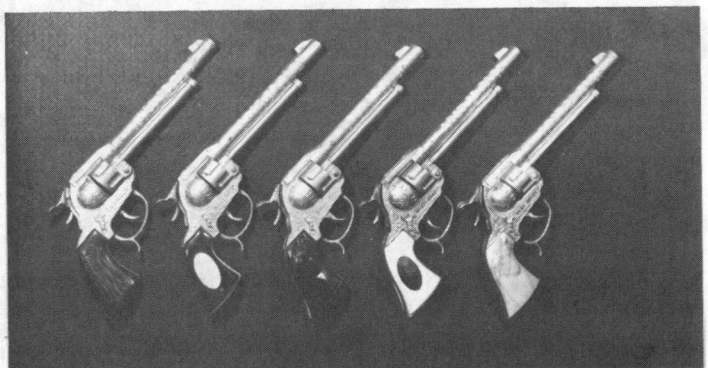

Rare Leslie-Henry Long Barrel Varieties, L-R: Bonanza, Maverick, Wagontrain, Wyatt Earp and Gene Autry.

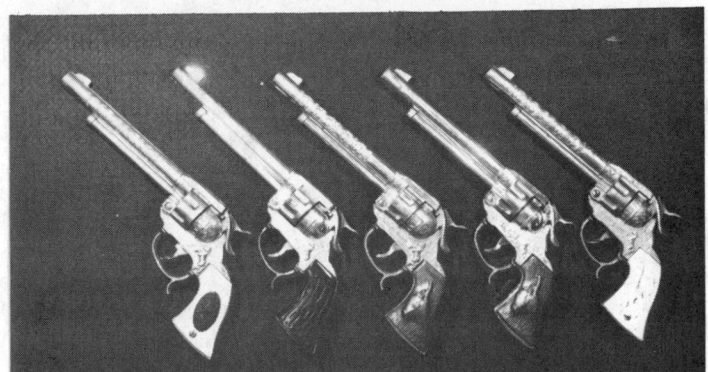

Rare Leslie-Henry Long Barrel Varieties, L-R: Texas, Unmarked, Wild Bill Hickok, Unmarked and Wyatt Earp with stag grips.

Mustang 250, 9 1/2", Nichols, N..$65
Mustang, 9", Nichols, Rep, N, Button Release, (Rare)............$85
Mustang, 9", Nichols, Rep, N, Button R., Jewels in Grips.........$95
No Name 44, 11 1/4", Leslie-Henry, RC, N & AB.....................$65
No Name, 10 1/2", Leslie-Henry, Long Barrel, Break-top........$80
No Name, 9", Leslie-Henry, Rep., Break-top...........................$65
No Name, 10 1/2", Classy Prod., Scroll Grips, N & BK............$50
No Name, 10 1/2", Classy, Wrap-Around Grip, N & BK.........$45
Annie Oakley, 9", Leslie-Henry, Rep., Rare........................$150
Annie Oakley, 32", Daisy Lever Pop Rifle, Gold, Rare...........$100
Paint, 3", Nichols (Miniature), G, BE & N., Bul., SS..............$20
Pal, 3", Kilgore SS, (Very common small pistol).......................$5
Paladin, 9", Leslie-Henry, Rep...$85
Paladin 45, 11", Halco, Break-top, RC, Bul., (Rare)..............$165
Panther, 4", Hubley Derringer, Gambler's Wrist Cuff, Rep........$75
Pathfinder, 12", G. Schmidt, RC, Secret Grip/Compass, (Rare)..$150
Patrol, 10 1/4", G. Schmidt, Rep. N & AB............................$65
Pecos Kid, 9 1/8", Lone Star, Rep.......................................$45
Peacemaker, 3 1/2", Marx Miniature Colt, RC, N & BK...........$25
Peacemaker, 5", Marx Buntline Colt Miniature, RC, N & BK...$85
Pepper Box, 6 1/4", Lone Star, 4 Shot Revolving Barrels.........$65
Pet, 6 1/2", Hubley SS..$25
Pet, 3 1/2", Kilgore SS (Very common small pistol).................$5
Pinto, 3", Nichols (Miniature), N & BE, Bul., SS...................$25
Pinto, 8 1/2", Hubley/Halco, SS...$15
Pinto, 9", Gabriel, Rep., N..$15
Pioneer, 10 1/4", Hubley, Black Grips with Compass, (Rare)..$95
Pioneer, 10 1/4", Hubley, Amber Grips, CW, N....................$50
Pioneer, 8", Stevens, SS, N...$45
Plainsman, 10 1/2", National, RC.......................................$35
Pony, 7", Nichols, SS, N & BE...$30

Pony, 7", Actoy, SS, N., All Metal......................................$25
Pony Boy, 10", Actoy, Rep. N & AB....................................$30
Potshot, 3", Mattel, "Shootin' Shell" Derringer...................$30
Rancho, 6", Nichols, SS, N & BE..$30
Ranger, 8", Lone Star, SS..$25
Ranger, 9 1/8", Kilgore, Rep, Cowboy on Grips....................$25
Ranger, 7 1/2", Buzz Henry, Rep., N & G............................$35
Range Rider MK II, 12 1/4", Lone Star, Bul., RC..................$115
Range Rider, 10 1/4", G. Schmidt, Rep., (Rare).....................$85
Red Ranger, 8", Marx or Wyandotte, Tin Clicker....................$25
Red Ranger, 9", Wyandotte, CW Dragoon Style......................$85
Red Ranger, 7 3/4", Wyandotte, Rep....................................$35
Rebel, 11 1/4", Lone Star, RC, N, BK, G, CW........................$95
Rebel Scattergun, 21", Double Barrel Shotgun, (Rare)..........$200
Red Rider, 10", Wyandotte RC, Pressed Steel........................$45
Remington 36, 8 1/4", Hubley, RC, Bul., CW.........................$50
Remington 36, 10", Hubley, RC, Long Barrel, (Rare)............$125
Restless Gun, 10", Actoy, Secret Compartment in Grip...........$65
Restless Gun, 9 1/2", Actoy, Rep...$45
Restless Gun 4 in 1, Actoy, Pistol-Carbine-Stock & Barrel...$200
Ric-O-Shay 45, 12 1/4", Hubley, RC, Bul.............................$85
Ric-O-Shay Jr., 10", Hubley, Rep...$65
Ricochet Rifle, 30", Daisy 660, Puffs Smoke.........................$65
Ruf Rider, 10 1/2", Classy-Latco, Metal Scroll Grips..............$50
Ring Rifle, 32", Hubley, Lever Rifle, Large Ring.....................$85
Rin Tin Tin, 9", Actoy, Rep., N & AB....................................$65
Rodeo, 8", Hubley, SS, Steerhead Grips................................$25
Rodeo, 7 1/4", Hubley, SS, N & BK......................................$20
Roy Rogers, 5", Classy, SS...$25
Roy Rogers, 10 1/4", G. Schmidt, RR Metal Stag Grips..........$125
Roy Rogers, 10 1/4", G. Schmidt, RR & Trigger Grips...........$130
Roy Rogers, 10 1/2", Classy Prod., Metal Scroll Grips..........$135
Roy Rogers, 9", G. Schmidt, Engd., Jewel in Grip, (Rare).....$200
Roy Rogers, 8 1/2", G. Schmidt Small Frame. (Rare)............$165
Roy Rogers, 2 1/2", Tuck-A-Way Derringer, N & G................$50
Roy Rogers, 9", Classy, Rearing Horse Grip...........................$85
Roy Rogers, 7 1/2", B. Henry, Insert Grips, N & G..................$85
Roy Rogers, 9", Leslie-Henry, Break-top, N & G....................$125
Roy Rogers, 10 1/2", Lone Star, RC, Indian Chief Grips.........$165
Roy Rogers, 8 1/2", Lone Star, RR & Steerhead Grip.............$100
Roy Rogers, 10 1/4", Kilgore RC, RR & Horsehead................$150
Roy Rogers, 9", Kilgore Rep., RR & Horsehead......................$90
Roy Rogers, 8 1/4", Kilgore RR & Horsehead.........................$75
Roy Rogers 45, 10 1/2", Balantyne Mfg. Co., RC, (Rare)........$165

L-R: Hubley Dagger-Derringer, Halco Swivel O/U, Hide-A Mite, Nichols O/U, Esquire Hide-A-Way-AB, same-Gold and Kusan O/U.

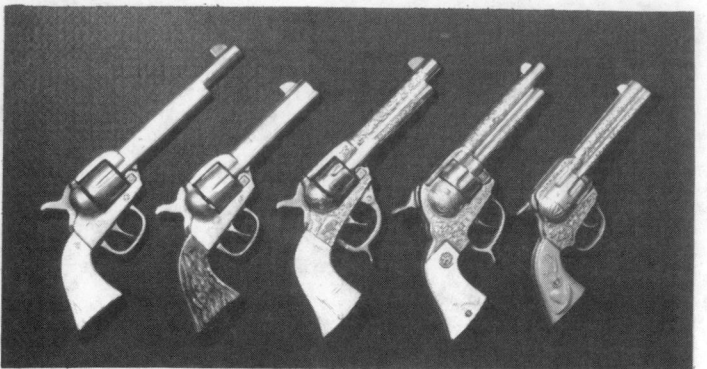

Classic Cast Iron L-R: Kilgore Long Tom, Kilgore Big Horn, Kilgore American, Hubley Texan and Kenton Gene Autry engraved.

Classic Cast Iron L-R: Hubley Texan, Jr., Kilgore Lone Ranger, Hubley Cowboy, Stevens Cowboy King and Kenton Gene Autry LB.

Roy Rogers, 24", Marx, Plastic Clicker Win. Rifle............$75
Roy Rogers, 35", Marx, Win. 348 Deluxe Rifle with Sling, Cap......$125
Roy Rogers, 26" Marx Cap Shooting Win. Rifle........................$95
Rustler 45, 12", Crescent, RC, Bul. Wolfhead Grip................$100
Scout Rifle, 32", Hubley Winchester Lever............................$65
Sharps Civil War Carbine, 27", Marx, Cap Shooter.................$85
Sheriff, 7 1/2", Wyandotte SS...$30
Sheriff's Derringer, 3 1/4", Ohio Art Co., Bul........................$20
Shotgun Slade, Marx, Double Barrel Shotgun, Cap.................$85
Silver Colt, 8", Nichols, Rep., Steer or Horse Grip................$75
Silver Pony, 8", Nichols, SS., All metal, (Rare)....................$75
Six Gun, 10 1/2", Lone Star, RC, Bul., N & G.......................$85
Smoky Joe, 9", Leslie-Henry, Rep. N & G.............................$75
Smoky Joe, 9", Leslie-Henry, AB Steerhead Grip..................$85
Smoky Joe, 8", Hubley, Rep., Steerhead Grip........................$45
Sniper, 22", Hubley, Extra Long Buntline Colt, Clicker.........$35
Special, 11", Actoy, Rep., Long Barrel.................................$65
Spitfire, 8 1/2", Nichols SS, Mini Rifle N & BE....................$30
Spittin' Image Six Gun, 10", Daisy, RC, BK........................$45
Stallion 22, 7 1/4", Nichols, 5 Shot, RC, Single Action.........$35
Stallion 22, 7 1/4", Nichols, 5 Shot, RC, Double-Action........$45
Stallion 32, 8", Nichols, RC, Bul., G & N............................$50
Stallion 38, 9 1/2", Nichols, RC, Bul..................................$75
Stallion 41-40, 10 1/4", Nichols, Flip-out RC, Bul................$135
Stallion 45, 12", Nichols 1st Mod. Jewel-Horse Grip.............$175
Stallion 45 Mark II, 12", Nichols, RC, Bul...........................$130
Stallion 45 Mark II, 12", Nichols, G & BE, (Very Rare)..........$500
Stallion 45 Mk II, 12", N-Kusan, No Bul. Transparent Grips....$200
Stallion 30-30 Saddle Gun 28", Nichols Lever, Bul...............$100
Stallion 61, 10 1/2", Nichols CW, RC, N & BE.....................$185
Star, 7", Hubley SS, All Metal..$10
Sure Shot, 8 1/4", Hubley, Rep...$10
Tex, 8", Hubley, Rep., Side Lever-Opening..........................$35
Texan, 9 1/2", Hubley, Rep., RC, N & G..............................$90
Texan Jr., 9", Hubley, Button Release, N, G, BK & AB..........$50
Texan Jr., 10", Hubley, Side-Opening, Rep...........................$35
Texan Jr., 9", Hubley, WW II Composition, Non-Working.......$45
Texan .38, 10 3/4", Hubley, RC, Bul...................................$100
Texas, 9", Leslie-Henry, Rep..$65
Texas, 10 1/2", Leslie-Henry, Long Barrel, (Rare)................$90
Texas, 9", Long Island Die Cast Co., Rep., N.......................$65
Texas, 11", L.I. Die Cast Co., Long Barrel, (Rare)................$100
Texas, 4", Halco, Spur Trigger Derringer..............................$25
Texas, 6 1/2", Hubley, All Metal...$20

Texas Ranger, 11", Leslie-Henry, RC, N & AB......................$65
Texas Ranger, 11", Lone Star, CW, RC, BE and AB...............$65
Texas Ranger, 8", Halco, Rep., Stag Grips............................$30
Texas Ranger, 8 1/4", Leslie-Henry, Rep., N........................$45
Texas Ranger, 8 1/2", Stevens, Rep, N & G..........................$35
Texas Ranger, 27", Leslie-Henry, Lever Rifle........................$65
Texas Ranger 44, 11 1/4", Leslie-Henry, RC, N & AB............$100
Texas Smoker 77, 10", Leslie-Henry, (Rare).........................$100
Texas 45 Colt, 13 1/2", Hubley, RC, Bul, N., (Very Rare).....$200
Thundergun, 12 1/2", Marx, Rep-2 Roll, N & BE...................$125
Tophand 250, 10", Nichols, Rep..$65
Trail Boss, 30", Daisy, Lever Pop Rifle.................................$65
Trigger, 8 1/2", Stevens, Rep..$50
2 in 1, 6" & 8 1/2", Hubley, Two Barrels, Rep......................$40
250 Shot, 10", Actoy, Rep..$35
38 Daisy, 9 1/2", Kusan, BE & N, RC, Bul...........................$85
38 Repeater, 6", Best, Victory Clicker/Whistle, Plastic...........$15
U.S. Marshal. 11 1/4", Leslie-Henry 44, RC, N & AB.............$85
Wagon Train, 9", Leslie-Henry, Rep.....................................$85
Wagon Train, 10 1/2", Leslie-Henry, Long Barrel, (Rare).......$125
Wagon Train, 11 1/4", Leslie-H. 44, RC, N & AB...................$120
Wagon Train "5 in 1", L-H 44 Carbine Stock & Brl. Extension.$200
Wagon Train, 10 1/2" L-H, Pop-Up Cap Box.........................$125
Wanted Dead or Alive, 19" Actoy Lever Car., Bul..................$125
Wells Fargo, 9", Actoy, Rep., N & AB..................................$65
Wells Fargo, 11", Actoy Rep., Long Barrel, N & AB...............$85
Wells Fargo Guard, 26" Sawed-Off Dbl. Brl. Shotgun, Darts..$85
Johnny West, 26", Marx, Ranch Lever Rifle...........................$65
Western, 9", Hubley, Rep..$35
Wild Bill Hickok, 9" Leslie-Henry, Rep., N & G....................$85
Wild Bill Hickok, 10 1/2" Leslie-Henry, Long Barrel, (Rare)..$125
Wild Bill Hickok, 10 1/2", L-H, Pop-Up Cap Box, (Rare).......$125

CW Remington-Style L-R: Halco Texas Ranger-Bronze, Lone Star Apache-Nickel, Lone Star Apache-black finish and Gold-Unmarked.

Wild Bill Hickok, 11 1/4", L-H 44, RC, Bul.........................$100	Cowboy King, 9", Stevens, Rep., Engraved, Classic Cap Gun..$150
Wild Bill Hickok, 7 1/2", B. Henry, N & G, (Rare)...............$100	Custer, 10", Kenton, SS, Long Barrel...................................$90
Winchester Saddle Gun, 33", Mattel, Bul...........................$85	Deadshot, 8 3/4", Stevens, SS, Long Barrel, (Rare)................$125
Winchester Saddle Gun, 26", Mattel "Shootin' Shell"..........$75	Dude, 5 3/4", Kenton, Rep., N & BK...................................$85
Winner, 8 3/4", Hubley, Plastic & Metal Rep........................$45	Fargo Express, 9 3/4", Kilgore, Cast Iron & Steel, (V. Rare)....$350
Y & Dot Ranch, 8", Wyandotte Clicker................................$35	49-ER, 9", Stevens, RC, Rep., N,G & AB, Classic Cap Gun....$125
Young Buffalo Bill, 8", Stevens, Rep...................................$25	Lasso Em Bill, 9", Kenton, RC., Bul., (Rare).........................$125
Young Buffalo Bill, 8", Halco, SS, Stag Grips.....................$25	Lasso Em Bill, 9", Kenton, RC., Bul., Jewels, (Very Rare)......$200
Young Buffalo Bill, 7 1/2", L-H/Halco, Rep.........................$25	Lawmaker, 8 3/8", Kenton, Rep., Engraved, N & BK.............$100
Young Buffalo Bill, 26", Leslie-Henry Lever Rifle..................$45	Lone Ranger, 8 1/4", Kilgore, Rep., Classic Gun, (Rare).........$165
Zorro, 8", Lone Star (Similar Hubley Coyote).......................$45	Long Tom, 10 3/8", Kilgore, Steel RC., Classic Gun, Rare.......$275
	Long Tom, 10 3/8", Kilgore, Cast Iron RC., Classic Gun,Rare..$300
Cast Iron Western Toy Guns	101 Ranch, 11 1/2", Hubley, SS, LB., (Rare).......................$165
American, 9 3/8", Kilgore, Steel RC., Rep.,Classic Cap Gun.....$250	Pawnee Bill, 7 5/8", Stevens, Rep., N & G, All Metal..............$100
American, 9 3/8", Kilgore, Cast Iron RC., Classic Cap Gun.....$275	Peacemaker, 8 1/2", Stevens, Rep., N, G, AB & BK..............$100
Gene Autry, 8 3/8", Kenton, Rep., N & BK, LB., Classic.......$125	Ranger, 8 1/2", Kilgore, Engraved, Rep., (Rare)...................$110
Gene Autry, 8 3/8", Kenton, LB, Engraved, N & BK, (Rare)..$225	Ranger, 8 1/2", Kilgore, Rep...$85
Gene Autry, 6 1/2", Kenton, N & BK., Classic Cap Gun...........$85	Rodeo, 11", Hubley, SS, Long Barrel, (Rare)........................$150
Gene Autry, 6 1/2", Kenton, Engraved, N & BK, (Rare)........$200	Roy Rogers, 8 1/4", Hubley, (Similar to Cowboy), (V. Rare)...$400
Bango, 7", Stevens, Rep., Some Grips Have Jewels...................$65	Roy Rogers, 10 1/4", Kilgore, (Similar to Long Tom), (Rare)..$450
Big Horn, 8 5/8", Kilgore, Steel R. Cylinder, Classic Cap Gun....$200	Sharpshooter, 6 1/4", Kilgore, Rep., (Rare)........................$125
Big Horn, 8 5/8", Kilgore,C. Iron Cylinder, Classic Cap Gun...$225	Six Shooter, 6 1/2", Kilgore, RC., Rep..............................$75
Billy The Kid, 6 3/4", Stevens, Rep...................................$125	Smokey Joe, 8 1/4", Hubley, (Similar to Cowboy), Rep. (Rare).$150
Buc-A-Roo, 7 3/4", Kilgore, SS...$50	The Sheriff, 8 1/2", Stevens, Rep., N................................$75
Buffalo Bill, 11 1/2", Kenton, SS, Wide & Narrow Hammer..$150	The Fortyfive, 11 1/8", National, Rep., Long Barrel................$85
Buffalo Bill, 13 1/2", Kenton, SS, Extra Long Barrel, (Rare)...$275	Texan, 9 1/4", Hubley, RC, Rep, N & BK., Classic Cap Gun..$125
Buffalo Bill, 7 3/4", Stevens, Rep.....................................$75	Texan, Jr., 8 1/8", Hubley, N & BK., Rep., Classic Cap Gun...$100
Bull's Eye, 6 1/2", Kenton, Rep., Engraved, N & BK.............$100	Texas Jack, 9 3/8", Ives, SS..$150
C-Boy, 6 1/2", Kenton, Rep., Some with Jewels on Frame......$100	Texas Ranger, 9 1/4", Kilgore, Rep., (Rare).......................$200
Cowboy, 7 5/8", Ives, SS...$125	Western, 7 1/4", Kenton, SS..$65
Cowboy, 8", Hubley, Rep, N & BK, Classic Cap Gun...............$75	Western Boy 7 3/4", Stevens, Rep....................................$125
Cowboy, 12", Stevens, SS., Long Barrel, (Rare)......................$175	Wild West, 11 1/2", Kenton, SS, Long Barrel.......................$150

Value Guide Notes

All prices quoted are for average condition guns that have no broken or missing parts, most of the original finish and work properly. Mint guns are double the quoted price and those with broken or missing parts and minimal finish are worth half or less than the price listed.

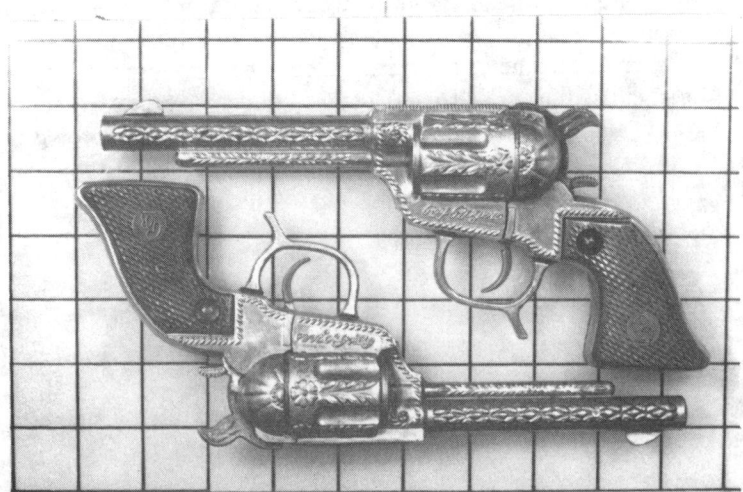

A pair of rare, George Schmidt, Roy Rogers guns with short barrels, engraved with red and yellow jewels in the copper grips.

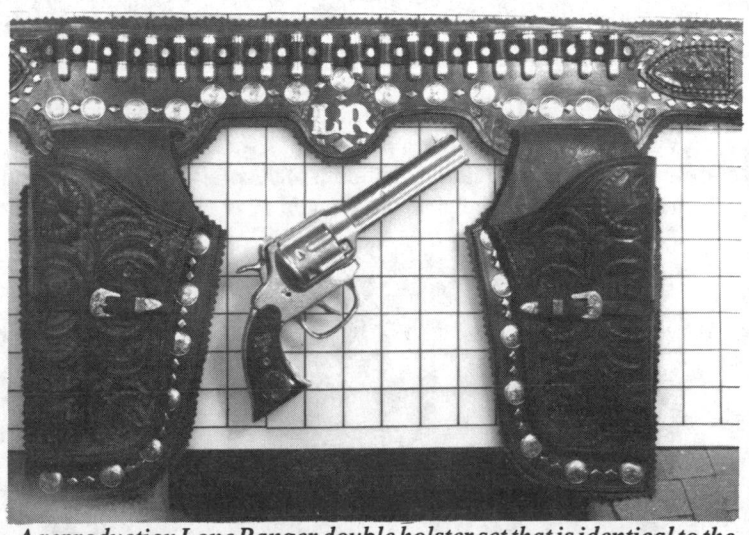

A reproduction Lone Ranger double holster set that is identical to the set worn by Clayton Moore on TV, except for the smaller size.

Toy Gun Holsters
by James Schleyer

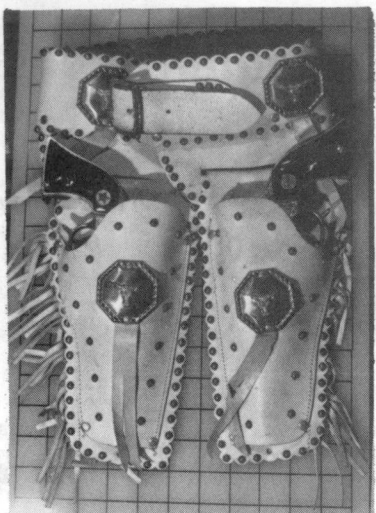

Studs & Jewels-(Girls)-$150

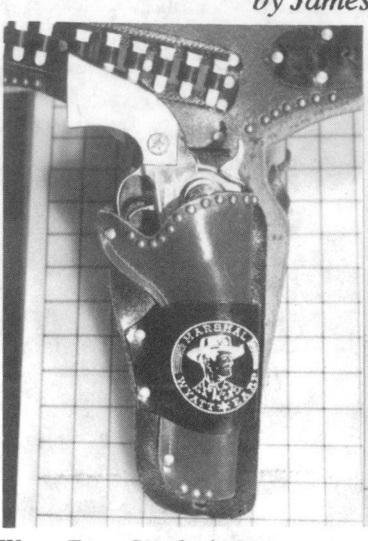

Wyatt Earp-Single-$150

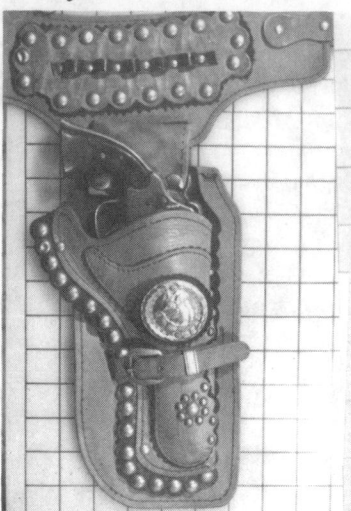

Conchos & Studs-Sgl.-$75

Studs & Jewels-Dbl.-$175

Prices are for holsters only and do not reflect the value of the guns.

The collectors of western toy guns are equally excited about the holster sets used to carry the guns! Toy guns and holsters were made to go together, so the demand for high quality, leather holsters is continuing to escalate like guns. The leather and synthetic materials used to make holsters, were more fragile than the metal guns, so fewer examples exist due to the ravages of time and rough play.

First class leather holster sets with gleaming metal studs, colorful jewels, pictoral cut-outs, metal conchos, fake bullets, fringe and character names are eagerly sought by both the toy and authentic cowboy or western collectors. The current market value of many toy gun holsters is surpassing those of real holsters. Obviously, the value is directly proportional to the amount of decoration, the fine quality, the rarity and famliarity of the character name. Holsters of non-leather materials, minimal decoration, poor quality or generic names are considerably less desirable.

The highest values are reserved for mint condition holsters in their original boxes, with maximum decoration, or important character name. The larger, double holster sets are more desirable than single ones or those of smaller size. Any famous western character name adds considerable appeal and value to a quality set. Names, such as; Hopalong Cassidy, Gene Autry, Roy Rogers, Dale Evans, Annie Oakley, Bat Masterson, Wild Bill Hickok, Wyatt Earp, Matt Dillon, Bonanza, Wagontrain, Gunsmoke, Lone Ranger, Buffalo Bill, etc., are eagerly sought. Generic western names, such as; Pony Boy, Cowboy, Ranger, Cowpoke, Sheriff, Marshal, Scout, etc., are less desirable unless the quality or amount of decoration are outstanding! Many of the toy gun holsters were made by real holster makers and

are of superb quality. Numerous small factories utilized women workers to produce thousands of holsters for the toy gun manufacturers. It was common practice to make the holsters over-sized to accomodate a larger selection of gun sizes, so in some instances a smaller size gun might be virtually lost in a large holster! Many mail-order companies and distributors, purchased toy guns from several manufacturers and holsters from various other sources, so those that could accomodate a wider range of gun sizes were more economical. Like all collectibles, the rarity and condition are prime factors affecting value. We are fortunate to have many fine leather preservatives and conditioners to protect our holsters. Use caution in storing fine guns in your holsters as salts used in leather tanning could damage or discolor their finish. Check you guns regularly to ensure protection.

As the demand for holster sets increases, so do their values. It is not uncommon for high quality toy holster sets to be priced from $100 to $350, without any guns! Remember that the proper display of holster sets requires additional space, so plan accordingly. The prices listed under each holster indicate their value in excellent to mint condition, with no tears, broken stitches, or missing decorations. The prices are for the holsters only, and do not reflect the value of the toy guns in them. A number of new, limited edition, and reproduction toy holster sets are presently being offered and should be advertised and priced to reflect this. White holster sets with red or gold hearts, jewels and fringe were normally intended for cowgirls. They are more difficult to acquire and usually demand a premium price, especially, a Dale Evans, Sally Starr or Annie Oakley.

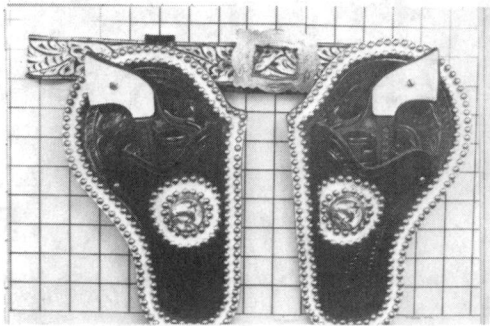

Early Generic-Dbl.-$150

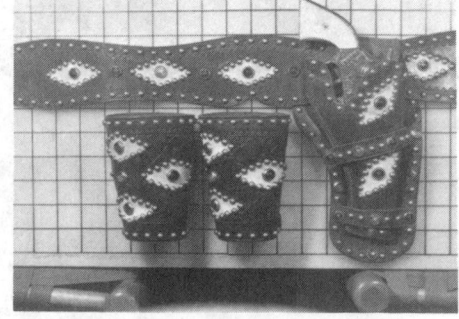

High Decoration-Sgl.& Cuffs-$165

Boxed Roy Rogers Spurs by Classy-$150.

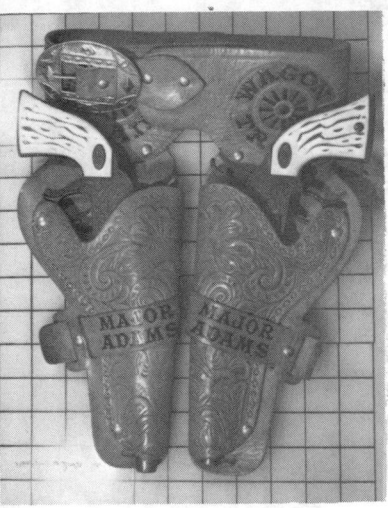

Wagontrain-Dbl.-$175

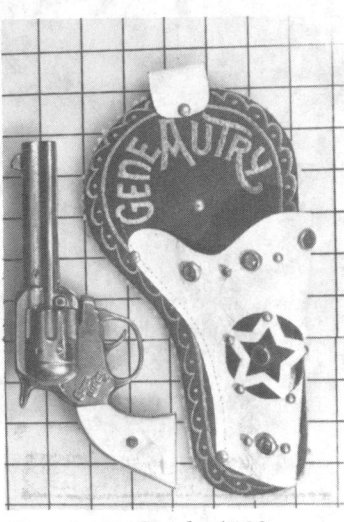

Gene Autry-Single-$100

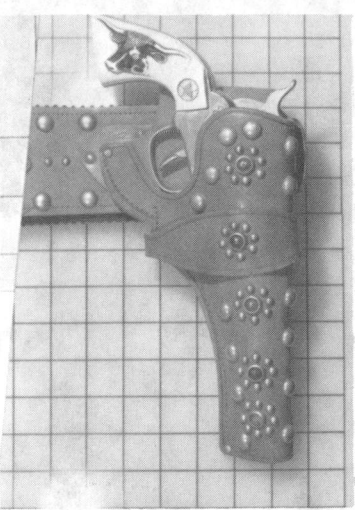

Multi-Studded-Single-$95

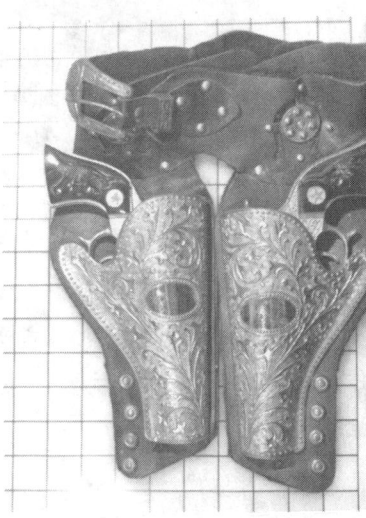

Metalic-W.B. Hickok-Dbl.-$250

Prices are for holsters only and do not include the guns.

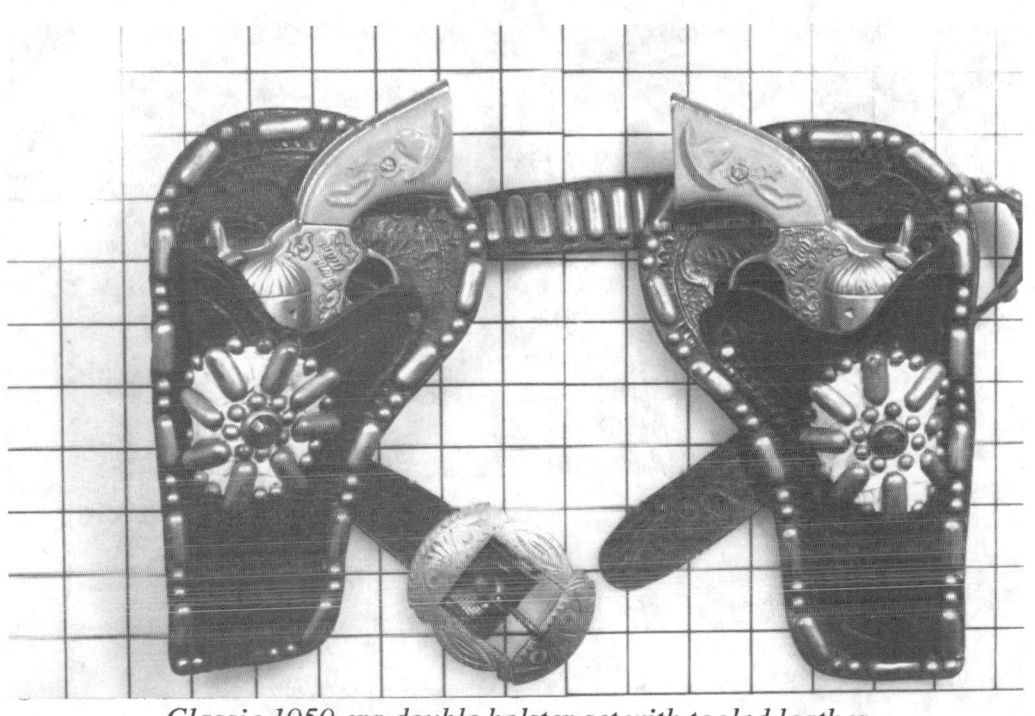

Classic 1950 era double holster set with tooled leather, glass jewels, silver studs and conchos. $150.

Gene Autry-Single-$165

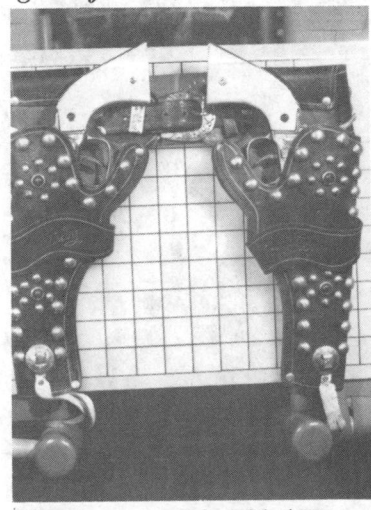

Hopalong Cassidy-Dbl.-$275

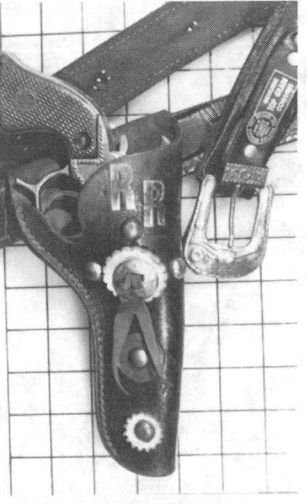

Roy Rogers-Single-$125

High Decoration-Dbl.-$225

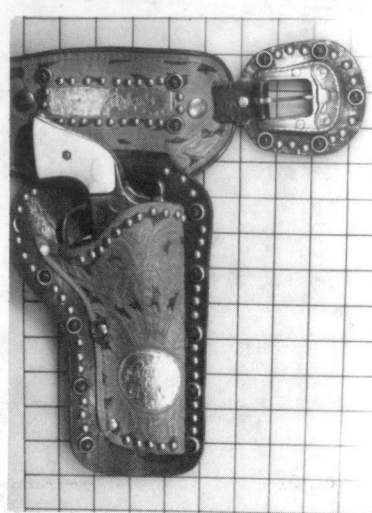

Roy Rogers-Dbl.-$300

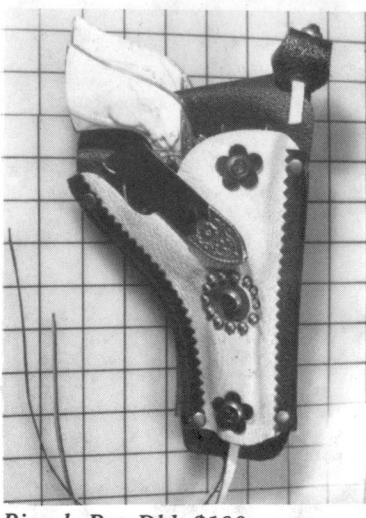

Bicycle Bar-Dbl.-$100

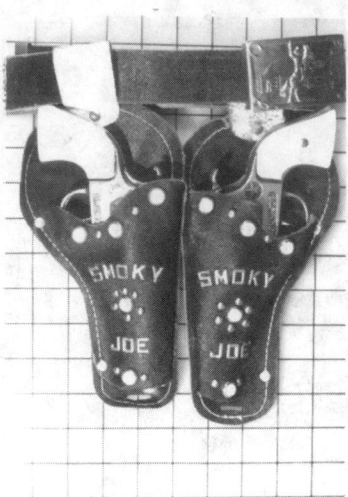

Smokey Joe-Dbl.-$150

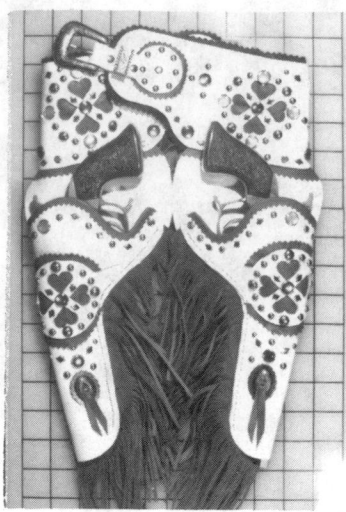

Annie Oakley-(Girls)-Dbl.-$250

Prices are for holsters only and do not include the guns.

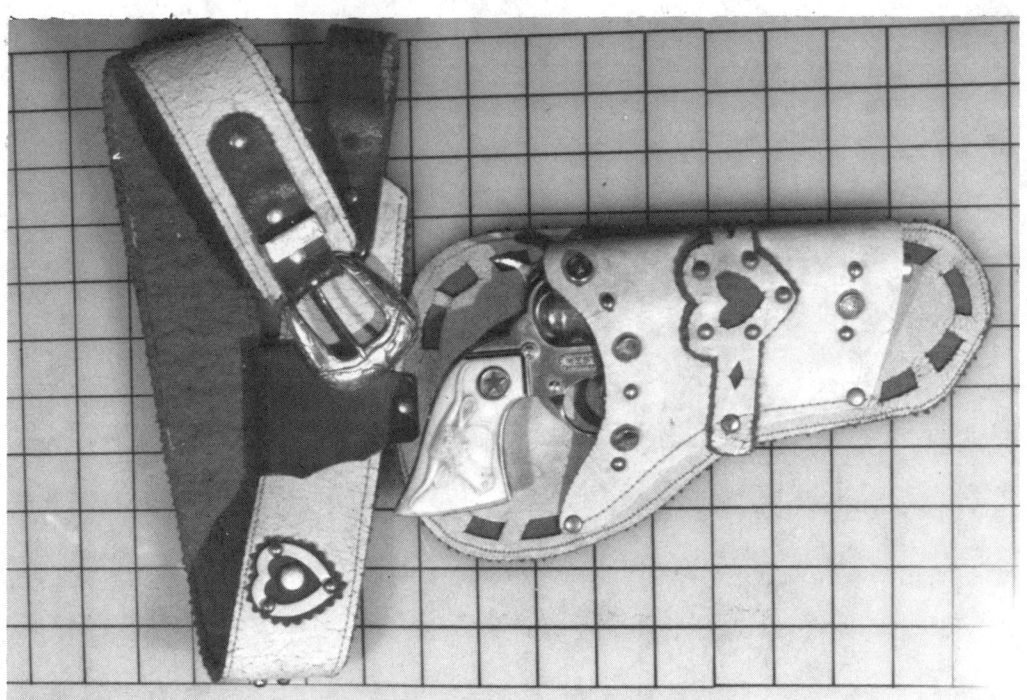

*Charming 1950 era Cowgirl's holster in red and white
leather with red hearts, silver studs and red jewels.$120*

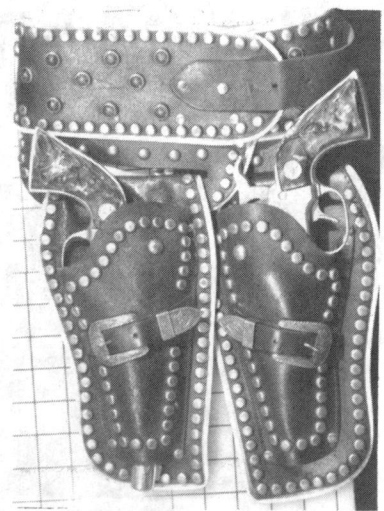

Classic '50s-Dbl.-$165

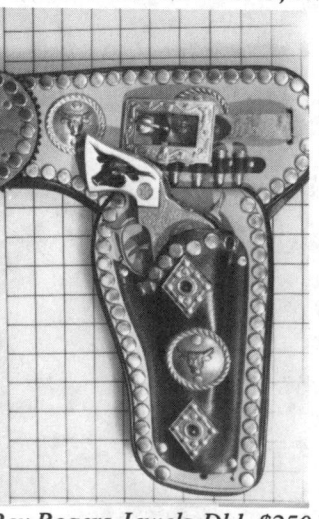

Roy Rogers-Jewels-Dbl.-$250

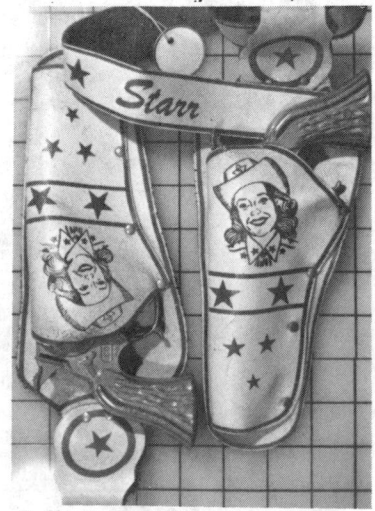

Sally Starr (Girls)-Dbl.-$125

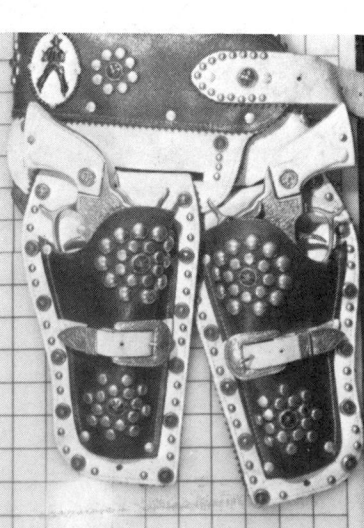

Jewels & Studs-Dbl.-$200

552

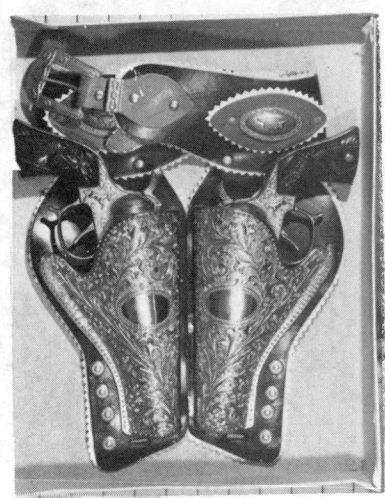

Metalic-G. Autry-Dbl.-$350

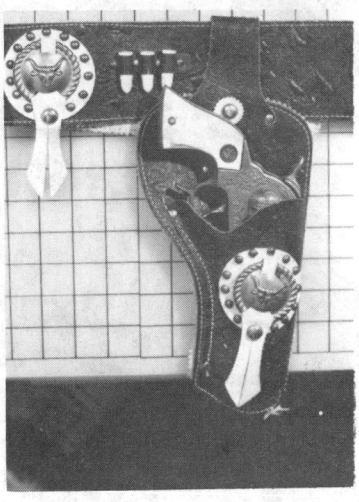

Generic-Single-$100

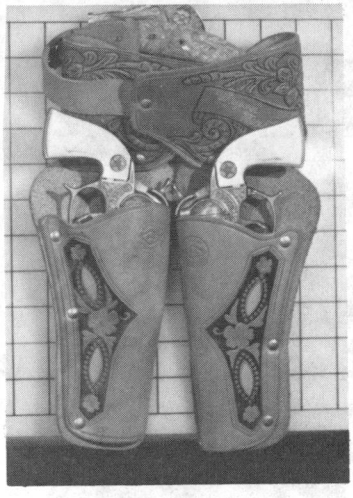

Tooled-Dbl-$100

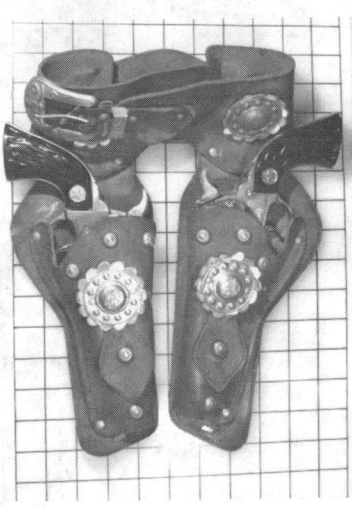

Conchos & Studs-Dbl.-$125

Prices arc for holsters only and do not include the guns.

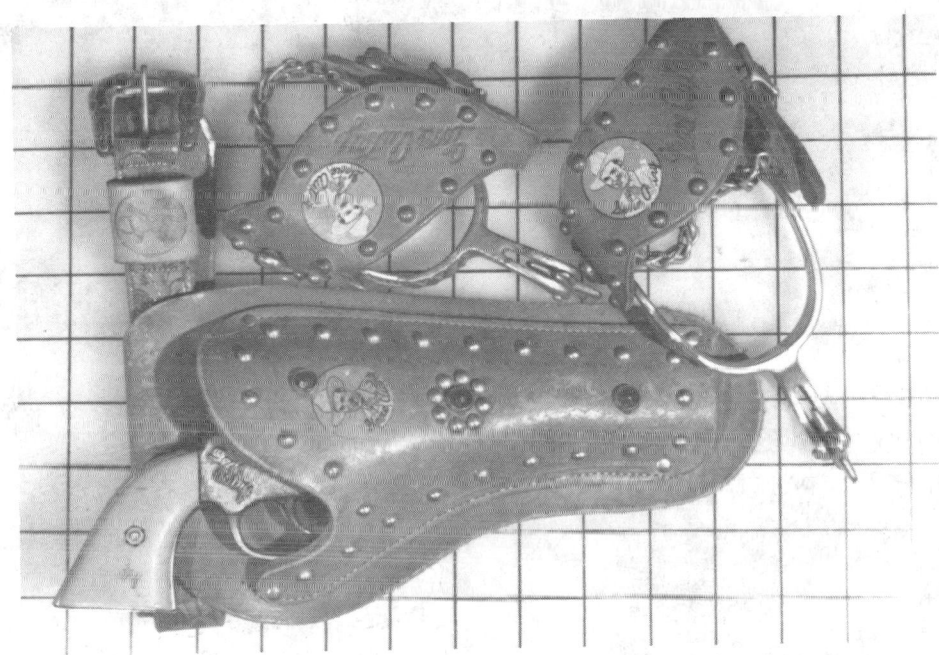

Classic pre-1940, Keyston Bros. "Gene Autry" single set with matching cast iron spurs. Gene's picture is on all pieces, as well as, silver studs and red jewels. $250 Set.

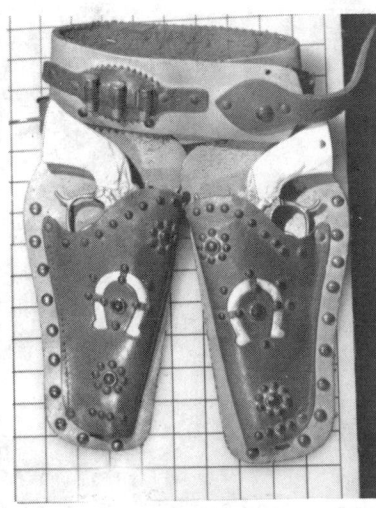

Early Generic-Dbl.-$125

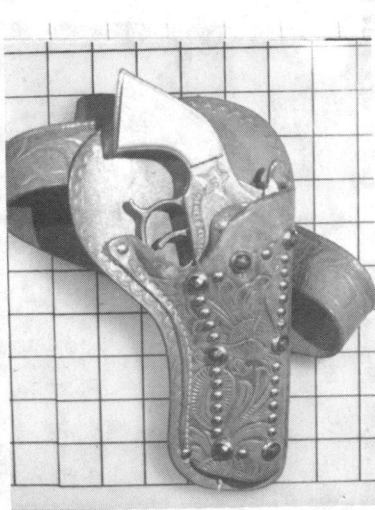

Tooled & Jewels-Single-$85

Roy Rogers-Sgl.-$200

Tooled & Studs-Dbl.-$125

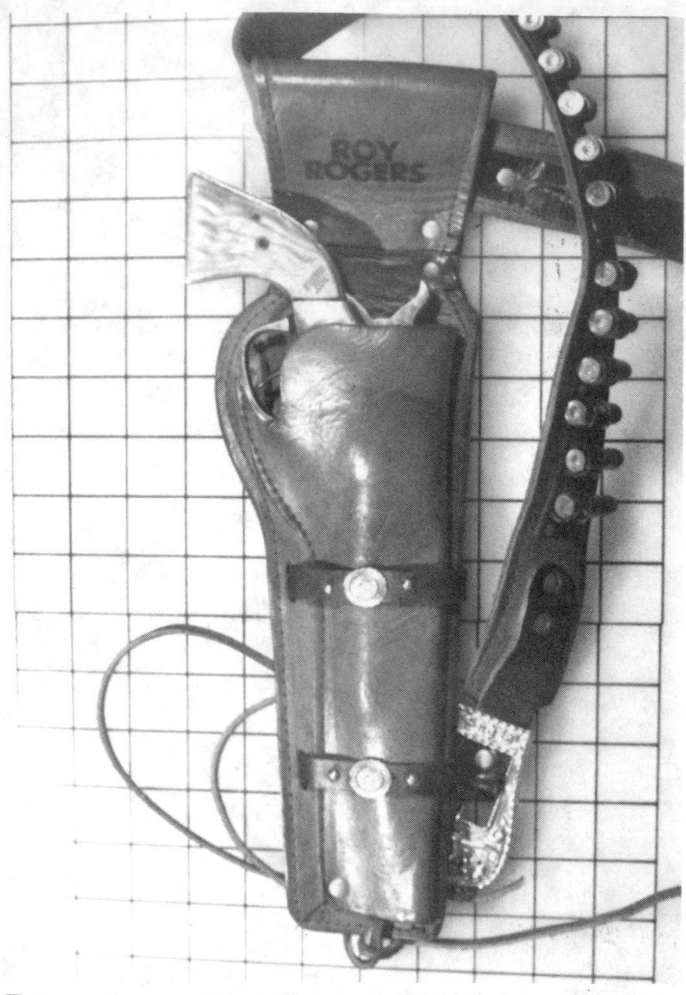

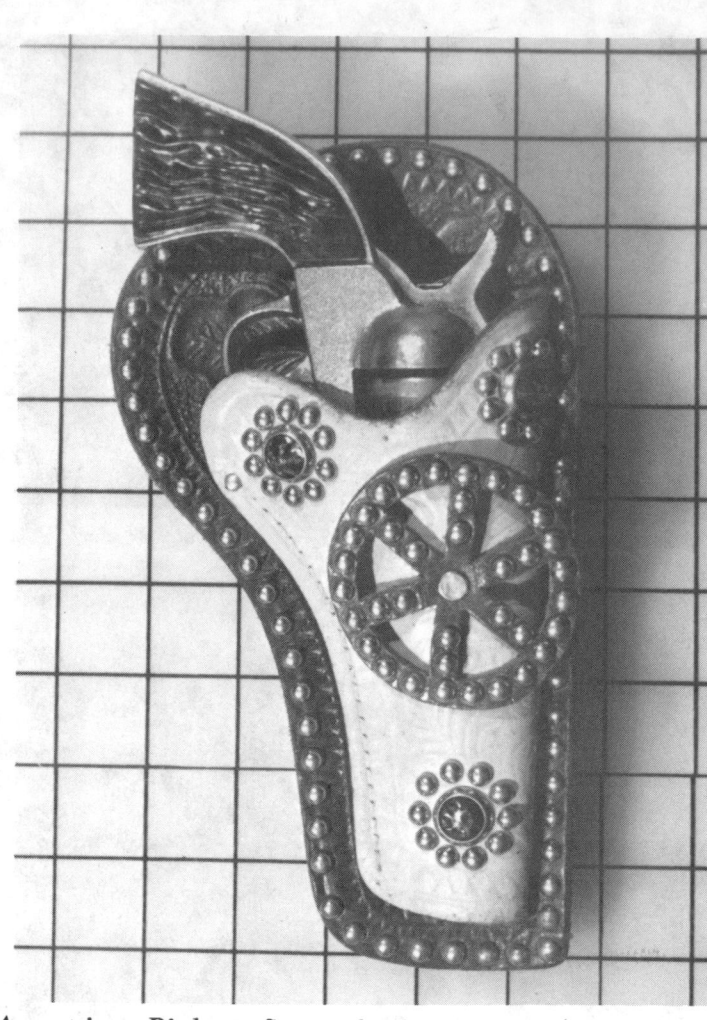

Extremely rare "Roy Rogers" single holster for the long barreled, cast iron Kilgore cap gun. $225.

A cast iron Bighorn fits perfectly into this early holster with wagon wheel cutout, tooled leather, silver studs and red jewels. $95.

Hopalong Cassidy-Dbl.-$175

Prices are for holsters only and do not include the guns.

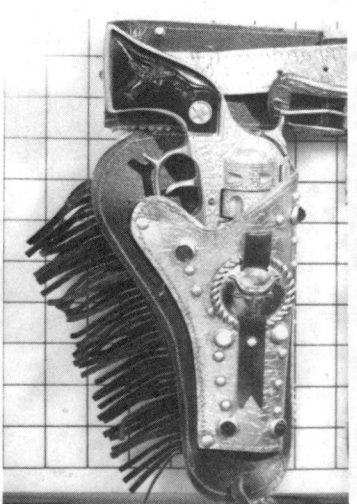

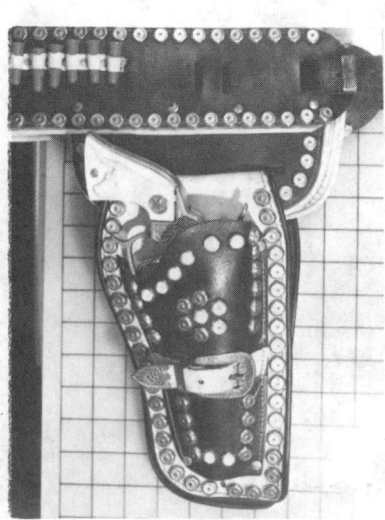

Generic Cowboy-Dbl.-$165   *Buckin' Bronc-Dbl.-$100*   *Metalic-Dbl.-$125*   *Multi-Studded-Sgl.-$135*

DAISY AND MARKHAM/KING SPRING-AIR BB GUNS

by Jim Buskirk

Definition

Spring Air BB guns, sometimes referred to as Air Rifles, are simple in design and operation. They cannot be pumped up to high pressures and their muzzle velocity is usually in the neighborhood of 400 FPS, give or take. Operation is simple; a one-stroke cocking action compresses a spring and draws a piston back through a cylindrical air chamber. Locked in this position the BB gun is ready to fire. Meanwhile a BB has been placed in the breach, either manually or by some kind of automatic feed mechanism. When the trigger is pulled the piston is driven forward, forcing the air in the cylinder out through the barrel, driving the BB ahead of this blast of air.

Is It A Toy?

A BB gun is not a toy in the traditional sense. If improperly handled it can be dangerous and can cause injury. And yet it was conceived, designed, manufactured and advertised for use by children. Common sense tells us that a BB gun should not be placed in the hands of a child too young to understand its dangers or who has not been properly instructed in its safe use. When I hear the BB gun criticized because of its dangers I like to compare it to the ordinary childrens' bicycle. A recent television news report stated that during the period from 1983 to 1993 over six hundred thousand children were seriously injured or killed in bicycle accidents.

A Brief History

Daisy and Markham/King both went into the BB guns business in the late 1880s. Located just across the railroad tracks from one another in Plymouth, Michigan they were in vigorous competition for years. By the early 1930s Daisy not only owned King but the King guns were being produced in the Daisy plant. During that period of about forty years as many as thirty companies tried their hand at the BB gun business. Few made a great success of it, none have survived. By the 1930s "Daisy" and "BB Gun" had become pretty much synonymous terms.

Daisy started life as the Iron Windmill Company in 1882. Iron windmills weren't great sellers and when windmill designer C. J. Hamilton brought in a small prototype BB gun to be considered for manufacture the Board of Directors was cool, at best. Eventually it was decided that the little gun would be made as a premium, not to be sold, but to be given to windmill purchasers. But as Cass Hough, grandson of one of Daisy's founders, said, in his 1976 book It's A Daisy, "It didn't take long for the tail to begin to wag the dog". A few months later production started in earnest and the first Daisy was on the market.

The people who were running the Iron Windmill Company didn't realize that their BB gun was only the first of hundreds of models that would be produced over the next century. Neither that first Daisy or the variations and new models that followed over the next few years was assigned a letter or number designation. Finally in 1900 Daisy produced a variation with the designation "Model B". The designations such as "First model, Second model" etc. are informal terms used by collectors and the BB guns are not so marked. The first Daisy was simply marked "DAISY MFD. BY IRON WIND MILL CO. PLYMOUTH MICH. PAT, APD. FOR". After that Daisy produced BB guns with names, letters, numbers or combinations of same. Their system, or more correctly, lack of system, is confusing to the average collector and even the advanced collector cannot answer questions about the chronology of Daisy BB guns with absolute certainty every time. Daisy didn't know they were making "collectibles", or that anyone would care a hundred years later when a particular model was manufactured. Some guns have no special marking except a name, which may be shared with several models. Some have a single letter or number designation, still others may have a combination of letter and number and many of Daisy's guns from the late 30s have a number and model number such as "No. 111 Model 40", in addition to a name, in this case "Red Ryder". A classic case is the No. 50 Golden Eagle of 1936. This out of sequence number was used because the gun was made to commemorate Daisy's 50th anniversary. To make it easy for the reader we have broken the Daisy listing down into several sections. **Name-only guns are in the first section. Those identified by a letter (Alphabet guns) are next, followed by numbered guns. Guns with a combination of letters and numbers will be listed according to whichever appears first, the letter or the number.**

Time Period Listed 1888-1942

With a few exceptions we have limited our listing to guns made between 1888 and the halt of BB gun production in early 1942, at the onset of WW II. BB guns made after WW II have not yet aroused much collector interest. That is not to say that none of the post WW II are collectible or that some collectors do not collect these later models, but most collector interest is focused on the pre-WW II era. This will eliminate most of the plastic-stocked guns from our list and also most of the guns from Daisy's facility at Rogers, Arkansas. Daisy switched to plastic stocks around 1950 and moved to Rogers in 1958. We have included some of the later Red Ryder guns and the Double Barrel Model 21 of 1968.

BB Gun Values

Like the prices of all collectibles, BB gun prices are somewhat subjective and actual prices paid can vary widely. Many factors have to be considered. Supply-and-demand, nostalgia, condition, how badly the buyer wants the item and the thickness of his wallet are all important factors in the collectibles game. There is no "Book" on BB gun values. The prices we have listed are based on our own experience in collecting, buying and selling BB guns over the past few years and may not reflect prices in every area, but we believe they are a fair representation of the current market. And one last word on the listing method used in this book. The term C10 means a piece that is exactly in the condition it was in on the day it was made. In the case of many of the early BB guns, no such piece will ever be found. Just because it is the best example you have ever seen or heard of does not make it a C10!

My contacts with other BB gun collectors from all over the country have been an important part of my BB gun education. There have been many contributors, far too many to list here, and my thanks go out to each one of them. I must, however, mention two of them in particular. Jim E. Thomas of Tulsa, Oklahoma, has long been my mentor in learning the intricacies of Daisy BB gun chronology. Jim, whom I often refer to as "Mr. Daisy", and his wife Elouise have always made us welcome by phone or in person at their beautiful home where Jim has shared his seemingly endless wealth of BB gun knowledge. In addition Bill and Lynn Johnson of Rosamond, California have been a great assistance in sorting out the very early Daisys and Kings. Much of this early information is very obscure. Daisy didn't know they were making "collectibles" or that anyone would care when or how many of the early models were made. They did not bother to keep complete records of early model changes or production. Bill, who has studied the subject for many years, and has a fine collection of old Daisy/King ads and other paper, was nice enough to go over the evaluations and to give us his own personal input prior to publication.

Two other important sources of information have been Arni Dunathan's 1971 book The American BB Gun, and It's A Daisy, by Cass S. Hough. Hough, grandson of one of Daisy's founders, was mainly responsible for developing the great Daisy character guns of the 1930's. The Buck Jones, Buzz Barton, and that most famous of all BB guns, the Daisy Red Ryder, were all Hough creations.

Jim Buskirk, born in Peru, Indiana in 1930, came to California in an Aunt's Model-T Ford in 1934. He lived in Los Angeles and later Montebello where he completed high school in 1948. Jim enlisted in the USAF in January 1951 and upon his return from military service in 1957 received his degree in Fire Science from Santa Ana College and joined the Anaheim Fire Department where he served until retirement in 1987. He and his wife

Eleanor, a registered nurse who was born and raised in San Diego, California, moved to the small town of Windsor, California in early 1994. A casual collector for several years, Jim began serious collecting in 1985 and in 1989 began to publish the Toy Gun Collectors of America Newsletter, a quarterly magazine for toy gun buffs. His collection of cap guns, BB guns, and related items numbers several hundred pieces. The collection consists mostly of pre-WW II items with its main focus being the 1930s era. The Daisy Red Ryder BB guns are a special interest and his collection includes what is believed to be the first Red Ryder ever made, a factory prototype which was hand built on a King Model 5536 frame. Another star of his collection is one of the very rare first versions of the first model Daisy, one of the few examples known of the so-called "premium" gun which was never sold but was given to windmill purchasers in 1888.

Abbreviations Used:	
LA: Lever Action	WS: Wood Stock
BA: Break Action	PLAS: Plastic Stock
PA: Pump Action	NIC: Nickel Finish
SS: Single Shot	BLU: Blued Finish
RPTR: Repeater	PNTD: Painted Finish

Daisy with Names

	C6	C8	C10
"Daisy" first model 1889 marked "Daisy Pat Apd For" or "Daisy Pat Aug 13, 89", LA, SS, wire stock, NIC, cast metal grip frame....	360	420	600
"Daisy" second model 1890 marked "Daisy Imp'd Pat May 6, 90",BA, SS, wire stock, NIC, cast metal grip frame	300	350	500
"Daisy" third model 1891 marked "Daisy Pat May 6, 90", July 14, 91, BA,SS, stock may be wire or wood, NIC, cast metal grip frame may have checkering, wire stock may have wood insert	210	275	375
"Daisy" 1901, BA, SS, WDS, NIC, marked "Daisy" in indented rectangle on side of grip frame, also marked "Pat. Aug 13, 1889, July 14, 91, Jan. 21, 92, March 26, 1901", frame is all sheet-metal, referred to by collectors as the "20th Century sheet-metal", but <u>not so marked</u>	100	115	175
"Daisy" 1901, repeater variation of above gun	120	140	200
"20th Century" 1899 marked "20th Century" BA,SS, WDS, NIC, has cast metal grip frame	180	210	300
"1000 Shot Daisy" 1903 marked "1000 Shot Daisy" on top and/or side of			

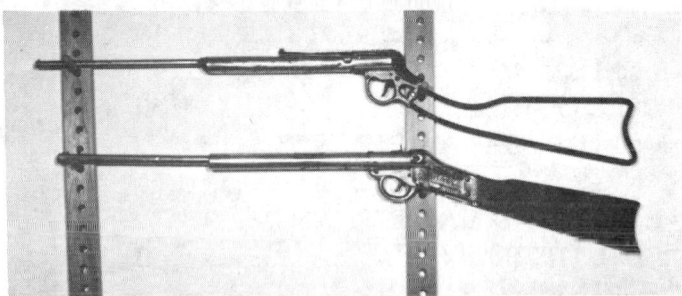

Top to Bottom: A Daisy First Model - 2nd variation of 1889. A product of the Iron Windmill Company of Plymouth, Michigan, the piece was marked "Daisy" on the cast iron top cocking lever. It is not marked with any model number or other designation; the 20th Century Daisy, sheet metal version, was not so marked. It is referred to in ads as "The Daisy 20th Century" model. The piece has a cast iron trigger guard.

	C6	C8	C10
frame, LA, RPTR, WDS, NIC	150	175	250
"500 Shot Daisy" 1905 marked "500 Shot Daisy" on top and/or side of frame, LA, RPTR, WDS, NIC	150	175	250
"Sentinel" 1899 marked "Sentinel", BA, SS, WDS, NIC, Daisy's first all sheet-metal gun, somewhat streamlined in appearance compared to the earlier guns, semi pistol-grip stock & grip frame.	100	115	175
"Sentinel" 1899 marked "Sentinel", BA, RPTR, WDS, NIC, repeater variation of the above gun	100	115	175

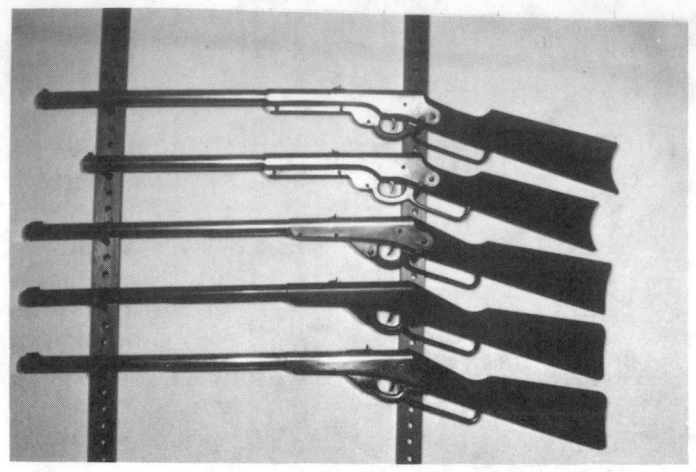

Top to Bottom: The "1000 Shot Daisy", generally referred to as the "Bennett" but not so marked, The "500 Shot Daisy"; The Model B - nickel plated version; The Model B - blued version; The Model 27.

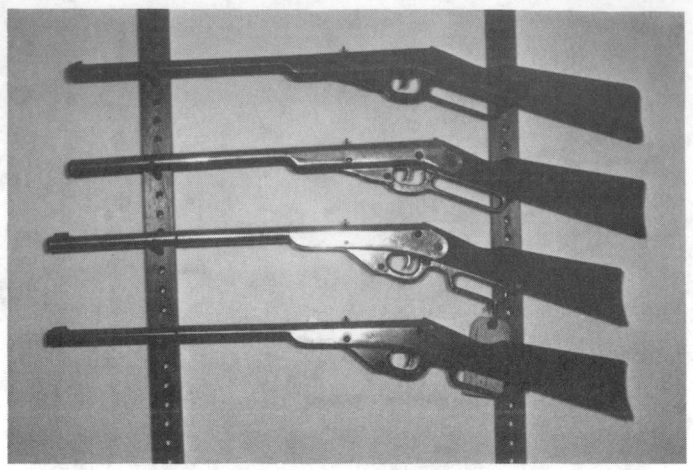

Top to Bottom: No. 101 Model 33 - blued finish; No. 102 Model 33 - nickel finish; No. 12 Model 29 - nickel finish; No. 11 Model 29 - blued finish.

Daisys with Letter Designations

	C6	C8	C10
"Model A" 1907, BA, SS, WDS, NIC..	120	140	200
"Model A" 1907, BA, RPTR, WDS, NIC, repeater variation of the above	90	105	150
"Model B" 1909, LA, RPTR, WDS, BLU (500 shot)	40	50	70
"Model B" 1909, LA, RPTR, WDS, NIC (500 shot)	55	65	90
"Model B" 1909, LA, RPTR, WDS, BLU (1000 shot)	35	50	75
"Model B" 1909, LA, RPTR, WDS, NIC (1000 shot)	60	75	120
"Model C" 1910, BA, SS, WDS, NIC	60	75	120
"Model C" 1912, BA, RPTR, WDS, NIC, repeater variation of the above (350 shot)	60	75	120
"Model H" 1913, LA, SS, WDS, BLU.	55	65	90
"Model H" 1913, LA, SS, WDS, NIC..	75	90	125
"Model H" 1914, LA, RPTR, WDS, BLU (350 or 500 shot)	55	65	90
"Model H" 1914, LA, RPTR, WDS, NIC (350 or 500 shot)	75	90	125

Daisys with Number Designations

	C6	C8	C10
"Number 3B" 1914 (1000 shot), LA, RPTR, WDS, Black Nickel finish, came in colorful lithographed box marked "Daisy Special"	90	105	150
"Number 11" 1917 (500 shot), LA, RPTR, WDS, BLU, may also have model number	55	65	90
"Number 11" 1917 (500 shot), LA, RPTR, WDS, NIC, may also have model number	75	90	125
"Number 12" 1918, LA, SS, WDS, BLU, may also have model number...	55	65	90
"Number 12" 1918, LA, SS, WDS, NIC, may aslo have model number.	75	90	125
"Number 20 Little Daisy" 1908, BA, SS, WDS, NIC (has no grip frame).	75	90	125
"Number 20 Little Daisy" 1912, BA, SS, WDS, NIC (two screws in grip frame)	75	90	125
"Number 20 Little Daisy" 1915, BA, SS, WDS, BLU (has three rivets in grip frame and "ring" trigger)	55	65	90
"Number 20 Little Daisy" 1915, BA, SS, WDS, NIC (has three rivets in grip frame and "ring" trigger)	70	80	110
"Model 21" 1968 (double barrel) BA, RPTR, PLAS, PNTD	180	210	300

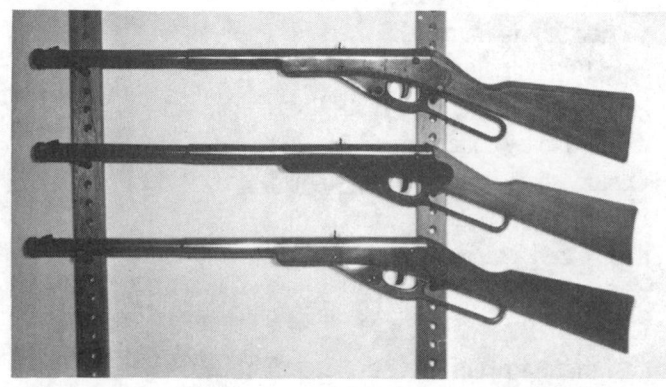

Top to Bottom: A King Model 2236 is identical to the two Daisys; Daisy No. 101 Model 36; Daisy No. 102 Model 36.

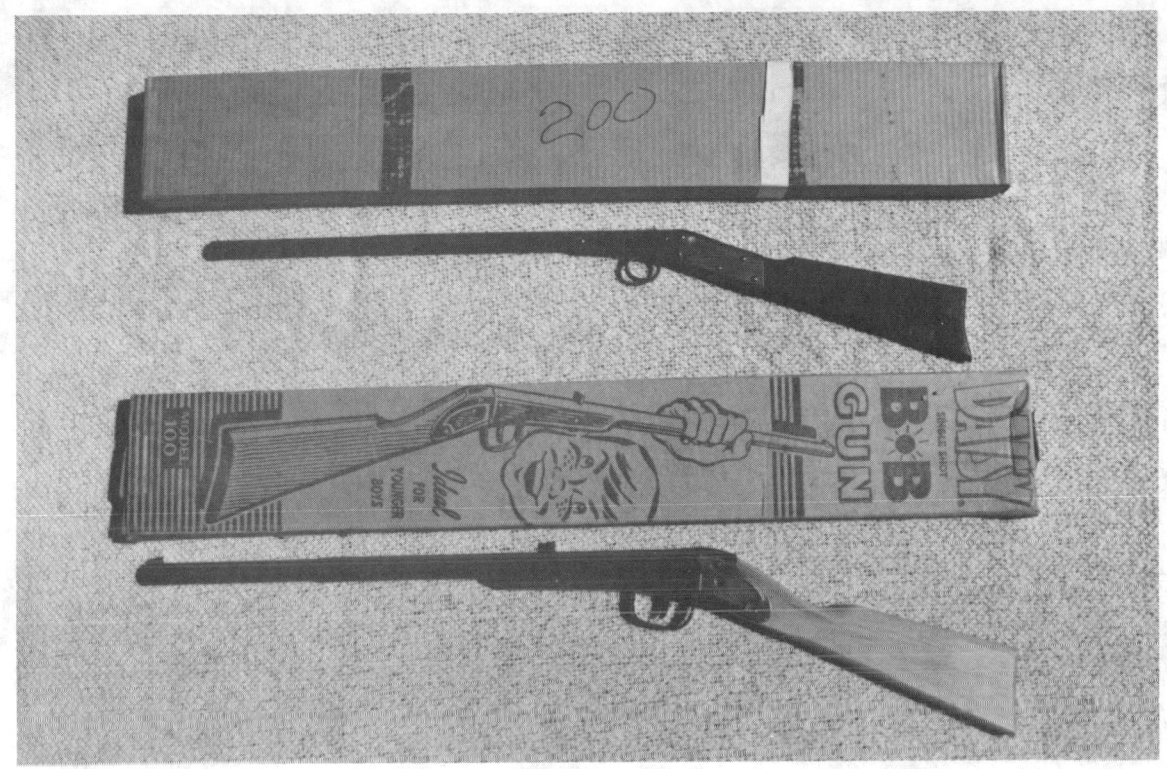

Top to Bottom:
A "Little Daisy No. 20" in near mint condition,
A No. 100 Model 38 with original box.

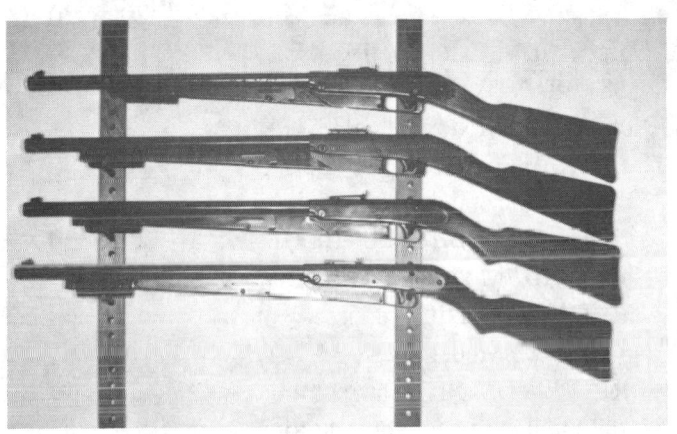

Four Daisy Number 25's. Top, early version with short cocking lever and straight stock, 2nd long lever and straight stock, 3rd long lever, pistol grip stock, 4th long lever, pistol grip stock with hunting scene stamped on frame.

Top: A Daisy Red Ryder, No. 111- Model 40. This early version has an iron cocking lever and has a Daisy No. 300 telescope sight attached. This sight could be added to most of the Daisy Lever Action BB Guns. Middle: A Daisy No. 4 "Military" shown with the cloth sling and detachable rubber tipped bayonet. Bottom: A Daisy No. 140 Defender shown with cloth sling.

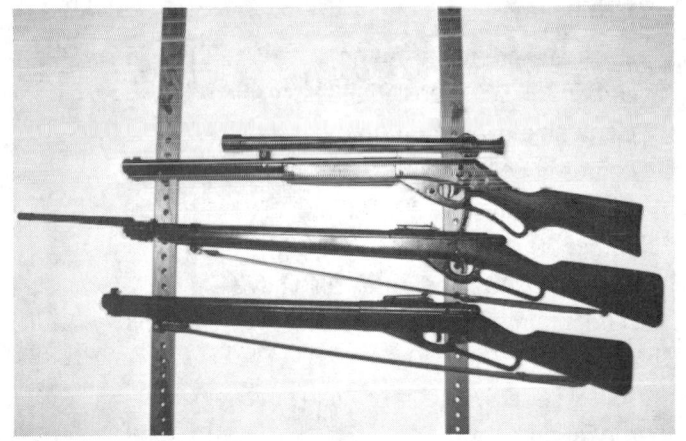

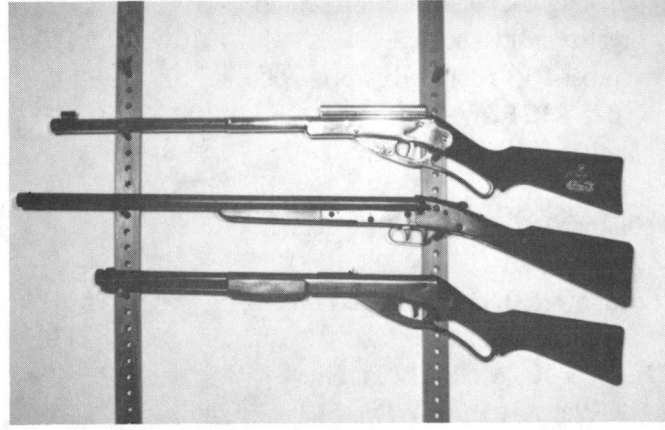

Top: The Daisy No. 50 Golden Eagle had a polished copper plated finish and a black painted stock with a special decal marking it as Daisy's 50 Anniversary Commemorative 1886-1936. Middle: The Daisy No. 104 double barrel had a blued finish and wood stock. Bottom: The Daisy No. 108 - Model 39 Carbine was a forerunner of the Red Ryder.

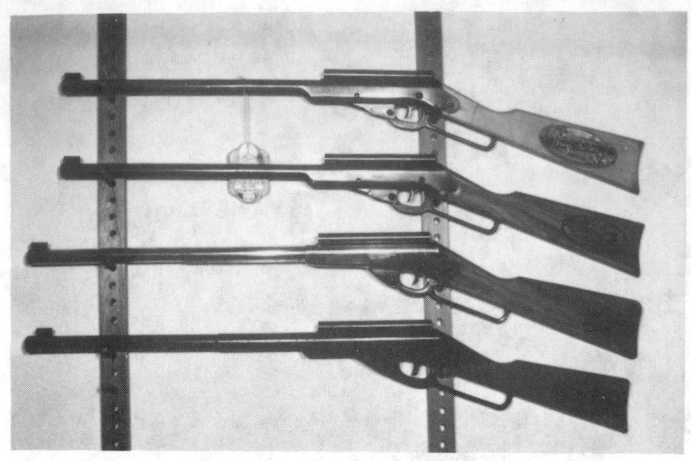

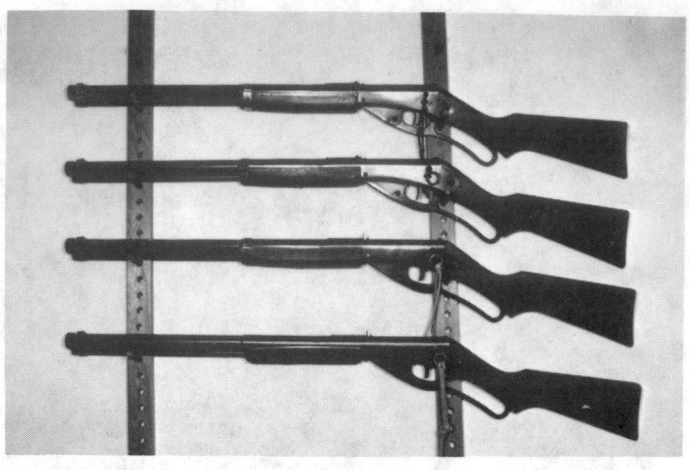

The four versions of the Buzz Barton Special. Top to Bottom: No. 195 with paper Buzz Barton stock label; No. 195 with Buzz Barton brand on stock; the No. 103 - Model 33 Buzz Barton Super Special was nickel plated and had a star shaped brand on the stock; No. 195 - Model 36 was blued and had the same oval brand as the first model. All models or variations of the Buzz Barton Guns had a non-optical tube, rear peep sight.

Four variations of the No. 111 - Model 40 Red Ryder. Top to Bottom: first two guns have iron levers, third gun has aluminum lever, fourth gun has plastic forestock.

	C6	C8	C10
"Number 25" 1914 (pump gun), PA, RPTR, WDS, BLU (has straight stock)	40	50	75
"Number 25" 1925 (pump gun), PA RPTR, WDS, BLU (has pistol grip stock)	40	50	75
"Number 25" 1936 (pump gun), PA, RPTR, WDS, BLU (has pistol grip stock and engraved frame)	30	35	50
"Number 25" BB Gun 1986, Daisy's Centennial Commemorative Model, comes in colorful litho box, has medallion in stock	40	50	75
"Number 30" 1925 (500 shot), LA, RPTR, WDS, BLU, may also have model number	34	38	40
"Number 30" 1925 (500 shot), LA, RPTR, WDS, NIC, may also have model number	44	48	60
"Number 40" 1916, LA, RPTR, WDS, BLU, Daisy's WW II military styled gun, has full length wood stock, sling and bayonet, lack of bayonet has serious effect on price!	150	175	250
"Number 50 Golden Eagle" 1936, LA, RPTR, WDS, entire gun is copper plated, stock painted black and has special eagle decal, has rear tube sight, lack of rear tube sight has serious effect on price!	75	90	125

	C6	C8	C10
"Number 94" Red Ryder, 1955, LA, RPTR, PLAS, PNTD (1000 shot)	28	32	40
"Number 100 Model 38" 1938, BA, SS, WDS, BLU	30	35	50
"Number 101 Model 33" 1933, LA, SS, WDS, BLU	18	20	30
"Number 101 Model 36" 1936, LA, SS, WDS, BLU	18	20	30
"Number 102 Model 33" 1933, LA, RPTR, WDS, BLU (500 shot)	18	20	30
"Number 102 Model 36" 1936, LA, RPTR, WDS, BLU (500 shot)	18	20	30
"Number 102 Model 36" 1936, LA, RPTR, WDS, NIC	28	32	40
"Number 103 Model 33" 1933, LA, RPTR, WDS, NIC, has rear tube sight which must be present to realize full value!	100	115	165
"Number 103 Model 33" 1934, LA, RPTR, WDS, NIC, "Buzz Barton" variation of the above gun, has star shaped Buzz Barton brand on stock, rear sight tube must be present to realize full value!	110	120	180
"Number 104" (double barrel), 1938 BA, RPTR, WDS, BLU	300	350	500
"Number 105 Junior Pump Gun" 1932, PA, RPTR, WDS, BLU	120	140	200
"Number 107 Buck Jones Special" 1934, PA, RPTR, WDS, BLU, engraved frame, compass and sundial stock	70	80	110
"Number 108 Model 39 Carbine" 1939, LA, RPTR, WDS, BLU	45	55	75

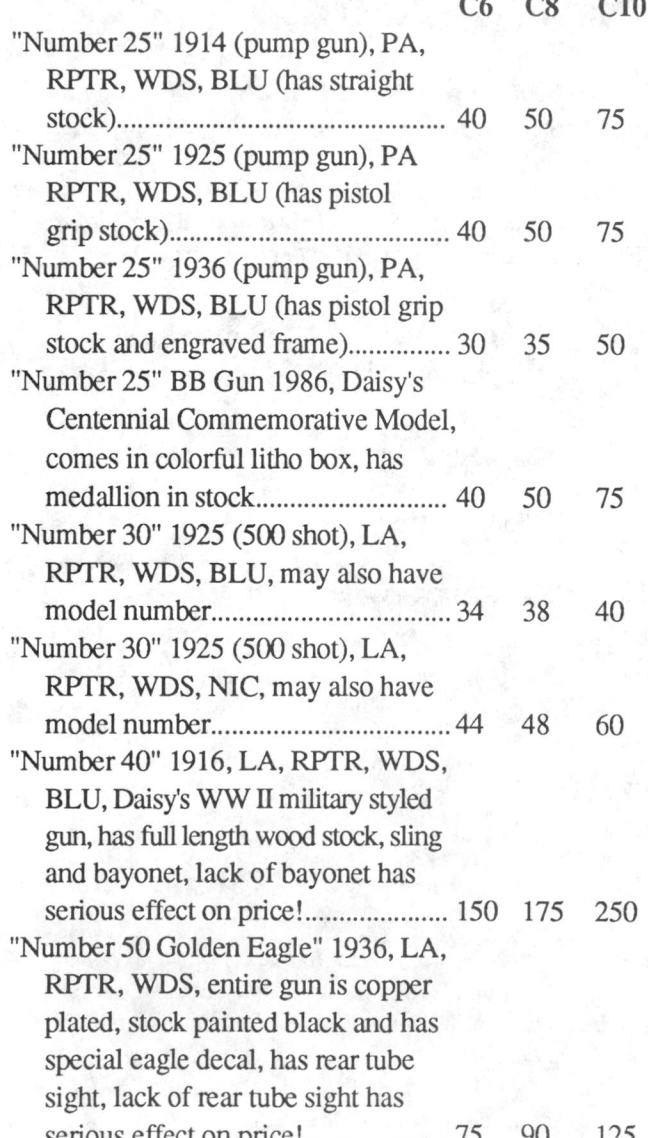

	C6	C8	C10

"Number 111 Model 40 Red Ryder"
1940, LA, RPTR, WDS, BLU, has
cast iron cocking lever and copper
plated barrel bands..........................75   90   125

"Number 111 Model 40 Red Ryder"
1941, LA, RPTR, WDS, BLU,
has cast iron cocking lever...............50   63   90

"Number 111 Model 40 Red Ryder"
1947, LA, RPTR, WDS, BLU,
has aluminum cocking lever............40   50   75

"Number 111 Model 40 Red Ryder"
1950, LA, RPTR, WDS, BLU,
has plastic forestock........................40   50   75

"Number 111 Model 40 Red Ryder"
1951, LA,RPTR, PLAS, BLU or
PNTD, both stock and forestock
are plastic..38   48   60

"Number 140 Defender" 1941, LA,
RPTR, WDS, BLU, has long
wooden forestock, dummy bolt
and bolt handle and sling...................120   140   200

"Number 195 Buzz Barton Special"
1932, LA, RPTR, WDS, BLU,
has oval Buzz Barton brand on stock.. 70   90   125

"Number 195 Model 36 Buzz Barton
Special" 1936, LA, RPTR, WDS,
BLU, has oval Buzz Barton brand
on stock..60   70   100

"Model 1938 Red Ryder" 1972, LA,
RPTR, WDS, PNTD, later variation,
similar in appearance to the earlier
variations, brand may be on left or
right side of stock.............................25   45   80

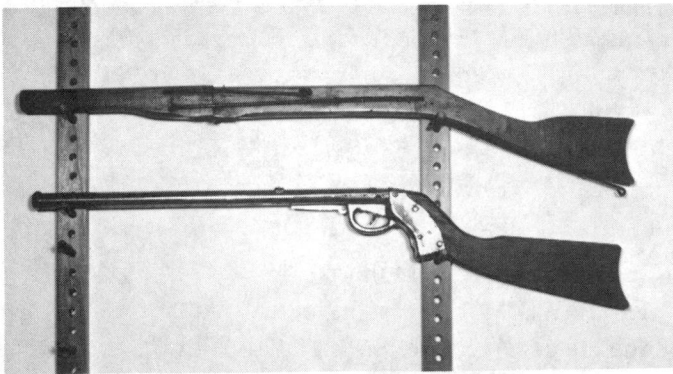

Two early Markham Guns, the all wood "Chicago" and the "New King".

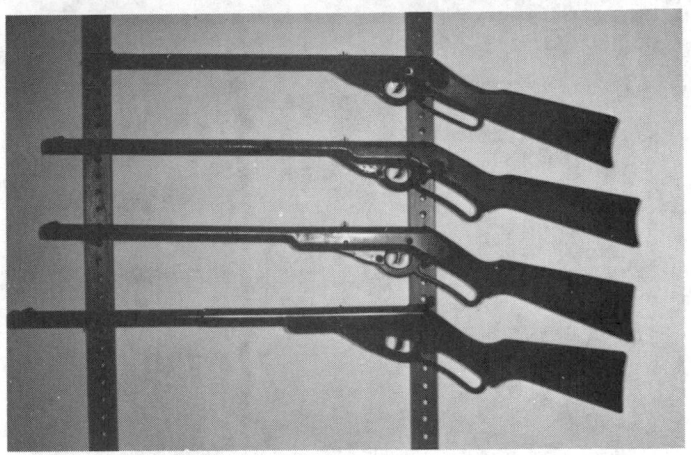

Top to Bottom: King No. 21, King No. 55, King No. 5533, King No. 5536.

MARKHAM/KING BB GUNS

	C6	C8	C10

Markham/King all Wood Guns

"Challenge" 1887, under-barrel cast
iron cocking lever, sheet metal
trigger guard, single shot, may have
no markings.....................................225   265   375

"Chicago" 1888, break action, single
shot, outside cocking rods on both
sides, oval Markham logo on stock. 90   105   150

Markham/King Metal Guns with Names

"New King" 1895, BA, SS, WDS,
NIC, stock stained red, pistol grip
stock is stamped "New King Patent
483153" in oval logo.......................80   95   135

"New King" 1896 (repeater), BA,
RPTR, WDS, NIC, repeater
variation of the above gun, has
small lever on muzzel cap used
to allow a BB to drop into the
shot tube...90   105   150

"Model D" 1905, BA, SS, WDS,
NIC, grip frame wraps around
wrist of stock, streamlined shape
without pistol grip stock...................45   55   75

"Model C" 1905, repeater variation
of the above gun................................45   55   75

"Prince" 1900, BA, SS. WDS, NIC,
has straight stock with wraparound
grip frame.. No Price Found

"Queen" 1900, BA,SS, WDS, NIC,
take down variation of the Prince.... No Price Found

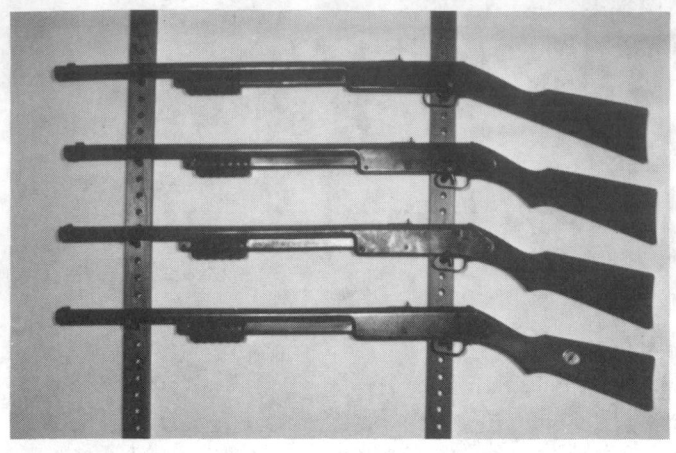

Four related guns. Top to Bottom: the "Sears & Roebuck Ranger" was made by King; the King No. 5 Pump Gun; the Daisy No. 105 Junior Pump Gun; the Daisy No. 107 Buck Jones Special with compass and sundial in the stock.

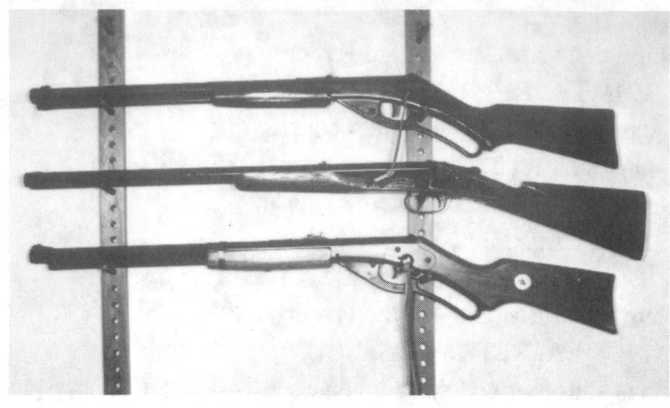

Three postwar Daisy's. Top to Bottom: The last version of the No. 111 - Model 40 Red Ryder had a plastic stock and forestock; the Model 21 Double Barrel of 1968 had a plastic stock and forestock and a painted finish; the "Christmas Story" Red Ryder was made to coincide with the movie "A Christmas Story" in 1983; due to the screenplay writer's error the Red Ryder was described in the movie as having a compass and sundial in the stock - which it never had, Daisy however went along with the error and not only made a special prop gun for use in the movie but also produced a limited number of these special Red Ryders for sale.

	C6	C8	C10

Markham/King guns with Number Designations

"Number 1" 1910, same as "Model D"
above, redesignated No. 1 in 1910.. 45   55   75

"Number 2" 1910, same as "Model C"
above, redesignated No. 2 in 1910.. 45   55   75

"Number 4" 1908 (500 shot), LA,
RPTR, WDS, NIC, frame has
octagon shape......................................100   115   175

"Number 5" 1908 (1000 shot), LA,
RPTR, WDS, NIC, frame has
octagon shape......................................100   115   175

"Number 5 Pump Gun" 1931, PA,
RPTR, WDS, BLU..........................75   100   150

"Number 5B" 1910, LA, RPTR,
WDS, BLU, a deluxe variation
of the No. 5 (above) came in a
lithographed box................................. 120   140   200

"Junior No. 10" 1910, BA, SS, WDS,
NIC.. 60   70   100

"Number 17" 1917, BA, SS, WDS,
BLU, has outside cocking rods........ 65   80   115

"Number 21" 1916, LA, SS, WDS,
NIC.. 60   70   100

"Number 22" 1916, LA, RPTR, WDS,
BLU.. 60   70   100

"Kadet No. 23" 1916, LA, RPTR,
WDS, BLU, had sling and bayonet. No Price Found

"New Chicago No. 24" 1923, BA,
SS, WDS, BLU............................... 75   90   125

"Number 2136" 1936, LA, SS, WDS,
BLU...18   21   30

"Number 2236" 1936 (500 shot), LA,
RPTR, WDS, BLU............................ 18   21   30

A near complete collection of Daisy Red Ryders makes a nice display on this office wall. There are several models displayed including No. 111 - Model 40's, Model 94's, Models 1938, 1938A and 1938B. Included are many variations of these models.

"Number 55" 1921 (1000 shot), LA,
RPTR, WDS, BLU, may have
straight or curved lever.................... 38   42   60

"Number 5533" 1933 (1000 shot),
LA, RPTR, WDS, BLU.................. 38   42   60

"Number 5536" 1936 (1000 shot),
LA, RPTR, WDS, BLU.................. 45   55   75

AIRCRAFT

by Capt. Perry R. Eichor USAF, Ret.
(See also Tin Wind-up, Comic Character, Premiums and Paper)

Aircraft in the last edition averaged $293.77 in mint condition, and this time
averaged $371.25, an increase of 26%.

The airplane, until the last several years, was one aspect of toy collecting that attracted little interest and even less enthusiasm. Prices of toy airplanes generally reflected this lethargy.

Then, suddenly, those of us born and raised during 1920-1940 (the golden age of aviation) had the time, the inclination and the means to acquire those objects on which our fantasies were transported during childhood. The scramble began, and demand and prices have been climbing steadily ever since.

Collecting toy aircraft and memorabilia has finally come into its own. As an investment, they seem a good risk, although I find few true collectors who get any joy from acquiring only objects that are guaranteed to appreciate in value. True value lies in the ability of an object to rekindle the fires of our memories and bring to mind those halcyon days of our youth when our ambitions were great, our desire simple and our potential unlimited.

The majority of us would never fly, at least not in the pilot's seat, but the future and the unknown were not limiting factors for young minds. We had not been exposed to the harsh realities of the world, and our concepts of truth, justice, freedom and opportunity were not yet jaded. Naivete was a mantle we wore proudly, for we knew the future was ours for the taking.

Pick up a Hubley Airacuda, a Tootsietoy Army Pursuit, an ID model of a P-38, or any number of other types. Make sure no one is looking. Then, with the toy in your hand, let your inner self, the child within, take over. With toy aircraft, you need not be constrained by earthly bonds, deteriorating eyesight, shortness of breath, or any of the other myriad aches and pains that announce the onslaught of middle age.

Those interested in collecting toy aircraft can limit themselves to diecast and will choose from Tootsietoy, Hubley, Erie, Manoil, Barclay, Dinky, Mercury, S.R., Solido, Tekno, C.I.J., and a host of others. Cast iron was used by numerous companies before WWII and included Hubley, Arcade, Dent and Kilgore, to name a few. Pressed steel seemed to be dominated by Wyandotte and Marx for the smaller types, while Keystone, Kingsbury and Steelcraft, among others, produced the larger types. Tin is unlimited, ranging from the pre-war types, made by Marx, Strauss, Chein, Kingsbury, Girard, American Flyer and numerous European makes, up to

the Japanese invasion of the 50's. Some of the later Japanese tin types were very accurate representations of actual aircraft, while others resembled real aircraft as much as Godzilla resembles Snow White.

Some of the nicest toy aircraft ever produced were the "Gnom" series made by Lehmann in the 1930's. These accurate small tin toys were based on two Heinkel aircraft and variations thereof. They are difficult to find and quite a nice display item.

In addition to the above, there are numerous examples of slush cast items from Barclay, Kansas Toy and Novelty, Tommy Toy, Ralstoy, etc., in addition to rubber facsimiles made by the Sun and Auburn companies. For obvious reasons, undistorted, well-preserved rubber toy aircraft are very rare.

Some excellent plastic types were produced immediately after WW II and into the 50's. Some items such as the P-38, B-25, B17 and P-40 by Renwal and the B-26 by Hubley were faithful copies, while others such as the P-39 by Ideal are so out of proportion that they lack even the symbiotic charm that often accompanies grotesqueness. Other toy manufacturers of plastic toy aircraft were Thomas, Acme, Premier, Lido, and Reliable.

Of course, if one collects toy aircraft, it follows that they must be displayed, and they really look best on the numerous toy airports depicting structures of the same time period. In addition to airfields and hangars, there were numerous ground support personnel and vehicles. As with other toys, related memorabilia begin to encroach into the aircraft collector's acquisitions.

Interest in aviation is on the rise, and the flight of the Voyager, along with numerous other record-setting craft, will have a dramatic effect on the interest in things related to flight. Consequently, prices will rise and availability will decrease out of the proportion to interest.

However, there will always be room for those of us who were excited during our youth by the sound of a rotary engine in a biplane passing overhead, doing slow rolls amoung cotton-ball clouds. We all still secretly yearn to fly with our youthful heros and perform daring feats of aerial combat. How many of you have a leather jacket in your closet? I rest my case.

Keep 'em Flying!

CAPT. PERRY R. EICHOR, USAF, RET. was born in Oklahoma and is currently living in South Carolina. His interest in aircraft toys was reborn when he was a young officer in the Air Force and his mother sent him several toys that had been his as a boy. Twenty-one years in the Air Force only served to deepen his interest in the subject. Today, when he is not out collecting, researching or writing about aeronautical toys, he works as a Criminal Justice Administrator as well as an appraiser and auctioneer.

American Flyer No. 560 Monoplane, "A.F. Lines Air Service", 1929. Courtesy Wilkinson Collection, Detroit Antique Toy Museum.

	C6	C8	C10
A. C. Gilbert "Erector" Biplane, with electric motor	150	250	500
Adam Bomb, circa 1946, wingspan approx. 11", wood and metal (also "Atom Bomb")	50	100	150
Airford, small, cast iron, two-passenger, steel wheels, single engine	45	65	125
Airplane, early 1900's, single wing, prop behind tail, pilot, open fuslage	300	450	600
Airplane, wood, ride-on	75	100	150
Airport Set No. 88 T. Cohn Co., circa 1940s, mechanical tin litho airport w/early plastic planes that fly, control tower controls for stunts, crash truck pumps water, airport bus, gasoline truck, etc.	50	100	200
American Flyer No. 560 Monoplane, "A.F. Lines Air Service", 1929, wingspan 24"	800	1200	1600
American Flyer Spirit of America, 1928, wingspan 18"	150	225	400
American Flyer Spirit of Columbia, "555", pressed tin friction, wingspan 18"	500	750	1000
American National air mail pedal plane, 1926	3000	5000	9000
"Ancient Art Metal Co., Brooklyn,N.Y." Spirit of St. Louis, c. 1927, "Pat. No. 74042", lead 5-1/8" wingspan	30	50	100
Arcade Airpane No. 361, cast iron, twin engine, "United Boeing", wingspan 4-7/8"	50	90	150
Arcade Airplane No. 3620, cast iron, tri-motor, pressed steel props, wingspan 4"	40	60	90

	C6	C8	C10
Arcade Airplane No. 3630, cast iron body, twin engine, pressed steel wing, 7" wingspan	50	90	150
Arcade Airplane No. 3640, cast iron body, single engine, pressed steel wing, body resembles Corsair, red and yellow, or blue and yellow, wingspan 10"	100	180	300
Arcade "Arcadia Airport"	650	1050	1600
Arcade Monocoupe No. 355, cast iron, steel wing, 8-1/2" wingspan	300	400	850
Arcade Monocoupe No. 357, cast iron, pull toy, 11" wingspan	250	400	850
Arcade "The Monocoupe" No. 353, 4-1/2" long	150	200	300
AA1 Auburn Rubber No. 1548 Boeing C-98 "Clipper", 8" wingspan	15	25	60
AA2 Auburn Rubber Consolidated A-11 light bomber, 4" wingspan	10	20	40
AA3 Auburn Rubber No. 586 Army Pursuit Plane, "US 1X2755" on wings, Curtiss P-37	10	15	35
AA4 Auburn Rubber Douglas DC2 Transport	20	40	75
AA5 Auburn "Jet 559"	10	15	35
AA6 Auburn Jet "XR577", 8"	35	52	70
Automatic Toy Co. Rocket and Space Ship No. 305, friction, tin litho w/rubber wheels, sparks, 9" long, 4-1/2" wide, 3" tall, late thirties	30	50	75
Automatic Toy Co. Silver Eagle, aluminum plane, wooden wheels, two-engine, 1930s, 13" wingspan	75	125	200

A.C. GILBERT "Erector" Biplane, incomplete in photo. Photo by Bill Kaufman. Courtesy Good Old Days Store.

Adam Bomb. Photo by Bill Kaufman. Courtesy Good Old Days Store.

"Ancient Art Metal Co." Lindy-type plane. Photo by Bill Kaufman.

Left to Right. Top: AA1, AA2; Bottom: AA3, AA4. Photo by Ed Poole.

American Flyer aircraft as advertised in the January, 1929 Playthings Magazine.

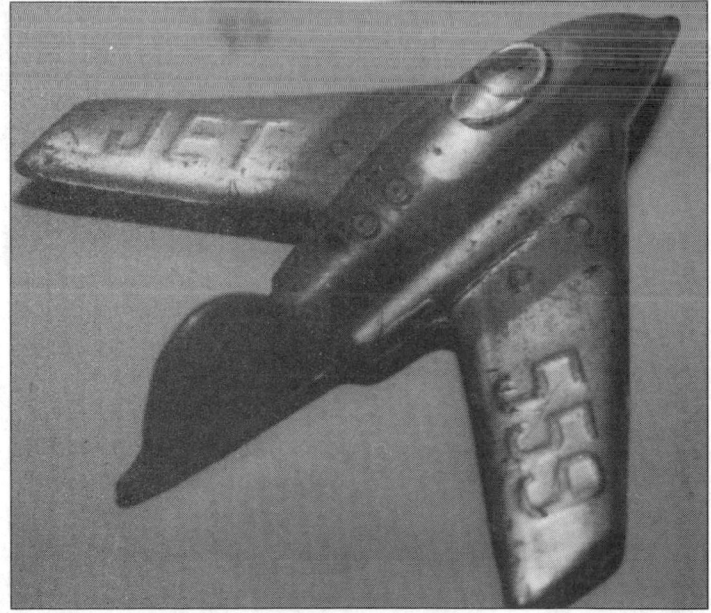

Auburn AA5 "JET 559". Photo by Max Heiss.

BARCLAY BA7. Photo by Bill Kaufman.

BARCLAY BA9. Courtesy Perry R. Eichor.

BARCLAY BA1, BA4a. Photo by Bill Kaufman. Courtesy Evelyn Besser.

BARCLAY (BA3) Monoplanes atop the firm's No. 372 Aeroplane Carrier. From the Barclay Catalog Book.

BARCLAY (BA5) No. 610 Rocket Ship. From the Barclay Catalog Book.

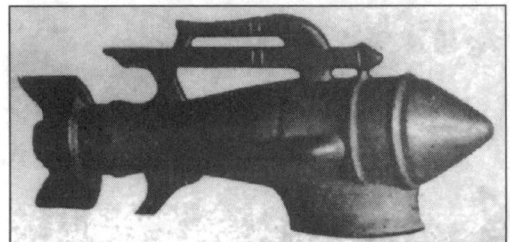

BARCLAY (BA6) No 611 Rocket Ship. From the Barclay Catalog Book.

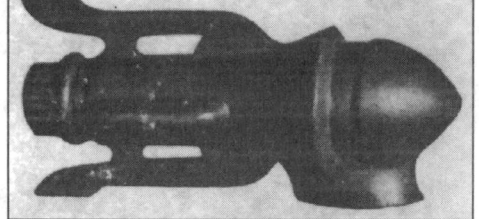

BARCLAY (BA8) "Old 307". From the Barclay Catalog Book.

BARCLAY (BA10) No. 52.

BARCLAY BA2. Photo by Bill Kaufman.

BARCLAY (BA4) No. 57 Giant Zeppelin. From the Barclay Catalog Book.

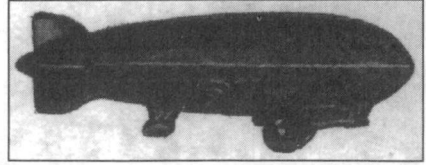

BARCLAY AIRCRAFT

	C6	C8	C10
BA 1 307 Lindy-type plane, early-mid 30s, wingspan approx. 4-3/8" long..	15	20	30
BA 1a 307 Monoplane, single engine..	15	20	30
BA 2 The Atlantic Bremen, c. 1928.....	20	30	50
BA 3 Monoplane, single engine, high wing, Crackajack size, one-piece, sold with Aeroplane Carrier and piggy-back on 195 Aeroplane..........	10	15	20
BA 4 No. 57 Giant Zeppelin.................	17	23	35
BA 4a Dirigible, early-mid 30s, 4-3/8".	25	40	60
BA 5 610 Rocket Ship...........................	25	40	60
BA 6 611 Rocket Ship...........................	25	40	60
BA 7 195 Aeroplane, "U.S.Army", single engine transport, 3-3/4" wingspan.......	17	25	40
BA 7a 195 Aeroplane w/BA3 monoplane piggy-backed on it..................	30	45	60

BARCLAY BA7b. Courtesy Hank Anton.

Big Bang Bombing Plane No. 11-P, steel propellor. Courtesy Sotheby's New York.

	C6	C8	C10
BA 7b 195 Aeroplane w/clip of bombs attached to it	25	35	60
BA 8 "Old 307"	15	20	30
BA 9 Thick-winged monoplane, approx. 2-1/2" long w/oversized wheels in 1935 Butler Bros. Catalog	20	25	35
BA 10 No. 52 Small Lindy-type plane	6	9	12

BEST - see KANSAS TOY & NOVELTY

	C6	C8	C10
Big Bang Bombing Plane No. 11-P, cast iron, single barrel, die-cast propellor, 13" long	600	900	1500
Big Bang Bombing Plane No. 11-P, cast iron, double barrel, steel propellor, 13" long	400	650	900

	C6	C8	C10
Biplane, wooden, tin tail, aluminum propellor, pull plane, propeller spins, approx. 7-1/2" wingspan	40	70	125
Boycraft "NX-130", high wing monoplane, pressed steel, 22" wingspan	350	525	850
Buddy L. No. 603 Transport Airplane (Ford), c. 1946, 27" wingspan	300	450	600
Buddy L. No. 959 Army Tank Transport Plane, 2 detachable tanks under wings, tanks have hum motor device, pressed steel, 1941, 27" wingspan	400	600	800
Buddy L. No. 2007 Monoplane and Catapult Hanger, 1930-31	750	1000	1500
Buddy L. No. 5000 single high wing monoplane, 1929-31	200	250	500
Buddy L. No. 5010 Triple Hangar and three planes, 1931, planes are monocoupes	750	1200	2250

C.A.W. NOVELTY COMPANY - THE INVISIBLE COMPANY

By Fred Maxwell, Slushmold Contributing Editor and Perry Eichor, Aircraft Contributing Editor, with the assistance of Gary Franson and The Clay Center Historical Society.

Charles A. Wood was known as the "Pioneer Birdman" in Clay Center, Kansas. Master aircraft mechanic, early pilot and aviation booster, his emphasis on aircraft in his toy line reflected his life-long love. And like aircraft, his toys have been too invisible. As a toymaker, did he fly too high?

Wood's line was heavy with miniature airplanes for he was a pilot, an aviation mechanic and an air enthusiast. It was even reported he flew his toys to Eastern markets; this could have been true under special circumstances only, for in its best years (over 60 employees and two million toys) the company output would have been too large to "ship by air". Perhaps he was more doer than publicist.

In comparing his toys and others, we see that he didn't take any shortcuts: a Ford Trimotor with the landing gear and outboard motors on struts; pilots' heads showing through open cockpit windows; a most realistic model of Ben Howard's famous stunt-plane with "Mr. Mulligan" prominently embossed. All of his pieces are more models than toys; miniature souvenirs of history; replicas of famous aircraft, local airliners and mailplanes.

A few years ago Fred found a neat little monoplane with initials "C.A.W." under the tail plane. Putting the pressure on his Kansas friends, he finally found a mint collection. Because Wood was such an activist a brief biography may be of interest. Born about 1891. Went to work for Longren Aircraft Mfg. Co., Topeka, Ks. in 1915. Opened the toy factory in Clay Center in 1925. Was influential in establishing a local airport in a wheat field in 1929. Received pilots license, bought a Waco F biplane, erected a Butler hangar and opened a repair service in 1930. He was active in persuading Midland Air Express and Western Air Express lines to make route stops there in 1931. This put this County Seat on the air map.

In 1938, during National Airmail Week, he flew a commemorative load (wish I had one of those First Day Covers) from Morganville to Kansas City. One mail sack was delivered to the airfield by a "Pony Express" horseman. During the war he was an instructor at a Naval Training Center. Later, he owned a Rearwin plane, was a Piper Cub dealer, and in 1955 designed and built a monoplane dubbed "Little Monster". He continued to fly until 1976 - a grand old man of early aviation.

Note: A sales flyer of C&H Mfg.Co. was issued about 1940. All evidence suggests this sheet covered only toys originally from C.A.W.

Note: Wood's early production had metal disk wheels with painted black "tires". Later toys had rubber or plastic wheels. All aircraft had cast propellers, tapered and rounded wings except C.W.A

C.A.W. NOVELTY CO.:
Back Row: CWA 1, CWA 2, CWA 8, CWA 6;
Front Row: CWA 5, CWA 9, CWA 7.
Photo by Perry Eichor.

C.A.W. NOVELTY CO., CWA 1. Courtesy of Gary Franson

	C6	C8	C10
CWA1 Small monoplane, high wing Lindy type, 6 cyl. radial engine, negative dihedral in wings, see #41 set, 2-3/8" x 2-1/8"	15	20	30
CWA2 Small monoplane, high wing racing type, V8 engine, closed cockpit in front of wing, 6 windows, "C A W" & "Pat, appld. for", under tailplane, 2-5/8" x 2-1/2"	30	45	60
CWA2b ? Small monoplane, similar to above, except no markings and			

	C6	C8	C10
stubbier wings (CAW copy?)	34	51	68
CWA3 Monoplane, high wing, Ford model 2 ?, V12 engine, 8 window + 2 restroom, crew of 2 in open cockpit behind wing, tail wheel, 3-5/8" x 3-1/2", C.A.W.?	20	25	40
CWA4 Monoplane, same as above with closed cockpit ahead of wing, no crew, C.A.W.?	10	20	35

C.A.W. NOVELTY CO., Left to Right: CWA 3, CWA 4, CWA 2. Photo by Fred Maxwell.

	C6	C8	C10
CWA5 Small monoplane, Amphibian, Douglas Dolphin?, bimotored, see #41 set, 2-1/4" x 2-1/2"	20	30	40
CWA6 Monoplane, larger version of CWA5, 3-1/4" x 3-5/8"	20	30	45

C.A.W. NOVELTY CO.: Top Row: CWA 13, CWA 9, CWA 8; Bottom Row: CWA 11, CWA 12. Photo by Perry Eichor.

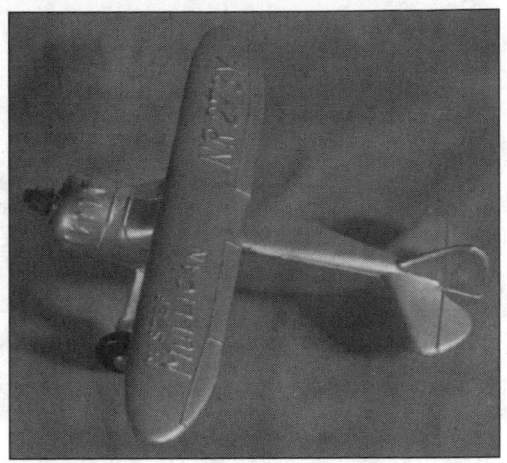

C.A.W. NOVELTY CO.: CWA 10. Courtesy Perry Eichor.

C.A.W. NOVELTY CO.: CWA7. Courtesy of Gary Franson.

	C6	C8	C10
CWA7 Monoplane, #12, Ford Trimotor model 4, 7 cyl. radial engines, outboards and landing gear on struts, tail wheel, complex molding, 3-1/8" x 4-3/8"	60	90	120
CWA8 Jr. LOW WING MONOPLANE #28, Lockheed or Northrop? Cowled radial engine, 6 windows, pilot in open cockpit near tail, (modern copy available, in different finish and "wire" wheels, 2-7/8" x 3")	20	40	60
CWA9 Sr.LOW WING MONOPLANE #29, larger version of above, tail wheel, 3-3/4" x 4"	20	40	60
CWA10 Mr. MULLIAGAN AIRPLANE #34, high wing, "Mr. Mulligan", "NR-273Y", cowled radial engine, 2 windows, 2 doors, circa 1936 production, 3" x 3-1/2"	40	80	120
CWA11 BOEING BOMBER #36,			

	C6	C8	C10
low wing "Boeing", "NC 13361", "Made in USA", bimotored, 3 bladed props, called a "bomber" (war was in the air), it looks like a Boeing mod. 247 airliner, 2-5/8" x 3-1/2"	20	40	60
CWA12 ARMY PURSUIT PLANE #37, low wing "Seversky" P-37 monoplane, under wings is Air Corps "star-in-circle", "37" and "Made in USA", cowled radial engine, 2-7/8" x 3-1/2"	30	60	80
CWA13 Monoplane, low wing cabin or pursuit plane, cowled radial engine, forward cockpit, divided windshield, open windows w/pilot's head inside, 3-1/2" x 3-5/8"	20	40	60
CWA14 ? Large monoplane, high wing Lindy Ryan type, but V8 engine, oversized propeller, 5 windows and door, probably C.A.W	No Price Found		
CWA15 Small biplane,(this from the maker's own mouth, but no description available)Has not been seen	No Price Found		
CWA16 THREE PIECE AIRPLANE SET #41, apparently 2 types, see CWA1 and CWA5, above	No Price Found		
"Champion" high wing monoplane, cast iron, 5" long	90	135	180
Dayton No. 700 high wing monoplane, open cockpit and pilot, red, yellow or blue, painted disc wheels, 13" wingspan	125	250	400
Dent "Air Express, cast iron, 12" wingspan	750	1200	1500

DENT "Air Express". Courtesy Wilkinson Collection-Detroit Antique Toy Museum.

DENT "Lucky Boy" Glider.

DENT "Los Angeles" dirigible.

	C6	C8	C10
Dent "Air Express", cast iron, trimotor, 11-1/2" wingspan	1500	2400	300
Dent "Airline" monoplane, "?" on fuselage, cast aluminum, stripes on rudder, 12-1/2" wingspan	700	1050	1400
Dent "Airline" monoplane, "X5043" cast on rudder, cast iron, 12-1/2" wingspan	500	750	1000
Dent Ford Trimotor, cast iron, #1417 cast on rudder above "Ford", 12" wingspan	800	1400	2000
Dent "Lindy", cast iron, 12-1/2" wingspan	1000	1700	2400
Dent "Los Angeles" dirigible, cast iron, circa 1925, 13" long	1000	1500	2000
Dent "Los Angeles" dirigible, cast iron, 1920s, 10-3/4"	1000	1700	2800
Dent "Los Angeles" dirigible, cast iron, circa 1925, 8-1/2"	450	675	900
Dent "Los Angeles", dirigible, circa 1932, 6-3/4"	130	200	300
Dent "Lucky Boy" 4" wingspan	300	450	600
Dent "Lucky Boy" cast iron, X6043 cast on rudder, 12-1/2" wingspan	600	1000	1400
Dent "Lucky Boy" trimotor, cast iron, 7" wingspan	500	750	1000
Dent "Lucky Boy Glider", cast iron, high wing, 6-1/2" wingspan	225	500	750
Dent "Question Mark" trimotor, cast iron, "?", on fuselage, 12" wingspan	1200	2000	3000

	C6	C8	C10
Dent "Zep" Zeppelin, cast iron, 6-1/2" long	150	280	375
Dent "Zep" Zeppelin, cast iron, 5"	100	150	200
Dent "Zep" Zeppelin, aluminum, 5" long	60	90	120

ERIE, Left to Right: E1, E2, E3. Photo by Perry R. Eichor.

	C6	C8	C10
Erie E1 Single seat open cockpit Northrup Gamma	40	75	100
Erie E2 2-place open cockpit, "U.S. Army" on wings	25	40	60
Erie E3 Northrup Delta single engine passenger airliner	30	60	125

ERIE, Left to Right, E4, E5. Photo by Perry R. Eichor.

	C6	C8	C10
Eric E4 Boeing 247 twin engine "U.S. Army"	25	45	70
Erie E5 Boeing B-17	25	60	125
Fighter, tin, circa 1940, single engine, 4 machine guns mounted on wing	20	30	60
"Flagship America" airplane, metal Ford Tri-Motor, pressed steel, 1930s, 25" wingspan	175	250	400
Girard High-wing Monoplane, pressed steel, 10" wingspan	125	250	470
Girard High-wing Monoplane, pressed steel, 18" wingspan	150	500	750
Girard Whiz Skyfighter biplane, early	85	130	170
Glass Airplane, candy container, 5" long	75	112	150
Helicopter, Army, tin litho, friction drive, spinning prop, 13" long	20	25	45

HUBLEY

	C6	C8	C10
H1 "America" cast iron, largest cast iron plane made, trimotor, open cockpit, pilot, copilot, 17" wingspan	2000	4000	6000

HUBLEY H1.

HUBLEY H2. Photo by Perry R. Eichor.

	C6	C8	C10
H2 Bell Airacuda, XFM-1, diecast, red and silver, folding landing gear, movable guns in front of twin pusher engines, 3-bladed props, new in 1940	100	150	250
H3 No. 377 "Lindy" cast iron, single engine, 3-1/2" wingspan	25	38	75
H4 No. 431 U.S. Army Plane, diecast, white rubber tires, enclosed in cast fairings, single engine, low wing monoplane, 5-1/2" wingspan	15	25	40
H5 No. 389 twin engine, cast iron, painted and nickle plate, "TAT NC 431", 5-5/8" wingspan	25	50	75
H6 Twin engine, silver and red or green, 3-3/8" wingspan	20	40	50
H7 No. 430 Jet, diecast, single engine, folding wings, retractable landing gear, cast cockpit, red and silver or blue and silver, 6" wingspan	12	20	40
H8 "U.S.N. 3-B-4" diecast, twin engine, twin vertical stabilizer, retractable landing gear, 5-1/8" wingspan	15	20	45

HUBLEY, Left: H3 and Right; H5. Photo by Perry R. Eichor.

HUBLEY H9. *Photo by Perry R. Eichor.*

HUBLEY H17, *cockpit variations. Photo by Perry R. Eichor.*

HUBLEY H19. *Photo by Perry R. Eichor.*

	C6	C8	C10
H9 "Lindy", cast iron, 10" wingspan....	500	900	1200
H10 "Lindy", cast iron, prop turns via gear attached to wheel, 10" wingspan.	750	1200	3000
H11 "Lindy", cast iron, w/"Spirit of St. Louis" decals, ratchet drive action noisemaker, has wing struts..	1200	2500	4000
H12 "Bremen", aluminum, 6-1/2" wingspan..................................	250	500	1000
H13 "Bremen", cast iron, 6-1/2" wingspan..	200	500	1000
H13A "Bremen", cast iron, 7" wingspan.	500	1000	1500
H14 "Bremen", cast iron, "Junkers Bremen" on fuselage, open cockpit w/2 pilots, prop turned by wheels, 10" wingspan.....................................	1000	5000	10,000
H15 "America", cast iron, single engine, wire spring drive, w/2 pilots in open cockpit, 17" wingspan......................	2000	7500	12,000
H16 "Friendship", cast iron seaplane, "Fokker" embossed on fuselage, 13" wingspan..................................	1500	3250	6000
H17 "U.S. Army" diecast, low wing, single engine monoplane, folding wheels, silver and red (early versions had red wood hubs w/white rubber tires - cast cockpit may have openings or be cast or solid), introduced in 1939, 8" wingspan..	25	40	80
H18 "U.S. Army", plastic, like above, folding wheels, "U.S. Army" embossed on horizontal stabilizer, 6" wingspan...	15	25	40
H19 No. 326 Attack Bomber, plastic, retractable landing gear Martin B-26 Marauder copy, 7-7/8" wingspan....	20	30	60

	C6	C8	C10
H20 P-39, diecast and tin, "U.S. Army" imprinted on rear horizon stabilizers, tin wings are 5-1/2"........	20	30	55
H21 No. 495 on wings, single engine, diecast, folding wings, retractable landing gear, sliding plastic cockpit (numerous versions, and later packaged as "American Eagle" or "Flying Circus), 11-1/2" wingspan:			
Early - red & silver, 4-bladed prop, no airscoop on top of engine cowl...	38	60	100
Mid - two tone blue, red cowl, large airscoop atop engine cowl, 4-bladed prop...	25	38	50
Late - orange & yellow, large airscoop, either 4 or 2-bladed prop..	15	22	30
H22 No. 433 Piper Club, red, also in olive drab L-4 version, 7-7/8" wingspan	10	20	40
H23 P-40, diecast, early version was silver & red w/3-bladed prop, later version orange & yellow w/2-bladed prop, 8" wingspan.............................	20	35	50

HUBLEY planes, as shown in the December, 1929 Butler Bros. Catalog.

HUBLEY, Left to Right: H7, H20, H22. Photo by Perry R. Eichor.

HUBLEY H21, early and later versions. Photo by Perry R. Eichor.

	C6	C8	C10
H24 P-38, diecast, red & silver, retractable landing gear, later versions are yellow & green camouflage, 12-5/8" wingspan	45	80	125
H25 No. 467, diecast, folding wings, retractable landing gear, plastic cockpit, resembles Brewster Buffalo, red & silver w/4-bladed prop in early version, later version was green & yellow w/2-blade prop, 8-5/8" wingspan	15	35	60
H26 No. 751 folding delta wing jet, diecast, retractable landing gear, red & silver plastic cockpit, 6-1/8" wingspan	12	20	40
H27 No. 427 Crusader, diecast, twin engine, twinboom "TAT NC-31", 5-1/8" wingspan	25	45	80
H28 No. 303 cast iron, low wing single engine monoplane, nickel plate wings & prop w/various colored body, 5" wingspan	40	75	100
H29 No. 305 cast iron, low wing single engine monoplane, nickel plate wings & prop, 3-3/4" wingspan	20	40	60
H30 No. 304 Giro plane, cast iron w/nickel plate rotor, prop & engine.	40	60	125

HUBLEY H24, two variations. Photo by Perry R. Eichor.

HUBLEY, Left to Right: H25, H23. Photo by Perry R. Eichor.

HUBLEY, Left to Right:
H28, H29, H8, H4.
Photo by Perry R. Eichor.

HUBLEY, Left to Right: H33, H18. Photo by Perry R. Eichor.

HUBLEY H31, DO-X.

HUBLEY H27. Photo by
Perry R. Eichor.

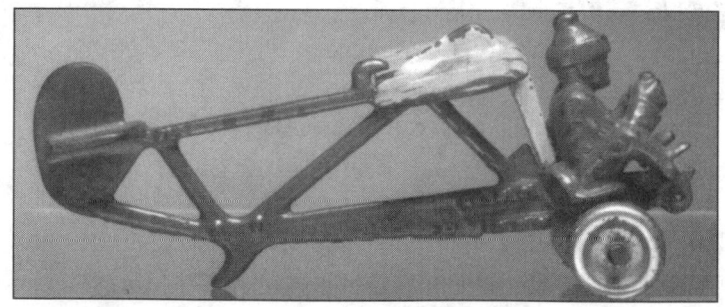

HUBLEY H34. Courtesy Sotheby's New York.

	C6	C8	C10
H31 302 DO-X, cast iron, high wing seaplane, 6 engine, 4" wingspan.....	50	75	125
H32 DO-X cast iron, larger version of above, 5" wingspan....................	70	100	200
H33 Hellcat, plastic, 9-1/4" wingspan..	10	15	20
H34 "Lindy" Glider, cast iron, 6-1/4" long...	300	700	1200

	C6	C8	C10
H35 Helicopter......................................	55	82	110
H36 "Question Mark" Trimotor, 12-1/2" wingspan.............................	1500	2750	4250
H37 Lockheed Sirius, "Lindy NR-211", 9" long..	1200	2200	3500
H38 "Air Ford" cast iron, 2 open cockpits, 4" long.................................	100	150	200

I.D. PLANES

The popularly called "black I.D. planes" were manufactured during World War II primarily as training aids initially for the U.S. Navy and then U.S. Army. The WW II airplanes covered in this section were all made in 1/72 scale (1" - 6'), all were colored black, and usually marked on the bottom in raised lettering with (1) the country of ownership/design (U.S., British, German, etc), (2) the aircraft type (P-38, Spitfire, FW 189, etc), and date of model issue (7-42, 8-42, 5-42, etc.).

While the program reportedly started the day after Pearl Harbor, the earliest marking on any of the known models is 5-42. (The dates so marked on the planes are dates of model issue or copright, not the date the actual plane became operational) Some of the early WW II attempts at manufacturing these identification aircraft used materials such as reinforced plaster (too lumpy), paper-mache (too little detail), a hard rubber-like material (too pliable for long sections like wings), Wood's metal and even cast iron (too heavy for shipping and perhaps needed elsewhere).

The vast majority of these I-D aircraft were molded by the Cruver Company of Chicago. The master molds were made by either the Comet Engraving Company or H & H Specialty Company, also both of Chicago. A few models were produced (molded) by Design Center and Leominster as noted in the listing.

While these airplanes were manufactured for our Armed Forces, Polk's Hobbies of New York did sell some domestically under the Aristo-Craft name. Most of the surviving WW II types, though, were probably midnight requisitioned by pilot or gunner trainees. The quantity produced during the War was staggering. *Flying* magazine of February, 1944 states that Cruver had manufactured over 2,000,000 model aircraft since the spring of 1941 (sic-they meant spring of 1942). Not many remain today.

The following listing of WW II model planes was taken from the most complete compilation known; it may not be totally inclusive nor may all of these planes have been made in quantity. The best story of all types of I.D. aircraft made from different materials and in different scales as well as those of the later Korean War vintage was well covered by Robert C. Mikesh in his excellent article in the May/June 1984 issue of *Fine Scale Modeler* magazine.

You will note in the guide that not much distinction is made between the values for similar size models. There is just not enough buying and selling nor large enough collections to accurately determine which plane is more rare than another. They could all be equally hard to find today.

As to grading, C10 is just that - no scuffs, no warpage, no "prune-skin", no repainting or, in other words, a brand new 45-year-old airplane. C8 covers models that are very nice; planes should be complete with wheels or floats if on originally; free of serious defects like "prune-skin" or missing parts, and not repainted (restored maybe). The C6 grade covers everything else and likely includes the majority of the models still in existence.

A special thanks is due to master modeler Ray ".43 Magnum" Wheeler of Lilburn, GA for his help in identifying some of the more obscure types listed.

Comments and especially documented corrections are always welcome.

WW II IDENTIFICATION MODELS
1/72 SCALE
(Black I.D. Airplanes)

Reproductions of many of these planes can be purchased from Classic Aircraft Collections, Ltd., of Fort Worth, Texas. A free brochure may be ordered by calling 1-800-245-0576.

Each model is identified by type and date marked.

	C6	C8	C10
UNITED STATES			
A-20 Havoc, 6-42	25	37	50
A-24 Dauntless, SBD - 3, 7-42	15	22	30
A-26 Invader, 2-44	25	37	50
A-29 Hudson (PBO-16), none	25	37	50
A-30 Baltimore, 2-43	25	37	50
A-31 Vengeance, 7-42	15	22	30
A-31 Vengeance, 7-44	15	22	30

	C6	C8	C10
A-35 Vengeance, 4-44	15	22	30
AT17 Bobcat*, 7-43	25	37	50
B-17 Flying Fortress, 7-42	50	75	100
B-24 Liberator, 7-42	50	75	100
B-25 Mitchell, 7-42	25	37	50
B-26 Marauder, 10-42	25	37	50
B-26 Marauder, none	25	37	50
B-29 Super Fortress, 3-44	50	75	100

ID PLANE, U.S. B-29 Super Fortress, 9/44. MacNary Collection. Courtesy RLM.

ID PLANE, U.S. P-38 Lightning. MacNary Collection. Courtesy RLM.

	C6	C8	C10
B-29 Super Fortress, 9-44	50	75	100
B-29 Super Fortress, none	50	75	100
B-32 Dominator, 12-44	50	75	100
C-46 Commando, 3-43	25	37	50
C-47 Skytrain, 3-43	25	37	50
C-47 Skytrain**, 5-43	25	37	50
C-54 Skymaster, 3-43	50	75	100
C60A Lodestar, 3-43	25	37	50
C69 Constellation, 4-44	50	75	100
C78 Bobcat, 6-44	25	37	50
C87 Liberator, 3-44	50	75	100
CG-4A Waco Glider, 6-43	15	22	30
F4F-4 Wildcat, 5-43	15	22	30
F4U-1 Corsair, 3-43	15	22	30
F6F Hellcat, 4-43	15	22	30
GH-1 Nightingale*, 5-43	25	37	50
J2F-4 Duck, 12-42	30	45	60
JRF OA-09 Goose*, 7-43	30	45	60
JRS-1 (S43), 11-42	30	45	60
JR2S-1 (S44) Excalibur, 11-44	60	90	120
L-1 Vigilant, 3-43	25	37	50
L-2 Grasshopper, 7-44	25	37	50
L-4 Grasshopper, 2-43	25	37	50
L-5 Sentinel, 1-44	25	37	50
OS2U (on floats)*, 2-43	25	37	50
OS2U (on wheels)*, 2-43	25	37	50
OS2U-1 (on floats), 7-43	25	37	50
PBM - 3 Mariner, 6-43	30	45	60
PBY-5 Catalina, 5-43	30	45	60
PB2Y-3 Coronado, 4-43	60	90	120
PV-1 (B-39) Ventura, 5-43	25	37	50
PV-2 Harpoon, 5-43	25	37	50
P-38 Lightning, 7-42	25	37	50
P-39 Airacobra, 6-42	15	22	30
P-40 Warhawk, 9-42	15	22	30
P-40 Warhawk, 4-44	15	22	30
P-43 Lancer, 5-43	15	22	30

	C6	C8	C10
P-47 Thunderbolt, 9-42	15	22	30
P-47 (D) Thunderbolt, 2-44	15	22	30
P-47 (N) Thunderbold, 4-45	15	22	30
P-47 Thunderbolt*, none	15	22	30
P-51 Mustang, 6-42	15	22	30
P-51D Mustang, 4-45	15	22	30
P-61 Black Widow, 2-44	25	37	50
P-63 King Cobra, 5-44	15	22	30
P-80 Shooting Star, 4-45	15	22	30
SB2A-2 Buccaneer, 5-43	15	22	30
SB2C-1 Helldiver, 3-43	15	22	30
SB2C-2 Helldiver, 2-45	15	22	30
SB2C-2 Helldiver, (floats)*, 3-43	25	37	50
SB2C-2 Helldiver, (wheels)*, 3-43	25	37	50
SB2U-3 Vindicator, 6-43	15	22	30
SNJ-2 Texan, 7-42	15	22	30
SNJ-3 Texan, 7-42	15	22	30
S03C-1 Seagull (floats), 3-43	25	37	50
S03C-2 Seagull (wheels), 3-43	25	37	50
SR-10B Reliant, 10-42	25	37	50
TBD-1 Devastator, 5-43	15	22	30
TBF Avenger, 7-43	15	22	30

* - molded by Design Center
** - molded by Leominster
All other molded by Cruver

ID PLANE/JR2S1 (S44) Excalibur. MacNary Collection. Courtesy RLM.

ID PLANE, British, Left to Right: Spitfire 9B (10/44), Spitfire 8/42. MacNary Collection. Courtesy RLM.

BRITISH

	C6	C8	C10
Albacore, 8-42	30	45	60
Albemarle, 9-44	25	37	50
Barracuda, 2-43	15	22	30
Beaufighter 1, 9-42	25	37	50
Beaufighter 2, 9-42	25	37	50
Beaufighter 6, 5-44	25	37	50
Beaufort, 9-42	25	37	50
Beaufort, none	25	37	50
Blenheim IV, 8-42	25	37	50
Boomerang (Aust.)*, none	15	22	30
Botha, 8-42	25	37	50
Defiant, 8-42	15	22	30
Firefly, 2-43	15	22	30
Fulmar, 8-42	15	22	30
Halifax, 9-42	50	75	100
Hampden, 8-42	25	37	50
Hastings, none	50	75	100
Horsa, 9-44	25	37	50
Hotspur, 6-43	15	22	30
Hurricane, 8-43	15	22	30
Lancaster, 4-43	50	75	100
Lerwick, 9-42	30	45	60
Lysander, 7-43	25	37	50
Manchester, 8-42	25	37	50
Maryland, 2-43	25	37	50
Mosquito, 3-43	25	37	50

	C6	C8	C10
Roc, 8-42	15	22	30
Skua, 8-42	15	22	30
Spitfire, 8-42	15	22	30
Spitfire, 1-44	15	22	30
Spitfire 9A, 10-44	15	22	30
Spitfire 9B, 10-44	15	22	30
Spitfire 22, 7-45	15	22	30
Stirling, 5-42	50	75	100
Sunderland, 9-42	60	90	120
Swordfish, 9-42	30	45	60
Tempest 2, 3-45	15	22	30
Tempest 5, 10-44	15	22	30
Typhoon, 6-43	15	22	30
Walrus, 4-44	25	37	50
Wellington 2, 9-42	25	37	50
Wellington 3, 9-42	25	37	50
Whirlwind, 8-43	25	37	50
Whitley, 9-42	25	37	50
York, 9-44	50	75	100

GERMAN

	C6	C8	C10
Arado Ar196, 12-43	25	37	50
Blohm & Voss BV138, 5-44	50	75	100
Blohm & Voss HA139, 11-42	60	90	120
Blohm & Voss BV222, 2-44	60	90	120
DFS 230, 8-43	15	22	30
Dornier DO 172, 9-42	25	37	50
Dornier DO 215, 9-42	25	37	50
Dornier DO 217E, 8-42	25	37	50
Fi 156 Storch, none	25	37	50
Focke Wulf FW 187, 8-42	25	37	50
Focke Wulf FW 189, 5-42	25	37	50
Focke Wulf FW 190, 7-42	15	22	30
Focke Wulf FW 190, 12-42	15	22	30
Focke Wulf 200, 3-44	50	75	100
Focke Wulf FW 200K, 9-42	50	75	100
Gotha Go 242, 7-42	25	37	50
Heinkel He 111, 9-42	25	37	50

ID PLANE, German, Focke Wulf FW189, with box. MacNary Collection. Courtesy RLM.

FW 189

	C6	C8	C10
Heinkel He 112, 7-42	15	22	30
Heinkel He 113, 5-42	15	22	30
Heinkel He 113, 9-42	15	22	30
Heinkel He 115K, 9-42	30	45	60
Henschel Hs 126, 10-42	25	37	50
Henschel Hs 129, 8-44	25	37	50
Junkers Ju 52, 8-42	50	75	100
Junkers Ju 86K, 9-42	25	37	50
Junkers Ju 87B, 8-42	15	22	25
Junkers Ju 88, 9-42	25	37	50
Junkers Ju 90, 9-42	50	75	100
Junkers Ju 188, 7-44	25	37	50
Messers. Me 109E, 7-42	15	22	30
Messers. Me 109F, 7-42	15	22	30
Messers. Me 110, 8-42	25	37	50
Messers. Me 210, 7-43	25	37	50

* - Molded by Design Center
** - Molded by Leominster
All others molded by Cruver

ITALIAN

	C6	C8	C10
Cantiere Z. 506B, 9-42	50	75	100
Cantiere Z. 1007, 9-42	30	45	60
Caproni CA. 133, 9-42	50	75	100
Fiat BR. 20, 6-42	25	37	50
Fiat CR. 42, 9-42	30	45	60
Fiat CR. 42, 1-43	30	45	60
Fiat G. 50, 8-42	15	22	30
Macchi C. 200, 8-42	15	22	30
Macchi MC. 202, 3-43	15	22	30
Piaggio P. 32 BIS, 9-42	15	37	50
Reggiane Rc. 2000, 9-42	15	22	30
Reggiane Re. 2001, 3-43	15	22	30
Savoia Marchetti 79, 9-42	30	45	60
Savoia Marchetti 81, 9-42	50	75	100
Savoia Marchetti 82, 9-42	30	45	60
Savoia Marchetti 84, 4-43	30	45	60

JAPANESE

	C6	C8	C10
(Adam) Naka. 97, 11-42	25	37	50
(Ann) Mitsu. T-98, 7-42	25	37	50
(Babs) Mitsu. T-97, 6-42	25	37	50
Betty (G4M1), 9-43	25	37	50
Betty (G4M2), 4-45	25	37	50
(Claude) Mitsu. T-96, 6042	25	37	50
(Dave) Naka. T-95-NOB, 7-42	25	37	50
Dinah (Ki46), 8-44	25	37	50
Emily (H8K2), 3-45	25	37	50
Francis (PIY), 3-45	25	37	50
Frank (Ki84), 5-45	15	22	30
	C6	C8	C10

	C6	C8	C10
George (NIKI-J), 5-45	15	22	30
Hamp (T-00, Zeke 32), 7-43	15	22	30
Helen (Ki49), -44	25	37	50
(Ida) Mitsu. T-98 ALB, 6-42	25	37	50
Irving (J1N1), *5-45	25	37	50
Jack (J2M1), 12-44	15	22	30
Jake (E13A), 9-44	25	37	50
Jill (B6N)*, 5-45	15	22	30
Judy (D4Y), 3-45	15	22	30
(Kate) Naka. T-97, 6-42	15	22	30
Lily (Ki48), 9-43	25	37	50
(Mary) T-97 ALB, 6-42	25	37	50
(Mavis) Kawa., 11-42	60	90	120
Myrt (C6N), 3-45	15	22	30
(Nate) "97" Fighter, 9-42	25	37	50
(Nell) Mitsu. T-96, 6-42	25	37	50
Nell (G3M), 1-44	25	37	50
Nick (Ki45), 8-44	25	37	50
Oscar T-01 (Ki43), 9-43	15	22	30
Paul 14, Exp*, 12-44	25	37	50
Pete (F1M2), 6-43	30	45	60
Rufe (A6M2-N), 8-43	25	37	50
(Sally) Mitsu. T-97, 6-42	25	37	50
(Sonia) Mitsu. T-99, 7-42	15	22	30
Tojo (Ki44), 6-44	15	22	30
Tojo (Ki44), 3-45	15	22	30
Tony (Ki61), 4-45	15	22	30
(Topsy) Mitsu. MC-20, 10-42	25	37	50
(Val) Aichi T-99, 6-42	25	37	50
Val T-99 MK2, 8-43	25	37	50
(Zeke) Mitsu. 00, 9-42	15	22	30
Zeke 52 (A6M5)*, 12-44	15	22	30

NOTE: *Japanese abbreviations used above:*
Kawa. - Kawanishi   Mitsu. - Mitsubishi   Naka. - Nakajima

NETHERLANDS

	C6	C8	C10
Fokker T8W, 11-42	30	45	60

RUSSIAN

	C6	C8	C10
DB-3F, 9-42	25	37	50
DB-3F, 4-44	25	37	50
I-16, none	15	22	30
IL-2, 9-42	15	22	30
IL-2, 12-43	15	22	30
MiG-3, 8-42	15	22	30
I-18 (MiG-3), 2-43	15	22	30
MiG-3, 2-44	15	22	30
Pe-2, 9-42	15	22	30
SB-3, 11-43	15	22	30
TB-7*, 4-44	15	22	30

End ID

	C6	C8	C10			C6	C8	C10
Ideal Electronic Fighter Jet, 1959	135	200	270		plastic windup, 10" wingspan	65	98	130
Ideal Globemaster	42	63	85		**Irwin** Helicopter, friction, circa 1950,			
Ideal "U.S. Navy" Rescue Float Plane,					15" long	30	45	60

KANSAS TOY & NOVELTY COMPANY

By Fred Maxwell, Slushmold Contributing Editor and Perry Eichor, Aircraft Contributing Editor,
with the assistance of Bob Condray and Lorene Sorell.

To Aviation the 1920-1940 period was decisive - an Era of ferment and growth. It was a time of barnstorming, excitement and record-breaking, including the conquering of the oceans and Lindbergh's impact on our consciousness. Kansas played a large part in the development of airmail and airlines with its manufacturing centers at Topeka and Wichita (Beach, Boeing, Cessna, Laird, Stearman and others). To Kansans this must have been a source of civic pride and we might have expected the toy industry to reflect it. Some did, but even Lindy's Flight of the Decade was poorly represented. Tootsietoy had a recognizable replica but called it Aero Dawn. The closest KT&N came to it was #32, probably already in production in 1927, with Army Air Corps insignia; (Years later Best Toy reproduced it with the name "Combat Airplane").

Kansas Toy barely got the fever, settling for a few basic designs, yet they must have been aware of diversity in cast-iron toys and Tootsietoy and other slushmolders. KT&N #6 and its versions of mailplanes are reminiscent of the Stout-Ford predecessors of the famous "Tin Goose". #45 and #47 are probably Fokkers, although of foreign origin, these fine aircraft were more prominent in building US aviation than most of us remember. These and #56 glider are not easy to rationalize; Best Toy later named #47 a "Seaplane" - with its engine on its prow? OK for kids but good for a chuckle from adult collectors.

Listed below are the aircraft said to have been made by KT&N from 1924 to circa 1931, using metal disk or wire wheels. Reproductions from Best Toy and Ralstoy will be found with later wheels. KTA4, below, has not been positively identified; it could have been made by others or been a sample.

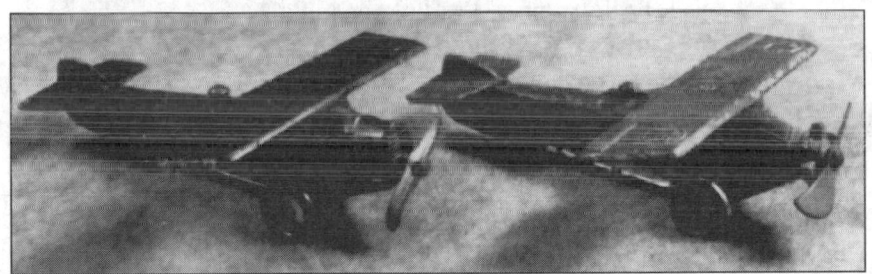

KANSAS TOY Aircraft: KTA2, KTA1. Photo courtesy of Perry R. Eichor.

	C6	C8	C10
KTA1 Cabin plane, "6", high wing with flaring positive dihedral, Army Air Corps star-in-circle insignia, 6 cyl. radial engine, pilot head in open cockpit, 8 oval windows, cast prop., lacquer finish, also unnumbered version with large tin propeller, 3-3/4" x 3"	14	21	35
KTA2 Cabin plane, no #, similar to above, Air Service dot-in-circle insignia, V-8 engine, cast propeller, 3-5/8" x 3"	14	21	35

KANSAS TOY (later BEST)
KANSAS TOY KTA9. Drawing by Deb Eccles.
KANSAS TOY KTA11. Drawing by Deb Eccles.

579

KANSAS TOY Aircraft: KTA3, unnumbered version "U.S. Mail" on both sides. Photo by Perry R. Eichor.

KATZ TOYS "The Red Arrow" No. 137. Photo by Perry R. Eichor.

KANSAS TOY KTA8. Photo by Bill Conover.

	C6	C8	C10
KTA3 Large cabin plane, "24", high wing, larger "U.S. Mail" version of above, dot-in-2-circles insignia, V-8 engine, cast propeller, white disk wheels w/painted black "tires", also an unnumbered version, 5-5/8" x 4-3/8"	20	35	50
KTA4 ? Large cabin plane, no #, Lindy type, high negative dihedral wing w/large stars, 6 cyl. radial engine, wheels w/black "Tires", Kansas Toy ?, about 5"	20	35	50
KTA5 Small cabin plane, "32", high, positive dihedral wing, Air Corps star insignia, 6 cyl. radial engine, 6 oval windows, 3 metal "wire" wheels, large tin or cast propeller, 2-3/8" x 2-1/8"	10	20	30
KTA6 Small cabin plane, no #, similar to above, w/o "windows" and diff. rudder, or wingtip, 2-3/8" x 2-1/8"	10	20	30
KTA7 Zeppelin, "44", front and rear cabins, 3 tail planes, mooring loop on nose, rear axle through rear cabin (unusual design), 4-1/4"	50	75	100

	C6	C8	C10
KTA8 Airliner, "45", Fokker ?, high, oval, corrugated wing and tail, 9 circular cabin windows, 9 rectangular flightdeck windows, 6 cyl. radial engine, large tin propellor, 2-1/2" x 2-1/2"	20	35	45
KTA9 Airliner, "KTN 47", Fokker, similar to #45, sometimes called a "seaplane", Why?, 3-5/8" x 3-1/2"	20	35	45
KTA10 Airliner, "KTN 47", larger version of above, 4" x ?"	20	30	40
KTA11 Glider, "56", high oval wing w/"GLIDER", pilot in front, flat lattice fuselage, 2-5/8" x 2-3/8"	15	25	40

NOTE: *Best Toys later reproductions will have "Made in U.S.A." embossed; and may have small white rubber wheels.*

	C6	C8	C10
Jet, USAF, friction powered, tin litho, 5" wingspan	15	20	35
Katz Toys "The Pathfinder", trimotor monoplane, 22" wingspan	350	600	900
Katz Toys "The Red Arrow" No. 137 single monoplane, pull toy	300	450	750
KD-1 Mak-a-plane - 4" long, all metal w/rubber wheels, mechanical, 1940s	40	50	70

KANSAS TOY Aircraft: KTA6, KTA5. Photo courtesy of Perry R. Eichor.

KENTON "Air Mail", wingspan approx. 8". Courtesy Chic Gast.

KEYSTONE Riding plane, 28" wingspan, No. 293 "Ride 'Em" Fighter. Courtesy Bob Black, Jr.

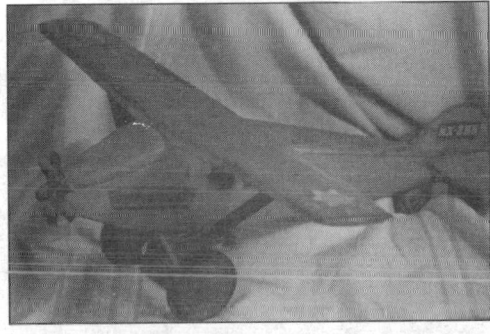

KEYSTONE Mail 27" wingspan. Photo by Calvin L. Chaussee.

KINGBURY "Trans Atlantic" Monoplane. Courtesy Lloyd W. Ralston Auctions.

KILGORE Sea gull, approx. 9" wingspan. Courtesy Chic Gast.

	C6	C8	C10
Kenton "Air Mail", wingspan approx. 8"	100	200	400
Kenton "Los Angeles" dirigible, 8" long	500	750	1050
Kenton "Pony Blimp", cast iron, 6"long	125	200	400
Kenton "United Boeing" twin engine, cast iron	112	168	225
Keystone "Airmail" plane, pressed steel, "NX-265", 24" wingspan	900	1350	1800
Keystone "Airmail", "NC-263"	500	750	1000
Keystone Ridem Mail Plane, 1930s	435	652	870
Keystone riding plane, scat over tail, steering bar over cabin, single wing, high, one engine, 23-1/2" long	500	750	1000
Keystone riding plane, No. 293, "Ride 'Em" fighter, 28" wingspan	400	600	850
Keystone Tri-motor, 1920s	900	1400	2200
Kilgore "Bullet" open cockpit monoplane, cast iron, 4" long	100	150	225
Kilgore Ford Trimotor, cast iron, "TAT", 13-1/2" wingspan	2000	3000	6000
Kilgore Hi wing Monocoupe, 5-1/2"	125	188	250
Kilgore High wing Monoplane, 3-1/2" long	50	75	100
Kilgore "N4", open cockpit monoplane, cast iron, 4" long	112	168	225
Kilgore, Seagull, high wing, pusher prop, 8-1/4" wingspan	300	700	1200
Kilgore Seagull, like above, but 4" wingspan	250	375	500
Kilgore "TAT No. 401", twin engine passenger monoplane, 4-1/2" long	150	250	325
Kilgore "Travel Air Mystery", double open cockpits, cast iron, 6" long	250	400	550
Kingsbury Biplane, steel windup, cast iron pilot, 16" long	300	500	700
Kingsbury Monoplane, high wing, trimotor, clockwork, 15" wingspan	200	350	650
Kingsbury Tin Goose, tri-engine, 1930s, 21" wingspan	600	900	1500
Kingsbury "Trans Atlantic" monoplane, painted pressed steel wind-up, 1930, 11" long	200	300	450
Kingsbury "U.S. Airmail" biplane, steel wind-up, 15" long	200	500	900

LINCOLN WHITE METAL LWA1. Photo by Fred Maxwell.

LINCOLN WHITE METAL AIRCRAFT

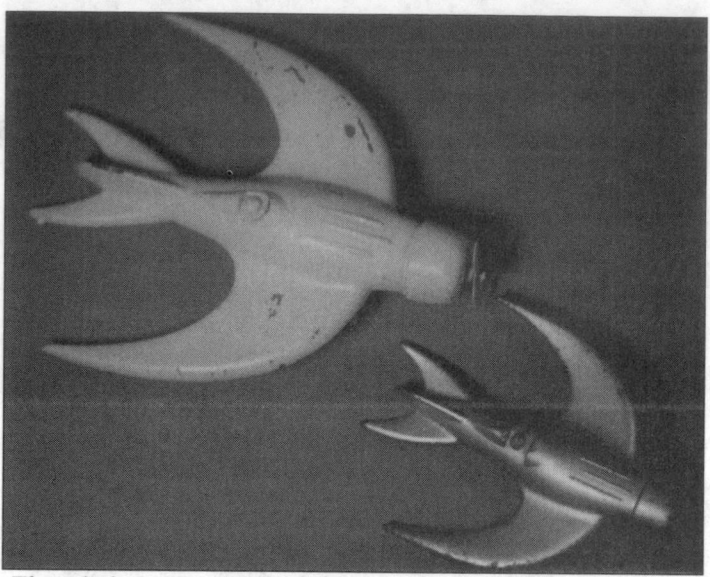

Though there is no hard evidence as yet, these two "Batplanes" have been attributed to Lincoln White Metal. Left to Right: LWA3, LWA4.

	C6	C8	C10
LWA1 Airplane, tri-motored, Fokker F-11 ?, tapered high wings w/wings symbol embossed, 7 cyl. radial engines, outboards mounted on landing gear struts, tin propellers, metal wheels, no windows, 3-1/4" x 4-1/2"............	25	50	100
LWA2 Airplane, tri-motored, similiar to above but outboard engines mounted in wings, unrealistic window patterns, metal wheels, 2-1/2" x 2-1/2"...........	20	30	55

	C6	C8	C10
LWA3 Airplane, streamlined, swallow-shaped, pilot, cowled radial engine, tin, propeller. It would be called "Batplane" today, c.4-1/2" x 3"........	40	60	100
LWA4 Airplane smaller version of above, c.3" x 2-1/2".........................	30	45	60
"Lindy" cast iron, nickel prop and wheels, 3-1/2" wingspan..................	40	60	100
Lindy type plane, lead, 2-1/4" wingspan..	10	20	30
Lionel No. 55 Airplane and Pylon........	300	450	1100
Luscombe Airplane, 4" long.................	30	45	60
Manoil No. 517, Lockheed F90............	20	30	50
Manoil No. 518 Navion........................	20	30	50
Manoil No. 519 Bonaza B-35...............	20	30	50
Manoil No. 520 Ercoupe......................	20	30	50
Marx American Airlines Flagship........	105	175	250
Marx "Army Bomber" No. 1025, tri-motor, c. 1935, 26" wingspan..........	75	150	250
Marx Astrojet Airport Set, planes, copter, etc...	150	250	375

LINCOLN White Metal: LWA1, LWA2. Photo by Perry R. Eichor.

MANOIL Airplanes, Left to right: 517, 518, 519, 520. Courtesy Peter and Marjorie Ruben.

MARX Pan American 4-motor, 1940, 27" wingspan. Courtesy Lloyd W. Ralston Auctions.

MARX Bomber, 14¾" wingspan, 4 engine, drops wooden bombs. Photo by Perry R. Eichor.

MARX Crop Duster Plane. Photo by Perry R. Eichor.

MARX DC-6 Transport Plane, plastic. Photo by Perry R. Eichor.

MARX Hangar, tin litho, circa 1941. Photo by James Apthorpe.

MARX P-35, 13½" wingspan. Photo by Perry R. Eichor.

MARX P35 - type 2 engine bomber, Photo by Bob West.

MARX Pan American Super 7 Clipper, 17½" wingspan, also as American Airlines. Photo by Perry R. Eichor.

MARX, Left to Right: Trimotor Biplane, 9½" wingspan, Gyroplane. Photo by Perry R. Eichor.

CONSTRUCTION AIRPLANES

METAL CAST No. 66 Aeroplane. Photo by Norbert Schachter.

Metalcraft Aircraft Construction Sets, as shown in a December 1929 Butler Bros. Catalog.

METALCRAFT Spirit of St. Louis, 9" long. Courtesy Mapes Auctioneers & Appraisers.

	C6	C8	C10
Marx Bomber, 4 engines, drops wooden bombs, 14-3/4" wingspan...	75	120	200
Marx Bomber, tin litho, sparkling mechanism, camouflaged, 4 engine, 18" wingspan...	60	140	200
Marx City Airport Set...	300	500	750
Marx Crop Duster Plane...	20	40	80
Marx Curtiss Transport, khaki, pressed steel, 9-1/2" wingspan...	60	90	120
Marx DC-3 Transport, pressed steel, circa 1939, 10" wingspan...	80	120	175
Marx DC-4 type, 4-motor passenger, circa 1930s, pressed steel...	60	125	250
Marx DC-6 Transport plane, plastic...	75	120	150
Marx "Electric Lighted Radio Airport", 1930s, 5" x 2-1/2" x 3-1/2"...	200	300	400
Marx Friction-powered 4-motor transport w/whirling propellors, tin litho.	60	90	200
Marx Futuristic Airport...	225	338	450
Marx Gyroplane...	40	75	100
Marx Hangar, tin litho, c. 1941...	50	75	100
Marx "Little Lindy Aeroplane", 1930s, friction, 6" wingspan...	100	150	200
Marx Lockheed Prop Jet...	125	188	250
Marx Mainstream Airport, c. 1930s...	110	165	220
Marx P35, pressed steel, w/and w/o wheel skirts, 13-1/2" wingspan...	60	90	120
Marx P35-type, 2-engine bomber, 15-7/8" wingspan...	70	105	140
Marx Pan American 4-motor, propellor-driven, also as PAA, 1940, pressed steel, 27" wingspan...	60	100	200
Marx Pan American Super 7 clipper,			
also as American Airlines, 17-1/2" wingspan...	150	225	300
Marx "Pioneer Air Express", tin litho, high wing monoplane, 25-1/2" wingspan...	75	100	200
Marx "Sky Cruiser" 2-motored Transport Plane w/siren and whirling propellors, Stratoliner 700, rubber wheels, 1940s, 18" wingspan...	45	75	150
Marx "Skycruiser Stratoliner 700", 4 engine...	45	75	125
Marx Sparkling Rocket Fighter No.1425, tin litho...	37	56	75
Marx Trimotor Biplane, 9-1/2" wingspan.	40	75	100
Marx TWA Mail Plane...	90	135	180
Marx Universal Airport w/2 metal planes, 1940s, 12" long...	55	90	200
Metal Cast No. 43 twin engine bomber, B-25?, 5-1/4" wingspan...	10	15	20
Metal Cast No. 66 Aeroplane, 2-engine,			

MID-WEST, Left to Right: MWA?2, MWA?1. Photo by Fred Maxwell.

	C6	C8	C10
c. 1940s, lead (some marked "Fred Greene"), approx. 4-1/2" wingspan.	5	10	20
Metal Cast No. 321, Aeroplane, "U.S. 256", Air Corps star insignia, 3-1/4" long	10	15	20
Metalcraft Build-A-Zep, builds 21 different 18" zeppelins	152	225	400
Metalcraft Northrup Alpha Monoplane, "PURE the Pure Oil Company", wingspan approx. 17"	300	1000	2000
Metalcraft Riding Rocket, 24" long	35	75	200
Metalcraft Spirit of St. Louis, came as kit, 9" long	150	225	300
Metalcraft Zeppelin	300	500	700

MIDWEST

(listing by Fred Maxwell)

MWA?1 Monoplane, 2 pilots in open cockpit (early record breakers?), Liberty V-12 engine, cast propellor,

	C6	C8	C10
8 oval & 2 round windows, 2 painted main gear disc wheels, 3-1/8" x 3-5/8". No Price Found			
MWA?2 Monoplane, same as above but no crew, ailerons and tail surfaces detailed & 3 disc wheels w/those black painted "tires", 3-3/16" x 3-5/8"			No Price Found
Ohio Art "Sea Patrol Plane", pontoons, moves on water, early 40s wind-up 9" long	45	68	90
Ohio Art Seaplane "Hot Job", tin litho, checkerboard wings, spinning prop. 1950s, 10" wingspan, 3-1/2" long	20	30	40
P-38 glass candy container	50	75	100
Passenger Plane, high-wing, 4-engine, 3 wooden wheels, approx. 9" wingspan	9	13	18
Pedal Car, Biplane, 2-motor, 54" long.	500	900	1800
Pedal Car, Pursuit Plane	400	600	1200

RALSTOY AIRCRAFT

By Perry Eichor, Aircraft Contributing Editor, and Fred Maxwell, Slushmold Contributing Editor

Ralstoy issued new aircraft and reproduced popular Kansas Toy numbers issued during the 1920s. The late 1930s toy reflected the growing awareness of the war in Europe.

	C6	C8	C10
RAA1 Small cabin plane, "32", "Ralstoy", wings positive dihedral, (See Kansas KTA5), 2 1/2" x 2-1/4"	5	10	20
RAA2 Cabin Plane, "NC414", "Ralstoy" midwing, V-12 engine, tin propellor, 3-3/8" x 3-3/8"	20	30	40

RALSTOY: RAA4, RAA2, RAA3. Photo by Perry R. Eichor.

RALSTOY? RAA5. Photo by Perry R. Eichor.

Top Left: Savoye Blimp, Top Right: What may have been the version sold by Tommy Toy. Bottom: Savoye Monoplane. Photo by Fred Maxwell.

	C6	C8	C10
RAA3, Cabin Plane, high wing, cowled radial engine, 2 doors, 6 windows, "Ralstoy", "Made in USA", 3-5/8" x 3-1/2"	20	30	40
RAA4 Pursuit plane, P40", Curtiss "U.S. Army", midwing, Air Corps star-in-circle insignia, V-12 engine, 2 machine guns, 3-bladed propellor, "Made in USA", "Ralstoy" in diamond, 3" x 3-1/4"	20	30	40
RAA5 Cabin Plane, slim midwing, cowled radial engine, pilot, tin propellor, underside is "Scout", "Made in USA", 3" x 3-3/4"	20	30	40
RAA6 ? Large cabin plane, Lindy type, high wing, 6 cly. radial engine, metal wheels, Ralstoy?	20	30	40
Remco Flying Boxcar	35	52	70
Remco Kennedy Airport	42	63	85
Remco WWI "Air Aces" Playset, 1965	150	250	325
Renwal B-17, small	5	10	20
Renwal B-17, plastic, c. 1944, 9-1/4" wingspan	15	30	60

	C6	C8	C10
Renwal B-25, plastic, circa 1944, 6-3/4" wingspan	12	25	40
Renwal B-29, No. 29	12	25	40
Renwal C54 Transport, large, plastic	10	25	40
Renwal P38, plastic	10	25	40
Renwal P40, plastic	10	15	20
Renwal P47, plastic	15	20	30
Renwal PB2Y Flying Boat	15	20	40
Savoye Blimp, "U.S.N.", 4" long	20	30	40
Savoye Monoplane, 3" long	20	30	40
Schieble Biplane, c. 1920s, 15-1/2" long	300	450	600
Schieble Ford Trimotor, steel, 29-1/2" long	200	600	1500
"Sky Cruiser", tin litho, 2 motor transport, engines turn w/friction mechanism, 18" wingspan	40	75	100
"Spirit of America" pull toy aeroplane, steel and litho, 14" long	12	18	24
Spirit of St. Louis glass candy container 4-3/8" long	150	225	300

RENWAL; Left to Right, Top: B-17 No. 777, P-38; Middle: B-25 No. 25, B-29 No. 29, C54 Transport; Bottom: B-17 (small) No. 17, P-40. Photo by Perry R. Eichor.

Schieble Ford Trimotor, 26-1/4" wingspan, No. 30. Courtesy Wilkinson Collection - Detroit Antique Toy Museum.

STEELCRAFT "Graf Zeppelin", 30" long.
Restored and Photographed by Tim Oei.

STEELCRAFT Lockheed Sirius. Courtesy Christie's East.

STEELCRAFT "NX130 U.S. Mail Plane", one engine.
Photo by Calvin L. Chaussee.

	C6	C8	C10
Steelcraft "Akron" blimp pull toy, 25" long	75	112	150
Steelcraft "Army Scout Plane" single engine, high wing monoplane, 1920s, 22-1/2" wingspan	100	200	400
Steelcraft "Army Scout Plane" trimotor, single high wing, 1920s	200	600	1000
Steelcraft Army Scout Plane, green and orange, 23" wingspan	100	200	400
Steelcraft "Graf Zeppelin", pressed steel pull toy, 30-1/2"	100	150	250
Steelcraft Graf Zeppelin, pull toy, 32" long	125	225	350
Steelcraft Lockheed Sirius, pull toy, 21-1/2" wingspan	300	600	1000
Steelcraft Monoplane, 2 open cockpits, 1930s, 16" wingspan	250	375	600
Steelcraft No. 79 pedal plane, high wing monoplane, 32" wingspan, 48" long	700	1250	3000
Steelcraft NX107, "Little Jim" 23" wingspan	200	400	600
Steelcraft NX130, blue eagles on wings, 23" wingspan	200	400	600
Steelcraft "NX130 U.S. Mail Plane", one engine	200	400	600

	C6	C8	C10
Steelcraft NX131, Tri-motor, U.S. Mail plane, pull toy, 26-1/2" wingspan	200	700	1500
Steelcraft Pedal Plane "Pursuit", 1940	1000	1700	3000
Strauss "Chicago" Dirigible, tin litho, 10"	125	188	250
Strauss "Flying Airship" (boxtop description) aluminum windup	275	350	550
Strauss Graf Zeppelin, 16" long	240	360	480
Sun Rubber "Pursuit Ship", "25-P75", circa 1940-41, 4-1/4" wingspan	15	20	30

SUN RUBBER, Left to Right: No. 12009, Pursuit Ship, No. 12010. Courtesy Ed Poole.

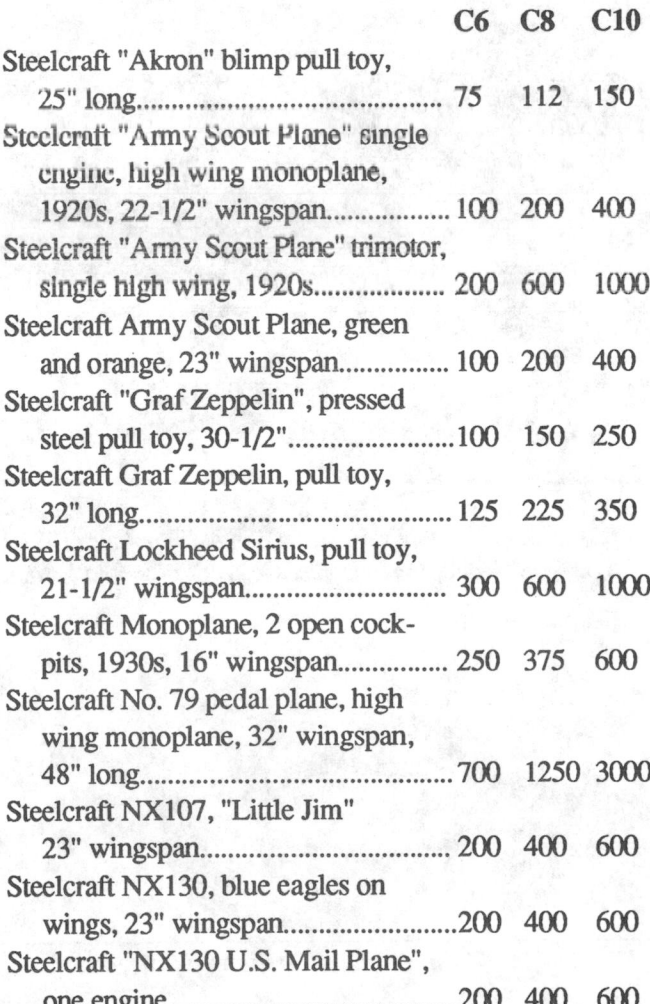

THOMAS TOYS F-80 Jet Action Rocket Launcher. Courtesy Islyn Thomas.

	C6	C8	C10
Sun Rubber **No. 12008 Racing Plane**, circa 1947, also called "Scout", both same plane as "Pursuit Ship"...	15	20	30
Sun Rubber No. 12009 Transport, 4" long............	15	30	40
Sun Rubber No 12010 Dual-Control Plane, 4-1/2" long............	20	30	40
Tip Top Giant Flyer monoplane, c. 1920s, 23" long............	200	350	500
Theodore Hahn Aeroplane No. 187, lead alloy, 1920's............	20	40	75

Theodore Hahn Aeroplane.

	C6	C8	C10
Thomas Toys Defiant, plastic, 4" long	10	15	20
Thomas Toys F-80 Jet Action Rocket Launcher............	10	15	20
Thomas Toys Warhawk, plastic, 4" long............	10	15	20
Tommy Toy Dirigible, "USN" slush lead, 1930s............	20	30	50
Tootsietoy 106 Lockheed Sirius, tin low wing............	20	25	40

TOMMY TOY "U.S.N." Dirigible.
Photo by Bill Kaufman.
Courtesy Charles W. Weldon, Jr.

	C6	C8	C10
Tootsietoy 107 Bellanca, high tin wing monoplane............	25	30	40
Tootsietoy 119 Northrup Alpha "U.S. Army" Pursuit............	15	20	40
Tootsietoy 125 Lockheed Electra, twin engine............	10	20	40
Tootsietoy 717 DC-2, "TWA"............	20	40	75
Tootsietoy 718 Waco, "U.S. Navy", C model Biplane............	35	50	90
Tootsietoy No. #, Waco "Dive Bomber" model Biplane............	40	60	100

TOOTSIETOY, Left to Right: No. 106 Low Wing Monoplane (1932); No. 107 High Wing Monoplane (1932). Collection & Photo John Gibson.

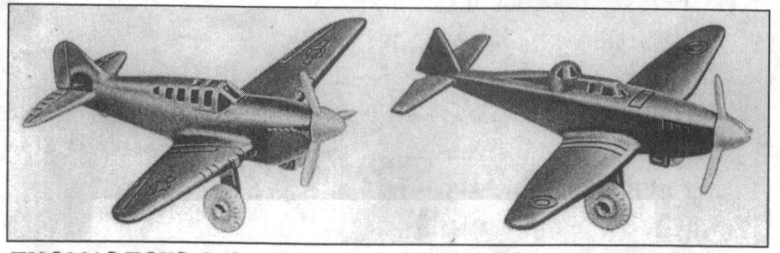

THOMAS TOYS, Left to Right: Warhawk, Defiant, plastic, 4" long.

588

TOOTSIETOY: Unnumbered Waco "Dive Bomber" biplane. Collection and photo John Gibson.

TOOTSIETOY P-38 Lightning Fighter Plane (1950), 5-1/4" wingspan. Collection & Photo John Gibson.

TOOTSIETOY: Unnumbered P-39 Airacobra Fighter Plane (issued postwar). Collection & Photo John Gibson.

	C6	C8	C10
Tootsietoy 719 Crusader, twin boom, twin engine	25	40	60
Tootsietoy 720 "Fly-N-Giro" Auto-gyro, small version	50	100	300
Tootsietoy 721 "Curtis P-40" Pursuit, silver	100	200	400
Same as above, olive	125	250	500
Tootsietoy 722 Military DC-4 "Army Bomber"	30	75	120
Tootsietoy DC-4 "Super Mainliner"	20	30	40
Tootsietoy 722 Military DC-4, "Army Transport"	40	75	100
Tootsietoy 4482 Bleriot, 67mm long	20	30	50
Tootsietoy 4491 Bleriot, 25mm long	15	20	25
Tootsietoy 4649 Ford Trimotor, tin wing	25	50	100
Tootsietoy 4650 Biplane, Jenny type	30	50	100
Tootsietoy 4659 Auto-Gyro, tin wing, large version	25	60	100
Tootsietoy 4660 AC Aero-Dawn, high wing monoplane, tin wing	15	25	50
Tootsietoy 4660 Aero-Dawn, sea-plane version	20	30	55
Tootsietoy 4675 Wings, Biplane, tin wing	25	35	55
Tootsietoy 4675 Wings, Seaplane version	30	40	60
Tootsietoy P-38	20	50	100
Tootsietoy P-39, tin wing, 2-bladed prop	30	60	120
Tootsietoy S-58, Sikorsky Helicopter	20	30	40

	C6	C8	C10
Tootsietoy Lockheed 749 Constellation, "PAA N88846"	30	60	120
Tootsietoy Boeing 377 Stratocruiser "PAA N102SV"	30	50	100
Tootsietoy Corvair CV-240 twin engine	20	40	80
Tootsietoy "Piper Cub", low wing monoplane	5	10	20
Tootsietoy Navion	5	10	20

TOOTSIETOY: Unnumbered P39 Airacobra Fighter Plane (issued postwar), rarer color combination. Collection & Photo John Gibson.

TOOTSIETOY U.S. Coast Guard Amphibian (resembles Sikorsky S-43), 1950. Collection & Photo by John Gibson.

TOOTSIETOY MINIATURE AIRPLANES
(list by John Gibson)

	C6	C8	C10
Tootsietoy Beechcraft Bonanza	5	10	20
Tootsietoy P-80 "Shooting Star" Jet	10	20	40
Tootsietoy F7V-3 "Cutlass" Jet	10	15	20
Tootsietoy "F-86 Sabre" Jet, 2-piece casting	20	35	60
Tootsietoy "F-86 Sabre" Jet, 1-piece casting	5	10	15
Tootsietoy F9F-2 Panther Jet, 2-piece casting	25	35	60
Tootsietoy F9F-2 Panther Jet, 1-piece casting	5	10	15
Tootsietoy F4D Douglas Skyray	5	10	15
Tootsietoy "Delta", 2-piece casting	20	35	60
Tootsietoy "F-94 Starfire" Jet	10	15	20
Tootsietoy Boeing 707	10	15	20
Tootsietoy Sikorsky S-43	40	60	100
Tootsietoy "Tootsietoy Airport", hangar and two planes	300	600	1000
Tootsietoy U.S. Moon Rocket, 3 types, all have 2 wheels to run on string, mid-1960s replicas of original Buck Rogers spaceships (see Comic Character)	40	75	100
Tootsietoy "U.S.N. Los Angeles" dirigible, two grooved wheels on top to run on string (also was sold as part of Buck Rogers set)	40	60	80

	C6	C8	C10
1353 High Wing Monoplane	8	12	16
1407 Air Defense 10pc. carded set	75	100	150
1636 DC2 TWA	6	9	12
1637 Atlantic Clipper	6	9	12
1639 P38	15	23	30
1743 Aeroplane Whistle Tin Litho (Crackerjacks)	20	30	40
1744 High Wing Monoplane Tin Litho, (Crackerjacks)	20	30	40
1746 Aerodawn Tin Litho (Crackerjacks)	20	30	40
1747 Low Wing Monoplane Tin Litho (Crackerjacks)	20	30	40
1812 Sky Fleet 5pc carded set (1946) contains 3 - #1636 TWA planes and 2 - #1637 clippers	38	56	75
4550 DC4 (charm)	2	3	4
9951 Pursuit Plane	6	9	12
Turner High Wing Monoplane, one engine, 1930s,18-1/2" wingspan	400	600	800
Turner High Wing Monoplane, pressed steel, 22-1/2" wingspan	400	600	800
United Electric "Spirit of St. Louis", go around tower, 2 planes, pressed steel, electrical	800	1200	1600
"U.S." high wing monoplane, single engine, open ironwork body, spool wheel works, prop, 8" wingspan	200	300	400

TOOTSIETOY No. 1030 Los Angeles dirigible (1934), with box. Collection & Photo John Gibson.

TOOTSIETOY, Left to Right: Top: 4679 Tri-Motor Plane, 4660 Aero-Dawn, 4650 Biplane, 4675 Wings, High-Wing Floatplane. Middle: 4659 Autogyro, 718 Waco Bomber, 719 Crusader. Bottom: 119 Army Plane, 125 Lockheed Electra. 717 TWA Douglas Airliner, DC4 Super Mainliner. Photo by Ed Poole.

TOOTSIETOY DC4 "Super Mainliner", three versions. Photo by Perry R. Eichor.

TOOTSIETOY, Left to Right: Top: P-39, 720; Bottom: Sikorsky S-43, 721, 722. Photo by Perry R. Eichor.

WYANDOTTE high wing passenger monoplane, No. 2 Lockheed Vega. Photo courtesy Dick and Nancy Dice.

591

VINDEX FOKKER, cast iron, Photo by Perry R. Eichor.

WYANDOTTE Crusader, two variations. Photo by Perry R. Eichor.

	C6	C8	C10
Vindex Fokker, 1929, cast iron, high wing, single engine,10" wingspan. Auctioned in mint condition in May 1994, with salesman's tags and original pullstring and ball attached for $24,000.			
Watrous single engine biplane, pressed steel bell toy, c. 1915, 8-1/4" wingspan.	200	300	600
Williams, A.C. UX83, cast iron, 3-1/4" wingspan	30	60	80
Williams, A.C. "UX-99", cast iron, wingspan approx. 4-1/2"	80	120	160
Williams, A.C. "UX-166", Lindy type plane, cast iron, nickeled engine and wheels, wingspan approx. 5-3/4"	40	80	150

	C6	C8	C10
Wyandotte Airliner, Circa WW II, two-engine, wooden wheels	55	82	110
Wyandotte Bomber, Army, pressed steel, two-engine	90	135	180
Wyandotte China Clipper, No. 207, 13" wingspan	75	150	200
Wyandotte City Airport, American Airlines, two hangars, control tower, etc., lights up	100	150	250
Wyandotte Crusader, 9-3/4" wingspan.	20	30	40
Wyandotte Crusader, 12-window version	30	40	60
Wyandotte Gyrocopter, twin engine passenger plane, circa 1930s, 12-1/2" wingspan	60	90	200
Wyandotte High Wing Passenger monoplane, No. 2 Lockheed Vega, single engine, bullet nose, 18" wingspan	50	75	150
Wyandotte Military Air Transport, 13" wingspan	25	40	60
Wyandotte Mystery Plane No. 101, twin engine, wings trail backward, 4-1/2" wingspan	30	50	100

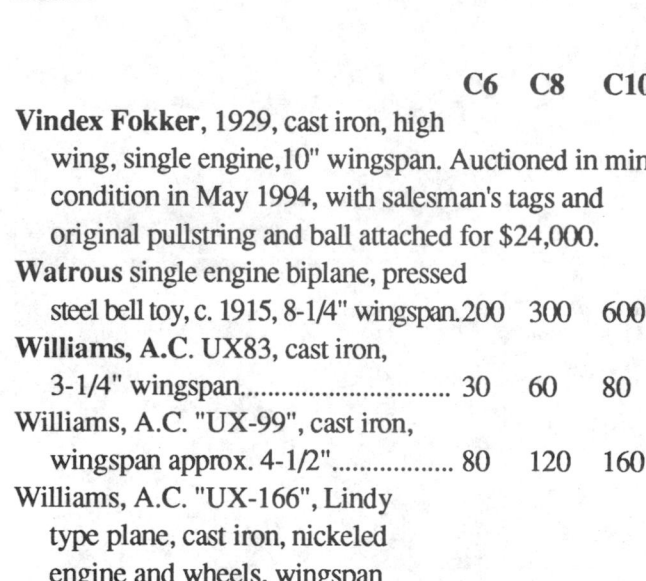

WYANDOTTE Airliner, 12-3/4" wingspan, four-engine, pressed steel. Photo by Perry R. Eichor.

	C6	C8	C10
Wyandotte Airacuda, pressed steel, twin vertical stabilizers, twin pusher engines, blue or red, 8-1/2" wingspan.	20	40	65
Wyandotte Airliner, 4 engine, pressed steel, 12-3/4" wingspan	50	75	100

WYANDOTTE, Left to Right: Airacuda, Airliner, circa WW II, two engine, Photo by Perry R. Eichor.

WYANDOTTE China Clipper. Courtesy Wilkinson Collection - Detroit Antique Toy Museum.

WYANDOTTE Gyrocopter, 12-1/2" wingspan. Photo by Perry R. Eichor.

WYANDOTTE Stratocruiser, 13" wingspan. Photo by Perry R. Eichor.

ZEPPELIN, "Graf Zeppelin", A.C. Williams, cast iron, 5-1/4" long (1932 ad).

WYANDOTTE "Rocket Racer #319" Rocket Ship, from an August, 1935 ad in Toys and Novelties magazine.

	C6	C8	C10
Wyandotte Rocket Racer No. 319, rocket ship sold in 1935	50	75	100
Wyandotte Stratocruiser, 13" wingspan	40	60	100
Wyandotte Super Jet	80	120	160
Zeppelin, cast iron, approx. 3" long	40	60	80
Zeppelin, "Akron" Marx, 1930s, 28" long	100	140	250
Zeppelin, "EPL 1", Lehmann No. 651	300	600	1000
Zeppelin, "EPL 2", Lehmann No. 652, 1907	225	400	800
Zeppelin, "Graf Zeppelin", aluminum, Strauss, 16" long	175	250	350
Zeppelin, "Graf Zeppelin", A.C. Williams, cast iron, 8" long	75	150	250
Zeppelin, "Graf Zeppelin", A.C. Williams, cast iron, 5-1/2" long	50	75	150
Zeppelin, "Graf Zeppelin", A.C. Williams, cast iron, 5" long	50	75	125

	C6	C8	C10
Zeppelin, "Los Angeles", cast iron, 12" long	300	750	1500
Zeppelin, pull-toy "Little Giant"	50	100	200
Zeppelin, pull-toy "Macon"	50	100	200
Zeppelin, "Pony DE107", cast iron, 5-1/2" long	50	100	250
Zeppelin, "U.S. Akron", potmetal, circa 1932, 6" long	25	40	75
Zeppelin, "ZEP", cast iron, 4" long	40	80	150
Zeppelin, "Goodyear" decals, hatch opens, 25" long	125	190	300
Zeppelin, pull toy, silver, circa 1920-30s, cast iron, 6" long	60	90	120
Zeppelin, metal, 25 " long	42	64	85
Zeppelin, metal, 26-1/2" long	45	68	90
Zeppelin, metal, 27-1/2" long	50	75	100

SHIPS

(See also Tin Wind-Up, Paper)

Mint prices in this category averaged $1032.80 in the last edition, and in
this edition averaged $995.60, a decrease of 4%.

AUBURN RUBBER Battleship and Submarine. Photo by Ed Poole.

*Left to Right: Arnold Ocean Liner, tin keywind, c. 1930; Falk
"Bremen". Middle: Ives Merchant Marine Ship; Fleischmann
Oil Tanker, "Esso". Bottom: Bing Ocean Liner; Ives
"New York". Courtesy Christie's East.*

	C6	C8	C10
"Adirondack" Sidewheeler, cast iron, approx. 13" long	500	750	1000
Admiral Dewey's Flagship from the White Fleet, wood and paper, 6" long	100	150	200
Admiral Dewey Flagship, paper litho on wood, c. 1900, 30" long	300	450	600
Aircraft Carrier "65", tin litho, large, circa 1950s	50	75	100
Althof-Bergmann "America", painted tin sidewheeler, c. 1874, 20" long	7000	11,000	18,000
Arcade "Showboat", cast iron, 1929, approx. 10-3/4" long	500	750	1050
Argo Aircraft Carrier, steel, w/3 6" jet planes which fire rockets, shell or drop bombs, 36" long	85	130	175

	C6	C8	C10
Arnold Ocean Liner, tin keywind, circa 1930, 11-1/2" long	400	650	900
"Automatic Submarine", remote-controlled, tin litho	40	60	80
Atwood Motors, California "Amazon Side-Wheeler", plastic and metal, circa 1950s	135	200	275
Atwood Jungle Boat	75	113	150
Auburn Rubber Battleship, circa 1940, No. 1582, 8-1/4" long	22	33	45
Auburn Rubber Dreadnaught, new in 1941, extremely rare, 9-1/8" long	30	50	70
Auburn Rubber Freighter, new in 1941, 9-1/4" long	22	33	45

ARCADE "Showboat", 1929.

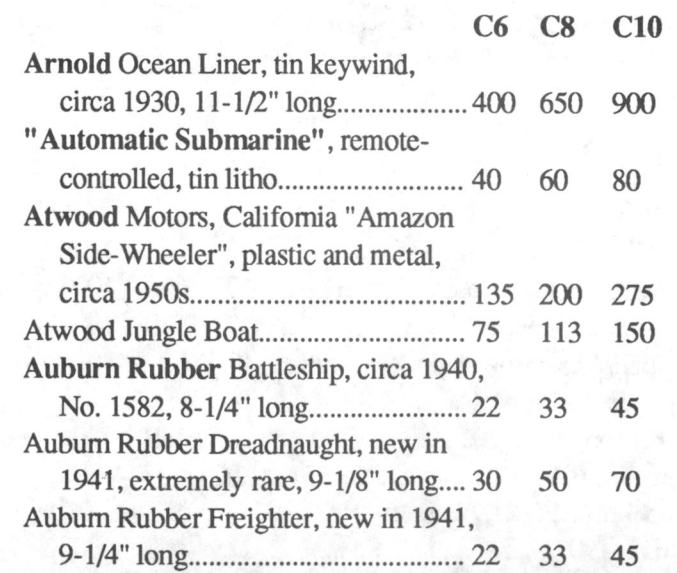

AUBURN RUBBER freighter (damaged).

AUBURN RUBBER Dreadnaught, 9-1/8" long. Courtesy Dave Leopard, from his book "Rubber Toy Vehicles".

"Baby" cast iron racing boat. Photo by Bill Kaufman. Courtesy Good Old Days Store.

	C6	C8	C10
Auburn Rubber Submarine, c. 1941, 6-1/2" long	20	30	40
Authenticast French Warships, incl. Richelieu, Algiers, Fantasque and others, each	30	45	60
Authenticast German Warships, scale models including Narvik, Galster and others, each	30	45	60
Authenticast Japanese Warships, incl. Fuso, Kaga, Mogani and others, each	30	45	60

Top: BARCLAY 372 Aeroplane Carrier; Bottom: BARCLAY 373 Battleship. Photos by Ed Poole.

	C6	C8	C10
Authenticast U.S. scale model warships, World War II including: Iowa, Enterprise, Sims and Farragut and submarine Sarge, each	30	45	60
B-LO submarine, metal, pat. no. 1318048	75	112.50	150
"Baby" cast iron racing boat, c.1930, wheeled, Hubley?, 4-1/2" long	60	90	120
Barclay 372 Aeroplane Carrier	39	58	78
Barclay 373 Battleship	60	95	125
Battleship "Admiral" paper litho, 1890, 20" long	600	900	1200
Battleship, cast iron, 14-1/2" long	300	450	600
Battleship, glass, candy container, approx. 3" long	60	90	120
Battleship, Hillclimber, pressed steel, 15" long	200	300	400
Battleship Oregon, paper litho and wood, 25" long	700	1050	1400
Battleship "Rover" paper litho and wood, 20" long	600	900	1200
Battleship, Tin Friction, circa 1920s, 9-1/2" long	200	300	400
Big Bang Navy Gun Boat No. 9B, cast iron, 8-1/4" long	125	200	250
Bing Battleship, tin clockwork, 16"	800	1300	1800
Bing Destroyer, tin clockwork, 22-1/2" long	1500	2400	3500
Bing "Leviathan" Ocean Liner, circa 1915, tin keywind, 40" long	No Price Found		
Bing Ocean Liner, tin keywind, circa 1925, 13-1/2" long	400	650	900

BING "Leviathan". Courtesy Christie's East.

Top, Left to Right: Bliss "Conqueror"; Bliss "Rover"
torpedo boat. Middle: Reed "Ocean Queen".
Bottom: Converse Battleship "Indiana".
Courtesy Christie's East.

BLISS Battleship "New York", 36" long. Courtesy
Lloyd W. Ralston Auctions.

Battleship
"Admiral", 1890,
20" long.
Courtesy
Lloyd W. Ralston
Auctions.

BLISS "St. Louis", litho on wood.
Courtesy Christie's East.

BOAT, tin friction, 13" long, two smokestacks, four lifeboats. Courtesy PB 84 New York (probably D. P. Clark or Schieble, circa 1908-1924).

BUCKMAN Steamboat, circa 1872, 11" long. Courtesy Christie's East.

	C6	C8	C10
Bliss "Battleship New York" paper litho and stained wood, 1890, 36" x 22"	450	675	900
Bliss "Conqueror" paper litho on wood, 20" long	900	1400	2000
Bliss "Marguerite" Sailing Schooner, 22" long	350	525	700
Bliss "Rover" Torpedo Boat, paper litho on wood, c. 1896, 20" long	850	1375	1900
Bliss "St. Louis" litho on wood liner, circa 1895, 34-1/2" long	800	1300	1800
Bliss? "Union" ferry, sidewheel, circa 1900, 24" long	225	375	450
Boat, Hot Air, tin with driver, 9" long	100	150	200
Boat, pull motor, metal	100	150	200
Boat, tin friction, lithographed	100	150	200
Boat, tin friction, painted, early	100	150	200
Boat, tin friction, painted, early	150	225	300
Boat, tin friction, two smokestacks, four lifeboats, 13" long	90	135	180
Boucher "Gee Whiz" speedboat, painted sheetmetal, heavy clockwork motor, bronze propellor, 25" long	550	825	100

	C6	C8	C10
Bradley "Columbia" side paddle-wheeler, paper litho on wood, c. 1890, 24" long	400	600	800
Bramwell-Smith, tin sidewheeler, pat. 1872	2000	3500	5000
Buckman "Pike" steam launch	2500	3800	5500
Buckman Steamboat No. 55, c. 1870, 19" long	1500	2500	3500
Buckman Steamboat, circa 1872, 11" long	1300	2000	3000
Buckman twin sidewheeler steamboat, "Patented May 7, 1872", steam engine, 11" long	2000	3500	5000
Buddy L "49 LST", 12" long	37	56	75
Buddy L No. 3000 Tugboat, 1929-30	3000	5000	7000
"C.C. JR" Brass-mounted Wood Boat, windup motor concealed within the rudder controlled from the wheel in the circular cockpit with a start-stop lever, 14-1/2" long	90	135	180

BUDDY L "49 LST". Photo by Ed Poole.

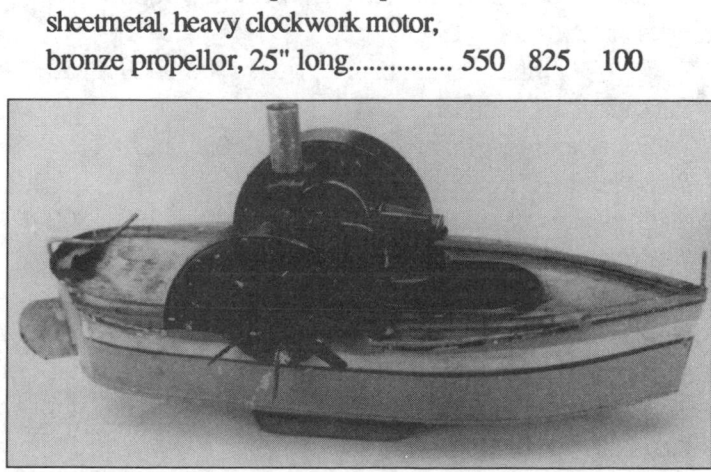

BUCKMAN twin sidewheeler steamboat, 11" long. Courtesy Wilkinson Collection, Detroit Antique Toy Museum.

BUDDY L No. 3000 Tugboat. Photo courtesy Thomas W. Sefton.

"Columbia" riverboat, 1890, 2' long. Courtesy Lloyd W. Ralston Auctions.

FALLOWS "Jumbo" riverboat, 14" long. Courtesy Lloyd W. Ralston Auctions.

GEORGE BROWN "Atlantic" sidewheel riverboat, 14" long. Courtesy Lloyd W. Ralson Auctions.

FLEISCHMAN Ocean Liner, 1930, 20-1/2" long. Courtesy Lloyd W. Ralston Auctions.

DENT Battleship "New York". Courtesy Christie's East.

	C6	C8	C10
Canoe, wood, 6" long	15	22	30
Cass Tugboat, wood, c. WW II?, 15" long	37	56	75
Cass Yacht, c. WW II?, wood, 15" long	37	56	75
Chein Hercules "Peggy Jane" sailboat, 23" long	250	375	500
Chein "Peggy Jane" speedboat, 14-1/2" long	115	175	235
Chein Sailboat, wheeled	112	168	225
Cohn Naval Base #888 Playset	210	315	425
"Columbia" riverboat, 1890, paper litho, tin litho, wood, working walking beam, 2' long	650	975	1300
Converse Battleship "Indiana", circa 1900, litho on wood, 32" long	650	1100	1600
Converse Battleship "Oregon", tin litho, wood, "1900"	500	750	1000
Cruiser, glass, candy container, approx. 3" long	50	75	100
Dayton Battleship, friction, c. 1920, 16" long	200	300	400
Dent Adirondack, cast iron, 15" long	1000	1700	2300
Dent Battleship "New York", c. 1900, largest cast iron boat made, 21"	2000	3200	4350
Destroyer, on wheels, cast iron, 12"long	1000	1500	2000
Eldon Aircraft Carrier, 22" long	40	60	80
Eldon Freighter, 20" long	40	60	80
Eldon L.C.T. Landing Craft, 10" long	17	26	35
Falk "Bremen" tin keywind, c. 1920, 18" long	1300	2100	3000

	C6	C8	C10
Fallows "Constitution" side-wheeler, 10" long	2000	3000	4000
Fallows "Jumbo" riverboat, side-wheel, painted tin, 1880, mechanical walking beam, 14" long	1000	1500	2000
Fallows "Volunteer IXL", 16" long	1800	2700	3600
"Ferry Go" twin paddlewheel ferry boat pull toy, tin litho, 14" long	125	185	250
Fleischmann Battleship	2000	3000	4000
Fleischmann Ocean Liner, 15-1/2" long	1000	1600	2250
Fleischmann Ocean Liner, 7-1/2" long	80	120	160
Fleischmann Ocean Liner, 1930, painted tin clockwork, working, 20-1/2" long	700	1350	1800
Fleischmann Oil Tanker, "Esso", 20" long	600	1000	1350
George Brown "Atlantic" sidewheel riverboat, painted and stenciled tin, 14" long	2250	3375	4500
Gunboat, tin friction, large wheel rises above deck, circa early 1920s, smokestack	300	450	600

Gunboat, tin friction, rocks back and
    forth on wheels, 10" long................. 250   375   500
Gunboat, friction, 19" long.................... 400   600   800
Gunboat, two guns, 2 small stacks, 2
    stories above deck, wheeled, fric-
    tion, 1920s or earlier........................ 300   450   600
Hess Voyager Tanker, 1966, price mint in box $2100
Hill Climber pressed steel battleship,
    18" long... 300   450   600
Hubley "Baby" speedboat, cast iron..... 60   90   120
Hubley "Penn Yan" motorboat, very
    rare, 5 people, 15" long, unauthorized by Penn Yan, which
    stopped Hubley's production. Auctioned in 1994 in excellent
    condition for $13,500.
Hubley "Sea Horse", cast iron motor-
    boat... 1750 2625 3500
Hubley "Static" speedboat, cast iron
        auctioned in 1994 in good condition for $4200.
Ideal Destroyer, plastic, 15" long......... 125   188   250
Ideal Phantom Raider........................... 72   108   145
Ideal Pirate Ship, plastic, w/6 pirates,
    new in 1953..................................... 107   145   215
Ideal Pumping Fire Boat w/siren,
    1955, plastic..................................... 60   90   120
Ideal Slo Motion VI, windup motor-
    boat, 13" long.................................. 60   90   120
Ideal Sparking Torpedo Boat, plastic,
    windup, 12" long.............................. 50   75   100
Ideal "Treasure Hunter", plastic............ 62   93   125
Ideal Varsity Racing Scull, 8 rowers,
    coxswain, 1890, cast iron, oars move,
    14" long.. 2000 3000 4000
Ives Merchant Marine ship, tin
    keywind, 13" long.......................... 450   675   900
Ives "Miss Liberty" speedboat, steam-
    powered, 13-1/2" long..................... 750 1125 1500
Ives "New York" Ocean Liner,
    13" long....................................... 500   800 1100
Ives Submarine, dives, c. 1910, tin
    keywind, 10" long........................... 400   600   800

*IVES Merchant Marine Ship.
Courtesy Christie's East.*

*IVES U.S. Merchant Marine, painted pressed tin
clockwork.*

Ives U.S. Merchant Marine Boat,
    painted pressed tin clockwork,
    10-1/2" long................................... 250   375   500
Ives "Vim" speedboat, 10-1/2" long..... 650   975 1300
Ives "Vixen" speedboat, 12" long......... 650   975 1300
"Johnson's Sea Horse", cast iron speed-
    boat w/figure, 10-1/2" long............ 1750 2625 3500
"Kearsage" gunboat, cast iron,
    13-3/4" long................................. 1000 1500 2000
Kenton Speedboat, cast iron............... 90   135   180
Keystone Action Submarine................. 50   75   100
Keystone Aircraft Carrier, wooden,
    12" long.. 50   75   100
Keystone Battleship, wooden, approx.
    2' long with guns, airplanes take
    off from a spring on deck of ship..... 130   195   260
Keystone Battleship, early 1940s,
    under 2' length.............................. 64   96   128
Keystone Ferryboat, wooden, circa
    1930s, 2 wood cars, 2 wood trucks,
    14" long.. 40   60   80
Keystone Fishing Boat, wooden, c.
    1940s, 12" long.............................. 35   52   70
Keystone Racing Sailboat, wood.......... 30   45   60
Keystone Radar Rocket Ship................. 75   112   150
Kingsbury Boat, 10" long.................... 100   150   200

LIBERTY PLAYTHINGS

Liberty Playthings was in business in the late 1920s and early
1930s in Niagara Falls, New York. All its toys, which were
made of wood and metal, seem to have borne names with
some variations of the word "Liberty", and all seem to have
been sea-connected. Those advertised in 1929 were: No. 2
Tug and Scow; No. 5 Freighter; No. 6 Airplane Carrier; No.
7 Fire Boat; No. 8 Destroyer; No. 22 Seaplane. The carrier,
which in the ad was called "Liberator" sold for $10. The
"Libertania" aircraft carrier seems to be the same ship, or a
slight variation.

HILL-CLIMBER pressed steel Battleship. Courtesy Mapes Auctioneers & Appraisers.

IDEAL Varsity Racing Scull, 8 rowers, coxswain. Courtesy Wilkinson Collection, Detroit Antique Toy Museum.

KEYSTONE Action Submarine. Courtesy Jack Matthews.

"Kearsage" gunboat. Courtesy PB 84 New York.

HUBLEY "Sea Horse". Courtesy Ed Hyers Antique Toys.

KEYSTONE Aircraft Carrier, wooden, 12" long. Courtesy Mapes Auctioneers & Appraisers.

IDEAL Pirate Ship (missing pirate flag).

Aircraft Carrier "Libertania" (see Liberty Playthings). Courtesy Mapes Auctioneers & Appraisers.

	C6	C8	C10
Liberty Playthings Cruiser or Battleship	225	338	450
Liberty Playthings Destroyer No. 8	225	338	450
Liberty Playthings "Libertania" Aircraft Carrier, wood and tin litho with lead planes, 27-3/4" long	800	1200	1600
Life Boat, steel, simple design, circa late 1930s, 11" long x 5-1/4" wide..	20	30	40

MARKLIN "Columbus". Courtesy Christie's East.

LIONEL No. 43 windup speedboat. Courtesy Phillips New York.

	C6	C8	C10
Marklin "Priscilla" steam yacht, tin, 20-1/2" long	\multicolumn{3}{No Price Found}
Marx "Caribbean" friction Luxury Liner, sparkling, 15" long, 3-1/2" tall	85	127	170
Marx Mosquito Fleet Putt Putt Boat	80	120	160
Multiple Products Pirate Ship, plastic with pirates	60	90	125
"New Orleans" sidewheeler, cast iron, 11" long	600	950	1400
"New York" warship, metal, circa 1899, 17"	500	750	1000
Ohio Battleship, friction, painted pressed steel, 16" long	140	210	280

LIONEL No. 44 windup speedboat. Courtesy Sotheby's New York.

	C6	C8	C10
Lionel Craft No. 43 windup speedboat	340	510	680
Lionel Craft No. 44 windup speedboat	350	525	700
Manoil No. 79 Submarine, lead alloy, also No. 71	17	26	35
Marklin "Columbus" liner, tin, electrified, 42" long	\multicolumn{3}{No Price Found}

MARKLIN "Priscilla" Steam Yacht. Courtesy Christie's East.

MANOIL Submarine. Courtesy K. Warren Mitchell.

MARKLIN "Kronzprinz Wilhelm", tin, 37" long, offered at auction in 1994. It sold for $23,000. Courtesy Christie's East.

MARKLIN "New York" Battleship, circa 1910, 28" long, tin. Offered at auction in 1994, it sold for $33,350. Courtesy Christie's East.

MARKLIN U-Boat, tin clockwork, 30" long, offered at auction in 1994 in a suggested range of $4000-6000, but it failed to sell. Courtesy Christie's East.

MARKLIN "H.M.S. Resolution", tin, 36" long. Offered at auction in 1994, it sold for $14,950. Courtesy Christie's East.

ORKIN

ORKIN, of Cambridge, Massachusetts, was founded by Samuel Orkin about the end of World War One. His metal ships were modeled after the real thing. They were big, ranging from about 15 to 35", but relatively inexpensive.

	C6	C8	C10
Orkin Battleship B2, pressed steel, 36" long	3000	5000	8000
Orkin Battleship "Constitution", steel keywind, c. 1914, 25" long	500	750	1000
Orkin Battleship "Marcella", 18" long	600	900	1350

	C6	C8	C10
Orkin Battleship "Nevada", steel keywind, c. 1914, 22" long	550	825	1100
Orkin Battleship "New Jersey" tin and wood, circa 1920, 35" long	600	900	1400
Orkin Battleship "New Mexico", steel keywind, c. 1914, 25" long	500	750	1000
Orkin Battleship "Pennsylvania", steel keywind, c. 1914, 30" long	700	1100	1700

Top, Left to Right: Orkin Battleship "New Jersey"; Orkin Battleship "Nevada". Middle, Left to Right: Orkin Battleship "Pennsylvania"; Orkin Battleship "New Mexico". Bottom, Orkin Battleship "Constitution". Courtesy Christie's East.

ORKIN Battleship B2.
Courtesy Sotheby's New York.

ORKIN CRAFT

ORKIN CRAFT was owned by the president of the Waterman Pen Company, with manufacturing done by Calwis Industries Ltd. of Beverly Hills, California. The pleasure boats sold by the firm were too expensive for the era (the price was in the $15-20 range), which is probably why it failed about 1935 or 1936. All the boats were motor-driven. Some were all metal, and some had wood decks.

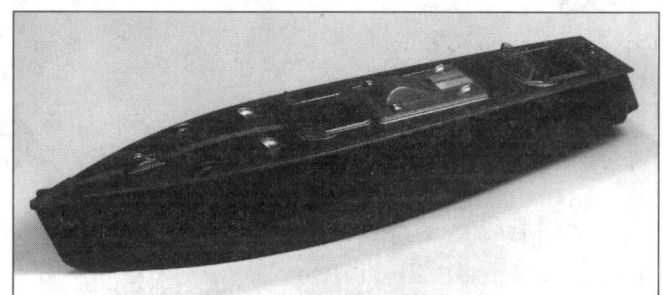

ORKIN Craft Speedboat, clockwork, 29" long. Courtesy Mapes Auctioneers & Appraisers.

	C6	C8	C10
Orkin Craft Cabin Cruiser, 30" long.....	900	1500	2075
Orkin Craft Speedboat, clockwork, 29" long..	1200	1900	2700
Payton Sea Raider, 34" long.................	20	30	40
"Priscilla" Side-Wheeler, Dent or Wilkins, cast iron, approx. 10" long	500	750	1000
PT107...	30	45	60
"Pull For The Shore", W.S. Reed, litho paper on wood........................	3500	8000	12000
Pull Toy boat by Hustilar Toy Corp., Sterling Ill., wood with some metal parts, oarsmen row in unison...........	75	112	150
"Puritan" Sidewheeler, cast iron, approx. 10-1/2" long......................	480	720	960
Reed "Ocean Queen" river boat, litho on wood, 23" long.......................	750	1300	1800
Reed Ocean Wave Freighter, c. 1883, with cargo, paper litho on wood, 35" long...	650	110	1500

	C6	C8	C10
Reed "Pilgrim" river boat, paper litho, 28-1/2" long............................	1000	1500	2000
Reed "River Queen" side-wheeler, litho on wood, c. 1895, 25" long......	1000	1500	2000
Remco Barracuda Sub., 23 man crew..	125	188	250
Remco "Big Caesar" Roman warship, with figures, 29" long.......................	125	188	250
Remco "Fighting Lady" battleship No. 710, 31" long....................................	115	172	230
Remco Gallant Gladiator Roman Warship, plastic, 17" long................	60	90	120
Remco Mighty Magee Carrier..............	80	120	160
Remco "Mighty Matilda" aircraft carrier, plastic, complete with all accessories, 35" long........................	75	113	150
Remco Showboat Theater......................	50	75	100
Renwal Drawbridge Set, bridge, 12 cars and boats...............................	55	82	110
Renwal Ocean Liner..............................	30	45	60
Renwal "Panama Canal", circa 1957, No. 273, 29" x 11".............................	55	82	110
Renwal Viking Ship No. 245, sold in 1955, 17" long................................	80	120	160
Row Boat with four men and oars, cast iron, mechanical, 9" long..........	1250	1875	2500
Row Boat, tin, rubber band driver, 9" long with man rowing..................	40	60	80
Schiebel Battleship, circa 1927, unpowered.......................................	1000	1500	2000
Schiebel Battleship, wood stacks and large wood guns and turrets, friction motor, circa 1920.......................	1250	1875	2500
Schoenhut Submarine and Dreadnought Naval War Toy, Pat. 4/6/15, torpedo explodes ship..........	100	150	200
Scull, 9-man crew, U.S. Hardware, wheeled, 14" long.............................	1600	2400	3200
Shore Patrol, battery operated, tin boat, 9" long....................................	10	15	20
Showboat, cast iron, 11" long..............	1000	1500	2000

REED "River Queen". Courtesy Wilkinson Collection, Detroit Antique Toy Museum.

RENWAL "Panama Canal", circa 1957. Courtesy Islyn Thomas.

SIDE WHEELER BOAT, tin, "The Star", 21" high with stand, 14-1/2" long.

"Speed Boat", A.C. Williams, 4" long, cast iron. (1932 ad)

Tillicum Battle Fleet No. 115. Courtesy John D. (Jack) Matthews.

RENWAL Viking Ship No. 245, sold in 1955. Courtesy Islyn Thomas.

Tillicum National Defense Set, Milton Bradley. Courtesy John D. (Jack) Matthews.

Tllicum Convoy Set, Milton Bradley. Courtesy John D. (Jack) Matthews.

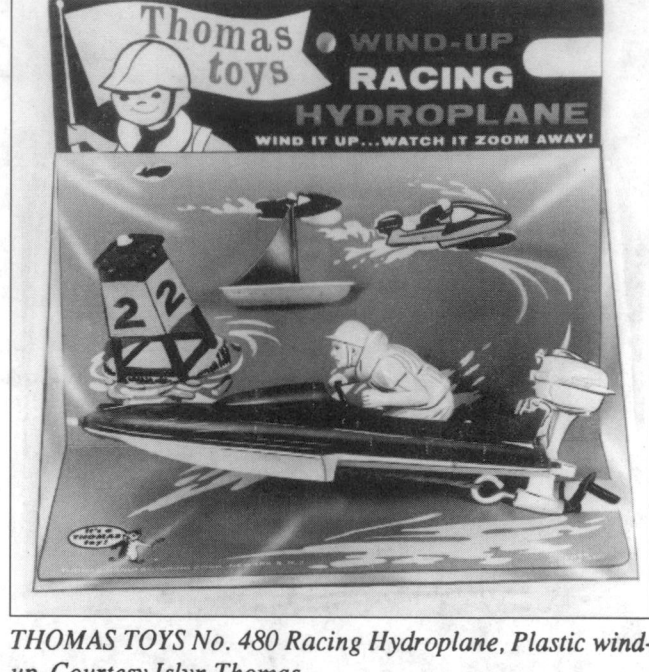

THOMAS TOYS No. 480 Racing Hydroplane, Plastic wind-up, Courtesy Islyn Thomas.

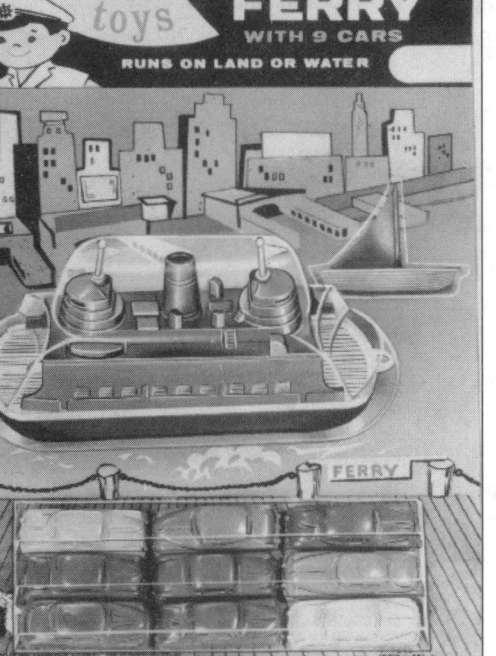

THOMAS TOYS No. 481 Ferry Boat with 9 cars and sailboat. Courtesy Islyn Thomas.

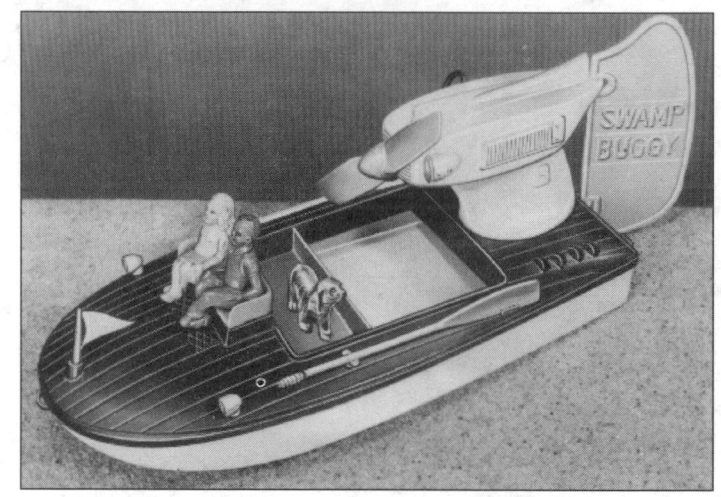

THOMAS TOYS No. 487 Swamp Buggy, motorized. Courtesy Islyn Thomas.

THOMAS TOYS, Top, Left to Right: Queen Mary, Battleship, Bottom: Left to Right: Aircraft Carrier, Freighter. All 5-1/2" long, plastic.

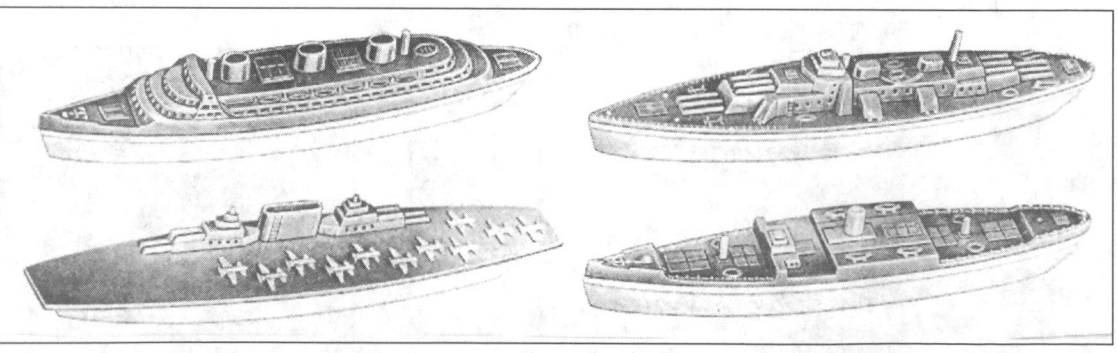

	C6	C8	C10
Side-Wheeler Boat, "The Star", tin, height with stand, 21", length 14-1/2"...............................	3500	5200	7000
Side-Wheeler, cast iron, approx. 5-1/2" long..........................	100	150	200
Side-Wheeler, cast iron, 8" long............	162	243	325

	C6	C8	C10
Side-Wheeler, cast iron, 10-1/2" long...	150	225	300
Side-Wheeler, tin clockwork, 11" long	90	135	180
"Sinking Battleship" Walbert Mfg., rubber band torpedo strikes die on ship and sinks it............................	250	375	500

TOOTSIETOY, Left to Right; Top: 1034 Battleship,
1036 Carrier, Middle: 1035 Cruiser, 1037 Liner,
Bottom: 127 Destroyer, 128 Submarine,
Photo by Ed Poole.

TOOTSIETOY, Left to Right; Top: 1037 Transport, 1039 Tanker,
Bottom: 129 Tender, 130 yacht. Photo by Ed Poole.

Steamship, alcohol burner, circa 1885, 19" long.
Courtesy Mapes Auctioneers & Appraisers.

	C6	C8	C10
"Speed Boat", A.C. Williams, cast iron, 5-1/4" long	60	90	120
"Speed Boat", A.C. Williams, cast iron with rider, 4-3/4" long	120	180	240
"Speed Boat", A.C. Williams, cast iron, 4" long	45	68	90
"Speed Boat", Kansas Toy & Novelty, "52", lead alloy, driver, 2-3/4" long	No Price Found		
Speed Boat, wood, rubber-band propelled	40	60	80
SS United States, tin friction, 6-1/2" long	50	75	100
Steam Boat "Memphis" Kansas Toy & Novelty "53", lead alloy, metal disc wheels, 2-7/8" long	No Price Found		
Steam Boat, tin, self-propelled, 17" long.	150	225	300
Steamer, litho paper on wood, 39" long, 22-1/2" high	450	675	900
Steamship, alcohol burner, c. 1885, 19" long	200	300	400
Sterling "56" scale model, all wood and metal Battleship Missouri, radio control, w/three electric motors	350	525	700
Submarine, "575", tin litho, remote-controlled, circa 1960	40	60	80
Submarine, glass	225	338	450

	C6	C8	C10
Submarine, steel, 6" long	40	60	80
Texaco Tanker	80	120	160
Thomas Toys Aircraft Carrier, plastic, 5-1/2" long	12	18	25
Thomas Toys Battleship, plastic, 5-1/2" long	12	18	25
Thomas Toys Freighter, plastic, 5-1/2" long	12	18	25
Thomas Toys Queen Mary, plastic, 5-1/2" long	15	22	30
Thomas Toys No. 480 Racing Hydroplane, plastic	12	18	25
Thomas Toys No. 481 Ferry Boat with sailboat, 9 cars, plastic	12	18	25
Thomas Toys No. 487 Swamp Buggy, motorized, plastic	12	18	25

TILLICUM

In 1930, Tillicum wood toys were made in Tacoma, Washington.

	C6	C8	C10
Tillicum Battle Fleet No. 115, Milton Bradley, c. late 1920s	31	46	62
Tillicum Convoy Set, Milton Bradley, 1940s, 2 destroyers, 3 freight boats, 3 ocean liners, 2 patrol boats, painted wood, destroyers 5-1/2" long, others about 4-1/2" long	350	525	700

	C6	C8	C10
Tillicum Harbor Set, Milton Bradley....	20	30	40
Tillicum National Defense Set, Milton Bradley....................................	40	60	80

TOOTSIETOY

(Compiled by Ed Poole and John Gibson)

	C6	C8	C10
127 Destroyer, 4".................................	8	11	15
128 Submarine, 4"...............................	7	10	13
129 Tender, 4"....................................	10	15	20
130 Yacht, 4"....................................	10	15	20
1034 Battleship, 6"............................	11	17	22
1035 Cruiser, 5-1/2".........................	11	17	22
1036 Aircraft Carrier, 6"...................	14	21	28
1037 Transport, 6"............................	12	18	24
1038 Freighter, 5-1/2".......................	11	17	22
1039 Tanker, 5-1/2"..........................	11	17	22

TOOTSIETOY MINIATURE SHIPS

	C6	C8	C10
196 Battleship....................................	4	6	8
1405 Fleet 9pc carded battleship assortment (1941): USS Idaho, USS Indiana, USS Tennessee, USS Texas, USS New Mexico, USS Maryland, USS Arizona, USS New York, USS Pennsylvania............................	50	75	100
1408 Naval Defense 14 pc carded assortment (1941).............................	70	105	140
1612 Cruiser......................................	3	4	6
1613 Destroyer..................................	3	4	6
1614 Submarine (smaller)....................	2	3	4
1618 Submarine.................................	3	4	6
1619 Destroyer..................................	3	4	6
1620 Aero Carrier..............................	4	6	8
1638 Battleship..................................	4	6	8
1811 Sea Champions 5 pc carded set (1946) contains: 2 #1638 battleships, 1 #1618 submarine, 1 #1619 destroyer, and 1 #1620 aero carrier.................	30	45	60
4519 Battleship..................................	8	12	16
4538 Tugboat....................................	2	3	4
4539 Speedboat.................................	2	3	4

End Tootsietoy

	C6	C8	C10
Turbo Boat, pressed tin, 10-1/2 long...	40	60	80
U.S. Naval Base, Superior......................	60	90	120
U.S. Hardware Rowers, circa 1890, 8 man crew and coxswain, cast iron, large wheels, 14-1/2" long................	2000	3200	4500
U.S. Hardware Rowers, circa 1890, 4 man crew and coxswain, cast iron			

U.S. HARDWARE Rowers, circa 1890. Courtesy Ed Hyers Antique Toys.

	C6	C8	C10
large wheels.................................	1250	1875	2500
"U.S.S. Maine" paper litho on wood, Reed?....................................	600	900	1200
"U.S.S. Narwahl", submarine, lead, mfg. unknown, 1930s, 7-1/2" long..	20	30	40
"U.S.S. New Mexico", battleship, lead, manufacturer unknown, 1930s.........	20	30	40
"U.S. Submarine", painted wood, fires torpedo for target set, 13" long.........	20	30	40
U.S. Wasp, carrier, wood storage under deck for planes, 27" long.......	50	75	100

WANNATOYS

WANNATOYS were manufactured by Dillon-Beck Manufacturing Company of Irvington, New Jersey from 1941 on. They were plastic.

	C6	C8	C10
Wannatoys Cruiser..............................	3	4.50	6
Wannatoys Freighter............................	3	4.50	6
Wannatoys Submarine.........................	3	4.50	6
Weeden "Dewey" Steamboat, circa 1900, 15-1/2" long...........................	500	750	1000
Weeden Launch, steam-driven, 18" long..	350	525	700
Weeden Steamboat, live steam, 15" long..	300	450	600
Wilkins Battleship, cast iron................	800	1400	2000
Wilkins "City of New York" river- boat, 15" long.................................	220	330	440
Wilkins "Puritan" riverboat, 10-1/2" long.................................	750	1300	1800
Wilkins Riverboat, 5-3/4" long............	140	210	280
Wilkins Riverboat, circa 1910, cast iron, 7-1/2" long................................	250	375	500
Wilkins Riverboat, cast iron, 10-1/2" long.................................	450	675	900
Wilkins Rowers, c. 1890, 4 man crew and coxswain in 10" long, big wheeled boat, cast iron....................	1250	1875	2500

WANNATOYS (Dillion-Beck) plastic ships, advertised in the July, 1941 Playthings. Plastic Toys, Inc. copied the submarine a few years later.

Top to Bottom: "U.S.S. New Mexico", "U.S.S. Narwahl". Courtesy Hank Anton.

WOLVERINE Diving Submarine. Courtesy Mapes Auctioneers & Appraisers.

WEEDEN Launch, steam-driven, 18" long. Courtesy Heinz Mueller, Continental Hobby House.

FERRY BOAT
No. 170—Boat travels rapidly along floor until either end strikes any solid object, then reverses automatically and travels in opposite direction. Has long running clockwork 13½ inches long
.... $3.50

WOLVERINE "Sandy Andy" Ferry.

	C6	C8	C10
Williams, A.C., Blue Speed Boat, cast iron, 4-3/4" long	120	180	240
Wolverine Diving Submarine, 13" long	115	172	230
Wolverine Ocean Liner	125	188	250
Wolverine "Sandy Andy Ferry", tin litho, 13-1/2" long	75	112.50	150
Wolverine Sandy Andy "Ferrygo", tin and wood, 11" long	150	225	300
Wyandotte Aircraft Carrier	55	82	110
Wyandotte Pocket Batleship, tin litho, wheeled, 7" long	60	90	120
Wyandotte "S.S. America", moves on metal wheels, 1930s, 7" long	50	75	100
Wyandotte "Sand-o'Land", tin litho sandtoy, wood wheels, 1940s, 10" long	40	60	80
Wyandotte Submarine	112	168	225
Wyandotte "U.S.S. Enterprise"	80	120	160
Yacht-type ship, either Ives or Bing, spring wind motor, 28" long	2000	3000	4000

WILKINS Riverboat, 10-1/2" long. Courtesy Mapes Auctioneers & Appraisers.

SCHOENHUT

By Blossom Abell with Jim and Patsy Carlson
C8 prices for Schoenhuts averaged $577.87 in the last edition. In this edition
they average $850.42, an increase of 47%.

The A. Schoenhut Company had a long history of toy manufacturing. Many items were produced, including animals, figures, moving pictures, Palmer Cox Brownies, children's musical instruments, and dolls. This section covers some of the items in the Humpty Dumpty Circus.

A brief chronological history of the A. Schoenhut Company follows:

- 1872 -Produced the first toy pianos
- 1903 -Began producing Humpty Dumpty Circus items
       -Began producing glass eyed animals, molded/two part head personnel
- 1909/11 -Produced Teddy Roosevelt figures
- 1910 -Produced bisque head ring master, lady circus rider, lion tamer, lady/gent acrobats
- 1918 -Produced painted eyed animals, wooden head personnel
- 1923 -Began producing reduced size circus
- 1927 -Produced miniature set (donkey, elephant, clown)
- 1935 -Company closed
- 1950 -Nelson Delavan purchased manufacturing rights and produced several figures and animals.

This history is not all inclusive, but should help the collector identify age for some animals/figures.

The Humpty Dumpty items covered in this section span the years of 1903 to 1935. Glass eyed animals and carved face personnel along with other rare examples are priced higher than painted eye animals and pressed head figures produced later. Delavan items are generally priced lower than reduced size figures.

In the past few years, popularity from toy collectors and folk art collectors have driven prices upwards. Particular interest in Teddy Roosevelt's "Adventures in Africa" series produced from 1909 to 1911 have led the price increase.

This price list should serve as a guideline for the collector. Several points deserve additional comment. Those comments are:

- Condition determines price (See photo of four horses for examples of condition C2 to C8)
- Mint condition Schoenhut toys are virtually non-existent. Mint condition means the toy was never played with. Toys found in this condition demand higher prices. Boxes increase value, and mint with the box commands a sizable premium.
- Glass eyed animals, early figures with plaster faces, and rare animals demand high prices also.
- It is acceptable to include rare figures and rare animals of lesser condition in a collection.
- Bisque headed figures and molded/two part head figures usually are priced higher than carved face figures.
- Condition on the majority of animals and figures found today is between C4 and C8.
- Skillful restoration can increase value. Anyone selling an animal or figure with restored sections should indicate where restoration has occurred.
- Prices in this guide have not been established for every style of animal and figure.

Because of the importance of condition and classification for the Schoenhut category of toys, the authors felt the need to enhance the existing definitions of Schoenhut categories and therefore assist pricing.

In addition, the authors call your attention to the prices shown. These prices reflect average prices realized at numerous auctions during the past year, and pricing factors applied to condition to determine prices for each category.

Private sales oftentimes differ from the prices shown.

Finally, many Schoenhut pieces found today are in the C4 to C7 category.

Exceptional condition remains difficult to find.

Definition of Terms

Rating	Definition
C1	Bits and pieces of Schoenhut toys.
C2	Poor quality with no paint or a "child's" effort to repaint, or, missing a major part. Definitely needs repair.
C3	Fair with no missing major part, but with little paint and moisture/moth/animal damage and soiling. Needs repair.
C4	Good with play wear, soiled/worn clothing, damaged paint/chips, missing leather and/or other attachable parts.
C5	Very good with either restored paint, clothes, and/or leather. Or could be good enough not to require restoration.
C6	Fine with good paint, new or worn leather and minor restorations. Could also have some soiling/wear/color loss and missing minor attached parts.

C7	Very fine with minor wear/color loss and fractional restoration.
C8	Almost perfect with no restoration but may have slight color loss. This is a wonderful piece.
C9	Perfect, meaning no damage or color loss of any kind. Almost new.
C10	Mint, meaning never played with and stored under ideal conditions. Factory new.

NOTE: Re-stringing is not considered restoration. If the re-stringing effort is not done properly however, wood damage can occur and reduce the value of the piece.

Additional information on Schoenhut figures or dolls can be obtained by joining the Schoenhut Collectors Club. For a membership application, please contact: Pat Girbach, 103 West Huron Street, Ann Arbor, MI 48103.

Jim and Patsy Carlson purchased a partial Schoenhut circus in 1988 as a rememberance to a deceased parent. That "rememberance" has now grown to include several specialized Schoenhut pieces, including an almost complete "Teddy Roosevelt's Adventures in Africa" play set.

The additional pieces would not have happened without the help of their dear friend Blossom Abell, who passed away in March, 1994. She openly shared her love and vast knowledge of Schoenhut with the Carlsons.

Jim and Patsy are members of the Schoenhut Collectors Club and Antique Toy Collectors of America.

In addition to collecting Schoenhut, the Carlsons actively collect platform animals, American rocking horses, early squeak toys, folk art and American primitive paintings, especially of children. They have one daughter in graduate school and reside in Clarkston, Michigan.

Prices below for regular size Circus animals that are most frequently seen. Not all animals have been included. Glass eyed animals are aged from 1903, when A. Schoenhut Company began to produce Circus animals and performers, to about 1918. Painted eyed animals are aged from about 1918 to 1933, the closing of the A. Schoenhut Company.

Circus Animals - Glass Eyed and Painted Eyed
Circus Animals
Regular Size

	C2	C4	C6	C8
Alligator, GE	100	175	350	475
Alligator, PE	75	125	250	385
Brown Bear, GE	175	325	425	600
Brown Bear, PE	75	120	250	375
Bulldog, GE	200	350	700	1000
Bulldog, PE	100	150	250	425
Buffalo, GE, cloth	100	200	325	500
Buffalo, GE, crvd	200	400	750	1050
Buffalo, PE	100	200	300	450
Burro, PE	100	175	275	400

SCHOENHUT Cloth Circus Tent, 34" high, with performers and animals. Courtesy Wilkinson Collection, Detroit Antique Toy Museum.

SCHOENHUTS, Left to Right: Glass-eyed Horse, missing leather belly strap, (C6), GE Horse, very worn paint and missing platform and belly strap, (C3), GE Horse, kid repainted, shipped wood and missing all attachable parts, (C2); foreground, GE Horse, good paint, missing attachable parts, (C4). Photo by Blossom Abell.

	C2	C4	C6	C8
Camel, 1 hump, GE	100	150	300	425
Camel, 1 hump, PE	95	120	250	375
Camel, 2 hump, GE	200	475	950	1400
Camel, 2 hump, PE	95	135	275	400
Cat, GE	500	1000	1600	2400
Cat, PE	200	360	725	1100
Cow, PE	50	125	250	385
Deer, GE	200	300	575	875
Deer, PE	175	325	425	600
Donkey, GE	30	60	120	175
Donkey, PE	20	30	50	75

	C2	C4	C6	C8
Elephant, GE	40	70	135	200
Elephant, PE	30	50	100	150
Gazelle, GE	400	1000	1600	2400
Gazelle, PE	300	400	775	1200
Giraffe, GE	100	175	350	500
Giraffe, PE	75	120	250	350
Goat, GE	75	200	275	350
Goat, PE	50	150	225	300
Goose, PE	75	150	350	475
Gorilla, molded ears	1000	1300	1600	2400
Hippoptamus, GE	100	275	550	800
Hippoptamus, PE	75	120	250	375

SCHOENHUT, Right to Left: Store Display-size Donkey, 14" tall, PE, C6; Donkey with Saddle, GE, C6 (Humpty-Dumpty Circus). Collection and Photo Jim and Patsy Carlson.

SCHOENHUT Cat, GE, C8, from Humpty-Dumpty Circus. Collection and Photo Jim and Patsy Carlson.

SCHOENHUT, Left to Right: Lion, PE (C6); Lion, GE, carved ears (C6). Both from Humpty-Dumpty Circus. Collection/Photo Jim and Patsy Carlson.

SCHOENHUT, Left to Right: Buffalo (C6) GE, cloth mane, mane worn; Buffalo (C8) GE, carved mane. Collection/Photo Blossom Abell.

SCHOENHUT, Left to Right: Giraffe (C8) PE, carved head; Giraffe (C8) GE. Collection/Photo Blossom Abell

SCHOENHUT, Left to Right: Camel (C9) reduced; Camel (C9), GE, Arabian, 1 hump; Camel (C8) GE, Bactrian, 2 hump. Collection/Photo Blossom Abell.

SCHOENHUT, Left to Right: Hippo, Style I, early, GE, (C7); Hippo, Style II, GE, (C7). Humpty-Dumpty Circus. Collection/Photo Jim and Patsy Carlson.

SCHOENHUT, Left to Right: Ostrich (C9) GE; Ostrich (C9) PE. Collection/Photo Blossom Abell.

SCHOENHUT, Left to Right: Pig (C9) reduced, fancy face; Pig (C8) GE, one piece head/neck; Pig (C5) ball joint head, body restoration. Collection/Photo Blossom Abell.

	C2	C4	C6	C8
Horse, Brown, GE	75	100	160	230
Horse, Brown, PE	30	50	100	150
Horse, White, GE	85	120	175	275
Horse, White, PE	40	75	125	190
Hyena, GE	1200	1400	1850	2600
Hyena, PE	400	500	950	1400
Kangaroo, GE	400	500	950	1400
Kangaroo, PE	200	350	700	1000
Leopard, GE	100	275	550	825
Leopard, PE	75	150	300	450
Lion, GE, crvd mane	300	475	850	1275
Lion, GE, cloth mane	100	200	400	600
Lion, PE	95	175	375	525
Monkey, blk face	100	200	400	600
Monkey, white face	125	225	500	750
Ostrich, GE	200	300	600	900
Ostrich, PE	100	225	300	425

SCHOENHUT, Left to Right: Tiger (C9) reduced; Tiger (C6) PE; Tiger (C9) PE (early). Collection/Photo Blossom Abell.

SCHOENHUT, Wolf, PE (C8), Humpty-Dumpty Circus. Collection/Photo Jim and Patsy Carlson.

SCHOENHUT, Left to Right: Leopard (C8) GE; Leopard (C9) reduced; Leopard (C7) PE, worn paint on face. Collection/Photo Blossom Abell.

615

SCHOENHUT, Left to Right: Hobo (C8) 2 part head; Chinaman Acrobat (C5) 2 part head, replaced felt on jacket. Collection/ Photo Blossom Abell.

SCHOENHUT, Left to Right: Clown (C7) wood hat/leather ears; Clown (C7) cloth hat over wood cone; Poodle (C7) reduced; Clown (C7) molded ears, all clowns reduced. Collection/Photo Blossom Abell.

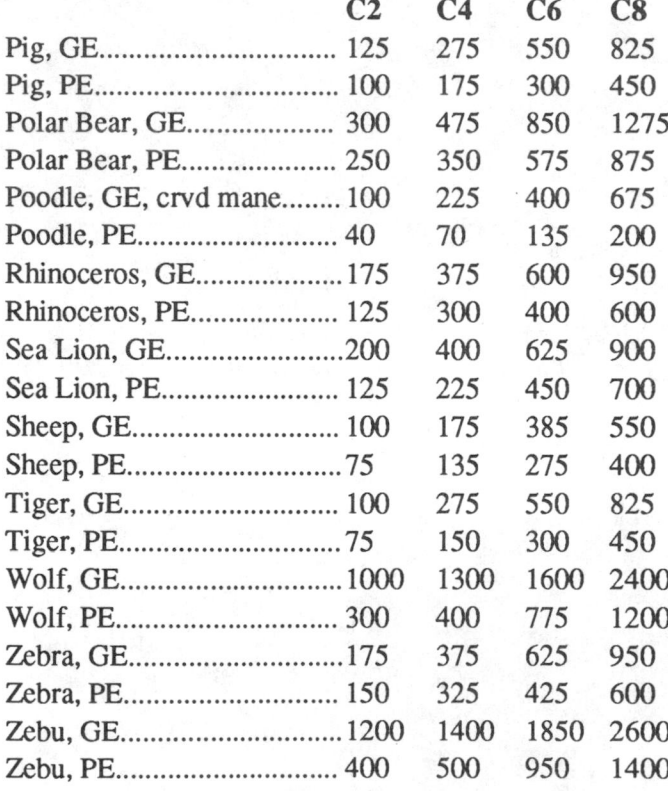

SCHOENHUT, Left to Right: Lady Rider, reduced (C8); Lady Rider Bisque Head (C8); Lady Rider, 2 part Head (C6), replaced skirt. Collection/Photo Blossom Abell.

	C2	C4	C6	C8
Pig, GE	125	275	550	825
Pig, PE	100	175	300	450
Polar Bear, GE	300	475	850	1275
Polar Bear, PE	250	350	575	875
Poodle, GE, crvd mane	100	225	400	675
Poodle, PE	40	70	135	200
Rhinoceros, GE	175	375	600	950
Rhinoceros, PE	125	300	400	600
Sea Lion, GE	200	400	625	900
Sea Lion, PE	125	225	450	700
Sheep, GE	100	175	385	550
Sheep, PE	75	135	275	400
Tiger, GE	100	275	550	825
Tiger, PE	75	150	300	450
Wolf, GE	1000	1300	1600	2400
Wolf, PE	300	400	775	1200
Zebra, GE	175	375	625	950
Zebra, PE	150	325	425	600
Zebu, GE	1200	1400	1850	2600
Zebu, PE	400	500	950	1400

The prices below are for regular size and a few reduced-size Circus Accessory Items. These items are most commonly found in "play wear" condition in the C4 to C7 category. Not all accessories have been included.

Accessories

Ball	10	20	40	50
Ball, reduced	10	15	30	40

SCHOENHUT, Left to Right: Lion (C10) GE, cloth mane; Monkey (C8), white face. Collection/Photo Blossom Abell.

	C2	C4	C6	C8
Barrel	2	4	6	10
Chair	2	4	6	10
Flexible Cage	75	175	375	500
Goblet	3	5	8	12
Hoop	10	15	25	40
Horizontal Bar	75	175	375	500
Ladder	2	4	6	10
Pedestal, short	10	20	30	45
Pedestal, tall	15	25	40	60
Table	15	25	40	65
Tent, 24"x16"(sml)	200	400	500	750
Tent, 24"x36" (lrg)	700	1100	1400	2200
Tent, litho w/panels	2000	3000	6000	9000
Tub	10	20	35	50
Weights 50/100/200lbs	75	150	200	325
Whip, 4-1/2" shaft	10	20	30	45
Whip, 5-1/2" shaft	15	25	40	65

SCHOENHUT, Left to Right: Clown (C7) plaster face, 2 part head, sunburst suit; Clown (C7) wood head; Clown (C7) wood head. Collection/Photo Blossom Abell.

SCHOENHUT, Left to Right: Polar Bear (C8) PE; (foreground) Polar Bear (C7) PE; 12" Wild Animal Cage Wagon (C8): Polar Bear (C7) GE; Lion Tamer (C9) 1 part head. Collection/Photo Blossom Abell.

The prices below are shown for regular size, wooden/pressed headed figures. Not all figures have been included, but where data is available, notation is made. The manufacturing sequence for figures was plaster face two-part head/faces, bisque heads and finally wooden/pressed one part head.

Prices shown below represent wooden/pressed one part head figures.

Performers Wooden/Pressed One Part Head

Performers, One Part Head	C2	C4	C6	C8
Chinaman	100	200	325	450
Clown	20	65	100	125
Hobo	45	145	250	325
Lady Acrobat	65	150	275	375
Lady Rider	45	145	250	325

SCHOENHUT, Left to Right: Top Row, earliest Clowns, plaster face, 2 part head with "footprint" or "snail" on front of uniform (C5), (C6), (C7). Bottom, wood head, striped suit, (C5); wood head, card suit (C6); 2 part head, sunburst suit (C7). Collection/Photo Jim and Patsy Carlson.

SCHOENHUT, Negro Dude, Style I, black coat (C6) from Humpty-Dumpty Circus. Collection/Photo Jim and Patsy Carlson.

	C2	C4	C6	C8
Lion Tamer	45	145	250	325
Negro Dude	100	200	325	450
Ring Master	65	150	275	375

The prices below are shown for reduced-size figures and animals. Not all figures and animals have been included, but where data is available, notation is made. Reduced-size figures and animals were first produced about 1927 by the A. Schoenhut Company to appeal to another market, and, perhaps by this production save the company. Even with this action the company still closed in 1933.

Reduced Size Figures and Animals

	C2	C4	C6	C8
Circus Figures, Reduced				
Clown	15	40	65	100
Hobo	55	130	280	410
Lady Rider	30	65	125	225
Negro Dude	65	140	370	500
Ring Master	30	60	120	200
Animals, Reduced				
Brown Bear	75	120	275	400
Buffalo	65	140	225	350
Camel, 2 hump	75	120	275	375
Donkey	20	30	40	50

	C2	C4	C6	C8
Elephant	25	45	95	125
Giraffe	75	120	275	400
Hippopotamus	100	240	325	500
Horse, Brown	30	50	100	135
Horse, White	30	50	100	135
Leopard	75	120	275	375
Lion	75	120	275	375
Ostrich	85	150	300	425
Pig	100	250	400	425
Poodle	75	120	275	400
Rhinoceros	85	150	300	425
Tiger	75	120	275	375
Zebra	150	325	450	600

Represented below are prices realized for "Teddy's Adventures in Africa". These figures were produced in low volume from 1909 to 1911 and represent "rare" or "scarce" toys.

Some of the animals were used in circus play-toys produced with Glass Eyes (GE) until 1918.

Teddy Roosevelt"s Adventures in Africa

	C2	C4	C6	C8
Teddy Roosevelt Figures				
Teddy Roosevelt	750	1000	1300	2000
Photographer (Kermit)	850	1300	1700	2450
African Native	700	1100	1400	2100
African Drummer	700	1100	1400	2100
African Chief	650	900	1200	1800
Arab Chief	900	1400	1800	2700
Doctor	950	1400	1800	2700
Naturalist	950	1400	1800	2700

SCHOENHUT, some personnel from Teddy's Adventures in Africa, Left to Right: Kermit (C6); Accessories - wire frame tent; bowl; barrel & jug; Great Guide (C10); African Drummer (C6); Teddy Roosevelt with rifle (C6); African Chief (C7). Collection/Photo Jim and Patsy Carlson.

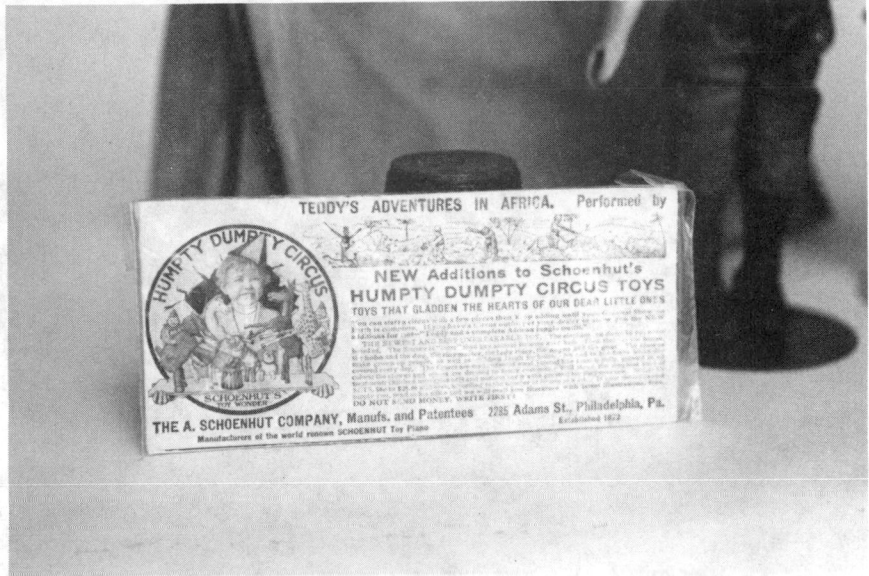

Magazine ad, 1910, for "Teddy's Adventures in Africa", 2-1/2" x 5-3/4". Collection/Photo Jim and Patsy Carlson.

SCHOENHUT, Great Guide (C10) from Teddy's Adventures in Africa. Collection/ Photo Jim and Patsy Carlson.

	C2	C4	C6	C8
Teddy Roosevelt Animals				
Alligator, GE	100	175	350	475
Camel, GE, 1 hump, closed mouth	100	150	300	425
Deer, GE	200	300	575	875
Elephant, GE	40	70	135	200

	C2	C4	C6	C8
Gazelle, GE	400	1000	1600	2400
Gorilla, leather ear	1100	1400	1700	2500
Hippopotamus, GE	100	275	550	800
Hyena, GE	1200	1400	1850	2600
Lion, GE, crvd mane	300	475	850	1275
Rhinoceros, GE	175	375	600	950
Zebra, GE, closed mth	175	375	625	950
Zebu, GE	1200	1400	1850	2600

SCHOENHUT, Gorilla, two part head, leather ears (C7) from Teddy's Adventures in Africa. Collection/Photo Jim and Patsy Carlson..

SCHOENHUT, African Chief, pouty lips & mouth (C7) from Teddy's Adventures in Africa. Collection/Photo Jim and Patsy Carlson.

SCHOENHUT Golfer in skirt. Photo courtesy PB 84.

SCHOENHUT Golfer Man. Courtesy Sotheby's New York.

The prices below are for a small number of Miscellaneous items produced by the A. Schoenhut company.

	C2	C4	C6	C8
Miscellaneous				
Doll House, small	100	150	250	375
Doll House, medium	125	175	375	425
Doll House, large	150	225	500	750
Golfer, Girl	125	200	375	475
Golfer, Man	125	175	350	425
Milk Wagon, horses and driver	1250	2400	3000	4000
Piano	No Information Available			
Railroad Station, large	125	175	350	475

This boxed SCHOENHUT Humpty-Dumpty Circus No. 2036, circa 1925, with jointed figures and glass-eyed animals, was auctioned in 1994 for $3680. Courtesy Christie's East.

A SCHOENHUT "Humpty-Dumpty Circus" circa 1915. It was auctioned in 1994 for $2185. Courtesy Christie's East.

The prices below are for a small number of Comic Characters produced by the A. Schoenhut company. Items shown as "rare" means not enough examples have been sold to determine prices.

Comic Character	C2	C4	C6	C8
Barney Google and Sparkplug	300	360	725	1100
Bonzo	Rare			
Boob McNutt	250	575	1050	1500
Felix, 4"	30	60	120	175
Felix, 6"	100	275	550	800
Felix, 8"	95	135	275	400
Happy Hooligan	250	575	1050	1500
Koko the Clown	Rare			
Maggie/Jiggs, rolling pin & bucket	200	400	775	1200
Max and Moritz, pair, early model	275	675	1100	1600
Rolly Dolly				
Dutch Girl	65	150	275	375
Foxy Grandpa, lge	100	275	550	800
Santa, medium	225	475	975	1350
Santa, large	500	1000	1600	2400

SCHOENHUT Felix the Cat, 6" (C7), 4" (C7), 8" (C8). Photo by Blossom Abell.

SCHOENHUT, Left to Right: Barney Google (early) 7-3/4" (C7); Sparkplug (C7); Barney, 7" (C7). Photo by Blossom Abell.

FISHER-PRICE TOYS

By John Murray

Fisher-Price toys in the last edition averaged $322.19 in mint condition
and this year average $352.38, an increase of 9%.

On October 1, 1930, in East Aurora, New York, the Fisher-Price Toy company began operation. Uniquely located on a small side street in a small town atmosphere, it would grow and eventually be considered one of the major manufacturers of toys.

Herman Fisher and Irving Price shared their names in developing a name for their new company. Herman Fisher, a past employee of the FairChild Company, a manufacturer of games, and Irving Price, who had sound experience with the Woolworth Company, would form the guidelines by which they would run their new company.

The first manufacturing facility was located on Church Street in East Aurora, New York. To date it still exists, but was sold by Fisher-Price in the 1970s due to lack of use for the facility.

The Church Street facility would be considered a small area for any type of manufacturing today, but would serve as the main and only facility for Fisher-Price toys for the first twenty years.

The most important factor in constructing this new company was to create a work force that could contribute their efforts towards a smooth, profitable venture. Among the most important employees would be Helen M. Schelle and Margaret Evans Price.

Helen M. Schelle was the first secretary and treasurer of Fisher-Price toys. She developed her skills in the retail management field through a business in which she operated, the Walker Toy Shop, in Binghamton, New York. Given the opportunity to manage the early company's activities, Helen proved to be a great asset to the advancement of Fisher-Price toys.

Margaret Evans Price was the company's first artist and designer for their new line of toys. She developed her early skills as a writer and illustrator for Rand McNally and Harper & Brothers, and by creating children's art for Strecher Lithography Company of Rochester, New York. Many of Margaret Evans Price's art work can still be found on early post cards, valentines, and children's books. These early paper collectibles are most often marked "M.E.P.".

Margaret created the early art work for the reproduction of color lithography for the toys. She was also talented in drawing, produced designs for early toys, and contributed in the development of her concepts to Fisher-Price's early line of toys. The Roycroft printers contributed their skills to produce the sales catalogs that prospective retailers would use to choose the toys that they would market.

The most important early development for the company was the forming of the labor force that would generate their efforts towards building the new toy line that would be sold to the public in 1931. The initial work force that first year was approximately 25 employees. As typical of any small town like East Aurora, most employees were neighbors, friends, and relatives, who contributed to a work force that took great pride in the product that they made, since many of the operations were done by hand labor.

Many of the early operations, such as band sawing, drilling, nailing, and painting were shared by these early employees. Quality control would be created by one employee checking the other and making any corrections immediately.

As Fisher-Price began toymaking, numbers were assigned to each toy. This number system started at Number 5 and went up into the thousands. To add to the confusion for collectors today, many of the numbers have been used more than once on various toys.

With the abundance of pine and its ease of workability, this was the main wood used in construction of Fisher-Price toys. During the 30s, another material was used, a heavy cardboard, in which brass eyelets were inserted to prevent wear from spinnning axles.

Creating action from child power was of great importance. The use of bellows was common to produce sound, and, as time passed, the introduction of bells was added to create sound and action.

Because of the immense amount of time required to assemble various toys, cottage-type industries were set up by employees, families, and residents of East Aurora. Toys such as the Pop-up Kritter were completely hand assembled in area homes. Because of the large demand, this would prove to be a quick and efficient method of assembly.

As the demand for Fisher-Price toys consistently rose, they began to use the skills of a freelance designer, Edward Savage, a mechanical engineer from the University of Minnesota. He created some of Fisher-Price's most successful toys. In his home in Rochester, New York, Savage created such toys as the Pop-up Kritters, Snoopy Sniffer, and many of the wind-up toys. The most popular of the toys that he created was the Snoopy Sniffer, which was produced from the 30s to the 80s, in four different versions.

After well over a decade of positive growth for Fisher-Price toys in the 30s and 40s, Fisher-Price would meet a major challenge of limited production.

With the United States entering World War II, Fisher-Price, like many companies, served its patriotic duty in a quite different type of manufacturing.

Because of the type of manufacturing that Fisher-Price was set up for, the ability to create and produce wood products set the basis for essential goods needed for war production. Ship fenders, first aid kits, cots, bomb crates, and glider ailerons were among the items produced from 1943-1946.

During this time of near non-existent toy manufacturing, very limited toy production continued on a material-availability basis. These toys were made from scraps of wood, with bells and some metal parts painted instead of plated. Toys made during this time sometimes used parts from similar toys, leaving odd and sometimes unusual variations.

As the World War came to an end, normal production began to resume. Well into the 50s, Ponderosa Pine, with a proven durability, was the main source of material in Fisher-Price toys. As wood became more difficult to obtain, the experimentation with plastics as a new material began. The first toy to use this new material successfully was the Busy Bee. Because of the ease of molding, durability, and bright colors, plastic was more prevalent in toys of the 50s.

In 1951, Fisher-Price moved to its new manufacturing facility on Girard Avenue in East Aurora, New York. The Girard Avenue facility handled most operations well into the late 50s.

In 1957, Tri Mold of Kenmore, New York, a plastics manufacturer, became a subsidiary of Fisher-Price and their main molding facility.

As the demand for plastics became greater and greater, a new molding facility was built in Holland, New York. This was completed in July 1962. The Holland Plant produced many of the plastic parts used in the construction of a more plastic-dominated toy line.

As the 60's advanced, plastic would eventually take over as the main material used to produce toys.

In 1969, the Quaker Oats Company acquired Fisher-Price toys. Three years prior to this acquisition, Herman Fisher resigned as president of the company, and was chairman of the board until the Quaker Oats acquisition. Since Fisher-Price was taken over by Quaker Oats, a plant in Medina, New York, was built, and numerous plants and facilities both nationally and internationally were created.

Considered one of the oldest and largest manufacturers of toys, Fisher-Price has its main offices at the Girard Avenue address in East Aurora, New York.

As I am sure many of you are aware, not only the earlier Fisher-Price are collectible, but the 1963 and newer has fast been an upcoming area of desirability of Fisher-Price toys.

TOYFEST TOYS:

One area of Fisher-Price that has created a large following of Fisher-Price is the limited edition (under 5,000) toys for the annual Toyfest celebration held in East Aurora, New York, each year since 1987.

This event attracts collectors of toys from all over the US and Canada, and frequent visitors from Europe. The toys manufactured for this event are as follows:

> #6550 Buzzy Bee, 1987
> #6558 Little Snoopy, 1988
> #6575 Toot Toot Engine, 1989
> #6590 Prancing Horses, 1990
> #6592 Teddy Bear Parade, 1991
> #6599 Molly Bell, 1992
> #6145 Jingle Elephant, 1993
> #6464 Gran'pa Frog, 1994

The second year toy has sold for well over $500, MIB and others are moving upwards in value because of the limited availability.

Fisher-Price also manufactured in 1991 a very limited (less than 4,000) toys of the traditional 1930s Snoopy Sniffer, #6588.

Fisher-Price Collector's Club

Since the last time I updated the Fisher-Price section, a Fisher-Price Collectors Club has begun. This is a great opportunity for fellow collectors to advance their knowledge, buy and sell, and communicate with other collectors.

I would encourage joining the club as information on new and old Fisher-Price is plentiful in the newsletter. For information, contact the Fisher-Price Collector's Club, Attention: Jeanne Kennedy, 1442 North Ogden, Meza, AZ 85205.

CONDITION

There are many factors that may contribute to values of Fisher-Price toys. The most important factor to consider is the paper lithography. Most Fisher-Price toys found have what I call "edge wear". Edge wear may be considered as wear only around the outer corners of edge of the toy. Most toys found with edge wear may also be called normal-wear toys. Any toys with this type of wear most often fall in a value class of good/very good. When determining condition of a toy, other areas of importance to the litho would be the amount of soil on the litho, and the extent to which it has faded and/or lost its color. These areas may be considered as less important, unless there is more than slight soiling or discoloration. When a Fisher-Price toy has advanced conditions of wear, soiling, or missing litho, the toy would be considered as less than good condition, and therefore, a value of less than good (poor) would be placed on it.

The next area that is of importance with regard to condition of the toy in determining value would be paint and originality. Toys with slight paint wear on wheels, bases, and handles would fall into the good/very good condition category, unless however, there is litho damage as stated above. Any parts missing also affect the value of the toy, especially lithography parts, such as arms, legs, and heads. These are especially important, since once the litho is gone, there is no means of replacement. Also lessening the value of a toy would be missing wheels and axles.

A toy which is mint is one that has absolutely no wear or damage on a complete basis. (Litho, paint, wheels, etc. in mint condition). These toy will reflect the highest of values. Boxes for older Fisher-Price toys may add up to 20% more for a mint toy, depending upon the condition of the box. Boxes from toys from the 1930s would be of the most value because of age, and are most often missing. Always consider condition of the box towards a value of a toy.

The last area that seems to have led the way demanding higher prices would be comic characters and the use of other company's names on Fisher-Price toys. Most often toys of this nature have much higher values placed on them than other Fisher-Price toys, due to the fact that there are many Disney, Popeye, and other comic-area collectors.

Because a toy may be a Disney, Popeye, or comic figure does not necessarily mean that it may be a rarer toy. There are many other Fisher-Price toys that are much rarer, since rarity is based on the amount of toys produced over a given period of time, and the amount still in existence.

Also, many toys that had accessories or figures that were often misplaced will bring higher values. Often these accessories and/or figures are difficult to locate separately from the toy itself. If a toy is found mint in the box with accessories, this most certainly will demand higher pricing. The prices reflected in this guide for Fisher-Price toys were established by taking an average of toys seen at toy shows, flea markets, dealers, and collectors.

JOHN J. MURRAY was born, raised, and educated in the Buffalo, New York, area. He presently resides in Eden, a suburb of Buffalo, withhis wife Mary and daugher Amanda. John, known to many as Jack, began his career in the printing industry and after serving in the Armed Forces, began his over 15-year career with Fisher-Price in the Research and Development Art Production Department. He is responsible for creating new color development and decoration for photo and TV models.

John pioneered the first documentation of Fisher-Price in Collecting Toys, volume 4 & 5, and has since completed the most extensive book on Fisher-Price. It is entitled FISHER-PRICE, 1931-1963, HISTORICAL, RARITY, VALUE GUIDE, by John J. Murray and Bruce R. Fox. The book is available from John by writing to him at Box 29,Eden, NY 14057. The cost is $24.95 plus $3.00 shipping.

In addition, John serves as Chairman of Toyfest in East Aurora, NY, which has become one of the largest antique toy gatherings in the U.S.

7 LOOKY FIRE TRUCK. Photo by Ross MacKearnin. Courtesy John J. Murray.

125 UNCLE TIMMY TURTLE. Photo by Ross MacKearnin. Courtesy John J. Murray.

110 KATY KACKLER. Photo by Ross MacKearnin. Courtesy John J. Murray.

	C6	C8	C10
7 Looky Fire Truck (see picture)	85	125	170
8 Bouncy Racer	40	60	80
10 Bunny Cart	85	125	170
11 Ducky Cart	85	125	170
16 Ducky Cart	85	125	170
28 Bunny Egg Cart	85	125	170
50 Baby Chick Tandem Cart	85	125	170
100 Musical Sweeper	175	225	350
120 Cackling Hen (white)	40	60	80
123 Cackling Hen (red)	40	65	80
123 Roller Chimes (with push stick)	85	125	170
125 Uncle Timmy Turtle (with glasses) (see picture)	85	125	170
131 Toy Wagon	225	325	450
132 Dr. Doodle	85	125	170
137 Pony Chime	40	60	80
138 Pony Chime	30	40	50
139 Tuggy Turtle	85	125	160
140 Katy Kackler (see picture)	85	120	150
145 Musical Elephant (with original ears)(see picture)	285	325	450
150 Timmy Turtle	85	125	170
151 Happy Hippo	85	125	170
155 Moo-oo Cow	85	125	170
156 F/P Circus Wagon (see picture)	375	562	750
161 Looky Chug-Chug (with tender)	200	250	350
164 Mother Goose	65	95	135
166 Bucky Burro (see picture)	225	295	395
168 F/P Chug Chug (with 2 cars)	55	70	80
168 Snorky Fire Engine (with all figures)	85	125	170
169 Snorky Fire Engine (with all figures)	85	125	170

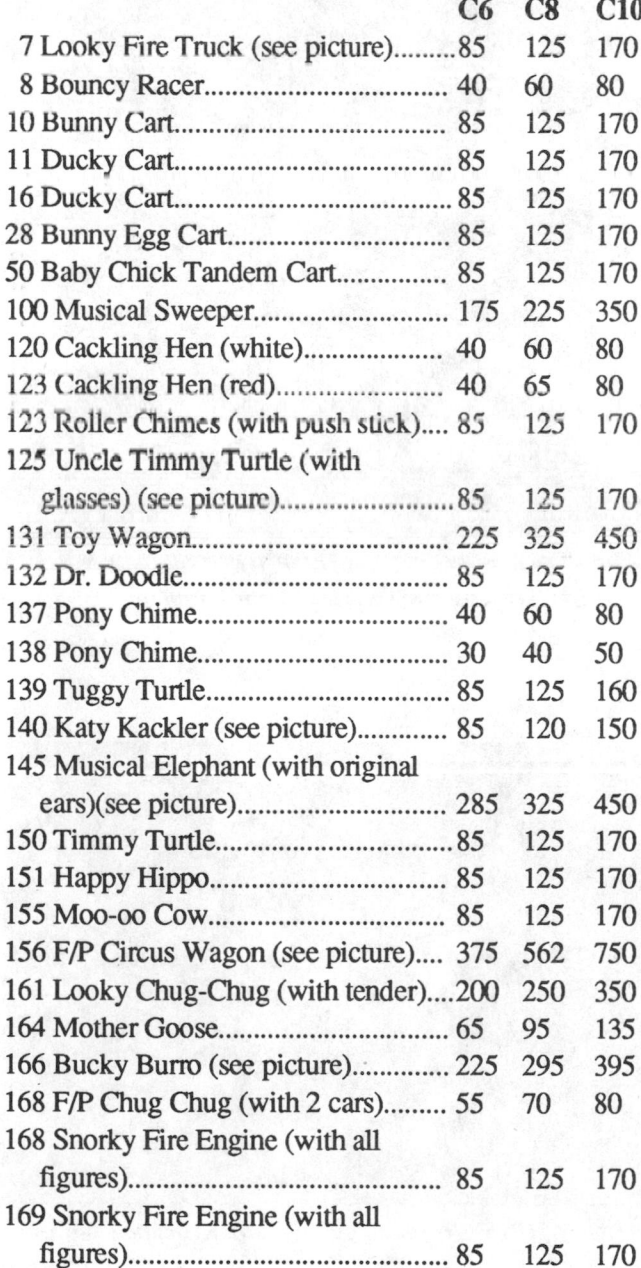

145 MUSICAL ELEPHANT. Photo by Ross MacKearnin. Courtesy John J. Murray.

	C6	C8	C10
170 American Airlines Flagship (with original propellors)	600	900	1200
175 Gold Star Stage Coach (with baggage-two)(see picture)	285	475	650
177 Donald Duck Xylophone (see picture)	265	425	575

156 FISHER PRICE CIRCUS WAGON. Photo by Ross MacKearnin. Courtesy John J. Murray.

166 BUCKY BURRO. Photo by Ross MacKearnin. Courtesy John J. Murray.

175 GOLD STAR STAGE COACH. Photo by Ross MacKearnin. Courtesy John J. Murray.

177 DONALD DUCK XYLOPHONE. Photo by Ross MacKearnin. Courtesy John J. Murray.

	C6	C8	C10
180 Snoopy Sniffer (see picture)..........	125	175	225
185 Donald Duck Xylophone..............	400	600	800
190 Molly Moo-Moo......................	225	275	350
191 Golden Gulch Express....................	85	125	170
192 Playland Express...........................	85	125	170
195 Teddy Bear Parade.......................	600	900	1200
200 Winky Blinky Fire Truck..............	85	125	170
210 Pluto the Pup.................................	350	475	600
211 Walt Disney's Elmer the Elephant...............................	350	475	600
215 Streamliner Express......................	800	1200	1600
220 Looky Chug-Chug (see picture)....	95	125	170
225 Musical Sweeper...........................	85	125	170
230 Musical Sweeper...........................	85	125	170
234 Nifty Station Wagon (with roof and four figures)(see picture)..........	225	325	450
237 Riding Horse (with original tail)....	600	900	1200

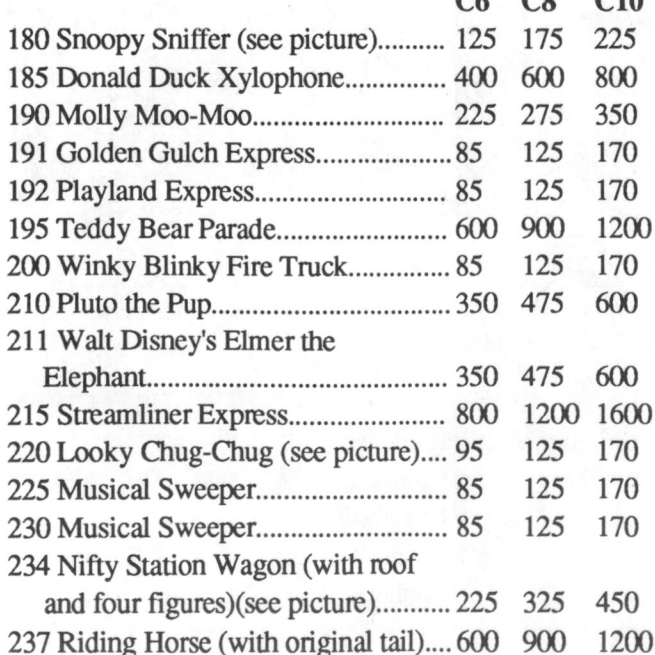

180 SNOOPY SNIFFER. Photo by Ross MacKearnin. Courtesy John J. Murray.

220 LOOKY CHUG-CHUG. Photo by Ross MacKearnin. Courtesy John J. Murray.

234 NIFTY STATION WAGON. Photo by Ross MacKearnin. Courtesy John J. Murray

314 QUEEN BUZZY BEE. Photo by Ross MacKearnin. Courtesy John J. Murray.

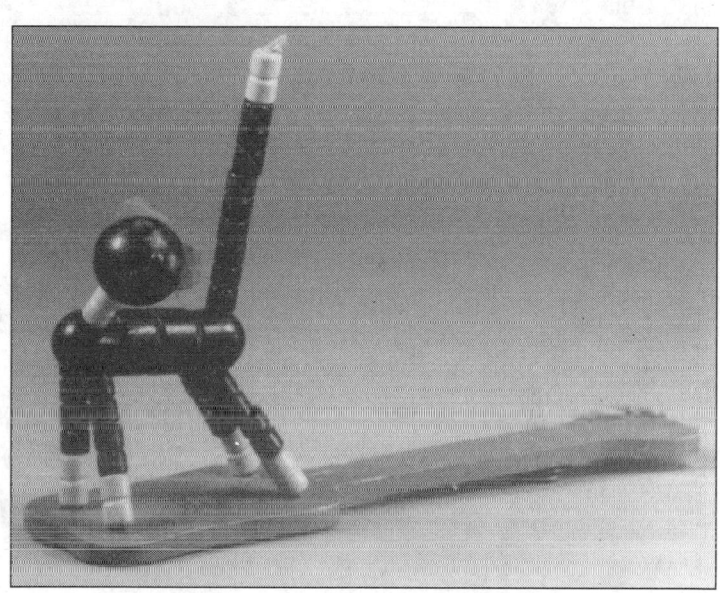

400 TAILSPIN TABBY. Photo by Ross MacKearnin. Courtesy John J. Murray.

415 SUPER JET. Photo by Ross MacKearnin. Courtesy John J. Murray.

415 LOP-EAR LOOIE. Photo by Ross MacKearnin. Courtesy John J. Murray.

	C6	C8	C10
301 Bunny Basket Cart	40	60	80
302 Chick Basket Cart	40	60	80
303 Bunny Basket Cart	85	125	170
305 Walking Duck Cart	45	60	90
307 Bouncing Bunny Cart	45	60	90
310 Mickey Mouse Puddle Jumper	90	135	180
314 Queen Buzzy Bee (see picture)	40	65	85
325 Buzzy Bee	40	65	85
333 Butch the Pup	85	125	170
350 Go'n Back Mule (with original ears)	700	1100	1400
400 Donald Duck Drum Major	225	325	450
400 Tailspin Tabby (original pull loops)(see picture)	90	135	180
401 Bunny Cart	200	300	400
406 Bunny & Cart	45	60	90
407 Chick & Cart	45	60	90
410 Stoopy Storky (with original cardboard feet)	280	375	550
415 Lop-Ear Looie (see picture)	300	400	500
415 Super-Jet (see picture)	200	300	400
432 Mickey Mouse Choo-Choo (early version)	650	775	1300
433 Dizzy Donkey (see picture)	85	125	170
434 Ferdinand the Bull (see picture)	600	900	1200
440 Goofy Gertie	300	425	575
440 Pluto Pop-Up	90	125	165
444 Puffy Engine	85	120	150
444 Fuzzy Fido (see picture)	225	325	450
445 Hot Dog Wagon (see picture)	225	325	450
445 Nosey Pup (see picture)	75	120	145
450 Donald Choo-Choo (see picture)	225	325	450
450 Jolly Jumper	85	125	170
454 Donald Duck Drummer (see picture)	225	325	450
455 Tailspin Tabby	85	125	170
462 Barky Dog	85	125	170
472 Peter Bunny Cart (see picture)	225	275	375
472 Jingle Giraffe	175	225	275
473 Merry Mutt	85	125	170
476 Mickey Mouse Drummer	225	235	450
476 Cookie Pig	40	50	60
477 Dr. Doodle	225	350	450
478 Pudgy Pig	40	60	80
479 Donald Duck & Nephews (with 2 nephews)(see picture)	400	500	600
480 Leo The Drummer (see picture)	225	280	375
485 Mickey Mouse Choo-Choo (see picture)	85	125	170
487 Bunny Cart	225	325	450

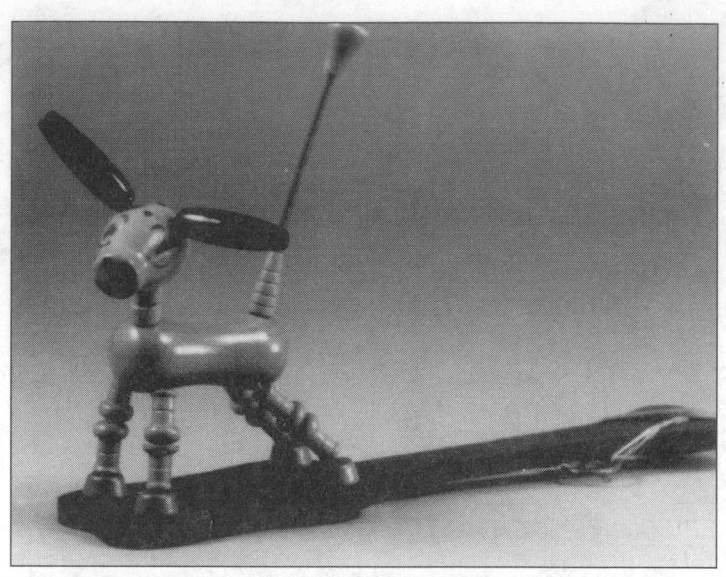

433 DIZZY DONKEY. Photo by Ross MacKearnin. Courtesy John J. Murray.

434 FERDINAND THE BULL. Photo by Ross MacKearnin. Courtesy John J. Murray.

444 FUZZY FIDO. Photo by Ross MacKernin. Courtesy John J. Murray.

445 HOT DOG WAGON. *Photo by Ross MacKearnin. Courtesy John J. Murray.*

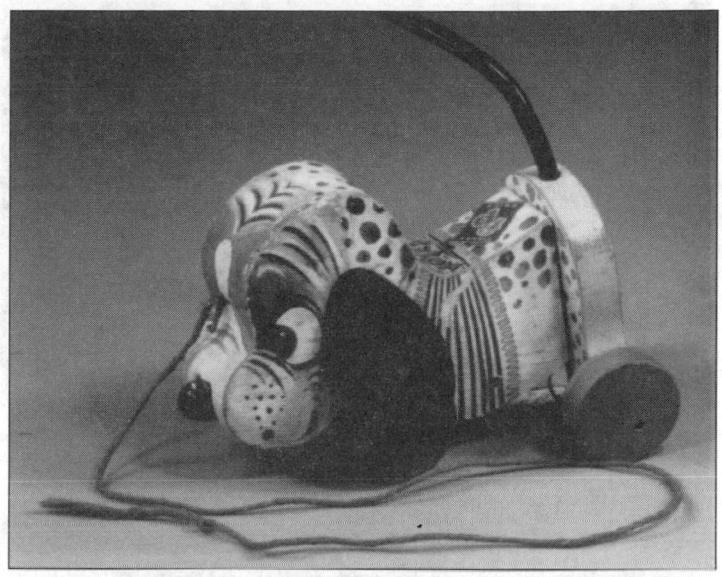

445 NOSEY PUP. *Photo by Ross MacKearnin. Courtesy John J. Murray.*

450 DONALD DUCK CHOO CHOO. *Photo by Ross MacKearnin. Courtesy John J. Murray.*

454 DONALD DUCK DRUMMER. *Photo by Ross MacKearnin. Courtesy John J. Murray.*

472 PETER BUNNY CART. *Photo by Ross MacKearnin. courtesy John J. Murray.*

479 DONALD DUCK & NEPHEWS. *Photo Ross MacKearnin. Courtesy John J. Murray.*

480 LEO THE DRUMMER. Photo by Ross MacKearnin. Courtesy John J. Murray.

485 MICKEY MOUSE CHOO CHOO. Photo by Ross MacKearnin. Courtesy John J. Murray.

491 BOOM BOOM POPEYE. Photo by Ross MacKearnin. Courtesy John J. Murray.

494 PLUCKY PINOCCHIO. Photo by Ross MacKearnin. Courtesy John J. Murray.

678 KRISS KRICKET. Photo by Ross MacKearnin. Courtesy John Murray.

698 TALKY PARROT. *Photo by Ross MacKearnin. Courtesy John J. Murray.*

703 POPEYE THE SAILOR. *Photo by Ross MacKearnin. Courtesy John J. Murray.*

	C6	C8	C10
488 Popeye Spinach Eater	600	900	1200
491 Boom-Boom Popeye (see picture)	600	900	1200
494 Plucky Pinocchio (see picture)	400	600	800
495 Sleep Sue	45	55	65
498 Happy Helicopter	225	275	325
508 Bunny Bell Drummer	85	125	160
533 Thumper Bunny	425	575	800
544 Donald Duck Cart	225	325	425
600 Tailspin Tabby Pop-up	225	275	325
610 Tailspin Tabby	85	125	160
616 Chuggy Pop-up	85	125	170
617 Whistling Engine	95	140	175
621 Suzie Seal (ball)	40	50	60
623 Suzie Seal (unbrella)	40	50	60
625 Playful Puppy	45	55	65
626 Playful Puppy	45	55	65
634 Tiny Teddy	85	120	140
635 Tiny Teddy	50	55	65
636 Tiny Teddy	50	65	80
640 Wiggily Woofer	85	120	145
642 Smokie Engine	35	55	70
653 Allie Gator	85	120	150
654 Tawny Tiger	85	120	150
656 Bossy Bell	35	60	80
658 Lady Bug	45	60	80
662 Merry Mousewife	40	60	80
674 Sports Car	85	125	150
678 Kriss Kricket (see picture)	85	120	150
686 Perky Pot	85	110	140

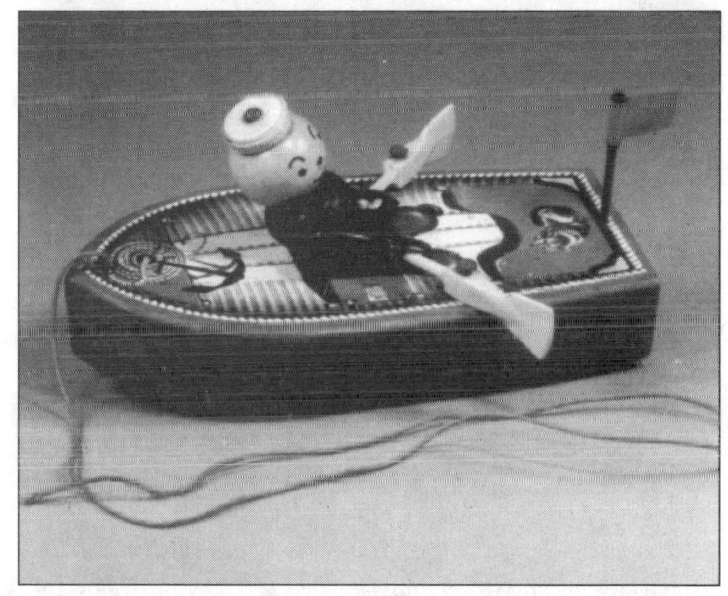

730 RACING ROWBOAT. *Photo by Ross MacKearnin. Courtesy John J. Murray.*

733 FISHER PRICE GENERAL HAULING. *Photo by Ross MacKearnin. Courtesy John J. Murray.*

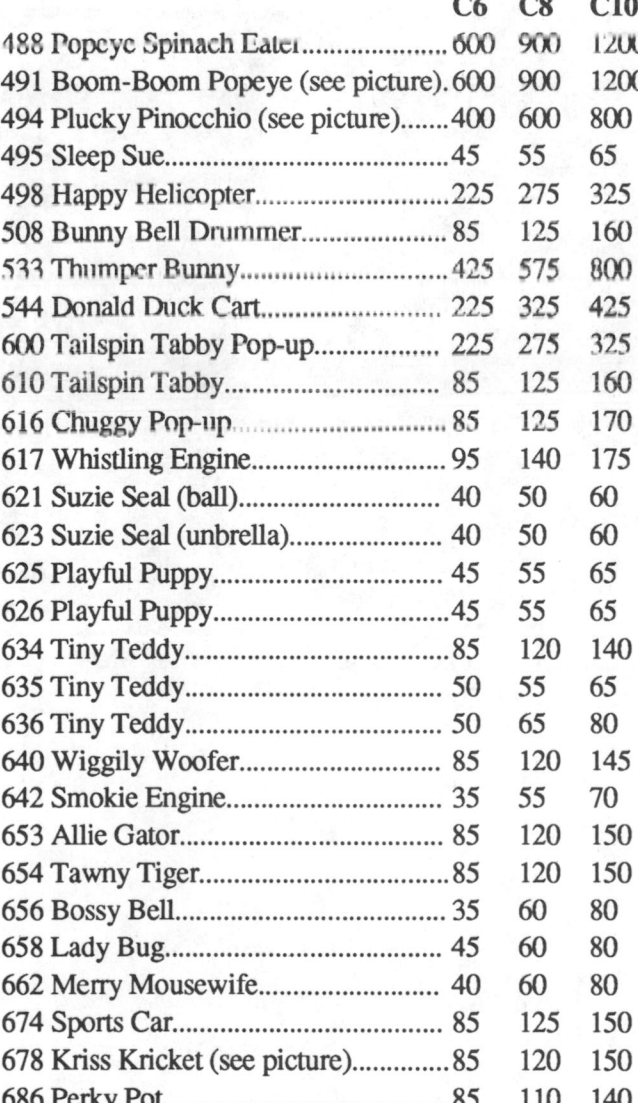

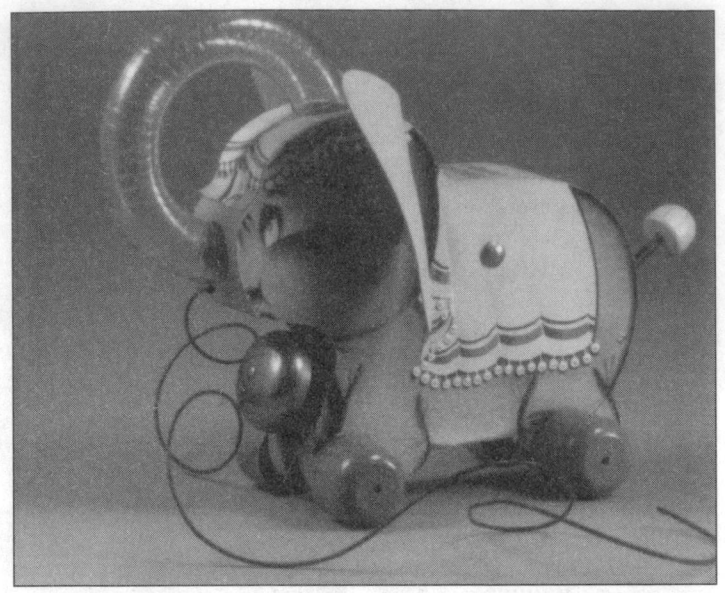

735 JUGGLING JUMBO. Photo by Ross MacKearnin. Courtesy John J. Murray.

745 ELSIE'S DAIRY TRUCK. Photo by Ross MacKearnin. Courtesy John J. Murray.

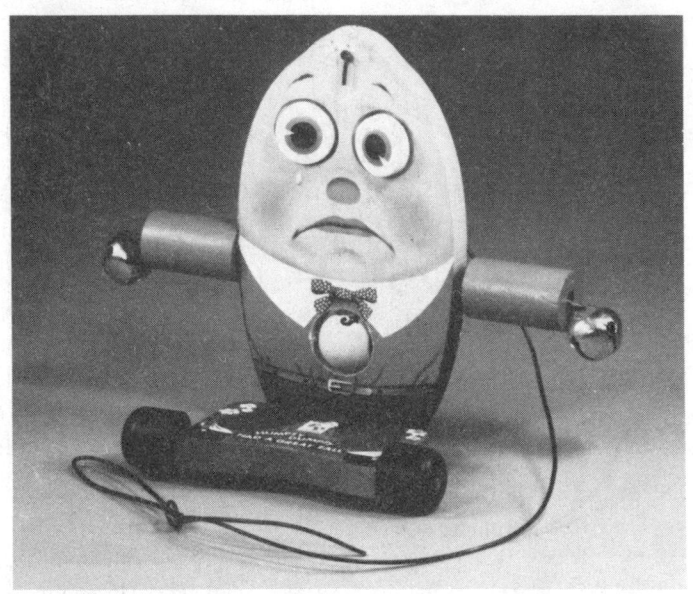

757 HUMPTY DUMPTY. Photo by Ross MacKearnin. Courtesy John J. Murray.

765 DANDY DOBBIN. Photo by Ross MacKearnin. Courtesy John J. Murray.

765 TALKING DONALD DUCK. Photo by Ross MacKearnin. Courtesy John J. Murray.

	C6	C8	C10
695 Pinky Pig.............................. 75		100	135
698 Talky Parrot (see picture)............. 90		125	160
703 Popeye the Sailor (see picture)....... 600		900	1200
707 Fido Zilo..............................85		110	150
712 Teddy Tooter...................... 245		375	485
720 Pinocchio Express.................600		800	1100
721 Peter Bunny Engine................. 225		325	450
728 Buddy Bullfrog........................ 85		120	150
730 Racing Rowboat (see picture)........ 225		375	450
733 Fisher-Price General Hauling (see picture)........................285		385	475
733 Mickey Mouse Safety Patrol.......... 250		375	500
735 Juggling Jumbo (see picture)........ 225		300	400
738 Dumbo Circus Racer (original arms)............................. 600		900	1200
738 Shaggy Zilo..........................85		120	180
739 Poodle Zilo..........................85		120	180
742 Dashing Dobbin...................... 400		500	675
745 Elsie's Dairy Truck with 2 milk bottles-deduct $25.00 for each missing bottle (see picture)............. 475		700	900
750 Hot Dog Wagon.....................400		600	800
750 Space Blazer 450		575	650
752 Teddy Xylophone.................... 225		300	400
755 Jumbo Rollo........................ 225		300	400
757 Humpty-Dumpty (see picture)...... 225		300	400
758 Pony Chime........................225		300	400
765 Dandy Dobbin (see picture).......... 200		275	400
765 Talking Donald Duck (see picture) 85		120	185
770 Doc & Dopey Dwarfs (see picture)............................. 750		1000	1500
775 Gabby Goofies...................... 40		60	80
776 Gabby Goofies,,,................... 40		60	80
777 Teddy Bear Zilo (see picture)........85		125	160
777 Squeaky the Clown (see picture)... 225		275	425
785 Blackie Drummer..................... 500		600	1000
794 Big Bill Pelican (with cardboard fish-add $20.00)............................... 65		85	120
795 Musical Duck...................... 85		130	160
798 Chatter Monk........................ 85		125	160
799 Quacky Family...................... 40		60	80
810 Timber Toter........................ 85		110	150
875 Looky Push Car (w/steering wheel push stick)..................... 75		95	145
900 Big Performing Circus (with all accessories)..................... 275		395	550
926 Cement Mixer.......................... 260		325	485
983 Safety School Bus (w/all figures).. 125		275	400
984 Safety School Bus (w/all figures).. 170		275	400
999 Huffy Puffy Train (with 4 cars)..... 90		130	160

770 DOC & DOPEY DWARFS. *Photo by Ross MacKearnin. Courtesy John J. Murray.*

777 SQUEAKY THE CLOWN. *Photo by Ross MacKearnin. Courtesy John J. Murray.*

777 TEDDY BEAR ZILO. *Photo by Ross MacKearnin. Courtesy John J. Murray.*

PLASTIC DOLLHOUSE FURNITURE

(1940s - 1960s)

By Mary Brett

The large number of babies born after World War II, giving a whole generation the nickname of "baby boomers", was just one side effect of the war. So was the birth of the plastic toy. The entire continent of Europe had been devastated. The importing of European toys, especially the once so popular German toys, ceased completely. For the first time American consumers turned solely to American toymakers. However, American toymakers had problems of their own. The war had created severe metal shortages as well as shortages of other materials previously used to create toys, such as wood, cloth and glass. A material was needed to fill the growing market demand that so many new babies were creating. It was then that these toy producers turned to a new product called plastic.

At first consumers were slow to respond to the new plastic toys, feeling them inferior and unsafe. But the Dow Chemical Company, who produced the polystyron plastic identified by the Styron label, spearheaded a large national campaign in 1948 to both make the consumer familiar with and completely confident in the Styron hallmark on toys.

Dow placed ads in National magazines and toy trade journals. They furnished window and counter displays as well as store banners to department stores, drug stores and dime stores featuring toys made from Styron. The campaign worked. Plastic caught on and sales soared.

Plastic proved to be everything Dow said it was: light, safe, sanitary, easy to handle, colorful and inexpensive. And even when metal and other materials were no longer scarce, plastic toys remained popular. Plastic dollhouse furniture continued as the top seller until the mid 1960s, when wood once again became the vogue.

There were several producers of plastic dollhouse furniture in the 1940s-1960s, such as Marx, Superior, Jayline, Jaydon and others, but the three top quality producers were Renwal, Plastic Art Toy Corporation of America (Plasco) and Ideal. Add to these three producers the "Little Deb/Little Hostess" line that Marx introduced in 1964 and you have the areas in which a serious collector should concentrate.

When purchasing plastic furniture, only accept perfect pieces. Any piece that is broken, chipped, warped, has a burn or melt spot or has a part missing is virtually worthless. Also, any time you are able to locate a mint in box (MIB) piece or set, purchase it, because its value is going up daily. Today collecting plastic dollhouse furniture is becoming more popular amoung antique dealers and collectors alike as "Baby Boomers" rediscover and repurchase thier youth. The prices are soaring. Plastic has proved to be everything Dow promised it to be in 1948, except today it is no longer inexpensive.

Photo by Ellen Shuler

Mary Brett has literally been involved with antiques her entire life, born into a family of antique dealers. She has published over a dozen articles in leading national toy and antique magazines on the subject of plastic dollhouse furniture and tin dollhouses and her personal collection is one of the largest and most complete in the country. Her book, A Tomart Price Guide To Tin Dollhouses and Plastic Dollhouse Furniture will be available soon. She currently lives in Midlothian, Virginia, with her husband Lee, and her two sons, Trey and Lee.

RENWAL

Renwal is the most highly collectable of all the plastic dollhouse furniture. In addition, the Renwal pieces are both categorally and sequentially numbered, making them both fun and a challenge to collect.

This furniture was produced between the 1940s and the mid 1960s. The furniture was sold in room sets or by individual piece. A child could furnish an entire dollhouse for less than $7.00 and individual pieces were sold in almost every dimestore, drug store or department store for about .29¢ each. Renwal furniture caught on quickly. In 1946 Renwal introduced the "Jolly Twins" line of dollhouse furniture. Collier's magazine (Toys for Tommorrow: March 1946) reported a Renwal spokesman as saying that their company expected to sell 150,000,000 pieces that year. There is every indication Renwal did just that. In the Christmas season of 1946 over 52,000,000 pieces sold, a fete made even more spectacular when we realize that the retail holiday season in 1946 was from the day after Thanksgiving until Christmas Eve.

The Renwal Manufacturing Company was founded in 1939 by Irving Lawner (Renwal backwards) who sold it to Irving Rosenblum 14 months later. Originally it was located in New York City. Later it moved to Mineola, New York but kept a showroom at the Toy Building on Fifth Avenue. Renwal became a division of Learning Aids Group, Inc. and on October 1, 1973, Learning Aids Group, Inc. merged into Chein Industries and later Chein merged into Revell. Renwal is also well known for their plastic cars, trucks and airplanes which they produced in the 40s-60s and also considered highly collectable. Today the great Renwal logo is no longer used.

Renwal Price Guide and Check List

These prices reflect only perfect pieces. (The exception being the Renwal family.) Any piece that is broken, chipped, has a part missing, is noticeably warped or has a burn/melt spot is virtually worthless.

MIB - Mint in Box
MP - Moveable Parts
NMP - Non-moveable Parts

No	Description		Value
5	Doll	MP	$35-45
7	Tricycle	MP	20 25
8	2" Baby	MP	10-15
9	5" Baby	MP	15-20
10	Bathroom Scale (paper dial)	NMP	10-15
11	Alarm Clock (paper dial)	NMP	10-15
12	Kitchen Stool	NMP	10-15
13	Pedestal Ashtray	NMP	10-15
14	Mantel Clock (paper dial)	NMP	10-15
16	Table Radio (paper dial)	NMP	10-15
18	Radio/Phonograph (paper dial)	MP	20-25
19	Swing	MP	$15-20
20	Slide	MP	10-15
21	Teeter-Totter	MP	15-20
22	Delux Sink (all parts)	MP	35-45
23	Motorcycle/Sidecar	MP	20-25
24	Delux Refrigerator (all parts)	MP	35-45
26	Delux Stove (all parts)	MP	35-45
27	Kiddie Cart	MP	20-25
28	Telephone	MP	10-15
30	Highchair	MP	15-20

Renwal's very popular accessory pieces. The broom, far right, is one of the rarest Renwals. Pictured is the flat-style broom. It also came rounded, and a rather witch's broom style. Photo by Mary Brett.

No.	Description		Value
31	Wringer Washer	MP	25-30
32	Ironing Board w/Iron	MP	15-20
33	School Desk	MP	15-20
34	Teacher's Desk	MP	15-20
35	Swivel Chair	MP	10-15

Renwal No. 20 Slide, No. 8 Baby in No. 19 Swing, No. 21 Teeter-Totter. The baby came in diaper only and in various color combination shirt and pants, and with and without shoes and socks. Photo by Mary Brett.

RENWAL's Father, Mother and Brother, mint in box (Sister not pictured). Renwal also made Doctor, Nurse, Policeman, and Mechanic Dollhouse Dolls. Photo by Mary Brett

No.	Descripton		Value
36	Potty Chair	MP	10-15
37	Vacuum Cleaner	MP	20-25
41	Sister	MP	25-30
42	Brother	MP	25-30
43	Mother	MP	$25-30
44	Father	MP	25-30
	Any Family Doll	MIB	40-45
44	Doctor w/Bag	MP	30-45
43	Nurse w/Cap	MP	30-45
	Any Doctor/Nurse Doll	MIB	45-60
44	Policeman	MP	45-50
44	Mechanic	MP	45-50
	Any Policeman/Mechanic	MIB	60-75
D51	Dining Table	MP	15-20
D52	Hutch	NMP	5-10
D53	Chair	NMP	5-10*
D54	Buffet	MP	15-20
	Buffet	NMP	5-10
D55	Sideboard	MP	15-20
62	Cabinet	MP	25-30
	Cabinet	NMP	5-10
K63	Chair	NMP	5-10*
64	Garbage Can	MP	15-20
65	Rocking Chair	NMP	10-15
K66	Refrigerator	MP	$15-20
	Refrigerator	NMP	5-10
K67	Table	NMP	5-10
K68	Sink	MP	15-20
	Sink	NMP	5-10
K69	Stove	MP	15-20
	Stove	NMP	5-10

No.	Descripton		Value
L70	Floor Lamp	NMP	10-15
L71	Table Lamp	NMP	10-15
L72	Coffee Table	NMP	5-10
L73	Round End Table	NMP	5-10
L74	Piano	NMP	20-25
L75	Piano Bench	NMP	5-10
L76	Club Chair (Men's)	NMP	5-10
L77	Ladie's Chair	NMP	5-10
L78	Couch	NMP	5-10
L79	Floor Radio (paper dial)	NMP	10-15
L80	Fireplace	NMP	20-25
B81	Twin Bed	NMP	5-10
B82	Vanity/Mirror/Bench	MP	20-25
	Vanity/Mirror/Bench	NMP	$10-15
B83	Dresser w/Mirror	MP	15-20
	Dresser w/Mirror	NMP	10-15
B84	Night Stand	NMP	5-10
B85	Chest	MP	15-20
	Chest	NMP	5-10

Renwal; Left to Right: No. 27 Kiddie Car, No. 7 Tricycle. Photo by Mary Brett.

Examples of the stenciled Renwal furniture. All three kitchen pieces have doors that open and shut. Photo by Mary Brett.

No.	Description		Value
87	Baby Push Cart	MP	$15-20
89	Sewing Machine	MP	40-45
T95	Tub	NMP	15-20**
T96	Sink	NMP	15-20**
T97	Toilet	MP	10-15
T98	Hamper	MP	15-20**
108	Folding Card Table	MP	20-25
109	Folding Chair	MP	10-15
114	Baby Carriage/Spread	MP	15-20
115	Baby Carriage	MP	15-20
(117)	Mop w/cloth		20-30
116	Carpet Sweeper	NMP	15-20
118	Playpen	MP	15-20
119	Cradle w/Spread	MP	$15-20
120	Molded Baby	NMP	10-15
(121)	Broom	NMP	45-75
122	Bathinette	MP	15-20
214	5 attached Hospital Cribs w/names Mary, John, Peter Irene, Alice (set)	NMP	25-30
No #	Cradle/Crib	MP	15-20
No #	Dustpan	NMP	10-15
No #	Mop (117)	NMP	20-30
No #	Broom (121)	NMP	45-75

* This piece bears two numbers
** This piece is dated

Rooms Mint in Box (MIB) - $135 - $165 (Original Room Box Sets - Cellophaned - Topped Boxes valued lower $95 - $125.)

Left to Right: Renwal Sewing Machine, Ideal Sewing Machine. Photo by Mary Brett.

LIVING ROOM (13 pieces): Couch (L78), Club Chair (L76), Ladies Chair (L77), Fireplace (L80), 2 Round End Tables (L73), 2 Table Lamps (L71), Floor Lamp (L70), Coffee Table (72), Floor Radio (L79), Piano (L74) and Piano Bench (L75).

DINING ROOM (8 pieces): Table (D51, 4 Chairs (D53/K63), Hutch (D52), Sideboard (D55) and Buffet (D54).

KITCHEN (8 pieces): Sink (K68), Stove (K69), Refrigerator (K66), Table (K67) and 4 Chairs (D53/K63).

BEDROOM (7 pieces): 2 Twin Beds (B81), Vanity Table (82) w/Bench (L75), Dresser (B83), Night Stand (B84) and Chest (B85).

BATHROOM (4 pieces): Tub (T95), sink (T96), Toilet (T97) and Clothes Hamper (T98).

NURSERY (9 pieces): Night Stand (B84 pink or blue), Chest (B85 pink or blue), Bathinette (122), Cradle Crib (no No. with the Molded Baby (120), Table Lamp (L71), Playpen (118), Carriage (115) and Highchair (30).

PLASTIC ART TOY CORPORATION OF AMERICA
(PLASCO)

Overshadowed by Renwal furniture and overlooked by collectors for years, Plasco plastic dollhouse furniture is finally being appreciated for the fine quality product that in reality it is.

The Plastic Art Toy Corporation of America was located at 1 Maple Street in East Rutherford, New Jersey in the 1940s and later moved to East Paterson, New Jersey. They manufactured the "Little Homemaker" furniture line and sold it by piece, each piece selling for about $.29, or in sets, each set originally selling for about $1.00 each. The first sets were packaged in a specially designed box with a lithographed interior simulating two walls of a room, complete with a pull out floor. The later sets were packaged in boxes, no room designs, and with a clear cellophane top. As with the Renwal line, a mint in box

(MIB) room set is valued higher because of the novelty of the box, and thus priced higher than the MIB cellophane box sets. An exception to the rule is the Plasco Nursery cellophane box which includes the 7" plastic record of nursery tunes. Also note that in 1950 Plasco changed their original cellophane boxes to a "new" look and included the Plasco baby with each set, not just with the Nursery Set.

There are seven original sets: Living Room (7 pieces), Dining Room (9 pieces), Kitchen (11 pieces), Bedroom (7 pieces), Bathroom (6 pieces), Nursery (6 pieces) and Garden (8 pieces) for a total of 54 pieces. Later sets varied the number and variety of pieces offered. The furniture was designed by Eugene J. Lux and was actually a 16 to 1 scale of real furniture of that day.

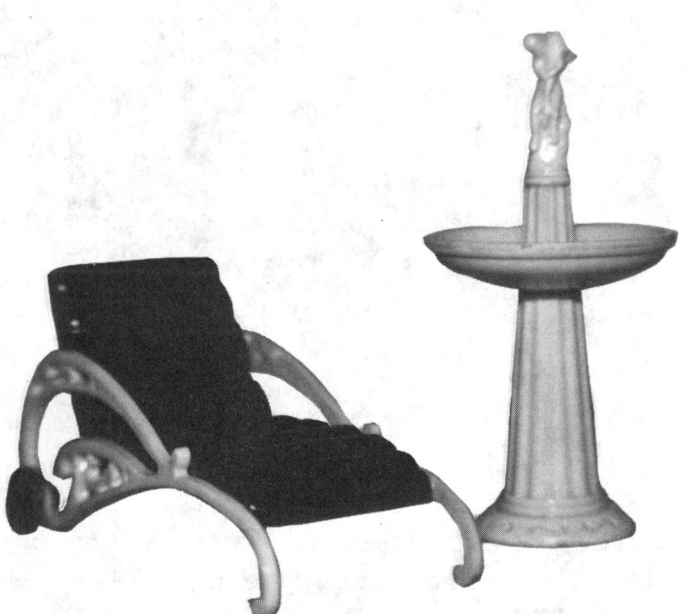

Plasco Chaise Longue and Fountain. Photo by Mary Brett.

Plasco Price Guide and Check List

The complete line of Plasco plastic furniture consists of 7 sets, 54 total pieces, 38 different pieces.

The prices listed reflect only perfect pieces. Any piece that is broken, chipped, has a part missing, is noticeably warped or has a burn/melt spot is virtually worthless.

MIB - Mint in Box
MP - Moveable Parts

Plasco TV, Living Room Chair, Grandfather's Clock. Photo by Mary Brett.

Item		Value
Living Room (7 pieces)		
Room Boxes	MIB	$125-150
Other Boxes	MIB	95-75
Sofa		10-15
Club Chair		5-10
Wing Chair		5-10
Fireplace		10-15
Grandfather Clock		15-20
Coffee Table		5-10
TV	MP	20-25
Dining Room (9 pieces)		
Room Boxes	MIB	$125-150

Item		Value
Other Boxes	MIB	75-95
Dining Table		15-20
2 Arm Chairs		5-10
Breakfront		15-20
2 Console Tables		10-15
Buffet		10-15
2 Straight Chairs		5-10
Kitchen (11 pieces)		
Room Boxes	MIB	125-150
Other Boxes	MIB	75-95
Table		5-10
4 Chairs		5-10
Stove		5-10
Refrigerator		5-10
Sink		5-10
Breakfast Bar		10-15
2 Cabinets		5-10
Bedroom (7 pieces)		
Room Boxes	MIB	125-150
Other Boxes	MIB	75-95
2 Twin Beds		5-10
Highboy	MP	15-20
Vanity with mirror		10-15
Dresser with mirror	MP	15-20
Night Table		5-10
Vanity Chair		2-5
Bathroom (6 pieces)		
Room Boxes	MIB	125-150
Other Boxes	MIB	75-95
Bathtub		5-10
Wash Bowl		5-10
Toilet		10-15
Hamper	MP	10-15
Vanity with mirror		10-15
Chair		2-5

PLASCO Baby in Plasco Crib. The sides of the crib go up and down and the baby has movable joints. One version of the baby has a movable head and the others do not. Photo by Mary Brett.

Item		Value
Nursery (6 pieces)		
Room Boxes	MIB	135-160
Other Boxes	MIB	75-95
w/Plastic Record of Nursery Tunes 7"	MIB	150-175
Crib with Mattress	MP	20-25
Doll's Bath	MP	15-20
Doll	MP	15-20
Highboy	MP	15-20
Chair		5-10
Night Table		5-10
Garden (8 pieces)		
Room Boxes	MIB	125-150
Other Boxes	MIB	75-95
Umbrella Table		15-20
4 Chairs		5-10
Sun Lounge		10-15
Refreshment Table		5-10
Fountain		5-10

IDEAL

The Ideal Novelty and Toy Company owes its start and success to the Teddy Bear.

In 1903 Rose and Morris Michtom owned a stationery and novelty store in Brooklyn, New York. Morris saw a politically staged newspaper picture of President Theodore (Teddy) Roosevelt with a small brown bear cub which the President had refused to shoot. Rose and Morris hand-made several plush bear toys with button eyes. They placed them in their store window for sale after obtaining permission from the President to call them "Teddy Bear". The demand was great. In fact the demand was so great that by 1907 the Michtoms moved to a larger store and the Ideal Novelty and Toy Company was started.

The Ideal 3/4" scale furniture was sold both separately and in boxed room sets. The most expensive individual piece was the combination TV/Radio/Record Player which retailed for $.75 in 1948. The table lamp, kitchen chair and dog retailed for $.05 each that same year. Boxed room sets sold for about $1.00 each.

The original boxed sets were sold in large, full colored cardboard boxes. These boxes, when opened, represented individual rooms and could be used for play in the absence of a dollhouse. The front of the original boxes proclaimed Ideal's "tiny plastic furniture" as "an educational toy" and featured an illustration of 2 little girls AND a little boy playing with the furniture.

The original room sets were: Living Room, Bedroom, Kitchen, Bath, Nursery, Dining Room and Garden.

In the early 1950s, the American post-World War II marketing trend turned towards self-service buying, requiring easy product identificaion. Ideal changed their dollhouse furniture packaging to cellophane-sided play cartons which became minature houses for the furniture when opened. When collecting dollhouse furniture, any MIB (Mint in Box) set is valuable, especially if the box as well as the furniture is in excellent condition. However, the earlier the packaging, the more valuable the product.

Ideal 3/4" Price Guide and Check List

MIB - Mint in Box

Item		Value
Set, Original Cardboard	MIB	$120-150
Set, Cellophane-sided, later	MIB	80-110

Original Room Sets:

Living Room

Sofa	5-10
Chair, Ladies	5-10
Chair, Men's	5-10
Coffee Table	5-10
Tilt-Top Table	15-20
Table Lamp	10-15
Floor Lamp	10-15
Floor Radio	10-15
TV/Radio/Record Player Combo	25-35
Piano	15-20
Piano Stool	5-10
Secretary	20-25
Mantle with Picture	20-25
Radiator	15-20

Bedroom

2 Twin Beds	$ 5-10
Sewing Machine	20-25
Night Stand	5-10
High Chest	10-15
Dresser	15-20
Stool	5-10
Pleted Chair	5-10

IDEAL TV Set with Stereo and Radio. Photo by Mary Brett.

Item	Value
Dining Room	
Table	$ 15-20
2 Armless Chairs	5-15
2 Armed Chairs	10-20
Buffet	15-20
Hutch	5-10
Bathroom	
Toilet	10-20
Hamper	5-10
Medicine Chest	20-25
Tub	5-10
Sink	5-10
Kitchen (Standard)	
Sink	5-10
Stove/Refrigerator	5-10
Table	5-10
4 Chairs	5-10
Kitchen (Deluxe)	
Table	5-10
4 Chairs	5-10
Sink	15-20
Stove	15-20
Refrigerator	15-20
Mangle	10-15
Washing Machine	20-25
Garden	
Table with Umbrella	20-25
Doghouse with dog	15-20

IDEAL: At left, the Young Decorator 1-1/2" scale Sectional Couch and Coffee Table. At right, the Ideal 3/4" Couch. Photo by Mary Brett

IDEAL's rare and much-sought-after Dollhouse Family. The father is approximately 5" high. Photo by Mary Brett.

IDEAL at left the Hallmarked Baby in a blue collapsible high chair. At right another style IDEAL Baby in pink collapsible high chair. IDEAL also made a high chair that didn't collapse. It is much rarer than the collapsible variety. Photo by Mary Brett.

Item	Value
2 Benches	10-15
Arbor	10-15
Birdbath	5-10
Reflecting Pool	15-20
Picnic Table	10-15
Chaise Longue	10-15
Androck Chair	10-15
Nursery (Original)	
Crib with Mattress	$ 15-20
Buggy	15-20
High Chair	15-20
Baby	10-15
Potty Chair with pot	10-15

Accessory pieces, pieces added to later room sets or pieces sold separately:

Tricycle	20-25
Kiddie Car	20-25
High Chair (collapses into Kiddie Chair)	15-20
Lawn Mower	20-25
Dishwasher	20-25
Card Table with four (4) folding Chairs	50-75

PETITE PRINCESS BY IDEAL

In 1964 Ideal brought out their line of plastic dollhouse furniture they termed "Fantasy Furniture". This furniture was, without a doubt, the most elaborate and ornate of all the Baby Boomers' dollhouse furniture.

This furniture was produced in Japan and fabric, paper, glass and metals were used along with the plastic to create this beautiful and detailed product. You will soon be able to recognize on sight the distinctive look of the Petite Princess line with its satins, lames', brocades and bright red velvet fabrics, its modern white antique furniture with "marble" tops and its gilded mirrors and frames.

PRINCESS PATTI BY IDEAL

In late 1965 Ideal brought out the Princess Patti line. It reproduced the Petite Princess line's look but at a more affordable production cost. The mirrors, for example, now had gold stripes of paper glued on instead of being contained in a gilded frame. Two additional room sets were added, the Kitchen Set and the Bathroom Set. Also added to the line was a TV, a 3-story, 5-room dollhouse and a vinyl room carrying case. This line was scaled to match the Petite Princess line so that all pieces were interchangeable. Both lines are hallmarked "Ideal" only and thus hard to differentiate. The boxes they are packaged in are very different, however. Ironically, today the Princess Patti TV, Kitchen Set and Bathroom are valued much higher than any piece or set from the Petite Princess line.

Petite Princess Price List and Checklist
These prices reflect only Mint in Box (MIB) or perfect pieces. Any piece that is broken, chipped, has a part missing, is noticeably warped or has burn/melt spot is virtually worthless.

IDEAL's Petite Princess Salon Drum Chair. Ideal produced the Petite Princess line only in 1964 and the Princess Patti line in 1965. Photo by Mary Brett.

Furniture		MIB	Main piece with no Accessories
4407-3	Salon Curved Sofa	30	15
4408-1	Boudoir Chair Lounge	30	15
4409-9	Guest Chair	30	15
4410-7	Salon Wing Chair	30	15
4411-5	Salon Drum Chair	30	15
4412-3	Occasional Chair/Ottoman	30	15
4413-1	Host Dining Chairs	20	10
4414-9	Guest Dining Chairs	20	10
4415-6	Hostess Dining Chairs	20	10
4416-4	Little Princess Bed	40	20
4417-2	Royal Dressing Table/stool	40	20
4418-0	Treasure Trove Cabinet	30	15
4419-8	Royal Buffet (MIB complete w/mirror, picture plate and 2 porcelain vases)	40	20
4420-6	Palace Chest	20	10
4421-4	Dining Room Table (MIB complete with picture)	30	15
4422-2	Regency Hearthplace (MIB complete w/2 Andirons, 2 pieces of firewood, bucket and mirror)	40	20
4423-0	Grandfather Clock and Folding Screen	40 each	20 each
4424-8	Rolling Tea Cart (MIB complete with wine bottle and 3 wine cups)	20	10
4425-5	Royal Grand Piano (MIB complete w/piano bench,		

Furniture		MIB	Main piece with no Accessories
	music and metrohome)	60	30
4426-3	Lyre Table Set (MIB complete with lamp & picture)	20	10
4427-1	Pedestal Table Set (MIB complete with lamp & flower vase)	20	10
4426-9	Heirloom Table Set (MIB complete with brass lamp, books & pair bookends)	20	10
4429-7	Tier Table Set (MIB complete w/lamp & fruit bowl)	20	10
4431-3	Palace Table Set (MIB complete w/porcelain decanter, 3 cups & leaf ashtray)	20	10
4437-0	Occasional Table Set (MIB complete w/cig. lighter, picture frame, Buddah statue & ash tray)	20	10
4432-1	Fantasy Telephone Set	20	10
4433-9	Salon Coffee Table Set (MIB complete w/flower vase, brass coffee pot, creamer and 2 bowls)	20	10
4439-6	Royal Candelabra	15	10
4438-8	Fantasia Candelabra	30	15
4440-4	Salon Planter	20	10
4450-3	Fantasy Room	30	15
9710-5	Fantasy Family	40 each	20 each

Accessories	Value
Painting	10
Mirror	10
Flower Vase	5
Lamp	10
Books, Bookends	5
Purfume Bottle	5
Ash Tray	5
Cigarette Lighter	5
Buddah Statue	5
Picture Frame	5
Wine Decanter	5
Wine Glasses (3)	5
Fruit Bowl	5
Picture Plate	5
Porcelain Base	5
Andirons (2)	5
Fireplace Bucket	5

Item	Value
Porcelain Decanter	5
Brass Coffee Pot	5
Brass Creamer	3
Brass Bowls (2)	3

PRINCESS PATTI

Price Guide and Check List

	MIB	EX	GD
Waste Basket, Stool and Mirror	35	15	10
Hamper	15	10	5
Oval Tub with Swans	75	55	20
Sink with attached Oval Mirror	65	45	15
Toilet	65	45	15
Linen Cabinet w/4 Towels	85	55	25
Television w/Stand	250	175	125
Round Kitchen Table w/Flowers	55	35	20
Kitchen Chairs (4) clear plastic	80	60	25
Range w/4 Utensils and Hood	150	100	35
Refrigerator-Freezer & Accessories	215	165	55
Sink & Dishwasher	95	65	35
Hutch with plates	55	35	20
Dollhouse	150	75	45
Vinyl Carrying Case	75	45	15

YOUNG DECORATOR BY IDEAL

After World War II there was a tremendous building boom in America. This building boom triggered the furniture boom and much of our country became engrossed in "modern" decorating. Many of the toy companies developed decorator-theme lines of toys and toy sets.

In 1950 Ideal introduced their 1-1/2" scale detailed high quality plastic dollhouse furniture line called "Young Decorator". The "Young Decorator" furniture is one of the most sought after of all the plastic furniture lines. It is also one of the most beautiful. It was produced from a high gloss hard plastic and many of the pieces were manufactured in up to two colors with moveable parts. The furniture was sold in sets and the six sets were: Living Room, Dining Room, Bedroom, Bath, Kitchen and Nursery.

Young Decorator Price Guide and Check List

	EX	GD
Living Room		
Tufted Couch - 4 pieces		
2 with arms, 2 without arms	35	30
Floor Lamp	20	15
Coffee Table	10	5
Television	45	35
Dining Room		
Dining Table	15	10
4 Chairs	8 each	5 each
Hutch	25	20
Buffet	20	15
Bedroom		
Twin Bed	20	15
Night Stand	10	5
Tall Chest of Drawers	25	20
Dresser	25	20
Dresser Stool	10	5
Bath		
Corner Tub	20	15
Vanity Sink	20	15
Toilet	30	20
Diaper Pail	20	15
Kitchen		
Kitchen Table	15	10
4 Chairs	8 each	5 each
Refrigerator	25	20
Sink	20	15
Stove	25	20
Nursery		
Crib	25	20
Playpen	25	20
High Chair	25	20
Bathinette	25	20
Tricycle	25	20

STEAM TOYS

By Richard Leach

Whenever I am asked about pricing older steam toys, the thought that always comes to mind is, "Whatever the seller is willing to take and the buyer is willing to pay". Obviously, this price is influenced by availability and condition of the toy and may vary greatly from place to place. However, good deals for both parties are not struck out of ignorance. I have learned a great deal about pricing in the last several years as I have bought, sold or traded mostly American-made steamers in the Midwest. It is my hope that these few notes may help you strike a deal in which both parties "win".

We need to remember there are three major companies still selling new steam toys in the U.S. They are Jensen Mfg. in Jeannette, PA, the British made Mamod engines and Wilesco from Germany. These products should not be confused with the earlier collectibles.

The more common vertical and horizontal boiler steam engines, in average condition, can usually be purchased between $50.00 and $75.00. These prices allow the novice to get into a very rewarding hobby with little cash outlay. The more unusual engines tend to be much higher in price. By unusual, I mean twin cylinders, double flywheels, hand rails, governors, double boilers or other unusual features. Larger, more elaborate engines with stair steps, catwalks, embossed brick chimneys, nickel plating or reverse levers are also more valuable. Engines with attached accessories like fire pumps, pile drivers, hoisting drums and saws are very desirable. I cannot, in good conscience, quote reliable prices for these more valuable engines in a short article.

Live steam boats have become very popular with collectors lately, and will bring $500.00 to $1000.00 or more depending on the condition and completeness of the model. The tractors and steam rollers are very desirable, although there are several by Mamod and Wilesco that are still in production for around $200.00. I have seen these confused with antiques, so know what you are buying. **Early** steam tractors should bring $250.00 to $600.00 depending on their condition. Burners are often missing on tractors, so look them over closely. Very nice repro burners and other parts are available at reasonable prices.

The horse-drawn, steam-operated fire pumper is the model of all models and the epitome for steam toy enthusiasts. They are very rare and if you are lucky enough to find one for sale, you can expect to pay between $2500.00 and $3000.00

Rarity or availability is determined by both the number of engines manufactured and their survival rates. Many elaborate but fragile models never survived the Christmas season. Condition is another important factor in pricing any steam toy. An engine that will run and has a burner, whistle, pressure valve, governor, etc. all in good shape will be worth much more than a rusty piece with missing parts. Look closely for repairs and parts that don't appear authentic. Excessive solder on steam pipes should tip you off that there was a problem.

Once you've purchased your steam toy, you may want to run it. Remember, these toys are very old. I always run mine on compressed air, which is much safer than steam. Compressed air can also be dangerous to you and your engine if too much pressure is used. So, build pressure slowly using a regulator (a few pounds should suffice) and always use a safety valve.

I have found this to be a rewarding hobby in terms of building both my collection of engines and friendships. I have also met a few less-scrupulous dealers so buyer, beware! but have fun. Happy steaming.

*Richard B. Leach has been building steam engines since 1975. He is perhaps best known for his tiny thimble steam engine with a .034 diameter cylinder and a paper clip wire piston. He enjoys building larger steam and Stirling model engines as well. Building engines quite naturally led to the repair of older toy steam engines and an extensive collection of mostly Weeden steam toys. Richard is kept busy today reprinting high quality early Weeden catalogs and other related historical information. He has consolidated much of the early information and illustrations from original Weeden advertising into his popular **Pictorial Guide To Weeden Steam Toys.***

Since the completion of the Weeden guide, Richard is actively collecting literature and historical data on early electric toy motors. Several repro catalogs have been finished and a Toy Electric Motor Guide is nearly complete.

WEEDEN No. 43, early. Value approximately $400-$500. Photo by Richard Leach.

WEEDEN No. 14, early, cast iron, 6 leg. Value approximately $125. Photo by Richard Leach.

WEEDEN No. 138 Walking Beam (late). Approximate value $250. Photo by Richard Leach.

WEEDEN No. 71, early, rare, approximate value $400-$500. Photo by Richard Leach.

Accessories (late) Back Row, Left to Right: Weeden No. 69 Stamp Mill; No. 67 Circular Saw; No. 68 Emery Wheel. Front Row, Left to Right: Marx Grindstone with Box, Marx Buffer, Marx Power Saw, Mamod Emery Wheel, Jensen Trip Hammer. Value about $35 each. Photo by Richard Leach.

WEEDEN National Playthings No. 42. Late, excellent condition value $125. Photo by Richard Leach.

WEEDEN No. 702, electric, early valve weight. Value approximately $100. Photo by Richard Leach.

ERECTOR SETS

By W.S. Harrison III

Erector Collecting! Why not? A. C. Gilbert was not only the inventor of Erector, but a Medical Doctor (graduate of Yale University 1908), winner of the Gold Medal at the 1908 World Olympics in London, UK for the pole vault....the quintessence of America...at that time an emerging nation!

While honoring the man responsible, we want to acquire his creations at fair and reasonable prices! Erector collecting has fairly recently come to the fore as folks tire of the endless nuance and trivia of modern toys. Very few stimulate and try the imagination as the toys of old. Imagine the questions posed by a Chemistry Set, an Erector Set, or the ability to examine the microcosm via a Microscope Set. If you think Nintendo can supply the mental stimulation that these "toys" of yesteryear could, well...you're just not in the right gear!

For many reasons, beyond the scope of this presentation, Erector an A.C. Gilbert ceased to be a major toy producer after 1962. Erector went through three development stages. First offered in 1913, it was an instant success! In addition to his many other skills, A. C. Gilbert was an accomplished professional magician and an outgoing, gregarious individual. With this background and a taste for hard work that he acquired overcoming boyhood deficiencies, there was no question of the outcome!

From 1913 to 1923, Stage I, the sets featured large, strong girders, and plenty of them! Ads showed boys sitting on the bridges built with Erector...and it was no exaggeration! After the trauma of WW I and the consequent inflation in this country (and worse in Europe), Erector was redesigned, and slimmed down. Girders were smaller, narrower, lighter, but Gilbert also introduced countless other shapes to make the Erector System more versatile.....more capable of building unique and beautiful models. Thus, in 1924, Stage II was born, and continued on until the advent of Stage III in 1963, which really signalled the end of the Gilbert company. While true collectors are interested in the total history of the once great company, most are more familiar with, and desire, the products of Stage II...1924 to 1962. One may, without much word inflation, call it the "shining hour" of the most successful scientific toy company in these United States. In truth, a tribute to the fine man that give it birth!

The decline was somewhat agonizing, ending with the acquisition of the rights to the famous name, "Erector", by the Meccano, SA of France, who, as one can see, also acquired Gilbert's old competitor in England. They produce a fine construction set, but it is not the set interesting to you now reading this analysis. Given all this, the question remains....

How to Buy, and What to Pay? Before launching into the endless statistics, consider some common sense rules. Of about 45 million Erector Sets produced through the years, 90% probably went to people who didn't take very good care of them...for whatever reason. That left about one million fairly nice sets in a good state of preservation...but, half of these were thrown out or otherwise disposed of. So we have a half million pretty nice Erector Sets left?? Where are they?

Most of us are inclined toward flea markets and garage sales, but this is probably not your best source. You may get lucky, but in most cases, this represents the "low end of the market". Many sets from these sources are what we, in the business, call "mixed trash". Either unintentionally, or on purpose, a set will be only fractionally complete and usually has a variety of (let's say) Type II or Type III parts mixed together. The idea is to make you think you are getting a bargain! No, if you are looking for fine quality sets in the "C10" category, carefully watch the estate auctions; alert high quality dealers; or buy from established collectors who are continually refining their collections.

Estate auctions are in your local big city newspaper. All of the avid collectors are members of one or both of the A.C. Gilbert Heritage Society (594 Front St., Marion, MA 02738) or the Southern California Meccano and Erector Club (Box 7653, Porter Ranch Sta., Northridge, CA 91327). The former is the larger of the two, together they represent 500 of the largest collections in the world. Some members have over 1000 Erector Sets, many have several hundred!

Keep in mind, unless a set was carefully preserved in a dry climate, there is little chance of acquiring a set that is truly "Mint", meaning as it left the factory! Though they do exist! We will stick with the very acceptable conventions of this book with these added qualifications.......

C10 - 100% complete, all parts pinned with the original "T" clips; all cardboards present, no rust or "white rust", manual present, near perfect, labels near perfect, only the lightest of scratches, parts may show very light cloudy oxidation (dingy).

C8 - 98 to 100% complete, some or all cardboards present but may not be all correctly pinned, manual present, may have folded corners, motor must be present and working; less than 5% of parts may show the very slightest real rust (like in corners, the type that auto chrome polish can easily remove).

C6 - 90 to 95% complete, probably no cardboard, motor there and working, acceptable manual, labels may show serious wear, considerable scratching on bottom, some on top; minor dents in metal box; some signs of rust on 5 to 10% of parts.

Anything of lesser quality is likely not a collectible of lasting value, and/or difficult, if not impossible, to restore. Most of what you will come across in flea markets is well below C6, we call it "mixed trash". Unless you have the facilities for electroplating and painting, you will have a problem on your hands. Fortunately, there are many small entrepreneurs making new parts for Erector Sets and one that does total restorations...read about them in the sources mentioned.

Note: "psnd" means prices not significantly different

W.S. Harrison III
Bill Harrison attended LaSalle Academy in New York City, where he graduated in 1947 as Valedictorian. He then attended Rensselaer Polytechnic Institute as a student of Chemical Engineering. This career path resulted from his extensive work in chemistry as a teenager; he was a finalist in the Westinghouse Science Talent Search. After marriage, Bill completed a degree in Mechanical Engineering at Polytechnic University of New York, where he was elected to Tau Beta Pi, the National Engineering Honor Society. Bill's engineering background spans over 40 years. He has engineered and designed machinery and special equipment in aerospace, executed project management assignments with Monsanto and was chief engineer in metal forging and rubber molding companies. He is retired Director of Technical Services with Engelhard Corportion, a major processor of precious minerals. He is a registered professional engineer in the states of New York and Massachusetts. Bill is the father of seven children and 12 grandchildren. His first love, after his wife, Judy, is engineering. His hobbies are woodworking and metalworking, and he buys, restores, trades and sells Erector sets and parts. After a nomadic engineering tour, he settled in the small town of Marion, Massachusetts on Buzzard's Bay, where he "plays" in a well-equipped 1300 sq. ft. workshop. Says Bill, "Please come and visit".

	C6	C8	C10
Erector #8, 3 layer WB sets..............	500	750	2500
Erector #8, 2 layer WB sets..............	300	450	800
Erector #10, 3 layer WB sets............	700	1000	2000

Type I - 1913 to 1923 the era of girders 1-1/8" wide

Most of the more valuable sets came in oak boxes with jointed corners. Smaller sets in cardboard boxes are not often seen, but can be quite valuable if discovered. Below the #4 set, condition is everything. 1913 sets, the first year, with a unique motor and girder, are most valuable.

Type II - 1924 to 1962 girders 5/8" wide,

greater variety of parts, sets capable of building more complex models. Sets from #4 up continued in wooden boxes (4 w/ cdbd cover) until 1933 when metal boxes were introduced to the larger sets except the Hudson which went metal in '34. Half numbers were introduced, confusing some collectors.

	C6	C8	C10
1913			
Mysto Erector, #1, cdbd......................	100	200	350
Mysto #4, w/motor, wood box..........	225	350	500
Mysto #8, largest, 3 layer, WB..........	1000	2200	5000
1914 - 16			
Mysto Erector, #1, cdbd......................	100	175	325
Mysto #4, w/motor, WB.....................	175	300	450
Mysto #8, largest, 3 layer, WB..........	800	1800	4000
1917 - 23			
Now called Gilbert Erector, #1..............	100	150	275
Erector #4, w/motor, WB....................	150	250	400
Erector #4, w/mo., WB, metal cover...	150	300	525
Erector #7, '23 EB, metal cover.........	250	400	700

	C6	C8	C10
1924 - 26			
Erector #00 (25¢ original).................	50	75	125
Erector #0 (50¢ original)....................	50	75	100
Erector #1.......................................	40	60	80
Erector #4, w/motor, WB...................	120	160	300
Erector #8.......................................	500	1000	2000
Erector #10.....................................	1000	2000	4500
Erec. #7, '26 Steam Shovel, brn box.....	200	350	450
Erec. #7-1/2 '26 White Trk.,br. box.....	300	500	750

Erector No. 1-1/2, 1952, "Beginner's" Set. Courtesy Marion Designs.

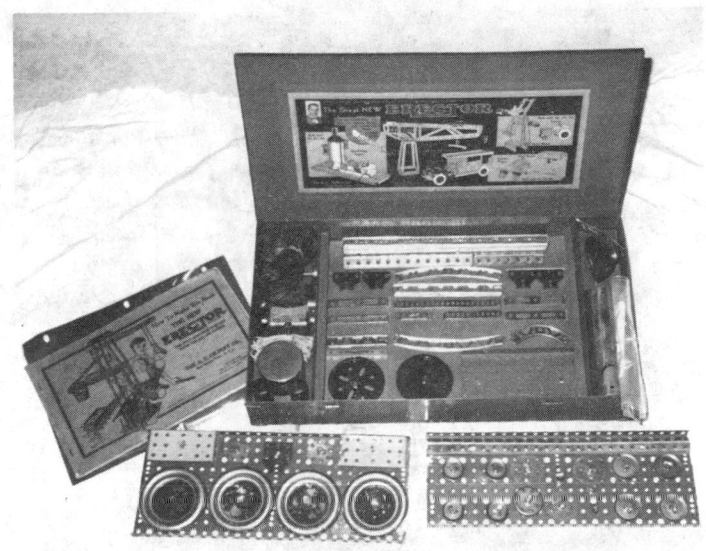

No. 6-1/2 Erector, 1935, "Super 6-1/2". Courtesy Marion Designs.

	C6	C8	C10
1927 - 28			
Erector #7-1/2, White Tr., red box....	250	450	700
Erector #7, Steam Shovel, red box....	200	350	500
Erector "B" giant red ferris wheel.....	300	550	900
Erector #10, multi drawer, WB..........	1400	2200	4500
1929 - 30			
Same as above except for #9 Mech. Wonders Set......................	600	1200	2000
1931 - 32			
Erector White Tr. rec. lid w/picture...	400	600	900
Erector Hudson Loco. "A" eng. only...	800	1000	1400
Erector Hudson #8 eng. only w/7 pts...	900	1300	1700
Erector Hudson #8-1/2 Eng & Tend +ot..........	1200	2400	5000
Erector #10 "Climax" largest set ever made, 150 lbs........	5000	10000	16-20,000
Erector #9 Zeppelin Set......................	1000	1600	2400
1933			
Erector Hudson #8-1/2, in WB..........	1500	2600	6000
Erector Super 6, w/P56G, 110V motor......................	175	275	500
Erector Sensa. 7, automotive parts....	250	400	600
1934			
Erector Super 6 as above, green box.	175	275	500
Erector Sensa. 7 no automotive parts, red box....................	200	350	550
Erector #7-1/2 Automotive Set..........	250	450	650
Erector #8 Hudson & Tend., blue met....................	1400	2800	5500
1935			

Sets this year only featured architectural panels. If present, sets are more valuable. Many new parts.

	C6	C8	C10
Erector Super 6-1/2, P51 motor, boiler.................	225	300	550
Erector 7-1/2, Classic Ferris Wheel..	275	400	600
Erector 8-1/2, Automotive Set..........	300	475	700
Erector 9-1/2, Hudson Set.................	1600	3200	6000
1936			
Erector 5-1/2, w/A52 110V motor....	200	275	425
Erector 8-1/2, Classic Ferris Wheel...	250	275	525
Erector 9-1/2, Automotive Set..........	275	400	600
Erector 10-1/2, Hudson Set................	1500	2800	5500

No. 7 Erector, 1929, "Steam Shovel". Courtesy Marion Designs.

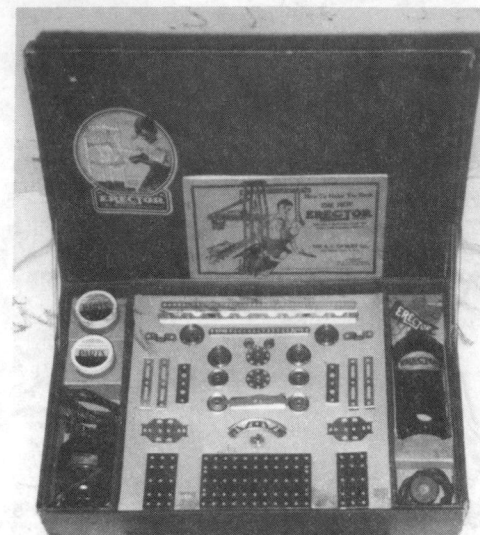

No. 7 Erector, 1946, "Sensational 7", a most unusual immediate postwar set. Courtesy Marion Designs

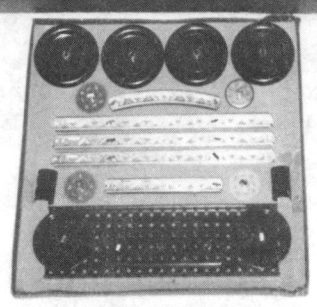

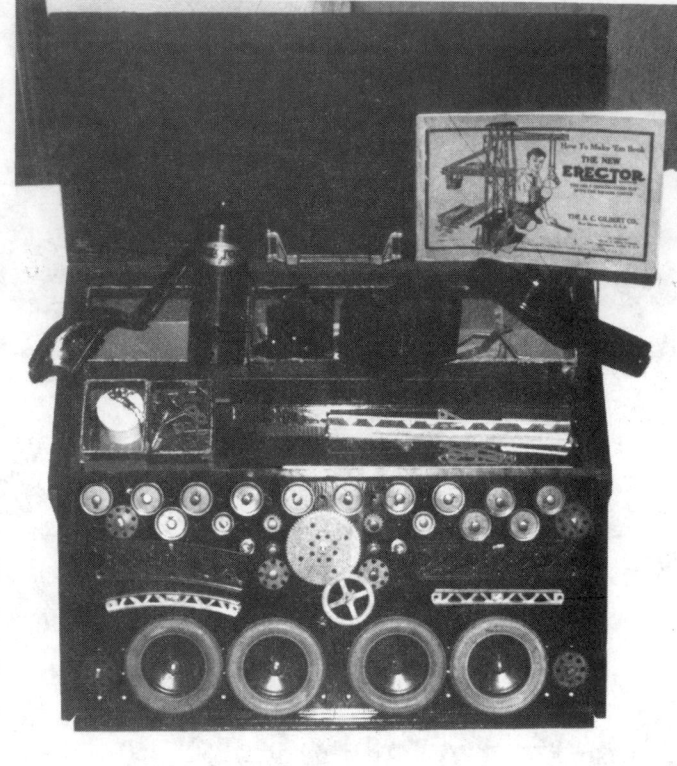

No. 7-1/2 Erector, 1929, "White Truck". Courtesy Marion Designs.

C6   C8   C10

1937

The last year of the Hudson Set, cdbd/metal top parts cans introduced, last year of P51 motor.

Prices not significantly different.

1938

Famous A-49 motor w/die cast housing introduced; "MX" house introduced.

Prices not significantly different.

10-1/2 becomes Electric Train Set

w/American Flyer engine and track..... 750   1500   300

1939

Whistle for A-49 intro.   pnsd

1940

Parachute Jump intro to 9-1/2,   pnsd

C6   C8   C10

1941

Little change. Royal Blue #556 in 10-1/2

1942

Sets before WW II conversion had black rim wheels, black boiler.   pnsd

1945 - 46

A confusing era. ACG brought out even numbered sets from '33, '34 era in a wild array of boxes. *Prices could be higher because of rarity.*

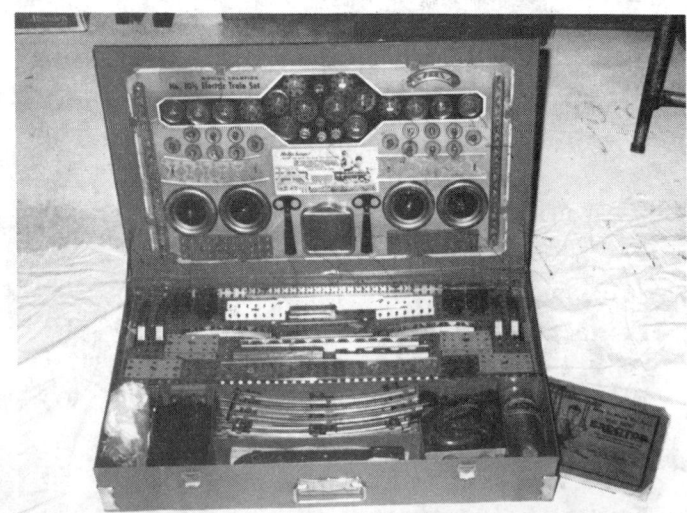

No. 10-1/2 Erector, 1941, "Electric Train" set. Courtesy Marion Designs

Erector No. 7-1/2, 1948, "Engineer's" Set, with aluminum parts. Courtesy Marion Designs

No. 8 Erector, 1916, largest set, has "Mysto" label. Courtesy Marion Designs.

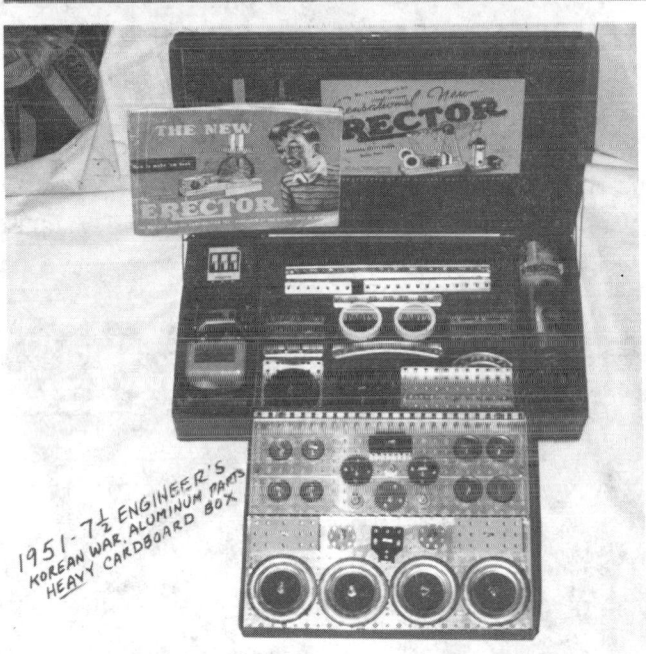

1951-7½ ENGINEER'S KOREAN WAR, ALUMINUM PARTS HEAVY CARDBOARD BOX

Erector No. 9-1/2, 1937, "Automotive" Set. Courtesy Marion Designs.

No. 7-1/2 Erector, 1951, "Engineer's" Set. Courtesy Marion Designs.

No. 8-1/2 Erector, 1939. "Ferris Wheel" Set. Courtesy Marion Designs.

Erector 10129, 1963, "Master Power" set (Type III). Courtesy Marion Designs.

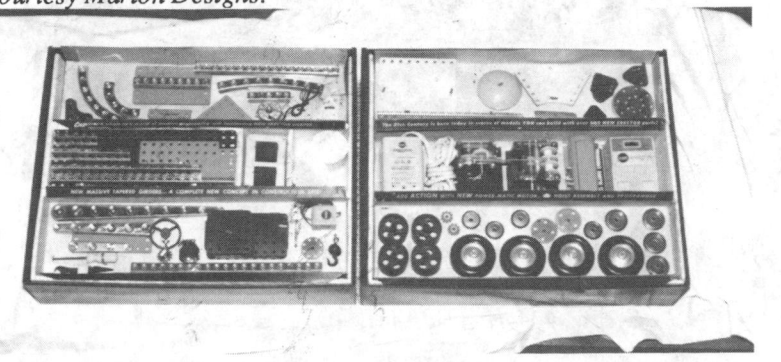

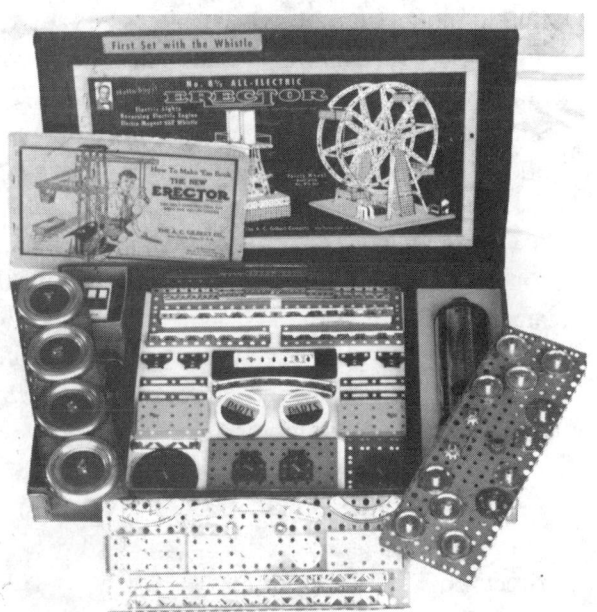

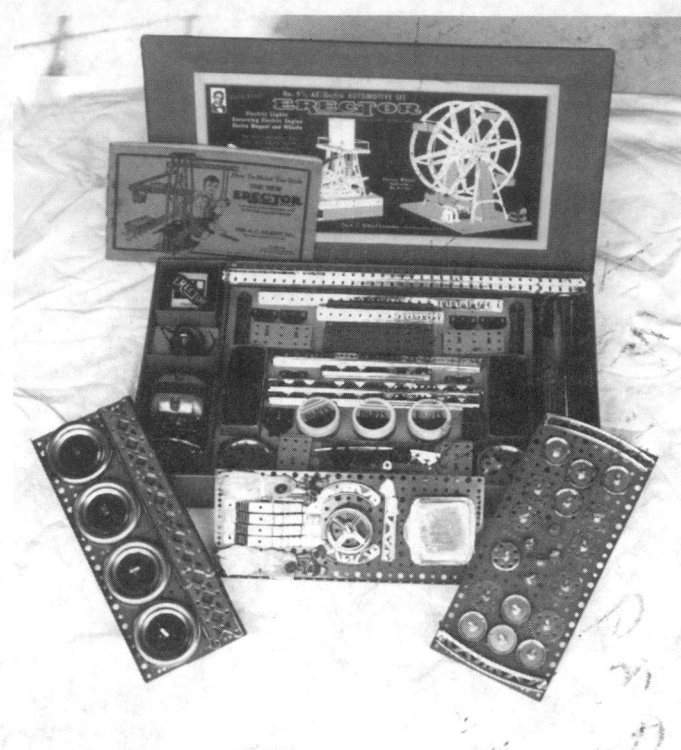

No. 9-1/2 Erector, 1948, "Automotive" Set. Courtesy Marion Designs.

	C6	C8	C10

1947 - 48

Except for old stock, brass metal corners gone; half sizes back; pnsd. Late '48 10-1/2 becomes the 12-1/2, remote control/robot set w/P55 motor,

A-48 and A-49 .... 500 900 1500

1949 Late

10-1/2 intro in 9-1/2 box w/Merry-

Go-Round capability 200 500 800

The era '46 through '52 is confusing. Many sets had aluminum parts, covers, and/or boxes due to the devastating effects of a long steel strike and later, the Korean War. Generally, sets with aluminum are not as valuable unless a rare collector wants one of everything ever made. Aluminum work hardens and splits, a metallurgical weakness. The 12-1/2 Set disappeared in '51 and reappeared again in '56 as the "Master Builder" with a clamshell bucket, no P55 motor. **pnsd**

1957

Two momentous changes occurred in '57, metal boxes up through 8-1/2 had lithographed covers with pictures of the featured model and the set numbers became a five digit computer code. Unfortunately, the gage of metal in the boxes was thinned out and these do not survive as well. '57 also saw the small plastic DC-3 motor of inadequate power.

	C6	C8	C10
Erector 5-1/2 "Motorized" (DC-3) (10041)	40	75	125
Erector 6-1/2 "Electric Engine" (10051)	60	90	140

	C6	C8	C10
Erector 7-1/2 "Engineer's" (10061)	70	110	190
Erector 8-1/2 "All Electric" Ferris Wheel (10071)	90	160	240
Erector 10-1/2 "Amusement Park" (10080)	110	250	450
12-1/2 "Master Builder" (10091)	400	750	1200

1958

Saw the introduction of the famous "musical parts". Very fragile, hence very valuable. They are scarce! The record alone brings $100. In the same order as preceding.....note "Name" changes.....

10041 "Power Model" (same as 5-1/2)

1052 "Rocket Launcher" (same as 6-1/2, additional
premium of $30)

1062 "Steam Engine"

10072 "Musical Ferris Wheel"

125 w/music 200 350

10082 "Amusement Park".... 200 w/music 400 600

10092 "Master Builder"........ 750 w/music 950 1500

1959

Saw only name changes, Rocket Launcher with 50th Anniversary label $30 premium.

10042 "Automatic Radar Scope" (same as 10041).....pnsd

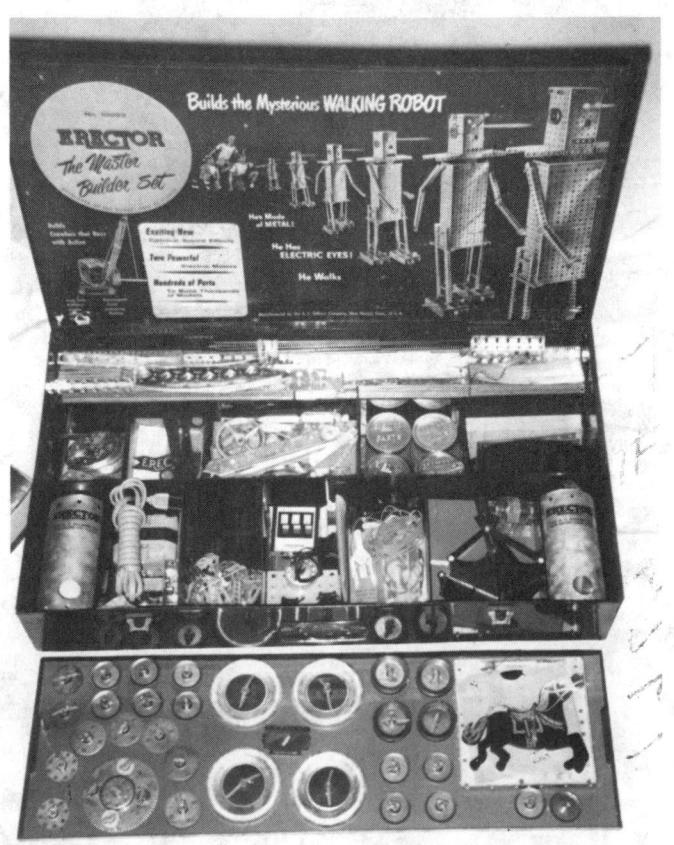

No. 12-1/2 Erector, 1958, "Master Builder" with musical parts. Courtesy Marion Designs.

10053 "Rocket Launcher"(same as 10051) $30 premium if gold label intact.

10063 "Automatic Conveyor" (same as 10062) premium $20 if two belts present.

10073 "Musical Ferris Wheel" (same as 10072) $20 premium if two belts present, music a must for 10072 price to apply.

10083 "Amusement Park" (same as 10082) $20 premium if two belts present, music a must for 10082 price to apply.

10093 "Master Builder" (same as 10092) $20 premium if two belts present, music a must for 10092 price to apply.

1960

Saw the musical parts dropped, styrofoam packing intro. A.P. & M. B. used metal boxes made by joining two smaller boxes. Sets retain earlier prices due to scarcity. Production and sales fell sharply in 1960.

10042 "Automatic Radar Scope"..................pnsd

10053 " Rocket Launcher"............................pnsd

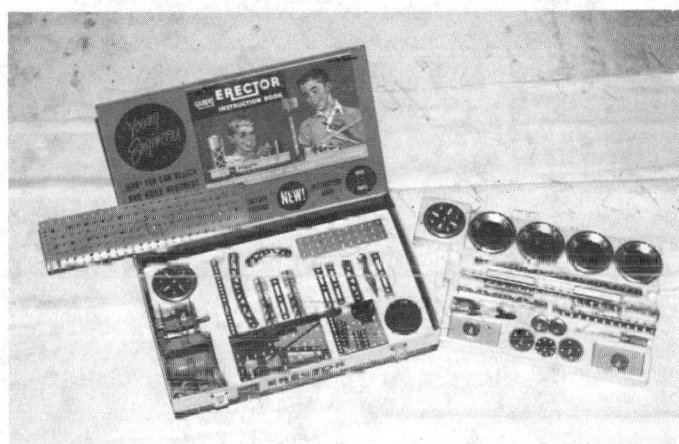

No. 10053 Erector, 1960, "Rocket Launcher". Courtesy Marion Designs.

C6 C8 C10

10063 "Automatic Conveyor".....................pnsd

10074 "Ferris Wheel"........................100 150 300

10084 "Amusement Park" (same as 1959 10083)
    double box.................................pnsd

10094 "Master Builder" (same as 1959 10093)
    double box.................................pnsd

1961

No real changes, no name change, no number changes. Price not significantly different. (pnsd)

1962

Saw the demise of the "classic" Erector Set with trussed girders. In the order as in 1959:

10181 "Action Helicopter" (same as 10042).........pnsd

10201 "Rocket Launcher" (same as 10053)..........pnsd

10211 "Cape Canaveral" (same as 10063)...........pnsd

10221 "Lunar Drilling Rig" (same as 10074).......pnsd

10231 "Astronaut" (same as 10084)
    double box...............................pnsd

10094 "Master Builder", double box.................pnsd

In 1962 the Gilbert Company was in receivership; production and sales continued to drop; tooling was worn out, with little money to replace it. The system was redesigned, eliminating the truss configuration. This easily cut the cost of new tooling in half as any tool engineer can tell you. Thus was born "TYPE III" Erector, a bit flimsier, not as true to life but still challenging to the young mind that hadn't become hooked on television. At present, sets from this era are not much in demand compared to the "classic" sets of type 1 & 2. This could change as more collectors dry up the supply. We will deal only with the three largest sets of 1963, 4 and 5. Most of the smaller sets were presented in corrugated boxes, tubes, etc...not given to survival.

C6 C8 C10

Type III 1963

10127 "Lunar Vehicle Set"................50   90   150

10128 "Planetary Probe Set".............80   150 200

10129 "Master Power Set"..................100 225 300

These sets were in metal boxes with a sliding plastic cover. An overcover of cardboard with colorful scenes of the models in action on the moon or somewhere in space. The C10 prices include these covers which did not survive well. If really nice, add 20% to C10 numbers. All three sizes had foam inserts to hold the parts, impossible to duplicate. 1964 and 1965 saw a continuation of these three sets. After '65 the company was sold to Gabriel Industries, hence type 3 sets are many times referred to as Gabriel Era trash....only time will tell!

Vital Parts & Accessory Sets

P-58 Motor, 6-12 volt AC/DC, "basket case" 10

P-56G Motor, 115 volt AC, running.........................80

A-52 Motor, 115 volt AC, running...........................65

P-51 Motor and Gearbox, 115 volt AC, running......90

A-48 Mechanical Motor w/Key,
    check for spring slip...............................35

A-49 Motor and Gearbox, 115 volt AC,
    running, EXC...40

P-55 Motor & remote control, 12 volt
    AC/DC, runs..125

P-58 Motor, "Joe Long" rebuild..............................50

1E Square Girder Kit, 20-"C", 8-"B",
    14-7/8" sc & nt......................................60

Illumination Kit..150

Whistle Kit, 7-15 volt AC....................................100

Smoke and Choo-Choo Kit, 7-15 volt AC..............125

Musical Parts-comp. reproducer,
    record, mech' ism...................................200

The Climax of Erector Glory

IT'S the giant DeLuxe No. 10 Erector, the set that combines all Erector thrills in one big red brass-bound chest. Think of it, boy! All the trail blazing Railroad Models! The sand-digging steam shovels and a hundred other big industrial machines. All the great ships of the sky, dirigible and airplanes. Automobiles and other fast moving vehicles of every kind and shape. The giant carnival ferris wheel and the circus Merry-Go-Round, which revolve just like the ponderous big giants of fun and pleasure. You can build everything you can think of with this Master set. It's the most gigantic, magnificent chest of sport ever offered to boys the world over. And it's so sturdy and rugged that you can hand it down to your own children when you grow up—the most treasured possession of two generations. It weighs 150 *pounds* in all and contains over 2500 engineering parts. Builds over 500 models. With the master 312-page and 72-page Locomotive "How to make 'em" books this enormous Erector set costs $69.75.

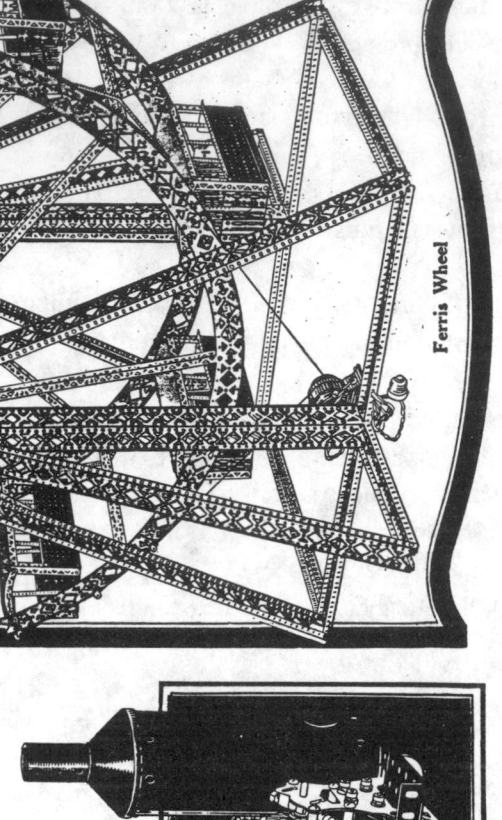

Ferris Wheel

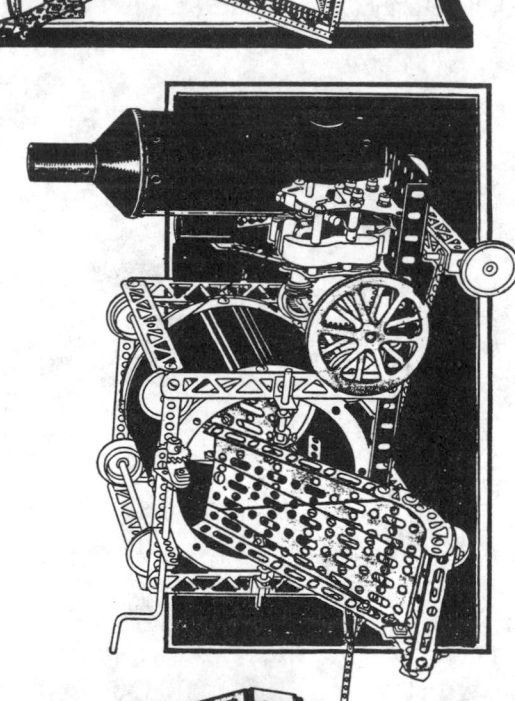

A flier for the Erector Climax set, 1931. It weighed an extraordinary 150 pounds. Courtesy Marion Designs.

654

MISCELLANEOUS

Average mint price in this category in the last edition was $580.00, and in this edition it is $649.33 an increase of 12%.

	C6	C8	C10		C6	C8	C10
"Acrobatic Monkey" John Henry Prod., 1950s, push toy, 10" long	60	90	120	American Metal Toys Animals, lead alloy, average price each	5	8	11
Air Raid Warden Junior Kit, felt hat, arm band, gas mask, whistle, window sign, forms and street-plan sheets, stethoscope, book of instructions, WW II era, rare	100	150	200	American Metal Toys Pillbox	41	63	82
				American Toy Co. Dancing Black Women, two	600	900	1200
All-Nu Horse, not made to have rider	15	22	30	Animate Toy Co. "Baby Haymaker", 1916 tin push toy playset	125	188	250
Alligator, cast iron, 9"	20	30	40	"Anti-Aircraft Rapid-Fire Machine Gun", cast iron, on wheels	275	363	550
Alligator, cast iron, two-part, 9" long	30	45	60	Arcade Bathroom Set, 3 piece, cast iron tub, stool, sink	425	638	850
American Badge ring, circa 1930s or 1940s, heavy metal, may have been premium	20	30	40	Arcade cast iron highway sign, "Curve"	50	75	100
American Logs - similar to Lincoln Logs, circa WW II, price includes box, instructions	30	45	60				

ARCADE Cast Iron Highway Signs. Courtesy Lloyd W Ralston Auctions.

AMERICAN METAL TOYS Animals.

ARCADE signs and tools; "Men Working Ahead", "Road Closed", "Slow". Courtesy Continental Hobby House.

AMERICAN METAL TOYS Pillbox.

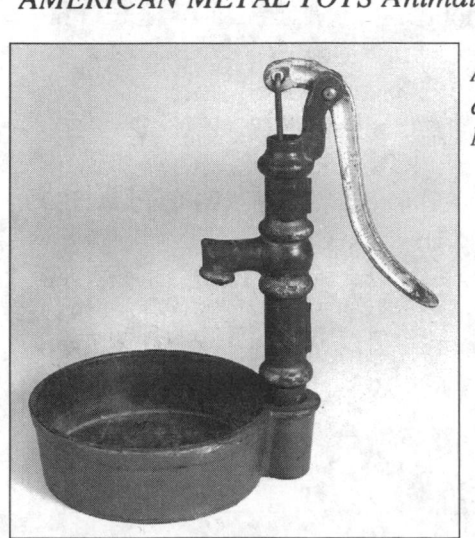

ARCADE Pump and Tub. Courtesy Mapes Auctioneers.

AMERICAN METAL TOYS Animals.

ARCADE "Don't Park Here" sign, 1920, 5" high. Courtesy Lloyd W. Ralston Auctions.

ARCADE Garage. Photo by Virginia Caputo. Courtesy James S. Maxwell/ Virginia Caputo.

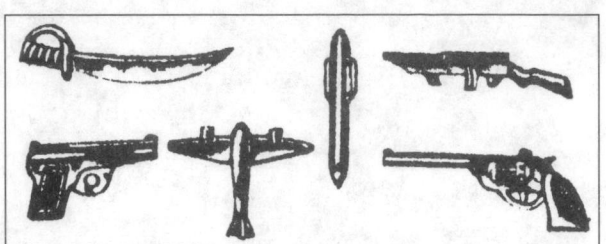

ARCADE Weapons.

	C6	C8	C10
small, nickel finish, cutlass, pistol, automatic, aerial bomb, tommy gun, airplane, came in set of 6, 1938, Price per each	10	15	20
Arcade Pump and Tub	60	90	120
Arcade Windmill, cast iron, 15-1/4" high	100	150	200
Arkitoy Play Lumber by G.B. Lewis Co., 1926, No. 3	20	30	40
Artascope, optical toy, circa 1920, pressed steel, spin base with multi-colors, see thru mirrors	60	90	120
Auburn Rubber Calf, circa 1937	6	9	12
Auburn Rubber Chicken, circa 1937	4	6	8
Auburn Rubber Collie, circa 1937	7	11	15
Auburn Rubber Colt, circa 1937	5	8	10
Auburn Rubber Cow, circa 1937	7	11	15
Auburn Rubber Duck, circa 1937	4	6	8
Auburn Rubber Farm Set, 40-plus pieces, post WW II	70	105	140
Auburn Rubber Fence Section, circa 1937	4	6	8
Auburn Rubber Firehouse Set No. 523	100	150	200
Auburn Rubber Horse, circa 1937	6	9	12
Auburn Rubber Pig, circa 1937	4	6	8
Auburn Rubber Piglet, circa 1937	4	6	8
Automatic Toy Co., "Rocket Space Ship No. 305", 1930s, tin, friction, sparks, 8-1/2" long	80	120	160
Automatic Toy Co., "Space Rocket Ship No. 306", 1930s, tin, friction, sparks, siren, 8-1/2" long	150	225	300
Automaton Dancer, 1800s, clockwork, I & W Co., black dancer	900	1500	2200
B & R Co., "Bossy The Moo Cow", 1930s, 11" long	80	120	160
Baby Buggy, cast iron, 4-1/2" high	48	72	95
Baby Carriage, Kilgore, 4-7/8" high	250	375	500
Baby Carriage, tin, w/folding cloth top, 7-3/4" long	40	60	80
Badge, "Dick Steel News Service"	20	30	40
Badge, G-Man, lead	5	7	10

	C6	C8	C10
Arcade cast iron highway sign, "Men Working Ahead"	26	39	52
Arcade cast iron highway sign, "Road Closed"	34	51	68
Arcade Dining Room Table, 2 chairs	245	368	490
Arcade "Don't Park Here" cast iron sign, 4-1/2" high	30	45	60
Arcade "Don't Park Here" sign, painted cast iron, 1920, 5" tall	30	45	60
Arcade Garage	300	450	600
Arcade Gas Pump, 6"	180	270	360
Arcade Grand Piano and bench, 3"	375	562	750
Arcade Kitchen Set, range, dinette, sink, refrigerator	500	750	1000
Arcade Refrigerator	212	318	425
"Arcade Service" gas station, No. 900, 1941	112	168	225
Arcade "Stop" sign, cast iron	30	45	60
Arcade "U.S. 30" highway sign	17	26	35
Arcade tools, cast iron, No. 779N, small, nickel finish, screwdriver, hammer, monkey wrench, pipe wrench, crescent wrench and S wrench, came in set of 6, 1938, Price per each	4	6	8
Arcade Weapons, cast iron No. 778N,			

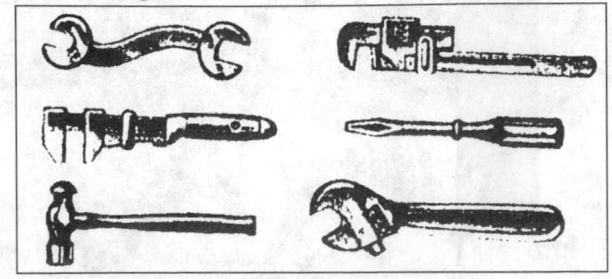

ARCADE Tools.

	C6	C8	C10
Badge, Jet Ranger	6	9	12
Badge, Junior Counter Spy Agent w/picture, No. 161731	10	15	20
Badge, "Junior Detective", heavy six-pointed star badge w/copper inset, nickel badge	10	15	20
Badge, Junior G-Man, circa late 1930s, brass, shield-shaped, eagle on top	10	15	20
Badge, Junior Secret Agent, metal	12	18	24
Badge, "The Purple Mask" detective badge	10	15	20
Badge, "Sheriff", six-pointed star, black oval insert and word "Oklahoma", nickeled metal	18	27	36
Baggage Cart, cast iron, 5" high	36	54	72

BALDWIN

Baldwin was located in Brooklyn, New York at 361 Stagg Street. Its material was pressed steel.

	C6	C8	C10
Baldwin Chicken on nest, marbles for eggs, 5" long	60	90	120
Baldwin Kingpin, spring action bowling	50	75	100
Baldwin "Little Red Hen", 1930s, crank action, 5" long	40	60	80

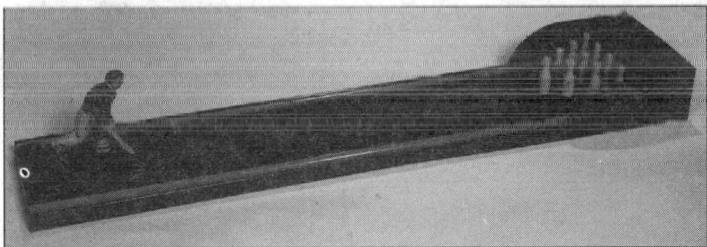

BALDWIN Kingpin, spring action. Courtesy Scott Smiles. Photo by Mike Adams.

	C6	C8	C10
Barbed Wire (Army), 8" long, for toy soldiers	7	11	14
Barbed Wire, mesh, for toy soldiers	12	18	25
Barclay Searchlight, swivels on base, 3".	20	30	40
Barclay No. 209 Work Horse	6	9	12
Barclay No. 210 Horse	5	8	10
Barclay No. 211 Grazing Horse	5	8	10
Barclay No. 212 Standing Cow	5	8	10
Barclay No. 213 Grazing Cow	5	8	11
Barclay No. 214 Lying Cow	6	9	12
Barclay No. 215 Bull	5	8	10
Barclay No. 216? Grazing Sheep	5	8	10
Barclay No. 217 Standing Sheep	5	8	10

	C6	C8	C10
Barclay No. 218 Resting Sheep	6	9	12

BARCLAY, L to R; Top: 209, 210, 213, 214. Bottom: 215, 217, 218, 219, 220, 216?.

	C6	C8	C10
Barclay No. 219 Ram	5	7.50	10
Barclay No. 220 Pig	5	7.50	10
Barclay Mess Table, two benches (wooden)	20	30	40
Beaut Mfg. Co., Wagon No. 50	6	9	12
Bell Toy, Acrobats holding bells, Gong Bell No. 54	310	465	620
Bell Toy, Alligator ridden by Black Boy, N.N. Hill, 1910, cast iron, 5-1/2" long	1000	1700	2300
Bell Toy, Alligator snapping at teasing boy, cast iron, 9-1/4" long	1500	2400	3500
Bell Toy, Althof Bergmann, tin, "Chime & Design Patd. May 19th 1874", 3 soldiers, one w/flag, 2 w/rifles	1600	2400	3200

BELL Toys, Top, L to R: "Tramp", cast iron, Gong Bell; Acrobats holding bells, Gong Bell. Bottom, L to R: "Mary and Her Little Lamb", Gong Bell; "Trick Pony", Gong Bell. Courtesy Christie's East.

BEAUT MFG. CO. Wagon. Courtesy George Buhler. Photo by Bill Kaufman.

BELL Toy, "Are You A Buffalo". Courtesy James S. Maxwell/ Virginia Caputo. Photo by Virginia Caputo.

BELL Toy, Billy Goat, Gong Bell No. 51. Courtesy Lloyd W. Ralston Auctions.

BELL Toy, Hunter and Rabbit. N.N. Hill. Courtesy Lloyd W. Ralston Auctions.

BELL Toy, Cat and Dog, Gong Bell. Courtesy James S. Maxwell/Virginia Caputo. Photo by Virginia Caputo.

BELL Toy Horse, FALLOWS, tin. Courtesy Lloyd W. Ralston Auctions.

BELL Toy, Clown & Pig, 1900. Courtesy Lloyd W. Ralston Auctions.

BELL Toy, Goat, FALLOWS. Courtesy Lloyd W. Ralston Auctions.

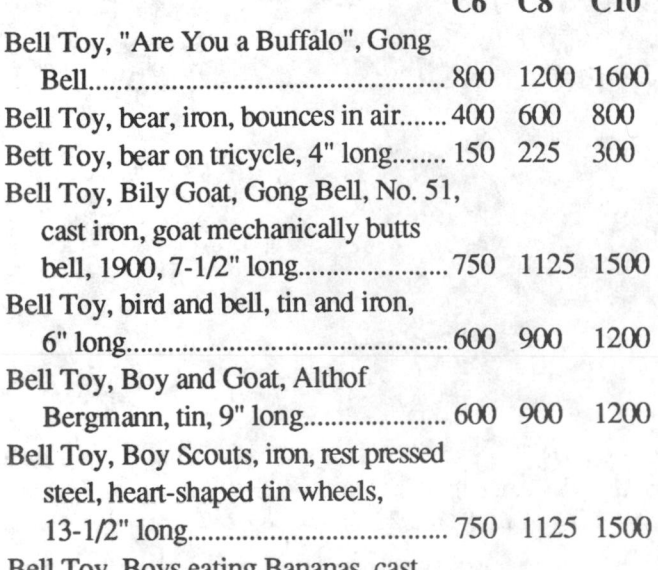

BELL Toy, Elephant on Platform, FALLOWS. Courtesy Christie's East.

	C6	C8	C10
Bell Toy, "Are You a Buffalo", Gong Bell	800	1200	1600
Bell Toy, bear, iron, bounces in air	400	600	800
Bett Toy, bear on tricycle, 4" long	150	225	300
Bell Toy, Bily Goat, Gong Bell, No. 51, cast iron, goat mechanically butts bell, 1900, 7-1/2" long	750	1125	1500
Bell Toy, bird and bell, tin and iron, 6" long	600	900	1200
Bell Toy, Boy and Goat, Althof Bergmann, tin, 9" long	600	900	1200
Bell Toy, Boy Scouts, iron, rest pressed steel, heart-shaped tin wheels, 13-1/2" long	750	1125	1500
Bell Toy, Boys eating Bananas, cast			

	C6	C8	C10
iron	700	1050	1400
Bell Toy, Camel with Rider, tin, Althof Bergmann, c. 1874, 9" long	1200	2000	2800

658

BELL Toy, Alligator ridden by Black Boy. Courtesy Ed Hyers Antique Toys.

BELL Toy, STEVENS, "Evening News Baby Quieter". Courtesy Christie's East.

BELL Toy, Goat, tin, circa 1890. Photo courtesy PB Eighty-Four.

BELL Toy, "Oriental Clown & Poodle". Courtesy Lloyd W. Ralston Auctions.

	C6	C8	C10
Bell Toy, Cat and Dog, Gong Bell........	2000	3200	4500
Bell Toy, Cinderella Chariot, 9-1/4" long	400	600	800
Bell Toy, Clown....................................	250	375	500
Bell Toy, Clown bell-ringers riding back to back on a mule....................	1000	1500	2000
Bell Toy, Clown and Black man on see-saw, c. 1905, 6 colors, Watrous, cast iron, 6-1/2" long...............	600	900	1200
Bell Toy, Comic Characters, two, pressed steel and iron, 3 bells, pierced heart wheels........................	700	1125	1400
Bell Toy, "Daisy", Gong Bell, 9" long.	600	1000	1400
Bell Toy, "Ding Dong Bell, Pussy's Not In The Well", cast iron, c. 1880, Gong Bell Co., 9-1/2" long..............	1100	1700	2700
Bell Toy, Dog on Platform...................	400	600	800
Bell Toy, Dog on Platform (Fallows)...	400	650	900
Bell Toy, "Eagle", c. 1906, Gong Bell, cast iron, 5-1/4" long........................	550	850	1200

	C6	C8	C10
Bell Toy, Elephant on Platform, Fallows, 6-3/4" long.........................	550	850	1200
Bell Toy, Elephant w/bell in trunk, N.N. Hill, circa 1905........................	700	1050	1400
Bell Toy, "Eskimo & Bear", pressed steel body, iron figures...................	750	1125	1500
Bell Toy, Francis, Field & Francis, Clown rotates, hits bell, 6" long.......	300	450	600
Bell Toy, Goat, Fallows, 1880, painted tin, 14" long x 14" tall......................	1100	1650	2200
Bell Toy, Goat, Lamb and Girl on platform, George Brown, tin, early 11" long...	550	850	1200
Bell Toy, Goat, tin, c. 1890, small woman at left leg of goat, either Althof Bergmann or Ives, 7-1/2" high.	500	750	1000
Bell Toy, Goats, two, butting, Gong Bell.	1200	2000	3000
Bell Toy, "Hello Hello Telephone Chimes" w/monkey, Gong Bell.......	2000	3000	4000
Bell Toy, Horse, Fallows......................	450	675	900
Bell Toy, Horse, tin, 9-1/4" long..........	287	430	575
Bell Toy, Horse on Rocker....................	375	562	750
Bell Toy, Horse, tin, pulling heart-shaped wheel...................................	200	300	400
Bell Toy, Ives, white horse pulling heart-shaped wheels, c. 1896, 9-1/2" long......................................	1000	1500	2000

Bell Toy, "Daisy". Courtesy Sotheby's New York.

Bell Toy, FRANCIS, FIELD & FRANCIS, Clown rotates. Courtesy Sotheby's New York.

Bell Toy, "Ding Dong Bell, Pussy's Not In The Well". Courtesy Sotheby's New York.

Bell Toy, "Hello, Hello Telephone Chimes". Courtesy James S. Maxwell/Virginia Caputo. Photo by Virginia Caputo.

Bell Toy, Elephant on Platform, FALLOWS, 6¾" long. Courtesy Wilkinson Collection, Detroit Antique Toy Mueum.

Bell Toy, Jonah & Whale, Hill. Courtesy James S. Maxwell/Virginia Caputo. Photo by Virginia Caputo.

Bell Toy, "Landing of Columbus". Courtesy Sotheby's New York.

660

Bell Toy, Monkey and Horse, Gong Bell. Photo by Virginia Caputo. Courtesy James S. Maxwell/Virginia Caputo.

Bell Toy, Liberty Bell Centennial. Courtesy Sotheby's New York.

Bell Toy, Monkey and Coconut, N,N, Hill. Courtesy Ed Hyers Antique Toys.

Bell Toy, Jack and Jill on seesaw, WATROUS. Courtesy Ed Hyers Antique Toys.

Bell Toy, Clown and Pig, Gong Bell. Courtesy Ed Hyers Antique Toys.

Bell Toy, Monkey in Wheeled Chariot. Photo by Virginia Caputo. Courtesy James S. Maxwell/Virginia Caputo.

BELL Toy, "Poodle Dog Bell Ringer" with Clown. Photo by Virginia Caputo. Courtesy James S. Maxwell/Virginia Caputo.

BELL Toy, Trick Pony, GONG BELL CO., 1893. Photo courtesy PB Eighty-Four.

BELL Toy, Trick Elephant, Gong Bell. Photo by Virginia Caputo. Courtesy James S. Maxwell/Virginia Caputo.

BELL Toy, Uncle Sam and the Don. Uncle Sam's bell is missing in photo. Photo by Virginia Caputo. Courtesy James S. Maxwell/Virginia Caputo.

BELL Toy, Monkey Riding Elephant, FALLOWS.

	C6	C8	C10
Bell Toy, Horse and Rider, heart-shaped wheels, tin, 9" long	750	1125	1500
Bell Toy, Hunter and Rabbit, N.N. Hill, 1900, cast iron rabbit pops out	750	1125	1500
Bell Toy, Jack and Jill on seesaw, cast iron and tin, Watrous, 7-1/2" long	600	950	1350
Bell Toy, Jockey on Horse, early, 7-1/2" long	200	300	400
Bell Toy, Jonah & Whale, Hill	600	1000	1400
Bell Toy, "Landing of Columbus", 7" long	500	750	1000
Bell Toy, Liberty Bell Centennial, Gong Bell Co., 8" long	800	1200	1600
Bell Toy, "Mary and Her Little Lamb", Gong Bell, 8" long	600	900	1250
Bell Toy, Monkey and Coconut, N.N. Hill, "Monkey Mobile", 6" long	500	850	1250

	C6	C8	C10
Bell Toy, "Monkey and Dog", heart wheels, cast iron and tin, 7" long	500	750	1000
Bell Toy, Monkey and Horse, Gong Bell, cast iron and tin, "No. 23"	1500	2250	3000
Bell Toy, Monkey in wheeled chariot (Gong Bell?)	2000	3000	4000
Bell Toy, Monkey on a Log, cast iron, Gong Bell Mfg. Co., circa 1900	750	1125	1500
Bell Toy, "Monkey on a Velocipede", cast iron, 8" high	1500	2400	3800
Bell Toy, Monkey riding Elephant, Fallows, tin, clockwork, 10" long	1400	2100	2800
Bell Toy, Mule kicks bell, No. 42	1400	2300	3200
Bell Toy, Nursery rhymes on drums, one horse	600	900	1200
Bell Toy, "Oriental Clown & Poodle", No. 44, painted cast iron, 1900, cloth in hoop, poodle jumps through hoop and back, 13" long	1250	1875	2500
Bell Toy, "Pig with Clown Rider", Gong Bell, 6" long	300	450	600
Bell Toy, "Poodle Dog Bell Ringer" with Clown, Gong Bell	850	1350	1900
Bell Toy, Rough Rider, Watrous, early, 6-1/2" long	90	135	180
Bell Toy, "Saw the Watermelon", Gong Bell, 8-1/2" long	1100	1700	2800
Bell Toy, Soldier & Sailor	550	825	1100

	C6	C8	C10
Bell Toy, Stevens, "Evening News Baby Quieter", 1890s cast iron, man reading paper to baby, 8" long.	1100	1700	2450
Bell Toy, "Teddy Roosevelt"	90	135	180
Bell Toy, "Tramp", cast iron, Gong Bell, 6" long	500	750	1000
Bell Toy, Trick Elephant, Gong Bell, 7-3/4" long	800	1200	1600
Bell Toy, Trick Pony, Gong Bell Co., 1893, cast iron "39", 8" long	700	1100	1600
Bell Toy, Uncle Sam and The Don, Gong Bell	2250	3375	4500
Bell Toy, Victory in a shell-form Chariot, cast iron, mounted with bell and eagle	1500	2250	3000
Bell Toy, Watermelon, N.N. Hill Brass Co., circa 1905, 8-1/2" long	600	900	1200
Bell Toy, Wild Mule Jack, cast iron	750	1125	1500
Bell Toy, "Young America", cast iron, Gong Bell, circa 1880, 6" long	450	675	900
Big Boy (Restaurants) vinyl doll	9	14	18
Bill Ding Clowns, boxed	50	75	100
Bilt-E-Z Skyscraper Building Blocks, Scott Mfg., Chicago, circa 1925	45	68	90
Bliss "Battle of the Toy Brigades", fort & soldiers, paper litho on wood, circa 1880	600	1000	1400
Bliss Brooklyn Bridge, 1880s, paper litho and stained wood, mechanical, 4' long x 11" tall	600	900	1200

BELL Toys, Top: "Saw the Watermelon". Bottom, Left to Right: Pig with Clown Rider; Monkey on a Velocipede. Courtesy Christie's East.

BLISS Brooklyn Bridge. Courtesy Lloyd W. Ralston Auctions.

	C6	C8	C10
Bliss Church building blocks, circa 1900, litho on wood, 8-3/4" high	500	750	1000
Blocks, Auburn Rubber building bricks, 1940s	17	25	34
Blocks, The Brownie, by McLoughlin Bros., 1891, 20 litho blocks	500	800	1100
Blocks, Chautauqua Architectural Building No. 510, circa 1920s	75	112	150
Blocks, Crandall's "Building Blocks" No. 3, pat. 1867	250	375	500

BLISS Church building blocks, circa 1900. Courtesy Wilkinson Collection, Detroit Antique Toy Museum.

Blocks, RICHTER'S ANCHOR BLOCKS No. 7. Courtesy Continental Hobby House.

	C6	C8	C10
Blocks, Halsam Logs, Senior Size 3/4", No. 815	17	26	35
Blocks, Hill's Alphabet Blocks, c. 1870s, miniset	62	93	125
Blocks, Leecraft Circus Blocks, 12 wooden blocks, painted w/lion, tiger, letters and numbers, contained in wooden pull-toy cage, 1930s	35	52	70
Blocks, Lincoln Bricks by Lincoln Logs	45	68	90
Blocks, Lincoln Logs, set No. 1A, John Wright, pat. 1920, complete	10	15	20
Blocks, Lincoln Logs set 1C, post WW II	35	52	70
Blocks, Lincoln Logs set 2-L	45	68	90
Blocks, Lincoln Logs set S-C	7	11	15
Blocks, Lincoln Logs, set No. 29, early	60	90	120
Blocks, Lincoln Logs, 1923	10	15	20
Blocks, Lincoln Logs, 1930	12	18	25
Blocks, Lincoln Logs, 1947	12	18	25

	C6	C8	C10
Blocks, Elgo American Plastic Bricks No. 705	17	26	35
Blocks, Elgo American Plastic Bricks No. 715	22	33	45
Blocks, Elgo American Plastic Bricks No. 725	30	45	60
Blocks, Elgo American Plastic Bricks No. 735	20	30	40
Blocks, Halsam American Blocks, wood, 1939, No. 60	27	41	55
Blocks, Halsam American Plastic Bricks	22	33	45

Blocks, MILTON BRADLEY, circa 1910, six nested. Courtesy Christie's East.

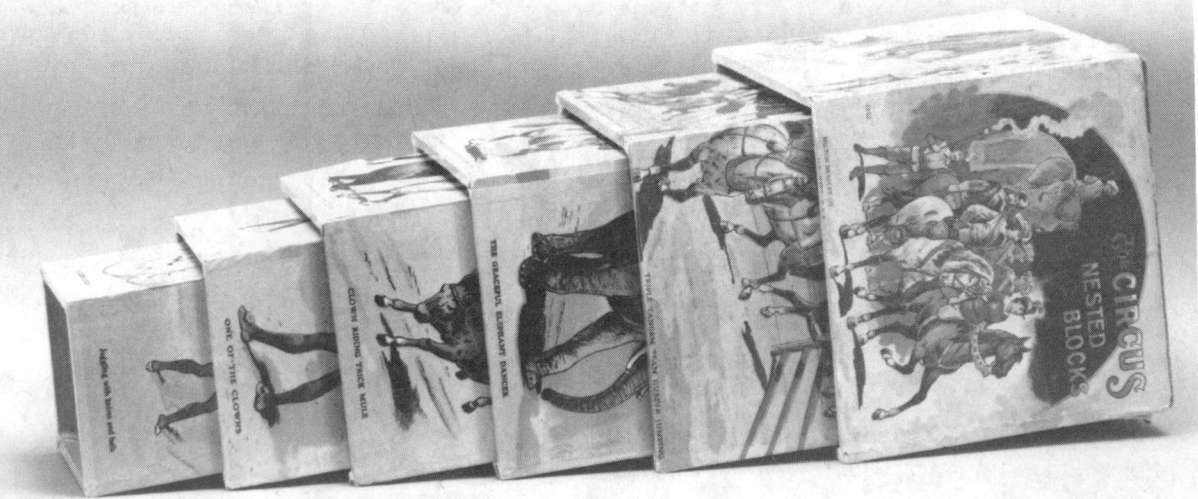

	C6	C8	C10

Blocks, Lincoln Timbers, pre WW
    II, with box, complete........................30   45   60

Blocks, Milton Bradley, circa 1910,
    six nested......................................262   393   525

Blocks, "Mother Goose Living Picture
    Blocks", circa 1890........................325   487   650

Blocks, Richter's Anchor Blocks
    No. 2-1/2.. 85   128   170

Blocks, Richter's Anchor Blocks No. 7. 100   150   200

Blocks, Richter's Anchor Blocks,
    No. 11A..175   262   350

Blocks, Richter's Anchor Blocks,
    No. 12..250   375   500

Blocks, "Stabuilt Blocks", The Em-
    bossing Co., 1916, 20 x 12"............ 42   63   85

Blocks, "Union Building Blocks"
    No. 7, early..................................... 75   112   150

Blocks, set of 6 puzzle blocks depicting
    The Three Bears, Old Mother
    Hubbard, Little Bo-Peep, Puss in
    Boots, Jack the Giant Killer and
    Red Riding Hood. Copyright 1892.. 35   52   70

Blocks, nested, 6, paper litho on card-
    board, picturing children and animals,
    1920, Cramer Publishing Co........... 20   30   40

Blocks, 16, embossed, wooden, 1-3/4"
    square, red and blue, alphabet and
    pictures, 7-1/2" square box, Dutch
    scene on cover, The Embossing
    Company's Toy Blocks, USA,
    price includes box............................. 20   30   40

Blocks, 64, wooden, 1-1/4" square,
    very colorful, letters and numbers
    on sides, box 6" square, price
    includes box.................................... 22   33   45

Bobsled, cast iron, 2 riders, 5" long...... 135   200   270

	C6	C8	C10

Bones Player, Secor, 1880, cloth-
    dressed, cast iron, wood and tin
    figure with hair, painted pot metal-
    head, clockwork mechanism in
    body..1250 1875 2500

Boo Berry, vinyl squeeze toy.............. 35   52   70

Boxers, Black, mechanical windup
    with Ives clockwork mechanism......1000 1500 2000

Boy climbing windmill, tin, wieght
    driven, 1900s, 16" high...................100   150   200

Boy on Sled friction toy, rear wheels
    have spokes, Dayton........................425   638   850

Boy on Tricycle, boy celluloid, trike
    tin, windup...................................... 185   280   370

Boy on Velocipede, paper mache, cloth
    and cast iron, windup, Stevens &
    Brown, or Althorp & Bergmann,
    circa 1870-1880, 10-3/4" long........ 2000 3500 5000

Boy on Velocipede, same as above,
    black boy (rarest), auctioned in 1994 for $6,820.00

Boy Scout Five-In-One Mystery Hid-
    den Compass.................................... 30   45   60

Bradley's Interchangeable Combination
    Circus in wooden box w/label. Pat.
    May 30, 1882, contains 35 3" x 5-1/4"
    interchangeable panels which make up
    a changeable 15-3/4" x 9" circus
    scene..400   600   800

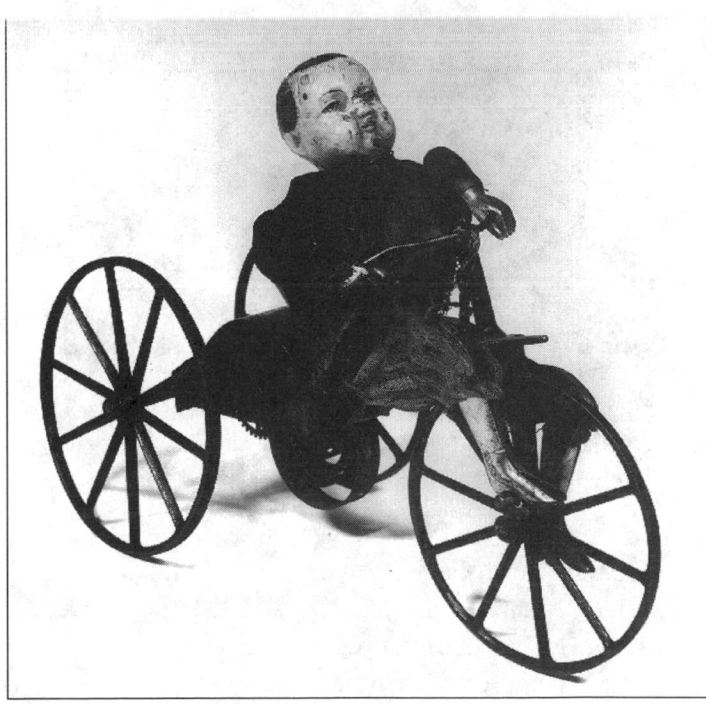

Boy on Velocipede, STEVENS & BROWN. Courtesy Phillips New York.

BONES Player. Courtesy Lloyd W. Ralston Auctions.

665

Boy on Velocipede. Courtesy Sotheby's New York.

	C6	C8	C10
Brownies, "Brownie Artillery", Brownies, cannon, etc., McLoughlin	650	1050	1500
Brownies, Brownie Glass Candy Container	500	750	1000
Brownies Ten-Pin Set, early	650	1100	1600
Buddy L Machine Gun, M101, fires caps	90	135	180
Buddy L Tool Chests, 1927-28, four different, per each, includes tools	125	187	250
Buffalo Toys "Mother Duck", 1930s windup (figure 8s), 9" long	60	90	120

BUFFALO TOYS "Mother Duck". Photo by Don Hultzman.

	C6	C8	C10
Bulldog, kid-covered windup, walks and turns head, German, rare, 7-1/2" long	200	300	400
Cackling Hen, cardboard, drum, w/brown plaster chicken standing on top of drum, metal side handle activates cackling, dated 1936 (also Rooster), 2-1/4" x 3-1/2"	20	30	40

	C6	C8	C10
Cap'n Crunch figure	22	33	45
Candy Container, tin, shaped like cannon, candy comes out barrel when crank is turned, "West Bros. Co. Grapeville, PA.", 7-1/2" long	45	68	90
Candy Container shaped like a desk phone, glass base with cast pewter mouthpiece and wooden receiver, paper labels "lines busy", 4-1/4" high	10	15	20
Cannon, "Admiral Dewey", cast iron, circa 1890s, 11" long	200	300	400
Cannon, Arcade Howitzer, c. 1941, 4" long	40	50	75
Cannon, Auburn Rubber (Aubrubr) Fieldpiece, 75 mm, 7" long	17	25	34
Cannon, Auburn Rubber Howitzer, 155 mm, 7" long	17	25	34
Cannon, Baldwin, No. 890, wood and metal, 16" long	52	78	105
Cannon, Barclay, barrel elevated, 2-1/2" long	6	9	12
Cannon, Barclay, circa 1931 (may be first Barclay cannon, from 1924)	25	38	50
Cannon, Barclay Coast Defense Rifle, 5-man, 4-1/2" long	60	90	120

Cannon, BARCLAY, circa 1931 (may be Barclay's earliest, from 1924). Courtesy Ed Poole.

BARCLAY, Left to Right; Top: Cannon, spring-firing, spoked wheels, 4" long; Cannon, barrel elevated; Cannon, spoked wheels, 3" long; Cannon, 7-3/4" long. Bottom: Coast Defense Rifle, Mortar, heavy, Searchlight. Photo by Ed Poole.

	C6	C8	C10
Cannon, Barclay, Howitzer, 4 wheels, loop hitch horizontal, 3" long	12	18	25
Cannon, Barclay, Howitzer, 4 wheels, loop hitch vertical, 3" long	12	18	25
Cannon, Barclay, Mortar, heavy, swivels on base, 3" long	60	90	120
Cannon, Barclay, Post WW II, very large wheels, 4" long	13	19	26
Cannon, Barclay, silver, black rubber wheels, 7-3/4" long	19	28	38
Cannon, Barclay, spoked wheels, 3" long	6	9	13
Cannon, Barclay, spring-firing, spoked wheels, 4" long	15	22	30

BIG BANG CANNONS

by Raymond V. Brandes

We seldom enjoy knowing where our path will lead and such was the case for Pennsylvania's James Hunter Wily, a Lehigh professor who was beat out by Westinghouse by a matter of hours filing his patent for an electric refrigerator. Two years later in 1912, the Gas Cannon Company was formed by Wily and W.S. Franklin, also a Lehigh professor. The cast iron Gas Cannon was the first product from the tiny company and it followed closely a 1907 patent held by Franklin. In 1915 they introduced "The Artillery Game" which had the outstanding feature of a cannon with a glass barrel!

About 1915, Franklin moved to M.I.T. and gave his interests in the cannon to Wily. Wily patented his own designs, which greatly simplified the toy and trademarked Bangsite, the powered calcium carbide that is key to the toy's success. In 1916 he changed the name of the company to The Toy Cannon Works and began production of the classic breech loading iron cannon. In 1924 the company was incorporated as The Conestoga Company, which survives today, producing six standard cannons and three re-issue brass and bronze collector's editions. In the company's eighty-plus-year history, no less than twenty-five different carbide toys have been documented, not to mention distinct variations that could add another ten items for a very complete collection.

means cannon still in production

Cannon, "Big-Bang", approx. 23" long. Photo by Bill Kaufman. Courtesy Good Old Days Store.

	C6	C8	C10
Cannon, Big-Bang No. 6F, 9" long		30	60*
Cannon, Big-Bang No. 7F, 9-3/4" long	75	125	200
Cannon, Big-Bang No. 7D, 8" long	35	50	150
Cannon, Big-Bang No. 8F, 12-1/2" long	75	125	200
Cannon, Big-Bang No. 10W, 9" long	50	100	150
Cannon, Big-Bang No. 11D, 12-3/8"	35	50	100
Cannon, Big-Bang No. 11F, 15"	150	200	300
Cannon, Big-Bang No. 12F, 16-3/8"	75	100	250
Cannon, Big-Bang No.16F, 22-1/4"	150	250	375
Cannon, Big-Bang No. 60mm, 9"		30	60*
Cannon, Big-Bang No.10FC, 17-1/2"		60	100*
Cannon, Big-Bang No. 15FC, 24"		50	125*
Cannon, Big-Bang No.15AC, 16-1/4"	100	150	250
Cannon, Big-Bang No.105mm, 17-1/2"		40	80*
Cannon, Big-Bang No.155mm, 24"		50	100*
Cannon, Big-Bang Gas Cannon, 9"	75	250	500
Cannon, Big-Bang The Artillery Game, 7" long	150	300	650
Cannon, Big Parade, cast iron	25	38	50
Cannon, "Big Victory", tin litho, 12" long	115	172	230
Cannon, "Boy Ranger", fires marbles, cast iron, Kilgore, 17-1/2" long	180	270	360
Cannon, "Boy Scout Machine Gun", 19" with 8-1/4" wheels	250	375	500
Cannon, C.A.W. Novelty Co., with limber, 2-piece, lead, 1930s, 6"	No Price Found		
Cannon, cast iron, 5" long	45	68	90
Cannon, cast iron on wood base, 5-1/2" long	45	68	90
Cannon, cast iron, 6" long	50	75	100
Cannon, cast iron, 6-1/2" long	55	82	110
Cannon, cast iron, early, 7" long	67	100	135
Cannon, cast iron, pat. 1894, 7" long	75	112	150
Cannon, cast iron, unusual design, 8" long	75	112	150
Cannon, cast iron, pat. 1888, 9" long	90	135	180
Cannon, cast iron w/turned barrel, "Hotchkiss", 9-1/2" long	100	150	200
Cannon, cast iron, 10" long, black	90	135	180
Cannon, cast iron, 11" long	90	135	180
Cannon, cast iron, Ives?, works on black powder, 12" long	100	150	200
Cannon, cast iron, 14" long	125	188	250
Cannon, cast iron, on 4-wheel platform, 14" long	75	112	150
Cannon, cast iron 15-1/2" long	100	150	200

	C6	C8	C10
Cannon, cast iron "Young America", "Rapid Fire Gun", 15-1/2" long	130	195	260
Cannon, Coast Defense Gun, litho tin, camouflaged, 5" long	44	66	88
Cannon, "Dainty" cast iron, on wood base, 10" long	175	263	350
Cannon, David Carlin mortar, circa WW I, cast iron, 15" long	60	90	120
Cannon, die cast, old type shoots, approx. 5-1/2" long	10	15	20
Cannon, "Disappearing Coast Defense Gun", Thomas & Skinner, Indianapolis, fires, 15" wood and steel	40	60	80
Cannon, field, World War I, cast iron, 15-3/4" long	32	48	65
Cannon, firecracker, cast iron, "Pat. Apr. 23, 1895", 4" long	40	60	80
Cannon, Grey Iron, 4-1/2" long	11	16	22
Cannon, Howitzer, c. 1930, double-barreled, woodhandled firing lever, 9" long	15	22	30
Cannon, howitzer type, die cast, shoots, spring mechanism, pre WW II, approx. 5" long	12	18	25
Cannon, Ideal Atomic Cannon	50	75	100
Cannon, Ives, muzzle-loader, 1900, cast iron, 2 wheels	150	225	300
Cannon, Ives, cast iron, brass barrel	200	300	400
Cannon, Ives, red wheels, brass cannon, 7" long	150	225	300
Cannon, Jolly Roger, metal, 1950s	8	12	16
Cannon, Kansas Toy "23", lead, 3-1/4" long	10	15	20
Cannon, Kansas Toy "34", lead, 2-1/4" long	10	15	20
Cannon, Kenton, Firecracker type	40	60	80
Cannon, Kilgore, 2" cast iron firecracker mortar, rubber cannon ball	40	60	80
Cannon, Kilgore, 4-1/2" cast iron firecracker cannon, rubber cannon ball	50	75	100
Cannon, Manoil 19 Metal Action Cannon, early version, "USA"	10	15	20
Cannon, Manoil 69, metal spoked wheels, early	12	18	24
Cannon, Manoil 69, metal spoked wheels, marked "M" left side, early 2nd version	12	18	25

	C6	C8	C10
Cannon, Manoil 69, solid wood wheels	9	13	18
Cannon, Manoil 69, solid wood wheels, variant	9	13	18
Cannon, Manoil, "Metal Action Cannon" No. 200, later version of 19, "Made in USA"	8	12	16
Cannon, Marx Anti-Aircraft Gun, No. 617	37	56	75

Cannon, MARX Anti-Aircraft Gun. Courtesy Joe and Sharon Freed.

Cannon MARX, litho tin, shoots wooden balls. Courtesy Charles D. Richards.

	C6	C8	C10
Cannon, Marx "Atomic Long Range Cannon", 25" long	35	52	70
Cannon, Marx, "Big Shot Cannon"	37	56	75
Cannon, Marx Howitzer Cannon, plastic, circa 1960s, 12" long	25	38	50
Cannon, Marx, litho tin, shoots wooden balls, 21" long	100	150	200
Cannon, Marx "Shell Shooting Long Tom Field Cannon", 1950s, plastic, 14" long	40	60	80
Cannon, Marx Twin Pom-Pom anti-aircraft cannon	50	75	100

Cannon, MARX Howitzer Cannon, plastic, circa 1960s.
Photo by Bill Holt.

	C6	C8	C10
Cannon, "Phoenix", brass barrel with touch hole, 8" long	100	150	200
Cannon, Premier, large thick barrel, large wheels, cast iron	20	30	40
Cannon, pressed steel base, 9-1/2"	15	22	30
Cannon, Ralstoy No. 23	8	12	16
Cannon, Ralstoy No. 34	8	12	16
Cannon, Ralstoy, 3-3/4" long	8	12	16
Cannon, Ranger Jr., cast iron, 10" long	125	188	250
Cannon, rapid fire, cast iron, embossed eagle	200	300	400
Cannon, "Remember The Maine", W.S. Hawkes Foundry, Dayton, Ohio, circa 1900, 13" long	250	375	500
Cannon, sheetmetal, shoots small marbles, blue with red wheels, 14" long	30	45	60
Cannon, Theodore Hahn, No. 189, 1920s, lead alloy	No Price Found		
Cannon, tin, camouflaged, early, 9"	37	56	75

Cannon, THEODORE HAHN No. 189.

	C6	C8	C10
Cannon, tin, pull lever for corks, 14" wood wheels	20	30	40
Cannon, tin, striped spring-loaded barrel with lever	20	30	40
Cannon, tin, two-wheel, circa 1915, 7-1/4", 4" high	40	60	80
Cannon, tinplate, spring action, 1950s, Japan, 7" long	20	30	40
Cannon, Tootsietoy, pre WW II, shoots, approx. 3-3/4" long	12	18	25
Cannon, Tootsietoy, 40 mm AA gun, pre WW II	17	26	35
Cannon, Tootsietoy, 155 mm gun, pre WW II	20	30	40
Cannon, Tootsietoy, 155 mm self-propelled howitzer, 1950s	20	30	40
Cannon, Tootsietoy, 1930s, shoots, approx. 5-1/2" long	30	45	60
Cannon, Victory Toy Co., 1943, Sure Fire Cannon, cardboard	37	56	75
Cannon, Wyandotte, shoots marbles, 14" long	40	60	80
Canoe, Kansas Toy and Novelty, slush lead, "50", two paddling Indians "Rain-In-The-Face" and "Chief Big Foot", 4 wheels, 3-1/2" long	No Price Found		

Carousel, ALTHOF BERGMANN, 1870. Courtesy Lloyd W. Ralston Auctions.

	C6	C8	C10
Carousel, Althof Bergmann, 1870, painted tin, wood base, cloth canopy, clockwork, bisque head doll, wood body, tin arms, turns, cranks and gives motion, 20" tall	2500	4200	6000
Carpet Sweeper, miniature Bissell	22	33	45
Cash Register, Buddy L, steel, 9" x 10-1/2" x 9"	275	363	550

	C6	C8	C10
Catalog: Aldens Xmas, 1946	45	68	90
Catalog: Arcade, 1889	100	150	200
Catalog: Arcade, 1900	115	172	230
Catalog: Arcade, 1901	375	562	750
Catalog: Arcade, 1902-03	85	128	170
Catalog: Arcade, 1917	500	750	1000
Catalog: Arcade, 1924	105	158	210
Catalog: Arcade, 1931	125	188	250
Catalog: Arcade, 1940	100	150	200
Catalog: Auburn Rubber, pre WW II	50	75	100
Catalog: Aurora, 1963, 1964, each	50	75	100
Catalog: Aurora, 1965, 1967, each	55	82	110
Catalog: Aurora, 1971, 1972, each	17	26	35
Catalog: Aurora, 1977	22	33	45
Catalog: Baltimore Price Reducer, 1928, illustrated w/toys, games, etc.	15	22	30
Catalog: Barclay, pre WW II	200	300	400
Catalog: Bilt E-Z, 1924	5	7.50	10
Catalog: Buddy L, 1926 flier	175	263	350
Catalog: Buddy L, 1929	275	352	550
Catalog: Buddy L Jr., 1930	150	225	300
Catalog: Buddy L, 1932 Robotoy flier	125	188	250
Catalog: Buddy L, 1935	175	262	350
Catalog: Buddy L, 1940	125	188	250
Catalog: Buddy L, 1941	135	202	270
Catalog: Buddy L, 1952, 1953, 1956, 1957, 1959, each	7	11	15
Catalog: Buddy L, 1961	22	33	45
Catalog: Butler Bros. 1889, tin toys squeak toys, etc.	30	45	60
Catalog: Butler Bros. 1891, illustrated w/mechanical banks, toys, dolls, etc.	30	45	60
Catalog: Butler Bros., Nov. 1899	40	60	80
Catalog: Butler Bros., Xmas 1930	35	52	70
Catalog: Butler Bros., 1935, 1936, each	22	33	45
Catalog: Butler Bros., Spring, 1941	60	90	120
Catalog: Carpenter, Francis, 1880s	900	1350	1800
Catalog: Champion, 4 pages & cover	150	225	300
Catalog: Daisy, 1975	22	33	45
Catalog: Dayton, 1929	150	225	300
Catalog: Dent Hardware Co., 1900, 40 pages	40	60	80
Catalog: Dent Hardware Co., 1905	37	56	75
Catalog: Dent Hardware, circa 1910	37	56	75
Catalog: Dent Hardware Co., Fullerton, Pa., undated	30	45	60
Catalog: Dent Hardware Co., Fulerton, Pa., iron toys, 1930	32	48	65
Catalog: Dinky No. 5, 7, each	6	9	12

	C6	C8	C10
Catalog: "Dunham", Buckley & Co., New York, 1895, toys, etc.	40	60	80
Catalog: Ehrich Bros., New York, 1892, illustrations of banks, toys, dolls, etc.	40	60	80
Catalog: Eldon, 1961, boats	20	30	40
Catalog: Erector Set, 1938, 38 pp	15	22	30
Catalog: Eureka Trick & Novelty Co., circa 1875, 32 pages	20	30	40
Catalog: A.J. Fisher, N. Y., 1877, illustrating cap pistols, etc.	18	27	36
Catalog: Fisher-Price, 1966	25	38	50
Catalog: Gendron, 1927	600	900	1200
Catalog: Gilbert, 1966	27	41	55
Catalog: Gould, L., 1922, Xmas	125	188	250
Catalog: Gould, L., 1940	40	60	80
Catalog: Grey Iron, c. 1920s, No. 24	115	172	230
Catalog: Hasbro, 1975	27	41	55
Catalog: Hasbro, 1987, 1989	20	30	40
Catalog: Hubley, 1939	60	90	120
Catalog: Hubley, 1974	22	33	45
Catalog: Ideal, 1973	12	18	25
Catalog: Ideal, 1976	12	18	25
Catalog: Ives, Blakeslee & Williams, two-sided broadside, circa 1890, 18" x 24"	70	105	140
Catalog: Ives Yachts, Ships and Shipping, circa 1915, 24 pages	50	75	100
Catalog: Illustrated brochure of cap pistols and animated cap pistols by Ives and Williams	20	30	40
Catalog: Jones & Bixler, 1912, N-8	100	150	200
Catalog: Kenton Hardware Co., No. 16, 1920s, 112 pages	70	105	140
Catalog: Kenton Hardware Co., 1934, illus. in color	50	75	100
Catalog: Kilgore 1977-78	22	33	45
Catalog: Kingsbury, 1919	55	82	110
Catalog: Kingsbury, circa 1920, circa 1925, each	32	48	65
Catalog: Kingsbury Toys, Motor Driven, 1936, 16 pages	40	60	80
Catalog: Knapp Electric Toys No. 35	10	15	20
Catalog: Manoil, circa 1935-1939	100	150	200
Catalog: Marx, 1966	100	150	200
Catalog: Marx, 1976	12	18	25
Catalog: Matchbox, 1964	25	38	50
Catalog: Matchbox, 1965	22	33	45
Catalog: Matchbox, 1966	15	22	30
Catalog: Matchbox, 1968	7	11	15

	C6	C8	C10
Catalog: Matchbox, 1969	6	9	12
Catalog: Matchbox, 1970	4	6	8
Catalog: Matchbox, 1973	11	16	22
Catalog: Matchbox, 1978	13	19	26
Catalog: Mattel, 1967	150	225	300
Catalog: "McCadden & Bros." Philadelphia, illustrated iron and tin toys, banks, mechanical toys, dolls, games, etc.	50	75	100
Catalog: Mego, 1967-69, each	50	75	100
Catalog: Mickey Mouse Merchandise Catalog, 1935, by Kay Kamen Co., 80 pages, hundreds of illustrations of Mickey Mouse items	300	450	600
Catalog: Montgomery Ward, 1935, Xmas	150	225	300
Catalog: Montgomery Ward, 1939, Xmas	25	38	50
Catalog: Montgomery Ward, 1955	45	68	90
Catalog: Montgomery Ward, 1941-1955, each	45	68	90
Catalog: Montgomery Ward, 1959	32	48	65
Catalog: Montgomery Ward, 1961	35	52	70
Catalog: Montgomery Ward, 1962	37	56	75
Catalog: Montgomery Ward, 1964	20	30	40
Catalog: Montgomery Ward, 1966	50	75	100
Catalog: Montgomery Ward, 1968	40	60	80
Catalog: Montgomery Ward, 1969	30	45	60
Catalog: Montgomery Ward, 1970	60	90	120
Catalog: Montgomery Ward, 1971-1976, each	20	30	40
Catalog: Montgomery Ward, Xmas, 1976	40	60	80
Catalog: Montgomery Ward, 1977	37	56	75
Catalog: Nicol & Co. 1895, illustrating banks, etc.	10	15	20
Catalog: Penney's Xmas 1964, 65 each	62	93	125
Catalog: Penney's Xmas 1971-75, each	15	22	30
Catalog: Popsicle Pete Radio News and Premium catalog, early	40	60	80
Catalog: Popsicle Pete's 1949 four page gift list	10	15	20
Catalog: Revell, 1957-58	37	56	75
Catalog: Schoenhut, 1903	100	150	200
Catalog: Schoenhut, 1918, Circus	112	168	225
Catalog: Schoenhut Circus, 1928	100	150	200
Catalog: Schoenhut Humpty Dumpty Circus Toys (other toys as well), circa 1915, many illustrations	100	165	220
Catalog: Sears, 1943, 1945, 1946, 1948,1949, 1951, 1952, 1955, each	37	56	75
Catalog: Sears, 1956-70, each	45	68	90

	C6	C8	C10
Catalog: Sears, 1971-80, Xmas, each	17	26	35
Catalog: Selchow & Righter, 1894-5, games and toys, illustrated trains,boats, bell toys, mechanical banks, etc.	120	180	240
Catalog: Selchow & Righter, 1908-1909, 108 pages	80	120	160
Catalog: Selchow & Righter, 1921	32	48	65
Catalog: Shure, N. 1940	37	56	75
Catalog: Smith-Miller, 1954	40	60	80

Catalog: SMITH-MILLER (Smitty), 1954. Photo by Bill Kaufman. Courtesy Ray Funk.

	C6	C8	C10
Catalog: Spiegel, 1966, Xmas	55	82	110
Catalog: State, Adams & Dearborn Sts., Chicago, illustrated	10	15	20
Catalog: Steelcraft, 1934, 44 pp.	300	450	600
Catalog: Steelcraft, 1936	350	525	700
Catalog: Carl P. Stern, illustrating cap pistols, etc.	15	22	30
Catalog: J. E. Stevens Co., 1906, illustrations of iron toys and mechanical banks	40	60	80
Catalog: J. E. Stevens Co., No. 51, Export	40	60	80
Catalog: Structo Toys, 1931, 8 pages	10	15	20
Catalog: Supplee-Biddle of Philadelphia, 1930, 174 pages, many toys	90	135	180
Catalog: Thorsen & Cassady, 1894, guns, etc.	20	30	40
Catalog: Tom Mix, 1936 Premium Catalog	30	45	60
Catalog: Vindex, circa 1932	80	120	160
Catalog: Walt Disney Character Merchandise, 1930s	250	375	500
Catalog: Walt Disney Character Merchandise, 1940-41	250	375	500
Catalog: A.C. Williams, 1908	125	188	250

	C6	C8	C10
Catalog: A.C. Williams, c. 1930, c. 1934, each	45	68	90
Catalog: A.C. Williams Co., Ohio, illustrating still banks, cast iron toys, airplanes, etc	100	150	200
Catalog: Williams, Charles, 1928	22	33	45
Catalog: Woolworth's Christmas Catalogs, pre WW II	30	45	60
Catalog: Woolworth's Christmas, 1951	30	45	60
Catalog: Woolworth's Christmas, 1952	15	22	30
Cathedral Music Box, tin litho, of organ pipes and cherubs, plays loud or soft according to speed of cranking, no markings, German, 5" x 5" x 7"	325	488	650
Charlie Tuna rubber squeeze toy	9	13	18
Chein "Busy Mike" sand seesaw, 1940s, 7-1/2" high	90	135	180

CHEIN "Busy Mike" sand seesaw. Courtesy Calvin L. Chaussee.

	C6	C8	C10
Chein Cathedral Organ	72	108	144
Chein Drum, 6" x 3-1/2"	22	33	44
Chein Easter Egg w/chicken on top, opens up to hold candy, circa 1938, tin, 5-1/2"	15	22	30
Chein "Sand Chute" No. 45	80	120	160
Chein Sand Pail, circa early 1940s, 7" diameter	21	32	42
Chein "Sand Loader"	75	112	150
Chein "Sand Mill", 1930s, 7" wide, 11" high	50	75	100
Chein Sand-Toy, monkey bends and twists, 7" high	20	30	40

	C6	C8	C10
Chein Windmill sand toy, tin litho, 8" high	15	22	30
Chemcraft No. 5 Chemistry Set, wooden box	37	56	75
Chemcraft No. 418 Master Deluxe Laboratory, wooden box	175	263	350
Chemcraft Beginners Chemistry Set No. 602 by Porter, 1956	12	18	25
Chicago Printing Press, No. 15, complete	20	30	40
Children's Telephone (set of two), 1920	10	15	20
Chimes Bell-Ringer with Elephant, 7" long	40	60	80
Climbing Monkey brings coconuts down from palm tree, tin, "Monkey Shines, Emporium Specialist", 18" high	60	90	120
Clown, balancing, copper, clown holding arched balancing pole weighted at both ends with lead balls, standing on one leg on small round platform on stationary metal ladder. Move clown in any direction and he won't fall off platform, 6-1/2" high	50	75	100

Clown, balancing on pedestal, painted wood, circa 1920, 15" high. Courtesy Mapes Auctioneers & Apraisers.

	C6	C8	C10
Clown, balancing on pedestal, painted wood, circa 1920, 15" high	100	150	200
Clown, clockwork, early, cloth suit, German, 9-1/2" high	300	450	600
Clown, windup, papier mache and cardboard, 43" high	90	135	180
Coffee Grinder, cast iron, 4" high	40	60	80
Cohn T. Inc. "Superior Space Port No. 75", 1950s, playset includes: space drome, space cannon and plastic accessories, 17" long	350	525	700

	C6	C8	C10
"Consul", the educated monkey, tin hand toy, monkey automatically adds, subtracts, multiplies and divides, dated June 27, 1916, 5-1/2" x 6"	40	60	80
Cot, Army, canvas with steel frame, circa early 1940s	10	15	20
Count Chocula, rubber squeeze toy	27	41	55

COURTLAND TOYS

(Numerical Order)

List by Joe and Sharon Freed

	C6	C8	C10
800 Zylo-P-ano. 1946 retail -79¢, 1947 retail - 69¢, 13-1/4" long, 5-1/2" wide	75	100	135
1000 Walt Reach Toys G-Man Pocket Siren Signal, 3-1/2" long, 2-3/8" wide, 1-3/4" high	75	100	125
1050 Courtland Walt Reach Toys Halloween Pocket Siren Signal, 3-1/2" long, 2-3/8" wide, 1-3/4" high	75	100	125
1060 Courtland Walt Reach Toys New Years Pocket Siren Signal, 3-1/2" long, 2-3/8" wide, 1-3/4" high	100	125	150
9000 Mechanical 3 pc. Train set, 24" long, 2-1/4" wide, 3-1/4" high	75	100	125
9050 Fire Department w/automatic garage door, found to have a non-powered fire chief car w/the Courtland Toy Co., Phila. Pa.,			

COURTLAND 9050 Fire Department. Courtesy Joe and Sharon Freed.

markings, it is quite possible that some of the 9050 garages were also manufactured in Philadelphia, 7-3/4" x 10-1/8" x 6-3/4" 125 150 175

9075 Private Garage w/automatic door. Since the non-powered car which accompanies this garage is found w/Courtland Toy Co., Phila. Pa. markings, it is quite possible that some of the 9075 garages were also manufactured in Philadelphia, 7-3/4" x 10-1/8" x 6-3/4" 125 150 175

COZZONE

(from information developed by Larry Giancola)

The Cozzone Corporation was founded by John A. Cozzone during the 1930s. The company made fishing reels, and during WWII components for incendiary bombs, etc. Located at 18 Nuttman Street in Newark, NJ, the firm decided to diversify after the war, and spent a great deal of money developing a construction set. Although a number of different sets pictured in the firm's catalog, only the No. 500 was actually produced. Production seems to have been in the 1948-1950 period. A crayoned price of $12.99 on a surviving set suggests the very high price for the time is why relatively few sets were sold. John Cozzone died in 1968 and his son Tom took over, changing the name to Tomrette Corp. However, toymaking by the family seems to have begun and ended with the construction set.

	C6	C8	C10
Cozzone No. 500 Construction Set, machined metal parts, electric motor, in box	200	300	400

	C6	C8	C10
Crackle (Kellogg's Rice Krispies) handpuppet	17	26	35
Crackle (Kellogg's Rice Krispies) squeeze toy, 8-1/2"	27	41	55

CRANDALL

At 16, Charles M. Crandall took over his family's woodworking business after the death in 1849 of his father. Crandall made croquet sets after the Civil War. They were packed in thin wooden boxes that had tongue-and-grove corners. When his boys were ill, he took home a bag of the grooved scraps. The buildings they made with them inspired "Crandall Building Blocks". The success of the interlocking blocks led to production of "Acrobats", with grooved parts. Crandall, who died in 1905, produced toys into the turn of the century.

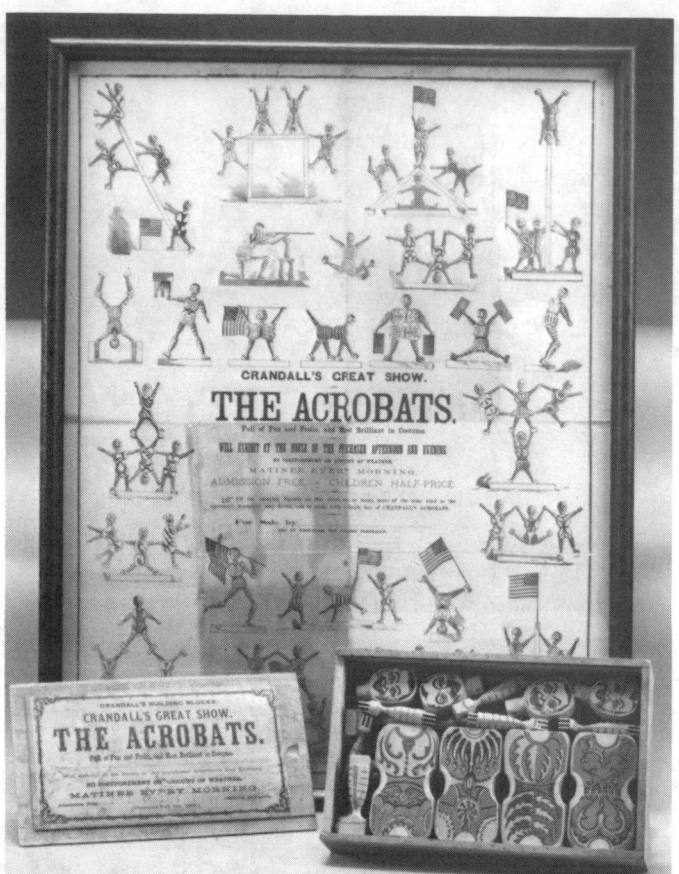

CRANDALL "Acrobats", 4 acrobats, with framed directions in backgound. Courtesy Christie's East.

CRANDALL, "Crandall's District School". Courtesy Wilkinson Collection, Detroit Antique Toy Museum.

	C6	C8	C10
Crandall "Acrobats", 4 acrobats	500	800	1200
Crandall "Crandall's District School", circa 1875	600	950	1300
"Crandall's Heavy Artillery", soldiers, blocks	750	1250	2000
Crandall "John Gilpin's Ride"	500	800	1200
Crandall, Man in Cap on Donkey, wheeled pull toy	275	413	550
Crandall Masquerade Blocks	320	528	976
Crandall Menagerie	500	800	1200
Cupboard, cast iron, open work has diamond and heart pattern, two doors and one drawer	40	60	80
Dancers, black, Automatic Toy Works, New York City, 1870, on box, clockwork, carved wood and jesso bodies, clothes, 6-1/4"w x 10-1/4"t	600	900	1200
"Davy Crockett Alamo Express Fix-It Stage Coach", 1950s, Ideal, 13" long push toy	62	93	125

	C6	C8	C10
Davy Crockett Indian Target Set by Keystone Wood Company, David Crockett rifle, all wood and hardboard litho set that pre-dates Davy popularity of the 50s, made about 1949. Wood stagecoach and horses, wood covered wagon and horses, Indians, bear, etc.	40	60	80
Doctor's Set, Transogram, 1948, Little Country Doctor, full doctor set, chest and bag	32	48	65
Do-Do Toy Co. - "Do-Do Clown", 1930s, squeeze toy, 5-1/2" long	70	105	140
Doepke No. W-11 Freddie Fireplug			

Dancers, black, AUTOMATIC TOY WORKS, 1870. Courtesy Lloyd W. Ralston Auctions.

	C6	C8	C10
wooden, comes apart........................	No Price Found		
Dragon, lead alloy, Kansas Toy, circa 1920s, early 1930s, 2-5/8" long.......	No Price Found		
Drum, Indian motif, tin litho, 11-3/4" diameter.............................	175	263	350

Drum, Indian Motif, tin litho, 11-3/4" diameter. Courtesy James S. Maxwell/Virginia Caputo. Photo by Virginia Caputo.

Ferris Wheel, "DRGM". First bought in 1895. Courtesy Calvin L. Chaussee.

	C6	C8	C10
Drum, metal body, litho, red, white and blue design, varnished wooden hoops, leather "ears", sheepskin head and fiber bottom, w/wooden drumsticks, circa 1910.....................	20	30	40
Drum, about 1920, circus decor, tin,litho..	40	60	80
Drum, metal w/drumsticks,13" diameter..	10	15	20
Drum, wooden w/harness, 13" diameter...	10	15	20
Duncan Yoyo, 1960s.............................	12	18	24
Electric Stove, works, 1930s................	42	63	85
Elephant in Hoop, tin, Fallows?, circa 1880, 12" diameter.................	No Price Found		
Emenee Accordion...............................	12	18	25
Fallows Buffalo Hunt, tin, c. 1886, 9".....	1200	2000	2700
Fallows Elephant on Rocker, tin,8"......	475	712	950
Ferris Wheel, "DRGM", four figures, tin, 1895, 11-1/2" high....................	600	1000	1400

	C6	C8	C10
Flagpole, wooden, w/flag that raises and lowers, approx. 8" high.............	6	9	13
Flying Propeller Ring, heavy metal, c. 1930s-40s, could have been a premium...	10	15	20

Elephant in Hoop, tin, FALLOWS?, circa 1880. Courtesy Christie's East.

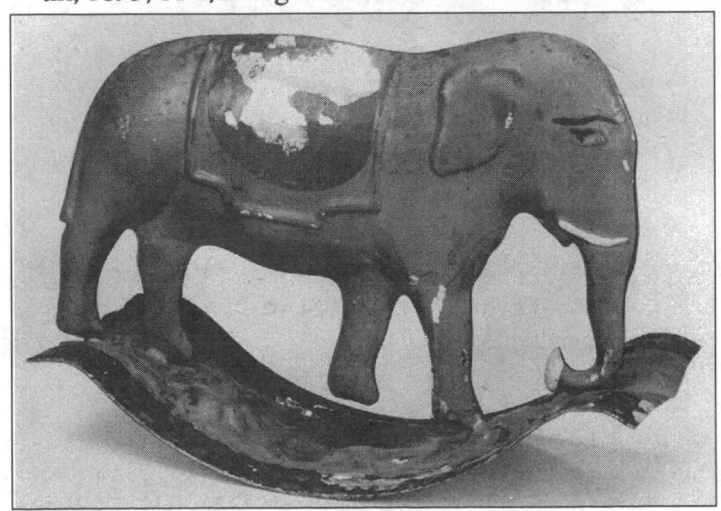

FALLOWS, Elephant on Rocker. Courtesy Wilkinson Collection, Detroit Antique Toy Museum.

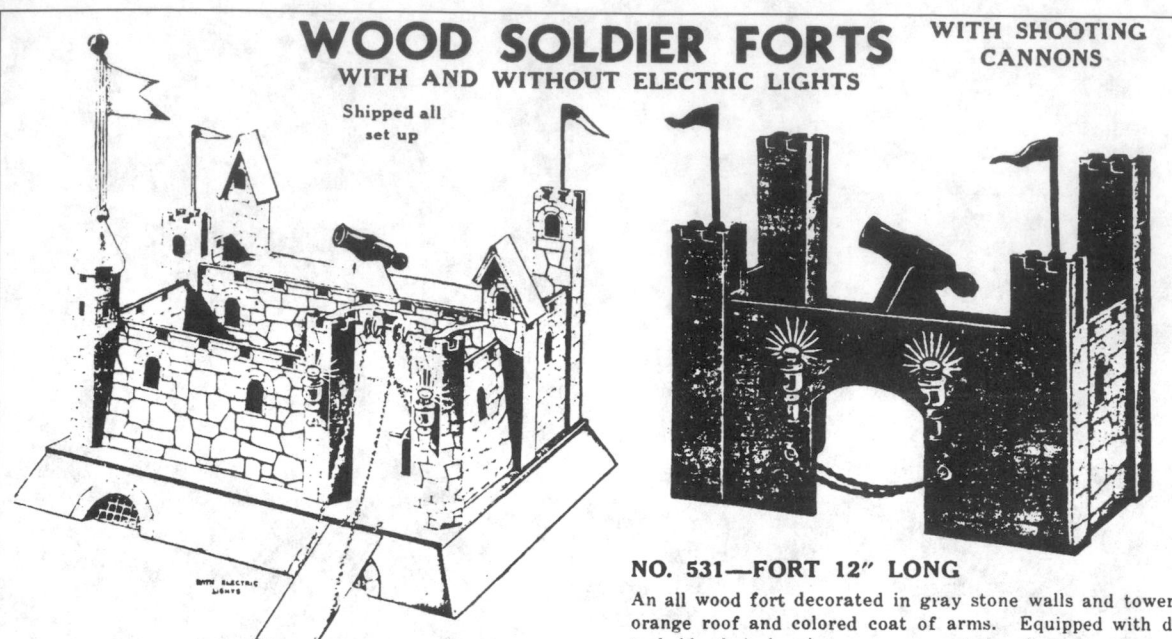

WOOD SOLDIER FORTS

WITH AND WITHOUT ELECTRIC LIGHTS

WITH SHOOTING CANNONS

Shipped all set up

Forts by KEYSTONE, showing No. 535 and 533. Original catalog illustration courtesy Ron Fink.

NO. 535—FORT 20″ LONG with Electric Light

An all wood fort mounted on wood base, decorated in gray stone walls and towers, green base, orange roof and colored turrets tops and shield. Equipped with draw-bridge, winch, swivel shooting cannon, pennants, movable flag, fire step in court yard, moat gratings and electric entrance lamps connected to batteries and operated by switch in tower tops. Size: 20″ long, 17″ wide and 19″ high. Weight when packed in Mullen-test carton 12 lbs. No battery furnished.

NO. 531—FORT 12″ LONG

An all wood fort decorated in gray stone walls and towers, orange roof and colored coat of arms. Equipped with detachable chain barrier, pennants and shooting swivel cannon on roof. Size 12″ long, 7½″ wide, 11″ high. Weight when packed for shipment 4 lbs.

NO. 533—FORT with Electric Light

Same as No. 531 with electric entrance lamps connected to battery and operated by switch on the roof. Weight when packed in Mullen-test carton 5 lbs. No battery furnished.

KEYSTONE MFG. CO., BOSTON, MASS.

New York Showroom, 200 Fifth Avenue

	C6	C8	C10
Fort, Keystone No. 523 U.S. Coast Defense Fort	35	50	70
Fort, Keystone No. 525 U.S. Coast Defense Fort, with accessories, circa 1942	40	55	80
Fort, Keystone No. 527 U.S. Coast Guard Defense Fort, w/accessories, circa 1942	40	70	100
Fort, Keystone No. 531, 12" long	40	60	85
Fort, Keystone No. 533, same as 531, but 2 electric lights at entrance	50	75	100
Fort, Keystone No. 535, w/2 electric lights at entrance, 20" long	60	90	120
Fort, Keystone Exploding Fort with Shooting Tank	46	69	92
Fort, Rich Toys No. 245 Siege Gun with Stone Fort	25	40	75
Fort, Rich Toys No. 246 Siege Gun with Stone Fort, two guns	30	50	80
Fort, Rich Toys No. 247 Siege Gun with Stone Fort, three guns	40	60	80
Fort, Rich Toys No. 260, 26-3/4" long.	35	50	75
Fort, Rich Toys No. 261, 26-1/2" long.	50	75	100
Fort, Rich Toys No. 262, 27" long	100	200	300
Fort, Rich Toys No. 263, 29" long	275	363	550

Fort, RICH TOYS No. 245. Courtesy Don Pielin.

	C6	C8	C10
Frankenberry vinyl squeeze toy	37	56	75
Froggie, rubber squeeze toy, Rempel, 1940s	12	18	24
Fruit Brute, rubber squeeze toy	27	41	55
Gibbs Girl on Swing, c. 1910	150	225	300
Gibbs Service Station No. 81, new in 1924	250	375	500
Girard "Knife Sharpener", crank action, 1930s, 8" high	60	90	120
Glass Candy Container, shaped like Biplane	500	750	1000
Glass Candy Container, shaped like dog	36	54	72
Glass Candy Container, Dolly's milk bottle	4	6	8

Fort, RICH TOYS No. 260. Courtesy Ron Fink.

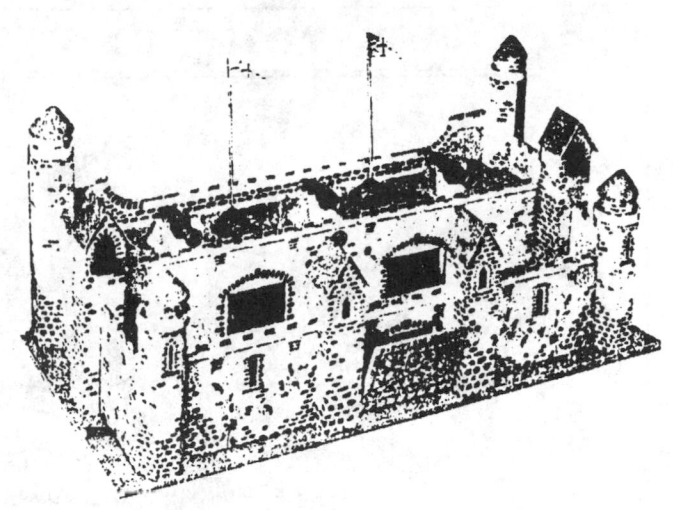

Fort, RICH TOYS No. 262. Courtesy Ron Fink.

Fort, RICH TOYS No. 261. Courtesy Ron Fink.

Fort, RICH TOYS No. 263. Courtesy Ron Fink.

	C6	C8	C10
Glass Candy Container, shaped like rabbit, Victory Glass	50	75	100
Glass Candy Container, shaped like train engine, 3" long	26	39	52
Glass Candy Container, shaped like a train lantern, 3-1/2" high	26	39	52
Glass Candy Container, shaped like the Spirit of St. Louis airplane	325	488	650
Glass Candy Container, Stop and Go, glass, etc. traffic signal	100	150	200
Glass Candy Container, shaped like a train lantern, tin top and base, "Victory Glass Inc.", 3-1/2" high	26	39	52
Glass Candy Container, shaped like Zeppelin	100	150	200
Grandfather's Clock, tin, has weights that make hands rotate and pendulum swing, but is not a working clock, transfer decorated, 8-3/4" high	40	60	80

Glass Candy Containers, as seen in a December, 1929, BUTLER BROS. Catalog.

KEYSTONE U. S. COAST DEFENSE FORTS

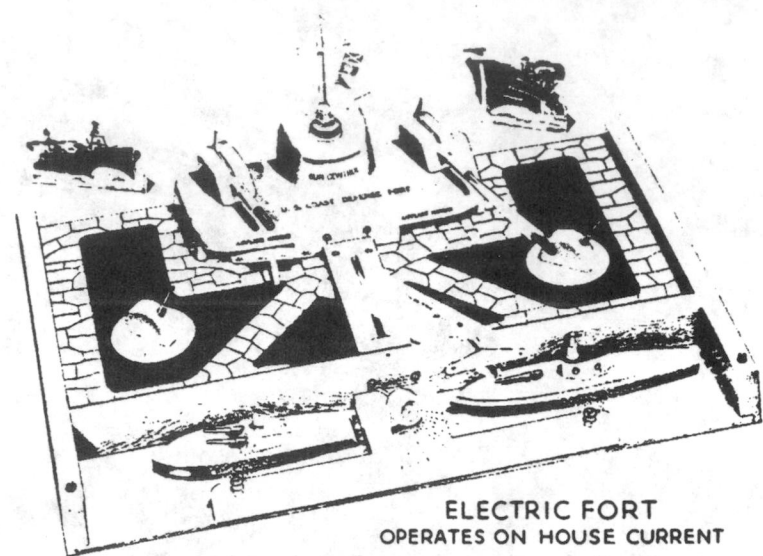

ELECTRIC FORT
OPERATES ON HOUSE CURRENT

- *Planes That Fly!*
- *Swivel Guns That Shoot!*
- *Electric Flashing Signals!*
- *Electric Searchlight!*
- *Electric Pier Lights!*
- *Turret Guns That Turn!*
- *Two Boats That Float!*
- *Two Airplane Hangars!*
- *Soldier Housing in Rear!*
- *Played From Front or Back With or Without Soldiers!*

No. 527 — U. S. COAST DEFENSE FORT

Two Flying Planes operated with catapult. *Pier and signal lights work off regular house current A.C.* Target and patrol ships and shells furnished for shooting cannons. Made of wood and fibre board. No assembling. Finished in gray, tan, green base and blue trim. Each boxed in shipping carton. Weight 175 lbs. per dozen. Size 24 x 17.

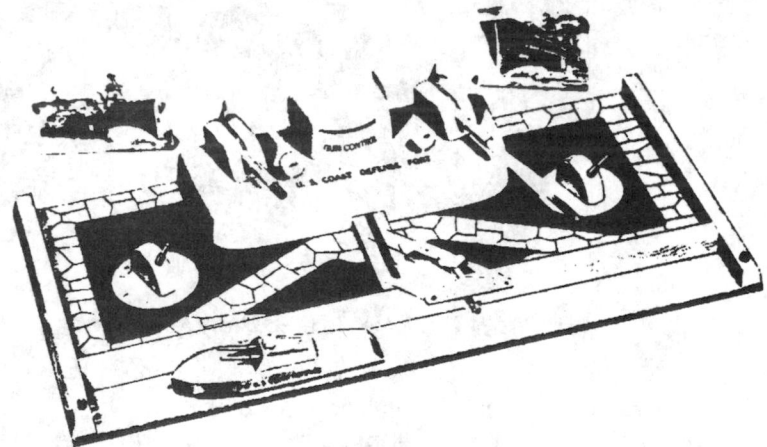

- *Plane That Flies!*
- *Swivel Guns That Shoot!*
- *Turret Guns That Turn!*
- *Boat That Floats!*
- *Soldier Housing in Rear!*
- *Battleship Target for Cannons!*
- *Play From Front or Rear With or Without Soldiers!*

No. 525 — U. S. COAST DEFENSE FORT

One Flying Plane operated with catapult. Target and scout ship and shells furnished for shooting cannons. Made of wood and fibre board. No assembling. Size 24 x 12. Finished in gray, tan, green and blue trim. Each in shipping carton. Weight 65 lbs. per dozen.

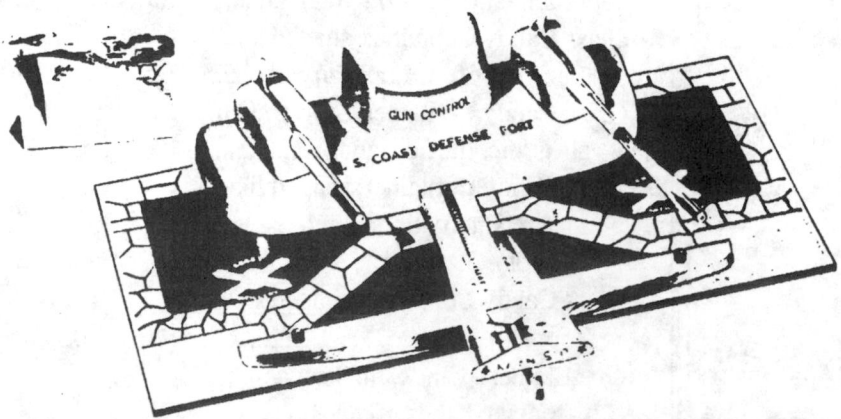

- *Plane That Flies!*
- *Swivel Guns That Shoot!*
- *Soldier Housing in Rear!*
- *Battleship Target for Cannons!*
- *Played From Front or Rear With or Without Soldiers!*

No. 523
U. S. COAST DEFENSE FORT

All wood and fibre board fort 16" x 8". Equipped with flying plane and catapult, ship target and shells for swivel shooting guns. All assembled each in a carton. Colors same as other models. Weight 30 lbs. per dozen.

KEYSTONE MFG. CO., BOSTON, MASS.
NEW YORK SHOW ROOM, 200 FIFTH AVENUE

GREY IRON Clever Clowns.

Horse, American painted tin, 1870, 4-1/2" long. Courtesy Lloyd W. Ralston Auctions.

Horses in Hoops, ALTHOF BERGMANN. Courtesy Lloyd W. Ralston Auctions.

	C6	C8	C10
Grey Iron Automatic Cap Machine Gun, 9" long	275	363	550
Grey Iron Clever Clowns Trapeze Set	275	363	550
Grey Iron Clever Clowns large set	500	750	1000
Grocery Store, tin, scales, cash register, wrapping paper, order pad and pencil, "Little Toy Town Grocery Store", shelves with small boxes of products, 14" long	100	150	200
Grocery Store, wood, "Pet's Grocery Store"	400	600	800
H.K. Electric Engine, patented 1908, used DC current	50	75	100
Handwashing Machine with wringer	10	15	20
Hasbro Mr. Potato Head No. 2000	35	52	70
Hasbro "Mr. Potato Head", 1950s, plastic car and boat trailer, plus all the parts to create different faces	75	112	150
Hasbro Mr. & Mrs. Potato Head Set, No. 2004	25	38	50
Hasbro Mrs. Potato Head	60	90	120
Hasbro Mrs. Potato Head w/car	40	60	80

	C6	C8	C10
"Historoscope", Milton Bradley, c. 1880, rolled panorama	238	355	475
Hobby Horse, "Black Beauty", wooden, 34" long	25	37	50
Horse, American painted tin, 1870, 4-1/2" long	175	263	350
Horse in Hoop, George Brown, early	550	850	1200
Horse, sheet metal, with cast iron jointed legs, full form, 10-3/4" long, 11" high	200	300	400
Horse Race, circular track within retangular box, c. 1900, lever-activated	100	150	200
Horses in Hoops, Althof Bergmann, American painted tin, 1880, 4-1/2" diameter	800	1200	1600
Hubley Duck, pull toy, c. 1930s, 9-3/8" long	800	1400	2000
Hubley Ferris Wheel, early, cast iron, brass and tin, clockwork, 17" high	1750	2625	3500

HASBRO "Mr. Potato Head". early.

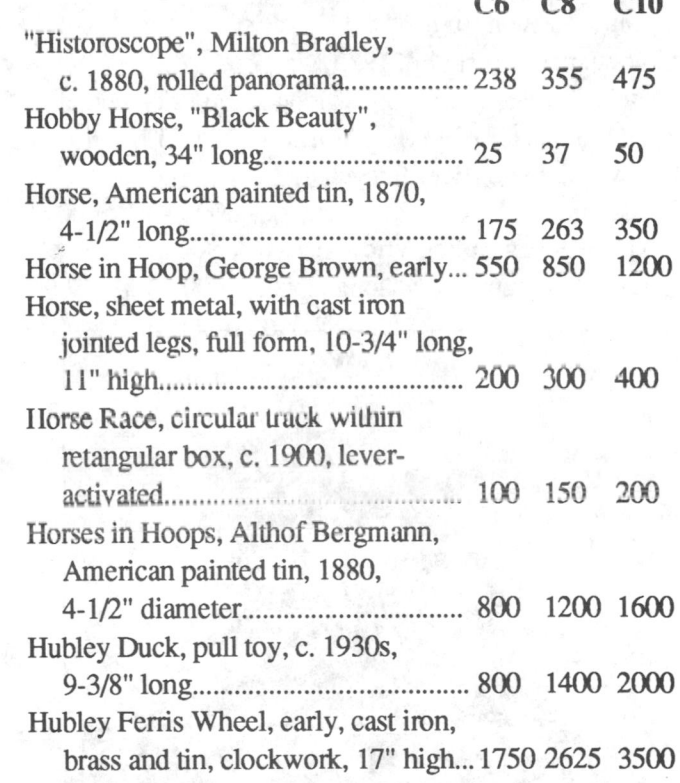

HUBLEY Ferris Wheel, early.

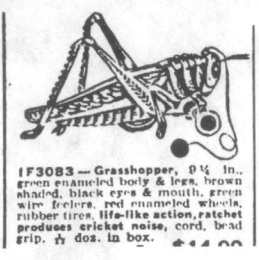

*HUBLEY
Grasshopper, 1929.*

*HUBLEY Jantzen Surf Girl.
Photo courtesy Lloyd W.
Ralston Auctions.*

	C6	C8	C10
Hubley grasshopper pull toy, cast iron..	290	435	580
Hubley Jantzen Beach Patrol, circa 1932, man on surfboard riding through waves, 8" long, auctioned in 1994 in near mint condition for $14,000			
Hubley Jantzen Surf Girl, 1932, girl surfboard rider, cast iron, 8" long....	No Price Found		
Hubley Jumbo the Elephant, on wheels...	25	37	50
Hubley Marathon Rider (bicyclist) cast iron............	300	450	600
Hubley Monkey Riding Tricycle, cast iron, aluminum, 6-1/4" long............	2000	3500	5500

HUBLEY Monkey Riding Tricycle. Courtesy James S. Maxwell/Virginia Caputo. Photo by Virginia Caputo.

	C6	C8	C10
Hubley Old Dutch Cleanser Woman, cast iron............	2200	3800	6000
Hurdy-Gurdy, turn crank and play tune, shows animal playing cello.....	30	45	60
Ice Box, "Alaska" cast iron, has glass cube of ice in top, 5" high............	200	300	400

IVES Black Dancers, clockwork, circa 1873. Photo courtesy Ed Hyers Antique Toys.

	C6	C8	C10
Ideal "Mr. Machine", first version, can be taken apart and put together, 18" high..............	170	255	340
Ideal "Mr. Machine", 1972 version, whistles, 17-1/2" high..............	32	48	65
Ideal "Mr. Machine", 1977 version......	22	33	45
Iron and Trivet, cast iron......	20	30	40
Iron, tin, 5" high..............	7.50	11.25	15
Iron, tin, 3-1/2" high..............	10	15	20
Irwin "Round-Up Tex the Whirling Cowboy", plastic windup, 1950s, 10" high..............	40	60	80
Ives Acrobat, hand over hand, 10-1/2" high overall..............	2000	3000	4000
Ives Automatic Toy Boxers, circa 1876, 11" high..............	4000	7000	12,000
Ives Automatic Dancer Circus Rider, standing on horse, 15" high, auctioned in 1991 in excellent to near mint condition for $38,500.			
Ives "Autoperipateticos" walking doll..	700	1050	1400
Ives Barrel Walkers, circa 1890, wood and paper litho balance toy, acrobat, ballerina, monkey..............	200	300	400
Ives Black Dancer, 1870s, clockwork..	800	1300	1800
Ives Black Dancers, circa 1873............	2400	3600	4800
Ives Black Dancers, clockwork, circa 1880, 11" high..............	1100	1800	2600
Ives Black Mechanical Walking Man, circa 1875, 9-1/2" high..............	1400	2100	2800

IVES Preacher. Courtesy Sotheby's New York.

IVES Struktiron set, 1915. Courtesy Lloyd W. Ralson Auctions.

IVES BLAKESLEY & WILLIAMS Mule Dancers. Courtesy Lloyd W. Ralston Auctions.

IVES Mechanical Bear. Courtesy PB Eighty-Four, New York.

	C6	C8	C10
Ives Boy on Rocking Horse, c.1874, wood and tin, 8-1/2" high, auctioned in 1991 in excellent condition for $57,200.			
Ives Boy smoking cigar and holding stomach, cast iron	195	263	350
Ives Chinese, "John Chinaman", windup walker, 9-1/2" high, auctioned in 1991 in excellent condition for $9,900.			
Ives Crawling Baby, circa 1871	2000	3000	4000
Ives "Crawling Baby", 1893	1500	2250	3000
Ives Elephant Ramp Walker	(See Ramp Walkers)		
Ives "Elephant Car", circus cage, cast iron, "serpent eggs" magic trick can be burnt in elephant's trunk, "Greatest Show on Earth"	790	1125	1500
Ives Fire Engine House, circa 1890, cast iron and wood, 16" long	2000	3000	5000
Ives General Butler windup walker, 9-1/2" high	2750	4125	5500
Ives General Grant, smoking, auctioned in 1991 in excellent condition with one side of wood base missing for $22,000.			
Ives Hot Air Toy, Circa 1870	250	375	500
Ives Jackass windup walker, 9-1/2" high, auctioned in 1991 in very good condition, missing one hand, for $22,000.			
Ives Judge, clockwork, circa 1880	1500	2300	3500

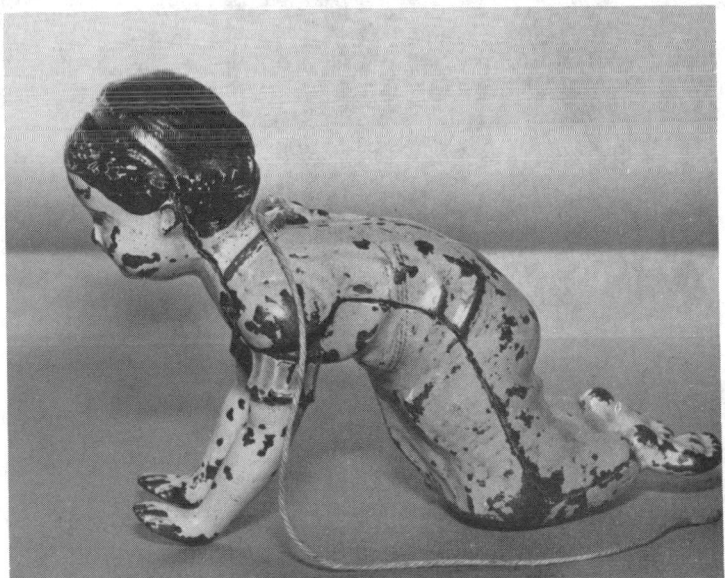

IVES "Crawling Baby", 1893. Courtesy Ed Hyers Antique Toys.

	C6	C8	C10
Ives Juggler, clockwork early	1000	1500	2000
Ives Mechanical Bear, patent 1872	600	900	1200
Ives Mechanical Performing Monkey, No. 49-10, 5-1/2" high	2250	3375	4500

681

IVES Crawling Baby, circa 1871. Courtesy Phillips New York.

Uncle Tom Walking Toy, IVES? Circa 1875. Courtesy Phillips New York.

Uncle Tom Walking Toy, IVES? Variation. Courtesy Phillips New York.

IVES General Grant, smoking. Courtesy Sotheby's New York.

IVES "Old Mammy Washing Clothes". Courtesy Christie's East.

	C6	C8	C10
Ives "Old Mammy Washing Clothes", clockwork, 11" high, auctioned in 1993 for $13,800.			
Ives Old Woman in a Shoe, pull toy, 9" long.	3000	4500	6000
Ives Platform Horse, pull toy, 9-1/2" long	1400	2100	2800
Ives Preacher, clockwork, 10-1/2" high.	1500	2400	3800
Ives Rower, "Pat. Feb. 9", 13" long, "U.S.Grant" auctioned in 1991 in excellent condition for $7,150.			
Ives Rower, 2 drive wheels protrude from bottom, wheel attached to rudder, 13" long.	3000	5500	8750

"Kid Flyer". Courtesy PB Eight-Four, New York.

	C6	C8	C10
Ives See-Saw, 18" long, auctioned in 1991 in excellent condition with one upper leg replaced for $13,200.			
Ives Scottish Jigger	1250	1875	2500
Ives Struktiron set, 1915	100	150	200
Ives Struktiron, 1916, nonmotorized, with box	75	112	150
Ives Vctran (sic) of '76, auctioned in 1994 for $5,175 (resembles Georgc Washington).			
Ives Walking Horse, circa 1890s, 10" long	800	1300	1800
Ives Walking Santa, 9-3/4" high	1200	2200	3500
Ives Zouave windup walker, 10-1/2" high	1500	2250	3000
Ives, Blakesley & Williams, 1890, Mule Dancers, mechanical revolving, paper litho, painted tin, wooden box, clockwork, 8" tall	1600	2400	3200
Jane Francis "Gulf Truck Service" Station	500	750	1000
"Jolly Jungleers", Milton Bradley, 1932, derringer type pistol shoots over animal targets	40	60	80
Judy Toys Farm Set, cardboard and rubber	62	93	125
Jumping Jack, composition and wood	70	105	140
Junior Mechanic Construction Set, circa 1940	48	72	95
Junior WAC set, Hassenfeld Bros., hats, gas mask, bandages, etc	40	60	80
Junior G-Man Whistle	20	30	40
Kaleidoscope "C. Bush, Prov. R.I., 1874", wood, brass & glass, 14" high	220	330	440
Kaleidoscope, Stevens, 1950s	10	15	20
Kangaroo, cast iron "Jumps", 6-1/4" long	125	187	250
Kenner Easy Bake oven, 1960s	22	33	44
Kenner Give A Show Projector, 112 slides	33	50	66
Kenton Baggage Cart, 6"	30	45	60
Kenton Drag Wagon, litho paper on			

	C6	C8	C10
sides, driver, 15-1/2" long	200	300	400
Kenton Egyptian Toys-Rhino, Lion, Elephant, offered at $175 each, condition unspecified			
Kenton Elephant - "Land-on Roosevelt 1936"	80	120	160
Kenton Stove, cast iron marked "Oak" on door	30	45	60
Kenton Stove, with warming shelves and stove plates, high back for smokestack, "Royal" on door and shelves, 10" high	40	60	80
Keystone Bus Terminal	92	138	189
Kcystone Firestone Station	112	168	225
"Keystone Garage", 1940s or 50s, 8" x 8" x 6"	100	150	200
Keystone "Keystone Fire Department"	90	135	180
Keystone Radiopticon, 1920s	75	112	150
Kcystone Service Statlon	137	205	275
Keystone Warehouse	237	355	475
"Kid Flyer" boy on scooter, tin litho, string-wound, 8-1/2" long	300	450	600
Kingsbury Fire Station, No. 8, clockwork bell and door, 9" x 10" x 13"	150	225	300
"Knockout Target Shooting Gallery", litho tin with rifle, many targcts	40	60	80
Laddcr for fire trucks, cast iron	3	4.50	6
Ladders, stamped steel, from Hubley and Arcade trucks	10	15	20
Lawnmower, Arcade, circa 1920, iron and wood	20	30	40
Lehmann "Climbing Monkey"	90	135	180
Lehmann "Tom Tom" spiral drive top No. 677, 1920	125	188	250
Lehmann "Toy-Kadi", 1920s friction	500	750	1000
"Lindstrom's Little Show", cardboard and wood theatre with seven show strips	250	375	500
Lion in Hoop, tin, 6-1/4" high	200	300	400
Lionel Science Kit, circa 1960	20	30	40
Machine Gun, Baldwin "Coast Defense Gun", wood & steel	55	82	110
Machine Gun, Grey Iron, rapid fire, cast iron, 1930s, 9" long	125	188	250
Machine Gun, McDowell, tin litho	70	105	140
Magic Lantern	55	82	110
Magic Lantern, Keystone, "Radioptocin"	40	60	80
Magic Lantern Projector, tin, embossed deer on door and side, 8" long	60	90	120

MANOIL Targets, "4 5 6", 7 8 9". Photo by Don Pielin.

	C6	C8	C10
Man on Bicycle, animated, tin, high wheel bike, bell on top of bicycle, 10-1/2" high	360	540	720
Manoil Target, lead either "4-5-6" or "7-8-9". "1-2-3" doesn't appear to exist, except in a version produced by collectors Ed Poole and Ron Eccles. Manoil's order number for the targets, without specifying which, was 76	45	68	90

MARBLES

Marbles are known to date back as far as ancient Rome, when they were made of clay and pottery. Marbles are divided into types, such as "Indian Swirls", "Clambroth", "Lutz Type Swirls", etc. Size numbers range from 000, which equals 1/2 inch to 8, which equals 1-1/8". There are estimated to be 40,000 to 50,000 current collectors of marbles in the U.S., about 1,700 of whom belong to the Marble Collectors' Society of America (see Leading Collectors and Dealers).

	Value
Sulphide, bust of Jenny Lind, size 1-7/8", near mint	$1,100.00
Sulphide, Standing Bear, size 1-1/2", mint	125.00
Handmade Swirl, size 1-1/2", mint	175.00
Handmade Swirl, size 3/4", mint	20.00
Ribbon Lutz, size 3/4", mint	400.00
Clambroth, size 5/8", mint	150.00
Indian Swirls, size 5/8", mint	100.00
Mica, size 3/4", mint	25.00

	C6	C8	C10
Marky Maypo rubber squeeze toy, 1960s	24	36	48
Marx Air-Sea Power bombing set	110	165	220
Marx "Allstate Terminal & Warehouse", Sears, 1960s, 23"x15"x2"	150	225	300
Marx Arcade Shooting Gallery	50	75	100
Marx Army and Navy Mechanical Target No. G169	20	30	40

	C6	C8	C10
Marx Army Code Sender, Morse key and phone, pressed steel, 9-1/2"	10	15	20
Marx Ballerina, operated by sawtooth bar, pulled through, 1930s, 6" high	85	128	170
Marx Bear Cyclist, metal, lever action	100	150	200
Marx "Brightelite Filling Station"	270	405	540
Marx Bust 'Em Target Game No. G38	20	30	40
Marx Cat with Ball, cable-operated, tin litho	40	60	80
Marx "Champion Skater" ballet dancer, pull spinning rod out of motor, place skater in upright position and she spins	100	150	200
Marx "Climbing Fireman", tin and plastic	150	225	300
Marx Co. A Barracks, tin litho building, 6" x 8" x 12"	20	30	40

MARX Colonial Doll House No. 4052. Photo by Mary Brett.

	C6	C8	C10
Marx Colonial Doll House No. 4052	60	90	120
Marx "Colonial Service Station", 1960s, 27" long, 15" wide, 4" high	90	135	180
Marx "Day & Nite Service Service Center"	75	112	150
Marx Deluxe Dial Typewriter, 1930s	24	36	48
Marx Dial Typewriter No. 1000A, 1930s	32	48	65
Marx Dishwasher K54, circa 1950s	60	90	120
Marx Doll House No. 4021	20	30	40
Marx Doll House No. 4030	30	45	60
Marx "Electric Lighted Filling Station", tin litho, 1930s, 10 x 13-1/2" long see "Sunnyside Service Station",			
Marx Gas Island, 1930s	220	330	440

	C6	C8	C10
Marx "General Alarm Fire House", 1940s, 17" long, 11" wide, 3" high.	375	562	750
Marx Gobbling goose, plastic windup, 9" long	70	105	140
Marx "Gulf" Service Station	300	450	600
Marx Happitime Service Station	112	168	225
Marx Headquarters, tin litho, U.S. Army Training Center, 5"x8"x11"	20	30	40
Marx "Hometown Drug Store", "F.W. Woolworth", tin litho, 5x2x3-1/2"	120	180	240
Marx "Hometown Favorite Store", "F. W. Woolworth", tin litho, 5x2x3-1/2".	120	180	240
Marx "Hometown Favorite Store" "S.S. Kresge Co.", tin litho	100	150	200
Marx "Hometown Firehouse", tin litho, 1930s, 5-1/2" x 2-1/2" x 3-1/2"	200	300	400
Marx "Hometown Grocery Store", tin litho, 1930s, 5" x 2-1/2" x 3-1/2"	60	90	120
Marx "Hometown Meat Market", tin litho, 1930s	60	90	120
Marx "Hometown Movie Theatre", tin litho, 1930s	62	93	125
Marx "Hometown Police Station"	46	69	92
Marx "Hometown Savings Bank", tin litho building,1930s,5x2-1/2x3-1/2".	60	90	120
Marx "Honeymoon Cottage Village", 1930s, tin litho, 17" long x 11" wide.	133	200	266
Marx "Honeymoon Garage", 1930s, tin litho, 6-1/2" x 7" x 3"	20	30	40
Marx "Ice Skater", 1930s, sawtooth bar operates it, 5-1/2" high	90	135	180

MARX "Honeymoon Garage". Photo by James Apthorpe.

	C6	C8	C10
Marx Junior Dial Typewriter No. 2109, circa 1930s	20	30	40
Marx Kitchen Sink K47, circa 1950s	10	15	20
Marx King Arthur sword and shield, tin litho	25	38	50
Marx "Knockout Champs", celluloid, 1930s	325	488	650
Marx "Loop the Loop", 1930s gravity toy, track 12" long, car 1-1/2" long	50	75	100
Marx Magic Barn w/tractor	130	195	260
Marx "Magic Garage and Car", 1950s, garage 10" long, car 7" long, wind-up	125	188	250
Marx Mechanical Gorilla	187	290	375
Marx Midtown Service Center	112	168	225
Marx Minit Car Wash	175	262	350
Marx Newlywed Library, lin litho, 1930s, 5" x 2-1/2" x 3-1/2" long	75	112	150
Marx Pathe News Movie Camera, tin litho	200	300	400
Marx Practice Target Ranger, 1950s, 11" long	30	45	60
Marx "Pretty Maid Washing Machine", circa 1930s, 4-1/2" high	50	75	100
Marx Refrigerator, K42, circa 1950s	15	22	30
Marx Rex Mars Planet Patrol 45 Cal. machine-gun, tin and plastic, winds up, 22" long	55	82	110
Marx "Rex Mars Space Target Game", 1950s, 14" long	100	150	200
Marx Roadside Rest, four pumps, car, garage, 1930	350	525	700
Marx Rock'em, Sock'em Robots	50	75	100
Marx Seachlight, tin litho, 3-1/2" high.	20	30	40
Marx Son of Garloo plastic and tin windup	105	158	210
Marx Stove K39, circa 1950s	20	30	40
Marx "Sunnyside Service Station", 1930s, complete	375	562	750
Marx "Super Service" Center	175	263	350
Marx Swinging Arm Target Game No. G52 and Gun	40	60	80
Marx Swinging Arm Target Game No. G55 and Gun	40	60	80
Marx Suburban Colonial Dollhouse, metal	60	90	120
Marx Trixo Monkey string climber	35	52	70
Marx Tunnel, tin litho, depicts farm scene, rolling hills, houses, 8" x 10" x 7"	10	15	20

MARX Mechanical Gorilla, with box. Courtesy James S. Maxwell/Virginia Caputo. Photo by Virginia Caputo.

MARX Cat with Ball, cable operated. Courtesy Mapes Auctioneers & Appraisers.

MARX Roadside Rest. Courtesy Thomas G. Nefos, Federal Shipping Network.

MARX Ballerina. Courtesy Scott Smiles. Photo by Mike Adams.

MARX Sunny Side Service Station. Photo by Ron Chojnacki. Courtesy Don Hultzman.

MARX "Pretty Maid Washing Machine". Photo by Bill Kaufman Courtesy Good Old Days Store.

MARX "Climbing Fireman", tin and plastic. Courtesy Mapes Auctioneers & Appraisers.

MATTEL "Farmer In The Dell", tin, crank, 7" high. Courtesy Calvin L. Chaussee.

	C6	C8	C10
Marx Typewriter No. 1110, metal and plastic, circa 1950s-1960s	10	15	20
Marx "Universal Gas Service Station", 1940s, 6-1/2" high, base 12" long	150	225	300
Marx Vertical Steam Engine	57	84	115
Mattel "Farmer In The Dell", tin, crank, 1951, 7" high	87	130	175
Mattel "Four & 20 Blackbirds", 1950s, crank action, musical toy, 9" diameter	100	150	200
Mattel Jack in the Music Box, 1961	22	33	45
Mattel Mad Scientist Dissect - An Alien	6	9	12
Mattel Mad Scientist Monster Lab	10	15	20
Mattel Mad Scientist Operating Room	5	8	10
Mattel Music Box Carousel	75	112	150
Mattel "Musical Man on the Flying Trapeze"	90	135	180
Mattel Thingmaker Creepy Crawlers Pak, 1960s	27	41	55
Mattel Thingmaker Fang 'n Claw Kit, 1967	20	30	40
Mattel Thingmaker People Makers Pak	35	52	70
Mattel Thingmaker Slitherees Kit, 1967	45	68	90
Mattel Vacuform with molds	30	45	60
Meat Grinder with clamp, die cast	7	11	15
Meccano Set 0	70	105	140
Meccano Set 00	47	70	95
Meccano Set 1	12	18	25
Meccano Set 1A	10	15	20
Meccano Set 1X	75	112	150
Meccano Set 2	600	900	1200

	C6	C8	C10
Meccano Set 2A	10	15	20
Meccano Set 3	10	15	20
Meccano Set 3A	10	15	20
Meccano Set 4	50	75	100
Meccano Set 4A	25	37	50
Meccano Set 11	600	1000	1400
Meccano Microscope Set, 1933	10	15	20
Merry-Go-Round, windup, litho paper and wood, w/four bisque figures riding four fur-skinned papier mache horses	600	900	1200
Merry-Go-Round, wood and litho paper Jenny musical windup with five horse-form seats	200	300	400
Microphone, Ward Toy	40	60	80
Mr. Machine	*See Ideal*		
Mr. Potato Head	*See Hasbro*		
Monkey, mechanical, in red pants, red-checked shirt, squeeze metal lever attached to 34" spiral wire and monkey jumps alongside you, hitting cymbals, 10" high	62	93	125
Monkey, stuffed, red felt cap and jacket, glass eyes, moveable arms and legs, move his tail and head moves from side to side, and up and down, c. 1910, 9-1/2" high	60	90	120
Mound of Earth, tin litho, (for toy soldiers), 4" long	12	18	25
Mound of Rocks, tin litho (for toy soldiers)	12	18	25
Movie-Jector, hand crank	40	60	80
Movie Projector, "Flip Movies", turn crank and flip cards from "Midgette" movies, with film, circa early 1930s	56	84	112
"Movie Projector Gun", film only, 1937, Box 1 contains Chaplin, Gasoline Alley, Babe Ruth, Buffalo Bill, Harold Teen; Box 2 contains Dick Tracy, Terry & Pirates, Smitty, Orphan Annie, Winnie Winkle; Box 3 contains Clyde Beatty, Gumps, Little Joe, Tiny Tim, Buffalo Bill; Box 4 contains Gasoline Alley, Chaplin, Tracy, Lone Ranger, Harold Teen. Price per box	10	15	20
Movie Projector, "Uncle Sam", hand cranks, circa 1930s	125	188	250
Mucis Box, tin, shaped like coffee grinder, German, 3" high	80	120	160

NOAH'S ARK, German, circa 1895, 15" long. Courtesy Christie's East.

NOAH'S ARK. Courtesy Continental Hobby House.

	C6	C8	C10
Myrioptican, optical toy, Milton Bradley	100	150	200
Mysto Erector Set No. 1	75	112	150
Mysto Erector Set No. 1A	50	75	100
Mysto Erector Set No. 2, circa 1915	50	75	100
Mysto Erector Set No. 2A	50	75	100
Mysto Erector Set No. 3A	50	75	100
Noah's Ark, wooden, 12 animals, Noah, 6-1/2" long	50	75	100
Noah's Ark, 27 animals, 11" long	115	172	230
Noah's Ark, Bliss, 10 animals, wooden, 13-1/4" long	150	225	300
Noah's Ark, cardboard, with animals, 14" long	100	150	200
Noah's Ark, Converse, carved wooden animals, 14" long	450	675	900
Noah's Ark, German, circa 1895, hand-carved animals, 15" long	450	750	1100
Noah's Ark, Peter-Mar, wood, no animals	275	363	550
Noah's Ark, Pyro, plastic w/animals	20	30	40
Noah's Ark w/wooden village blocks	20	30	40
Noah's Ark, wood litho, w/animals, 10" long	30	45	60
Noise Maker, tin, shaped like old-fashioned phone mouthpiece, 2-1/4" high	6	9	12
Nutty mads figures, Marx, 1963 issue, vinyl, each	11	16	22

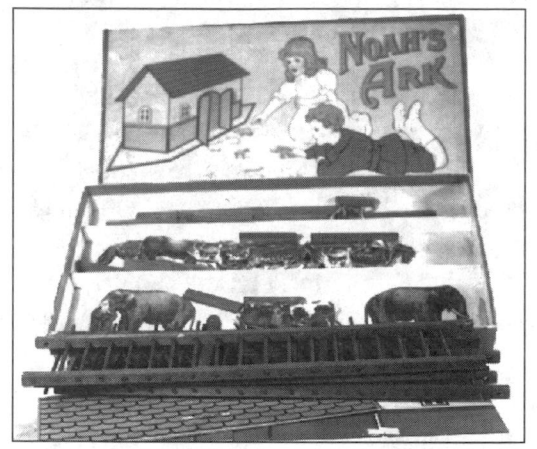

OHIO ART

Ohio Art was started in October, 1908 by a dentist, H.S. Winzeler. Originally its intent was to make metal picture frames (thus its name), but in 1917 the firm bought C.E. Carter (Erie Toy Plant) and began producing metal toys, including a climbing monkey on a string for Ferdinand Strauss. Winzeler later sold the plant to Louis Marx, but continued making tin toys, while Marx, according to Ohio Art history, used the former Carter plant as the foundation of his own company. Ohio Art is still making toys in Bryan Ohio.

	C6	C8	C10
Ohio Art Barrel Organ, musical, 5-1/2" tall	40	60	80
Ohio Art Beach Toy Water Pumper, circa 1939, signed "Elaine Ends Hileman", 8-1/2" high	17	26	35
Ohio Art Children's Tea Set, tin, 1950s, 14 pieces	75	112	150
Ohio Art Drum, 6" x 4" + 2 sticks	22	33	45

	C6	C8	C10
Ohio Art "Fido's Musical Dog House", 1960s, 8" high	36	54	72
Ohio Art "Mini Farm Set", 1960s playset, 12" long, 5" high	80	120	160
Ohio Art "Realistic Farm Set" No. 197, 1960s playset, 16" long, 7" high	80	120	160
Ohio Art Sandpail, 1940s, tin litho	7	11	15
Ohio Art Shooting Gallery, key wind-circus	50	75	100
Ohio Art Sunnyfield Farms Barn and Silo set w/animals, tin litho, 1950s	80	120	160
Ohio Art Toyland Band, drums, bass and snare, cymbals, triangle and sticks, 7-1/2" high	20	30	40
Ohio Art Washtub, tin litho, wood and metal scrubboard, 1940s	16	24	32
Ohio Art Watering Can, tin litho, 1940s	7	11	15
"Old Kentucky Home" wood litho action toy, six dancers, singer-musicians, moved by handcrank, 15-1/2" long	366	549	732
Organ Grinder, monkey, push bottom, squeaks and dances, Kohner Bros., 6" wooden	20	30	40
Paddle Wheel and Tower on base, tin, 14" high	20	30	40
"Paris Coaster", wood-wheeled cart	30	45	60
Parker Bros., 1910, Toy Town Garage, 3 litho tin penny cars, paper litho garage	1200	2000	3000

PARKER BROS. Toy Town Garage. Courtesy Lloyd W. Ralston Auctions.

	C6	C8	C10
Parker Bros., "Toy Town Grocery Store"	220	330	440
Phonograph, toy, Genola, cranks with sound horn	100	150	200
Phonograph, toy, Nerona, cranks, sound comes from horn connected to needle, early	100	150	200
Pig and Piglet in cage, wood, cloth and lithographed paper, spring-loaded squeak toy	50	75	100
Pillsbury Poppin' Fresh, 5" high	14	21	28
Pillsbury Poppin' Fresh, 6-1/2" high	2.50	3.75	5
Pillsbury Poppin' Fresh, 10" high	13	19	26
Pillsbury Poppie Fresh, 5" high	8	12	17
Plarola Corporation Organ, tin litho, with six organ rolls	300	450	600

PLASTICVILLE

(from information developed by Mark Schulz)

Plasticville Buildings and accessories were produced by Bachmann Bros., which dates back to 1833. In its early history Bachmann produced ivory cane handles and combs. In 1907 the firm purchased the second injection molding machine made, and began making eyeglass frames. After World War II, the growth in the toy train market led Bachmann to create plastic picket fences to enclose toy train platforms. This evolved into building kits, the first of which was the Log Cabin. Production continued into the late 1960s, with HO and N scale by then the main emphasis. In recent years, Bachmann has reintroduced some of the old O/S scale buildings. During its heyday the Plasticville line boasted over 100 items. C8 and C10 include box. All prices assume that no glue has been used.

	C6	C8	C10
Airport Admin Bldg	20	30	40
Airport Hangar	17	26	35
Apartment House	30	38	45
Apartment Add-a-Floor	10	15	20
Autumn Trees	25	35	50
Bank	10	20	28
Barn	12	18	24

PLASTICVILLE Birdbath, French Section, Trellis. Photo by Gary Linden.

PLASTICVILLE Barnyard Animal Set. Photo by Gary Linden.

PLASTICVILLE Billboard. Photo by Gary Linden.

PLASTICVILLE Fence and Gate. Photo by Gary Linden.

PLASTICVILLE Cape Cod House. Photo by Gary Linden.

PLASTICVILLE Police Dept. 0 scale. Photo by Gary Linden.

PLASTICVILLE Frosty Bar. Photo by Gary Linden.

PLASTICVILLE Fire House Kit. Photo by Gary Linden.

	C6	C8	C10
Barbecue	1	2	2
Barnyard Animal Set (18)	7	11	15
Billboard	1.25	1.88	2.50
Birdbath, Fence Section, Trellis	6	10	14
Bungalow	10	15	20
Cape Cod House Kit	10	15	21
Cathedral	14	21	28
Cattle Loading Pen	8	11	15

690

PLASTICVILLE Diner. Photo by Gary Linden.

PLASTICVILLE Hobo Shacks. Photo by Gary Linden.

PLASTICVILLE Log cabin, Rustic Fence & Tree. Photo by Gary Linden.

PLASTICVILLE 5 & 10. Photo by Gary Linden.

PLASTICVILLE Diner Kit Box. Photo by Gary Linden.

PLASTICVILLE Mobile Home. Photo by Gary Linden.

PLASTICVILLE House Under Construction. Photo by Gary Linden.

PLASTICVILLE Plasticville Citizens. Photo by Gary Linden.

PLASTICVILLE Outhouse, Telephone Booth, Well, Barbecue, Pump. Photo by Gary Linden.

PLASTICVILLE Police Dept. Kit, HO scale box. Photo by Gary Linden.

PLASTICVILLE Police Dept. Kit box, 0 scale. Photo by Gary Linden.

PLASTICVILLE Supermarket, large. Photo by Gary Linden.

PLASTICVILLE Trailer. Photo by Gary Linden.

PLASTICVILLE Railroad Signal Bridge. Photo by Gary Linden.

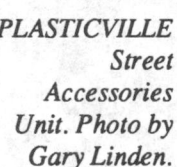

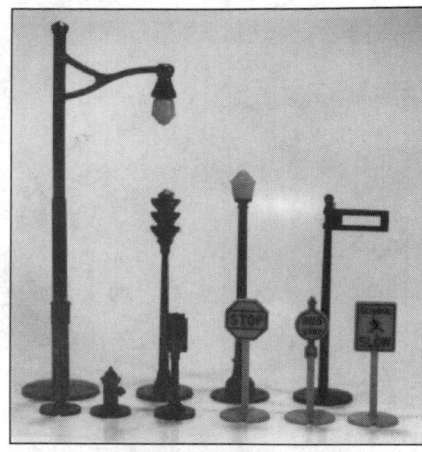

PLASTICVILLE Street Accessories Unit. Photo by Gary Linden.

PLASTICVILLE Supermarket Box, small size. Photo by Gary Linden.

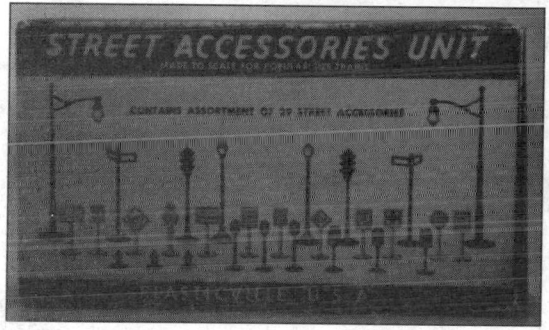

PLASTICVILLE Street Accessories Unit box. Photo by Gary Linden.

PLASTICVILLE Supermarket, small. Photo by Gary Linden.

PLASTICVILLE Trees and Fern. Photo by Gary Linden.

PLASTICVILLE Trees. Photo by Gary Linden.

PLASTICVILLE Water Tank. Photo by Gary Linden.

	C6	C8	C10
Cattle Loading Pen	8	11	15
Church/Parish Church	15	22	30
Coaling Station	8	10	12
Colonial Church	14	21	28
Colonial Mansion	15	22	30
Corner Store	10	15	20
Country Church	3	4	6
Covered Bridge	4	6	8
Dairy Barn	5	8	10
Diner Kit	4	6	8

PLASTICVILLE Suburban Station. Photo by Gary Linden.

PLASTICVILLE Switch Tower. Photo by Gary Linden.

	C6	C8	C10
Factory	15	20	25
Fence and Gate (12 pcs)	3	4.50	6
Fire House Kit	14	21	28
5 & 10	15	22	30
Frosty Bar	12	15	18
Gas Station, small	16	24	33
Greenhouse	31	47	62
Hobo Shacks (two bldgs)	30	37	42
Hospital (w/furniture)	27	41	55
House under Construction	15	20	25
Log Cabin Rustic Fence & Tree	14	21	28
Mobile Home	15	22	30
Motel	5	7	9
New England Ranch House	14	21	28
Outhouse	4	7	9
Pharmacy/Hardware	14	21	28
Plasticville Citizens (24 or 16)	15	22	30
Police Dept., HO scale	8	11	15
Police Dept., 0 scale	14	21	28
Post Office	14	21	29
Pump	2.50	3.75	5
Railroad Signal Bridge	4	6	8
Railroad Work Car	9	13	18
Ranch House	12	18	24
Roadside Stand	7	11	15
Schoolhouse	15	22	30
Split Level House	6	8	10
Street Accessories Unit (15 pcs)	22	33	45
Suburban Station	3	4	6
Supermarket, large	14	21	28
Supermarket, small	4	6	8
Switch Tower (Railroad)	8	12	16
Telephone Booth	4	6	8
Town Hall	10	15	20
Trailer	15	22	30
TV Station	6	9	12
Union Station	7	10	14
Water Tank (Railroad)	3	5	7
Well	3	5	7
Windmill	22	33	45

	C6	C8	C10
Roadrace Accessories			
Grandstand	15	20	25
Officials' Stand	8	11	15
Pit Stop	15	20	25
Sitting People	10	15	20

End Plasticville

	C6	C8	C10
"Play Store Register", tin and brass, Durable Toy and Novelty Co., 4" high	18	27	36
Pop (Kellogg's Rice Krispies) squeeze toy, 8-1/2" high	32	48	65
Pop (Kellogg's Rice Krispies) hand puppet	17	26	35
Pull Toy, "Buffalo Bill" on horse, tin, 15" long	600	1000	1400
Pull Toy, Camel on Platform, tin, Althof-Bergmann	600	900	1200

Pull Toy, Buffalo Bill on Horse, tin (Miscellaneous). Courtesy Sotheby's New York.

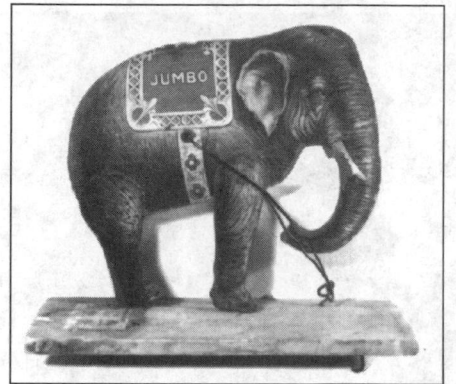

Pull Toy, Jumbo Elephant (wheels missing), GIBBS. Courtesy Continental Hobby House.

Pull Toy, Elephant, tin, 4-1/2" long, 1870, nothing on back. Courtesy Lloyd W. Ralston Auctions.

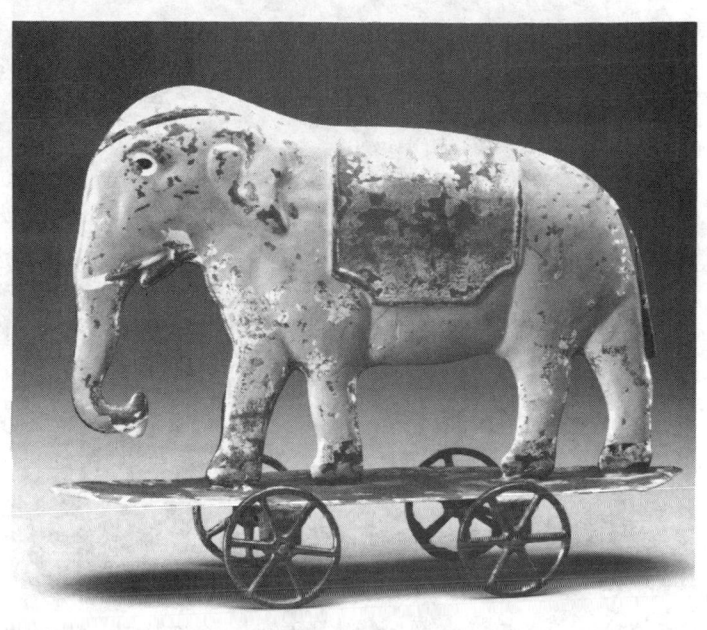

Pull Toy, Elephant, tin, 8-1/2" long, circa 1890. Courtesy Christie's East.

	C6	C8	C10
Pull Toy, Clown on Elephant, Kenton, 1911	400	600	800
Pull Toy, Elephant, hide-covered with bisque head, native	150	225	300
Pull Toy, Elephant, tin, 1870, nothing on back, 4-1/2" long	140	210	280
Pull Toy, Elephant, tin, with blanket, iron wheels, 4-1/2" long	170	255	340
Pull Toy, Elephant with saddle, tin, iron wheels, 4-1/2" high	75	112	150
Pull Toy, Elephant, tin, circa 1890, 8-1/2" long	400	600	800
Pull Toy, Elephant, tin, early, 9" long	850	1275	1700
Pull Toy, Elephant with howdah, cast iron	600	900	1200
Pull Toy, Elephants, two, on platform, tin, 12" long	300	450	600
Pull Toy, Gibbs, jockeys on horses, wood and paper litho, 10" long	750	1125	1500

Pull Toy, horse on platform, 6-1/2" long. Courtesy Lloyd W. Ralston Auctions.

Pull Toy, Rooster on platform. Courtesy Lloyd W. Ralston Auctions.

	C6	C8	C10
Pull Toy, Goat, tin, early, 9 1/2" long	150	225	300
Pull Toy, four race horses and riders, tin w/cast iron wheels, 8-1/4" long.	400	600	800
Pull Toy, horse, galloping, tin, 7" long.	250	375	500
Pull Toy, horse, tin, Harwood, circa 1876, 8-1/2" long	2500	3750	5000
Pull Toy, horse, leather reins, metal stirrups, felt saddle, circa 1880, 13-1/4" high	125	187	250
Pull Toy, horse and animated figure w/composition head and tin arms playing drum and cymbal, horse is tin, wheels, wooden platform, 13-1/2" long	500	750	1000
Pull Toy, horse and cart w/chicken-shaped sides, iron wheels, tin, 5-1/4" long	125	187	250
Pull Toy, horse and covered delivery wagon, tin, 5-1/4" long	150	225	300
Pull Toy, horse and polo player on horse's back, tin, 4-1/4" long	75	112	150
Pul Toy, horse and rider, tin, iron wheels, 4-1/2" long	80	120	160
Pull Toy, horse and rider, tin, iron wheels, 11" long	150	225	300
Pull Toy, horse (white) and water wagon, tin, 6-3/4" long	250	375	500
Pull Toy, horse (dark) and water wagon, tin, 7-1/4" long	150	225	300
Pull Toy, horse and wagon, tin, 9-1/4" long	150	225	300

Pull Toy, Jockey on Horse, tin, Fallows, 7" long. Courtesy Christie's East.

Pull Toy, Rider on Horse, tin, 10" long. Courtesy Sotheby'sNew York.

	C6	C8	C10
Pull Toy, horse on platform, George Brown, 1880, American painted tin, 6-1/2" long	250	375	500
Pull Toy, horsewoman riding side-saddle on pony, cast iron	225	337	450
Pull Toy, jockey on dog, tin, early, Ives, 10-1/4" long	1000	1500	2000
Pull Toy, jockey on goat, Ives, 9-1/2" long	3500	5200	7000
Pull Toy, Jockey on Horse, tin, c.1875, Fallows, 7" long	500	800	1200
Pull Toy, Jockey on Horse, early 1900s	500	800	1200
Pull Toy, Jockey on Horse, tin, hair tail, 9" long	600	900	1200
Pull Toy, Jonah & Whale, cast iron	400	600	800
Pull Toy, Jumbo Elephant on wheels, Gibbs, 10" long	200	300	400
Pull Toy, Mary & Lamb, tin, Fallows, circa 1890, 6-1/2" long	1000	1600	2400
Pull Toy, Rider on Horse, tin, 10" long	500	750	1000
Pull Toy, rooster, tin, 3-1/4" long	400	600	800

	C6	C8	C10
Pull Toy, rooster on platform, 1890, painted tin, 4-3/4" long	100	150	200
Pull Toy, sheep, tin, circa 1890, 6-1/4" high	150	225	300
Pull Toy, Swan Chariot	6000	9000	12,000
Pull Toy, three bears by Toycraft	30	45	60
Pull Toy, Two Frogs, painted tin, Fallows, 1898, 7-1/2" long	900	1350	1800
Pump, tin, with round trough, transfer of puppies, 7" high	15	22	30
Punch and Judy Puppet Theatre with 6 puppets: Punch, Judy, Devil, Princess, Sailor, Workman	400	600	800

Pull Toy, Sheep, tin, circa 1890. Photo courtesy PB Eighty-Four.

Pull Toy, Swan Chariot. Courtesy James S. Maxwell/Virginia Caputo. Photo by Virginia Caputo.

Pull Toy, Two Frogs, 7-1/4" long, painted tin, FALLOWS, 1898. Courtesy James S. Maxwell/Virginia Caputo. Photo by Virginia Caputo.

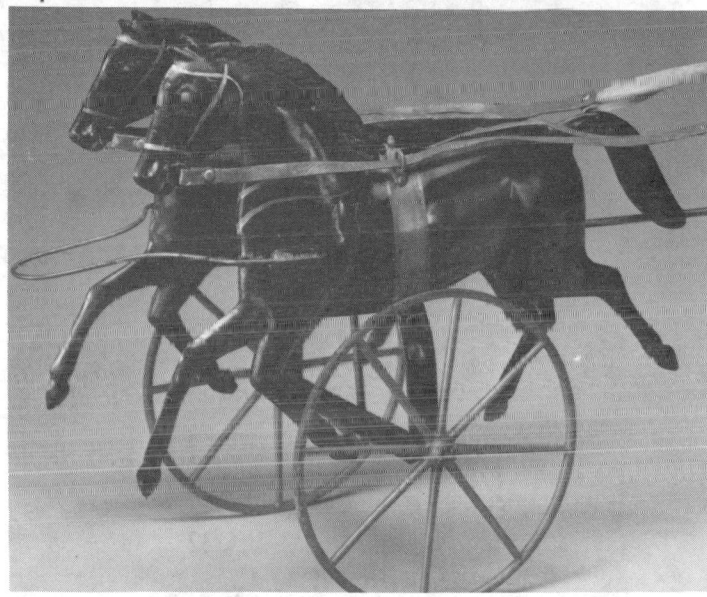

Push Toy, large running horses, FALLOWS, tin. Courtesy Christie's East.

	C6	C8	C10
Push Toy, butterfly that flaps its wings	40	60	80
Push Toy, clown on log, bell toy, cast iron	500	750	1000
Push Toy, horse and rider, Wilkins, circa 1910, cast iron and wood, 29" long	200	300	400
Push Toy, large running horses, tin, Fallows, cast iron wheels, 30" long	1000	1600	2300
Push Toy, horse, wooden, walks	40	60	80
Q.R.S. Playasax, uses paper rolls, Devry Corp., 12" long	175	262	350

Push Toy, Horse and Rider, WILKINS. Courtesy Wilkinson Collection, Detroit Antique Toy Museum.

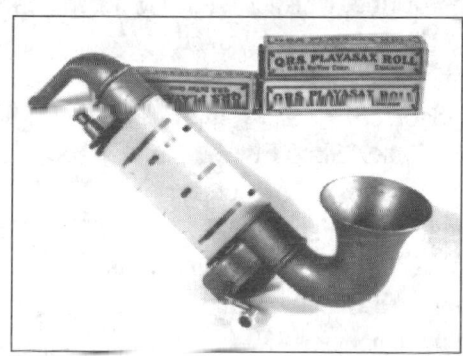

Q.R.S. Playasax, with music rolls. Courtesy Continental Hobby House.

	C6	C8	C10
Quake rag doll, 1960s, 12" high	100	150	200
Quisp rag doll, 1960s, 11" high	100	150	200
Rabbit, moves ears, small	110	165	220
Rabbits, two, mashing ingredients in small bowl, tin, animated by squeezing, 6" high	15	22	30
Ranger Steel "Drive Safely" set	112	168	225
Ranger Steel Co. "Gas Station- Auto Laundry", 1940s, 3"x5"x13" long	130	195	260
Reddy Kilowatt plastic figure, 1940s	125	188	250
Reed "Mammoth Hippodrome" circus ring, 19" diameter	600	1000	1500
Refrigerator, cast iron, Hubley, "GE", 7" high	150	225	300
Remco B-52 Ball Turret	60	90	120
Remco Johnny Reb Cannon	50	75	100
Remco Movieland Drive-In Theatre	82	123	175
Remco Naval PomPom Gun	27	41	55

	C6	C8	C10
Remco Space Commander Walkie Talkies..............	25	38	50
Renwal Drawbridge, plastic, 2 plastic autos, 2 boats, cardboard river scene, early 50s, 27" long............	79	119	158
Renwal Globe Trotter Set No. 305-150, 4 boats, 3 cars, train, jet plane..	19	28	38
Renwal "Visible Dog, The".................	30	45	60
Renwal "Visible Man, The".................	19	28	38
Renwal "Visible V-8"........................	47	70	95
Renwal "Visible Woman, The"............	16	24	32
Ripley's Believe It or Not Disk-O-Knowledge, round piece of cardboard w/another piece attached on top, turn to reveal questions and answers, 1932, 9-1/2" diameter........	10	15	20
"Rocket Ring", with futuristic rocket on top of ring, whistles, 1930s.........	30	45	60
Rocking Horse, hand carved, all wood, 1890s..........................	425	638	850
Rocking Horse, 1930s, 24" high..........	112	168	225
Rocking Horse, "Shoo Fly"..................	100	150	200
Rocking Toy, tin, girl on horse, German-Penny Toy, 3-3/4" long.....	220	330	440
Rolmonica, harmonica that plays rolls of tunes, "Blow, crank and play", with three songs, 1930s................	80	120	160
Roly Poly, Boy on Horse, circa 1900....	140	210	280
Roly Poly Clown, circa 1900, 13" high...............................	250	375	500
Sand Toy Set, Chick Art Co., 1942, includes tin litho frog, sailboat, shovel and round sieve.................	36	54	78
Sandbags, variously marked, for toy soldiers................................	2.50	3.75	5
Sand Pail, tin litho, circa 1940..............	15	22	30
Scales, cast iron, tin tray and four brass weights, 5-3/4" long...............	26	39	52
Scales, cast iron, "Dayton", 3-1/2" high	40	60	80
Secor Banjo Player, black man, early, auctioned in 1993 for $25,300.			
Secor Bones Player, blackman, early windup, auctioned in 1993 for $12,650, clothes replaced			
Seiberling Latex Prod. Panda, rubber squeak toy........................	60	90	120
Sewing Machine, circa 1920, 6" high...	85	127	170
Shooting Gallery Chickens, cast iron, 10-1/4" long.........................	75	112	150
Signal Jr. R-70 Twin Wireless Practice Set, two beginner's sending keys,			

Rolmonica

Sewing Machine, circa 1920. Photo by Bill Kaufman. Courtesy Good Old Days Store.

	C6	C8	C10
and one advanced key, circa 1920...	30	45	60
Simplex Typewriter No. 300, tin..........	32	48	65
Slinky, 1947, with box...........................	12	18	25
Snap (Kellogg's Rice Krispies) squeeze toy, 8-1/2" high.................	32	48	65
Snap (Kellogg's Rice Krispies) hand puppet.........................	17	26	35
Squeak Toy, Bird, c. 1884, composition, 7-1/2" long........................	100	150	200
Squeak Toy, Cat & Kitten, c. 1880, composition, 4"........................	200	300	400
Stitchwell Sewing Machine, child's floor model, circa 1920s..................	80	120	160
Stove, cast iron, "American".................	100	150	200
Stove, "Daisy", cast white metal, 4-1/4" high..........................	15	22	30
Stove, "Eagle", cast iron, 4-1/4" high...	50	75	100
Stove, "Eagle", cast iron, 11-1/2" high.	100	150	200
Stove, "Eagle", cast iron, 13-1/2" high.	125	187	250
Stove, cast iron, 13"x11-1/2" high........	75	112	150
Stove, cast iron, Ark, 4" x 5".................	25	37	50

Stove, "Eagle", cast iron, 11-1/2" high. Courtesy Mapes Auctioneers and Appraisers.

	C6	C8	C10
Stove, electric, one burner, two ovens, chrome-finished steel, porcelain on oven doors, 16" wide, 14" tall	75	112	150
Stove, "Lancaster", "Eagle", on door and shelf, cast iron, 10-3/4"	60	90	120
Stove, wood-burning cast iron, "The Queen"	45	67	90
Stove, Roper, Arcade gas burner, cast iron, 6" high	100	150	200
Stove, "Royal", cast iron, 4-1/2"	67	100	135
Stove, wood-burning cast iron, "The Triumph Range"	100	150	200
Stove, tin, with four plate covers, four pans and one skillet, 5" high	150	225	300
Stretcher for 3" toy soldiers, pre-WW II	6	9	12
Structo Erector Set, 1910	50	75	100
Structo No. 3	70	105	140
Sulky, cast iron, single casting	30	45	60
Superior Service Station Playset, 1950s	200	300	400
Swing, animated, cast iron and pressed steel, for doll, with eagle, wheel	600	900	1200
Swinging Clown, tin, base marked "C.D. Kenny Co.", 4-1/4" high	120	180	240
"The Symmetroscope", wood and tin type of kaleidoscope, F.P. Irving, Troy, N.Y., 6-1/4" high	60	90	120
Tea kettle, cast iron, 3-1/4" long	30	45	60

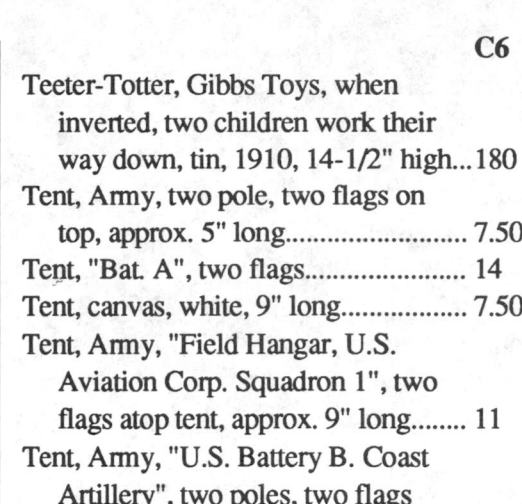

	C6	C8	C10
Teeter-Totter, Gibbs Toys, when inverted, two children work their way down, tin, 1910, 14-1/2" high	180	270	360
Tent, Army, two pole, two flags on top, approx. 5" long	7.50	11.25	15
Tent, "Bat. A", two flags	14	21	28
Tent, canvas, white, 9" long	7.50	11.25	15
Tent, Army, "Field Hangar, U.S. Aviation Corp. Squadron 1", two flags atop tent, approx. 9" long	11	16	22
Tent, Army, "U.S. Battery B. Coast Artillery", two poles, two flags on top	11	16	22
Tent "Guard Tent Co. A", 4-1/4" high	5	7.50	10
Tent, "Inf. Co. C"	9	13	18
Tent, "Medical Unit"	12	18	24
Tent, "Mess Hall", wood base	12	18	25
Tent, "Sail-Me" Co., 6 w/box, c. 1931, paper	40	60	80
Tent, "U.S. Infantry Co. A", two flags on top, 4-1/2" high	11	16	22
Tent, "U.S. Infantry Co. B"	6	9	12
Tent, paper, "State Camp Co. A", 5" high	1.50	2.25	3
Tent, No. 76, small pup, white with cardboard base, center support	4	6	8
Tin dog with boy rider, on wheeled platform, 13-1/2" long	600	900	1200
Tinker Toys, round box, 1940s, 12" high	12	18	24

Teeter-Totter, GIBBS. Courtesy Garth's Auctions Inc.

	C6	C8	C10
Tinker Toys, Electric ET-1	30	45	60
Tinker Toys No. 104	12	18	25
Tinker Toys No. 136	8	12	16
Toledo Scales, cast iron, 4"x4"	25	37	50
"Tom Thumb" cash register, metal, 6-1/2" x7-1/2"x8-1/4" by Western Stamping co.	18	27	36
Tools, Grey Iron, 1933, price per set	15	22	30
Tool Set, Greycraft (Grey Iron), 1940, cast iron, steel and wood	12	18	25

"Uncle Sam's Cash Store Register". Courtesy James S. Maxwell/Virginia Caputo. Photo by Virginia Caputo.

TOOTSIETOY, Bathroom Set. Courtesy Continental Hobby House.

TOOTSIETOY, Dining Room Set. Courtesy Continental Hobby House.

	C6	C8	C10
Tootsietoy Bathroom set	80	120	160
Tootsietoy Bedroom set	50	75	100
Tootsietoy Dining Room set	60	90	120
Tootsietoy furniture, six chairs, moveable bar, two side tables and a dining table.	50	75	100
Tootsietoy living room set, two chairs, lamp, gramophone, sofa secretaire, table	50	75	100
Tootsietoy metal kitchen and bathroom furniture, sink, bathtub, toilet, stove, table and cupboard	45	67	90
Tootsietoy Music Room set	110	165	220
Top, Carnival Whistling Top, tin litho circus decor, spring-wound, Lupor, 1930s, 4" diameter	30	45	60
Top, gyro style, 1918	16	24	32
Top, wooden, circa 1940	4	6	8
Transworld Airlines, Jr. Pilot Wings	10	15	20
Tricycle, iron, Kilgore, 2-3/4"	30	45	60
Trix Rabbit, rubber squeeze toy	20	30	40
Turner Firehouse, heavy sheet metal, 12" x 15" x 21"	200	300	400
Turner Garage, heavy sheet metal, one window on each side, divided into four panes	100	150	200

	C6	C8	C10
The Twister, in black cloth pants and red stripe shirt w/porkpie hat, reminiscent of outfits worn at the Peppermint Lounge where the Twist was born. Stands on a 7" sq. platform, 3-1/2" high, inscribed "Let's Twist!", which is exactly what he does, early 60s, 12" high	90	135	180
"Uncle Sam's Cash Store Register", Durable Toy and Novelty, steel 5" high	42	63	85
Waffle Iron, cast iron, Wagner	25	37	50
Wagon, Champion Express Coaster, 8" with handle	80	120	160
Wagon, "Express" wood spoke wheels	250	375	500
Wagon, Express Flyer, cast iron	125	187.50	250
Wagon, "Kiddie Kart", c. 1925, H.I. White, 20" long	50	75	100
Wagon, "Pioneer", tin, circa 1870	750	1300	1700
Wagon, "Pony Express", 38" long	100	150	200
Wagon, "Radio Flyer, No. 94, 29" long	85	130	175
Wagon, wood, for child, 1900	75	112	150
Walking Horse, metal and papier mache windup, early, 8-1/4"	400	600	800
Washing Machine, tin, works, circa 1940, seashore scene on side	32	48	65
Water Tank Wagon, 1910, painted pressed steel, 26" long	250	375	500
"Western Union" telegraph key, battery powered, code printed on front	22	33	44
Wheelbarrow, cast iron, 1930, 4-1/2"	25	37	50
Wheelbarrow, cast iron, approx.5-1/2".	30	40	60
Wheelbarrow, cast iron, 6-1/2" long	35	52	70

Whirligig of Life.
Courtesy Lloyd W. Ralston Auctions.

Water Tank Wagon, 1910. Courtesy Lloyd W. Ralson Auctions.

	C6	C8	C10
Wheelbarrow, cast iron, w/tools, 1915, 7" long	50	75	100
Wheelbarrow, steel, 9" long	25	38	50
Whirligig of Life, McLoughlin, 1870s, illusion of motion	600	1000	1400
Wilkins Fire House No. 8, tin, 18-1/2" long	600	900	1200
Wilkins Horse and Jockey, 1900, cast iron, wheeled pull toy, 10"	600	900	1200
Windmill, metal, with pumping apparatus	800	1300	1800

WOLVERINE

Wolverine, of Pittsburgh, Pa., was founded in 1903 by B.F. Bain. The company got its name from Bain's Michigan hometown. In later years Wolverine became a subsidiary of Spang Industries, and in 1970 moved to Boonville, Arkansas. The "Sandy Andy", in all its variations, was probably Wolverine's most successful and famous toy. The firm's name is now Today's Kids.

	C6	C8	C10
Wolverine-"Adding Machine No. 39", 1940s, 7" long	25	38	50
Wolverine Auto Magic Sand Loader, 1947, 11" high	87	130	175

	C6	C8	C10
Wolverine "Automatic Coal Loader", 1940s, 10" high	55	83	110
Wolverine "Automatic Sand Crane", tin	112	168	225
Wolverine Bizzy Andy, pat. 1914, steel and tin, 11" high sand toy	80	120	160
Wolverine Bizzy Andy Trip Hammer, 1917	100	150	200
Wolverine "Captain Sandy Andy" No. 63C sand toy, 1930s, 13" high	90	135	180
Wolverine "Corner Grocer", tin litho store	375	562	750
Wolverine "Dumping Sandy", 1916, 12" high	80	120	160
Wolverine Farm Wagon, plastic windup, 10" long	40	60	80
Wolverine "General Grocery", 1930s, includes 10-1/4" tin counter, scale, phone, paper dispenser and groceries, 20-1/4" opened and 10-1/4" closed	150	225	300
Wolverine Kitchen Cabinet No. 178	39	58	78
Wolverine Merry Masons sand toy, 16" high	40	60	80
Wolverine "Music Box. No. 38, 1930s, (crank action), 6" high	30	45	60
Wolverine Organ, tin, turn crank to make organ-like sounds	120	180	240

WOLVERINE Automatic Sand Loader, 1947. Courtesy Calvin L. Chaussee.

WOLVERINE sand and other toys, as shown in a December, 1929 Butler Bros. Catalog.

WOLVERINE "Sunny Andy Kiddie Kampers". Courtesy Mapes Auctioneers & Appraisers.

WOLVERINE Automatic Coal Loader. Photo by Don Hultzman.

WOLVERINE Captain Sandy Andy 63C. Photo by Ron Chojnacki. Courtesy Don Hultzman.

	C6	C8	C10
Wolverine "Panama Pile Driver" No. 54	175	263	350
Wolverine "Post Office" with cardboard accessories	125	188	250
Wolverine Refrigerator No. 183	35	52	70
Wolverine "Sandy Andy No. 60 Automatic Sand Toy", Patented 1909 and 1911	87	130	175
Wolverine "Sandy Andy Full Back", 1920	275	363	550
Wolverine Sandy Andy Sand Loader, 1912	65	98	130
Wolverine Sandy Andy Trick Animals, seal, polar bear pull toy	350	525	700

WOLVERINE "General Grocery". Photo by Ron Chojnacki. Courtesy Don Hultzman.

	C6	C8	C10
Wolverine "Shell" Service Station with 3 vehicles	175	263	350
Wolverine "Ski Jumper", 1940s, catapult action, 18" long	60	90	120
Wolverine "Skyscraper Elevator", 1915, 24" high with "2000 lbs" counterweight	150	225	300
Wolverine "State Capital Quiz No. 43", 1940s, 7" long	40	60	80

WOLVERINE "The Corner Grocer". Photo by Ron Chojnuckl. Courtesy Don Hultzman.

WOLVERINE Sandy Andy.

	C6	C8	C10
Wolverine "Streamline Railway No. 129", 17" long - pull toy	210	315	420
Wolverine "Sunny Andy" Cable Car Set No. 53, circa 1920-30s, 12" high	80	120	160
Wolverine "Sunny Andy Fun Fair No. 65", 1930s, action toy gravity activated by steel balls, 14" long	180	270	360
Wolverine Sunny Andy "Kiddie Kampers", action toy, color litho, three boy scouts and two girl scouts in backdrop camp setting; boys chop and saw wood and girls signal w/flags, marbles drop down chute, circa 1929, 5-5/8" x 3-1/2"	225	338	450
Wolverine "Sunny Andy Rabbit Chase", 1930s, 9-1/2" diameter	150	225	300
Wolverine "Texaco Service Station", 1960s, 25" x 15"	90	135	180
Wolverine "The Corner Grocer No. 182",1930s, includes 16" tin counter, scale, phone, paper dispenser and groceries, 31" long - opened; 15-3/4" - closed	400	600	800
"Wonder Clown" No. 110, 1950s, Nesco Co., spinning top action, 5-3/4" high	80	120	160
Wood Cage with horse, when gate is opened horse pops out and whinnies	125	187	250
Wood Cage, mechanical, rooster flies out when door is open	50	75	100
Wooden Music Maker, "Auto Phone Co. H.B. Horton's, Ithaca, N.Y.",			

	C6	C8	C10
uses player rolls, 9-1/2" high	100	150	200
Wyandotte Air Raid Defense Target Game	42	63	85
Wyandotte Black Sambo target game, tin, has gun	70	105	140
Wyandotte "Carnival", with ferris wheel, carousel and airplane ride, metal	325	488	650
Wyandotte "Flash Strat-O-Wagon", 6" long	42	63	85
Wyandotte hen, chubby, tin, lays egg when body pressed down, with eight eggs, 8-1/2" long	62	93	125
Wyandotte "Musical" push top, circa 1939	30	45	60
Wyandotte "Posse" Shooting Gallery, windup gallery, 14" wide	75	112	150
Wyandotte " Shooting Gallery", 1930s, windup, 14" long, 11" high	112	168	225
Wyandotte Wagon, streamlined, steel, 1930s, 8"	55	82	110
"Zoetrope", wood and cardboard, illusion of motion game, Milton Bradley	350	525	700
"Zulu Blow Gun", copright 1925, 4 arrows, target, instructions, etc. mfd. Battle Creek, Michigan, 2' long	50	75	100
"Zulu Blow Gun" same as above, different coloring and target, no instruction sheet	45	68	90

WYANDOTTE "Carnival". Courtesy Joe and Sharon Freed.

WYANDOTTE "Musical" Push Top. Photo by
Bill Kaufman. courtesy Good Old Days Store.

WYANDOTTE "Posse" Shooting Gallery. Photo by
Bill Kaufman. Courtesy Good Old Days Store.

Zoetrope. Photo Courtesy Milton Bradley.

GERMAN COMPOSITION CIVILIAN FIGURES

By James Theobald

German composition soldiers have long been popular among collectors, but until recently, modern collectors have not strongly focused on civilian figures, including zoo and farm figures and scene accessories.

Composition figures were manufactured from the late 1890s until the early 1960s. The materials and production method were used by doll makers in the latter half of the eighteenth century. Brass molds were hand filled with a mixture of wood flour, fine white clay, and glue. While the mixture was soft, a wire or wood armature was embedded into the mold. The mold pieces were then joined and dried. The figure was removed while warm and flexible, trimmed and painted. The result was an inexpensive, relatively durable toy figure of impressive detail.

Tipple-Topple, a branch of the Pfeiffer doll company of Vienna, Austria was the first commercial producer of composition soldiers, circa 1898. Composition figures were subsequently produced by many companies across the European continent, but the two most prominent manufacturers were Elastolin and Lineol. Elastolin was founded in 1904 by brothers Otto and Max Hausser in Ludwigsberg, Germany, and Lineol in 1905 by Oskar Wiederholz in Brandenburg/Havel, Germany. Elastolin and Lineol introduced civilian production lines about 1914. They were major competitors in both German and export markets.

In the 1930s, corrsponding with the rise of Hitler, Elastolin relocated to Neustadt bei Coburg, nearer the German doll and toy manufacturing hub of the era. During the period, heavy emphasis was placed on military soldier production. The company ceased production in 1943 due to the ravages of W.W.II, but resumed limited production of civilian and foreign soldier figures in 1946 under cooperative agreement with postwar occupational forces. In the 1950s, Elastolin began producing plastic figures, which completely replaced composition production by the early 1960s. Elastolin produced high-quality, detailed civilian and soldier figures.

Lineol figures were generally more accurate and detailed than Elastolin figures. Lineol took over Tipple-Topple in the 1920s. Production continued throughout W.W. II, but the company was nationalized in 1949 and relocated to Dresden, East Germany. Very limited production of plastic figures was continued in East Germany, but they were not available to Western markets.

This section of the book focuses primarily on Elastolin (E) and Lineol (L) figures. The two prices listed for each figure approximate current collector value of figures in good condition (minor leg crack, paint chip acceptable) and in near mint condition (bright paint, no cracks or chips). As with virtually all toy collectible categories, price is significantly influenced by rarity, condition, and demand by collectors.

Because Elastolin and Lineol manufacturing records were destroyed during W. W. II, early production documentation does not exist. Without such records, it is impossible to know precisely how many or what figures were produced. Sales catalogues and price lists published during production are today invaluable records, although sometimes inaccurate, of company production. Of those manufactured, there is no way to estimate how many figures survived the destruction of the war and the elements of time. It is, nonetheless, obvious to any collector of composition toys that figures in excellent condition are now quite rare. German composition civilian figures are frequently of greater rarity than soldiers from the same production periods. Although causes are speculative, it is believed soldier production was much greater than animal production in the war and prewar years. Animal figures were often larger than soldiers and were designed with more fragile parts, i.e., ears, antlers/horns, legs, and tails. The result was more frequent cracks and breaks than their soldier counterparts. Also, soldiers of the German Reich era were preserved as "mementos" of W.W. II, but animals did not have the same socio-political association and were, therefore, seldom preserved. Regardless of the actual reasons, many civilian figures are quite difficult to locate in today's collector market.

Condition of any composition toy, civilian or soldier, will greatly affect the value of the figure. Mint or near-mint specimens of composition figures are highly prized and difficult to locate. Humidity and temperature changes caused more damage to figures than children playing with them. Storage in uninsulated attics or damp basements in Europe and the U.S. have made mint examples quite rare. Pieces often cracked and warped when subjected to moisture as the interior wire armature rusted and expanded. Expansion and contraction in extreme temperatures would also cause the rigid figures to crack apart. In the modern market, minor damage, such as a small crack in a leg or a paint chip, reduces the value of a figure unless exceedingly rare or uncatalogued. Major damage, such as missing or badly deteriorated sections, repaint or reconstruction of a figure, or broken and bent legs that affect the upright standing position of a figure, of course render all but the very rare figure virtually valueless.

During recent decades, civilian figures have lagged behind

toy soldiers in popularity and interest among collectors. This was not only true for German composition figures, but for toy figure collecting in general, including W.B. Britains, Barclay, Grey Iron, and other manufacturers of both civilian and soldier lines; however, in very recent years, civilian figures have gained significant recognition and appreciation. Although not as popular as toy soldier collecting (yet), there are compelling new reasons for preserving animal toys that will likely increase the popularity of civilian figure collecting in the future. As German toy soldiers were keepsakes of a past period in history following the end of W.W. II, animal and farm toys have become a part of preserving the fading heritage of rural life styles, threatened animal species, and a rich natural environment.

In the U.S. and Germany, composition animals are now prized additions to many toy collections. Despite the fact that extensive collections of figures are rarely available for sale in the modern collector's market, individual civilian figures continue to surface at antique shops, flea markets, and auctions. Persistence and patience reward new and advanced collectors with the find of German composition civilian figures.

James Theobald, a native of Bloomington, Illinois, is a Lieutenant Colonel in the U.S. Air Force, currently stationed at the Pentagon in Washington DC. He lived in Germany for six years with his wife, Marge, and children, Jon and Katy. While there, he assembled an extensive German composition civilian figure collection. A dedicated, if eclectic, private collector of toy figures, cast iron cars, electric trains, political memorabilia, Viennese bronzes, and other interesting artifacts, Jim aspires to be an educator and antique dealer after retirement from military duty.

2E Farm Display

3L Circus Display

1E Farm display   All Photos by James Theobald

		Price
1E	Farm display (house/barn/fence)............220	340
1E	House Only.............................. 110	190
2E	Farm display (house/barn/fence).............70	110
3L	Circus display (performance ring/ stands/step)....................................160	270
4L	Circus tiger performing.......................... 18	35
5L	Animal Keeper.. 22	35

4L Circus Tiger Performing

5L Animal Keeper. 6L Circus Animal Wagon.

5L Animal Keeper. 6L Circus Animal Wagon (with Animal).

Left to Right: 7L Circus Bear Cub w/milk bottle, 8L Circus Orangutan (young) with ball, 9L Circus Monkey w/mirror, 10L Circus Tiger Cub w/ball.

Top, Left to Right: 11L Indian Elephant, 12L Elephant Calf, 13E Raging African Bull Elephant. Bottom, Left to Right: 14L Indian Elephant, 15L Elephant Calf, 16L Raging African Bull Elephant.

16L Raging African Bull Elephant.

	Price	
6L Circus Animal Wagon (w/o animal)	90	140
6L Circus Animal Wagon (w/animal)	115	180
7L Circus Bear Cub w/milk bottle	35	60
8L Circus Orangutan (young) w/ball	16	25
9L Circus Monkey w/mirror	35	60
10L Circus Tiger Cub w/ball	15	28
11L Indian Elephant	180	240
12L Elephant Calf	70	110

11L Indian Elephant. 14L Indian Elephant.

	Price	
13E Raging African Bull Elephant	245	325
14L Indian Elephant	180	240
15L Elephant Calf	55	80
16L Raging African Bull Elephant	320	425
17L Snake	35	55
18L Crocodile	20	35

Left to Right: 12L Elephant Calf, 13E Raging African Bull Elephant, 15L Elephant Calf.

Top, Left to Right: 17L Snake, 18L Crocodile, 19L Tortoise, 20L Tortoise. Middle Row, Left to Right: 21E Llama (young), 22E Llama, 23L Guinea Pig, 24L Zebra, 25E Zebra Colt, 26E Zebra. Bottom Row, Left to Right: 27L Cobra Snake, 28L Anteater, 29L Sable Antelope, 30L Orynx (gembok), 31L Kudu.

Left to Right: 17L Snake, 19L Tortoise, 20L Tortoise, 18L Crocodile.

Left to Right: 30L Orynx (gembok), 31L Kudu, 29L Sable Antelope.

Left to Right: 24L Zebra, 25E Zebra Colt, 26E Zebra.

	Price	
19L Tortoise	20	35
20L Tortoise	16	25
21E Llama (young)	18	30
22E Llama	28	45
23L Guinea Pig	14	20
24L Zebra	40	65
25E Zebra Colt	28	45

Top Row, Left to Right: 32L Armadillo, 33L Porcupine, 34L Beaver, 35E Badger, 36E Badger, 37L Wild Boar. Middle Row, Left to Right: 38L Yak, 39L Gnu, 40L Water Buffalo, 41L Kangaroo. Bottom Row, Left to Right: 42E Caribou, 43L Hyena eating meat, 44L Bison, 45L Bison.

Left to Right: 40L Water Buffalo, 38L Yak, 39L Gnu.

Left to Right: 37L Wild Boar, 34L Beaver, 28L Anteater.

Left to Right: 23L Guinea Pig, 27L Cobra Snake, 33L Porcupine, 32L Armadillo.

Left to Right: 45L Bison, 44L Bison.

	Price	
26E Zebra	40	65
27L Cobra Snake	40	65
28L Anteater	24	40
29L Sable Antelope	45	75
30L Orynx (gembok)	60	110
31L Kudu	65	110
32L Armadillo	14	20
33L Porcupine	14	20
34L Beaver	14	20
35E Badger	8	12
36E Badger	8	12
37L Wild Boar	24	40
38L Yak	70	130
39L Gnu	40	65
40L Water Baffalo	70	130
41L Kangaroo	20	35
42E Caribou	40	65
43L Hyena eating meat	18	30
44L Bison	80	140
45L Bison	65	110
46E Squirrel on branch	12	18
47L Squirrel on branch	12	18

Top Row, Left to Right: 46E Squirrel on branch, 47L Squirrel on branch, 48E Wolf, 49E Wolf, 50E, Fox, 51L Marten on branch, 52L Wolf running. Middle Row, Left to Right: 53L Hippopotamus, 54L Hippopotamus (young), 55L Hippopotamus, 56L Tapir, 57E Ibex. Bottom Row, Left to Right: 58L Moose, 59E Moose, 60L Chamois, 61L Rhinoceros.

	Price	
48E Wolf	12	18
49E Wolf	10	16
50E Fox	14	20
51L Marten on branch	12	18
52L Wolf running	10	16

Left to Right: 41L Kangaroo, 56L Tapir.

Left to Right: 53L Hippopotamus, 61L Rhinoceros.

Left to Right: 58L Moose, 59L Moose.

Top Row, Left to Right: 62L Bactrian Camel (young), 63E Bactrian Camel, 64L Bactrian Camel, 65L Dromedary Camel. Bottom Row, Left to Right: 66L Dromedary Camel, 67L Dromedary Camel (young), 68L Bactrian Camel, 69L Giraffe (young), 70E Giraffe, 71L Giraffe.

Left to Right: 69L Giraffe (young), 70E Giraffe, 71L Giraffe.

Left to Right: 67L Dromedary Camel (young), 66L Dromedary Camel, 62L Bactrian Camel (young), 68L Bactrian Camel.

	Price	
53L Hippopotamus	95	155
54L Hippopotamus (young)	20	35
55L Hippopotamus	40	65
56L Tapir	24	40
57E Ibex	18	30
58L Moose	75	120
59E Moose	55	95
60L Chamois	28	45
61L Rhinoceros	80	135

	Price	
62L Bactrian Camel (young)	24	40
63E Bactrian Camel	35	55
64L Bactrian Camel	35	55
65L Dromedary Camel	35	55
66L Dromedary Camel	45	75

	Price	
67L Dromedary Camel (young)	24	40
68L Bactrian Camel	45	75
69L Giraffe (young)	40	60
70E Giraffe	95	155
71L Giraffe	110	180
72E Ostrich	15	22
73E Peacock	16	25
74L Peacock	14	20
75L Marabou Stork	12	18
76L Pelican	10	16
77L Penguin	14	20
78L Emperor Penguin	18	30
79E Emperor Penguin	14	20
80L Auk Penguin	16	25
81E Ostrich	18	30
82L Ostrich	16	25
83E Eagle	24	40
84E Emu	18	30
85L Eagle	24	40
86L Swan	12	18
87E Vulture with lamb	14	20

Top Row, Left to Right: 72E Ostrich, 73E Peacock, 74L Peacock, 75L Marabou Stork, 76L Pelican, 77L Penguin, 78L Emperor Penguin, 79E Emperor Penguin, 80L Auk Penguin. Bottom Row, Left to Right: 81E Ostrich, 82L Ostrich, 83E Eagle, 84E Emu, 85L Eagle, 86L Swan, 87E Vulture with lamb.

Left to Right: 80L Auk Penguin, 79E Emperor Penguin, 77L Penguin, 78L Emperor Penguin.

Top Row, Left to Right: 88L Elk bellowing, 89E Deer, 90E Polar Bear, 91L Brown Bear Cub sitting, 92E Brown Bear, 93E Brown Bear standing. Bottom Row, Left to Right: 94E Deer Stag, 95L Deer, 96L Deer Stag, 97L Deer grazing, 98E Deer Fawn grazing, 99E Deer.

Left to Right: 73E Peacock, 85L Eagle, 84E Emu, 72E Ostrich.

	Price	
88L Elk bellowing	40	65
89L Deer	16	25
90E Polar Bear	20	35
91L Brown Bear Cub sitting	18	30
92E Brown Bear	18	30
93E Brown Bear standing	28	45
94E Deer Stag	18	30
95L Deer	40	60
96L Deer Stag	45	70
97L Deer grazing	40	60
98E Deer Fawn grazing	24	40
99E Deer	35	55
100L Elephant Seal	45	70
101E Sea Lion	20	35
102E Panther	16	25

Left to Right: 57E Ibex, 88L Elk belowing, 60L Chamois.

Left to Right: 90E Polar Bear, 91L Brown Bear Cub sitting, 93E Brown Bear standing, 92E Brown Bear.

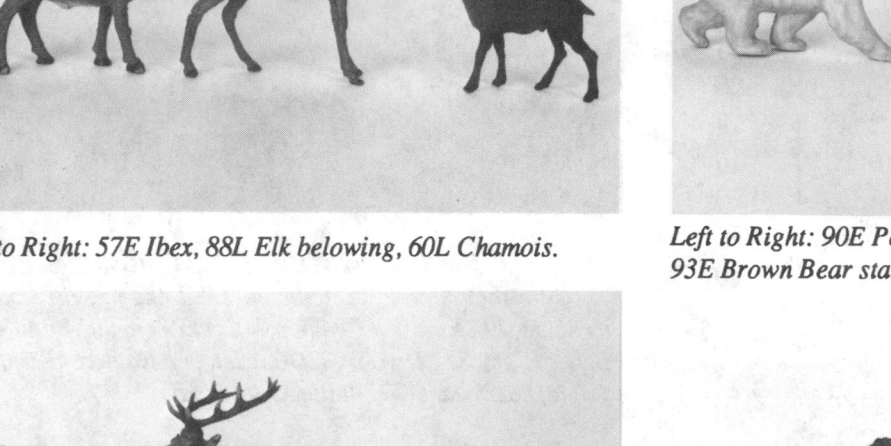

Left to Right: 95E Deer, 96E Stag, 97E Deer grazing.

Top Row, Left to Right: 100L Elephant Seal, 101E Sea Lion, 102E Panther, 103E Leopard. Bottom Row, Left to Right: 104L Seal, 105L Gorilla, 106L Mandrill Baboon, 107L Monkey, 108L Monkey, 109L Monkey grooming, 110E Orangutan on branch.

Left To Right: 109L Monkey grooming, 107L Monkey, 105L Gorilla, 106L Mandrill Baboon.

Left to Right: 104L Seal, 100L Elephant Seal, 101E Sea Lion.

	Price	
103E Leopard	16	25
104L Seal	14	20
105L Gorilla	40	65
106L Mandrill Baboon	40	60
107L Monkey	6	10
108L Monkey	15	22
109L Monkey grooming	18	30
110E Orangutan on branch	40	60

Top Row, Left to Right: 111E Tiger, 112E Tiger, 113L Tiger Cub, 114L Tiger Cub, 115E Tiger. Middle Row, Left to Right: 116L Lioness, 117L Lion Cub standing, 118L Lion Cub lying, 119L Lion Cub, 120L Lion, 121L Lion, 122E Lion, 123L Lion, 124L Lion.

Top, Left to Right: 125E Tree (pine), 126E Crow, 127E Tree (aspen). Bottom, Left to Right: 128E Collie Dog, 129L Saint Bernard Pup, 130E Dog, 131E Pup, 132E German Shepherd Dog.

Left To Right: 124L Lion, 116L Lioness, 118L Lion Cub lying, 117L Lion Cub standing, 119L Lion Cub, 122L Lion.

Left to Right: 125E Tree (pine), 126E Crow, 127E Tree (aspen), 189E Rabbit running.

	Price	
111E Tiger	18	30
112E Tiger	18	30
113L Tiger Cub	12	18
114L Tiger Cub	12	18
115E Tiger	18	30
116L Lioness	18	30
117L Lion Cub standing	12	18
118L Lion Cub lying	12	18
119L Lion Cub	12	18
120L Lion	16	24
121L Lion	14	20
122E Lion	16	25
123L Lion	28	45
124L Lion	28	45
125E Tree (pine)	16	25
126E Crow	12	18
127E Tree (aspen)	65	90
128E Collie Dog	12	18

	Price	
129L Saint Bernard Pup	12	18
130E Dog	10	16
131E Pup	10	16
132E German Shepherd Dog	15	22
133E Rooster	12	18
134L Hen	8	12
135E Hen	8	12
136E Hen on nest	14	20
137E Chick	5	8
138L Woman feeding birds	24	40
139L Goose	8	12
140E Goose	10	16
141E Goose	10	16
142E Goose	10	16
143E Ram	8	14
144E Sheep	8	14
145L Goat	18	28
146E Goat Kid	10	16
147L Goat Kid playing	10	16
148E Goat	18	28

Top Row, Left to Right: 133E Rooster, 134L Hen, 135E Hen, 136E Hen on nest, 137E Chick, 138L Woman feeding birds, 139L Goose, 140E Goose, 141E Goose, 142E Goose. Middle Row, Left to Right: 143E Ram, 144E Sheep, 145L Goat, 146E Goat Kid, 147L Goat Kid playing, 148E Goat, 149E Duck, 150L Duck. Bottom Row, Left to Right: 151L Sheep, 152L, Sheep lying, 153L Lamb lying, 154L Lamb, 155L Sheep lying, 156L Shepherd, 157L Sheep grazing, 158L Ram.

Left to Right: 150L Duck, 138L Woman feeding birds, 135L Hen, 137E Chick, 139L Goose, 187L Turkey.

Left to Right: 145L Goat, 147L Goat Kid playing, 148E Goat.

Left to Right: 153L Lamb lying, 156L Shepherd, 157L Sheep grazing, 158L Ram.

Top Row, Left to Right: 159L Cow lying, 160L Calf, 161E Calf lying, 162L Calf feeding, 163E Calf lying. Second Row, Left to Right: 164L Cow mooing, 165E Bull, 166L Calf, 167L Cow lying. Third Row, Left to Right: 168E Cow lying, 169L Woman milking, 170E Calf, 171E Cow, 172E Cow. Bottom Row, Left to Right: 173L Cow grazing, 174L Cow mooing, 175L Cow, 176L Cow.

		Price
149E Duck	10	16
150L Duck	8	12
151L Sheep	16	24
152L Sheep lying	15	22
153L Lamb lying	15	22
154L Lamb	15	22
155L Sheep lying	15	22
156L Shepherd	28	45
157L Sheep grazing	15	22
158L Ram	18	28
159L Cow lying	24	40
160L Calf	16	25
161E Calf lying	15	22
162L Calf feeding	20	34
163E Calf lying	12	18
164L Cow mooing	28	45

	Price	
165E Bull	40	60
166L Calf	16	25
167L Cow lying	24	40
168E Cow lying	20	35
169L Woman milking	24	40
170E Calf	15	22
171E Cow	28	45
172E Cow	24	40
173L Cow grazing	28	45
174L Cow mooing	28	45
175L Cow	28	45
176L Cow	28	45
177L Pig	18	30
178E Pig	15	22
179E Pig running	18	28
180E Piglet	8	12
181E Piglet	6	10

Left to Right: 166L Calf, 167L Cow lying, 164L Cow mooing.

Left to Right: 174L Cow, 169L Woman milking, 175L Cow, 162L Calf feeding.

Left to Right: 165E Bull, 170E Calf, 171E Cow.

Top Row, Left to Right: 177L Pig, 178E Pig, 179E Pig running, 180E Piglet, 181E Piglet, 182E Piglet sitting, 183E Pig. Middle Row, Left to Right: 184L Donkey, 185E Donkey, 186L Donkey in halter, 187L Turkey, 188E Turkey, 189E Rabbit running, 190E Rabbit running. Bottom Row, Left to Right: 191L Pony, 192L Work Horse, 193L Work Horse grazing, 194E Work Horse, 195E Work Horse Colt.

Left to Right: 179E Pig running, 180E Piglet, 178E Pig.

	Price	
182E Piglet sitting	8	12
183E Pig	10	16
184L Donkey	18	30
185E Donkey	12	18
186L Donkey in halter	20	35
187L Turkey	12	18
188E Turkey	14	20
189E Rabbit running	8	12

	Price	
190E Rabbit running....................	10	16
191L Pony..................................	20	35
192L Work Horse.......................	40	60
193L Work Horse grazing............	40	60
194E Work Horse.......................	40	60
195E Work Horse Colt................	20	34
196E Horse...............................	18	28
197L Horse trotting....................	18	28
198L Horse trotting....................	18	28
199L Horse...............................	20	35
200E Horse grazing....................	15	22
201E Horse grazing....................	18	28
202L Horse grazing....................	18	28
203L Horse running....................	20	35
204E Horse...............................	20	32
205E Horse...............................	18	28
206E Horse...............................	18	28
207L Colt..................................	15	22

Left to Right: 191L Pony, 186L Donkey with halter, 184L Donkey.

Top Row, Left to Right: 196E Horse, 197L Horse trotting, 198L Horse trotting, 199L Horse. Middle Row, Left to Right: 200E Horse grazing, 201E Horse grazing, 202L Horse grazing, 203L Horse running. Bottom Row, Left to Right: 204E Horse, 205E Horse, 206E Horse, 207L Colt.

Left to Right: 192L Work horse, 194E Work Horse, 193L Work Horse feeding.

Left to Right: 196E Horse, 207L Colt, 199L Horse.

208L Indian Elephant with Rider.

	Price	
208L Indian Elephant with Rider..................	220	320
209L Dromedary Camel with Rider..............	175	260
210E Alligator (large scale)........................	17	26
211E Turtle (large scale)............................	15	22
212E Chimpanzee (large scale)....................	10	16

209L Dromedary Camel with Rider.

	Price	
213E Anteater (large scale)	20	35
214E Wild Boar (large scale)	15	22
215L Baboon (large scale)	18	30
216L Badger (large scale)	10	16
217E Polar Bear (large scale)	18	30
218L Polar Bear Cub standing (large scale)	10	16
219L Polar Bear Cub (large scale)	10	16
220L Brown Bear (large scale)	12	18
221E Elephant (large scale)	28	45
222E Zebra (large scale)	18	30
223E Gnu (large scale)	20	35
224E Llama (large scale)	18	30
225E Elephant (miniature scale)	28	45
226E Alligator (miniature scale)	22	30
227E Brown Bear (miniature scale)	18	26
228E Polar Bear (miniature scale)	18	26
229E Bactrian Camel (miniature scale)	22	34
230L Horse on wheels	45	80

Top Row, Left to Right: (these animals are all large scaled) 210E Alligator, 211E Turtle, 212E Chimpanzee, 213E Anteater, 214E Wild Boar. Middle Row, Left to Right: 215L Baboon, 216L Badger, 217E Polar Bear, 218L Polar Bear Cub standing, 219L Polar Bear Cub, 220L Brown Bear. Bottom Row, Left to Right: 221E Elephant, 222E Zebra, 223E Gnu, 224E Llama.

Displaying size comparison of miniature to full scale.

All these animals are miniature scale, Left to Right: 225E Elephant, 226E Alligator, 227E Brown Bear, 228E Polar Bear, 229E Bactrian Camel.

230L Horse on wheels.

	Price				**Price**	
231E Wood Fence section..............................	8	12		237E Cow lying (early plastic)......................	8	14
232E Wood Fence section with gate..............	20	30		238E Cow (early plastic)................................	10	16
233E Wood Fence section..............................	8	12		239E Cow mooing (early plastic)..................	10	16
234E Zoo Fence section with gate..................	12	18		240E Cow grazing (early plastic)..................	10	16
235E Donkey (early plastic)...........................	8	14		241E Bull (early plastic)................................	14	22
236E Calf (early plastic)................................	8	14				

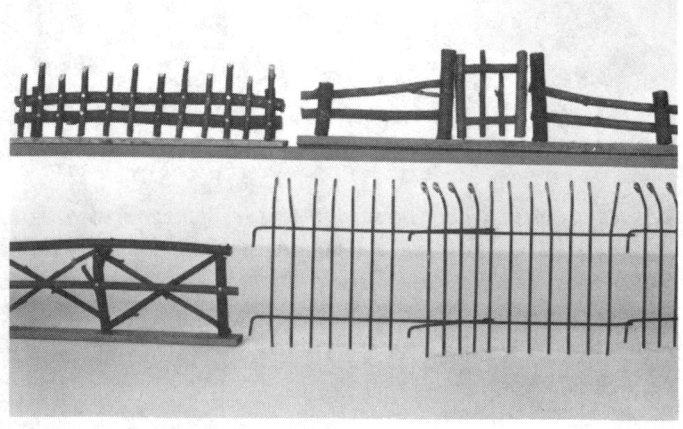

Top Row, Left to Right: 231E Wood fence section, 232E Wood fence section with gate. Bottom Row, Left to Right: 233E Wood fence section, 234E Zoo fence section with gate.

All these animals are early plastic. Top Row, Left to Right: 235E Donkey, 236E Calf, 237E Cow lying, 238E Cow. Bottom Row, Left to Right: 239E Cow mooing, 240E Cow grazing, 241E Bull.

TOY MUSEUMS AND MUSEUMS THAT FEATURE TOYS

AUBURN-CORD-DUSENBERG MUSEUM
Auburn, Indiana 46706
(Auburn toys and Cord and Dusenberg automobiles)

MUSEUM OF THE CITY OF NEW YORK
5th Avenue and 103rd Street
New York, NY

SMITHSONIAN
Washington, DC

DAISY GUN MUSEUM
U.S. 71 South
Rogers, Arkansas
(The world's most complete collection of air rifles, dating from the 18th century)

NASHVILLE TOY MUSEUM
(Next to Opryland USA)
2613 McGavok Pike
Nashville, Tennessee

MARGARET WOODBURY STRONG MUSEUM
One Manhattan Square
Rochester, New York 14607

LAWRENCE SCRIPPS WILKINSON COLLECTION
c/o Detroit Antique Toy Museum
6325 West Jefferson
Detroit, Michigan 48209
(383) 843-9775
(Available only for traveling exhibitions)

TOY TRAIN MUSEUM
Paradise Lane
Strasburg, Pennsylvania

THE STERLING COLLECTION
Stone Castle
804 North Third Street
Bardstown, Kentucky

BAUER TOY MUSEUM (Donald A. Bauer)
233 E. Main
Fredericksburg, Texas
(512) 997-9394

MUSEUM OF CHILDHOOD
8 Broad Street
Greensport, New York

ISLIP TOWN MUSEUM
Montauk Highway
Oakdale, New York

SAN FRANCISCO INTERNATIONAL TOY MUSEUM
2801 Leavenworth Street
San Francisco, CA

SULLIVAN-JOHNSON MUSEUM
(Kenton Toys exhibit)
223 North Main Street
Kenton, Ohio

WASHINGTON DOLL'S HOUSE & TOY MUSEUM
5236 44th Street, NW
Washington, DC 20015

THE TOY MUSEUM
42 Bridge St. Row
Chester, Cheshire
England

THE LONDON TOY & MODEL MUSEUM
23 Craven Hill
London, England

TOY AND SOLDIERS MUSEUM
1100 Cherry Street
Vicksburg, Mississippi

ANTIQUE TOY MUSEUM
Exit 230, I-44
P.O. Box 175
Stanton, Missouri 63079
(314) 927-5555

REMEMBER WHEN TOY MUSEUM
Box 226A
Canton, Missouri 63435
(314) 288-3995 or 288-3176

LAKE ERIE TOY MUSEUM (Aaron Roy)
P.O. Box 860
Kelleys Island, Ohio 43438
(419) 746-2451

BIBLIOGRAPHY AND RECOMMENDED PUBLICATIONS

Antique Toy World - Monthly, $29.95 for one year subscription, payable to Dale Kelley, PO Box 34509, Chicago, IL 60634

U.S. Toy Collector (Vehicles Only) - Monthly, $18 per year, 231 S. Grove St., Missoula, MT 59801

Cast Iron Toy Guns and Capshooter. Heavily illustrated book by Samuel H. Logan and Charles W. Best. $55 from Sam Logan, 1200 Harvard Drive, Davis, CA 95616

Radio Mystery and Adventure by Jim Harmon, McFarland & Company, Inc., Jefferson, North Carolina & London.

Big Bang Cannons by Raymond V. Brandes, Ray-Vin Publishing, 2964-R Brookshire Way, Duluth, Georgia 30136.

A.C. Gilbert Heritage Society Newsletter (Quarterly), Marion Designs, 594 Front St., Marion, MA 02738. $6 a year. Trial issue $1.50.

Rubber Toy Vehicles by Dave Leopard, $26.95 from Dave Leopard, 2507 Feather Run Trail, West Columbia, SC 29169-4915.

Toy Gun Collectors of America Newsletter, 16-page quarterly, $16 per year payable to Jim Buskirk, 175 Cornell St., Windsor, CA 95492

Pictorial Guide to Weeden Steam Toys. $10 from Richard B. Leach, 26146 Redfield Road, Edwardsburg, MI 49112.

Die Cast & Tin Toy Report. Monthly, $36 per year. Payable to: Shoreline Publishing, PO Box 301, Easton, CT 06612

Plastic Toys by Bill Hanlon. All-color, 288 pp. $72.90 from Schiffer Publishing, 77 Lower Valley Road, Atglen, PA 19310.

Toy Shop, monthly newspaper of toy ads, free copy on one-time basis; 700 E. State Street - Sample Copy Department, Iola, WI 54990.

Plastic Figure & Playset Collector, bimonthly, $18 a year, Specialty Publishing Company, PO Box 1355, LaCrosse, WI 54602-1355.

Fisher-Price 1931-1963 (1991 edition) Books Americana, P.O. Box 2326, Florence, AL 35630 $24.95.

Old Toy Soldier Newsletter, $21 for one-year subscription (bimonthly), payable to Steve Sommers, 209 North Lombard, Oak Park, IL 60302.

Toy Soldier Review, $12 for four issues , Vintage Castings Inc., 127-74th Street, North Bergen, NJ 07047.

Arcade Toys by Al Aune, 1990, published by Robert F. Mannella, 4441 Shari Ann Lane, Brooklyn Park, MN 55443.

The Barclay Catalog Book - Early Barclay catalogs, drawings, photos, etc. $16 from Richard O'Brien, 705 Greene Street, Beaufort, SC 29902.

The Second Catalog Book - Reprints of catalogs by Manoil, Barclay, Warren, All-Nu, Authenticast, Beton, Grey Iron. $16 from Richard O'Brien, 705 Greene Street, Beaufort, SC 29902.

The Story of American Toys by Richard O'Brien, 1990. Abbeville Press, $24.95.

National Toy Connection, Vehicles Bimonthly, $11.95 annually, P.O. Box 615, Brigantine, NJ 08203-0615.

The Toy Cannon News, Journal for Cannon Collectors and Shooters. Bimonthly, $25 a year. Ray-Vin Publishing Co., P.O. Box 2052, Norcross, GA 30071-2052.

AUCTIONEERS

These are established firms experienced in disposing of large collections of toys by auction.

SOTHEBY'S
1334 York Avenue
New York, NY 10021
(212) 606-7000

PHILIPS NEW YORK
406 E. 79th St.
New York, NY 10021

CHRISTIE'S EAST
219 East 67th Street
New York, NY 10021
(212) 606-0400

MAPES AUCTIONEERS & APPRAISERS
1600 Vestal Parkway West
Vestal, NY 13850
(607) 754-9193

HAKE'S AMERICANA & COLLECTIBLES
Sample catalog $3.00
P.O. Box 1444N
York, Pennsylvania 17405
(717) 848-1333

LLOYD W. RALSTON
173 Post Road
Fairfield, Connecticut 06430
(203) 255-1233

CONTINENTAL AUCTIONS (Mail)
P.O. Box 193
Sheboygan, Wisconsin 53082

SMITH HOUSE (Mail)
P.O. Box 336
Eliot, Maine 09903
(207) 439-4614

BILL BERTOIA AUCTIONS
2413 Madison Ave.
Vineland, NJ 08360
(609) 692-1881
FAX: 609-692-8697

TOYSENSATIONS (Barry Goodman)
P.O. Box 218
Woodbury, NY 11797
(516) 338-2701

CHICAGO ANTIQUE TOY AUCTION
by Just Right, Inc.
6582 RFD
Long Grove, IL 60047
(708) 949-0059

RICHARD OPFER AUCTIONEERING, INC
1919 Greenspring Drive
Timonium, MD 21093

REX & KATHY BARRETT (Mail)
P.O. Box 254
Medinah, Illinois 60157

NOEL BARRETT ANTIQUES & AUCTIONS
P.O. Box 1001-T
Carversville, PA 18913

TED MAURER
1003 Brookwood Dr.
Pottstown, Pensylvania 19646
(215) 323-1573 or 367-5024

DEBBIE & MARTY KRIM'S NEW ENGLAND AUCTION GALLERY (Mail)
Box 2273-T
West Peabody, MA 01960
(508) 535-3140

BUTTERFIELD & BUTTERFIELD
1244 Sutter Street
San Francisco, CA 94109

MID-HUDSON AUCTION GALLERIES
One Idlewild Avenue
Croton-On-Hudson, NY 12520

JEFF BUB
1658 Barbara Drive
Brunswick, Ohio 44212
(216) 225-1110

HENRY KURTZ, LTD.
163 Amsterdam Ave. Suite 136
New York, NY 10023
(212) 642-5904
FAX: 212-874-6018

SOME LEADING COLLECTORS AND DEALERS

(It is suggested that, when writing to any of the following, you enclose a stamped, self-addressed envelope.)

JIM HARMON
Radio premiums and tapes, comic books and strips
634 S. Orchard Dr.
Burbank, CA 91506

BARBARA & JONATHAN NEWMAN
Paper toys, old and new
The Paper Soldier
8 McIntosh Lane
Clifton Park, NY 12065

CHARLES W. BEST
Old toy pistols, etc.
11523 Pine Valley Drive
Franktown, CO 80116

BIZARRE BAZAAR
Quality collectible toys
130 1/4 East 65th St.
New York, NY 10021-7007
(212) 517-2100
FAX: 212-517-2283

JOHN MURRAY
Fisher-Price
Box 29
Eden, NY 14057

BARRY GOODMAN
GI Joes, Barbies, Robots, Pez, all
1950s-60s character toys
P.O. Box 218
Woodbury, NY 11797
(516) 338-2701

JIM BUSKIRK
Spring-Air BB guns, cast iron pistols
c/o TGCA
175 Cornell St.
Windsor, CA 95492

BILL BERTOIA
Mechanical banks, antique toys
2413 Madison Avenue
Vineland, NJ 08360
(609) 692-1881

EDWARD K. POOLE
Toy soldiers, 1/36 scale ID vehicles and
old wooden military vehicle kits
926 Terrace Mtn. Drive
Austin, TX 78746

DON PIELIN
Toy Soldiers
1009 Kenilworth
Wheeling, IL 60090

PERRY R. EICHOR
Aircraft toys and literature
703 North Almond Dr.
Simpsonville, SC 29681

JOE & SHARON FREED
Vehicles
6209 Sandy Forks Rd.
Raleigh, NC 27615

JAMES S. MAXWELL - VIRGINIA CAPUTO
Old toys, all types, buy and sell
Box 367
Lampeter, PA 17537

SECOND CHILDHOOD
Antique Toys
283 Bleecker Street
New York, NY

GARY J. LINDEN
Marx and other plastic toys
P.O. Box 243
River Forest, IL 60305
(708) 453-0470

RICHARD MacNARY
Marx trains, Coca-Cola vehicles, wood,
cardboard, paper toys, soldiers
4727 Alpine Drive
Lilburn, GA 30247

ECCLES BROTHERS
Toy soldiers, Comic figures and vehicles from original molds, Catalog $3.00
R.R. 1, Box 253-D
Burlington, IA 52601

BILL LANGO
Barclay vehicles, animals and soldiers from original and new molds - Send for flyer
127 74th Street
North Bergen, NJ 07047

K. WARREN MITCHELL
Soldiers of all types, regular lists at no charge
1008 Forward Pass
Pataskala, OH 43062

STEVE BALKIN
Toy soldiers including Warren
BURLINGTON ANTIQUE TOYS
1082 Madison Avenue
New York, NY 10028

BOB LOWE'S TOONERVILLE JUNCTION
Classic American and European Toys
7 E. Church Street
Bethlehem, PA 18018
(215) 691-6736

LONDON BRIDGE COLLECTOR'S TOYS
Britains soldiers, etc. and Britains replacement parts
East Penn Plaza
1325 Chestnut Street
Emmaus, PA 18049
(215) 967-6887

RON SMITH
Tin plate cars & planes, plastic promotional cars
33005 Arlesford
Solon, OH 44139
(216) 248-7066

BUDDY K TOYS
Buddy L Toys, etc.
RD 9 Box 322
Bingen Road
Bethlehem, PA 18015

MARBLE COLLECTORS SOCIETY OF AMERICA
P.O. Box 222
Trumble, CT 06611

EXCALIBUR HOBBIES LTD
Toy soldiers, all types
63 Exchange Street
Malden, MA 02148-5523
(617) 322-2959

BRAD KREWSON
Beany & Cecil toys
588 Lindford Drive
Bay Village, OH 44140

DON HULTZMAN
Tin wind-up and battery-operated, also repairs, restorations
5026 Sleepy Hollow Road
Media, OH 44256

SCOTT SMILES
Tin wind-ups, etc.
848 S. Atlantic Dr., E.
Lantana, FL 33462

CONTINENTAL HOBBY HOUSE
Toys and Trains, regualr catalogs
P.O. Box 193
Sheboygan, WI 53082

FRED THOMPSON
New designs of Smitty vehicles
Smith-Miller Inc.
P.O. Box 139
Canoga Park, CA 91305

JOHN D. (JACK) MATTHEWS
World War II toys, etc.
13 Bufflehead Dr.
Kiawah Island, SC 29455

DUTKINS' COLLECTABLES
Tin toys, soldiers, etc.
1019 W. Route 70
Cherry Hill, NJ 08002
(609) 428-9559

DANNY FUCHS
Superman toys, games, etc.
209-80 18th Avenue
Bayside, NY 11360

STEVE LEONARD
Antique Mechical Toys, etc.
Box 127T
Albertson, LI, NY 11507
(516) 742-0979

DAVID M. LEOPARD
Old toy cars and trucks
2507 Feather Run Trail
West Columbia, SC 29169-4915

DARROW'S FUN ANTIQUES
Old toys of all types
309 E. 61st Street
New York, NY 10021
(212) 838-0730

FRED MAXWELL - COLLECTOR-RESEARCHER
Slush mold cars, planes, novelties, literature, toys
4722 No. 33 Street
Arlington, VA 22207

CHARLES FRANCIS WILDING
Secretary, Capitol Miniature Auto Collectors Club
10207 Greenacres Dr.
Silver Springs, MD 20903

FREDINAND ZEGEL
Antique toys, postwar, Corgi, Dinky
P.O. Box 589
Ft. Belvoir, VA 22060

FRED & MARGARET WILHELM
Disney, Popey, Comic, Barclay, Manoil soldiers
W & F Collectibles
Box 2054
Leucadia, CA 92024

CLASSIC TOYS
New and old toys; military, vehicles, zoo, etc.
69 Thompson St.
New York, NY 10012

PHIL SAVINO
Mail Auctions in various toy categories-send SSAE
Rt. 2, Box 76
Micanopy, FL 32667

TONY AND JACKI GRECCO
Toy soldiers and related items
P.O. Box 3490
Poughkeepsie, NY 12603
(914) 462-8829

DAVID WELCH
Pez, Cereal boxes, Model kits, TV, Disney, Premiums
P.O. Box 714
2308 Clay Street
Murphysboro, IL 62966
(618) 687-2282

CALVIN L. CHAUSSEE
Antique Toy Buyer - Any Quantiy
Box 22
Calhan, CO 80808
(719) 347-2000
FAX: 719-347-2780

THOMAS G. NEFOS
FEDERAL SHIPPING NETWORK
Investment quality transportation toys
P.O. Box 707
Brigantine, NJ 08203-0707

JIM & PATSY CARLSON
Schoenhut Collectors
7939 Caberfae Trail
Clarkston, MI 48348-3708

LARRY BRUCH
Old Toys Wanted & For Sale
P.O. Box 121
Mountaintop, PA 18707
(717) 474-9202

CARL LOBEL
Toys of all eras
Box 74A
Warren, VT 05674
(802) 496-4025

RAY FUNK
Toys, Bicycles
P.O. Box 5019
Upland, CA 91785

CHARLIE-BRESLOW
Toys of all Types
971 Canton Drive
Toms River, NJ 08753
(908) 286-7618

BLYSTONE'S
Specialists in Books on Toys
2132 Delaware Ave.
Pittsburg, PA 15218
(412) 371-3511
FAX (412) 244-8028

JAMES L. THEOBALD
German Composition Figures, etc.
P.O. Box 701
Bloomington, IL 61702-0701

RICHARD LEACH
Old Steam Engine toys, literature
26146 Redfield Rd.
Edwardsburg, MI 49112

NEW ERA TOYS
Restorations service for pressed steel toy, pedal cars
P.O. Box 10
Lambertville, NJ 08530
(609) 397-2113

MARK SUOZZI
Antique Penny Banks & Toys
Box 102
Ashfield, MA 01330
(413) 628-3241

RONALD L. SIMKOFF
Holgate Toys
5171 Mayfield Rd.
Lyndhurst, OH 44124
(216) 461-2660

BILL HELLIE
ALL AMERICAN TOY COMPANY
American Toy Company parts and limited editions; buy
sell, restore antique toys
P.O. Box 4266
Salem, OR 97302

A. (GUS) HANSEN
Mignot, Dimestore, Britains, etc.
4645 Lilac Avenue
Glenview, IL 60025

JAMES SCHLEYER
Toy Guns
Box 243-C
Burke, VA 22015

MARY BRETT
Plastic doll Furniture, Tin dollhouses
3607 Nuttree Woods Drive
Midlothian, VA 23112
(804) 744-9170

RANDY WELCH
Ramp Walkers, Tin Windups & Sparklers
Raven' Tiques
1100 Hambrooks Blvd.
Cambridge, MD 21613
(410) 228-5390

W.S. (BILL) HARRISON III
Erector Sets, buy and sell
Marion Designs
594 Front Street.
Marion, MA 02738

MARK McMANUS
Matchbox, Pez, GI Joe, Tonka, etc.
120 Main Street
Boonville, NY 13309
(315) 942-2185

INSURANCE FOR COLLECTIBLE TOYS
Debbie Riley
Reeves & Melvin
P.O. Box 229
Millville, NJ 08332
(609) 825-0713

SALUNGA (Don Eckel)
Cast iron parts for toys
P.O. Box 369
Talmage, PA 17580
(717) 656-4857

TIM OEI - OEI ENTERPRISES, LTD.
Buys, sells, trades, restores old toys
241 Rowayton Ave.
Rowayton, CT 06853-1227
(203) 866-2470

JOHN GIBSON
Tootsietoy Restoration, Parts & Services
9857 Dockside Terrace
Gaithersburg, MD 20879
(301) 527-0076

RAY BRANDES
Big Bang Cannons Collector-Dealer
2964 Brookshire Way
Duluth, GA 30136
(404) 476-8259

BOB SMITH
Sells toys of all types, Toy Show
62 West Ave.
Fairport, NY 14450
(716) 377-8394

KENT M. COMSTOCK
Motorcycles, all types
507 Vine St.
Ashland, OH 44805

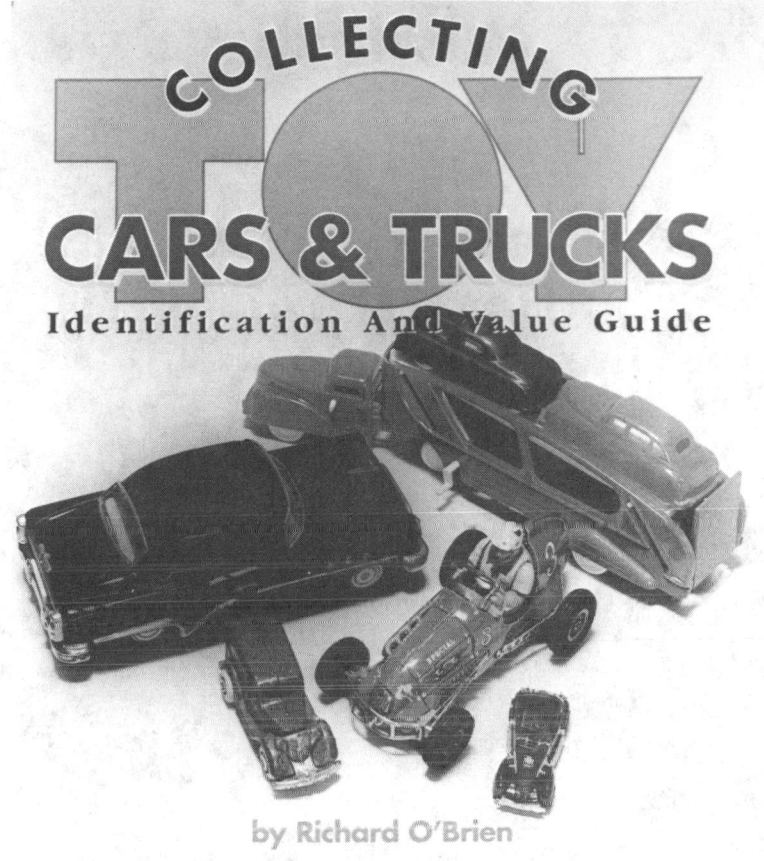

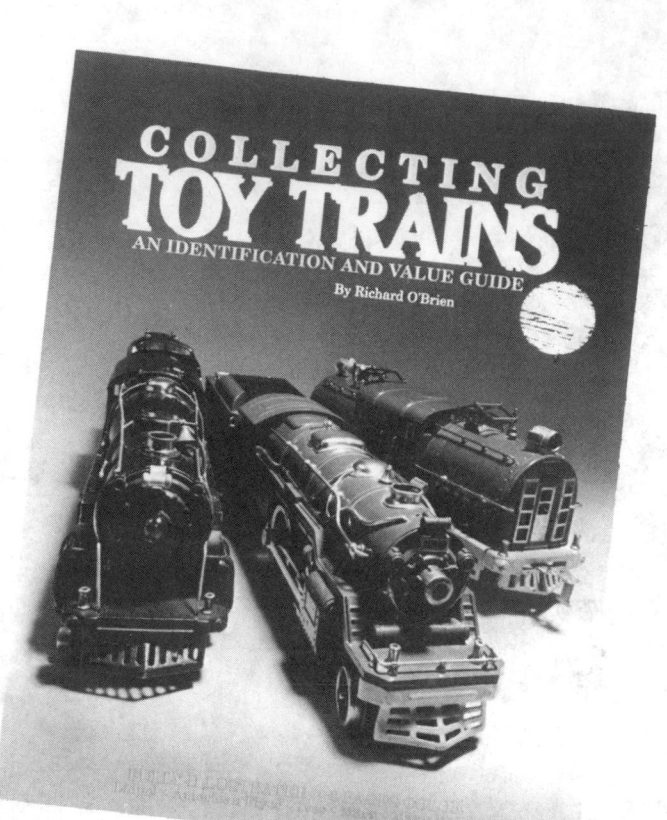
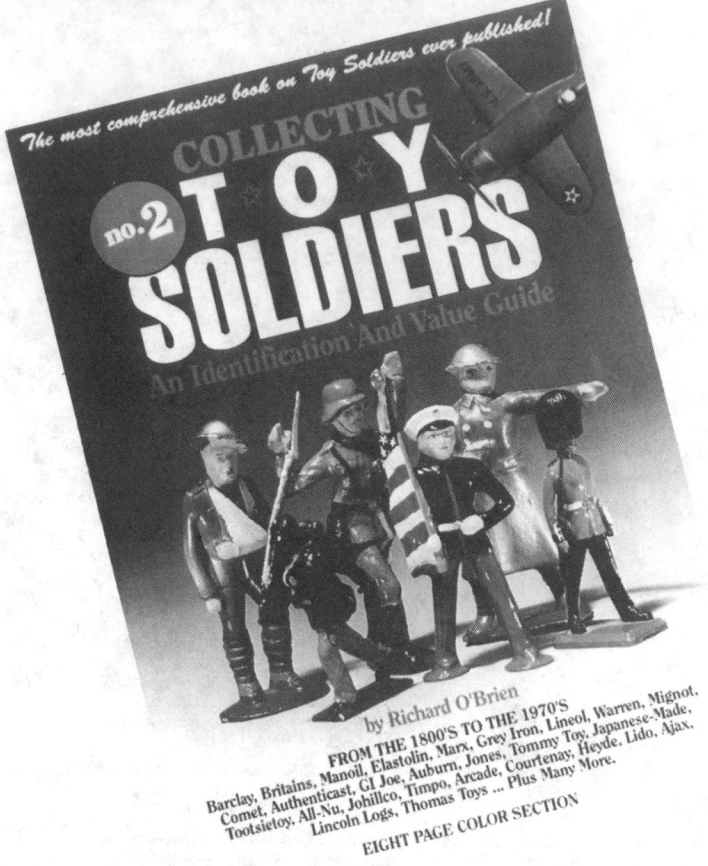
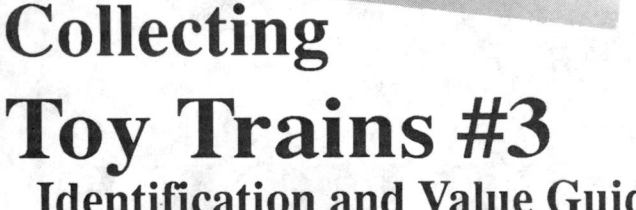